WORD
BIBLICAL
COMMENTARY

WORD

BIBLICAL

COMMENTARY

VOLUME 18B

Job 38—42

DAVID J. A. CLINES

THOMAS NELSON
Since 1798

NASHVILLE DALLAS MEXICO CITY RIO DE JANEIRO

To my granddaughters
Megan and Elsie and Esther

ἑκάστῃ ἔδωκεν δέκα τάλαντα
To each he gave ten talents.

Published in Nashville, Tennessee, by Thomas Nelson. Thomas Nelson is a trademark of Thomas Nelson, Inc.

Thomas Nelson, Inc., titles may be purchased in bulk for educational, business, fund-raising, or sales promotional use. For information, please e-mail SpecialMarkets@ThomasNelson.com. Scripture quotations in the body of the commentary marked NRSV are from the New Revised Standard Version of the Bible, copyright 1989 by the Division of Christian Education of the National Council of the Churches of Christ in the USA and are used by permission. The author's own translation of the text appears in italic type under the heading *Translation*.

Library of Congress Cataloging-in-Publication
Data Main entry under title:
Word biblical commentary.
Includes bibliographies.
1. Bible—Commentaries—Collected works.
BS491.2.W67   220.7′7   81-71768
ISBN-10: 0785252673 (v. 18B) AACR2
ISBN-13: 9780785252672

Printed in Mexico
3 4 5 6 7 EPAC 16 15 14 13 12

Contents

Editorial Preface

The launching of the Word Biblical Commentary brings to fulfillment an enterprise of several years' planning. The publishers and the members of the editorial board met in 1977 to explore the possibility of a new commentary on the books of the Bible that would incorporate several distinctive features. Prospective readers of these volumes are entitled to know what such features were intended to be; whether the aims of the commentary have been fully achieved time alone will tell.

First, we have tried to cast a wide net to include as contributors a number of scholars from around the world who not only share our aims, but are in the main engaged in the ministry of teaching in university, college, and seminary. They represent a rich diversity of denominational allegiance. The broad stance of our contributors can rightly be called evangelical, and this term is to be understood in its positive, historic sense of a commitment to Scripture as divine revelation and to the truth and power of the Christian gospel.

Then, the commentaries in our series are all commissioned and written for the purpose of inclusion in the Word Biblical Commentary. Unlike several of our distinguished counterparts in the field of commentary writing, there are no translated works, originally written in a non-English language. Also, our commentators were asked to prepare their own rendering of the original biblical text and to use the biblical languages as the basis of their own comments and exegesis. What may be claimed as distinctive with this series is that it is based on the biblical languages, yet it seeks to make the technical and scholarly approach to a theological understanding of Scripture understandable by—and useful to—the fledgling student, the working minister, and colleagues in the guild of professional scholars and teachers as well.

Finally, a word must be said about the format of the series. The layout, in clearly defined sections, has been consciously devised to assist readers at different levels. Those wishing to learn about the textual witnesses on which the translation is offered are invited to consult the section headed *Notes*. If the readers' concern is with the state of modern scholarship on any given portion of Scripture, they should turn to the sections on *Bibliography* and *Form/Structure/ Setting*. For a clear exposition of the passage's meaning and its relevance to the ongoing biblical revelation, the *Comment* and concluding *Explanation* are designed expressly to meet that need. There is therefore something for everyone who may pick up and use these volumes.

If these aims come anywhere near realization, the intention of the editors will have been met, and the labor of our team of contributors rewarded.

General Editors: *Bruce M. Metzger†*
David A. Hubbard†
Glenn W. Barker†
Old Testament Editor: *John D. W. Watts*
Associate Editor: *James W. Watts*
New Testament Editor: *Ralph P. Martin*
Associate Editor: *Lynn Allan Losie*

Publisher's Note

It is with great joy that Thomas Nelson brings you the concluding volume of David J. A. Clines' definitive commentary on the book of Job.

The staff of Thomas Nelson would like to thank Professor Clines for his patience and graciousness as we worked to bring his exhaustive research to an eager audience. Professor Clines delivered the manuscript for *Job* 18B to Thomas Nelson in August of 2008. Due to unforeseen production issues and through no fault of Professor Clines, publication was delayed until October 2011.

We would like to thank Dr. Kevin A. Wilson of Upper Case Textual Services for stepping into the middle of the production process to rebuild lost files. We would also like to thank Melanie McQuere for her tireless work editing this final volume despite difficult circumstances.

Thomas Nelson, Inc.

Testimonia

This is the most singular Book in the whole of the Sacred Code: though written by the same inspiration, and in reference to the same end, the salvation of men, it is so different from every other book of the Bible, that it seems to possess nothing in common with them; for even the language, in its construction, is dissimilar from that in the Law, the Prophets, and the Historical Books. But on all hands it is accounted a work that contains "the purest morality, the sublimest philosophy, the simplest ritual, and the most majestic creed."

Adam Clarke
Preface to his *Commentary* on the Bible (1813)

I call it, apart from all theories about it, one of the grandest things ever written with pen. ... [S]uch a noble universality, different from noble patriotism or noble sectarianism, reigns in it. A noble Book; all men's Book! It is our first, oldest statement of the never-ending Problem,—man's destiny, and God's way with him here in this earth. And all in such free flowing outlines; grand in its sincerity, in its simplicity; in its epic melody, and repose of reconcilement. Sublime sorrow, sublime reconciliation; oldest choral melody as of the heart of mankind;—so soft, and great; as the summer midnight, as the world with its seas and stars! There is nothing written, I think, in the Bible or out of it, of equal literary merit.

Thomas Carlyle
On Heroes, Hero-Worship and the Heroic in History (1841)

The Book of Job is perhaps the Greatest Masterpiece of the Human Mind.
Victor Hugo (1802–1885)

The pencil of the Holy Ghost hath labored more in describing the afflictions of Job than the felicities of Solomon.
Francis Bacon (1561–1626)
Of Adversity

The greatest poem of ancient and modern times.
Alfred Lord Tennyson (1809–1892)

If you want a story of your own soul, it is perfectly done in the book of Job.
D. H. Lawrence (1885–1930)

The most tragic, sublime and beautiful expression of loneliness which I have ever read is the Book of Job.
Thomas Wolfe (1900–1938)

Nowhere in the world has the passion of anguish found such expression.
Søren Kierkegaard (1813–1855)

Through the All-disposing providence of God, and the importunate call of not a few worthy friends, I began this Work; and now, after twenty-four years travel ... I am come to the end of it; And truly, I might justly be reproved, at least, for dullness and indiligence, or counted a very slow-paced Traveller, had I spent that twenty-four years (the best of my time and strength) in measuring so short a journey. But, as I have to say towards an Apology for my over-long stay in this work, that I have had frequent diversions, for a considerable part of that time, quite from it; so the whole time which I have spent in it, hath been but a diversion, or time (I hope, honestly) stolen, either from my rest, or from that which was my more proper work.

And, now that I have, at last, ended what I began, all that I shall say of it, is, that I have ended it. Whether I began it well, or have ended it well, and whether or not the end be better than the beginning, is not for me to say.

Joseph Caryl
Preface to *An Exposition with Practical Observations upon the Book of Job* (1666)

Abbreviations

Arab.	Arabic
Aram.	Aramaic
ArOr	*Archiv orientalní*
AS	Alonso Schökel, L. *Diccionario bíblico hebreo-español.* Madrid: Editorial Trotta, 1994.
ASEs	*Annali di storia dell'esegesi*
AsiaJT	*Asia Journal of Theology*
Ass.	Assyrian
ASTI	*Annual of the Swedish Theological Institute*
ASV	American Standard Version
ATAbh	Alttestamentliche Abhandlungen
ATANT	Abhandlungen zur Theologie des Alten und Neuen Testaments
ATD	Das Alte Testament Deutsch
ATR	*Anglican Theological Review*
ATSAT	Arbeiten zu Text und Sprache im Alten Testament
Aug	*Augustinianum*
AUMLA	*Australasian Universities Languages and Literatures Association*
AusBR	*Australian Biblical Review*
AusCathRec	*Australasian Catholic Record*
AUSS	*Andrews University Seminary Studies*
AV	Authorized Version, King James Version
BA	*Biblical Archaeologist*
Bab.	Babylonian
BAC	Biblioteca de autores cristianos
Ball	Ball, C. J. *The Book of Job. A Revised Text and Version.* Oxford: Clarendon Press, 1922.
Barr	Barr, J. *Comparative Philology and the Text of the Old Testament.* Oxford: Clarendon Press, 1968.
BASOR	*Bulletin of the American Schools of Oriental Research*
Bauer–Leander	Bauer, H., and P. Leander. *Historische Grammatik der hebräischen Spraches des Alten Testaments.* Halle: Niemeyer, 1922.
BBB	Bonner biblische Beiträge
BCPE	*Bulletin du centre protestant d'études*
BDB	Brown, F., S. R. Driver, and C. A. Briggs. *A Hebrew and English Lexicon of the Old Testament.* Oxford: Clarendon, 1906.
BEATAJ	Beiträge zur Erforschung des Alten Testaments und des antiken Judentums
Beer, BH^2	Beer, G. Textual notes to Job in *Biblia hebraica.* Ed. R. Kittel. 2nd ed. Stuttgart: Württemburgische Bibelanstalt, 1909. 1062–1112 [only mentioned when it differs from *BHK*].
Beer, *BHK*	Beer, G. Textual notes to Job in *Biblia hebraica.* Ed. R. Kittel. 3rd ed. Stuttgart: Württemburgische Bibelanstalt, 1937. 1105–54.
Beer, *Text*	Beer, Georg. *Der Text des Buches Hiob.* Marburg: N. G. Elwert, 1895–1897.
Ben Yehuda	Ben Yehuda, Eliezer. מלון הלשון עברית הישנה והחדשה. *Thesaurus totius hebraitatis et veteris et recentioris. Complete Dictionary of Ancient and Modern Hebrew.* New York: Yoseloff, 1960.

BeO	*Bibbia e oriente*
BETL	*Bibliotheca ephemeridum theologicarum lovaniensium*
BEvTh	Beiträge zur evangelischen Theologie
BHK	Beer, G. Textual notes to Job in *Biblia hebraica*. Ed. R. Kittel. 3rd ed. Stuttgart: Württemburgische Bibelanstalt, 1937.
BHS	Gerleman, G. Textual notes to Job in *Biblia hebraica stuttgartensia*. Ed. K. Elliger and W. Rudolph. Stuttgart: Deutsche Bibelstiftung, 1966–1967.
BHT	Beiträge zur historischen Theologie
Bib	*Biblica*
BibB	Biblische Beiträge
BibBash	*Biblebashyam*
BibFe	*Biblia y fe*
BibInt	*Biblical Interpretation*
BibOr	Biblica et orientalia
BibRes	*Biblical Research*
BibRev	*Bible Review*
Bickell	Bickell, G. "Kritische Bearbeitung des Iobdialogs." *WZKM* 6 (1892) 136–47, 241–57, 327–34; 7 (1893) 1–20, 153–68.
Bickell[2]	Bickell, G. *Carmina Veteris Testamenti metrice. Notas criticas et dissertationem de re metrica Hebraeorum adjecit.* Innsbruck: Libraria Academica Wagneriana, 1882. 151–87.
Bickell[3]	Bickell, G. *Das Buch Job nach Anleitung der Strophik und der Septuaginta auf seine ursprüngliche Form zurückgeführt und in Versmasse des Urtextes übersetzt.* Vienna: Carl Gerold's Sohn, 1894.
BIFAO	*Bulletin de l'Institut Français d'Archéologie Orientale*
BIJS	*Bulletin of the Institute of Jewish Studies*
BIOSCS	*Bulletin of the International Organization for Septuagint and Cognate Studies*
BiTod	*The Bible Today*
BiTrans	*Bible Translator*
BJ	*Bible de Jérusalem*
BJRL	*Bulletin of the John Rylands University Library of Manchester*
BK	*Bibel und Kirche*
BKAT	Biblischer Kommentar: Altes Testament
Bleeker	Bleeker, L. H. K. *Job.* Tekste en uitleg: Praktische Bibelverklaring. Groningen: J. B. Wolters, 1935.
BLit	*Bibel und Liturgie*
Blommerde	Blommerde, A. C. M. *Northwest Semitic Grammar and Job.* BibOr 22. Rome: Pontifical Biblical Institute, 1969.
BMik	*Beth mikra*
BMJ	*British Medical Journal*
BN	*Biblische Notizen*
BO	*Bibliotheca orientalis*
Böttcher	Böttcher, F. *Neue exegetisch-kritische Aehrenlese zum Alten Testamente.* Leipzig: J. A. Barth, 1863–1865.
BOT	De Boeken van het Oude Testament

BotAT	Die Botschaft des Alten Testaments
Brockelmann	Brockelmann, C. *Lexicon syriacum.* 2nd ed. Halle: M. Niemeyer, 1922–1928.
Brockelmann, *Syntax*	Brockelmann, C. *Hebräische Syntax.* Neukirchen: Buchhandlung des Erziehungsvereins, 1956.
Brockington	Brockington, L. H. *The Hebrew Text of the Old Testament: The Readings Adopted by the Translators of the New English Bible.* Oxford: Clarendon, 1973.
BSac	*Bibliotheca sacra*
BSOAS	*Bulletin of the School of Oriental and African Studies*
BullSocFranNumis	*Bulletin de la société française de numismatique*
BTB	*Biblical Theology Bulletin*
BThSt	Biblisch-theologische Studien
BTS	*Bible et terre sainte*
Budde	Budde, K. *Das Buch Hiob übersetzt und erklärt.* HAT 2/1. Göttingen: Vandenhoeck & Ruprecht, 1896.
Budde²	Budde, K. *Das Buch Hiob übersetzt und erklärt.* 2nd ed. HAT 2/1. Göttingen: Vandenhoeck & Ruprecht, 1913.
BulBibRes	*Bulletin for Biblical Research*
BulMusBeyrouth	*Bulletin du musée de Beyrouth*
BurHist	*Buried History*
Buttenwieser	Buttenwieser, M. *The Book of Job.* London: Hodder & Stoughton, 1922.
Buxtorf	Buxtorf, J. *Lexicon hebraicum et chaldaicum.* Basel, 1600.
BWANT	Beiträge zur Wissenschaft vom Alten und Neuen Testament
BZ	*Biblische Zeitschrift*
BZAW	Beihefte zur *ZAW*
BZAW	*Beihefte zur ZAW* (when book title is not also cited)
CAD	[Chicago] *Assyrian Dictionary.* Chicago: University of Chicago Press, 1956–2007.
CahArch	*Cahiers archéologiques*
CalvTJ	*Calvin Theological Journal*
CamB	Cambridge Bible
CanRevCompLit	*Canadian Review of Comparative Literature*
Carey	Carey, C. P. *The Book of Job Translated … on the Basis of the Authorized Version, Explained in a Large Body of Notes … and Illustrated by Extracts from Various Works.* London: Wertheim, Macintosh, & Hunt, 1858.
CAT	Dietrich, M., O. Loretz, and J. Sanmartín. *The Cuneiform Alphabetic Texts from Ugarit, Ras Ibn Hani and Other Places.* Münster: Ugarit-Verlag, 1995 [2nd ed. of *KTU* (*q.v.*)].
CB	Century Bible
CBQ	*Catholic Biblical Quarterly*
CBQMS	*CBQ* Monograph Series
CBR	*Currents in Biblical Research*
CCAR Journal	*Central Conference of American Rabbis Journal*
CCSL	Corpus christianorum. Series latina

CDA	*A Concise Dictionary of Akkadian.* Ed. J. Black, A. George, and N. Postgate. Wiesbaden: Harrassowitz, 2000.
CenB	Century Bible
Charles	Charles, R. H. *The Apocrypha and Pseudepigrapha of the Old Testament.* 2 vols. Oxford: Clarendon Press, 1913.
Cheyne	Cheyne, T. K. *Job and Solomon, or the Wisdom of the Old Testament.* London: Kegan Paul, Trench & Co., 1887.
ChrCent	*Christian Century*
ChrLit	*Christianity and Literature*
ChrPädBl	*Christliche pädagogische Blätter*
ChrSchRev	*Christian Scholar's Review*
ChrTod	*Christianity Today*
CiTom	*Ciencia tomista*
CiuD	*La ciudad de Dios*
CivCat	*La civiltà cattolica*
CiVit	*Città di vita*
CJT	*Canadian Journal of Theology*
CleR	*Clergy Review*
CML	Driver, G. R. *Canaanite Myths and Legends.* Old Testament Studies 3. Edinburgh: T. & T. Clark, 1956.
CML²	Gibson, J. C. L. *Canaanite Myths and Legends.* 2nd ed. Edinburgh: T. & T. Clark, 1978.
Coccieus	Coccieus (Coch), J. *Commentarius in librum Ijobi.* Franeker, 1644.
Cohen, *Biblical Hapax Legomena*	Cohen, H. R. (C.). *Biblical Hapax Legomena in the Light of Akkadian and Ugaritic.* SBL Dissertation Series 37. Missoula, MT: Scholars Press, 1978.
ColBG	*Collationes brugenses et gandavenses*
ColcTFu	*Collectanea theologica universitatis Fujen*
ColctMech	*Collectanea mechliniensia*
CommSpok	*Communio,* Spokane
ConBNT	Coniectanea biblica: New Testament Series
ConBOT	Coniectanea biblica: Old Testament Series
Conc	*Concilium*
ConcJ	*Concordia Journal*
ConcRev	*Concilium-Revue,* French edition of *Concilium*
ConsJud	*Conservative Judaism*
Cox	Cox, D. *The Triumph of Impotence. Job and the Tradition of the Absurd.* AnGreg 212. Rome: Università Gregoriana Editrice, 1978.
CPL	Clavis patrum latinorum
CQ	*Church Quarterly*
CRBS	*Currents in Research: Biblical Studies*
CSCO	Corpus scriptorum christianorum orientalium
CSEL	Corpus scriptorum ecclesiasticorum latinorum
CSRBull	*Council for the Study of Religion Bulletin*
CTA	Herdner, A. *Corpus des tablettes en cunéiformes alphabétiques découvertes à Ras-Shamra-Ugarit.* Paris: Imprimerie Nationale, 1963.
CTM	*Concordia Theological Monthly*

CTQ	*Concordia Theological Quarterly*
CuadTe	*Cuadernos de teología*
CuBíb	*Cultura bíblica*
CurTM	*Currents in Theology and Mission*
DAC	*Dictionnaire d'archéologie chrétienne et de liturgie.* Ed. F. Cabrol and H. Leclercq. Paris: Letouzey & Ané, 1907–1953.
Dahood, *Psalms I*	Dahood, M. *Psalms I: 1–50.* Garden City, NY: Doubleday, 1966.
Dahood, *Psalms II*	Dahood, M. *Psalms II: 51–100.* Garden City, NY: Doubleday, 1968.
Dahood, *Psalms III*	Dahood, M. *Psalms III: 101–150.* Garden City, NY: Doubleday, 1970.
Dalman, *Arbeit und Sitte*	Dalman, G. *Arbeit und Sitte in Palästina.* Gütersloh: C. Bertelsmann, 1928–1942.
Dathe	Dathe, J. A. *Jobus, Proverbia Salomonis, Ecclesiastes, Canticum Canticorum ex recensione textus hebraei et versionum antiquarum latine versi notisque philologicis et criticis illustrati.* Halle: Sumtibus Orphanotrophei, 1789.
Davidson	Davidson, A. B. *The Book of Job, with Notes, Introduction and Appendix.* CamB. Cambridge: Cambridge University Press, 1884.
DB	*Dictionnaire de la Bible.* Ed. F. Vigouroux. Paris: Letouzey & Ané, 1895–1912.
DBAT	*Dielheimer Blätter zum Alten Testament*
DBSup	*Dictionnaire de la Bible, Supplément.* Ed. L. Pirot and A. Robert. Paris: Letouzey & Ané. 1928–.
DCH	Clines, D. J. A. (ed.). *The Dictionary of Classical Hebrew.* Vols. 1–8. Sheffield: Sheffield Phoenix Press, 1993–2011.
DDD	Toorn, K. van der, B. Becking, and P. W. van der Horst. *Dictionary of Deities and Demons in the Bible.* 2nd ed. Leiden: Brill Academic Publishers, 1999.
Delitzsch	Delitzsch, Franz J. *Biblical Commentary on the Book of Job.* Trans. F. Bolton. 2 vols. Edinburgh: T. & T. Clark, 1866.
Delitzsch, Friedrich	Delitzsch, Friedrich. *Das Buch Hiob, neu übersetzt und kurz erklärt.* Leipzig: J. C. Hinrichs, 1902.
Dhorme	Dhorme, E. *A Commentary on the Book of Job.* Trans. H. Knight. London: Thomas Nelson & Sons, 1967 [original *Le livre de Job.* Paris: Gabalda, 1926].
DictSpir	*Dictionnaire de spiritualité ascétique et mystique.* Ed. M. Viller. Paris: Beauchesne, 1932–1995.
Dillmann	Dillmann, A. *Hiob.* 4th ed. Leipzig: S. Hirzel, 1891.
DissAbstr	*Dissertation Abstracts*
DJD	Discoveries in the Judaean Desert
DNWSI	*Dictionary of the North-West Semitic Inscriptions.* Ed. J. Hoftijzer and K. Jongeling. 2 vols. Leiden: E. J. Brill, 1995.
Doederlein	Doederlein, J. C. *Scholia in libros Veteris Testamenti poeticos Jobum, Psalmos et tres Salomonis.* Halle, 1779.
Dor	*Dor le Dor*

Dozy	Dozy, R. *Supplément aux dictionnaires arabes.* 2 vols. Leiden: E. J. Brill, 1881.
DPB	*Deutsches Pfarrerblatt*
Driver	See Driver–Gray
Driver–Gray	Driver, S. R., and G. B. Gray. *A Critical and Exegetical Commentary on the Book of Job together with a New Translation.* ICC. Edinburgh: T. & T. Clark, 1921.
Driver, *Tenses*	Driver, S. R. *A Treatise on the Use of the Tenses in Hebrew and Some Other Syntactical Questions.* 2nd ed. Oxford: Clarendon, 1881.
DTT	*Dansk teologisk tidsskrift*
Duhm	Duhm, B. *Das Buch Hiob erklärt.* KHC. Tübingen: J. C. B. Mohr, 1897.
DukeDivSchRev	*Duke Divinity School Review*
DUL	Olmo Lete, G. del, and J. Sanmartín. *A Dictionary of the Ugaritic Language in the Alphabetic Tradition.* 2nd ed. Leiden: Brill, 2004.
EB	*Encyclopaedia biblica.* Ed. T. K. Cheyne and J. Sutherland Black. London: A. & C. Black, 1899–1903.
EC	*Enciclopedia cattolica.* Città del Vaticano: Ente per l'Enciclopedia cattolica e per il libro cattolico, 1949–.
EchB	Echter-Bibel
ed.	edited by, edition
EglTh	*Eglise et théologie*
EHAT	Exegetisches Handbuch zum Alten Testament
Ehrlich	Ehrlich, A. B. *Randglossen zur hebräischen Bibel.* VI. *Psalmen, Sprüche, und Hiob.* Leipzig: J. C. Hinrichs, 1918.
EHS	Europäische Hochschulschriften
EI	*Eretz Israel*
Eitan	Eitan, I. *A Contribution to Biblical Lexicography.* New York: Columbia University Press, 1924.
ELH	*English Literary History*
Enc	*Encounter*
EncBib	*Enciclopedia de la Biblia.* Ed. A. Díez-Macho and S. Bartina. 6 vols. Barcelona: Garriga.
EncJud	*Encyclopaedia judaica.* Jerusalem: Macmillan, 1972.
EphLit	*Ephemerides liturgicae*
ErbAuf	*Erbe und Auftrag*
ERE	*Encyclopaedia of Religion and Ethics.* Ed. J. Hastings. 13 vols. Edinburgh: T. & T. Clark, 1908–1926.
EstBíb	*Estudios bíblicos*
EstEcl	*Estudios eclesiásticos*
EstFranc	*Estudios franciscanos*
ETL	*Ephemerides theologicae lovanienses*
ETR	*Etudes théologiques et religieuses*
EuntDoc	*Euntes docete*
EvErz	*Der evangelische Erzieher*
EvQ	*Evangelical Quarterly*
EvTh	*Evangelische Theologie*

EVV	English versions
Ewald	Ewald, G. H. A. von. *Commentary on the Book of Job.* Trans. J. F. Smith. London: Williams & Norgate, 1882.
Exp	*Expositor*
ExpB	Expositor's Bible
ExpT	*Expository Times*
FAT	Forschungen zum Alten Testament
Fedrizzi	Fedrizzi, P. *Giobbe: La Sacra Bibbia, traduta dai testi originali illustrata con note critiche e commentata.* Turin: Marietti, 1972.
fem.	feminine
FF	*Forschungen und Fortschritte*
fl.	flourished
Fohrer	Fohrer, G. *Das Buch Hiob.* KAT 16. Gütersloh: Gütersloher Verlagshaus Gerd Mohn, 1963.
FoiTemps	*La foi et le temps*
FoiVie	*Foi et vie*
FolOr	*Folia orientalia*
FOTL	The Forms of the Old Testament Literature
frag.	fragment
FreibRu	*Freiburger Rundbrief*
Freytag	Freytag, G. W. *Lexicon arabico-latinum praesertim ex Djauharii Firuzabaiique et aliorum Arabum operibus adhibitis Golii quoque et aliorum libris confectum.* Halle: C. A. Schwetschke & Filius, 1830–1837.
FRLANT	Forschungen zur Religion und Literatur des Alten und Neuen Testaments
frt	*forte*, perhaps
FrThSt	Freiburger theologische Studien
FundJ	*Fundamentalist Journal*
G	Greek translation of the OT, Septuagint
Galling, *Reallexikon*	Galling, K. *Biblisches Reallexikon.* 2nd ed. Tübingen: Mohr, 1977.
Gard	Gard, D. H. *The Exegetical Method of the Greek Translator of the Book of Job.* SBLMS 8. Philadelphia: Society of Biblical Literature, 1952.
GeistL	*Geist und Leben*
GerefTTs	*Gereformeerd theologisch tijdschrift*
Gerleman	Gerleman, G., textual notes to Job in *BHS*
Germ.	German
Ges[18]	*Wilhelm Gesenius Hebräisches und aramäisches Handwörterbuch über das Alte Testament.* Ed. R. Meyer and H. Donner, with U. Rütersworden. 18th ed. 6 vols. Berlin: Springer Verlag, 1987–2010.
Gesenius	Gesenius, W. *Thesaurus philologico-criticus linguae hebraeae et chaldaicae Veteris Testamenti.* 2nd ed. Leipzig: Vogel, 1829.

Gesenius–Buhl	Gesenius, W., and F. Buhl. *Hebräisches und aramäisches Handwörterbuch zum Alten Testament.* 17th ed. Leipzig: Vogel, 1915.
GGA	*Göttingische gelehrte Anzeiger*
Gibson	Gibson, J. C. L. *Canaanite Myths and Legends.* 2nd ed. Edinburgh: T. & T. Clark, 1978.
Gibson, E. C. S.	Gibson, E. C. S. *The Book of Job.* WC. London: Methuen, 1899.
Giesebrecht	Giesebrecht, Friedrich. *Der Wendepunkt des Buches Hiob.* Greifswald, 1879.
Gill	Gill, J. *An Exposition of the Whole Old Testament, Critical, Doctrinal and Practical.* London: George Keith, 1778–1781.
GJ	*Grace Journal*
GKC	*Gesenius' Hebrew Grammar.* Ed. E. Kautzsch and A. E. Cowley. 2nd ed. Oxford: Clarendon Press, 1910.
GNB	Good News Bible
Golius	Golius, J. *Lexicon arabico-latinum, contextum ex probatioribus orientis lexicographis.* Leiden: Typis Bonaventurae & Abr. Elseviriorum, 1653.
Good	Good, Edwin Marshall. *In Turns of Tempest: A Reading of Job, with a Translation.* Stanford: Stanford University Press, 1990.
Gordis	Gordis, R. *The Book of Job: Commentary, New Translation, and Special Notes.* New York: Jewish Theological Seminary of America, 1978.
Grabbe	Grabbe, L. L. *Comparative Philology and the Text of Job: A Study in Methodology.* SBLDS 34. Chico, CA: Scholars Press, 1977.
Graetz	Graetz, Heinrich. "Lehrinhalt der 'Weisheit' in den biblischen Büchern." *MGWJ* 35 (1886) 289–99, 204–10, 544–49 (pp. 402–10, 544–49 often cited as "Register der corrumpierten Stellen in Hiob und Vorschläge zur Verbesserung").
GratzCollJewSt	*Gratz College Jewish Studies*
Gray	Gray, J. *The Book of Job: A Commentary.* Sheffield: Sheffield Phoenix Press, 2010.
Greg	*Gregorianum*
Grimme	Grimme, H. "Metrisch-kritische Emendationen zum Buche Hiob." *ThQ* 80 (1898) 295–304, 421–32; 81 (1899) 112–18, 259–77.
GSAI	*Giornale della Società Asiatica Italiana*
Guillaume	Guillaume, A. *Studies in the Book of Job with a New Translation.* ALUOSSup 2. Leiden: E. J. Brill, 1968.
Guillaume, *Lexicography*	Guillaume, A. *Hebrew and Arabic Lexicography: A Comparative Study.* Leiden: E. J. Brill, 1965.
Gunkel	Gunkel, H. *Schöpfung und Chaos in Urzeit und Endzeit: Eine religionsgeschichtliche Untersuchung über Gen 1 und Ap Joh 12.* Göttingen: Vandenhoeck & Ruprecht, 1895.
Habel	Habel, N. C. *The Book of Job.* OTL. London: SCM Press, 1985.
Hahn	Hahn, H. A. *Commentar über das Buch Hiob.* Berlin: J. A. Wohlgemuth, 1850.

Ḥakham	Ḥakham, A. ספר איוב מפורש [The Book of Job, a Commentary]. Jerusalem: Kook, 1970.
HALOT	*The Hebrew and Aramaic Lexicon of the Old Testament.* Ed. L. Koehler and W. Baumgartner. Trans. M. E. J. Richardson. 5 vols. Leiden: E. J. Brill, 1994–2000.
HAR	*Hebrew Annual Review*
HAT	Handbuch zum Alten Testament
HBT	*Horizons in Biblical Theology*
HDB	*A Dictionary of the Bible.* Ed. J. Hastings. 5 vols. Edinburgh: T. & T. Clark, 1899.
Heath	Heath, T. *An Essay towards a New English Version of the Book of Job, from the Original Hebrew, with a Commentary, and Some Account of His Life.* London: A. Miller and S. Baker, 1756.
Heb.	Hebrew
Hen	*Henoch*
HervTS	*Hervormde teologiese studies*
Hesse	Hesse, F. *Hiob.* Zürcher Bibelkommentar. Zurich: Theologischer Verlag, 1978.
HeythJ	*Heythrop Journal*
HibJ	*Hibbert Journal*
Hirzel	Hirzel, L. *Hiob erklärt.* KEH 2. Leipzig: Weidmann, 1839.
Hitt.	Hittite
Hitzig	Hitzig, F. *Das Buch Hiob übersetzt und ausgelegt.* Leipzig: C. F. Winter, 1874.
HKAT	Handkommentar zum Alten Testament
Hölscher	Hölscher, G. *Das Buch Hiob.* HAT. Tübingen: J. C. B. Mohr (Paul Siebeck), 1937.
Hoffmann	Hoffmann, J. G. E. *Hiob.* Kiel: C. F. Haeseler, 1891.
Hontheim	Hontheim, J. *Das Buch Hiob als strophisches Kunstwerk nachgewiesen, übersetzt und erklärt.* BibS 9.1–3. Freiburg i.Br.: Herder, 1904.
Horst	Horst, F. *Hiob.* Vol. 1. BKAT. Neukirchen: Neukirchener Verlag, 1960–1963.
Houbigant	Houbigant, C. F. *Biblia hebraica cum notis criticis.* 4 vols. Paris, 1753.
Houtsma	Houtsma, M. T. *Textkritische Studien zum Alten Testament. I. Das Buch Hiob.* Leiden: Brill, 1925.
HS	*Hebrew Studies*
HSAT	*Die Heilige Schrift des Alten Testaments.* Ed. A. Bertholet. 4th ed. Tübingen. 1922–1923.
HSM	Harvard Semitic Museum; Harvard Semitic Monographs
HSS	Harvard Semitic Studies
HTR	*Harvard Theological Review*
HUCA	*Hebrew Union College Annual*
Hufnagel	Hufnagel, W. F. *Hiob neu übersetzt mit Anmerkungen.* Erlangen, 1781.
Hupfeld	Hupfeld, H. *Quaestionum in Jobeidos locos vexatos specimen. Commentatio.* Halle: E. Anton, 1853.
IB	*The Interpreter's Bible.* Ed. G. A. Buttrick. 12 vols. Nashville: Abingdon Press, 1951–1957.

IBD	*Illustrated Bible Dictionary.* Ed. N. Hillyer et al. Leicester: Inter-Varsity Press, 1980.
ibn Ezra	Commentary printed in Rabbinic Bibles (*Miqra'ot Gedolot*)
ICC	International Critical Commentary
IDB	*Interpreter's Dictionary of the Bible.* Ed. G. A. Buttrick. 4 vols. Nashville: Abingdon Press, 1962.
IDBS	*IDB, Supplementary Volume.* Ed. K. Crim. Nashville: Abingdon Press, 1976.
IEJ	*Israel Exploration Journal*
'Ilu	*'Ilu: Revista de ciencias de las religiones*
IndJT	*Indian Journal of Theology*
IndTSt	*Indian Theological Studies*
Int	*Interpretation*
Interp	*Interpreter*
IntJPolPhilos	*Interpretation: A Journal of Political Philosophy*
IntJPsychRel	*International Journal for the Psychology of Religion*
IntJSysTheol	*International Journal of Systematic Theology*
ISBE	*The International Standard Bible Encyclopedia.* Ed. G. W. Bromiley. Rev. ed. 4 vols. Grand Rapids: Eerdmans, 1979–1988.
Itin	*Itinerarium*
ITQ	*Irish Theological Quarterly*
IZT	*Internationale Zeitschrift für Theologie* [*Concilium*, German edition]
JA	*Journal asiatique*
JAAR	*Journal of the American Academy of Religion*
JAC	*Jahrbuch für Antike und Christentum*
JANES	*Journal of the Ancient Near Eastern Society of Columbia University*
Janzen	Janzen, J. G. *Job.* Interpretation. Atlanta: John Knox, 1985.
JAOS	*Journal of the American Oriental Society*
Jastrow	Jastrow, M. *A Dictionary of the Targumim, the Talmud Babli and Yerushalmi, and the Midrashic Literature.* London: Luzac, 1903.
JB	Jerusalem Bible
JBC	*The Jerome Bible Commentary.* Ed. R. E. Brown et al. London: Geoffrey Chapman, 1968.
JBibSt	*Journal of Biblical Studies*
JBL	*Journal of Biblical Literature*
JBLMS	*Journal of Biblical Literature*, Monograph Series
JBQ	*Jewish Biblical Quarterly*
JBR	*Journal of Bible and Religion*
JCS	*Journal of Cuneiform Studies*
JDTh	*Jahrbücher für deutsche Theologie*
JETS	*Journal of the Evangelical Theological Society*
JewEnc	*The Jewish Encyclopedia.* Ed. I. Singer. New York: Funk & Wagnalls Co., 1901–1906.
JHI	*Journal of the History of Ideas*
JHisp/LatTh	*Journal of Hispanic/Latino Theology*
JHS	*Journal of Hebrew Scriptures*
JJewThPhilos	*Journal of Jewish Thought and Philosophy*
JJS	*Journal of Jewish Studies*

JMA	*Journal of Mediterranean Archaeology*
JMEOS	*Journal of the Manchester Egyptian and Oriental Society*
JNES	*Journal of Near Eastern Studies*
JNSL	*Journal of Northwest Semitic Languages*
Joüon	Joüon, P. *Grammaire de l'hébreu biblique*. Rome: Pontifical Biblical Institute, 1947.
Joüon–Muraoka	Joüon, P., and T. Muraoka. *A Grammar of Biblical Hebrew*. 2 vols. Subsidia biblica 14. Rome: Pontifical Biblical Institute, 1991.
JPOS	*Journal of the Palestine Oriental Society*
JPS	Jewish Publication Society version of the Bible
JPsychJud	*Journal of Psychology and Judaism*
JPsychTheol	*Journal of Psychology and Theology*
JPTh	*Jahrbücher für protestantische Theologie*
JQR	*Jewish Quarterly Review*
JR	*Journal of Religion*
JRAS	*Journal of the Royal Asiatic Society*
JRelHealth	*Journal of Religion and Health*
JRelThought	*Journal of Religious Thought*
JScrReas	*Journal of Scriptural Reasoning* (http://etext.lib.virginia.edu/journals/ssr/)
JSem	*Journal for Semitics*
JSJ	*Journal for the Study of Judaism*
JSNTSup	*Journal for the Study of the New Testament*, Supplement Series
JSOR	*Journal of the Society of Oriental Research*
JSOT	*Journal for the Study of the Old Testament*
JSOTSup	*Journal for the Study of the Old Testament*, Supplement Series
JSP	*Journal for the Study of the Pseudepigrapha*
JSS	*Journal of Semitic Studies*
JThSAfr	*Journal of Theology for Southern Africa*
JTS	*Journal of Theological Studies*
JüdSHRZ	*Jüdische Schriften aus hellenistischer und römischer Zeit*
Jud	*Judaica*
JZWL	*Jüdische Zeitschrift für Wissenschaft und Leben*
Kaltner	Kaltner, J. *The Use of Arabic in Biblical Hebrew Lexicography*. CBQMS 28. Washington, DC: Catholic Biblical Association of America, 1996.
Kamphausen	Kamphausen, A. *Die Bibel, oder, die Schriften des Alten und Neuen Bundes nach den überlieferten Grundtexten übersetzt und für die Gemeinde erklärt*. III. *Die Schriften*. Ed. C. C. J. Bunsen. Leipzig: F. A. Brockhaus, 1858–1868.
KAT	Kommentar zum Alten Testament
KatBl	*Katachetische Blätter*
KB	*Lexicon in Veteris Testamenti libros*. Ed. L. Koehler and W. Baumgartner. Leiden: E. J. Brill, 1953.
Keel	Keel, O. *Jahwes Entgegnung an Ijob: Eine Deutung von Ijob 38–41 vor dem Hintergrund der zeitgenössischen Bildkunst*. FRLANT 121. Göttingen: Vandenhoeck & Ruprecht, 1978.

Keel, *Dieu répond*	Keel, O. *Dieu répond à Job: Une interprétation de Job 38–41 à la lumière de l'iconographie du Proche-Orient ancien.* Paris: Cerf, 1993.
Keel, *Symbolism*	Keel, O. *The Symbolism of the Biblical World: Ancient Near Eastern Iconography and the Book of Psalms.* New York: Seabury, 1978.
KEH	Kurzgefasstes exegetisches Handbuch zum Alten Testament
KHC(AT)	Kurzer Hand-Commentar (zum Alten Testament)
King	King, E. G. *The Poem of Job, Translated in the Metre of the Original.* Cambridge: Cambridge University Press, 1914.
Kissane	Kissane, E. J. *The Book of Job Translated from a Critically Revised Hebrew Text with Commentary.* Dublin: Browne & Nolan, 1939.
KJV	King James Version, Authorized Version
KKAT	Kurzgefasster Kommentar zu den Heiligen Schriften Alten und Neuen Testaments
Knox	[Knox, R.] *The Holy Bible. A Translation from the Latin Vulgate in the Light of the Hebrew and Greek Originals.* London: Burns, Oates & Washbourne, 1945–1949.
König	König, E. *Hebräisches und aramäisches Wörterbuch zum Alten Testament, mit Einschaltung und Analyse aller schwer erkennbaren Formen, Deutung der Eigennamen sowie der massoretischen Randbemerkungen und einem deutsch-hebräischen Wortregister.* Leipzig: Dieterich'sche Verlagsbuchhandlung (Theodor Weicher), 1910.
König (followed by §)	König, E. *Historisch-kritisches Lehrgebäude der hebräischen Sprache.* III. *Historisch-comparative Syntax der hebräischen Sprache.* Leipzig: Hinrichs, 1897.
Kroeze	Kroeze, J. H. *Het Boek Job, opnieuw uit de grondtekst vertaald en verklaard.* Korte verklaring der Heilige Schrift. Kampen: J. H. Kok, 1960.
Kt, K	Kethiv, consonantal Hebrew text of Hebrew Bible
KTU	Dietrich, M., O. Loretz, and J. Sanmartín. *Die keilalphabetischen Texte aus Ugarit.* AOAT 24. Kevelaer and Neukirchen: Butzon & Bercker, 1976. This edition is used for its numbering of Ugaritic texts; page references are usually given to the second edition, *CAT* [*q.v.*].
KuD	*Kerygma und Dogma*
KV	Korte Verklaring
Lamparter	Lamparter, H. *Das Buch der Anfechtung, übersetzt und ausgelegt.* BotAT. Stuttgart: Calwer. 1951.
Lane	Lane, E. W. *An Arabic–English Lexicon.* London: Williams & Norgate, 1863–1893.
Larcher	Larcher, C. *Le Livre de Job.* BJ. Paris: Cerf, 1950.
Lat.	Latin
LCQ	*Lutheran Church Quarterly*
Leigh	Leigh, E. *Critica sacra, in Two Parts: The First Containing Observations on All the Radices, or Primitive Hebrew Words of the Old Testament, in Order Alphabetical … The Second, Philologicall and Theologicall*

	Observations upon all the Greek Words of the New Testament, in Order Alphabetical. 3rd ed. London: Thomas Underhill, 1650.
Leqach	*Leqach: Mitteilungen und Beiträge der Forschungsstelle Judentum*
Lesh	*Leshonenu*
Lévêque	Lévêque, J. *Job et son Dieu. Essai d'exégèse et de théologie biblique.* Paris: Gabalda, 1970.
Levy	Levy, J. *Neuhebräisches und chaldäisches Wörterbuch über die Talmudim und Midraschim.* 4 vols. Leipzig: Brockhaus, 1876–1889.
Ley	Ley, J. "Die metrische Beschaffenheit des Buches Hiob." *TSK* (1895) 635–92; (1897) 7–42.
Ley²	Ley, J. *Das Buch Hiob nach seinem Inhalt, seiner Kunstgestaltung und religiösen Bedeutung. Für gebildete Leser dargestellt.* Halle: Waisenhaus, 1903.
LingBib	*Linguistica biblica*
lit.	literally, literal
LitTheol	*Literature and Theology*
Löw, *Flora*	Löw, I. *Die Flora der Juden.* I. *Krytogamae, Acanthaceae, Graminaceae.* Veröffentlichungen der Alexander Kohut Memorial Foundation 4. Vienna: R. Löwit, 1928. II. *Iridaceae, Papilionaceae.* Veröffentlichungen der Alexander Kohut Memorial Foundation 2. Vienna: R. Löwit, 1924. III. *Pedaliaceae, Zygophyllaceae.* Veröffentlichungen der Alexander Kohut Memorial Foundation 3. Vienna: R. Löwit, 1924.
LS	*Lebendige Seelsorge*
LTP	*Laval théologique et philosophique*
LTQ	*Lexington Theological Quarterly*
LTR	*Lexington Theological Review*
LUÅ	Lunds universitets årsskrift
Lugt, van der	Lugt, Pieter van der. *Rhetorical Criticism and the Poetry of the Book of Job.* OTS 32. Leiden: E. J. Brill, 1995.
LumVie	*Lumière et vie*
LuthQ	*Lutheran Qiuarterly*
LXX	Septuagint, Greek translation of the OT
MAA	*Medelelingen der koninklijke nederlandse Akademie van Wetenschappen, Amsterdam*
MastSemJ	*Master's Seminary Journal*
MemphThSemJ	*Memphis Theological Seminary Journal*
Merx	Merx, A. *Das Gedicht von Hiob. Hebräischer Text, kritisch bearbeitet und übersetzt, nebst sachlicher und kritischer Einleitung.* Jena: Mauke's Verlag (Hermann Dufft), 1871.
MEstArabH	*Miscelanea de estudios arabes y hebraicos*
MethQR	*Methodist Quarterly Review*
MethRev	*Methodist Review*
mg	margin
MGWJ	*Monatsschrift für Geschichte und Wissenschaft des Judentums*
MH	Mishnaic Hebrew
Michaelis	Michaelis, J. D. "Varianten im Buch Hiob." In his *Orientalische und exegetische Bibliothek* 7 (1774) 217–47; 8 (1775) 179–224.

Michaelis, *Deutsche Übersetzung*	Michaelis, J. D. *Deutsche Übersetzung des Alten Testaments, mit Anmerkungen für Ungelehrte.* 2nd ed. 13 parts. Göttingen: Dieterich, 1773–88.
Michaelis, *Supplementa*	Michaelis, J. D. *Supplementa ad lexica hebraica.* Göttingen: J. G. Rosenbusch, 1792.
Michel	Michel, W. L. *Job in the Light of Northwest Semitic.* Vol. 1. Rome: Pontifical Biblical Institute, 1987.
MittSeptU	Mitteilungen des Septuaginta-Unternehmens
ModTh	*Modern Theology*
Moffatt	Moffatt, J. *A New Translation of the Bible.* London: Hodder & Stoughton, 1926.
MP	*Monatsschrift für Pastoraltheologie*
ms, mss	manuscript, manuscripts
MT	Masoretic Text
MTZ	*Münchener theologische Zeitschrift*
Murphy	Murphy, R. E. *Wisdom Literature: Job, Proverbs, Ruth, Canticles, Ecclesiastes and Esther.* FOTL 13. Grand Rapids: Eerdmans, 1981.
MUSJ	Université Saint-Joseph, Beyrouth (Syrie), *Mélanges de la Faculté Orientale*
Muss-Arnoldt	Muss-Arnoldt, W. *A Concise Dictionary of the Assyrian Languages.* Berlin: Reuther & Reichard, 1905.
MVAG	Mitteilungen der vorderasiatisch-ägyptischen Gesellschaft
NAB	New American Bible
NBD	*The New Bible Dictionary.* Ed. J. D. Douglas. London: IVF, 1962.
NBL	*Neues Bibel-Lexikon.* Ed. Manfred Görg and Bernhard Lang. Zurich: Benziger Verlag, 1991.
NCB	New Century Bible
n.d.	no date
NEB	New English Bible
NedGTT	*Nederduitse gereformeerd teologiese tydskrif*
NedTTs	*Nederlands theologisch tijdschrift*
Newsom	Newsom, Carol A. "The Book of Job." In *The New Interpreter's Bible.* Ed. Leander E. Keck et al. Vol. 4. Nashville: Abingdon Press, 1996. 317–637.
N.F.	Neue Folge, new series
NICOT	New International Commentary on the Old Testament
NIDTTT	*The New International Dictionary of New Testament Theology.* Ed. C. Brown. 2 vols. Grand Rapids: Eerdmans, 1979.
NIV	New International Version
NJB	New Jerusalem Bible
NJDTh	*Neue Jahrbüche für deutsche Theologie*
NJPS	New Jewish Publication Society Version
NovT	*Novum Testamentum*
N.R.	Nieuwe Reeks, new series
NRT	*Nouvelle revue théologique*
ns	new series
NTS	*New Testament Studies*

NTT	*Norsk teologisk tidsskrift*
NZSysTh	*Neue Zeitschrift für systematische Theologie und Religionsphilosophie*
OBO	Orbis biblicus et orientalis
OED	[Oxford English Dictionary] Murray, J. A. H. *New English Dictionary on Historical Principles.* Oxford, 1888–1928. Cited from http://dictionary.oed.com/.
OLA	Orientalia lovaniensia analecta
OLP	*Orientalia lovaniensia periodica*
Olshausen	Olshausen, J. *Hiob erklärt.* 2nd ed. KEH 2. Leipzig: S. Hirzel, 1852.
OLZ	*Orientalische Literaturzeitung*
opp.	opposite (to)
Or	*Orientalia*
OrChr	*Oriens christianus*
OrdKor	*Ordens-Korrespondenz*
orig.	original, originally
OTEss	*Old Testament Essays*
OTL	Old Testament Library
OTS	*Oudtestamentische studiën*
OTWSA	*Die Ou Testamentiese Werkgemeenskap in Suid-Afrika*
PacJT	*Pacific Journal of Theology*
PalCl	*Palestra del clero*
ParSpV	*Parola, spirito e vita*
PastBl	*Pastoralblätter*
PastPsych	*Pastoral Psychology*
PatrTStud	Patristische Texte und Studien
Payne Smith	Payne Smith, R. *Thesaurus syriacus.* 2 vols. Oxford: Clarendon Press, 1879–1901.
Payne Smith, J.	Payne Smith, J. *A Compendious Syriac Dictionary, Founded upon the Thesaurus Syriacus of R. Payne Smith.* Oxford: Clarendon Press, 1903.
Peake	Peake, A. S. *Job, Introduction, Revised Version with Notes, and Index.* CB. Edinburgh: T. C. & E. C. Jack, 1905.
PEFQS	*Palestine Exploration Fund, Quarterly Statement*
PEQ	*Palestine Exploration Quarterly*
Perles	Perles, F. *Analekten zur Textkritik des Alten Testaments.* Munich: Theodor Ackermann, 1895.
Perles[2]	Perles, F. *Analekten zur Textkritik des Alten Testaments.* N.F. Leipzig: Gustav Engel, 1922.
pers.	person
PerspRelSt	*Perspectives in Religious Studies*
PerspT	*Perspectiva teológica*
Pesh	Peshitta, Syriac version of the OT
Peters	Peters, N. *Das Buch Hiob übersetzt und erklärt.* Münster: Aschendorff, 1928.
PG	*Patrologiae cursus completus. Series graeca.* Ed. J. P. Migne. 161 vols. in 166. Paris: Imprimerie catholique, 1856–1866.

PL	*Patrologiae cursus completus. Series latina.* Ed. J. P. Migne. 217 vols. Paris: Imprimerie catholique, 1844–1855.
PO	Patrologia orientalis
Pope[1]	Pope, M. H. *Job.* AB. Garden City, NY: Doubleday, 1965.
Pope	Pope, M. H. *Job.* 3rd ed. AB. Garden City, NY: Doubleday, 1973.
POTT	*Peoples of Old Testament Times.* Ed. D. J. Wiseman. London: Oxford University Press, 1973.
PrakT	*Praktische Theologie*
PrAmAcJewRes	*Proceedings of the American Academy of Jewish Research*
PrGLM	*Proceedings of the Eastern Great Lakes and Midwest Biblical Societies*
PrIrBibAss	*Proceedings of the Irish Biblical Association*
Prot	*Protestantesimo*
prp, prps	*propositum,* suggested (of a textual emendation)
PrSemBull	*Princeton Seminary Bulletin*
QDAP	*Quarterly of the Department of Antiquities in Palestine*
Qr, Q	Qere, Masoretic vocalized Hebrew text of Hebrew Bible
q.v.	*quod vide,* which see
RA	*Revue d'assyriologie*
RAC	*Reallexikon für Antike und Christentum.* Ed. T. Klauser et al. Stuttgart: A. Hiersemann, 1950–.
Rashi	Commentary printed in Rabbinic Bibles (*Miqra'ot Gedolot*)
Ravasi	Ravasi, G. *Giobbe, traduzione e commento.* Rome: Borla, 1979–1984.
RazF	*Razón y fe*
RB	*Revue biblique*
RBen	*Revue bénédictine*
RBibArg	*Revista biblica,* Buenos Aires
RBibIt	*Rivista biblica italiana*
RCatalT	*Revista catalana de teologia*
RE	*Realencyklopädie für protestantische Theologie und Kirche.* Ed. J. J. Herzog. 3rd ed. Leipzig: J. C. Hinrichs, 1896–1913.
REArmén	*Revue des études arméniennes*
RefTR	*Reformed Theological Review*
Reiske	Reiske, J. J. *Coniecturae in Jobum et Proverbia Salomonis.* Leipzig, 1779.
REJ	*Revue des études juives*
RelHum	*Religious Humanism*
RelLit	*Religion and Literature*
RelSRev	*Religious Studies Review*
RelStud	*Religious Studies*
Renan	Renan, E. *Le livre de Job, traduit de l'hébreu.* Paris: Calmann Lévy, 1860.
repr.	reprinted
RestQ	*Restoration Quarterly*
Reuss	Reuss, E. *Hiob.* Braunschweig: Schwetschke & Sohn, 1888.
RevApol	*Revue apologétique*
RevArch	*Revue archéologique*

RevEcclLiège	*Revue ecclésiastique de Liège*
RevEspTeol	*Revista española de teologia*
RevEtAug	*Revue des études augustiniennes*
RevEtGr	*Revue des études greques*
RevEthThéolMor	*Revue d'éthique et de théologie morale*
RevEtIsl	*Revue des études islamiques*
RevExp	*Review and Expositor*
RevNouv	*Revue nouvelle*
RevPhil	*Revue philosophique*
RevQ	*Revue de Qumran*
RevSémBib	*Revue sémiotique et Bible*
RevUnivOtt	*Revue de l'Université d'Ottawa*
RGG	*Die Religion in Geschichte und Gegenwart.* Ed. K. Galling. 6 vols. Tübingen: J. C. B. Mohr, 1957–1965.
RHE	*Revue d'histoire ecclésiastique*
RHPR	*Revue d'histoire et de philosophie religieuses*
RHR	*Revue de l'histoire des religions*
RHS	*Religionsunterricht an höheren Schulen*
RIBLA	*Revista de interpretação bíblica latino-americana*
Richter	Richter, G. *Textstudien zum Buche Hiob.* BWANT 3/7. Stuttgart: W. Kohlhammer, 1927.
RicR	*Ricerche religiose*
RivB	*Rivista biblica*
RL	*Religion in Life*
Rosenmüller	Rosenmüller, E. F. C. *Scholia in Vetus Testamentum. Editio secunda auctior et emendatior.* Pars V. *Jobus.* Leipzig: J. A. Barth, 1824.
Rossi, de	Rossi, G. B. de. *Variae lectiones Veteris Testamenti.* Parma: Ex regio typographeo, 1784–1798.
Rowley	Rowley, H. H. *Job.* NCB. Thomas Nelson & Sons, 1970.
RPäB	*Religionspädagogische Beiträge*
RR	*Review of Religion*
RRel	*Review for Religious*
RS	Ras Shamra
RSO	*Rivista degli studi orientali*
RSP	*Ras Shamra Parallels: The Texts from Ugarit and the Hebrew Bible.* Ed. L. R. Fisher and S. Rummel. AnOr 49–51. Rome: Pontificium Institutum Biblicum, 1972–1981.
RSPT	*Revue des sciences philosophiques et théologiques*
RSR	*Recherches de science religieuse*
RSV	Revised Standard Version
RTAM	*Recherches de théologie ancienne et médiévale*
RTL	*Revue théologique de Louvain*
RTP	*Revue de théologie et de philosophie*
RuBi	*Ruch biblijny i liturgiczny*
RV	Revised Version
S	Syriac version of the OT, Peshitta
SAB	*Sitzungsberichte der Deutschen Akademie der Wissenschaft zu Berlin*
SacDoc	*Sacra doctrina*

SANT	Studien zum Alten und Neuen Testament
SBFLA	*Studii biblici franciscani liber annuus*
SBL	Society of Biblical Literature
SBLDS	Society of Biblical Literature Dissertation Series
SBLMS	Society of Biblical Literature Monograph Series
SBLSCS	Society of Biblical Literature Septuagint and Cognate Studies
SBOT	Sacred Books of the Old Testament
SBT	Studies in Biblical Theology
sc.	scilicet, that is to say
SC	Sources chrétiennes
ScEs	*Science et esprit*
Schultens	Schultens, A. *Liber Jobi cum nova versione ad hebraeum fontem et commentario perpetuo.* Leiden: J. Luzac, 1787.
SchwTZ	*Schweizerische theologische Zeitschrift*
ScrB	*Scripture Bulletin*
ScrHieros	*Scripta hierosolymitana*
SEÅ	*Svensk exegetisk årsbok*
Sef	*Sefarad*
Selms, van	Selms, A. van. *Job.* 2 vols. Die Prediking van het OT. Nijkerk: Callenbach, 1982–1983.
Sem	*Semitica*
SémBib	*Sémiotique et Bible*
Sicre Díaz	Alonso Schökel, L., and J. L. Sicre Díaz. *Job, comentario teológico y literario.* Madrid: Cristiandad, 1983.
Siegfried	Siegfried, C. [G. A.] *The Book of Job. Critical Edition of the Hebrew Text.* SBOT. Baltimore: Johns Hopkins Press, 1893.
si v.l.	*si vera lectio,* if the reading is correct
SJT	*Scottish Journal of Theology*
Skehan	Skehan, P. W. *Studies in Israelite Poetry and Wisdom.* CBQMS 1. Washington, DC: Catholic Biblical Association of America, 1971.
Skehan–Di Lella	Skehan, P. W., and A. A. Di Lella. *The Wisdom of Ben Sira. A New Translation with Notes by Patrick W. Skehan; Introduction and Commentary by Alexander A. Di Lella.* AB 39. New York: Doubleday, 1987.
SMSR	*Studi e materiali di storia delle religioni*
Snaith	Snaith, N. H. *The Book of Job: Its Origin and Purpose.* SBT 2/11. London: SCM Press, 1968.
SNTSMS	Society for New Testament Studies Monograph Series
Soden, von	Soden, W. von. *Akkadisches Handwörterbuch.* Wiesbaden: Harrassowitz, 1965–1971.
Sokoloff	Sokoloff, M. *The Targum to Job from Qumran Cave XI.* Ramat-Gan: Bar-Ilan University Press, 1974.
SOTSMS	Society for Old Testament Study Monograph Series
SR	*Studies in Religion/Sciences religieuses*
SRSup	*Studies in Religion/Sciences religieuses* Supplements
SSEA	Society for the Study of Egyptian Antiquities
ST	*Studia theologica*
StAns	*Studia anselmiana*

StANT	Studien zum Alten und Neuen Testament
STDJ	Studies on the Texts of the Desert of Judah
Steinmann	Steinmann, J. *Job. Texte français, introduction et commentaires.* Connaître la Bible. Bruges, Paris: Desclée de Brouwer, 1961.
Steuernagel	Steuernagel, C. "Das Buch Hiob." In *Die Heilige Schrift des Alten Testaments.* Ed. E. Kautzsch and A. Bertholet. 4th ed. Tübingen: J. C. B. Mohr, 1923. 2:323–89.
Stevenson	Stevenson, W. B. *The Poem of Job. A Literary Study with a New Translation.* London: Oxford University Press, 1947.
Stevenson[2]	Stevenson, W. B. *Critical Notes on the Hebrew Text of the Book of Job.* Aberdeen: Aberdeen University Press, 1951.
Stier	Stier, F. *Das Buch Ijjob hebräisch und deutsch. Übertragen ausgelegt und mit Text- und Sacherläuterungen versehen.* Munich: Kösel, 1954.
StGen	*Studium generale*
STK	*Svensk teologisk kvartalskrift*
StLuke	*St Luke's Journal of Theology*
StOr	*Studia orientalia*
StPatr	*Studia patristica*
Strahan	Strahan, J. *The Book of Job Interpreted.* Edinburgh: T. & T. Clark, 1913.
Strauss	Strauss, Hans. *Hiob.* BKAT 16/2. Neukirchen–Vluyn: Neukirchener Verlag, 2000.
StSemNed	*Studia semitica nederlandica*
StTh	*Studia theologica,* Romania
StudMonast	*Studia monastica,* Montserrat
SUNT	Studien zur Umwelt des Neuen Testaments
s.v.	*sub verbo,* under that word
SvTK	*Svensk teologisk kvartalskrift*
SWJT	*Southwestern Journal of Theology*
Symm	Symmachus
Syr.	Syriac (language)
Szczygiel	Szczygiel, P. *Das Buch Job, übersetzt und erklärt.* HSAT. Bonn: Hanstein, 1931.
Tarb	*Tarbiz*
Taylor	Taylor, J. *The Hebrew Concordance, Adapted to the English Bible, Disposed after the Manner of Buxtorf.* London: J. Waugh & W. Fenner, 1754.
TBT	*The Bible Today*
TDig	*Theology Digest*
TDNT	*Theological Dictionary of the New Testament.* Ed. G. Kittel and G. Friedrich. Trans. G. W. Bromiley. 10 vols. Grand Rapids: Eerdmans, 1964–1976.
TDOT	*Theological Dictionary of the Old Testament.* Ed. G. J. Botterweck, H. Ringgren, and H.-J. Fabry. Trans J. T. Willis, G. W. Bromiley, and D. E. Green. 15 vols. Grand Rapids: Eerdmans, 1974–2006.
Tem	*Temenos*
Ter	*Teresianum*

Terrien	Terrien, S. L. "Job." *IB*. New York and Nashville: Abingdon Press, 1954. 3:877–1198.
TEV	Today's English Version [= Good News Bible]
Textual Notes	*Textual Notes on the New American Bible*. Paterson, NJ: St Anthony's Guild, n.d. [Pp. 325–451 of some editions.]
TGegw	*Theologie der Gegenwart*
TGl	*Theologie und Glaube*
TGUOS	*Transactions of the Glasgow University Oriental Society*
ThB	Theologische Bücherei
ThBeitr	*Theologische Beiträge*
ThBl	*Theologische Blätter*
Theod	Theodotion
Theol	*Theology*
TheolVersuche	Theologische Versuche
ThEv	*Théologie évangélique*
ThEx	*Theologische Existenz heute*
Thomas, *Lexicon*	Thomas, D. W. *A Revised Hebrew and English Lexicon of the Old Testament*. 11 vols. (*aleph* to *kaph*). (Unpublished at the author's death in 1970.)
ThRev	*Theological Review* (Beirut)
ThSz	*Theológiciai szemle*
THWAT	*Theologisches Handwörterbuch zum Alten Testament*. Ed. E. Jenni and C. Westermann. 2 vols. Munich: Kaiser, 1971.
ThZ	*Theologische Zeitschrift*
TLOT	*Theological Lexicon of the Old Testament*. Ed. E. Jenni and C. Westermann. Trans. M. E. Biddle. 3 vols. Peabody, MA: Hendrickson, 1997 [translation of *THWAT*].
TLZ	*Theologische Literaturzeitung*
TOB	*Traduction oecuménique de la Bible*
Torczyner	Torczyner, H. [Tur-Sinai, N. H.]. *Das Buch Hiob. Eine kritische Analyse des überlieferten Hiobtextes*. Vienna: R. Löwit, 1920.
TOTC	Tyndale Old Testament Commentaries
TPM	*Theologische-praktische Monatsschrift*
TPQ	*Theologische-praktische Quartalschrift*
TQ	*Theologische Quartalschrift*
TRE	*Theologische Realenzyklopädie*. Ed. G. Krause and G. Müller. 36 vols. Berlin, 1977–2006.
TRev	*Theologische Revue*
TrierThStud	Trierer theologische Studien
TrinJ	*Trinity Journal*
Tristram, *Natural History*	Tristram, H. B. *The Natural History of the Bible: Being a Review of the Physical Geography, Geology and Meteorology of the Holy Land; with a Description of Every Animal and Plant Mentioned in Holy Scripture*. 9th ed. London: Society for Promoting Christian Knowledge, 1898 (orig. 1867).
TRu	*Theologische Rundschau*
TS	*Theological Studies*
TSK	*Theologische Studien und Kritiken*
TTijd	*Theologische tijdschrift*

TTKi	*Tidskrift for teologi og kirche*
TTod	*Theology Today*
TTQ	*Tübinger theologischer Quartalschrift*
TTZ	*Trierer theologische Zeitschrift*
Tur-Sinai	Tur-Sinai, N. H. *The Book of Job, A New Commentary.* Jerusalem: Kiryath-Sepher, 1957.
TVers	*Theologische Versuche*
TWNT	*Theologische Wörterbuch zum Neuen Testament.* Ed. G. Kittel and G. Friedrich. Stuttgart: Kohlhammer Verlag, 1932–1979.
TynB	*Tyndale Bulletin*
TZ	*Theologische Zeitschrift*
UF	*Ugarit-Forschungen*
Ugar.	Ugaritic
Ugaritica V	Nougayrol, J. *Ugaritica V: Nouveaux textes accadiens, hourrites et ugaritiques des archives et bibliothèques privées d'Ugarit: Commentaires des textes historiques (première partie).* Bibliothèque archéologique et historique 80; Mission de Ras Shamra 16. Paris: Imprimerie Nationale, 1968.
Umbreit	Umbreit, F. W. C. *Das Buch Hiob: Übersetzung und Auslegung nebst Einleitung über Geist, Form und Verfasser des Buchs.* 2nd ed. Heidelberg: J. C. B. Mohr, 1832.
USQR	*Union Seminary Quarterly Review*
VD	*Verbum domini*
VerbEccl	*Verbum et ecclesia*
VetChr	*Vetera christiana*
VF	*Verkündigung und Forschung*
Vg	Vulgate
VigChr	*Vigiliae christianae*
v.l.	*varia lectio,* alternative reading
Voigt	Voigt, C. *Einige Stellen des Buches Hiob.* Leipzig: W. Drugulin, 1895.
Volz	Volz, P. *Weisheit (Das Buch Hiob, Sprüche und Jesus Sirach, Prediger).* 2nd ed. Göttingen: Vandenhoeck & Ruprecht, 1921.
VS	*Vie spirituelle*
VT	*Vetus Testamentum*
VTSup	*Vetus Testamentum,* Supplements
VTSup	*Vetus Testamentum,* Supplements (when book title is not also cited)
VyV	*Verdad y vida*
Wagner	Wagner, M. *Die lexikalischen und grammatikalischen Aramaismen im alttestamentlichen Hebräisch.* BZAW 96. Berlin: Alfred Töpelmann, 1966.
Waltke and O'Connor	Waltke, B. K., and M. O'Connor. *An Introduction to Biblical Hebrew Syntax.* Winona Lake, IN: Eisenbrauns, 1990.
Watson	Watson, W. G. E. *Classical Hebrew Poetry: A Guide to Its Techniques.* JSOTSup 26. Sheffield: JSOT Press, 1984.
WC	Westminster Commentaries

Webster	Webster, E. C. "Strophic Patterns in Job 3–28." *JSOT* 26 (1983) 33–60; "Strophic Patterns in Job 29–42." *JSOT* 30 (1984) 95–109.
Wehr–Cowan	Wehr, Hans. *A Dictionary of Modern Written Arabic.* Ed. J. Milton Cowan. Beirut: Librarie du Liban, 1980.
Weiser	Weiser, A. *Das Buch Hiob übersetzt und erklärt.* ATD. Göttingen: Vandenhoeck & Ruprecht, 1951.
Westermann	Westermann, C. *The Structure of the Book of Job: A Form-Critical Analysis.* Trans. C. A. Muenchow. Philadelphia: Fortress Press, 1981.
Whybray	Whybray, Norman. *Job.* Readings. Sheffield: JSOT Press, 1998.
Wilde, de	Wilde, A. de. *Das Buch Hiob eingeleitet, übersetzt und erläutert.* OTS 22. Leiden: E. J. Brill, 1981.
WMANT	Wissenschaftliche Monographien zum Alten und Neuen Testament
WO	*Die Welt des Orients*
Wolfers	Wolfers, D. *Deep Things out of Darkness. The Book of Job: Essays and a New English Translation.* Kampen: Kok Pharos and Grand Rapids: Eerdmans, 1995.
Wor	*Worship,* Collegeville, MN
Wright	Wright, G. H. B. *The Book of Job.* London: Williams & Norgate, 1883.
WTJ	*Westminster Theological Journal*
WuD	*Wort und Dienst*
WZ…	*Wissenschaftliche Zeitschrift …*
WZKM	*Wiener Zeitschrift für die Kunde des Morgenlandes*
Yellin	Yellin, D. הקרי־מקרא. Jerusalem, 1927.
ZA	*Zeitschrift für Assyriologie*
ZAC	*Zeitschrift für antikes Christentum*
ZAR	*Zeitschrift für altorientalische und biblische Rechtsgeschichte*
ZAW	*Zeitschrift für die alttestamentliche Wissenschaft*
ZDMG	*Zeitschrift der deutschen morgenländischen Gesellschaft*
ZDMGS	*Zeitschrift der deutschen morgenländischen Gesellschaft,* Supplement
ZDPV	*Zeitschrift des deutschen Palästina-Vereins*
ZeichZt	*Die Zeichen der Zeit*
ZKT	*Zeitschrift für katholische Theologie*
Zorell	Zorell, Franz. *Lexicon hebraicum et aramaicum Veteris Testamenti.* Rome: Pontifical Biblical Institute, 1984 (original 1946).
ZRGG	*Zeitschrift für Religions- und Geistesgeschichte*
ZST	*Zeitschrift für die systematische Theologie*
ZTK	*Zeitschrift für Theologie und Kirche*
ZZ	*Zwischen den Zeiten*

Biblical (including Apocryphal) Books

Gen	Genesis	Num	Numbers
Exod	Exodus	Deut	Deuteronomy
Lev	Leviticus	Josh	Joshua

Judg	Judges	Sus	Susanna
Ruth	Ruth	1–2 Esd	1–2 Esdras
1–2 Sam	1–2 Samuel	Tob	Tobit
1–2 Kgs	1–2 Kings	Jdt	Judith
1–2 Chr	1–2 Chronicles	Wisd	Wisdom of Solomon
Ezra	Ezra	Ecclus	Ecclesiasticus or Wisdom
Neh	Nehemiah		of Jesus son of Sirach
Esth	Esther	Bar	Baruch
Job	Job	1–2 Macc	1–2 Maccabees
Ps(s)	Psalm(s)	Matt	Matthew
Prov	Proverbs	Mark	Mark
Eccl	Ecclesiastes	Luke	Luke
Cant	Canticles	John	John
Isa	Isaiah	Acts	Acts
Jer	Jeremiah	Rom	Romans
Lam	Lamentations	1–2 Cor	1–2 Corinthians
Ezek	Ezekiel	Gal	Galatians
Dan	Daniel	Eph	Ephesians
Hos	Hosea	Phil	Philippians
Joel	Joel	Col	Colossians
Amos	Amos	1–2 Thess	1–2 Thessalonians
Obad	Obadiah	1–2 Tim	1–2 Timothy
Jonah	Jonah	Titus	Titus
Mic	Micah	Phlm	Philemon
Nah	Nahum	Heb	Hebrews
Hab	Habakkuk	James	James
Zeph	Zephaniah	1–2 Pet	1–2 Peter
Hag	Haggai	1–2–3 John	1–2–3 John
Zech	Zechariah	Jude	Jude
Mal	Malachi	Rev	Revelation

JEWISH LITERATURE

1QBer	*Berakot*	*Ber.*	*Berakot*
1QH	*Hymn Scroll* from Qumran	*Gen. Rabb.*	*Genesis Rabbah*
1QM	*War Scroll* from Qumran	*Midr.*	*Midrash*
1QpHab	*Pesher Habakkuk*	*Midr. Rabb.*	*Midrash Rabbah*
1QS	*Manual of Discipline*	*Mo'ed Qat.*	*Mo'ed Qatan*
4QBark[a]	*Barkhi Nafshi[a]* (4Q434)	*Qidd.*	*Qiddushin*
4QShirShabb[d]	*Songs of the Sabbath Sacrifice*	*T. Job*	*Testament of Job*
	(4Q403)	*T. Jos.*	*Testament of Joseph*
4QWiles	*Wiles of the Wicked Woman*	*T. Levi*	*Testament of Levi*
	(4Q184)		
11QtgJob	Targum of Job from		
	Qumran, Cave 11		
1 Enoch	*1 Enoch (Ethiopic Apocalypse)*		
2 Bar.	*2 Baruch (Syriac Apocalypse)*		
b.	Babylonian Talmud		
B. Bat	*Baba Bathra*		

Hebrew Grammar

abs	absolute	juss	jussive
acc	accusative	masc	masculine
cohort	cohortative	neut	neuter
consec	consecutive	niph	niphal
constr	construct	obj	object
fem	feminine	pass	passive
fut	future	perf	perfect
gen	genitive	pers	person
haplog	haplography	pilp	pilpel
hiph	hiphil	pl	plural
hithp	hithpael	pron	pronoun
hithpo	hithpolal, hithpolel	ptcp	participle
hoph	hophal	sg	singular
impf	imperfect	subj	subject
impv	imperative	suff	suffix
inf	infinitive	trans	transitive
intrans	intransitive	vb	verb

Yahweh's First Speech (38:1–40:2)

Bibliography: 38:1–40:2; 40:6–41:34 (26) (Yahweh's Speeches)

Alonso Schökel, L. "La respuesta de Dios." *Conc* 19/189 (1983) 392–402. **Alter, Robert.** "The Voice from the Whirlwind" [poetry of Job 38–41]. *Commentary* 77 (1984) 33–41 [see also rejoinder by Robert Gordis]. **Amu, Ifeoma C. M.** *Voice from Heaven and Earth: A Literary and Conceptual Exploration between Job 3 and 38:1–41:34.* Diss. Candler, Atlanta, 2000. **Balentine, Samuel E.** "'What are human beings, that you make so much of them?' Divine Disclosure from the Whirlwind: 'Look at Behemoth'." In *God in the Fray: A Tribute to Walter Brueggemann.* Ed. Tod Linafelt and Timothy K. Beal. Minneapolis: Fortress Press, 1998. 259–78. **Bergfalk, Bradley J.** "When God Speaks: God and Nature in the Divine Speeches of Job." In *To Hear and Obey: Essays in Honor of Fredrick Carlson Holmgren.* Ed. Bradley K. Bergfalk and Paul E. Koptak. [= *Covenant Quarterly* 55 (1997)] 75–83. **Bochart, Samuel.** *Hierozoicon sive bipartitum opus de animalibus Sacrae Scripturae.* London: Thomas Roycroft, 1663. **Boecker, H. J.** *Redeformen des Rechtslebens im Alten Testament.* WMANT 14. Neukirchen–Vluyn: Neukirchener Verlag, 1964. **Bonora, Antonio.** "Le ragioni di Giobbe e la ragione di Dio. Il discorso di Dio in Gb 38–42." *Humanitas* 48 (1993) 179–91. **Brenner, Athalya.** "God's Answer to Job." *VT* 31 (1981) 129–37. **Brüning, C.** "Kleine Schule des Staunens. Die Gottesrede im Ijobbuch." *Erbe und Auftrag* 72 (1996) 385–413. **Burrows, Millar.** "The Voice from the Whirlwind." *JBL* 47 (1928) 117–32. **Clements, Ronald E.** "Wisdom." In *"It Is Written": Scripture Citing Scripture. Essays in Honour of Barnabas Lindars, SSF.* Ed. D. A. Carson and H. G. M. Williamson. Cambridge: Cambridge University Press, 1988. 67–83. **Dailey, Thomas F.** "Theophanic Bluster: Job and the Wind of Change" [Job 38:1–42:6]. *SR* 22 (1993) 187–95. **Dick, Michael B.** "The Neo-Assyrian Royal Lion Hunt and Yahweh's Answer to Job." *JBL* 125 (2006) 243–70. **Fadeji, Samuel Olaniran.** *A Critical and Interpretative Study of the Yahweh Speeches in Job 38–41.* Diss. Southern Baptist Theological Seminary, 1980. **Fohrer, G.** "Gottes Antwort aus dem Sturmwind (Hi 38–41)." *TZ* 18 (1962) 1–24 [= his *Studien zum Buche Hiob (1956–1979).* BZAW 159. Berlin: de Gruyter, 1963. 2nd ed., 1983. 114–34]. **Fuchs, Gisela.** *Mythos und Hiobdichtung: Aufnahme und Umdeutung altorientalischer Vorstellungen.* Stuttgart: W. Kohlhammer, 1993. 189–264. **Gordis, Robert.** "The Lord out of the Whirlwind: The Climax and Meaning of Job." *Judaism* 13 (1964) 48–63. **Gowan, Donald E.** "God's Answer to Job: How Is It an Answer?" *HBT* 8 (1986) 85–102. **Greenstein, Edward L.** "A Forensic Understanding of the Speech from the Whirlwind." In *Texts, Temples, and Traditions: A Tribute to Menahem Haran.* Ed. Michael V. Fox, Victor Avigdor Hurowitz, and Avi Hurvitz. Winona Lake, IN: Eisenbrauns, 1996. 241–58. **Han, Jin Hee.** *Yahweh Replies to Job: Yahweh's Speeches in the Book of Job, A Case of Resumptive Rhetoric.* Diss. Princeton Theological Seminary, 1988. **Illman, Karl-Johan.** "Did God Answer Job?" In *"Lasset uns Brücken bauen ..." Collected Communications to the XVth Congress of the International Organization for the Study of the Old Testament, Cambridge 1995.* Ed. Klaus-Dietrich Schunck and Matthias Augustin. BEATAJ 42. Frankfurt a.M.: Peter Lang, 1998. 275–85. **Jakubiec, C.** "Objawienie Boze w Ksiedze Hioba [The Theophany in the Book of Job]." *RuBi* 26 (1973) 248–61. **Keel, Othmar.** *Jahwes Entgegnung an Ijob: Eine Deutung von Ijob 38–41 vor dem Hintergrund der zeitgenössischen Bildkunst.* FRLANT 121. Göttingen: Vandenhoeck & Ruprecht, 1978 [= *Dieu répond à Job: une interprétation de Job 38–41 à la lumière de l'iconographie du Proche-Orient ancien.* Paris: Cerf, 1993]. **Keel, Othmar, and Max Küchler.** "Wilde Tiere." In their *Orte und Landschaften der Bibel: Ein Handbuch und Studien- Reiseführer zum Heiligen Land.* Zurich: Benziger; Göttingen: Vandenhoeck & Ruprecht, 1982. 1:143–64. **Kegler, Jürgen.** "'Gürte wie ein Mann deine Lenden! ...': Die Gottesreden im Ijob-Buch als Aufforderung zur aktiven Auseinandersetzung mit dem

Leid." In *Nachdenken über Israel, Bibel und Theologie. Festschrift für Klaus-Dietrich Schunck zu seinem 65. Geburtstag*. Ed. H. Michael Niemann, Matthias Augustin, and Werner H. Schmidt. BEATAJ 37. Frankfurt a.M.: Peter Lang, 1994. 217–34. **Köhlmoos, Melanie.** *Das Auge Gottes: Textstrategie im Hiobbuch*. FAT 25. Tübingen: Mohr Siebeck, 1999. 66–68, 321–54. **Kubina, Veronica.** *Die Gottesreden in Buche Hiob. Ein Beitrag zur Diskussion um die Einheit von Hiob 38,1–42,6*. FrThSt 115. Freiburg i.Br.: Herder, 1979. **Kutsch, Ernst.** "Unschuldsbekenntnis und Gottesbegegnung. Der Zusammenhang zwischen Hiob 31 und 38ff." In his *Kleine Schriften zum Alten Testament*. Ed. Ludwig Schmidt and Karl Eberlein. BZAW 168. Berlin: Walter de Gruyter, 1986. 308–35. **Lang, Bernhard.** "Ein Kranker sieht seinen Gott. Leidenswelt und Leidenswende im Buch Ijob [38–41]." In *Der Mensch unter dem Kreuz: Wegweisung, Erfahrungen, Hilfen*. Ed. Reinhold Bärenz. Regensburg: Pustet, 1980. 35–48 [= "Ein Kranker sieht seinen Gott." In Bernhard Lang. *Wie wird man Prophet in Israel? Aufsätze zum Alten Testament*. Düsseldorf: Patmos Verlag, 1980. 137–48]. **Lévêque, Jean.** "L'interprétation des discours de YHWH (Job 38,1–42,6)." In *The Book of Job*. Ed. W. A. M. Beuken. BETL 114. Leuven: Leuven University Press, 1994. 203–22. **Lillie, William.** "The Religious Significance of the Theophany in the Book of Job." *ExpT* 68 (1956–57) 355–58. **Luc, A.** "Storm and the Message of Job." *JSOT* 87 (2000) 111–23. **Lundberg, Marilyn Jean.** *"So that hidden things may be brought to light": A Concept Analysis of the Yahweh Speeches in the Book of Job*. Diss. Claremont, 1995. **MacKenzie, R. A. F.** "The Purpose of the Yahweh Speeches in the Book of Job." *Bib* 40 (1959) 435–45. **Martin-Achard, Robert.** *Et Dieu crée le ciel et la terre: trois études: Esaïe 40–Job 38–42–Genèse 1*. Essais bibliques 2. Geneva: Editions Labor & Fides, 1979. **Mettinger, Tryggve N. D.** "Söderlund och Job ännu en gång" [reply to his "Den svårupptäckta kaoskampen"]. *SvTK* 64 (1988) 139–40. **Morriston, Wesley.** "God's Answer to Job." *RelSt* 32 (1996) 339–56. **Müller, Hans-Peter.** "Gottes Antwort an Ijob und das Recht religiöser Wahrheit." *BZ* ns 32 (1988) 210–31. **Muñoz [Mu Hung-chich], J.** "Yüehposhuchung 'Yawei hsienhsien' de shenhsüeh [Theology of the Theophany in the Book of Job]." *ColcTFu* 5/20 (1974) 155–63. **Nel, P. J.** "Cosmos and Chaos: A Reappraisal of the Divine Discourses in the Book of Job." *OTEss* 4 (1991) 206–26. **Nel, P. J., and N. F. Schmidt.** "The Rhetoric of the Theophany of Job." *OTEss* 16 (2003) 79–95. **Newsom, Carol A.** "The Moral Sense of Nature: Ethics in the Light of God's Speech to Job." *PrSemBull* 15 (1994) 9–27. **Nicholson, E. W.** "The Limits of Theodicy as a Theme of the Book of Job." In *Wisdom in Ancient Israel: Essays in Honour of J. A. Emerton*. Ed. John Day, Robert P. Gordon, and H. G. M. Williamson. Cambridge: Cambridge University Press, 1995. 71–82. **O'Connor, Daniel.** "The Futility of Myth-Making in Theodicy: Job 38–41." *PrIrBibAss* 9 (1985) 81–99. **Oeming, Manfred.** "'Kannst du der Lowin ihren Raub zu jagen geben?' (Hi 38:39): Das Motiv der 'Herrn der Tiere' und seine Bedeutung fur die Theologie der Gottesreden Hi 38–42." In *"Dort ziehen Schiffe dahin ...": Collected Communications to the XIVth Congress of the International Organization for the Study of the Old Testament, Paris, 1992*. Ed. Matthias Augustin and Klaus-Dietrich Schunck. Frankfurt a.M.: Peter Lang, 1996. 147–63. **Oorschot, Jürgen van.** *Gott als Grenze: Eine literar- und redaktionsgeschichtliche Studie zu den Gottesreden des Hiobbuches*. BZAW 170. Berlin: de Gruyter, 1987. **Parke, Ivan David.** *The Literary Role of the Yahweh Speeches in the Book of Job*. Diss. New Orleans Baptist Theological Seminary, 1997. **Patrick, Dale.** "Divine Creative Power and the Decentering of Creation: The Subtext of the Lord's Addresses to Job." In *The Earth Story in Wisdom Traditions*. Ed. N. C. Habel and S. Wurst. Earth Bible 3. Sheffield: Sheffield Academic Press, 2001. 103–15. **Pidcock-Lester, Karen.** "'Earth has no sorrow that earth cannot heal': Job 38–41." In *God Who Creates. Essays in Honor of W. Sibley Towner*. Ed. William P. Brown and S. Dean McBride, Jr. Grand Rapids: Eerdmans, 2000. 125–32. **Pleins, J. David.** "'Why Do You Hide Your Face?' Divine Silence and Speech in the Book of Job." *Int* 48 (1994) 229–38. **Preuss, Horst Dietrich.** "Jahwes Antwort an Hiob und die sogenannte Hiobliteratur des alten Vorderen Orients." In *Beiträge zum alttestamentliche Theologie: Festschrift für W. Zimmerli zum 70. Geburtstag*. Ed. Herbert Donner,

Robert Hanhart, and Rudolf Smend. Göttingen: Vandenhoeck & Ruprecht, 1977. 323–43. **Priest, John.** "Job and J.B.: The Goodness of God or the Godness of Good?" *Horizons* 12 (1985) 265–83. **Richter, Heinz.** "Die Naturweisheit des Alten Testaments in Buche Hiob." *ZAW* 70 (1958) 1–20. **Rowley, H. H.** "The Book of Job and Its Meaning." *BJRL* 41 (1958–59) 167–207 [= his *From Moses to Qumran: Studies in the Old Testament*. London: Lutterworth, 1963. 139–83]. **Rowold, Henry Lawrence.** *The Theology of Creation in the Yahweh Speeches of the Book of Job as a Solution to the Problem Posed by the Book of Job.* Diss. Concordia Seminary in Exile (Seminex), 1977. **Sacks, Robert D.** "The Book of Job: Translation and Commentary on Chapters 32 through 38." *IntJPolPhilos* 25 (1998) 293–329. ———. "The Book of Job: Translation and Commentary on Chapters 39 through 42." *IntJPolPhilos* 26 (1998) 21–63. **Sarrazin, Bernard.** "Du rire dans la Bible? La théophanie de Job comme parodie." *RSR* 76 (1988) 39–56. **Sawicki, M.** "Technological Imagery in the Yahweh Speeches: What Did Job See?" *TBT* 91 (1977) 1304–10. **Scholnick, Sylvia Huberman.** "Poetry in the Courtroom: Job 38–41." In *Directions in Biblical Hebrew Poetry*. Ed. Elaine R. Follis. JSOTSup 40. Sheffield: JSOT Press, 1987. 185–204 [= Roy B. Zuck (ed.). *Sitting with Job: Selected Studies on the Book of Job*. Grand Rapids: Baker Book House, 1992. 421–40]. **Skehan, Patrick W.** "Job's Final Plea (Job 29–31) and the Lord's Reply (Job 38–41)." *Bib* 45 (1964) 51–62 [= his *Studies in Israelite Poetry and Wisdom*. CBQMS 1. Washington, DC: Catholic Biblical Association of America. 1971. 114–23]. **Smick, Elmer B.** "Architectonics, Structured Poems, and Rhetorical Devices in the Book of Job" [incl. 13:28–14:6; 27–31; 38–41]. In *A Tribute to Gleason Archer*. Ed. Walter C. Kaiser, Jr, and Ronald F. Youngblood. Chicago: Moody Press, 1986. 87–104. **Söderlund, Rune.** "Den svarupptäckta kaoskampen: Svar tillk Tryggve Mettinger angaende Jobsbokens gudsbild." *SvTK* 64 (1988) 91–92. **Spieckermann, Hermann.** "Der Satanisierung Gottes. Zur inneren Konkordanz von Novelle, Dialog und Gottesreden in Hiobbuch." In *"Wer ist wie du, Herr, unter den Göttern?" Studien zur Theologie und Religionsgeschichte Israels für Otto Kaiser zum 70. Geburtstag.* Ed. Ingo Kottsieper, Jürgen van Oorschot, and Diethard Römheld. Göttingen: Vandenhoeck & Ruprecht, 1994. 432–44. **Swanepoel, M. G.** "Job 12—An(other) Anticipation of the Voice from the Whirlwind?" *OTEss* ns 4 (1991) 192–205. **Terrien, Samuel L.** "The Yahweh Speeches and Job's Responses." *RevExp* 68 (1971) 497–509. **Tsevat, Matitiahu.** "The Meaning of the Book of Job." *HUCA* 37 (1966) 73–106 [= his *The Meaning of the Book of Job and Other Biblical Studies: Essays on the Literature and Religion of the Hebrew Bible*. New York: Ktav, 1980. 1–37; *Studies in Ancient Israelite Wisdom: Selected with a Prolegomenon*. Ed. James L. Crenshaw. New York: Ktav, 1976. 341–74; *Sitting with Job: Selected Studies on the Book of Job*. Ed. Roy B. Zuck. Grand Rapids: Baker Book House, 1992. 189–218; also *The Fourth World Congress of Jewish Studies*. 1967. 1:177–80]. **Unsvag, H. H.** "Gudstalene i Jobs bok—monolog eller dialog?" *TTKi* 65 (1994) 81–96. ———. "Men nå har jeg sett med egne Øyne." *TTKi* 64 (1993) 21–37. **Vaage, L. E.** "Do meio da tempestade: a resposta de Deus a Jó: sabedoría bíblica, ecologia moderna, vida marginal: uma leitura de Jó 38,1–42,6." *RIBLA* 21 (1995) 199–213. **Vermeylen, Jacques.** "'Connais-tu les lois des cieux?' Une lecture de Job 38–41." *FoiTemps* 20 (1990) 197–210. **Viviers, Hendrik, and L. M. Jacobs.** "Pinksterhantering van lyding in die lig van die godsredes in die boek Job (Job 38:1–42:6)." *Ekklesiastikos Pharos* 83/1 (2001) 1–14 . **Viviers, Hendrik, and R. Maarschalk.** "Die godsredes in die boek Job, ideologie en eko-teologie." *VerbEccl* 23/1 (2002) 125–40. **Viviers, Hennie.** "How Does God Fare in the Divine Speeches (Job 38:1–42:6)?" *OTEss* 10 (1997) 109–24. **Webster, Edwin C.** "Strophic Patterns in Job 29–42." *JSOT* 30 (1984) 95–109. **Weigart, Mazal.** "God's Reply to Job." *Dor* 3 (1974) 25–29. **Westermann, Claus.** *Der Aufbau des Buches Hiob.* Tübingen: J. C. B. Mohr (Paul Siebeck), 1956; 3rd ed., Stuttgart: Calwer Verlag, 1978. 108–24 [= *The Structure of the Book of Job: A Form-Critical Analysis*. Trans. Charles A. Muenchow. Philadelphia: Fortress Press, 1981]. **Williams, J. G.** "Deciphering the Unspoken: The Theophany of Job." *HUCA* 49 (1978) 59–72 [= *Sitting with Job: Selected Studies on the Book of Job*. Ed. Roy B. Zuck. Grand Rapids: Baker

Book House, 1992. 359–72]. ———. "Job's Vision: The Dialectic of Person and Presence." *HAR* 8 (1984) 259–72 [= *Biblical and Other Essays in Honor of Sheldon H. Blank*. Ed. Reuben Ahroni]. **Wolfers, David.** "Science in the Book of Job." *JBQ* 19 (1990–91) 18–21. **Würthwein, E.** *Gott und Mensch in Dialog und Gottesreden des Buches Hiob.* Habilitationsschrift, Tübingen, 1938. **Zamodi, J.** "מענה אלהים לאיוב"—The Answer of God to Job." *BMik* 119 (1988–99) 302–11.

Bibliography: 38:1–40:2 (Yahweh's First Speech)

Anon. *A Paraphrase of the Thirty-Eighth Chapter of Job.* Chesterfield: J. Bradley, 1778; London: J. Parker, 1779. **Are, Tom, Jr.** "Between Text and Sermon: Job 38:1–7." *Int* 53 (1999) 294–98. **Bekar, Shlomo.** "מענה י׳ לאיוב" [Yhwh's Reply to Job]." *BMik* 25,80 (1979) 25–29. **Bezuidenhout, L. C.** "Struktuur en strekking van Job 38:39–39:30." *HervTS* 43 (1987) 709–22. **Broome, William.** "Part of the 38th and 39th Chapters of Job: A Paraphrase." In his *Poems on Several Occasions.* London: Henry Lintot, 2nd ed., 1739. **Crenshaw, James L.** "When Form and Content Clash: The Theology of Job 38:1–40:5." In *Creation in the Biblical Traditions.* Ed. Richard J. Clifford and John J. Collins. CBQMS 24. Washington, DC: Catholic Biblical Association of America, 1992. 70–84 [= his *Urgent Advice and Probing Questions: Collected Writings on Old Testament Wisdom.* Macon, GA: Mercer University Press, 1995. 455–67]. **Dahood, M. J.** "Hebrew-Ugaritic Lexicography X." *Bib* 53 (1972) 386–403. ———. "Is Eben Yiśrā'el a Divine Title?" *Bib* 40 (1959) 1002–5. ———. "Northwest Semitic Philology and Job." In *The Bible in Current Catholic Thought: Gruenthaner Memorial Volume.* Ed. J. L. McKenzie. St Mary's Theological Studies 1. New York: Herder & Herder, 1962. 55–74. ———. "Philological Notes on Jer 18,14–15." *ZAW* 74 (1962) 207–9. **Driver, G. R.** "Birds in the Old Testament. I. Birds in Law." *PEQ* 87 (1955) 5–20. ———. "Birds in the Old Testament. II. Birds in Life." *PEQ* 87 [1955] 129–40. ———. "Problems in Job." *AJSL* 52 (1936) 160–70. ———. "Problems in the Hebrew Text of Job." In *Wisdom in Israel and in the Ancient Near East, Presented to Professor Harold Henry Rowley … in Celebration of His Sixty-Fifth Birthday.* VTSup 3. Leiden: E. J. Brill, 1955. 72–93. ———. "Two Astronomical Passages in the Old Testament." *JTS* ns 7 (1956) 1–11. **Duguet, [J. J.] and [J. V. Bidel] d'Asfeld.** *Explication de l'ouvrage des six jours, où on a joint les explications des chapîtres XXXVIII et XXXIX de Job, et des pseaumes [sic] XVIII et CIII, qui traitent de la même matière.* Paris: François Babuty, 1736. 263–344. **Dunphy, Graeme.** "Rabengefieder–Elefantengezisch: Naturdeutung in der mitteldeutschen Hiob-Paraphrase." In *Natur und Kultur in der deutschen Literatur des Mittelalters (Proceedings of the 1997 Exeter Colloquium).* Ed. Alan Robertshaw and Gerhard Wolf. Tübingen: Niemeyer, 1999. 91–102. **Fox, M. V.** "Job 38 and God's Rhetoric." *Semeia* 19 (1981) 53–61. **Horne, Milton.** "From Ethics to Aesthetics. The Animals in Job 38:39–39:30." *RevExp* 102 (2005) 127–42. **Jamieson-Drake, David W.** "Literary Structure, Genre and Interpretation in Job 38." In *The Listening Heart: Essays in Wisdom and the Psalms in Honor of Roland E. Murphy, O. Carm.* Ed. Kenneth G. Hoglund, Elizabeth F. Huwiler, Jonathan T. Glass, and Roger W. Lee. JSOTSup 58. Sheffield: Sheffield Academic Press, 1987. 217–35. **Kaltner, John.** *The Use of Arabic in Biblical Hebrew Lexicography.* CBQMS 28. Washington, DC: The Catholic Biblical Association of America, 1996. **Keel, Othmar.** "Die höchsten Berge sind dem Steinbock: über das Verständnis von Natur und Boden im Alten Testament" [interview]. *Reformatio* 37 (1988) 34–39. **Kis, A. Zaradija.** "Particularités des traductions de l'Ancien Testament dans le glagolisme croate (Job 38–39)." In *The Interpretation of the Bible: The International Symposium in Slovenia.* Ed. Jože Krašovec. JSOTSup 289. Sheffield: Sheffield Academic Press, 1998. 1015–29. **Lévêque, J.** "'Et Jahweh répondit à Job'–Job 38,1." *Foi vivante* 7,28 (1966) 72–77. **Lüling, Alfred.** … *Als ich die Erde gründete. Hiob 38,4.* Wuppertal: Brockhaus, 1953. **Malchow, Bruce.** "Nature from God's Perspective: Job 38–39." *Dialog* 21 (1982) 130–33. **Miller, James E.** "Structure and Meaning of the Animal Discourse in the Theophany of Job (38,39–39,30)." *ZAW* 103 (1991) 418–21. **Passoni dell'Acqua,**

Anna. "La Sapienza e in genere l'elemento intermedio tra Dio e il creato nelle versioni greche dell'Antico Testamento: Giob. 28 e 38." *EphLit* 98 (1984) 270–322. **Pellauer, David.** "Reading Ricoeur Reading Job." *Semeia* 19 (1981) 73–83. **Rad, G. von.** "Hiob 38 und die altägyptische Weisheit." In *Wisdom in Israel and in the Ancient Near East, Presented to Professor Harold Henry Rowley ... in Celebration of His Sixty-Fifth Birthday, 24 March 1955.* Ed. M. Noth and D. Winton Thomas. VTSup 3. Leiden: E. J. Brill, 1955. 292–301 [= "Job xxxviii and Ancient Egyptian Wisdom." In his *The Problem of the Hexateuch and Other Essays.* Edinburgh: Oliver & Boyd, 1966. 281–91; "Job 38 and Ancient Israelite Wisdom." In *Studies in Ancient Israelite Wisdom: Selected with a Prolegomenon.* Ed. J. L. Crenshaw. New York: Ktav, 1976. 267–77.] ———. *From Genesis to Chronicles: Explorations in Old Testament Theology.* Ed. K. C. Hanson. Minneapolis: Fortress Press, 2005. **Reymond, Philippe.** *L'eau, sa vie, et sa signification dans l'Ancien Testament.* VTSup 6. Leiden: E. J. Brill, 1958. **Ritter, Petra.** "Die Verben der Gottesrede in Ijob 38 und 39: Eine formal-statistische Untersuchung." In *Liebe zum Wort: Beiträge zur klassischen und biblischen Philologie, P. Ludger Bernhard OSB zum 80. Geburtstag dargebracht von Kollegen und Schülern.* Ed. Friedrich V. Reiterer and Petrus Eder. Salzburg: Otto Müller Verlag, 1993. 215–37. **Ritter-Müller, Petra.** *Kennst du die Welt? Gottes Antwort an Ijob. Eine sprachwissenschaftliche und exegetische Studie zur ersten Gottesrede Ijob 38 und 39.* Altes Testament und Moderne 5. Münster: LIT, 2000. **Rowold, Henry.** "Yahweh's Challenge to Rival: The Form and Function of the Yahweh-Speech in Job 38–39." *CBQ* 47 (1985) 199–211. **Sadler, Ralph.** "A Translation of Job XXXVIII." In his *Vox clamantis ...* London: K. Paul, Trench, Trübner, & Co., 1891. **Schneider, Thomas.** "Hiob 38 und die demotische Weisheit (Papyrus Insinger 24)." *TZ* 47 (1991) 108–24. **Schroer, Silvia.** "In die Enge getrieben—in die Weite geführt. Hiobs Klage und die erste Gottesrede (Hiob 3 und 38–39)." In *Hiob. Ökumenischer Arbeitskreis für Bibelarbeit.* Ed. Regina Berger-Lutz. Bibelarbeit in der Gemeinde 7. Basel: F. Reinhardt, 1989. 128–60. **Tönsing, Detlev L.** "The Use of Creation Language in Job 3, 9 and 38 and the Meaning of Suffering." *Scriptura* 59 (1996) 435–49. **Vinel, Françoise.** "Job 38: Le commentaire de Julien l'arien et les interprétations cappadociennes." In *Le Livre de Job chez les Pères.* Cahiers de Biblia patristica 5. Strasbourg: Centre d'Analyse et de Documentation Patristiques, 1996. 163–75. **Wheeler, David.** "Job 38:1–40:2. Rain on a Land Where No One Lives, Oxen Who Won't Plow Your Field." *RevExp* 96 (1999) 441–50. **Williamson, H. G. M.** "A Reconsideration of עוש II in Biblical Hebrew." *ZAW* 97 (1985) 74–85. **Wilson, Lindsay.** "Job 38–39 and Biblical Theology." *RefTR* 62 (2003) 121–38. **Wolde, Ellen van.** "Ancient Wisdoms, Present Insights. A Study of Job 28 and Job 38." *SEÅ* 71 (2006) 55–74. ———. "Towards an 'Integrated Approach' in Biblical Studies, Illustrated with a Dialogue between Job 28 and Job 38." In *Congress Volume: Leiden, 2004.* Ed. André Lemaire. VTSup 109. Leiden: Brill, 2006. 355–80.

Bibliography: Chaps. 38–39 (Rhetorical Questions)

Craig, Kenneth M. "Questions outside Eden (Genesis 4.1–16): Yahweh, Cain and Their Rhetorical Interchange." *JSOT* 86 (1999) 107–28. ———. "Rhetorical Aspects of Questions Answered with Silence in 1 Samuel 14:37 and 28:6." *CBQ* 56 (1994) 221–39. **Koops, Robert.** "Rhetorical Questions and Implied Meaning in the Book of Job." *BiTrans* 39 (1988) 415–23. **Kuntz, J. Kenneth.** "The Form, Location, and Function of Rhetorical Questions in Deutero-Isaiah." In *Writing and Reading the Scroll of Isaiah: Studies of an Interpretive Tradition.* Ed. Craig C. Broyles and Craig A. Evans. VTSup 70. Leiden: E. J. Brill, 1997. 1:121–41. **Regt, L. J. de.** "Discourse Implications of Rhetorical Questions in Job, Deuteronomy and the Minor Prophets." In *Literary Structure and Rhetorical Strategies in the Hebrew Bible.* Ed. Lénart J. de Regt, J. de Waard, and J. P. Fokkelman. Assen: Van Gorcum, 1996. 51–78. ———. "Functions and Implications of Rhetorical Questions in the Book of Job." In *Biblical Hebrew and Discourse Linguistics.* Ed. Robert D. Bergen. Winona Lake, IN: Eisenbrauns, 1994. 361–73. ———. "Implications of Rhetorical Questions in

Strophes in Job 11 and 15." In *The Book of Job*. Ed. W. A. M. Beuken. BETL 114. Leuven: Leuven University Press, 1994. 321–28.

Bibliography: Job 38:2–3 (Proem)

Bimson, John J. "Who Is 'This' in 'Who is this ... ?' (Job 38.2)? A Response to Karl G. Wilcox." *JSOT* 87 (2000) 125–28. **Wilcox, Karl G.** "'Who is this ... ?' A Reading of Job 38.2." *JSOT* 78 (1998) 85–95.

Bibliography: Job 38:4–7 (Earth)

Cunchillos, J. L. "Le dieu Mut, guerrier de El" [on the sons of God (Job 1–2; 38:7)]. *Syria* 62 (1985) 205–18. **Whyte, William.** *Scripture Geology. Being a Comparison of Job, xxxviii. 4–11, with Genesis, i. 1, 19. Part II, or, Summer Walks along the Margin of Sea and Land, for All Ages and Both Sexes*. Edinburgh: Bell & Bradfute, 1843.

Bibliography: Job 38:8–11 (Sea)

Caspari, Wilhelm. "Eine Dittographie in Hiob 38, 8 und ihre Begleiterscheinungen." *ZDMG* 63 (1909) 688–98.

Bibliography: Job 38:12–27 (Morning, Light, etc.)

Begg, Christopher T. "Access to Heavenly Treasuries: The Traditionsgeschichte of a Motif." *BN* 44 (1988) 15–20. **Burns, John Barclay.** "Is the Ibis Yet Wise? A Reconsideration of Job 38:36." *PrGLM* 21 (2001) 131–36. **Cornelius, Izak.** "The Sun Epiphany in Job 38:12–15 and the Iconography of the Gods in the Ancient Near East— The Palestinian Connection." *JNSL* 16 (1990) 25–43. **Michel, Walter L.** "Ṣlmwt, 'deep darkness' or 'shadow of death'?" [Job 38:17]. *BibRes* 29 (1984) 5–20. **Zurro Rodríguez, Eduardo.** "La raíz *kw/yl*y siete textos bíblicos" [incl. Job 38:18]. *EstBíb* 57 (1999) 777–86.

Bibliography: Job 38:28–30 (Rain, Ice, Frost)

Ashbel, D. "On the Importance of Dew in Palestine." *JPOS* 16 (1936) 316–21. **Gilead, M., and N. Rosenan.** "Ten Years of Dew Observation in Israel." *IEJ* 4 (1954) 120–23. **Humbert, Paul.** "La rosée tombe en Israël. A propos d'Esaïe 26, 19." *TZ* 13 (1957) 487–93. **Meijer, Diederik J. W. (ed.).** *Natural Phenomena: Their Meaning, Depiction and Description in the Ancient Near East*. Verhandelingen Koninklijke Nederlandse Akademie van Wetenschappen. Afd. Letterkunde; Nieuwe reeks 152. Amsterdam: North Holland, 1992. **Milik, J. T.** "Giobbe 38, 28 in siro-palestinese e la dea ugaritica Pdry bt ar." *RivB* 6 (1958) 252–54. **Stadelmann, Luis I. J.** *The Hebrew Conception of the World: A Philological and Literary Study*. AnBib 39. Rome: Pontifical Biblical Institute, 1970. 114–26. **Vall, Gregory.** "'From Whose Womb Did the Ice Come Forth?' Procreation Images in Job 38:28–29." *CBQ* 57 (1995) 504–13. **Vattioni, F.** "La rugiada nell'Antico Testamento." *RivB* 6 (1958) 147–65.

Bibliography: Job 38:31–33 (Astronomy)

Ammon, Franz. *Über die Bedeutung der im Buche Hiob vorkommenden Sternnamen: Ein Beitrag zur Astrognosie*. Passau, 1838. **Burney, C. F.** "Stars." *EB* 4:4779–86. **Driver, G. R.** "Two Astronomical Passages in the OT" [Job 38:31]. *JTS* ns 7 (1956) 1–11. **Galter, Hannes D.** "Die Rolle der Astronomie in den Kulturen des Zweistromlandes." In *Die Rolle der*

Astronomie in den Kulturen Mesopotamiens: Beiträge zum 3. Grazer Morgenländischen Symposion (23.–27. September 1991). Ed. Hannes D. Galter. Grazer morgenländische Studien 3. Graz: GrazKult, 1993. 149–59. **Gaster, T. H.** *Thespis. Ritual, Myth, and Drama in the Ancient Near East*. New York: Doubleday, rev. ed., 1961. 320–27. ———. *Myth, Legend, and Custom in the Old Testament*. London: Duckworth, 1969. 790. **González Núñez, Angel.** "El rocío del cielo." *EstBíb* 22 (1963) 109–39. **Halpern, Baruch.** "Assyrian and Pre-Socratic Astronomies and the Location of the Book of Job." In *Kein Land für sich allein: Studien zum Kulturkontakt in Kanaan, Israel/Palästina und Ebirnâri für Manfred Weippert zum 65. Geburtstag*. Ed. Ulrich Hübner and Ernst Axel Knauf. OBO 186. Freiburg, Switzerland: Universitätsverlag; Göttingen: Vandenhoeck & Ruprecht, 2002. 255–64. **Herz, N.** "The Astral Terms in Job ix 9, xxxviii 31–32." *JTS* 14 (1913) 575–77. **Hess, J.-J.** "Die Sternbilder in Hiob 9:9 und 38:31f." In *Festschrift Georg Jacob zum siebzigsten Geburtstag 26. Mai 1932 gewidmet von Freunden und Schülern*. Ed. Theodor Menzel. Leipzig: Harrassowitz, 1932. 94–99. **Hirschberg, J. W.** "Job xxxviii, 31." *REJ* 99 (1935) 130–32. **Hodson, F. R. (ed.).** *The Place of Astronomy in the Ancient World: A Joint Symposium of the Royal Society and the British Academy [1972]*. London: Oxford University Press, 1974. **Houtman, Cornelis.** *Der Himmel im Alten Testament: Israels Weltbild und Weltanschauung*. OTS 30. Leiden: E. J. Brill, 1993. **Hunger, Hermann, and David Pingree.** *Astral Sciences in Mesopotamia*. Handbuch der Orientalistik 1/44. Leiden: E. J. Brill, 1999. **Lansing, John G.** "Pleiades, Orion and Mazzaroth: Job xxxviii., 31, 32." *Hebraica* 1 (1884–85) 236–41. **Maunder, E. Walter.** *The Astronomy of the Bible: An Elementary Commentary on the Astronomical References of Holy Scripture*. London: T. Sealey Clark, 1908. **Mesnard, R.** "Les constellations du livre de Job." *Revue belge de philosophie et d'histoire* 30 (1952) 1–11. **Mowinckel, Sigmund Olaf Plytt.** *Die Sternnamen im Alten Testament*. Oslo: Gröndahl, 1928 [= *NTT* 5 (1928)]. **Neugebauer, O.** "The History of Ancient Astronomy: Problems and Methods." *JNES* 4 (1945) 1–38. **Parpola, Simo.** "Mesopotamian Astrology and Astronomy as Domains of the Mesopotamian 'Wisdom'." In *Die Rolle der Astronomie in den Kulturen Mesopotamiens: Beiträge zum 3. Grazer Morgenländischen Symposion (23.–27. September 1991)*. Grazer morgenländische Studien 3. Graz: GrazKult, 1993. 47–59. **Puhvel, Jaan.** "Names and Numbers of the Pleiad." In *Semitic Studies in Honor of Wolf Leslau on the Occasion of His Eighty-Fifth Birthday*. Ed. Alan S. Kaye. Wiesbaden: Otto Harrassowitz, 1991. 1243–47. **Robbins, Ellen.** "The Pleiades, the Flood, and the Jewish New Year." In *Ki baruch hu: Ancient Near Eastern, Biblical, and Judaic Studies in Honor of Baruch A. Levine*. Ed. Robert Chazan, William W. Hallo, and Lawrence H. Schiffman. Winona Lake, IN: Eisenbrauns, 1999. 329–44. **Rochberg, Francesca.** "The Cultural Locus of Astronomy in Late Babylonia." In *Die Rolle der Astronomie in den Kulturen Mesopotamiens: Beiträge zum 3. Grazer Morgenländischen Symposion (23.–27. September 1991)*. Grazer morgenländische Studien 3. Graz: GrazKult, 1993. 31–45. ———. *The Heavenly Writing: Divination, Horoscopy, and Astronomy in Mesopotamian Culture*. Cambridge: Cambridge University Press, 2004. **Rochberg-Halton, Francesca.** "Astrology in the Ancient Near East." *ABD*, 1:504–7. **Schiaparelli, G.** *Astronomy in the Old Testament*. Oxford: Clarendon Press, 1905. **Stern, M. A.** "Die Sternbilder in Hiob Kp. 38, V. 31 und 32." *JZWL* 3 (1864–65) 258–76. **Waldman, N. M.** "The Heavenly Writing [Job 38,33]." *GratzCollJewSt* 6 (1977) 93–97. **Weinfeld, Moshe.** "Divine Intervention in War in Ancient Israel and in the Ancient Near East." In *History, Historiography and Interpretation: Studies in Biblical and Cuneiform Literatures*. Ed. H. Tadmor and M. Weinfeld. Jerusalem: Magnes Press, 1984. 121–47. **Zalcman, Lawrence.** "Astronomical Allusions in Amos [5:9]." *JBL* 100 (1981) 53–58. **Zatelli, Ida.** "Astrology and the Worship of the Stars in the Bible." *ZAW* 103 (1991) 86–99.

Bibliography: Job 38:34–38 (Clouds)

Alfrink, Bern. "Die Bedeutung des Wortes בֶּרֶק in Job 21, 33 und 38, 38." *Bib* 13 (1932) 77–86. **Brentjes, Burchard.** "Nutz- und Hausvögel im Alten Orient." *Wissenschaftliche*

Zeitschrift Halle–Wittenberg 11 (Gesellschafts- und sprachwissenschaftliche Reihe 6; 1962) 635–702 (643–46). **Keel, Othmar.** "Zwei kleine Beiträge zum Verständnis der Gottesreden im Buch Ijob (xxxviii 36f., xl 25)." *VT* 31 (1981) 220–25.

Bibliography: Job 38:39–40 (Lion)

Benzinger, Immanuel. "Jagd bei den Hebräern." *RE* 8:520. **Botterweck, G. J.** *TDOT,* 1:374–88. **Brentjes, Burchard.** "Mensch und Katze im Alten Orient." *Wissenschaftliche Zeitschrift Halle–Wittenberg* 11 (Gesellschafts-´und sprachwissenschaftliche Reihe 6; 1962) 595–634 (595–99). **Cassin, Elena.** "Le roi et le lion." *RHR* 198 (1981) 353–401. **Cornelius, Izak.** "The Lion in the Art of the Ancient Near East: A Study of Selected Motifs." *JNSL* 15 (1989) 53–85. **Velden, Adria Schouten van der, and Adrian Schouten van de Velden.** *Tierwelt der Bibel.* Stuttgart: Deutsche Bibelgesellschaft, 1992.

Bibliography: Job 38:41 (Raven)

Angerstorfer, A. *TDOT,* 11:341–43. **Ciccarese, Maria Pia.** "Filippo e i corvi di Giobbe 38,41: alla ricerca di una fonte perduta." *Aug* 35 (1995) 137–59. **Toynbee, J. M. C.** *Animals in Roman Life and Art.* London: Thames & Hudson, 1973.

Bibliography: Job 39:1–4 (Mountain Goats)

Bochart, Samuel. *Hierozoicon sive bipartitum opus de animalibus Sacrae Scripturae.* London: Thomas Roycroft, 1663. 1:879–95. **Bok, Willy.** "Le bouc et le nomade: essai sur le symbolisme du bouc dans la Bible." In *Mélanges Armand Abel.* Ed. A. Destrée. Leiden: E. J. Brill, 1978. 3:1–15. **Brentjes, Buchard.** "Die Caprinae." In *Wildtier und Haustier im alten Orient.* Lebendiges Altertum 11. Berlin: Akademie-Verlag, 1982 [= *Wissenschaftliche Zeitschrift Halle–Wittenberg* 11 (Gesellschafts- und sprachwissenschaftliche Reihe 6; 1962) 549–94]. **Firmage, Edwin.** *ABD,* 6:1109–67 (1127–29). **Hirsch, Henricus Albertus Christianus.** *Dissertatio philologico-physica de generationi ceruarum ad Jobi cap. XXXIX, 4–6.* Diss. Altdorf. Altdorf: J. W. Kohlefius, 1706. **Stek, John H.** "The Bee and the Mountain Goat: A Literary Reading of Judges 4." In *A Tribute to Gleason Archer.* Ed. Walter C. Kaiser, Jr, and Ronald F. Youngblood. Chicago: Moody Press, 1986. 53–86.

Bibliography: Job 39:5–8 (Wild Ass)

Bailey, Kenneth E., and William L. Holladay. "The 'Young Camel' and 'Wild Ass' in Jer ii 23–25." *VT* 18 (1968) 256–60. **Bochart, Samuel.** *Hierozoicon sive bipartitum opus de animalibus Sacrae Scripturae.* London: Thomas Roycroft, 1663. 1:867–79. **Brentjes, Burchard.** "*ANŠE.gi.ga.ŠU.MUL* = parû = Onager." In *Studia orientalia in memoriam Caroli Brockelmann.* Ed. Manfred Fleischhammer [= *Wissenschaftliche Zeitschrift der Martin-Luther-Universität Halle–Wittenberg* 17 (Gesellschafts- under sprachwissenschaftliche Reihe 2–3; 1968) 29–34. ———. "Onager und Esel im Alten Orient." In *Beiträge zu Geschichte, Kultur und Religion des Alten Orients. In memoriam Eckhard Unger.* Ed. Manfred Lurker. Baden-Baden: Verlag Valentin Koerner, 1971. 131–45 (and two unnumbered pages of plates). **Cohen, Amos.** "יתור הרים מרעהו" [Job 39:8]. *BMik* 29 (1966–67) 105–6. **Dahood, Mitchell.** "Four Ugaritic Personal Names and Job 39:5, 26–27." *ZAW* 87 (1975) 220. **Fensham, F. Charles.** "The Wild Ass in the Aramean Treaty between Bar-Ga'ayah and Mati'el." *JNES* 22 (1963) 185–86. **Firmage, Edwin.** *IDB,* 6:1137–38. **Helck, Wolfgang.** *Jagd und Wild im alten Vorderasien.* Hamburg: Paul Parey, 1968. 20–23. **Iran Zoo.** www.iranzoo.cjb. net (photos). **Keller, Otto.** "Wildesel und Wildpferd." In his *Die antike Tierwelt.* Leipzig: Engelmann, 1909–13. 271–74. **McCullough, W. S.** "Wild Ass." *IDB,* 4:843.

Bibliography: Job 39:9–12 (Wild Ox)

Buren, E. Douglas van. *The Fauna of Ancient Mesopotamia as Represented in Art.* AnOr 18. Rome: Pontificium Institutum Biblicum, 1939. 69–74. **Cansdale, George.** *Animals of Bible Lands.* Exeter: Paternoster Press, 1970. 82–84. **Godbey, Allen H.** "The Unicorn in the Old Testament." *AJSL* 56 (1939) 256–96. **Hilzheimer, Max.** *Die Wildrinder im alten Mesopotamien.* Mitteilungen der Altorientalischen Gesellschaft 2/2. Leipzig: E. Pfeiffer, 1926. **Keller, Otto.** *Die antike Tierwelt.* Leipzig: Engelmann, 1909–13. 1:341–43. **Klotz, John.** "Notes on the Unicorn." *CTM* 32 (1961) 286–87. **Ley, Willy.** *The Lungfish, the Dodo and the Unicorn.* New York: Viking, 1948. 19–34. **Müller, H.-P.** "רְאֵם." *THWAT,* 7 (1990) 267–71 [= *TDOT,* 13 (2004) 243–47]. **Velden, Adria Schouten van der, and Adrian Schouten van de Velden.** *Tierwelt der Bibel.* Stuttgart: Deutsche Bibelgesellschaft, 1992. 24–25.

Bibliography: Job 39:13–18 (Ostrich)

American Ostrich Association. www.ostriches.org. **Bochart, Samuel.** *Hierozoicon sive bipartitum opus de animalibus Sacrae Scripturae.* London: Thomas Roycroft, 1663. 2:238–62. **Boehmer, Julius.** "Was ist der Sinn von Hiob 39:13–18 an seiner gegenwärtigen Stelle?" *ZAW* 53 (1935) 289–91. **Brentjes, Burchard.** "Nutz- und Hausvögel im Alten Orient." *Wissenschaftliche Zeitschrift Halle–Wittenberg* 11 (Gesellschafts- und sprachwissenschaftliche Reihe 6; 1962) 635–702 (640–41). **Cansdale, George.** *Animals of Bible Lands.* Exeter: Paternoster Press, 1970. 190–93. **Driver, G. R.** "Birds in the Old Testament. I. Birds in Law." *PEQ* 87 (1955) 5–20 (12–13). ———. "Birds in the Old Testament. II. Birds in Life." *PEQ* 87 (1955) 129–40 (137–38). **Firmage, Edwin.** *ABD,* 6:1144. **McCullough, W. S.** "Ostrich." *IDB,* 3:611–12. **Müller, Hans-Peter.** "Die sog. Straussenperikope in den Gottesreden des Hiobbuches." *ZAW* 100 (1988) 90–105. **Nau, François.** "Etude sur Job, xxxix, 13 et sur les oiseaux fabuleux qui peuvent s'y rattacher." *JA* 215 (1929) 193–236. **Walker-Jones, Arthur.** "The So-Called Ostrich in the God Speeches of the Book of Job (Job 39,13–18)." *Bib* 86 (2005) 494–510. **Wyper, G., and Nola J. Opperwall.** "Ostrich." *ISBE,* 3:620.

Bibliography: Job 39:19–25 (Horse)

Anon. *Bellicus equus: ex Jobi cap. 39, ad vers. 19.* London, 1685 (?). **Ap-Thomas, D. R.** "All the King's Horses? A Study of the Term פָּרָשׁ (I Kings 5.6 [EVV., 4.26] etc.)." In *Proclamation and Presence: Old Testament Essays in Honour of Gwynne Henton Davies.* Ed. John I. Durham and J. R. Porter. London: SCM Press, 1970. 135–51. **Avi-Yonah, M.** "Oriental Elements in Palestinian Art" [incl. figurines of horses and riders]. *QDAP* 10 (1944) 105–51 (127–30). **Barclay, Harold B.** "Another Look at the Origins of Horse Riding." *Anthropos* 77 (1982) 244–49. **Barkay, Gabriel.** "'The Prancing Horse'—An Official Seal Impression from Judah of the 8th Century B.C.E." *Tel Aviv* 19 (1992) 124–29. **Boer, P. A. H. de.** "וּמֵרָחוֹק יָרִיחַ מִלְחָמָה—Job 39:25." In *Words and Meanings: Essays Presented to David Winton Thomas.* Ed. Peter R. Ackroyd and Barnabas Lindars. Cambridge: Cambridge University Press, 1968. 29–38. ———. "וּמֵרָחֹק יָרִיחַ מִלְחָמָה—Job 39:25." In his *Selected Studies in Old Testament Exegesis.* Ed. C. van Duin. OTS 27. Leiden: E. J. Brill, 1991. 80–89. **Borger, R.** "Hiob 39,23 nach dem Qumran-Targum." *VT* 27 (1977) 102–5. **Crespo, M.** "La faune biblique. Le cheval." *BTS* 12 (1976) 250–66. **Firmage, Edwin.** *ABD,* 6:1136–37. **Görg, Manfred.** "Die Göttin auf dem Kriegspferd." *BN* 13 (1980) 32–34. **Hyland, Ann.** *Equus: The Horse in the Roman World.* London: Batsford; New Haven: Yale University Press, 1990. ———. *The Horse in the Ancient World.* Stroud: Sutton, 2002. **Kletter, Raz.** "Pots and Polities: Material Remains of Late Iron Age Judah in Relation to Its Political Borders" [incl. horse and rider figurines]. *BASOR* 314 (1999) 19–54. **Kreyssig, Joannes**

Gottlieb. *Observationes philologico-criticae in Jobi cap. XXXIX. vers. 19.–25.* Leipzig: Goethio Commissum, 1802. **Littauer, M. A., and J. H. Crouwel.** *Wheeled Vehicles and Ridden Animals in the Ancient Near East.* Handbuch der Orientalistik 2B/1. Leiden: E. J. Brill, 1979. **Morgan, D. F.** *ISBE,* 2:759–60. **Mowinckel, S.** "Drive and/or Ride in the O.T." *VT* 12 (1962) 278–99. **Odell, David.** "Images of Violence in the Horse in Job 39:18–25." *Prooftexts* 13 (1993) 163–73. **Olds, L. P.** "Job's War-Horse." *MethQR* 14 (1860) 581–87. **Slotki, Israel W.** "A Study of רעם" [Job 26:14; 37:4; 39:19]. *AJSL* 37 (1920–21) 149–55. **Smith, Charles W. F.** "The Horse and the Ass in the Bible: An Essay on Zechariah 9:9, 10." *ATR* 27 (1945) 86–97. **Stendebach, F. J.** *TDOT,* 10:178–87. **Thompson, J. A.** *IDB,* 2:646–48. **Zissu, Boaz.** "A Graffito Depicting a Horseman from the Judaean Foothills" [probably Hellenistic]. *PEQ* 128 (1996) 52–56.

Bibliography: Job 39:26–30 (Hawk and Eagle)

Bochart, Samuel. *Hierozoicon sive bipartitum opus de animalibus Sacrae Scripturae.* London: Thomas Roycroft, 1663. 2: chap. 19. **Bodenheimer, F. S.** *Animal and Man in Bible Lands.* Leiden: E. J. Brill, 1960. 53–55. **Brown, Leslie H.** *Eagles of the World.* Newton Abbot: David & Charles, 1976. **Brown, Leslie, and Dean Amadon.** *Eagles, Hawks and Falcons of the World.* Feltham, Middlesex: Country Life Books, 1968. **Cansdale, George.** *Animals of Bible Lands.* Exeter: Paternoster Press, 1970. 142–46. **Dahood, Mitchell.** "Four Ugaritic Personal Names and Job 39:5, 26–27." *ZAW* 87 (1975) 220. **Driver, G. R.** "Job 39:27–28: The *Ky*-Bird." *PEQ* 104 (1972) 64–66. **Ferguson-Lees, James, and David A. Christie.** *Raptors of the World.* London: Christopher Helm, 2001. **Firmage, Edwin.** *ABD,* 6:1144. **Grelot, Pierre.** "Note de critique textuelle sur Job xxxix 27." *VT* 22 (1972) 487–89. **Kronholm, T.** *TDOT,* 10:77–85. **Leshem, Y.** "Trails in the Sky: Fall Migration of Raptors over Israel." *Israel Land and Nature* 10 (1984–85) 70–77. **McCullough, W. S.** "Vulture." *IDB,* 4:794. **Vogel, Dan.** "Ambiguities of the Eagle." *JBQ* 26 (1998) 85–92.

Bibliography: Job 40:1–2 (Peroration)

Fullerton, Kemper. "On the Text and Significance of Job 40:2." *AJSL* 49 (1932–33) 197–211. **Johnson, Timothy.** "Implied Antecedents in Job xl 2b and Proverbs iii 6a." *VT* 52 (2002) 278–84. **Zimmermann, Frank.** "Supplementary Observations on Job 40:2." *AJSL* 51 (1934–35) 46–47.

Translation

> [1] [a]*And Yahweh answered Job from the tempest,*[b] *and said:*

> [2] *"Who is this*[a] *who obscures*[b] *the Design*[c]
>   *by words without knowledge?*
> [3] *Gird up your loins*[a] *like a man*[b]*;*
>   *I will question you,*[c] *and you shall answer me.*[d]

> [4] [a]*Where were you when I founded the earth?*
>   *Tell me, if*[b] *you have insight.*[c]
> [5] *Who fixed*[a] *its dimensions*[b]*? Surely*[c] *you know!*
>   *Who stretched the measuring cord across it?*
> [6] *Into what were its bases sunk,*[a]
>   *or who set*[b] *its capstone,*[c]
> [7] *when the stars of the morning rejoiced*[a] *together,*[b]
>   *and all the sons of God shouted for joy*[c]*?*

^{8}Who shut in^a the sea^b with doors^c?–
   when it broke forth from the womb,^{d}
^{9}when I made clouds its garment,
   and thick darkness its swaddling band,^{a}
^{10}when I prescribed^a bounds^b for it,
   and set up a bar and doors,^{c}
^{11}and said,^{a} 'Thus far shall you come,^{b} and no further,^{c}
   and here^d your proud waves^e must stop.'^{f}

$^{12\ a}$Since your days began,^{b} have you called up the morning,
   and assigned^c the dawn its place,
^{13}so as to seize^a the earth by its fringes^b
   ^{c}so that the Dog-stars^d are shaken loose?
$^{14\ a}$It is transformed^b like clay under a seal^c
   and all becomes tinted^d like a garment,^{e}
$^{15\ a}$as the light of the Dog-stars fades,^{b}
   and the Navigator's Line^c breaks up.^{d}

$^{16\ a}$Have you journeyed down^b to the springs^c of the sea,
   or walked about^d in the remotest parts^e of the abyss?
^{17}Have the gates of death been revealed to you,
   or have you seen^a the door-keepers^b of death's darkness^c?
^{18}Have you gazed on^a the furthest expanse^b of the underworld^c?
   Say if you know its extent^d!

$^{19\ a}$Where is the realm^b of the dwelling of light,^{c}
   and as for darkness, where is its place?
$^{20\ a}$Could you take them^b to their domain,^{c}
   escort them^d on their homeward paths?
$^{21\ a}$You know,^{b} for you were born in ancient times,^{c}
   and the number of your days is great^d!

^{22}Have you entered the storehouses of the snow?
   Or have you seen the arsenals^a of the hail,
^{23}which I have reserved^a for a time of calamity,^{b}
   for a day of battle and war?
$^{24\ a}$Where is the realm^b where heat^c is created,^{d}
   which^e the sirocco^f spreads^g across the earth?

^{25}Who cuts^a a channel for the torrent of rain,
   a path for the thunderbolt,^{b}
^{26}to bring rain on a land uninhabited,
   on the unpeopled desert,
^{27}to satisfy^a a waste and desolate land,^{b}
   making the thirsty^c ground sprout with grass?

$^{28\ a}$Has the rain a father?
   Who sires the dewdrops^b?

^{29 a}*From whose womb comes the rime*^b*?*
   Who is the hoar-frost's^c *mother*^d*?*
^{30 a}*The waters become hard*^b *as stone,*
   and the face of the deep is captured [by the ice].^c

^{31 a}*Can you bind*^b *the cluster*^c *of the Pleiades,*
   or loose Orion's belt^d*?*
³²*Can you bring out Mazzaroth*^a *in its season,*
   or guide^b *Aldebaran*^c *with*^d *its train*^e*?*
³³*Do you determine*^a *the laws of the heaven?*
   Can you establish its rule^b *upon earth?*

³⁴*Can you lift*^a *your voice to the clouds,*
   and make a flood of waters answer you^b*?*
³⁵*Can you send lightning bolts on their way,*^a
   and have them report to you, 'Ready!'^b*?*
^{36 a}*Who gave the ibis*^b *its wisdom*
   or endowed the cock^c *with its intelligence?*
³⁷*Who can disperse*^a *the clouds with skill,*
   and tilt over^b *the water jars*^c *of the heavens,*
³⁸*so that the soil*^a *fuses*^b *into a solid mass,*^c
   ^d*and the clods*^e *of earth stick fast together*^f*?*

³⁹*Do you hunt prey*^a *for the lion,*^b
   do you satisfy the appetite^c *of its cubs,*^d
⁴⁰*while they crouch in their dens,*^a
   lie in their lairs^b *in the thickets*^c*?*
⁴¹*Who provides*^a *nourishment*^b *for the raven,*^c
   ^d*when its young cry to God,*^e
   and croak^f *for lack of food*^g*?*

^{39:1}*Do you know*^a *the birthing*^b *of the mountain goats,*^c
   do you watch^d *when the doe*^e *bears her kids*^f*?*
²*Can you count*^a *the months they must complete*^b*?*
   Do you know^c *the time when they give birth,*
³*when they crouch down*^a *to give birth*^b *to their young*^c
   and deliver their offspring^d*?*
⁴*When the young grow*^a *and thrive*^b *in the wild,*^c
   they go off and never return to them.^d

⁵*Who let the wild ass*^a *go free*^b*?*
   Who loosed the onager's^c *bonds,*
⁶*to whom I gave the steppe*^a *as its home,*
   the saltings^b *as its dwelling*^c*?*
⁷*It laughs at*^a *the tumult of the city,*
   and hears^b *no shouts*^c *from a donkey-driver.*^d
⁸*It ranges*^a *over the hills for pasture,*^b
   searching^c *for anything green.*^d

⁹*Would the wild ox*^a *agree to serve you*^b*?*

> Would it take up its residence[c] in your stall[d]?
> [10] Can you bind it[a] with ropes to the furrow,[b]
> and will it harrow[c] the plains[d] after you[e]?
> [11] Can you rely on it because of its massive strength,[a]
> and leave your heavy work[b] to it?
> [12] Can you depend on it to[a] bring in[b] your grain,[c]
> gathering it to your threshing floor[d]?

> [13] [a] The wings[b] of the ostrich[c] are beautiful,[d]
> but are they[e] the pinions[f] of stork[g] or falcon[h]?[i]
> [14] For she leaves[a] her eggs on the ground,[b]
> and lets them warm[c] in the dust,
> [15] [a] forgetting[b] that a foot may crush them,[c]
> and that a wild animal[d] may trample them.
> [16] She is harsh[a] with her chicks, as if they were not hers[b];
> she has no fear[c] that her labor may be in vain,[d]
> [17] [a] because God made her forget[b] wisdom
> and gave her no share in understanding.[c]
> [18] But the moment[a] she spreads her plumes[b] aloft,[c]
> she laughs[d] at the horse and its rider.

> [19] Do you give the horse its might?
> Do you clothe its neck with a mane[a]?
> [20] Do you make it quiver[a] like locusts[b]?
> [c] The majesty[d] of its neighing[e] is terrible.[f]
> [21] It paws[a] the plain,[b] exulting in its strength[c];
> then it goes off[d] to meet the battle.[e]
> [22] It laughs at fear,[a] and is not deterred[b];
> it does not flinch[c] before the sword.
> [23] A quiverful of arrows[a] rattles[b] past it,
> and the flashing[c] spear and javelin.[d]
> [24] Stamping[a] and raging,[b] it swallows[c] the ground,[d]
> [e] when the trumpet[f] sounds,[g] it cannot stand still.[h]
> [25] [a] When the trumpet sounds,[b] it cries, 'Hurrah!'[c]
> [d] From afar it scents[e] the battle,
> [f] the thunder[g] of the captains and the shouting.[h]

> [26] [a] Is it by your understanding[b] that the hawk[c] takes flight,[d]
> and spreads its wings toward the south[e]?
> [27] Is it at your command that the eagle[a] soars[b]
> and[c] makes its nest on high?[d]
> [28] [a] On the cliff it dwells[b] and spends the night,
> on a rocky crag[c] is its eyrie.[d]
> [29] From there it watches for prey;
> its eyes can see it afar off.
> [30] Its young feed[a] on blood,
> for wherever the slain are, there it is.[b] "

[40:1] [a] And Yahweh answered Job, saying:

² *"Will the disputant*ᵃ *with the Almighty*ᵇ *correct him*ᶜ*?*ᵈ
     *Let God's critic make his answer!*ᵉ*"*

Notes

1.a. LXX adds at the beginning of the verse, "And after Elihu had finished speaking." This addition shows that if the theory adopted in this commentary is correct, that the Elihu speeches originally preceded Job's final speech in chaps. 20–31, the misplacement of the Elihu speeches took place prior to the translation of the LXX.

1.b. סערה is, like סופה at 37:9, "tempest" (JB, NJPS, NEB) or "storm" (NAB, NIV, GNB) rather than "whirlwind" (as KJV, RSV). A whirlwind is properly a tornado. Ehrlich and Hölscher delete "from the tempest," as a secondary link to chap. 37. LXX adds "and the clouds" after "tempest." Strahan remarks that the article is generic, so "out of a storm" would be correct. K מן הסערה apparently read the two words as one; Q מן is the normal or "correct" form (as, e.g., Beer [*BH*²]).

2.a. The reference must be to Job. But in the present shape of the Book of Job, the last person to have spoken before Yahweh opens his mouth here is Elihu (chaps. 32–37), and "this" would most naturally refer to him.

Indeed, Karl G. Wilcox ("'Who is this … ?' A Reading of Job 38.2," *JSOT* 78 [1998] 85–95) has recently argued that "this" does indeed refer to Elihu, the line being Yahweh's immediate dismissal of Elihu and his opinions. Wilcox notes the apparent mismatch of the third-person question "Who is this?" in v 2 with the second-person summons "Gird up your loins" in v 3. He concludes that while it is Job who will be challenged to gird up his loins for debate with Yahweh (38:3), it is not he who has "darkened counsel by words without knowledge" (38:2) for he will shortly be certified in 42:7 as having spoken of Yahweh "what is right." Against Wilcox is the fact that at 42:3 Job acknowledges, with very similar words, "Who is this that hides counsel without knowledge?," that he is the one Yahweh had in mind when he asked "Who is this who darkens counsel?" in 38:2; see further, John J. Bimson, "Who Is 'This' in '"Who is this … ?"' (Job 38.2): A Response to Karl G. Wilcox," *JSOT* 87 (2000) 125–28; David J. A. Clines, "Putting Elihu in His Place: A Proposal for the Relocation of Job 32–37," *JSOT* 29 (2004) 115–25.

2.b. חשׁך hiph "make dark," i.e., obscure, make invisible; KJV, RSV, NIV, NJPS, REB have "darken," NAB, JB "obscure." Though the metaphor is somewhat different from that of the vb עלם "conceal" which Job uses when he quotes Yahweh's words in 42:3, both חשׁך and עלם could well be translated "obscure." Gordis says the vb is "declarative," i.e., "declare my plan to be dark, obscure," but his Translation does not reflect that, and the suggestion seems improbable. Andersen's suggestion, that בלי "without" is to be understood before עצה "advice, counsel" in the first colon as well as before דעת "knowledge" in the second, and that מחשׁיך "darkens" has no obj (yielding a translation such as "who is in the dark without good advice, with words without knowledge") is strained.

An emendation, to מכחישׁ "denies," i.e., "declares to be false," is made by Tur-Sinai (so too Pope¹, though not Pope²), but כחשׁ is not used elsewhere in hiph, and for Job to declare God's עצה "plan" to be false would imply that he understands what it is—which is precisely what Yahweh is denying.

2.c. עצה is "counsel, plan," and, being without the article, it could mean counsel in general (as RSV, NJPS, REB "darkens counsel"). But it seems clear that the reference here is to the *divine* counsel or plan, and many translations reflect that understanding. Thus NAB "divine plans," NJB "my intentions," NIV "my counsel," Gordis "my plan," NEB, JB "my design(s)." Since it appears to be Yahweh's design for the universe as a whole (see further, *Comment*), it seems fit to give the term a capital letter.

3.a. On the idiom, see *Comment*. It seems a pity to abandon the image, as JB, NEB, and NIV do with "brace yourself."

3.b. גבר means an adult male, without any special reference to strength, as is sometimes supposed (cf. *Comment* on 3:3). Since, however, it is indeed a contest of strength that is envisaged here, some emend to כגבר "like a warrior, hero," the word occurring elsewhere in Job only at 16:14 (*q.v.*); so Bickell, Budde², Beer [*BH*² גבור], Driver–Gray, Beer (*BHK*), Hölscher, Larcher, Tur-Sinai, apparently Pope (the reading is supported by one ms; cf. Gerleman [*BHS*]), JB. But the word גבר "man" is quite adequate in the context, since strength is an expected characteristic in a man, even though the term does not itself imply that.

3.c. ואשׁאלך "and I will ask you" has a prefatory ו "and," which many delete (e.g., Beer [*BHK*], Driver–Gray, Hölscher, Fohrer) or else ignore in translation (KJV has "for").

3.d. והודיעני lit. "and inform me" (impv).

4.a. Kissane moves to this place vv 31–32, on the rather feeble ground that we should expect the opening line to concern the heavens.

4.b. אם "if." It is tempting to take it as "since" (cf. JB "since you are so well informed"), but parallels to such a sense are absent. Perhaps we could render "surely you have understanding" (see *DCH*, 1:304a §2b).

4.c. אם־ידעת בינה "if you know understanding," בינה referring to the object of knowledge rather than to the faculty of understanding (BDB, 108a; Duhm). The idiom "to know understanding" (ידע בינה) is paralleled at Isa 29:24; Prov 4:1; 1 Chr 12:33; 2 Chr 2:11, 12. Dahood, thinking Understanding and Wisdom to be personified, rendered "if you are acquainted with Understanding" (*Psalms III*, 266, on Ps 136:5). Andersen suggests that בינה here may be a quite different word, meaning something like "building," from בנה "build"; but the noun form points rather to a derivation from בין "understand" (cf. GKC, §84c). Gray emends to קומה "its establishment" (no doubt the inf of the vb with a suff), i.e., how it was established; but this reading is no improvement on the MT.

5.a. שם "set, fixed." Mitchell Dahood, "The Metaphor in Job 22,22," *Bib* 47 (1966) 108–9, and "Hebrew-Ugaritic Lexicography X," *Bib* 53 (1972) 386–403 (399), argued that שם "set" sometimes has the specialized meaning of "set down in writing," as at 22:22; Ps 56:8 [9], or "trace out, draft" as here and at v 33; Prov 8:29. He is followed by Pope and Hartley; but there is nothing in the text to require that view.

שם is emended ingeniously, but not convincingly, by Ehrlich to שם "name"; vocalizing ממדיה as piel ptcp of a new vb מדה "measure" (equivalent to the more usual מדד), he translates "What is the name of him who measured it?"

5.b. ממד "measurement" occurs only here, but the root מדד "measure" is well attested. Joüon proposed we should read מוסדיה "its foundations" ("Notes de critique textuelle [suite]," *MUSJ* 6 [1913] 184–211 [209]) (so too Tur-Sinai, reading מסדיה [*frt*]), but "measurements, dimensions" suits the parallelism better.

5.c. כי is usually "for, since," but "since you know" is a little awkward here (though followed by Kissane). Very occasionally it is an interrogative particle (cf. *DCH*, 4:389a §12; Gordis on 37:20), which would permit the translation "Do you know?" (as NAB, JB). Perhaps it is best to take it as an emphatic "surely" (cf. *DCH*, 4:388a §9; for other examples, see the list in the *Note* on 22:26); so RSV, NIV, NEB, Pope, de Wilde; there is a close parallel at Prov 30:4. There are many cases where כי means "if, supposing that, in the case that" (cf. *DCH*, 4:386b §5), but this does not seem appropriate following the direct question (against Delitzsch, Dhorme, Fohrer, Gordis, Hartley); Dhorme appeals to the use of כי "if" in 7:13, but there it seems rather to be the כי frequentative.

6.a. טבע "sink" is used of sinking mountains at Prov 8:25, foundations here. The English idiom is "sink into, or, in" (as NAB), not "sink on" (RSV) or "onto" (NJPS); the prep על here signifies "into" rather than "upon." It is better to preserve the term "sink" rather than to use the somewhat different image "on what were its footings set?" (NIV), "on what do its supporting pillars rest?" (NEB), "whereupon are the foundations thereof fastened?" (KJV). For "sinking" implies that the structure extends below the surface of what it appears to rest upon; and NIV, NEB, KJV do not convey that image.

6.b. ירה is usually "throw," but its specialized use in Gen 31:51 of setting up or erecting a pillar is a good parallel to what we have here. Parallels in other languages of a vb for "throw" meaning "lay (a foundation)" (cf. Aram. רמה at Dan 7:9, Akk. *šubta ramû* [*CDA*, 297b], Lat. *fundamentum iacere*) may be misleading, but cf. Felix Perles, "Babylonisch-biblische Glossen," *OLZ* 8 (1905) 125–29 (129).

6.c. On the precise sense of פנה, translated "cornerstone" by the modern translations (as also by de Wilde), see *Comment*. Pope, while translating "cornerstone," allows that it could be a capstone. Kissane and Tur-Sinai, however, are clear that it is the crowning stone of the edifice; Newsom appears to assume it also. The case was made out in a series of articles by J. Jeremias: "κεφαλὴ γωνίαι–ἀκρογωνιαῖος," *ZNW* 29 (1930) 264–80; "Eckstein–Schlussstein," *ZNW* 36 (1937) 154–57; "γωνία, ἀκρογωνιαῖος, κεφαλὴ γωνίας," *TWNT* 1:792–93 (= *TDNT* 1:791–93); "λίθος," *TWNT* 4:275–83 (= *TDNT* 4:268–80). He was followed by Edwin E. le Bas, "Was the Corner-Stone of Scripture a Pyramidion?," *PEQ* (1946) 103–15 (105).

7.a. רנן "rejoice" designates a loud cry, a shout, just like רוע "shout" in the next colon; there is no evidence that it is a term for music or singing, despite the translations (KJV, RSV, JB, NAB, NIV, NJPS, NEB, Moffatt, Dhorme, Pope, Gordis, Habel "sing"; NJB "the joyful concert of the morning stars").

7.b. יחד is certainly "together," but since רנן does not mean "sing," translations such as "as a choir, in chorus" (Dhorme, Terrien, de Wilde) are inappropriate.

7.c. רוע is simply "shout," sometimes perhaps in distress (Isa 15:4; Mic 4:9, though the text may be doubtful in both cases), often as a war-cry, sometimes in triumph, and clearly with applause or joy at 1 Sam 10:24; Zech 9:9 (|| גיל "rejoice"), Isa 44:23 (|| רנן "rejoice"). It is normal that the finite vb should follow the inf ברן "in the rejoicing of" in the first colon (GKC, §114r).

8.a. ויסך "and [who] shut in?," is commonly understood as סכך I hiph "shut off" (so, e.g., HALOT, 2:754a; but the verb means more correctly "screen"; see *DCH*, 6:153a). But it is better to derive it from סוך II "hedge about" (BDB, 692a, Dhorme, *DCH*, 6:130a). We might have expected the subj of the vb at the beginning of this new strophe to be expressed, and so Bickell, Budde read וּמִי סָךְ "and who shut up?" Further, the initial ו "and" seems inappropriate for the head of the new strophe, so it seems best to emend, as in the *Translation* above, to מִי סָךְ "who shut up?" (Merx, Duhm, Driver–Gray, Dhorme, Hölscher, Kissane, Larcher, Fohrer, Sicre Díaz, Gray, JB; Vg apparently supports this reading, but it may simply be smoothing the text). MT, however, is retained by Gordis, Guillaume, Good. Some translations render the initial *waw* as "and" (NAB) or "or" (KJV, RSV), but we cannot tell if the others emended the text.

Hartley suggests the vb was סכך II "weave, knit," as in Ps 139:13 of "knitting" a fetus in its mother's womb; he translates, "Who knit the sea together behind doors [i.e., the labia]?" Similarly Andersen. But the movement from the bringing forth of the sea to its control in vv 10–11 is hard to trace on this understanding.

Among emendations, we may note: (1) NEB reads וּמִי סָכָה "who watched [over the birth of the sea]?" (Brockington), and REB presumably the same with its rendering "who supported [the sea at its birth]?" A verb סכה is, however, unknown to the lexica, and must be a proposal of G. R. Driver that I have not been able to trace. (2) Beer (*BH²frt*) reads סָכַר בְּלִדְתּ "(who) shut in [the sea] at its birth?" (3) In *BHK* he reads אֵפֹה הָיִתָ "where were you [at the birthing of the sea]?" (as in v 4) instead of וַיָּסֶךְ. Both his proposals are rather radical, but they do address the oddity that the doors of the sea are mentioned both here and in v 10a. (4) Blommerde read וַיֻּסַךְ lit. "and it was poured out" (hoph or passive qal), i.e., "and it [the sea] poured out [of the two doors]," from נסך "pour," connecting the line with what precedes as a depiction of creation (following Driver–Gray). He takes the initial ב of בדלתים as "from." It is much more likely, however, that the whole of vv 8–11 concerns the control of the sea. (5) Tur-Sinai read וַיֻּסַךְ "and it (the heavenly sea) was shut up [in sheets; see below]," from סכך hoph; but it suits the sequence of the poem better if Yahweh is the subj of the vb, with מי being supplied.

8.b. Wilhelm Caspari, "Eine Dittographie in Hiob 38, 8 und ihre Begleiterscheinungen," *ZDMG* 63 (1909) 688–98, removes ים "sea" as a dittograph, and argues that vv 8–11 have nothing to do with the sea.

8.c. דלתים "double doors," with the dual ending, which for this word is as common as the pl (not an intensive, as Gordis). Tur-Sinai maintains that it means "sheets," for wrapping the infant, arguing that דלת can also mean "sheet" of papyrus for writing on. But the evidence is rather that this specialized sense of דלת is not "sheet" but "column of a scroll" (as at Jer 36:23; cf. *HALOT*, 1:224a) or "tablet" (as at Lachish ost. 4:3; cf. *DCH*, 2:442a §5; *DNWSI*, 1:250).

Beer (*BHK*), followed by Driver–Gray, de Wilde, would emend, to בְּהִלָּדֶ יָם "[where were you (implied from v 4a)] at the birthing of [the sea]?" (wrongly written in *BHK* as בְהִלָּדֶת). NEB and REB followed a similar emendation, to בְּלִדְתּוֹ "at its birth," translating "who watched over the birth of the sea?" (NEB), "who supported the sea at its birth?" (REB). Neither of these readings is superior to the MT.

8.d. בְּגִיחוֹ מֵרֶחֶם יֵצֵא, lit. "in its breaking out of the womb that it came from" (Gordis), with a relative particle אשׁר understood before יצא. Or is it "which came forth from the womb with a rush," a relative being understood before בְּגִיחוֹ? Andersen, followed by Hartley, read יוֹצִיא "[who] brought [it] forth [gushing from the womb]?," God being understood as the subj.

9.a. חתלה "swaddling bands" occurs only here, but the vb חתל "swaddle" is found at Ezek 16:4; the noun חתול is "bandage" for a broken arm (Ezek 30:21), so the noun here and the vb are not specifically related to wrapping up infants.

10.a. וָאֶשְׁבֹּר is "and I broke," from שׁבר (so KJV). Most think the text is improbable. Gordis (followed by Sicre Díaz, Habel [apparently], and Hartley) argues that the sense "break" has developed to "decree, decide," but he has no other examples of this quite common word with such a meaning. BDB, 990, suggests implausibly "broke it for my boundary," in reference to the abrupt ending of the mainland where it meets the sea (so too Strahan). Gesenius–Buhl, 804b, has "form a boundary, i.e., a rugged broken off boundary." *HALOT*, 4:1403a, to similar effect, makes the unparalleled and far-fetched supposition of a technical sense "break into, make a mark in the ground," meaning "I fixed my boundary for him." This may lie behind RSV "prescribed [bounds]," NEB "established [its bounds]."

W. G. E. Watson, "Problems and Solutions in Hebrew Verse: A Survey of Recent Work," *VT* 43 (1993) 372–84 (377), has an interesting suggestion, that we have a case of what he calls "metathetic parallelism," in which terms are placed in a colon to which they do not apparently belong; thus "When I shattered my bounds upon it, I imposed bolts and doors" means "When I imposed my bounds upon it, I shattered bolts and doors" (a possible parallel in Isa 29:10). This proposal is identical in effect with the emendation of Dhorme mentioned below. The problem is that there is no point in Yahweh's shattering bolts and doors; at creation he is more likely to be establishing them.

Tur-Sinai, arguing that vv 8–10 contains only the imagery of birthing, connects the word with שבר hiph at Isa 66:9 "bring to the birth," i.e., presumably "break open the womb" (as *HALOT*, 4:1404b) or "cause to break out (from the womb)" (as BDB, 991a); he translates "and made its womb [i.e., the womb of its mother] give birth to it" (see also on חק below). But the bars and doors of v 10a are sufficient evidence that we are here outside the realm of birthing.

There is plainly a case to be made for a different vb שבר. Two suggestions have been made: (1) T. H. Gaster (*Thespis: Ritual, Myth, and Drama in the Ancient Near East* [New York: Henry Schuman, 1950] 456; but not in the 1961 edition) proposed a new vb cognate with Arab. *sabara* "prescribe boundaries." But *sabara* means "measure, determine," usually a thing already in existence (see the examples in Lane, 1293b), not by way of prescription for the future. (2) A. Guillaume, followed by Gray, proposed a new שבר "span" (better, "measure"; cf. Arab. *šabara* [Lane, 1495c]), translating "measured it by span [by my decree]" ("The Arabic Background of the Book of Job," in *Promise and Fulfilment: Essays Presented to Professor S. H. Hooke in Celebration of His Ninetieth Birthday* [ed. F. F. Bruce; Edinburgh: T. & T. Clark, 1963] 106–27 [123]; *Studies* 130). The same word is recognized by Dahood, *Psalms I*, 89–90 (though he does not correctly distinguish between *sabara* and *šabara*). This well-supported proposal is adopted in the *Translation* above.

Among emendations may be mentioned: (1) וָאָשִׁית "and I set" (Perles, *Analekten*, 87; Beer [*BHK*]), to which LXX ἐθέμην δέ would correspond. (2) אָסֹר "I shut it [within its bound]" (Fohrer). (3) וָאֶשְׂכֹּר "and I shut" (Hoffmann, Beer [*BH²prps*]), שׂכר being understood as a byform of סכר "shut." (4) Beer (*BH²frt*) suggests a new word וָאֶשְׂטֹר "and I inscribed, wrote," apparently cognate with Akk. *šatāru* [*CDA*, 364a]), while (5) Ehrlich read וָאֶשְׁמֹר "and I kept," neither suggestion being very appealing. (6) Dhorme transposed the two vbs, reading אשׂים "I set, imposed [my limit on it]" in the first colon, and אשׁבר "I shattered [bolts and doors]" in the second. His argument, that the word of God, his "limit" expressed in the command of v 11, supplants the need for a bar and doors, is extremely improbable. (7) Gray transposed the second and third words of the colon, reading וָאֶשְׁבֹּר חֻקִּי עָלָיו "and I gauged (שבר II "measure, gauge") the bounds to which he might come up," lit. "of his coming up." But he does not explain the form עָלָיו, which does not occur; "his coming up" would be עֲלֹתוֹ.

10.b. חקי is "my decree, limit." It can hardly be that God would be imposing a limit upon himself, and it would have to mean "the limit set by me" (Gordis, Habel, Hartley); cf. Kissane "I set up my bound against it." Dillmann, Duhm, Beer (*BH²prps*), Beer (*BHK*), Hölscher, Fohrer read חֻקּוֹ "its limit," but Dahood defended the suff of חקי as third person (*Psalms I*, 90), as also Blommerde (for other examples, see on 21:16), rendering "its limit"—which is unlikely. Sicre Díaz, following Peters, read חק "a limit."

Tur-Sinai, in line with his rather forced interpretation of the verse as representing the birth of the sea, takes the word as חֵיק "lap, womb," translating "and made its womb [read חֵקֹן, i.e., the womb of its mother] give birth to it." But there is no evidence that חֵיק can mean "womb" (it is "lap" or "fold" of a garment according to *HALOT*, 1:312b, "bosom" according to BDB, 300b).

10.c. Tur-Sinai thinks the דלתים are not "doors" but swaddling "sheets" for the newborn child (as in v 8), and, most improbably, that the בריח is not a "bar" but a "board," supposedly to keep the back of the infant straight.

11.a. Some delete, thinking the line is too long (Driver–Gray [*frt*], Beer [*BHK frt*]). It is often acknowledged as an anacrusis, outside the meter (Dhorme, Gordis); Dhorme notes 33:24, 27 as other possible examples.

11.b. Some delete תבוא "you shall come" to shorten the line (so Duhm, arguing that the word weakens the effect, and Beer [*BH²*]; thus too Moffatt "Thus far and no further!").

11.c. ולא תסיף, lit. "and you shall not add (to come)." Some delete, thinking the line is too long (Bickell, Beer [*BHK al*], de Wilde; Gray would delete either this phrase or ואמר "and I said"). Hölscher proposed we shorten the vb by one syllable by reading the form at Prov 30:6 תּוֹסְף.

11.d. אפ occurs nowhere else in Job, though the forms פֹּה, אֵפֹוא, אֵיפֹה, and אֵפֹו are attested in Job for "here." Either we should regard אפ as a byform of פֹּה or else actually emend to פֹּה (as Beer [*BHK*], Fohrer, NAB). Beer (*BH²*) read וּבְכֹה, but that means "thus, in this way," and not "here."

11.e. גאון גליך, lit. "the pride of your waves." But perhaps גאון has a physical meaning here, "height" (cf. גאה "rise up") rather than the emotional sense "pride." This may also be the significance of גְּאוֹן הַיַּרְדֵּן "the height of Jordan," usually translated "the thicket, jungle of Jordan" (Jer 12:9; 49:19; 50:44; Zech 11:3). Perhaps we should also compare קוֹל גְּאוֹנוֹ "his [God's] mighty voice" (37:4). No doubt the term גֵּאוּת הַיָּם at Ps 89:9 (10) should be rendered "[you rule] the rising up of the sea" (BDB, 145a; NJPS "swelling").

Most delete the initial *beth* of בגאון, reading גְּאוֹן and making "the pride of your waves" the subj of the vb (so, e.g., Beer [*BHK*], KJV, RSV, NAB, NIV, NEB). This emendation is adopted in the *Translation* above.

11.f. יָשִׁית "it will set" is unintelligible (NEB mg offers "[here] one shall set on [your surging waves]"), though Adolphe Lods took it to mean "set in place," i.e., make it return to its bounds ("Quelques remarques sur les poèmes mythologiques de Ras Chamra et leurs rapports avec l'Ancien Testament," *RHPR* 16 [1936] 101–30 [114]). Gerleman (*BHS*) wonders whether בּ שׁית might mean "resist," presumably reading אָשִׁית "and I shall resist [your proud waves]"; but the idea of Yahweh resisting the waves seems improbable.

Various emendations have been proposed, of which the last mentioned is to be preferred: (1) A common emendation is to וְאָשִׁית "and I set [its boundary for it]" (so Kissane, de Wilde, NAB), though this would still be a strange use of שׁית. (2) Duhm read שִׁית "stop!" (impv), but this sense of שׁית still needs to be defended. (3) Some read גְּאוֹן יִשָּׁבֵר "the pride of [your waves] shall be broken" (Ewald [*vel*], Merx, Driver–Gray, Kissane [*vel*]) or יִשְׁתַּבֵּר "shall be broken, destroyed" (Dhorme, Larcher [presumably], Gray, JB); so too apparently Hartley "will break" (there may be some support from Pesh), and presumably JB "here your proud waves shall (NJB must) break." (4) Ewald (*vel*) thought an even better proposal might be יִשְׁלָק "shall be hushed"; but שׁתק (BDB, 1060b) means "be still" without any sense of being constrained to be still. (5) Kissane suggested יִשּׁוֹבֵב "shall be turned back," שׁוב polel (*vel*); but this is not an attested sense of שׁוב polel. (6) Blommerde, keeping the consonants as they stand, offered an emendation of יָשִׁית ב- to יִשָׁתַב "shall be broken," supposedly an infixed -*t*- form from the vb שׁבב "break" (cf. Ugar. *ṯbb*) proposed by Dahood, "Is *Eben Yiśrā'el* a Divine Title?" It seems an elaborate way of defending the MT.

(7) More commonly יִשְׁבֹּת (qal) "shall cease" is read (Bickell, Beer [*BHK*], Driver–Gray [*vel*], Hölscher, Fohrer, Fedrizzi, Gerleman [*BHS frt*], de Wilde, Sicre Díaz, van der Lugt; Gordis "be stayed," NEB "halt" [Brockington]) or else יִשָׁבֵר (niph) with the same meaning (Driver–Gray [*vel*], Beer [*BHK vel*]), or perhaps יַשְׁבִּית (hiph) "put an end to" (Beer [*BH²vel*]), but it is not clear in that case how the colon is to be translated. It is not easy to determine what modern versions are reading when they translate "be stayed" (KJV, RSV), "be stilled" (NAB), "halt" (NIV), "stop" (NJPS), "shall not pass" (Moffatt). It is best to take the vb in a modal sense, "must cease," as is done in the *Translation* above, where that present emendation is adopted.

Suggestions that a new Heb. word is to be found here are far from convincing. Among them, (1) Pope suggested that a Ugar. *št*, apparently meaning "destroy," might be cognate with the שׁית here (followed by Hartley, who translates "[your proud waves] will break)." (2) Guillaume's proposal of a new שׁית "come to an end" cognate with סוף "end" is far from plausible (he argues that *s* and *f* frequently interchange in Arabic).

12.a. Duhm believed two distinct stanzas had been mistakenly combined in vv 12–15. The first, equivalent to vv 12, 13a, 14a, read: "Have you since your days began commanded the morning, and directed the dawn to its place, to take hold of the edge of the earth so that it should change as in the clay of a seal?" The second read: "Then the wicked are hidden by it, and they stand ashamed; and light is denied to the wicked, and the raised arm is broken." Terrien moves the whole strophe (vv 12–15) to follow vv 19–21, both about the light, thus connecting vv 8–11 with vv 16–18, both about the sea.

12.b. מִיָּמֶיךָ, lit. "from your days"; cf. 1 Kgs 1:6; but מִיָּמַי "from my days" in 27:6 (though see *Note*) and מִיָּמֶיךָ "from your days" in 1 Sam 25:28 do not appear to be analogous (against Gordis). Duhm and Strahan think the term ironical, Job's short life being contrasted with the age of the earth; but the parallel usage in 1 Kgs 1:6 would not support that view.

12.c. יִדַּעְתָּה "have made to know," the only occurrence of ידע "know" in piel, though it has also been proposed for v 33 and for Ps 104:19 (cf. *DCH*, 4:108a). The Q regards the final *he* of the vb as the article before שָׁחַר "the dawn"; but it is probably better to read the K with a fuller writing of the vb form (as also Beer [*BH²*], Gray).

13.a. לֶאֱחֹז "to seize" most naturally connects with צִוִּיתָ "you commanded" and יִדַּעְתָּה "you assigned" in v 12, which makes Job the subject of the inf here (so too Gordis, Habel). Others think the morning is the subj (so RSV "that it might take hold" and most modern versions, Tur-Sinai). Pope does not seem to be correct in thinking that "night cloaks the earth like a garment" (similarly Strahan, Kissane, Andersen, Habel), for it is the earth itself that is the cloth or garment.

13.b. כַּנְפוֹת are "wings, corners, edges, fringes"; Duhm, being a little too literal-minded, read בְּכְנַף "by the fringe of" in the sg, since the dawn touches only the eastern edge of the earth.

13.c. The colon is deleted by Hoffmann, Siegfried, Voigt, Duhm, Beer, *Text*, on the ground that at creation there were no wicked. But it is more likely that the line refers to the creation of each new morning, and moreover that רשעים does not mean "wicked" (see *Comment*).

13.d. For this understanding of רשעים, which apparently means "wicked," see *Comment* on vv 12–15, 13, 15. Guillaume believes that both the traditional interpretation and Driver's astronomical interpretation are correct. The emendation mentioned by Beer (*BH²prps*), רְשָׁפִים "flames," is forced.

14.a. Tur-Sinai moved the verse to follow v 38 on the basis of his idiosyncratic interpretation of the language.

14.b. הָפַךְ hithp is elsewhere "turn this way and that" (37:12; Gen 3:24; Judg 7:13), but BDB, 246a, *HALOT*, 1:254a, and *DCH*, 2:581b, offer "transform oneself" for this passage. Terrien "it changes its color [to sealed clay]" imports more than is justified into the vb, though it creates an exact parallel with the second colon.

14.c. JB "it changes the earth to sealing clay" takes the verb as transitive, and, following Dhorme, understands the words חֹתָם חֹמֶר as a construct phrase "clay of the seal," the reddish clay used for seals; similarly NJB "she [the earth] turns it as red as a clay seal." Tur-Sinai awkwardly reads חַוָּתָם "their pool [was turned as clay]" (cf. Arab. *ḥawiyy*), i.e., the water of the rain clouds that threaten the wicked; *ḥawiyy*, however, is attested only in the sense "a small watering trough, or tank, which a man makes for his camel" (Lane, 679a), and it does not appear to be a general word for "pool."

14.d. וְיִתְיַצְּבוּ "and they stand" is hard to fit into the context (KJV "and they stand as a garment" is not very intelligible). The pl is a difficulty, since there has been no pl referent since רְשָׁעִים "wicked (?)" in v 13, and one cannot see how they would be standing like a garment (though see Gordis below). NEB is very attractive with its rendering "until all things stand out like the folds of a cloak" (similarly NIV, Hartley "its features stand out like those of a garment"; Habel "and they stand out like a garment" understands "they" as "the features of"), but "all things" is no more than a good guess (it is adopted in the *Translation* above), and the "folds," which are crucial for the image, have nothing to represent them in the Hebrew. Good thinks כְּמוֹ לְבוּשׁ "like one clothed" means "as if in uniform," the vb יָצַב often having a military sense and the earth being thought of as taking its station at dawn; but did ancient armies wear uniforms? Fedrizzi is content to change the pl to a sg, omitting to change the gender also if וְתִתְיַצֵּב is to mean "and [the earth] presents itself as a garment."

Gordis has an elaborate interpretation, which, however, fails to carry conviction: he reads תֵּתְהַפֵּךְ כַּחֹמֶר חַיָּתָם וְיִתְיַצְבוּ כֻלָּם יֵבֹשׁוּ "their soul, i.e., they, is turned round and round in the mire, they all stand (i.e., are arraigned, in judgment), they are put to shame." The emendation of חֹתָם "seal" to חַיָּתָם "their life" is plausible enough, but the other usages of הָפַךְ hithp do not support "turn round and round" (it means rather "turn this way and that"). כְּחֹמֶר "like clay" is revocalized to כָּחֹמֶר, a contraction of כְּבַחֹמֶר "as in the mire." The second colon is much less persuasive a reconstruction since it represents a declination from the elevated poetry of the chapter, and there is no apparent connection with the theme of the coming of the morning. Tur-Sinai has "they [the dark rain clouds threatening the wicked] stood (as if contained in) a garment"—an extraordinarily implausible suggestion.

An emendation is usually adopted here, as in the *Translation* above. Most common is וְתִצְטַבַּע hithp or וְתִצָּבַע niph "and it [the earth] is dyed" (from צבע "dye," which does not occur elsewhere, though there is a noun צֶבַע "dyed stuff"); so Ehrlich, Beer [*BH² frt*], Dhorme, Kissane, Larcher, Pope, Gerleman (*BHS prps*), Sicre Díaz, van der Lugt, Newsom, Gray; RSV, NAB, Moffatt "in all its colours like a robe." JB "and dyes it as a man dyes clothes," and NJB "she [morning] tints it as though it were a dress" presumably read וְתִצְבַּע qal.

14.e. Duhm, following Hoffmann, read לְבֹשׁ "as (if) in shame"; so too Beer (*BH² al*), Hölscher.

15.a. The verse, understood as "from the wicked their light is withheld and their high arm is broken," is deleted by Hoffmann, Duhm, Hölscher for the reason that the wicked are not destroyed each morning. Gordis finds that an extremely prosaic objection, understanding the text to say that "the light of day deprives the evil-doers of the light they need to carry on their nefarious plans." Nonetheless, the astronomical sense adopted in the *Translation* above and in the subsequent *Notes* is preferable.

15.b. מִנַע "withhold, restrain" could in reference to light mean "be withdrawn" (NEB) or "be dimmed" (REB).

15.c. רָמָה זְרוֹעַ "high arm" (as KJV) is a phrase that occurs nowhere else, though explained by Gordis as meaning "arrogant power"; RSV has "uplifted arm," Moffatt "uplifted arms," NIV, NJPS "upraised arm," NAB "the arm of pride," NJB "the arm raised to strike." "With a high hand" (יָד רָמָה) generally means "in triumph" or "deliberately, defiantly" (P. R. Ackroyd, *TDOT*, 5:393–426 [415]), but such a sense would not be relevant here. The explanation of G. R. Driver that there is a reference to a star name here (see *Comment*) is attractive in avoiding the difficulty of the phrase.

15.d. Rather than תִּשָּׁבֵר "is broken," Duhm read תִּשְׁבַּת "is brought to an end, vanishes."

16.a. Beer (*BH²*) moves vv 16–18 to precede v 21.

16.b. בָאתָ, lit. "have you come?," but בוֹא, unlike English "come," is not strictly confined to the perspective of the focalized place, and can sometimes mean "go." The occurrences in 23:3; 37:8; 38:22; 41:13 (5) may be considered as possible parallels. The springs of the sea are no doubt *beneath* the sea, so NEB's "descended" (REB "gone down") is perhaps more correct than the usual "entered" (KJV, RSV, NAB), "penetrated" (NJPS), or "journeyed" (NIV).

16.c. נֵבֶךְ "spring" occurs only here (BDB, 614a), though it has been proposed also for Prov 8:24 and Jer 48:32 (see *DCH*, 5:592a); נְבוֹךְ "spring" is found at 1QH 11:15 (*DCH*, 5:584b), and a vb נבך "pour out" has been inferred on the basis of Ugar. *nbk* (George M. Landes, "The Fountain at Jazer," *BASOR* 144 [1956] 30–37 [31–34]; M. Dahood, *Ugaritic-Hebrew Philology: Marginal Notes on Recent Publications* (BibOr 17: Rome: Pontifical Biblical Institute, 1965) 65–66; *Psalms II: 51–100* (AB 17; Garden City, NY: Doubleday, 1968; 3rd ed., 1979), 158, 281; *DCH*, 5:592a). Cf. also מִבָּךְ "source" at 28:11 (*q.v.*). KJV, RSV, NIV, NEB render "springs," NAB, JB, NJPS "sources," with the same meaning. G. R. Driver saw a new נֵבֶךְ "sandy depths" (cf. Arab. *nabk* "shifting sands"); see his "Studies in the Vocabulary of the Old Testament. VI," *JTS* 34 (1933) 375–85 (379); *DCH*, 5:592b. But his only source for the Arabic is Dozy, 2:637a (Driver admits that the word is cited only from Algiers), which is notoriously unreliable evidence for the classical language.

16.d. הלך hithp is "walk about, walk to and fro" (NAB "walked about"; cf. *DCH*, 2:557b) rather than, as in the qal, simply "walk" (as most other translations).

16.e. חֵקֶר is properly "(act of) searching," and only here and at 11:7 refers to the thing searched for (cf. KJV "walked in the search of the depth"); cf. *DCH*, 3:305a. The "searched thing" of the deep is its remotest part, such as would require a lot of effort to reach. If תהום is translated "the Deep," "the remotest part of the Deep" may seem to be its deepest part (NAB "the depths of the abyss," NEB, REB "the unfathomable deep," GNB "the floor of the ocean"); but the term חקר does not itself suggest "depth" and it could well imply the remotest parts of the Abyss on a linear scale (which is perhaps what "the recesses of the deep" in ASV, RSV, NRSV, NJPS means).

17.a. תראה "you have seen" is a preterite, a single action in the past parallel to the perf tense vb נגלו "have been revealed" in the first colon; so too in v 22 (an emendation to the perf רָאִיתָ "you have seen" [Gray] is unnecessary). Quite interesting is the emendation to יֵרְאוּ "[have the door-keepers] been alarmed by you?," suggested by LXX πυλωροὶ δὲ ᾅδου ἰδόντες σε ἔπτηξαν "have the door-keepers of Hades been terrified when they caught sight of you?"; Duhm thought it might well be correct, and Moffatt catches the sense exactly with "Have the warders cowered before you?" Emendation to רָאִתָה "have you seen?," the perf tense (as Beer [*BHK*]), seems unnecessary.

17.b. Instead of שַׁעֲרֵי "gates of," a mere repetition of the term in the first colon, some revocalize as שֹׁעֲרֵי "gatekeepers of" (cf. LXX πυλωροί); so Duhm, Beer (*BH² frt*), Larcher, Terrien, de Wilde, NEB (cf. JB with its wonderful phrase "the janitors of Shadowland"); cf. also the repetition in v 22. The emendation is adopted in the *Translation* above. It could be, however, that LXX's rendering was for the sake of variety. Dhorme's objection that to "see" the gatekeepers of death is "too insipid" is not decisive. There is some justification for Blommerde's view of a custom of repeating a word at the beginning of the second colon, prefaced by emphatic *waw* (as also in v 22; for other examples of the emphatic *waw*, see *Note* on 28:21).

Guillaume finds here a new Hebrew שֶׁעַר "boundary" (cf. Arab. *taghr*) ("The Arabic Background of the Book of Job," in *Promise and Fulfilment: Essays Presented to Professor S. H. Hooke in Celebration of His Ninetieth Birthday* [ed. F. F. Bruce; Edinburgh: T. & T. Clark, 1963] 106–27 [123–24]; *Studies* 130–31). Kaltner, however, argues that the Arab. evidence does not support such a translation (*The Use of Arabic in Biblical Hebrew Lexicography*, 79–80), since *taghr* properly means "gap" or a breach in a wall that gives access. Lane, 339a, however, offers the senses "the frontier of a hostile country" and "boundary between countries," which would support Guillaume adequately (though "frontier" would be a better translation than "confines"). Kaltner's distinction between giving or precluding access seems somewhat beside the point, and perhaps arises from a misunderstanding of the term "confines," which denotes a borderland without a connotation of containment. Guillaume's proposal is nevertheless not to be preferred to the revocalization to שֹׁעֲרֵי noted above.

17.c. On צלמות as "darkness of death" (KJV, NIV "shadow of death"; similarly NJB "shadow dark as death"), rather than simply "deep darkness" (RSV, NJPS) or "darkness" (NAB, NEB) or "Shadow" (Dhorme) or "Shadowland" (JB), see *Note* a on 3:5.

18.a. בין hithpo is in Job "consider" (as at 11:11; 23:15; 37:14; and even at 26:4) (so too Dhorme; cf. KJV "perceive," and perhaps NJPS "survey"), not "understand" or "comprehend" (as RSV, NEB, NAB, NIV). The interrogative הֲ should be prefixed to the word or else understood (Tur-Sinai, Gordis); cf. on 39:13.

18.b. The translation "furthest expanse" attempts to render both the sense of עַד "as far as" and the pl of רחבי lit. "expanses of," no doubt a pl of intensity; cf. NIV "vast expanses," Tur-Sinai "the vast expanse." G. R. Driver made the interesting suggestion that עַד is not the preposition but a new noun meaning "extent" ("Mistranslations," *PEQ* 80 [1948] 64–65 [64]). Duhm, however, thought that עַד should be emended to עַל "upon" (as at, e.g., 31:1); Beer (*BHK*) agreed, noting that עַל would be meant in the sense of אֶל "unto."

18.c. אֶרֶץ of course is usually "earth," but I follow here the suggestion of some that it here means "underworld" (Andersen, Hartley); cf. Jer 17:13; Jonah 2:6 (7); Ps 22:29 (30) (Exod 15:12; Ps 71:20 are not such good examples). See *HALOT*, 1:91a.

18.d. כלה is apparently "[if you know] all of it." Emendations to מִלָּה "a word" (Graetz), גְּבֻלָה "its frontier" (Budde, though translating "all of it"), and כַּמֶּה "how much" (Duhm, Beer [*BH*²], Strahan, Gray ["its extent"], and Moffatt "how large," following LXX πόση) are not especially attractive (Duhm thought "all of it" childish). Tur-Sinai thought we might have here a second vb כול "measure," reading כָּלָה. More probably, we have a little-recognized noun כֹּל "measure, extent" (*DCH*, 4:413b [כֹּל III]; noted for Prov 28:5 by Mitchell Dahood, "Qoheleth and Northwest Semitic Philology," *Bib* 43 [1962] 349–65 [359–60], and for this passage by Eduardo Zurro Rodríguez, "La raíz *kw/yl* y siete textos bíblicos," *EstBib* 57 (1999) 777–86 [778–79]).

19.a. Hölscher and Fohrer delete vv 19–20 as an explanatory gloss; Duhm, followed by Moffatt, moved them to follow v 15.

19.b. אֵי־זֶה הַדֶּרֶךְ "where then is the way?," the זֶה functioning as an enclitic (see BDB, 261a §4). Although this reading is perfectly intelligible, Andersen is perhaps correct in understanding דֶּרֶךְ rather as דֶּרֶךְ II "power, dominion, realm" (cf. *DCH*, 2:472b), a closer parallel to מָקוֹם "place" in the second colon. The repeated phrase אֵי־זֶה הַדֶּרֶךְ in v 24 would be a further example of דֶּרֶךְ II. Beer (*BH*²) suggested deleting the article of הַדֶּרֶךְ, though it is not clear why.

19.c. הַדֶּרֶךְ יִשְׁכָּן־אוֹר lit. "the way (to where) light dwells."

20.a. כִּי at the beginning of this line is usually taken as introducing a result clause (cf. *DCH*, 4:386a §4), thus, e.g., RSV "that you may take it to its territory." But, as Gordis points out, there are two problems here: (1) it is illogical to say in v 10 "Where is the way … so that you may take them?"; logically, the verse would have to say "Do you know … the way so that you may take them." (2) Even so, it makes a poor connection to say "Do you know the way to the dwelling of light (v 19a) … so that you may perceive the paths to their home? (v 20b)." It is better, with Gordis, to regard the initial כִּי as an interrogative particle (see on 37:20, and cf. *DCH*, 4:389a). NIV also makes of v 20 two separate questions unconnected syntactically with v 19, but one cannot know if that is because they adopt the explanation of כִּי as interrogative. NEB "And can you then take" seems to imply that it begins a result clause.

20.b. תִּקָּחֶנּוּ "you could take it," the sg suff referring to both light and darkness in v 19; translations need to say "them" to show that both light and darkness are referred to. גְּבוּלוֹ "its domain" must likewise be translated "their domain," as also בֵּיתוֹ "its home." נְתִיבוֹת "paths" is however pl. Even if both light and darkness are conceived of as sharing the same dwelling turn and turn about, that would not explain the suffs (as de Wilde suggests) since although there may be only one "house," the suffs refer to two entities.

לקח "take" is only rarely used in the sense "lead to," but the idiom לקח אל with such a meaning can be paralleled in Esth 2:8, 16; Num 11:16; 23:14, 27. Emendation to תַּנְחֶנּוּ "will you set it [at its boundary (?)]?" (נוח hiph B), as Beer (*BH*²), is awkward; תַּנְחֶנּוּ "will you lead it?" (נחה hiph) would be much more likely.

20.c. גְּבוּל is usually "boundary" (as NAB, REB; KJV, NEB "bound," Pope "bourne"), but also "territory within a boundary," thus "domain" (BDB, 147b), as NJPS (RSV "territory," NIV "places," JB "proper places"). Moffatt, with "Can you conduct them to their fields," suggests that the גְּבוּל is the field of operation.

20.d. בִּין "understand, discern" is perhaps not the most obvious vb to use with "path" as the obj, but it does occur in the qal at Prov 20:24; 21:29 (Q) with דֶּרֶךְ "way," and Prov 2:9 with מַעְגַּל "way," and in the hiph at Prov 14:8 with דֶּרֶךְ "way." Tur-Sinai and presumably Pope (Pope "show it the way to go home") explain תָּבִין as hiph, thus "teach, show."

On the other hand, there is much to be said, not least from the point of view of the parallelism, for the revocalization of Hoffmann from תָּבִין "you discern" to תְּבִיאֶנּוּ, a defective spelling of תְּבִיאֵנּוּ "you should bring it," from בוא hiph (so too Duhm, Strahan, Peake, Beer [*BHK*], Hölscher, Larcher, Fohrer, Gerleman [*BHS prps*], de Wilde, Gray [תְּבִיאֵנּוּ], Moffatt "lead them home again," NAB "set them on their homeward path," JB "put them on the path to where they live (NJB their home)," NEB "escort it on its homeward path"). The revocalization is accepted in the *Translation* above.

21.a. De Wilde moves this verse to follow v 18; it concludes, he thinks, the first section of the speech, dealing with the creation and ordering of the world (similarly Bickell, Duhm).

21.b. It is possible that the interrogative particle הֲ should be prefixed or assumed for יָדַעְתָּ, thus "Do you know?" (so Duhm), just as it is almost certainly is at the beginning of v 18. If that were so, כִּי might need to be understood as "surely" (cf. on v 5).

21.c. אָז "then" is awkward, since no notation of time has preceded. Dhorme, NIV, REB "you were already born" (NEB "born already") is no improvement. NAB has "you were born before them," JB "you must have been born with them (NJB when they were)," Moffatt "you, born when it was made," do not address the problem of the Hebrew. Unless the line is misplaced, we should probably emend to מֵאָז "from of old" (as at Isa 44:8; Ps 93:2; Prov 8:22; cf. *DCH*, 1:168a). Unlike most commentators we should be cautious about defining the moment referred to as the time of creation; the text speaks only of great antiquity.

21.d. רבים "great" is pl, by attraction to ימים "days," though strictly it should agree with מספר "number."

22.a. אצרות "storehouses" is the same word as in the first colon. As in v 17, Duhm, Beer (*BH² prps*), want to create variety in the line by reading אוֹצְרֵי "the treasurers of [the hail]," i.e., those appointed to distribute the hail. De Wilde preferred to emend to a new word for Biblical Hebrew, אֲגוּרָה "store-house" (as in MH). Guillaume proposed another Heb. אוֹצָר "huge hailstone" (cf. Arab. *waḍrā* "large rock") ("The Arabic Background of the Book of Job," 124 [*waḍra* or *waḍrā'u* "large rock"; *Studies*, 131 [*waḍrā'u*]). Others (e.g., Beer [*BHK frt*]) suggest מִזְוֵי "storehouses of" (from מָזוּ), as at 37:9. Gray proposes צְפֻנוֹת "hoards," but the other uses of that term in Isa 48:6 and 65:4 are not very apposite (it seems to mean either "hidden things" or "secret places"). Blommerde's suggestion that the repetition of a word at the beginning of the second colon prefaced with emphatic *waw* is a normal feature of Hebrew poetry (cf. above on v 17) may well be the best solution. The adoption in the *Translation* above of "arsenals" in the second colon is merely for the sake of the English, which prefers not to have simple repetition.

23.a. חשׂך was "spare" at 21:30, but "hold back, reserve" here.

23.b. עת־צר "a time of calamity," though the idiom is elsewhere always עֵת צָרָה (Judg 10:14; Isa 33:2; Jer 14:8; 15:11; 30:7; Ps 37:39; Dan 12:1; Neh 9:27; 2 Chr 28:22). צר could be צר II "calamity," from צרר I "bind up," or צר III "enemy," from צרר II "be hostile." "The day of the enemy" seems less likely than "the day of calamity," but if עֵת is used in the special sense of "doom" (as apparently at Ps 81:15 [16]; Eccl 9:12), "for the fate of the enemy" becomes a more plausible suggestion.

24.a. De Wilde moves to this point vv 29–30, concerning the ice.

24.b. הדרך יחלק אור is apparently "the way (to where) lightning is dispersed"; a relative such as לַאֲשֶׁר is presupposed. But perhaps we have here דֶּרֶךְ II (cf. also v 19) "realm," thus "where is the realm (from which) lightning is dispersed?" Some storehouse from which stored lightning is distributed is presumably in mind. This suggestion is adopted in the *Translation* above. Pope also saw here דרך II, but, less probably, in the sense "power," translating "by what power is the flood [אָר, the cosmic water reservoir] divided?" If דרך is "way, path," it will refer to the way to the storehouse of lightning, not the path that lightning follows when it is dispersed from the storehouse (as Dhorme "in what path are … dispersed," or NEB "by what paths is … spread abroad"). Beer (*BH²*) suggested deleting the article of הדרך, though it is not clear why.

24.c. אור is usually "light," but here, especially because of the parallel with the east wind, it is more likely to be "lightning" (as 36:32; 37:3, 15); so also JB, NIV, Habel, van der Lugt, Newsom, Strauss; this would perhaps yield a good sense for חלק "divide," i.e., "from which direction does the lightning fork?" (JB).

A better suggestion, however, is that of G. R. Driver, followed by NEB, Guillaume, de Wilde, Sicre Díaz, Gray, to revocalize to אוּר "heat" (BDB, 22a, "flame"), comparing Arab. *'uwār* "heat (of sun or fire)" (cf. Freytag, 1:69b; Wehr–Cowan, 34a; but not apparently in Lane), finding the same word also at Isa 31:9; 44:16; 47:14; 50:11; Ezek 5:2; and emending to it at Zech 14:6; see "Problems in Job," *AJSL* 52 (1936) 160–70 [166, though it is not clear that the vocalization intended is אוּר]; "Problems in the Hebrew Text of Job," in *Wisdom in Israel and in the Ancient Near East, Presented to Professor Harold Henry Rowley … in Celebration of His Sixty-Fifth Birthday* (VTSup, 3; Leiden: E. J. Brill, 1955) 72–93 [91–92]). I do not regard this word as the same word as אוּר I "flame" in BDB, 22a, since BDB does not use the term "heat" or cite Arab. *'uwār* as a cognate; but the same passages are cited by BDB, though without our Job reference or Zech 14:6. Fedrizzi also translated "heat," but without revocalizing to אוּר. The two halves of the line fit together better if the storehouse is that of the heat which the east wind spreads over the earth.

Tur-Sinai thought it was the "west wind" (cf. Akk. *amurru* [*CDA*, 16a], Bab. *awurru* "land of the west wind"), parallel to קדים "east wind"; he is followed by NJPS, Hartley. Gordis thought it another word meaning "air, air currents" (perhaps the origin of Greek ἀήρ "air, wind").

Others have emended, to רוּחַ "wind" (Merx, Wright, Bickell², Budde, Driver–Gray, Beer [*BHK*], Hölscher, Fohrer, NAB "[the parting of] the winds"), קְטוֹר "smoke" (Beer [*BH²*], weakly claiming the support of LXX πάχνη "hoar-frost"), כְּפֹר "hoar-frost" (Siegfried, also comparing LXX πάχνη), or אֵד "mist, cosmic flood" (Hoffmann, Bickell, Duhm, Peake, Pope, Moffatt; also Dhorme and Terrien, who, however, understand אד as "mists" or "fog").

24.d. יחלק is usually derived from חלק "divide, share, distribute." G. R. Driver, however, found here a new חלק VI "create" (cf. Arab. *ḥalaqa*); see "Problems in the Hebrew Text of Job," 91–92); Dahood, *Psalms III*, 180–81; *DCH*, 3:242b; the vb has been suggested for Ecclus 31:13; 38:1; Jer 10:16 ∥ 51:19; Lam 3:24. It is hard to see what would be intended by the "apportioning" of the heat, since only one conveyance for it (the east wind) is mentioned; so the proposal for חלק VI "create" is adopted in the *Translation*.

24.e. Guillaume, understanding אור as "heat," translates "which the sirocco scatters over the earth," which is to be preferred to NEB's interpretation of the verse: "By what paths is the heat spread abroad or the east wind carried far and wide over the earth?" For the east wind is obviously the carrier of the heat rather than a second source of heat.

24.f. Duhm's emendation (followed by Peake, Beer [*BH²prps*]) of קדים "east wind" to קרים "cold, i.e., fresh (water)," as in Jer 18:14, is no improvement; Moffatt, however, adopted it, with "How are the mists marshaled, that scatter water on the earth?" Kissane saw here a parallel to אור "lightning," and read יקדים "burnings, flames" (as in Isa 10:16), translating "to where the lightning is parted, that scatter flames upon the earth"; he is followed by Larcher and thus by JB also, though not by NJB. This is an attractive suggestion, which brings the two cola together, but lightning is not usually connected with burning.

24.g. פוץ hiph is usually trans., and an implied relative pronoun אשר could well be the obj, thus "the heat, which the sirocco spreads." Those, however, who do not agree that the subj of the first colon is "heat" need to take the vb as intrans, "scatter, be scattered" (as also at Exod 5:12; 1 Sam 13:8). Beer (*BHK*), Hölscher, NEB read qal יפץ, i.e., יפוץ "[the east wind] is spread" (NEB "is carried"), but to be "spread" is not a natural word to use of the wind.

25.a. We are not hearing about creation here, but about the regular cycle of nature, so the present tense "cuts" (NIV), "carves" (JB), "bores out" (NJB) is to be preferred to "hath divided" (KJV), "has cleft" (RSV, Kissane), "cleft" (Pope, Habel), "has cut" (NRSV, NEB; similarly Terrien), "cut" (Moffatt, NJPS, Habel, Good), "has laid out" (NAB). It seems unlikely then that the channel is cut in the solid vault of heaven (as Peake, Strahan, Kissane), for that can hardly be imagined as an everyday occurrence. The second colon refers to a path through the air, and so, we may expect, does the first colon.

25.b. חזיז קלות, lit. "the lightning of thunder" (so KJV), i.e., the thunderbolt (Moffatt, RSV, REB, Hartley), a single discharge of lightning accompanied by its thunder, not "thunderstorm(s)" (NAB, NIV, NJPS, GNB, Kissane, Habel) or "thunder" (JB) or "thundershower" (Pope) or "thunderclouds" (Terrien) or "thunderclap" (Good), all of which remove the element of the lightning. The term has occurred at 28:26; on its meaning, see *Note*.

27.a. שבע hiph "satisfy"; that emotional term should probably be maintained (Moffatt "gladden" is on the right lines) rather than rendering "water, irrigate" (as Dhorme; cf. JB "give drink") or "saturate" (NJPS, Habel). NJB "to meet the needs" is far too prosaic. NEB "clothing lands waste and derelict with green," though pretty enough, loses sight of the metaphor.

27.b. שאה ומשאה, lit. "desolation and devastation." Israel Eitan, "Biblical Studies," *HUCA* 14 (1939) 1–22 (3–4), reads שאה משואה, שאה being in his view a verbal noun from a new vb ישה "shoot forth plants" (cf. Arab. *waša(y)* "increase"), and translates "to cause shoots to spring up from the waste." He finds the vb also in Hos 10:1 and Prov 8:21, and he explains the noun תושיה "success" from the same root.

27.c. דשא is lit. "source of grass." Contrary to common opinion, דשא does not mean "green, greenness" (as also BDB, 205b, *s.v.* דשא, KB, 220a, *s.v.* דשא, *HALOT*, 1:233b) but simply "grass" or other edible vegetation (cf. *DCH*, 2:476b). מוצא, a noun from יצא "go out," thus a going forth, what goes forth, or a place of going forth, has occurred at 28:1 as the "mine," i.e., source, for silver; it is harder to identify its meaning here. BDB, 425b, understands "the growing place [of grass]," which would be a strange circumlocution for "ground" (though adopted by RSV). *DCH*, 5:184a–b, suggests "growing-place" or "crop" (as NJPS). KJV "the bud [of the tender herb]" is not implausible, though unparalleled. *HALOT*, 2:559b, accepts the emendation to מציה "from the thirsty land" (so Dhorme, Beer [*BHK*], Hölscher, Larcher [apparently], Sicre Díaz, Habel, Hartley, van der Lugt, Gray, NAB, JB "making grass spring where everything was dry"). More commonly, as in the *Translation* above, the emendation to מצמא "from the thirsty (land)" is accepted (so NJB, NEB "thirsty ground," NAB "till the desert blooms"; Wright, Duhm, Peake, Driver–Gray, Beer [*BHK vel*], Kissane, Pope). NIV "make it sprout with grass" seems to omit the word מצא.

28.a. The verse is omitted by Bickell, Duhm, Peake, Beer (*BH²frt*), Strahan, Hölscher, de Wilde, arguing that rain has been dealt with in v 25. Driver–Gray, however, correctly note that it is torrential rain there and ordinary rain here; there is no repetition.

28.b. אגלי-טל "drops of dew." אגל "drop" occurs only here; the noun may be related to אגר "gather." Tur-Sinai, remarking that Arab. *ma'jal* is "accumulation of waters, pool" (cf. Freytag, 1:16a; not in

Lane), thinks the reference is to a storehouse of dew; but vv 28–29 seem rather to have left the idea of the storehouses behind and to be considering the various kinds of moisture on earth.

29.a. De Wilde moves vv 29–30 to follow v 23 (for the reason, see *Comment* on vv 22–24). Terrien regards them as secondary.

29.b. קרח is both "frost" (as at Gen 31:40 and Jer 36:30) and "ice" (as at 6:16; 37:10), probably "hail" at Ps 147:17, and perhaps "crystal" at Ezek 1:22. Here in vv 28–29 we plainly have atmospheric phenomena, and "rime" is chosen for the *Translation* as a variant to "hoar-frost" in the next colon. Rime is strictly a "deposit formed by the rapid freezing of supercooled droplets of water when they are brought by air currents into contact with a cold surface," whereas hoar-frost is "a crystalline deposit of ice formed by the sublimation of water vapour" (*OED*), in the form of interlocking crystals in the pattern of a feather, fern, or flower. Tur-Sinai improbably argues that קרח always means "storm" in Biblical Hebrew.

29.c. כפר שמים is lit. "frost of heaven," a phrase that may suggest that כפר, like קרח, can mean both "frost" and "ice," שמים כפר being reserved for the frost that occurs in the air. All the occurrences of כפר in the Hebrew Bible in fact mean "frost," but at Ecclus 3:15 it could perhaps mean "ice."

29.d. מי ילדו lit. "who gave birth to it?" Duhm, having deleted v 28, took ילד as the act of the male parent, which the vb does sometimes refer to (BDB, 408b §2; *DCH*, 4:216a §2); but most take both vbs in this verse in reference to the mother, "give birth to."

30.a. Fedrizzi thinks the verse is an explanatory gloss on v 29, and encloses it in brackets.

30.b. חבא is "hide"; hithp is "keep oneself hidden, be hidden" (cf. *HALOT*, 1:284b; *DCH*, 4:147b); thus KJV "are hid," NAB "lie covered." But "hidden like a stone" is not a plausible sense. Perhaps כאבן "like a stone" is an abbreviated form of כְּאָבֶן "as with a stone" (so KJV, RV, NAB, Gerleman [*BHS*], Grabbe, Sicre Díaz; cf. NEB "which lays a stony cover over the waters"; the usage is noted in GKC, §118s). Even so, the image seems strained. Tur-Sinai even more implausibly thought of the *heavenly* waters being hidden "as (behind) stone."

Some lexica and versions attempt to mend matters by understanding חבא as "draw together, thicken, harden" (so BDB, 285a); so too the translations "become hard" (RSV, NIV; JB, no doubt, follows Larcher's emendation, but we do not know what exactly that is), "harden" (Bickell, Hartley), and "congeals" (NJPS; similarly RV mg, Strahan). But these are simply impossible senses for the unproblematic vb חבא "hide" (though see further at the end of this *Note*).

One route to a solution, not involving an emendation, is to propose a new root: thus (1) חבא "harden" (not in *DCH*; perhaps a byform of an otherwise unattested חמא, evidenced in the noun חֶמְאָה "curd" (an Arab. cognate is often cited as *ḥamaʔa* "be hard" [so Pope], or *ḥamaʔ* [so Kissane], but it is rightly *ḥamā* [so BDB, 326a, citing Freytag (1:527b)], though it is not in Lane). This proposal is adopted by Siegfried, Hitzig (who thinks חבא is also related to כפא "thicken, condense, congeal"), Hoffmann, Dhorme, Hölscher, Larcher (apparently), Pope. (2) חבא "contract" (not in *DCH*); so Guillaume, invoking Arab. *ḥabā* "contract," and translating "become solid." The word is actually *ḥabā* (Lane, 507b), which in the VIII form has the specialized sense "drew the legs together against the body"; it is not a general word for "contract," and there is not the slightest evidence that it means "be solid." Though "become hard" is presumably the general sense that is required, the cognates can offer little support.

An initially plausible emendation is to transpose the two verbs, making the first colon "[like a stone the waters] are compacted together (יתלכדו)" (so Bickell[2], Merx, Budde, Peake, Beer [*BH*[2] *frt*], Driver–Gray, Moffatt, Rowley, Gordis, de Wilde; Habel thinks of the two vbs being cumulative). לכד is "capture"; hithp occurs only elsewhere at 41:17 (9), where the scales of Leviathan "clasp" one another. The parallel is not close enough, however, for while it is understandable that discrete items like scales should mutually "capture" one another, water (מים) does not consist of discrete particles "capturing" or cohering with one another; moreover, they would not capture one another "like stone," since stone is not formed of discrete particles either. "Stone" here must refer to the hardness of the ice that forms, not to the manner of the cohesion of the water into ice.

Other emendations are: (1) יְתְחַמְּאוּ "are hardened" (Duhm, Beer [*BH*[2] *al*], Kissane, Gray [יִתְחַמְּאוּ], JB), an otherwise unknown vb. Grabbe, 118–20, however, doubts the existence of a vb *ḥmʔ* in Semitic. (2) יְתְחַבְּרוּ "are joined together" (Beer [*BHK*]; Zorell, 218b).

Even though we may not be able to identify the vb, plainly some word meaning "harden" is required here to describe how water becomes like stone; the *Translation* represents the required sense rather than a specific textual reading.

30.c. On the assumption that the two vbs of the line should be transposed (see previous *Note*), the face of the deep would here be said to be "hidden" (יתחבאו), i.e., by the ice that forms on it. An objection might be that it is the deep, and not its face, that would be hidden; Peake, however, explains ingeniously that "the face of the deep is the surface of the water that flows under the ice" (cf. Moffatt "the ice hides the depth below").

If the MT יתכלדו is maintained, lit. "is captured," a conformable translation is hard to find: Pope has "imprisoned," NAB "stone that holds captive the surface of the deep," but it is not the "surface of the deep" that is imprisoned, rather what is below the surface. KJV, RSV, NIV, Hartley have "is frozen," NEB "freezes," JB "congeals," NJPS "compacts," Dhorme "becomes a solid mass," but there is no parallel for such a sense of לכד. Perhaps the best solution is to maintain the precise sense of לכד, "capture," and supply "by the ice" to make clear what the image is—as in the *Translation* above.

Tur-Sinai proposed an emendation to יִתְלַבָּדוּ "they stick together," from a new לבד "stick together" (cf. Syr. *lbad*), which he saw also at 41:17 (9); Isa 5:8.

31.a. Kissane moves vv 31–32 to follow v 3, since he regards them as concerning the creation of heavenly phenomena.

31.b. קשר piel "bind" occurs elsewhere at Isa 49:18, of binding on clothes or ornaments. Merx has the interesting translation "Wilt thou engirdle thyself with the beauty of the Pleiades?," meaning that they are the delightful girdle that encircles Yahweh, not Job. But there would then be no satisfactory parallel with the second colon.

31.c. מַעֲדָן II "bond, chain" seems to be a different word from מַעֲדָן I "delicacy," which was how KJV interpreted the word ("the sweet influences [of Pleiades]"), apparently in reference to the spring fruits and flowers that they were thought to stimulate (following the Jewish interpreters Nachmanides and Gersonides; so too apparently NIV "the beautiful Pleiades"). מעדן II may occur also at 1 Sam 15:32, if the sense is "Agag came towards him in chains" (for other possibilities, cf. *DCH*, 5:381a–b). It is probably a metathesis of מַעֲדָך "chain" (the vb is ענד "bind"); so too Duhm, Dhorme, Beer (*BHK*), Hölscher, Terrien, Tur-Sinai, Fedrizzi, Sicre Díaz, Habel, Hartley, Gray. "Bands" is a frequent translation (so, e.g., Dhorme, Terrien). However, as Driver points out, there is no evidence in ancient mythology for "bonds" of the Pleiades, and to translate "fetters" (Pope, Habel, de Wilde) conjures up a myth we know nothing of. The Pleiades are a close-knit group of stars, a "cluster" in modern scientific parlance, so perhaps they were thought to be bound together with chains (so RSV). Presumably RV's and Moffatt's "cluster" conveys the same idea. Other translations adopt variations on this interpretation: JB "Can you fasten the harness of the Pleiades?," NAB "Have you fitted a curb to the Pleiades?," NJPS "Can you tie cords to Pleiades?" But all three renderings presuppose some wholly speculative mythological tale.

G. R. Driver proposed a new word מַעֲדָת "company, group" on the basis of Ugar. *'dn* (*DUL*, 151) and Arab. *'adānat* "company, party" (Lane, 1976c) ("Two Astronomical Passages in the Old Testament," *JTS* ns 7 [1956] 1–11 [3]; cf. *DCH*, 5:381b). This is apparently followed by NEB "cluster"; the same rendering is arrived at on a different basis by RV and Moffatt, as we have seen above. To similar effect is Guillaume's proposal of a מַעֲדָן V "army, host" (on the same Ugar. basis).

31.d. משכה, which occurs only here, is apparently "belt, cord" from משך "draw, drag." In some ancient mythology, Orion is girded with a belt from which his sword hangs (thus NEB "loose Orion's belt"). But others understand it of a "cord" by which he is dragged along (cf. RSV, Driver–Gray "cords") or "bonds" (NAB) or "bands" (KJV, JB) or "reins" (NJPS, Habel). משכות is pl, but Orion has only one belt; hence some read מֹשְׁכַת "belt" (NEB [*vel*]) or מִשְׁכַת (NEB [*vel*]). The same sense is obtained by an emendation to מֹסְרוֹת "bonds" (so Beer [*BHK*], Gray), but it is questionable whether the author was aware of a myth of the binding of Orion (see *Comment*); Gray agrees, but explains the bonds as the fixedness of the constellations.

32.a. מַזָּרוֹת "Mazzaroth," occurring only here, appears to be the name of a star or constellation. Though the form is pl, the sg suff of עתו "its season" suggests that it is a single star or constellation, though the sg could perhaps be distributive: "the Mazzarot, each in its season." Dhorme thinks the pl is a plural of majesty (cf. Mitchell Dahood, "Philological Notes on Jer 18,14–15," *ZAW* 74 [1962] 207–9 [208]); Blommerde explains the ending ־וֹת as a "Phoenician singular."

Mazzaroth has been variously identified as: (1) *Arcturus*; so KJV "Arcturus"; Sigmund Mowinckel, *Die Sternnamen im Alten Testament* (Oslo: Grøndahl, 1928) 27–29. Arcturus, the Bear Watcher, in the constellation Boötes, the Herdsman, is just below Ursa Major and Minor (the Bear, also known as the Big and Little Dipper). It is the brightest star of the northern hemisphere and the fourth brightest star of the entire night sky, after Sirius, Canopus, and Alpha Centauri.

(2) *The Hyades*; so Duhm (*frt*), Hölscher, Tur-Sinai, Dahood, comparing זור "flow" ("Philological Notes on Jer 18,14–15," 208; *Proverbs and Northwest Semitic Philology* [Scripta pontificii instituti biblici 113; Rome: Pontificium Institutum Biblicum, 1963] 33). But the Hyades are the "sons" of Aldebaran that are mentioned in the next colon, so it would be strange if they appeared in this colon as well. Nevertheless, wider considerations may point to this identification (see *Comment*).

(3) *The planets*; so Menahem Mansoor, *The Thanksgiving Hymns* (STDJ 3; Leiden: E. J. Brill, 1961) 109, *HALOT*, 2:566b, Hartley. Sometimes the word is thought to be a variant of מַזָּלוֹת "planets" or "constellations of the Zodiac" (BDB, 561a, *HALOT*, 2:565b).

(4) *Venus* in its two phases; so G. Schiaparelli, *Astronomy in the Old Testament* (Oxford: Clarendon Press, 1904) 74–89; JB "the morning star."

(5) *Sirius*, the Dog Star, in Canis Major, the brightest star in the night sky, whose rising coincides with the rising of the Nile at Memphis (de Wilde).

(6) *The Corona Borealis*, the Northern Crown, visible in the northern hemisphere in the spring and summer; so Dhorme, Terrien, NJB. The term מַזָּרוֹת may be connected with נֵזֶר "crown."

(7) *The Zodiac*; so Duhm (*frt*), Moffatt, Driver, "Two Astronomical Passages in the Old Testament," 4–8; Thomas, *Lexicon*, 1:272; NEB "the signs of the Zodiac." So too Gordis, regarding it as a byform of an unattested מַאְזָרוֹת "girdle" from אזר "bind"; alternatively, *the southern Zodiac* (as J. J. Hess cited by KB, 510b; Fohrer). Against the interpretation of Mazzaroth as the Zodiacal circle is the fact that those stars and constellations do not come out "at their time" (בְּעִתּוֹ) but for the most part are visible every night (de Wilde).

(8) *The constellations* in general; so NIV. Cf. GNB "the stars."

(9) *The Guard*; so Tur-Sinai, comparing Akk. *maṣṣartu* (*CDA*, 200b) "guard." But he does not suggest which star or constellation that may refer to.

(10) Some translations and commentators just use the term Mazzaroth (so KJV, RSV, NJPS, Pope), though no star or constellation is of course known by that name. Since the identification of the term is so uncertain, it seems best to adopt this solution.

32.b. תַנְחֵם "will you lead them?," from נחה "lead"; since the vb has the suff, עַיִשׁ עַל בָּנֶיהָ will be *casus pendens*. Merx, Hitzig, Beer (*BHK prps*), following Michaelis, revocalized to תְּנַחֵם, from נחם piel "comfort," thus "will you console [the Bear for her children]?," in reference to a myth attested in the Talmud (*b. Ber.* 58b) that God took two stars from the Bear to plug the gap in the firmament caused by the Flood. This reading is perhaps supported by the Qumran Targum; cf. Pope. But the strophe as a whole does not appear to be alluding to myths (see *Comment* on v 31). Another possible revocalization is to תְּנִחֵם "will you give rest to them?," from נוח hiph (cf. Driver–Gray), presumably in reference to settling the constellations in their places.

32.c. On the identification of עַיִשׁ, see *Comment*. Hölscher vocalizes עָיֵשׁ on the basis of Syr. *'⁽e⁾yūtā*.

32.d. For עַל "with," cf. Gen 32:12; 1 Sam 14:32; BDB, 755b §c; *DCH*, 6:392a §8a–b.

32.e. בָּנֶיהָ lit. "its sons, children." If עַיִשׁ is understood as the Bear, translations may have "its cubs" (so JB, NIV, Pope), but sometimes "its train" (NAB). If it is Aldebaran, it may be "its train" (NEB) or "its satellite stars" (REB).

33.a. הֲיָדַעְתָּ "do you know?" If the "laws" are the associations of the constellations with the seasons, perhaps Job could answer, Yes—which is not what is intended by the rhetoric. So some prefer to read the piel, הֲיִדַּעְתָּ "do you inform, proclaim?" (Duhm, Peake, Strahan, Beer [*BHK*], de Wilde, NEB "determine," Terrien "promulgate," Moffatt "control") (though piel of ידע occurs elsewhere only at v 12) or הֲיָעַדְתָּ "do you ordain" (so Gray, though יעד is not common in qal). The resulting parallelism would be more strict, but that should not be a persuasive reason for adopting the revocalization.

33.b. מִשְׁטָר occurs nowhere else, but there is a noun שֹׁטֵר "official." BDB, 1009b, suggests "rule, authority" (thus RSV, Driver–Gray, Pope, Hartley, Good "rule"; cf. KJV, NIV "dominion," NJPS "authority," Moffatt "sway," Habel "order"), comparing Akk. *šaṭāru* (*CDA*, 364a), Arab. *saṭara* "write" (Lane, 1357c); JB's "[make] their writ [run]" is a nice play on the meaning of the root. Gordis proposes "ordinance, law," while NEB has "laws of nature" and NAB "[put into effect] their plan." GNB "Do you know the laws that govern the skies, and can you make them apply to the earth?" is more interesting than lucid. *HALOT*, 3:645a, and *DCH*, 5:520a, however, hew closer to the sense "write" and regard מִשְׁטָר as the "writing" in the sky, i.e., the pattern of the stars (cf. Akk. *siṭir šame* "the writing of heaven, sky-writing," i.e., pattern of stars in the firmament); so Friedrich Delitzsch, *Assyrisches Handwörterbuch* (Leipzig: J. C. Hinrichs, 1896) 652b; N. H. Tur-Sinai (Torczyner), "*šiṭir šamê*, die Himmelsschrift," *ArOr* 17/2 [1949] 419–33; *CAD*, 17:146a; Piotr Michalowski, "Presence at the Creation," in *Lingering over Words: Studies in Ancient Near Eastern Literature in Honor of William L. Moran* (ed. Tzvi Abusch, John Huehnergard, and Piotr Steinkeller; HSS 37; Atlanta: Scholars Press, 1990) 381–96 (395). It remains unclear how Job could "set" (שׂים) that writing "upon earth" (if that is what בָאָרֶץ means); Tur-Sinai argued that the meaning of the celestial writing was the law that Moses "brought down from the sky"—an unlikely suggestion in the present context. In the absence of a better interpretation, perhaps the safest solution is to create a close parallel with the first colon, thus "Can you impose its rule?"

The sg suff of מִשְׁטָרוֹ is a problem. It could refer to God (thus NIV "God's dominion," and apparently Pope "[determine] his rule"), or to heaven considered as a single object though the Hebrew שָׁמַיִם is dual (so NJPS "its authority," Dhorme, Hartley). Gordis thinks the form is a scribal abbreviation of מִשְׁטָרוֹת "decrees" (he sees the same form of abbreviation at 39:10); he translates "order." Gray reads rather מִשְׁטָרִים "rules."

Less probably, Tur-Sinai emended to מִשְׁטָרִי "my writing," others to מִשְׁטְרֵי אָרֶץ "the ordinances of the earth," i.e., for the earth (so Beer [*BHK*]).

34.a. רוּם קוֹל hiph "lift up the voice" is a standard phrase (more commonly with נשׂא "lift up") for loud or, more probably, high-pitched, speaking or weeping (Gen 39:15; Isa 40:9; of weeping, Ezra 3:12); it is not related to the comparative positions of the speaker and the addressee, for although Job is below the clouds, Yahweh, who *can* lift up his voice to the clouds, is no doubt above them.

34.b. תְּכַסֶּךָ "shall cover you," Dhorme "submerge you," REB "envelop you in a deluge of rain." For reasons outlined in the *Comment,* we should emend to תַּעֲנֶךָ "shall answer you" (Bickell[2], Duhm, Strahan, Ehrlich, Beer [*BHK*], Kissane [*frt*], Gerleman [*BHS frt*], following LXX ὑπακούσεταί σου); thus too JB "make the pent-up waters do your bidding." Hölscher's emendation to תְּכַסֶּה "shall cover it [the earth]" (Gray תְּכַסֶּהָ) has as its antecedent the last word of the previous verse, but the difficulty is that we have begun a new strophe, and the antecedent is no longer very firmly in mind (similarly Fohrer).

35.a. יֵלְכוּ lit. "that they should go." NIV has "on their way," NJPS "on a mission."

35.b. הִנֵּנוּ lit. "behold us," usually translated "here we are" (KJV, RSV, NAB, JB), but preferable for the response of an emissary is "I am ready" (NJPS, NEB) or "at your service" (GNB).

36.a. NAB, following Skehan, 121, transposes the verse to precede v 41, so that, being about birds, it will form part of the second half of the speech. Tur-Sinai moves it to follow v 38. The explanation below will, however, show that the verse is perfectly intelligible in its present place.

36.b. The term מַחֹת is very problematic.

(1) According to BDB, 376a, it is "inward parts" (thus KJV, NRSV, Guillaume; NJPS "hidden parts," NAB, NIV "heart"), a formation from טוּח "over-spread, over-lay"; this does seem to be the sense at its other occurrence, Ps 51:6 (8), but that cannot be conclusive.

(2) טוּח "overlay" and טִיחַ "coating" led Duhm to translate "feathery clouds," cirrus clouds that overlay the blue sky as with white, chalky plaster, signalling a change in the weather; so too Strahan, Moffatt, RSV, Kissane, Rowley.

(3) טוּח "overlay" is the source also of Fedrizzi's view that it means "plaster (of a wall)" (cf. Lev 14:42, 43, 48; Ezek 13:10–15; 22:28). The metaphor of plaster would be an indication of the dryness or humidity of the atmosphere.

(4) Gunkel, *Die Psalmen* (Göttingen: Vandenhoeck & Ruprecht, 1926) 227, proposed a מָחֹה II "darkness"; so too G. R. Driver, "Problems in Job," *AJSL* 52 (1936) 160–70 (167), comparing Arab. *taḥā* "be dark" (Freytag, 3:44a; Lane, 1832c); hence NEB "depths of darkness," Habel "cloud canopy." The form, Driver thinks, should probably be מֻחֶה or מוּחֶה. From the same Arab. vb Umbreit, Hitzig, Dillmann, RVmg, Peake derived the sense "dark clouds." See also S. Mowinckel, "מחות und שׂכוי: Eine Studie zur Astrologie des Alten Testaments," *AcOr* 8 (1930) 1–44.

(5) Hoffmann thought it the name of Thoth, the Egyptian god of wisdom, known among the Greeks as Hermes Trismegistos; Pope, Good, and W. F. Albright, *Yahweh and the Gods of Canaan: A Historical Analysis of Two Contrasting Faiths* (London: Athlone Press, 1968) 212–14, saw rather here the Phoenician form of the name, Tauut, which would suggest the Hebrew be vocalized מָחֹת. Cf. Otto Eissfeldt, *Taautos und Sanchunjaton* (Sitzungsberichte der Deutschen Akademie der Wissenschaften zu Berlin, Klasse für Sprachen, Literatur und Kunst, 1952, No. 1; Berlin: Akademie Verlag, 1952).

(6) Schultens, 1101a, followed by de Wilde, related it to Arab. *ṭāḥa* "go astray" (Lane, 1888c; de Wilde wrongly *ṭaḥa*), thus things that err or go astray, such as lightning, thunderclaps, rainstorms (though there is nothing in the Arabic evidence specifying such subjs). De Wilde translates "lightnings."

(7) Duhm offered an emendation to שׂוחות "spiders" (the word would be fem ptcp of שׂוּח "spin") if שׂכוי in the next colon is "cock."

(8) Tur-Sinai thought מָחוֹת a word for "bird," specifically one that flies high (cf. Arab. *ṭawāḥi* or *ṭaḥāwi* "bird of prey"); but the reference to Arabic is doubtful, and may perhaps be a misunderstanding of an entry in Lane, 1832c.

(9) מַחֹת is understood by Baruch Halpern as the name of a constellation, perhaps Ares or Andromeda, but he has no philological evidence for such a connection ("Assyrian and Pre-Socratic Astronomies and the Location of the Book of Job," in *Kein Land für sich allein: Studien zum Kulturkontakt in Kanaan, Israel/Palastina und Ebirnâri für Manfred Weippert zum 65. Geburtstag* [ed. Ulrich Hübner and Ernst Axel Knauf; OBO 186; Freiburg, Switzerland: Universitätsverlag; Göttingen: Vandenhoeck & Ruprecht, 2002] 255–64 [261]).

(10) A מָחֹת III "ibis," the symbol of the Egyptian god of wisdom, is, however, much more probable in this context; so *HALOT*, 2:373b; Dhorme, Hölscher, Fohrer, Gordis, Sicre Díaz, van der Lugt, Newsom, Whybray, Gray, JB, GNB. This is the view adopted in this commentary.

36.c. שְׂכוִי, which occurs only here in Biblical Hebrew, also is variously explained:

(1) By BDB, 967b, as "perh. a celestial appearance, phenomenon," i.e., from a presumed vb שׁכה "look" (cf. מַשְׂכִּית perhaps "object to look at," and Aram. סכא "look out, hope"); thus Duhm "Aurora Borealis" (*Nordlicht*), Moffatt, RVmg "meteor," Dillmann "mass of clouds," Merx "shaft of light" (*Lichtblitz*), Hitzig, Budde "airy shapes" (*Luftgebilde*), RSV "mists."

(2) By Buxtorf, 803, following a rabbinic tradition (e.g., Kimchi) it was understood as "intelligence, mind"; thus KJV "heart," NRSV, NIV, Guillaume "mind."

(3) Zorell, 799b, suggested the meaning "eye," comparing Samaritan סכוי; cf. Aram. סכא "look, look forward"; Sokoloff, 377a, notes סכוי "prospect" in Jewish Palestinian Aram.

(4) Driver, "Problems in Job," 167, vocalizing it as שִׂכּוִי, takes it as "object of hope" (cf. Aram. סכוי, סיכוי "hope, object of hope").

(5) NEB "[veiled understanding in] secrecy" reads לְכָסוִי, a byform of כְּסוִי "covering" (BDB, 492a).

(6) De Wilde compares the root שׂכך IV (BDB, 968a) "be sharp" (cf. שְׂכָּה "barb"), and translates "lightning flashes."

(7) Kissane read שֻׂכִּי "my covert," from שֻׂך "booth" (Lam 2:6); so too Habel "my pavilion."

(8) Fedrizzi thought it might be "(massive) rock," comparing סֻכָּה "thicket, booth"; it is hard, however, to see any connection between thickets and rocks. Certain rocks, he says, signal the imminence of rain or of a dry season.

(9) Hoffmann (cf. on טחות above) understood it as the god Hermes (Roman Mercury), σουχι being in Coptic the name for Mercury; so too Pope, though he renders simply Sekwi.

(10) Good simply identifies it as a proper name, Sekwi.

(11) Halpern, "Assyrian and Pre-Socratic Astronomies," 260–61, thinks it is the constellation Perseus (Sumerian *šu.gi*), known in Assyrian astronomy as the "elder" of the sky, but the connection of such a star with wisdom is hard to sustain.

(12) Beer (*BH²prps*) mentions an emendation to כֵּסֵא "full moon," but how could the moon be said to have בינה "intelligence"?

(13) More commonly now, however, it is taken as "cock, rooster" (as in MH; cf. Vg *gallus*; so *HALOT*, 3:1327a; Dhorme, Othmar Keel, "Zwei kleine Beiträge zum Verständnis der Gottesreden im Buch Ijob [xxxviii 36f., xl 25]," *VT* 31 [1981] 220–25 [220–23]; *Entgegnung*, 60 n. 219; Hölscher, Fohrer, Tur-Sinai, Sicre Díaz, Hartley, van der Lugt, Newsom, Whybray, Gray; NAB, NJB, GNB). This view is adopted in the *Translation* above. The cock is apparently at Prov 30:31 זָרְזִיר, and at Neh 5:18 צִפּוֹר. For a famous depiction of a cock on a seal, see William F. Badè, "The Seal of Jaazaniah," *ZAW* 51 (1933) 152–56 (with plate).

37.a. סָפַר seems to be "number, count" (so KJV, RSV, NAB, NIV), yet the piel form, as here, almost always means "recount, narrate" rather than "count" (Ps 22:17 [18] seems the one exception), and, more importantly, it is hard to grasp the image: why should God want to first count the number of clouds before letting their contents fall on the earth? (It is different at Isa 40:26 and Ps 147:4, where the stars are counted and called out by name since all the known stars must be present each evening in the sky.) Dhorme says it is in order that only the exact and correct amount of water should be poured out (similarly Kissane, Fohrer), but could that be determined by counting the *number* of the clouds? Sensing the difficulty, some have translated "give an account of" (NJPS, and apparently JB "whose skill details every cloud"). But why would an account of the heavens be a prerequisite to bringing rain on the earth, and to whom would such an account be given? We need not stress in addition the weakness of the parallelism of "count" with "tilt over."

For these reasons, the *Translation* above adopts the proposal for a new סָפַר II "disperse" (cf. Arab. *safara* [Lane, 1370a]), offered by Ehrlich (as also at 37:20) and by Driver, "Problems in the Hebrew Text of Job," 92; cf. *DCH*, 6:189b. NEB "Who is wise enough to marshal the rain-clouds?" professes to follow this interpretation (it reads the qal יִסְפֹּר), but "marshal" seems the very opposite of "disperse"; the point is the spreading of the clouds across the sky, not their gathering together. Dahood had argued that it is natural to connect "wisdom" (חכמה) with counting (ספר), but it is even more appropriate to connect it with the spreading of the clouds; see *Comment*. It should be noted that Arab. *safara* does not unequivocally mean "disperse"; its normal senses are "sweep, remove, uncover," but Lane, 1370b, cites an example that is translated "the wind dispersed the clouds from the sky." Yet this example could equally well be translated "the wind removed the clouds from the sky," so we should not lay too much weight on the precise sense "disperse"; it may be that "disperse" is appropriate only if the place from which things are removed is also mentioned.

Other philological proposals are these: (1') Guillaume appeals to the same Arab. *safara* in its II form *saffara*, which he translates "send forth." However, in Lane's entry (1370b), the II form has several very diverse meanings, only one of which is "he sent him to go a journey," so the evidence for this sense is not strong. (2) Gordis, following Doederlein and Dathe, wonders if we may have another ספר equivalent to שפר "be beautiful" (ספר III, *DCH*, 6:189b), thus "[who] beautifies [the clouds]." But his explanation of "beautifies" as "i.e., clears" is hard to accept: are clouds made more beautiful by being removed? (3) Gordis's own preferred solution is to suppose yet another ספר "spread out" (not in *DCH*), a byform of the שפר he suggested for 26:13 and cognate with Akk. *šuparruru* "spread out (a canopy)" (*CDA*, 386a). (4) Tur-Sinai thinks a primary meaning of Heb. ספר is "fill [in this case, worn-out clouds]" but the evidence is thin if not non-existent. (5) Equally improbable, because of its inappropriate meaning, is Joseph Reider's proposal of another ספר "probe," cognate with Aram. סבר and Arab. *sabara* (Lane, 1293b) ("Etymological Studies in Biblical Hebrew," *VT* 2 [1952] 113–30 [127]), which he found also at 28:27 (ספר IV, *DCH*, 6:189b).

Among emendations, BDB, 708a, Piel §3, recommends reading the qal, יספר "counts"; so too Driver–Gray (*frt*), Beer (*BHK*), NAB. Wright reads ישבר "breaks up," Duhm יסב "brings them around," or יפרש (perhaps spelled יפרס) "spreads out" (so also Beer [*BH²prps*]), Beer (*BH²frt*) ישפר "beautify," though שפר nowhere else occurs in the hiph. Moffatt's "to mass the clouds" is unexplained.

37.b. שכב hiph is "lay down, make lie down," hence KJV "stay [the bottles of heaven]." Most, however, translate "tilt" (Moffatt, RSV, NAB, JB, NJPS, GNB) or "tip over" (NIV), or, less poetically, "empty" (NEB), with the image of water jars, designed to be kept upright, being lain flat so that they discharge their contents. For "tilting" (צעה) jars to empty them, cf. Jer 48:12.

H. M. Orlinsky, "The Hebrew Root *škb*," *JBL* 63 (1944) 19–44 (37), proposed a new שכב "pour out" (cf. Arab. *sakaba* [Lane, 1388b]), rendering "the bottles of the heavens who can pour out?"; cf. also Num 5:13 and perhaps Exod 16:13. So too Guillaume (without reference to Orlinsky), thinking there may be a play on this vb and שכב I hiph "make to lie down." The same Arab. vb no doubt lies behind NEB's "empty." Cf. also Barr, *Philology*, 137. Tur-Sinai implausibly thought it referred to pouring water *into* water bottles.

37.c. נבל is normally "amphora" (*DCH*, 5:594b) or "water jar" (NAB, NIV; KJV, NJPS, Guillaume, Habel "bottles," JB "flasks," Moffatt "pitchers"), not (cf. *HALOT*, 2:664a) "water skin" (as RSV, NJB, Kissane), and certainly not "cistern" (NEB). See further, *Comment*.

38.a. עפר could be dry soil, i.e., dust (as KJV, RSV, NAB, NJB, NIV; NEB "dusty soil"), or "soil" (JB) or "earth" (NJPS) simply. Since it is no longer dust when the rain "fuses" the particles together, the translation "soil" is preferred. It can hardly be the firmament, for there is no evidence that it is a mixture of earth and water (as Tur-Sinai thinks).

38.b. בצקת, inf constr of יצק "pour, cast, flow," thus "[when] it flows." Beer (*BH²*) wonders if we have a form from בצק "swell."

38.c. מוצק "solid mass"; see *Note* on 37:10.

38.d. Grimme, thinking the colon short, read ורגבים ברגבים ידבקו "and clods stick fast to clods"; so too Budde², Beer (*BHK*).

38.e. רגב "clod"; cf. *Note* on 21:33.

38.f. דבק "cling, keep close," as also at 41:9, 15 (17, 23). NJB "the cracks in the ground close up" is not the same image.

39.a. טרף is normally "prey," killed and devoured by wild animals (e.g., 4:11; Gen 49:9; Num 23:24; Amos 3:4; Ps 104:21; Ecclus 11:30), but sometimes also "food" of humans (Mal 3:10; Ps 111:5; Prov 31:15) or of beasts (Job 24:5) that is not hunted. Here the combination with the vb צוד "hunt" makes it plain that the former meaning is in mind.

39.b. לביא is clearly "lion" (BDB, 522b; so too Duhm) but not all agree that it is specifically "lioness" (as *HALOT*, 2:517a, Moffatt, Dhorme, Kissane, Pope, Guillaume, Hartley, Good, NAB, JB, NIV, NEB). The interpretation "lioness" goes back at least to Samuel Bochart, *Hierozoicon sive bipartitum opus de animalibus Sacrae Scripturae* (London: Thomas Roycroft, 1663) 1:719.

39.c. חיה "life" here in the special sense of "appetite" (as BDB, 312b §3). We should perhaps add 33:20 as another occurrence in this sense (as *HALOT*, 1:310b; *DCH*, 3:209b). Certainly it is common for נפש (cf. *DCH*, 5:725a §3).

39.d. כפיר is usually understood as "young lion" (KJV, RSV, NJB; NAB, Pope, "cubs," JB, Habel "whelps," Kissane "lion-cubs"; Duhm thinks the כפירים are distinct from the "young" [ילדים] of v 41), though the evidence that כפיר does not mean just "lion" in general (as NIV; NJPS "king of beasts") is slim. Joshua Blau relates the term to Arab. *jafr* "young mountain goat" ("Etymologische Untersuchungen auf Grund des palästinischen Arabisch," *VT* 5 [1955] 337–44 [342]), but it is hard to know if that is enough to settle the meaning in Hebrew. In any case, Arab. *jafr* is said by Lane, 433a, to mean "lamb, kid, that has become large"—not "young mountain goat," and not, in any case, "lion." M. Dahood, even less probably, related the word to Eblaite *kàparu* "copper" and translated "tawny lion" ("Love and Death at Ebla and Their Biblical Reflections," in *Love and Death in the Ancient Near East: Essays in Honor of Marvin H. Pope* [ed. John H. Marks and Robert M. Good; Guilford, CT: Four Quarters Publishing Company; Los Angeles, CA: Western Academic Press, 1986] 93–99 [95]).

40.a. מעונה is a general term for "dwelling"; in reference to the lair of wild animals, see *Note* on 37:8. Beer (*BHK*) reads בִּמְעוֹנֹתָם "in their dens," claiming the support of LXX ἐν κοίταις αὐτῶν, but we cannot know what LXX actually read.

40.b. אֶרֶב is "lair" of a wild animal; the noun occurs only here and at 37:8. Though the vb means "lie in wait, ambush," the noun does not convey any thought of attack in these two passages (so too Kissane, as against KJV, RSV, NAB, NIV, NEB, GNB, Pope, Habel "lie in wait"; NJPS "lie in ambush," Dhorme, Fedrizzi, Hartley, Good). למו־ערב is "in their lairs"; at 37:8 it was במו־ערב. For ל "in, at," cf., e.g., לפתח "at the entrance of" (Gen 4:7) and examples in *DCH*, 4:481b §4.

40.c. סכה is everywhere else a "booth," made by humans from twigs and matting (*HALOT*, 2:753a), the word being connected with סכך "screen, cover." Since we have had already in this colon a word for the lions' dwelling (מעונה), it is likely that סכה here, not being made by human hands, means "thicket, brake, covert," i.e., a dense growth of shrubs and small trees that provides screening (KJV, RSV, NEB "covert"; NAB, NIV "thicket"; NJB "bushes"); JB "lurk in their lairs" conflates the two terms מעונה and סכה (similarly Moffatt "couching in their coverts"). Beer (*BHK*) reads בַּסְּבָךְ "in the thicket," a word attested at Gen 22:13; Isa 9:18 (17); 10:34 (BDB, 687b, *HALOT*, 2:740b, spell the word סְבָךְ).

41.a. כון hiph is usually "establish, fix, prepare" but the sense "provide" is well enough attested (BDB, 466b §2b; cf., e.g., Ps 147:8).

41.b. BDB, 844b, 845a, recognizes two nouns from which צֵידוֹ might be derived: (1) צַיִד "hunting, game" (as at Gen 25:28; 27:3) from צוד "hunt" (thus RSV "prey," NEB "quarry"), and (2) צֵיד "provision, food" cognate with Akk. ṣidītu (*CDA*, 338a) and Aram. זְוָדָה "provisions" (as at Josh 9:14; Ps 132:15) (thus NAB "nourishment," NJPS, JB "provision," NIV, Moffatt "food"). The latter is more appropriate here since ravens feed on dead flesh and do not hunt game (Dhorme).

41.c. Some eliminate the raven from the verse altogether by reading לְעֶרֶב "at evening" for לָעֹרֵב "to the raven" (Wright, Beer, *Text*, Duhm [*frt*]), making the verse a continuation of the depiction of the lion (cf. Moffatt "Who furnishes the lion's food at evening?"). But, as Budde[2] and Gordis point out, the interrogative phrase מִי יָכִין suggests a new theme (cf. also vv 25, 29, 36, 37). De Wilde also remarks that the suff of צֵידוֹ cannot refer to the לביא "lioness" (if indeed that is what the word signifies) or the pl כפיריה "cubs"; but of course לביא may be masc, and there is no difficulty in referring the suff back so far (against Driver–Gray).

41.d. Duhm and Dhorme, followed by Strahan, Kissane, Rowley, commented that this verse probably had four lines originally. De Wilde undertakes to supply the missing line after v 41a, suggesting וּמִי יַמְצִיאֵהוּ צְלָלוֹ "and who makes it find its prey?" Hölscher, followed by Fohrer, thought the missing colon followed v 41b. Instead of the last three words of the line, יתעו לבלי־אכל "they wander without food," Duhm created a whole new line on the basis of Ps 104:21, הַכְּפִירִים יִשָּׁאֲגוּ לַטָּרֶף יִתְעוּ לְבַקֵּשׁ אֹכֶל "the young lions growl for their prey, and roam about seeking their food" (the reference to ravens is deleted), and Moffatt reproduces this in part with "seeking their prey."

41.e. NEB omits אֶל־אֵל יְשַׁוֵּעוּ "they cry to God" from the second colon, making the verse a bicolon.

41.f. תעה is "wander," and (in a moral sense) "err." Dhorme thought it meant "stagger," from weakness (certainly it is used of a drunkard staggering, as at 12:25); Good has, loosely, "frantic [for want of food]." Most, however, envision the parent and not the young roaming around seeking food (for they are not likely to have left the nest in search of food, despite KJV, RSV, NJPS, Hartley), and adopt one of the following emendations; the fifth is to be preferred, and is used for the *Translation*.

(1) יִתְעֶה "it (the parent bird) wanders" (Bickell, Budde, Driver–Gray). (2) יִתְעוּ "they (the young) stagger" from weakness, lacking food (Gray). (3) יְפֹעוּ "they (the young) cry out" from פעה "groan" (also "bleat" in MH); so Driver–Gray "pipe," Beer (*BHK prps*), de Wilde. (4) JB "crane their necks in hunger" accepts Larcher's emendation to יִתְעַלּוּ "they stand up." עלה "go up" occurs elsewhere in the hithp only at Jer 51:3, and Sicre Díaz thinks the emendation unpoetic, though the translation is certainly not.

(5) Guillaume read יְתֹעוּ "repeat the same thing over and over," from תעע, otherwise only in pilp and hithp "mock" (Gen 27:12; 2 Chr 36:16) (BDB, 1073b; cf. Arab. *ta'ta'a* "stammer" [Lane, 307a]). Driver, "Problems in Job," 167–68, "Glosses in the Hebrew Text of the Old Testament," in *L'Ancien Testament et l'orient. Etudes présentées aux VIes Journées Bibliques de Louvain (11–13 septembre 1954)* (Orientalia et biblica lovaniensia 1; Louvain–Leuven: Publications Universitaires/Instituut voor Orientalisme, 1957) 123–61 (139 n. 61), and "Another Little Drink'—Isaiah 28:1–22," in *Words and Meanings: Essays Presented to David Winton Thomas* (ed. Peter R. Ackroyd and Barnabas Lindars; Cambridge: Cambridge University Press, 1968) 47–67 (51–52), thought that young ravens are hardly likely to be "wandering around" (תעה), and invoked the same Arab. root *ta'ta'a*, cognate with תעע,

which he understood to mean "guffaw" ("stammer" in his "Glosses in the Hebrew Text"); he therefore translated the vb תעה here "twitter" or "croak"; hence NEB "when its fledglings croak for lack of food." In Isa 28:7 he rendered "cackle, croak, guffaw," of the shouting of drunken men (NEB "clamouring"). Kaltner, *The Use of Arabic in Biblical Hebrew Lexicography*, 78–79, thinks the sense Driver advances is not supported by genuine Arab. sources, but the evidence of Freytag, 1:192b, essentially a translation of the *Qāmūs*, seems adequate (Freytag has "stammered, stuttered" [*balbutivit*]). Lane, 307a, is not so plain, rendering "he reiterated in speech, by reason of an impediment, or ability to say what he would"—which may not be stammering exactly.

41.g. לבלי־אכל "without food," the initial *lamedh* being the *lamedh* of condition (BDB, 516a §i); cf. Isa 5:14.

39:1.a. The MT has, after ידעת "do you know?," עת "season, time"; the word does seem to overload the line, it could well be a dittograph of the end of הידעת, and more importantly, it makes v 1a totally equivalent to v 2b. Many therefore delete it (so Bickell[2], Budde, Peake, Beer [*BH² frt*], Strahan, Dhorme, Beer [*BHK vel*], Ehrlich, Kissane, Rowley, Gerleman [*BHS frt*], Moffatt, NAB "Do you know about the birth of the mountain goats?," JB "Do you know how mountain goats give birth?"); this emendation is adopted in the *Translation* above.

Others delete the phrase עת לדת "the time of birthing" (so Driver–Gray, de Wilde). Budde[2], and Hölscher, on the other hand, omitted לדת "birthing" (see next *Note*).

Since Job may be presumed to know something about the habits of the mountain goats, even though they are wild creatures, the question "do you know?" seems to some inappropriate, and they prefer to revocalize to הֲיָדַעְתָּ "do you fix?," piel of ידע (so Beer [*BHK frt*]). Duhm also reads the same, but by emending its obj to עֲשָׁתְרוֹת he arrives at the rendering "have you taught (ידע piel) sexual desire to the ibex?" (for עַשְׁתְּרוֹת cf. Jer 2:24); but the word in Jer is now understood as עַשְׁתְּרֹת "offspring of young animals" or perhaps "mother animal" (*HALOT*, 2:899b; *DCH*, 6:625b, is somewhat different). Alternatively, an emendation may be considered, to תְעָדֵר "do you determine?" (Duhm, Strahan, Gray); cf. also יְדַעְתָּ in v 2b.

1.b. לֶדֶת, inf constr of ילד, thus "giving birth." Since ילד can also be used of the father, thus "beget" (cf. BDB, 408 §2; *DCH*, 4:216a), perhaps the term refers to the he-goat here, and that is why the masc יעל is used. The word is deleted by Budde[2] and Hölscher, understanding the עת יעלי־סלע "time of the mountain goats" (masc) as the time of the male arousal. Beer (*BHK*) deletes either לדת or עת "time," for the sake of the meter.

Beer (*BH²vel*) mentions the proposal תַּאֲנַת "the lust of (the mountain goats)" for עת לדת "the time of birthing"; for the term תַּאֲנָה, cf. Jer 2:24 (also of the wild ass, but the female).

1.c. The form יעל "mountain goat" we would expect to denote a male (there is a fem form יַעֲלָה, as at Prov 5:19); but here it must be fem (cf. the fem personal name יעל "Jael"). יעל refers to the ibex (*Capra nubiana*) or mountain goat (*Capra sinaitica*) (*HALOT*, 2:420b). An identification with the antelope (as Dhorme), one member of the class of Bovidae that is generally recognized as the Arabian Oryx, is not favored. The domesticated goat is עז.

1.d. שמר "watch" is attested as "observe" (BDB, 1036b §1d), at, e.g., 1 Sam 1:12; Eccl 11:4; Jer 8:7. Is it perhaps "watch over" (as Strahan, Newsom), or "watch for" (as NAB)? NEB has "attend [the wild doe when she is in labour]," as a midwife might, though this translation does not appear justified. Nor is "control" (Moffatt) a suitable sense for שמר. The interrogative particle ה is to be understood from the first colon as applying also to this vb.

1.e. אילה is according to BDB, 19a, "hind, doe," *HALOT*, 1:40b, "doe of a fallow deer," and *DCH*, 1:212a, "hind." KJV, RSV, NAB, JB, NJPS have "hind(s)," NRSV, NJB "deer," GNB "wild deer," NIV "doe" with a "fawn"; in all these cases, the animal in question is the deer. The deer is of course a totally different animal from the goat of the first colon, and it lives in a quite different locale. It would make more sense of the present passage if, against the lexica, אילה here were used of the female goat (which is also known as a "doe" in English, as are the females of the rabbit and the hare too); so Driver–Gray, Hölscher, comparing Arab. *'ijjal* (perhaps NEB "wild doe" also signifies that). The *Translation* above uses the term "doe" in reference to the female of the mountain goat.

If we should be recognizing here the deer (as Duhm, Kissane, Pope, Tur-Sinai, Fohrer, Terrien, Sicre Díaz, Habel, Hartley, Good, Newsom, Whybray, Strauss), which is what אילה usually refers to, admittedly, here are some details: Two deer species are known for Palestine: (a) The fallow deer, the male of which reaches a height of 3 feet or more at the shoulder and weighs between 140 and 230 pounds (the female can be 2.5 feet high, and weigh between 60 and 120 pounds). Gestation takes about 8.5 months, and new births take place at the beginning of summer. The fallow deer roam in separate herds of males and females, the fawns with the mothers. (b) The (smaller) roe deer, the male of which has a height of 2 to 3 feet, and weighs 35–50 pounds. The roe deer form small herds of the two parents and the young, several families joining together during the winter. Gestation takes about 11 months, and offspring are usually twins. Deer were never domesticated, though they are known to have been kept in captivity in some places. These details are from Edwin Firmage, *ABD*, 6:1109–67 (1142).

1.f. חלל is polel inf of חול "whirl, twist," several times in reference to writhing in pain in childbirth (Isa 26:17; 51:2; cf. Job 15:7). It is possible that עת "time" from the first colon is to be understood before חלל in the second colon; thus NJPS "Can you mark the time when the hinds calve?"

2.a. תספר "you count," with the interrogative particle ה understood from v 1a, thus "do you count?" Similar omissions of ה at 41:1, 6 (40:25, 30).

2.b. מלא piel "complete (a period of time)," as at Gen 29:27 (qal at Gen 25:24).

2.c. ידעת "you know"; perhaps it should be revocalized to the piel יַדַּעְתָּ "you fix" (so Duhm, Driver–Gray, de Wilde, Moffatt, NAB "and fix the time of their bringing forth"), since knowing the number of months of their pregnancy (or rather, we should say, the season of their foaling) requires no superhuman capacity (de Wilde). On the other hand, "counting" (ספר in the first colon) the months of their pregnancy is perhaps not all that difficult either. In either case, the interrogative particle ה is to be understood from v 1a, thus "do you know?" or "do you fix?" Strahan, Beer [*BHK prps*], NAB adopt a not unattractive emendation to וְיָעַדְתָּ "and have you appointed?" (for יעד with "time" [מוֹעֵד] as the obj, cf. 2 Sam 20:5; at 1QM 1:10 יום "day" is the obj [*DCH*, 4:240b]).

3.a. כרע "crouch down (in childbirth)," as at 1 Sam 4:19.

3.b. פלח is "cleave open," of opening up kidneys by piercing in 16:13, liver in Prov 7:23, of cutting up gourds in 2 Kgs 4:39 (uncertain referent in Ps 141:7); it is used exceptionally here of opening the womb in childbirth, i.e., "they open (the womb)," which is strange, since ילדיהן "their young" seems to be the object. To the same effect, Pope translates "they squeeze out their young," but that is a strange rendering of פלח. Driver, "Problems in the Hebrew Text of Job," 92–93, defends the MT by regarding פלח as an Aramaism for פתח "open (the womb)"; but he silently omits ילדיהן "their young" in his translation (so too NEB). The same omission is suggested by Bickell[2], Duhm, Strahan, as a gloss on חבליהם "their offspring." An emendation to תְּפַלְּטְנָה "they cast forth, i.e., give birth" (as also at 21:10) has been proposed by Olshausen, Driver–Gray, Dhorme, Beer [*BHK*], Hölscher, Kissane, Tur-Sinai (*frt*), de Wilde, Gray. Theod, Symm διασώσεις αὐτά "will you save them?" perhaps read תמלטנה, which could be evidence that the Heb. original had תפלטנה.

3.c. Houbigant, Wright, Beer (*BH²al*), and Ehrlich transpose the places of ילדיהן "their off-spring" and חבליהם, understood by Ehrlich as "their cords" (חֶבֶל), thus "they break their umbilical cords." But פלח means "open," not "cut, sever." Beer (*BH² frt*) is inclined to delete ילדיהן as a dittograph.

3.d. There are several ways of reading חבל. (1) There is a well-attested word חֵבֶל "pang, pain, labor pains"; it was formerly connected by BDB, 286b, with חבל "bind," but is now related rather to חבל "be pregnant" (*HALOT*, 1:286b; *DCH*, 3:151a). According to *HALOT*, 4:1514b, §2b, the phrase שלח חבלים piel, lit. "send out pains," means "be rid of the pains of childbirth" (and similarly NJB "they get rid of their burdens," NIV "their labor pains are ended," KJV "they cast out their sorrows"; so too Fohrer). But שלח is an awkward vb to use with this obj. שלח piel is "put forth, produce" (branches are the obj in Jer 17:8; Ps 80:11 [12]; Ezek 31:5; but there are no parallels for offspring as the obj); Gray's strange translation "shooting out their foetus" is sign enough of the awkwardness of the vb.

(2) Alternatively, we may have a secondary meaning of that word, "fetus" and thus "offspring" (so *HALOT*, 1:286b; *DCH*, 3:151a; Strahan, Hölscher [חֵבֶל], Kissane, Tur-Sinai, Gordis, Sicre Díaz, Habel, Gray). This is the view adopted in the *Translation* above.

(3) Perhaps, however, Gordis is right in thinking that חֵבֶל "fetus" should be regarded as a separate word from חֵבֶל "birth pang."

(4) Driver, "Problems in the Hebrew Text of Job," 93, suggests that the word be vocalized חֶבֶל, as also Driver–Gray, Beer [*BHK* חֶבְלֵיהֶם].

(5) Mitchell J. Dahood saw here rather חֶבֶל "cord," in its special sense "band, company," here "herd (of goats and hinds)" ("Northwest Semitic Philology and Job," in *The Bible in Current Catholic Thought: Gruenthaner Memorial Volume* [ed. J. L. McKenzie; St Mary's Theological Studies 1; New York: Herder & Herder, 1962] 55–74 [73]; "Hebrew-Ugaritic Lexicography II," *Bib* 45 [1964] 393–412 [407]).

(6) Terrien also derives the word from חֶבֶל "cord," translating "they dispose of their cords," i.e., their umbilical cords; similarly Good, "expel their cords."

חבליהם "their young" strangely has a masc suff, whereas ילדיהן "their offspring" has a fem suff. Some mss have the fem חבליהן, but the oddity is not without parallel (cf. GKC, §135o). Some emend to חַבְלֵיהֶן "their progeny" (so NAB).

NAB adds, at the end of the line, "in the desert"; so too JB "in the open desert," and Pope, transferring בבר from the next colon (v 4a) to here.

4.a. חלם "be, become strong," generally said to be an Aramaism, though it it is found also in MH; it occurs also at Isa 38:16 (hiph). Guillaume translates "put on flesh." An emendation to יִגְמְלוּ "are weaned" (Beer [*BH²frt*]) is not generally adopted.

4.b. רבה "be, become much, great" in the sense "grow great" is said to be a Aramaism (also at Ezek 16:7); גדל would be the normal Hebrew (cf. Gen 21:8; 25:27), while רבה is more usually "be numerous," as at 27:14. Beer (*BHK*) deletes either this word or בר for the sake of the meter.

4.c. בָּר "open field," an Aramaism, occurring only here. Perhaps it should be regarded as the first word of the second colon, as NJB "go off into the desert"; so too Hölscher, Fohrer, Fedrizzi, Sicre Díaz, de Wilde. חוץ would be the normal Hebrew (Gordis; cf. 2 Kgs 10:24; Isa 42:2). KJV "(they grow up) with corn" takes the word as בָּר III "corn" (BDB, 141a), which is inappropriate. Gray deletes the word בבר as a dittograph of ירבו.

4.d. לָמוֹ "to them," i.e., the mothers (Dhorme, Habel), or perhaps it is an ethic or reflexive dative, "for themselves," as in 12:11.

5.a. פרא "wild ass"; cf. on 24:5. Ludwig Köhler identified it as the zebra (*Equus Grevyi*, Grevy's zebra); see his "Archäologisches. Nr. 21. פֶּרֶא = Equus Grevyi Oustalet," *ZAW* 46 (1926) 59–62; "Das Zebra im Alten Testament," in *Kleine Lichter: Fünfzig Bibelstellen erklärt* (Zurich: Zwingli, 1945) 64–70; KB, 775b; so too Hölscher, Fohrer. But the traditional interpretation has been defended by Paul Humbert, "En marge du dictionnaire hébraïque," *ZAW* 62 (1949–50) 199–207 (202–6), followed by Keel, *Entgegnung*, 67 n. 231; so too *HALOT*, 3:163b.

5.b. שלח חפשי "let go free," "set at liberty," as at, e.g., Exod 21:26–27; Isa 58:6.

5.c. ערוד "wild ass" (BDB, 789a; *DCH*, 6:753a, "wild ass, onager"), according to some the Aram. equivalent of פרא (attested also in MH), *Asinus hemippus* according to *HALOT*, 2:882b, the same as NJPS "onager." The term occurs only here, though it has been conjectured for Jer 48:6. Most think the פרא and the ערוד are the same creature, but NEB thinks the former is the Syrian wild ass and the latter the Arabian wild ass. ערוד "wild ass" is thought by some to be cognate with Arab. *gharada* "cry out, bray" (Lane, 2245b; hence Driver–Gray, NJB "the brayer") or else with Arab. *'arada* "flee," thus "the swift" (de Wilde); *HALOT*, 2:881b, compares Arab. *'ard* "wild ass."

6.a. ערבה is properly "steppe" (as RSV; Moffatt "steppes"), an open plain that is not always sandy or waterless (cf. *HALOT*, 2:880a; *DCH*, 6:552a) and that is not devoid of vegetation; this translation is preferable to "wilderness" (KJV, NAB, NJPS, NEB) or "desert" (JB, GNB) or "wasteland(s)" (NJB, NIV). For wild asses of the steppe, cf. also 24:5.

6.b. מלחה (also at Jer 17:6; Ps 107:34) "salt land" (RSV, NJPS, Kissane), "salt flats" (NAB, NIV, Pope, Habel), "salt plain(s)" (JB), "salt barrens" (Good), though the last of these terms refers properly to land beyond the reach of the highest high tides, and the preferable term is "saltings" (NEB), i.e., strictly the land overflown by the sea except at low tide. Beer (*BHK*) inserts אֶרֶץ before מלחה, thus "the salt land," for the sake of the meter.

6.c. משכנותיו "its dwelling," the pl being common with nouns for dwellings even if only one is meant (Hölscher, Blommerde); cf. *Note* on 18:21; and cf. 21:28.

7.a. ישחק "it laughs at" (NIV) means "it does not fear" (see *Comment*), not "scorns" (RSV, JB, Moffatt, Pope; KJV, Tur-Sinai "scorneth"), "scoffs at" (NAB, NJPS), "disdains" (NEB).

7.b. שמע "hear" could perhaps be "obey, give heed" (as NJB, REB; cf. BDB, 1034a §1j), but that sense is more usually with ל or ב (cf. *HALOT*, 4:1572a §4). For KJV, Tur-Sinai "regardeth not," i.e., "pay no attention," cf. BDB, 1033b §1f.

7.c. On תְּשֻׁאָה "loud noise," see on 36:27.

7.d. נגש is "press, drive, oppress"; the ptcp here plainly means "driver," not "taskmaster" (Habel); see further, *Comment*. The reading is correctly נֹגֵשׂ, as in BHK. BHS נֹגֵשׁ is a mistake, since נגשׁ means "draw near," which does not make sense in the context; the correct reading is clearly shown in *The Leningrad Codex: A Facsimile Edition* (ed. David Noel Freedman; Grand Rapids: Eerdmans, 1998) 828.

8.a. יְתוּר would seem to be a noun (Gordis), thus "the range of the mountains is his pasture" (presumably from תור "seek, explore"), or "the outcrop of the mountains" (apparently from יתר "exceed"), as Gillis Gerleman, "Rest und Überschuss. Eine terminologische Studie," in *Travels in the World of the Old Testament: Studies Presented to Professor M. A. Beek on the Occasion of His 65th Birthday* (ed. M. S. H. G. Heerma van Voss, Ph. H. J. Houwink ten Cate, and N. A. van Uchelen; Studia semitica neerlandica 16; Assen: Van Gorcum, 1974) 71–74 (74); so too Gerleman (*BHS*); cf. *DCH*, 4:342b. But most read יָתוּר, i.e., 3 masc sg impf of תור "seek out, explore" (so, e.g., Driver–Gray, Beer [*BHK*], Kissane, Tur-Sinai, Gray, RSV, NAB, NEB, JB; Dhorme agrees it is a vb, but with unusual spelling; Tur-Sinai and Pope that the first vowel is a Aramaic-like reduction). This emendation is followed in the *Translation* above. Some support may be offered by Theod κατασκέψεται "will spy out, inspect" and Vg *circumspicit* "looks around." תור and דרשׁ "seek" are used together also at Eccl 1:13.

8.b. מרעהו lit. "as its pasturage," in apposition to הרים "mountains."

8.c. דרשׁ "search" usually takes a direct obj; the אחר "after" (found only here with דרשׁ; cf. *DCH*, 2:476a) may suggest that it is "following a certain track with the greatest care" (Dhorme).

8.d. ירוק "green thing" occurs only here, but the meaning is clear (cf. יֶרֶק "green, greenness").

9.a. רֵים "wild ox" is spelled elsewhere רְאֵם (Num 23:22), רְאֵים (Ps 92:10 [11]), plural רְמִים (Ps 22:21 [22]) and רְאֵמִים (Isa 34:7; Ps 29:6). LXX rendered μονοκέρως "unicorn" (hence KJV), and Vg "rhinoceros." Modern translations usually have "wild ox," though Dhorme, Hölscher, Terrien, Pope, Fedrizzi, de Wilde (*frt*) have "buffalo"; but that identification is not generally accepted. Some older commentators saw here the antelope (so, e.g., Duhm).

9.b. עָבְדֶךָ, inf constr of עבד "serve." Duhm expects it to be prefixed with ל.

9.c. לין is not necessarily "spend the night" (cf. BDB, 533b, "lodge, spend the night"), but also "lodge, dwell" (cf. *Note* a on 41:22 [14]).

9.d. אבוס is usually said to be a trough for feeding cattle, a manger (BDB, 7a [*s.v.* לון]; KB, 4a; *HALOT*, 1:4a; *DCH*, 1:102b); thus "manger" (NAB, JB, NIV, Hartley), "crib" (KJV, RSV, NJPS, Dhorme, Pope, Habel, Good). But an ox, wild or tame, could not lodge—or even spend the night—in a manger, and the term must mean here "stall" (NEB), or "stable" (GNB, Moffatt). If it is retorted that עַל־אֲבוּסֶךָ should mean "at your manger" rather than "in your stall," I reply that it is not "lodging" (לין) that an animal does at a manger but eating. It may be significant that the Akk. cognate *abūsu* means "storehouse, stable" (*CDA*, 3b).

10.a. MT repeats רֵים "wild ox." Hence Budde (הֲתִקְשְׁרֵהוּ), Duhm, Peake, Strahan, Beer (*BHK* הֲתִקְשְׁרֵנּוּ), Driver–Gray, Kissane, Pope (apparently), Rowley, de Wilde, Sicre Díaz, NAB read הֲתִקְשְׁרֵנּוּ "will you bind him" (Siegfried הֲתִקְשְׁרֵם "will you bind them"), deleting רֵים. Dhorme deletes only רֵים, taking עבת "rope" as the obj of the vb. The *Translation* above simply omits the term for the sake of smoothness, without necessarily accepting the deletion.

Gray emends רים to נִיר "yoke," following LXX ζυγόν; but such a נִיר is unknown to the lexica (it can hardly be נִיר II "tillable, untilled, fallow ground" [BDB, 644b]).

10.b. בחלם עבתו, lit. "in the furrow its rope," תלם "furrow" as at 31:38; Hos 10:4; 12:12, and עבת being well attested as "cord, rope" for binding (e.g., Judg 15:13), or pulling a cart (Isa 5:18), or as cordage of twisted chains (Exod 28:14). The phrase could mean "bind to the furrow with its cord" (Hakham, cited by Gordis, a satisfactory sense adopted in the *Translation* above), or else "in the furrow of its cord," i.e., the furrow to which its cord limits it (Dillmann); but this latter sense is awkward. Gordis thinks עבתו an abbreviation for the pl עֲבֹתוֹת "[to the furrow] by ropes" (he saw the same abbreviation at 38:33), עבתו being an acc of specification.

Emendations, none of them a real improvement on the MT, include: (1) בְּעֲבֹות תְּלָמוֹ "by the cord of its furrow" (Duhm). (2) בְּעָרְפּוֹ עֲבֹת "[do you bind] about its neck a rope" (Beer [*BH²*], proposing a new word עֹרֶף "neck" (not in *DCH*; but cf. עֲנָק "necklace," and cf. Aram. עַנְקָא [Levy, 1096b]); Dhorme's reading בְּעֲנָקוֹ seems rather to follow the attested form עֲנָק "[men of] Anak," i.e., supposedly, long-necked men. (3) בְּעָרְפּוֹ עֲבֹת "[do you bind] its neck with a rope" (Hölscher). (4) בתלם בְּעֲבֹתוֹ "to the furrow with its cord" (Budde²[*vel*], Beer [BHK], Fedrizzi, de Wilde, Hartley). (5) בתלם בְּעֲבֹתוֹת "to the furrow with cords" (Siegfried [בְּעֲבֹתֹת], Driver–Gray). (6) בתלם בְּעֲבֹת "to the furrow with a cord" (Budde²[*vel*]). (7) בְּבֶלֶם עֲבֹת "with a halter of cord," supposing a new word בֶּלֶם "halter" (the vb בלם "curb, hold in" occurs at Ps 32:9) (Kissane, followed by Rowley); it is an ingenious suggestion, but perhaps the two terms are tautologous. (8) Moffatt "Can you rope him to your plough?" understands תלם "furrow" as referring to the plow that cuts the furrow, but this sense is not paralleled. (9) Dahood read בתלם עֲבֹת "[Do you bind him] in the fertile furrow, lit. furrows of fertility, or [does he harrow]," taking עָבֹה as "fertility, fatness" (cf. עבה "be thick, fat," and מַעֲבֵה הָאֲדָמָה "the fertile ground" in 1 Kgs 7:46; see *DCH*, 6:231b) ("Northwest Semitic Philology and Job," 73–74). (10) Gray proposes to delete תלם as a gloss on the Aram. word for "your furrows" that he detects in the second colon, חֲרָתֶיךָ; thus in this first colon he reads התקשר נִיר עֲבֹתוֹ "Will you bind a yoke on his massive bulk?," appealing like Dahood to the vb אבה "be thick." (11) Tur-Sinai reads, in place of the word רים, בֶּהָרִים "on the hills"; but this is most unlikely, since we know that the ox is harrowing "the valleys" (עמקים). (12) An excellent solution is that proposed by NEB, "Can you harness its strength with ropes, or will it harrow the furrows after you?," reading בְּעֲבֹתוֹ רִים עָמְקִי התקשר, lit. "will you bind the strength of the ox with its rope?," i.e., transposing תלם "furrow" and עמקים, interpreted as the new word "strength" (עֹמֶק II cognate with Ugar. *'mq*, Akk. *emūqu* [*CDA*, 73a]; cf. *HALOT*, 2:842b; *DCH*, 6:488b; Gordon, *Ugaritic Grammar*, 105; *UT* §19:1874; G. R. Driver, "Difficult Words in the Hebrew Prophets," in *Studies in Old Testament Prophecy Presented to Professor Theodore H. Robinson* [ed. H. H. Rowley; Edinburgh: T. & T. Clark, 1950] 52–72 [61]; Joseph Reider, "Etymological Studies in Biblical Hebrew," *VT* 2 [1952] 113–30 [129]; W. F. Albright, "Some Canaanite-Phoenician Sources of Hebrew Wisdom," in *Wisdom in Israel and in the Ancient Near East, Presented to Professor Harold Henry Rowley ... in Celebration of His*

Sixty-Fifth Birthday [VTSup 3; Leiden: E. J. Brill, 1955] 1–15 [14]; Anton Jirku, "Eine Renaissance des Hebräischen," *FF* 32 [1958] 211–12; M. Dahood, "The Value of Ugaritic for Textual Criticism," *Bib* 40 [1959] 160–70 [166–67]); Arnold A. Wieder, "Ugaritic-Hebrew Lexicographical Notes," *JBL* 84 (1965) 160–64 (162–63); Giovanni Rinaldi, " '*mq*," *BeO* 10 (1968) 196. Grabbe, 124–26, however, calls the existence of a עמק II into question, noting that there is only one example of the supposed Ugar. '*mq*, (13) NFB reads עֻמְקֵן רֵים "strength of the wild ox," but עֻמְקֵו "its strength" would be preferable, and indeed "Can you harness its strength with ropes?" is its translation (see [12] above). The difficulty with this solution, however, lies in its treatment of the second colon (see below).

10.c. שׂדד "harrow," as at Isa 28:24; Ecclus 38:25, 26 (of humans), Hos 10:11 (of an animal, as here); the term for "plow" is חרשׁ. BDB, 961a, relates the vb to Akk. *šadādu* "draw, drag" (*CDA*, 344a). Some, however, say that the harrow was unknown in ancient Palestine (so Hölscher, thinking the vb refers to plowing boundary furrows, connected it with Aram. שׂד "furrow"); similarly Gray, connecting the word rather with Arab. *sadda* "be straight." Part of the evidence that שׂדד "harrow" is a different operation from חרשׁ "plow" lies in the fact that in harrowing (שׂדד) the farmer leads the animal (though see *Note* on אחריך below), whereas in plowing he follows the animal.

10.d. עמק is always (over sixty occurrences) "plain (between hills)," but traditionally though misleadingly translated "valley." Beer (*BH²*), followed by Dhorme, having removed תלם from the first colon, read תְּלָמִים "furrows" or תְּלָמֶיךָ "your furrows," corresponding to LXX σου αὔλακας. So too Moffatt, NEB (reading the sg תֶּלֶם). JB also has "will he harrow the furrows?," but it is not clear what their reading of the Hebrew is. The translation is impossible, in that one does not "harrow" (שׂדד) "furrows" (תלמים), since furrows are made with a plow, while a harrow scratches the soil without making regular incisions like a furrow; nonetheless, quite what שׂדד means remains problematic.

10.e. אחריך "after you" either refers to the farmer leading the ox or else, less probably, means "at your command." Gray, having decided that שׂדד means "plow" rather than "harrow," cannot have the ox following the farmer (אחריך), and makes the ingenious proposal that the word was originally חֲרָתֶיךָ "your furrows." His reading of the second colon is thus אִם־יִשַׂדֵּד בְּעֵמֶק חֲרָתֶיךָ "Will he draw your furrows straight in the plain?" He says that חֲרָתֶיךָ is Aram., comparing Syr. *ḥrat* "spit" and Ugar. *ḥrt* "score" (*DUL*, 371, renders *ḥrt* "plow"); no comparable Aram. noun or vb is to be found in Jastrow.

11.a. רב כחו, lit. "its strength is great."

11.b. יגיע is attested, though rarely, in the sense of "toil" (elsewhere v 16; Gen 31:42; Isa 55:2); thus KJV, RSV, NEB "labo(u)r," JB, NIV, REB, GNB "heavy work," NJPS "toil," Moffatt "field-work." But because the word usually means "product of labor, property" (as at Deut 28:33; Isa 45:14; Ps 128:2), some prefer "[leave to him] the fruits of your toil" (NAB), "your produce" (Gordis; similarly Driver–Gray, Fohrer); however, the thought of the wild ox inheriting the farmer's property is bizarre. It can hardly be simply that the crops would not be left for the aurochs to graze on (Guillaume).

12.a. כי "that [it will bring in]." אמן hiph "trust" with such a כי of the object of trust is paralleled at 9:16; Exod 4:5; Lam 4:12.

12.b. K ישׁוב "that he will return" makes poor sense, since the ox has not been away; the Q ישׁיב "that he will bring back [your grain]" seems far preferable. But the K, having no obj for the vb, would carry the caesura, yielding a line of 3 + 3, which would be better than the Q, which needs זרעך "your grain" as its obj, yielding an unusual line of 4 + 2. It is a difficult decision. The K is followed by RSV, NEB, Duhm, Moffatt, Dhorme, Beer (*BHK*), Hölscher, Fohrer, Pope, Guillaume, Rowley, Fedrizzi, Gordis, de Wilde, Sicre Díaz, Hartley, Good, Gray, while the Q is followed by KJV, NIV, NJPS, Habel, van der Lugt.

NAB accepts an emendation to יָדוּשׁ "threshes," i.e., "[Can you rely on him] to thresh out [your grain]?" But this would duplicate the second colon. NAB's "gather in the yield of your threshing floor," presumably into barns, makes גרן mean not just the threshing floor but also its "yield," which is unparalleled (though see Gordis in next *Note* but one).

12.c. If the K ישׁוב is read, זרעך must be vocalized זַרְעֶךָ (the non-pausal form); some would also prefix it with *waw* (so, e.g., Duhm, Hölscher).

12.d. וגרנך "and your threshing floor" has no prep before it, so what is implied could be "to" (as most translations, a locative use), or "from" (as NJPS, GNB, Habel), i.e., from the threshing floor to the barn. Gordis, exceptionally, argues that גרן here means "fruit of the threshing floor, i.e., harvest" (cf. תבואת הגרן, Num 18:30; and cf. perhaps also Ruth 3:2 זרה את־גרן "he is winnowing the threshing floor," i.e., the produce on the threshing floor), and that the second colon means "will he gather in your seed and your harvest?," or else "the seed of your harvest" (as a hendiadys like Gen 3:16; similarly Hartley, Good. Others suggest that we read אֶל־גָּרְנְךָ (Merx [אֶל גרנך (!)], Fohrer) or גָּרְנְךָ (Bickell², Beer [*BH²*], Hölscher, Gray) or גָּרְנָה (Budde, Duhm, Beer [*BHK* וְזַרְעֲךָ גָּרְנָה], Gerleman [*BHS prps*] de

Wilde, NEB; Gerleman [BHS prps גָּרְנֶךָ וְזֶרַע]]) or לְגָרְנֶךָ (Beer [BH² vel], Dhorme, Kissane, Fedrizzi), all meaning "to your threshing floor." Pope read גָּרְנֶךָ וְזֶרַע "and the grain of your threshing floor."

Guillaume thinks גֹּרֶן here means, not "threshing floor" but "corn," as the product that is threshed there; he compares Arab. jarīn "ground corn."

13.a. Many delete vv 13–18 about the ostrich because (1) the passage is missing from the LXX, (2) there are in it apparently no questions of the kinds typical of this first divine speech, (3) though the speaker is Yahweh, God is referred to in the third person (v 17), and (4) a bird seems out of place among the quadrupeds. Against these arguments, (1) there are many passages in the Hebrew text missing in the LXX, and it may even have been because of the difficulties of the text that the passage was not translated (Dhorme), (2) v 13b is pretty clearly the second half of a double question, and v 13a may well be understood as its first half, (3) God is referred to in the third person in the divine speeches also at 38:41; 40:2, 9, 19, and (4) the principle of organization in this speech is hard to identify, and in any case a misplacement does not impugn the originality of a passage. However, Duhm, Beer (BH²), Moffatt, Hölscher bracket these verses, Moffatt locating them at the end of the speech. Fedrizzi moves them to follow v 25. Strauss thinks the passage was originally an independent little poem. Tur-Sinai attempted to reconstruct from the materials here a fable about two birds, which no one except F. S. Bodenheimer, *Animal and Man in Bible Lands* (Leiden: E. J. Brill, 1960) 59–60, has found plausible.

13.b. כְּנַף "wing of" is sg, but it is more natural in English to speak of "wings" when both are meant. Some prefix the interrogative הֲ, thus הַכְנַף "Is the wing of" (so Driver–Gray, Beer [BHK], Kissane); the second colon begins with אִם, which is ordinarily a signal of the second part of a question. GKC, §150f, notes a few parallel examples, which it ascribes to "suppression of the first member of a double question," so the present text may yield the same meaning (so too Hartley). Another example of the omission of an initial הֲ has been noted at 38:18. Yellin, followed by Gordis, proposed הֲיָדַעְתָּ "do you know?" (as in v 1); but the suggestion has little to recommend it.

13.c. רְנָנִים, found only here, means, according to BDB, 943b, "[bird of] piercing cries" (cf. רִן "give a ringing cry," רָנָה "cry"), generally identified as the ostrich (so too *HALOT*, 3:1249a). Its short, sharp cry warning of danger from predators such as hyenas has been noted; Tristram, *Natural History*, 234, compared it to "the hoarse lowing of an ox in pain." Dhorme's interpretation of רנן as "be jubilant, sing," and thus of the "song" of the female as distinct from the shrill clamor of the male, is probably incorrect (רנן in 38:7 probably means "shout," not "sing"). The usual term for the ostrich is יָעֵן (Lam 4:3 K), and more often בַּת הַיַּעֲנָה "daughter of greed (?)" (so BDB, 419a), allegedly because of the ostrich's habit of swallowing all kinds of objects, or "daughter of the stony desert" (cf. Arab. *wa'nat* "stony country," Zorell, 319a), or "daughter of singing, screeching" (cf. ענה IV "sing," BDB, 777a). Some, however, consider יָעֵן to be the owl (e.g., George Cansdale, *Animals of Bible Lands* [Exeter: Paternoster Press, 1970] 190–92). KJV had "peacocks."

Some emend to the usual word for "ostrich," יְעֵנִים, as at Lam 4:3 (so Hoffmann, Budde [יְעֵנִים], Duhm, Beer [BHK], Gray).

13.d. עלס niph is here understood as "be enjoyed, be delightful" (so Tur-Sinai), the plumes of the male ostrich being famously beautiful; the vb is niph only here (qal at 20:18, hithp at Prov 7:18), and a niph of a word for "rejoice," though a difficulty, may perhaps have that meaning (neither of its byforms עלז or עלץ has a niph). עלס is "rejoice" according to BDB, 763a, KB, 709a, *DCH*, 6:429b, Zorell, 603b, Habel "rejoices," Dhorme "is gay," Good "are glad" (cf. עלז and עלץ "rejoice"); most, however, relate the beauty, or, rejoicing, to the movement of the wings: thus Gordis "beating joyously," Strahan "flap joyously," NIV "flap joyfully," NJPS, Hartley "beat(s) joyously"; similarly Fohrer, Fedrizzi. The translations "wave proudly" (ASV, RSV) and "flaps her wings in pride" (Moffatt) are not substantiated, still less "flap wildly" (Pope, NRSV).

HALOT, 2:836, we may note, does not allow the sense "rejoice," distinguishing only עלס I "taste" (Job 20:18; Prov 7:18; cf. Arab. *'alasa* [Freytag, 3:207b]) and II "be agitated, vivacious" (only here; cf. Arab. *'aliza* "be disturbed" [Freytag, 3:207b]); similarly Hölscher.

Guillaume, comparing the same Arab. *'aliza* in its IV form, "be weak" (Freytag, 3:207b), proposed a new עלס "be weak" (עלס IV, *DCH*, 6:429b) and rendered "Is the wing of the ostrich weak, or is it strong like that of the stork and hawk?" To this suggestion it may be objected that it would be strange if the first question expected the answer "Yes," and the second expected "No" (Rowley). See also D. F. Payne, "Old Testament Exegesis and the Problem of Ambiguity," *ASTI* 5 (1966–67) 48–68 (65), who points to the difficulty that the supposed Arabic cognate has a different sibilant (z rather than s).

Emendations include: (1) נֶעֱלָזָה "is weak," following Guillaume but supposing a Heb. vb עלז rather than a homonymous עלס; so Gray (cf. עלז II, *DCH*, 6:419b). (2) נָלוֹזָה "crooked," niph ptcp of לוז; so Duhm, Beer (*BHK prps*), Ehrlich. (3) נֶעֱצָלָה "lazy, sluggish," from עצל niph; so Hoffmann, Budde²,

Beer (*BHK al*), de Wilde, NAB "beat idly." (4) וְעֶרְכָה "be compared," ערך in this sense being found at 28:17, 19; Isa 40:18; Ps 40:5 [6] (Kissane). Thus JB "Can the wing of the ostrich be compared with the plumage of the stork or falcon?" The niph, however, is found nowhere else, and the expected form would be the qal תֵּעָרְךָ. (5) וְקִלְסָה "is mocked" (Ley, Beer [*BH*² *frt*]) (as at Ezek 16:31 [piel]; Hab 1:10; Ezek 22:5; 2 Kgs 2:23 [hithp]); the vb is not found elsewhere in the niph, and the reading is awkward.

(6) וְסֻעְלָה "are stunted" (NEB) depends on the proposal of a new word סעל "be little" (cf. Arab. *saʿila*; *DCH*, 6:174b) (G. R. Driver, "Birds in the Old Testament. II. Birds in Life," *PEQ* 87 [1955] 129–40 [138], rendering "atrophied"). Driver took v 13 as a double question ("Is the wing of the hen-ostrich atrophied, or are pinion and feather lacking?"), which formally expects the answer "No." It is only if the answer could be "Yes" that this could be the reason why the hen leaves her eggs on the ground; even so, it is not true that the ostrich lacks feathers. NEB avoids the difficulty by making both cola statements rather than questions. Kaltner, *The Use of Arabic in Biblical Hebrew Lexicography*, 85–86, notes that the Arab. vb referred to by Driver, *saʿila*, does not mean "be little," but "be brisk, lively, sprightly" (Lane, 1365b). He suggests that Driver intended the vb *ṣaʿila* "be small." Even so, that vb in reference to humans or animals means only to be small in the head and long in the neck (thus of ostriches commonly and of a tall palm tree); cf. Lane, 1690c. So the view that סעל can mean "be little" in any context at all is unsubstantiated; and if Driver was indeed referring to *ṣaʿila* his proposal has the added difficulty that Arab. *ṣ* (*ṣād*) usually corresponds to Heb. צ *ṣade*, not ס *samekh*.

13.e. אם is apparently the sign of the second half of a double question (cf. GKC, §150f; similarly Fohrer); see above on the first colon. Brockelmann, *Syntax*, §54f, however. thinks a prior question is not presupposed (so too Strauss). Sicre Díaz thinks it is an emphatic particle, but parallels are lacking. Others emend: Kissane reads אֶל־ "[compared] with [the pinions of the stork and the falcon]," but that also requires his emendation of נעלסה. Dhorme, followed by Habel, unconvincingly read אם "the mother (i.e. possessor) of [gracious plumage]." Ehrlich carries no more conviction with his reading אם אכזָרִיָּה חסידה "a cruel mother is the stork" (omitting ונצה as a gloss on אברה), since it is the ostrich that is supposed to be cruel. NEB simply omits אם. Gray emends אם to עם, which he understands as a preposition of comparison, thus "in comparison with [the wing of the stork or the hawk]." A עם of comparison is not known to BDB, but *DCH*, 6:460b (§10), mentions numerous examples, including Job 9:26; 37:18; 40:15; in many if not all of these examples, however, the vb contributes something to the sense of comparison, and a vb is here conspicuous by its absence.

13.f. אֶבְרָה "pinion" (as at Deut 32:11; Pss 68:13 [14]; 91:4). Gordis read אֶבְרָה "[is] her wing [the wing of the stork or the falcon]?" Others (e.g., Budde, Hölscher, Kissane, Fohrer, van der Lugt, Strauss, Gray) read אֶבְרַת "pinion of"; this emendation is adopted in the *Translation* above. Sicre Díaz's argument that the abs can sometimes stand for the constr is not very likely. Guillaume emended to אַבִּירָה "[is it] strong?," but with resultant problems for the exegesis.

13.g. חֲסִידָה is generally recognized as the "stork" (as Lev 11:19; Deut 14:18; Jer 8:7; Zech 5:9; Ps 104:17), rather than the "heron" (Vg, KB, 319a, Fohrer) or "ostrich" (KJV). The form, however, could be the fem of the adj חָסִיד "kindly, pious" (though the fem does not occur elsewhere); so BDB, 339b, RV "are her pinions and feathers kindly?," Moffatt "but is the feathered creature kind?," Duhm "is it a pious pinion?" Dhorme translated "gracious [plumage]," but חסיד does not have an aesthetic meaning. Tur-Sinai, however, thought it could, suggesting חסיד was equivalent to חָסוּד in MH "beautiful," and parallel therefore to נעלסה "is delightful" in the first colon; but the verse would then lack any connection with the following.

Beer (*BHK*) reads (*prps*) חֲסֵרָה "lacking" (from חָסֵר). Pope adopts the emendation, rendering "though her pinions lack feathers" (deleting the *waw* of ונצה), though that is not consistent with his comment that "The ostrich's wings, though absurdly small, are beautifully plumed"; similarly NEB "her pinions and plumage are so scanty" (which is true of the wings but not of the plumage), NRSV "its pinions lack plumage" (which does not appear to be true at all), NAB, the other way about, "her plumage is lacking in pinions" (reading נֹצָה: "her plumage"; it is true enough, but it seems strange to say that her *feathers* lack *wings*). Hoffmann, Budde², and Hartley adopt the same reading, but, taking it as a question, get the opposite sense, "Do her pinions lack feathers?" (answer expected, No!). It is hard then to see what the point of the two questions is, and improbable that the first expects the answer Yes, while the second expects No. De Wilde's version is no improvement: "Is the wing of the ostrich sluggish, or does it lack wings and feathers?" For it seems rather meaningless to ask whether the ostrich lacks wings after asking whether its wing is sluggish.

13.h. נֹצָה "plumage" (of eagle, Ezek 17:3). Beer (*BH*²*frt, BHK*), Fohrer, Sicre Díaz, NAB read נֹצָתָהּ "its feathers" (so too apparently NIV, NJPS). But there would be merit in reading with Hölscher, Guillaume, Fedrizzi, Gordis, Gray (נֹצָה), JB, following Aq and Vg, נֵץ "falcon," fem of נֵץ (v 26; Lev 11:16; Deut 14:15), thus "is it the wing of the stork or the falcon?" This revocalization is adopted in the *Translation* above. To the same effect, Kissane reads the masc נֵץ "falcon." See further, *Comment*. Moffatt appears to omit the word.

13.i. Other interpretations of the colon as a whole are: (1) "Do you give wings to the ostrich and feathers to the stork?" (ibn Ezra, cited by Gordis; hence KJV "Gavest thou the goodly wings unto the peacocks? Or wings and feathers unto the ostrich?" This can hardly be the meaning since the ostrich does not have wings. (2) Terrien understands "[the ostrich] has the feathers of the stork and the falcon," but it is hard to see what point the sentence would then be making. Similarly Sicre Díaz translates "her feathers are like the plumage of the stork," attractively linking vv 14–16 together: "when (כי) she leaves her eggs ... she is harsh with her young." But again, why should we be told that the plumage of the ostrich resembles that of the stork?

14.a. תעזב, fem sg in agreement with the presumed subj "the ostrich" rather than with the grammatical subj רננים "[daughters of] piercing cries" (v 13) (cf. GKC, §124b). Mitchell Dahood, "The Root עזב in Job," *JBL* 78 (1959) 303–9 (307–8), sees here another עזב "repair, set, arrange" (cf. S. Arab. *'db*, Ugar. *'db*; cf. *DCH*, 6:332a; and BDB, 738a, for Neh 3:8 only), as also at 10:1; 18:4; 20:19—which would restore the ostrich's reputation! The suggestion is followed by Pope, Andersen, Hartley; it was anticipated by Julius Boehmer, "Was ist der Sinn von Hiob 39:13–18 an seiner gegenwärtigen Stelle?," *ZAW* 53 (1935) 289–91. But at none of these places has the suggestion been accepted in this commentary; see also the adverse judgment of H. G. M. Williamson, "A Reconsideration of עזב II in Biblical Hebrew," *ZAW* 97 [1985] 74–85; and cf. *DCH*, 6:866a.

14.b. For לארץ "on, in the ground," cf. 2:13; 15:29; 16:13. It is not "leaves her eggs to the earth" (RSV; similarly NEB, but not REB).

14.c. תחמם "she warms." The piel may suggest that she herself is warming them (so too Kissane), rather than that she leaves them for the sun to warm (as RSV, NIV, NJPS, NEB, Moffatt, Fohrer, Pope, Good, Habel, Strauss); but the latter interpretation must be right, for if she is incubating them herself, there would be no question of a foot or wild animal (v 15) crushing them. An obj "them" is understood, or else we should emend to תְּחַמְּמֵם "she warms them" (Gordis). Dhorme thinks a final *mem* is omitted for the sake of euphony. Others emend to תַּנִּחַם or תַּנִּיחֵם "she deposits them," from נוח hiph (Beer [*BH²*], Budde², Driver–Gray [at 1:345; not 2:318], Beer [*BHK*], NAB).

Tur-Sinai thought the form could be related to a new word חמא "neglect" (cf. Aram. חמא, חמי; not in *DCH*), thus "she neglects them in the dust," which indeed creates a closer parallelism with the first colon, but at the cost of making the two cola say the same thing.

15.a. Fohrer deletes the verse as introducing a new motif.

15.b. וְתִשְׁכַּח lit. "and she forgot," but we might expect simple rather than consec *waw*; hence Budde, Beer (*BHK*), Gray, NAB תִּשְׁכַּח. Good parallels for the consec *waw* for logical rather than temporal connection exist, however; cf. GKC, §111t.

15.c. זור III "press down" (BDB, 266b; זור I, *HALOT*, 1:267a; זור II, *DCH*, 3:100a). The sg suff must refer to בציה "her eggs" as a collective (cf. GKC, §135p).

15.d. חית השדה "wild animal," lit. "living creature of the open country," as in 5:23 (חית הארץ "living creature of the earth" in 5:22).

16.a. קשה hiph "make hard, treat hardly" (BDB, 905a), as in Isa 63:17 (make the heart hard). The masc is a problem, since the subj appears to be the female ostrich; it frequently happens, however, that a masc vb is used with a fem subj (see GKC, §145o). Nevertheless, the form is often emended to the fem תַּקְשִׁיחַ (some mss, Dillmann [*vel*], Beer [*BHK*], Hölscher, Fohrer, Gray, NAB) or הַקְשִׁיחַ (Bickell²; inf abs, cf. GKC, §113z) (Ewald, Dillmann [*vel*], Driver–Gray, Driver, "Birds in the Old Testament. II. Birds in Life," 138 n. 5, van der Lugt) or הִקְשִׁיחָה (perf; so Hitzig, Siegfried, Duhm, Hartley) "she treats harshly"—which is how most versions render it, whether or not they accept an emendation.

Gordis less probably thinks קשה should be understood as "grow tough," with בניה "her chicks" as the subj, thus "Her young ones grow tough without her."

16.b. ללא־לה ought to mean "(making them) into none of hers" (as Driver–Gray note); similarly NAB "She cruelly disowns her young," i.e., makes them not hers. But most agree that the sense is rather "as if they were none of hers," in which case perhaps כְלֹא־לָה should be read (as also Beer [*BHK*], Driver, 138 n. 6, Gray, NEB).

16.c. פחד "dread" is a common word. Dahood, however, sees here another פַּחַד "flock" (cf. Ugar. *phd*), thus "without a flock" ("Northwest Semitic Philology and Job," 74; cf. פַּחַד III, *DCH*, 6:675b). De Wilde, alluding to the custom of the female ostrich of running away from the nest when she is threatened (in order to draw off her attackers) and of destroying her own nest if she has had to be absent from it for a long time, thinks we should read בלי־פֶּשַׁע "without fault" rather than בלי־פחד "without fear," which he sees as a "dogmatic correction." The ostrich is not at fault, because the blame is ascribed to God in v 17. Beer (*BHK frt*) reads לְהַפְרִחַ "[her labor] to make them flourish" (פרח hiph as at Isa 17:11; Ezek 17:24), which seems rather weak. Gray would read פֶּרַח "chick," a sense he postulates for פֶּרַח "bud, sprout" (BDB, 827a; cf. *DCH,* 6:765a) parallel to Arab. *farḥ* (Lane, 2362b).

16.d. The syntax of the colon is somewhat cryptic, and there are two main ways of taking it. The second alternative is adopted in the *Translation* above. (1) On the one hand, the emphasis may be on the real or probable vanity of her labor: the Hebrew is lit. "her toil is in vain; there is no fear" (so Driver–Gray); similarly KJV "her labour is in vain without fear," NJPS "Her labor is in vain for lack of concern." So too apparently RSV "though her (NRSV its) labor be in vain, yet she (NRSV it) has no fear." (2) On the other hand, the emphasis may be on her lack of fear that her labor may be in vain: thus Gordis "that her labor is in vain she has no fear," i.e., "that her labor may be in vain gives her no concern." Others have, for example, "little she cares if her labor goes for nothing" (JB), "not caring if her labour is wasted" (NEB), and similarly Moffatt, Pope, Hartley. But it should be insisted that בְּלִי־פַחַד means "without fear," not "unheeding" (Moffatt), or "not caring" (NEB).

17.a. Kissane, Fohrer delete the verse as a gloss. Hartley accepts that this verse may be an addition because it is strange to have Yahweh speaking about "God" (אֱלוֹהַ) in the third person. But parallels do exist; see 40:2 (also אֱלוֹהַ); 38:41; 40:9, 19 (with אֵל); 1:8; 2:3 (with אֱלֹהִים); 38:7 (though here it is a fixed phrase, בְּנֵי אֱלֹהִים "sons of God"; cf. also Isa 40:8.

17.b. הִשָּׁה is נשׁה hiph "cause to forget"; the hiph occurs elsewhere only at 11:6, where it means "cause to be forgotten, i.e., overlooked."

17.c. בְּבִינָה lit. "in understanding." The initial ב is partitive (GKC, §119m), thus "no part of understanding," i.e., "no understanding at all"; so, e.g., Driver–Gray, Blommerde, Hartley. For other examples of *beth* partitive, see *Note* on 21:25.

18.a. כָּעֵת lit. "at the time [when]," i.e., as soon as (a relative pron being understood). Some prefer to read כְּעֵת "while" (cf. כְּעֵת מוּתָה "at the moment of her death," 1 Sam 4:20; so Duhm, Beer [*BH*²], Driver, "Birds in the Old Testament. II," 138 n. 7, NEB, though its claim of support from LXX is dubious).

18.b. The verb מרא is problematic, and the following meanings have been suggested: (1) "beat" (the air with the wings), cognate with Arab. *marā* "whip (a horse)"; so BDB, 597a (מרא I) "flap away," Duhm, Dhorme, Hölscher, Kissane, Fohrer, Guillaume "speeds"; thus too Strahan "she scours along," and Moffatt "she will scour the plain." Some, hewing closer to the Arab. sense, understand "spurs herself" (Driver–Gray, Kissane, Sicre Díaz) (the vb is מרא II in *HALOT,* 2:630a, and *DCH,* 5:474a).

(2) "strike" (the ground with the foot); cf. *HALOT,* 2:630a, and *DCH,* 5:474a.

(3) "be manly, act the man" (cf. Arab. *maru'a* [Lane, 2702c]); so Driver, "Birds in the Old Testament. II. Birds in Life," 138 (מרא IV in *DCH,* 5:474a). Thus NEB "like a cock she struts."

(4) Dhorme, de Wilde propose a distinct new vb מרא "rebel," a byform of מרה (so too KB, 563a, *HALOT,* 2:630a, but for Zeph 3:1, *DCH,* 5:474a [מרא I]). Similarly, apparently, Habel, "rear up, rise up, be roused."

(5) Gordis sees it as a metathesis for תַּאֲמִיר "goes aloft," i.e., a new vb אמר that may be inferred from אָמִיר "top, summit" of tree (Isa 17:6, 9; Gen 49:21 emended); such an אמר II "act proudly" may be recognized at Isa 61:6; Ps 94:4; and perhaps hiph at Deut 26:17, 18. Here Gordis translates "now she soars aloft"; but how can that be said of the ostrich, which cannot fly?

(6) "when she runs fast" (J. Boehmer, "Was ist der Sinn von Hiob 39:13–18 an seiner gegenwärtigen Stelle?," *ZAW* 53/12 [1935] 289–92 [290]).

(7) a new word מרא V "wing up" (cf. מֶרְאָה "wing, bird's tail," Aram. מָרֵא "master," lit. "high one"; not in *DCH*) (Tur-Sinai). Pope accepts the connection with מֶרְאָה, translating "up she spreads her plumes"; cf. NRSV "spreads its plumes aloft," NIV "when she spreads her feathers to run." This is the solution adopted in the *Translation* above.

Among emendations are: תְּמַהֵר "she hastens" (Hontheim, Beer [*BH*²*frt*], NAB "in her swiftness of foot"), which is too vague, תַּאֲמִיר "she rises" (Graetz; Gordis had the same idea but did not emend), and a form of רום "be high" (Strauss). Least appealing of all is that reported by Beer (*BHK prps*), תַּאֲבִיר, apparently hiph of אבר "fly," which is attested only elsewhere in qal, at v 26, of the hawk; but if there is one thing certain about the ostrich, it is that it cannot *fly.*

18.c. בַּמָּרוֹם "on high" (so KJV) is more than a little strange, since the ostrich is earth-bound (contrast Hab 2:9, where a nest is set רוֹם "on high" to be safe from harm). The word is effectively omitted by RSV "rouses herself to flee," NAB "in her swiftness of foot," NIV "when she spreads her feathers to run." JB "if she bestirs herself to use her height" is forced. NJPS "Else she would soar on high, scoffing at the horse and its rider" is a poor sense. NEB "over the uplands" and Good's "on the heights" are ways of coping with the Hebrew, but they fail to convince since the ostrich typically flees its pursuers on the plains. The only time when the ostrich is high is when it is not sitting on the ground, so we may suspect that the image is of the female bird rising from her nest, spreading her feathers, and running off at great speed.

Emendation to בְּמָרוֹץ "when she runs" (Hitzig, Duhm, Beer [*BHK al*], NAB "in her swiftness of foot") is attractive; less so is the quite ingenious בֹּא מֹרִים "[when] archers arrive" (Wright [in part], Budde, Strahan, Beer [*BHK prps*], Moffatt "let hunters come").

18.d. For שׂחק "laugh" signifying absence of fear, cf. v 7. It is not a question of "mak[ing] sport of the horse and its rider" (NAB), or "mak[ing] fools" of them (JB), or even "scorning" (NEB, similarly KJV) them.

19.a. רעמה, which occurs only here, is understood by BDB, 947b, as "vibration (?)," apparently connecting it with רעם "thunder" (so too RV, Guillaume "quivering mane," Moffatt "tossing mane"). KJV actually translated "thunder," taking the word as a byform of רַעַם "thunder"; so too Good, Habel, who thinks "mane" is "a prosaic leveling of the poetic language," and Newsom, who regards the translation "mane" as a "domestication" of the horse, and defends the retention of the "striking image" of thunder, the horse being presented effectively as a warrior deity. Dahood, "Hebrew-Ugaritic Lexicography X," 393, also attempts to retain a connection with רעם "thunder."

KB, 901a, followed by *HALOT*, 3:1268a, offers "mane," comparing Arab. *ri'm*; and NRSV, JB, NIV, NEB, GNB, Dhorme, Hölscher, Kissane, Fohrer, Pope, Rowley, Hartley follow suit, with simply "mane." This view is adopted in the *Translation* above.

Driver–Gray argued for "strength" as the meaning of רעמה, purely on the ground of its parallelism with גבורה "strength" in the first colon, a sense perhaps supported by Tg (so too RSV); the mane is no doubt a symbol of its strength, but that is not to say that the word *means* that.

The sense "glory" for רעם and רעמה was argued for by Israel W. Slotki, "A Study of רעם," *AJSL* 37 (1920–21) 149–55 (154), the "glory" of the horse being its mane.

Among emendations are these: (1) Hontheim, Beer (*BHK frt*) read עָצְמָה "strength." (2) Duhm reads רִקְמָה (*frt*) "motley, variegated stuff." (3) De Wilde reads רוֹמָה "haughtily" (as at Mic 2:3), thus "do you clothe its neck with pride?" He compares Homer, *Iliad* 15.266 "high it carries its head." (4) NAB replaces רעם with הוֹד "splendor," moved to this place from v 20b. (5) Tur-Sinai, rather weakly, reads עֹז "strength," and moves רעמה to v 20a.

20.a. רעשׁ "shake, quake"; Habel, who is maximizing the mythic aspect of the language, has "quake." Gordis thinks the image is of a plague of locusts descending on crops and making the whole field appear to be quaking. But the best translation would seem rather to be "make him quiver" (NJPS, NEB, similarly NAB, Andersen; cf. the "waving" of fields of grain in Ps 72:16) or "shake" (Good), i.e., with excitement. Less appropriate are "make him leap" (RSV, JB, NIV; cf. Dhorme, Hölscher, Kissane, Fohrer, Pope, Guillaume, Hartley; Moffatt "leap forward") or "make him afraid" (KJV). Rowley notes that in Joel 2:4 locusts are compared to horses running, and suggests that perhaps here, contrariwise, horses' galloping is compared to the movement of locusts (cf. also Rev 9:7); but galloping would not be referred to as "shaking" or "quivering" (רעשׁ).

Among emendations, Ehrlich's הֲתַעֲשִׁנֶּנּוּ כָאָרֻבָּה "do you make it smoke like a chimney?," i.e., with the steam rising from its flanks, is quite brilliant: ארבה elsewhere usually means "lattice, window, sluice," but at Hos 13:3 may well mean "[smoke from] a chimney" (so KJV, NEB); so also Theodor H. Gaster, "Short Notes," *VT* 4 (1954) 73–79 (79). עשׁן "smoke" is only used in qal elsewhere, but the hiph is no doubt acceptable. Tur-Sinai's "Does thunder frighten him as the locusts?" (removing to this colon רעמה from the previous) is on the other hand not at all attractive. Gray proposes הן תריעשׁו, rendering the whole colon, "Lo! you may send him hurtling on his way like locusts," thinking of the use of רעשׁ in 41:29 (21) for the "hurtling" of a spear (though the word there perhaps rather means a sound, viz. "rattle").

20.b. ארבה is the commonest term for locust, referring to the adult, winged insect. The term is probably used here as a collective (Habel "locust swarm"). NAB emends to כָּאַבִּיר "like a stallion," translating "Do you make the steed to quiver?"; but while אביר appears in this sense at Jer 8:16; 47:3; 50:11, how can the horse be "like" a stallion?

20.c. Duhm thought this colon belonged after v 19a.

20.d. הוֹד "majesty" is recognized by most here, some taking הוֹד נחרו "the majesty of its snorting" as "his majestic snorting" (RSV, NJPS; similarly Good); cf. הוֹד קוֹלוֹ "the majesty of his voice" for "his majestic voice" (Isa 30:30). Some tone down the term "majesty," thus "its proud neighing" (cf. Terrien; Moffatt "snorting bravely, furiously."

Gordis, however, sees a new word הוֹד "echo," a byform of הֵד "shout, echo" (as at Ezek 7:7; similarly Tur-Sinai; Ehrlich actually reads הֵד). For that word, הֵד, *HALOT*, 1:238, curiously offers the translation "thunderbolt (?)," though explicitly dissenting from that very proposal by Godfrey Rolles Driver, "Problems of the Hebrew Text and Language," in *Alttestamentliche Studien Friedrich Nötscher zum*

sechzigsten Geburtstage 19. Juli 1950 gewidmet (BBB 1; ed. Hubert Junker and Johannes Botterweck; Bonn: Hanstein, 1950) 46–61 (56) (= הֹד II, in *DCH*, 2:489b). (KB, 225a, had not recognized a הֹד, recommending either that הוד be deleted or that הֵידָד "cry" be read.) Guillaume proposes another הוד cognate with Arab. *hadd* "rough, harsh noise" (Lane, 2882c). It is perhaps the same הוד that NEB "his shrill neighing" accepts with its reading הַד (Brockington). De Wilde reads הֲלֹא "is not [its snorting terrible]?," arguing that "majesty" is too formal a term for the snorting of a horse; NAB, interchanging the places of רַעְמָה in v 19 and הוד in v 20, reads רַעַם נַחְרוֹ "the thunder of his snorting," thus "his thunderous snorting."

20.e. נַחַר occurs only here, though the חֲרָה of horses appears at Jer 8:16 and is proposed for Ezek 32:2 (of a dragon); BDB, 637b, thinks it is "snorting," but several think rather of "neighing" (JB, NEB, Dhorme, Andersen). Although there is another vb usually translated "neigh" (צהל), in the present context this seems to be the appropriate sense (on the sounds made by horses, see further, *Comment*). KJV "[the glory of] his nostrils" identified נחר with נְחִיר "nostril" at 41:20 (12). A vb נחר, though not recognized by BDB, seems to be attested at Jer 6:29 (of bellows snorting), and is proposed for Isa 41:11; 45:24 (cf. *DCH*, 5:667a; *HALOT*, 2:690a); in piel perhaps also at Cant 1:6 (if not from חרה "be angry"). BDB, however, derives the vb in Jer 6:29 from חרר "be hot." On the vb נחר (cf. Aram. נחר, Akk. *naḥāru* "snort" [*CDA*, 231b]), see Driver, "Studies in the Vocabulary of the Old Testament. VI," 381; "Studies in the Vocabulary of the Old Testament. VII," *JTS* 35 (1934) 380–93 (393); "Linguistic and Textual Problems: Isaiah xl–lxvi," *JTS* 36 (1935) 396–406 (398–99); "Two Misunderstood Passages of the Old Testament," *JTS* ns 6 (1955) 82–87 (85).

Tur-Sinai's supposition that נחר may refer to the "snorting" of thunder has nothing to recommend it, nor does his proposal to read פַּחַד "[the noise of] fear [and terror]" in its place.

20.f. אֵימָה lit. "[is] terror." For the use of the noun instead of an adj, cf. Driver, *Tenses* §189. The emendation of Bickell, Duhm, Beer (*BH²prps*) הוד נַחְרָה אֲיָמָה (perhaps בְּהוֹד) "(in) the majesty of (its) terrible snorting" (חֲרָה as at Jer 8:16) is only an improvement if we think the whole verse should be a question. Thus Driver–Gray "Dost thou cause him to quiver like a locust, in the majesty of his terrible snorting?" (similarly NAB, NIV).

21.a. חפר is "dig, search for," only here of a horse pawing the ground (Arab. *ḥāfir* "hoof" means "that which digs"). The pl יחפרו is read as a sg יַחְפֹּר or יַחְפּוֹר "he paws" by most (Bickell, Budde, Duhm, Peake, Dhorme, Driver–Gray, Beer [*BHK*], Hölscher, Fohrer, Pope, Fedrizzi, Gerleman [*BHS frt*], de Wilde, Sicre Díaz, van der Lugt, NAB, NEB); the ancient versions (LXX, Pesh, Vg) all have a sg, but that is not much evidence of the text they had before them. Gray also translates "he paws," but he reads rather יַחְפִּיר, hiph of a different vb חפר, which he understands as a denominative of a noun for "paw" cognate with Arab. *ḥāfir* (Wehr–Cowan, 188a). Blommerde unconvincingly explains the final *waw* as "the old indicative ending." Tur-Sinai found חפר an unacceptable term to use of the horse, and decided instead that the subj must be the birds of prey (as in 38:36); but he has no followers.

21.b. בעמק looks like "in the valley" (KJV, RSV; JB "the soil of the valley"). Many, however, think this a good example of a new עֶמֶק "force, strength" (cf. Akk. *emūqu* [*CDA*, 73a], Ugar. *'mq*), as in 29:10; Jer 47:5; 49:4 (cf. *DCH*, 6:488b); for bibliographical references, see *Note* on 39:10 above. So too for the present verse Blommerde, Rowley, Gordis, Habel; cf. NIV "he paws fiercely," NJPS "with force," Pope, Andersen "violently," Guillaume "vigorously."

But since עמק means—rather than "valley"—"plain" (as NAB) or "lowland," as the site of battles and the deployment of chariots (see further, *Comment*), this may well be the appropriate sense here.

21.c. וישיש בכח "and it exults in strength." Some versions link the vb with the previous vb, יחפרו "they paw" or יחפר "it paws," thus NAB "he jubilantly paws," JB "Exultantly he paws." NEB "he shows his mettle as he paws and prances" is hard to derive from the MT. Many retain the Masoretic vocalization, which ends the first colon with "[exults] in strength." Some, however, join בכח with יצא, thus "he goes out mightily" (so Wright, Bickell, Budde, Duhm, Driver–Gray, Beer [*BHK*], Hölscher, Kissane, Fohrer, Fedrizzi, Gerleman [*BHS prb*], Guillaume). Beer (*BHK*) reads יָשִׂישׂ without the *waw*, "he exults," and so too Gray, explaining the vb as an impf of attendant circumstances. Moffatt "He paws the valley proudly, facing the clash of arms" does not do justice to both ישיש "it exults" and בכח "in might."

21.d. יצא "go out" is a colorless vb. What is the translator to do? Simply reproduce it, hoping it will not be noticed (KJV "he goeth on," RSV "goes out"), or brighten it up to "rushes" (NAB), "prances" (JB), "charges" (NJB, NIV, NEB; similarly NJPS), "charges out" (Good), "charges headlong" (Habel)? There seems no right or wrong in this matter.

21.e. נֶשֶׁק is usually "weapons, military equipment," but it may, metonymically, be "battle" here and at Ps 140:7 (8) (*HALOT*, 2:731b; *DCH*, 5:781a). RSV, NAB have "weapons," whereas NIV has "the fray," NJPS, Gordis "battle," JB "the clash of arms," NJB "battle-line," NEB "the armoured line" (KJV "the armed men").

22.a. פחד "fear." Some mss, however, read לפחת "at the pit" (so Beer [BH²]), which sometimes means "calamity" and is associated with פחד at Lam 3:47. Some LXX manuscripts have βασιλεῖ "at the king," conceivably reading the same לפחת, which it understood as "to the governor, ruler" (so Beer); but it is more likely that βασιλεῖ is a corruption of βέλει "at the weapon," read by other manuscripts, which would parallel the sword in the second colon, though it cannot otherwise be explained.

22.b. יחת, from חתת, lit. "is shattered, dismayed." RSV has "is not dismayed," NEB "knows no dismay," JB, NIV "(is) afraid of nothing," NJPS "cannot be frightened," KJV "is not affrighted," Pope, Habel, Hartley "undaunted."

22.c. ישוב lit. "returns." RSV, NAB have "does not turn back" (similarly KJV), JB, NJPS, Hartley "recoil(s)," NIV, REB "shy away," Pope "shies," NEB "flinch."

23.a. אשפה is "quiver"; the meaning could be that the quiver is strapped to the horse's back (JB, Terrien) or side (NIV, NEB, Moffatt, Habel, Guillaume, Andersen, Hartley) or is just, in some loose way, "upon" it (RSV, Strahan, Fohrer, Good) (it is hard to see how it could be "around" it, as NAB, or "about" it, as Pope). Those who think of the quiver as borne by the horse include Dhorme, Rowley. But here, since the sword (v 22) must be a weapon that it confronts, and the spear and javelin seem also to be assaulting it rather than carried by it (so too Gill, Sicre Díaz), it will probably be, by metonymy, "arrows" (DCH, 1:418a; NJPS "a quiverful of arrows," Gordis, Gray).

23.b. תרנה must be derived from a vb רנה, occurring only here, "rattle" (BDB, 943a, HALOT, 3:1246b); it could describe the rattle of arrows in the quiver (so, e.g., Dhorme, Kissane) or the rattle of arrows flying past the horse (so, e.g., Gordis). Some think, however, that the noun should be ascribed to the vb רנן "cry out," in which case it would have to be vocalized תרלנה (Driver–Gray [frt], Hölscher; so too Dahood, "Northwest Semitic Philology and Job," 74, with the energic ending -nna; followed by Pope, Blommerde) or תרלן (Beer [BHK prps], attaching the final ה to אשפה as the article). Gray also adopts the reading תרנה, rendering "twangs," like Arab. ranna "to twang (of a bowstring, for example)" (Lane, 1164a, but it should be noted that ranna is not specifically of "twanging" but of making many different kinds of sound).

23.c. להב lit. "the flash of"; cf. להב חרב וברק חנית "the flash of the sword and the lightning of the spear" (Nah 3:3). At Judg 3:22, a prose text, it is plainly the "blade" of the sword. Most have "flashing spear" (RSV, JB, NIV, NJPS) or "glittering spear" (KJV), though Good translates literally "flame of spear." It would be possible to take להב as the predicate (cf. Driver, Tenses §189), i.e., "the spear and javelin are a flash." Budde read the vb לְהַב "flash" or the ptcp לֹהֵב "flashing," though, as Driver–Gray say, we might have expected the impf; so too NEB "the spear and sabre flash."

23.d. כידון is, because of its connection with the arrows and the spear (חנית), probably "javelin" (BDB, 475b, "dart, javelin"; DCH, 4:391b; RSV, NAB, JB, NJPS, Moffatt, Kissane, Tur-Sinai [but "lance" in his translation], Guillaume, Habel), a light spear that is thrown, rather than "lance" (NIV), a weapon for piercing that is held by a horseman, or "sabre" (NEB), or "scimitar" (HALOT, 2:472a), or "sword" (Pope, Hartley), weapons for cutting that are held (not thrown) by the warrior. KJV "shield" understood the term in the same sense as at 1 Sam 17:6, 45 (where it has "target," i.e., shield), though it translated the term with "lance" at Jer 50:42 and "spear" at Josh 8:18, 26; Jer 6:23 (|| 50:42!), Job 41:29 (21); F. M. Cross and D. N. Freedman suggest the word means "breastplate" at 1 Sam 17:6 ("The Blessing of Moses," JBL 67 [1948] 191–210 [205 n. 40]), while acknowledging that elsewhere it seems rather to be a weapon. On כידון (or perhaps the form at Qumran should be registered as כידן, as DCH, 4:391b, 601a) meaning "scimitar," i.e., a heavy sword with a curved flat blade and an outer, convex, cutting edge, in Qumran texts (which does not automatically determine its meaning in earlier Hebrew), see G. Molin, "What Is a Kidon?," JSS 1 (1956) 334–37. Cf. A. Dupont-Sommer, "«Règlement de la guerre des fils de lumière»: traduction et notes (suite)," RHR 148 (1955) 141–80 (143 n.); Karl Georg Kuhn, "Beiträge zum Verständnis der Kriegsrolle von Qumran aus dem Qumran-Arbeitsgemeinschaft," TLZ 81 (1956) 25–30 (29–30).

24.a. רעש is "quaking, shaking," e.g., of the earth by the tramping of warriors (Isa 9:5 [4]) or by chariots (Jer 47:3); at Jer 8:16 the neighing of stallions makes the whole land shake. Sometimes, however, רעש seems to be not a movement but a sound, a "roar" or "din" (HALOT, 3:1272a), associated with a noise (קול), e.g., Jer 10:22; Nah 3:2. Pope thinks the phrase ברעש ורגז depicts the battle, thus "mid rattle and roar"; similarly Tur-Sinai "'midst fright and fear," Good "in clatter and clamor." But it is more probable that it describes the horse's eagerness for battle (Gordis); he translates "shaking with excitement." Most believe that רעש is descriptive of the horse's own feeling: "frenzied" (NAB), "quivering" (JB, Kissane, Guillaume), "trembling" (NJB, NJPS, NEB), "he quakes and shakes" (Habel). But the term may be better understood as referring to the horse's effect on the earth, thus "stamping" in the Translation above.

24.b. רְמ is "agitation, excitement, raging" (BDB, 919b), "rage, agitation, wrath" (*HALOT*, 3:1183b). "Rage" (KJV, RSV), "impatience" (JB), "excitement" (NIV, NJPS; similarly Kissane, Guillaume), "eagerness" (NEB), "trembling" (NAB) are typical renderings. Both רַעַשׁ and רְמ, as Rowley points out, indicate excitement rather than anger.

24.c. גמא is usually taken as the vb "swallow" (as Gen 24:17 [hiph]); thus "swallow" (KJV, RSV, NJPS, Dhorme, Kissane, Guillaume, Habel), "devour" (NAB, NEB, Hartley), "eats up" (NIV), "races" (Pope). The same idiom is frequent in Arabic, where a swift horse is called a "swallower" and to "swallow the ground" is to devour distance. JB "he eats up the miles" uses an idiom more familiar in our culture. Cf. Catullus 35.7 *viam vorabit* "he [a person] will eat up the road."

Gordis, on the other hand, argues for a new word גמא II "make holes in" (cf. גוּמָץ "pit" in Eccl 10:8 and Aram. גוּמָץ "hole"); but he somewhat prosaically translates "stamps (the ground)." We might prefer "he dents the ground." Tur-Sinai's "plungeth" is not explained.

24.d. אֶרֶץ "earth" seems unproblematic, but Andersen suggests we have here another noun meaning "grace, pleasure," as at 37:13 (*q.v.*), thus "willfully."

24.e. De Wilde inserts a complete colon here, הַסָּעֵר יִסְתָּעֵר קָדִימָה "impatiently he storms forward," thus creating two bicola instead of the tricolon of v 25.

24.f. שׁוֹפָר "trumpet" strangely appears both here and in the next colon as well. Duhm not unreasonably thought one occurrence a mistake, and read here שׁוֹמֵר "guard" (as in Judg 7:19), adding a vb יֵעֹר "he is roused" or יִרְקַד "he skips," thus "when the guard calls he sets off." But if the MT is in error, this is hardly an improvement.

24.g. כִּי־קוֹל lit. "when the sound" is strange, for it is a clause without a vb. Some emend to בְּקוֹל "at the sound of" (Bickell, Budde), but, as Driver–Gray note, כ temporal ("when") is rare except with an inf or verbal noun. Others read בְּקוֹל "at the sound of" (Beer [*BHK*]), while Driver–Gray think לְקוֹל would be the normal idiom. Gray reads for the second colon יַאֲמִין כִּי בְקוֹל־שׁוֹפָר, deleting וְלֹא and rendering "his whole trust is in the sound of the trumpet" (he rather awkwardly explains כִּי as "exceptive," i.e., "only"). Gordis explains קוֹל as the inf or, preferably, an archaic qal ptcp of a new vb קוֹל "speak" (cf. Arab. *kāla* [Lane, 2994c]), thus "the trumpet is sounding." Terrien's "without waiting for the sound of the trumpet" is not explained.

24.h. אמן hiph is always "trust, believe," and some render it so; thus, e.g., "neither believeth he [that it is the sound of the trumpet]" (KJV), Gordis "(he) cannot believe that the trumpet is sounding," meaning presumably that the horse can hardly believe its own ears (so Rowley, similarly Habel)—which seems forced ("surely a fanciful idea, even for our extravagant author," says Andersen), and worse, over-anthropomorphic. Kissane ingeniously translated "he believeth not in the sound of the trumpet," meaning that it does not need the trumpet's call to tell it of the battle since its own instinct is a surer guide; but would that thought be expressed as "not believing" in the trumpet? Good thought that not to believe meant not to obey ("he does not heed the trumpet call"), but this depends on his interpretation of the trumpet as the signal for retreat (see on v 25). The eighteenth-century commentator John Gill took it that it will not trust to its ears, but must see with its eyes whether the battle is ready.

The *Translation* above, "stand still," adopts a sense for אמן hiph that is inferred also by BDB, 43a, *DCH*, 1:316b; RSV, NIV, GNB, Dhorme, Sicre Díaz, Hartley. It must be admitted, however, that there is no parallel (Guillaume compares the sense of the Arab. cognate *'amina* "be quiet" [Lane, 100a], but that is not a good indication of the meaning of the Hebrew, and in any case, *'amina* can just as well mean "be safe" or "trust"). Pope's rendering "unchecked by trumpet sound" is hard to accept, since it implies, implausibly, that a horse might be *held back* by the sound.

Emendations include: (1) לֹא יִמָּנַע "it cannot be held back" (Beer [*BH²al*]; similarly JB, NEB). (2) NAB "he holds not back" (similarly de Wilde) seems to read יִמָּנַע, but מנע always has an obj or is followed by the prep מִן, and is not used absolutely, as it would be here. (3) לֹא יִמִּין וְלֹא יַשְׂמִאִיל "he turns neither to the right or the left" (Duhm, Budde², Beer [*BH²prps*], Hölscher, Moffatt "straight ahead, never swerving"); Tur-Sinai and NJPS accepted the first part of the emendation, translating "he does not turn aside." The emendation is arbitrary. (4) NAB reads וְלֹא יְמָאֵן בְּקוֹל "he does not refuse at the sound [of the trumpet]," thus "he holds not back at the sound of the trumpet." (5) Since the sense is pretty plainly "it cannot be made to stand still," and the natural Hebrew for that would be לֹא יַעֲמִיד "one cannot make it stand," perhaps that is the reading we should adopt.

25.a. Kissane transfers this colon to follow v 20a, but that seems no improvement in sense. It does, however, enable him to arrange the whole of the strophe (vv 19–25) as five tricola, describing in turn the horse's physical qualities, its restiveness, its courage, its speed, and its instinct for the battle. Hölscher thought a colon was missing before v 25a.

25.b. דַי is "sufficiency," and בְּדַי "sufficient for" (Nah 2:12 [13]), "in exchange for" (e.g., Hab 2:13), and supposedly here "as often as" (BDB, 191b §2aβ; *DCH*, 2:432b), which מִדֵּי certainly can mean (e.g., 1 Sam 1:7; Jer 48:27). Driver–Gray, Beer (*BHK*), NAB think that we should actually read מִדֵּי. Good proposes that דַי "Enough!" is the title of a bugle call, summoning warriors to retreat; but that would set the trumpet in the height of battle whereas מֵרָחוֹק "from afar" (v 25b) would suggest that the horse is not yet in the battle.

Others, however, find here a new word דְּוִי "echo, sound" (cf. Arab. *dawiyy* [Lane, 940c]); so I. Eitan, *A Contribution to Biblical Lexicography* (New York: Columbia University Press, 1924) 36–38; "Studies in Hebrew Roots," *JQR* ns 14 (1923–24) 31–52 (36–38); G. R. Driver, "Hebrew Studies," *JRAS* (1948) 164–76 (168); Samuel I. Feigin, "The Captives in Cuneiform Inscriptions," *AJSL* 50 (1933–34) 217–45 (219 n. 4); Guillaume, Sicre Díaz; cf. *DCH*, 2:425b; thus "at the sound of the trumpet"; NEB "at the blast of [the horn]" and REB "at the trumpet-call" read בְּדַוֵּי. Gordis takes the Arabic to mean "faint sound" and so understands the word here of the *distant* sound of the trumpet. Pope, less persuasively, connects בְּדַי rather with Ugar. *bd* "song," reading בַּד or בַּדֵּי, and rendering "at the call of [the trumpet]," the word being used adverbially. Gray offers a somewhat tame emendation to בְּיָד "to the accompaniment of," comparing עַל־יְדֵי כְלֵי דוּד "to the accompaniment of David's instruments" in Amos 6:5. The emendation to בְּדַוֵּי "at the sound of" is adopted in the *Translation* above.

25.c. הֶאָח "hurrah!" (so JB), a cry of satisfaction, rather than "Aha!" (as RSV, NAB, NIV, NJPS, NEB), which tends to be a cry of surprise (though the English term can suggest triumph, satisfaction, mockery, or irony, according to *OED*). KJV's "Ha, ha" is not necessarily a cry of laughter (though the horse does "laugh" [שׂחק] in v 22a), but may be a cry of surprise; cf. Shakespeare, *The Tempest*, V.i.263 "Ha, ha! What things are these, my lord Antonio?"

25.d. Fohrer thinks a colon has been omitted here.

25.e. רִיחַ "smell, scent" (BDB, 926a; s.v. רוח in *HALOT*, 3:1197a). P. A. H. de Boer, however, has argued that the vb here is intrans, thus "he smells of the battle" ("וּמֵרָחוֹק יָרִיחַ מִלְחָמָה Job 39:25," in *Words and Meanings: Essays Presented to David Winton Thomas* [ed. Peter R. Ackroyd and Barnabas Lindars; Cambridge: Cambridge University Press, 1968] 29–38; he is followed by Good. But elsewhere (e.g., Gen 27:27; Amos 5:21) it is plainly trans. Others are not so happy with the idea of "scenting" battle, and read יָרִיעַ (better תָּרִיעַ) "[the battle] sounds" (Wright, with one ms); but a word for battle is never the subj of רוע hiph.

25.f. NEB omits the colon.

25.g. רַעַם is always "thunder" (previously at 26:14), obviously here "thunderous shouting." It is a good idea to keep the metaphor, "the thunder of the captains" (KJV, RSV; JB "thundering") rather than to dissipate it to a mere "roar" (NAB, Pope; cf. NJPS) or "shout" (NIV, Hartley; cf. REB). רַעַם and תְּרוּעָה are, along with מִלְחָמָה "battle," objs of רִיחַ "smell"; strictly speaking, only "battle" is appropriate, and the combination is to be explained as the rhetorical figure of zeugma. Moffatt avoids the zeugma by translating "scenting the battle from afar, where captains thunder, 'mid the thoughts of war."

Gordis finds here, however, רֵעַ "shouting" (as at Exod 32:17; Mic 4:9; and perhaps at Job 36:33), with enclitic *mem*. Duhm too thought the cries of the captains could hardly be "scented," so read בְּרֵעַ "at the shout." Neither proposal is very attractive.

25.h. תְּרוּעָה can be "blast (of a trumpet)" (as, e.g., Num 10:5) or a human shout (as, e.g., Josh 6:5; Amos 1:14), often in the context of battle. Since we have heard already of the trumpet in vv 24b, 25a, it is most likely to be human "shouting" here (as against Gordis).

26.a. De Wilde moves the whole strophe about the hawk and eagle (vv 26–30) to follow 38:41, i.e., immediately after the line about the other raptor, the raven. Budde[2] moved it to follow 39:18, i.e., between the horse and the ostrich.

26.b. הֲמִבִּינָתְךָ "is it from your understanding," i.e., from understanding derived from you. Moffatt nicely has "Does your wit send the hawk to soar?," followed by "Does your word make the eagle mount?" (v 27a).

26.c. נֵץ "hawk," includes many species of falcon. Good has "peregrine," a type of hawk, but we cannot be specific about which type is meant.

26.d. אבר "fly, soar," occurs only here, but the existence of the noun אֶבְרָה "pinion" puts its general sense beyond doubt (BDB, 7b; *HALOT*, 1:9a); it could perhaps mean "grow feathers" (Dhorme) or "grow wings" (cf. *DCH*, 1:115a). Vg had "become feathered," i.e., either when fully fledged, or when, as it is said (Aelian, *On Animals* 12.4), it grows new feathers each year. But it does not take "understanding" to grow feathers, whereas it does require some kind of "understanding" to fly up and away in seasonal migration.

26.e. תֵּימָן is "south," the point of the compass; though the word could also refer to the south wind (תֵּימָן, mentioned in Ps 78:26; Cant 4:16), it is unlikely that the reference is to "the strength of wing that enabled it to fly in the teeth of the south wind" (Peake, after Duhm; similarly Fedrizzi, Strauss). If the hawk were spreading its wings "against" the south wind, we should expect על, not ל. Exceptionally, Fohrer envisages the birds being in the south, and spreading their wings for the south wind to carry them northwards to their breeding grounds.

27.a. נשר can refer both to the eagle and to the vulture (Pope). There are three possibilities for the bird referred to here: (1) "eagle"; so G. R. Driver, "Birds in the Old Testament. I. Birds in Law," *PEQ* 87 (1955) 5–20 (8–9); "Once Again: Birds in the Bible," *PEQ* 90 (1958) 56–58 (56–57).

(2) "griffon-vulture" (*Gyps fulvus*); so Driver, "Birds in the Old Testament. I. Birds in Law," 8–9; J. Milgrom, *Leviticus 1–16: A New Translation with Introduction and Commentary* (AB 3; New York: Doubleday, 1991) 662; John Tamulénas, "Översättningen av fågellistorna i Lev 11:13–19 och Deut 14:11–18," *SEÅ* 57 (1992) 28–59 (36–37).

(3) "eagle and vulture"; so Keel, *Entgegnung*, 69 n. 234; T. Kronholm, "נשר; *nešer*," *TDOT*, 10:77–85; Hans-Peter Müller, "Die Funktion divinatorischen Redens und die Tierbezeichnungen der Inschrift von Tell Deir 'Allā," in *The Balaam Text from Deir 'Alla Re-Evaluated* (ed. J. Hoftijzer and G. van der Kooij; Leiden: E. J. Brill, 1991) 185–205 (195–96); Meindert Dijkstra, "Response to H.-P. Müller and M. Weippert," in *The Balaam Text*, 206–17 (211).

27.b. Duhm, Beer (*BH*²), Driver–Gray (*frt*), Hölscher, Fohrer, de Wilde delete נשר וכי יגביה, thus removing reference to the eagle and leaving "Is it at your command that it [the hawk] makes its nest on high?" There may be some contamination of the text by the very similar passages at Jer 49:16 (כי תגביה כנשר קנך) "though you make your nest high as the eagle") and Obad 4 (אם תגביה כנשר ואם בין כוכבים שים קנך) "though you mount up like the eagle and though your nest be set among the stars"). However, the lofty dwelling of the bird of vv 27–29 suggests the eagle rather than the hawk. De Wilde thinks the hawk in question must be Eleonora's Falcon (*Falco eleonorae*), which both nests on cliffs and migrates (www.eurobirding.co.uk); but its diet is insects and small birds, and it does not feed on carrion, so it is not a suitable candidate for the bird described here. Fohrer and de Wilde acknowledge this problem, and argue, unsuccessfully, that חלל does not mean "slain" (נבלה is indeed the term for "corpse") but simply "wounded," and envisage the falcon sucking the blood from wounded warriors and feeding it to its young.

G. R. Driver, noting the apparently unnecessary repetition of סלע "crag" and the use of both ישכן "dwell" and יתלנן "lodge" for the same thing, reads, for the whole of vv 27–28, אם־על־פיך כיורים קנו ויתלנן על־שן־סלע ומצודה "does the *ky*-bird (i.e. vulture) at thy bidding build its nest high up and perch on a crag of a cliff and (i.e. as) a look-out?," the *waw* before מצודה being explicative (see next *Note*).

27.c. וכי "and that"; the syntax is a little strange, but not impossible. BDB, 472a §1d, notes 2 Sam 9:1; Gen 29:15; 27:36; Job 6:22 for cases of וכי, which is analogous. Dhorme explains the כ as expletive after the interrogative אם. NAB omits the *waw* before כי. Beer (*BH*²) deletes וכי altogether.

Joseph Reider and G. R. Driver, however, saw here the name of another bird, the *ky*-bird, perhaps a vulture (cf. Arab. *kuy* "pelican, ibis"); so Reider, "Etymological Studies in Biblical Hebrew," *VT* 4 (1954) 276–95 (294); Driver, "Job 39:27–28: The *Ky*-Bird," *PEQ* 104 (1972) 64–66; Mitchell Dahood, "Four Ugaritic Personal Names and Job 39:5, 26–27," *ZAW* 87 (1975) 220 (on the basis of a personal name *bn ky* in Ugar.); Grabbe, 126–28; Keel, *Entgegnung*, 69 n. 234l; Sicre Díaz ("vulture"); cf. *DCH*, 4:391a. Kaltner, *The Use of Arabic in Biblical Hebrew Lexicography*, 57–58, however, points out that the Arab. word is attested only in the dictionary of Dozy (2:503), which cites only medieval and later texts for the word; Reider's proposal is not thereby disproved, but the grounds for it are "very shaky" (Kaltner).

LXX reads γύψ "vulture." To the same effect, Pierre Grelot, "Note de critique textuelle sur Job xxxix 27," *VT* 22 (1972) 487–89, noting the Qumran Tg's translation by עוזינא, some kind of eagle (Jastrow, 1049a), thinks כ is an error for כדר "bird of prey." Pope also thinks that כ could be the first letters of a word כידור "bird of prey"; there is a Syr. *kudrā* "bird of prey," and a Arab. *kadara* VII "rush down" (of a hawk, but also of rain and a star; but there is nothing to suggest that a noun from *kadara* would mean a bird of prey, since *kadara* I is "be dark" and its noun *kudr* refers to a bird of dusky color [Lane, 2596a–c]). Gray also sees כידור "bird of prey" here, but he does not delete כ "for." Pope and Gray find the same word כידור in 15:24, but there it seems rather to have the meaning "attack" (as BDB, 461b; KB, 433b; *DCH*, 4:391b; *HALOT*, 2:172a, has "sparks").

27.d. The colon has been emended to וכי יכין בהרים קנו "and that it establishes its nest in the mountains" (Steuernagel, Budde², Driver–Gray [*frt*], Moffatt "to nest aloft among the hills"; but perhaps GNB "high in the mountains" is not dependent on this emendation). It seems rather superfluous, however, to say the eagle's nest is "in the mountains" when the next line will say it is "on the cliff" and "on a rocky crag." NAB inserts מרום "on high" before ירים "makes high," which seems unnecessary; its translation is simply "to build his nest aloft." Strahan suggests, instead of ירים קנו "makes its nest on high," יקנן "makes its nest" (as, e.g., at Ps 104:17; Jer 48:28).

28.a. Strahan, deleting what he called "pleonasms," read the whole verse as simply יתלנן על־שן־סלע "and she hath her lodging upon the crag of the rock." Andersen suggests, with some plausibility, that the verse is just two parallel cola, with the parallel vbs in the first colon and the parallel nouns in the second; it means "On the cliff he dwells, and spends the night on the crags" (similarly Moffatt).

28.b. Duhm, Beer (BHK), Fohrer, de Wilde delete the first two words, ישכן סלע "on the cliff it dwells," as a gloss on שן־סלע "rocky crag." On לין "dwell, lodge," rather than just "spend the night," see Note on 41:22 (14).

28.c. שן־סלע lit. "tooth of a rock," as at 1 Sam 14:4.

28.d. מצודה II is, according to BDB, 845a, "fastness, stronghold," from צוד "hunt"; מצודה I is "prey," from the same root. Driver thought it was rather a sense of מצודה I "net, prey," thus the "outlook" from which it watches for prey rather than the fastness where it makes itself secure ("Job 39:27–28: The Ky-bird," 66); cf. DCH, 5:445b. HALOT, 2:622b, has, however, "mountain stronghold," connecting it with an Arab. maṣd or maṣād "mountain peak, place of refuge."

The waw prefixing מצודה is odd, as kjv shows: "upon the crag of the rock, and the strong place" (similarly Dhorme "on the crag of a rock and a fastness," nab "on the spur of the cliff or the fortress"; similarly Kissane). G. R. Driver explains it as explicative (see Note on v 27a above), Blommerde as "emphatic." Most take the colon as a noun-clause (niv "a rocky crag is his stronghold"; similarly Hartley; neb "its station is a crevice in the rock," jb "with an unclimbed peak as her redoubt," njb "with a needle of rocks as her fortress"). rsv "[makes his home] in the fastness of the rocky crag" and njps "[lodging] upon the fastness of a jutting rock" cannot be justified syntactically from the Hebrew—unless perhaps they are invoking the figure of zeugma. Cf. Good, who renders "on the tooth of rock and stronghold" by "on the sharp, craggy fastness." Hölscher read וממצודה "and from the fastness," Beer (BHK frt) and de Wilde וממצודתו "and from its fastness," replacing the משם "from there" of v 29a with it (similarly Duhm).

30.a. יעלעו would seem to be from a עלע "drink"; there is a Syr. la'"lick, lap up." But most, including BDB, 763a, think it a defectively written ילעלעו "they drink" from לוע I "swallow" (BDB, 534a) or לע II pilp "lick up avidly" (HALOT, 2:533b; DCH, 4:556b; it would be a byform of לקק "lap, gulp up," as at Judg 7:5 [Gray]); so too, e.g., Duhm, Driver–Gray (vel), Beer (BHK), Hölscher, Fohrer, Terrien, Gerleman (BHS), de Wilde, Sicre Díaz, Habel (vel), Gray, nab; it is not a "quadriliteral" (Gordis) but the pilp of a regular triliteral vb. We could of course read ילעו (Kissane) or ילעו qal "they swallow" or "they lap up," from לוע (Driver–Gray [vel], Dhorme, Hölscher [vel], Gordis [vel], Habel [vel]); cf. the dogs lapping up (לקק) the blood of Jezebel in 1 Kgs 21:19, of an Israelite king in 22:38. Tur-Sinai related it to עול "suck (mother's) milk" and read יעלעלו; but עול is always "give suck" and even in pilp it is not likely to mean "suck." Pope proposed another עלע "extract" (cf. Arab. 'ld "shake so as to pull out"; DCH, 6:429b), which seems unlikely. Grabbe, 128–30, thought עלע might be a byform of עלל "enter," thus "the young plunge into blood."

30.b. neb, reb rather idiosyncratically insert here six verses about Leviathan, 41:1–6 (40:25–30), which they identify as the whale, the last of the wild animals. Similarly Gray, the remainder of the Leviathan material being regarded by him as a secondary expansion.

40:1.a. On the authenticity of this verse, see also Comment. Most translations render the sentence literally, but njb attempts to explain its significance with "Still speaking to Job, Yahweh said." The verse is deleted by Duhm, Strahan, Driver–Gray, Moffatt, Hölscher, Fohrer; and effectively by gnb.

2.a. רב is usually explained as inf abs of ריב "contend," thus "will he contend?," the inf substituting for the impf (cf. Jer 3:1; GKC, §113cc); so Duhm, Budde, Driver–Gray, Fohrer, Tur-Sinai, Sicre Díaz. But it may be a ptcp, whether with this form as an old form of the qal ptcp of hollow vbs (Gordis), or emended to the normal form רב, thus "one contending" (Dhorme, Hölscher, Kissane, Terrien, Pope, Fedrizzi, Habel, Good, Gray, neb). This is the view adopted in the Translation above. The ptcp רב in the first colon would then balance the ptcp מוכיח "reproving, arguing," in the second. Ehrlich read רב "contention." The view adopted here is broadly that of Kemper Fullerton, "On the Text and Significance of Job 40:2," AJSL 49 (1932–33) 197–211; cf. also Frank Zimmermann, "Supplementary Observations on Job 40:2," AJSL 51 (1934–35) 46–47.

2.b. שדי is certainly "Shaddai," traditionally translated, "the Almighty"; njb apparently proposes an emendation to יהוה "Yahweh."

2.c. יסור is often thought to be an adj used as a noun, "reprover, faultfinder" (BDB, 416a; HALOT, 2:417b); it would occur only here in this sense, though the word is common enough in the sense "punishment, pain" or "instruction" in the Dead Sea Scrolls (DCH, 4:234b). So rv "caviller," rsv "faultfinder," Strahan, Driver–Gray, Fohrer, Tur-Sinai, Sicre Díaz.

But the view is adopted in the *Translation* above that it is a vb יִסּוֹר "will instruct," qal impf of יסר (so too KJV, Gordis, Andersen; on the form, cf. Francis I. Andersen, "Biconsonantal Byforms of Weak Hebrew Roots," *ZAW* 32 [1970] 270–74); the qal of יסר is rare, but it does seem to be attested; Habel, Hartley render "correct." Another possibility from the same vb is יִוָּסֵר niph "will he be corrected?" (Kissane [*vel*], following Tg); this reading seems to be followed by NJPS "one who should be disciplined."

Others suggest יָסוֹר "yield, cease," from the verb סוּר "turn aside" (so Ehrlich, Dhorme, Hölscher, Kissane [*vel*], Terrien, Pope, Fedrizzi, Good, Gray, following Theod and Vg), thus "will the contention cease?," or "will the disputant cease?," though these are not normal meanings of סור "turn aside" (but cf. Isa 11:13). Similarly JB, "Is Shaddai's opponent willing to give in (NJB give way)?"

Another, more remote, possibility is that יָסוֹר means "is stubborn," from סרר (so de Wilde, NEB "Is it for a man who disputes with the Almighty to be stubborn?"). But that would not harmonize so well with the second half of the verse.

2.d. The whole colon has several possible senses, depending on how the key term יָסוֹר is understood. (1) If יָסוֹר means "faultfinder, reprover," we could translate "Will the reprover contend with the Almighty?" (Driver–Gray), i.e., will Job, who has made himself God's critic or "reprover," continue the dispute? In that case, the second colon would go on to say, he must answer Yahweh's questions, or else he has no right to reprove. Among those who adopt such an understanding are RV "Shall a caviller contend with the Almighty?," and NAB "Will we have arguing with the Almighty by the critic?" Moffatt generalizes the thought: "Will critics still dispute with the Almighty?"; but there seems no good reason to move Job from the spotlight by introducing plural "critics." (2) If יָסוֹר is a verb meaning "instruct, correct," we could translate "Will one who contends with Shaddai correct him?" (Habel, Hartley; similarly KJV, NIV), i.e., does Job, God's reprover, now intend to offer a correction to Yahweh's argument? The second colon would then be parallel to that; if its verb יַעֲנֶנָּה is to be understood as a jussive ("let him answer it"), it would mean: let Job make a reasoned reply to Yahweh, if he can; if the verb is an indicative ("he will answer it"), the second colon would be a question like the first colon, and it would mean, Does Job intend a reply? (3) If יָסוֹר is a verb meaning "yield," we would translate "Will the contender with Shaddai yield?" (Dhorme, Pope), i.e., does Job, who has been contending with Yahweh, now concede defeat? The second colon could be understood then in either of the senses mentioned in the previous point.

2.e. יַעֲנֶנָּה "let him answer it," the fem sg suff referring "in a general sense to the verbal idea contained in a preceding sentence" (GKC, §135p; Waltke and O'Connor, 305 §16.4f, speak of the neutrum or vague referent), thus to the questions Yahweh has posed (Gordis "all this"). The issue has recently been discussed by Timothy Johnson, "Implied Antecedents in Job xl 2b and Proverbs iii 6a," *VT* 52 (2002) 278–84, who suggests that the referent of the suff is the *implied* word תּוֹכַחַת "reproof," i.e., "the one who reproves God must answer the reproof"; this suggestion does not seem as good as that mentioned first in this *Note*. Pope's "let him answer for it" and Habel's "answer me" cannot be justified from the Hebrew. In Dhorme's "Will he who criticises Eloah answer that?" the "that" can only refer to the question in the first colon, i.e., Job is being asked if he will answer whether he will concede defeat.

Most take the vb in a modal sense, "let him answer" or "he should answer": thus NRSV "anyone who argues with God must respond" (i.e., to the foregoing speech) (presumably RSV "let him answer it" intended the same meaning), NAB "Let him who would correct God give answer!," NIV "Let him who accuses God answer him!," NJPS "He who arraigns God must respond," Gordis "Can he who reproves God answer all this?" NEB, however, offers a different sense: "Should he that [REB who] argues with God answer back?" Others take the vb as a simple future, thus Dhorme, as a second question, "Will he who criticises Eloah answer that?"

Tur-Sinai revocalizes the vb to create a masc suff, יַעֲנֶנּוּ "will he answer him?"

Form/Structure/Setting

The *structure* of this first speech of Yahweh is straightforward. It is prefaced by a two-line proem in 38:2–3, and concluded by a peroration in 40:1–2. The body of the speech is divided into two almost equal halves: 38:4–38 (35 lines) concerning the physical universe, and 38:39–39:30 (33 lines) concerning the world of animals (it is strange that the chapter division was placed where it was, and not three verses later).

The *strophic structure* is also very neat:

Chapter	Verses	Section	Strophe	Lines	Topics
38	2–3			2 lines	proem
	4–7	I	1	4 lines	foundation of earth
	8–11		2	4 lines	sea
	12–15		3	4 lines	morning
	16–18		4	3 lines	extent of the earth
	19–21		5	3 lines	light and darkness
	22–24		6	3 lines	storehouses
	25–27		7	3 lines	rain
	28–30		8	3 lines	other moisture
	31–33		9	3 lines	stars
	34–38		10	5 lines	clouds
	39–41	II	1	3 lines, the last a tricolon	lion and raven
39	1–4		2	4 lines	mountain goats
	5–8		3	4 lines	wild ass
	9–12		4	4 lines	wild ox
	13–18		5	6 lines	ostrich
	19–25		6	7 lines	war horse
	26–30		7	5 lines	hawk and vulture
40	1–2			1 line, with prose preface	peroration

The clear distinction of topics in the speech ensures that most commentators and translators identify the same strophic divisions (RSV and Murphy, for example, have exactly the same divisions as in the table above; so too REB except that it combines 38:34 with the preceding strophe, vv 31–33). NIV and NJPS strangely make 38:22–30 a single strophe; it is true that the topics are closely related, but ten-line strophes are not in evidence here. Van der Lugt's analysis is similar, except that he joins 38:16–21, 22–27, 28–32, which means connecting v 33 with what follows). NAB differs from the above table in joining, in Section I, strophes 1 and 2 (38:2–3, 4–7), 4 and 5 (vv 16–18, 19–21), and in Section II, strophes 5 and 6 (39:13–18, 19–25), none of which can be well justified. There may well be some typographical error in the NAB, since Skehan, whose authority NAB followed on this matter, was clearly in accord with the divisions noted above, except that he (and NAB) moved 38:36 to follow 38:40 (*Studies*, 121). JB marks divisions after 38:11, 21, 30, 38; 39:4, 8, 12, 18, 25—which is to say, without especial regard to strophic structure in chap. 38 (NJB does not mark a division after 39:4). NEB does not indicate strophes as such, and makes only a division after 38:21; 39:12, 18; there is no accounting for marking pauses at these points and not at others.

Among the commentators, Terrien identifies, in Section I, 5 large strophes, each consisting of two substrophes: 38:2–7 (2 + 4 lines), 8–11 + 16–18 (4 + 3 lines, with a rearrangement of the place of vv 16–18), 19–21 + 12–15 (3 + 4 lines, with a rearrangement of vv 19–21), 22–28 (3 + 4 lines, with the omission of vv 29–30), 31–38 (3 + 5 lines). In Section II he finds the same pattern, 38:39–39:4 (3 + 4 lines), 39:5–12 (4 + 4 lines), 13–18 (3 + 3 lines), 19–25 (3 + 4 lines), 26–30 (3 + 2 lines). Apart from the problematic rearrangements and the omission, there is little difference between this schema and that laid out above, except that strophes are linked together in pairs—which is arguable but not compelling.

De Wilde, as is usual, identifies mostly couplets, but he makes a number of rearrangements to establish that pattern: he moves 38:21 to follow v 18, vv 29–30 to follow v 23, 39:26–29 (hawk) to follow 38:41 (raven), 40:15–24 (Behemoth) and 41:1–12 (Leviathan) to follow 39:25 (horse), he adds a colon about the horse after 39:24a, and he regards 41:13–34 (Leviathan) as secondary. Though he also identifies a number of larger units (38:2–18 + 21; 38:19–20 + 22–23 + 29–30 + 24–27 + 31–38), the divisions seem determined by content rather than on poetic-structural grounds.

The *genre* of the speech as a whole is that of the *disputation speech*. The proem (38:2–3) and the peroration (40:2) display typical features of this genre, viz. the challenge to the opponent (38:3; 40:2b), and rhetorical questions (38:2; 40:2a). The setting of the disputation remains the lawsuit; hence the language of "questioning" and "answering" (38:3b; 40:2b), and the reference to Job as a "disputant" (40:2a); "correction" (if that is the meaning of the word יסור, 40:2a) is also a law court activity. Further, it is the legal controversy that is referred to with the metaphor of the engagement of warriors in a trial of strength (38:3a). Throughout the body of the speech, the feature of the rhetorical question remains dominant, uniquely so within the Hebrew Bible: the only material in the body of the speech that is not in the form of a rhetorical question is 38:4b, 5aβ, 14–15, 18b, 21, 30; 39:4, 7–8, 13–18, 21–25, 28–30—that is, 21 lines out of a total of 68 lines. Ten of these 21 lines are descriptive elaborations of the material of the rhetorical questions, and could be regarded as syntactically part of the questions they follow. The only lines that are certainly not rhetorical questions or descriptions have the form of the disputation itself (38:18b, 21).

On the categorization of the speech as disputation, see also Heinz Richter, *Studien zu Hiob* (Berlin: Evangelische Verlagsanstalt, 1959) 125–26, speaking of the genre of the "legal disputation" (*Rechtsstreit*), and Fohrer, 496, using the term *Streitrede* ("controversy speech"). See also M. B. Dick, "The Legal Metaphor in Job 31," *CBQ* 41 (1979) 37–50. Less probable is the proposal of Henry Rowold that the form should be specified as that of a challenge to a rival, such as he finds notably in Second Isaiah ("Yahweh's Challenge to Rival: The Form and Function of the Yahweh-Speech in Job 38–39," *CBQ* 47 [1985] 199–211); the framework in Job is more clearly that of the lawsuit disputation. Veronica Kubina has drawn attention to the similarity of the questions in the divine speeches to the trial speeches in Second Isaiah where false understandings of God are being challenged (*Die Gottesreden in Buche Hiob. Ein Beitrag zur Diskussion um die Einheit von Hiob 38,1–42,6* [FrThSt 115; Freiburg i.Br.: Herder, 1979] 131–43); the metaphor of the lawsuit is the common element.

A notably variant perception of the genre of the divine speech is that of C. Westermann, who, in line with his overall view of the Book of Job as an elaborate individual lament, saw the two divine speeches as a *praise* of the God of creation in chaps. 38–39 and of the God of history in chaps. 40–41, together corresponding to the priestly oracle that is often found at the end of an individual lament (*Structure*, 109–10). His thesis is, however, far from persuasive, since there are no elements of praise in the verbal content of the speeches.

Within the genre of the disputation speech, the most noticeable subgenre is that of *descriptions of the natural world* or *Naturweisheit* (so Heinz Richter, Fohrer, Murphy). Gerhard von Rad saw in it influence from the Egyptian onomastica such as the famous Onomasticon of Amenemope, an extensive list of hundreds of features of the created universe; such a form in found also in various other lists in the Old Testament (Ps 148, Ecclus 43, Song of the Three Children) ("Job xxxviii and Ancient Egyptian Wisdom," in *The Problem of the Hexateuch and Other Essays* [Edinburgh: Oliver & Boyd, 1966] 281–91).

Others have seen in the incessant questioning of Job signs of a teacher–pupil relationship, and have spoken of a *catechetical form* lying behind the divine speeches. Von Rad ("Job xxxviii," 287–91) recognized an ironic cast in such a catechesis, and compared the ironic and almost polemical tone in the Egyptian instruction of Papyrus Anastasi I. See further, James G. Williams, "Deciphering the Unspoken: The Theophany of Job," *HUCA* 49 (1978) 59–72 (= *Sitting with Job: Selected Studies on the Book of Job* [ed. Roy B. Zuck; Grand Rapids: Baker Book House, 1992] 359–72). It is doubtful, nevertheless, that the teacher–pupil relationship is at all apt for the Book of Job, and the legal framework for the divine speeches seems much more appropriate.

The *function* of the speech is, in the first place, for Yahweh to accede to Job's demand for a response. In the second place, it appears, from the content of the speech, that Yahweh is refusing to accept Job's agenda, and is redefining the issue between them as that of the "plan" or "design" of the universe (38:2) rather than that of the justice or otherwise of Job's experience.

The *tonality* of the speech is notoriously difficult to pin down. Yahweh's address has seemed to many supercilious, patronizing, or bullying. "Tell me, if you have insight" (38:4), "Surely you know!" (38:5), "You know, for you were born in ancient times, and the number of your days is great" (38:21) are all sentences that can hardly be kindly spoken. And it is hard to resist the impression that the relentless hail of unanswerable questions is designed to be intimidating. Yet Yahweh's opening challenge to Job to "gird up [his] loins like a man" (38:3) at least recognizes Job as a worthy combatant, and it seems clear enough that Yahweh's ambition is to defeat Job in a contest and by no means to avoid the contest by humiliating his opponent. We should, no doubt, hesitate in using our own standards of polite behavior as we listen in on this ancient disputation, but there is little denying that the tone of Yahweh's speech tends more toward the severe, if not the savage, than toward the gracious. What matters very much more, though, than the tone Yahweh adopts is the argument he proffers, and the teasing out of that argument will be the substance of the commentary that follows. On the tonality of the speech, see further the *Comment* on 38:1–41:34.

The *nodal verse* is evidently the opening and headline sentence, "Who is this who obscures the Design by words without knowledge?" (38:2). It leads us immediately to the essence of Yahweh's argument, that Job's appeal for justice has been a gross misunderstanding of Yahweh's design for the universe, in which justice is far from being the supreme value.

Comment

38:1–41:34 (26) For so long now Job has been calling on God for a reply, wistfully, hopefully, despairingly, tauntingly, aggressively; but we have had the feeling that he has never had much confidence that his appeal would be answered. It is no doubt a shock to him when Yahweh's voice addresses him from the tempest; and even readers who have grown old with the Book of Job can still feel a frisson when the moment of divine utterance comes. If the proposal made in this commentary is correct, that the Elihu speeches of chaps. 32–37 originally preceded Job's last speech in chaps. 29–31 (see *Comment* on 32:1–37:24), then the divine speeches follow immediately upon the last sentence of chap. 31, "The words of Job are ended"—almost as if Job's last words have been swallowed up in the noise of the tempest that accompanies the theophany. It will be perhaps the longest speech of Yahweh in the Hebrew Bible (it is hard to tell where some of the speeches delivered by prophets in his name begin and end, to be sure), and, strange to say, he will comport himself like one of the interlocutors in the book, with a discourse that is addressed to Job and yet ignores, apparently, all his concerns.

The question of the *tone* of Yahweh's speeches is an intriguing one (see also the comments on the tonality of the speeches under *Form/Structure/Setting* above). Most readers and commentators think Yahweh is severe, and some would say condescending, sarcastic, and bullying.

But Yahweh's tone does not strike all readers in the same way. Terrien, for example, thinks that Yahweh speaks with a "courteous and slightly wistful irony," and Andersen finds a "kindly playfulness in the Lord's speeches which is quite relaxing." Carl Heinrich Cornill, in contrast, spoke of their "unparalleled brutality, which is usually palliated and styled divine irony, but which, under such circumstances and conditions, should much rather be termed devilish scorn (*teuflischer Hohn*)" (*Einleitung in das Alte Testament mit Einschluss der Apokryphen und Pseudepigraphen* [Grundriss der theologischen Wissenschaften, 1/2/1; Freiburg i.B. and Leipzig: Mohr, 2nd ed., 1896] 232). For further examples, see David J. A. Clines, "Job's Fifth Friend: An Ethical Critique of the Book of Job," *BibInt* 12 (2004) 233–50 (243–44).

We should admit that to judge what is etiquette in a culture different from our own is always difficult. It may well be that no disrespect or aggression is intended by parties to a lawsuit who address each other as Yahweh does Job. There does not seem to be much benefit in attempting to identify Yahweh's exact tone of voice, and it is better by far to pay attention to his words. But, for what it is worth, my own view is that the tone is indeed severe and not at all gracious, yet not offensive and by no means cruel.

What then is the *meaning* of the divine speeches? It is a crucial question for the book as a whole, and, unsurprisingly, a plethora of answers has been given. I will distinguish between what I take to be the meaning of the speeches in themselves and their meaning when viewed as Yahweh's response to Job.

The most important clue to the meaning of the divine speeches is given in their opening question, "Who is this who obscures the Design by words without knowledge?" (38:2). Job has not been allowing the divine Design, or plan for the universe, to become evident. Yahweh's purpose in his speech to Job is therefore to make his Design plain. Above all, the divine speeches are to be read as Yahweh's statement of his strategy for cosmic order. The issue here is, let us note, an issue of knowledge, and Yahweh's intention in the speech is essentially to provide knowledge, correcting misunderstanding of his purposes. In order to do so, he will present a comprehensive, though selective, survey of the world, first of its infrastructure—the creation and then the maintenance of the physical universe—and secondly of its life forms. From these sketches he expects that his listener will be able to deduce the general principles on which the world is founded, the great Design.

We never should forget that the divine speeches are poetry; even though they are didactic, they are lightly impressionistic and lyrical and suggestive as well, and their meaning does not lie on their face. It is for the wise and sympathetic reader to discern principles and generalities that lie beneath the surface of the scenes the speaker paints. All readers will not agree on what those principles are, but here is one reader's perception of some elements in the picture.

(1) The world, according to these speeches, has been neatly and tidily organized by Yahweh. The formal structure of the first divine speech, with its set of ten strophes about the physical universe followed by its set of seven strophes about the wild animals creates that impression at the outset. There is no chaos in the universal structure; everything that exists evidences forethought, planning, and wisdom.

(2) There is evidently a great deal of power at Yahweh's disposal, which one would expect from the creator of a universe. Yet his power is not the principal thing about him, according to these speeches. It is rather his skill and his insight. He is omnicompetent rather than omnipotent.

(3) In this discourse, Yahweh knows his universe intimately. He knows how broad the earth is (38:18), the directions to the dwellings of light and darkness (38:19), the system of the stars (38:33), the birth cycle of mountain goats (39:1–3); he implants migratory instincts into birds (39:26) and maternal fecklessness into ostriches (39:16–17). "Nature for the Job poet is not a Newtonian clock operating with automatic mechanisms" (Robert Alter, "The Voice from the Whirlwind," *Commentary* 77/1 [1984] 33–41 [38]). This God loves the detail, and, even when he is taking the broadest view, he only ever works with examples.

(4) Sustenance and nurture are key objectives of the universal order. Whether it is the physical universe or the animal world, the divine intimacy is directed to sustaining life. Creation is not just a past event according to this worldview; every day the morning has to be remade by its creator, calling up the dawn, grasping the fringes of the earth, shaking the Dog-star from its place, bringing up the horizon in relief as clay under a seal till everything stands out like folds in a cloak and the light of the Dog-star is dimmed as the stars of the Navigator's Line go out one by one (38:12–15). According to this worldview, the god of all the earth is counting the months of pregnancy of each doe of the mountain goats (39:2), imbuing horses with their strength (39:19), training hawks in flight (39:26), providing fresh meat for young lions in their lairs (38:39–40), directing the raven to its quarry when its fledglings croak for lack of food (38:41).

(5) In this discourse, the world is hugely various. "World is crazier and more of it than we think, / Incorrigibly plural"; Yahweh himself revels in "the drunkenness of things being various" (Louis MacNeice, "Snow"). It lives for itself, and if anything is instrumental, if anything serves a purpose other than itself, that is coincidental. The purposes of the universal structure are infinitely multiple, each of its elements with its own quiddity and its own mission—whether it is the sea, the clouds, light, darkness, rain, stars, mountain goat, ostrich, war horse, or eagle. See further Ellen van Wolde, developing the theme of biodiversity in the divine speeches, in her "Towards an 'Integrated Approach' in Biblical Studies, Illustrated with a Dialogue between Job 28 and Job 38," in *Congress Volume: Leiden, 2004* (ed. André Lemaire; VTSup 109; Leiden: Brill, 2006) 355–82.

(6) This is a discourse without abstracts, without oppositions, without propositions, without generalizations. It works with images, and maximizes impact and affect. It has little time for clarity or logic. It is not the language of the *Summa* or the *Institutes*, or even of Deuteronomy—or of the Joban dialogues themselves.

(7) There is no problem with the world. Yahweh does not attempt a justification for anything that happens in the world, and there is nothing that he needs to set right. The world is as he designed it. The sea does not breach its eternal bounds (38:8–11); the onager ranges freely over the hills for pasture, oblivious to the shouts of the donkey-driver (39:7–8); Behemoth lies forever somnolent under the lotus plants in the river (40:21, 23). There is no dereliction from an original state of perfection; there is no eschaton toward which the universal order tends. God's in his heaven; all's well with the world.

(8) Not only is there no problem with the world: every element in it is a source of constant delight to its maker. As the divine speeches move towards their climax, Yahweh candidly confesses, "I will not keep silence about its limbs, and I will tell of its incomparable might" (41:12 [4]), as if he cannot refrain from composing an ode of praise to the crocodile. In a similar exclamation of satisfaction with the hippopotamus he exclaims, "What strength it has in its loins, what

vigor in the muscles of its belly!" (40:16). It is hard to miss the equal delight he feels in the freedom of the onager (39:5–8), the independence of the aurochs (39:9–12), and the confidence of the war horse (39:19–25).

(9) There is nothing about humans in the divine speeches. Job is of course addressed, and, in a way, that marks humans out as something special in the divine economy. It is true that the sea also is addressed at 38:11, and the clouds at 38:14, and the eagle is commanded to soar into the sky at 39:27; from the side of creation, the lightning bolts report to Yahweh at 38:35, and the fledglings of the raven cry to him at 38:41. But, unlike these creatures, Job is not incidentally present in the divine speeches; throughout, he is the focus of Yahweh's attention, and both speeches are formally addressed to him. Nonetheless, apart from the direct forensic addresses to Job himself (38:2–3; 40:7–14), the human world and its concerns are totally ignored by the divine speeches (the reference to the "wicked" in 38:13 is probably a scribal error, the wicked and haughty in 40:11–14 belong to Job's program, not to God's, and the intersection of the world of the crocodile with humans in 41:1–11 [40:25–41:3] focalizes the crocodile rather than humans). In other words, Yahweh can give a considered and comprehensive account of his purposes in creation without considering the topic of humans! If there is one place where Job the man may stand for humankind in general, it is when the creation of humanity is equated in some sense with the creation of hippopotami: "Consider now Behemoth, whom I made as I made you" (40:15). Perhaps even more challenging to any human notion of supremacy in God's scale of values is the stunning remark that it is Behemoth (and not the human race) that is God's masterpiece, "the first of the ways of God" (40:19). The absence of reference to humans is not to teach Job that the universe can survive without him (as James L. Crenshaw, *Old Testament Wisdom: An Introduction* [Atlanta: John Knox Press, 1981] 110), but to show that the principles on which it is founded should be discerned from the realities of the natural world rather than from some artificial theology.

(10) And yet, though humanity is never the explicit subject, humans are, surprisingly, the measure of all things in the divine plan. The physical universe is systematically anthropomorphized: its creation was the building of a house fit for habitation (38:5–6); the primeval sea was a lusty infant (38:8–9); the morning is imaged as a seal being rolled over clay by an unseen human hand (38:14); the underworld is a city with gates and doorkeepers like any terrestrial town. And in the animal world it is no different: the raven's starving young are crying to God for food as if in prayer (38:41), the wild ox can only be a wild ox if it does not enter the human sphere (39:9–12), and the war horse is a sentient being that desires and laughs and cries out, with anthropoid will and self-determination (39:19–25). Even Behemoth is made like humans (40:15), and Leviathan is its own unique self because it will not be a human plaything or target or comestible (40:25–31 [41:1–7]). Watching its wake, one would think the deep hoar-headed (41:24 [32]); the human observer, though invisible, is always present. Above all, we are conscious that the divine speeches are being listened to by their addressee; the human mind is the context of the divine plan. And, there is nothing in the divine speeches that has not been conceived by a human intelligence and written by a human's pen. The substance of the universe is grander than the measure of it, and Yahweh's speeches concern the substance; but not so as to belittle or negate the measure by which it is comprehended.

These have been some reflections on the significance of the divine speeches in and of themselves. What is their meaning, however, when they are read as Yahweh's *response* to Job, which is of course what their position in the book leads us to believe they are? In the lawsuit Job is bringing against God, his final request has been for a statement of the charges that God would make against him, which he is confident he could defend himself against (31:35–37). With that as the background to the divine speeches, the most important thing about them is that such a statement is denied Job by Yahweh in his speeches. And why did Job want such a statement? Because he believed he was being treated unjustly, and that there was nothing in his life that deserved the punishment being meted out to him by God. What becomes then of his demand for justice? Not a word is said of the justice or injustice of Job's treatment; Yahweh's silence can only be understood as a deliberate denial of Job's demand. Then what of Job's wider claim, that the world itself is not being governed in justice by God, in that the wicked live long and prosperous lives, and the righteous die prematurely? Again, the matter is not so much as mentioned (except perhaps in the rather cryptic passage in 40:10–14), and the absence of a response is itself a most telling response.

In short, Yahweh refuses Job's claim for justice—not explicitly, but equally effectively, implicitly. The world that God has created, if its "Design" (38:2) is properly understood, does not contain a principle of retribution. As Matitiahu Tsevat puts it so well: "No retribution is provided for in the blueprint of the world, nor does it exist anywhere in it. None is planned for the nonhuman world and none for the human world. Divine justice is not an element of reality. It is a figment existing only in the misguided philosophy with which you have been inculcated" (*The Meaning of the Book of Job and Other Biblical Studies* [New York: Ktav, 1980] 1–37 [31]).

38:1–39:30 This first speech of Yahweh is, after the proem in 38:2–3, and before the peroration in 40:1–2, divided into two almost equal halves: 38:4–38 (35 lines) concerning the physical universe, and 38:39–39:30 (33 lines) concerning the world of animals.

The Structure of Section I (the World), 38:4–38. There are, many would agree, 10 strophes, of 3, 4, or 5 lines, in this Section; their topics are pretty clearly distinguished from one another. But is there any larger structuring device in the Section? David W. Jamieson-Drake has suggested that there are two main elements: vv 4–21, concerning the earth, and vv 22–38, concerning the heavens ("Literary Structure, Genre and Interpretation in Job 38," in *The Listening Heart: Essays in Wisdom and the Psalms in Honor of Roland E. Murphy, O. Carm.* [ed. Kenneth G. Hoglund, Elizabeth F. Huwiler, Jonathan T. Glass, and Roger W. Lee; JSOTSup 58; Sheffield: Sheffield Academic Press, 1987] 217–35). But it is not so evident that vv 19–21 (the dwellings of light and darkness) concern the earth, or that vv 25–27 (rain on the uninhabited land) concern the heavens. Van der Lugt, 372–76, on the other hand, finds a tripartite structure: vv 4–15, 16–27, 28–38. Each of these units concludes, he believes, with a statement of the benefits for humans of God's ordering of the universe; yet, as far as vv 13, 15 are concerned, the *Translation* above suggests that there is no reference to the removal of the wicked from the earth, and in vv 26–27 the point is the divine provision of rain precisely for regions where no human dwells, and in vv 34–38, though the ibis and the cock can predict the coming of the rain, humans are conspicuous by their absence. It is difficult therefore to argue that the quintessential thought of the poem is the beneficial effects of the divine creation in the human domain (van der Lugt, 375). The only patterning device that can be discerned in the Section seems to be the grouping of elements about the world's structure in strophes 1–5, and elements about the world's functioning in strophes 6–10; yet the position of the strophe about the morning (38:12–15) apparently runs counter to even this simple pattern.

The Structure of Section II (the Animals), 38:39–39:30. Is there any rationale for the sequence of animals here passed in review? It is hard to find one. Westermann thought there was a distinction between 38:39–39:8, where there is an emphasis on Yahweh's activity in the lives of the animals, and 39:9–30, where the focus is more on the qualities of the animals themselves. But it is not at all clear in the case of the lion and the raven (38:39–41) that Yahweh is doing anything at all for them beyond perhaps establishing the world order that provides prey for their sustenance. It is questionable also whether Yahweh does anything for the mountain goats (39:1–4), though he does know about their birthing habits, and in the case of the wild ass (39:5–8) it is not even clear that it is he who has given it its freedom (see *Comment* on 39:5).

Keel, *Entgegnung*, 37–38, argued that the animals are arranged in pairs: lion and raven, ibex and hind, wild ass and wild ox, ostrich and horse, hawk and vulture. However, while this analysis is true of the opening and closing strophes (38:39–41; 39:26–30; 3 lines and 5 respectively), the *Comment* will show that there is no hind (deer) in 39:1–4, and it is doubtful if we should link together other material into much longer poetic units (8 lines if we combine ass and ox; 13 lines for ostrich and horse).

James E. Miller, "Structure and Meaning of the Animal Discourse in the Theophany of Job (38,39–39,30)," *ZAW* 103 (1991) 418–21, saw both a linear and a chiastic arrangement in the speech. In the linear sequence, the animals at the beginning (lion, raven, 38:39–41) are in search of prey, which includes the animals of 39:1–18; then the ostrich laughs at the war horse (v 18), which carries its rider off to war, where the eagle of vv 27–30 dines on the corpses. In the chiastic arrangement, the animal section of the speech begins with a beast and a bird of prey (lion, raven) and ends with an animal of war and birds of prey (horse, hawk and vulture), while in the center are the wild versions of two domesticated animals (ass, ox). Against this analysis, there is nothing in the text to suggest that the lion preys especially on the animals mentioned in 39:1–18 (and it would be surprising if the wild ox were among its prey), there is no evident connection between the ox and the ostrich, and the horse of v 18 is for hunting rather than for war. Moreover, the lion and the horse do not seem to form a parallel.

Van der Lugt, 386–89, identifies a structure of two main sections, 38:39–39:12 and 39:13–25, followed by a smaller section in 39:26–30. In all sections he sees a systematic alternation of two motifs: Yahweh's care for young animals, and the unbounded freedom or passion of certain animal species. The weakness of this analysis is that there is no rationale for the conjoined presence of the two themes; further, it is questionable whether, or how far, it is implied that Yahweh cares for the animal young. While Yahweh might be saying that he provides nourishment for the raven (38:41) in the sense of creating the system of hunting for food, he by no means says that he "hunts" prey for the lion and its cubs (38:39–40).

Nor is it implied that though the ostrich may neglect its young Yahweh protects them (39:14–16); and the vulture's prey (39:27–30) is not said to be Yahweh's provision.

All that can be safely said about the structure of the animal section of the speech (38:39–39:30) is this: (a) There is an inclusio of sorts between the beast and bird of prey (lion and raven at the beginning, 38:39–41) on the one hand, and the birds of prey (hawk and vulture at the end, 39:26–30) on the other; but it is doubtful whether this structuring device has any symbolic significance. (b) The strophes about the ostrich and the horse would seem to be in climactic position; coming as they do toward the end of the speech and having 6 and 7 lines respectively as compared with the typical 4 lines for the other animals, they are obviously given more prominence; but that need not mean that these creatures have any special significance that the other animals do not.

1   An answer from Yahweh is what Job has so often been hoping for or demanding—perhaps we should say, hoping for and fearing (Habel); cf. 9:34–35; 10:2; 13:3, 15, 18, 22; 23:3–6; 31:35–37. The friends also have been hoping for some exchange between God and Job (5:8 [Eliphaz]; 8:5–6 [Bildad]; 11:5–6 [Zophar]). But on Job's part it has been a hope against hope, for a personal communication from God is a rarity in the Hebrew Bible, granted only to exceptional figures like Abraham, Moses, and the prophets. In a way, Yahweh is doing just what Job had asked: answering him. But in another way, he is not at all fulfilling Job's expectation, for he does not respond to Job's accusations, but rather forces Job on to the defensive from the start (Whybray).

This appearance of Yahweh is an unusual theophany, in more than one way. First, as Cox points out (D. Cox, "Structure and Function of the Final Challenge: Job 29–31," *PrIrBibAss* 5 [1981] 55–71 [65]), "theophanies have no real function in wisdom literature, where reason and experience, not revelation, are normative." So this may be called a "stunted" theophany in that it is more of an answer than of an appearance. Secondly, it is characteristic of the depiction of theophanies in the Hebrew that the accompanying disturbance of nature is elaborated, but here only a single word, "the tempest," suggests the natural world (see also Jörg Jeremias, *Theophanie: Die Geschichte einer alttestamentlichen Gattung* [WMANT 10; Neukirchen–Vluyn: Neukirchener Verlag, 1965]). A storm (סערה) is elsewhere not uncommonly an accompaniment of a theophany (cf. the same term in Ezek 1:4; Nah 1:3; Zech 9:14; cf. Ps 50:3 with the verb שׁער "whirl away," and in addition, without a specific word for "storm," Pss 18:7–15 [8–15]; 68:7–8 [8–9]; Hab 3:5–6; Exod 19:16). It is language generally thought to be derived from the cult of the weather-god (Pope). For thunder as an accompaniment of a theophany in the classical world, cf. Homer, *Odyssey* 20.102–3, 112–33, 120–21; 21.413; Virgil, *Aeneid* 2.692–94. The significance of the tempest as an accompaniment of the theophany may be that the appearance of God constitutes a disturbance in the normal course of events, both in the lives of humans and in the course of natural events—which is not the same as saying "the thunderstorm represented absolute power which could be both malevolent and beneficent" (Theodore Hiebert, *ABD*, 6:505–11 [509]), since there is no hint here of value judgments.

The tempest is not only an accompaniment of the divine presence; it is also the manifestation of the divine presence. So Yahweh's appearance is not only an audible experience for Job but also a visible one, for the tempest can be both seen and heard (42:5; so Whybray). It would be uncanny if Job's fear in 9:16–17 should have been that God would crush him "with a tempest" (as RSV, NAB, NIV have); more probably the word there should be understood as "for a hair" (see *Comment*). No matter; Job has already had an uncomfortable brush with a tempest: the "great wind" that killed his children (1:19). So it is rather shocking that his quest for justice should lead him, at its end-point, to a god who dwells in a tempest, who knows only how to speak out of a tempest, who is, in effect, himself the tempest. If we have been hoping, along with Job, that his lawsuit with the divine being will be patiently and punctiliously conducted within the august halls of a solemn lawcourt, we will be disappointed; we would do better to prepare ourselves for bluster.

Further aspects of the storm are explored by Thomas F. Dailey, "Theophanic Bluster: Job and the Wind of Change," *SR* 22 (1993) 187–95 (e.g., it moves the dispute from Job's demand for a judicial setting to a context of Yahweh's choosing), and further allusions to theophany in the speeches of Yahweh are identified by Donald E. Gowan, "God's Answer to Job: How Is It an Answer?," *HBT* 8 (1986) 85–102 (94).

The divine name Yahweh is used in the prose prologue and epilogue of the book, as also in the prose introductions to the divine speeches and to Job's responses to God (40:1, 3; 42:1), but it never occurs within the dialogues of the friends (for the one exception, see *Comment* on 12:9). Here it is a further sign of the presence of the narrator, who introduces all the characters of the book, even the deity, and who will have the privilege of the last word in chap. 42. Job and the other characters in the book know God as El, Eloah, and Shaddai; it is the Israelite readers of the book who are familiar with the term Yahweh.

2 It is obviously Job to whom God refers as obscuring his plan, but if the speeches of Elihu had immediately preceded—as they do in the present form of the book—one might have thought that "Who is this?" should refer to Elihu (see further, *Note* a). This is a further minor argument for the theory proposed in this commentary that the Elihu speeches were originally located prior to chap. 28 and that Job's final speech in chaps. 29–31 was followed directly by Yahweh's speeches from the tempest. Obviously, the question "who?" is not seeking to know the identity of the person who is obscuring the divine plan, but to ask rhetorically what kind of a person it is who would dare do so.

The sentence has the form of a reproach to a foolish person. The question "Who is this?" expresses surprise at how far Job's accusations have been from the truth about the divine design, and its formulation in the third person suggests that Yahweh is coming to the conversation from a great distance (there are no good parallels to the form of the question, since "Who is this?" is usually not a rhetorical but an information-seeking question, as in Isa 63:1; Pss 24:8; 25:12, in each case with the answer being supplied). The question is condemnatory, and puts Job in the wrong at the very start. It is no way to begin a pleasant conversation or even a dispute between equals, for it shows a superior person expressing annoyance at an inferior's lack of comprehension. It is not the language of legal argument, such as Job has been hoping for; it is not measured or deliberative language, but more of an outburst against Job personally. Job will not know from this sentence whether Yahweh intends to take his summons to formal litigation seriously. Terrien remarks that the question of Yahweh, while ironic, is without cruelty.

The divine Design (עצה) that Job's words have been obscuring must be Yahweh's principles for running the creation, what we might call the Universe Project; these principles are implicit in the descriptions of the universe that follow in Yahweh's speech. The "plan" is not God's plan in history, as Lévêque argues, 510–12, or the course of providence in history, as Veronica Kubina, *Die Gottesreden in Buche Hiob. Ein Beitrag zur Diskussion um die Einheit von Hiob 38,1–42,6* (FrThSt 115; Freiburg i.Br.: Herder, 1979) 122–23, or his designs for the future, as Terrien. It is not so much a "plan" that God has in mind—since that term suggests a purpose or an end in view—as a grand design for how the universe should be structured and managed. So vast a scheme, it might be suggested, might well have been termed in the heavenly councils "the Design" or "the Project," "[a] mighty maze! but not without a plan" (Alexander Pope, *Essay on Man*). Job's quest for justice, and his complaint that he is being denied it, obscure the fact that, according to these speeches, Yahweh does not undertake to ensure that justice reigns in the world. Yahweh has created the world, with its physical and moral systems, but he does not monitor the detail of what goes on in it and he does not serve as a cosmic policeman. See further, *Explanation*.

It is obscuring the divine plan, and speaking without knowledge, that is Job's crime. This important headline statement by Yahweh means, in the first place, that Job is not suffering for some fault or misdemeanor committed prior to his testing by God. And secondly, therefore, obscuring the divine plan cannot be the reason for Job's suffering, since he has been doing that only since he started to speak in the book. Thirdly, Job's wrong has not been his rebelling against God, or his charging him with injustice in ordering the world; it has been his insistence on justice to the neglect of other values. He has not been destroying anything, he has not been, it appears, mistaken in what he has been affirming (see further, *Comment* on 42:2–6); but he has been ignoring, and so obscuring, the grand design to which God is operating. It is not so much that Job is wrong as that he lacks adequate or appropriate understanding of the broader picture.

To "darken" (חשׁך hiph) or "obscure" the divine Design is to prevent God's intentions from becoming apparent; Job is not of course in any position to damage or thwart the divine plan. Words that create a divergent worldview from that of Yahweh, words such as we have been hearing in the book hitherto, have had the effect of covering over the divine intentions; being misguided, they are "words without knowledge" (cf. *Comment* on 35:16; a parallel phrase "hides counsel without knowledge" occurs in 42:3 when Job is quoting Yahweh's words).

3 Girding the loins means tying a belt around the loins and tucking into it the skirt of the outer garment, the robe, like the modern *qumbaz,* to prevent it from getting in the way of vigorous activities (it is not a matter of tensing the muscles of the loins, as Dhorme, nor does the phrase derive from girding on a sword, as Pope). Loin girding is a gendered activity; only men gird the loins for the strenuous work of fighting (2 Sam 20:8; 1 Kgs 2:5; Isa 5:27); sometimes girding the loins is in preparation for running (1 Kgs 18:46) or for traveling (Exod 12:11; 2 Kgs 4:29). In Hebrew, the loins (חלצים) are that part of the body between the waist and the upper thighs; they include the belly, the buttocks, the hips, and the genitals. In English, however, the loins are more narrowly defined: they are that part of the lower back between the ribs and the pelvis.

Yahweh's call to Job to gird up his loins is a call to combat, to the combat between warriors, to the combat of heroes. If he is to gird up his loins, he must be expected to fight, or at least, to be attacked. Though what v 3b portrays is the onset of a verbal dispute, to be precise a legal controversy, such as Job had envisaged in 13:22 and 14:15, v 3a severely modifies that picture of what will take place: God tells Job without qualification that he regards him as his opponent, and enemy, who will need courage and strength—not a just cause—to be able to confront him. God, in short, makes no secret that the legal dispute will only be the form of their encounter; a trial of strength will be its substance. It is all metaphorically speaking, of course; the conflict will still be a matter of words, and the trial of strength will be a trial of knowledge. But Job had better understand that summoning God to trial will not lead to a calm, rational, orderly legal process. God takes Job's summons personally, and he intends to fight. A superior male has been injured by an inferior and he intends to get his revenge.

Some have seen here an allusion to a supposed ancient custom of belt-wrestling, the winner being the one who can strip the other of his belt (see Cyrus H. Gordon, "Belt-Wrestling in the Bible World," *HUCA* 23/1 [1950–51] 131–36, with Plates I–V; previously in "Western Asiatic Seals in the Walters Art Gallery," *Iraq* 6 [1939] 3–34 [4–5]; thus too Tur-Sinai, Fohrer). H. L. Ginsberg, however, rightly doubts that wrestling belts are alluded to in the Hebrew Bible ("Interpreting Ugaritic Texts," *JAOS* 70 [1950] 156–60 [158]; similarly Gordis). See also David J. A. Clines, "Loin-girding and Other Male Activities in the Book of Job" (www.shef.ac.uk/bibs/DJACcurrres/Loingirding.html).

Hartley observes with some truth that Yahweh shows respect for Job by addressing him as a "man," a "male" (גבר). "[N]either his affliction nor his inflamed rhetoric has diminished his intrinsic worth as a human being," he says; but it is not Job's humanity that God recognizes, but his maleness, which means, in the context, his capacity for fight. There is no question of Job being God's equal, of course, but he is a worthy sparring partner. Job has already proved himself a doughty combatant, and Yahweh relishes an engagement with a human who is no wimp. Yahweh will make the running: he is the one who will be doing the questioning (Job will hardly be surprised that of the two choices he offered God at 13:22 his opponent has accepted the former); but he anticipates, even demands, response from Job. As it happens, he will not get much out of Job, who, perhaps surprisingly easily, abandons his case (see *Comment* on 40:4–5; 42:2–6). But it would seem wrong in the light of the present verse to suggest that Yahweh's principal intention is to browbeat and humiliate Job. He wants to *defeat* him in a *contest*, not to bypass the contest by simply scorning his opponent.

4–38 *Section I: The physical world.* The first half of the first divine speech consists of ten strophes concerning different aspects of the physical world: (1) the structure of the world (vv 4–7), (2) the sea (vv 8–11), (3) the new day (vv 12–15), (4) the underworld (vv 16–18), (5) light and darkness (vv 19–21), (6) the heavenly storehouses (vv 22–24), (7) rainstorm and lightning (vv 25–27), (8) rain, dew, rime, hoar-frost, ice (vv 28–30), (9) the four constellations (vv 31–33), (10) the clouds (vv 34–38). Possible rationales for the arrangement of these topics have been discussed above (see *Comment* on 38:1–39:30).

4–15 In these first three strophes, the key word stands in each case at the end of the first colon of the first verse (van der Lugt): "Where were you when I

laid the foundations of the *earth*?" (v 4); "Who shut in with doors *the sea*?" (v 8);
"Since your days began, have you called up *the morning*?" (v 12).

4–11 These ironical questions are not all of the same kind. The first (v 4) is a
regular rhetorical question expecting a negative answer: "Where were you when
I laid the foundations of the earth? Nowhere." But it is immediately followed
by others to which the answer is "God": "who fixed [the earth's] dimensions?"
(v 5), "Who laid its cornerstone?" (v 6b), "Who shut in the sea with doors?" (v 8).
And there is within this strophe one question that calls for yet a different answer:
"Into what were its [the earth's] bases sunk" (v 6a), namely "I do not know."

It is not the first time that Job has heard such questions. Eliphaz has asked him,
"Were you the first human ever born?" (15:7–8), and from Elihu he has heard
such impossible questions as "Will you, with him, hammer out the sky, hard as
a metal mirror?" (37:15–18). But there is much more to the divine speech than
questions to Job. Whether or not the style is that of self-praise (Keel, *Entgegnung*,
55), what Yahweh achieves through these questions is to paint an impressionistic
panorama of the totality of creation. It begins in these verses with a sketch of the
founding of the universe.

4–7 *Strophe 1: The structure of the world.* The work of creation is conceived as
the erection of a building. There is the outlining of its shape with a measuring
line (v 5b), and the laying of foundations (v 4) viewed as the sinking of pillar-
bases into underlying material (v 6a) and, finally, the setting of a capstone on
the work (v 6b). Yahweh is architect (v 5a), surveyor (v 5b), and engineer (v 6)
(Habel). De Wilde observes that there is hardly a parallel in ancient Near Eastern
literature to this picture of the founding of the earth (cf., however, the foundation of Esharra in *Enuma elish* [*ANET*, 67b]); even in the Hebrew Bible, where the
image of creation as a building is frequent, there is no occasion where the image
is so fully developed (Newsom). Building the universe, as it is described here,
perhaps also includes by implication instituting all its structures and systems,
moral as well as physical; so there is a close connection between the picture here
and the comprehensive "design" or "plan" (עצה) of God in v 2, though, more
generally, the divine design refers to everything in the two speeches of Yahweh.

4 Clearly this question, "Where were you when I laid the foundations of the
earth?," is crucial in the conflict between God and Job. It is not a question about
the justice of Job's claim against God, but a denial of Job's competence to raise
any question about the way the world is ordered. This is what makes the interchange with God in these chapters a trial of strength rather than a judicious
debate. From the very outset, it becomes clear that Job has no right to speak, and
so every argument he can bring against God is marginalized.

To understand the workings of the world, Yahweh implies, one needs to have
seen how it was constructed. The problem is not exactly that Job was not present at the moment of creation; it is rather that, not having been present and
seen its making for himself, he cannot possibly understand the purposes and
designs God has built into it. We might hesitate over the logic of this claim. Is
it really impossible to understand God's purposes in the universal order if one
did not witness the moment of creation? Does the poet not intend his readers,
who certainly were not present at creation, to come to a proper and adequate
understanding of God's purposes from reading the divine speeches? Is Job
being treated entirely fairly?, we wonder.

There seems at first a mismatch between the two halves of this line. For the question "Where were you at creation?" stands alone perfectly well, demanding the admission, "Nowhere," i.e., Job had not yet been born. Perhaps there is an allusion to a myth of the First Man, who was thought in some circles to have come into being prior to the creation (cf. *Comment* on 15:7); Job is certainly not that man. Then how does that answer depend on whether he has "insight" or not? He should know the answer without any special insight, we would have thought. A question that would require insight on Job's part would be, for example, "How was the earth founded?" But perhaps there is an explanation. If the idea found in Prov 8:30, that wisdom was "beside" God throughout all the work of creation, is in the background here (it is not in chap. 28, which does not concern divine wisdom but the wisdom for humans devised at creation), the verse will mean: If you really know Insight (בינה is equivalent to חכמה "Wisdom") then you must have been present at creation as my assistant. Since you were not there, you cannot lay claim to Insight.

Can Job possibly "know insight" if he has already been damned by Yahweh for his "words without knowledge"? Or is Yahweh's "Tell me, if you know insight" simple sarcasm (Good)? It is hard to deny it is sarcasm, but there is a difference between v 2 and v 4. In v 2 Job is criticized for what he has said; but perhaps his mouth has led him astray, perhaps he knows more of the world order than his unremitting focus on the question of justice has suggested. But the second chance he is given, here in v 4, to show his understanding only reveals that he lacks the fundamental insight he would need to have to answer Yahweh.

The concept of the founding of the world is an important theme in wisdom, psalmody, and prophecy, for it enshrines what Hebrew thinkers understand to be the fundamentals of existence (cf. the verb יסד "found" in Isa 48:13; Zech 12:1; Prov 3:19; Pss 24:2; 78:69; 102:25 [26]; 104:5; cf. Matt 13:35). It means that the world has not always been in existence; it once came into being, as a creation, and the creator God is not an element of the world order but beyond and before it. One would have thought, however, that the fixing of the dimensions and the stretching of the measuring line, which are mentioned in the following verse (v 5), would have taken place before the laying of the foundations. We should therefore assume that the term יסד here is a comprehensive one for all the activities of creation, not itself the first creative act. On the term, see W. H. Schmidt, *TLOT*, 2:547–48; R. Mosis, *TDOT*, 6:109–21; F. I. Andersen, "Who Built the Second Temple?," *AusBR* 6 (1958) 3–35 (10–22); "A Short Note on Psalm 82,5," *Bib* 50 (1969) 393–94.

5 "It is an important truth that God 'wrought by weight and measure' [William Cowper, *Olney Hymns*], that law and order are visible in all that He has made. Of course, no metaphor should be unduly pressed, and mechanical ideas of nature need always to be supplemented by vital and spiritual conceptions" (Strahan). On "measurement" (ממד) as a creatorial activity, cf. H.-J. Fabry, *TDOT*, 8:118–34 (131–32). To stretch out a measuring line (נטה קו) is a first step in undertaking building works; cf. Zech 1:16 of the rebuilding of Jerusalem; Isa 44:13 of drawing the design for an image. The קו "line" is sometimes accompanied by the משקלת, which is either a "level" or a "plumb-line" (2 Kgs 21:13; Isa 28:17; 1QH 8:22). It is as though builders' plans had been drawn up beforehand (Rowley). For marking out (חק) the foundations of the earth, see Prov 8:29. Jer 31:37 has

Yahweh saying that it is not possible to measure (מדה) the heavens, but that is from a human point of view.

6 The construction of the building that will become the universe must begin of course with the digging of foundations, as with any building. "Bases" (אדן) are usually metal supports for pillars (cf. *DCH*, 1:133a), which of course extend below the surface of what the pillars appear to be resting on. Here they are supports for the pillars that hold up the earth; those pillars are not explicitly mentioned here, but they are referred to at 9:6, Ps 75:3 (4) (the term is עמוד), 1 Sam 2:8 (מצוק), and Ps 104:5 (מכון). The pillars of heaven at 26:11 are completely different; they support the sky (so too Homer, *Odyssey* 1.53–54). The bases of the earth themselves must rest upon something, as a house must rest on the rock: they are sunk (טבע) into some primeval matter, unspecified here (and, apparently, unknown to Job). Perhaps it is the underworld sea, in conformity with Ps 24:2, where the earth is founded (יסד) on the seas. There is a different (against Duhm) cosmological conception at 26:7 where the earth is suspended upon nothing.

Immediately after the first task of sinking the bases has been mentioned, we reach the completion of the building. The term for the "capstone" (אבן פנה) of the world is commonly translated "cornerstone"; but, in building generally, each course has its own cornerstone(s), and what seems to be referred to here is not that but the very last stone to be laid, as the final stage of the work. In Ps 118:22 the capstone is called "the head of the corner" (ראש פנה), and in Jer 51:26 the capstone (אבן לפנה, lit. "stone for the corner") is distinguished from the foundation stone (אבן למוסדות, lit. "stone for the foundations"). The capstone (האבן הראשה, lit. "the stone, the head") of the Second Temple is mentioned in Zech 4:7. For this correct understanding of the term, see most recently M. Cahill, "Not a Cornerstone! Translating Ps 118,22 in the Jewish and Christian Scriptures," *RB* 106 (1999) 345–57. We might note that while we can identify the pillars of the earth and their bases and the matter into which they are sunk as elements of a traditional Hebrew cosmological picture, there is nothing we know of in Hebrew cosmology to which the capstone corresponds. It must be here an extension of the metaphor of building.

7 The start of a great work or a great building deserves celebration, as does its completion. So when the foundation of the Second Temple was laid, there was music and singing according to Ezra 3:10–11; similarly, the finishing of Solomon's temple was celebrated with music and song according to 2 Chr 5:13 (in Ezra 6:16, 22 the completion of the Second Temple is celebrated with "joy," music not being specifically mentioned). If v 6 has been rightly understood in reference to both the beginning and finishing of the work of creation, the rejoicing and shouting here may be conceived as accompanying both events. The two verbs here signify loud shouting: רנן is "cry aloud," usually in joy, but occasionally in distress or as a summons (cf. R. Ficker, *TLOT*, 3:124–43). רוע similarly is "shout," often as a war-cry, but sometimes with applause or joy. Despite the modern translations, which generally have the heavenly beings *singing* at creation, there is no reference here to music.

On the theme of celebration at the completion of buildings, cf. the building of Babylon as a sanctuary for the gods (*Enuma elish* [*ANET*, 68b–69a]), and the building of Baal's temple in the Ugaritic Baal myth (*ANET*, 134). The theme of rejoicing, often specifically with music, at creation, is known in many cultures. From Egypt we have the hymn to Amon-Re (*ANET*, 365b); from Babylonia, *Enuma elish* (*ANET*, 67b). Cf. also Milton's lines, "Such music (as 'tis said) / Before was never made, / But when of old the sons of morning sung, / While the Creator great / His constellations set, / And the well-ballanc't world on hinges hung, / And cast the dark foundations deep, / And bid the welt'ring waves their oozy channel keep" (*Hymn on the Morning of Christ's Nativity* [1645], lines 89–96).

The "sons of God" were in chap. 1 the attendants at the heavenly court (cf. *Comment* on 1:6). But here they seem rather to be the stars. The "stars of the morning" are the "stars of the (morning) twilight" at 3:9, the planets Venus and Mercury, harbingers of the coming day, which would also have been conceived of as living beings. In Gen 1:6 the stars are created *after* the earth, but the sequence of creation in Genesis 1 may not have been known to the author of Job. Are the morning stars named because the events celebrated took place in the morning (Peake)?

8–11   *Strophe 2: The sea.* The creation of the world is not enough to make it habitable: the dry land must yet be separated from the seas (Whybray). The scene is developed more elaborately in Ps 104:5–9, where the earth is first set (יסד) upon its foundations (מכון), the deep (תהום) still covering it as with a garment, the water being higher than the mountains; thereafter God issues a "rebuke" (גערה) to the waters (for covering the earth) and they flee, whereupon God sets a "bound" (גבול) for them that they should not pass.

This second strophe concerning the ordering of the world focuses on God's primeval control of the sea as a threatening element in the cosmos. Since Yahweh has been warning Job that their present encounter is going to be a trial of strength (v 3), it is unsurprising that he should choose as a parade example of his power his primeval control of the forces of disorder. Job in his small way has been threatening to be a latter-day Sea.

"Who shut in the sea with doors?" is not a very difficult question, for anyone can tell that its answer is "God." Job is not being tested for his religious knowledge, and he is not being mocked for his ignorance; he is being warned that his opponent has a history of suppressing conflict.

8   In an unmistakable allusion to the common Semitic myth of a struggle of the deity with the sea at creation (like that of Marduk with Tiamat in *Enuma elish* [*ANET*, 63–67]), the poet depicts God taking the mastery of this unruly element in the world order, a symbol no doubt of all threats to order. Here, exceptionally, the aggressive sea is portrayed as a violent brawling infant (not exactly a child who is likely to develop into a dangerous monster unless restrained, as Kissane; Rowley, less probably, sees rather the combination of two images, the infant bursting from the womb and an unruly flood). It is an infant, for it is said to come from the womb, and it is provided with clothes and swaddling bands; but its birth is called a "breaking forth" (גיח), a term used elsewhere of a raiding party (Judg 20:33) or the rushing of the Jordan (Job 40:23), and its clothing is more of a restraint than a covering. For the safety of the earth it must be held fast, as if in a prison, behind barred doors (as also in v 1). The whole image is deliberately absurd (Habel).

The Semitic myth depicted a life and death struggle between the deity and the sea, which came to a conclusion with the deity's victory. Other allusions to it in the Hebrew Bible in Pss 74:13–14; 89:9–10 (10–11); Isa 51:9–10 evince more of a conflict than this quite enfeebled version of the myth, where there is no real struggle and so no real victory.

The "doors" (דלתים) are literally "double doors," the idea being of two leaves of a door fastened by a bar (v 10). Doors will not serve to hold in water, so the doors here are not an item in the cosmology but a metaphor for whatever it is that restrains the sea.

What is the origin of the sea? From whose womb did it break forth? Dhorme says the earth, but if the phrase has a more specific meaning than just "when it was created" (as Kissane), it is much more probably the cosmic abyss (Pope, Habel; Moffatt translates "from the womb of chaos"). The sea can hardly be the heavenly ocean (as Tur-Sinai). Whatever its mother is, it is not depicted as God's handiwork at creation, but as an independent being.

9 The clothing of the sea by God is perhaps not so much a representation of him as a nurturing midwife (as Newsom), but of his effective control of it: some have suggested that swaddling bands were essentially "restraints to prevent the baby's arms and legs from moving about and were believed to calm the child" (Newsom), though others think they were just for warmth and to ensure that the limbs grew straight (D. E. Garland, *ISBE,* 4:670). Wrapping a child in swaddling bands is referred to also at Ezek 16:4; Wisd 7:4; Luke 2:7, 12. The sea is greeted at birth with a "decree" (חק) prescribing its bounds, it is hemmed in with bolts and doors, and laid under a charge that its "proud waves" should not exceed their stated domain. This violent infant is depicted in the language of mythology, as also are the allusions to the sea at 7:12; 9:13; 26:12.

Thick darkness (ערפל) is traditionally what cloaks the presence of God (see also 22:13; and cf. Exod 20:21; Deut 4:11; 2 Sam 22:10; 1 Kgs 8:12; cf. M. J. Mulder, *TDOT,* 1:371–75). Why should it be wrapped around the sea? It can hardly be the water bound up in the clouds (Kissane), such as Zophar has spoken of (26:8). Rather, the reference is to the mists that often gather over the seas.

10 The sea is prevented from encroaching on the dry land. In Jer 5:22 the sand of the shore is seen as the boundary of the sea, a perpetual barrier (חק) that it cannot pass, but it is unlikely that there is a specific reference here to the sand (as Gordis). Rather we have a general statement of the sea's confinement to its own place, by a divine decree that is at the same time a law (חק) of nature (the Hebrew idiom is "laws of heaven and earth"), as in v 33; 28:26; Jer 33:25; Ps 148:6; Prov 8:29.

Doors or gates (usually double) with a bar, mentioned already in v 8, are part of the usual defense works of a city; they are met with at Deut 3:5; 1 Sam 23:7; Isa 45:2; Jer 49:31; Ezek 38:11; 2 Chr 8:5; 14:7 (6). See Keel, *Symbolism,* fig. 41, with a drawing of a boundary stone (*kudurru*) apparently representing the city gates of the underworld. Whether the doors and the bar are conceived of more as "a barrier to keep the sea out than part of a prison to keep it in" (Andersen) is hard to say; they are of course both. In the Babylonian creation epic, *Enuma elish,* Marduk places a bar and a guard to keep back the waters of the sea (IV.137–39 [*ANET,* 67).

11 The sea may not be a rival to Yahweh, and he may not have had to fight a hard-won primeval battle against it, but it is personified enough to be addressed, and its hostile inclinations and intentions are manifest even if kept under restraint. The divine word is all it takes to keep the power of the sea under control. The firm and unambiguous "thus far and no further," combining both permission and restraint, is perhaps reminiscent of a parent's direction (similarly Tur-Sinai).

The sea's "proud waves" (lit. "the pride of your waves") is a dramatic phrase, but it means perhaps no more than the "swelling" of the waves (see *Note* c).

12–15 *Strophe 3: The new day.* In this third four-line strophe, after the creation of the universe as a whole (vv 4–7), and the ordering of it by the control of the unruly waters (vv 8–11), we move to the daily renewal of creation with the assignment of the morning to its place, every morning being an image of the morning of creation in miniature (Fohrer), a recapitulation of creation, or rather, part of the continuing work of creation (Newsom). Though the Hebrew is not especially difficult, the meaning of this stanza is extremely problematic.

To be familiar with the design (עצה, v 2) of the universe, it is not absolutely necessary to have been present at the world's foundation, which Job plainly was not. Some creative acts recur daily, such as the calling forth of each new morning. Perhaps Job has some experience as the marshal of the dawn? The strophe seems to be saying that when the morning has been given the command (v 12), it (or perhaps it is implied that God is the subject) takes hold of the edges of the earth and shakes it, as if to remove loose objects, which are apparently the "wicked" (v 13). The earth then, no doubt with the growing light in the sky, becomes more visible and increasingly three-dimensional, like the impression in a clay seal as light shines on it from an angle (v 14), while the light is kept from the wicked and their power is broken (v 15).

But there are some serious difficulties with this sequence of ideas. First, we would expect the strophe to concern only cosmological matters, as does everything else in this first section (vv 4–38) of the first divine speech, and not to refer to humans. Secondly, the presence of the wicked is surprising, for there is very little about humans in the whole of the Yahweh speeches, and even less about any moral government there may be of the world (the only moral language in the speeches is at 40:12; משפט, רשע, and צדק at 40:8 are used in a forensic, not an ethical, sense, and mean respectively, "legal case," "condemn," "prove right"). Thirdly, in the Masoretic text the word for "wicked" (רשעים) in vv 13 and 15 is written abnormally, with the middle letter elevated above the line—which is probably a sign that the scribes thought there was something odd about the word). Fourthly, the relation between the cosmological material (vv 12–13a, 14) and the references to the wicked (vv 13b, 15) is hard to determine. Fifthly, the phrase "high arm" (זרוע רמה), used apparently of the wicked (v 15), occurs nowhere else. Given the disparity between the two themes of cosmology and the wicked, the idea of Duhm, that two completely different stanzas have been mistakenly combined, had a lot to recommend it.

For these reasons, G. R. Driver (followed by NEB, REB) appears to have been on the right track when he argued that all the references to the "wicked" cloak original allusions to stars and constellations, even if his identifications of the heavenly bodies concerned are not certain. In vv 13b and 15a, he argued, what is referred to is not the human "wicked" but the constellations Canis Major and Minor, of which Sirius is the brightest; in v 15, he argued that the "high arm" is the line of stars in the shape of a crooked arm, known formerly as the Navigator's Line, from Sirius to Procyon to Castor and Pollux. See his "Two Astronomical Passages in the Old Testament," *JTS* ns 4 (1953) 208–12 (210–12), and cf. *Comment* on vv 13 and 15 for further details.

12 A mythological scene is here depicted, in which the high deity summons the lesser (male) deity Dawn to take its station and bring the new day into being. Dawn (שַׁחַר, *šaḥar*) is known from the Ugaritic texts as one of the two "beautiful and gracious gods," Dawn and Dusk. For Job to assign Dawn to its prescribed post "would mean that he knew the ordering principle ... which established the 'place' of each component in the cosmos" (Habel). Has he ever in his life played such a part in the life of the world?

13 The earth is compared to a blanket (Driver–Gray, Newsom) or cloak (Rowley, Gray) or carpet (Dhorme, Fedrizzi) or tablecloth (Fohrer, Gordis, Hartley), which is shaken out to remove dust (Dhorme, Gray) or crumbs or flies (Strahan) or vermin (Habel, Gray) or bedbugs (Newsom). The "corners" or "fringes" of the earth, which the morning seizes, are romantically defined by Budde (followed by Fohrer) as the tips of the mountains lit up by the rays of the dawn; but the other occurrences of the phrase make clear that the earth has four corners, all of course in distant places (37:3 [*q.v.*]; Isa 11:12; 24:16; Ezek 7:2; in the last two references, the word "four" is explicit). The shaking out is done either by the morning, or, more dramatically, by the one who summons the morning to appear (see *Note* a)—who is God, or, if he could answer the question, Job.

If the "wicked" (רְשָׁעִים) are what is shaken out, what is being suggested is that, though they have been active in the hours of darkness, they never get to see the light of day and carry out their acts of violence once the sun is up. The association of the wicked with darkness has previously been brilliantly depicted in 24:13–17, the strophe on the "rebels against the light"; to them "morning is as the darkness of death" (24:17), meaning either that morning is the time of danger for them, or that darkness is their morning, the time when they are most full of energy (cf. *Comment* on 24:17).

On the other hand, it is decidedly odd to find in this chapter a reference to the "wicked"; the term would be much more likely to have a reference to a feature of the cosmos. Driver offered two possibilities: (1) the "evil ones" (רְשָׁעִים) are not humans but the constellations of Canis Major and Minor; Sirius, the Dog Star, also known as Orion's Hound, the brightest star in these constellations and in the whole sky, had a reputation in antiquity for bringing pestilence, fire, and fever (cf. Homer, *Iliad* 22:29–30, where Sirius is called "an evil omen"). The "Dog Days," named for the constellations of Canis "the dog," were the twenty or so sultry days before and after the heliacal rising of Sirius, that is to say, in July and early August in Mediterranean countries. The Masoretic writing of the word could indicate that the scribes recognized that it had such a specialized reference here. (2) Alternatively, the word רְשָׁעִים "wicked" may be a scribal error for שְׂעִירִים "hairy ones," which is a term used in Arabic for the two constellations of Canis (though according to de Wilde the Arabic term is derived from the Greek for Sirius); this variant explanation of the word would, however, lead to the identification of the same stars. Following this proposal, NEB translates "and shake the Dog-star from its place" (REB "from the sky"). It is indeed not at all an obvious metaphor to have the stars shaken from the sky by the morning; yet it is hardly stranger than having the wicked shaken from the earth like crumbs from a carpet. And the image may be that the stars have attached themselves to the earth overnight, like bedbugs to a blanket, so that Dawn, like a busy housewife, must shake out the earth in the morning to rid the earth of those accretions. We should notice that the Dog-stars are shaken, not from the sky, but "from it" (ממנה), i.e., from the earth, the feminine noun mentioned in the first colon; NEB and REB do not understand that, and are obliged to translate "from its place" and even "from the sky."

It is perhaps a weakness in Driver's theory that whereas the ancient evidence is that it is Sirius, not the whole constellation to which it belongs, that is "wicked," the term for "wicked" is in the plural both here and in v 15. No doubt recognizing this difficulty, Driver originally translated the term as "the Dog-stars" in the plural, but NEB and REB have transformed that into the singular.

14 Just as a seal stamps on a flat and featureless piece of clay a design in relief, so the light of the morning changes the featureless dark earth: what in the darkness had no shape becomes three-dimensional, contoured features appear, and the landscape takes on its varied colors. Peake reminds us that dawn in biblical lands is a much more rapid event than in higher latitudes, seeing here not only the "perfect clearness with which the light throws up the innumerable features that go to make up the landscape, but the suddenness of its action, the seal stamps the impression on the clay all at once."

15 Following his astronomical interpretation of these verses, G. R. Driver understood the term "the wicked" (רשעים) as the constellations of Canis Major and Minor (as in v 13) and the "high arm" here as the Navigator's Line joining Sirius to Procyon to Castor and Pollux (in Arabic "the arm" or "the arm of Leo" or "the extended arm" refers to the Twins, Castor and Pollux, and "the contracted arm" to Canis Major and Minor). Thus he translates "and the light of the Dog-stars is withdrawn from it [NEB; REB 'is dimmed'] and the Navigator's Line is broken up" (NEB, REB "and the stars of the Navigator's Line go out one by one"), as one star after another fades before the dawning light. The resulting translation is one of the most beautiful passages in the NEB of Job, and though it cannot be pronounced certain, it deserves more attention than it has been given in modern scholarship. De Wilde's objection that Israel was not a seafaring nation and so would not have been interested in the "Navigator's Line" is beside the point, since the Hebrew author does not know the presumed star formation by that name but as "the high arm."

If, after all, the verse concerns the wicked, it must be saying that they, who thrive in the dark, do not benefit from the coming of the day. "Their light," i.e., the daylight they might have expected to share with other humans, is withheld, and they live out a murky existence. Though there is no parallel to the phrase "a high arm" (the usual idiom is "a mighty hand and an outstretched arm," as at Deut 4:34; 1 Kgs 8:42; Ps 136:12), there are many parallels to the arm being broken as a symbol of the destruction of power; cf. 31:22; Jer 48:25; Ezek 30:21, 22, 24; Pss 10:15; 37:17. It is hard to believe that this sentence constitutes Yahweh's response to Job's complaint that the wicked are allowed to prosper (chaps. 21, 24) (cf. Hartley).

16–21 In these two strophes Job is asked by God whether he has experience of the world's dimensions: first, the underworld—its depth (v 16), its breadth (v 18), and its city (v 17)—, and the heavens (vv 19–20). They conclude with an ironic admission that Job knows all these things since he was born long ago and he has therefore accumulated enormous wisdom (v 21).

As Newsom has pointed out, the vocabulary here evokes a journey: travel, walk, see, gaze upon; depths, gates, expanse, realm, place, domain, path. We are reminded inevitably of the underworld journey of the Mesopotamian hero Gilgamesh who crossed the world, traveled through the underworld passage of the sun at night, and crossed the waters of death. Of him it was said that "he saw everything to the ends of the earth, he experienced all things, considered all" (*ANET*, 73b, adapted). Job has not undertaken such a heroic journey; and yet neither did Gilgamesh, of course, for his adventure is a fiction, and his experience lies entirely in the imagination of the epic poet. There is nothing in the divine speeches to Job either that is not known to the Hebrew poet, and if Job has never before traveled to the depths of the abyss, to the realm of the dwelling of light, or the treasury of the hail, he is traveling such a journey now in imagination. The benefit of his "virtual" journey will be identical with that of any "real" but impossible one: he will have surveyed the world in its totality, abandoning any myopic and self-centered vision.

16–18 *Strophe 4: The underworld.* This strophe concerns three distinct features of the underworld (if the term ארץ in v 18 is rightly understood as "underworld" rather than, as usually, "earth"; see *Note* c): the depths of the sea (v 16) as the location of the underworld, the city of the underworld (v 17), and the furthest extent of the underworld (v 18). If Job has not traveled to these places, he can hardly have a comprehensive knowledge of the world; without such knowledge, how can he claim to understand the principles by which the world functions? (Whybray does not think the strophe is about Job's travel through the underworld, remarking that Job is "not an underwater diver," but about whether Job has entered the realm of the dead and returned to life.)

16 The "springs" (נבך) of the sea are the underworld depths that feed the sea (not the heavenly ocean, against Tur-Sinai) with its water; see Gen 7:11 and 49:25, where the "deep" (תהום) provides life-giving water for the earth (at 1QH 1:15 [1QHᵃ11:16] the ocean depths [תהום] "boil" over the springs of water [נבוך]). The "remotest parts" (חקר; see *Note* e) of the abyss are apparently its furthest reaches rather than its deepest floor. The question to Job concerns both the depth and the extent of the underworld ocean: whether he has ever traveled, downwards, to its bottom, or, having journeyed across its expanse to its remotest extent, found himself "walking about" (הלך hithp) admiring the scenery (the verb does carry a hint of the touristic).

The destructive and life-threatening "abyss" or "deep" that must be restrained has been pictured as little ago as vv 8–11, but its danger was dealt with definitively at creation, and it is now little worse than mysterious.

17 Job knows nothing of the realm of the dead, though it is open before God (26:6). The land of Sheol is naturally mentioned in connection with the sea and its sources, for it is thought to be located immediately beneath the sea, and accessed from earth by the river of death (cf. 33:18). It is a land, but also a city, with gates ("the gates of death," Isa 38:10; Jonah 2:6 [7]; Pss 9:13 [14]; 107:18; Wisd 16:13; 1QH 3:17; 6:24; 4QWiles 1:10; Matt 16:18), which prevent its inhabitants from ever leaving. It is presided over by a ruler, the King of Terrors (18:14), who is surrounded by demons as his courtiers.

In the Babylonian underworld, the realm of the dead was a city with seven gates, built upon the ocean that surrounds and supports the earth (see also John F. Healey, "Das Land ohne Wiederkehr: Die Unterwelt im antiken Ugarit und im Alten Testament," *TQ* 177 [1997] 94–104). A similar conception prevails in the Hebrew Bible: for the waters under the earth as providing the originals for cultic images, cf. Exod 20:4. Sheol is "deep" (Job 11:8), Abaddon and Death being apparently deeper than Sea and Ocean (28:14, 22). Likewise in other ancient thought: according to Hesiod, Pegasus was born "at the sources of Ocean" (*Theogony* 282). Aristotle's *Meteorologica*, Book 2, Chap. 1, is devoted to denying that the sea has sources.

The gatekeepers are mentioned in several ancient sources: in Sumer, in *Inanna's Descent to the Nether World*, Neti is the head gatekeeper (*ANET*, 54b, lines 113–14); in Akkadian literature, in the *Descent of Ishtar to the Nether World*, there is reference to the gatekeepers at the seven doors of the underworld (*ANET*, 107). On gates, see especially E. Otto, "שַׁעַר," *TDOT*, 15 (2006) 359–405 (392–95); and on the gates of the underworld, A. S. Kapelrud, "The Gates of Hell and the Guardian Angels of Paradise," *JAOS* 70 (1950) 151–56.

18 After vv 16–17, asking Job about his knowledge of the depths of the earth, v 18 is generally understood as concerning the extent of the earth: has he "considered," or better, since the verb is followed by the preposition "as far as" (עַד), "looked to" or "gazed on" (בִין hithpo) the "expanses" (רַחֲבֵי) of the earth? It may be more suitable to see here the special sense of אֶרֶץ, i.e., the "underworld," which would continue the theme of Sheol in v 17 (so Andersen, Hartley, Habel "the vast netherworld domain of which the ground is but the visible surface")— even though the "extent" (רַחֲבֵי) of Sheol is nowhere else a matter of interest.

19–21 *Strophe 5: Light and darkness.* Job has evidently no experience of the underworld. What of the upper world, then, where the light and the darkness reside?

19 Light and darkness are elements that have existed since the creation, independently of the heavenly bodies (as also in Genesis 1). Darkness is regarded as not merely the absence of light, but an entity in its own right. As is already suggested by 26:10, light and darkness alternate, as day and night, in the same physical space. But, in addition, there appears to be beyond the horizon a permanent area of darkness, with a boundary (תַּכְלִית) separating it from the region of light. It is likely that light and darkness are conceived of as inhabiting the same dwelling, using it in turns (de Wilde), as is depicted in Hesiod, *Theogony* 745–57, where Night and Day greet one another as they cross one another's path at the door of their house: "one is always outside the house passing over the earth, while the other stays at home and waits until the time for its journeying comes" (cf. also Gisela Fuchs, *Mythos und Hiobdichtung: Aufnahme und Umdeutung altorientalischer Vorstellungen* [Stuttgart: W. Kohlhammer, 1993] 207). The home of Night and Day will be in the east, since daylight obviously comes in from the east, and darkness likewise creeps over the earth from the east (against Hartley). Pope says simply: "Light and darkness were separated on the first day of Creation … and thus have different abodes"; but it is not clear that the author of Job was thinking of Genesis 1.

The Hebrew seems to ask, "Where is the way to the dwelling of light?," lit. "Where is the way [to where] light dwells?" But it may be that we have here דֶּרֶךְ

II, not "way" but "realm" (see *Note* b), as Andersen suggests (which seems also to be the case in the repetition of the same phrase in v 24).

20   Light and darkness would hardly need a guide to see them to their home, since they travel the same route every day. What might be called for, however, is a ceremonious escort that would accompany them with dignity. To serve as such an escort, Job would need to know either the "path" to their home or their "realm" (v 19). It is possible, though it does not seem likely, that this verse begins the irony that is explicit in v 21, as Kissane: "For thou takest it to its domain" (similarly Strauss).

21   If the usual translation is correct, "You know, for you were born then," this is irony that verges on sarcasm, for there is no subtlety in its double meaning. It is simply untrue that Job was born "then," whenever that may have been. It seems like a sarcasm far more severe in tone than the ironical rhetorical question of v 4: "Where were you when I laid the foundations of the earth?" But perhaps this too is a question (so Andersen), the initial interrogative particle *he* being omitted, as it is at the beginning of v 18. As Andersen says, "Since Job had never pretended to have such knowledge, he is quite undeserving of the sarcasm which many commentators find in this verse"—though the matter is not settled by whether Job deserves the sarcasm or not.

When is Job alleged to have been born? The Hebrew says, "You were born then (אָז)," but no time in the past has been mentioned (for אָז "then" in reference to primordial times, cf. 28:7). Perhaps we should read instead מֵאָז "of old," which does not refer back to some specific moment. The point is, however, not Job's age but the wisdom that comes with age (cf. on 32:9; 36:26). Many find here an allusion to the myth of the First Man, born from a divine being before creation and endowed with supernatural wisdom (see further on 15:7). Eliphaz has there asked ironically whether Job is the First Man, and now Yahweh would be affirming, equally ironically, that he is. But of course in reality he is not, and his wisdom has not had untold ages to mature and develop.

22–38   We move now in these strophes (the second set of five strophes in the first divine speech) from fundamental cosmic structures to aspects of the world order that impinge on the daily life of its inhabitants: snow, hail, and heat reserved in storehouses (strophe 6, vv 22–24), torrential rain (strophe 7, vv 25–27), other forms of moisture (strophe 8, vv 28–30), the constellations that affect or determine the seasons (strophe 9, vv 31–33), and the clouds and their rains (strophe 10, vv 34–38).

22–24   *Strophe 6: The heavenly storehouses.* The heavenly storehouses contain a variety of items: snow, hail, and heat. To some extent they cause damage on earth, and yet (Newsom) they are "associated ... with words of regulation and control: storehouses, proper times, way, place, reserve, distribute, disperse."

There may be here the beginning of a sequence of strophes organized according to the course of the seasons (de Wilde): winter in vv 22–23, 29–30, spring in vv 24–27, summer in vv 31–32, and autumn in vv 34–38; but it would be unwise to rearrange the position of vv 29–30 on the basis of this structure, which is not very strongly marked.

22   The word for "storehouses" (אוֹצָר) can refer either to the contents, whether valuables or supplies of food, or, as here, to the place where wealth or other items are stored. It is well known that there are heavenly storehouses, but how many are they? There is a variety of opinions in the Hebrew Bible: for heaven as a storehouse of rain, cf. Deut 28:12; of wind, cf. 37:9; Jer 10:13 || 51:16 || Ps 135:7; of clouds, Ecclus 43:14; perhaps of the heavenly sea, cf. Ps 33:7; of darkness, cf. 1QS 10:2; of winds, snow, mist, thunder, *1 Enoch* 41:3–4; 60:11–12; of fire, snow, and ice, in the second heaven, cf. *T. Levi* 3; of winds, meteors, lightning, cf. 1QH 1:12; 11QBer 2:7; and apparently of manna also, cf. Ps 78:23–24. Here in Job we find the only reference to storehouses of snow and hail. It appears also that there is mention of yet another storehouse, that of the heat (v 24). On the heavenly storehouses, see further, C. Houtman, *Der Himmel im Alten Testament: Israels Weltbild und Weltanschauung* (OTS 30; Leiden: E. J. Brill, 1993) 253–55.

Hail appears as an instrument of divine punishment against evildoers (Isa 28:17; Ezek 13:11, 13; Ecclus 39:29), against crops (Exod 9:22; Hg 2:17), and against enemies (Josh 10:11; Isa 30:30; Rev 8:7; 11:19; 16:21). It is an accompaniment of a theophany in Isa 30:30; Ps 18:12–13 (13–14).

23 It is the hail, and not the snow as well, that is stored up for use in warfare. KJV, NAB, NJB, Moffatt make that clear, but other translations could suggest that snow also is kept for times of calamity—for which there seems no supporting parallel except perhaps the dubious reference in Ps 68:14 (15): "When the Almighty scattered kings there, snow fell on Zalmon" (NRSV). The sense of that verse may rather be "When Shaddai scattered the kings, it seemed like a snowstorm in Zalmon" (NJPS; similarly NAB, NIV).

24 Some of our versions suggest that the first question concerns the "light," which is the literal meaning of אוֹר (so KJV, RSV). But it is much more likely, since the light has already been dealt with in v 19, and since the parallel is with the east wind, that אוֹר here means "lightning," as it does at 36:32; 37:3, 15 (so too Whybray, Newsom). A better suggestion, however (G. R. Driver, Guillaume), is that אוֹר *ʾôr* "light" should be revocalized to אוּר *ʾûr* "heat," so that the question becomes one about the storehouse of heat, which is spread across the earth by the hot sirocco (in *T. Levi* 3, fire is kept in a storehouse in the second heaven). This is an improvement on having to conceive of a single storehouse both for the light (or lightning) and for the east wind; there is just one storehouse (in addition to those in v 22 for snow and hail). It is possible that the idea is that in this storehouse heat is "created" (חלק VI; see *Note* d), rather than being "apportioned" or distributed from it as from a warehouse; apportioning or dividing is not the most natural thing to be happening in an arsenal or warehouse or factory. It remains uncertain whether Job is being asked "what is the way" to such a storehouse, or "where the realm is" where heat is kept and from where it is then apportioned to various parts of the earth. It depends on whether the word דרך is the usual word for "way" or whether we have דֶּרֶךְ II "realm" (cf. *Note* b); the same issue has arisen in v 19.

The heat created or produced in the heavenly storehouse is a source of heat additional to the sun and so must have a separate origin; coming from the storehouse it is spread across the earth by the hot east wind. The sirocco or "east wind" (קָדִים), the hot, violent wind from the desert, has been referred to at 15:2; 27:21, and perhaps also at 37:17 as the "south wind" (דָּרוֹם).

25–27 *Strophe 7: Rainstorm and lightning.* In the heavenly storehouses of vv 22–24 God keeps reserves of snow, hail, and heat for distribution over the earth (vv 22–24). In this next strophe, nothing is said explicitly about a storehouse for rain, but vv 34, 37 will shortly show that rain is stored in the clouds, along with lightning. Our strophe here depicts the delivery of water to the earth—indiscriminately, in torrents (v 25), and even onto land where it apparently serves no useful purpose for humans (vv 26–27).

There is nothing about creation here, let us notice; the picture is of the regular cycle of nature, so the main verb should be translated in the present tense "cuts" (NIV), "carves" (JB), or "bores out" (NJB)—rather than the past tense "hath divided" (KJV), "has cleft" (RSV), "has cut" (NRSV, NEB), or "has laid out" (NAB).

25 The idea of a "channel" forms a transition from the storehouses of vv 22–24 to the atmospheric or meteorological phenomena of the next four strophes (the rainstorm and thunderbolt in vv 25–27, the various kinds of moisture in vv 28–30, the influences of the stars on the seasons of the year in vv 31–33, and the clouds with their rains and lightnings in vv 34–38). This metaphorical channel, the path that the rain takes through the atmosphere, links heaven and earth. The term (תעלה) elsewhere always refers literally to a watercourse in the earth (e.g., 2 Kgs 18:17; Isa 7:3) or a trench (1 Kgs 18:32). It is a strange term to use of rain, which of course falls in drops rather than as an unbroken stream, but that is just the point: the focus here is on the rainstorm, the "downpour" or "flood" (שׁטף; cf. פלג אלהים "stream of God" for the rain in Ps 65:9 [10]), accompanied by thunderbolts. Aqueducts, a symbol of civilization in the ancient world, are a means of both ensuring and regulating the supply of water; this airy aqueduct may be reminiscent of the rivers of Eden (Gen 2:10–14). E. F. Sutcliffe, "The Clouds as Water-Carriers in Hebrew Thought," *VT* 3 (1953) 99–103, thought that the idea here may be, as in *Ber. Rab.* 13.10, that each drop of rain has its own path to follow, so that each reaches the earth separately from its fellows; but we are not hearing in this verse about the normal fall of rain (which is מחר) but about torrential rainfall.

The lightning has been depicted already in detail by Elihu at 36:30, 32; 37:3, 15. And in 28:26 the same speaker (so it has been argued) has referred to the "path for the lightning of the thunder," the very phrase we have here. The idea is that "[e]very bolt has its track, along which it shoots to its mark" (Strahan). See further, Philippe Reymond, *L'eau, sa vie, et sa signification dans l'Ancien Testament* (VTSup 6; Leiden: E. J. Brill, 1958) 204; Luis I. J. Stadelmann, *The Hebrew Conception of the World: A Philological and Literary Study* (AnBib 39; Rome: Pontifical Biblical Institute, 1970) 111–14.

26 In speaking of the channeling of rain and the prescribed path for the lightning to the waste and uninhabited places, the poet does not of course mean such places are the only recipients of the rain; he seems to have in mind downpours of rain, along with the accompanying lightning, upon the earth in general, and in particular even upon places where no human dwells. The principal clause in this long sentence (vv 25–27) concerns Yahweh's sending of rain (v 25), and it is only secondarily that the uninhabited land as a destination is mentioned. So it is only incidentally that God's concern for parts of his cosmos unusable by humans is referred to, but it is nevertheless an important implicit theme of the divine speeches. Though animals are not referred to explicitly, they may be in mind as the beneficiaries of such rain, which produces their foodstuff (v 27). Whybray also sees that these verses introduce a new theme for the speech: "that Yahweh performs many of his activities in ways that appear to human beings to be sheer waste, but which demonstrate the unimaginable scope of his concerns and, by implication, the insignificance of purely human concerns in his sight."

It would be unwise, however, to put too much weight on the theme of the uselessness of such rain to humans, or on the contrast between the sown and the unsown as representing order and chaos (as Keel, *Entgegnung*, 58, Newsom), since land that is not strictly settled may still be used by humans, for example for grazing their herds.

27 The phrase "waste and desolate land" is the same at 30:3, where it denotes land that provides inadequate sustenance for the poor. More commonly the word "waste" (שאה, *šōʾa*, which is now used, in the form Shoah, as the technical term for the Holocaust) refers to destruction, e.g., the desolation of cities after enemy attack (e.g., Isa 10:3; 47:11; Ezek 38:9; Zeph 1:15; Ps 35:8), but here it is of land that is simply unusable, comparatively speaking, by humans. We are viewing snapshots here, not a panorama or a systematic survey: just as torrential rain on the desert is only one example of Yahweh's provision, so the blossoming of the dry ground is a quite temporary occurrence (on the coming of fresh growth to the desert and steppe lands, cf. Ps 65:13; Joel 2:22).

28–30 *Strophe 8: Rain, dew, rime, hoar-frost, ice.* The focus in this strophe shifts from the dramatic downpours of rain, accompanied by thunderbolts (v 25), to the more placid provision of moisture in five forms, those of rain (מטר, v 28a), dewdrops (אגלי־טל, v 28b), rime (קרח, v 29a), hoar-frost (כפר) (v 29b), and ice (depicted but not named in v 30).

28 Here we have a new kind of question, which may not at first seem to have an obvious answer. Has the rain a father? Here is the fusion of cosmogony and cosmology, for the answer to the question of origins is also the answer to a question about the arrangement of the natural order. Does the rain have a father? It is a rhetorical question expecting the answer, No! Yahweh does not mean that it is he who is the "father" of the rain (the question is not, as Moffatt would have it, "Have showers a human sire?"), but that the rain, along with all the other forms of moisture, has no (mythological) father or mother (Hartley), being nothing but the product of divine acts or, less probably, the operation of natural laws (cf. v 33). The language of begetting and birthing, of father and mother, as Whybray rightly points out, reflects an older theogony, in which these phenomena were seen as the offspring of divine unions; cf. the references in the Ugaritic literature to female deities named Pidrya, "daughter of mist," and Taliya (Dew), "daughter of showers" (*Baal* II.1.14–15 [*CML*, 93a]). Jer 14:22, more forthrightly, denies the ability of foreign gods to bring rain. Here, however, there is no polemic against foreign gods, but a resistance to any idea that these beneficent features of the world were brought into being once and for all in a primordial time, as the language of begetting and child-bearing might suggest. Rain and dew, rime, hoar-frost, and ice—all forms of moisture that are here ranged beside rain torrents—are perpetually created anew by Yahweh in his daily care for his universe (cf. the description of the coming of each new day in vv 12–15). See further, Gregory Vall, "'From Whose Womb Did the Ice Come Forth?' Procreation Images in Job 38:28–29," *CBQ* 57 (1995) 504–13. On dew as a significant element in precipitation in the region of Palestine (on the coastal plain it can contribute up to 55 mm annually), see M. Gilead and N. Rosenan, "Ten Years of Dew Observation in Israel," *IEJ* 4 (1954) 120–23.

29 If v 28 has asked after a supposed male parent of the moisture, this verse enquires after a female parent. From whose womb comes the rime? Who is the hoar-frost's mother? Rime (קרח) occurs when the water droplets in fog freeze;

it is the ice that is often seen on trees. Hoar-frost (כְּפוֹר) is the ice that occurs when water vapor settles on an object, often the ground (as at Exod 16:14). Hoar-frost is scattered like ashes from heaven, according to Ps 147:16, or poured on the earth like salt, according to Ecclus 43:19. Manna is reminiscent of it (Exod 16:24). Cf. also Ecclus 3:15; Dalman, *Arbeit und Sitte*, 1:230, 237–38.

30 It is perhaps suggested that the ice that forms on water is no different from the frost that settles on solid objects. The frost is normally a white deposit, but its effect on water is another matter. There it hardens what it falls upon—an extreme example of the workings of frost.

We have heard before of the wadis that become "dark with ice" (6:16), so the formation of ice is a phenomenon well known to the poet. But if the "deep" (תְהוֹם) here means the ocean, there will be no freezing of its surface anywhere near the author's home. It is more than "interesting to ask where our author traveled to observe freezing on such a grand scale" (Andersen), although, of course, he did not need to have first-hand acquaintance with everything he wrote about. Much more probably, the term "deep" does not refer to the sea but is used loosely for pools of fresh water (so too Sicre Díaz); in 41:32 (24) it appears to be in reference to a river or lake.

31–33 *Strophe 9: The four constellations.* This strophe in which four heavenly constellations feature may seem to be out of place among more earth-bound strophes concerning rainstorms and lightning (vv 25–27) and other forms of moisture (vv 28–30) preceding it, and one concerning clouds with their rains and lightnings (vv 34–38) following it. But the three constellations that can be identified with some certainty (the Pleiades, Orion, and Aldebaran) are all connected with the coming of rains, so they may well owe their presence here to their importance for the supply of water on earth; and the fourth, Mazzaroth, may also be connected with rain (see on v 32). Job would then be asked if he is able to establish or affect these constellations; if he were to be in charge of the governing of the universe, he would at least need to manage the rain-bringing stars, whose operation is vital for life on earth. What Job cannot do is to bind the Pleiades together in a cluster and fasten a belt around Orion's waist; but that is what Yahweh has done. He too is the one who brings out Mazzaroth into the night sky in its season and guides Aldebaran and its Hyades to their accustomed places. Is Job capable of such undertakings, "binding" and "loosing" (v 31), "bringing out" and "guiding" (v 32), acts of control and direction? Has he set himself up as shepherd of the stars (cf. Keel, *Entgegnung*, 59)?

As for the sequence in which the four constellations are mentioned, Pleiades, Orion, Mazzaroth, and Aldebaran with the Hyades, G. R. Driver (who thinks Mazzaroth is the Zodiacal circle) explains that the author's "starting point is the Pleiades, a constellation which has always attracted attention by its conspicuous light … and Orion, one of the largest and most brilliant constellations in the skies …. [T]hese two constellations … situated almost at the beginning of the Zodiac circle, are natural starting points for a survey of the heavens. He then speaks of the Zodiac belt, whose constellations take him round the pole, and comes back lastly to Aldebaran and the Hyades, which lie between the two constellations from which he set out on his journey" ("Two Astronomical Passages in the Old Testament," *JTS* ns 7 [1956] 1–11 [8]). Even if Mazzaroth is not the Zodiac, the same plan will have governed the sequence.

31 The point of this series of references to the stars is not that "they are all bound and fettered by God, who leads them around the sky as he pleases" (Andersen). Rather, "[t]he stars in their constellations are mentioned here, probably because they were believed to exert influence on the seasons and the weather" (Gordis).

For the identification of כימה as the Pleiades and כסיל as Orion, cf. on 9:9. The Pleiades, also often known as the Seven Sisters (though only six are visible to the naked eye), are a cluster of stars in the constellation of Taurus. For observers in the northern hemisphere, like the author of Job, the cluster is above and to the right of Orion the Hunter as one faces south. The brightest Pleiad is Alcyone, 1,000 times more luminous than our own sun would be at the same distance. The name כימה for the Pleiades probably means "herd," as a cognate noun in Arabic.

The constellation of Orion is one of the most easily recognized in the northern sky. In mythology, Orion the Hunter is accompanied by his dogs, Canis Major and Minor. Together they hunt various celestial animals, including Lepus, the rabbit, and Taurus, the bull. Orion's Belt is formed by three bright stars (known by their Arabic names, Alnitak, Alnilam, and Mintaka) in a straight line. Hanging down from Orion's belt is his sword that is made up of three fainter stars.

It is probably a mistake to seek here allusions to ancient mythology about these constellations (against, e.g., Tur-Sinai), since the issue here is not how they come to be in the sky but how they function as Yahweh's mechanism for producing rain on the earth. According to some sources, Orion, called in Hebrew כסיל "the fool," was represented as a foolish giant who rebelled against God and after his death was lashed to the sky. See E. Walter Maunder, *The Astronomy of the Bible: An Elementary Commentary on the Astronomical References of Holy Scripture* (London: T. Sealey Clark, 1908) 232–41; C. F. Burney, *EB*, 4:4782; W. Brueggemann, *IDB*, 3:609. But this myth is found only in classical sources, and even if this were to be the explanation of Orion's bonds, it would nevertheless remain uncertain whether the question implies that Job could not release one whom Yahweh had imprisoned, or that "in spite of his turbulent character the Almighty relaxes his bands, because, however dangerous he may be, God can, when He will, contemptuously leave him at large. Job, if he could, would not dare to do this" (Peake).

What does it mean to "bind" (קשׁר) the Pleiades and "loose" (פתח) Orion's belt? In cosmogonic terms, it would presumably mean to establish these constellations in their places, clustering the stars of the Pleiades together as with cords or slackening off the belt of Orion. But it does seem that chap. 38 has by now moved on from thoughts of creation to speak of repeated phenomena in the world's cycles (as, e.g., the storehouses in vv 22–24, the rain in vv 25–27, and the other forms of moisture in vv 28–30). G. R. Driver therefore may well be correct in seeing here the seasonal influences of the stars: the Pleiades are the harbingers of spring and Orion is the herald of winter. To "bind" the Pleiades would thus be, functionally, to check the spring floods that they unleash, and to loose Orion's belt would be to disable the autumn rains ("Two Astronomical Passages in the Old Testament," *JTS* ns 7 [1956] 1–11). De Wilde, on the other hand, followed by Newsom, thinks the binding of the Pleiades refers to their becoming invisible at the beginning of April, when the rainy season is over and the hot season begins. When Orion's belt is loosed, it is from early July onward, when his arrows of heat and dryness have been discharged over the earth. Whatever the precise reference of binding the Pleiades and loosing Orion may be, the point is that Job cannot alter the structure of the cosmos; the functions of the constellations are a matter of divine decree (v 33).

There is some evidence that in some parts of the ancient world the stars were thought be suspended from the sky with cords, which could be used also to move them around (cf. Keel, *Symbolism,* fig. 239; and for later Arab thought, cf. J. W. Hirschberg, "Job 38, 31," *REJ* 99 [1935] 130–32). This does not, however, appear to be the idea here. Hartley suggests that the stars were believed to be restrained by chains and that each day God would loosen their cords so that they could make their journey across the sky. Ḥakham, however, thought that when a constellation rises it is harnessed to its course, and when it sets the harness is loosed.

32 Job is asked if he can "bring out" (יצא), i.e., into the night sky, the star or constellation known as Mazzaroth. Cf. Isa 40:26 for the idea of God "bringing out" the stars one by one, calling each one by its name; יצא is used also at Neh 4:15 for the "coming out" of the stars. "Leading" (נחה) or "guiding" stars will also no doubt refer to bringing them out into the night sky and shepherding them across the sky in the course of the night. As v 33 will expound, the appearance of the stars follows a divinely determined pattern or law, each star or constellation having its own "right time" (עת; cf. also *Comment* on 39:1).

Mazzaroth is a name that occurs only here in the Hebrew Bible; it has been variously identified with the Zodiacal circle, with Arcturus, Sirius, Venus, and the Northern Crown (for details, see *Note* a). In view of the association of the other three stars with the coming of rain, perhaps the best identification is with the Hyades, which are preeminently the harbingers of rain. If that is so, the two cola of this line would refer to the same constellation: the Hyades.

Aldebaran (עיש) is the bright star that forms the eye of Taurus, the bull. Its "sons" are the Hyades, forming the head of Taurus. Thus NEB "Aldebaran and its train," REB "and its satellite stars." So G. Schiaparelli, *Astronomy in the Old Testament* (Oxford: Clarendon Press, 1904) 54–60; G. R. Driver, "Two Astronomical Passages in the Old Testament," *JTS* ns 7 (1956) 1–11 (1–2), de Wilde. A more common, though probably erroneous, identification of עיש has been with the Bear (Ursa Major, the Big Dipper, also known as Charles's [i.e., Charlemagne's] Wain); so most modern versions (JB has "the Bear and its cubs"; similarly NIV; TEV "the Big and the Little Dipper") and commentators (Terrien, Gordis, Habel, Hartley). Good calls it the Lioness.

33 Behind the question here is the belief that the stars determine certain events on earth, especially seasonal changes. It is not the same as the astrological determination of historical events mocked in Isa 47:13. The "laws of the heavens" (חקות שמים) are here not so much the laws governing the movements of the heavenly bodies (Peake, Kissane, Gordis), as they may well be at Jer 31:35–36 (perhaps cf. also Ps 148:6); rather, they are the regularities that associate a given constellation with a rainy season, for example (the "laws of heaven and earth" in Jer 33:25 have a broader scope). In this way, the two cola come together in meaning: these laws of association constitute the "rule" (משטר) of the heavens upon earth. It is not so likely (against van der Lugt) that the verse is to be connected without what follows, the laws of the heavens then pertaining not to the stars but simply to the production of clouds and lightning.

As against Job's perception that the world is chaotic and out of control (see esp. chap. 24), Yahweh points to the cosmic order that sustains life: earth and sky are united by a design, by "laws" written in the heavens that exercise their "rule" over the earth.

And what is it that Job is asked about these constellations? If it is, Do you know (ידעת) these laws? (as RSV, NAB, NIV; cf. JB "have you grasped the celestial laws?"), perhaps Job can answer that he does; certainly the poet of Job seems to know them. If Job does know them, that would rather spoil the effect of the rhetorical question. Perhaps therefore we should revocalize the verb to the piel יִדַּעְתָּ "Can you determine the laws?" or even "Did you proclaim the rules?" (NEB), which would as well create a closer parallel with the next colon.

34–38 *Strophe 10: The clouds.* In this final strophe about the cosmos, longer than all the others because of its climactic position, we are reminded that what Job cannot do, God can, and does. These verses envisage the falling of rain from the clouds as a response (ענה) to the voice of Yahweh. The lightning likewise does not drop of its own accord, but reports for duty to its master; each bolt is directed on its way individually by God. The law of nature, according to this cosmology, is that nature does what it is told.

In this strophe, Yahweh is not speaking of the clouds with their lightning and rain as a benefit and a warning for humans, as Elihu was in 36:27–33; 37:11–13. Rather, they are manifestations of his intricate involvement with his universe and his skill in its maintenance. The present strophe continues the theme of the rain that has begun at v 25; vv 25–27 have focused especially on downpours of rain, vv 28–30 on the other forms of moisture, vv 31–33 on the influence of the heavenly bodies on the coming of the rains. Now we have a powerful statement of the authority of Yahweh over the rains (vv 34–35), an allusion to his provision of earthly witnesses to their arrival (v 36), and an exceptional image of the sending down of the rains and their effect on the earth (vv 37–38). As so often in the poetry of the book, the touch is amazingly light and impressionistic, and the effect vivid in the extreme. The key concepts are authority (vv 34–35) and "wisdom" (vv 36–38).

34 Job is no sorcerer (Fohrer) who can bring down rain with his invocations. Even if he possessed the authoritative words, his voice would not even travel as far as the clouds, the divine pavilion (36:29), nor could he command the obedience of the lightning as its dispatcher (v 35). In the second colon, the MT has "a flood of waters shall cover you." The selfsame phrase has appeared also at 22:11, where it was a punishment on the wicked; so it is strange to find it here as if it were something Job could perhaps wish for (even stranger is the other parallel, in Isa 60:6 "A flood of camels shall cover you"). Presumably Yahweh is asking Job whether he can imitate the divine actions: when he asks "Can you lift your voice to the clouds?" he means that he can and Job cannot (it was not even so simple for Elijah in 1 Kings 18). "God has merely to raise his voice and the rain pours down" (Gordis). But it cannot be imagined how a flood of waters could cover Yahweh (against Andersen), so we must have recourse to the (admittedly less dramatic) reading suggested by LXX "and make a flood of waters answer you."

35 Dispatching lightning is equally outwith Job's competence. Lightning bolts, referred to as God's arrows, are "sent" (שלח) like messengers also at Ps 18:14 (15). The wording of the verse seems to be closely imitated by Bar 3:33–34 (35), where God is "he who sends forth the light, and it goes; ... he called [the stars], and they said, 'Here we are!'" "Here am I" (הננו, here in the plural) is a typical response of servants (cf. 1 Sam 3:4–6; Isa 6:8). For the lightning as God's servant, accomplishing his will, cf. 36:32; 37:11–13. Terrien and Andersen, not without cause, find a little touch of the ridiculous in this picture of the lightning reporting to Yahweh for duty.

36 This has been an obscure verse, with many variant translations. Thus KJV had "Who hath put wisdom in the inward parts? Or who hath given understanding to the heart?" RSV, on the other hand, has "Who has put wisdom in the clouds, or given understanding to the mists?" NEB has "Who put wisdom in depths of darkness, and veiled understanding in secrecy?" And JB has "Who gave the ibis wisdom and endowed the cock with foreknowledge?"

Since we have been reading about meteorological and atmospheric phenomena, the RSV interpretation is at first sight the most plausible. But it must be admitted that it is a strange idea to attribute wisdom and understanding to the clouds and mists (clouds may seem to have a mind of their own [Hartley], but that is not exactly wisdom, nor is it wisdom by which the thunder-cloud "moves unerringly towards its goal" [Kissane]). The NEB reading sounds profound, but it refers to nothing in the present context. The KJV, supported to some extent by the use of the term שחות at Ps 51:6 (8) for "inward parts," likewise seems entirely out of place in a strophe about clouds, lightning, and rain. A reference to birds, such as we find in JB, and TEV, seems no more relevant, and might moreover seem to belong rather to the depiction of the animals in the second half of this speech of Yahweh's (38:39–39:40).

However, there is a good reason why these birds should be mentioned here: they are both associated with the coming of the rains as foretellers of their imminent arrival. The ibis (שחות) was famous in antiquity for its ability to foretell the rising of the Nile (Dhorme, Gordis). This foretelling was apparently conceived of as a precondition for the rising of the Nile, and to kill an ibis was punishable with death (though whether for that reason is not known); cf. Herodotus, *Hist.* 2.65.2. Egyptian amulets with a Thoth ibis figure were known in Israel; and we have from Ashkelon a bronze figure of a seated ibis (J. H. Iliffe, "A Hoard of Bronzes from Askelon," *QDAP* 5 [1936] 60–68 [65 no. 8]; cf. Keel, *Dieu répond,* 46 n. 203). On the ibis, cf. also M. Görg, *NBL* 1 (1991) 211.

The cock (שכוי) was apparently believed to have the ability to forecast the rain (for the same belief in the modern period, cf. J. A. Jaussen, "Le coq et la pluie dans la tradition palestinienne," *RB* 33 [1924] 574–82). Othmar Keel has drawn attention to a striking illustration of the language of vv 36–37, a seal cylinder from Nimrud that associates a cock with water jars in heaven ("Zwei kleine Beiträge zum Verständnis der Gottesreden im Buch Ijob [xxxviii 36f., xl 25]," *VT* 31 [1981] 220–25; also in *Dieu répond,* 47). A cock figures on the well-known seal of Jaazaniah (W. F. Badè, "The Seal of Jaazaniah," *ZAW* 51 [1933] 150–56 [152–54]; *ANEP,* fig. 277). Cranes prophesy rain in Virgil, *Georgics* 1.373–75. On the cock in the Ancient Near East, cf. Burchard Brentjes, "Nutz- und Hausvögel im Alten Orient," *Wissenschaftliche Zeitschrift Halle–Wittenberg* 11 (Gesellschafts- und sprachwissenschaftliche Reihe 6; 1962) 635–702 (643–46).

These birds, heralds of the rain and of the rising waters, have a wisdom (חכמה) and intelligence (בינה) greater than the ordinary, implanted in them by Yahweh. As TEV has it: "Who tells the ibis that the Nile will flood, or who tells the rooster that rain will fall?" It is Yahweh, of course. Job, by contrast, who cannot summon down a cloudburst or dispatch a lightning bolt, has never possessed the skill himself to set upon earth these animate forecasters of the rains.

Many other data about the ibis and the cock mentioned by commentators are extraneous to the present setting. For example, the wording of the second colon has been incorporated into the Jewish morning service, which begins a blessing to God with "who gives to the cock understanding (בינה) to distinguish between day and night." That was indeed perceived in antiquity as a sign of the cock's wisdom, but it does not seem to be in view here at all. Nor is there an implicit rebuke to "man's pretensions to wisdom" and a tribute to the animal creation by contrast with humans (Gordis). Nor should we pay any special attention to the fact that the ibis was a bird sacred to Thoth, the Egyptian god of wisdom, for it would be far-fetched to see here any allusion to that deity.

37 What Yahweh must do in order to bring rain on the earth—and what Job is incapable of doing—is first to "disperse" (ספר, see *Note* a) the clouds over the surface of the earth, and then to "tilt" (שכב hiph, lit. "make lie down") these containers or water jars so that their contents spill out and fall on the earth. Only here and at Ecclus 43:8 (נבלי מרום "the jars of the Height") are the clouds referred to as "jars" (cf. also Houtman, *Der Himmel*, 259–62). A "water jar" (נבל) is normally a ceramic amphora, with two or four handles and a narrow neck; in Lam 4:2 it is explicitly said to be the work of a potter. A נבל may be used for the storage of wine (1 Sam 1:24; 10:3; 2 Sam 16:1; Neh 5:18; Jer 13:12) or oil (only in the Samaria ostraca, where there are many references also to jars of wine; see *DCH*, 5:594b). It may be accidental that there is no reference to water jars in Classical Hebrew. On jars, cf. A. M. Honeyman, "The Pottery Vessels of the Old Testament," *PEQ* (1939) 76–90 (84–85); K. Seybold, *TDOT*, 9:172–74.

The metaphor of the clouds as water jars is quite different from that in v 25 where the rainstorms are envisaged as kept in storehouses above the firmament, reaching the earth via a channel in the air. For the idea of the clouds as containers of the regular rain, cf. also 26:8; 36:27–28. The dispersal of the clouds across the sky is regarded as an exercise of the divine "skill" or "wisdom" (חכמה), since no human can understand the operation of the clouds, as Elihu has stressed: God's wisdom is demonstrated by his production of clouds of rain from the evaporation of water (36:26–28), the spreading of the clouds being beyond human comprehension (36:29), and one of the "wonderful deeds of God," a "marvel of one who is perfect in knowledge" (37:14–16).

38 The rain here is the early rain of October–November, falling after the heat of summer has cracked open the ground (cf. the depiction in the Ugaritic Baal myth, "Cracked are the furrows of the field, O Shapash [goddess of the sun], cracked are the furrows of the vast fields" (*Baal* III.iv.1–2, 12–13 [*CML*, 113a]). What is depicted is the agglomeration of the dust into a compact mass by the rain (Duhm, Strahan, Dhorme, Hölscher, Kissane, Rowley, Habel). Others, however, think that what is described are the dry clods of earth prior to the coming of the rains (Budde, Fohrer, Pope, Fedrizzi, Keel, *Dieu répond*, 47, Hartley), perhaps with reference to the standard phrase "the heavens brass and the earth iron" (Deut 28:23; in the reverse order at Lev 26:19). The former is more suitable to the verb "flow, fuse" (יצק), which happens as a result of the rain.

38:39–39:30 *Section II: The world of animals.* The second half of this first divine speech, in seven strophes, concerns nine animals: the lion (38:39–40), the raven (38:41; together, strophe 1), unless this line also concerns the lion, the mountain goats (strophe 2, 39:1–4), the wild ass (strophe 3, vv 5–8), the wild ox (strophe 4, vv 9–12), the ostrich (strophe 5, vv 13–18), the horse (strophe 6, vv

19–25), the hawk (v 26), and the eagle (vv 27–30, together strophe 7). With the exception of the war horse, these are all wild animals that live their lives totally independently of humans: they are of no service to humans, and humans are comparatively ignorant of their ways (though obviously the poet knows enough about them to portray them). The "very pointed omission of any reference to human beings, with their obsession with their own problems and their demands that God should conform to their own notices of justice, cannot but be intentional" (Whybray).

On God's provision of food for animals, cf. Gen 1:30; Pss 104:14, 21, 27; 145:15–16; 147:9; Matt 6:26; Luke 12:24. The esoteric knowledge about wild animals contained in these verses must reflect an interest in ancient Israel. See further, H. Richter, "Die Naturweisheit des Alten Testaments im Buche Hiob," *ZAW* 70 (1958) 1–20.

39–41 *Strophe 1: The lion and the raven.* The poet's eye turns first, not unnaturally, to the lion, long recognized as the king of beasts, and the wild animal *par excellence,* so common indeed in ancient Israel as to be a pest; cf. 2 Kgs 17:25–26. Associated here with the lion is the raven, though it is a little uncertain why that should be so (see further, *Comment* on v 41).

The lion is of course mostly portrayed in the Hebrew Bible as a creature hostile and dangerous to humans (Judg 14:5; Isa 31:4; Jer 2:15; Ezek 19:3); see also Keel, *Symbolism,* 79–80. Though humans of ancient times especially would rather eradicate the lion than feed it (Duhm, Strahan), God ensures its survival by providing food for it. Here, however, the focus is not on the adult lions but rather on the lion's cubs (so it appears) in vv 39b–40, who are utterly dependent on their parents for their sustenance (the adult lion is more than capable of finding its own food). A lioness will usually have two or three cubs, who are helpless in the first weeks of their life, begin to run around in their second month, but continue to need protection for the first six months. Job 4:11 has alluded to the fate of the cubs if the parent cannot find food.

The question to Job is whether he hunts (or can hunt) prey for the lions, and the answer is obvious. But does Yahweh mean to imply that he himself does? The theme of God providing food for the animals is a common enough topos (cf. on 38:39–39:30 above). But here, some would argue, he does not just "give" or "provide" (כון, v 41) the lions' food; rather, he becomes a lion himself and "hunts prey" (צוד טרף), an image that would hardly appeal to Hebrew shepherds whose flocks were not infrequently the victims of attack by lions (1 Sam 17:34–37; Isa 31:4). God the hunter would be an exceedingly rebarbative image, no doubt (Job had complained of it in 10:16). Newsom wonders if there may be an "oblique parody" of Job in these pictures of the lion and the raven, in that he has represented himself as a provider who delivered the poor when they cried out (שוע, as of the raven's young in v 41). If so, he will find it hard to accept that human society as constituted by God contains metaphorical lions and ravens—who are not checked by God.

Nevertheless, this line of interpretation is open to question. The rhetorical questions in this speech do not necessarily imply that what Job cannot do, Yahweh himself does. Because Job has not "walked in the depths of the abyss" (38:16), does it mean that Yahweh has? If the wild ox does not agree to "serve" Job and spend the night in his stall (39:9), does it mean that it labors in the fields for Yahweh's sake? In short, it may well be a mistake to envision Yahweh here as a hunter; he "provides" food for the lions, as he does for the ravens (v 41)—but by way of creating a world with a balanced system of provision for all its creatures. Lions hunt, ravens feed on carrion—but, we may aver, Yahweh does not. Nevertheless, he acknowledges, in the world he has made, lions kill for food—and he is not apologizing. Robert Alter has made the point well when he writes: "[T]he sharp paradoxes [the animal realm] embodies make us see the inadequacy of any merely human moral calculus—not only that of the friends, learned by rote, but even Job's spoken out of the integrity of suffering. In the animal kingdom, the tender care for one's young may well mean their gulping the blood of freshly slain creatures" ("The Voice from the Whirlwind," 38).

39 It is hard to know whether the "young lions" (כְּפִירִים) here are the "cubs" and "whelps" of the lion or lioness (לָבִיא) of the first colon. Is the parent lion out hunting prey for its young, in just the same way as the raven will be in v 41? Or are the "young lions" here mature beasts who need their appetite satisfied and are lurking in their lairs before going out in quest of prey? We seem to have the former picture at 4:11, and in the light of the reference to the raven in v 41 (and all the more so if that verse continues the depiction of the lioness, and not the raven at all; see *Note* c) we should probably see that here too.

40 Lions do not use caves as their dens, but lie in scrub and thickets (cf. Ps 10:9). The lurking of a lion in its covert is a metaphor in Ps 10:8–9 for the operations of the wicked, much of the same language being used: they "sit" (יֵשֵׁב, as here) "in ambush" (מַאְרָב; it is argued in *Note* b that the related noun אֹרֶב here means "lair" rather than "ambush"), in their "thicket" (סֻכָּה, as here). The picture of the lions couching in their lairs until the coming of dark when they will begin their hunting is alluded to also in Akhnaton's Hymn to the Sun (*ANET*, 370a).

41 Some have thought that the raven does not belong at this point, and might be better located together with the other birds, the hawk and the eagle (39:26–30). It would not be difficult textually to remove the raven altogether, since the letters of עֹרֵב *'ōreb* "raven" are the same as those of עֶרֶב *'ereb* "evening," and with the change of one vowel the line could be read "Who provides nourishment for it in the evening?" However, such an alteration is by no means obligatory. See further, *Note* c.

The connection with the lion in vv 39–40 (if one is to be sought) will probably be not so much that both are carnivorous (so Dhorme, Kissane) but that both, whether huge or small, need to hunt to feed their young (there is a striking contrast between the fearsomeness and savagery of the mighty lion and the comparative harmlessness of the quite small raven). For God as providing food for the young of the ravens, cf. Ps 147:9 (for the ravens in general, Luke 12:24); it should not be forgotten that the raven is ritually unclean (Lev 11:15; Deut 14:14), but Yahweh's provision of food transcends ritual law. The raven eats fruit, grain, insects, eggs, small birds; it does not capture its prey, but feeds on carcasses. A family of ravens includes three to six young. The parents take great care with their young, rarely leaving them alone. This contrasts with the popular ancient belief that ravens hate their young (cf. Tur-Sinai, 537–39; Pliny, *Natural History* 10.15.31, says they drive their young out of their nests). A patristic interpretation was that God feeds the young of the ravens with dew (Chrysostom, Gregory, Isidore), but of course, as everywhere in this speech, the activity of God does not supplant the natural processes but rather lies behind them. It remains the parents of the young birds that feed them.

For אכל "food" as the nourishment of birds of prey, cf. 9:26; 39:29.

39:1–4   *Strophe 2: The ibex.* Unlike the lion and the raven (38:39–41), the mountain goat or ibex (*Capra ibex nubiana*) is a shy, elusive creature (Habel). It is a graceful animal, and well suited for life in a harsh mountain environment; its light tan coloring provides good camouflage. Wild goats are about 30 inches high at the withers, bucks weighing 130–200 pounds, does 65–110 pounds. The male of the wild goat has long scimitar-shaped horns up to 3 feet long; the female has much shorter horns. In biblical lands there are several varieties of goat, from the large Syrian mountain goats to the dwarf goats of the Arabian peninsula. The Nubian ibex has a gestation period of 5 to 6 months; there are usually one or two young in a birth, and most kids are born in March. They form small herds of eight to ten. For the high mountains as the home of the wild goats, cf. Ps 194:18; and cf. also the place name Wildgoats' Rocks at 1 Sam 24:2 (3) (RSV). The ibex is to be found in modern Israel around Qumran, En-Gedi, and Sinai (Hartley).

The second colon of v 1 is thought by many to refer to another animal altogether, the deer, which belongs to the woodland fauna, rather than living on exposed mountains. It seems probable, however, that the term אילה here does not mean, as everywhere else in the Hebrew Bible, "hind" (female deer)—despite the lexica, the main English versions and many commentators (see *Note* e)—but "she-goat." In English too, a "doe" is usually a female deer, but in the context of goats, the term can be used for a she-goat (a "buck" is a he-goat). Its young are "kids." Although a "lovely hind" (אילת אהבים) and a "graceful she-goat" (יעלת־חן) are mentioned together at Prov 5:19 as metaphors of a wife, and it is not impossible that the two different animals appear side by side in the present verse, it seems more likely that we are reading of just one species.

1   Some have thought that Yahweh is represented as the "unseen midwife" (Habel) of these animals, overseeing the period of gestation and the delivery of the offspring. But, as noted above (*Comment* on 38:39–41), the fact that Job cannot do something does not imply that Yahweh does it. Here it is a matter of Yahweh's "knowing" (ידע) their giving birth (MT the "time" of their giving birth), "observing" or "marking" (שמר) when they bear their kids, "counting" (ספר) the months of their pregnancy, and "knowing" (ידע again) the time of their delivery. All these actions could be said of a relatively detached observer, though perhaps they represent the concern of an involved carer (de Wilde thinks that "know" really means "take care for"). Either way, however, Yahweh is being said to have a very intimate knowledge of this species—which is of course only one example of his relation with the world of the wild animals. There is no doubt an implicit contrast with the world of domesticated animals, such as sheep and cattle—a world that Job knows well (strangely, he does not seem to keep goats)–, where the human owners know the details of the animals' gestation, take a close interest in the birthing process, and sometimes need to assist it; the wild animals on the other hand benefit from no human concern—but they do have Yahweh's.

2   Job does not know how long their term of pregnancy is, or when the season of their foaling is. The latter is perhaps surprising, since one would expect it to be well known that the young of wild animals are generally born in the spring or early summer. So perhaps the term "count" (ספר) does not imply simply "in order to learn the number" but "take account of, consider, reckon" (cf. BDB, 707b; *DCH*, 6:185b; de Wilde), or perhaps even "prescribe" (Duhm; cf. Ezek 4:26). The question whether Job knows the "time" (עת) when the she-goats give birth should not be taken to imply that everything in the cosmos has its own fixed "time" (as Habel, Whybray). On counting months, we might compare the Ugaritic hero Aqhat, who apparently counts months till his wife should bear a child (II.ii.43; *CML*, 51b); this is no doubt different from *Aqhat* II.vi.26–22 (*CML*, 55a), "I will make you count years with Baal, months with the sons of El," which must refer to longevity. Job 3:6 has spoken of the "number of the months," but probably not with reference to gestation (against Tur-Sinai).

3 Some think that the language implies that for the she-goats "the process of parturition is speedy and uncomplicated" (Gordis; similarly Duhm, Driver–Gray, Fohrer, Strauss), others that it signifies the opposite. The rapid sequence of verbs without connective particles (asyndeton) suggests the former. There are many references in rabbinic and classical sources to wild goats, first collected by Samuel Bochart, *Hierozoicon sive bipartitum opus de animalibus Sacrae Scripturae* (London: Thomas Roycroft, 1663), 1.3.17.

4 These goats quickly become independent of their mother and her nurture. But the text does not actually say that it is Yahweh who looks after them in their lonely habitats. There is a lot of over-interpretation about in the commentaries by writers eager to extract moral and religious truths from these depictions of the animals. Strahan, for example, writes "If He is so kind to the wild goats, is it likely that He is the malignant Foe of man?" The purpose of this section of the divine speech seems rather to expound the diversity of life forms brought into being by Yahweh than to offer banal observations about his paternal care (note also, for example, the absence of any positive statement of Yahweh's concern for the ostrich, vv 13–18).

5–8 *Strophe 3: The onager.* Two main species of wild ass or onager were to be found in the region of the Bible: the Syrian (*Equus hemionus hemippus*), now extinct, and the Persian (*Equus hemionus*), now an endangered species. The onager was never domesticated, being temperamentally unsuitable. It feeds on small bushes and hardy grasses. Its color is reddish brown in the summer, lightening to yellowish brown in the winter; the belly is white or buff. The wild ass is said to be faster than all but the swiftest horses; speeds of up to 43 miles per hour have been recorded. It grazes on highland or lowland steppe.

To roam like a wild ass on the steppe is a familiar idiom (cf. 24:5). References to the wild ass in the Hebrew Bible allude to its quest for food (Job 24:5; Ps 104:11; Jer 14:6), its speed (Jer 48:6), its independence (Hos 8:9), and its avoidance of human society (Gen 16:12; Jer 2:24; Dan 5:21; Ecclus 13:19). In Assyrian culture, the fate of a violator of a treaty is to roam the desert "like an onager" (D. J. Wiseman, *The Vassal-Treaties of Esarhaddon* [London: British School of Archaeology in Iraq, 1958 (= *Iraq* 20)] 60, lines 419–21). It "stands for everything opposed to the world of human order and culture" (Newsom). A saying from the wisdom of the sage Ahiqar enshrines the stubborn independence of the onager: "He said to a wild ass, Let me ride you, and I will feed you. The wild ass replied, Keep your food, and spare me your riding" (*ANET*, 430b). For other examples of the symbolic significance of the onager, see F. Charles Fensham, "Common Trends in Curses of the Near Eastern Treaties and *kudurru*-Inscriptions Compared with Maledictions of Amos and Isaiah," *ZAW* 75 (1963) 155–75 (163–64). For the ass as an enemy of the gods in Egypt, see E. Brunner-Traut, "Esel," *Lexikon der Ägyptologie*, II (Wiesbaden: Otto Harrassowitz, 1977) 27–30 (28–29).

If Yahweh's interest in the lion and the raven (38:39–41) could be called solicitous, and in the wild goats (39:1–4) tender, it is hard to miss a certain delight in, perhaps almost an envy for (Andersen), the independence and freedom of the wild ass (so too Habel); Peake thinks that "the poet's sympathy throbs in his scorn and enthusiasm," but perhaps Strahan goes a little far in seeing here the poet's sympathy for wild nature and even perhaps "his own weariness of the conventions of civilization." Newsom, however, is no doubt correct in seeing here the "resistance of the sphere of the wild to incorporation within Job's organizing categories." What we might call "natural" is seen by the poet as God-given: it is Yahweh who has "freed" the onager, and "given" it certain environments as its home. All these details are part of the divine design.

5 The terms "wild ass" (פרא) and "onager" (ערוד) refer to the same animal. Who "set free" (שלח) and "loosed" (פתח) the onager? The answer here is not Yahweh (against Fohrer), but rather "no one" (so too Duhm). It is not that the onager is conceived of as "really a domestic ass, that patient drudge, released from bondage" (Rowley); it is an animal that by definition has not been tied with cords, and that therefore has never been loosed (loosing bonds [מוסר] also in 12:18). The language is very reminiscent of that in 3:17–19 for the freedom enjoyed in Sheol, though there it is a case of being loosed from bonds: there the slave too is "free" (חפשי) from his master, and the prisoner (אסיר, cf. מסרות "bonds" here) does not "hear" (שמע) the voice of the "taskmaster" (נוגש).

6 Unlike the domesticated ass, who knows its master's stall for sleeping (Isa 1:3; on this sense of אבוס see *Note* d on 39:9 below), the wild ass makes its home far from any human dwelling. Though salty soil is comparatively infertile (cf. turning a fruitful land into a salty waste, Ps 107:34, and sowing a city with salt, Judg 9:45), saltings (מלחה), i.e., marshes covered by the sea at high tide, are often suitable for grazing and thus are not necessarily "barren land" (KJV). In fact the salt is needed by herbivorous animals to supplement their diet. But such salt lands are uninhabited by humans (cf. Jer 17:6). The Great Rann of Kutch in northwestern India, a saline clay desert of more than 10,000 square miles, remains the prime habitat of the Asiatic wild ass. Inhospitable though such lands may be to humans, the "steppe" (ערבה) is "home" (בית) for the onager, "his place in the order of things" (Habel); there is probably not a specific reference to the Arabah, the Jordan valley and rift valley from the Dead Sea southwards to the Gulf of Aqaba (against Hartley).

Is there perhaps a hint of a special affection of Yahweh's for the onager that he speaks of himself in the first person as the one who gave it the steppe as its home? It is quite a rare thing in the divine speeches for Yahweh to use the "I" form, if we exclude proems and peroration (38:4, 9, 10 [*bis*], 11, 23; 40:15; 41:11 [3] [?], 12 [4] [rhetorical]; "God" in the third person at 39:17).

7 Why does the wild ass "laugh at" (שחק) the din of the city, "far from the madding crowd's ignoble strife" (Thomas Grey)? Not so much because the "freedom of the open country is more exciting to the wild ass than all the hubbub of the city" (Rowley), or because it "finds exhilarating exercise for his powers in fleet scouring of the mountain ranges" (Peake), or because it pities or scorns its domesticated cousin (cf. Driver–Gray "a contempt for man's angry shoutings"), but because it need not *fear* the city's noise (Driver–Gray, Fohrer). The term "laugh," with the same sense of "not fear," is used also of the ostrich at v 18, of the war horse at v 22, of Leviathan at 41:21 (29), and of a restored Job at 5:22.

A נֹגֵשׂ is usually an oppressor (e.g., Isa 14:4; Zech 9:8) or "taskmaster" (e.g., Exod 3:5; Isa 60:17); this is the only place where the term refers to the driver of an animal, though cf. Isa 9:3, where deliverance from oppression is conceived metaphorically as the release of an animal from hard service under a yoke, a staff for the shoulder, and a rod of a driver.

8 There is little pasture on the hills, so the wild ass must paradoxically "pay the price of its freedom" (Rowley) in searching high and low for its food. The point is not so much that it is not fastidious about what it eats (Kissane), but that given the aridity of the mountain steppe land it must make do with anything edible. Even here, though, there is no pathetic element in the depiction; rather the onager's total freedom to go where it likes is being brought to the fore. Davidson notes that Arab poets "compare a deep ravine or abyss to the 'belly' of the wild ass, which is often lank and empty from want of food." For the mountains as the habitat of the wild ass, cf. Ps 104:10–11; on its hunger for green herbage, cf. 6:5; Jer 14:6.

9–12 *Strophe 4: The wild ox.* The domestic ox and ass are often mentioned together (e.g., Exod 20:17; 21:33; Isa 1:3; usually the ox is first, but not in 6:5; 24:3), so here too their wild counterparts form a pair. The wild ox (רֵים) was understood as the unicorn by the LXX (so too KJV), and the rhinoceros by Aquila and the Vulgate, but is now generally identified with the aurochs (*Bos primigenius*), the ancestor of most of our modern cattle, but now extinct (the last specimen is said to have died in 1627). This massive animal was about 10 feet long, and could weigh over a ton, half the size of a rhinoceros; it had two thick, long, curved horns. Like all oxen, the aurochs was herbivorous, and frequented woods and hills; it was usually found in small herds, though males were sometimes solitary.

The aurochs was hunted in Egypt, Palestine, and Babylonia. It is usually identified with the *rimu* mentioned often in the annals of the Assyrian kings. On the Ishtar Gate at Babylon (*ANEP*, fig. 760), the blue tile decoration is of alternating rows of aurochs and dragons. In Palestine, Baal hunts aurochs in the marshes of Lake Huleh (*Baal* I.i.19 [*CML*, 109b]; III.vi.18 [*CML*, 115a]; *Aqhat* II.vi.20 [*CML*, 55a]). In classical literature, see Herodotus, *Hist.* 7.126 (in Macedonia); Aristotle, *Hist. anim.* 1.1 (488a); 2.1 (499a); Pliny, *Natural History* 8.30.72 (in Ethiopia).

In the Hebrew Bible the huge and dangerous horns of the aurochs are especially mentioned (Num 23:22; 24:8; Deut 33:17; Pss 22:21 [22]; 92:10 [11]); cf. also Pss 29:6; 34:7. In Deut 33:17 the horns of a domesticated ox are praised as being like those of an aurochs. Here, since it is a wild beast, not only is the aurochs untameable (vv 9–10), but it is unreliable also (vv 11–12).

In the background of all that is said about the aurochs is the life of its cousin, the domesticated ox, which is a byword for docility and obedience. Unlike the farmer's ox, the aurochs would not be "willing" or "agreeable" (אבה) to "slave" (Moffatt) for a human master, it would not stand all night in a stall, it would not submit to be bound with ropes and set to work in plowing, it could not be relied on to carry out the heavy work of the farm, it could not be trusted to trudge from field to threshing floor pulling a cart piled high with sheaves. The implied comparison is striking, and even perhaps intended to be amusing (so, e.g., Fedrizzi).

This depiction is another site in the chapter where there is a danger of overinterpretation. Whybray remarks that "the freedom of the life of the wild ox from human servitude is clearly seen as one of Yahweh's most glorious achievements."

Newsom, noting that domestication involves domination (v 10) but also a relationship of trust (vv 11–12), deduces that "These categories, so evocative of Job's hierarchical and paternalistic moral world, break down when confronted with the wild ox. The aurochs's utter alienness confounds Job's customary ways of thinking." And Andersen comments, "Is there a hint that its Creator might be more fearsome and unmanageable?" In fact, the aurochs figures here primarily, and perhaps exclusively, as a further demonstration of the almost unimaginable diversity of the world Yahweh has created.

9 It is the aurochs that is focalized, not Job. It is not a question of whether Job would be able to bring the aurochs into submission to human desires, but whether the mighty beast would be agreeable to spending a life of drudgery.

10 In modern times a harrow is used for scouring the earth, as distinct from the plow, which turns up the earth in furrows. Whether true harrows were known in ancient Palestine is unclear (cf. N. H. Richardson, *IDB*, 2:526). The Palestinian plow was a "scratch plow," which did not turn over the soil; the ground needed to be cross-plowed (i.e., at right angles to the first plowing) for a second time, a month later than the first plowing in December. The picture here is of the ox following the farmer ("after you"); in plowing, it would precede. For oxen plowing, cf. 1:14. On שׂדד "harrow," cf. G. Wallis, *THWAT*, 7:710.

Keeping the ox in the furrow when plowing is an effort for the farmer; de Wilde reports Palestinian farmers calling out to their beasts, *'uq'od* "stay in the furrow!" and *'inzil* "go in the furrow!" Can Job imagine tying an aurochs with cords to keep it plowing straight furrows? On plowing, see Dalman, *Arbeit und Sitte*, 2:81–115; Oded Borowski, *Agriculture in Iron Age Israel* (Winona Lake, IN: Eisenbrauns, 1987) 47–56; Borowski, "Observations on Terracing, Plowing, Fallowing, etc. in the Early Iron Age," in *Early Israelite Agriculture: Reviews of David C. Hopkins' Book The Highlands of Canaan* (ed. Olystein Sakala LaBianca and David C. Hopkins; Occasional Papers of the Institute of Archaeology, Andrews University 1; Berrien Springs, MI: Andrews University Press, 1988) 9–16.

11 Presumably the strength of the aurochs was greater even than that of the domesticated ox, the principal draft animal in ancient times (Edwin Firmage, *ABD*, 6:1129), even though the ox's strength and endurance was less than that of the horse, and oxen typically worked in pairs. The domesticated ox is very clearly a reliable worker, which will perform onerous routine tasks unflinchingly on behalf of the farmer who has left to it his "toil, heavy work" (יגיע).

12 Not being at all domesticated, the aurochs could not be relied on to dutifully bring in the grain from the fields to the threshing floor on a cart (as Amos 2:13; carts pulled by cattle also at 1 Sam 6:19; 2 Sam 6:3, 6; asses and camels do not pull carts but bear burdens).

13–18 *Strophe 5: The ostrich.* The theme of this marvelous cameo about the ostrich seems to be its paradoxical nature (similarly Fohrer). A bird that cannot fly is almost a contradiction in terms; it is no elegant stork or high-flying falcon (v 13). And there is a second paradox: although it is reputedly a stupid creature, negligent of its young (vv 14–17), it has no difficulty escaping its predators because of its astonishing speed (v 18).

Once again, as in vv 4, 9–12, there is tendency among commentators to over-interpretation. Andersen, for example, asks whether Job is "being reminded that some of his behaviour might be equally lacking in understanding." And Habel thinks that "the ostrich's lack of 'discernment' and wisdom places her in the same category as Job whom Yahweh challenged to demonstrate 'discernment' (38:4)." Newsom too finds "symbolic associations" in the depiction, such as the connection of the uninhabited wastelands where it lives with the demonic, the sense of exclusion from human society (as in 30:29), and the opposition between culture and nature. All these are examples of thinking too laterally; it is preferable to focus the mind's eye on what is central in the description of this strange bird.

The ostrich (*Struthio camelus*) is the largest of birds, the males reaching as high as 8 feet and weighing between 200 and 300 pounds. Ostriches live in flocks of five to 50, normally in the company of grazing animals like antelope and zebra. The ostrich is, after the cheetah, the fastest land animal in the world, capable of running with 11-foot strides (Tristram, *Natural History*, 237, measured strides of up to 28 feet) at speeds over 30 miles per hour for as long as half an hour, with a top speed of 50 miles per hour; it can change direction abruptly at full speed. As it runs, its wings are outspread but it is too heavy to lift itself off the ground. In biblical times it was found in semi-desert regions of Syria, Arabia, and Africa, and, within Palestine, both in desert regions, where it is often depicted in rock art, and on the coastal plain (ostrich eggs from the Chalcolithic period at Gilat; cf. Avraham Negev and Shimon Gibson, *Archaeological Encyclopedia of the Holy Land* [London: Continuum, 1972] 201). The ostrich is in levitical law an unclean bird (Lev 11:16; Deut 14:15).

It should be noted that much questionable information about the ostrich is contained in Bible encyclopedias, especially the older ones. And there is a dubious tradition among commentators to represent the ostrich as a comic figure, which is to be deplored (as Andersen's "This comical account suggests that amid the profusion of creatures ... some are there just for God's entertainment and ours"; similarly Habel, Hartley, Whybray).

13 In this very difficult verse, the one thing that seems clear is that the ostrich is being contrasted with the stork and the falcon (for alternative views, see *Notes* g, f). The most striking difference among these birds is the fact that the ostrich, despite its impressive display of wings and feathers (its wings beat joyfully [עלס]), cannot lift itself from the ground, whereas the stork (חסידה) is famous for its elegant and apparently effortless flight (cf. Zech 5:9), while the falcon (נץ) is equally proverbial for the height and the speed of its flight (the peregrine falcon can fly at 100 miles per hour and dive at 200 miles per hour). On the use of this verse among the Syrian commentators especially, see François Nau, "Etude sur Job, xxxix, 13 et sur les oiseaux fabuleux qui peuvent s'y rattacher," *JA* 215 (1929) 193–236.

14 Most birds make nests above ground for their eggs, but the ostrich, being unable to fly up to a tree, lays its eggs in a shallow depression in the soil, making them very vulnerable. In the wild, up to 90% of ostrich nests are destroyed by predators (Brian C. R. Bertram, *The Ostrich Communal Nesting System* [Princeton: Princeton University Press, 1992]). The nest is made by the cock scooping out a hollow in the ground. A hen will typically lay 10 eggs, but the other hens in the same family unit (one cock and 2 to 6 hens) may lay in the same nest, so that a nest may contain as many as 50 eggs; but only 20 or so of them will be incubated. The incubation period of 45 days is shared by the male and the major female, the male incubating during the night, the major hen during the day (Bertram found that the male spent 70% of the incubating time on the nest). The secondary hens do not incubate the eggs, and the major hen will give preference to her own eggs, ensuring that they are always being incubated at the center of the nest. The eggs that are not incubated will rot or be destroyed. On warm days the major female might leave the nest for periods, especially during the early days of incubation (when she is still laying eggs, one every two days), though she will never go far from it; and she will cover the eggs with sand as protection against the sun.

There was an ancient belief that the female ostrich actually abandoned her eggs, and let the heat of the sun hatch them (so the *Physiologus* of the second century BCE, cited by Pope; for the text, see Dimitris Kaimakis, *Der Physiologus nach der ersten Redaktion* [Meisenheim am Glan: A. Hain, 1974] 147b [no. 540]), but the belief is not substantiated by observation; in fact the hen sits on the eggs not to warm them but to protect them from the heat of the sun. The text may suggest that the hen "warms" (חמם) the eggs herself, but if she is sitting on them, no foot or wild animal (v 15) could crush them. We should understand the verb to mean that she "lets them be warmed," and thus incubated, by the sun (as, e.g., RSV, NIV), even though this image is apparently counterfactual.

15 It seems very risky to leave the eggs on the ground, but as it happens, the ostrich's eggs weigh up to 3 pounds and are hard enough, it is said, for a human to stand on one without breaking it, the shell being a quarter of a inch thick (Bertram has a photo of himself with his wife on his back standing on an egg). So it would be an exceptional foot that could crush the egg (it is apparently a human foot that is in view here, since wild animals are dealt with in the next colon). In saying that the female ostrich "forgets" (שכח) that a foot may crush the eggs, it is not implied that she once knew it; it is a heightened way of saying that she never knew or realized it (cf. "forget" [נשׁה] in v 17).

16 In accord with the popular belief, the ostrich is said to deal harshly (קשׁה) with its young; in Lam 4:3 also it is said to be "cruel" (אכזר). Here the reference may be exclusively to its treatment of its eggs (so, e.g., Peake), rather than to its hatched chicks (as Duhm), perhaps with a reference to the habit of female ostriches of running away from their young (or, from the nest) when hunters approach (George Cansdale, *Animals of Bible Lands* [Exeter: Paternoster Press, 1970] 193)—though this is no doubt in order to distract the hunters from the young. Wetzstein reported that when the ostrich finds its nest has been discovered it tramples on the eggs itself—and that would no doubt seem a callous act (but would the ostrich herself be able to break the shells?). Her labor that may be in vain is that of laying her eggs (a similar idiom in Isa 49:4).

17 It is not implied that the female ostrich once had wisdom, and that God has taken it from her. Just as the loosing of the bonds of the wild ass (v 5) meant that it never had bonds, so here too the deprivation of wisdom means that the ostrich has never had wisdom. In folk culture the stupidity of the ostrich is famous (there is an Arab proverb, "more stupid than an ostrich"), but it not certain why. Pliny thought it was because it would thrust its head into a bush and think its whole body was concealed (*Natural History* 10.1.2), but Diodorus Siculus (2.50.6) thought that was a sign of wisdom, to protect the weakest part of the body. Contrary to the popular belief, ostriches do not hide their heads in the sand, though an incubating female that is disturbed may stretch out its neck and head flat on the ground, merging in color with the dusty gray of the landscape. Others say the ostrich is stupid because it will eat anything offered to it, such as stones or iron (Aelian, *On Animals* 14.7; Pliny *Natural History* l. 10.1; cf.

Shakespeare's "I'll make thee eat iron like an ostrich" [*Henry VI, Part 2* 4.10.30]); but in fact these hard objects (stomach stones or gastroliths) are explained by naturalists as an aid to its digestion, facilitating the breaking up of tough, fibrous foods.

Once again, it is over-interpretation to claim, on the ground that the ostrich has no share (חלק) in understanding, that "[e]ach creature apparently had an allocated 'portion' (*ḥlq*) of natural 'discernment' (*bīnā*) to enable procreation and preservation" (Habel). The "forgetting" of the ostrich is explicit in v 15, where it is restricted to its apparent carelessness about leaving its eggs in the nest, and there is no grand theory about animals' intelligence in the background here.

18 Though the ostrich may appear stupid, in one respect at least it is superior to most other animals: its speed. "[T]he fleeing ostrich spreads out the feathers of its tail like a sail, and by constantly steering itself with its extended wings, it escapes its pursuers with ease" (Wetzstein, cited by Delitzsch). With that facility, it has no cause to fear any predator, animal or human. As has been observed, the female will, when attacked, often get up from the nest, spreading out its tail feathers (the whole action seems to be described as "spreading [its plumes] high," מרא מרום), and make off at high speed, drawing its attackers away from the eggs. Pliny chimes with the Joban author in remarking that its speed exceeds that of a mounted horseman (*Natural History* 10.1.2). Its laughter at its pursuers (שׂחק), perhaps a reference to its startled cries, shows its lack of fear (cf. the same word of the wild ass in v 7). Obviously the verse refers to the hunting of ostriches, as is depicted in Egypt (Keel, *Entgegnung*, 72 fig. 1). An Assyrian cylinder seal (9th–8th cent. BCE, Pierpont Morgan Library) shows a man throttling an ostrich, which is delivering a powerful kick to him (*ISBE*, 3:620). Another fine seal depicts a rider on a galloping horse hunting an ostrich with a lance (Cyrus H. Gordon, "Western Asiatic Seals in the Walters Art Gallery," *Iraq* 6 [1939] 3–34 [27–28, and Plate X, 86]). M. E. L. Mallowan presents a drawing of a glazed vase depicting a rider on a horse hunting ostriches in his *Nimrud and Its Remains* (London: Collins, 1966), 1:119–20 fig. 61. See also Armas Salonen, *Vögel und Vogelfang im alten Mesopotamien* (Helsinki: Suomalainen Tiedeakatemia, 1973) 165. The same phrase, "the horse and its rider," is found in the song of Moses in Exod 15:1.

Many say that the last phrase forms a transition to the next cameo about the horse (e.g., Dhorme, Fohrer). But it is questionable whether the poet cares about "transitions," and, more than doubtful whether in any case the horse used for hunting ostriches is the same as the war horse of vv 19–25.

19–25 *Strophe 6: The war horse.* This vignette of the horse has been called by many the most brilliant of all the animal depictions in these chapters. Longer than all the other animal descriptions, as if the poet could not restrain himself, the strophe is remarkably vivid. Andersen suggests that "the nervous energy of this mettlesome steed can be felt more effectively when the poetry is arranged in short staccato lines," each colon as a line in its own right. The horse is nowhere in the Hebrew Bible so much the object of appreciation as here; prophets and wisdom teachers are more prone to warn of the folly of amassing stables of horses and of trusting in the prowess of horses (Isa 30:15–16; 31:1, 3; Prov 21:31; Ps 33:17; cf. 147:10). Israel's memory includes some bad experiences with horses, such as the pursuit by the pharaoh's chariots (Exod 14:9, 23; 15:19, 21), and defeats at the hands of foreign armies with their chariots (cf., e.g., Judg 1:19; 2 Kgs 13:7).

The horse appears to have been originally a native of central Asia. In biblical times, it was used mostly for pulling chariots (for agriculture the ox was much preferred, and for transport the donkey), especially in Mesopotamia and Egypt; in the Bible, cf. Gen 14:9; Deut 20:1. Of the c. 140 references to horses in the Hebrew, not many more than a score may be references to their being ridden; very rarely are they said to be used for transport (of a corpse, 2 Kgs 14:20 || 2 Chr 25:28; for display, Esth 6:8–11; 8:10). Here the horse may perhaps be ridden by an archer, but it is even more likely to be a chariot horse (see Sigmund Mowinckel, "Drive and/or Ride in O.T.," *VT* 12 (1962) 278–99, who allows as references to riding only Gen 49:17; Isa 62:13; Esth 8:10, 14; Zech 1:8, 9, 11; 10:5; 12:4 [*si v.l.*]; Jer 6:23; 50:42; Ezek 38:15. See further, Joseph Wiesner, *Fahren und Reiten in Alteuropa und im alten Orient* (Der Alte Orient 38, 2–4: Leipzig: J. C. Hinrichs, 1939); M. A. Littauer and J. H. Crouwel, *Wheeled Vehicles and Ridden Animals in the Ancient Near East* (Handbuch der Orientalistik 2B/1; Leiden: E. J. Brill, 1979). For a depiction of a (female) deity riding a horse, see Manfred Görg, "Die Göttin auf dem Kriegspferd," *BN* 13 (1980) 32–34. For a collection of horse and rider figurines, many of the eighth century BCE, see Raz Kletter, "Pots and Polities: Material Remains of Late Iron Age Judah in Relation to Its Political Borders," *BASOR* 314 (1999) 19–54 (38–41). A fine seal impression from the same period depicting a prancing horse is studied by Gabriel Barkay, "'The Prancing Horse'—An Official Seal Impression from Judah of the 8th Century B.C.E.," *Tel Aviv* 19 (1992) 124–29.

Some think that the presence of the horse here is odd, in that the horse is not a *wild* animal (cf. Andersen, Newsom, Whybray), but one used by humans and evidently trained for a human purpose. But unless we argue that the strophe was not an original part of the poem (as, e.g., Strauss), we should accept that what the animals here (and in chaps. 40–41) have in common is not precisely that they are *wild* but that they are not *tamed* or domesticated, like the ox or ass or like sheep or goats; the war horse may be *trained*, but it is not domesticated (Aristotle already discussed the classification of animals as wild and tame, pointing out how the categories overlap [*Hist. anim.* 1.1 (488a)]).

Habel suggests that a heightened language is used of the horse, as if it were pictured as a "magnificent godlike figure" whose appearance is like a theophany. The horse has the "might" (גבורה) of a god (cf. 12:13; 26:14), its neck is adorned with "thunder" (רעמה), its body "quakes" (רעש), its snort is full of "majesty" (הוד), its voice spreads "terror" (אימה), it "quakes" (רעש) and "shakes" (רגז)—both expressions associated with earthquakes—, it "swallows" (גמא) the earth as if in an earthquake. But closer philological study does not support this estimation: for "might" is not only ascribed to gods, the horse's neck is more probably adorned with a "mane" than with "thunder," "quaking" does not only refer to the movement of the earth, but also, for example, to the waving of fields of grain (Ps 72:16), the "majesty" of the horse's snort might only be its "sound" (see *Note* 20.d), "shaking" is often used of humans in many different circumstances, and "swallowing" the ground is an idiom frequently attested for swift horses (if indeed the word does not simply mean "stamp").

What is special about the war horse is its will, which drives its energy. Humans may think that horses they use in battle are doing their bidding and are subservient to their needs; the poet knows differently, that this creature acts from its own self, reaching ecstatic heights of pleasure in the midst of awful and lethal danger.

19 The strophe opens with another of those questions to Job that imply "You did not, but I did." It is not Job, but Yahweh, who in his creation of the horse, endowed it with its strength, and, therewith, all its other qualities as well. The horse's "strength" (גבורה) is not often alluded to, but what is meant here is no doubt not just its physical strength but also its "valor," as of a warrior (Judg 8:21; Isa 28.6); at Ps 147:10 it is said, in a reflection of the typical negative evaluation of horses, that Yahweh does not delight in the strength of a horse; but here, where the focus is much more on the horse as a creature of Yahweh's, he evidently does. The hair of the horse's mane, the clothing of its neck, is the symbol of its strength, just as Samson's hair was of his strength (Judg 16:17).

20 Horses can "quiver" (רעשׁ) with their whole body when excited, appearing to become bigger than their real size. But how are they like locusts? Horses are also compared to locusts in Jer 51:27, where the point of comparison is their number; but that cannot be at issue here, where the focus is on a single horse. In Joel 2:4 locusts are compared to horses running, but that does not evoke the image of "quivering" (there is in Rev 9:7 a surreal picture of locusts like horses). Gordis has perhaps solved the problem by picturing a plague of locusts descending on crops and making the whole field appear to quake.

The one sound made by a horse that could be called "terrible" is most probably the neigh or whinny, the longest and loudest of horse sounds. It is terrible only to those unfamiliar with it, since it is no more than a call to other horses to identify themselves. The horse will neigh with its head held high, looking around for others, and will repeat the neigh several times if not answered. The horse is not a warlike creature, and, being a herd animal, is more excited in a battle situation by the prospect of meeting other horses than by any bloodlust or excitement for battle (contrast David Odell, "Images of Violence in the Horse in Job 39:18–25," *Prooftexts* 13 [1993] 163–73, who sees here strains of the presence of evil in the world). The horse's interest in the horses of the enemy is interpreted by the humans, incorrectly though not unnaturally, as a desire to be engaged in the battle.

The only other horse sound that could be referred to here (it is not the blow, the nicker, the squeal, or the scream) is the snort. A snort is produced when the horse holds its head high and exhales through the nose with its mouth shut, creating a vibration in the nostrils for a second (it can be heard up to 30 feet away); it is the horse's sign that it senses danger. Such a sound would be relevant to the context of battle, but it could hardly be called "terrible." It is a little strange to speak of the "majesty" or "splendor" (הוד) of a horse's neigh; the term is almost always used of the majesty of God or the king (cf. G. Warmuth, *TDOT*, 3:352–56).

21 The first colon depicts the impatience of the horse, the second its eventual charging off into the battle. Pawing the ground (חפר lit. means "dig") is a well-known sign of equine impatience, some horses putting a lot of energy into producing the loud clap their hoof makes on contact with the ground, scooping up the earth with the toe of their hoof. Perhaps that could be called "rejoicing in strength," though some think that "in strength" fits better with the second colon (see *Note* c). The "plain" or the "lowland" (עמק) often features in the Hebrew Bible as the location for battles, especially since it is only on relatively flat ground that the chariot can be deployed (cf. Gen 14:8; Josh 17:16; Judg 7:1; Isa 22:7; 28:21). The verb to "go out" (יצא) is especially used for setting out for war (e.g., 1 Sam 8:20; Isa 42:13).

22 From the human point of view the horse is courageous, but the image here is rather of its "unrestrained eagerness" (Newsom) or perhaps rather reckless abandon in the face of danger. From the horse's point of view the excitement and exhilaration is mostly the prospect of a wild rendezvous with other horses (Jer 8:26 speaks of a horse plunging [שׁטף] into battle). On laughter (שׂחק) as signifying the absence of fear, see above on vv 7, 18. The horse does not "flinch" (שׁוב, lit. "turn back"), as is said also of the lion in Prov 30:30. The horse will obviously have been trained not to startle at the noises of war; Aelian speaks of the Persians so training their horses (*On Animals* 16.25). The "sword" is a metonym for the whole business of "battle."

23 Though there is no reference to any chariot being drawn by the horse, we should not assume that the horse is being ridden by a bowman. In fact, the absence of any human rider or driver is a remarkable feature of the depiction. If, as is more likely, the horse is drawing a chariot, the weapons—arrows in a quiver (אשׁפה), spear (חנית), javelin (כידון, unless it is a short sword; see *Note* d)— will all form part of the charioteers' equipment; one charioteer will concentrate on driving, the other one or two on deploying their weapons. If, on the other hand, the horse is being ridden, the "quiver" with its rattling arrows may be the bowman's, strapped to the side of his horse. But to add to the quiver, with its bow (not mentioned) and its arrows, also a spear and a javelin flashing in the sunlight, would seriously encumber the archer, who is finding it hard enough to draw his arrows from the quiver, fasten them to his bow and then aim and shoot them while riding bareback without stirrups (as riders did in the ancient world). It would seem better in that case to see the spear and javelin as weapons hurled at the archer (and his horse), like the spear of v 22b, before which the horse does not flinch. If that is so, we may wonder whether the "quiver" is not rather the "quiverful of arrows," i.e., the arrows themselves (rather than their container) that the horse and its rider encounter as they enter the battle (see *Note* a and *Translation* above). On the rattling quiver, cf. Homer, *Iliad* 20.71; Virgil, *Aeneid* 9.660; Ovid, *Metamorphoses* 6.332.

24 The previous two verses (vv 22–23) are set within the battle, following the horse's "charging out" (יצא) in v 21b to meet the enemy. Now it appears that in vv 24–25 we are back with the scene before the battle, for the trumpet has yet to sound (vv 24b, 25a), and the battle will be scented "from afar" (v 25b).

The horse's "stamping" makes the earth shake, as if in an earthquake; in parallel passages the earth is shaken by the tramping of warriors (Isa 9:5 [4]) or by chariots (Jer 47:3) or by the neighing of stallions (Jer 8:16). To the same effect, Virgil speaks of the war horse's hoof "shaking with galloping tread the crumbling plain" (*Aeneid* 8.596). Its "raging" (רגז) is its excitement or impatience, not its anger, which is a rare emotion in horses, and not at all relevant to the present context.

To "swallow" (גמא) the earth is a well-attested idiom for devouring distance; in Arabic a swift horse is called a "swallower." But these verses seem to be about the horse's impatience for the moment of battle to come rather than its speed in getting to it, so there is something to be said for an alternative interpretation of the verb as "denting" the ground. Virgil's description of the war horse likewise has its hoof "scooping out the ground" (*Georgics* 3.87–88).

The war horse has obviously been trained to recognize the trumpet blast as the signal to charge forward. It is the same in Virgil's description: "If even from afar the battle sounds he cannot stand still; he pricks up his ears, quivers in his limbs, and snorts the gathered heat from his nostrils" (*Georgics* 3.83–85).

On the sounding of the trumpet to begin battle, cf. Judg 3:27; Jer 4:19; Amos 3:6. Cf. also Aeschylus, *Seven against Thebes* 393–94, where the war horse "chafes while it awaits the trumpet's blare." Virgil, *Aeneid* 9.503–4, has the trumpet "ringing out from afar its terrible cry" (cf. also 11.474–75).

25 The depiction of the horse has on the whole avoided anthropomorphism, and that has no doubt been one of its strengths poetically. But here, in a climactic position, human speech is attributed to the horse, when it "says" (אמר) "Hurrah!" (האח), an ejaculation that is found elsewhere as a cry of satisfaction, at Pss 35:21, 25; 40:16; Isa 44:15 (16); Ezek 25:3; 26:2; 36:2.

Horses have a excellent sense of smell; in the battle situation they will no doubt smell the blood and the adrenaline, but the main attraction, as noted above, will be the presence of other horses. Cf. for horses snorting in anticipation of a battle, Homer, *Iliad* 4.227; Ovid, *Metamorphoses* 3.704–5 "a brave horse snorts and shows his love for the fight, when the trumpeter's brass gives the signal for attack"; horses snorting after a battle are mentioned in *Iliad* 16.506; Lucretius, *De rerum natura* 5.1076 "with nostrils wide open it snorts at the battle" (though there it is a battle between stallion and mares). It is of course the humans rather than the horses who are excited by the distant sounds of officers shouting orders and of warriors' battle-cries.

The thunder (רעם) of the captains is their shouting of orders during the battle (cf. Horace, *Odes* 2.1.17–22, though he imagines the cries striking terror into the horses); the shouting (תרועה) will refer to the war-cries of the combatants, rather than to their shouts of victory.

26–30 *Strophe 7: The hawk and the vulture.* The final animal depiction in this first divine speech brings together two birds of prey that were probably not carefully distinguished from one another in the world of the Bible, the hawk (נץ) and the eagle or vulture (נשׁר). Here the hawk's migratory instinct is the theme in v 26, and the eagle's inaccessible home and predatory habits in vv 27–30.

There may be an implicit contrast of these birds with the ostrich: here we have birds that can fly (vv 26–27), that make their nests in places where predators cannot reach them (vv 27b–28), that are directed by wisdom (v 26a), and that care for their young by providing food for them (v 30).

26 The hawk (נץ), an unclean bird according to Lev 11:16 and Deut 14:15, is found in a variety of species; hawks are small- or medium-sized birds of prey, some of which are well known as migratory. The two halves of this verse are to be taken closely together: the "understanding" (בינה) that has been implanted in the hawk—though not by Job—is its knowledge of seasonal migration. The migration of large soaring birds, especially birds of prey, in the Middle East is still observed today, over 100,000 migrants being recorded in one late summer period of six weeks. The Levant sparrow-hawk (*Accipiter brevipes*), for example, breeds in the Balkans and southern Russia, and winters in southwest Iran, Syria and the southeastern Mediterranean as far as Egypt. The young are hatched in early June, and leave the nest in August, after a fledging period of about six weeks. A couple of weeks later they migrate to the south, "spreading their wings to the south" in the language of the poet, and covering 100 or 150 miles in a day. It is said that most of the world's population of sparrowhawks in dense swarms pass down the Arabah valley and over Eilat during a few days in mid-April (www.birdingisrael. com; www.osme.org). The migration of hawks was already noted by ancient writers such as Aelian (*On Animals* 2.43) and Pliny (*Natural History* 10.9.22).

Habel maintains that the presence of "understanding" (בינה) in this strophe forms a deliberate inclusio with the use of the term in 38:4, where Job is asked to say where he was when Yahweh laid the foundations of the earth—if he knows "insight" or "understanding" (בינה). Yet בינה is not the only word for wisdom used in the opening of this divine speech (cf. דעת "knowledge" in 38:4 and ידע "know" in 38:4, 5), and the knowledge possessed by migrating hawks is hardly to be compared with the knowledge that Job lacks.

27 Associated with the hawk is another bird of prey, the eagle or vulture (the one Hebrew term, נשר, does duty for both species; there is an unfortunate tendency, since the time of the Greeks, to use "eagle" when the reference is positive and "vulture" when it is negative, as Keel, *Entgegnung,* 69 n. 234, notes). This estimation was unknown in ancient Egypt or Mesopotamia, where the vulture was either venerated or at least frequently depicted (Kronholm, *TDOT,* 10:80). If the lion is the king of the earth, the eagle is the king of the air (Shakespeare's "feather'd king" [*The Phoenix and the Turtle,* 11]); cf. 2 Sam 1:23, where Saul and Jonathan are eulogized by David as "swifter than eagles, stronger than lions." It is the swiftness of the eagle that is referred to at Deut 28:49; Jer 48:40; 49:22; but here it is perhaps the wisdom of the eagle in making its dwelling and nest in inaccessible places (unlike the ostrich!), from which vantage point it can locate its prey without fail. The hawk has been pictured soaring aloft in order to start its annual migration; the eagle here flies into the sky in order to attain its mountain home. In an Assyrian inscription of Sennacherib, an inaccessible fortress is said to be "like the nest of the eagle" (N. Na'aman, "Sennacherib's 'Letter to God' on His Campaign to Judah," *BASOR* 214 [1974] 25–39).

The species of eagle or vulture referred to here has been identified by G. R. Driver as the griffon vulture (*Gyps fulvus fulvus*) (see *Note* a for details). It feeds on the carcasses of large animals, mostly on what has been left by wolves and bears.

28 Other biblical references to the nest of the eagle or vulture in inaccessible places are Jer 49:16, where Yahweh threatens the Edomite enemy that "Though you make your nest as high as the eagles, I will bring you down from there," and Obad 4, where Yahweh says to the same enemy, "Though you soar aloft like the eagle, though your nest is set among the stars, thence I will bring you down." Cf. also Num 24:21, where it is said of the Kenites, living in much the same region as the Edomites, that their "nest is set in the rock." Aristotle (*Hist. anim.* 8 [9].32 §619a) and Pliny (*Natural History* 10.3.6) already noted that eagles make their nests on high rocks. Cf. also Milton, *Paradise Lost* 7.424: "The Eagle and the Stork / On Cliffs and Cedar tops thir Eyries build." For שכן "dwell" parallel with לין "dwell," not specifically "spend the night," cf. Ecclus 14:26.

29 The eagle's or vulture's stoop on its quarry we have already met with at 9:26 (*q.v.*), but here it is only suggested, not described. Here we read only of the eagle's keen eyesight. The term "watches" is lit. "digs" (חפר), as if it were search-ing for something hidden like treasure. Some vulture species rely on their sense of smell to find prey, but the griffon vulture, if that is what we have here, is com-pletely reliant on its excellent sight.

Aelian, *On Animals* 1.42 (cf. 2.26), says the eagle is the most sharp sighted of birds; cf. Homer, *Iliad* 17.674–75; Apuleius, *Florida* 2; Shakespeare, *Love's Labour's Lost* 4.3: "A lover's eyes will gaze an eagle blind." On the eagle's quest for food, cf. Shakespeare's "empty eagle" (*Henry VI, Part I*, 3.1; *Venus and Adonis*, 55).

30 The prey taken by the eagle/vulture is brought back to the young in the nest. The young of the griffon vulture mature very slowly, and stay in the nest for the first seven weeks (www.animal-information.com).

Raptors do not of course distinguish between the carcasses of humans and of other animals; but the poet, perhaps drawing upon a proverbial phrasing (cf. Matt 24:28; Luke 17:37 "Where the corpse is, there the eagles will be gath-ered") focuses on the corpses of humans who are slain (חלל "slain" always refers to humans; cf. *DCH*, 4:236a). For ancient knowledge of the eagle feeding on flesh and blood, cf. Aelian, *On Animals* 10.14 (specifically as food for its young). The picture of the fledgling eagles feeding on human carcasses is a grim note of conclusion to this carnival of the animals. Whybray comments: "The inclusion of these unpleasant and even repulsive beasts side by side with the 'harmless' ones in the list of his creatures reflects a concept of the breadth of the 'wisdom' of the creator-god which leaves the reader in wonderment."

Nothing is said explicitly here about the food of the eagles' young being pro-vided by Yahweh, as had been said about the young of the raven (38:41). If it is implied, it is nevertheless no doubt not the main point of the description. The central point of all the animal descriptions seems rather to be that Yahweh has filled his created world with a vast variety of life forms, each with its own qualities and peculiarities, in which he evidently takes a delight. That is the substance of his reply to Job's demand for justice; it can only mean that the interests of the human being Job cannot be a top priority for Yahweh.

40:1–2 This first divine speech concludes with a peroration, addressing the hearer Job directly in the context of the legal disputation. Whatever the argu-ment may be that has been presented by Yahweh in his accounts of the structures of the universe and of the world of the wild animals, it has all been in the service of the lawsuit in which he is engaged with Job.

40:1 It is more than a little strange that this verse, which apparently marks the beginning of a new speech, should come just before what is seemingly the last verse of the first divine speech. LXX does not have it, and some commenta-tors (e.g., Driver–Gray) delete it. But perhaps it is no more strange than those headings in the Elihu speeches (34:1; 35:1; 36:1) that seem only to indicate that Elihu continues to speak, not that a new speech begins. The effect of the verse is to restore attention to the speech as an address by Yahweh to Job, a fact that has rather fallen into the background as the sketches of the animals have come more and more into the limelight. When Yahweh is about to begin his second speech, a fuller heading will be used: "And Yahweh answered Job *from the tempest* and said" (v 6).

The proposal has sometimes been made to remove these verses (40:1–2) of the divine speech, together with Job's first response (40:3–5), to the end of the second divine speech, viz. following 41:34 (26). The second divine speech is indeed remarkable for the absence of any final address to Job, but there is no pressing reason for rearranging the material at this point.

2   Job has demanded a lawsuit with God, and now he is getting it. At the beginning of Yahweh's speech, it was more a trial of strength that Job was led to expect ("gird up your loins like a man," 38:3), and throughout the speech the didactic flavor may have seemed more that of the schoolroom than of the courtroom; but now the naked legal language shows what is really going on. Job has a "legal dispute" (ריב, *rîb*) against God (9:3; 31:35), which makes him God's "legal accuser" (מוכיח, *mōkîaḥ*). Talk about "strength" or "knowledge" is no more than metaphoric; the bottom line is that Job has arraigned God, and the issue is simply justice. Now that Job has made the final statement of his dispute (chap. 31) and now that his opponent has answered (chaps. 38–39), it will be for Job to say how he responds. As in any lawsuit, at this point either he will have to admit the truth of his opponent's reply or else he will have to offer new arguments. What we have before us is not a moral issue, as if it had become a matter of whether Job still felt competent to criticize Yahweh, but a legal issue, of whether he will concede his case or continue to maintain it. A formulation like that of Rowley's incorrectly makes the meaning of v 2 revolve about moral rights rather than matters of legality: "Either Job must show his competence to criticize God by answering the questions that have been put to him or he must forfeit his right to criticize." No, it is not a matter of whether Job has the right to criticize, but of whether—in view of how Yahweh has responded to Job's accusation of divine injustice—Job intends to continue pressing his case, whether he still believes there is a case for Yahweh to answer.

The legal significance of the verse, as a critical stage in the progress of the lawsuit, is beyond doubt; but it is not so certain what precise point the lawsuit has now reached. It may be that Yahweh is asking directly whether Job now intends to capitulate and concede his case ("Will the contender with the Almighty yield [סור]?," as Dhorme, Pope). If so, the second half of the verse would be best rendered, "Or will God's accuser answer [the foregoing speech]?" That would be stating the two possible responses that Job could now make. But it is perhaps marginally better to suppose that in the first half of the verse Yahweh urges Job to correct (יסר) him—if he thinks his argument is at fault. In that case, the second half of the verse would be equivalent to the first half. Either way, the ancient Hebrew legal procedure is in force: there is no judge, but the parties continue to argue until one or other of them concedes.

Explanation

It might be possible to imagine a book of Job in which there was no reply from heaven to Job's insistent demand for justice. It would indeed be a dismal book if Job were shut up to the sound of his own voice and that of his friends, but it is conceivable. It would be a great tragedy, but it would not be untrue to real life, where a voice from the tempest rarely breaks through the clouds, and the cries of sufferers are not commonly met with a theophany. The appearance of Yahweh, though ardently longed for by Job, and craved by the readers who are inevitably sympathetic to the character Job, is not utterly indispensable.

Yet Yahweh speaks. Surprisingly, we might say, if we could ever come at this book as if for the first time. Surprising, too, is the speech both for what it contains and for what it omits. It might be possible to imagine a divine speech more brusque, or more brief, or else more defensive than this one. But it is not possible to imagine a speech more worthy of its speaker. The poet has excelled himself in composing for Yahweh a speech that is grand and elegant—and at the same time, one that conveys an unrivalled perception of the purposes of God in his creation of the universal order.

In this speech, Yahweh presents himself as the master architect of a world order that is astonishing in its profusion. In two sets of strophes, one of ten and one of seven, no two of them alike, he sketches features of the world—its mysterious physical structure and its strange life forms—that lie beyond human comprehension. The scope is vast, but it is not in the least comprehensive, for everything here is impressionistic and suggestive: everything Yahweh depicts carries with it hints of an untold variety in the grand design.

Yet there is one thing about this speech we may be sure of: whatever is said in this speech is not what it means, it is not the purpose and point of it. Everything here is by way of illustration—but of what? The principles of the world order that lie behind the vivid cameos are never stated, but are left unspoken, for the readers to discern and construct for themselves. Earlier, in the *Comment* on 38:1–41:34 (26), I suggested ten such principles, though other readers will undoubtedly read differently. I remarked that the speeches imply, though they never state, that (1) the world has been neatly and tidily organized by Yahweh; (2) though he is immensely powerful, it is his skill and insight rather than his power, that is the principal thing about him; (3) Yahweh knows his universe intimately; he loves the detail, and, even when he is taking the broadest view, he only ever works with examples; (4) sustenance and nurture are key objectives of the universal order, creation being not just a past event, but a daily repeated process; (5) the world is hugely various, and the purposes of the universal structure are infinitely multiple; (6) the world order is described without abstracts, without oppositions, without propositions, without generalizations; it works with images, and maximizes impact and affect; (7) there is no problem with the world; there is nothing that Yahweh needs to set right; (8) not only is there no problem with the world, but every element in it is a source of constant delight to its maker; (9) the universal order can be described without reference to humans; (10) and nevertheless humans are, surprisingly, the measure of all things in the divine plan.

If such are the meanings of the first divine speech (or some of them), where does that leave Job? None of them is a matter with which he has been concerned in his speeches, for he has been focused, not to say fixated, on a single issue, that of justice in the governance of the world. The issue of justice had come to a head in his speech of chaps. 23–24, where it took two forms: there was the question of justice for himself, a man gravely wronged, and there was the broader question of justice in the world at large, in a world where the wicked prospered and the innocent came to an untimely end. And then in his final speech, in chap. 31, he had reviewed every aspect of his life, given himself a clean bill of health, and challenged God to justify his cruel handling of him by proving him a sinner. Now when Yahweh speaks, Job will expect, and we will expect, that in some way or another Yahweh will address Job's complaints.

Yet all that Job has been striving for is totally ignored, and everything that Job has spoken is castigated as an ignorant obscuring of the divine plan for the universe (38:2). Yahweh's speech, both on its surface and in its hidden meanings, has been hugely attractive, but when we realize that it has only been so at the cost of ignoring the concerns of the suffering Job we are inevitably much less sympathetic. How can Job respond?

Job's First Reply (40:3–5)

Bibliography

Curtis, John Briggs. "On Job's Response to Yahweh." *JBL* 98 (1979) 497–511. **Dailey, Thomas F.** "The Wisdom of Divine Disputation? On Job 40.2–5." *JSOT* 63 (1994) 105–19. **Glazov, Gregory Yuri.** "The Significance of the 'Hand on the Mouth' Gesture in Job xl 4." *VT* 52 (2002) 30–41. **Maher, Seán.** "The Answer of Job to God." *PrIrBibAss* 28 (2007) 48–65.

Translation

3 a *Then Job answered Yahweh, and said:*

4 a *Behold, I am of little account*[b]*; what*[c] *can I answer you?*[d]
I put my hand over my mouth.
5 *I have spoken once, but I shall not speak again,*[a]
twice,[b] *but I shall say no more.*[c]

Notes

3.a. The verse is deleted (*frt*) by Beer (*BH²*).

4.a. De Wilde and others (see *Comment*) move vv 4–5 to precede 42:2, combining the two responses of Job into one.

4.b. קלל is "be light," and so "be contemptible" (rather than "be swift," as it is at 7:6; 9:25; 2 Sam 1:23; Jer 4:13; Hab 1:8; Good finds a hint of this sense here, but such a use of both meanings at the same time cannot be paralleled). It is used elsewhere of persons at Gen 16.4–5; 1 Sam 2:30; Nah 1:14; Ecclus 8:16, but always in reference to the judgment of one person upon another. Here it is Job's assessment of himself.

Some have doubted this understanding, however. Symm had ἰδοὺ κούφως ἐποίησα "behold, I have acted lightly," and Vg *leviter locutus sum* "I have spoken lightly." Hence Dhorme "if I have been thoughtless," JB "my words have been frivolous." Similarly Hölscher "I was rash." But these senses of קלל are not attested elsewhere, and do not suit the remainder of the colon.

4.c. מה is understood by Curtis, "On Job's Response," 506, as a relative, not an interrogative pron (cf. *DCH*, 5:159b §8), thus "[I was too light in respect of that] which [I answered you]." This is not only very awkward, but it also overlooks the presumptively temporal contrast between the perf of קלתי "I was light" and the impf of אשיבך "I will answer." Ehrlich, followed by Gray, reads, instead of מה אשיבך "what shall I answer you?," מהשיבך "[I am too insignificant] to answer you," with מן and the inf constr of שוב hiph.

4.d. The verb is שוב "return," in the causative as here "make return, answer."

5.a. ולא אענה, lit. "and I will not answer." Hitzig, followed by Budde, Duhm, Ehrlich, Strahan, Driver–Gray, Dhorme, Beer (*BHK*), Hölscher, Fohrer, Gray, JB, reads אשנה (from שנה "repeat"); the vb has been used in this sense at 29:14, and it would be more natural here, in parallelism with the second colon "I shall say no more," lit. "I shall not add" (לא אוסיף). NAB "I will not do so again" appears to accept that reading, but it is not noted in its *Textual Notes*, and the translation may be just a free rendering of the MT. The emendation is accepted in the *Translation* above. Rowley defends the MT as meaning that Job "declines to answer" God; similarly Kissane, Gordis.

5.b. Driver–Gray, Gordis, JB rightly recognize that "twice" (שתים) here really signifies "more than once" (though not "too often," as Kissane suggests)—for Job has by no means only two speeches to his credit! It is the same sense in 33:14.

5.c. לא אוסיף, lit. "I shall not add." Andersen thinks RSV's "I will proceed no further" suggests giving up and NEB's "I will do so no more" suggests the renunciation of an admitted fault. See further, *Comment.*

Form/Structure/Setting

This is the shortest speech of the book, obviously forming a single strophe. In genre it belongs with the legal disputation, with its language of "speaking" (דבר, v 5), "replying" (שוב hiph, v 4), and "answering" (ענה, v 5, if the text is sound). The "ascending numeration" (Gordis's term) in "once, twice" (v 5) belongs rather to wisdom.

The function of the speech is to signal Job's intention to give up the prosecution of his case. Its tonality, however, is not a little ambiguous: has Job reached a moment of enlightenment, or does he feel that all his worst fears—that he is destined never to receive an adequate response—have been realized? The absence of any note of regret and the reference to his previous speeches without any qualification of them suggest that he still stands by what he has said. Here the tonality seems in conflict with the literary form, for in the legal disputation it is usual for a resolution to be achieved by one of the parties abandoning the case (cf. Fohrer). Job, however, both gives up speaking and at the same time draws attention to his previous speeches as if they are still valid.

There is little point in designating one of the verses as a nodal verse, but it is obvious that it is v 6 that carries the weight of the speech.

Comment

40:3–5   This is a crucial passage for the development of the book as a whole, for here it might appear that Job announces the withdrawal of his complaint—or, to be more exact, his decision not to proceed further with it. If he did, it would be an astonishing moment, for nothing in Job's complaint against God has been addressed in the divine speech of chaps. 38–39, and capitulation on Job's part is almost inexplicable (Tur-Sinai thought the original text must have contained some motivating explanation).

Yet the wording of Job's brief reply does not suggest capitulation; if anything, it is a re-affirmation of his previous speeches. It is probably best to regard it as a first indication of how he will respond. Only in 42:4–6 will we hear his final decision; here he merely says that he will not further prosecute his case. Hartley remarks that "the loquacious Job has been reduced to a few words," but the point is rather that it is his own autonomous decision to make no further statement of his case.

Some have argued that the second speech of Yahweh was not originally part of the book, and that the two short speeches of Job in 40:3–5 and 42:4–6 belonged together (so, e.g., Driver–Gray). Duhm, Peake, Strahan, Hölscher, Fohrer, and de Wilde move 40:3–5 to the beginning of Job's second response in 42:4–6. Not many support that view today, but it does highlight effectively the question why Job should here respond to Yahweh before the deity has finished speaking.

3   The line is a formal parallel to v 1, where "Yahweh addressed Job and said."

4–5   Job's response to Yahweh's first speech makes us wonder whether Job has been listening very carefully to Yahweh. Yahweh's chief concern has been to sketch his conception of the universe, and Job responds by saying, "Behind, I am of little account." He has taken the divine speech personally, and heard nothing in it but the admittedly reproachful and belittling remarks of Yahweh. Yet making Job feel small has not been Yahweh's main intention. If Yahweh wrongs Job by ignoring the matter of justice, Job wrongs Yahweh by discarding the main thrust of Yahweh's speech. Perhaps it has been hard for the "greatest of the Easterners" (1:3) to acknowledge that he also can be "of small account," but it should not have come as a surprise to Job.

In acknowledging that he is "of small account" (RSV), "unworthy" (NIV), and "carry[ing] no weight" (NEB), Job uses the term קלל, lit. "be light." It is the opposite of כבד "be heavy," i.e., be invested with honor (כבוד), and signifies Job's recognition of the vast difference in status and honor between God and himself (Terrien, Newsom, Matitiahu Tsevat, "The Meaning of the Book of Job," *HUCA* 37 [1966] 93–106 [91]). The wording may not even express Job's own evaluation of himself, but be his assessment of how Yahweh evidently regards him—as if to say, I can see that in your eyes I am of small account. It would certainly be wrong to infer that Job thinks of himself as "contemptible," and any talk of human "nothingness" in comparison with the divine (as, e.g., Fohrer) is out of order. It has not been Yahweh's purpose in his speech to humiliate Job, nor even to stress Job's incapacity. His purpose seemed rather to expound his intentions for the universe he created (see further, *Comment* on 38:1–41:34 [26]). But he has said enough about Job's ignorance and lack of power for Job's response here to be a reasonable inference. Even if Yahweh did not intend to put Job down, that has been the effect of his words.

The gesture of laying the hand on the mouth has appeared at 21:5 to represent silence brought about by involuntary horror or amazement; but here, as also at 29:9, it shows only a conscious restraint as a mark of deference. So understood, there is a close parallelism between the two cola: his sense of inferiority in honor is expressed by his gesture of deference (cf. Gregory Yuri Glazov, "The Significance of the 'Hand on the Mouth' Gesture in Job xl 4," *VT* 52 [2002] 30–41). Mayer I. Gruber, *Aspects of Nonverbal Communication in the Ancient Near East* (Studia Pohl 12; Rome: Biblical Institute Press, 1980) 289 n. 1, rightly points out that the gesture itself signifies no more than silence, and that any connotations such as reverence or astonishment are supplied by the context.

In saying that he has spoken once, indeed more than once (an example of "number parallelism"; cf. Watson, 145), Job seems to be affirming what he has previously said, not rescinding it. In saying that he will speak no more, he may only mean that he has said all that needs to be said. "He continues to stand behind his avowal of innocence" (Hartley). He certainly does not indicate any regret for what he has said.

It is striking that Job does not capitulate (against Weiser); he does not withdraw a word he has said, he does not abandon his case, he does not admit that God is in the right or that he is in the wrong, he does not confess his sins or apologize for what he has said. He only announces that he will not reiterate his case. And that means that his words remain spoken, his criticism of God is still in force, his sense of injustice is as great as ever; he is still "sticking to his guns" (Andersen). Even if it is going too far to see defiance here (as Good suggests) or even a reiterated complaint that God has still not answered his accusations, it is more than doubtful that this is the mark of a dawning recognition in Job that Yahweh is right, a gradual discovery of his place in the universe (Terrien), "a dogged submission to authority, a sad acceptance of the inevitable" or even "the silence of satisfaction ... mingled with awe" (Strahan, quoting T. K. Cheyne, *Job and Solomon, or, The Wisdom of the Old Testament* [London: Kegan Paul, Trench &

Co, 1887] 54). Jung perceptively remarked: "Guileless as Job's speech sounds, it could just as well be equivocal" (C. J. Jung, *Answer to Job* [trans. R. F. C. Hull; London: Routledge & Kegan Paul, 1954] 31). And Andersen is probably right that "Job's reply is somewhat evasive [though not feigning submission, as David Robertson, *The Old Testament and the Literary Critic* (Philadelphia: Fortress Press, 1977) 52] and not at all a satisfactory end to the matter." Wilson too rightly recognizes that Job both refuses to press his case or to withdraw it, depicting Job's refusal to speak as the biblical equivalent of "taking the fifth" (invoking the Fifth Amendment in the US Constitution in order to avoid self-incrimination). The second divine speech will be by no means superfluous.

Explanation

Job's first response seems at first timid and insipid, as well as surprisingly brief; it is a far cry from the passion and the scope of his previous speech in chaps. 29–31. Yet the position he adopts is quite subtle, and not at all without bravery. He admits to feeling humiliated by Yahweh, and yet he does not concede that he is in the wrong. If anything, he wants what he has said, over and over again (which is what "once ... twice" [v 4] means), to stand on the record. He is adding nothing to what he has said, but he is withdrawing nothing.

If Yahweh has slighted Job by paying no attention to the question of justice that has occupied Job, Job reciprocates by paying no attention to the substance of Yahweh's speech and referring only to the feeling it has provoked in him ("I am of little account," v 5).

At the end of this first reply by Job the two parties to the dispute are in a stand-off, and it is by no means evident how their debate can continue. Neither has conceded any ground to the other. Nor has either, it appears, really been listening to the other.

Yahweh's Second Speech (40:6–41:34)

Bibliography

Boerhave, Jakob. *Aandagtig beschouw, naauwkeurig ondersoek, ende uitvoerige verklaaring van den Behemoth, en den Leviathan: afgetekend van den Heere God in het XLsten en XLIste hoofdstuk van het Boek Jobs, als de Heere Job uit een onweder andermaal antwoordde.* Leiden: Luchtmans, 1737. **Caquot, André.** "Leviathan et Béhémoth dans la troisième «Parabole» d'Hénoch." *Semitica* 25 (1975) 111–22. **Cohen, Matityahu.** "More on the Subject 'Behemoth and Leviathan' in God's Second Lecture to Job." In *Proceedings of the Twelfth World Congress of Jewish Studies, Jerusalem, July 29–August 5, 1997, Division A: The Bible and Its World.* Ed. Ron Margolin. Jerusalem: World Union of Jewish Studies, 1999. 65–78. **Dahood, Mitchell.** "Hebrew-Ugaritic Lexicography II." *Bib* 45 (1964) 393–412. ———. *Ugaritic-Hebrew Philology: Marginal Notes on Recent Publications.* BibOr 17. Rome: Pontifical Biblical Institute, 1965. **Driver, G. R.** "Difficult Words in the Hebrew Prophets." In *Studies in Old Testament Prophecy Presented to Professor Theodore H. Robinson.* Ed. H. H. Rowley; Edinburgh: T. & T. Clark, 1950. 52–72. ———. "L'interprétation du texte masorétique à la lumière de la lexicographie hébraïque." *ETL* 26 (1950) 337–53. ———. "Mythical Monsters in the Old Testament." In *Studi orientalistici in onore di Giorgio Levi della Vida,* I. Pubblicazioni dell'Istituto per l'Oriente 52. Rome: Istituto per l'Oriente, 1956. 234–38. ———. "Presidential Address" [Job 41.21]. In *Volume du Congrès, Strasbourg 1956.* VTSup 4. Leiden: E. J. Brill, 1957. 1–7. ———. "Problems in Job." *AJSL* 52 (1936) 160–70. **Ebach, Jürgen.** *Leviathan und Behemoth: Eine biblische Erinnerung wider die Kolonisierung der Lebenswelt durch das Prinzip der Zweckrationalität.* Philosophische Positionen 2. Paderborn: Schöningh, 1984. **Engseth, Jerome M.** "The Role of Behemoth and Leviathan in the Book of Job." In *Church Divinity, 1987.* Ed. John H. Morgan. Bristol, IN: Wyndham Hall Press, 1987. 119–37. **Erikson, Gösta, and Kristina Jonasson.** "Jobsbokens juridiska grundmönster." *SvTK* 65 (1989) 64–69. **Gammie, J. G.** "Behemoth and Leviathan: On the Didactic and Theological Significance of Job 40:15–41:26." In *Israelite Wisdom: Theological and Literary Essays in Honor of Samuel Terrien.* Ed. John G. Gammie. Missoula, MT: Scholars Press, 1978. 217–31. **Gibson, John C. L.** "On Evil in the Book of Job" [as represented by Leviathan and Behemoth]. In *Ascribe to the Lord: Biblical and Other Studies in Memory of Peter C. Craigie.* Ed. Lyle M. Eslinger and Glen J. Taylor. JSOTSup 67. Sheffield: JSOT Press, 1988. 399–419. **Gutmann, Joseph.** "Leviathan, Behemoth and Ziz: Jewish Messianic Symbols in Art." *HUCA* 39 (1968) 219–30. **Kinnier Wilson, J. V.** "A Return to the Problem of Behemoth and Leviathan." *VT* 25 (1975) 1–14. **Spangenberg, I. J. J.** "Om te teologiseer oor God en lyding: Opmerkings na aanleiding van Harold Kushner se interpretasie van Job 40:9–14." *HervTS* 50 (1994) 990–1004. **Whitney, Kenneth William, Jr.** *Two Strange Beasts: A Study of Traditions Concerning Leviathan and Behemoth in Second Temple and Early Rabbinic Judaism.* Diss. Harvard, 1992. Cf. *HTR* 85 (1992) 503–4. **Wolfers, David.** "The Lord's Second Speech in the Book of Job." *VT* 40 (1990) 474–99.

Bibliography: 40:6–14 (Introduction)

Cheyne, T. K. "The Text of Job." *JQR* 9 (1896–97) 573–80. **Dahood, M.** "*HDK* in Job 40,12." *Bib* 49 (1968) 509–10. **Driver, G. R.** "Leviathan and Behemoth." In H. H. Rowley, "The Istanbul Congress of Orientalists and the Old Testament." *VT* 1 (1951) 313–18 (314). **Gradl, Felix.** "Ijobs Begegnung mit Gott: Anmerkungen zu Ijob 40,6–8.9–14." In *Ein Gott, eine Offenbarung: Beiträge zur biblischen Exegese, Theologie und Spiritualität: Festschrift für Notker Füglister zum 60. Geburtstag.* Ed. Friedrich V. Reiterer. Würzburg: Echter, 1991.

65–82. **Mettinger, Tryggve N. D.** "The God of Job: Avenger, Tyrant, or Victor?" In *The Voice from the Whirlwind*. Ed. Leo G. Perdue and Clark Gilpin. Nashville: Abingdon Press, 1992. 39–49. **Patton, Corrine L.** "The Beauty of the Beast: Leviathan and Behemoth in Light of Catholic Theology." In *The Whirlwind. Essays on Job, Hermeneutics and Theology in Memory of Jane Morse.* Ed. Stephen L. Cook, Corrine L. Patton, and James W. Watts. JSOTSup 336. Sheffield: Sheffield Academic Press, 2001. 142–67. **Poliakoff, Michael B.** "Jacob, Job, and Other Wrestlers: Reception of Greek Athletics by Jews and Christians in Antiquity." *Journal of Sport History* 11/2 (1984) 48–65.

Bibliography: 40:15–24 (Behemoth)

Balentine, Samuel E. "'What are human beings, that you make so much of them?' Divine Disclosure from the Whirlwind: 'Look at Behemoth'." In *God in the Fray: A Tribute to Walter Brueggemann.* Ed. Tod Linafelt and Timothy K. Beal. Minneapolis: Fortress Press, 1998. 259–78. **Beal, Timothy K.** "Behold Thou the Behemoth: Imaging the Unimaginable in Monster Movies." In *On Imag(in)ing Otherness: Filmic Visions of Living Together.* Ed. S. Brent Plate and David Jasper. Minneapolis: Fortress Press, 1998. 197–211. **Behrmann, Almuth.** *Das Nilpferd in der Vorstellungswelt der Alter Ägypter.* Europäische Hochschulschriften 38/52. Frankfurt a.M.: Peter Lang, 1989–1996. **Bernat, David.** "Biblical *Waṣfs* beyond Song of Songs." *JSOT* 28 (2004) 327–49. **Bochart, Samuel.** *Hierozoicon sive bipartitum opus de animalibus Sacrae Scripturae.* London: Thomas Roycroft, 1663. 5:753–69. **Botterweck, G. J.** *TDOT,* 2:17–20. **Brentjes, Burchard.** "Gelegentlich gehaltene Wildtiere des Alten Orients." *Wissenschaftliche Zeitschrift Halle–Wittenberg* 11 (Gesellschafts- und sprachwissenschaftliche Reihe 6; 1962) 703–32 (708–9). **Caquot, André.** "Behémot." *Sem* 45 (1966) 49–64. **Cheyne, T. K.** "Behemoth." *EB* (1899) 1:519–23. **Couroyer, B.** "Béhémot = hippopotame ou buffle?" *RB* 94 (1987) 214–21. ———. "Le «glaive» de Béhémot: Job xl,19–20." *RB* 84 (1977) 59–79. ———. "Qui est Béhémot?" *RB* 82 (1975) 418–43. **Davis, Simon.** "The Large Mammal Bones." In *Excavations at Tell Qasile, Part Two.* Ed. Amihai Mazar. Qedem 20. Jerusalem: Institute of Archaeology, Hebrew University, 1985. 148–50. **Day, John.** *God's Conflict with the Dragon and the Sea. Echoes of a Canaanite Myth in the Old Testament.* University of Cambridge Oriental Publications 35. Cambridge: Cambridge University Press, 1985. **Drewer, Lois.** "Leviathan, Behemoth and Ziz: A Christian Adaptation." *Journal of the Warburg and Courtauld Institutes* 44 (1981) 148–56. **Gordis, Robert.** "Job and Ecology (and the Significance of Job 40:15)." *HAR* 9 (1985) 189–202 [= *Biblical and Other Studies in Memory of S. D. Goitein.* Ed. Reuben Ahroni]. ———. "Job xl 29—An Additional Note." *VT* 14 (1964) 491–94 [= *The Word and the Book.* New York: Ktav, 1976. 355–57]. **Gutmann, Joseph.** "Leviathan, Behemoth and Ziz: Jewish Messianic Symbols in Art." *HUCA* 39 (1968) 219–30. **Haas, Georg.** "On the Occurrence of Hippopotamus in the Iron Age of the Coastal Area of Israel (Tell Qasîleh)." *BASOR* 132 (1953) 30–34. **Herrmann, Wolfram.** "Eine notwendige Erinnerung." *ZAW* 104 (1992) 262–64. **Horwitz, Liora Kolska, and Eitan Tchernov.** "Cultural and Environmental Implications of Hippopotamus Bone Remains in Archaeological Contexts in the Levant." *BASOR* 280 (1990) 67–76. **Jackson, Wayne.** "Was the 'Behemoth' of Job 40:15 a Dinosaur?" http://www.apologeticspress.org/rr/faq/r&r8612b.htm. **Kaiser, Otto.** *Die mythische Bedeutung des Meeres in Ägypten, Ugarit und Israel.* BZAW 78. Berlin: A. Töpelmann, 1959. 140–52. **Keel, Othmar.** "Zwei kleine Beiträge zum Verständnis der Gottesreden im Buch Ijob (xxxviii 36f., xl 25)." *VT* 31 (1981) 220–25. **Kees, Hermann.** "Zu den Krokodil und Nilpferdkulten des Ägyptens." In *Studi in memoria di Ippolito Rosellini nel primo centenario della morte (4 guigno 1843).* Ed. Evaristo Breccia. Pisa: Lischi, 1949–1955. 2:143–52. **Keller, Otto.** "Nilpferd." In his *Die antike Tierwelt.* Leipzig: Engelmann, 1909–13. 1:406–7. **Lang, Bernhard.** "Job xl 18 and the 'Bones of Seth'." *VT* 30 (1980) 360–61. **Mathis, Claudia.** "'Sieh doch den Behemot!' Die zweite Gottesrede Ijob 40,6–41,26." *BN* 112 (2002) 74–86. **Nowak, Ronald M.** *Walker's Mammals of the World.* Baltimore: Johns Hopkins University Press,

6th ed., 1999. 1347–50. **Perdue, Leo G.** *Wisdom in Revolt: Metaphorical Theology in the Book of Job.* JSOTSup 112. Bible and Literature Series 20. Sheffield: Almond Press, JSOT Press, 1991. 221–26. **Rinaldi, Giovanni.** "L'ippopotamo" [photo of Egyptian tomb of Meruruka, c. 2420 BCE]. *BeO* 14 (1972), Table IX, after p. 208. **Ruprecht, Eberhard.** "Das Nilpferd im Hiobbuch. Beobachtungen zu der sogennanten zweiten Gottesrede." *VT* 21 (1971) 209–31. **Thomas, D. Winton.** "Job xl 29b: Text and Translation." *VT* 14 (1964) 114–16. **Wakeman, Mary K.** *God's Battle with the Monster: A Study in Biblical Imagery.* Leiden: E. J. Brill, 1973. 113–17. **Wolfers, David.** "Is Behemoth Also Jewish?" *Dor* 14 (1985–86) 220–27. ———. "Bulrush and Bramble" [Job 40:26]. *JBQ* 19 (1990–91) 170–75. **Wolters, Al.** "Text and Script of the LXX Vorlage of Job 40:17b." *Textus* 17 (1994) 101–15.

Bibliography: Chap. 41 (Leviathan)

Allen, Ronald Barclay. *The Leviathan-Rahab-Dragon Motif in the Old Testament.* Diss. Dallas Theological Seminary, 1968. **Bernat, David.** "Biblical *Waṣfs* beyond Song of Songs." *JSOT* 28 (2004) 327–49. **Bochart, Samuel.** *Hierozoicon sive bipartitum opus de animalibus Sacrae Scripturae.* London: Thomas Roycroft, 1663. 5:769–95. **Brentjes, Burchard.** "Gelegentlich gehaltene Wildtiere des Alten Orients." *Wissenschaftliche Zeitschrift Halle–Wittenberg* 11 (Gesellschafts- und sprachwissenschaftliche Reihe 6; 1962) 703–32 (709–10). **Caquot, A.** "Le Léviathan de Job 40, 25–41, 26." *RB* 99 (1992) 40–69. **Cheyne, T. K.** "Leviathan." *EB*, 3:2770. **Day, John.** *God's Conflict with the Dragon and the Sea. Echoes of a Canaanite Myth in the Old Testament.* University of Cambridge Oriental Publications 35. Cambridge: Cambridge University Press, 1985. ———. "Leviathan." *ABD*, 4:295–96. **Day, John N.** "God and Leviathan in Isaiah 27:1." *BibSac* 155 (1998) 423–36. **Drewer, Lois.** "Leviathan, Behemoth and Ziz: A Christian Adaptation." *Journal of the Warburg and Courtauld Institutes* 44 (1981) 148–56. **Duin, Kees van.** "Der Gegner Israels: Leviatan in Hiob 3:8." In *Give Ear to My Words: Psalms and Other Poetry in and around the Hebrew Bible. Essays in Honour of Professor N. A. van Uchelen.* Ed. Janet Dyk. Amsterdam: Societas hebraica amstelodamensis, 1996. 153–59. **Emerton, J. A.** "Leviathan and *ltn*: The Vocalization of the Ugaritic Word for the Dragon." *VT* 32 (1982) 327–31. **Fishbane, Michael.** "Rabbinic Mythmaking and Tradition: The Great Dragon Drama in b. Baba Batra 74b–75a." In *Tehillah le-Moshe: Biblical and Judaic Studies in Honor of Moshe Greenberg.* Ed. Mordechai Cogan, Barry L. Eichler, and Jeffrey H. Tigay. Winona Lake, IN: Eisenbrauns, 1997. 273–83. **Gibson, John C. L.** "A New Look at Job 41.1–4 (English 41.9–12)." In *Text as Pretext: Essays in Honour of Robert Davidson.* Ed. Robert P. Carroll. JSOTSup 138. Sheffield: JSOT Press, 1992. 129–39. **Gray, George Buchanan.** "Crocodiles in Palestine." *PEQ* (1920) 167–76. **Gregg, Tresham Dames.** *Leviathan: The Iron-Clads of the Sea Revealed in the Bible: An Exposition of Job XLI.* London: William Macintosh, 1864. **Groenbaek, Jakob H.** "Jahves kamp med dragen: om baggrunden for kampmotivet i de gammeltestamentlige skabelsesforestillinger." *DTT* 47 (1984) 81–108. ———. "Baal's Battle with Yam: A Canaanite Creation Fight." *JSOT* 33 (1985) 27–44. **Gunkel, Hermann.** "Leviathan." In his *Schöpfung und Chaos in Urzeit und Endzeit: Eine religionsgeschichtliche Untersuchung über Gen 1 und Ap Joh 12.* Göttingen: Vandenhoeck & Ruprecht, 1895. 41–61. **Gutmann, Joseph.** "Leviathan, Behemoth and Ziz: Jewish Messianic Symbols in Art." *HUCA* 39 (1968) 219–30. **Hamilton, Mark W.** "In the Shadow of Leviathan: Kingship in the Book of Job." *RestQ* 45 (2003) 29–40. **Huntington, Ronald M.** "Leviathan." In *Tradition as Openness to the Future: Essays in Honor of Willis W. Fisher.* Ed. Fred O. Francis and Raymond Paul Wallace. Lanham, MD: University Press of America, 1984. 45–53. **Kaiser, Otto.** *Die mythische Bedeutung des Meeres in Ägypten, Ugarit und Israel.* BZAW 78. Berlin: A. Töpelmann, 1959. 140–52. **Keller, Otto.** "Krokodil." In his *Die antike Tierwelt.* Leipzig: Engelmann, 1909–13. 2:260–70. **Kline, Meredith G.** "Death, Leviathan, and Martyrs: Isaiah 24:1–27:1." In *A Tribute to Gleason Archer.* Ed. Walter C. Kaiser and Ronald F. Youngblood. Chicago: Moody Press, 1986. 229–49. **Kubina, Veronica.** *Die Gottesreden in Buche Hiob. Ein Beitrag zur Diskussion um die Einheit von Hiob*

38,1–42,6. FrThSt 115. Freiburg i.Br.: Herder, 1979. 68–75. **Maag, Victor.** "Leviathan."
RGG, 4:337–38. **Norin, Stig I. L.** *Er spaltete das Meer: Die Auszugsüberlieferung in Psalmen
und Kult des Alten Israel.* ConBOT 9. Lund: Gleerup, 1977. 67–70. **Patton, Corrine L.**
"The Beauty of the Beast: Leviathan and Behemoth in Light of Catholic Theology."
In *The Whirlwind: Essays on Job, Hermeneutics and Theology in Memory of Jane Morse.* Ed.
Stephen L. Cook, Corrine L. Patton, and James W. Watts. JSOTSup 336. Sheffield:
Sheffield Academic Press, 2001. 142–67. **Perdue, Leo G.** *Wisdom in Revolt: Metaphorical
Theology in the Book of Job.* JSOTSup 112. Bible and Literature Series 20. Sheffield: Almond
Press, JSOT Press, 1991. 227–32. **Philonenko, Marc.** "Romains 7,23, une glose qoum-
rânisante sur Job 40,32 (Septante) [Engl. 41:8] et trois textes qoumrâniens." *RHPR* 87
(2007) 257–65. **Pitard, Wayne T.** "The Binding of Yamm: A New Edition of the Ugaritic
Text *KTU* 1.83." *JNES* 57 (1998) 261–80. **Podella, T.** "Der 'Chaoskampfmythos' im Alten
Testament. Eine Problemanzeige." In *Mesopotamica–Ugaritica–Biblica: Festschrift für Kurt
Bergerhof zur Vollendung seines 70. Lebens-jahres am 7. Mai 1992.* Ed. Manfried Dietrich and
Oswald Loretz. Kevelaer: Butzon & Bercker; Neukirchen–Vluyn: Neukirchener Verlag,
1993. 283–329. **Qimron, Elisha.** "תחתיו חַדּוּדֵי חָרֶשׂ (Job 41,22)." *Lesh* 37 (1972–73) 96–98, 1.
Rendsburg, Gary A. "*UT* 68 and the Tell Asmar Seal." *Or* 53 (1984) 448–52. **Ringgren,
Helmer.** "Jahvé et Rahab–Leviatan." In *Mélanges bibliques et orientaux en l'honneur de M.
Henri Cazelles.* Ed. A. Caquot and M. Delcor. AOAT 212. Kevelaer, Neukirchen–Vluyn:
Butzon & Bercker, 1981. 387–93. **Rowold, Henry.** "מִי הוּא? לִי הוּא!": Leviathan and Job in
Job 41:2–3." *JBL* 105 (1986) 104–9. **Schellhorn, Johann Georg.** *Dissertatio ṣalṣel dagim
ad Job XL, 31.* Ugolini's Thesaurus antiquitatum sacrarum 29. Venice, 1765 [EVV 41:7].
Steadman, John M. "Leviathan and Renaissance Etymology." *Journal of the History of
Ideas* 28 (1967) 575. **Toynbee, J. M. C.** *Animals in Roman Life and Art.* London: Thames
& Hudson, 1973. 218–20. **Uehlinger, C.** "Drachen und Drachenkämpfe im alten
Vorderen Orient und in der Bibel." In *Auf Drachenspuren: Ein Buch zum Drachenprojekt des
Hamburgischen Museums für Völkerkunde.* Ed. Bernd Schmelz and Rüdiger Vossen. Bonn:
Holos, 1995. 55–101. ———. "Leviathan." *DDD* 511–15. ———. "Leviathan und die Schiffe
in Ps 104, 25–26." *Bib* 71 (1990) 499–526. **Vansittart, William.** *A New Translation of the
Forty-Ninth Psalm, in a Sermon Preached before the University of Oxford, at St Mary's, on Sunday,
June 3, 1810; to Which Are Added Remarks, Critical and Philological on Leviathan, Described
in the Forty-First Chapter of Job.* Oxford: University Press, 1810. **Vattioni, F.** "Un nome
punico e Giob. 3,9: 41,10." *Aug* 8 (1968) 383–84. **Wakeman, Mary K.** *God's Battle with the
Monster: A Study in Biblical Imagery.* Leiden: E. J. Brill, 1973. 62–65. **Wilson, Penelope.**
"Slaughtering the Crocodile at Edfu and Dendera." In *The Temple in Ancient Egypt: New
Discoveries and Recent Research.* Ed. Stephen Quirke. London: British Museum Press,
1997. 179–203. **Young, W. A.** "Leviathan in the Book of Job and Moby-Dick." *Soundings*
65 (1983) 388–401.

Translation

⁶ ᵃ *Then Yahweh answered Job out of the tempest*[b]*:*

> ⁷ ᵃ *"Gird up your loins like a man,*[b]
> *I will question you,*[c] *and you shall answer me.*[d]
> ⁸ ᵃ *Will you indeed*[b] *annul*[c] *my cause*[d]*?*
> *Will you put me in the wrong*[e] *so that you may prove yourself right*[f]*?*
> ⁹ *Have you an arm like God's*[a]*?*
> *Can you thunder with a voice like his?*
>
> ¹⁰ *Adorn yourself*[a] *with majesty*[b] *and dignity,*[c]
> *clothe yourself with splendor*[d] *and glory.*[e]
> ¹¹ *Pour out*[a] *the fury*[b] *of your wrath,*

^{c}*look out*^{d} *all who are haughty and bring them*^{e} *low.*^{f}
^{12}*Look out*^{a} *all*^{b} *who are haughty*^{c} *and humble them,*^{d}
$\quad$ ^{e}*and crush*^{f} *the wicked where they stand.*^{g}
^{13}*Hide them together in the dust,*^{a}
$\quad$ *imprison*^{b} *them*^{c} *in the Dungeon.*^{d}
^{14}*And I myself*^{a} *will praise you,*
$\quad$ *because your own right hand has brought salvation*^{b} *for you*^{c}*!*

^{15}*Consider now Behemoth,*^{a} *which I made as*^{b} *I made you*^{c}*;*
$\quad$ *it feeds on grass like an ox.*^{d}
^{16}*What*^{a} *strength it has in its loins,*
$\quad$ *what vigor in the muscles*^{b} *of its belly!*
^{17}*It stiffens*^{a} *its tail*^{b} *like a cedar*^{c}*;*
$\quad$ *the sinews*^{d} *of its thighs*^{e} *are intertwined.*^{f}
^{18}*Its bones are tubes*^{a} *of bronze,*^{b}
$\quad$ *its frame*^{c} *like bars*^{d} *of iron.*

^{19}*It is the first*^{a} *of the ways*^{b} *of God*^{c}*;*
$\quad$ ^{d}*only its maker*^{e} *could approach it with a sword.*^{f}
^{20} ^{a}*The rivers*^{b} *bring*^{c} *to it their produce,*^{d}
$\quad$ *where*^{e} *all the wild animals play.*^{f}
^{21}*Under*^{a} *the lotus plants*^{b} *it lies,*
$\quad$ *hidden among the reeds*^{c} *in the swamps.*^{d}
^{22}*The lotus covers it for shade,*^{a}
$\quad$ *around it are the river*^{b} *poplars.*^{c}
^{23}*Even if*^{a} *the river is in spate,*^{b} *it is not disturbed,*^{c}
$\quad$ *it is tranquil*^{d} *even if*^{e} *the torrent*^{f} *surges*^{g} *at its mouth.*^{h}
^{24} ^{a}*Can it be captured*^{b} *with a fork*^{c}*?*
$\quad$ *Can you pierce*^{d} *its nose*^{e} *with hooks*^{f}*?*^{g}

$^{41:1 (40:25)}$ ^{a}*Can you drag*^{b} *Leviathan out with a fishhook*^{c}
$\quad$ *or slip a noose*^{d} *round its tongue*^{e}*?*
$^{2 (40:26)}$*Will you put a reed*^{a} *through its nose,*^{b}
$\quad$ *or pierce its jaw with a hook*^{c}*?*
$^{3 (40:27)}$*Will it keep begging you for mercy*^{a}*?*
$\quad$ *Will it plead with soft words?*
$^{4 (40:28)}$*Will it enter into a pact with you,*
$\quad$ *to be taken as your slave for life?*
$^{5 (40:29)}$*Will you play*^{a} *with it as with a bird,*^{b}
$\quad$ *will you put it on a leash*^{c} *for your little girls*^{d}*?*

$^{6 (40:30)}$*Will*^{a} *the guild of fishers*^{b} *haggle over*^{c} *it?*
$\quad$ *Will they divide it up*^{d} *among*^{e} *the merchants*^{f}*?*
$^{7 (40:31)}$*Will you riddle*^{a} *its hide with darts,*^{b}
$\quad$ *or its head with fishing spears*^{c}*?*
$^{8 (40:32)}$ ^{a}*You have only to lay*^{b} *your hand on it;*
$\quad$ *you will never forget*^{c} *the struggle or risk it again!*^{d}

$^{9 (41:1)}$ ^{a}*One's hope*^{b} *is disappointed*^{c}*;*
$\quad$ *one is overwhelmed*^{d} *at the mere*^{e} *sight of it.*^{f}

10 (2) ^a*There is none so fierce*^b *as to*^c *rouse it,*^d
    who is the man who can stand before it^e*?*
11 (3) *Who ever attacked it*^a *and survived*^b*?*
    No one^c *under the whole heaven!*

12 (4) ^a*I will not keep silence*^b *about its limbs,*^c
    and I will tell^d *of its incomparable might.*^e
13 (5) ^a*Who could strip off*^b *its outer garment,*^c
    or penetrate its double corselet^d*?*
14 (6) *Who dare open*^a *the doors of its face*^b*?*
    Terrible^c *are the rows*^d *of its teeth.*

15 (7) *Its back*^a *is rows*^b *of shields;*
    it is enclosed^c *by a firm seal.*^d
16 (8) ^a*Each is so close to the next*
    that not a breath of air^b *can come between.*
17 (9) ^a*They stick fast*^b *to one another,*
    they cling together^c *and cannot be parted.*^d

18 (10) *Its sneezes*^a *flash*^b *with lights,*^c
    its eyes are like the eyelids^d *of the dawn.*
19 (11) *Out of its mouth come flaming torches,*^a
    sparks of fire^b *escape.*^c
20 (12) *From its nostrils*^a *comes steam,*^b
    as from a pot^c *fanned*^d *and seething.*^e
21 (13) *Its breath*^a *could kindle*^b *coals,*^c
    so hot a flame^d *comes from its mouth.*

22 (14) *Strength has made its home*^a *in its neck,*
    and terror^b *dances*^c *before it.*
23 (15) ^a*Its underbelly*^b *is taut,*^c
    ^d*cast hard*^e *and immovable.*^f
24 (16) ^a*Its chest*^b *is firm*^c *as*^d *a rock,*^e
    hard^f *as a nether*^g *millstone.*^h
25 (17) ^a*When it jumps,*^b *heroes*^c *are terrified;*
    at its splashes^d *they are beside themselves.*^e

26 (18) *If a sword should strike it,*^a *it can have no effect;*
    no more can spear^b *or dart*^c *or javelin.*^d
27 (19) *Iron it counts as straw,*
    and bronze as rotten wood.^a
28 (20) *No arrow*^a *can make it take flight*^b*;*
    sling-stones hurled at it are turned into^c *chaff.*^d
29 (21) *A club*^a *it thinks of*^b *as a straw*^c*;*
    at the rattle^d *of javelins*^e *it laughs.*

30 (22) ^a*Beneath it*^b *are the sharpest of potsherds*^c*;*
    it leaves a mark^d *like a threshing sledge upon the mud.*^e
31 (23) *It makes the deep*^a *boil*^b *like a cauldron;*
    it makes^c *the water*^d *[bubble] like an ointment-pot.*^e

32 (24) *Behind,*[a] *it leaves a shining wake*[b]*;*
    one would think[c] *the deep*[d] *hoar-headed*[e]*!*

33 (25) *Upon earth*[a] *there is not its like,*[b]
    a creature[c] *born to know no fear.*[d]
34 (26) *All that are lofty fear it*[a]*;*
    it is king over all proud beasts.[b] "

Notes

40:6.a. Strahan, Hölscher, Fohrer delete vv 6–7 as a gloss that repeats 38:1, 3.

6.b. On the translation of סערה as "tempest" rather than "whirlwind," see *Note* b on 38:1.

7.a. The verse is deleted by Beer (*BH²*) on the ground that it has already occurred at 38:3, a rather inadequate reason. Likewise de Wilde, regarding it as a gloss.

7.b. On גבר "man, male," cf. on 38:3, where the proposed emendation to גבור "warrior" is also discussed.

7.c. The verse differs from 38:3 only in the absence of the copula *waw* from this vb.

7.d. Beer (*BHK*) inserts אתה "you" after the *waw* of והודיעני "and tell me," supposedly on the basis of LXX; but the presence of the personal pron in LXX is no evidence that it appeared in its Hebrew original.

8.a. Verses 8–14 are transposed by Beer (*BH²*) to follow 40:2.

8.b. האף, the אף strengthening the interrogative, always introduces an "inadmissible hypothesis" (Dhorme), as also at 34:17 (*q.v.*).

8.c. פרר hiph is "break," thus "frustrate, make ineffectual" (BDB; cf. *DCH*, 6:781b), "disannul" (Strahan), as also at 5:12; 15:4; for other analogous terms, see *Comment*. פרר is more commonly used of breaking a covenant (Lev 26:44; Isa 33:8; Jer 11:10; Zech 11:14), the combination with משפט "judgment" occurring only here. Hartley regards the hiph form as declarative (cf. GKC, §53c, and רשע and צדק in the next colon), translating "impugn, discredit," but that would only be preferable if משפט meant "ordinance," in reference to the world order (see *Note* d). "Pervert [my justice]" (Habel) is not an appropriate rendering of פרר.

8.d. It is hard to know how משפטי should be understood. It could be (1) "my cause" in the legal sense (BDB, 1048b §1d; *DCH*, 5:558a §1c), i.e., the case in which Yahweh is involved thanks to Job's accusations, or perhaps (2) his (legal) "right" (BDB, 1049a §5; *DCH*, 5:564a §5) to fair treatment or the presumption of innocence (cf. NAB "Would you refuse to acknowledge my right?," Driver–Gray "disallow my right"). Conceivably it is (3) his "ordinance" (BDB, 1048b §3; *DCH*, 5:561a §3), i.e., the order he has established for the world (cf. Jer 8:7) (so Good); on the divine order, see too John Gray, "The Book of Job in the Context of Near Eastern Literature," *ZAW* 82 (1970) 251–69 (253). But since the vbs in the second colon (רשע, צדק) plainly belong in the realm of legal judgment, it seems preferable to take משפט in this sense also. Some suggest that the term is intended to allude to both "cause" and "ordinance," but the parallelism seems rather to prescribe the former.

What the phrase פרר משפטי cannot mean is "put me in the wrong" (RSV); the term for that is רשע hiph, as in the next colon. Not likely either is "judgment" (as JB "Do you really want to reverse my judgment?," KJV "Wilt thou also disannul my judgment?"; similarly Dhorme, Kissane, Pope), for there has been no formal "judgment" of Yahweh against Job, has there? Nor is the more abstract "justice" plausible (as NIV "Would you discredit my justice?," NJPS, Hartley "Would you impugn My justice?," NEB "Dare you [REB Would you] deny that I am just?," Gordis "Will you deny My justice?"; similarly Terrien), since it would be unusual to have a personal suff on an abstract (משפט often has a suff when it means "command").

8.e. רשע hiph is here declarative, "declare to be wrong, wicked" and thus "condemn," as also at 9:20; 10:2; 15:6; 32:3; 34:17 (at 34:12 it is not declarative but "do wickedly").

8.f. Parallel to רשע hiph, צדק hiph is also declarative, "declare to be right," thus "justify," as also at 27:5.

9.a. כאל is lit. "like God," but it obviously means "like that of God." The absence of an expected prep after כ is well attested (cf. Joüon–Muraoka, §133h; BDB, 455a), as also at Isa 28:21; 63:2; Cant 5:12 (but not Job 29:2, *q.v.*)

10.a. עדה "adorn" (*DCH*, 6:273a) is used of finery and decoration additional to normal clothing (as at Ezek 16:11). Elsewhere it is used most commonly of a woman putting on jewelry and other ornaments (e.g., Isa 61:10; Jer 4:30; Ezek 23:40; Hos 2:15); at Isa 61:10 it is also used of a bridegroom decking himself with a garland. The sequence of 7 impvs in vv 10–13 is to be understood as uses of the impv as an "ironical challenge" (GKC, §110a), or, equally well, as a "hypothetical imperative" (GKC, §, §110f; see also *Note* b on "lay" at 41:8 [40:32] below).

10.b. גאון is elsewhere in Job the "pride" of the wicked (35:12), the "pride" (or perhaps it is the "height") of the waves (38:11), and the "majesty" of God's voice in the thunder (37:4). Here it is of course used in a morally neutral sense. On the term, see S. Loffreda, "Raffronto fra un testo ugaritico (*2 Aqht VI*, 42–45) e Giobbe 40, 9–12," *BeO* 8 (1966) 103–16.

10.c. גבה is elsewhere simply "height," of trees (Ezek 19:11; Amos 2:9), of Goliath (1 Sam 17:4), of buildings (2 Chr 3:4; and frequently at Qumran [cf. *DCH*, 2:299a]), of heaven (Job 11:8), or else, in a morally negative sense, "pride" (Jer 48:29; Ps 10:4; Prov 16:18; 2 Chr 32:26). Only here is it in the morally neutral sense, "grandeur."

10.d. הוד is at 37:22 apparently the "majesty" of God, and in 39:20 the "majesty" of the horse's neighing (if the word is rightly understood there). Normally the word denotes the majesty of God or of the king.

10.e. הדר occurs only here in Job; it is well attested in the senses of "adornment," "splendor" (BDB, 217a).

11.a. This is probably not פוץ I "scatter" (as *HALOT*, 3:919b; *DCH*, 6:667b; NJPS; KJV "cast abroad," Good "strew about," Pope "let loose," Tur-Sinai "spread about," perhaps also NIV, NEB "unleash," NAB "let loose"), but פוץ II "cause to overflow, pour out" (as ASV, RSV), as at 37:11 (*q.v.*). *DCH*, 6:667b, fails to note the passage under this vb.

11.b. עברה is not, as generally thought, "overflow" (from עבר "pass over"; so BDB, 729b), as "the overflowings of your anger" (RSV, Dhorme), "the spate of your anger" (JB). The word here is עֶבְרָה II "rancour, indignation" (*DCH*, 6:245a, from עבר II "be angry"). The use of two synonyms in a construct chain often expresses a superlative (Gordis), but Beer (*BH²*) would rather delete the word (though it does not appear correct to say that LXX omitted it; they seem rather to have read it differently).

11.c. The colon is omitted by NAB as a dittograph of material in v 12a (though hardly of v 10b, as it suggests).

11.d. De Wilde, following Duhm, deletes וראה "and look upon," as weakening the series of severe impvs in vv 11–12. He omits to mention that the initial *waw* of והשפילהו would also need to be deleted. ראה would seem to be used in the sense of "observe, watch" (as 1 Sam 6:9; 17:28; BDB, 907b §6e, with some other less convincing examples) or "look out, select" (as 2 Kgs 9:2; Gen 41:33; 1 Sam 16:17; BDB, 907b §6g), which is more or less "identify."

11.e. MT has sg for "haughty" (גאה) and the suff of "bring low" (השפילהו); the pl is used in the *Translation* to avoid referring to the haughty as males exclusively.

11.f. The vb שפל hiph "bring low, humiliate" has appeared already at 22:29, though the exact reading is open to question. Beer (*BH²*) deletes the initial *waw* of והשפילהו, which corresponds to LXX and has the support of several mss.

12.a. De Wilde deletes וראה "and look upon" for the same reason as in v 11b; similarly Beer (*BH²*).

12.b. כל "all" is deleted by Duhm.

12.c. For גאה "proud," which was used in the previous colon (v 11b), Duhm, followed by Dhorme, Beer (*BHK*), Hölscher (*frt*), de Wilde, read גָּבֹהַּ "high, haughty" (used pejoratively also at Ps 138:6; Isa 5:15; 10:33; etc.). Gray prefers to read גֹּבַהּ in v 11, retaining גאה here, thinking that גבה "high" fits better with שפל "be low." Beer (*BHK vel*) also suggests an alternative, זֵד "haughty (one)."

12.d. As in v 11b, the MT has sg for "haughty" (גאה) and the suff of "humble" (הכניעהו); the pl is used in the *Translation* to avoid referring to the haughty as males exclusively.

12.e. NAB transposes the colon to follow v 11a (it deletes v 11b).

12.f. הדך occurs only here. It is explained by BDB, 213a, as "cast or tread down" (similarly *DCH*, 2:490b), and by *HALOT*, 1:239a, as "tread down" on the basis of Arab. *hadaka* "tear down (a building)" (Freytag, 4:376b; not in Lane). KJV, RSV render "tread down" (Good "trample," Hartley "trample down") but the Arab. cognate does not support that sense. If the cognate is determinative, NAB's and NJPS's "bring down" and NAB's "throw down" would be more suitable. Alternatively, NIV's and REB's "crush" (as also Dhorme, Habel) no doubt understands the vb as a byform of דכא, דכה, דוך, and רכך, all meaning "crush" (cf. also Ben Yehuda's *Thesaurus*, 2:1043, where our הדך "crush" is registered as a MH word).

Among emendations, Hoffmann, Beer (*BHK prps*) read הֲדֹךְ "crush!," hiph impv of דכך (or of דוך, according to Tur-Sinai). Graetz, Duhm, Beer (*BHK al*) read הֲדֹף "push!" (as perhaps also Aq, Pesh), but that means "push aside," which is rather feeble in the context. Dahood's proposal to read וְהֹדֵךְ *HDK* in Job 40,12," *Bib* 49 [1968] 509–10) is lame, not least because בּ must be understood.

12.g. תחתם is lit. "under them," which not infrequently means "in their place," "where they stand" (RSV), "on the spot" (Dhorme); cf. BDB, 1065b §2 and 36:20 (*q.v.*). NAB "with a glance" apparently adopts LXX παραχρῆμα "suddenly," though that reading is not mentioned in their *Textual Notes*. Dahood reads תחתם "[by your splendor] you will terrify (חתת) them," the final *mem* being either a resumptive suff following רשעים "wicked" or the enclitic (see the foregoing *Note*). Beer (*BH²prps*) mentions emendations to מתחתם "from under them" (so too Gray), which is plausible (Zech 6:12 could be an analogy), and תחתיך "under you," which is lame.

13.a. עפר "dust" is "the grave and the world of the dead" (*HALOT*, 2:862b).

13.b. חבש "bind" is not elsewhere used of imprisonment, but Dhorme and Gordis compare the Arab. cognate *ḥabasa* with that sense (Lane, 500b, "confine, imprison, restrain, withhold"); so too NAB, Fedrizzi "imprison." An alternative rendering is "veil [their faces]," as BDB, 289b (NIV "shroud their faces," NEB "shroud them," Good "bind their faces in concealment"; similarly Habel); cf. חבש in Exod 29:9 of binding round the head. Tur-Sinai's emendation הבש "shame [their faces into hiding]" (for בוש as the obj of פנים, cf. 2 Sam 19:6) is good, but does not suit the previous colon.

13.c. פניהם, lit. "their faces," i.e., their persons (Dhorme, Fohrer).

13.d. טמון is "concealed thing"(qal pass ptcp), thus perhaps "obscurity" (NJPS; cf. KJV "in secret," ASV "the hidden place"), but more likely "the dungeon" (JB) or rather "the Dungeon" (NJB) as a name for the underworld; so too RSV "the world below," NAB "the hidden world," NIV "the grave"— though not "an unknown grave" (NEB), which is not what the Heb. means.

Among emendations, Beer (*BHK prps*) mentions Ehrlich's בדמן "in the dung," which seems unlikely. De Wilde more attractively suggests בדומה or בדומיה "in quietness," i.e., of the world of the dead (for the idea of silence in the grave, cf. Pss 31:18; 94:17; 115:17; and perhaps 51:16 if מדומה "from silence" is read instead of מדמים "from blood"; and cf. also the "tents of silence" in 4QWiles 1:7). Alternatively, he proposes תעמם "darkness," an otherwise unattested noun from עמם II "be dark." Guillaume tentatively suggested a תמון "grave," cognate with Arab. *tamnun* "low, depressed ground."

14.a. וגם־אני "and also I," almost as if to say "I will be the first [to praise you]."

14.b. ישע hiph is certainly "save, deliver," though some translations render, less probably, "give you victory" (RSV), "assure your triumph" (JB); cf. NJPS "the triumph your right hand won you," GNB "you won the victory yourself," Good "your right hand won you victory." It is arguable that ישע hiph never refers to "victory," even, for example, at Judg 7:2; 1 Sam 25:33.

14.c. תושע לך is not precisely "saved you," but "brought salvation for you," the use with the prep ל being rather rare (e.g., Isa 59:16; 63:5; Ps 98:1; cf. *DCH*, 4:337a). Gordis suggests the original reading may have been לי "[your right hand could save] me," implying that Job would have succeeded where God had not; but there seems no hint here of any goal that God "has not been able to achieve completely."

15.a. Most take בהמות as a proper name, Behemoth, though NIV has "the behemoth," for reasons unknown. In that the form is the pl of בהמה "beast," it may of course be a "plural of majesty," i.e., an intensive pl (GKC, §124e), signifying "the supreme beast," "the enormous beast"; it is not likely to be a Phoenician sg ending in *-ot* (as Blommerde). An interesting, but rather far-fetched, proposal was made by Richter, and followed by G. R. Driver, that there is no beast Behemoth, but only a crocodile. They emend בהמות אשר־עשיתי עמך to ראשית בהמות אמשך "the firstborn of beasts (Driver: the chief), the crocodile," אמשך "crocodile" being a new addition to the Hebrew vocabulary, cognate with Egyptian *msḥ*, Coptic *emsah* (so Driver, "Mythical Monsters," 235; so too NEB "the chief of the beasts, the crocodile." For the word, see also *HALOT*, 2:850b; *DCH*, 6:491a.

An alternative etymology for בהמות has often been proposed, that it is the Egyptian *p3-iḥ-mw* "the ox of the water," the hippopotamus; this view, taken by Duhm, Hölscher (cf. also Terrien), is to be found also in the *OED*. Since T. K. Cheyne and W. Max Müller, *EB* (1889) 1:519, most now, however, are clear that no such word existed in Egyptian; further, Eg. *ḥ* does not correspond to Heb. *h* (so Driver). Cf. Eberhard Ruprecht, "Das Nilpferd im Hiobbuch. Beobachtungen zu der sogennanten zweiten Gottesrede," *VT* 21 (1971) 209–31.

15.b. עמך "with you" might mean (1) "just as I made you" (NRSV; similarly NJPS, Gordis; Driver-Gray "equally with thee," de Wilde "your fellow-creature"), or (2) "with you," i.e., at the same time as you (KJV "which I made with thee," NIV, Hartley "which I made along with you"), or "in addition to you" (ASV, "as well as you," NAB "besides you"), or (3) "as well as you" (ASV), i.e., in addition to you (NAB "besides you"), or (4) "like you," עם being the alleged עם comparative (for other examples, see *Note* c on 29:18). Merx and Siegfried omit עמך as well as אשר־עשיתי, but then the line becomes too short.

J. V. Kinnier Wilson, "A Return to the Problem of Behemoth and Leviathan," *VT* 25 (1975) 1–14 (7), translated "which I have made with thy help," the clumsiness of the creature Behemoth being a result of Job's unskilled participation in its creation. But, while the Heb. would allow this rendering, there is no suggestion elsewhere that Job may have been involved, even in fantasy, in a creative act.

15.c. אֲשֶׁר־עָשִׂיתִי "which I made" is deleted by many (the phrase does not appear in the LXX, and it makes for an exceptionally long first colon; so Duhm, Strahan, Moffatt, Dhorme, Beer (*BHK*), Hölscher, Fohrer, Gray, NAB. Deleting "which I made" makes עִמָּךְ "with you" somewhat problematic. Dhorme has "Behold now Behemoth before you!" (similarly Gray), but עִמָּךְ seems an unnatural way of expressing "before you" (17:3; 36:4; 1 Kgs 2:8 are hardly parallel). NAB's "See, besides you I made Behemoth" follows an emendation to הִנֵּה בְהֵמוֹת עֲשִׂיתִי עִמָּךְ, i.e., omitting the enclitic נא and the relative אֲשֶׁר. Gordis argues that הִנֵּה־נָא, lit. "behold," could lie outside the metrical scheme, but it does not do so in the next verse.

15.d. NEB's "who devours cattle as if they were grass" follows G. R. Driver's reading כֶּחָצִיר בָּקָר יֹאכַל ("Mythical Monsters," 236), a purely conjectural emendation on the basis that, unlike the hippopotamus, the crocodile is carnivorous. Even so, crocodiles do not eat cattle.

16.a. הִנֵּה, lit. "see, [its strength ...]." NIV, NJB, NEB, Hartley suggest the rendering used in the *Translation*. Kissane has a good point in taking בְמָתְנָיו "in its loins" as a relative clause, for the marvel lies not in the location of its strength in its loins, but in the strength itself.

16.b. שָׂרִיר occurs only here, but cf. שֹׁר "navel string," שֵׁרָה "bracelet," and שְׁרִרוּת "firmness, stubbornness"; it is usually translated "sinew, muscle" (BDB, 1057a). Wetzstein (in Delitzsch) renders "supports" of its belly, comparing Arab. *sarîr* (Lane, 1339b, wrongly cited by Driver–Gray as 1338b); but Driver–Gray properly object that "a thing on which one lies or sits," i.e., a bedstead, throne, etc., is not semantically equivalent to "supporting bones." Tur-Sinai stresses, perhaps correctly, that שָׂרִיר ought to mean "strong, solid" (like Aram. שְׁרִיר [Jastrow, 1631b]), and translates "in the masses [of his belly]." Pope, though he translates "massive [belly]," thinks rather of Arab. *sirr* "secret" (Lane, 1338a), thus "genitals" of male or female (as also noted by Lane, 1338b); it may be attested also, in the form שְׁרֵרֵךְ "your vulva" (?), at Cant 7:3. Guillaume, though translating "muscles," thinks the word perhaps rather means "low parts" (cf. Arab. *'asārīr*), the vulnerable underbelly, which, however, seems somewhat beside the point. Wolfers, 167–69, offers a thoroughgoing sexual interpretation of vv 16–17: that the hippopotamus's strength in its loins implies that it concentrates, or wastes, its strength in reproduction, the otherwise unknown word שְׂרִיר, usually translated "muscles," means "genitals," while its "tail" (זָנָב) is its penis and חפץ means that it "delights" in its erection; curiously, he does not combine with these renderings the sense of פַּחַד as "testicles" (cf. פַּחַד VI "testicle," in *DCH*, 6:676a), preferring rather "his sinews of fear (פַּחַד I) are intertwined"—which he takes to be a symptom of paralysis in the face of danger.

17.a. חפץ II is "bend down" (trans) according to BDB, 343b, comparing Arab. *ḥafaḍa* "lower, depress" (Lane, 773a; so too Driver–Gray), but it is hard to see how the tail could be "bent down *like a cedar*." NEB mg has "he bends his tail like a cedar" (similarly Driver–Gray), but the Arab. cognate certainly does not mean "bend" but "lower, make low," and in any case bending is not what cedars are noted for. *DCH*, 3:287b, "stretch out, let hang" is not much improvement, though it also sees the vb as transitive. KB, 321b, and *HALOT*, 1:340a, take the vb as intrans, "his tail hangs down" (Arab. *ḥafaḍa* is an error in KB, and *ḥafaṣa* an error in Gordis); similarly Pope's "arches" is hardly justified by the Arab. cognate. Ball has recourse to another sense of Arab. *ḥafaḍa* attested by Lane, "remain, stay" (Lane, 773b), and translates "is rigid," i.e., is firm, inflexible; but this is a very unusual meaning of *ḥafaḍa* and in any case there is insufficient semantic overlap between "remain" and "be rigid."

Most commonly, the word is understood as "stiffens," though, as far as can be seen, there is no philological evidence for this meaning: RSV has "makes stiff," NJB "His tail is as stiff as a cedar," NEB "His tail is rigid as a cedar," Gordis "stiffens," Habel "when erect his tail is like a cedar." The *Translation* above adopts this sense, purely on the basis of the context.

Other philological proposals are: (1) Though he translates "stiffens," Gordis derives the word from חפץ I, usually "desire," but here, he thinks, in the concrete meaning of "stretch out" (similarly Dhorme, Hölscher); evidence for such a meaning is, however, lacking. (2) Terrien thinks it might mean "takes its pleasure," the normal meaning of חפץ, but here in a sexual sense. (3) Tur-Sinai postulates another vb חפץ meaning "be strong," which also leads to the translation "stiffens"; unconvincingly, he finds the same vb also at Cant 2:7; 3:5; 8:4, arguing that the woman is not to be awakened until she is "strong" after her lovesickness. (4) Guillaume, translating "is rigid," suggests a חפץ cognate with Arab. *ḥaṣif* (correctly *ḥaṣīf*; Lane, 584c) "strong." (5) KJV "moveth" depends upon the annotation in the lexicon of Buxtorf, 251, following ibn Ezra and Gersonides, that חפץ here is like חפז "move quickly" (BDB, 342a). Buxtorf also offered the translation "erected" (*erigit, arrigit*), likewise attributed to ibn Ezra, and an independent rendering, "when he wishes, his tail is like a cedar, i.e., upright and immobile," i.e., taking the vb יַחְפֹּץ as a temporal clause.

Three other translations may be noted, even though it is unclear what Hebrew they depend on: NJPS has "makes stand up" (cf. LXX ἔστησεν, which is however intransitive). NAB has "carries his tail like a cedar," and NIV "his tail sways like a cedar."

17.b. זנב "tail" is attested in post-biblical Hebrew also as "penis" (Jastrow, 406a). Terrien and Habel incline to a sexual meaning of זנב and פחד, and Newsom admits the sense at least for זנב. So too David Bernat, "Biblical *Waṣfs* beyond Song of Songs," *JSOT* 28 (2004) 327–49 (335–36). The tail of the hippopotamus is indeed rather insignificant (see *Comment*).

17.c. ארז is undeniably "cedar," but because of the problem of likening the hippopotamus's tail to a cedar, de Wilde suggests that the word here is rather אֶרֶז, which he renders "what is tied fast, a rope." Now ארוז occurs once, at Ezek 27:24, apparently as an adj "secure"; if we infer a vb ארז "make fast" we are still a long way from "rope." And if the tail "hangs down like a rope" that is rather banal and not very distinctive of the hippopotamus.

17.d. גיד "sinew" or "tendon," the fibrous cord that connects muscle to bone or to another part of the body. Tur-Sinai claims it means "ligaments" (also at 10:11), the flexible tissue that connects one bone to another; but it seems that Hebrew did not distinguish tendons and ligaments.

17.e. פחד II "thigh" (BDB, 808b) is in its Arab. cognate *afhādh* both "thighs" and "testicles," according to Gordis, but Lane, 2349a, does not recognize the second sense; there is, however, a Syriac cognate meaning "testicles." Tg and Vg render "testicles." So too Bernat, "Biblical *Waṣfs*," 338. The testicles of the hippopotamus are, however, internal, and so could hardly form a topic for the poet's description.

17.f. שרג is "intertwine"; it occurs elsewhere only at Lam 1:14, of sins being fastened together. KJV had "wrapped together," ASV, RSV, NJPS "knit together," NIV "close-knit," NEB "closely knit," NJB, REB "tightly knit." NAB "like cables" adopts the rendering of LXX συμπέπλεκται "are wrapped together" in an attempt to visualize what intertwined sinews might look like. Though the wording is similar at 10:11, "with bones and sinews [you] knit (תשׂכני) me together," the image there of weaving the body as a whole is rather different. Beer (*BH*²) would read שֹׂרְגוּ perf "intertwined."

18.a. אפיק is usually "stream," as at 6:15, but here apparently "tube" (as English versions); at 41:15 (7) it is the "furrows" between the scales of the crocodile.

18.b. נחושה is either the naturally occurring mineral "copper" (cf. 28:2) or the alloy of copper and tin, "bronze." Since bronze is harder than copper, it is presumably bronze that is meant here.

18.c. גרם is normally "bone" (BDB, 175a; *DCH*, 2:375b). At Gen 49:14 גרם חמר "an ass of bone" is obviously "a strong ass," unless we should read גרים חמר "ass of sojourners" (as Samaritan); at 2 Kgs 9:13 גרם מעלות, lit. "the bone of the steps" (? the bare steps), we should perhaps recognize as a different word גרם II "landing," as John Gray (*I and II Kings: A Commentary* [OTL; London: SCM Press, 1964] 489; cf. *DCH*, 2:376a), comparing Arab. *jarama* "cut off, complete" (Lane, 412b). What גרם never means is "limb," though this is the rendering here of ASV, RSV, NJPS, NEB, NIV, NEB, no doubt to avoid using the same English word twice in the one verse (KJV had "bones" in both cola). Driver has "vertebrae" ("Mythical Monsters," 236), and RV mg, Moffatt have "ribs"; but this is to limit the reference unnecessarily. The best solution may be to adopt "frame" (in the sense of the framework of bones) from Kissane, NAB, NJB. Arab. *jirm* "body" (Lane, 413b) is of little use as a cognate, for it would not explain the pl גרמיו.

18.d. מטיל, only here, is apparently "rod" (cf. Arab. *maṭala* "forge iron" [Freytag, 4:190a; Wehr–Cowan, 914a; not in Lane). Chaim Rabin, less probably, thought it meant "strong," i.e., "like strong iron," on the basis of a supposed cognate in Hittite (cf. Akk. *mutallu* "noble"; "Hittite Words in Hebrew," *Or* 32 [1963] 113–39 [131–32]).

19.a. ראשית may be "first" in time, or "chief" in importance. The former view is adopted by NAB "He came at the beginning of God's ways," Pope "He is a primordial production of God," the latter by KJV, NEB "chief," NIV "He ranks first among the works of God," JB "He is the masterpiece of all God's work" (similarly Moffatt), Strahan, Kissane. The translation of RSV, NJB "He is the first of the works of God" (similarly NJPS) is perhaps intended to be understood in either sense. Fedrizzi suggests that ראשית essentially means "authenticity," so that the colon proper means simply that "Behemoth is truly a project (דרך) of God's"; but no parallels are offered.

19.b. דרך is unambiguously "way," not "work," though the latter, which many translations have (RSV, NJPS, NIV, JB, NEB; similarly Rowley), may be the better rendering (see also *Note* c on 26:14). In a very similar phrase in Prov 8:22, Wisdom was created as the "first of [God's] way" (ראשית דרכו), the second word is perhaps to be vocalized דְּרָכוֹ "his ways").

It is not very likely that we should be thinking here of דֶּרֶךְ II "power" (cf. *DCH*, 2:472b, 633a), though the translation "he is the chief (manifestation) of divine power" has a certain plausibility; cf. Mitchell Dahood, review of Gustav Hölscher, *Das Buch Hiob*, *TS* 13 (1952) 593–94 (593); Johann

Bapt. Bauer, "«Initium viarum suarum» = Primitiae potentiae Dei? (Iob 40,19, cf. 26,14, et Prov 8,22," *VD* 35 (1957) 222–27; but see Hans Zirker, "דרך = potentia?," *BZ* 2 (1958) 291–94. ראשית by itself, however, can hardly mean "chief manifestation."

19.c. It is a little odd to find Yahweh referring to himself as "God," but the usage is not unparalleled (e.g. 2:3; 38:7). Kissane offers an ingenious but entirely speculative solution: we should move to this point 41:17 "At his rising mighty men are afraid, And panic-stricken hide themselves," and then v 19 is the speech of the mighty men at the sight of the monster.

19.d. The line appears in LXX as "made [reading no doubt עשׂו; see next *Note*] to be played with (ἐγκαταπαίζεσθαι) by his angels," which is repeated at 41:25 with reference to Leviathan (with the variant "by my angels").

19.e. העשׂו with the article and a suff is anomalous (though paralleled by forms with a verbal suff at Isa 9:13 [12]; Ps 18:32 [33]; GKC, §127i, denies the relevance of these examples to the present text); if it means "its maker" (as Gerleman [*BHS*]), the form should be either עשׂו (or עשׂהו), the ptcp with a suff, or העשׂו, the ptcp with the article and without a suff for "its."

LXX πεποιημένον "what is made" presumably read העשׂו (or העשׂוי, though the form without the final *yodh* occurs several times in the Ketiv [Gordis]) "what is made," which would refer to Behemoth; this is read by Duhm, Beer (*BHK*), Hölscher, Tur-Sinai, Driver, "Mythical Monsters," 237, Gray. The form עשׂו "a creature, what is made" occurs at 41:33 (25) in reference to Leviathan.

Gordis also reads העשׂו, but, in a rather far-fetched proposal, derives it from עשׂה III "cover" (he spells it עשׂו; cf. *DCH*, 6:603a), and translates "only the one well-covered (with armor) [may bring his sword near to attack him]." Guillaume offers an initially more attractive rendering, "the creatures do not fear his tusks. For the pools bring him their produce"; but to do so he must take the ה of העשׂו as the interrogative (reasonable), and עשׂו as "created things" (unparalleled), read the vb as יָגֵשׁ, i.e., a new word נגשׁ "fear" (cf. Arab. *wajasa* [Freytag, 4:439b; Wehr, 1050b; not apparently in Lane]) (questionable), and adopt the explanation of חרב "sword" as "the formidable array of long spear-like incisors and curved chisel-edged canines or tusks" (so Driver–Gray) (dubious). Still, he does explain the כי "for" at the beginning of the next verse: it would mean that the other animals are unafraid of the hippopotamus because as a herbivore it does not threaten them.

19.f. יַגֵּשׁ is 3ms impf of נגשׁ hiph "bring near"; חרב "sword" is nowhere else the obj of נגשׁ hiph, but the sense "draw (a sword)" is by no means implausible. RV mg "He that hath made him hath furnished him with a sword" introduces a note of aggression into the depiction of the hippopotamus that is otherwise quite absent; some have thought it is the hippopotamus's teeth that are supposed to be like a scythe or sword (e.g., Davidson, B. Couroyer, "Le «glaive» de Béhémoth: Job xl,19–20," *RB* 84 [1977] 59–79), but "it is hard to think of a sword as an instrument of mowing" (Rowley). Rowley thinks it is "the sharp, chisel-edged tusks with which the hippopotamus attacks its enemies when aroused," and that the sword is Behemoth's own, a sign of its power over its enemies (Newsom is tempted by this suggestion); but the hippopotamus does not have any enemies it must keep at bay, except perhaps for human hunters who are more afraid of it than it is of them. The simplest explanation is that the hippopotamus is so fearsome a creature that only God, who made it, can dare to approach it; "only" is supplied in the *Translation* to make this sense clear (so too Sicre Díaz, NRSV, NJPS, GNB). JB "but his Maker threatened him with the sword" suggests a sense for נגשׁ hiph that is not paralleled.

Nevertheless, many prefer an emendation. (1) Gunkel, *Schöpfung und Chaos*, 62 n. 3, proposed הֶעָשׂוּי יִגַּשׁ חָרְבוֹ "which was made so that it might govern the desert" (there is no word from which חָרְבוֹ may be derived, and it is perhaps a mistake for חֶרְבָּה); but this proposal is hardly likely given that the hippopotamus lives in the water not in the desert! (2) Giesebrecht (*GGA* [1895] 595) suggested חֲבֵרָיו "his fellows," i.e., the other animals, and Peake (*frt*), Beer (*BH²*), and Driver, "Mythical Monsters," 237, accept this emendation. (3) Duhm, followed by Strahan, Driver–Gray (*frt*), Dhorme, Beer (*BHK frt*), Hölscher, Fohrer, de Wilde, modified it slightly to the participial form נֹגֵשׂ חֲבֵרָיו "the tyrant of his companions" (so NAB "was made the taskmaster of his fellows," NEB "made to be a tyrant over his peers [REB his fellow-creatures]," Moffatt "made to be lord of his fellows"). On נגשׁ "oppressor, tyrant, taskmaster," cf. *DCH*, 5:614b; it seems that in some late texts (Zech 10:4; Isa 60:17) the term has a neutral meaning, "governor," in which case "taskmaster" and "tyrant" would perhaps be out of place here. But is the general idea plausible? No; the hippopotamus's fellow-creatures in chaps. 38–39 apparently live in total ignorance of the hippopotamus, and it is hard to conceive of any sense in which the hippopotamus could be their tyrant or ruler or taskmaster or governor. (4) Gray prefers to read נגשׁ בְּרֵכָה "[made to] lord it over the pool," the "pool" being the area where the hippopotamus is indisputably king; but a pool is not a river, and Behemoth is plainly disporting himself in the river (v 23).

Merely ingenious is Tur-Sinai's translation "that he [Leviathan, according to Tur-Sinai] might fetch his [Yahweh's] sword," Leviathan being God's weapon-bearer. Even less attractive is Ehrlich's emendation to גֵּשָׁה רַבָּה "[he who is made of] giant stature," גֵּשָׁה being a new Heb. word cognate with Arab. *juṯṯa* "body" (Lane, 379a).

20.a. The line begins with כִּי "for," but it is difficult on most interpretations to make sense of this connective—unless perhaps it is emphatic, "indeed" (Gordis). Even so, it is hard to see why an emphatic particle should be wanted here. Gray took the *kaph* as the final letter of v 19 as he reconstructed it, (ה)ברכ "pool" (see previous *Note*).

20.b. The Hebrew has הרים "mountains" as the subj of this clause, but why are mountains mentioned in connection with the hippopotamus, which never strays more than a couple of miles from water? Dhorme explains that it is because the mountains are the habitat of the wild animals, who also, like the mountains, "bring tribute" to Behemoth; but how do they do that? Gordis thinks the tribute is the waterfalls and streams that flow down from the mountains. Kissane thinks that v 20 is concessive: "though the mountains yield him food, And all the beasts of the field play there, Beneath the lotus-trees he lies"; but this does not explain what the hippopotamus is doing in the mountains. Rowley, following Driver–Gray, thinks they may be "lower hills," which the hippopotamus could scale in search for food; Fohrer even regards the "hills" as merely the banks of the river. Pope thinks that the herbage of the mountains is delivered to Behemoth, but he does not suggest how we should visualize that (he is reminded of the midrashic interpretation of Ps 50:10 which envisages the monster Behemoth lying on a thousand hills and feeding on them; cf. 4 Ezra 6:51). All these explanation are strained, and it is perhaps more reasonable to doubt a reading that connects mountains with hippopotami.

Among emendations, Wright suggests יארים "Niles," and, better, Siegfried suggests נְהָרִים "rivers," which is a very simple and very tempting alteration, accepted by Moffatt and in the *Translation* above (though according to Pope it doesn't merit serious consideration, while Driver–Gray object that the beasts of the field do not play in the rivers). The reference to rivers would fit well with the next colon's picture of other animals at play in the streams where the hippopotamus is at home (cf. Ps 104:26, where the place where Leviathan "sports" [שׂחק as here] is also watery: the sea). Guillaume does not emend the text but interestingly suggests a new word הר "pool" (cf. Arab. *haur* [Freytag, 417a]).

20.c. נשׂא makes sense as "carry," thus "bring"; but the text is somewhat questionable, and several emendations have been proposed. Duhm, Beer (*BHK frt*), reading ישׂא "he takes," understand that the hippopotamus takes the "produce" of the mountains for himself (similarly Driver–Gray, Driver, "Mythical Monsters," 137). Driver regards the crocodile (as he understands Behemoth) to be taking the "creatures" of the hills for himself (thus NEB "he takes the cattle of the hills for his prey"). Beer (*BH²prps*) mentions an emendation to ישׁעו "gaze at" (Ball ישְׁתָּעוּ hithp), i.e., "[the cattle of the hills] gaze at him (in wonder)," which has a lot of merit (similarly Moffatt "wild animals are all amazed at him"); G. R. Driver pronounced it a brilliant suggestion (review of C. J. Ball, *The Book of Job* [1922], *The Oxford Magazine* 40 [1921–22] 423–24). Pope, who is followed by Gray, makes the very interesting proposal of ישְׁלְיוּ "they are at ease" (from שׁלה; the form is attested at 12:6), which would be a nice parallel to שׁחק in the next colon. The only problems are that there is no reason why the other beasts should be mentioned, and there is no referent for שׁם "there"—and those are insuperable problems. Gray moves שׁם to the end of the first colon, translating "where the beasts of the mountains take their ease."

Gordis thinks ישׂאו "they lift up" is elliptical for קול ישׂא "lift up the voice, i.e., sing" (so ibn Janah; and so too Kinnier Wilson, "A Return to the Problem of Behemoth and Leviathan," 9), which would then be parallel to שׂחק "play" in the next colon (cf. רנו נשׂא "rejoice," Isa 42:11) (Habel is tempted to follow); but Gordis retains "bring him their tribute" in his Translation.

20.d. בול is very problematic. BDB, 385a, takes it as an abbreviation or error for the more common word יבול "produce (of soil)"; similarly *HALOT*, 1:115a, NAB, Hartley. *Faute de mieux*, this is the interpretation adopted in the *Translation* above. Beer (*BH²prps*) mentions an emendation to יבולי "products of [the mountains]." Some have suggested that the old month name Bul may be the same word, as the month of "produce." KB, 113b, followed by Fohrer, takes it to mean in Isa 44:19 "dry wood" (cf. Akk. *bulû* [*CDA*, 48a]), and perhaps here "drift-wood" (which would no doubt be *wet* wood, and equally unattractive as food to hippopotami). Dhorme, followed by Hölscher, Gordis, Habel, Sicre Díaz, understands it, however, as "tribute," cognate with Akk. *biltu* (*CDA*, 44a), developing further the notion of the hippopotamus as lording it over its fellows in v 19a. Ball, Tur-Sinai, Driver, "Mythical Monsters," 137, Gordis, Pope, Gray, Kinnier Wilson, "A Return to the Problem of Behemoth and Leviathan," 9, invoke Akk. *būlu* "beasts," especially in the phrase *būl ṣēri* "the beasts of the open country," which would be parallel to חית השׂדה "the wild animals of the open field" in the second colon; so Driver, "he takes the creatures of the hills for himself," but this could only be right if we agree with Driver that Behemoth is the crocodile, for the hippopotamus is herbivorous.

20.e. The colon is understood as a relative clause, with the relative pron omitted; שם "there" then becomes "where." Duhm however, followed by Beer (*BHK frt*), Hölscher, Driver, "Mythical Monsters," 137, removed שם to the beginning of the next colon, "There in the fields (Duhm) or under the lotus plants (Driver) ..." Habel imagines that "there" is deeply mysterious, and is impressed by LXX's rendering "in Tartarus," i.e., in the mythological underworld. He also notes the use of שם "there" in 1:21; 3:17 as a euphemism for the underworld, but is very questionable whether such a sense can be attributed to שם in those places.

20.f. Dhorme understands the colon "as do all the wild beasts which play there," comparing Ps 104:26, "Leviathan, which you created to play there."

Among emendations may be noted: (1) Beer (*BHK*) reads ישׁחק, sg because the subj is חית שדה "beasts (collective) of the field," and in pause because he removes שם to the beginning of the next colon. Gray too reads the sg vb. (2) NAB reads בם ישׂחק "[and of all wild animals] he makes sport," but that does not fit with the previous colon at all. (3) Emendation to ישׁחק "he crushes" (Duhm, Hölscher, Driver, "Mythical Monsters," 137), as in 2 Sam 22:43, is unsuitable in the context, and "would obliterate the emphasis ... on the peaceful, nonpredatory character of this massive beast" (Gordis). Driver translates "he crunches up all the beasts of the field"; but whereas "crunch" means "crush with the teeth, or, underfoot" שׁחק means "pulverize," a quite different concept. (4) Terrien's proposal מגבול הרים ישׁא־לו "he [God] puts it outside the limits of the mountains," i.e., denies it access to "the plateaus and steppes of the Fertile Crescent," demands unparalleled senses of גבול "border" and נשׂא "bear, carry." JB "forbidding him the mountain regions where all the wild animals have their playground" (NJB "and all the wild animals that play there") similarly reads גבול הרים ישׁא־לו, but how can נשׂא mean "forbid"? Perhaps the sense "take away" is in mind (cf. *DCH*, 5:766b §7), but the following ל does not fit with that. (5) De Wilde proposed כבוד ראמים ישׁאו־לו "the buffaloes pay him respect," and for the next colon וכל־חית השׂדה ישׁתחוו "and all the wild animals revere him"; but there is no parallel for כבוד "honor" as the obj of נשׂא "lift up, bear" and חוה hithp is only used of human subjects (except in Joseph's dream, Gen 37:7, 9).

21.a. The sequence of the "heavy" prep תחת "under" in the first colon and the "light" ב "in" in the second is a case of "ballast prepositions reversed" (Watson, 345).

21.b. צאלים, which occurs only here and in v 22, is not an aquatic plant, the water lily (*Nymphaea lotus*). It is understood by BDB, 838a, as "lotus," specifically the thorny lotus (*Rhamnus lotus, Zizyphus lotus*), a bush or plant producing berries known as "jujubes." Most English versions follow this identification, NEB even affirming that we know which kind of lotus is in question, the "thorny lotus." Hölscher thought rather it was the near relative *Zizyphus spina Christi* (Christ's-thorn; cf. Dalman, *Arbeit und Sitte*, 1:373; 2:322; photo: www.pbase.com/image/1588576). Cognates cited are Arab. *ḍāl* (Lane, 1816c; not *ṣa'l*, as Gordis) and Syr. *sā'lā'* (so KB, 790a; Driver–Gray [comparing ארץ = ארעה], Dhorme, Gordis have *'ālā*; so too *HALOT*, 3:992b; Löw, *Flora*, 3:134–35; Payne-Smith has for that "bramble"). Paul Humbert, "En marge du dictionnaire hébraïque," *ZAW* 62 (1949–50) 199–207 (206), comparing Copt. *čal*, Eg. *ḏ3rt*, thought it just meant "bough" (as Driver, "Mythical Monsters," 137, also recognizes); hence *HALOT*, 3:992b offers both "bramble bush" and "bough" (cf. Barr, *Philology*, 105).

KJV "the shady trees" obviously connected the term with צל "shade."

21.c. קנה refers to all kinds of reeds, and cannot be specified as the papyrus (as Driver–Gray).

21.d. בצה "swamp, marsh" ("waterlogged ground" according to *HALOT*, 1:147b) has occurred already at 8:21, as a place where reeds grow.

22.a. יסכהו צאלים צללו lit. "the lotus bushes cover it, its shade." צללו or צללי is attested as a suff form of צל "shade." When צל has a suff, that suff usually refers to the obj that gives shade, not that which receives it (thus, e.g., Ps 121:5; Lam 4:20), but at Num 14:9 צלם "their protection" is the protection they are afforded; so here צללו could be "the shade it enjoys." Gordis translates "as his shadow," an adv accus of specification. Gray proposes reading צללם "their shade," i.e., the lotus bushes cover it with their shade, which is not a bad idea.

The text is undoubtedly suspicious, with the repetition of צאלים in 21a and 22a, and the similarity of צאלים and צללו in 22a and of יסכהו and יסבובו in 22a and b. Dhorme, followed by Hölscher, transposes צאלים צללו and reads צללי צאלים "the shades of the lotus [cover it]." So too Driver, "Mythical Monsters," 137, and perhaps also Moffatt's "in the shade of thorny thickets." Less persuasively, Beer (*BHK prps*) and Fohrer read וסך נעצוצים "and a thicket of thorn-bushes" for יסכהו צאלים "lotus covers it." De Wilde suggests סך חבצלת צללו "a covering of meadow saffron (or, asphodel) is its shade," חבצלת as in Isa 35:1; Cant 2:1. Guillaume, believing that "the author hardly ever repeated himself," sought a homonym, and proposed "beneath the warm mud he lies," צאלים being cognate with Arab. *ṣallaṭ*; similarly Gray, referring to Arab. *ṣalālu(n)*, which he glosses as "dry mud," understanding תחת as "in the place of" (cf. on 30:7). תחת seems an odd choice of prep in such a context, however, and, more important, according to Freytag, 2:510b, and Lane, 1710c, *ṣallat* means "dry ground."

22.b. נחל is either the "wadi," which may often be dried up, or, as here, the "brook" or "stream" that flows through the wadi (*DCH*, 5:657b). Use of the term suggests strongly a Palestinian or Arabian background rather than an Egyptian one, where the one "river" dominates.

22.c. ערבה may be the "willow" (*Salix*; so *HALOT*, 2:879b), as Dhorme, KJV, RSV, NJPS, JB, or the "poplar" (*Populus euphratica*; so BDB, 788a; Löw, *Flora*, 3:322–23; Dalman, *Arbeit und Sitte*, 1:101; J. V. Kinnier Wilson, "Hebrew and Akkadian Philological Notes," *JSS* 7 [1962] 173–83 [175–77]; *DCH*, 6:553a, prefers the latter), as NIV, NEB, both of which favor well-watered locations (Lev 23:40; Isa 44:4; Ps 137:2). The name "Brook of the Willows, or, Poplars" (נחל הערבים, cf. ערבי-נחל "willows of the brook" here) occurs in Isa 15:7.

23.a. For הן "behold" as translationally equivalent to "if," see *Note* b on 23:8.

23.b. עשק is normally "oppress"; although the vb is almost always transitive, many attempt to devise an intransitive sense that will suit here, such as "grows violent" (NAB; RV mg "be violent"), "rages" (NIV), "swells violently" (Dhorme), "rages" (Habel), "is turbulent" (RSV), "is strong" (Hölscher, similarly Sicre Díaz), or simply "overflow" (JB), though a river may well be swollen without actually overflowing; but the absence of any parallel leads us rather to suspect either our lexica or the text. Tur-Sinai strains for a sense with his "If the river cheated him [of expected food], he cared not, he felt sure that the stream would thrust (food) into his mouth."

Among emendations, (1) the most attractive is ישפע "overflows" (Beer [*BHK frt*], Fohrer, "very plausible" according to Driver–Gray), though the vb does not occur elsewhere; the nouns שפע "abundance" and שפעה "abundance, quantity," however, do occur; and cf. 22:11; 38:34 where we find the clause "a flood (שפעה) of water covers you." (2) The emendation ישקע "sinks" (Gunkel, Budde, Beer [*BHK al*]) envisages the Nile as the river in question, but the Nile could hardly be called a נחל "wadi" (v 22b), and it is hard to see why the hippopotamus should be disturbed by the sinking of the Nile, which still leaves it plenty of water. (3) Duhm and Beer (*BHK prps*) suggest ישוק "gushes forth" (from שוק "rush," as of a bear in Prov 28:15; BDB, 1003a, 1055a, and Driver–Gray distinguish שוק "be abundant, overflow" from שקק "run about, rush"); Hartley follows this suggestion. (4) Gerleman (*BHS prps*) mentions an emendation to יפשע, which could only mean "[if the river] transgresses, revolts," which hardly seems possible, and it is perhaps more likely that the form in his critical apparatus to *BHS* is an error for ישפע "overflows." (5) Blommerde vocalizes the word as עשׁק (qal pass) "he is oppressed [by the river, בהר being adv accus!]," but he does not say how the hippopotamus could be "oppressed" by the river.

Among philological proposals, (1) G. R. Driver proposes a new word עשק II "gush, pour" (cf. Akk. *ešqu* "strong, violent" [*CDA*, 83a "solid, massive"], Arab. *ghasaqa* "be dark, pour forth" [Lane, 2257c]; cf. *DCH*, 6:620b; the objection of Guillaume [see below] that *ghasaqa* is used only of tears, pus, or light rain is belied by the evidence in Lane); see his "Difficult Words in the Hebrew Prophets," in *Studies in Old Testament Prophecy Presented to Professor Theodore H. Robinson* (ed. H. H. Rowley; Edinburgh: T. & T. Clark, 1950) 52–72 (60); thus NEB "if the river is in spate." So too Kinnier Wilson, "A Return to the Problem of Behemoth and Leviathan," 9. Ehrlich and Hölscher had already proposed this solution, which is adopted in the *Translation* above. (2) A. Guillaume ("The Arabic Background of the Book of Job," in *Promise and Fulfilment: Essays Presented to Professor S. H. Hooke in Celebration of His Ninetieth Birthday, 21st January, 1964* [ed. F. F. Bruce; Edinburgh: T. & T. Clark, 1963] 106–27 [126]; *Studies*, 136) proposes yet another new word, עשק III "come and go" (*DCH*, 6:623b; cf. Arab. *'afaqa* [Freytag, 3:186a: form IV "come and go repeatedly beyond necessity"; not in Lane], the correspondence between Arab. *f* and Heb. *š* being explained by him in "A Contribution to Hebrew Lexicography," *BSOAS* 16 [1954] 1–12 [3, 8]); thus "though (הן being "if") the river rise and fall." This suggestion is rather far-fetched.

Other interpretations are these: (1) NJPS has a distinctive interpretation of the verse: "He can restrain the river from its rushing; He is confident the stream will gush at his command." But (a) עשק can hardly mean "restrain," (b) "at his command" would require an emendation from אל-פיהו "to his mouth" to על-פיהו "at his mouth, i.e., command," and (c) there is no reason within the depiction of the hippopotamus here to think that it can restrain a river or send it gushing again. (2) Tur-Sinai has "when the river cheats him (of his prey) he is not concerned," but the hippopotamus, being herbivorous, has no prey properly speaking, and it is hard to imagine how the river could rob the hippopotamus of its food, since it can always clamber up a river or marsh bank and find plants. (3) Gordis, following ibn Ezra, thinks the hippopotamus "robs the river [of its water] without haste," but the idea of "oppressing" a river is too strange (עשק always has a person as the obj). (4) KJV "he drinketh up a river" follows Vg *absorbebit fluvium*, but it is not clear how Vg arrived at that translation.

23.c. חפז is usually "hurry" (1 Sam 23:26; 2 Sam 4:4), but sometimes, as here, expresses the emotion of anxiety, e.g., Deut 20:3 (beside ירא "fear" and ערץ "tremble"), Ps 48:6 (beside תמה "be astonished" and בהל niph "be terrified").

23.d. בטח is usually "trust" (as KJV), but that translation raises the unanswerable question of whom Behemoth would be trusting. Better are RSV, NJPS "is confident," NAB "tranquil," i.e., the opposite of חפז "be disturbed" in the previous colon (so too the *Translation* above). NIV "secure" is not quite right since בטח must express Behemoth's own sense of security, not the objective fact of its security. JB "A Jordan could pour down his throat without his caring" is a vivid translation, but "caring" is quite some way from the thought of בטח.

Perhaps, however, we here have בטח II "fall down, lie down" (*DCH*, 2:141a), suggested, on the basis of Arab. *baṭaḥa*, also for Jer 12:5; Prov 14:16; Ps 22:9 (10) (hiph), i.e., "it lies flat," NEB "he sprawls at his ease." So Samuel L. Skoss, "The Root בטח in Jeremiah 12.5, Psalms 22.10, Proverbs 14.16, and Job 40.23," in *Jewish Studies in Memory of George A. Kohut 1874–1933* (ed. Salo W. Baron and Alexander Marx; New York: Alexander Kohut Memorial Foundation, 1935) 549–53; G. R. Driver, "L'interprétation du texte masorétique à la lumière de la lexicographie hébraïque," *ETL* 26 (1950) 337–53 (341–42); other bibliography in *DCH*, 2:606b, to which add Johann August Dathe, *Prophetae majores ex recensione textus hebraei et versionum antiquarum latine versi notisque philologicis et criticis illustrati* (Halle: Sumtibus Orphanotrophei, 1779) 267; Benjamin Kennicott, *Remarks on Select Passages in the Old Testament* (Oxford: Prince & Cooke, 1787) 231 (in reference to Ps 22:10 [9]); G. R. Driver, "Linguistic and Textual Problems: Jeremiah," *JQR* 28 (1937–38) 97–129 (111–12); Driver, "Difficult Words in the Hebrew Prophets," in *Studies in Old Testament Prophecy Presented to Professor Theodore H. Robinson* (ed. H. H. Rowley; Edinburgh: T. & T. Clark, 1950) 52–72 (59–60). Driver is followed by Kinnier Wilson, "A Return to the Problem of Behemoth and Leviathan," 9. Similarly Guillaume, who regards this sense as the "literal meaning" of בטה I "trust."

Pope removes the word ובטח altogether as overloading the line.

23.e. כי introducing a concessive clause, i.e., "if" rather than "that"; KJV's "he trusteth that he can draw up Jordan into his mouth" does not make much sense.

23.f. ירדן is usually "Jordan." It is strange to find a Palestinian place name in Job, and it may be that the term means "river" (lit. "the descender," from ירד "go down") in the first place and was applied only secondarily to the River Jordan as the most notable river in the region. At Gen 32:10 (11) also it does not seem to mean "Jordan"; similarly Driver, "Difficult Words in the Hebrew Prophets," in *Studies in Old Testament Prophecy Presented to Professor Theodore H. Robinson* (ed. H. H. Rowley; Edinburgh: T. & T. Clark, 1950) 52–72 (60). It is "merely an illustration of a swift running current" (Rowley; similarly Terrien, Tur-Sinai, Guillaume, Gordis). On the other hand, it could be that "Jordan" is used poetically for "a mighty river" in general; we might then translate "a Jordan." Some are tempted to delete the word, since the colon is long (so Budde, Driver–Gray, Beer [*BHK frt*], Hölscher, Fohrer, de Wilde). Beer (*BH²*; *BHK prps*) thinks of יאר "stream," though that is used generally of the Nile, which may not be appropriate here.

23.g. גיח "burst forth," as also at 38:8. The vb does not seem wholly appropriate here; Graetz proposed הגיע "approaches," which, however, is too tame.

23.h. אל־פיהו "against its mouth" is transferred by Beer (*BH²*), Guillaume, and Gray to the beginning of v 24; so also G. R. Driver, "Difficult Words," 60, emending to הבאפל עיניו "is it by darkening [i.e., blinding] its eyes that one takes it?," an allusion to one method of catching a crocodile in Egypt noted by Herodotus (*Hist.* 2.70): after dragging it to the river bank the hunter throws mud in its eyes to blind it (it is not a matter of "stuffing the eyes of the animal with clay" as Dhorme reports and Pope and Gordis believe! Terrien reports Herodotus more faithfully). The vb אפל "darken" is not, however, attested in Biblical Hebrew (though cf. אפל "darkness").

24.a. On this sequence of sixteen rhetorical questions (40:24–41:7 [40:28]), the longest such series in the Hebrew Bible, cf. Watson, 339.

24.b. יקחנו "one will take it," without any interrogative; but an interrogative must be understood (as also RV, RSV, NJPS, NIV, JB, NEB). Some think we should insert at the beginning of the line as the subj מי־הוא "who indeed [will take it]?" which perhaps fell out following the similar פיהו "its mouth" (so too Ehrlich, Peake, Beer [*BHK frt*], Driver–Gray [*frt*], Ball, Dhorme, Hölscher, Fohrer, Pope, Rowley, Fedrizzi, Gordis, de Wilde, NAB). Others think that מי הוא "who indeed" should be read instead of אל־פיהו (Duhm, Moffatt, Kissane, Habel). Another nearby example of a rhetorical question without an interrogative has occurred at 38:8; see further, Lénart J. de Regt, "Functions and Implications of Rhetorical Questions in the Book of Job," in *Biblical Hebrew and Discourse Linguistics* (ed. Robert D. Bergen; Winona Lake, IN: Eisenbrauns, 1994) 361–73 (362).

24.c. בְּעֵינָיו "with its eyes," hence JB "So who is going to catch him by the eyes?" (similarly NIV, NAB, NJPS)—not a very transparent translation. The hippopotamus's eyes are lodged in bulges protruding from the head (as de Wilde notes), but it is hard to imagine capturing the beast by them. RV "Shall any take him when he is on the watch?" (similarly Davidson) strains the sense uncomfortably. Duhm thought that smaller animals might be captured in this way (he omits to mention any example), and that the idea of using this technique for Behemoth is palpably absurd. Ehrlich had the intriguing idea of the hunter's eyes ensnaring Behemoth by staring him down; but in the next colon the suff refers to Behemoth, and so it probably does here too. It is most unlikely that "capture it by its eyes" could refer to blinding the creature (cf. also Driver's emendation noted above on אֶל־פִּיהוּ). Guillaume, followed by Gray, moves אֶל־פִּיהוּ "into its mouth" to the beginning of this verse, and translates "Into his mouth with open eyes he receives it" (the river); but why does it matter whether its eyes are open or not? Pope ventures to compare the effect of grasping a large fish (once landed) by its eyes and so paralyzing it; but would that be called "capturing by the eyes"? An emendation seems called for, and there is no shortage of proposals.

(1) Beer (*BH²*) deleted the word, substituting אֶל־פִּיהוּ "to its mouth" from the end of the previous colon. (2) Kissane read בִּמְעוֹנוֹ "in his lair," but hippopotami do not have lairs, and in any case how would a hunter enter such a lair? (3) Better is Ball's proposal of צִנִּים (or the form צִנּוֹת) as "fishhooks, barbs," as in Amos 4:2; Prov 22:5 (followed by Moffatt [apparently], Driver–Gray [*frt*], Beer [*BHK al*] [apparently], Rowley, RSV). (4) Equally acceptable would be Ball's other proposal בְּצַמִּים "in a snare" (cf. 5:5, though there it should be emended; 18:9, where it is parallel to פַּח "trap"), though it is less similar to the MT graphically. (5) Gordis suggested that עֵין is the name of a trap, which he finds also at Hos 10:10 בְּאָסְרָם לִשְׁתֵּי עֵינוֹתָם (Kt) "when they are caught by the double ring"; Habel accepts this, rendering "El takes him by the mouth with rings" (moving אֶל־פִּיהוּ from v 23b to here), and so too Hartley.

(6) The best solution, however, seems to that suggested by Reiske: בְּשִׁנָּיו מִי יִקָּחֶנּוּ "who will take it by its teeth?" (בְּשִׁנָּיו "by its teeth" is also read by Beer [*BHK frt*], and Peters), but though, on the one hand, that does not seem very practical (which is what is required here), on the other hand it does not have enough absurdity to fit the present context. There is, however, a sense of שֵׁן "tooth" that might suit: at 1 Sam 2:13 it means the tooth or "tine" of a (three-pronged) meat fork (BDB, 1042a; *HALOT*, 4:1595b; an illustration in G. E. Wright, *Biblical Archaeology* [Philadelphia: Westminster Press, 1957] 143 fig. 95), so perhaps the absurd image is of plunging a kitchen fork into the river to haul Behemoth to the bank; hence the *Translation* above. בְּשִׁנָּיו would be a better reading.

24.d. נקב "pierce" is elsewhere used with these body parts as objs: יָד "hand" (2 Kgs 18:21 ‖ Isa 36:6), לְחִי "cheek" (Job 41:2 [40:26]), רֹאשׁ "head" (Hab 3:14) (*DCH*, 5:747a). Duhm and Beer (*BH² frt*) think the form should be piel, יִקֹּב.

24.e. אַף "[its] nose"; the suff is unnecessary, but Duhm, Beer (*BHK*), Hölscher, and Driver, "Mythical Monsters," 237 (*frt*), say it should be emended to אַפּוֹ "its nose," Gordis that אַף should be "read" אַפּוֹ (similarly Blommerde).

24.f. מוֹקֵשׁ is plainly "snare," though the term may in some cases refer specifically to the "striker" of the snare, i.e., the part of the trap that falls on its victim, or the "bait" or "decoy" placed in the snare (*DCH*, 5:186a; see also G. R. Driver, "Reflections on Recent Articles," *JBL* 73 [1954] 125–36 [131–36]). Whatever exactly it means, however, a snare cannot be used for piercing (נקב)! Gordis's notion (following Delitzsch and Driver–Gray) that it is "a metal tooth or trigger on which the bait was placed," which then pierced the nose of the hunted animal, is entirely fanciful (nor can we say מוֹקֵשׁ means "hooks," as Habel). Ehrlich therefore proposed emending בְּמוֹקְשִׁים "with snares" to בְּקִמּוֹשִׁים "with hooks" (followed by Dhorme [translating "thorns," but explaining it as "barbs"], Driver, "Difficult Words," 60, Driver, "Mythical Monsters," 237, Terrien, Pope "barbs," NJPS); קִמּוֹשׁ, however, elsewhere always means "thorns, nettles," and there is no direct evidence that it can mean also "hook" (though some analogy may be provided by צָנִין "thorn" alongside צִנָּה "hook" and by חוֹחַ I "thorn" and, in 41:2 [40:26], "hook"). This emendation is adopted in the *Translation* above.

NIV tried to solve the difficulty with "or trap him and pierce his nose," making the piercing a subsequent operation to the trapping; but that is an unnatural way of taking the Hebrew. It points the way, however, to the likelihood that בְּמוֹקְשִׁים "with snares" should be taken with the vb לקח, i.e., "can one capture it with snares?" De Wilde proposes an emendation to מוֹרָשִׁים "ropes" (cf. Syr. *maršā*; מוֹרָשׁ III "string" in *DCH*, 5:189a), which some see at 17:11 (*q.v.*), but *piercing* with ropes does not seem very natural. Guillaume, who thinks the first colon does not refer to capturing the hippopotamus and translates it "Into his mouth with open eyes he receives it (the river water)," offers for the second colon the ingenious rendering "alone among the river animals his snout is dry," postulating a new מקש, cognate with Arab. *māqasa* "vie in diving with," the ptcp מוֹקֵשׁ "diver" thus meaning amphibians, and a new נקב "be dry" (cf. Arab. *qabba* "become dry" [Lane, 2477b]); unlike other amphibians, he says, the hippopotamus's nose remains dry. Gray accepts the proposal for מקש "dive," but emends

יקֹב אַף to אָפוֹ יקֹב "his snout protrudes," from a new קבב cognate with Arab. *qabba* V "protrude." But the sense "vie in diving with" for Arab. *maqasa* cannot be substantiated (Freytag, 4:197b, has "pour out, immerse").

24.g. The description of Behemoth is thought by some to end too abruptly; Duhm suggested that 41:9–12 (41:1–4) originally formed its conclusion.

41:1 (40:25).a. NEB, with REB, transposes 41:1–6 (40:25–30) to follow 39:30, identifying Leviathan as the whale. Duhm transposes vv 9–12 (1–4) to this point.

1 (40:25).b. The interrogative particle הֲ is presumably to be understood (as also de Wilde, NAB), as previously in v 24 (it appears in one MT ms, and is in the Qumran Tg; Beer [*BH² vel*; BHK] and Gray insert it here). Alternatively, Budde[2], Gunkel, Beer (*BH² frt*) may be right in restoring אִם, the interrogative particle, perhaps omitted by haplography after אִם at the end of v 24. משׁךְ can be "drag along, drag away" or, better in this context, "draw up" vertically (cf. *DCH*, 5:523b §2), from the water. NAB, however, has "lead about [Leviathan with a hook]," which does not seem to be what משׁךְ signifies.

Budde[2] and Hölscher, followed by Gordis, noted that the word for "drag up" (תִּמְשֹׁךְ, *timšōq*) may be a pun on the Egyptian word for the crocodile, Egyptian *pemsaḥ* (Arab. *timsāḥ* [Freytag, 1:200b]; in the Greek of Herodotus χάμψαι, *champsai*). De Wilde, following Delitzsch and Budde, even thinks that an original תְּמְשָׁךְ "crocodile" (unattested in Biblical Hebrew) was later replaced by לִוְיָתָן "Leviathan."

1 (40:25).c. חכה "fishhook" in Isa 19:8; Hab 1:15 (cf. Dalman, *Arbeit und Sitte*, 6:359). NEB, having decided that Leviathan is the whale, renders "with a gaff."

1 (40:25).d. תשׁקיע is usually derived from שׁקע "sink, sink down" (BDB, 1054a; *HALOT*, 4:1645a "restrain, thrust down" [in a trick to catch it]); thus KJV "or his tongue with a cord which thou lettest down?" (i.e., with a fishing line), RSV, NJPS "press down his tongue," NJB "hold his tongue down," NIV "tie down." Tur-Sinai thought it was a matter of "sinking" a hook into Leviathan's tongue; but the omission of a prep before לשׁנו is a difficulty (and certainly not "usual in the poem"), and "by means of a cord" for בחבל is very awkward.

But already Michaelis (cf. Gesenius–Buhl, 861b) recognized a different שׁקע II "bind," which stands in the Samaritan text of Lev 8:13 for the MT חבשׁ "bind," and which was understood by Theod δήσεις, Aq συνδήσεις, Vg *ligabis*; this view is followed by Beer (*BH²*), Dhorme, JB "run a line round his tongue," NEB "slip a noose round its tongue," and is adopted in the *Translation* above. Beer (*BH² prps*) mentions an emendation that achieves the same sense, to תְּקְשׁר "can you bind?," but it is preferable to suppose a second שׁקע. It is hard, however, to know which of these vbs is in view in NAB's "curb his tongue with a bit."

Gray's solution invokes a שׁקע II "vie, contend" cognate with Arab. *šaqa(y)* (Lane, 1582a), and reads תִּשְׁקֶה "will you contend with him?"

1 (40:25).e. MT לשׁנו "its tongue" could conceivably be vocalized as לְשִׁנָּי "to its teeth" (so Hoffmann, Beer [*BH² prps*]), which might be preferred if the ancient belief that the crocodile lacked a tongue was shared by the Joban poet (see *Comment*). But the ל is hard to explain on this suggestion. Gray would obviate the difficulty by reading תִּשְׁקֶה עַל־שִׁנָּיו, rendering "[or] contend with him [with a line] in despite of his teeth."

2 (40:26).a. אגמון "rush" or "reed," usually as something weak (Isa 9:13; 19:15; 58:5), only here for binding (the occurrence in v 20 [41:12] is problematic). No doubt it is a cord made of rushes that is meant here, "either made of rushes, or spun of rush-fibre" (Driver–Gray). It is an ironic thought of course. There is no evidence that it can mean "hook" (as Tur-Sinai). Gray adopts the reading of the Qumran Tg זְמַם "bridle" (not otherwise known in Heb., but cf. Syr., Arab. *zimām* [Lane, 1249a]), but that is probably no more than an interpretation. David Wolfers, "Bulrush and Bramble," *JBQ* 19 (1991) 170–75, urges that אגמון be translated "bulrush" and חוח "bramble," conceived of as absurdly unsuitable weapons for capturing Leviathan; but the idea of attempting to capture it with a rope and a hook is absurd enough.

2 (40:26).b. אף is "nose," not "gills" (Moffatt), since the crocodile, being a reptile, has no gills.

2 (40:26).c. חוח is usually "thorn, briar," but also "hook" here and at 2 Chr 33:11 (so BDB, 296a; unless there is it is חוֹח II "hole," as *HALOT*, 1:296b, *DCH*, 3:170b); cf. חח "hook, ring, fetter." Tur-Sinai is over-confident in insisting that it is "an iron bridle-ring put through the horse's nose." Moffatt's "carry him with a gaff [a barbed fishing spear] between his jaws" attempts to make plain what the purpose of piercing its jaw would be.

3 (40:27).a. הירבה אליך תחנונים, lit. "will it make many supplications to you?" (similarly RSV). The rendering in the *Translation* "will he keep begging you for mercy?" is borrowed from NIV; it expresses the continued image of Leviathan as a prisoner.

5 (40:29).a. שׂחק is understood by most to mean "play," i.e., with the captured Leviathan, but by Tur-Sinai to mean "sport" in the sense of hunting (of chasing birds for sport, cf. Lam 3:52). But the

topic of hunting seems not to belong in this verse, and it certainly does not fit with the subject of the next colon, the playing of girls with Leviathan.

5 (40:29).b. כצפור lit. "as a bird," when what is meant is "as with a bird"; the omission of ב following כ is well known (cf. GKC, §118s–w; and cf. 5:14). A צפור is a bird of any kind, not necessarily a sparrow.

5 (40:29).c. קשר is "bind" (as at 39:10), and frequently "conspire," but not "cage" (as Moffatt); even "bind" (kjv) gives the wrong impression, as does "tie him down" (njps). "Put him on a leash" (rsv, niv; similarly nab, jb, neb) is to be preferred. Tur-Sinai improbably thinks of Leviathan, like a bird, being caught and bound and then handed to maidservants to be cooked; killing, rather than binding, would be a more appropriate step between catching and cooking.

5 (40:29).d. Though the Qumran Targum supports the mt לנערותיך "for your little girls," D. Winton Thomas, "Job xl 29b: Text and Translation," *VT* 14 (1964) 114–16, suggests we have here a word for "sparrow," נֻעְרָה (not otherwise attested in Hebrew, but cf. Arab. *nugharat* [Lane, 2817b]; see *DCH*, 5:712b), translating "tie him with a string like a young sparrow"; but he needs to emend away the suff and the pl ending, and to alter the prefixed preposition from ל to כ; similarly Robert Gordis, "Job xl 29—An Addition," *VT* 14 (1964) 491–94 (= *The Word and the Book* [New York: Ktav, 1976] 355–57), preferring the form נֶעְרָה, identical to the word for "little girl," and explaining the ל as indicating movement from one state to another, and the pl as "distributive" ("tie him up like one of your birds"); thus also Sicre Díaz. Gordis defends his interpretation by remarking that Job no longer has any daughters; but even if they were still alive, they would hardly be נערות "little girls," so the rhetoric is not supposed to be very realistic. Tur-Sinai insists that the term means "maidservants," which is certainly possible.

lxx ὥσπερ στρούθιον παιδίῳ, incorporating both "sparrow" and "child," supports the view of Winton Thomas and Gordis that such a word existed in Hebrew, but does not settle the reading here. John Day (*God's Conflict with the Dragon and the Sea. Echoes of a Canaanite Myth in the Old Testament* [University of Cambridge Oriental Publications 35; Cambridge: Cambridge University Press, 1985] 63), however, argued that the rendering of lxx resulted from their reading כנענים "merchants" in the next verse in this place also, but as ישׁעני "sparrows" here; although at Lam 4:3 lxx has στρούθιον for ישׁעני, the Hebrew means rather "ostriches." Gunkel tried to reproduce lxx by inserting כָּחוֹר "like a dove," and Beer (*BHK*) כַּיוֹנָה "like a dove" (Driver–Gray are tempted to follow; Driver, "Mythical Monsters," 242, does follow).

6 (40:30).a. As in v 1 (40:25), the interrogative is to be understood (similarly at 39:2).

6 (40:30).b. חברים is not the common word חָבֵר "companions" (as kjv), but a related word חַבָּר, occurring only here (BDB, 289a; *DCH*, 3:155a); its formation suggests a permanent trade or occupation [like גַּנָּב "thief" and טַבָּח "butcher, cook"], thus "partners" [Dhorme], "trading partners" [neb], "guildsmen" [cf. Gordis], "the fishing guild" [njb], "partners in the fishing" [reb], "fishing syndicates" [Terrien]; cf. the "guildsmen" of fishers in Luke 5:7). It is not a general word for "traders" (as rsv, niv, njps, nab; Good "salesmen"). Alternatively, Tur-Sinai has suggested the term may be related to a new word חֶבֶר "granary, warehouse" (cf. Ugar. *bt ḥbr*; but this term is no longer recognized), which he finds also at Prov 21:9; 25:24; Pope is inclined to follow this proposal, with his translation "mongers," i.e., wholesalers.

In view of the occurrence in Isa 23:8 of כְנַעְנֶיהָ "its traders" in parallelism with סֹחֲרֶיהָ "its merchants," Beer (*BHK frt*) proposed reading סֹחֲרִים "the merchants" here. The problem with that is that then the כנענים and the סחרים would be the same people, and it would be strange to have the merchants dividing it among the merchants. Beer's solution was to read בְּנֵי כְנַעֲנִים "the sons of the traders" as the subj of יחצוהו "they divide it up" in the second colon, but that has its own difficulty; see *Note* on בין below. Gunkel's suggestion was to read חֹבְלִים "sailors" (as in Ezek 27:29); but sailors are not necessarily fishers.

6 (40:30).c. כרה II "trade" must mean, with a following על, "bargain over" (Dhorme), "chaffer over" (Peake). Moffatt's "Will fishermen make a meal of him?" has recourse to כרה III "give a feast" (BDB, 500a; *HALOT*, 2:497a; cf. *DCH*, 4:459b, recognizing this as a possible sense here), as apparently at 2 Kgs 6:23; but fishers are not the most likely persons to be eating Leviathan, and it would be strange to have the eating before the dividing up (in the next colon). Tur-Sinai proposed another כרה "heap up" (as in MH; cf. Jastrow, 666a), which he found also at 6:27; but there is no evidence that it implies the obj "money" if that is not specified. Duhm, unlike most others, thought the bargaining of the fishers could well be with the merchants, not with one another.

6 (40:30).d. חצה, lit. "cut in half" (cf. חֵצִי "half"), can occasionally mean simply "divide" (as at Judg 9:43, where it is a division into three, and Dan 11:4, a division into four). Dhorme renders "offer for sale," but that is not justified by the evidence. Nor is Habel's suggestion that it means "divide the

proceeds of the sale." The image is of Leviathan being cut up like a large fish (Rowley), not of "a huge ferocious creature no one would want to buy" (Habel).

6 (40:30).e. בֵּין is lit. "between," but it can often mean "among" (e.g., Isa 2:4; Jer 25:16; Zech 3:7; Prov 14:9; Cant 2:2, 3; Esth 3:8). Gunkel, as also Beer (*BHK*), saw in בֵּין an original בְּנֵי "the sons of [the traders]" (so too Driver, "Mythical Monsters," 242), but why mention their sons and not themselves?

6 (40:30).f. כְּנַעֲנִים, lit. "Canaanites," but without the article the term has probably become just "traders" (כְּנַעֲנִי II in BDB, 489a; *DCH*, 4:438a), as at Zech 14:21; Prov 31:24 (so too, e.g., Gordis); Pope has "hucksters." Cf. W. F. Albright, "The Role of the Canaanites in the History of Civilization," in *The Bible and the Ancient Near East: Essays in Honor of William Foxwell Albright* (ed. G. Ernest Wright; London: Routledge & Kegan Paul, 1961) 328–62.

7 (40:31).a. מִלֵּא, lit. "fill," but "fill his skin, hide [with darts]" (as KJV, RSV, NAB, NIV, NJPS, NEB, GNB, Gordis) seems rather unidiomatic in English. Dhorme's "stab his skin all over" is good, but best is "riddle his hide" (JB). Kinnier Wilson, "A Return to the Problem of Behemoth and Leviathan," 11, has the interesting proposal to understand מלא as "load," like Akk. *malû* IV "fill, load" (*CDA*, 194a) and translate the line "Will you load his skin into a boat, or his head into a fishing vessel?" See further the two *Notes* below on "darts" and "fishing spears."

7 (40:31).b. שֻׂכָּה, occurring only here, is understood by BDB, 968a, as "barb, spear" (from שׂכך IV, an unattested root perhaps meaning "pierce"), by *HALOT*, 3:1326b, more specifically as "harpoon" (as also RSV, NIV, NEB). KJV had "barbed iron," NAB "barbs," JB, NJPS "darts." We may compare שִׂכִּים "thorns" (Num 33:55). Kinnier Wilson, "A Return to the Problem of Behemoth and Leviathan," 11, follows LXX πλωτόν "floating," and translates "Will you load his skin into a boat [שְׂכִית; cf. שְׂכִיּוֹת in Isa 2:16], or his head into a fishing vessel [צלצל; see next *Note*]?" G. R. Driver preferred the form שְׂכָה "ship" ("Difficult Words," 52). Tur-Sinai, ever ingenious, proposed that שׂכות are "cloves" (cf. Akk. *šikkatu* "pin, nail," though the word does not mean that according to *CDA*) and that בצלצל is the Mishnaic בְּצַלְצוּל "chive" (*Cepa pallacana*) or "shallot" (Jastrow, 184b), thus "Couldst thou stud his body with cloves, with fish-onions his head?," turning Leviathan by culinary magic into gefilte fish!

7 (40:31).c. צלצל דגים, lit. "spear of fish." צלצל is derived precariously (Gordis) from צלל "tingle, quiver," a reference to the whizzing sound of a spear in the air (cf. צְלָצַל "whirring, buzzing"). It would be hard to justify the translation "fish-hooks" (Driver, "Difficult Words," 56; NEB; REB has "fishing spears"). LXX ἐν πλοίοις ἁλιέων "in ships of fishers" mistook צלצל for another צלצל "ship" (cf. Driver, "Difficult Words" 56), but Kinnier Wilson, "A Return to the Problem of Behemoth and Leviathan," 11 n. 1, thinks that "ship" is the right sense here (as also in Isa 18:1); he translates "[will you load] his head into a fishing vessel?"

8 (40:32).a. Dhorme thought the verse out of place, and proposed moving it to follow the next verse, 41:9 (1); he is followed by de Wilde.

8 (40:32).b. שִׂים is impv, "lay [your hand]." For parallels to this hypothetical impv, see GKC, §110f, Driver, *Tenses*, §§188–91, and cf. Prov 20:13 "open your eyes, be filled with food" for "if you open your eyes ... ," Isa 8:10; 55:2 (similarly Gordis). See also *Note* a on "adorn yourself" at 40:10 above.

8 (40:32).c. זכר is "remember"; Budde suggested that the word here points not to the past but to the future, "consider." Cf. Peake: "remember beforehand the fatal issue a battle with him would involve."

8 (40:32).d. זְכֹר מִלְחָמָה אַל־תּוֹסַף, lit. "remember the battle, do not add." Gordis, however, thinks זְכֹר is not the impv "remember" but an inf with תוסף, thus "you will not continue to remember the battle," because you will be dead.

9 (41:1).a. Dhorme moves this verse to follow v 10 (41:2) (so also NAB, Driver, "Mythical Monsters," 237), so as to identify a suitable antecedent for the third-person suff of תחלתו "his hope," which can hardly be Job, the "you" of v 8 (40:32). Gordis argues in return that "It is characteristic of the poet's style to introduce a new subject through a pronoun without an explicit antecedent, thus creating a challenge for the reader to discover from the context who is intended." We could compare the opening of chap 28. Sicre Díaz transposes vv 9–11 (41:1–3) to the end of the chapter, but it is hard to agree that they form a better climax than vv 33–34 (25–26).

Pope rightly remarks of vv 1–3 (9–11) that the Hebrew is difficult, but is on less safe ground when he maintains that "the text has suffered some sabotage intended to obscure gross pagan allusions."

9 (1).b. תחלתו "one's hope" is often emended to תֹּחַלְתְּךָ "your hope" (Gunkel, Budde, Steuernagel, Beer [*BHK*], Hölscher, Kissane, Fohrer, Terrien), in order to make the verse follow naturally upon the second-person vbs of the previous verse (v 8 [40:32]). But perhaps the "you" in v 8 (40:32) is not specifically Job, but anyone—which would make it equivalent to an indefinite third person. RSV has "the hope of a man." תחלתו is maintained also by Duhm, Driver–Gray.

9 (1).c. כזב (usually piel) is "lie"; niph is "be proved a liar" (Prov 30:6) in its only other occurrence. Here it must rather be "be proved deceptive, disappointing" as of a revelation (Hab 2:3) or a spring

(Isa 58:11) (both piel). Thus RSV, NJPS "disappointed," NIV "false," JB "vain," NJB "futile." NEB more loosely has "such a man is in desperate case" (REB "Anyone who tackles him has no hope of success").

9 (1).d. מול, usually in hiph, is "hurl, cast," and here, in hoph, no doubt "hurled down," i.e., "over-whelmed" (as BDB, 376b); some keep the metaphor, as NEB "hurled headlong at the very sight of him" (but REB "is overcome"), RSV "is laid low" (but NRSV "overwhelmed"), JB "the mere sight of him would stagger you" (but NJB "overwhelm").

Emendations are proposed: (1) If תחלתו "one's hope" is to be given a second-person suff, יֻטָּל "it is overwhelmed" should become תֻּטַּל 2ms impf "you are overwhelmed" (Budde, Steuernagel, Beer [BHK prps], Hölscher), or perhaps תֻּטַּל 3fs impf "it is overwhelmed," תּוֹחֶלֶת being fem. (2) Others suggest יָטִיל "he overwhelms," with the obj אֵל "a god" (Gunkel, *Schöpfung und Chaos*, 55–56), i.e., "his appearance casts down even a god," or אֵלִים "the gods" (T. K. Cheyne, "The Text of Job,"*JQR* 9 [1896–97] 573–80 [579]) with the subj מַרְאוֹ "his terror," i.e., the terror of it overwhelms even the gods; similarly Pope "Were not the gods cast down at sight of him?," NRSV "were not even the gods overwhelmed at the sight of it?" (3) Merx read וְגַם מַרְאִי יָטֵל, translating "Will he even hurl, i.e., fight, against my appearing?," which has little to recommend it. (4) Wright, with more reason, reads "Will he even hurl, i.e., fight, against those who shoot at him?" (מֹרָאיו, as at 2 Sam 11:24; the hunters with darts and harpoons have just now been in view in v 7 [40:32]). However, מול hiph is hardly the natural word for "fight." (5) It could be that it is "hope" that is overwhelmed, if we emend יָטֵל to תֻּטַּל (as Beer [BHK prps], Hölscher).

9 (1).e. גַם in the sense "even" (BDB, 169a §2). Most agree that the prefixed interrogative ה should be deleted (so, e.g., Driver–Gray, Dhorme, Beer [BHK], Terrien, Gerleman [BHS], de Wilde, Gray; and NAB, who transfer it to the beginning of v 10 [41:2]). Gordis, however, argues that ה is an abbreviated form of הֲלֹא, thus "indeed, even at his mere sight ..."

9 (1).f. מַרְאִי "its sight," i.e., the sight of it. Some suggest an emendation to מוֹרָא "its fear," i.e., the fear of it (thus Gunkel [vel], Beer [BHK prps מֹרָא]). Kissane ingeniously suggested אַיִל מַרְאִי "(even) a mighty man [is flung down] at the sight of him," אַיִל being presumably a miswriting for אַיִל III "leader, chief" (BDB, 18a, *DCH*, 1:211a, and *HALOT*, 1:40a, take this as a sense of אַיִל I "ram").

10 (2).a. Many (e.g., Driver–Gray, Dhorme, de Wilde) insert the interrogative ה, translating "Is he not cruel, as soon as awakened?"

10 (2).b. אכזר is elsewhere "cruel," as at 30:21; 34:6 (emended); Lam 4:3. Dhorme defends the sense "cruel" (of Leviathan when it is awakened). But here it seems rather to be "fierce" (as BDB, 470a; *DCH*, 1:240a; against *HALOT*, 1:45b), whether of Leviathan itself (Driver–Gray, Dhorme, Pope, Terrien, Habel, de Wilde, NAB, JB, NEB) or of the attacker of Leviathan (KJV, RSV, NIV, NJPS, Moffatt). Hölscher, Gordis, taking it of the attacker, thought it means "cruel to oneself," i.e., "foolhardy" (cf. אַכְזָרִי in Ecclus 8:15); Hartley thought it was "brave." Guillaume thinks rather that it is "weakling" (cf. Arab. *kasīr* "broken" [Wehr–Cowan 826b]); thus "He is no weakling that one dares stir him up."

Among emendations, we may mention: (1) Gunkel, followed by Beer (*BH²prps [?]*), "modestly" emended to מַלְאָךְ זָר "an angel shrinks" (but זור is rather "become estranged"). (2) Cheyne took up his proposal, with מַלְאָךְ יֵשַׁע "an angel shudders" ("The Text of Job," 579). But there is elsewhere no parallel to angels shrinking or shuddering. (3) Beer (*BH²prps*) noted another emendation, to לֹא יִזְכֹּר "he will not remember," but it is hard to see what that might mean in the context.

10 (2).c. Taking כִּי as "so that"; Dhorme thinks rather it is "when, as soon as." Either way, the message is, Let sleeping crocodiles lie.

10 (2).d. יְעוּרֶנּוּ is not a possible form, for עוּר qal is "be awake," and cannot have a suff (though contrast *DCH*, 6:315a). Most emend to יְעִירֶנּוּ hiph "arouses it/him" (so, e.g., Beer [*BH²*], Dhorme, Hölscher, Gerleman [BHS prb], Gray); Beer (*BH²vel; BHK*) prefers יְעֹרְרֶנּוּ pilp, which occurs only at Isa 15:5, and Gordis explains the MT as a contraction of that form.

10 (2).e. לְפָנַי "before me" does not make sense in the context (though it is accepted by KJV, RSV [not NRSV], NIV, NJPS, Terrien, Habel, Hartley, Rowold [see below]), and most accept an emendation to לְפָנָיו "before it (Leviathan)" (so, e.g., Dhorme, Beer [BHK], Pope, Gordis, de Wilde, Gray, NEB, NAB); not so likely is the suggestion that the suff is really third person (Mitchell Dahood, review of G. Garbini, *Il Semitico di Nord-Ovest* (1960), *Or* 32 [1963] 498–500 [499]; *Psalms I*, 115, 168; "Hebrew-Ugaritic Lexicography VIII," *Bib* 51 [1970] 391–404 [399, where he reads לְפָנָיו]; Blommerde; for other examples, see on 21:16). Yahweh is indeed the speaker, but the issue is not who can stand before God, but before Leviathan.

H. Rowold, "מִי הוּא? לִי הוּא: Leviathan and Job in Job 41:2–3," *JBL* 105 (1986) 104–9, has mounted a defense of the MT לְפָנַי "before me," arguing that it is a confrontation of Leviathan with Yahweh that is in view, not of Leviathan with an attacker. Thus he translates, "Who is he that he will take his stand over against me?" and in v 3 renders "Who has confronted me that I should sue for peace?" (following E. Ruprecht's translation of וְאַשְׁלֵם ["Das Nilpferd im Hiobbuch," 209–31]) and "Under the whole of heaven, he is mine!" The objection to this view is that "under the whole of heaven" does not make sense alongside the ejaculation "He is mine!"

11 (3).a. הקדימני is "has confronted me" (NJPS "Whoever confronts Me I shall requite"; similarly Habel), but it is better to understand the whole verse as envisaging an encounter, not with Yahweh but with Leviathan. Thus Graetz, Gunkel, Cheyne, Duhm, Beer (BH^2), Dhorme, Hölscher, Rowley, Fedrizzi, Gordis, NAB, followed by the *Translation* above, read הקדימו "has confronted it" (NEB הקדימו); Ball, Driver, "Mythical Monsters," 237, and Gray read the piel impf יקדמנו, and Beer (*BHK*) and de Wilde the piel perf קדמו, with the same sense. For קדם hiph "confront (an opponent)," cf. Amos 9:10 (piel in Isa 37:33; Ps 18:5, 18 [6, 19]).

RV has "Who hath first given unto me, that I should repay him?," which is followed by RSV (similarly Terrien), and by NIV with "Who has a claim against me that I must pay?" But קדם does not mean "give," and in any case it is hard to understand what the sentence would mean in the context. Rom 11:35 appears to quote the colon in the traditional sense: "who has given a gift to him that he might be repaid?" (RSV).

Blommerde read הקדימני as הקדימנו, the suff being supposedly third person (another example in v 10 [2] above), and translated "Whomosoever [sic] dares to approach him, I shall reward, What is under all the heavens shall be his." But this seems irrelevant to the concerns of Yahweh and Job in this speech.

11 (3).b. ואשלם is apparently "and I paid" (שלם piel; so BDB, 1022b §3); RSV "that I should repay him," NIV, Hartley "that I must pay," NJPS " I will requite," Habel "whoever confronts me I require." TOB and Peters translate "I leave him in health." But many prefer, as in the *Translation* above, to understand Leviathan as the subj and to read the qal, וישלם "and remained safe" (as the word means in 9:4); so Merx, Wright, Gunkel, Budde, Beer (*BHK*), Hölscher, Fohrer, Fedrizzi, de Wilde, Gray, NEB, NAB, *HALOT,* 4:1533b; perhaps rather the sequence of vbs might lead us to expect וישלם (as Driver–Gray).

11 (3).c. לי־הוא is "it is mine" (KJV "whatsoever is under the whole heaven is mine"; similarly RSV, NIV, NJPS, Hartley). Improbably, Dahood and Blommerde take the *yodh* of לי as a 3 sg suff (for other alleged examples, see on 23:14), Dahood translating "Whatever is under the whole heaven will be his alone" ("The Phoenician Contribution to Biblical Wisdom Literature," in *The Role of the Phoenicians in the Interaction of Mediterranean Civilizations* [ed. William A. Ward; Beirut: American University in Beirut, 1968] 123–52 [140]). On the more probable assumption that the subj of the verse is Leviathan, we should read לא אחד "not one" as in 14:4 (so T. K. Cheyne, *EB* 1:521, Beer [*BHK*]). This reading is adopted in the *Translation* above. Others prefer לא הוא "none" (Gunkel, Beer [*BH²*; *BHK al*], Hölscher, Gordis, de Wilde, Driver, "Mythical Monsters," 237, NEB) or מי הוא "who is it?" (Beer [*BH² frt*], Pope, Gray, NAB), or, less probably לא היה "there has not been (one)" (Ehrlich). One or other of these emendations is accepted by NRSV, JB, NAB, Rowley.

12 (4).a. The verse is lacking in the LXX proper.

12 (4).b. אחריש is unproblematically "I will keep silence." Duhm, however, thinking the subj continues to be the hunter of Leviathan, emended to יחדש "he will not renew [his boastings]"; so too Beer (*BHK frt*) and apparently Moffatt "No hunter would survive to boast." Merx thought God was the subj ("I will not silently endure his [Job's] idle talk"; but such a remark is inappoite (Merx transposed vv 9–12 [1–4] to precede 39:1). Hölscher thought the crocodile was the subj, "Does it not reduce his [the hunter's] boasts to silence?" (הלא יחריש דברי בדיו), acquiring דברי from the ודבר of the second colon. Fohrer took the subj as indefinite ("no one can bring its power to silence"). De Wilde reads הלא יחריש בדיו "did it not bring his boasting [the hunter's] to silence?"; but this sits poorly with the next colon. Tryggve N. D. Mettinger, "The God of Job: Avenger, Tyrant, or Victor?," in *The Voice from the Whirlwind* (ed. Leo G. Perdue and Clark Gilpin; Nashville: Abingdon Press, 1992) 39–49, translates "Did I not silence his boasting, his mighty word and his persuasive case?"

Dahood (*Psalms III,* 67) read לא as the presumed divine title אל "the Almighty" (for further examples, see *Note* on 21:16), thus "I the Almighty fashioned his limbs" (חרש "engrave, devise").

12 (4).c. בד "limb" as at 18:13 (בד II in BDB, 94b; *DCH,* 2:93b; בד I in *HALOT,* 1:108b). Merx, Duhm, Hölscher, Pope, Habel, JPS saw rather בד III "boasting" (BDB, 95a; *DCH,* 2:94a; בד IV in *HALOT,* 1:109b), as at 11:3. Beer (*BHK*) mentions the proposals עדיו "its ornaments, trappings" and מדיו "its garments." Gerleman (*BHS frt*) reads בדי, suggesting that בדי means "in the presence of" (at 11:3 he had read [*frt*] בדיך with that meaning), thus presumably "I will not keep silence in its presence"; but there seems no good reason why this praise of Leviathan should be uttered in its *presence*.

12 (4).d. MT ודבר־גבורות וחין ערכו is apparently "and the word of might and the grace of its arrangement," a phrase from intelligible phrase massaged by RSV to read "or his mighty strength, or his goodly frame." Houbigant reads the first two words as וַאֲדַבֵּר גְּבוּרֹתוֹ "and I will tell of its might," followed by

Dhorme, Beer (*BHK prps*), Rowley, Fedrizzi, Gray. This emendation is followed in the *Translation* above.

גְבוּרוֹת "mighty deeds" is commonly emended to גְבוּרָתוֹ "its might" (so Driver–Gray, Beer [*BHK*], Kissane, Gordis, Hartley, NAB), more rarely to גְבוּרֹתָיו [*BHK vel*], Fedrizzi).

דבר is understood differently by, e.g., Dahood (*Psalms III*, 67), who translates דְבַר־גְבוּרוֹת as "his powerful back," דבר perhaps being connected with דבר III "turn the back" (*DCH*, 2:396b). Hölscher moved דבר, and read דִּבְרֵי to precede בְּדָיו, thus "words of his boastings." Duhm, thinking that the verse concerns the hunter for Leviathan, understands דְבַר־גְבוּרוֹת as his talk about valiant deeds, and reads הִין עֶרְכּוֹ "his practical and comfortable equipment for the expedition" (taking הִין as Aram. הִין; but that means "mind, reason" rather than "comfort"); similarly Moffatt "brag of his exploits and his fine arms." Kissane suggests רֹב "the greatness of [its strength]" for דבר.

12 (4).e. חִין is perhaps "grace" and עֶרֶךְ "arrangement." חִין, occurring only here, has been thought a byform of חֵן "grace" (Gordis, Hartley; BDB, 336b "meaning not very appropriate in context ... but nothing better has been proposed"; *DCH*, 3:216a; *HALOT*, 1:312b, offers no meaning, and simply cites Ehrlich's emendation). Some object that the crocodile is not famed for its grace; Kissane retorts that "grace" means "nothing more than the marvelous arrangement of the different parts," but that is not a little lame. Habel translates "his persuasive case," taking עֶרֶךְ in a legal sense (as, e.g., in 13:18; 23:4; 33:5); but the idea of Leviathan as a litigant is far-fetched.

Guillaume thinks חִין is simply a byform of חֵיל "strength of." Among emendations, Beer (*BHK frt*) and Driver–Gray actually read חֵיל "might," and Tur-Sinai הִין "defiance," a new word proposed on the basis of Deut 1:41. Beer (*BH²al*) mentions emendations to הוֹן "wealth, sufficiency" and הוֹד "splendor." Pope, who is out to maximize the mythological references in this description of Leviathan, reads הִין עֶרְכּוֹ and offers "Did I not silence his boasting by the powerful word Hayyin prepared?," Hayyin being a title for the Ugaritic deity Koshar who allegedly devised enchantments before Baal's battle with Yam, the sea; but Day, *God's Conflict*, 63 n. 8, points out how rare the name Hayyin is in Ugaritic.

The most appealing emendation of חִין, however, is to אִין "not, none," as will become plain in what follows.

עֶרֶךְ is "arrangement" (of showbread, Exod 40:23), and so perhaps "form, structure" of body (so Driver–Gray, Fedrizzi, Gordis); KJV has "comely proportion." But it is much more likely that the term here, following the particle אִין (as emended) has to do rather with comparison. Ehrlich reads וְדִבֶּר גְבוּרָתוֹ אִין עֶרֶךְ "and as for its strength, it is unequaled," עֶרֶךְ being the inf of ערך "arrange, set in order" (BDB, 789a); de Wilde would read rather the noun עֵרֶךְ meaning "valuation, i.e., comparability" (cf. Ps 55:14, עֶרְכִּי "my equal"). Similarly Hölscher, though he moves ודבר back to the previous colon. It is better still to follow Houbigant's proposal mentioned in the previous *Note* and begin the colon with וְאַדֶּבֵּר "and I will tell"; thus Dhorme, Beer (*BHK prps*), Rowley, Fedrizzi, Gray read וַאֲדַבֵּר גְבוּרָתוֹ אִין עֶרֶךְ "and I will tell of its might [that is] without compare." G. R. Driver, however, "Problems in Job," *AJSL* 52 (1936) 160–70 (168), notes that there is no good parallel to עֶרֶךְ meaning "comparison," and makes the same proposal as Ehrlich (though without reference to him), אִין עֲרוֹךְ "there is no comparison" as in Ps 40:5 (6). The emendation וְאֲדַבֵּר גְבוּרָתוֹ אִין עֶרֶךְ "and I will tell of its incomparable might" is adopted in the *Translation* above.

13 (5).a. De Wilde regards vv 13–34 (5–26) as a secondary insertion elaborating the original poem about Leviathan.

13 (5).b. גלה picl "uncover," sometimes, as here, in reference not to the thing uncovered (e.g., eye [Num 22:31], thigh [Isa 47:2]) but to the thing that has been covering (e.g., veil [Isa 47:2], hem of garment [Nah 3:5]). Most translations retain the metaphor of the Hebrew, but Moffatt more concretely has "Who can strip him of his hide?" Less plausibly, Gray thinks rather of the sense of גלה "go into exile" (BDB, 163a §3), i.e., going beyond a certain point (cf. Arab. *jala/y* "emigrate, pass over" [Lane, 446b]), and thus "pass within his outer covering."

13 (5).c. פְּנֵי לְבוּשׁוֹ, lit. "the face of its garment." Dhorme thinks this means the face of the garment as opposed to the back (as also KJV, JB, Kissane, de Wilde), but others think rather of the "outer" garment (so RV, RSV, NAB, NIV, NJPS, NEB, Driver–Gray, Pope, Gordis, Habel). Peake strangely thought the face was the inner surface of the scales, next to the flesh.

13 (5).d. רִסְנוֹ is "its jaw" or "its bridle," but כֶּפֶל רִסְנוֹ "the double of its jaw, bridle" seems improbable (KJV "double bridle," NJPS "the folds of his jowls"), and there would be no parallel with the first colon. NIV "Who would approach him with a bridle?" means that he cannot be tamed and ridden; the translation is sensible, but there is no connection with the preceding.

Many therefore adopt the emendation, adopted in the *Translation* above, to סִרְיוֹ "its coat of mail, cuirass" suggested by LXX εἰς δὲ πτύξιν θώρακος αὐτοῦ "and to the fold of its breastplate" (so Wright,

Budde[2], Duhm, Strahan, Driver–Gray, Dhorme, Beer [BHK], Hölscher, Kissane [סִרְיוֹנוֹ], Fohrer, Gerleman [BHS prb], Gordis, Habel, Hartley, Gray, RSV, NAB; Guillaume would say that it is not really an emendation but simply a "metathetic" form of רסן). Dhorme thinks that כבל, elsewhere used only in the dual, must refer specifically to the lining or inside part of the coat of mail; but it may just be "double coat of mail" (so RSV; NAB "double corselet," JB "double armour of his breastplate," NEB "his doublet of hide"). De Wilde thinks the emendation needless, understanding כפל רסנו as "its double barrier," i.e., the rows of its teeth; but this would be an unparalleled sense of רסן.

14 (6).a. פתח is lit. "[who] opened?," but the vb is quite possibly used modally (thus "could open," "dare open"), since the issue is not exactly the fact that no one has opened a crocodile's mouth (as NEB "Who has ever opened?"), but that no one would, or would dare to do so (thus JB "Who dare open?"; similarly NIV).

14 (6).b. פניו is "its face," but many follow Pesh in emending to פיו "its mouth" (so Budde, Ehrlich, Beer [BHK], Hölscher, Kissane, Fohrer, Gray, RSV, NAB, NIV, JB), though Duhm, Driver–Gray, Rowley, Gordis, de Wilde, Hartley, KJV, NJPS, NEB retain "face." The expression "the doors of the mouth" occurs in Mic 7:5 ("doors of the lips" in Ps 141:3), but "doors of the face" is unparalleled. The mouth is the door of the face, of course, though hardly the upper and lower jaws (Strahan, Moffatt, Kissane).

14 (6).c. אימה, lit. "terror." For the noun used instead of an adj, cf. on 39:20.

14 (6).d. סביבות, lit. "circuits, the parts round about" (BDB, 687a; HALOT, 2:740b; DCH, 6:109b). Dhorme translates "Around his teeth, terror reigns!"

15 (7).a. גאוה "its pride" does not fit the context too well (KJV "His scales are his pride," NJPS "His protective scales are his pride"), and most accept an emendation to גוה "its back," as in the Translation above, following LXX τὰ ἔγκατα αὐτοῦ "its entrails" (no doubt it misunderstood the word as גו "midst" [BDB, 156a], but it did attest the letters of גו "back"); so Hoffmann, Houbigant, Dillmann, Bickell, Budde, Peake, Ehrlich, Driver–Gray, Beer (BHK), Hölscher, Kissane, Pope (גוֹ), Fedrizzi, Gerleman (BHS prps), Gordis (גוה), de Wilde, Habel, Hartley, Gray, RSV, NAB, JB, NIV, NEB.

Dahood ("Hebrew-Ugaritic Lexicography II," Bib 45 (1964) 393–412 [398–99]) maintains that גַּאֲוָה itself can mean "back," being no more than a byform of גו); he finds the form also at Deut 33:26. Guillaume too thinks that גאוה is no more than a writing variant of גוה.

15 (7).b. אפיק is properly "furrow, channel," i.e., in this case, the grooves between the scales of the crocodile; thus Driver–Gray "his back is (made of) channels of shields." It seems more intelligible, however, to speak of the scales themselves as being arranged in rows (thus "rows" in RSV, NAB, JB, NEB; Kissane "lines of shields"). Gray suggests a new אֲפִיק "tanned work," cognate with Arab. 'afaqa "tan leather"; אפיקי מגנים would thus be "tanned shields."

15 (7).c. סגור lit. "shut, closed," i.e., closely joined (BDB, 689a); it is the back that is thus "enclosed," though Driver–Gray remarks that "the implicit reference will be to the individual scales of which the back consists." Kissane has "stamped with a seal of flint," i.e., each scale is like the impression of a seal on clay; but this does not explain why the seal should be "of flint," for its substance makes no difference to the firmness of the seal. Rowley thinks it means that the scales are "as alike as a row of seal impressions"; but that seems to have little relation to the Hebrew.

Some prefer to emend: thus (1) Bickell, Duhm, Beer (BHK), Hölscher, Kissane, Gray (סֵגֹרה) read סְגֹרוֹ "its chest," comparing Hos 13:8, where סְגוֹר may be the "membrane of the heart" (NJB) or "breast" (RSV) (cf. סָגוֹר I "enclosure, membrane, enclosing tissue," DCH, 6:117a); LXX σύνδεσμος is not, however, a strong support, since it means "bond, ligament." (2) Hölscher also reads סְגֹרוֹ, but not in the sense of "breast," which he denies, but as "fastening, lock" (a new word from סגר "shut"; cf. סֶגֶר II "fastening," DCH, 6:121a), thus "a seal of flint is its fastening." (3) Dhorme's proposal of סָגַר אֹתָם "it shut them up," i.e., which it enclosed (he renders "made firm") is too prosaic; and it is doubtful that סגר can mean "make firm" even though French fermer "shut" is from Latin firmare "make firm."

15 (7).d. צר חותם "a narrow, tight seal," though צר never means "tight" elsewhere and חותם "seal" is not qualified elsewhere by an adj. KJV, RV "shut up together as with a close seal" implies a questionable relation between סגור and חותם as adv accus (Driver–Gray). Driver–Gray's own translation "(Each) [i.e. each shield] shut up closely, (as) a compressed seal" is far from clear; it is hard to imagine a seal any more compressed than seals usually are. RSV "shut up closely as with a seal" and NAB, NIV "tightly sealed together" make sense, but they do not appear to translate צר. Moffatt's "sealed close and tight" is rather general. NJPS "locked with a binding seal" seems more appropriate. The scales, as a whole, form a seal over the crocodile's back.

It is often suggested that צר חותם should be emended to צֹר חֹתָם "a seal of flint" (as at 22:24) (cf. LXX σμιρίτης λίθος "emery stone"); so Merx, Hoffmann, Bickell, Budde, Dhorme, Beer [BHK], Hölscher, Kissane, Fohrer, Pope ("adamant"), Fedrizzi, Good, JB "a seal of stone." But how could flint be used as a seal? "Knives of flint" (Josh 5:2–3) are a different matter altogether. NEB "[enclosed in] a wall of flints" presupposes סָגוּר חוֹמַת צֹר; similarly de Wilde translates "enclosed by a wall of pebble (צֹר)" (or צוּר "rock"). Dahood ("Hebrew-Ugaritic Lexicography II," *Bib* 45 [1964] 393–412 [399]) proposes a new word צוּר "back, top" (cognate with Ugar. *ẓr* [*DUL*, 1005]), thus "the spine a closed seal"; but it is hard to believe that סְגוּר modifies חוֹתָם, for are not seals generally "closed"? Best of all the emendations is Gray's, to צֹר חָתוּם גָּאֲלָה "his breast is sealed with flint," its only weakness being the uncertainty of סְגוּר "chest, breast" (see previous *Note*).

16 (8).a. Verses 16–17 (8–9) are absent from LXX, but that does not necessarily mean that they are secondary (as Duhm and Hölscher).

16 (8).b. רוּחַ "wind, air" is unproblematic; but Hontheim, Budde[2], Beer (*BHK frt*), Pope, Gerleman (*BHS prps*) read רֶוַח "space, interval" (so too NAB "no space intervenes"). Dahood (*Psalms I*, 107; *Psalms III*, 35) found רֶוַח "space" also at Pss 18:10 (11); 104:3. There is admittedly an apparent mismatch between רוּחַ "wind," which is usually fem, and the vb יָבֹא, which is masc; but רוּחַ is sometimes masc (cf. 1:19; 4:15), and lack of agreement in gender is not uncommon.

17 (9).a. The verse is absent from LXX, but this need not mean that it is secondary. Merx, Bickell, Duhm, Beer (*BH²*), Hölscher, Fohrer, Terrien, de Wilde delete this verse as merely repetition of the previous verse, which is indeed the case, but not necessarily a reason for deletion.

17 (9).b. רבק "cling" occurs in pual only here and at 38:38; "joined" (KJV, RSV, NAB; NIV "joined fast") is weak, "sticking" (JB) little better. NJPS "clings" is superior, as are "firmly clamped" (NEB), "fastened firmly" (GNB), and "welded" (Moffatt).

17 (9).c. לכד "capture" occurs in hithp only here and at 38:30; "clasp" (RSV; similarly Moffatt), "cling together" (NIV), "are interlocked" (NJPS), and even "stick together" (KJV) are preferable to "hold fast" (NAB) and "hold" (NEB), and certainly than "to make an indivisible whole" (JB), or "making an impervious whole" (NJB).

17 (9).d. פרד "divide" occurs in hithp only here in Biblical Hebrew in the sense of "be separated," at 4:11 and Ps 92:9 (10) in the sense "be scattered," and at Ps 22:14 (15) in the sense of "be loosened" (of bones); cf. *DCH*, 6:755b.

18 (10).a. עטישה "sneeze" (obviously onomatopoeic) occurs only here, though the vb is attested in Arab. *'aṭasa* [Lane, 2078c] and Aram., as well as in later and modern Hebrew (KJV "neesings" is a now obsolete word with the same meaning). Because the vb תהל is sg, some think we should read a sg subj עֲטִישָׁתוֹ "its sneezing" (so Siegfried, Duhm, Dhorme, Beer [*BHK*], Hölscher, Kissane, Terrien, de Wilde, Gray, as also LXX, Aq, Vg, Tg); but the pl, though anomalous, can stand (for the sg vb with a pl subj of names of things, see GKC, §145k). Tur-Sinai is alone in denying that עטישה means "sneeze"; he thinks rather it is a word for "nose" (cf. Arab. *ma'ṭas* [Lane, 2079a]).

18 (10).b. הלל qal is "shine" (as at 29:3); in hiph, "flash forth light" (as 31:26; Isa 13:10).

18 (10).c. אוֹר lit. "light," explained by BDB, 237a, as "shining water-drops"—which is rather more specificity than the word itself can bear. Mitchell Dahood, *Ugaritic-Hebrew Philology: Marginal Notes on Recent Publications* (BibOr 17; Rome: Pontifical Biblical Institute, 1965) 41 (13.105), rendered "like the sun," supposing that the *kaph* in the second colon is to be understood with this noun in the first as well; similarly Blommerde. Gray takes אוֹר as the obj of תהל, thus "his sneezing makes the sunlight flash," explaining it as "the reflection of the sun in the humid sneezing of the crocodile"; but the natural meaning of the Heb. would be "makes the sun to shine," which is absurd. For אוֹר as "sun," see on 37:11.

18 (10).d. Whether עפעפים are "eyes" (as NAB; so too *HALOT*, 2:861b), "eyelids" (as KJV, RSV, JB; *DCH*, 6:514b), or "eyelashes" (as NJPS), see on 3:9. There is no good evidence that the term means "beams" or "rays," despite KB, 723b, de Wilde "beams," NIV, Moffatt, Hartley "rays," NJPS the "glimmerings" of dawn, NEB the "shimmer" of dawn; similarly Newsom. Less probably, Dahood, *Ugaritic-Hebrew Philology*, 41, rendered "the twinklers of dawn," and Habel thinks they may be the stars at dawn rather than the rays of dawn, while Tur-Sinai supposes that the שׁחר עפעפי are the "wings of the dawn" (as also at 3:9).

19 (11).a. לפיד is a "torch" (literally, Judg 7:16; 15:4), "burning lamps" (KJV), "flaming torches" (RSV), "fiery torches" (JB), "firebrands" (NIV, NJPS, NEB), "flames" (Moffatt); explained by BDB, 542a, as "flashing water-drops expelled by snortings of crocodile"—which, like its definition of אוֹר in the previous verse, is rather more florid than we might expect of a dictionary meaning. Chariots are said to have the appearance of torches (Nah 2:4 [5]), which BDB says means "flashes (reflected) from darting chariots." In Exod 10:18 לפיד clearly means "lightning."

19 (11).b. כידוד, occurring only here, is usually said to mean "spark" (so BDB, 461b; KB, 433a). BDB related it to Arab. *kadda* "toil severely" (Lane, 2594c), Dhorme and Gordis to Arab. *kāda(y)* "make a spark shoot forth from a stone" (Lane, 2639b, but this seems a very rare and questionable sense of a vb meaning "deceive"). We might also compare כַּרְכֹּד "precious stone" as something that

sparkles (Gordis). *HALOT*, 2:472a, on the other hand, relates it to Ugar. *kdd* "child" (*DUL*, 430), sons of fire being equivalent to the בְּנֵי רֶשֶׁף "sons of Resheph, i.e., sparks" in 5:7 (following Mitchell Dahood, "Hebrew-Ugaritic Lexicography III," *Bib* 46 [1965] 311–32 [327]; cf. *DCH*, 4:391a).

19 (11).c. מלט hithp, lit. "escape," as מלט consistently means. BDB, 572a, identifies its basic meaning as "slip away" (as in 1 Sam 20:29; 2 Sam 4:6), and thus in hithp "slip forth, escape"; but it is better to think first of "escape" in the sense of "go out of a confined or restricted place," in this case of the sparks escaping from the crocodile's mouth (as NJPS "escape"). Versions sometimes find the image a bit too startling, and offer a tamer translation such as "leap out" (KJV, NRSV), "leap forth" (RSV, NAB, Driver–Gray), "fly out" (Moffatt, JB; DCH, 5:299b), "shoot out" (NIV), "come flying out" (NEB), "spew forth" (*HALOT*, 2:589b), but it better to preserve the Hebrew image.

The term is admittedly a little strange here, so it is understandable that some prefer an emendation, commonly to יִתְלַהֲטוּ "are kindled" (so Pope), but the reading is much tamer than MT.

20 (12).a. נחיר "nostril" is found only here, but its meaning is not in doubt (cf. נַחַר "neighing" of the horse at 39:20 and נַחְרָה with the same meaning at Jer 8:16 and perhaps Ezek 32:2 [of a dragon]; and cf. Arab. *manḥar* "nostril" [Lane, 2777b]).

20 (12).b. עשן is everywhere "smoke," but since a boiling pot (as in the second colon) does not emit smoke but steam, and the fire beneath it, if it is fanned, is not likely to be smoky, there is some attraction in Moffatt's "steam pours out of his nostrils," REB's "his nostrils gush forth steam like a cauldron on a fire fanned to full heat"; similarly NAB "from his nostrils issues steam." Dhorme also insists that עשן is "vapor"; similarly Driver–Gray.

20 (12).c. כדוד is lit. "like a pot," but we have here yet another case, no doubt (cf. 40:29), of a single prefixed preposition serving for a compound one, in this case for כְּמִדּוּד "as from a pot" (so Gordis, Sicre Díaz). Pope, followed by Habel, however, sees here the word כִּידוֹד "flame," which occurred in the previous verse, thus "From his nostrils issues smoke, flame blown and blazing." Fohrer and de Wilde, however, would emend to כְּכוּר "as [from] an oven" (cf. LXX καμίνου).

20 (12).d. נפח is "breathe, blow," the niph ptcp being "blown," thus "[a cooking pot with the fire under it] fanned," or, more loosely, "a boiling pot" (RSV); a "boiling pot" (סִיר נָפוּחַ) is found at Jer 1:13, and a "heated furnace" (כוּר נפוּחַ) at Ecclus 43:4 (B) (with the niph at 4Q416 4:2).

20 (12).e. אגמן is "rush" (BDB, 8b; DCH, 1:117a), which would be a suitable fuel for a cooking pot, but the syntax (lit. "like a pot and rush[es]") hardly allows that sense; NIV "a boiling pot over a fire of reeds," while making good sense, cannot be justified from the Hebrew. RSV "as from a boiling pot and burning rushes" unconvincingly applies נפוּח "fanned" to אגמן "rush" as well as to דוּד "pot." KJV, following Buxtorf (*Lexicon*, 6), whose rendering goes back to Saadia and Rashi, saw the term as equivalent to דוּד "pot" and translated "cauldron" (similarly NAB "a seething pot or bowl").

Many prefer to emend. Possibilities are (1) וְאֹגֵם "and seething," a vb not otherwise attested, but Arab. *'ajama* "be hot, angry" (Freytag, 1:16b; according to Lane, 26a, however, it means rather "loathe"), Akk. *agāmu* "be angry" (*CDA*, 6a), may be compared (so KB, 9b; *HALOT*, 1:10b; not in *DCH*); so Bickell, Duhm, Ehrlich, Strahan, Driver–Gray, Dhorme, Beer (*BHK*), Hölscher, Kissane, Tur-Sinai, Fohrer, Pope, Fedrizzi, Gerleman (*BHS prps*), de Wilde, Habel, Hartley, Gray; Moffatt, NEB. This suggestion is adopted in the *Translation* above. (2) Guillaume would prefer to see an adjective here, cognate with Arab. *'ajmun* "intensely hot," but he forbears to suggest its form. (3) Less plausible is the reading אַגָּן "bowl" (as NAB), partly because אגן is not elsewhere used for cooking (Exod 24:6; Isa 22:24; Cant 7:2 [3]; and see also A. M. Honeyman, "The Pottery Vessels of the Old Testament," *PEQ* [1939] 76–90 [78–79]), and partly because "like a pot fanned and a bowl" is awkward syntactically. (4) Gordis ingeniously proposes וְאֲגַם "and a swamp," thinking of the mist rising from a swamp as parallel to the steam from a boiling pot. But the close combination of two distinct similes is hard to parallel, and intrinsically unlikely.

21 (13).a. נפש is here obviously not "life, vitality" but "breath" (as modern translations generally); cf. *DCH*, 5:728a §5, and 11:20; 31:39 (this is not the only possible occurrence in this sense, against Driver–Gray). Tur-Sinai idiosyncratically translates "throat"; how would the *throat* do that?

21 (13).b. תלהט is "kindle, set on fire" (Deut 32:22; Isa 42:25; Ps 83:14 [15] [?]), "devour by fire" (Joel 1:19; Mal 3:19 [4:1]; Pss 97:3; 106:18), "burn" (intrans) (Joel 2:3; Ps 104:4) and apparently simply "devour" without any reference to fire (Ps 57:4 [5]). With "coals" as the obj, only the sense "kindle" will be appropriate. No doubt the poet means rather that its breath is hot enough to kindle coals, not that as a matter of fact it *does* kindle coals (raising the question, Where would a crocodile encounter coals?). This modal use of the impf is recognized by Moffatt, JB "his breath could kindle coals," and is preferable to "kindles" (RSV), "sets coals afire" (NAB), "sets coals ablaze" (NIV, NEB), "ignites coals" (NJPS).

21 (13).c. נֶחָלִים are elsewhere "burning coals," but it is perhaps a little hypercritical to insist on reading כְּנֶחָלִים "like burning coals" on the ground that one cannot "kindle" what is already burning (as Siegfried, Budde, Duhm, Beer [*BHK*], Terrien [apparently], de Wilde; there appears to be only one ms of LXX that prefixes "coals" with ὡς "like," contrary to the notations in Beer [*BHK*], de Wilde); of course, if the vb is intrans, it would need to be rendered with "scorches" or the like. NEB "his breath sets burning coals ablaze" offers a way of taking the Hebrew literally, but it weakens the image, for any breath of air, cold or hot, will stir embers into life, and the point here is the (hyperbolical) heat of the crocodile's breath. It is probably best to understand "kindle burning coals" as "kindle charcoal into burning coals."

21 (13).d. Lit. "and a flame," but JB's rendering, showing the logical link between the cola, is followed here.

22 (14).a. לִין is traditionally thought to mean basically "spend the night" (cf. BDB, 533b), the sense "remain, dwell, abide" being regarded as figurative. But it is better to think of the vb as meaning "lodge" in general, "lodge overnight" being a sense specified by particular contexts (cf. *DCH*, 4:543a). It refers then to dwelling, but does not specify whether permanently (as at 17:2; 19:4; 29:19; 39:9, 28) or temporarily (as at 31:32, and probably 24:7 "pass the night"). KJV has "remaineth," RSV, NAB "abides," NJB, NIV, NJPS, REB "resides," NEB "is lodged," but best of all is JB "has made a home."

22 (14).b. דָּאֲבָה "terror, dismay" occurs only here (BDB, 178a, "faintness, failure of mental energy, dismay"); the vb דאב means "be dry, languish." "Terror" is the rendering of RSV, NAB, "dismay" of NIV, REB, Gray, and "fear" of JB. KJV "sorrow" derives from Buxtorf's rendering *moeror* "sadness." "Languor" (Good) is most implausible.

On the other hand, Frank M. Cross, Jr, "Ugaritic *db'at* and Hebrew Cognates," *VT* 2 (1952) 162–64, saw here a new word דְּבָאָה "strength" (*HALOT*, 1:208a; *DCH*, 2:383b), cognate with Ugar. *dbat* (*DUL*, 260), and apparently supported by the Qumran Targum's translation עלימו "its vigor"; he is followed by Pope and Terrien ("violence"), and by de Wilde and Hartley. While this would certainly create a close parallelism with עֹז "strength" in the first colon, the similarity is really too close, since the terms would be strictly synonymous. Others have seen here the דְּבָא attested at Deut 33:25; BDB, 179a, wondered if the word meant "rest" (cf. Arab. *dabā*, but that vb usually means "collect, prepare" [Lane, 849c]), KB, 198a, that it was "leisurely walk, gait" (cf. Arab. *dabay* "walk gently" [Lane, 850c]), but *HALOT*, 1:208a, that it was "strength," on the basis of the LXX rendering ἰσχύς (so too *DCH*, 2:383b). One or other of these two suggestions is followed by NJPS "power leaps before him," and apparently also by NEB "untiring energy dances ahead of him" (REB, however, has "dismay"). LXX has ἀπωλεία "destruction," which led Houbigant, followed by Beer (*BH²*), to propose that the original reading here was אֲבַדּוֹן "Abaddon, destruction"; but, as Driver–Gray and Dhorme point out, Abaddon is a place, not a general term for destruction.

22 (14).c. דּוּץ is, according to BDB, 189a, "spring, leap, dance," on the basis of Syr. *dāṣ* "leap, dance, be joyous," Aram. דּוּץ "be joyous," Arab. *dāṣa(y)* "decline, slip, glide to and fro" (Lane, 941c); the versions have "danceth" (RV), "dances" (RSV, NEB), or "leaps" (NAB, JB, NJPS, Hartley). NIV "goes" is too weak. KJV "sorrow is turned into joy" depends on the sense "leaps, springs" (as in Buxtorf, 137), but the translation is very free. Some emend to תָּרוּץ "runs" (Houbigant, Beer [*BH²*], and curiously Tur-Sinai), since that is read by some mss and apparently by LXX τρέχει and the Qumran Targum תרוט; Gordis thinks this reading much less poetic, but the image would be of a squire running before a warrior. Hölscher compares Hesiod's picture of Terror (δειμός) and Fear (φόβος) running before the chariot of Ares, god of war.

23 (15).a. NJB removes to this place v 25 (17) "for the sake of the context," but it is hard to see the point. NAB deletes the line as a dittography of v 24 (16), though there is in fact little overlap. Nevertheless, the removal of the line enables Skehan, 122–23, followed by NAB, to discern in the Leviathan material a complete sequence of strophes alternating in length between five and six lines.

23 (15).b. מַפָּל occurs elsewhere only at Amos 8:6, of the "refuse of the wheat," lit. "what falls [out]." Here it is suggested it means "the hanging (falling, drooping) parts" of the crocodile (BDB, 658b), its "fleshy paunch" (KB, 552b), or its "folds of flesh" (*HALOT*, 2:618a; *DCH*, 5:431b; similarly RSV, JB, NIV, Dhorme "flaps," de Wilde "dewlaps" [*Wampen*], Terrien "dewlaps" [*fanons*], Pope "the normally flabby and pendulous parts of the flesh and skin," Good "sagging flesh," Hartley, Gray). KJV "the flakes of his flesh" (followed by Moffatt, and by Gray's translation) took מַפָּל as "the falling off parts" literally, perhaps thinking of how reptiles shed their skin in flakes. But while it would be true that the scales or flakes of the crocodile's skin are cast hard and do not move, it would be a little strange to refer to them as the "falling off" parts, since the main point is that they are immovable. It seems preferable therefore to take מַפָּל of the "hanging" part of a beast, i.e., the underbelly (so NEB); in the crocodile, unlike many other creatures, the belly is not soft but covered with scales. It is not

easy to see what NJPS's "the layers of his flesh" and NJB's "the strips of his flesh" refer to, or how they would be reasonable interpretations of the Hebrew.

Tur-Sinai goes his own way in finding in מפל an equivalent to משׁיגהו at the head of v 26 (18); thus he reads מַפִּלוֹ "one causing to fall," and renders "When someone came to throw him down, his flesh cleaved (to the ground, so that he could not be moved)." The suggestion is altogether unacceptable: the crocodile's legs are so short that one would never speak of it being "thrown down," and why should we supply "to the ground" to explain "cleaved"?

23 (15).c. דבקו "cleave together, keep close"; thus KJV "are joined together," NIV "are tightly joined," RSV, Habel "cleave together," NRSV "cling together," JB, NJPS "stick together," NEB "close knit." LXX and Tg use a passive vb, so Duhm, Beer (*BH²*) emend to the pual דֻּבְּקוּ "are joined together," like the pual יְדֻבָּקוּ in v 17 (9), also of the scales of the crocodile.

23 (15).d. Beer (*BH²*) deletes this colon, and replaces it with לבו יצוק כפלח תחתית "its chest is hard as a nether millstone," all that he thinks should survive from v 24 (16). This excision is adopted by NAB, and by Moffatt with the further deletion of תחתית "nether." Duhm similarly deletes בל־ימוֹט "it does not move" from the end of v 23 (15) and all of v 24 (16) except פלח תחתית "like a nether millstone"; he is right that it is what is visible that is being described, but wrong not to see that לבו "its chest" is not the internal organ, "its heart."

23 (15).e. יצוק "cast hard," an image from pouring molten metal (only in 22:16 is it used of pouring out water); the vb יצק has been used in 11:15 ("secure, firmly established," of a person), and in 38:38 of hard earth (cf. the noun מוצק "solid thing," of ice in 37:10, and of a mirror of cast metal in 37:18); it occurs twice in the next verse. Habel infers that Leviathan's body is imagined as made of solid metal, but that seems unjustifiable in light of the uses of the term. Dhorme, however, takes the form here as 3 sg impf qal of צוק "press" (otherwise used only in hiph) and its clause as a conditional: "if one presses on it [its flesh], it does not yield"; this is apparently followed by NEB "no pressure will make it yield." But who would be applying pressure to the "chest" of a crocodile? De Wilde is troubled by the sg vb with a pl subj, and proposes reading יַחֲזִיקוּ "they [the folds of flesh] stick fast to it [its flesh]" (חזק hiph as in Neh 10:30); Duhm thinks rather to make מפלי into the sg מַפֵּל "the fold of [its flesh]." Gray reads יוּצְקוּ, hoph pl of יצק, "they are welded."

23 (15).f. Gray would read the pl יָמוֹשׁוּ "they do [not] move," in harmony with the pl of הוּצָקוּ (see previous *Note*).

24 (16).a. Hölscher and Fohrer delete the line as largely repetitious of the previous verse.

24 (16).b. לב is usually "heart," of course; but sometimes apparently also "chest" (cf., e.g., Exod 28:29; 2 Sam 18:14; Hos 13:8; Nah 2:7 [8]; Cant 8:6; perhaps Pss 37:15; 45:5 [6]; cf. *DCH*, 4:499a §4), which would fit much better here in a description of the visible aspects of the crocodile (so too NIV, Tur-Sinai, Gordis, Newsom; de Wilde "trunk, body," Hartley, Gray "breast").

24 (16).c. It is curious that יצוק "firm" should be used again after its appearance in the previous colon (v 23b [15b]) and that it should occur yet again in the second colon of the verse. Peake, Hölscher, and others have thought it a sure sign that the text has been damaged.

24 (16).d. כמו is the "heavy" form of the comparative particle; when two parallel cola both have the comparative, usually the "light" form is in the first colon, the "heavy" in the second, but here we have a case of "ballast prepositions reversed" (Watson, 345).

24 (16).e. Beer (*BH²*) deletes כמו־אבן "like a rock" as a gloss.

24 (16).f. ויצוק "yes, hard." Blommerde is very likely correct in seeing here another example of the emphatic *waw* at the beginning of a second colon, prefixing a word repeated from the first colon (as also in 3:17; 17:15 [though an emendation may well be required here]; 34:28; 38:17, 22); for other examples of emphatic *waw*, see *Note* on 28:21. The use of *waw* in the sense of "yea" has long been recognized (BDB, 252b §1c), but observation of its use with repetition at the head of the second colon is Blommerde's own. Similarly Driver–Gray, "yea, firm as the nether millstone." Beer (*BH²*), on the other hand, would delete the *waw* as repetitious. NAB thinks that it is ויצוק that should be deleted, and replaced with בִשָׂרוֹ "its flesh," thus "his flesh, as the nether millstone." Gray thinks this repetition of יצוק should be a different word from the יצוק in v 15, so he views it as the impf of צוק "be pressed hard," rendering "his breast is … tight as a nether millstone." But צוק is elsewhere used only in the hiph, meaning "constrain, press upon" (BDB, 847b), and if there were a qal it could hardly mean "be pressed hard"; moreover, millstones are not renowned for their "tightness" or "compactness."

24 (16).g. Tur-Sinai is alone in maintaining that תחתית should not be taken with פלח as "nether millstone" but as a term for the underpart of the crocodile's body, thus "the lower part of his body was solid as a millstone" (though his translation differs). There is some sense in this suggestion, since תחתית would then be parallel to לבו "its chest" in the first colon; the objection would be that תחתית and לבו would mean the same thing, and so not be simply parallel but repetitious.

24 (16).h. De Wilde moves to this place v 30 (22), which also concerns the underparts of the crocodile, and which can be argued to be out of place there.

25 (17).a. Kissane transfers this verse to follow 40:18, which speaks of the bones and limbs of the hippopotamus.

25 (17).b. מִשֵּׂתוֹ lit. "at its rising," which is usually translated "when he raises himself, or itself, up" or "rears up" (NJPS, REB) or simply "comes up" (Moffatt) or "comes up on land" (Gray). It may be better to see here a reference to the crocodile's "jump"; see the *Comment*. The word may be a defective spelling of inf constr of שׂא:, viz. שְׂאֵתוֹ (cf. GKC, §23f), or else it may be the noun שְׂאֵת "uprising, dignity," with the suff. The latter is favored by Dhorme, Habel, Hartley with the rendering "at (or, before) his majesty." Kinnier Wilson, "A Return to the Problem of Behemoth and Leviathan," 9, thinks this is a case of נשׂא having the obj קוֹל "voice" understood (as also at 40:20; Isa 42:11), thus "at the lifting up of his voice"; but it is not clear how a voice could be parallel to שֶׁבֶר, whatever that means, in the second colon.

Among emendations, we may note: (1) Ehrlich offered an emendation to מִשֵּׁתוֹ "at its hinder part" (שֵׁת "buttock" at 2 Sam 10:4; Isa 20:4; BDB, 1059b); the objection of Driver–Gray and Pope, that שֵׁת (which probably suggests "foundation") refers only to humans, is not strong; the hinder part of the crocodile, which we would call its tail (half the length of the entire body), is especially terrifying. (2) Gunkel, 55, read מִשְׁאֵתוֹ "at its raging," but שְׁאֵת is rather "devastation, waste" (BDB, 996a), perhaps also "storm" and "desert" (*HALOT*, 4:1427a). (3) De Wilde read מִשַּׁאֲתוֹ "from its roaring"; but crocodiles are not famous for their cries; only one of the communicatory cries of the crocodile, a courtship bellow, could possibly be called a roar (audio clip at www.flmnh.ufl.edu/cnhc/croccomm.html).

25 (17).c. אֵלִים is most often "gods" (thus NRSV; NJPS "divine beings"; Beer [*BHK*], Tur-Sinai, Pope, Gordis, Good); most, however, take the word as a variant spelling of אַיִל "ram; chief" (as Ezek 31:11, where Nebuchadnezzar is called "the אֵל (*BHS* אַיִל) of the nations"; cf. also 17:13; 32:21; Exod 15:15; 2 Kgs 24:15 Q); Budde[1] and Sicre Díaz have "heroes," Gray "strong men." Beer (*BHK vel*) also allows it might mean "chiefs" (reading אֵילִים).

The emendation has sometimes been offered to גַּלִּים "billows (of the sea)" (so Budde[2], Ehrlich, Steuernagel, Dhorme, Beer [*BHK al*], Hölscher, Terrien), but the crocodile is usually associated with rivers, not with the sea, and in any case, such language seems irrelevant at this point.

25 (17).d. שֶׁבֶר is "breaking," a word that occurs frequently, but what could it mean here? BDB, 991a, suggests without much confidence that it is the "breaking" of the strong men with terror (cf. Vg *territi* "terrified," RV "by reason of consternation"). It is perhaps more likely that it is something to do with the crocodile, perhaps the crashing noise it makes as it falls into the water from its jump pictured in the first colon; hence the *Translation* above has "splashes." Habel too thinks it "at (his) crashings" (cf. the שֶׁבֶר גָּדוֹל "loud crash" in Zeph 1:10), though he relates that to the "frightening clatter of his 'cast hard' body"; but that would be the body of the dragon Leviathan, not of the crocodile, which Habel does not recognize here. Good has "crashing down." NEB has "[bewildered (REB panic-stricken)] at the lashings of his tail." Moffatt "the swirl in the water" is a good guess, but hardly represents the Hebrew vb.

Among emendations are the following: (1) Kissane has a small and simple suggestion, מָשְׁבָּרִים "broken," i.e., panic-stricken (hoph of שׁבר elsewhere only at Jer 8:21, also in a psychological sense). (2) Giesebrecht, Driver–Gray, Beer (*BHK*) emend to מִשִּׁנָּיו גִּבֹּרִים "at its teeth mighty men [are dismayed]," but the crocodile's teeth are not here in view (though Driver–Gray think this the best emendation, they do not adopt it in their translation). De Wilde also read גִּבֹּרִים "[at its roar] mighty men [hide]." (3) Others, following Rashi, suggest מִשְׁבָּרִים "the breakers, waves" or, better, יָם מִשְׁבְּרֵי "the breakers of the sea" (as in Ps 93:4; so *HALOT*, 4:1405b, Reiske [מִשְׁבַּר יָם], Gunkel, Budde, Dhorme, Beer [*BHK al*], Hölscher, Fohrer, Terrien, Gordis, NAB); Gray explains such a reading as referring to "the waves caused by the crocodile's rising out of the water." (4) Gunkel, 33, suggested בִּשְׁמֵי מָרוֹם "in the high heavens"; but the phrase is unparalleled (though cf. the two words in parallelism at 16:19). (5) Duhm proposed מִשְׁמָרִים "guards" (cf. *DCH*, 5:545b §2), though the masc pl of that word does not elsewhere refer to persons; 7:12 is an excellent parallel for the idea of guards being posted over a sea monster. (6) Tur-Sinai suggests רוֹם מִשַּׁב "[in] their lofty abode," lit. "abode of height"; but מוֹשָׁב is never used with רוּם or any equivalent term, and the omission of the prep, though not unparalleled, is a weakness. (7) Pope thought it an ellipsis for מָתְנַיִם שֶׁבֶר "breaking of the loins" (cf. מָתְנַיִם שִׁבָּרוֹן in Ezek 21:6 [11]), i.e., loss of bladder control at a time of severe fright (cf. Anat in the Ugar. text 'Anat iii 29–32; followed by Hartley, and Veronica Kubina, *Die Gottesreden in Buche Hiob. Ein Beitrag zur Diskussion um die Einheit von Hiob 38,1–42,6* [FrThSt 115; Freiburg i.Br.: Herder, 1979] 101). (8) Guillaume would vocalize מֻשְׁבָּרִים "driven away," from a postulated new שׁבר "drive away," cognate with Arab. *zabara*; but this vb cannot be traced, since *zabara* means "write" (Freytag, 2:81a; Lane, 955b); see further *Note* on

חמא. (9) Gray sees here a new word שֶׁבֶר "(open) jaws," cognate with Ugar. ṯbrn "opening" (*DUL*, 898) (and cf. Arab. ṯabaratu[n] "cavity"); he emends to מִשְׁבָּרָיו and renders "from his gaping jaws they turn back" (for this sense of חמא, see next *Note*).

25 (17).e. חמא is the common word for "miss, sin." The hithp is rare, eight times in Numbers for "purify oneself," and here only in an uncertain sense. BDB, 307b, suggests "miss oneself, lose oneself, fig. for be bewildered, beside oneself"; this seems the best suggestion, though not entirely convincing. Budde rendered "[the waves of the sea] get out of rhythm, become confused," but that is a forced interpretation of חמא.

Several other vbs have been invoked: (1) The translation "withdraw, retire" proposed by Dhorme (so also KB, 289; Ges[18], 339a; *DCH*, 3:197a) and followed by Hölscher, Fohrer, Habel, Hartley (Good "shrink away") implies a different vb חמא cognate with Eth. ḫṭ', whether or not such is acknowledged. (2) Pope, translating "they are prostrate," supposes yet another vb חמא "cast down," cognate with Arab. ḫṭ'. Guillaume also invoked this root, but with the unlikely interpretation that the mighty are "driven away" (see above on שברים) by fear and then "throw themselves down" in exhaustion. Gordis objected that the Arab. root is ḥaṭṭa, a geminate vb and not one ending in 'alif. (3) Gordis himself translates "make supplication" on the basis of an attestation of חמא in MH (Jastrow, 448b) in the possible sense of "act petulantly"; but if the supplication of the waves is petulant and in sport, why should the fear of the "gods" be any more serious? The suggestion has little to recommend it. Tur-Sinai had recourse to the same vb in suggesting "they tried to placate [him in their high seat]," but the difficulties with this view are spelled out in the *Note* on 35:3, where also he finds this vb. (4) Eitan, 38–42, postulated a vb חמא "step, walk," cognate with Arab. ḫaṭā V, thus "[billows] pass over, pass away from him" (he found the noun חֶטְאָה "step, walk" at Prov 13:6; Job 14:16); he is followed by Day, *God's Conflict*, 64 n. 14.

Two emendations have been suggested: (1) Gunkel, followed by Beer (*BHK al*), Kissane (*vel*), de Wilde, read יִתְחַבָּאוּ "[in the high heavens] they hide." (2) P. Joüon, followed by Beer (*BHK*), Kissane (*vel*), emended to יֵחַתּוּ "[and strong men] are terrified" (from חתת) ("Notes de lexicographie hébraïque (suite)," *MUSJ* 5/2 [1912] 416–46 [432]), but that creates not parallelism to the first colon but simple repetition. This is, however, probably the basis of Moffatt's translation "scared" and NEB's "bewildered (REB panic-stricken) [at the lashings of his tail]."

26 (18).a. מַשִּׂיגֵהוּ is as it stands "one reaching it [with a sword]" (hiph ptcp of נשׂג "reach, overtake," with two accusatives); cf. KJV "him that layeth at him." Though it would be awkward ("horrible," says Duhm), the verse can perhaps be understood as a conditional, with the protasis being expressed by a ptcp: "If anyone reaches for him with a sword, it [the sword] will not succeed" (Gordis, following ibn Ezra, and comparing Gen 4:15; 1 Sam 2:13; cf. also his "Note on General Conditional Sentences in Hebrew," *JBL* 49 [1930] 200–203); so too Fohrer, Tur-Sinai, Hartley, Gray. Most, however, take the sword as the subj, translating, e.g., "Though the sword reaches him" (RSV) or "Sword may strike him" (JB), "the sword that reaches him [has no effect]" (NIV); similarly Driver–Gray, Kissane, de Wilde. Conceivably the masc ptcp is acceptable with the fem noun חרב "sword," but it is no doubt more probable that we should read תַּשִּׂיגֵהוּ "reaches it" (so one Heb. ms, Beer [*BHK*], NAB). Guillaume translated "if one lay at him with the sword" (*Studies*, 74, 138; cf. *HALOT*, 2:727a), invoking the sense of Arab. našaja "hunt"; but našaja seems rather to mean "sob" (Lane, 2792c).

Emendations proposed are less probable: (1) Budde has מִמָּגִנָּיו "because of its shields [i.e., its scales]." (2) Duhm suggests מִשִּׂיאוֹ "because of his height" (שׂיא as at 20:6).

26 (18).b. חנית "spear" has occurred previously at 39:23 as one of the weapons used against the war horse. Tur-Sinai is alone in supposing, rather improbably, that this colon refers, not to three kinds of weapon, but to three means of attack: a camp, journeying, or staying. חֲנִית he consequently explains as a noun "camp" from חנה "encamp" (cf. מַחֲנֶה "camp"), or perhaps, with the final *mem* of תקום being regarded as haplography, מַחֲנוֹת "camps."

26 (18).c. מסע II "dart" occurs only here (*DCH*, 5:368b). BDB, 652b, glosses it as "missile, dart," hesitantly comparing Arab. nasagha "throw, puncture, wound" (but Freytag, 4:274a, does not recognize a sense "throw," and the word seems to mean "wound" as with a whip rather than "pierce" [the word is not in Lane]); Gray thinks it is from נסע I "pull out," which seems unlikely. KB, 543a, leaves it unexplained, while *HALOT*, 2:607a, suggests "weapon," cryptically treating it as the same word as מַסָּע "quarry (?)," which it understands as "outcrop (of rocks)"; Hartley, though translating "dart," considers the possibility that it means "stone." De Wilde takes it as a stone hurled as a weapon (*Fauststein*). Dhorme, followed by Sicre Díaz, connects it rather with Arab. *minza'* "arrow hurled to a distance" (Wehr–Cowan, 945a; it is not clear why it is hurled "to a distance"). Zorell, 453a, thinks it is "spear." KJV, RSV, NIV, NEB have "dart," JB "javelin," NJPS, Fohrer "missile," NEB "dagger." Tur-Sinai, in accord with his view of the colon as a whole (see *Note* above), reads מַסָּע "journey" (BDB, 652b; *DCH*, 5:368b). The emendation mentioned by Beer (*BHK prps*), חָסָף "sets forth (?)" is unintelligible.

26 (18).d. שְׁרֵיה occurs only here; the context and the probable connection with שְׁרָה "throw" make clear that it is a weapon for throwing, thus "lance, javelin" (BDB, 1056a); less probable is "arrowhead" (KB, 1011a) or "small arrow, arrow head" (*HALOT*, 4:1654b, both appealing to Arab. *sirwat* "short arrow" [Freytag 2:312b; Lane, 1354a [not 1345a]). RSV, NIV, NEB, Gordis, Hartley have "javelin," JB, NJPS "lance," RV, ASV, Driver–Gray "pointed shaft," Dhorme "dart," Good "catapult." KJV "habergeon" (a sleeveless coat or jacket of mail or scale armor [*OED*]), following Buxtorf, 847, understood the term as equivalent to שִׁרְיוֹן "body-armor" (RV mg "coat of mail"); but that is wholly inappropriate in a list of weapons.

Hoffmann, Budde (*vel*), Duhm, Beer (*BHK prps*) read שְׁרֵיָה "spear," which does not occur in Hebrew but might be presumed on the basis of Syr. *šdîtā* (so Hoffmann). Others read מִשִּׁרְיֹנָה "from its armor" (Beer [*BHK al*]). Tur-Sinai, following his interpretation of the whole colon (see *Notes* above), postulated a new שְׁרָיָה "rest" cognate with Aram. שְׁרִי "rest (after traveling), of an armed camp" (Jastrow, 1630a). But this word would be exactly equivalent to his first term חֲנִית, which rather negates his whole hypothesis.

27 (19).a. עֵץ רִקָּבוֹן "wood of rottenness," the word רִקָּבוֹן occurring only here. Beer (*BHK*) suggests (*frt*) רָקָב "rotting [wood]," the final *nun* of רִקָּבוֹן being explained as a dittograph; but nothing is gained by the emendation (as also M. Dahood, "Hebrew-Ugaritic Lexicography X," *Bib* 53 [1972] 386–403 [395]).

28 (20).a. בֶּן־רֶשֶׁף, lit. "son of the bow" ("bow's child" [Good] is twee). See further, *Comment*. But Hölscher says the poet does not use poetic periphrases for weapons, and takes the term rather to mean "marksman, bowman."

28 (20).b. ברח is usually "flee," and hiph "put to flight" makes good sense here. But in Exod 36:33 ברח qal and in 26:28 ברח hiph apparently mean, of a bar (a derived noun, בְּרִיחַ) of wood, "pass through." BDB, 137b, seems to have treated the sense "pass through" as "basic" to the root; and KB, 149a, and *HALOT*, 1:156a, acknowledge that sense. Since a bar of wood passing through holes in timber may be said to "pierce" that timber, Kissane not unreasonably suggests that "pierce" should be the meaning here (so too Ehrlich, 6:263). But the meaning "pass through" or "pierce" is probably erroneous, and it is better to understand the wooden bar not as "piercing" but as "running" from side to side of the frame it supports.

It was then suggested by G. R. Driver that a second vb ברח "wound" should be postulated for Heb., cognate with Arab. *baraḥa* (not *baraḥa*) "bruise" and attested in the hiph here ("the arrow does not wound it") and in the qal at Prov 19:26; Job 20:24; 27:22. See his "Proverbs xix. 26," *TZ* 11 (1955) 373–74; "Problems in the Hebrew Text of Job," in *Wisdom in Israel and in the Ancient Near East, Presented to Professor Harold Henry Rowley ... in Celebration of His Sixty-Fifth Birthday* (VTSup 3; Leiden: E. J. Brill, 1955) 72–93 (81; the support of Ehrlich is wrongly claimed); *HALOT*, 1:156b; *DCH*, 2:263a; Eduardo Zurro, "La raíz *brḥ* II y el hápax **mibrāḥ* (Ez 17,21)," *Bib* 61 (1980) 412–15. Arab. *baraḥa* (Freytag, 1:104a; Lane, 181a), however, means (in form II) "distress, annoy, molest" (as *HALOT* also notes), but not the more physical "bruise" or "wound" claimed by Driver; likewise the noun *barḥ* is "difficulty, distress, affliction" and not "blow of a sword." Such a sense would not suit 20:24. For full discussion, concluding that ברח is "flee" in all of its occurrences, see David J. A. Clines, "Was There a ברח II 'vex' or ברח III 'wound, bruise, pierce' or ברח IV 'bar' in Classical Hebrew?," in *Shai le-Sara Japhet: Studies in the Bible, Its Exegesis, and Its Language* (ed. Moshe Bar-Asher, Dalit Rom-Shiloni, Emanuel Tov, and Nili Wazana; Jerusalem: The Bialik Institute, 2007) 285*–304*.

28 (20).c. הפך niph is 1. "turn oneself, turn back," 2. "change oneself, be changed," 3. "be turned over, overthrown" (*DCH*, 2:581a). Here it is the second sense, "are transformed" (as at 30:21; 38:14; cf. Isa 63:10) or "turned into, or, to" (KJV, RSV, Gordis, Habel, Hartley). It is unfortunate that some translations omit this rather powerful vb; thus NAB "are but straws," NIV "are like chaff to him," REB "are so much chaff," Moffatt "to him are merely stubble," or substitute another for it, as JB "he treats as wisps of hay," even the delightful NJB "a sling-stone tickles him like hay."

28 (20).d. קשׁ stands both for "stubble," i.e., the lower, worthless part of stalks of grain left standing in the field (e.g., Exod 5:12, where stubble is gathered to make bricks) and "chaff," i.e., the stems or stalks of grain crops, cut into short lengths and used for feeding cattle but not for human consumption ("straw" refers to longer pieces of the same material, while "hay" is quite different, viz. grass cut or mown or ready for mowing). קשׁ "chaff" is frequently used of what is light and easily carried by the wind (e.g., 13:25; Isa 41:2; Jer 13:24; Ps 83:13 [14]), and this must be the sense here. The translation "stubble" (KJV, RSV, NJPS, Dhorme, Guillaume, Gordis, Good) is quite inappropriate, surprisingly so for KJV, since its precise meaning, "properly that strawe with leues and hosen that is lefte in the felde after that repers haue repen the corn" (John of Trevisa [1398]) (*OED*), was apparently in force in the seventeenth century. "Chaff" (NRSV, NIV, NEB, Hartley) and "straws" (NAB) are correct, but "hay" (NJB) and "wisps of hay" (JB) are not. BDB, 905b, correctly offers "stubble, chaff" as the senses, but KB, 858,

and *HALOT,* 3:1150b, have only "stubble" (*Strohstoppeln*) and "straw stubble" (a term rarely used in English, and then in reference to stubble in the field).

Duhm thought קשׁ had replaced an original שָׁחַק "dust, cloud"; but it is hard that see what that would mean.

29 (21).a. תוֹתָח, which occurs only here, is evidently the name of a weapon, a "club" or "mace" according to BDB, 450b, and *HALOT,* 4:1715a, who also consider "cudgel" (so Good). The Arab. vb *wataha* "strike with a club or cudgel" (Freytag, 4:431b; not in Lane) is adduced as cognate. Cf. Driver, "L'interprétation du texte masorétique," 339–40. Tur-Sinai explained תותח from Arab. *watih,* *watih* "negligible, insignificant" (Freytag, 4:431b), thus "they [the arrow and sling-stones of v 29 (19)] are reckoned [by it] as straw and chaff" (reading ותוחה).

29 (21).b. נחשׁבו lit. "are considered." Because the subj is sg and the vb pl, some would read נֶחְשָׁב לוֹ "is reckoned by it" (so Houbigant [*vel*], Dillmann, Budde, Duhm, Driver–Gray, Dhorme, Beer [*BHK*], Hölscher, Kissane, Fohrer, de Wilde). Blommerde would read נֶחְשְׁבוּ, the suff being either a dative, "seems to it," or signifying the agent of the passive vb, "is considered by it"; he supports this view with a reference to König, §21 (p. 9); cf. also M. Bogaert, "Les suffixes verbaux non accusatifs dans le sémitique nord-occidental et particulièrement en hébreu," *Bib* 45 (1964) 220–47 (243 n. 3); and he is followed by Good. For other examples of dative suffs in Job, see *Note* on 22:21.

29 (21).c. To avoid the repetition of קשׁ "straw," which has been used in the previous colon, Beer (*BH²*), Driver–Gray, Hölscher (*frt*), Kissane, de Wilde propose כְּקָנֶה "like a reed," appealing to the Greek (Theod, not original LXX) ὡς καλάμη. καλάμη, however, means "straw" or "stubble," not "reed" (it commonly translates קשׁ but never קנה), and it is κάλαμος that means "reed." Guillaume nevertheless maintains that קשׁ can mean "reed," but there is no Heb. evidence of that. NAB's translation "splinters" cannot be justified.

29 (21).d. רעשׁ is "quaking, shaking," usually of an earthquake (e.g., 1 Kgs 19:11; Zech 14:5), but also of the shaking of the ground by the tramping of warriors (Isa 9:5 [4]) or by chariots (Jer 47:3). Once it is a person's "quaking" or "trembling" (Ezek 12:18), and at Job 39:24 (*q.v.*) it may mean a "roar," though in the *Note* to 39:24 the translation "stamping" (of the horse's feet) is preferred. Here it could be the "shaking" of a javelin that is meant (as KJV, Tur-Sinai, Habel; cf. NJPS "the quivering javelin," Dhorme "vibration, whirr"); but, although there is no unequivocal evidence that it can signify a sound, most understand it as such: RSV, Gordis "rattle," NIV "rattling," NAB "crash," JB, Hartley "whirring," Moffatt "whizzing," NEB "swish," Good "clatter."

29 (21).e. כידון has occurred previously at 39:23 (*q.v.*), where it was debated whether it meant a missile or a weapon held by a warrior. Here the missile "javelin" is preferred by RSV, JB, NJPS, whereas the hand-held weapon "lance" is favored by NIV, "spear" by KJV, NAB, "sabre" by NEB, "battle sword" by Good.

An emendation, mentioned by Beer (*BHK prps*), has been suggested, to כִּידוֹר "onset (of battle)" (BDB, 461b; *HALOT,* 2:472a, "onslaught, battle"; *DCH,* 4:391b, "attack"), which otherwise occurs only at 15:24 (*q.v.*). LXX πυρφόρου "of the fire-bearing" may perhaps have read כידור "spark" (BDB, 461b); although this cannot be right, it may suggest that the text originally had כידור "attack."

30 (22).a. De Wilde moves this verse to follow v 24 (16), which is also about the scales of the crocodile.

30 (22).b. תחתיו "beneath it" is said by Gordis to be used as a noun, "its underparts." Instead of תחתיו, Duhm, Beer (*BH²prps*), thinking the whole verse continues the theme of weapons useless against Leviathan, read החַת "he breaks" (החת hiph), and instead of חרשׂ "sherd," חָרָשׁ "worker in metal, blacksmith," thus "he breaks the sharp tools of the blacksmith," i.e., the metal weapons he has forged (see further on "leaves a trail" and "threshing sledge" in the next colon). Moffatt's "his lair is the sharp rocks" seems something of a guess.

30 (22).c. חרשׂ is both "earthenware, earthen vessel," and a piece of a broken vessel, a "sherd." חדוד is an adj "sharp," here used effectively as a noun, "the sharp ones of sherd," i.e., "the sharpest of potsherds" (BDB, 292b); it is found only here, but its meaning is not in doubt since it is from חדד "be sharp." This seems better than taking it as a noun, "points, spikes" (as KB, 277b; *HALOT,* 2:292a; Dhorme), since it is whole sherds, and not just their points, that are fitted to threshing sledges; the same criticism applies to Gordis's "sharp fragments of potsherds." Most translations are content with "sharp potsherds" (RSV, JB, Hartley), "sharpest potsherds" (Driver–Gray, Gordis), "sharpened shards" (Good, but that would suggest deliberate sharpening), "sharp shards" (Habel), "jagged potsherds" (NIV), "jagged shards" (NJPS); NAB, to no apparent advantage, avoids the obvious term "potsherd" with "sharp as pottery fragments." NEB nicely has "armoured beneath with jagged sherds," but there is of course no Heb. word corresponding to "armoured."

Tur-Sinai divides the words differently to read חֲדוּד יַחֲרֹשׁ "[its underparts, belly] is a coulter, which plows [the ground]." A coulter is "the iron blade fixed in front of the share in a plough; it makes a vertical cut in the soil, which is then sliced horizontally by the share" (*OED*). This creates a nice parallelism with the second colon, but there is no reason to regard חדוד as having such a specific sense (though Tur-Sinai refers to Arab. *ḥadīd* with such a meaning [Freytag, 1:351b]). Gray offers a very similar reading, יַחֲרֹשׁ חָדוּד תחתיו "his underpart (belly) is as a plough sock [the iron tip of the plow] making a furrow."

30 (22).d. רפד is "spread" a couch at 17:13; it is a byform of רבד "spread" (Prov 7:16; 1 Sam 9:25 [em.]; cf. מַרְבָד "coverlet" at Prov 7:16; 31:22). Driver, "Problems in Job," 169, argues that the vb is intrans, like Akk. *rapādu* "be stretched out, run at a gallop" (though *rapādu* means rather "roam" [*CDA*, 298a]); thus also Habel's "he spreads out like a threshing sledge" (similarly Sicre Díaz). Tur-Sinai urges that רפד should mean "make one's bed," and thus "lie down"; but the use at 17:13 of an explicit term for "couch" (יְצוּעַ) makes that unlikely. (Against the lexica, רפד "support, sustain" with food at Cant 2:5 is quite probably a separate word, cognate perhaps with Arab. *rafada* "help" [Lane, 1119a], as Gordis proposes; cf. also רְפִידָה "support" in Cant 3:10.) Here it seems to be "spreads [a threshing sledge in the mud]." kjv strangely has just "sharp stones," since Buxtorf's lexicon, which they used, gave "pot, sherd" (*testa*) (p. 270). The obj is חרוץ, presumably "threshing sledge," but it is awkward to say "it spreads a threshing sledge upon the mud" (as njps) when the threshing sledge is itself. Nor can rsv's "he spreads himself like a threshing sledge in the mire" or neb's "he sprawls on the mud like a threshing sledge" (similarly nab, Gordis, Good) be counted successful translations, since threshing sledges are not noted for sprawling or spreading themselves. Dhorme's "like a threshing sledge he leaves his mark on the mire" (similarly Hartley) is perhaps the best solution (assuming the crocodile has been lying in the mud, and then gets on its feet to walk away). niv's "leaving a trail in the mud like a threshing sledge" would be excellent if we could be sure that the picture is of the crocodile in motion. gnb's "they [the scales on its belly] tear up the muddy ground like a threshing sledge" is another interesting possibility. Moffatt's "he rests his loins on the mud" is hard to explain from the Hebrew.

A philological proposal that would not alter the mt is offered by Guillaume, who supposes another רפד "dig down," cognate with Arab. *raṭada* in the V form, thus "he digs down into the mud like a threshing sledge"; though this would make good sense, the philological foundation is weak, since that form *arṭada* is not cited as meaning "dig" but rather, in the context of one digging, "he reached the moist earth" (Lane, 1031a).

Among emendations, there is (1) a simple alteration to the piel יְרַפֵּד, which is what we have at 17:13 (mentioned by Beer [*BHK al*], and preferred by Driver–Gray). (2) The reading יִרְקֵד כְּחָרוּץ "it jumps about like a threshing sledge" is also proposed (Beer [*BHK frt*]), רקד being used of skipping and dancing (e.g., 21:11, of children; 1 Chr 15:29, of David before the ark; Eccl 3:4), but also of trees struck by lightning (Ps 29:6), and, most to the point, of chariots jolting (Nah 3:2). (3) Gray proposes another רקד "lie still," cognate with Arab. *rakada* "be still" (Lane, 1145b); he renders "he lies like a sharp-studded threshing-sledge on the mud." One would, however, expect the threshing sledge to be described as doing something, not just lying there. (4) Duhm, continuing his understanding of the verse as descriptive of weapons useless against Leviathan, reads דָּרְבָן חָרִיץ עָלָיו טִיט "a goad, a pick-ax against it are (as) mud," which is too radical to be very convincing, while "as mud" is quite unbelievable.

30 (22).e. חרוץ is recognized by BDB, 358b, only as an adj, "sharp," with מוֹרַג "threshing sledge" implied here and at Isa 28:27, Amos 1:3. But it seems safe to identify it rather as a (poetic, as Gordis?) noun for "threshing sledge" (so *HALOT*, 1:352a *s.v.* חָרוּץ III; *DCH*, 3:315b *s.v.* חָרוּץ II). At Isa 41:15 it may be left an open question whether it is the noun in apposition with מוֹרַג "threshing sledge" (as *DCH*), or a noun in constr relation (as *HALOT* "threshing sledge of incision"), or an adj modifying מוֹרַג "threshing sledge" (as BDB). If חרוץ is not identified as a noun, kjv's "sharp pointed things" is reasonable enough, but who could know what they are? jb's "moves across the slime like a harrow" is equally independent in recognizing the sharp pointed thing as a harrow, not a threshing sledge, but the translation is far from satisfactory, for it is not how the crocodile moves across the mud that is like a harrow, but the marks it leaves behind that are like the marks of a harrow.

Curiously, חרוץ occurs in the immediate vicinity of טיט "mud" also in Zech 9:3, but there it is pretty certain that it must be חָרוּץ I "gold" (BDB, 359a *s.v.* חָרוּץ V; *DCH*, 3:315b).

31 (23).a. מְצוּלָה means "deep water," not necessarily of the ocean (as it is in Exod 15:5; Mic 7:19; Jonah 2:3; Ps 107:24; Neh 9:11), but also of the Nile (Zech 10:11) and of a deep swamp (Ps 69:2 [3]), and of Sheol (Ps 88:6 [7]). Crocodiles are more usually encountered, in the world of the poet, in rivers and lakes.

31 (23).b. רתח "boil" has occurred earlier in pual of Job's inner body being in turmoil (30:27); its only other occurrence is at Ezek 24:5, in piel, of boiling meat.

31 (23).c. ישׂים "set, makes." Reiske, Budde[2], Beer (*BH*[2]*frt*), Sicre Díaz quite attractively read יַשִּׁים "makes it breathe, steam," from נשׁם "pant," though the vb occurs only once (Isa 42:14), and then in qal.

31 (23).d. ים is of course usually "sea," but it can also be "lake" and can even be used of the Nile (Nah 3:8; Isa 19:5) and the Euphrates (Jer 51:36), as well as of a large basin in the temple, the "molten sea" (1 Kgs 7:23). The term "water" has been used in the *Translation* above to avoid specifying more than the Hebrew does. We may note that Heb. מים "water" always means water as a substance, and never the surface of a sea or lake or water as an expanse (which is what ים seems to signify here). Most translate "sea," but NEB has "lake"; Duhm, Strahan, Fohrer, Gordis, Guillaume, and de Wilde think that ים is the Nile.

31 (23).e. מרקחה is, according to BDB, 955b, *HALOT*, 2:638a, *DCH*, 5:493a, "ointment-pot" (cf. רקח "mix," רֶקַח "spice-mixture, perfume," רַקָּח "perfumer"), or perhaps "spice" (at Ezek 24:10); in the context here it must mean a pot, or pan (Guillaume), in which ointment or perfume was mixed and boiled, not the vial or flask in which it was sold and kept (see further, *Comment*). Since the form at Isa 24:10 is probably corrupt, this is its only occurrence in this sense. A translation needs to go further than KJV, RSV "maketh [RSV makes] the sea like a pot of ointment" or Habel's "turns the sea into an ointment pot" and specify in what way the sea resembles an ointment-pot. NIV suggests "stirs up the sea like a pot of ointment," Gordis "stirs up the sea like a seething mixture," NJPS "makes the sea boil," GNB "makes it bubble," NEB "whips up [the lake] like ointment in a mixing bowl," NAB "churns" (Moffatt similarly "churning the deep like unguents in a pot"), JB "makes the sea fume like a scent burner." Rowley thinks of the foam on the top of boiling ingredients, or, less probably, the foam created as the perfumer beats the ingredients together (so Strahan). It is not said that Leviathan "transforms the sea into a ointment-pot" (Dhorme), and certainly not that "the sea reeks with sweet perfumes like a censer" (Dhorme), but that it makes the sea *like* an ointment-pot.

32 (24).a. אחריו, lit. "behind it." Duhm removes the word to the beginning of the second colon (see below on יחשׁב). Dahood finds a new word "snout," translating "with his snout he lights up his path" ("Ugaritic and the Old Testament," *ETL* 44 [1968] 35–54 [36]); but could its snout be said to "illuminate" the sea?

32 (24).b. נתיב יאיר, lit. "it illumines a path." יאיר hiph may be trans (as, e.g., Ps 119:135; Neh 9:19) or intrans (as, e.g., Gen 1:5; Isa 60:19), thus either "it lights up a path" or "a path lights up." Most take the first option. KJV has "maketh a path to shine," RSV, Gordis "leaves a shining wake (NAB path)," JB "glittering wake," NIV, Hartley "glistening wake," NEB "shining trail," NJPS "his wake is a luminous path," Moffatt "he leaves a shining furrow in his wake." Duhm reads יָאִיר נְתִיב חֹשֶׁךְ "it lights up the path of darkness." Gunkel reads נתיב יאור אַחֲרִית "the depths of the river are its pathway"; but this is an unparalleled sense of אחרית "end." Beer (*BH*[2]*prps*) adopts part of this idea, reading יָאוֹר נְתִיבוֹ "[after it (?)] the river is its pathway." Reading נְתִיבוֹ "its path" instead of נתיב "path" (Bickell, Gunkel, Budde, Beer [*BH*[2]*prps*]) is neither here nor there. Tur-Sinai also accepted the reading יאור "river," but improbably interpreted "the river behind him [turned into] a path," Leviathan's heat drying up the waters and turning them into a path.

32 (24).c. יחשׁב "one would think" (KJV, RSV, NIV) or "you would think" (NAB), a rather unusual use of the 3rd-person indefinite subj (GKC, §144d). JB has "[a white fleece] seems [to float]" and NJPS "[he makes the deep] seem [white-haired]." NEB "the great river is like white hair" loses the force of the Heb. A revocalization to יְחֻשַּׁב "[the deep] is thought" (Bickell, Budde, Beer, *Text, BH*[2] [*frt*]) is not an improvement (though it is necessary for Tur-Sinai's interpretation). Duhm replaces the word by אחריו, reading אַחֲרִית תְּהוֹם לְשָׁבִיב "behind him the deep (becomes) a flame."

32 (24).d. תהום, "the deep," has occurred in the cosmic sense of the "ocean" at 28:14; 38:16, but in a narrower sense of "pools of water" at 38:30; here the reference is most probably to the water of a lake or river, where the crocodile is typically to be found.

32 (24).e. שׂיבה is both "hoary head" and an abstract, "old age." KJV "one would think the deep to be hoary" is hard to surpass as a translation (Gordis "hoary-headed"); NAB thinks the Heb. needs spelling out, with "the hoary head of age." JB "a white fleece seems to float on the deeps" and GNB "white foam" abandon the metaphor, with no improvement in sense. NIV, NEB, Habel "white hair" (similarly NJPS) does not immediately convey the sense of "old age" that both the Heb. and "hoary" (cf. Old Eng. *hár* "old") have.

Gunkel reads לְשִׁבְיָה, thus "[it regards the abyss] as its booty," following LXX ὥσπερ αἰχμάλωτον, which read the word so. Tur-Sinai reads לְיַבָּשָׁה "to dry land," following Pesh, i.e., "the deep was thought as dry land," which harmonizes with his interpretation of the first colon. Most commentators are scornful of these attempts to discard what they see as the unsurpassed (Gordis) beauty of the MT. Certainly the proposal to read לְשִׁבְתּוֹ "for its dwelling" (Beer [*BH²prps*]) may be safely discarded.

33 (25).a. עָפָר is lit. "dust, mud" (Hölscher, Good "dust"), but עַל־עָפָר has meant "upon earth" at 19:25 (39:14 is different, against Dhorme). The combination of על and עָפָר is quite rare, strangely enough, nine of the eleven occurrences being in Job.

33 (25).b. מָשְׁלוֹ may be qal inf constr of משל II (BDB, *HALOT* משל I) "be like," thus "its being like, its likeness" or a noun מֹשֶׁל "likeness," occurring only here (so BDB, 605b; *HALOT*, 2:648a; *DCH*, 5:539b). The translation "upon earth there is not its like" is the KJV's, which can hardly be bettered (followed by RSV, and similarly NAB, though all three have "his"). "It has no equal" (NRSV; similarly JB, NIV, NEB), though it is quite correct, seems more prosaic.

Not a few have offered an emendation to מָשְׁלוֹ "its likeness" (Merx, Siegfried, Gunkel, Budde, Duhm, Beer [*BHK*], Gray, NAB), sometimes calling in support LXX ὅμοιον αὐτῷ "like it." But the noun מָשָׁל never means "likeness," only "proverb" and similar things, and LXX does not imply that noun.

Some have thought, however, that מֹשְׁלוֹ is a form of משל I (BDB משל III, *HALOT* משל II) "rule," i.e., "one ruling over it" (ptcp with suff), as NJPS "There is no one on land who can dominate him." So too Rashi, Hitzig, Hoffmann, Dillmann, Fedrizzi, Habel, Good. Newsom and Gray even think that both meanings ("no equal" and "indomitable") are intended.

33 (25).c. הֶעָשׂוּ is lit. "the one made," qal pass ptcp of עשה (GKC, §75v). Some think the form should be הֶעָשׂוּי (so Driver–Gray), but Gordis, followed by Hartley, defends the MT form as "archaic," finding it also in Hos 2:8 (10). Job 40:19 (*q.v.*) is a different matter.

33 (25).d. חַת "fear," though occurring elsewhere only at Gen 9:2, is certain in meaning (cf. חתת "be shattered, dismayed"). We should no doubt take the ל of לִבְלִי־חָת seriously, thus "made to be without fear," "a creature born to know no fear" (Moffatt), or even "created for fearlessness" (Duhm). Most translations have, less correctly, "a creature without fear" (KJV, RSV; similarly JB, NIV, NJPS, NEB).

Among emendations, Duhm (*frt*), Hölscher (*frt*), and Fohrer would prefer to read חֲתָת, which occurs at 6:21; the final *tau* might have become the את at the head of the next colon. Dahood, "Hebrew-Ugaritic Lexicography II," *Bib* 45 (1964) 393–412 (410), followed by Blommerde, sees here a new word חֲמָאת "flaw" cognate with Ugar. *ḫtu* "scatter, crack" (not recognized by *DUL*), thus "made as he is without a flaw"; but the issue of Leviathan's perfection has never been raised in the description.

In addition, several bolder emendations have been proposed: (1) Giesebrecht, Beer (*BHK*) attractively read לְבַעַל חַיָּה "[made to be] lord of the beasts," corresponding to מלך על־כל־בני־שחץ "king over all the sons of pride" in the next verse. Driver–Gray thought this might be right. (2) Gunkel has לְבַעַל תָּחַת "like a lord of the underworld," not an attested sense of תחת. (3) Cheyne, "The Text of Job," 579, proposes similarly לבעל תַּחְתִּיּוֹת "like a lord of the infernal regions"—which is at least Hebrew, as Driver–Gray caustically remark (implying that Gunkel's proposal is not). None of these emendations has gained much approval.

34 (26).a. The straightforward meaning of אֵת־כָּל־גָּבֹהַּ יִרְאֶה is "it sees all that is proud." But what could it mean for Leviathan to "see" (NJPS "sees," KJV "beholdeth," RSV "beholds," NRSV "surveys") the lofty beasts? It can hardly be that it sees them passing by on the riverbank, for that would not be related to his being king of the proud beasts in the next colon (it can hardly be "when he sees the lofty creatures, he is king," since he is king of the beasts whether or not he is observing them). ראה can have a variety of specialized meanings, including "look upon with pleasure" (Ps 128:5; Eccl 2:1; so BDB, 908a §8.a.5, though most of its examples are questionable), "enjoy" (Job 20:17 [*q.v.*]; 33:28), and "gloat over" (as Ezek 28:17; Mic 7:10; Obad 12, 13; Pss 22:17 [18]; 54:7 [9]; 112:8; 118:7; so BDB, 908a §8.a.6). But although these senses are worth considering for the present passage, they do not impose themselves. Many think it should mean "look down on" (as NIV, NEB, GNB), but that is one sense that is not attested. JB "he looks the haughtiest in the eye" would mean that he feels the equal of the tallest animals, which ראה can hardly mean (though the view is supported by Sicre Díaz).

Two relatively small emendations transform the sentence. Giesebrecht and Gunkel, followed by Budde, Duhm, Strahan, Peake, Beer (*BHK*), Driver–Gray, Moffatt, Hölscher, Fohrer, Rowley, Gordis, de Wilde, Hartley, Gray, NAB read יִירָא or יְרָא "fears" and אֹתוֹ "it" for את at the beginning of the verse (which is always open to suspicion in poetry anyway), thus "all that are lofty fear it"—which would harmonize perfectly with the next colon, without robbing it of its climactic force. These emendations are adopted in the *Translation* above. Ehrlich's emendation to יְרָאֵהוּ "[all that is lofty] fears it" is a little variant on the same idea. Guillaume also reads יִרְאֵהוּ, but explains את as "as to" (BDB, 85a §3; cf. *DCH*, 1:445b §4a, "את before subject of active verb"). Dahood, followed by Blommerde, obtains the same sense with his reading הוא יִרְאֶה "fears it," הוא being allegedly an accus pronoun. All these suggestions are inferior to those mentioned at the beginning of this paragraph.

The objection can only be that in 40:11, 12 the vb ראה is used with כָּל־גֵּאֶה "all who are proud" in the sense "look upon" or perhaps rather "identify." Yet there it is a matter of selecting or identifying the proud so as to bring them low; here there is no apparent purpose why Leviathan should "look" upon the lofty. Furthermore, in 40:11, 12 the "proud" are morally at fault; here the "proud" or lofty are impressive animals and the word has no moral connotation. So the objection is not sustainable.

34 (26).b. בְנֵי־שָׁחַץ, lit. "sons of pride" (as RSV, JB; KJV "children of pride") has occurred previously at 28:8 (q.v.), in parallelism with שָׁחַל, apparently "lion." The term may refer to large or tall animals ("all the larger beasts of prey, of course," says Duhm), or perhaps to wild animals in general; it is hard to tell if translations such as "king over all proud beasts" (as NAB, NJPS, NEB) intend to exclude other beasts that are not "proud," or whether they regard all wild beasts as "proud" by nature (cf. GNB "king of all wild beasts," and perhaps NJB "of all the lordly beasts he is king"). It is probably as well not to omit a word for beasts, as NRSV's and NIV's "king over all that are proud," since proud humans are surely not included (though Hartley thinks the reference is to "great rulers")! The ancient versions took the phrase to refer to fish or reptiles (LXX πάντων τῶν ἐν τοῖς ὕδασιν "of all those in the waters," Tg בני כוורי "the little fish," Pesh rḥmʾ "reptiles," Qumran Tg רחש presumably "creeping things"), no doubt reading שֶׁרֶץ "swarming things" rather than שָׁחַץ "pride." Leviathan is naturally perceived as a water animal or a reptile, so the reading is not as strange as at first appears; Beer (BHK) and de Wilde (frt) adopt it.

Form/Structure/Setting

The *structure* of this second speech of Yahweh is simple. After a proem in 40:7–14, the body of the speech consists of two unequal parts: 40:15–24 on the subject of Behemoth (explicitly announced at 40:15), and 41:1–34 (40:25–41:26) on Leviathan. The structure invites comparison with that of the first speech: here the proem consists of eight couplets, compared with the two of the first speech. Unlike the varied subject matter in the first speech (ten strophes about various features of the natural world, then seven about various animals), here we have depictions of only two creatures. And there is no peroration here, a somewhat strange aspect since one might have expected the divine speeches to conclude with an address to Job.

The *strophic structure* is not so evident as that of the first divine speech, but it is nevertheless reasonably transparent. In the proem, we should probably identify two strophes, of 3 and 5 lines respectively (vv 7–9, 10–14; the series of seven imperatives in vv 10–14 compels us to keep those lines together). In the lines about Behemoth, there is a clear transition at the end of v 18; we should therefore identify one 4-line strophe in vv 15–18, followed by a 6-line strophe in vv 19–24, or two strophes of 4 and 2 lines (vv 19–22, 23–24). In the Leviathan material, there is a clear division of topic after 41:11 (3) and a less clear one after 41:24 (16) or 41:25 (17), corresponding to its themes, first of the impossibility of capturing it (41:1–11 [40:25–41:3]), secondly its physical characteristics (41:12–24 [4–16]), and thirdly the creature in motion (41:25–32 [17–24]), with a summary conclusion (41:33–34 [25–26]). It is not so easy to distinguish strophes within these larger units, but I would propose that we identify ten strophes in all: 41:1–5 (40:24–29, 5 lines), 6–8 (40:30–32, 3 lines), 9–11 (41:1–3, 3 lines), 12–14 (4–6, 3 lines), 15–17 (7–9, 3 lines), 18–21 (10–13, 4 lines), 22–25 (14–17, 4 lines), 26–29 (18–21, 4 lines), 30–32 (22–24, 3 lines), and 33–34 (25–26, 2 lines).

Fohrer does not attempt to identify strophes in this speech apart from in the Leviathan material, where he finds six strophes, of 6, 6, 5, 5, 5, and 5 lines respectively: 41:1–6 (40:25–30), 41:7–12 (40:31–41:4), 41:13–18 (5–10, deleting v 9 as a gloss), 19–23 (11–15, deleting v 16 as a gloss), 25–29 (17–21), and 30–34 (22–26). It seems a weakness in this scheme to separate 41:18 from 19–21 (10 from 11–13), since the flashing sneezes belong naturally with the nostrils and the breath.

Terrien sees strophes of 5, 6, and 7 lines, with sub-strophes of 2 or 3 lines, throughout the Behemoth and Leviathan material. Thus for Behemoth he identifies two strophes of vv 15–19 (2 + 3 lines), and 20–24 (3 + 2 lines), and for Leviathan six strophes of 41:1–5 (40:25–29) (2 + 3 lines), 41:6–11 (40:30–41:3) (3 + 3 lines), 41:12–17 (41:4–9) (3 +3 lines, though he would delete v 9), 41:18–22 (41:10–14) (2 + 3 lines), 41:23–29 (41:15–21) (2 + 5 lines), and 41:30–34 (41:22–26) (3 + 2 lines). But it is hard to justify a division between 41:5 (40:29) and the next verse 41:6 (40:30), since the sequence of rhetorical questions continues without pause.

Van der Lugt identifies in the proem three strophes (40:7–9, 10–12, 13–14), but it is probably better to keep vv 10–14 together because of the series of rhetorical questions. In the Behemoth material he sees strophes consisting of vv 15–18, 19–22, and 23–24. In the Leviathan material he finds four major units, 41:1–11 (40:25–41:3) (4 + 4 + 3), 41:12–17 (4–9) (3 + 3), 18–25 (10–17) (4 + 4), and 26–34 (18–26) (4 + 3 + 2), a division with which I am in accord.

De Wilde, as usual, identifies mostly couplets. This will work for the Behemoth material (40:15–24). Of the Leviathan material he regards only 41:1–12 (40:25–41:4) as original, the remainder being a gloss. It is implausible, however, that 41:11–12 (3–4) should constitute a single strophe, and very strange that the original poem on Leviathan should end with Yahweh's announcing that he will not keep silent about its limbs, and proceeding to do just that (de Wilde emends the text, however).

The standard translations usually divide the proem, as I have done, into 40:7–9, 10–14 (so RSV; but NAB has 7–8, 9–14), and the Behemoth material into vv 15–18, 19–24 (so RSV; but NAB makes no strophic division). The Leviathan material proves more of a problem for them: RSV simply has two units, too long to be regarded as strophes, 41:1–11, 12–34. NAB has 41:1–6 (40:25–30, 6 lines), 7–11 (41:31–41:3, 5 lines), 41:12–17 (4–9, 6 lines), 18–22 (10–14, 5 lines), 23–29 (15–21, 6 lines, merging vv 23 and 24 [15, 16]), and 30–34 (22–26, 5 lines). This arrangement was adopted from Skehan, 122–23, who noted the sequence of alternating strophes of 5 and 6 lines thus created.

JB, NJB, and NJPS merely divide the speech into its three main parts, proem, Behemoth, and Leviathan, and do not attempt to display strophes. NIV is not concerned either to identify strophes, but it does make of 40:7 a paragraph of its own (unlike all other translations), and in the Leviathan section inserts a break after 41:11 (3). NEB and REB make a break at the end of the address to Job (i.e., after 40:14), and then, strangely, only after 41:8 (40:32; REB does not insert a space here, however). Idiosyncratically, they have moved 41:1–6 (40:25–30) to follow 39:30, identifying Leviathan as the whale, the last of the wild animals of the first divine speech. In the second divine speech, they recognize only the crocodile.

The *genre* of the speech as a whole, like that of the first divine speech, is that of the *disputation speech*. We have the challenge to the opponent (40:7, exactly the same as 38:3), and the rhetorical questions (40:8–9; cf. 38:2; 40:2a). The language is still that of the legal disputation in the lawcourt: Job is accused of attempting to "annul" (פרר hiph) Yahweh's "cause" (משפט), and of trying to "put [Yahweh] in the wrong" (רשע hiph) and "prove [himself] right" (צדק hiph). As also in 38:3, it is the legal controversy that is referred to by the metaphor of the engagement of warriors in a trial of strength ("gird up the loins," 40:7).

Unlike the first divine speech, however, the feature of the *rhetorical question* is not so important in this second speech. We find such questions only in 40:8, 24, 41:11 (3), 13–14 (5–6), and in the long sequence in 41:1–7 (40:25–31). In other words, of the 52 lines of the second divine speech, only 12 have the form of rhetorical questions—as contrasted with the first divine speech, where only 11 lines out of 68 are neither rhetorical questions nor their elaborations. What has taken the place of the rhetorical questions in the second speech is the element of *descriptions of the natural world*, in this case solely of Behemoth and Leviathan. The term "description" is no doubt too prosaic for the lyrical, almost hymnic, depictions. David Bernat has with some justification called the Behemoth and Leviathan passages *waṣfs*, that is, examples of the ancient Near Eastern poetic form of praise of the beloved ("Biblical *Waṣfs* beyond Song of Songs," *JSOT* 28 [2004] 327–49; I do not agree however that they are in fact "enemy" *waṣfs*, since Behemoth and Leviathan have no negative overtones in Job. See further, *Explanation*, on the import of the lyrical in these descriptions.

The *function* of the speech is twofold: first, to deny Job's claim for justice by offering him the opportunity to execute his own kind of justice himself; and second, to elaborate further Yahweh's own plan for the universe, as it may be deduced from the nature of two of his wild animal creations.

The *tonality* is both more and less severe than that of the first divine speech. The proem is markedly more severe. The opening sentence, "Gird up your loins like a man" (40:7), identical with the second sentence of the first speech (38:3), is a challenge to combat, so we know that the confrontational aspect of the first speech has not been set aside. In the next sentence, "Will you indeed annul my cause? Will you put me in the wrong so that you may prove yourself right?" (40:8) attributes to Job intentions that are not his, in that it is not Job's purpose to attempt to deny Yahweh his rights, nor to seek to prove God is in the wrong so that he himself may be justified. Even more directly hostile is the challenge to Job in vv 10–14 to dress up like a god and execute justice in the world according to his own notions of good cosmic management. To encourage someone to attempt something they are plainly incapable of, and to offer that person praise for completing the task successfully (v 14), is sarcasm, and there is no way these verses can be meant kindly. On the other hand, in the remainder of the speech, there is no reproof for Job, and he is being invited to share in Yahweh's lingering contemplation of his wonderful creations Behemoth and Leviathan. The mood is far different from the battery of questions, impossible of answer, with which he was assaulted in the first speech. By the time we have reached the end of the Leviathan depiction it is hard to remember how savagely the speech began, and the overall effect of the poem is benign.

The *nodal verse* is plainly 40:15 "Consider now Behemoth, which I made as I made you." The principal purpose of the speech is to invite Job to reflect on the significance of the animal creation, and this headline sentence nicely encapsulates that purpose.

Comment

40:6–41:34 (41:26)   This second speech of Yahweh is very similar in structure and content to the first speech. Its purpose is plainly the same as that of the first speech, first to reprove Job for his misunderstanding of God's plan in devising the universe, and secondly to sketch that plan by means of depictions of various features of the created universe. Here there are three elements in the speech: (1) a proem (40:7–14), in which Job is addressed directly, and reproached for his words which Yahweh sees as an attempt to "annul" God's "cause," i.e., to make his legal position untenable; (2) a depiction of Behemoth (40:15–24), the hippopotamus, which is declared to be God's masterpiece ("the first of the ways of God," 40:19); and (3) a depiction of Leviathan (41:1–34 [40:25–41:26]), the crocodile, which is called "king over all proud beasts" (41:32 [26]). (The numbering of the verses in chap. 41 differs in the English versions from that of the Hebrew, so references are given below with the English numbering followed by the Hebrew.)

There are some interesting differences from the first speech. (1) The proem is lengthier (eight couplets compared with the two in the first speech), and its tone is sharper. The proem reminds us that however occupied Yahweh is in these speeches with the broad scope of his universe, the fact that Job is being addressed is never lost sight of. Yahweh will take more trouble to explain what his purposes in creation are than to reproach Job for his misunderstanding; but both elements are essential to his speeches. (2) Only two animals are depicted here, compared with the ten in the first divine speech, and at much greater length. The function of the animal descriptions is however the same. While Yahweh does not state explicitly what meanings these animals have in the divine purposes, the significance of Behemoth and Leviathan is no different from that of the other animals; these two are just prime examples of the animal creation. (3) There is no peroration or closing address to Job in this speech. It is hard to know why, but it is tempting to suppose that the positive exposition has occluded the faults of Job. (4) There are far fewer rhetorical questions in the second speech than in the first: 57 of the 68 lines in the first speech were rhetorical questions or elaborations of those questions; only 12 of the 52 lines of the second speech are rhetorical questions. We could perhaps say that Yahweh becomes more and more absorbed with the realities of his own creation as his speeches continue. Or we could say that we are witnessing the triumph of the lyrical over the didactic, as the didactic exposition and questions of the first speech give way to the more lyrical delight of the second (see further, *Explanation*).

Some have argued that the second divine speech was not original to the book. It has been argued, for example, (1) that Yahweh has already made his point in the first speech, (2) that these longer descriptions of Behemoth and Leviathan differ from the more succinct descriptions of animals in the first speech, and (3) that the animals of the first speech are plainly real creatures, whereas Behemoth and Leviathan, even if they are denizens of the real world, are described sometimes with mythological coloring. These difficulties are not hard to answer, nevertheless. (1) There is a dramatic dividend in having Job make a provisional reply at the end of the first divine speech, in having Yahweh resume his speech without our knowing in what direction it will move, and in making us wait for the final statement of Job's response to God. (2) It would be a literary failure if a second divine speech merely repeated the structure of the first; the movement in the two speeches from the brief surveys of the first to the extended lyrical fascination in the second is itself of dramatic import. (3) All the animals of the divine speeches are real animals, but the depictions are developed in an imaginative crescendo.

The question is sometimes raised whether this second speech of Yahweh is indeed a separate speech from the first, or whether the two should be viewed as a single speech, with 40:1–5 being wrongly removed from its presumed original place at the beginning of chap. 42. Curtis, for example, reckons with only one speech of Yahweh, consisting of 38:2–39:12; 39:19–30; 40:2, 7–14 (i.e., the two speeches without the ostrich poem and the Behemoth and Leviathan poems) (John Briggs Curtis, "On Job's Response to Yahweh," *JBL* 98 [1979] 497–511 [498]). The same responses would apply. An interesting proposal was made by Ronald M. Huntington, that the first divine speech portrays the orderliness of the creation, and the second its chaos, making Job aware of the ambivalence of ultimate reality ("Leviathan," in *Tradition as Openness to the Future: Essays in Honor of Willis W. Fisher* [ed. Fred O. Francis and Raymond Paul Wallace; Lanham, MD: University Press of America, 1984] 45–53). If this were so, it would seem that Yahweh has a decided preference for the chaos. But it seems more likely that no contrast is intended between the creatures of the first speech and those of the second.

40:6–14 Just as with the first divine speech (38:2–40:2), this second speech is prefaced with a reproachful address to Job.

The intention of this proem is in its own way as ambiguous as that of the animal descriptions in chaps. 38–41 generally. In summoning Job to play the role of a deity and exterminate the wicked from the world, Yahweh is speaking ironically—that is plain. For it is self-evident that Job can do no such thing. But can Yahweh mean that because Job cannot personally destroy the wicked he has no right to complain about their impunity? Surely if they deserve to die, they should die, regardless of who can carry out their sentence?

It seems promising to take as the key verses those at the beginning and end of the pericope, vv 8 and 14. In v 8, Yahweh's question "Will you annul my cause?" means that he has correctly heard Job's speeches as not merely a demand for personal vindication but, more far-reachingly, a critique of God's government of the world and as demanding an alternative world-order. Now Job has had two separate criticisms to make of the world-order he experiences: the one is that a righteous man like himself may suffer unjustly; the other is that the wicked, who ought to be punished, often prosper. Yahweh takes up only the latter point here, but no doubt it stands also for the former. In Job's theology there is no room for the prosperity of the wicked, though there is in Yahweh's world. Since Yahweh is not going to change his world order, let Job re-order the world to his own taste by crushing the wicked (vv 11–13); then he will have "delivered" himself from the risky role he has adopted as God's opponent (v 14).

6   It is the same formula as that which began Yahweh's first speech in 38:1. Its repetition means that Yahweh is still in the tempest. We might have thought that the tempest was merely the accompaniment of Yahweh's arrival, the signal of his becoming present for dialogue. We now know that the tempest is where Yahweh stands, and that the relentless force of Yahweh's address to Job will not diminish.

7   The verse is an almost exact repetition of the second line of Yahweh's first speech (38:3). Either the implication is that Job's response has seemed to Yahweh a feeble one, so that Job must be urged again to defend himself more vigorously, or that Yahweh is announcing that Job can expect no relaxation of the pressure Yahweh put upon him in the first speech.

8   These are questions of reproach, not purely rhetorical questions to which "no" is the expected answer (on the literary feature of the "cluster" of questions, cf. Watson, 339). In Yahweh's view, annulling God's legal cause and putting God in the wrong is exactly what Job has been doing. It is not exactly that Yahweh wants Job to acknowledge what he is up to, but to have him know that his disreputable plan has not escaped Yahweh's notice. If Job will charge Yahweh with running a disorderly universe, Yahweh will charge Job with gross impropriety in the pursuit of his petty personal dignity.

What is Yahweh's מִשְׁפָּט here that Job is allegedly annulling? *Mišpāṭ* is normally "(act of) judgment, decision" or else "justice" as an abstract concept, but what would be his judgment or justice in this setting? It seems more likely that it means his "cause" in the legal sense, i.e., his case under judgment (BDB, 1048b §1d; *DCH*, 5:558a §1c) or perhaps his (legal) "right" (BDB, 1049a §5; *DCH*, 5:564a §5). Conceivably it is his "ordinance" (BDB, 1048b §3; *DCH*, 5:561a §3), the order he has established for the world, but that sense would not form a good parallel with the legal language of the second colon (see further in *Note* d). The view that it means "world order" is, however, supported by Michael B. Dick, "The

Neo-Assyrian Royal Lion Hunt and Yahweh's Answer to Job," *JBL* 125 (2006) 243–70 (268).

To "annul" (פרר hiph) means lit. "break," and so "frustrate, make ineffectual." The term would be analogous to סור "remove" (as at 27:2 "deny me justice"; 34:5 "take away my rights"), or מאס "reject" (as at 31:13 "reject the cause"). It is not within Job's capacity actually to take away Yahweh's rights, or to make his case ineffectual, but it suits Yahweh's point to claim that such is Job's intention. It seems equally unfair, and little more than a debating point, to suggest that Job is declaring Yahweh to be in the wrong "so that" (למען) Job may be in the right: Job is indeed anxious to be shown to be an innocent man, but if he accuses Yahweh of mismanagement of the world order it is because he believes Yahweh is guilty, not in order to gain a verdict favorable to himself. On the other hand, Job does want to be judged undeserving of his suffering, and he does believe that Yahweh is in some sense at fault.

9 The connection with the previous verse seems to be that "[i]n order to annul God's judgment it would be necessary to wield power equal to His own" (Dhorme). Such language comes dangerously close to equating might with right, a trap that has faced the author of Job more than once already. But there is perhaps a more innocent exegesis: if anyone is to rule, it needs more than right and wisdom; it takes power also (de Wilde). "[N]one but an omnipotent Ruler could rule ... with perfect justice" (Driver–Gray). Even if Job is "in the right," that does not entitle him to arrange world affairs; a world governor must have "arm" and "thunder" as well.

On the arm as a symbol of strength, cf. also 22:8, 9; 26:2; 35:9; 38:15; elsewhere at Exod 6:6; 15:16; Deut 4:34; 9:29; 2 Kgs 17:36; Isa 30:30; 40:10; 51:5; 59:16; Jer 27:5; Pss 44:3 (4); 71:18; 77:15 (16); 89:10 (11), 13 (14); 98:1 (cf. A. S. van der Woude, *TLOT*, 1:392–93; F. J. Helfmeyer, *TDOT*, 4:131–40). Thunder is regarded here as an expression of the power of God (cf. also 37:2–4).

It is a little strange that Yahweh should speak of "God" in the third person: "Have you an arm like God's?," but it is by no means unparalleled (cf. Isa 40:11).

10–14 With a series of seven imperatives (which are not to be understood as commands), Yahweh ironically invites Job to take over the governing of the world, and especially to rid it of all its wicked inhabitants. It is not that Yahweh thinks it would be a good idea, for it lies outside the divine plan for the cosmos; but since it seems so important to Job, let him try!

10 The transition from v 9 is a little awkward: there it appeared that Job lacks the power of a god, but now he is being invited to clothe himself (עדה is "deck yourself") in the regalia of a deity; if he is going to act as a god, he had better look like one. Perhaps what is meant is that in reality Job is powerless, but let him in that case pretend to divine splendor by dressing in the accoutrements of divinity and see if his fury can crush the wicked and bring them down to Sheol.

Two euphonic pairs of nouns (cf. Watson, 224) provide the clothing: "majesty" (גאון, *gāʾôn*) and "dignity" (גבה, *gōbāh*) in the first colon, "splendor (הוד, *hôd*) and glory (הדר, *hādār*)" in the second (Good translates "pride and puissance," "glory and grandeur"). In the first pair there are no divine overtones, גאון usually being "pride," though occasionally, e.g., in Exod 15:7; Isa 24:14 (in Job 37:4 Yahweh's "majestic voice"), it is the "majesty" of Yahweh, while גבה is properly "height." But in the second pair, the language is very specifically used of God:

in Ps 104:1 Yahweh is clothed with "splendor and glory"; in 111:3 it is Yahweh's "work" that is splendor and glory, in 96:6 splendor and glory are "before" him, and in 21:5 (6); 45:3 (4) they are the attributes of the king.

11   The ironic language continues. Bringing low the haughty is a divine task, as in 5:11; 1 Sam 2:7; Isa 2:12–17; 5:15; 10:33; 13:11; 25:11; Ezek 17:24; 21:26, while the idea of "looking" (ראה) upon the proud may also suggest that Job is being invited to adopt a divine perspective (cf. 22:12, where Yahweh "looks down on the topmost stars"). Job has complained that the wicked go unpunished (e.g., 21:30; 24:1–17); why, asks Yahweh, does he not take in hand their punishment himself?

Interestingly, Yahweh speaks in these verses of the wicked as the "proud" or "haughty" (גאה, twice), who deserve to be "brought low" (שפל hiph) or "humbled" (כנע hiph) and "crushed" (הדך). These "proud" ones are the same as the "wicked" (רשעים), of course, but Yahweh sees them as challengers of his divine authority rather than as primarily evil persons.

"The irony implies," writes Strahan, "that this, after all, may not be the highest and wisest mode of procedure. He who finds a place in his world even for the birds and beasts of prey[,] does not 'tread down the wicked where they stand'—as the old theory of moral retribution required Him to do—and yet He may be none the less just. ... He does not act like a petty human prince who decrees the instant execution of all his enemies. God's retributive justice is slower in its action; may it not be because He takes so much longer views and works for so much higher ends?"

Some think that Behemoth and Leviathan are "clearly examples of the proud, whom Job is challenged to 'bring low'" (Newsom). But although Leviathan is said to be "king over all proud beasts" (41:34), and thus a proud beast himself, there is no hint that either Behemoth or Leviathan is evil or constitutes any threat to Yahweh. Nor are they positive role models for Job (as Samuel E. Balentine, "'What are human beings, that you make so much of them?' Divine Disclosure from the Whirlwind: 'Look at Behemoth'," in *God in the Fray: A Tribute to Walter Brueggemann* [ed. Tod Linafelt and Timothy K. Beal; Minneapolis: Fortress Press, 1998] 259–78 [269–73]). Rather, they are depicted as nothing other than creatures of God, in whose mysterious natures he takes a delight. It is no more part of the divine plan to remove the "proud" from the world than it is to remove Behemoth and Leviathan.

12   The first colon is almost a repetition of v 11b, except that the verb here is כנע hiph "abase" rather than שפל hiph "bring low." The text may have suffered some damage here.

13   It seems most likely that Job is ironically being exhorted to drive the wicked into the underworld, hiding them in the dust of death, imprisoning them in the Dungeon (טמון, lit. "the hidden place," an otherwise unattested term for the underworld; cf. Nicholas J. Tromp, *Primitive Conceptions of Death and the Nether World in the Old Testament* [BibOr 21; Rome: Pontifical Biblical Institute, 1969] 46–47). In the word "bind" (חבש) there may be an allusion to the trope of the chaining of creatures in the underworld (cf. *1 Enoch* 10:5; Jude 6). The "dust" is the netherworld also in Isa 29:4; Ps 22:29 (30); though the expression "hide in the dust" occurs in Isa 2:10, the sense does not appear parallel. Terrien saw in the phrase "bind their faces" an allusion to the preparation of mummies in Egyptian ritual, which seems rather improbable.

14 It is a final irony that Yahweh imagines himself being the first to admit (cf. TEV)—not that Job is God's equal (as Kissane)—but that Job has brought himself salvation: "I will praise you" is frequently the phrase of the psalmists in address to God (e.g., 18:49 [50]; 30:12 [13]; 35:18; 43:4; 108:3 [4]; cf. Isa 12:1), but God never praises (ידה hiph) anyone (the only apparent exception is 4QShir-Shabb^d 1:1.38 where the "gods," i.e., divine beings, are the subj of ידה; cf. *DCH,* 4:95a). Here it is the "right hand" that saves, as also (of Yahweh) at Exod 15:6; Pss 20:6 (7); 44:3 (4); 98:1; in Judg 7:2; 1 Sam 25:26 it is the "hand," and in Isa 59:16; 63:5; Ps 98:1 the "arm."

It is clear that the term ישע hiph means "deliver, save," usually from danger or oppression (cf. J. F. A. Sawyer, *TDOT,* 6:441–63; F. Stolz, *TLOT,* 2:584–87), and there is perhaps no passage where "be victorious" is a preferable sense, despite the translation "give you victory" of RSV and others (see *Note* b). Typically, though not exclusively, God is the subject of the verb (cf. *DCH,* 4:336a), and it is all part of the irony that Job should be envisaged as a "savior," accomplishing an act of deliverance single-handedly, with none to help (as the idiom means at Isa 59:16; 63:5). But what would Job be saved from? Well, his salvation will be achieved by wiping the wicked out of existence in a godlike manner (vv 10–13), so it must be their survival that is the greatest threat to him (it is not, as Hartley thinks, the absence of a vindicator). The continued existence of the wicked is a danger to Job from which he needs to be delivered because it is to Job perpetual evidence that God is neglecting his responsibilities of world governance and the ground for his reiterated claim that God is "in the wrong" (cf. v 8b). So, suggests Yahweh, Job should single-handedly and forthwith send the wicked posting to Sheol, and, by re-ordering the world according to his own standards of moral rightness, deliver himself from the dreadful danger he now finds himself in of "annulling [Yahweh's] cause" (v 8a). This is sarcasm rather than mere irony on Yahweh's part, since Job of course has no chance of dealing with the wicked, so he can never deliver himself or earn the praise that Yahweh holds out before him (v 14a).

15–24 *Behemoth, the hippopotamus.* Yahweh's ironic address to Job (vv 7–14) is now over, and he resumes the theme of his first speech, his exposition of the divine plan for the universe as a response to Job's complaints about the way the world seems to be managed. There is no close connection between the subject matter of the address to Job in vv 7–14 and the topic of the hippopotamus, as if to say, for example, How could a mere mortal hope to manage Yahweh's universe if that person is powerless against one of his creatures? Rather, the movement in thought is this: Job has been in effect, in the course of his speeches, denying the validity of the divine plan, which means, in legal terms, attempting to "annul [Yahweh's] cause" (v 8). Ironically, Yahweh invites him to execute a better plan for the universe (vv 10–14). Since that has no chance of success, Yahweh will return to his depiction of his own plan, describing some of the animals of his creation.

The general function of this depiction of the hippopotamus is disclosed by the lines that frame it: it is such a fearsome animal that no human could lightly undertake to capture it (v 24), yet Yahweh as its creator obviously has power over it (v 15a). In turn, the poet depicts (1) the strength of the hippopotamus (vv 15b–16), (2) its bodily frame (vv 17–18), (3) its superiority over other beasts (vv 19–20), and (4) its habitat (vv 21–24; de Wilde prefers to regard vv 21–22 as a separate strophe, and to designate vv 23–24 as a description of its unconquerability).

Nevertheless, what exactly the hippopotamus signifies is something of a mystery. It is obviously dangerous: the only one who could dare approach it with a sword is its Maker (v 19); yet the poet, rather than warning of the danger (contrast Leviathan in 41:8 [40:32]), stresses the absurdity of supposing one could capture it (v 24). So it is not so much dangerous as beyond being a danger: no one entertains thoughts of hunting it, so in a way it is no threat. Nor does it constitute a threat, despite its size, to the other animals: if v 21 is correctly rendered in the *Translation,* the other water animals "play" around it, knowing that they will not be harmed by this giant herbivore. So there is an implicit ambiguity about the hippopotamus: it is dangerous but also safe.

There is another paradox here too: it is immensely powerful but it does little. We are to admire the strength of its loins and the muscles of its belly (v 16), and to observe that its bones are like bronze tubes, its frame like iron bars (v 18). Yet the only things it actually does with all that strength are eat (v 15b) and procreate (v 17, if that is what is referred to); most of the time it is taking its ease in the water (it spends most of the day asleep), in the shade of trees and reeds (vv 21–22). Its most obvious characteristic is that it is "tranquil" and "undisturbed," even when a more prudent beast might take refuge from a surging torrent (v 23). When, then, this indolent beast is called God's "masterpiece" (v 19a) it is hard to be sure the poet is being serious; or at least we suspect that there is a deeply playful seriousness at hand.

By the standards of the animal kingdom, the hippopotamus would seem rather to be a beast without qualities. It has no practical use for humans, but neither does it have the admirable spirit of freedom of the wild ass (39:5–8), or the brave spirit of the war horse (39:19–25), the hunting skills of the lion and the raven (38:39–41), the farsightedness of the eagle (39:27–30), the fecundity of the mountain goats (39:1–4), or even the strange paradoxical nature of the ostrich (39:13–18). The wonder is that God has taken the trouble to create such a useless creature. Yet he has, and Behemoth is as much a creation of his as is humanity (v 15a). Can it be that it is Behemoth, rather than humanity, that is his masterpiece because Behemoth so well represents God's freedom—his freedom to refuse rules and rationality and principles of utility, even aesthetics?

Several objections against the literary authenticity of this description of Behemoth have been raised: (1) It is longer than the descriptions of other animals in chaps 38–39. (2) There are far fewer questions than in chaps 38–39. (3) In chaps 38–39 it is "the habits, actions and temper of the animals, and especially what is striking or strange in these, that are referred to," whereas here and in the description of Leviathan it is the body parts that are central (Driver–Gray). (4) It is "generally recognized to be of inferior poetic quality" (Rowley); Duhm thought the poetry "bombastic." (5) If Behemoth and Leviathan are the hippopotamus and crocodile, they are, unlike the other animals in the divine speeches, not Palestinian but Egyptian creatures.

These objections are easily answered: (1–3) There is no reason why in this second divine speech the descriptive patterns of the first speech should be used; in any case there is not such a big difference between the seven verses allocated to the horse in 39:19–25 and the ten verses for Behemoth in 40:15–24. (4) The poetic quality of the description is a matter of opinion, and many modern readers find the depiction impressive. (5) There is now evidence of the presence of hippopotami in Palestine, from the twelfth to the fourth centuries BCE, at Tell Qasileh near Tel Aviv, in northern Galilee, and in the Jordan valley (Georg Haas, "On the Occurrence of Hippopotamus in the Iron Age of the Coastal Area of Israel [Tell Qasîleh]," *BASOR* 132 [1953] 30–34; Simon Davis, "The Large Mammal Bones," in *Excavations at Tell Qasile, Part Two* [ed. Amihai Mazar; Qedem 20; Institute of Archaeology, Hebrew University, 1985] 148–50; Liora Kolska Horwitz and Eitan Tchernov, "Cultural and Environmental Implications of Hippopotamus Bone Remains in Archaeological Contexts in the Levant," *BASOR* 280 [1990] 67–76; even in third-millennium Syria, according to P. J. Riis, "Tell Sukās," *AfO* 21 [1966] 195). Crocodiles were also known not only in the Nile but also on the Mediterranean coast of Palestine (see further on 41:1-34 [40:25–41:26]).

Some have argued that Behemoth and Leviathan are not real beasts but mythological animals (e.g., Hermann Gunkel, *Schöpfung und Chaos in Urzeit und Endzeit: eine religionsgeschichtliche Untersuchung über Gen 1 und Ap Joh 12* [Göttingen: Vandenhoeck & Ruprecht, 1895]; Pope, comparing the monstrous bull of the Ugaritic myths and the "bull of heaven" in the Gilgamesh epic [*ANET*, 83–85]; André Caquot, "Behémot," *Sem* 45 [1966] 49–64; John Day, *God's Conflict with the Dragon and the Sea* [University of Cambridge Oriental Publications 35; Cambridge: Cambridge University Press, 1985] 75–83). They certainly became such in later interpretation (cf. *1 Enoch* 60:7-9; *4 Ezra* 6:49–52; *2 Bar.* 29:4; and cf. the dragon and the beasts of Rev 12:3–17; 13:1–8, 11–18). Newsom seems to regard Behemoth as essentially a mythological creature, even if modeled after the hippopotamus. Even when Behemoth and Leviathan were identified with real animals, as by Thomas Aquinas with the elephant and the whale, they represented diabolical power. The identification with the elephant is probably very ancient, since the term seems to be used of elephants in warfare in the Qumran *Commentary on Habakkuk* (1QpHab 3:10; cf. Ethelbert Stauffer, "Der gegenwärtige Stand der Erforschung der in Palästina neu gefundenen hebräischen Handschriften. 19. Zur Frühdatierung des Habakkukmidrasch," *TLZ* 76 [1951] 667–74 [667–70]).

Most scholars today, however, have no doubt that Behemoth and Leviathan are real creatures, though the descriptions are of course literary and not necessarily realistic, perhaps not entirely accurate. Since the work of Samuel Bochart in his *Hierozoicon* (1663), Behemoth has been almost universally identified with the hippopotamus (*Hippopotamus amphibius*); G. R. Driver has found few followers in arguing that it is the crocodile, reconstructing in v 15 the Hebrew word עֲמֻשָׁךְ, which he supposes to mean "crocodile" ("Mythical Monsters in the Old Testament," in *Studi orientalistici in onore di Giorgio Levi della Vida*, I [Pubblicazioni dell'Istituto per l'Oriente 52; Rome: Istituto per l'Oriente, 1956] 234–38 [235]). And B. Couroyer has persuaded only a few that Behemoth is to be identified with the species of the wild buffalo that is known to have lived in Upper Galilee, in the marshes around Lake Huleh ("Qui est Béhémoth?," *RB* 82 [1975] 418–43; "Behemoth = hippopotame ou buffle?," *RB* 94 [1987] 214–21, a rejoinder to the incisive criticisms of Keel, 127–31); Hartley and Newsom, however, seem open to this suggestion. B. D. Eerdmans thought it was the dolphin (*Studies in Job* [Leiden: Burgersdijk & Niermans, 1939] 29–30). Tur-Sinai is alone in denying that Behemoth is a particular animal: he claims that the term means "beasts" in general (בהמות, *bᵉhēmôt* is indeed the plural of בהמה "beast"), and that the singular subject of subsequent verses is Leviathan, a hunter who was Yahweh's weapon-bearer and aide. Ruprecht thinks that Leviathan is another name for Behemoth, not a separate animal such as the crocodile (E. Ruprecht, "Das Nilpferd im Hiobbuch. Beobachtungen zu der sogennanten zweiten Gottesrede," *VT* 21 [1971] 209–31). But these differing views have made little impact on the opinion of the majority that Behemoth is the hippopotamus and Leviathan the crocodile.

Characteristics of the hippopotamus that coincide with Behemoth are these: they are both herbivorous (v 15), amphibious (cf. vv 22–23), remarkable for the strength of their body (v 16), with solid bones (v 18); they live in swamps, among reeds, and seek shade (vv 21–22). It is, however, a little strange that no mention is made of the hippopotamus's enormous mouth, which can open as wide as 4 feet, and its terrifying teeth (the lower ones may be almost 2 feet long). The male hippopotamus weighs up to 7000 pounds, and stands about 5 feet high (the female weighs up to 5000 pounds, and is almost as tall).

It is sometimes claimed that a more sophisticated approach to the identity of Behemoth would resist a simple choice between "realistic" and "mythological." But to acknowledge that Behemoth the hippopotamus may have a symbolic value (as Terrien, Botterweck [*TDOT*], Newsom) does not break down the distinction between "realistic" and "mythological." Alter puts it well in saying "Not a single detail is mythological, but everything is rendered with hyperbolic intensity" (Robert Alter, "The Voice from the Whirlwind," *Commentary* 77/1 [1984] 33–41 [40]). Ruprecht ("Das Nilpferd im Hiobbuch," 209–31) goes a step further and sees Behemoth as an enemy of the creator god, while Habel sees Behemoth as a monster Yahweh overcame and controlled, and Kubina envisages Behemoth as a Hebrew equivalent of the Canaanite god Yam (*Die Gottesreden in Buche Hiob. Ein Beitrag zur Diskussion um die Einheit von Hiob 38,1–42,6* [FrThSt 115; Freiburg i.Br.: Herder, 1979] 89); but the reference to the "sword" of the hippopotamus's Maker does not amount to an allusion to a primeval conflict between Yahweh and the hippopotamus. The Behemoth of Job is merely a creature (v 15).

In the history of interpretation, Behemoth has often figured as the per-sonification of evil. A striking example is the miniature of the devil riding Behemoth in the Bestiary of the *Liber floridus* by Lambert of Saint Omer (repro-duced in Samuel Terrien, *The Iconography of Job through the Centuries: Artists as Biblical Interpreters* [University Park, PA: Pennsylvania University Press, 1996] 46). Another illumination, in a Patmos manuscript of the Book of Job, shows Behemoth and Leviathan as a single androgynous monster, representing sensu-ality and fertility, the navel (cf. on v 16) being especially focused on (Terrien, 41). In Blake's *Illustrations of the Book of Job*, however, both Behemoth and Leviathan are much less threatening creatures; if they are still personifications of evil, they perhaps represent forces within Job himself rather than in the world around him (cf. Terrien, *The Iconography of Job*, 215–16). In the context of the Book of Job, it would be wrong to say that Behemoth and Leviathan have no symbolic value, but it is not as representations of evil or of danger to the divinely established order.

15 "Consider Behemoth" (הִנֵּה־נָא בְהֵמוֹת, lit. "behold now Behemoth"). This is the only time in the divine speeches that Job is explicitly encouraged to consider what Yahweh is passing before his eyes, though considering is of course the pur-pose of the whole parade of natural phenomena and of creatures. It is not just a matter of observing, but of reflecting on the significance of what is seen, for the meaning of the divine response will only be discerned beneath the level of the visible. To Job's quest for a universal order, the deity can hardly respond with a "Consider the hippopotamus" unless the hippopotamus has a significance that Job (and the readers) will be able to figure out for themselves.

The hippopotamus and the crocodile were well-known creatures in antiquity, even if most people knew of them by hearsay rather than by personal experience. Herodotus gives an account of the two in his *History* 2.68–70, 71; so too Pliny, *Natural History* 8:37–39; Diodorus 1:35.

The size and strength of the hippopotamus might well suggest that it is a fearsome carnivorous animal, but in fact this huge monster eats only grass and aquatic plants. In a single night's grazing, however, a hippopotamus may consume over 100 pounds of grass. Herodotus noted the similarity between the hippopotamus and the ox (*Hist.* 2:71), and Pliny that it feeds on crops and has the same kind of hoof as the ox (*Natural History* 8:39).

There is one other possible occurrence of the term Behemoth in the Hebrew Bible: at Ps 73:22, where the psalmist says, "I was stupid and ignorant; I was like a Behemoth to you." It is not the expected singular form of the noun *bᵉhēmâ*, "a beast," but the plural form that occurs both here and in the psalm. If there is a link between the two texts, it may suggest that Behemoth, for all its strangeness and awesomeness, is also conceived of as a clumsy creature. Though the hippopotamus moves gracefully in the water, its bulk and weight make it ungainly on land, and such may be the point of comparison.

16 Some think it strange that its strength should be said to be in its loins, since the loins are so commonly the seat of strength (e.g., Ps 69:23 [24]; Deut 33:11) (Driver–Gray). But the strength of the hippopotamus is legendary: to move a body mass of up to 7000 pounds up muddy river banks requires an enormous musculature.

In the history of interpretation, the LXX rendering "and its strength is in the navel (*omphalos*) of its belly" has been influential, even appearing in KJV. Among modern scholars also it is sometimes thought that the allusion is to the hippopotamus's reproductive powers, with explicit reference in v 17 to its penis and testicles (see *Notes* 17.b, e).

17 The tail of the hippopotamus is some 20 inches in length, and not unlike that of a pig, "hairless, very thick near the root, about the thickness of a finger at the end" (Driver–Gray); so to compare it with the cedar, famed for its height and nobility (cf. Ezek 17:22–24; 31:2–18), is strange, if not absurd. It has seemed to some a simple error (the poet's "only serious zoological error," according to W. S. McCullough, *IDB*, 2:606b), as if the writer was not very familiar with the hippopotamus; but perhaps it is no more than a poetic exaggeration. The point of comparison must be its stiffness, since it cannot be its length. Or perhaps rather it is the strength of the tail, which is used powerfully by the hippopotamus as a paddle to scatter its excrement by way of aggression or of advertising its territory (www.nature-wildlife.com/hipptxt.htm; cf. Ruprecht, "Das Nilpferd im Hiobbuch," 218 n. 2).

Some have seen here rather a reference to the virility of the hippopotamus, understanding "tail" (זנב) as the penis and "thighs" (פחד) as the testicles (Pope, Hartley [perhaps]); see *Notes* 17.b, e.

18 Habel suggests that the image of the hippopotamus's bones being "woven" or "intertwined" is intended to be reminiscent of the description in 10:9–11 of Job's own creation as a "weaving together" (סכך there, שׂרג here) of "bones" (עצמה,

as here) and "sinews" (גיד, as here also); Job and Behemoth, he concludes, "are similar mysterious creations of God." However, the point does not seem to be any identity between Job and Behemoth but the fact that Behemoth, for all its fearsomeness, is a deliberate creation of God—just as much as Job is.

For bronze as a metaphor for solidity, cf. 6:22; 41:27 (19). For iron and bronze (or copper) as a pair, cf. also 20:24; 28:2; 41:27 (19). Bernhard Lang has noted that in Egypt iron was known as "the bones of Seth," the hippopotamus god ("Job xl 18 and the 'Bones of Seth'," *VT* 30 [1980] 360–61), but, despite Habel's approval of the idea, it is hard to see more than a coincidence here.

19   There does seem to be a reference here to Gen 1:24, where the first of the animals to be created are בהמה, *bᵉhēmâ*, "cattle," the collective singular form of the term Behemoth. Whether the word ראשית, lit. "head," means "first" (as RSV, NAB) or "chief" (as KJV, NEB, de Wilde "masterpiece") is very hard to say, for the first is very likely also to be the chief example. Strangely, in Prov 8:22 Wisdom is called "the beginning of [Yahweh's] way" (ראשית דרכו, the same phrase as here). Perhaps the two texts have no knowledge of one another, and the identity of the phrases may be entirely coincidental; or perhaps we may reflect on the relation between Wisdom and the hippopotamus: the nature of the hippopotamus as God's masterpiece (40:19) means that it may contain some of the secret of the universe—and thus be a kind of personification of wisdom, not totally unlike the figure of Wisdom in Proverbs. If it is the first of God's works, it is remarkably similar to Wisdom, which was "the first of his acts of long ago" (Prov 8:22 NRSV), even "the forerunner of his prodigies of long ago" (NAB). It is curious that in Prov 8 Wisdom is found "at play" (שׂחק) on the earth (8:31), while in this depiction of the hippopotamus, it too, along with the other wild animals, is to be seen "at play" (שׂחק, the same verb) in its watery habitat (v 20); perhaps then there is a hint that the deepest secrets of the universe are not solemn truths so much as delightful games. Still, we need to notice that Wisdom in Proverbs is created before there were watery depths or springs, before mountains, fields, or mud (8:24–26), whereas the hippopotamus in Job is no ethereal abstraction, but indefeasibly of the earth, earthy (cf. 1 Cor 15:47). Nonetheless, the massive corporeality of the hippopotamus evokes a whimsical conceit of its inner spirituality, leading T. S. Eliot to envisage the hippopotamus "take wing / Ascending from the damp savannas, / And quiring angels round him sing / The praise of God, in loud hosannas … / He shall be washed as white as snow, / By all the martyr'd virgins kist, / While the True Church remains below / Wrapt in the old miasmal mist" (*Poems* [New York: Alfred A. Knopf], 1920).

It is mere speculation to find in the language of the Maker's sword an allusion to a myth of a struggle between Behemoth and God (as Pope; cf. also T. N. D. Mettinger, "God the Victor," in *The Voice from the Whirlwind: Interpreting the Book of Job* [ed. Leo G. Perdue and W. Clark Gilpin; Nashville: Abingdon Press, 1992] 45–46; J. C. L. Gibson, "On Evil in the Book of Job," in *Biblical and Other Studies in Memory of P. C. Craigie* [JSOTSup 67; Sheffield: JSOT Press, 1988] 399–419); we should not read back into this text the midrashic portrait of Behemoth and Leviathan being hunted for food by the righteous (*Midr. Rabb.*, Lev 13:3). The fact that Yahweh is here called "its Maker" suggests that from the beginning Behemoth was nothing but a creature of God, and that God did not need to defeat it to gain control of the world (Habel).

To conjure up from this passing reference to Yahweh approaching Behemoth with a sword the theme of the Divine Warrior is over-interpretation. The text does not actually say Yahweh does take a sword to Behemoth, but only that he alone could do so. Nevertheless, some writers are clear that this theme lies behind the wording here; cf. Patrick D. Miller, *The Divine Warrior in Early Israel* (HSM 5; Cambridge, MA: Harvard University Press, 1973); Marc Z. Brettler, "Images of YHWH the Warrior in Psalms," *Semeia* 61 (1993) 135–65; Martin Klingbeil, *Yahweh Fighting from Heaven: God as Warrior and as God of Heaven in the Hebrew Psalter and Ancient Near Eastern Iconography* (OBO 169; Göttingen: Vandenhoeck & Ruprecht, 1999); David Bernat, "Biblical *Wasfs* beyond Song of Songs," *JSOT* 28 (2004) 327–49 (337).

Since the hippopotamus is herbivorous, the other animals can disport themselves around it without fear.

20 The hippopotamus may look fearsome, and humans are well advised not to get too close. But it is not aggressive; it does not go hunting for prey, but waits for its plant food to be brought to it by the streams. That, at least, is how it may appear to the human observer by day; in fact, the hippopotamus mainly survives on its foraging for food by night.

21–22 Much is made of the hippopotamus's need for shade. Its thin skin, not covered by hair, is prone to sunburn and drying, and to avoid dehydration the hippopotamus must spend a considerable time submerged, with only its eyes, ears, and nostrils above water.

The lotus tree (*Zizyphus lotus*, a low shrub) is found throughout Africa and in Syria, especially in hot, damp valleys. In Syria it is said to grow to a height of over 20 feet, but more in Africa. It has no connection with the famous lotus (*Nymphaea lotus*) of Homer's *Odyssey* (9.91–97), where the companions of Odysseus who ate it fell into a dreamy forgetfulness, and lost all desire to continue their journey toward their home. The poplar (ערבה) is common on the banks of the Jordan and beside most watercourses in the region.

Habel sees an allusion to the Dragon (Tannin) of Ezek 29:3, where the Egyptian pharaoh is depicted as a dragon "lying in the midst of the streams (of the Nile)"; but the hippopotamus here is more probably a Palestinian beast, and there is no sign of hostility in it toward the deity.

23 We are to picture the hippopotamus lying in a fast-flowing river, with only its head above the water. In reality, hippopotami prefer still waters, but this is an image of its imperturbability.

24 The depiction of the hippopotamus comes to a formal conclusion with a pair of rhetorical questions (Watson, 342). It is self-evident that hunting a hippopotamus must be a dangerous undertaking. The text does not say that it is impossible to capture a hippopotamus, but alludes to the magnitude of the task by comparing it lightheartedly to fishing a piece of meat out of a cooking pot or catching a fish with a hook and line. Hippopotami have been hunted in ancient and modern times for their flesh, fat, tusks, teeth, and hide. Davis, "The Large Mammal Bones," 148, mentions cut marks on hippopotamus bones from Tell Qasile that indicate the animal was butchered for meat.

Hippopotamus hunting was a sport of Egyptian pharaohs, many illustrations showing a king about to hurl a harpoon into the beast's mouth (see Keel, 132–39). In the realm of ideas, the hippopotamus in Egypt was symbolic of hostile power, and a manifestation of Seth, the god of Upper Egypt. At a festival of "Harpooning the Hippopotamus" a hippopotamus representing the king's enemies was ritually slain. Cf. T. Säve-Söderbergh, *On Egyptian Representations of Hippopotamus Hunting as a Religious Motive* (Horae soederblomianae 3; Uppsala: C. W. K. Gleerup, 1953).

41:1–34 (40:25–41:26) *Leviathan, the crocodile.* This section on Leviathan deals first with the impossibility of capturing it (41:1–11 [40:25–41:3]), secondly with its physical characteristics (41:12–24 [4–16]), and thirdly with the creature in motion (41:25–32 [17–24]); the last two verses are a summary conclusion about Leviathan as the king of beasts (41:33–34 [25–26]). The depiction is both parallel to and distinct from the description of Behemoth (40:15–24). Behemoth was indolent and unthreatening; Leviathan is nothing but violence and turmoil.

It is the consensus that Leviathan here is the crocodile, though B. D. Eerdmans thought it was the dolphin (*Studies in Job*, 27–34; G. R. Driver, review of H. H. Rowley, *The Book of Job, JTS* ns 22 [1971] 176–79 [177–78], also entertains the possibility), though dolphins are hardly fearsome. G. R. Driver identified Leviathan as the whale ("Mythical Monsters in the Old Testament," in *Studi orientalistici in onore di Giorgio Levi della Vida*, I [Pubblicazioni dell'Istituto per l'Oriente 52; Rome: Istituto per l'Oriente, 1956] 234–38; so too NEB for vv 1–6 [40:25–30] which it transposes to follow 39:30), though 41:8–34 (40:32–41:24) he allows to be the crocodile, his identification for Behemoth; but large whales are not found in the Mediterranean or the Red Sea or the Persian Gulf (de Wilde). Eerdmans thought that only 41:1–8 (40:25–32) referred to Leviathan, and that thereafter the topic of Behemoth was resumed. Gunkel (*Schöpfung und Chaos*, 55–56) thought vv 8–11 (40:32–41:3) were misplaced, and originally referred to Behemoth. Ruprecht ("Das Nilpferd im Hiobbuch," 209–31) has recently argued a similar case, that 41:1–7 (40:25–31) properly refers to Behemoth, a view vigorously resisted by Keel (p. 141).

Even if the whole passage refers to the one beast, it is still arguable that there is more than one poem here about Leviathan. Thus Fohrer distinguishes 41:1–12 (40:25–41:4), which is characterized by its use of rhetorical questions addressed to Job and its fairly naturalistic depiction of the creature, from 41:13–34 (5–26), which lacks second-person questions and which depicts Leviathan in more mythological and fabled language; in the first, struggle with the beast is dangerous, in the second, fruitless; furthermore, the first poem contains strophes of six lines, the second strophes of five lines. Fohrer infers two different poets. Driver–Gray distinguished 41:1–11 (40:25–41:3), describing Leviathan, a sea monster, from 41:12–34 (4–26), concerning the crocodile, the inhabitant of the Nile. Westermann, 117–22, regards vv 9–11 (1–3) as the original conclusion of the second divine speech, and the account of Leviathan's activity (vv 12–34 [4–26]) as a secondary addition. Terrien thinks that vv 12–29 (4–21) may well represent "literary exercises from the Joban school." For those less disposed to postulate various authors and a history of literary expansion, these acknowledged differences in the depiction can be comfortably ascribed to the inspiration of the poet.

The crocodile (*Crocodylus niloticus*), of the class of reptiles, has the shape of a large lizard and a scaly skin, which, unlike most reptiles, it does not shed. Its eyes and nostrils are on the top of its head, so that it can see and breathe while almost totally submerged. Its "third eye," the mictating membrane, keeps its eyes functioning while it is under water. It swims by moving its huge tail from side to side. Its back feet are webbed. On land it looks ungainly, since its legs are short, but it can attain speeds of up to 30 miles per hour. It grows to up to 16 feet in length. The crocodile eats most living creatures: insects, crustaceans, fish, and larger mammals such as baboons, and hyenas, even young hippopotami, buffalo, giraffes, and lions.

Crocodiles are well attested in ancient Egypt, and, more rarely, in Palestine; a town north of Caesarea even had the name Crocodilopolis according to Strabo (*Geography* 16.2.27), and a stream nearby, perhaps the Yarkon (Nahr ez-Zerqa), was known as Crocodilion (Pliny, *Natural History* 5.17.75). Cf. G. B. Gray, "Crocodiles in Palestine," *PEQ* (1920) 167–76; Penelope Wilson, "Slaughtering the Crocodile at Edfu and Dendera," in *The Temple in Ancient Egypt: New Discoveries and Recent Research* (ed. Stephen Quirke; London: British Museum Press, 1997) 179–203. Crocodiles, however, are not mentioned elsewhere in the Bible (the "land crocodile" in Lev 11:30 [RSV] is a type of lizard).

The points of connection between the Leviathan pictured here and the crocodile are principally its terrifying jaws and teeth (v 14 [6]), its interlocking scales that cannot be penetrated (vv 13, 15–17, 23 [5, 7–9, 15]), the strength of its neck (v 22 [14]), the traces it leaves in the mud (v 30 [22]), and the fact that it is equally at home on land or sea (vv 30–33 [22–25]). On the other hand, the Leviathan of the poem appears to possess some of the characteristics of a fire-breathing dragon (vv 18–21 [10–13]); the LXX even calls it a "dragon" (δράκων). There is plainly a heightened, if not exaggerated, depiction of the crocodile here; Strahan rightly remarked that "The writer is not a natural historian, and his poetical licences and humorous sallies are not to be treated as grave and sober prose."

Unlike the term Behemoth, which we meet with nowhere else in the Hebrew Bible (though see on 40:15), Leviathan is found in several places in the Hebrew Bible as the name of a mythological creature. It is represented as a violent seven-headed sea-monster, personifying the waters of chaos, which was subdued by God in primeval times (cf. on 3:8); thus Ps 74:14; Isa 27:1 (eschatological). It is no doubt the same mythological figure that is called Lotan, or more correctly *Lītān*, in the Ugaritic literature, a sea-monster that threatens Baal (*KTU* 1.5.1.1 = *CTA* 5.1.1; *KTU* 1.3.III.4–42 = *CTA* 3.III.D.37–39). It may be significant that Leviathan is to be found in the "sea" and the "deep" (vv 31, 32 [23, 24]) rather than in the rivers or pools like Behemoth (though see *Comment* on these verses). Here in Job, however, while Leviathan is fearsome, there is no thought of a battle with God, and Leviathan is God's creature, not his rival. It is incorrect to say simply that Leviathan here is a "supernatural" being (as Pope), or that it is not a real but a mythological creature (as Day), or even an imaginary creature with the features of a crocodile (Good); it seems best to see it as a real creature depicted with mythological features or overtones. We should certainly not jump to the conclusion that Leviathan is a symbol of evil (as Keel, 143–44) or of chaos (as Newsom).

The mythological interpretation of Leviathan seems to have first been argued by Gunkel (*Schöpfung und Chaos*, 48–58), and taken up by Cheyne (*EB*, 3:2770). It is adopted in the commentaries of Tur-Sinai, Weiser (261–63), Pope, and Habel, as well as by Day, *God's Conflict*, and A. Caquot, "Le Léviathan de Job 40, 25–41, 26," *RB* 99 (1992) 40–69. Keel, 143–56, and Kubina, *Gottesreden*, 68–75, have argued that Leviathan is the Egyptian god Seth, who is represented as a crocodile in his conflict with Horus.

It is different in the post-biblical literature, where Leviathan is clearly mythological: so 2 Esd 6:49–52 and *2 Bar* 29:4, where Leviathan along with Behemoth is devoured at the Messianic banquet, Leviathan's skin being used to build huts for the most righteous to sit in; see further, Joseph Gutmann, "Leviathan, Behemoth and Ziz: Jewish Messianic Symbols in Art," *HUCA* 39 (1968) 219–30, and Jeremy Schonfield, *The North French Hebrew Miscellany (British Library Add. MS 11639), Companion Volume* (London: Facsimile Editions, 2003) 97–98, commenting on the brilliant miniatures on fols. 519r and 518v of the manuscript. Though Leviathan is not mentioned by name in the NT, the seven-headed dragon (Satan) in Rev 12:3 and the seven-headed beast (Rome) in Rev 13:1 and 17:3 are obviously modeled on it, as is the seven-headed dragon of *Odes Sol.* 22:5; *Pistis Sophia* 66; *b. Qidd.* 29b.

In this depiction of Leviathan the emphasis seems to lie less on Job's inability to master it (Day, Hartley) or on Job's helplessness by comparison with it (Andersen) as on its sheer otherness that lies outside normal human experience. From the viewpoint of this poem, indeed, humans are almost denizens of another world: they may invade Leviathan's sphere in the hope of capturing it, but they will soon retreat disappointed (41:7–10 [40:31–41:2], 26–29 [18–21]). The impossibility of bringing Leviathan within the world of humans is made into a joke: imagine, if you can, the poet says, Leviathan as a fishing trophy (v 1 [40:25]), a prisoner pleading for his life (vv 2–3 [40:26–27]), a faithful old retainer (v 4 [40:28]), a plaything for little children (v 5 [40:29]), a slab of seafood haggled for in the market (v 6 [40:30]). Each image of Leviathan in the human realm is ludicrous. Leviathan is other: it is self-contained and self-assured, kitted out with its armor of scales and its terrifying rows of teeth (vv 13–17 [5–9]), and fending off all assailants with the fire constantly emanating from its nostrils and mouth (vv 18–21 [10–13]). It is deadly dangerous to approach, but it is not threatening, nevertheless. It does not go on rampages, it does not seek out victims, it does not invade human space even if humans might attempt to intrude on its sphere. It is not companionable, and it wants to be left alone; it is always in the singular, and (unlike Behemoth) it cannot even be imagined mating. It expects to be respected and feared, though it itself is without fear, "made for fearlessness" (v 33 [25]). It is king of all proud beasts, which must mean that it is the proudest of all. And yet it is a creature, "made" by a creator who is otherwise absent from the poem.

41:1 (40:25)   The poet obviously thinks it impossible to capture a crocodile with a fishhook, but Herodotus has a story about such a method of taking the creature (2:70); you dangle in the river a lump of pork attached to a rope while beating a live pig on the bank to attract the crocodile's attention; when the crocodile seizes the pork it swallows the rope as well and can then be hauled to the bank. De Wilde thinks that Ezek 29:4 is about hunting the crocodile.

Why would anyone want to "press down" Leviathan's tongue with a cord, and what would that do to the beast? Hartley, for example, following Herodotus's account, explains that the tongue would be pressed down by the rope, but it is hard to see why that would be worth mentioning. Herodotus also tells us that the crocodile has no tongue (2:68), and so too Aristotle, Plutarch, Pliny, and Ammianus. In fact it has an immobile tongue attached to the lower jaw (Rowley), but the ancients perhaps did not know of that. Unlike other game, the poet means to say, you cannot hope to catch Leviathan with its tongue—and perhaps he means, Because it has none!

An alternative explanation is offered by Davidson, Duhm, and Peake, who think the line refers to a rope fastened around the tongue and lower jaw, which would then enable the captor to lead the beast around as if it were a bull or some other animal of that kind; but that would seem rather to be the theme of v 2 (40:26).

Yet another suggestion is that the reference is to the method of carrying fish, with a line through their jaws (illustration: J. Gardner Wilkinson, *The Manners and Customs of the Ancient Egyptians* [London: John Murray, 1878] 2:118, fig. 373), or of keeping caught fish alive by passing a cord through their gills and returning them to the water (Dalman, *Arbeit und Sitte*, 8:338, 360). Or the image may be of the treatment of captives in war; a famous stele of Esarhaddon, for example, shows two of his captives, Tirhakah (Taharka), the Egyptian king, and Ba'lu, king of Tyre, with rings through their lips, attached to a cord that Esarhaddon holds in his left hand (*ANEP*, fig. 447). From Egypt, a depiction of King Narmer shows a prisoner attached by a rope through his nose (*ANEP*, fig. 296). Similarly in the Mesopotamian creation epic *Enuma elish*, the god Ea lays hold of his captive Mummu, "holding him by the nose-rope" (*ANET*, 61b, line 72).

41:2 (40:26) Here the fancy is that the crocodile is being treated as a human captive (for hooks in the nose or jaws of captives, see *Comment* on the previous verse, and cf. 2 Kgs 19.28 || Isa 37:29; Ezek 38:4). But real-life crocodiles are also represented as tied with a rope: Othmar Keel has drawn attention to an Egyptian vignette (in the Papyrus of Cha, c. 1430 BCE) showing a crocodile being led by a rope; its captor threatens it with a knife held over the crocodile's head ("Zwei kleine Beiträge zum Verständnis der Gottesreden im Buch Ijob (xxxviii 36f., xl 25)," *VT* 31 [1981] 220–25; *Jahwes Entgegnung*, 144–56; cf. fig. 83c).

3 (40:27) The absurd picture of capturing Leviathan is continued. If it became your prisoner, Job is asked, would it fall to begging you for mercy, to have its life spared, or to be treated kindly, or perhaps (Hartley) to have its cords eased? Without a tongue, it will have some difficulty! It would be a tragic loss of its fearsome reputation if it were reduced to mouthing "soft, tender" (רך) words (the opposite of the "harsh" [קשה] words of Joseph in Gen 42:7). Perhaps Leviathan's soft (רך) answer will turn away Job's wrath (Prov 15:1), perhaps its soft (רך) tongue will break a bone (Prov 25:15). In an Egyptian myth cited by Kubina (*Gottesreden*, 74), Isis warns Horus not to listen to the crocodile if it speaks sweetly to him (Newsom).

Some commentators have seen here an allusion to the old belief that crocodiles weep, first found in English in the medieval book *The Voyages and Travailes of Sir J. Mandeville, Knight* (c. 1400): "In that contre ... ben gret plentee of Cokadrilles. ... Theise Serpentes slen men, and thei eten hem wepynge" (chap. 31; also in Spenser's *Fairie Queene*, 1.5.18; Shakespeare, *Othello*, 4.1.257). Richard Blackmore's famous verse paraphrase of Job (1700) contains the lines "His plighted Faith the Crocodile shall keep, / And seeing thee, for Joy sincerely Weep." Crocodiles cannot in fact cry, because they have no tear ducts; but the glands that moisten their eyes are so near the throat that the effort of swallowing forces moisture from them, giving the impression of tears. Interesting though this tradition may be, there is nothing about weeping in the present text.

4 (40:28)   The irony continues. Would the captured Leviathan be so in awe of Job as to sue for peace with the suzerain Job, undertaking to become Job's servant, in return for a daily food allowance? Would it be found "making a covenant" (כרת ברית) with Job to become his servant in perpetuity (obviously it would be a covenant between Job as the sovereign and Leviathan as the vassal)? The term "servant of eternity" (עבד עולם), meaning a person who has renounced one's liberty permanently, occurs in Deut 15:17 (cf. Exod 21:6); 1 Sam 27:12; it is also found in the Ugaritic texts (in the Baal myth, I*.B.ii.12 [*ANET*, 138b]). In 39:9 there was a similar ironic picture of the wild ox being unwilling to become a "servant." We are reminded too of the "covenant" or "league" with the stones of the field in 5:23.

5 (40:29)   It is a nice touch to feminize the mighty Leviathan by imagining it as a plaything for little *girls,* so safe and tame as to belong to their world. For a sparrow as a toy for a girl or young woman, cf. Catullus 2; and for a quail, Plautus, *The Captives* 5.4.1002–3; *The Comedy of Asses* 3.692–93. The only being who could dare take Leviathan as a plaything is God himself: Ps 104:26, in depicting the sea, speaks of Leviathan whom God made "to play with" (שׂחק, the same word as here), if that is the correct translation (as in NJPS, NJB). No doubt in dependence on this verse, a rabbinic tradition had it that God plays with Leviathan every day, from the ninth to the twelfth hour (*b. Aboda Zara* 3b).

6 (40:30)   Or, if Leviathan is not to become a plaything, can it perhaps be a source of low-fat, low-calorie protein? Crocodile meat has half the fat of lean beef, the calories of chicken breast, and 31 grams of protein per 100 grams when roasted as a fillet. This next absurd picture is, first, of the guild of fishers (not "traders," as RSV) who have been out hunting for the larger-than-life Leviathan, who is at this moment at least not simply the down-to-earth crocodile. Now that they have caught it, they must agree on the price they will sell it for, and then they will have to cut up the carcass to parcel it out to retail traders. The second group are the traders who run market stalls; Leviathan will be too big a purchase for any of them individually, and they will have to buy portions of it by weight. For a glimpse of (Tyrian) merchants bringing fish (probably salted) to markets in Jerusalem, cf. Neh 13:16.

7 (40:31)   Of course, if Leviathan is to be traded in the market, it must first be caught. We are back to the setting of vv 1–2 (40:25–26), where the hunting of Leviathan is in view. Here the question is whether, if fishhooks will not serve, darts and harpoons will assist Job in conquering it. The crocodile was indeed hunted with spears and harpoons in Egypt, but the mere fact that some Egyptians did it does not put it within the capacity of a Job. Various kinds of spears are attested for fishing in Egypt; see Erika Feucht, "Fishing and Fowling with the Spear and the Throw-Stick Reconsidered," in *The Intellectual Heritage of Egypt: Studies Presented to László Kákosy by Friends and Colleagues on the Occasion of His 60th Birthday* (ed. Ulrich Luft; Studia aegyptiaca 14; Budapest: La Chaire d'Egyptologie, 1992) 157–69.

8 (40:32)   With ironic thoughtfulness, Yahweh warns Job against too close a contact with Leviathan. The sentence seems a little odd, nevertheless. Job is hardly disposed to "lay [his] hand" on a crocodile, so a warning is out of place. If "lay the hand" means only "attack, hunt," then, regardless of Job's own interest in big game hunting, it is by no means absurd to hunt crocodiles, and many have done so for a living. So either the poet does not know of crocodile hunting, or he does not believe that Job would be capable of it.

9 (41:1) In v 8 (40:32), an attempt to capture Leviathan is said to be ill advised. Here things are even worse: The mere sight of the creature is enough to frighten off a would-be captor.

11 (3) Rowold's supposition (Henry Rowold, "מִי הוּא לִי הוּא?!: Leviathan and Job in Job 41:2–3," *JBL* 105 [1986] 104–9) that this verse is Leviathan's reply to God in the previous verse, i.e., "Whoever confronts me, I will repay. Under all the heavens, he is mine!" is far from probable (though Newsom is attracted by it).

12 (4) Hartley thinks the reason why Yahweh will not be silent is that "he who stops speaking concedes his opponent's point" (cf. 9:3). It seems rather that Yahweh takes such delight in the prowess of his creature that he cannot restrain himself from praising it.

13–17 (5–9) "Yahweh now revels in flamboyant description [of Leviathan]... The body of this monster is completely impenetrable. There is no way one can get beneath his skin, prise open his jaws, or penetrate behind the interlocking pieces of armor which cover his body" (Habel). On the one hand, it is hugely self-contained and autonomous. But on the other, it has a quite special beauty about it, as Leo G. Perdue has rightly noted (*Wisdom in Revolt: Metaphorical Theology in the Book of Job* [JSOTSup 112; Bible and Literature Series 20; Sheffield: Almond Press, JSOT Press, 1991] 230 n. 5).

14 (6) The crocodile has thirty-six teeth in the upper jaw, thirty in the lower. Since the crocodile's mouth has no lips, the teeth are all the more prominent. Several teeth in the upper jaw lie outside the lower jaw even when the mouth is closed.

15 (7) Each of its scales is a shield in itself, and they are formed in rows, of which there are said to be seventeen. The scales, which are hard and bony, tessellate, i.e., they fit together without leaving spaces in between. These scales are connected to one another and move as the crocodile moves. They do not grow, so as the animal grows it sheds its skin and grows a new one.

18–21 (10–13) If it is truly the crocodile that is being described, these verses are certainly hyperbolical. But it is no more than a fanciful and amusing hyperbole, which all rests on a single conceit, that the crocodile's breath is hot as fire. From that central idea come the depictions of the spray from its nostrils like flashing lights (v 18 [10]), sparks of fire from its mouth (v 19 [11]), smoke or steam from its nostrils (v 20 [12]), and a hot flame from its mouth that can kindle coals (v 21 [13]). The same tendency to hyperbole is to be found in the description of the hippopotamus in Achilles Tatius, *Leucippe and Clitophon* 4.2. Some, however, for example Dhorme, Pope, and Habel, see here the strongest evidence that the creature is indeed a supernatural mythological being. Here, says Habel, is depicted the "inner fire which emanates from this sea monster."

18 (10) How do the crocodile's sneezes "flash with light"? The usual answer may be correct, that "[t]he vapour or spray that issued from the nostrils of the crocodile flashed in the sunlight" (Rowley; similarly Peake, Dhorme, Gordis), or, as Moffatt picturesquely translates it, "the light plays on his snorting snout." Others, who think Leviathan is more of a mythological creature, see here a dragon breathing out flames of fire (Pope, Habel).

In fact, there does not seem to be any zoological evidence that crocodiles actually sneeze. As Pope has rightly pointed out, the passages from Strabo (17.39), and others that have frequently been cited (since Bochart's *Hierozoicon* of 1663) as evidence of the crocodile sneezing, refer not to sneezing but only to the crocodile yawning or gaping in the sun. But it does seem that crocodiles snort. And when they vomit, as part of their normal digestive process, they seem to sneeze, snap their jaws together, and then shake their heads from side to side.

As for the eyes of the crocodile, while they are exceptionally interesting from a biological point of view, the opening of the crocodile's eye with its mictating membrane that sweeps across the eye as it opens (video clip at www.junglewalk. com) just conceivably being likened to the coming of dawn, a reasonable view is that what we have here is an embroidering of the picture of the real crocodile with fanciful or mythological material about a dragon. From the eyelids of the dawn come rays of light (as in 3:9, the eyelids of the dawn are the first light in the east that heralds dawn); the eyelids (or, eyes; see *Note* d) of the crocodile, on the other hand, emit nothing. Habel, regarding the creature as a mythological dragon, explains its red eyes as an expression of the intense heat within its body.

It is unlikely that the reference is to "the reddish eyes of the crocodile" (Rowley, similarly Gordis), since its eyes are not especially red. No more probable is the explanation of Hartley, that "[t]he reflection of the light in its reddish eyes makes them appear *like the rays of dawn.*" Equally fanciful are the reports of Achilles Tatius (4.2), regarding the hippopotamus as "opening its nostrils wide and snorting out a reddish smoke as if from a fire," and of Bochart, who speaks of its "vomiting" flames from its mouth and nostrils.

The eye of the crocodile is in Egyptian hieroglyphic the sign for the dawn, but it is doubtful whether that fact has any significance here. Pope reports Bochart citing the fourth-century Greek grammarian Horapollo from Egypt that "the Egyptians used the crocodile's eyes as the symbol of dawn because the crocodile swims with his whole body submerged except for the eyes which appear above the surface. The reddish eyes, or eyelids, of the crocodile are said to glow through the water." Pope compares the account of the messengers of Yam, the Ugaritic sea-god, who intimidate the gods with their fiery appearance: "Fire, burning fire, doth flash, A whetted sword [are their e]yes" (*ANET,* 130).

19 (11)   Rowley explains: "When the crocodile issues from the water, it expels its pent-up breath together with water in a hot stream from its mouth, and this looks like a stream of fire in the sunshine." On the other hand, perhaps this depiction of flaming torches and sparks of fire emanating from the mouth of the crocodile is no more than an elaboration of the image of the fire-breathing dragon, as also in v 21 (13) below.

20 (12)   We would certainly be in the realm of the mythological—or at least it would be mythological language applied to a real-life crocodile—if "smoke" came from this creature's nostrils.

But perhaps עָשָׁן means here, though it never does elsewhere (but cf. *Note* a on 38:20), "steam" (as Moffatt, NAB, REB), which is still not literally true but an acceptable metaphor for the jet of water from the crocodile's nose. Such a translation would improve the sense of the second colon, for it is not "smoke" that comes from a boiling pot, but steam. Fanning a fire under a cooking pot is in any case not designed to produce smoke, but to increase the temperature (for fanning a fire with bellows, cf. Isa 54:16; Jer 1:13; Ezek 22:20; Ecclus 43:4).

21 (13)   The language of the crocodile's breath setting coals on fire is certainly hyperbolical, even mythological (similarly Peake). That is, the language is mythological, but that does not settle the question whether the creature described is or is not a mythological creature. Everyone knows, of course, that dragons have fiery breath, and supporters of the mythological interpretation of Leviathan are much affirmed by this description. Habel notes how fire blazes from the mouth of Marduk when he manifests his glory (*ANET*, 62), and how the messengers of the sea god Yam flash fire when they arrive (Baal III*.B.30). And we could compare the bulls in Virgil's *Georgics* that "breathe fire from their nostrils," which Jason yoked together at Colchis in order to sow the teeth of the dragon (2:140). We do not need to go outside the Hebrew Bible, however, for a picture of the deity with smoke from the nostrils, fire from the mouth, and glowing coals flaming forth (2 Sam 22:9 || Ps 18:8 [9]). Mineral coal is not known in Palestine, and the reference is to wood coal, i.e., charcoal (נחלה), used for heating (Isa 47:14; John 18:18), for cooking (Isa 44:19; John 21:9), and for forging (Isa 44:12); specifically charcoal of broom is mentioned at Ps 120:4 (cf. Dalman, *Arbeit und Sitte*, 4:4–5).

22 (14)   The crocodile's neck is not very obvious, but it certainly exists, as Aristotle already knew (*Hist. animal.* 9.6). Whether it is correct that the neck is in general regarded as a seat of strength (so, e.g., Rowley, de Wilde) is doubtful: 15:26 is probably not a mention of the human neck, and the phrase "a stiff neck" (as, e.g., in Ps 75:5 [6]) has more to do with obstinacy than with strength. It is certainly correct to focus on the strength of the crocodile's neck (with the hippopotamus, its strength was in its loins, 40:16), for it is the muscles of its neck that enable it to smash its prey by tossing it from side to side.

The terror or dismay the crocodile provokes in onlookers is said to "dance" (דוץ), if the text is sound, before it. Is this a matter of the dancing being "transferred from the panic stricken victims to the dismay itself" (Rowley), though? It is a good thought on Hartley's part that the terror is provoked by the sight of the crocodile in motion; one has only to see a crocodile covering the ground at a gallop to be aware of its formidable power. But it is surely more than an ironic description of the "convulsive movements of terrified creatures when leviathan suddenly shows his head" (Strahan), though Moffatt's wonderful rendering "all creatures twitch in terror at him" begs to be adopted. Dhorme is reminded of David dancing and leaping before the ark (2 Sam 6:14–16), but it is perhaps more relevant to think of righteousness going before Yahweh as a herald in Ps 85:13 (14) (cf. 89:14 [15]), or of fire going before him (Ps 97:3), or of pestilence going before him at his theophany and plague following close after (Hab 3:5). De Wilde notes references in Greek literature where qualities are pictured as comrades in battle: thus Homer, *Iliad* 15.119 (of Terror and Rout); Hesiod, *Shield of Heracles* 195 (Fear and Flight), 463 (Panic and Dread). That said, we should note that the idiom here stresses the beauty or at least the fascination of the crocodile and its effect on its watchers. Driver–Gray thought it a "beautiful and expressive figure ... which it is an injustice to emend away" and Duhm found it a "truly poetic verse."

23 (15)   The description now turns from the appearance of Leviathan, with its adoption of motifs from the mythical dragon, to a much more down-to-earth depiction of the flesh of the beast's body, specifically its underneath parts. Newsom nicely remarks that what is described in vv 23–24 (15–16) is visible only when Leviathan raises itself up—which is not mentioned until v 25 (17). "It is as though the visual description itself introduces motion into the picture," she says. Unlike the bodies of other animals, its flesh is solid, hard, and immovable. Three times the term "firm" (יָצוּק) is used in vv 23–24 (15–16), more probably an intentional repetition by the poet than a sign of a disordered text (as, e.g., Duhm).

24 (16) In comparing the chest or body of the crocodile to the nether millstone, the poet does not have in mind the commercial kind of millstone that has a rotating stone (as probably at Matt 24:41), but the domestic mill, or saddle quern, used for the daily preparation of grain (as at Exod 11:5): it consists of a lower stone, slightly concave, perhaps 30 inches in length, and a lighter stone held in the hand. The person milling, usually a woman, would kneel in front of the lower stone (the term שֶׁכֶב, lit. "the lier," is attested in Mishnaic Hebrew [Levy, 2:1571a]) and move the upper stone, "the rider" (רֶכֶב, as in Deut 24:6; Judg 9:53; 2 Sam 11:21), back and forth across the lower, thus grinding the grain (H. N. Richardson, *IDB*, 3:381–82, with an illustration from the Egyptian Old Kingdom of the device in operation [= *ANEP*, fig. 149]; Karel van der Toorn, *ABD*, 4:831–32; Dalman, *Arbeit und Sitte*, 3:208–11). The nether millstone, which received the harder wear, would commonly be basalt, or sometimes limestone.

25 (17) When the crocodile "raises itself up" (נשא), one might have expected it to expose the less well protected parts of its body. Not so, for as we have just seen, its nether parts are covered by armor no less than its back is.

There is more than one possible explanation of the crocodile "raising itself up." It could be a reference to its behavior when about to eat its prey: it is quite a terrifying sight to see it tip its head back and throw its food to the back of its mouth with a flick of the head. But perhaps more likely still is a reference to its jumping out of the water to catch low-flying birds or bats. It positions itself with the tail underneath the body and the head pointing up into the air. Thrusting the tail and paddling with the back feet, it swims up and projects itself into the air, until half or more of its body is out of the water (video clip at www. junglewalk.com).

The text seems to say that it is the "gods" (אלים) who are terrified of the crocodile, since that is the normal meaning of אל. Pope correctly observes that the motif of the cowering of the gods in fear is widespread in Near Eastern literature (e.g., in the Gilgamesh Epic [*ANET*, 94, lines 113–14] and in the Baal myth when the messengers of Yam arrive [Baal III*.B.22–24]). But it is hard to see how gods come to be spectators of the crocodile; it seems preferable to take the word in its rarer sense of "chiefs, mighty men," who are to be envisaged as out hunting the crocodile.

26 (18) Here begins a striking example of the literary form of the "tour," in which the poet lists a number of terms with a similar meaning. In vv 26–29 (18–21), no fewer than ten weapons are named: sword, spear, dart, javelin, iron weapon, bronze weapon, arrow, sling-stone, club, javelin (a second word). On the "tour," cf. Watson, 348–49 (Duhm's pejorative remark, "as if the poet were working with a dictionary," is now outmoded). This verse itself contains in its second colon a "triple synonym" that is "expletive" of the term "sword" in the first colon (Watson, 174; cf., e.g., Jer 51:27b; Hos 2:11 [13]).

27 (19) Weapons from iron and bronze for hand-to-hand fighting are useless against Leviathan. For straw as something of little substance, cf. 21:18 (straw before the wind); for wood that is *not* rotten, and so desirable for making an image, cf. Isa 40:20.

28 (20) Equally useless are weapons deployed from a distance like arrows and slingstones. Arrows are here called "sons of the bow" (בני־קשת); in Lam 3:13 the term is "sons of the quiver" (בני אשפה), while in Arabic poetry, as Dhorme notes, they can be called "daughters of the quivers." It is a picturesque image to have slingstones turning in flight into harmless pieces of chaff (הפך ל "turn into," as KJV, RSV, should not be overlooked, as it is by most modern translations).

29 (21) To Leviathan, "bludgeons are mere bulrushes" (Moffatt). The term "laugh" (שחק) occurs also of the wild ass at 39:7, of the ostrich at 39:18, of the war horse at 39:22, and of a restored Job at 5:22. In each case, the laugh is a display of the absence of fear. (In 40:20 the verb is used somewhat differently, of the wild beasts "playing" beside the hippopotamus, and in 41:5 [40:29] of little girls "playing" with Leviathan as with a pet bird.)

30 (22) Here we move from the description of Leviathan's stout body as proof against attack (vv 26–29 [18–21]) to a depiction of the marks it leaves as it moves across the mud (v 30 [22]) and then across the water (vv 31–32 [23–24]). Imagining its nether parts as a threshing sledge fitted with sharp potsherds, the poet envisages how it will leave a deep imprint as it walks away from lying in a comfortable spot in the mud (or perhaps the picture is of it scoring a groove in the mud as it slides across it). Poetic though the depiction is, there is nothing mythological about the creature here.

Peake offers an instructive, and amusing, piece of metacommentary on the matter: "Duhm objects to this that the scales on the underpart are smooth. Dillmann says they are smaller than those on the back, but equally sharp. Davidson says that though smoother than those on the back, they are still sharp. If modern commentators can differ like this on a plain matter of fact, one cannot expect too great precision in a poet, who may have known the crocodile only from reports or reading." In fact, the scales on the underparts of the crocodile are not sharp.

A threshing sledge was a flat heavy wooden board, bent upward at the front and with projecting stones or pieces of iron fixed into its under side; as it was dragged over the threshing floor, weighted down with stones or workers, it tore the husks from off the grain and cut the straw into chaff. See further, Dalman, *Arbeit und Sitte*, 3:83; Robert L. Webb, "The Activity of John the Baptist's Expected Figure at the Threshing Floor (Matthew 3.12 = Luke 3.17)," *JSNT* 43 (1991) 103–11 (105–8); William A. Fox and David A. Pearlman, "Threshing Sledge Production in the Paphos District, Cyprus," in *Western Cyprus: Connections: An Archaeological Symposium* (ed. David W. Rupp; Studies in Mediterranean Archaeology 77; Gothenburg: Paul Aström, 1987) 227–34 (on the manufacture and use of such sledges in modern times, with an impressive photograph of the under side of such a *dhoukani*).

31 (23) As it makes its way across the water, Leviathan disturbs its surface, making it boil like a cooking pot and bubble like a pot in which ointment is prepared. As Newsom very aptly remarks, "A pot of boiling ointment is also an image of agitation, yet is one not associated with danger. The small size of such a pot subtly introduces an element of visual distance into the picture, as though one were watching the sea from far away."

As it happens, though the crocodile often moves gently through the water, it leaves a very distinct and characteristic wake (videoclip at www.flmnh.ufl.edu/natsci/herpetology/brittoncrocs/images/cp-swim1.mpg). A cooking pot or cauldron (סיר, as at Exod 16:3, the "flesh pots" of Egypt; 2 Kgs 4:40 "death in the cooking pot") has boiling water in it, an ointment-pot (מרקחה), which would be much smaller, would contain the ingredients of ointments or perfumes. The base for ointment and perfume was olive oil, to which was added various plant materials or animal secretions during a process of steeping and boiling (Victor H. Matthews, *ABD*, 5:226–28; J. A. Thompson, *IDB*, 3:593–95). One would not say the mixture "boiled" but "bubbled" (see further, *Note* e). The vials and flasks, containers in which ointments and perfumes were kept and traded (e.g., 1 Sam 10:1; 2 Kgs 9:1; illustration in *IDB*, 3:594 = *ANET*, fig. 69), were of course much more elaborate and expensive than vessels used in their manufacture.

It has long been known that crocodiles have a strong scent of musk, and the extract from its musk glands has been used in the manufacture of perfume (cf., e.g., de Wilde); but it is hard to believe that its smell is what suggested the comparison here (as Duhm; cf. Rowley).

To judge by many translations, vv 31–32 (23–24) depict Leviathan's progress across the *sea*: the terms מצולה "deep," ים "sea," and תהום "deep" appear. Yet none of these refers unambiguously to oceans, and each is attested in reference to smaller bodies of water such as lakes or rivers (see further, *Notes* a and d on v 31 [23] and *Note* d on v 32 [24]). NEB in particular, in using "deep water," "lake," and "great river" for the three terms, expresses the view that Leviathan is not a sea creature, but the freshwater crocodile (*Crocodylus niloticus*).

32 (24)   Before the final summarizing encomium on Leviathan (vv 33–34 [25–26]), we bid it farewell as it swims off into the distance, leaving only a shining wake behind it (Newsom). In a delightful metaphor, which brings the reader into the sphere of Leviathan's activities ("one would think," says the poet), the foaming water is compared to the white hair of old age. Who can the "one" of "one would think the deep hoar-headed" be if not the reader in unison with the poet? "The image with which the wake is visualized is no longer one of agitation, but a calm image of the deep" (Newsom). Homer also speaks of the "hoary deep" and the "hoary sea" (*Iliad* 1.350; 4.248; *Odyssey* 5.410; 6.272); cf. Aristophanes, *Birds* 350. Among the Roman poets, cf. Apollonius, *Argonautica* 1.545; Manilius, *Astronomica* 1:708, Ovid, *Heroides* 3.65 (the seas foam). Milton's depiction of Leviathan as "haply slumbering on the Norway foam" (*Paradise Lost,* 7:203) may have been inspired by the same image.

33–34 (25–26)   In these last two verses the poet stands back from his marveling scrutiny of Leviathan, and ponders its significance in the divine economy. With Behemoth, the depiction had been prefaced with the evaluation "which I made as I made you" (40:15), which was supplemented by a second evaluation in the middle of the depiction: "It is first of the works of God" (40:19). The description of Behemoth had then drawn to an end on the note of how impossible it is to capture the beast (40:24). The Leviathan passage began on exactly that note, "Can you drag Leviathan out with a fishhook?" (41:1 [40:25]), but throughout the lengthy description not a word has been said of the beast's significance until we arrive now at the conclusion. If Behemoth was God's masterpiece, Leviathan is king of beasts, without a peer on earth, fearsome to others but above all fearless itself.

34 (26) While Leviathan itself is fearless—perhaps we should even translate "created for fearlessness" (Duhm)—it inspires fear in others (the Hebrew "it sees [יראה] all that is lofty" should probably be emended to "all that are lofty fear [ייראו] it"; see *Note* a). Though it is not what one would call a "lofty" animal, it is more than a match for other much larger and taller beasts of prey, and rightly feared by them. The term גבה, "lofty" or "proud," refers primarily to height and metaphorically to high status. It is not in itself a pejorative term, being used of mountains (e.g., Gen 7:19) and trees (e.g., Ezek 31:3). The verb גבה "be high" is used of God (Isa 5:16). The other term for "pride," שחץ, occurs only here and in 28:8, also in reference to beasts; there is no hint of censure in the term.

The "lofty" or "proud" over which Leviathan is king must surely be other beasts, since it is self-evidently untrue that it rules over humans. Some have seen a deliberate allusion to 40:11–12, at the beginning of this second divine speech, where Yahweh taunts Job to "look upon all who are haughty (גבה) and humble them, bring them low." Newsom even calls v 34 (26) an *inclusio* with 40:11–12; but those verses are not exactly at the beginning of the poem, and they are found in the address to Job, not in the accounts of the two beasts. The problem would be to see what the significance of the allusion would be: Job is incapable of "treading down the wicked" (40:12c), i.e., of managing the moral universe, but that seems little related to Leviathan's kingship, which is only one of status, not of function, and which subsists in fear, not in judgment. The language is the same, but the spheres in which the two passages live are totally different.

It is no accident that in Egypt the crocodile was frequently used as a metaphor for the king. The victory hymn of Thutmosis III, for example, has the god Amon-Re saying to the pharaoh, "I cause them [the king's enemies] to see thy majesty as a crocodile, the lord of fear in the water, which cannot be approached" (*ANET*, 374b; the king is also likened to a shooting star, a young bull, a fierce lion, a "lord of the wing," and a "jackal of the Southland"). In Roman times the crocodile appeared on coins as a royal symbol.

Pope, a strong supporter of the mythological nature of Leviathan, admits that its kingship over all the "sons of pride" would suggest that it belongs to the world of real-life animals; he can counter this natural implication only be pointing again to the many mythological features he has already noted in the depiction.

There is no sly implication here of Job's pride or any inadequacy of his by comparison with the crocodile, or any suggestion that he should not struggle with the victims of hybris (as Terrien). Leviathan is here in its own right, as king of beasts, a source of pleasure and pride for its maker, just like Behemoth his masterpiece (40:19). Whatever it signifies, whatever it implies, is about Yahweh and his relations with his created world.

The absence of any concluding address to Job at the end of the divine speeches is surprising, but it is not clear what inference, if any, we should draw from it. Patrick W. Skehan is clear that the omission is "deliberate, to indicate that the theme could be pursued indefinitely" ("Job's Final Plea [Job 29–31] and the Lord's Reply (Job 38–41)," *Bib* 45 (1964) 51–62 [= his *Studies in Israelite Poetry and Wisdom* (CBQMS 1; Washington, DC: Catholic Biblical Association of America, 1971) 114–23 (123)]). Certainly, the dramatic effect is to leave Job face to face with the figure of Leviathan, paraded by Yahweh as in some sense the key to the meaning of the universe.

Explanation

This second speech of Yahweh has contained two unequal, and unalike, parts. The first (40:7–14) has been a frankly unattractive baiting of Job, a sarcastic challenge to him to dress up like a god, and act like the kind of god he expects the universal ruler to be, executing absolute authority and sweeping away the wicked from the world. There has been an edge in this reproof of Job that we did not hear in the first speech, almost a bitterness. Yahweh has been needled, as well he might be, by Job's unambiguous and reiterated charges that he does not know how to do his job. It has not helped matters that after the first divine speech Job has not capitulated. Yahweh cannot forbear from saying to Job, Well, let's see you do it better! He does not mean that it would be too difficult, even for him, to carry out the kind of program of extermination of the wicked that Job has in mind, but rather that Job has no idea what he is asking. It has not been Yahweh's way in these speeches to spend much time on pointing out where Job is wrong; he has been much more interested in expounding his own vision of the cosmos. But here at least he confronts Job's notion of justice head-on, and says, implicitly, Feel free to do it your way; it is not my way of managing the universe. Job is of course powerless to "crush the wicked where they stand" (40:12) and therefore his criticisms of Yahweh will not wash.

Yahweh, however, as we have seen in this speech, will not linger with his sarcasm. He prefers to accentuate the positive, and is only too happy to return to his theme of his creation, confining himself to depiction and leaving to Job the task of discerning, beneath the data, the principles that make up the grand divine Plan (38:2). The transition from Job's misprisions to the proper perspective on the universe comes with the phrase "Consider Behemoth" (40:15, lit. "Behold now Behemoth"), the only time in the divine speeches that Job is explicitly encouraged to view, and thus to ruminate on, the parade of universal phenomena that Yahweh passes before his eyes. Beholding is everything, of course. What Job has lacked is any perception of God's purposes; that is where he has been wrong. He has not been wicked, he has not been offensive (well, not so as to earn reproof on that account), he has simply been speaking "words without knowledge" (38:2). It has been an intellectual fault, and it can be remedied by better knowledge, a considered knowledge of Behemoth (standing here, we may suppose, for all the facets of the world Yahweh has created).

Something has happened in the course of this speech that has moved the book on to a new plane. The subject matter seems much the same as in the first divine speech, in that Behemoth and Leviathan are no more than two further wild beasts, like those of 38:39–39:30. The argument is not different, for Yahweh is continuing his program of expounding his plan for the universe, leaving Job (and us) still somewhat in the dark about the underlying meaning of the depictions. What has happened is that the didactic has given place to the lyrical, as the sustained argument of the greater part of the book issues at the end in an entire concentration on, absorption in, one amazing creature, Leviathan the crocodile.

In finally settling for the lyrical over the didactic the poem proffers a wholly conscious realignment of the issue under debate in the book: it changes the discourse from that of rationality and argument to that of delight and praise. From a more intellectual point of view, we might say that the divine speeches have refused the categories of the dialogues, and in particular the complaints of Job that the world is not being governed with justice. What they have left in their place is the suggestion that God does not put himself forward as world governor, and that his acts toward his creation are not to be judged in the scales of justice. Such a perception could no doubt have been expressed in didactic poetry—it can be stated quite prosaically, in fact—but it is the achievement of the poet that he handles it by means of a major shift in the poetic form, from the didactic to the lyrical. There were two things that had been lacking from the realm of the didactic: understanding and wonder. In the didactic, there had been no room for wonder, since everything was already known; but also, ironically, the knowledge with which the dialogues abounded had left no space for understanding either. There is, in the poet's vision, an understanding that comes through indirection, a worldview that arises from a wondering (rather than an analytical) contemplation of reality.

Can the divine speeches really represent the triumph of the lyrical over the didactic? Are not the divine speeches the most didactic of all the speeches in the book, a paean to didacticism? Do they not emulate an encyclopaedia, replete with the questions of an ironic schoolmaster to the classroom dunce Job? Did any of the friends ever stifle Job with a greater display of erudition?

Or does it not belong to the poet's achievement that the seeming didacticism of the divine speeches is only a front, that in these lines the form of the didactic entirely undermines the intentions of the didactic? How can these speeches be didactic when Yahweh is teaching Job nothing, is telling Job nothing he does not know already, is not interested in what he might answer? How can they be didactic when the further they proceed the more the formally didactic elements drop away, until the Leviathan poem at their end abandons the questioning altogether and the poet's imagination revels in pure depiction?

And yet, to come back to earth, what has happened to Job's question? It is all very well for the poet of Job to change the discourse from rationality to delight, but humans are rational beings as well as participants in delight, and what, at the end of the day, has happened to justice? Should we not be wary of poets who sweep questions of justice under carpets of delight? And what kind of a God has our poet almost succeeded in passing off on us? Does he need to be so supercilious, so self-defensive, so prolix, so unsympathetic, and—above all—so utterly unaware of the gratuitous injustice he has done Job in putting him in the Satan's hands with all the resultant damage to Job's family and life and reputation? Has our poet set before us, in the magnificent sweep of the cosmic Plan, a deity who is in the end unlovely and not a little chilling? Has this deity perhaps a little too much attachment to crocodiles?

Job's Second Reply (42:1-6)

Bibliography

Boer, P. A. H. de. "Haalt Job bakzeil? (Job xlii 6)." *NedTTs* 31 (1977) 181–94 [= "Does Job retract? (Job xlii 6)." In his *Selected Studies in Old Testament Exegesis*. Ed. C. van Duin. OTS 27. Leiden: E. J. Brill, 1991. 179–95]. **Copenhaver, Martin B.** "Risking a Happy Ending [Job 42:1–6, 10–17]." *ChrCent* 111 (1994) 923. **Dailey, Thomas F.** "And Yet He Repents—On Job 42,6." *ZAW* 105 (1993) 205–9. ———. "The Aesthetics of Repentance: Re-Reading the Phenomenon of Job." *BTB* 23 (1993) 64–70. ———. "'Wondrously far from me.' The Wisdom of Job 42,2–3." *BZ* 36 (1992) 261–64. **Gruber, Mayer I.** *Aspects of Nonverbal Communication in the Ancient Near East.* Studia Pohl 12. Rome: Biblical Institute Press, 1980. **Harrop, G. Gerald.** "'But now my eye seeth thee.'" *CJT* 12 (1966) 80–84. **Kaplan, L. J.** "Maimonides, Dale Patrick, and Job xlii 6." *VT* 28 (1978) 356–58. **Krüger, Thomas.** "Did Job Repent?" In *Das Buch Hiob und seine Interpretationen: Beiträge zum Hiob-Symposium auf dem Monte Verità vom 14.–19. August 2005.* Ed. Thomas Krüger, Manfred Oeming, Konrad Schmid, and Christoph Uehlinger. ATANT 88. Zurich: Theologische Verlag Zürich, 2007. 217–29. **Kuyper, Lester J.** "The Repentance of Job." *VT* 9 (1959) 91–94. **MacKenzie, R. A. F.** "The Transformation of Job." *BTB* 9 (1979) 51–57. **Maher, Seán.** "The Answer of Job to God." *PrIrBibAss* 28 (2007) 48–65. **Morrow, William.** "Consolation, Rejection, and Repentance in Job 42:6." *JBL* 105 (1986) 211–25. **Muenchow, Charles.** "Dust and Dirt in Job 42:6." *JBL* 108 (1989) 597–611. **Newell, B. Lynne.** "Job: Repentant or Rebellious?" *WTJ* 46 (1984) 298–316 [= *Sitting with Job: Selected Studies on the Book of Job.* Ed. Roy B. Zuck. Grand Rapids: Baker Book House, 1992. 441–56]. **O'Connor, Daniel J.** "Job's Final Word—'I am consoled ...' (42:6b)." *ITQ* 50 (1983–84) 181–97. ———. "The Comforting of Job." *ITQ* 53 (1987) 245–57. **Patrick, Dale.** "The Translation of Job xlii 6." *VT* 26 (1976) 369–71. **Pippin, Tina.** "Between Text and Sermon: Job 42:1–6, 10–17." *Int* 53 (1999) 299–303. **Shelley, John C.** "Job 42:1–6: God's Bet and Job's Repentance." *RevExp* 89 (1992) 541–46. **Taylor, John B.** "Job's Confession" [Job 42:1–6]. *ExpT* 107 (1996) 374–75. **Tilley, Terrence W.** "God and the Silencing of Job." *Modern Theology* 5 (1989) 257–70. **Vaage, L. E.** "Do meio da tempestade: a resposta de Deus a Jó: sabedoría bíblica, ecologia moderna, vida marginal: uma leitura de Jó 38,1–42,6." *RIBLA* 21 (1995) 199–213. **Wilde, A. de.** "Jobs slotwoord." *NedTTs* 32 (1978) 265–69. **Willi-Plein, Ina.** "Hiobs Wiederruf?—Eine Untersuchung der Wurzel נחם und ihrer erzähltechnischen Funktion im Hiobbuch." In *Essays on the Bible and the Ancient World: Isac Leo Seeligmann Volume.* III. *Non-Hebrew Section.* Ed. Alexander Rofé and Yair Zakovitch. Jerusalem: E. Rubinstein, 1983. 273–89. **Wolde, Ellen J. van.** "Job 42,1–6: The Reversal of Job." In *The Book of Job.* Ed. W. A. M. Beuken. BETL 114. Leuven: Leuven University Press, 1994. 223–50. **Wolters, Al.** "»A child of dust and ashes« (Job 42,6b)." *ZAW* 102 (1990) 116–19.

Translation

^{1a}*Then Job answered Yahweh:*

^{2}*I know^a that you can do anything,*
   and that no purpose^b of yours can be thwarted.^{c}
^{3a}*"Who^b is this who obscures^c the Design^d without knowledge?," you ask.^{e}*
   To be sure,^{f} I made my depositions^g—without understanding^h—
   concerning things too wonderful^i for me—which I did not know.^{j}

4 a *"Listen, and I will speak," you said,*[b]
  "I will question you, and you shall answer me."
⁵ *I have heard you with my ears,*[a]
  and[b] *my eyes have now seen*[c] *you.*
6 a *So I submit,*[b] *and I accept consolation*[c]
  for[d] *my dust and ashes.*[e]

Notes

1.a. Beer (*BH²*), Peake, Moffatt, Fohrer, and de Wilde delete this verse, in the interests of the theory that there was originally only one response from Job, and that these verses followed directly after 40:5.

2.a. יָדַעְתָ (Kt) is, as it stands, יָדַעְתָ "you know," but, despite Merx, that does not make sense (except as a defective spelling of the first person sg, as GKC, §44i, Gordis), and the Qr יָדַעְתִּי "I know" is universally accepted as the preferable reading.

2.b. מזמה is frequently "wicked plan, plot," but is adequately attested in the morally neutral sense "purpose, intention, thinking" (cf. *DCH*, 5:209a); the negative connotations that sometimes accompany it derive from the context, not the term itself (S. Steingrimsson, *TDOT*, 4:88–89), so there is no problem in ascribing מזמה to Yahweh. On the other hand, Habel is tempted to find an echo of the negative sense here, with a sidelong glance to the original "scheme" of Yahweh to test Job. On the sense "private thoughts, caginess," cf. Michael V. Fox, "Words for Wisdom: תבונה and בינה; ערמה and מזמה; עצה and תושיה," *ZAH* 6 (1993) 149–65 (159–60). Most modern translations have "purpose" (RSV, NEB) or "plan" (NIV) or some such phrase as "what you conceive, you can perform" (JB), "nothing You propose is impossible for You" (NJPS). KJV "no thought can be withholden from thee" is inappropriate. For מזמה as the purpose of *Yahweh*, cf. Jer 23:20.

LXX has ἀδυνατεῖ δέ σοι οὐθέν "nothing is impossible for you," which has led some to read מאוּמה "a thing" (so Hoffmann, Graetz, Beer [*BH²*]) or מָה "anything" (Bickell), but which is more likely to be simply an idiomatic translation of the same text as MT. Duhm ingeniously proposed that מזמה, which is not represented in LXX, was an abbreviation of מי זה מחשיך "who is this that darkens" in 38:2; here he read כי יָכֹלְתָ וכל לא "[I know] that you are capable, superior (*überlegen*) and nothing is [too high for you]" (explaining בצר by Ps 139:6). But the usual rendering is entirely satisfactory.

2.c. בצר is "cut," but also "restrain," and in the niph, as here, "be cut off, be withheld" (*DCH*, 2:246b) or "be inaccessible, impossible" (*HALOT*, 1:148b; *HALOT* distinguishes this בצר III, cognate with Aram. *baṣura*, from בצר I "cut"). A parallel expression is Gen 11:6: "nothing that they plan (זמם) to do will be withheld (בצר) from them." Moffatt "nothing is too hard for thee" weakens the force of the Hebrew. Kissane's "no design is hidden from Thee" suggests a design of humans, but בצר does not mean "hide."

3.a. The colon, which is omitted by LXX S*, is thought secondary by Budde, Duhm, Peake, Beer (*BH²*), Strahan, Driver–Gray, Moffatt, Dhorme, Hölscher, Fohrer, Pope, Tur-Sinai, de Wilde. It is omitted also by NAB, NEB (not REB).

3.b. Klostermann (cited by Peake) suggests אני זה מעלים "I am the one who has been darkening"; thus JB "I am the man who obscured your designs," NJB "I was the man who misrepresented your intentions."

3.c. עלם is "conceal," the hiph being usually employed for the active (as here). One Hebrew ms has מחשיך, in conformity with 38:2. But "conceal" is a different metaphor from "darken" even if we translate עלם with "obscure." Conceivably, however, we may have here another vb, עלם II "darken," like עולם III "darkness" at 22:15 (*q.v.*); cf. *DCH*, 6:307a.

3.d. On this translation of עצה "plan," see *Note* on 38:2. Some would insert במלים "by words," which is what we have (with the form מלין) in 38:2, which Job is obviously citing here. This reading is supported by LXX and Pesh, and is read by one Masoretic ms, and is adopted by Beer (*BHK*), Driver–Gray, Kissane, Sicre Díaz, Gray.

3.e. "You ask" is not in the Hebrew, but implied (added also by REB, TEV, and by NIV "You asked").

3.f. לכן is usually "therefore" (as KJV, RSV), but that is not an appropriate link between the quotation in v 3a and Job's own words in v 3b-c (it is omitted by NAB, JB, and effectively by NEB, REB "but"). לכן is attested sometimes as "surely, assuredly" (cf. *DCH*, 4:548b §2); cf. 1 Sam 28:2; Jer 2:33. Thus NIV "surely," NJPS "indeed," and "to be sure" in the *Translation* above. Blommerde, followed by Sicre Díaz, explains it rather as emphatic *lamed* plus כן, thus "indeed." Alternatively, it may just be the use of לכן to begin a response to the words of another, as in Gen 4:15; 30:15 (B. Jongeling, "*Lākēn* dans l'Ancien Testament," in *Remembering All the Way: A Collection of Old Testament Studies Published on the Occasion of the Fortieth Anniversary of the Oudtestamentisch Werkgezelschap in Nederland* [ed. A. S. van der Woude; OTS 21; Leiden: E. J. Brill, 1981] 190–200 [193, 200]).

3.g. On the exact sense of הגדתי, see *Comment.* Most have "uttered" (KJV, RSV), "spoke of" (NJPS, NIV; similarly NEB), "talked" (Pope); JB senses that the term is a little richer than that, and renders "I have been holding forth," and NAB "I have dealt with." In the *Translation* above it is understood in a more legal sense, "make a deposition" (see *Comment*). Some would insert גְּדֹלוֹת "great things" as the obj of הגדתי "I spoke" (Beer [*BHK*], Stier; so also NAB "I have dealt with great things that I do not understand"; similarly NEB, but not REB); LXX has μεγάλα "great things," but perhaps not as the obj of הגדתי. נגד hiph, however, does not need to have an obj expressed or a dative of the person addressed; cf., e.g., 15:18; 38:18.

The *Translation* above takes נפלאות "wonderful things" as the obj (as also Peters, NJPS "I spoke without understanding of things beyond me"). Others are more inclined to take ולא אבין, though it is not a noun, as the first obj, and "wonderful things" as a second, parallel obj (so KJV "therefore have I uttered that I understood not, things too wonderful for me, which I knew not"; similarly RSV, NAB, JB, NIV, REB). Moffatt's "I thoughtlessly confused the issues; I spoke without intelligence" appears to offer a double translation.

Instead of MT הִגַּדְתִּי "I have uttered," Stier reads הִגַּדְתָּ‌נִי "you have made known to me," inserting also גְּדֹלוֹת "great things" as the obj; he is followed by C. Westermann, *The Structure of the Book of Job: A Form-Critical Analysis* (Philadelphia: Fortress Press, 1981) 125–26.

3.h. ולא אבין "and I did not understand," and ולא אדע "and I did not know," are circumstantial clauses meaning "without understanding," "without knowing" (GKC, §156f).

3.i. On נפלאות "wonderful things," see the *Comment.* William Morrow, however, "Consolation, Rejection, and Repentance in Job 42:6," *JBL* 105 (1986) 211–25 (222–23), argues that נפלאות ממני may mean simply "things too difficult for me" (cf. Gen 18:14; Deut 17:8; 30:11; Jer 32:17, 27; Ps 131:1; Prov 30:18), but the interpretation of the verse is not much altered if that were so. The argument of T. F. Dailey, "'Wondrously Far From Me.' The Wisdom of Job 42,2–3," *BZ* 36 (1992) 261–64, that נפלאות is adverbial, qualifying the manner of Job's speech as "wondrously far" from himself, is grammatically unacceptable.

3.j. Moffatt nicely renders the colon "of wonders far beyond my ken."

4.a. Budde, Duhm, Peake, Beer (*BH*²), Strahan, Driver–Gray, Moffatt, Dhorme, Hölscher, Fohrer, Pope, Tur-Sinai, de Wilde omit the verse. NEB (not REB) and NAB omit it as a gloss. JB puts the whole verse in parentheses. And likewise NJB, saying it is probably a gloss.

4.b. "You said" is not in the Hebrew, but implied (added also by NIV, REB, TEV).

5.a. לשמע־אזן שמעתיך is lit. "with the hearing of the ears I have heard you." A very similar phrase occurs in Ps 18:44 (45), לשמע־אזן ישמעו לי lit. "at the hearing of the ears, they obeyed me" (|| 2 Sam 22:45 has the variant לשמוע) but with quite a different sense, i.e., "the moment they heard" (so too in Ecclus 43:24)—which is not at all relevant to the present verse. In Ps 18 || 2 Sam 22 the vb שמע is niph, which apparently means "obey" but is poorly attested (cf. BDB, 1034a §3). There is no reason to affirm that "with the hearing of the ears" means "by hearsay" (against, e.g., Dhorme, Gordis, de Wilde; Duhm, who gives the phrase this sense, acknowledges that this is the only place where it would have that meaning). We should note that the Hebrew here says "I heard you" (שמעתיך), as NJPS, not "I heard about you," though most English translations say or imply that (so KJV, RSV, NAB, NIV; cf. JB "I knew you only by hearsay," NEB "I knew of thee then only by report"; similarly Moffatt, Dhorme, Pope, König, §22, even arguing that the suff is dative; for other examples of the datival suff, see *Note* on 22:21). Admittedly, שמע could be said to mean "hear of" in Exod 18:1 ("Jethro heard all God had done for Moses and Israel"); 2 Kgs 19:11 ("you have heard what the kings of Assyria have done to all lands"); 1 Kgs 4:34 (all the kings of the earth had heard of Solomon's wisdom); Ps 132:6; but in none of these places is a person the obj, and in all of them the idea of a report is quite transparent.

5.b. Translations uniformly understand the *waw* as contrastive, "but." See, however, the *Comment*, for arguments that the two cola of the verse are to be regarded as parallel.

5.c. For "seeing" (ראה) as a form of perception, and thus of knowing, cf. *HALOT*, 3:1157b. For examples, see Gen 2:19 ("He brought them to the man to see what he would call them"); 42:1 "When Jacob saw that there was grain in Egypt ..."; see further D. Vetter, *TLOT*, 3:1178. Cf. Samuel Terrien, "The Yahweh Speeches and Job's Responses," *RevExp* 68 (1971) 497–501 (498): "[T]he expression 'to see God' refers in Biblical Hebrew not to the actuality of a sensorial perception of sight but to the immediacy and directness of divine presence."

6.a. It must be confessed that the meter of the MT text is odd, apparently 2 + 3, which would suggest that there has been some omission. Driver–Gray reach the frustrating conclusion that the verse is "probably corrupt." The metrical problem has usually been addressed by supposing that an obj has dropped out or that the text should be emended in some other way (see below).

6.b. אמאס, as it stands, appears to be from מאס "reject," which, however, usually has an obj expressed. Can it be used absolutely, as it appears to be here? That seems to be the case at 7:16, where, however, the obj "my life" is present as a concept in the verse (it is explicit in 9:21); at 34:33 (q.v.), which is, however, very problematic; and at Ps 89:38 [39], where the obj "my anointed" is present in the verse, though not as the direct obj of this vb. BDB, 549b §2, also regards the vb as capable of being used absolutely, with the sense "despise," though without indicating how it can be translated here (the English "despise" needs an obj).

Various senses have been proposed for the term understood absolutely: (1) "feel loathing, contempt, revulsion"; see Walter D. Michel, *Job in the Light of Northwest Semitic* (BibOr 42; Rome: Biblical Institute Press, 1987) 1:174; John Briggs Curtis, "On Job's Response to Yahweh," *JBL* 98 (1979) 497–511 (503, 505), translating "Therefore I feel loathing, contempt and revulsion [toward you, O God]." (2) "yield" or "retract"; so Ehrlich, Fohrer "I retract" (*ich widerrufe*), Bleeker "I retract" (*herroep ik*), similarly Kroeze, KB, 490a. (3) "reject, despise, repudiate," and thus "have had enough of"; so "I have mourned enough" or "I have had enough of it all" (P. A. H. de Boer, "Haalt Job bakzeil? (Job xlii 6)," *NedTTs* 31 (1977) 181–94 [= "Does Job Retract? Job xlii 6," in P. A. H. de Boer, *Selected Studies in Old Testament Exegesis* (ed. C. van Duin; OTS 27; Leiden: E. J. Brill, 1991) 179–95 (193–94)]).

Others argue that an obj, though not expressed, is understood. Such an obj could be: (1) "myself" (so KJV "I abhor myself," Moffatt, RSV, NIV "I despise myself," Gordis "I abase myself"; cf. LXX ἐφαύλισα ἐμαυτόν "I have held myself cheap," similarly Vg *ipse me reprehendo* "I rebuke myself"). (2) "my words" (so ibn Ezra, Peake, Strahan, Steuernagel, NAB "I disown what I have said," Guillaume "I repudiate what I have said," JB "I retract all I have said"; similarly Fohrer; Whybray "his earlier misapprehension"; Lester J. Kuyper, "The Repentance of Job," *VT* 9 [1959] 91–94; NJPS, Pope "I recant"; so too apparently *HALOT*, 2:540b §2a, "reject what one has said previously, revoke"). (3) "my life." One MT ms (Kenn 601) actually reads אמאס חיי "I despise, reject my life," a phrase that occurs at 9:21 and is probably implied at 7:16. Delitzsch and König supply "my former activity." (4) "my wealth." No modern commentators accept this, but Tg has אמאס עתרי "I despise my wealth." (5) "dust and ashes." Though the phrase "upon dust and ashes" cannot be the direct obj of the vb, Patrick regards that as the implied obj, translating "I repudiate dust and ashes," i.e., I forswear mourning (Dale Patrick, "The Translation of Job xlii 6," *VT* 26 [1976] 369–71); the difficulty with this is that מאס nowhere takes על. (6) If an obj of מאס is implied, the most probable term in my opinion is משפט "my case, my suit," since it appears that Job is making his response within the framework of the legal dispute between himself and Yahweh; it would make perfect sense for him to acknowledge that now he is withdrawing or retracting his case. It is interesting that מאס does on one occasion have משפט in the sense of "case" as its obj, at 31:13 where Job denies that he has "rejected" or "dismissed" the case of a servant. Now to dismiss someone else's case is no doubt not the same thing as to retract one's own, but the parallel remains striking. So too Habel.

Another approach is to appeal to another vb מאס. There is a מאס II "flow, melt," a byform of מסס "flow" (BDB, 549b; *DCH*, 5:121c; see also David A. Diewert, "Job xxxvi 5 and the Root *m's* II," *VT* 39 [1989] 71–77), which should be considered. This is the source of NEB's "I melt away," Dhorme, Terrien ("sink down," *je m'abîme*). So too Buttenwieser, Stier, Richter, Daniel J. O'Connor, "Job's Final Word—'I am consoled …'" (42:6b)," *ITQ* 50 (1983–84) 181–97 (193–94). Perhaps it should be understood with the sense "flow with tears" (as Hölscher, de Wilde suggest); or with the sense "abase myself" (as Hartley); or with the sense "yield," REB; or with the sense "submit" (William Morrow, "Consolation, Rejection, and Repentance in Job 42:6," *JBL* 105 [1986] 211–25 [214–15]). This is the interpretation followed in the *Translation* above, with the rendering "I submit." מאס II "flow, melt" is accepted by BDB, 549b (for 7:16, not for this passage); KB, 490b (for 7:16); *DCH*, 5:121b (mentioning also Job 36:5 [q.v.]); but it is not accepted by *HALOT*, 2:540b. This understanding is supported by LXX ἐτάκην "I melted" (from τήκω "melt"), though we should note that LXX offers a double translation: before ἐτάκην it had ἐφαύλισα ἐμαυτόν (see above, and further, Morrow, "Consolation, Rejection, and Repentance in Job 42:6," 212–13). The Qumran Tg also apparently understood אמאס as "flow," since it renders אתנסכ "I am poured out." Perhaps Pesh *'štwq* "I am silent" was also understanding אמאס as "I submit." See also the proposed emendation to אמס below. Thomas Krüger also accepts the sense of מאס as "I will waste away," understanding that Job believes that his encounter with the deity will inevitably lead to his death ("Did Job Repent?," in *Das Buch Hiob und seine Interpretationen: Beiträge zum Hiob-Symposium auf dem Monte Verità vom 14.–19. August 2005* [ed.

Thomas Krüger, Manfred Oeming, Konrad Schmid, and Christoph Uehlinger; ATANT 88; Zurich: Theologische Verlag Zürich, 2007] 217–29).

Emendations have also been proposed, of course. (1) One of these simply involves reading אֶמַּס "I melt," from מסס "melt," which has the same effect as taking אמאס from the vb מאס II "melt." The verb is used at 2 Sam 17:10, where a valiant man melts with fear, and at Isa 10:18, where נֹסֵס means "the melting of a sick person," which G. R. Driver, "Isaiah i–xxxix: Textual and Linguistic Problems," *JSS* 13 (1968) 36–57 (41–42), suggests means "the collapse of a person in convulsions" (NEB "as when a man falls in a fit") (the finite vb is נסס IV, perhaps cognate with Akk. *nasāsu* "wail, moan" [*CDA*, 243a]; cf. *DCH*, 5:701b). Similarly Terrien, translating "I sink into the abyss" (*The Iconography of Job through the Centuries: Artists as Biblical Interpreters* [University Park, PA: Pennsylvania State University Press, 1996] 219). (2) A variant on this suggestion is that of Böttcher, הִמֵּס אֶמַּס "I must pine away" (from מסס "dissolve, melt"), as at 2 Sam 17:10. Beer (*BHK*) likewise read הִמֵּס אֶמַּס "I melt." (3) De Wilde would read נִמְאָס אֶמְאָס "I strongly reject myself" (niph inf and impf of מאס), which he translates "I recognize my nothingness" (the niph inf should, however, be נִמְאֹס or הִמָּאֵס); see also his "Jobs slotwoord," *NedTTs* 32 (1978) 265–69. Although de Wilde says that the niph makes the vb reflexive, all the occurrences of מאס niph (three in Hebrew Bible, six in Ecclesiasticus, one in Qumran) are passive, "be rejected, despised" (*DCH*, 5:121b). (4) Gray prefers, ingeniously, calling upon the double rendering of LXX (ἐφαύλισα ἐμαυτόν, "I have abased myself," and ἐτάκην, "I have melted"; a not dissimilar double rendering in the Qumran Tg) to read אֶמְאַס וְאֶמַּס "I demean myself and yield, lit. melt," the first vb being from מאס and the second from מסס.

Another set of emendations aims at providing an obj for the vb אמאס, understood as "I despise, reject." Thus (1) Budde proposes אֲשֶׁר דִּבַּרְתִּי "what I have said" after אמאס "I reject (?)," which is both prosaic ("insipid" he called it himself in his second edition) and not without its own problems (see *Comment*). This proposal seems to be followed by Driver–Gray. (2) עַל כָּל דְּבָרָי "concerning all my words" (Tur-Sinai), which he understands as the obj both of אמאס and of נחמתי. (3) לְעוֹתִי "my stammering" (Bickell, Budde²). (4) מִרְצָתִי "my violence," a dubious form (Cheyne, Budde² [*vel*]). (5) Kissane thinks that "my words" or "my folly" have dropped out of the text, but he is so uncertain that he renders simply "I repudiate ...."

6.c. נחם niph is (1) "regret, be sorry, repent, relent," (2) "be moved to pity, have compassion," (3) "comfort oneself, be comforted, be consoled" (*DCH*, 5:663a) (although the form נִחַמְתִּי could equally well be piel, which is almost always "comfort, console," the piel does not make sense in the context).

(1) The sense "repent" has been the traditional translation (so KJV, RSV, NAB, JB, NIV, NEB, Moffatt, Dhorme, Kissane, Pope; BDB, 637a §2; KB, 608b §3; *HALOT*, 2:688b §1c). נחם niph in the sense "repent" is frequently used absolutely, i.e., without a following phrase indicating what is being repented of; so Exod 13:17; 1 Sam 15:29; Jer 4:28; 20:16; Ezek 24:14; Jonah 3:9; Joel 2:14, Zech 8:14; Pss 106:45; 110:4. In all these cases it is Yahweh who is "repenting," i.e., changing his mind, about planned evil. Only in Jer 31:19 is the vb used of a human ("after I had turned away, I repented"), which does seem to concern repentance in the usual sense. However, the translation "repent" is in most cases inappropriate, and it would be better to understand it as "retract a declared action," as H. Van Dyke Parunak puts it ("A Semantic Survey of NHM," *Bib* 56 [1975] 512–32). Thus NJPS "I recant and relent," Hartley "I recant"; Tur-Sinai thinks it is rather "repent and cease doing." Janzen prefers "I change my mind."

(2) The sense "be moved to pity" is inappropriate here.

(3) The sense "be comforted, be consoled" is well attested, at Gen 24:67; 2 Sam 13:39; Ezek 14:22; 31:16; 32:31; Ecclus 38:17, 23; 1QH 14:17; 17:13; 4QBarkᵃ1.1.1. Of special interest are Gen 38:12 where it refers to a point in time after the death of Judah's wife when he "is consoled," i.e., has completed his period of mourning, and Jer 31:15, where Rachel "refuses to be comforted," i.e., to accept the consolation a mourner would usually receive (the same language in Ps 77:2 [3]). With that as a background, it is possible to see Job here as "accepting consolation," i.e., deciding that his period of mourning has come to an end (so also de Boer, "Haalt Job bakzeil? (Job xlii 6)," "comfort oneself after a period of mourning," i.e., desist from it, leave it behind; see on מאס above). Now that he has abandoned his lawsuit with Yahweh, he is ready to return to normal life. The translation "I am consoled" is also favored by O'Connor, "Job's Final Word," 181, 195.

A different approach is that of Hölscher, who understands נחם as "sigh," in line with the sense of the Arab. *naḥama* (the word is unknown to Freytag and Lane, while Wehr–Cowan, 948a, renders "clear one's throat; wheeze, pant, gasp"; so it is by no means clear that the Arab. word means "sigh"). The Qumran Tg has אחוא "I shall become [dust and ashes]." Emendations of נחם are rare: (1) Tur-Sinai, while retaining נחמתי, thought it concealed another word also, וְנָחֵת "and I shall go down [to dust and ashes]," from נחת I "go down"; but a longing for death at this point seems unlikely. (2) Gray, taking a hint from the Qumran Tg with its rendering ואתמהא "and I am diluted," reads here

וְנִחַמְתִּי "I am reduced [to dust and ashes]," supposing a Heb. מהא "dilute" cognate with Aram. מחא; the root, Pope notes, is attested in MH in the sense "dissolve, dilute, make threadbare (of clothes)" (Jastrow, 736b), and has an Arab. cognate *mahā* "beat violently, be thin and watery"; it may perhaps be the same word as Aram. מחי "rub, wipe out, destroy, dissolve" (Jastrow, 759a) and perhaps also the common Semitic *mḥṣ* "strike, slay" (Akk. *maḫāṣu* [*CDA*, 190a], Ugar. *mḥṣ* [*DUL*, 541], Heb. מחץ); cf. M. Held, "*mḥṣ/*imḫš* in Ugaritic and Other Semitic Languages (A Study in Comparative Lexicography)," *JAOS* 79 (1959) 169–76 (171 n. 37). This is an intelligent proposal, but not to be preferred to the MT נִחַמְתִּי understood as "I accept consolation."

6.d. On the possible nuances of על, see the next *Note*. Here it is only reported that Al Wolters, "»A child of dust and ashes« (Job 42,6b)," *ZAW* 102 (1990) 116–19, offers the original suggestion that, against all previous interpreters, על is not to be taken as the prep, but as the attested noun על "child," as at Isa 49:15; 65:20 (BDB, 732a). It is supportive of this view that על "upon" at 24:9 is emended by most to the same word על (or עול). Wolters also claims the support of the Tg, which reads "I comfort myself for my children (מבניי) who are dust and ashes," observing that the MT has no word for "child, children" unless such is the meaning of על. The difficulty with the last point is that if the Tg understood על as "child, children" they could not have translated "comforted myself for," since the "for" would require that על be understood as the prep על; one would have to postulate that the text originally had something like על על, which would be decidedly odd. The other problem is that in its other occurrences על fairly clearly means "suckling" (as BDB, 732a), being derived from עול "give suck." Wolters demurs that Hebrew children were not weaned until the age of three or four, but even so there are no parallels for an adult being spoken of, even metaphorically, as an על. The case of עולל, עולל "child" is perhaps not relevant, since it seems to be connected with a quite different root (so BDB, 760b; KB, 688a, and *HALOT*, 2:798a, however, connect it with עול "give suck").

6.e. על־עפר ואפר "upon dust and ashes" has been variously understood as "[I repent while sitting] upon dust and ashes" (Driver–Gray), or "[I console myself for my sins], who am dust and ashes" (Tg), or "[I console myself] for dust and ashes" (Merx), "[I comfort myself and am content that] dust and ashes [are my portion]" (Bickell[3]), "I will repent unto dust and ashes," i.e., until death (Szczygiel), "[sinking down] upon dust and dirt" (as a ritual act of self-abasement) (Charles A. Muenchow, "Dust and Dirt in Job 42:6," *JBL* 108 [1989] 597–611). The Tg, as mentioned in the previous *Note*, had "I comfort myself for my sons, who are dust and ashes." Most translations have "I repent in dust and ashes" (KJV, RSV, NAB, JB, NIV, NEB), which can only suggest that dust and ashes are being regarded as clothing and that the phrase is analogous to "in sackcloth and ashes." This translation is almost certainly wrong, since על must denote what Job is (in some sense) "upon," not what is "upon" Job.

The phrase נחם על is often translated "repent for"; so at Exod 32:12, 14; 2 Sam 24:16 (mss); 1 Chr 21;15; Jer 18:8; 26:3 (mss), 13 (mss); Joel 2:13; Jonah 3:10; 4:2 (all of Yahweh "repenting" of harm he has been planning; similarly Amos 7:3, 6 (though here the term רעה "evil" is not used); and also Isa 57:6 (apparently of Yahweh "relenting"); Jer 18:10 (of Yahweh repenting of *good* he is about to do). As has been noted above, "repent" seems an inappropriate term for what is essentially a change of plan on Yahweh's part. Only in one case, in Jer 8:6, is the phrase used of a human "repenting" of wickedness; but that would not seem to be relevant here, for Job can hardly be repenting of his dust and ashes since they are nothing to be ashamed of.

Patrick, however, followed by Habel, thinks that is exactly what the phrase means, translating "I repent of dust and ashes," i.e., he forsakes his position of lamentation among the dust and ashes and forswears remorse (Dale Patrick, "The Translation of Job xlii 6," *VT* 26 [1976] 369–71; similarly Thomas F. Dailey, "And Yet He Repents—On Job 42,6," *ZAW* 105 [1993] 205–9). L. J. Kaplan points out that Maimonides had the same understanding ("Maimonides, Dale Patrick, and Job xlii 6," *VT* 18 [1978] 356–58). Along the same track is the interpretation "I have changed my mind concerning" (Whybray; this seems also to be Newsom's preferred interpretation). Such an interpretation fails to carry conviction, however. For the rituals of mourning are a wholly appropriate response to bereavement, and are nothing to be repented of, or even changing one's mind about; when they come to an end, it is because a new phase of life is being entered upon, not because the mourning has been in any way rejected.

The *Translation* above, "I accept consolation for my dust and ashes," does not adopt the sense "repent" or even "change one's mind," but rather depends on the attestations of the phrase נחם על as "comfort oneself for, be comforted for." It occurs also in v 11, and at 2 Sam 13:39 (David for Amnon); Jer 31:15 (Rachel refuses to be comforted for her children); Ezek 32:31 (Pharaoh comforted for his slain army); 14:22 (Jerusalem comforted for the evil Yahweh has brought on it); Isa 22:4 (the mourner comforted for the destruction of the city); similarly 1 Chr 19:2 (|| 2 Sam 10:2 has אל rather than על); Jer 16:7; 31:15; Ezek 14:22; 32:31; 1QH 14:7; 17:13; 4QBark[a]1.1.1 (*DCH*, 5:663b). Job is announcing that he is ending his period of mourning (see further, *Comment*).

An emendation was proposed by T. K. Cheyne (*EB* 2:2481), הִמֵּס אָמֵס וְנָמַקְתִּי "I must pine away [from מסס], and dissolve [to dust and ashes]"; עַל could only be suitable here if it is regarded as equivalent to אֶל. LXX has ἥγημαι δὲ ἐγὼ ἐμαυτὸν γῆν καὶ σποδόν "and I think myself earth and ashes," but, as Driver–Gray say, "it is doubtful whether this is anything but a paraphrase of [MT]." In the same vein, Houtsma proposes reading וְאֵפֶר עַל־עָפָר נִמְשַׁלְתִּי "I liken myself to dust and dirt [see below on the exact translation of אֵפֶר]." De Wilde followed the same track with his proposal נֶחְשַׁבְתִּי "I regard myself [as dust and dirt]."

The Qumran Tg's וְאִתַּמָּא "and I am boiled up" apparently read נִחַמְתִּי as if derived from הָמַם "be hot."

עָפָר וְאֵפֶר "dust and ashes" is commonly thought to be a term for the refuse-heap (*mezbala*) on which Job is sitting in 2:8 (the same phrase in Ecclus 40:7 [3]). However, it does not seem that one sits both on dust and on ashes, for the normal rituals of mourning are apparently to have dust on the head and to sit in ashes: so typically Ezek 27:30 "they cast dust on their heads and wallow in ashes," while in Job 2:8, 12 Job sits "among" ashes while his friends put dust upon their heads; from Isa 58:5 we gather that on a fast day one would spread sackcloth and ashes under one, and from Jer 6:26 that mourning involves rolling in ashes (cf. lying in ashes in Esth 4:3); from Neh 9:1 that a national ritual of mourning would involve "earth" (אֲדָמָה) upon the head. The evidence does not, however, all run in one direction: in 2 Sam 13:19 Tamar puts ashes on her *head* (as also in Jdt 4:11 of Jerusalemites), while in Mic 1:10 mourners roll in *dust*, not ashes. It is hard to say exactly what is meant when in Esth 4:1 Mordecai "puts on" sackcloth and ashes; are the ashes on the sackcloth? The phrase "sackcloth and ashes" occurs as well at *T. Jos.* 15:2; Luke 10:13; Matt 11:21. But as a whole, the evidence suggests that עַל־עָפָר וְאֵפֶר is unlikely to mean "[sitting] upon dust and ashes."

The picture becomes more complicated when we review the terms more closely. Perhaps the word פָּלַשׁ is not the usual פָּלַשׁ I "roll one (in)" (as BDB, 814a; *HALOT*, 2:935b) but a פָּלַשׁ III "sprinkle," cognate with Ugar. *plṯ* (though *DUL*, 673, thinks the word means "humiliation"), as G. R. Driver argues for Jer 6:26; 25:34; Ezek 27:30; Mic 1:10 ("Ezekiel: Linguistic and Textual Problems," *Bib* 35 [1954] 145–59, 299–312 [157–58]; so too Mayer I. Gruber, *Aspects of Nonverbal Communication in the Ancient Near East* [Studia Pohl 12; Rome: Biblical Institute Press, 1980] 457–58, who cites Umberto Cassuto as the first proponent of this idea, in his "The Death of Ba'al [Table I*AB from Ras-Shamra," *Tarb* 12 [1941] 179). And perhaps also the word יָצַע "lay, spread out" (BDB, 426b; *HALOT*, 2:428a) does not necessarily refer to what is *beneath* one, in which case Esth 4:3 may mean, literally, that sackcloth and ashes were "spread" for many (יֻצַּע לְרַבִּים) *over their heads*. Isa 58:5, we may note, does not specifically say that the sackcloth and ashes are *under* the penitents, despite the translations. If these suggestions are correct, only Job 2:8, 12 would be left, of the passages mentioned in the previous paragraph, to suggest that sitting on ashes is a normal mourning custom; and it can easily be argued that Job's is a special case, since he is sitting on the town refuse heap anyway, where ashes are usually disposed of. What is clear is that עַל־עָפָר is unlikely to mean "upon dust" in a locative sense.

If then the phrase does not mean "[sitting] upon dust and ashes," it could satisfactorily mean "[consoled] for (my) dust and ashes, i.e., the symbols of mourning I must necessarily surround myself with." On mourning rituals, see further E. Kutsch, "'Trauerbräuche' und 'Selbstminderungsriten' im Alten Testament," in Kurt Lühti, Ernst Kutsch, and Wilhelm Dautine, *Drei Wiener Antrittsreden* (Theologische Studien 78; Zurich: EVZ-Verlag, 1965) 25–37 (= his *Kleine Schriften zum Alten Testament* [ed. Ludwig Schmidt; BZAW 168; Berlin: de Gruyter, 1986] 78–95). See further, *Comment*.

We should note that the traditional translation of עָפָר וְאֵפֶר as "dust and ashes" is in any case by no means assured, though it is accepted in the *Translation* above. BDB, 68a, is clear that the term אֵפֶר means "ashes," doubtfully connecting the word with an Arab. cognate *'afara* "leap" (Freytag, 1:43a, but the word has many other meanings also; it is not in Lane) as describing ashes, and noting first Num 19:9, 10, concerning the disposal of the ashes of the red heifer. Many other authorities, however, regard אֵפֶר as equivalent in meaning to the first word of the phrase, עָפָר "dust, earth," to which it is said to be related etymologically; KB, 79a, for example, gives the meaning as "dust," with a sense "ashes" noted only for Num 19:9, 10 (the red heifer). *HALOT*, 1:80a, adds, with a question mark, Ezek 28:18, where the king of Tyre is consumed by fire and turned to ashes (Ges[18], 90a, and *TLOT*, 2:940, also accept only these two passages for the sense "ashes"). According to Zorell, 75b, only Num 19:9, 10 and Ezek 28:18 are certainly "ashes," while only Mal 4:3 (3:21) is certainly "dust" (though even here RSV, NAB, NIV, JB, NEB are happy with "ashes"). De Wilde thinks that Lam 3:16 is also a clear example of the sense "dust," though here RSV has "made me cower in ashes" and NEB "fed on ashes." The same is argued by Gruber, *Aspects of Nonverbal Communication*, 457–58, and Muenchow, "Dust and Dirt in Job 42:6," 608. A strong support for the sense "ashes" in all the uses of אֵפֶר is Ezek 27:30 where mourners put אֵפֶר on their heads and "roll about" (פָּלַשׁ) in, or "sprinkle," עָפָר; if the two terms were equivalent, the line would be rather tautologous, though some might argue that it simply displays strict parallelism.

As for the two terms together, עפר ואפר, we should also note the special use referring to the composition of the human frame (Gen 18:27; Ecclus 10:9; 1QH 18:5; 4Q266 [4QD^a] fr. 1 a–b.22–23; 4Q227 [4QpsJub^c] fr. 7.ii.16 [Job 30:19 and Ecclus 40:7 do not belong here]). Whether we understand the phrase as "dust and ashes" or "thoroughly dust" (KB, 79b) it can hardly be relevant to the present passage, for it does not seem to be Job's frailty or mortality that is the issue. NJPS "I recant and relent, being but dust and ashes" is worth considering, nevertheless; presumably על would have to be understood as standing for על־אשר "on account of the fact that." But if this were the meaning one would have expected על־עפר ואפר אני "in that I am dust and ashes." Some others have argued that the phrase simply signifies humility or humiliation (Whybray); but that does not explain the prep על. Newsom thinks of "a consolation concerning the human condition," but it is not easy to see Job speaking here on behalf of humanity.

Form/Structure/Setting

This short speech, though longer than Job's previous speech (40:4–5), obviously constitutes a single strophe. Its *structure* is threefold: (1) Job acknowledges the omnipotence of Yahweh (v 2), (2) he accepts that he has intruded into an area in which he has no competence (v 3), and (3) having heard Yahweh's speeches, he abandons his case against God and determines to resume his normal life (vv 4–6). The second and third elements each begin with a quotation of words of Yahweh, to which Job responds. The first element does not begin with a quotation, and so may be seen as Job's response to the divine speeches as a whole, which have just now concluded.

The *genre* of the speech is, unsurprisingly, that of the *legal disputation*, though there is not very much of its typical language. In the quotation of Yahweh's words in v 4, there are the common terms "listen," "speak," "question," and "answer," which all belong in that setting. One important legal term occurs in v 3, where I have translated הגדתי "I made my depositions" (נגד hiph). The term has been used by Job in 31:37, where he said that if only he could encounter God face to face in a legal setting he would "give him an account (נגד hiph) of [his] steps," i.e., he would set out in detail the evidence of his life that would prove him an innocent man. It may be that the term מאס (or מסס) in v 6 should also be regarded as a legal term, meaning "submit"; but its use elsewhere is always in metaphorical contexts. The quotations of the opponent's words (vv 3a, 4) are also instances of the use of legal language.

The *function* of the speech is to present Job's response to the divine speeches (the first of Job's replies, in 40:4–5, was only a holding operation). At the end of a lawsuit, the plaintiff would be expected to accept or reject the case offered by the defendant, and the expectation of readers is that such will be the function of this speech. Job's position, however, appears to be ambivalent. On the one hand, he concludes with a statement that he is "submitting," or withdrawing from the case (if the interpretation of the term מאס in v 6 set out below is correct). On the other hand, he does not concede that his opponent is in the right or that he is in the wrong. He does concede that he made his depositions "without understanding" and regarding matters "too wonderful" for him (v 3), and yet he says no more of the divine speeches than that he has "heard" them. This sounds rather like a non-acceptance of their argument.

In short, it seems that Job has come to the realization that his case is hopeless. Yahweh is determined not to answer questions about justice, whereas justice is the one thing that Job is interested in. Job will therefore withdraw his suit—not because he has lost his case but because, given the attitude of his opponent, he finally despairs totally of ever winning it—or even of having it heard.

The *tonality* of the speech is low-key and cool. The one term with a possible emotional content is אמאס in v 6, which is understood here as "I melt, I submit," and which gives a helpful clue as to Job's tone of voice. His language is the language of concession, but there is a determination about his speech as well: it is Job who will define what Yahweh's speeches have really been about (power!, v 2), which is not at all what Yahweh was trying to convey; and his concentration in vv 4 and 5 on the mere process of the disputation rather than upon any substantive issues is no doubt to be understood as his refusal to accept the responses of Yahweh. Job's final word "I accept consolation" (נחמתי, v 6) shows that we do not leave Job in despair or misery or self-abasement; he is determined to bring his period of mourning to an end and resume his life. So the tone is ultimately forward-looking, preparing for the positive air of the prose epilogue that will ensue.

The *nodal verse* of Job's speech is inevitably the last (v 6), which faces two ways: in respect of the past, he has had no satisfaction, but he will draw a line beneath it; in respect of the future, he intends to live as a social being surrounded by his support group, no longer as an outcast on the ash heap.

Comment

2–6   In his reply to the first divine speech (40:3–5), brief though it was, Job has said that he stands by what he has previously argued, and he will not reiterate his case. This reply to the second divine speech goes one step further, in saying that he is abandoning his suit against Yahweh (if that is indeed how v 6a is to be read); but, just as in 40:3–5, he does not withdraw a word he has said, he does not admit that God is in the right or that he is in the wrong, he does not confess to any sins or apologize for what he has said. This reading, it must be admitted, is not accepted by all; given that this final reply by Job is hugely important for the understanding of the book as a whole, it is truly tantalizing that it is so cryptic and ambiguous. Jung perceptively remarked: "Guileless as Job's speech sounds, it could just as well be equivocal" (C. G. Jung, *Answer to Job* [trans. R. F. C. Hull; London: Routledge & Kegan Paul, 1954] 31). It is not that Job's speech is a "tongue-in-cheek" confession, as David Robertson suggested ("The Book of Job: A Literary Study," *Soundings* 56 [1973] 446–69 [466]), for it is not insincere; but it is a crafty and subtle speech that means more than it says. For an analysis of the many interpretational possibilities, see B. Lynne Newell, "Job: Repentant or Rebellious?," *WTJ* 46 (1984) 298–316 (= *Sitting with Job: Selected Studies on the Book of Job* [ed. Roy B. Zuck; Grand Rapids: Baker Book House, 1992] 441–56); Ellen J. van Wolde, "Job 42,1–6: The Reversal of Job," in *The Book of Job* (ed. W. A. M. Beuken; BETL 114; Leuven: Leuven University Press, 1994) 223–50. I do not follow Newsom's attractive suggestion, nevertheless, that the ambiguity may be "strategic," the poet involving readers even more than usual in the construction of the meaning, and deliberately creating more than one possibility for meaning (cf. also William Morrow, "Consolation, Rejection, and Repentance in Job 42:6," *JBL* 105 [1986] 211–25).

In this speech, Job has three remarks to make: (1) he acknowledges the omnipotence of Yahweh (v 2), (2) he accepts that he has intruded into the area of "marvels," in which he has no competence (v 3b), (3) now that he has heard the utterances Yahweh has addressed personally to him (v 5), he abandons his suit against God (v 6a) together with his mourning and he intends to resume his normal life (v 6b) (if that is what that verse means). Remarks 2 and 3 are preceded by quotations he makes of the words of Yahweh, so that his remarks are presented as responses to particular utterances of Yahweh. Remark 1 is not so preceded, which may suggest that it is Job's response to the divine speeches as a whole.

2 Job, we may presume, has a specific purpose in beginning his response to the divine speeches on this note. There is nothing novel about his point, which goes "no further than he had acknowledged all along" (Rowley). So why does he make it? It is no spontaneous "expression of unrestrained admiration" (Andersen). It is more deliberate than that. It can only be to signal how he has heard the speeches of Yahweh: he recognizes full well that whenever Yahweh has asked him whether he can do this or that, he has always been implying that Job can not but Yahweh can (that, we note, is not the only point of the divine speeches, and is certainly a minor element in the second speech). Job will not deny the force of that manifold truth. In that sense, he accepts the argument of the divine speeches: he is a mere mortal, unfitted by capacity or knowledge for the management of the universe; as he has said already, in comparison with Yahweh, he is of little account (40:4).

So there is a concessive note here: he will not resist the divine move to put him in his place and to underline his creatureliness.

And yet there is also perhaps a dimension to his words that remains resistant to that divine move: as Dhorme puts it, Job's words are "tantamount to a confession of the futility of discussions concerning divine intervention in human affairs." If demands for justice and a questioning of God's manner of governing the universe are only ever to be answered by an invocation of the divine almightiness, it is a sorry state of affairs, and every bit as bad as Job had been complaining all along (cf. 23:13–14). In short, Job's words are both a capitulation and, in a way, a reiteration of his complaint. And when Job says, "No purpose of yours can be thwarted," what purpose can he be thinking of if not Yahweh's designs against him? To be sure, Yahweh has illustrated in rich detail his cosmic purposes, but what bearing have those upon Job's case? What those divine designs in cosmology and meteorology and zoology have gone to show is that Yahweh's purposes always succeed, which means for the Job of the dialogues that he cannot ever be other than Yahweh's victim.

There is yet more to this response by Job. However we state the purpose of the divine speeches, there are few who would argue that they intend only to reassert the divine power. At the very least, they seem equally concerned to convey the divine wisdom, and, if the argument of this commentary is adopted, they go far beyond that in sketching Yahweh's program for the whole universe. His created order is not a rule-bound mechanism, sustained by principles of balance and equity and retribution and equivalence. Yahweh's universe is a vast array of differences held together by the divine intimacy with its manifoldness and the divine delight in the quiddity and the contrariness of its parts that are exemplified by Behemoth and Leviathan. This formal response by Job to the divine speeches ignores all that, and—as when Joseph says to his brothers, "It is as I said to you, You are spies" (Gen 42:14)—retorts in effect to Yahweh's subtle and engaging exposition of his vision for the cosmos, "I know, it is as I said, you are only interested in power." That ידעתי "I know" is very revealing: whether it means "I now know what I only guessed before, that you really are addicted to power" or "You don't need to tell me, I've known all along that you only ever follow your own desires, which are never thwarted" Job can hear nothing that is not addressed to his single issue of concern: the question of justice. From Yahweh's point of view, Job is being recalcitrant, but from Job's point of view, though he will have to submit and withdraw his case (v 6) he is not going to accept that he has received the shadow of an answer.

The foregoing remarks are by no means the received wisdom about this verse. Strahan, for example, thought that "This is no longer a recognition of God's arbitrary omnipotence. It does not mean, 'Thou canst do as Thou wilt, and never give an account of Thy doings,' but rather, 'Thou canst make the innocent suffer, yet … Thou art just and good." Fohrer observes that the term "know" (ידע) signifies an experience that embraces the whole of existence, a knowledge that liberates and supports. What such commentators do not explain is how the speeches of Yahweh can have led Job to this conclusion. At another extreme, it has been argued (by Good) that the sentence is almost infinitely ambiguous: it could be straightforwardly submissive, he says, or indignant, or sarcastic, or obsequious, or even falsely submissive. He is right that the tone is very difficult to determine, but the matter here must be settled by the meaning in the context, and especially the context of the immediate sequel to the divine speeches.

3 Job's second remark consists of a quotation of Yahweh's words followed by his own response to them; by the citation form, "Job is making quite explicit that he is responding formally to the challenge of Yahweh as his adversary" (Habel). The first colon repeats (with one omission) the words of 38:2, "Who is this who obscures the Design by words without knowledge?" Most translations make this into a quotation of Yahweh's words, to which Job responds in the remainder of the verse, but some commentators think it is an editorial gloss (cf. Rowley).

Job evidently has had ringing in his ears all through the divine speeches the charge with which the first of them began: "Who is this who obscures the Design by words without knowledge?" According to Yahweh, what Job has really been doing in all his quest for justice is to ignore the grand design Yahweh has for the universe. In 38:2 Yahweh had said that Job had been "darkening" (חשׁך) it, which Job quotes as "concealing" or "obscuring" (עלם) it—a minor change that seems to be without special significance.

Job's own response is intriguing. He says that he spoke "marvels" (נפלאות), things "too wonderful for me" (נפלאות ממני), which he did not "understand" (בין) and did not "know" (ידע). What in the Book of Job count as "wonders"? They have always been the inscrutable deeds of God in creation, which Eliphaz speaks of in 5:9, Job himself in 9:10, and Elihu in 37:5, 14—except for 10:16, where Job speaks ironically of the heroic deeds of God in battle against puny Job (see further, J. Conrad, *TDOT,* 11:533–46; R. Albertz, *TLOT,* 2:981–86; outside Job, God's "wonders" tend to be acts of deliverance in history). So what "wonders" has Job been speaking of, which have been "too wonderful" for him, which he did not "understand" (בין) or "know" (ידע)? All Job has been speaking of are the principles on which the world is, or should be, governed; he thought they were pretty straightforward matters of justice and fairness, but the way Yahweh tells it, everything in the world is a marvel, and Job had better accept that justice and fairness too, like the structure of the physical universe, and the ways of Yahweh in rain and wind, are "marvels" beyond his comprehension or understanding. Redefining cosmic justice as a "marvel" puts it outside any realm that humans can access or have rights in. "A confession of ignorance is appropriate when man is faced by divine mysteries" (Dhorme), and Job has to confess that he knows nothing, understands nothing now that it is clear that justice is one of those "marvels" or divine mysteries.

Now this is a capitulation indeed. If cosmic justice is God's business, then it is whatever he decides it is. It is not a principle to which he himself is subject, to which he gives his allegiance. It is not a rule, the knowledge of which is shared by Yahweh and humans. It is yet another sphere of divine might, another instance of the truth that Yahweh can "do anything," as Job began this speech by acknowledging. And Job has come to know that such is in fact the truth about the universe through the divine speeches, which have—in his understanding—made Yahweh's power and Yahweh's knowledge the only issue, and have steadfastly suppressed Job's questions about justice. Calling Yahweh's manner of administering the universe a "marvel" is not to praise it (as Dale Patrick thought ["The Translation of Job xlii 6," *VT* 26 (1976) 369–71]), but Job's ultimate act of despair.

Job has no choice now but to accept that this is the way things are, but he cannot be at all happy about it—because he has now had his worst fears confirmed (John Briggs Curtis, "On Job's Response to Yahweh," *JBL* 98 [1979] 497–511 [509], sees this point very clearly). All along he had suspected that, for God, might meant right, and he had wanted that suspicion to be corrected. Too late; Yahweh has assured him that the creator of the universe is indeed subject to no law or principle. Such is the Design, and Job's demands for justice have been adjudicated out of order as an obscuring of it.

Job is not going to press the matter further. He has been defeated in his case against God, but he has won a victory of sorts, as Gordis puts it: "God's admission that justice is not all-pervasive in the universe is a clear, if oblique, recognition of the truth of Job's position." As we saw on v 2 above, Job's words of capitulation are not the end of the matter for the observant reader.

We should note the term Job uses of his speaking without understanding. נגד hiph is not the ordinary word for "speak" or "utter," but refers rather to informing or declaring; it is especially used of announcing things not previously known before (as in 1:15; 12:7; 36:9) or things kept secret (as in 11:6; 38:18) (cf. BDB, 616b §2), and is thus almost like "reveal." One particular context is important for the present passage: 31:37, where in the very last verse of Job's final speech (as it has been regarded in this Commentary; cf. on 31:35–37) Job says that if only he could encounter God face to face in a legal setting he would "give him an account (נגד hiph) of [his] steps," i.e., he would set out in detail the evidence of his life that would prove him an innocent man. In using the same term here, he makes clear that the legal suit is still the framework of his thinking; what is different now is that he has come to a realization that the whole of that legal realm, with his self-defenses and his accusations against Yahweh, were outside his scope. At the time, the lawsuit had seemed a reasonable step for a man to take who suffered an injustice; now it transpires that justice is not a value in its own right, but, if anything, a minor element in a huge divine plan consisting of "wonders" (נפלאות). Though he did not understand it at the time, his "depositions" (הגדתי) concerned matters that belonged to the realm, not of the prosecution of justice, but of the "wondrous," a realm to which he recognizes himself an outsider, who knows nothing (ולא אדע "and I did not know").

4 Job again quotes Yahweh. But only the words "I will question you, and you shall answer me" have been spoken by Yahweh (at the beginning of both his speeches, 38:3 and 40:7). The words "Listen, and I will speak" are not Yahweh's, but Elihu's, in 33:31. Has Job then confused Yahweh with his self-avowed spokesman Elihu? Or has the poet forgotten what Elihu said? Or should we make nothing of this little discrepancy? Probably the last option is the best. Kissane's solution, that these are Job's words, falters because of the parallelism between the two cola of the verse.

Like v 3a, this verse is correctly presented by most modern translations as a quotation of the divine words, although some commentators think it is no more than a gloss, and NEB omits it altogether.

5–6 As with the previous citation of Yahweh's words, Job is formally follow-ing the routines of the dispute (*rîb*) process. Verse 4, however, unlike v 3a, has not been a charge against himself that he must deal with here. It was a sentence in Yahweh's mouth that dealt only with procedure and process: who will speak first, who will reply. It seems too trifling a matter to mention now, at the very cli-max of the interchanges between Job and Yahweh, does it not? And, more than that, it is all water under the bridge by now, is it not, now that the confrontation with Yahweh is drawing to a close? No, by no means; its function is to declare, in the coolest manner possible, that the process of the dispute has now come to a close. What it means is that Yahweh has spoken, Job is giving his reply, and that will be that. The debate, the lawsuit, has nowhere else to go. I hear you, says Job to Yahweh, as people say, I hear you, when they mean, I understand you per-fectly, but I don't agree.

But what does Job's reply amount to? He does not for a moment negate the words he has spoken, but he withdraws or abandons his case (so too Habel). Why so? Habel thinks that "Yahweh's appearance in person was sufficient vin-dication of Yahweh's integrity and clear evidence of his goodwill," but the Job we have come to know in the course of the dialogues cannot have drawn such a conclusion from the divine speeches. It would seem rather that Job has come to the realization that his case is hopeless: Yahweh is determined not to answer questions about justice. Job will withdraw his suit not because he has lost his case but because, given the attitude of his opponent, he finally despairs totally of ever winning it—and even of having it heard.

In these sentences lies the dénouement of the whole Book of Job. It is a climax that has rarely (in my opinion) been properly understood. It is not an upbeat, "comic," resolution, but it is not a tragedy either. Some may find it a deeply sad and cheerless outcome, but others may feel it rather a blessed release to recog-nize that there is no underlying principle of justice in the universe. However we may feel about the outcome of the book, in order to grasp the nature of that outcome there is much exegetical ground to cover.

5 It is usual to find a contrast between the two halves of this verse, between "hearing" and "seeing," between "hearing about" and "seeing (directly)," between "then" and "now," between (inferior) "hearing" and (superior) "see-ing." But all this is more than doubtful. First, Job has not actually *seen* Yahweh (there is no language of visual perception), but only heard him speak, so "my eyes have seen you" can only be an idiom for a close or authentic encounter (and the view that seeing is a higher form of knowledge than hearing [de Wilde; cf. also G. Gerald Harrop, "'But now my eye seeth thee'," *CJT* 12 (1966) 80–84] is without foundation, and probably a Western intellectualization of the privileg-ing of that particular sense). Secondly, Job does not say that he had previously heard "about" Yahweh, as distinct from now seeing him directly; the Hebrew has "I heard you with the hearing of the ears." It would be strange if he were describing his imbibing of traditions about God or his listening to the friends' theological statements as "hearing Yahweh." All the sententious remarks of commentators about a contrast between mere hearsay in the past and immediate perception at the present moment are an irrelevance. Thirdly, though Job says that "now" (עתה) his eyes have seen Yahweh, it is now also, just now, that he has heard Yahweh—for the first time; so in effect the "now" refers both to the hearing and the seeing (similarly Good). Fourthly, seeing and hearing in the Hebrew Bible are usually parallel forms of perception and not contrasted with one another (cf., e.g., 13:1; 29:11; Gen 24:30; Exod 3:7; 2 Kgs 19:16; Prov 20:12; Cant 2:14; and Ps 48:8 [9] "as we have heard, so have we seen," where the hearing and the seeing are consonant); 1 Kgs 10:7, where what the Queen of Sheba sees with her own eyes surpasses the reports she has heard of Solomon's wisdom and wealth, is only an apparent exception, for the contrast is not between hearing and seeing but between hearing a report and "seeing" for oneself (a seeing that must include hearing, since she is more likely to be hearing than seeing Solomon's *wisdom*).

An important consequence that flows from recognizing the two halves of the verse as essentially equivalent rather than contrastive is that only so does the connection of vv 5–6 with what precedes become clear. That is, in v 4 Job quotes Yahweh as undertaking to speak first himself and then give Job the opportunity of replying; then in v 5 Job acknowledges that Yahweh has indeed spoken and asked his questions, so now Job will give his reply (v 6). If on the other hand, we were to think that "I heard you with my ears" (v 5a) refers to the time before Yahweh's speeches and "my eyes have now seen you" (v 5b) to what Yahweh has said in his speeches, it would be difficult to discern (1) how v 5a is relevant at this point (i.e., why should Job go back earlier than the matter of chap. 38?), and (2) why he should speak of his hearing of the divine speeches as "seeing" Yahweh? It is only if we take "hearing" and "seeing" together as two essentially similar forms of perception that "seeing" can be an appropriate term for taking in the intentions of Yahweh in his speeches (so too, to some extent, Newsom, Good).

Even if the two halves of the verse were contrastive, it would still be important to consider what might be contrasted. It would have to be a distinction between distant and close experience of God, and though it may be portrayed as a contrast between ears and eyes, it is not really a contrast of verbal and visual communication. For, as it has been noted above, Job has not actually "seen" God (as, e.g., Driver–Gray agree), and what he has just now been doing is "hearing" God's speeches. It is common to make Job's declaration "now my eyes see you" into the statement of a mystical experience of the divine (cf., e.g., Terrien), but it is unlikely that Job is referring to any experience apart from what he has just had—that is, of the words of Yahweh and their import.

Job had uttered the hope in 19:27 that he might see God while he still lived: "to behold Eloah while still in my flesh—that is my desire, to see him for myself, to see him with my own eyes, not as a stranger." At that point it was very clear that for Job to see God would mean his vindication: he firmly believed that his "champion" or defending counsel would sooner or later "rise last to speak for me," even if it had to be a post-mortem vindication, after Job's skin had been "stripped" from him (19:26)—and then Yahweh would be compelled to acknowledge the right in Job's plea. Now that it is true that Job has "seen" Yahweh, which is to say, he has witnessed him speaking, we might think that he has attained all his desire. But it has not turned out as Job expected: the new question is, When he "saw" God, was it his Vindicator that he saw? Or was the Yahweh of the speeches not the very same deity that Job had imagined in his worst nightmares as a cosmic bully who cannot be held to account (9:12–20)? Now that he has seen Yahweh for himself, seen him with his own eyes, and heard him deny him the vindication he so craved, he can have no more hope. Sentence by sentence through the divine speeches his words in 14:19 have come true for him: "as water wears away stone and torrents scour the soil from the land—so you destroy a mortal's hope."

Job's sentence here has been invested with great significance by some commentators. Peake found it "the supreme lesson of the book ... Happy, even in his pain, that he has found himself and his God, he would rather suffer, if God willed it, than be in health and prosperity. He knows that all is well, he and his sufferings have their place in God's inscrutable design; why should he seek to understand it? In childlike reverence he acknowledges it to be far beyond him." Strahan beautifully commented: "From the dark and narrow field of personal experience he is led into a vast cosmos which is luminous with God ... He is content to take his place in the great scheme of things .... He is at once satisfied and awed into silence ... [T]here is a singular blending of rapture and pain,—the rapture of the consciousness of God, the pain of self-knowledge." More simply put, but in the same tradition, is Rowley's remark: "His intellectual problem is unsolved, for he has transcended it." The distance of such readings from the wording of the text is an adequate marker of their loss of perspective.

In another idiom, many speak of the "immediate personal encounter" of Job with God that he has now experienced (e.g., Fohrer), without recognizing that within the worldview of the book that is not so surprising an event as we today might count it. Job has often enough been expressing a desire for such a meeting (e.g., 23:3–4), but he never envisaged an existential encounter that would turn his world upside down and change all his values and priorities, and, as far as he is concerned, he has had no such encounter. He has wanted a meeting with God where his case for justice can be weighed; and now that he has heard from Yahweh a long and self-regarding speech that has never once mentioned justice for Job, he is not going to be impressed by attempts to bill it as a divine–human encounter that shakes the foundations of his universe.

6 This crucial verse, with the last words of Job (which did not end with 31:40, despite what is said there!), forms the climax of the whole dispute between Job and Yahweh. But sadly it contains three major uncertainties: (1) the meaning of אמאס (is it "I reject, despise" with perhaps "myself" or "my words" as the implied object, or "I melt, submit"?), (2) the meaning of נחמתי (is it "I repent" or "I am consoled, I accept consolation"?), and (3) the meaning of "dust and ashes" (is it a reference to the place and the situation of Job on the ash-heap, or a reference to Job's status as a mourner, or to his human mortality?). For the details, see also the *Notes*.

In a nutshell, the view that will be argued here is that (1) in a legal sense, Job "submits," i.e., he withdraws his lawsuit against Yahweh, (2) since he has done no wrong, he cannot "repent," but having been in mourning, he now brings the period of mourning to an end by "accepting consolation," for his lost children as well as for the loss of his honor, a consolation that is being offered to him both from the friends and (in his own way) from Yahweh, and (3) the consolation he accepts is "for" the "dust and ashes" that have been the visible expression of his state of mourning.

(1) The verb מאס at first sight appears to be the common verb for "despise, reject"; the difficulty with that understanding is that the verb has no object here. Perhaps, lacking an object, think some, it means "feel loathing, contempt, revulsion," as in a few other cases (Ps 89:38 [39]; Job 34:33; 36:5). But even these cases are questionable: in Ps 89:38 (39), the object is probably explicit in the term "your anointed," though that is not grammatically the object of the verb (it would be the object also of זנח "reject," which almost always has an object but oddly lacks one here); Job 34:33 (*q.v.*), which is very difficult, may have an explicit object in the subject or the object of the previous verb, and in any case can hardly mean "feel loathing"; and 36:5 is very problematic text-critically. Even more to the point, it would seem strange to have Job express a self-loathing for having raised his issue of justice. Where could such an attitude have arisen from? The divine speeches have ignored Job's complaint, but they have not suggested that it is in any way disgusting.

So is an object to the verb מאס implied? Judging by the possible parallels mentioned above, it does not seem likely; and in terms of the resulting sense there are difficulties also. Many have therefore proposed that an object should be restored to the text by emendation. The suggestions for filling such a gap have usually been "myself" or "my words." The problems with so doing are these: (1) we have seen no reason for Job to "despise himself," which would be much more emotional language than he has otherwise used in this rather low-key speech, and it would be hard to see what it would mean for him to "reject himself." And (2) there is no reason either why he should "despise" his words, while the clause "I reject my words" does not seem at all natural. Perhaps a better solution would be to suppose that the missing word is "my case," and that what Job is rejecting or retracting (though hardly "despising") is his claim against Yahweh that he has been unjustly treated.

But there is something rather too speculative about identifying an implied object for the verb or creating an object by emendation. There is another route that may be better: to seek another interpretation of the verb. A meaningful alternative is available in the verb מאס II "flow, melt," a homonym of מאס I "despise, reject," which occurs also at 7:16; Ps 58:7 (8). That sense might not at first sight seem very suitable here, but if we understand it as a metaphor for "yield" (as REB) or "submit" (as in the *Translation* above), it creates an excellent meaning at this point. For what we expect to hear from Job before he has finished speaking is an explicit capitulation and acknowledgment of the defeat of his lawsuit especially if it is correct that a Hebrew lawsuit was conceived to be still underway so long as one of the parties had not acknowledged that there was nothing more to be said in defense of their position. If this is so, then with this one word Job announces the end of his legal claim for justice, while in the rest of the verse he expresses where he now stands in personal and social terms.

There is one other plausible approach to the problem of the first verb: it is to accept a tiny emendation of the verb form itself, from אֶמְאַס "I melt" from the verb מאס II "flow, melt," to אֶמַּס, with exactly the same meaning, from the verb מסס "flow, melt" (which is in fact a byform of מאס); see further, *Note* b. The advantage of this proposal is that it brings two further texts into the discussion where the verb is used of humans, Isa 10:18, where מָסֹס נֹסֵס is "the melting of a sick person," which apparently means "the collapse of a person in convulsions" (NEB "as when a man falls in a fit"), and even more to the point, 2 Sam 17:10, where a valiant man melts (מסס) with fear. It is not with fear that Job is melting, but the example shows that it is not a very strange metaphor to speak of a person "melting" and that various English translations need to be sought to accommodate the senses of the Hebrew word.

(2) As for the second problematic word of this verse, the verb נחם has two different senses: in the niphal, as here, it can mean (a) "regret, be sorry, repent, relent," or (b) "comfort oneself, be comforted, be consoled."

(a) The sense "repent" has been the traditional translation (so KJV, RSV, NAB, JB, NIV, NEB). The problem is that נחם niph in this sense, when used absolutely (i.e., without a following phrase indicating what is being repented of), is almost always in reference to Yahweh's "repenting," i.e., changing his mind, about planned evil: Exod 13:17; 1 Sam 15:29; Jer 4:28; 20:16; Ezek 24:14; Jonah 3:9; Joel 2:14, Zech 8:14; Pss 106:45; 110:4. The translation "repent" in such contexts is in fact inappropriate, and it would be better to understand the verb as meaning "retract a declared action," as H. Van Dyke Parunak puts it ("A Semantic Survey of *NHM*," *Bib* 56 [1975] 512–32). Only in Jer 31:19 is נחם used of human repentance in the usual sense ("after I had turned away, I repented"). So it is not very likely that Job means that he "repents" or feels sorry for anything (so too Andersen); and it is unthinkable that he should say that he "repents" for his dust and ashes (whether that means his state of mourning or his existence as a mortal human being; but see *Note* c).

In addition to the evidence of the precise meaning of the term is the very important consideration that Job is no sinner; in his world it would not be regarded as a "sin"—a sin for which one would need to repent—to have spoken "without understanding," and there is no other wrongdoing of which Job would be able to repent.

(b) The sense "be comforted, be consoled" is preferable in the context. It is well attested, at Gen 24:67; 2 Sam 13:39; Ezek 14:22; 31:16; 32:31; Ecclus 38:17, 23; 1QH 4:17; 17:13; 4QBark[a] 1.1.1. Of special interest are Gen 38:12, where it refers to a point in time after the death of Judah's wife when he "is consoled," i.e., has completed his period of mourning, and Jer 31:15, where Rachel "refuses to be comforted," i.e., to accept the consolation a mourner would usually receive (the same language in Ps 77:2 [3]). To the same effect, Jacob "refuses to be comforted," and says that he will go down to Sheol to his son (Joseph), mourning (Gen 37:35). Others who are comforted, or allow themselves to be comforted, are Isaac, after his mother's death (Gen 24:67), Judah, after the death of his wife (Gen 38:12), David, after his son Amnon's death (2 Sam 13:39), and Jerusalem, after its ruin (Ezek 14:22) (in Ezek 32:31, Pharaoh comforts *himself* for his lost army). This is the sense in which the verb (נחם) and the related noun (נחמה) have been used elsewhere in Job (2:11; 6:10; 7:13; 15:11; 16:2; 21:2, 34; 29:25; 42:11). For such an understanding, see also Ina Willi-Plein, "Hiobs Wiederruf? — Eine Untersuchung der Wurzel נחם und ihrer erzähltechnischen Funktion im Hiobbuch," in *Essays on the Bible and the Ancient World: Isac Leo Seeligmann Volume* (ed. Alexander Rofé and Yair Zakovitch; Jerusalem: E. Rubinstein, 1983) 3:273–89 (= her *Sprache als Schlüssel: Gesammelte Aufsätze zum Alten Testament* [ed. Michael Pietsch and Tilman Präckel; Neukirchen–Vluyn: Neukirchener Verlag, 2002] 130–45); Daniel J. O'Connor, "The Comforting of Job," *ITQ* 53 (1987) 245–57; Thomas Krüger, "Did Job Repent?," in *Das Buch Hiob und seine Interpretationen:*

Beiträge zum Hiob-Symposium auf dem Monte Verità vom 14.–19. August 2005 (ed. Thomas Krüger, Manfred Oeming, Konrad Schmid, and Christoph Uehlinger; ATANT 88; Zurich: Theologische Verlag Zürich, 2007) 217–29.

What these passages make clear is that to be comforted is not a matter of being on the receiving end of comfort from others, but a decision one makes for oneself, that one will accept comfort and thus cease the period of mourning and resume a normal life. So too P. A. H. de Boer, "Does Job Retract? Job xlii 6," in his *Selected Studies in Old Testament Exegesis* (ed. C. van Duin; OTS 27; Leiden: E. J. Brill, 1991) 179–95 (192): "[T]o consider the period of mourning as closed is not the same as being compensated for it or denying the loss one has suffered: it means to live on, to turn a new page in the book of one's life." H. Simian Yofre has described it as a moment of "dissociation" from previous action or feelings (*TDOT*, 9:342), while Gary Anderson has stressed the behavioral aspect of being comforted, i.e., the change of behavior consequent upon returning to normal life (*A Time to Mourn, a Time to Dance: The Expression of Grief and Joy in Israelite Religion* [University Park, PA: Pennsylvania State University Press, 1991] 9–14). See also, especially on the role of consolation as a combating of grief through rational argument, Carol A. Newsom, "'The Consolations of God': Assessing Job's Friends across a Cultural Abyss," in *Reading from Right to Left: Essays on the Hebrew Bible in Honour of David J. A. Clines* (ed. J. Cheryl Exum and H. G. M. Williamson; JSOTSup 373; London: Continuum, 2003). And see also Xuan Huong Thi Pham, *Mourning in the Ancient Near East and the Hebrew Bible* (JSOTSup 302; Sheffield: Sheffield Academic Press, 1999).

(3) How now are we to understand the final phrase of the sentence, "upon dust and ashes"? For a defense of the traditional translation of the term אֵפֶר as "ashes," as against the claim of some that it is another word for "dust, earth," see the *Note*. The key question is how the "upon" (עַל) is to be understood in the present context.

It is often thought that "upon dust and ashes" refers to Job's present situation, that is, presumably, on the refuse-heap outside the town where he has been sitting "among the ashes" since the news of his children's deaths has been brought to him (2:8). The problem with this view is that the normal ritual of mourning seems to have involved sitting "upon" ashes but not sitting "upon" dust (which is where one would usually sit, and so is unlikely to be a ritual): in mourning the dust is usually sprinkled upon one's head (2:12; Josh 7:6; 1 Sam 4:12; 2 Sam 1:2; Ezek 27:30; Neh 9:1), while one is sitting upon ashes (2:8; Isa 58:5; Jonah 3:6) or rolling in ashes (Jer 6:26; Ezek 27:30) or lying in ashes (Esth 4:3) or sitting in sackcloth and ashes (Luke 10:13; cf. Matt 11:21). For some rarer exceptions to this practice, see *Note* e. Other references to the use of ashes in mourning ritual are Isa 61:3; Dan 9:3.

In that case, it is unlikely that Job is literally "upon" both dust and ashes, the dust being rather what is sprinkled on his head. So we should understand עַל not as "upon" in a spatial sense, but as "on account of" or "for," denoting the matter or the reason for which he is accepting consolation. The idiom is the same in 2 Sam 13:39, where David is comforted "in the matter of" (עַל) Amnon, and Isa 22:4, where the mourner is being comforted "for" (עַל) the destruction of the city (similarly 1 Chr 19:2 [|| 2 Sam 10:2 עַל]; Jer 16:7; 31:15; Ezek 14:22; 32:31; and some Qumran references mentioned in *Note* e)—as well as in v 11, where Job is comforted "over, in respect of" (על) all the evil that Yahweh had brought on him. Here Job says that he now accepts consolation for the dust and ashes (i.e., the mourning and the bereavement that was its cause) that he has been enduring.

This line of Job's, as thus construed, contains one of the biggest surprises of the book. We have not been prepared by the course the book has taken to witness Job abandoning his case against God. His arguments have been so cogent, his passion so sincere, that it is almost unthinkable that at the end of the day he should merely withdraw from the lawsuit. But he does; and we need to understand why he does. He has not been convinced by the divine speeches either that he is in the wrong or that Yahweh's cosmic concerns truly outweigh his own call for justice. On the contrary, he has made it plain that he has heard the divine speeches as nothing more than a reaffirmation of divine power (v 2)—which means inevitably a marginalization of the issues of justice he cares about so passionately. And he has not admitted to any fault—apart from not recognizing that in the divine counsels justice is subsumed into supranatural "wonders," which means that the discussion of cosmic justice is ultimately off limits to humans. Job will accept that he is not permitted to question the divine decision—he has no choice—but his complaints are still not answered, and he knows it. Now he knows what he had always feared, that he would never get justice; now he can no longer hope that his champion will in the end rise to speak on his behalf (19:25), for the judge before whom his champion would prosecute Job's claim has now dismissed the claim out of hand. And now the desire to "behold Eloah while still in my flesh" (19:26), a desire so intense that it has been consuming his inmost being (19:27), has proved the ultimate disappointment of his existence: it was no beatific vision of the deity that Job wished for, but a face-to-face confrontation that would lead to his exculpation. What has happened now is the worst of outcomes, worse even than being judged guilty—it is Eloah's definitive decision that Job's case amounts to nothing, given the cosmic scope of the grand Design.

With one word, Job announces his withdrawal from his lawsuit: אמאס "I submit." And then, in words that have nothing to do with the processes of law or his grievance against the deity, and as if he had never raised the issue of justice, he declares that he will bring to an end his period of mourning and return to his usual life—as if it could ever be normal again: "I accept consolation for my dust and ashes." We readers may have somewhat lost sight of his dead children in the course of the great drama of his struggle with God, but that word נחמתי "I accept consolation" is all the reminder we need that, in all his rage against heaven, he has also been a man in mourning. Now, in that word "I submit," he has bidden farewell to theology, and, like Candide, will retire to cultivate his garden. He will not again say a single word, by the evidence of the Epilogue, he will conduct no more theological disputations with his friends or summon God again to defend himself; he will devote himself to his family and his farm.

But what he leaves unsaid is as important as what he says. What he does not say is that he is accepting consolation for his loss of standing and dignity, and for the traducing of his character, for he has had no consolation on that score. He is not "content" (Whybray), he is not convinced, he is not now possessed of a totally new outlook on the world. He has submitted to the famous omnipotence of Yahweh (as in v 2), that is all. His eyes have been opened by his encounter with God, to be sure, but what he has seen has not been his vindication but his ultimate humiliation.

Finally, we may note the case for which William Morrow (followed by Newsom) has argued ("Consolation, Rejection, and Repentance in Job 42:6," *JBL* 105 [1986] 211–25 [223, 225]), that the verse may well be deliberately vague: "the writer has constructed the verse in such a way as to make it ring with several nuances ... Job 42:6 is a polysemous construction, which even its original readers would have heard differently, depending on their evaluation of the meaning of Yahweh's address to Job ... [T]he poet himself intended no explicit resolution to the tension that exists in the Yahweh speech(es) between the very fact of Yahweh's presence and the actual contents of the divine address." Attractive though this suggestion is, my own inclination is, without insisting that the text has only one specific sense or that I have correctly identified it, to order the interpretive suggestions that have been made according to their plausibility in my judgment, and to prefer one proposal over the others.

Explanation

If we had thought that the speeches of Yahweh would be the climax of the book, and that they would provide the solution to the problems of Job, we were mistaken. For the meaning of the Book of Job cannot be inferred without a full appreciation of the response of Job, the hero of the book, to those speeches, and an understanding of the nuances of this last short speech of his in reply.

As we have seen, there are three elements in Job's speech. In the first, Job acknowledges the omnipotence of Yahweh (v 2); in the second, he accepts that he has intruded into an area in which he has no competence (v 3); and, in the third, having heard Yahweh's speeches, he abandons his case against God and determines to resume his normal life (vv 4–6). Put like that, Job's intentions seem rather straightforward. But there is a subtlety in each of these responses.

First, when Job acknowledges Yahweh's omnipotence, there is nothing new in that, for he has always done so, and there is none of his companions who would deny it. But this avowal of Yahweh's omnipotence stands here as a response to Yahweh's speeches, which have by no means had that as their central theme. If this is Job's response, it means that he has failed to understand much of the divine speeches, whose purpose seems rather to have laid out the principles behind Yahweh's creation and maintenance of the world. Though Yahweh never mentioned justice, Job has not failed to notice its absence. Job declines to accept any worldview that does not prioritize justice, and so he effectively says, It is as I always said, Might is right with you!

Second, when he says he spoke of "marvels," matters beyond his comprehension, he gives the appearance of a humble acknowledgment of the wonders of the divine working. But throughout his many speeches, Job was never speaking of "marvels," only of the justice that he, and the world of humans, is denied, but that he believed is knowable and accessible even if not presently enjoyed. If now Yahweh designates such matters "marvels," that is, beyond human understanding, Job has no choice but to accede; he has made, in Yahweh's eyes, a category mistake. But not in his own, for his words were not some casual misspeakings, but his solemn and considered "depositions" (נגד hiph; see *Comment* on v 3). A lawsuit had seemed to him a reasonable step to embark on when he had suffered an injustice; now it turns out that justice is not a value in its own right, but merely a minor element in a huge divine plan consisting of "wonders"—a realm in which he recognizes himself an outsider, who knows nothing. So while he accepts he has spoken out of order according to the divine judgment, he has not accepted this reclassification of justice, which still remains unsatisfied.

Third, when he says he has "heard" and "seen" Yahweh, it is a stunning rejection of the divine speeches. There is not a word of how Job feels about the speeches of Yahweh, of the effect they have had on him, of how he might yet respond to them. Without insubordination or hostility, Job's last word coolly turns its back on the substance of Yahweh's speeches, and merely focuses on the process of the lawsuit. Yahweh, he says, has spoken, Job has given his reply, and that is all there is to it; the case is over. Job will not continue his lawsuit any longer. And that is not because he has been satisfied, and certainly not because he has lost the case, but because he now realizes definitively that there is no hope of having it heard. No hope, then, of the vindication he has always craved, of seeing his champion rise last to speak in court on his behalf and of Yahweh conceding defeat by falling silent (19:25–27). Line by line, the divine speeches have, as water wears away stone and torrents scour the soil from the land, destroyed Job's hope (14:19).

There is one more sentence, spoken more to himself than to Yahweh, perhaps. This too faces two ways. As for his lawsuit with Yahweh, he "melts" or "submits" to the state of affairs that has left the case without a resolution. As for the future, the words "I accept consolation" show that we do not leave Job in despair or misery or self-abasement; he is determined to bring his period of mourning to an end and resume his life.

Job is neither triumphant nor defeated. The divine speeches have in the end neither satisfied nor humiliated him. It is almost as if Yahweh had not spoken from the tempest, for Job has chosen not to hear in the divine speeches the sunny side of the world's structure and management, and he has learned nothing except to have his worst fears confirmed, that he will not get justice from God. No doubt he is better off knowing where he stands and having nothing left to hope for.

The book is not over yet. The Epilogue will demand that we revise yet again our assessment of the meaning of the book as a whole.

The Epilogue (42:7–17)

Bibliography

Balentine, Samuel E. "'My servant Job shall pray for you' (Conventional and Non-Conventional Views of Intercessory Prayer in Hebrew Wisdom Literature)." *TTod* 58 (2002) 502–18. **Batten, L. W.** "The Epilogue of the Book of Job." *ATR* 15 (1933) 125–28. **Ben-Barak, Zafira.** "פרשת בנות איוב"—The Daughters of Job." *EI* 24 (1993) 41–48 (*Avraham Malamat Volume*. Ed. S. Aḥituv and B. A. Levine. Jerusalem: Israel Exploration Society). **Berg, W.** "Gott und der Gerechte in der Rahmenerzählung des Buches Ijob." *MTZ* 32 (1981) 206–21. **Berges, Ulrich.** "Der Ijobrahmen (Ijob 1,1–2,10; 42,7–17): Theologische Versuche angesichts unschuldigen Leidens." *BZ* ns 39 (1995) 225–45. **Brenner, Athalya.** "Job the Pious? The Characterization of Job in the Narrative Framework of the Book." *JSOT* 43 (1989) 37–52. **Chittister, Joan.** *Job's Daughters: Women and Power.* New York: Paulist Press, 1990. **Christensen, Duane L.** "Job and the Age of the Patriarchs in Old Testament Narrative." *PerspRelSt* 13 (1986) 225–28. **Coogan, Michael David.** "Job's Children." In *Lingering over Words: Studies in Ancient Near Eastern Literature in Honor of William L. Moran.* Ed. Tzvi Abusch, John Huehnergard, and Piotr Steinkeller. HSS 37. Atlanta: Scholars Press, 1990. 135–47. **Costacurta, Bruno.** "'E il Signore cambiò le sorti di Giobbe.' Il problema interpretativo dell'epilogo del libro del Giobbe." In *Palabra, prodigio, poesía: in memoriam P. Luis Alonso Schökel, S.J.* Ed. Vicente Collado Bertomeu. AnBib 151. Rome: Editrice Pontificio Istituto Biblico and Jávea, Alicante: Huerto de Enseñanzas (ALAS), 2003. 253–66. **Costard, George.** *Two Dissertations:* I. *Containing an Enquiry into the Meaning of the Word Kesitah, Mentioned in Job, chap. 42. vers. 11 … II. On the Signification of the Word Hermes.* Oxford: Richard Clements, 1750. **Crouch, Walter B.** *Death and Closure in Biblical Narrative.* Frankfurt a.M.: Peter Lang, 2000. **Dulin, Rachel Zohar.** *Old Age in the Hebrew Scriptures: A Phenomenological Study.* Diss. Northwestern, 1982. **Ebach, Jürgen.** "Hiobs Töchter: Zur Lektüre von Hiob 42,13–15 (auch eine Art Brief an Luise Schottroff)." In *Für Gerechtigkeit streiten: Theologie im Alltag einer bedrohten Welt.* Ed. Dorothee Sölle. Gütersloh: Chr. Kaiser, 1994. 35–40 [= his *Hiobs Post. Gesammelte Aufsätze zum Hiobbuch zu Themen biblischer Theologie und zur Methodik der Exegese.* Neukirchen-Vluyn: Neukirchener Verlag, 1995. 67–72]. **Fishbane, Michael.** "The Book of Job and Inner-Biblical Discourse." In *The Voice from the Whirlwind: Interpreting the Book of Job.* Ed. Leo G. Perdue and Clark Gilpin. Nashville: Abingdon Press, 1992. 86–98. **Fleishman, Joseph.** "'Their father gave them *nahala* "an estate" among their brethren' (Job 42:15b): What Did Job Give His Daughters?" *ZAR* 13 (2007) 120–34 [= *Shnaton* 17 (2007) 201–11]. **Fontaine, Carole R.** "Folktale Structure in the Book of Job: A Formalist Reading." In *Directions in Biblical Hebrew Poetry.* Ed. Elaine R. Follis. JSOTSup 40. Sheffield: JSOT Press, 1987. 205–32. **Forrest, R. W. E.** "An Inquiry into Yahweh's Commendation of Job." *SR* 8 (1979) 159–68. **Gibson, J. C. L.** "The Book of Job and the Cure of Souls." *SJT* 42 (1989) 303–17. **Guey, J.** "Une glose pseudonumismatique incluse dans Job 42,11." *Bulletin de la Société française de numismatique* 19 (1964) 320–32. **Habel, Norman C.** "The Verdict on/of God at the End of Job." In *Job's God.* Ed. Ellen van Wolde. London: SCM Press, 2004. 27–38. **Hoffer, Victoria.** "Illusion, Allusion, and Literary Artifice in the Frame Narrative of Job." In *The Whirlwind: Essays on Job, Hermeneutics and Theology in Memory of Jane Morse.* Ed. Stephen L. Cook, Corrine L. Patton, and James W. Watts. Sheffield: Sheffield Academic Press, 2001. 84–99. **Ivanski, Dariusz.** *The Dynamics of Job's Intercession.* AnBib 161. Rome: Pontifical Biblical Institute, 2006. **Janowski, Bernd.** "Sündenvergebung »um Hiobs willen«: Fürbitte und Vergebung in 11QtgJob 38:2f und Hi 42:9f LXX." *ZNW* 73 (1982) 251–80. **Kottsieper, Ingo.** "'Thema verfehlt!' Zur Kritik Gottes an den drei Freunden in Hi 42,7–9." In *Gott und Mensch im Dialog: Festschrift für Otto*

Kaiser zum 80. Geburtstag. Ed. Markus Witte. BZAW 345. Berlin: Walter de Gruyter, 2004. 2:775–85. **Krieg, Matthias.** "Gegeben–genommen. Die Hiob-Novelle (Hiob 1–2 und 42)." In *Hiob. Ökumenischer Arbeitskreis für Bibelarbeit.* Ed. Regina Berger-Lutz. Bibelarbeit in der Gemeinde 7. Basel: F. Reinhardt, 1989. 97–127. **Kutsch, Ernst.** "Hiob und seine Freunde: Zu Problemen der Rahmenerzählung des Hiobbuches." In *Zur Aktualität des Alten Testaments: Festschrift für Georg Sauer zum 65. Geburtstag.* Ed. Siegfried Kreuzer and Kurt Lüthi. Frankfurt a.M.: Peter Lang, 1992. 73–83. **Legaspi, Michael C.** "Job's Wives in the Testament of Job: A Note on the Synthesis of Two Traditions." *JBL* 127 (2008) 71–79. **Lévêque, Jean.** "L'épilogue du livre de Job: essai d'interprétation." In *Toute la sagesse du monde: hommage à Maurice Gilbert, S.J., pour le 65e anniversaire de l'exégète et du recteur.* Ed. Françoise Mies. Le livre et le rouleau 7. Brussels: Lessius, 1999. 37–55. **Machinist, Peter.** "Job's Daughters and Their Inheritance in the Testament of Job and Its Biblical Congeners." In *The Echoes of Many Texts: Reflections on Jewish and Christian Traditions. Essays in Honor of Lou H. Silberman.* Ed. William G. Dever and J. Edward Wright. Brown Judaic Studies 313. Atlanta: Scholars Press, 1997. 67–80. **Mathew, Geevarughese.** *The Role of the Epilogue in the Book of Job.* Diss. Drew, 1995. **Morrow, William S.** "Toxic Religion and the Daughters of Job." *SR* 27 (1998) 263–76. **Moster, Julius B.** "The Punishment of Job's Friends." *JBQ* 25 (1997) 211–19. **Nam, Duck Woo.** *Talking about God: Job 42:7–9 and the Nature of God in the Book of Job.* Studies in Biblical Literature 49. New York: Peter Lang, 2003. **Newsom, Carol A.** "The 'Consolations of God': Assessing Job's Friends across a Cultural Abyss." In *Reading from Right to Left: Essays on the Hebrew Bible in Honour of David J. A. Clines.* Ed. J. Cheryl Exum and H. G. M. Williamson. JSOTSup 373. London: Sheffield Academic Press, 2003. 347–58. **Ngwa, Kenneth Numfor.** *The Hermeneutics of the "Happy" Ending in Job 42:7–17.* BZAW 354. Berlin: W. de Gruyter, 2005. **O'Connor, Daniel J.** "The Cunning Hand: Repetitions in Job 42:7, 8." *ITQ* 57 (1991) 14–25. ———. "The Keret Legend and the Prologue–Epilogue of Job." *ITQ* 55 (1989) 1–6. **Oeming, Manfred.** "'Ihr habt nicht recht von mir geredet wie mein Knecht Hiob': Gottes Schlusswort als Schlussel zur Interpretation des Hiobbuchs und als kritische Anfrage an die moderne Theologie." *EvTh* 60 (2000) 103–16. **Pinker, Aron.** "The Core Story in the Prologue–Epilogue of the Book of Job." *Journal of Hebrew Scriptures* 6 (2006) (www.arts.ualberta.ca/JHS/Articles/article_51.htm). **Porter, Stanley E.** "The Message of the Book of Job: Job 42:7b as Key to Interpretation?" *EvQ* 63 (1991) 291–304. **Reed, Annette Yoshiko.** "Job as Jobab: The Interpretation of Job in LXX Job 42:17b–e." *JBL* 120 (2001) 31–55. **Rudolph, Wilhelm.** "Lesefrüchte. I." *ZAW* 93 (1981) 291–92 [on the possible relevance of 1 Chr 7:20–29]. **Schwienhorst-Schönberger, Ludger, and Georg Steins.** "Zur Entstehung, Gestalt und Bedeutung der Ijob-Erzählung (Ijob 1f; 42)." *BZ* ns 33 (1989) 1–24. **Vattioni, Francesco.** "Il colofone del libro di Giobbe nel Vat. lat. 5729." In *Miscellanea Bibliothecae Apostolicae Vaticanae II.* Ed. Leonard E. Boyle. Studi e testi 331. Città del Vaticano: Biblioteca Apostolica Vaticana, 1988. 267–86. **Wagner, Siegfried.** "Theologischer Versuch über Ijob 42,7–9 (10a)." In *Alttestamentlicher Glaube und biblische Theologie: Festschrift für Horst Dieter Preuss zum 65. Geburtstag.* Ed. Jutta Hausmann and Hans-Jürgen Zobel. Stuttgart: Kohlhammer, 1992. 216–24. **Watty, William W.** "Man and Healing: A Biblical and Theological View" [World Council of Churches consultation on health and wholeness; Port of Spain, Trinidad, 1979]. *Point* 10 (1981) 147–60. **Willmington, Harold L.** "The Man Satan Wanted" [Job]. *FundJ* 5 (1986) 67.

Translation

[7] *After Yahweh had spoken these words to Job, he said to Eliphaz the Temanite, "My anger is roused against you and your two friends, for you all*[a] *have not spoken of me*[b] *what is right,*[c] *as my servant Job has.* [8] *So now take seven bulls and seven rams and go to my servant Job, and offer for yourselves a burnt offering. Then*[a] *Job my servant shall pray for you, for I shall accept him*[b] *not to treat you outrageously,*[c] *for you have*

not spoken of me[d] *what is right, as my servant Job has." *[9]*Eliphaz the Temanite and Bildad the Shuhite and*[a] *Zophar the Naamathite went and did as Yahweh had told them; and Yahweh accepted Job.*[b]

[10]*Yahweh restored the fortunes*[a] *of Job while he was praying*[b] *for his friends,*[c] *and gave him twice as much as he had had before.* [11]*All his brothers and sisters and all his former*[a] *acquaintances came to him and shared a meal*[b] *with him in his house. They showed grief for him and consoled him for all the misfortune that Yahweh had brought on him. And they each gave him a coin*[c] *and a gold ring.* [12]*And Yahweh blessed the later years*[a] *of Job's life more than the former years. Job had fourteen thousand sheep,*[b] *six thousand camels, a thousand yoke of oxen, and a thousand she-asses.* [13]*He also had seven*[a] *sons and three daughters.* [14]*He called the name of the first Jemimah,*[a] *the name of the second Keziah,*[b] *and the name of the third Keren-happuch.*[c] [15]*In all the land there were not to be found*[a] *women as beautiful as Job's daughters; and their father*[b] *gave them*[c] *an inheritance among their brothers.*

[16]*After this Job lived a hundred and forty years, and he saw*[a] *his children and their children*[b] *to the fourth generation.* [17]*Then Job died, an old man and full of days.*

Notes

42:7.a. "All" is added to make clear that the vb דברתם is pl, unlike the "you" of the previous clause.

7.b. אלי cannot mean "to me," but "concerning me," so we have another example of the interchange of אל and על (as, for example, with דבר at Jer 40:16); we do not necessarily have to emend to עָלַי "concerning me" (as Beer [*BH*²], Gray).

7.c. נכונה lit. "the established (thing)," niph ptcp of כון "establish," used elsewhere in the sense of "the truth" at Ps 5:9 (10); Deut 13:14 (15), and "what is proper" at Exod 8:26; at Gen 41:32 it means "fixed" (the event foretold by Joseph's dream), at Ps 57:7 (8) of the heart being "steadfast"—as well as "established" in more obvious contexts, e.g., of David's throne (2 Sam 7:16). Here it is translated "the thing that is right" (KJV), "what is right" (RSV, NIV), "truthfully" (JB), "correctly" (NJB), "truth" (NJPS), "as you ought" (NEB).

Duck Woo Nam, *Talking about God: Job 42:7–9 and the Nature of God in the Book of Job* (Studies in Biblical Literature 49; New York: Peter Lang, 2003), has argued that נכונה does not mean "right" but "constructively," i.e., it refers to the manner of Job's speech rather than its truth content. But such a sense cannot be justified from the Hebrew (see Edward L. Greenstein, www.bookreviews.org/pdf/3195_3573.pdf).

8.a. כי אם cannot be "for if," for it does not introduce a hypothetical clause. As a compound prep, it means "but rather," or "except" (*DCH*, 4:389a), which is equally inappropriate here. An emendation seems called for; by changing just one letter, we have כי אתו lit. "for [I will accept his face]," i.e., I will favor him (so Beer [*BHK*], Gerleman [*BHS prps*], Gray, NAB). This emendation is followed in the *Translation* above. Less probably, Dhorme reads כי־אז "for then [I will accept his face]."

8.b. שׂא את־פניו lit. "lift up the face" is "favor"; the phrase often refers to inappropriate behavior in a legal context, but that is not the case here. See further on 13:8. NAB would emend פניו "face" to פָּנָי "his face."

8.c. עשׂה עם נבלה is not a simple phrase. נבלה usually means "a sacrilegious act," i.e., a breaking of religio-social rules of conduct (as Wolfgang M. W. Roth, "Nbl," *VT* 10 [1960] 394–409), or perhaps simply of social norms (as Anthony Phillips, "*Nebalah*—A Term for Serious Disorderly and Unruly Conduct," *VT* 25 [1975] 237–42); the phrase עשׂה נבלה "commit sacrilege" or "engage in disorderly conduct" occurs in Gen 34:7; Deut 22:21; Josh 7:15; Judg 19:23; 20:6; 20:10; 2 Sam 13:12; Jer 29:23. נבלה is a term from the world of social relations; it is not to do with the world of mental processes and abilities, as the common translation "folly" (Gray "obtuseness") would imply. It is very strange to have Yahweh as the person contemplating נבלה, and even those translations like NAB "not to punish you severely," NJPS "not treat you vilely," NEB "by not being harsh with you," NJB "shall not inflict my displeasure on you," GNB "not disgrace you the way you deserve," Dhorme "inflict on you any disgrace" weaken the severity of the phrase. Yahweh is branding his instinctive reaction to the friends as a desire to exceed all the bounds of reasonable behavior; he is outraged and tempted to respond outrageously; hence the *Translation* above.

One traditional translation, "lest I deal with you after your folly" (KJV; RSV, NIV "not to deal with you according to your folly") is unjustifiable from the Hebrew, partly because נבלה never means "folly" and partly because there is no suggestion of "after, according to."

Surprisingly, there has been little attempt to emend the text. Gray offers the suggestion that we read עם נבלכם "according to your folly," or "obtuseness," as he prefers to render it. The rendering "according to" for עם, however, is problematic. Gray says it is "the comparative sense 'in proportion to', as regularly in Hebr. wisdom literature," but the evidence is thin. BDB, 768a §1f, notes an עם of "equality or resemblance generally," and *DCH*, 6:460b §10, has an עם of likeness, translatable as "(comparable) with, (likened) to, like, as." Other proposed examples in Job of a "comparative" עם have been noted at 29:18 (*q.v*.), but "like" is not the same as "in proportion to."

8.d. אלי "to me" meaning "concerning me," as in v 7; the emendation to עָלַי "against me" (*Beer* [*BH²*], Gray) is therefore otiose.

9.a. The "and" is missing in most mss of the MT, but it is generally restored (e.g., by Beer [*BHK*]); its presence in LXX, Pesh, Vg proves nothing about the text they had before them.

9.b. וישא יהוה את־פני איוב is unequivocally "and Yahweh accepted Job" (as KJV) or "listened to Job with favour" (JB), or "showed favour to Job" (NJPS, REB), but some find it necessary to expand the last word to "Job's prayer" (RSV, NIV, GNB), "the intercession of Job" (NAB). NEB's addition "when he had interceded for his friends" (though not explained in Brockington's notes) results from transferring בהתפללו בעד רעהו from the next verse to this point (so too de Wilde).

10.a. Kt שבית and Qr שבות are both attested spellings of the one word, "captivity." It would be strange to describe Job's experience as "captivity," and there is one parallel where the term seems rather to mean "fortunes" (Ezek 16:53), so that sense is gratefully adopted here (NAB has "prosperity," NIV "made him prosperous again," NJB "condition"). The phrase is still odd, not least in the use of the qal of שוב, which should mean "return" (intrans), not "bring back, cause to return" (which would be hiph). E. Preuschen, "Die Bedeutung von שוב שבות im Alten Testament," *ZAW* 15 (1895) 1–74, maintains the usual meaning "turn the captivity"; but Job has not in any real sense been a captive. E. L. Dietrich, שוב שבות: *Die endzeitliche Wiederherstellung bei den Propheten* (BZAW 40; Giessen: A. Töpelmann, 1925) 32–37, argued that שוב שבות properly means "render a restoration," which suits the present context, and that in some prophetic passages שבות was confused with שבית "captivity." Less persuasively, E. Bauman, "שוב שבות, eine exegetische Untersuchung," *ZAW* 47 (1929) 17–44, regarded the meaning as "do away with a sentence of imprisonment," which is inappropriate for Job's experience, especially in a simple prose narrative like the present. J. M. Bracke, "*šûb šĕbût*: A Reappraisal," *ZAW* 97 (1985) 233–44, concludes that the translation "restore the fortunes" is after all the best solution. See also R. Borger, "Zu ש(ו)ב שב(י)ת," *ZAW* 25 (1954) 315–16; J. A. Soggin, *TLOT*, 3:1314–15.

The את, the sign of a definite obj, is also odd, and not surprisingly often deleted.

Older explanations are not longer in vogue, such as Ehrlich's view that שבות was the qal pass ptcp of שבת "cease," yielding the translation "restore what has ceased to exist." That view could not in any case explain the syntax of את־איוב "Job."

10.b. בהתפללו is the inf constr of פלל prefixed by ב, which normally means "while" in such circumstances (e.g., 4:13; 6:17; 29:3). Most think that the meaning is "when he had prayed," but it would be better to keep to the usual sense of ב, translating "while he was praying" (as NJB "while Job was interceding"). JB's translation "Yahweh restored Job's fortunes, because he had prayed for his friends," cannot be justified as a translation of the prep ב, and it creates moreover a rather implausible sense.

10.c. רעהו is apparently "his friend" (from רֵע); GKC, §91k, explains the form as an alternative for רֵעֵיהו "his friends" or perhaps as a collective sg. Others suggest the small emendation to רֵעָיו "his friends" (so, e.g., Beer [*BHK*], Gerleman [*BHS prps*], Gray).

11.a. לפנים "formerly" usually refers to far distant times (e.g., Deut 2:10; Josh 14:15; 1 Sam 9:9; Ps 102:25 [26]; Ruth 4:7), and for that reason, no doubt, Dhorme calls the expression "ironical." But there is no call for irony here, and it may rather be a feature of the *faux-naïf* style of the Prologue and Epilogue.

11.b. After ויאכלו "and they ate," some insert וישתו "and they drank," following one Heb. ms and LXX; thus Beer (*BHK*), Gray. This reading would necessitate deleting לחם "food," as does LXX (unless perhaps וישתו followed that word). LXX and some Heb. mss also omit בביתו "in his house," as does Gray. The omission of וישתו בביתו is adopted by Beer (*BHK*).

11.c. קשיטה occurs elsewhere in Gen 33:19 and Josh 24:32 apparently as the name of a piece of silver or gold. Coinage proper is generally thought to have come into being in the seventh century BCE, in western Asia Minor, and to have become widespread in Palestine only in the fifth century. The Book of Job, whatever its date, clearly envisages a world more ancient than that, in which objects of precious metals, in the form of bars, amulets, rings and the like, were used as currency, but weighed rather than counted. The קְשִׂיטָה and the gold ring are two such forms of currency. Cf. H. Hamburger, *IDB*, 3:423–35; John Betlyon, *ABD*, 1:1076–89.

There is an old tradition, attested in LXX, Tg, Pesh, Vg (but not Symm), that the term meant "lamb" (cf. Levy, 4:396b; Jastrow, 1:654b); so too ibn Ezra. This is followed by NEB "sheep."

12.a. אחרית lit. "end, latter end," contrasted with ראשׁית "beginning" exactly as in 8:7.

12.b. צאן strictly means "small cattle" (as NEB), including both sheep and goats.

13.a. שִׁבְעָנָה occurs only here. It is explained by Beer (*BH²*), KB, 944b, as a mixed form, with שִׁבְעָה "seven" and a dual form שִׁבְעָן "twice seven, fourteen," which the Tg offers (as also Rashi). So too Ehrlich, Dhorme. Alternatively, שִׁבְעָנָה may be a corruption of שִׁבְעָתַיִם "sevenfold," i.e., שֶׁבַע with the adverbial ending ־ם (mentioned by Gray). *HALOT*, 4:1401a, thinks rather that the suff is an archaic form. Some manuscripts have שִׁבְעָה "seven," and this reading is sometimes adopted (e.g., by BDB, 988b, NAB).

14.a. יְמִימָה "Jemimah" is Arab. *yamamat* "turtle-dove" (Freytag, 4:523a; not in Lane) according to BDB, 410b, KB, 384a, *HALOT*, 2:414b (KB and *HALOT* speak of *Turtur senegalensis aegyptiacus*, which appears to be the Laughing Dove, *Streptopelia senegalensis*). Beer (*BHK*) reads the name as יְמוֹמָה "Jemomah" or יְמִימָה "Jememah."

14.b. The personal name is also the common noun קְצִיעָה "cassia," see *Comment*. G. R. Driver, "Technical Terms in the Pentateuch," *WO* 2 (1954–59) 254–63, discusses the difference between קְצִיעָה "powdered cassia" and קִדָּה "cassia in strips of bark."

14.c. This personal name means "horn of antimony." פּוּךְ "antinomy, stibium" is explained by BDB, 806b, as "black mineral powder, for increasing brilliance of eyes by darkening edges of lids." Jezebel uses it (2 Kgs 9:30), and Zion is depicted as a woman "enlarging (lit. tearing) her eyes with antinomy" (Jer 4:30). Antimony is a semi-metallic chemical element found in stibnite ore, and also in the ore of silver, lead, and copper. It is mixed with soot to make the eye cosmetic known especially in the Middle East as kohl. In Isa 54:11 and 1 Chr 29:2 it is apparently a dark substance used as a setting for precious stones. Werner Grimm understands it as a powder of malachite (*Fürchte dich nicht: Ein exegetischer Zugang zum Seelsorgepotential einer deuterojesajanischen Gattung* [EHS 23/298; Frankfurt a.M.: Peter Lang, 1986] 182 n. 1).

15.a. מצאן lit. "was found," a sg vb with the pl subj נָשִׁים "women" (examples in GKC, §121a). Some would prefer to emend to a pl נִמְצְאוּ "were found," as in two Heb. mss (so Beer [*BHK*], Gray); but the plurals of LXX, Pesh, Vg do not constitute evidence of their original (against Beer).

15.b. No subj for the vb וַיִּתֵּן "and he gave" is expressed, though it is obviously Job; it is inserted in the *Translation* for the sake of clarity. Some Heb. mss actually read אֲבִיהֶן "their father" and some commentators restore it in the text (e.g., Gray).

15.c. להם "to them" has the masc pl suff; though this is not unparalleled when the reference is to females, some Heb. mss read the more normal לָהֶן, which is followed by some commentators (e.g., Gray).

16.a. Kt ויירא implies וַיֵּרֶא, the usual apocopated form, but Qr וַיִּרְאֶה offers a full form such as is not infrequent after the *waw* consec (GKC, §75t).

16.b. Beer (*BHK*) suggests (with a ?) the insertion of וְאֶת־בְּנֵיהֶם not yet account for the four generations the text speaks of. Some (e.g., Rowley) surmise that something must have fallen out of the text.

Form/Structure/Setting

The *structure* of this epilogue to the book is not distinct (by contrast with that of the prologue). Clearly there is a scene about Job's praying for his friends (vv 7–9), a headline sentence in v 10 about the restoration of Job (vv 11–15), a scene about a visit from his family and friends (v 11), a description of the prosperity of Job (vv 12–15), and a notation about the later life of Job (vv 16–17).

The only real narrative in the epilogue comes in vv 7–9, 11 (his naming his daughters in v 14 and his giving them an inheritance in v 15 barely constitute a narrative); the remainder of the epilogue is description. Verse 10, despite appearances, does not narrate the restoration of Job, for the restoration comes about only in the events of vv 11–13, while v 10 serves as a headline sentence for those verses; in other words, Job's fortunes are not reversed before the family and friends come to offer him consolation (v 11).

The headline sentence of v 10 is developed by the narrative of the visit of the friends and family (v 11), and by the description of the numbers of Job's cattle (v 12) and of his children (vv 13–14). The notation about the inheritance given, exceptionally, by Job to his daughters (v 15) is apparently the final evidence of the restored wealth of Job.

A comparison of the paragraphing of the English versions shows a lack of agreement about the structure of the epilogue. RSV and NRSV demarcate only two elements, Job and his friends (vv 7–9), Job and his family and fortunes (vv 10–17); NJPS has vv 7–10, 11–17, and Moffatt vv 7–11, 12–17. NAB has three elements: vv 7–9, 10–11, 12–17, while NEB, REB have vv 7–10, 11–15, 16–17, and JB, NJB have vv 7–9, 10–15, 16–17. NIV has four elements: vv 7–9, 10–11, 12–15, 16–17. Verse 10 is understandably sometimes linked with the foregoing verses (vv 7–9) because of its reference to Job's praying for his friends; but that is no more than a temporal connective, and the main concern of the verse is with what follows (as against NJPS, NEB, REB). Since v 10 is the headline for vv 11–15, it is unwise to insert a paragraph division in those verses (as NAB, NIV, Moffatt). As for vv 16–17, about the later life of Job, they do not fall under the heading of v 10, and so belong in a paragraph of their own (against RSV, NRSV, NJPS, NAB, Moffatt). The best paragraph division would thus seem to be vv 7–9, 10–15, 16–17 (as also JB, NJB).

Unlike the prologue, which contains a good deal of speech, only the first scene of the epilogue contains speech, viz. that of Yahweh to the three friends (vv 7–8). There is no dialogue in the epilogue.

The *genre* of the epilogue, like that of the prologue, is *legend,* i.e., form-critically, an edifying story. Unlike the prologue, the epilogue is not amenable to analysis of exposition, complication, and resolution.

The *style* of the epilogue is, like that of the prologue, what may be called *faux-naïf*. Elements of false naivety may be identified as these: (a) the excessive anger of Yahweh against the friends, to the extent of his considering committing an "outrage" against them (v 7; see *Comment*); (b) the excessive size of the offering required from the friends (v 8); (c) the round numbers of seven bulls and seven rams; (d) the restoration of Job at the moment he is praying for his friends (v 10); (e) the impression given that Job's restoration happens in an instant (v 10); (f) the restoration of twice Job's former wealth (v 12); (g) the "perfect" numbers of his seven sons and three daughters (v 13); (h) the reporting of the names of his daughters (v 14). The naivety is termed "false" only because it seems probable that it masks the highly sophisticated content of the narrative.

Comment

7–17   A lot hangs upon this epilogue to the Book of Job. By the time we have reached the end of Job's second response (42:6), we readers may well feel, with Job, that nothing has been resolved, and that his cry for just treatment has gone unanswered. Perhaps that is the most realistic conclusion the story of Job can come to, and many modern readers would prefer it if the book were now over and they were spared the "happy ending" of the epilogue. That preference is often translated into scholarly opinion by the argument that the epilogue is a secondary addition to an original Book of Job (see further, *Comment* on vv 7–9). Even if that were so, the epilogue is a crucial part of the Book of Job as we have it and must be brought into any assessment of the meaning of the book as a whole. In fact, it will be argued below, at two key points it confounds readers' expectations and has the potential for changing traditional interpretations of the book: (1) the announcement by Yahweh that Job has spoken of him what is right (vv 7–8), and (2) the restoration of Job's wealth and status, with the implication that Yahweh acknowledges that Job has indeed been treated unjustly (vv 10, 12). It belongs to the "false naivety" of the epilogue that both crucial points are treated only incidentally in the narrative, Yahweh's announcement about Job being contained in a sub-clause of his speech to the friends (vv 7, 8), and the reference to the injustice of Job's treatment by heaven being an inference from the narrative of the doubling of his wealth, with perhaps an allusion to an ancient law of reparation (v 12).

7–9 In this speech by Yahweh, Eliphaz is the only friend who is addressed. Perhaps it is assumed that he is the eldest. But the speech is evidently intended for all three friends, since it is against all of them that Yahweh's anger is roused, and v 9 narrates that the three of them went and did as Yahweh had told *them*. Elihu is not mentioned. Those who think the Elihu speeches are an addition to the original book of Job, later than the epilogue, are not surprised. But it could well be that Elihu is not regarded as one of the "friends" of Job: he is not, like Job's interlocutors, a person of importance from a distant town, but a youth of Job's own city. Whether it is for this reason or because his speeches have been more acceptable to the divine mind that he does not fall prey to the divine anger is hard to tell.

The most surprising thing about this epilogue must be the announcement by Yahweh that Job has spoken of him "what is right." To which of Job's many speeches can Yahweh be referring? It cannot be simply to Job's earliest statement, "Yahweh has given and Yahweh has taken. May Yahweh's name be blessed" (1:21), for the narrative knows also of Yahweh's own speeches (42:7) and therefore of Job's many speeches hostile to God. If it were Job's speeches in the course of the dialogue that were "right," why was the theophany needed? If it is only Job's brief responses in 40:4–5 and 42:2–6 that are being called "right," has Job said enough of substance about God to elicit this evaluation? If the reference is to all Job's speeches in general, what is it about them that Yahweh now declares to be "right"? And how can Job be said to have spoken what is right about God when Yahweh has criticized him for "darkening" his Design by words without knowledge (38:2)?

The impression of readers may well be that throughout the book Job has been persistently castigating God for his cruelty towards him and his feckless irresponsibility as governor of the universe. It is not likely that Yahweh will be approving of such opinions. But what Yahweh can and does accept is that he does not govern the world according to the dictates of retributive justice. That was never his plan (as the divine speeches have just now shown, though indirectly; see *Comment* on 38:1–41:34 [26]), and he does not undertake to execute retribution for all the acts of humans. Though Job has not meant his remarks as a commendation of God, Yahweh recognizes in them Job's perception of the underlying truth. The friends, by contrast, have everywhere been affirming the principle of retribution, which casts God as a universal policeman, a role that Yahweh resists. And as for the apparent contradiction between obscuring the Design and speaking what is right (impossible to reconcile, according to Newsom, for example), Job stands reproached for focusing exclusively on the issue of justice rather than appreciating the whole scope of Yahweh's creative intentions, but he is praised for recognizing that Yahweh does not indeed govern the world according to the principle of retribution.

7–8 There is a strange opening to this narrative, "After Yahweh had spoken these words to Job." For it is Job who has most recently been speaking. It is as if the Yahweh of v 7 is ignoring what Job has said in his speech in vv 2–6; cf. Ellen J. van Wolde, "Job 42,1–6: The Reversal of Job," in *The Book of Job* (ed. W. A. M. Beuken; BETL 114; Leuven: Leuven University Press, 1994) 223–50.

The number of seven bulls and seven rams in atonement for the wrongdoing of the three friends is an astonishingly high one. We might compare the seven bulls and seven rams offered for the whole people of Israel on each of the seven days of Passover, according to Ezekiel's cultic calendar (Ezek 45:23). We find a sacrifice of seven bulls and seven rams in three other places in the Hebrew Bible: in the narrative of Balaam and Balak (Num 23:1, 29), at the installation of the ark of the covenant in David's time (1 Chr 15:26) and at the cleansing of the temple in Hezekiah's time (2 Chr 29:21). On all these occasions the stakes are much higher than they are in the case of Job's friends. Here again we seem to encounter the naivety of the folk narrative, with its large, round numbers, but the underlying suggestion is that the friends' error is no mere trivial verbal fault, but a fundamental wrong, which needs the most strenuous sacrificial effort to expunge.

The sacrifice is offered by the friends, for their own wrongdoing, and the sacrificial animals are provided at their expense (Job has no animals of his own now); but the presence of Job is essential (Dhorme compares the presence of Samuel that is apparently necessary at Saul's sacrifice [1 Sam 10:8; 13:8], but it is far from certain why that was so). Job functions as an intercessor in prayer, like Abraham (Gen 20:7), Moses (Num 21:7; Deut 9:20), Samuel (1 Sam 7:5; 12:19, 23), and Jeremiah (37:3).

The narrative of the epilogue has opened with Yahweh angry. We have seen anger in action once before, in Elihu's reaction to the incapacity of the other friends to refute Job adequately (32:2, 3, 5), and Job has inferred God's anger from his experience of the divine punishment (14:13; 16:9; 19:11), but this is the first and only exhibition of God's anger in the narrative of the book. We have not been prepared for it by the comparatively pacific air of the divine speeches; even if they have been caustic against Job's "obscuring" of the divine plan for the universe, they have never been angry. Indeed, when Yahweh has sarcastically invited Job to take upon himself the government of the world and remove the wicked from it by pouring out upon them the fury of *his* wrath (40:11), we are taken aback by the relative violence of the language.

So when we read of Yahweh's anger against the friends (he is never said to be angry with Job) we have to reckon that their fault is no small one; if Job has been obscuring the divine plan (38:2), they have been actively assaulting it. Job, in claiming that the world is not governed by justice, though he meant it as a complaint, had put his finger on the truth of the matter; they, in defending the doctrine of retribution, were advocates of a theology hostile to the divine designs.

So serious is their fault, and so outraged is Yahweh by it, that Yahweh imagines himself abandoning the norms of decent behavior and dealing with them outrageously (עשׂות עמכם נבלה). נבלה usually means "a sacrilegious act," i.e., a breaking of religio-social rules of conduct (as Wolfgang M. W. Roth, "Nbl," *VT* 10 [1960] 394–409), or perhaps rather simply a breaking of social norms (as Anthony Phillips, "*Nebalah*—A Term for Serious Disorderly and Unruly Conduct," *VT* 25 [1975] 237–42; see *Note* a on 30:8). It is not "folly," and the Hebrew does not permit the rendering "to deal with you according to your folly" (as RSV, NRSV, NIV; see further, *Note* c). Yahweh is tempted, or inclined, to break his own self-imposed bounds; if he is to control his anger he knows he will need to be persuaded by some outside agency.

In the *faux-naïf* style of the narrative, though Yahweh knows how he should act, he will need help to behave as he should, so strong is the impulse to throw over the traces. Only a supplication from his "servant" Job, that is, his devoted worshiper, who says all the right things about him, will suffice to hold him back from the improper behavior he contemplates. Samuel E. Balentine has rightly observed that Job is praying for God as much as for the friends; see his "'My servant Job shall pray for you' (Conventional and Non-Conventional Views of Intercessory Prayer in Hebrew Wisdom Literature)," *TTod* 58 (2002) 502–18. Without Job's intercession (the sacrifices of the friends will not in themselves be sufficient to avert his wrath), Yahweh might lose his self-control and do something dreadful to the friends; but he won't, for he knows he will let himself be prevailed upon by Job, and in any case he himself has engineered the friends' supplication to Job for his intercessory prayer.

Why should Yahweh assume that Job will be willing to pray for his friends? Job has called them "torturer-comforters" (16:2), asked how long they will torment him and try to crush him with their words (19:2), reproached them for offering him empty comforts that contain nothing but their perfidy (21:34). Now he learns that God regards them as false theologians, as having not spoken about him what is right, and implicitly as having systematically wronged Job in their speeches. What does Job owe them, that he should plead with God on their behalf? Is God counting on Job to resurrect his old loyalty toward his friends? Are some residual bonds between Job and the friends all that stand between them and God's anger? Or does he expect that at the end of the day, when there is conflict between the divine realm and the human, humans will stick together? Yahweh seems to be expecting more of Job than he has a right to, but Job will not fail him nevertheless.

It is interesting that in threatening to act outrageously against the friends Yahweh evidently does not recognize that he has acted against Job in that very way. Job has never been slow in expressing the disproportion between any wrong he is alleged to have committed and the extremity of the suffering God has imposed on him (e.g., 7:12–21; 16:7–14). But God has not admitted to "doing outrage" (עשׂה נבלה) against Job—which only adds insult to the injury he has done him.

There are several more striking features in the narrative of these verses, usually overlooked by commentators and other readers in their preoccupation with the admittedly crucial question of how it is that Job can be praised for speaking of Yahweh what is right. First is the fact that Yahweh addresses the friends. Job has been longing, all through the book, that God would speak to him, but never confident that it would happen. When Yahweh does open his mouth, it is a major event for the drama of the book, and its consequences are momentous. When his speeches are over, we might well expect heaven to fall silent again, but no, Yahweh has a word for the friends, as if it were the most natural thing in the world for them to hear a voice out of the sky setting them about their business. Yahweh speaks to no one else in the book, and we recall that the whole sorry business in the prologue was conducted without any communication from heaven to earth.

Second, the friends have to go to Job (which the text says) and ask him (which the text does not say) to pray for them. They can explain their request to Job only if they tell him what Yahweh has said to them—which is to say, they must confess to Job that they have been definitively put in the wrong by Yahweh, and have roused his fury. So, in a dramatic reversal of their superior attitude to Job throughout their speeches, they must now humiliate themselves before Job, acknowledging that all they have said was wrong.

Third, they are the bearers of a message to Job from Yahweh that Job has spoken what is right and that Yahweh is calling him "my servant." It may seem a little offhand for Yahweh to leave this all-important message to the friends to pass on to Job, when he could just as easily have told Job himself that Job was in the clear. On the other hand, it must be doubly galling for the friends to have both to confess their own wrong and to acknowledge aloud that Job has prevailed over them in matters of theology and in the sight of God.

Fourth, we must remember that Job has not yet been restored when the friends bring their request to him for his prayer. He is presumably still on the ash-heap. He has no inkling that Yahweh intends to reverse his fortunes. All he knows is that he is still suffering at Yahweh's hand, and, if it is difficult for the friends to acknowledge the divine judgment against them, it must be no less difficult for Job to accept this second-hand instruction to offer prayer for people he must be totally disenchanted with; he certainly owes them nothing. If he prays for them, is he reconciled with them, or does he just do what Yahweh has bid him do, out of his inexhaustible piety?

Fifth, it may be some consolation to Job to know in advance, this time, that his prayer will be answered. Maybe he would rather that it should not be answered, and that Yahweh should do something rash with the friends, as he is tempted to do. Is this yet another "test" that Job must undergo before he is restored?

We may note finally that this narrative of the prayer of Job for the friends presupposes that the epilogue (or vv 7–9 at least) has been composed in full knowledge of the dialogues. Only if there have been speeches of the friends can it have been possible for them to have spoken of Yahweh what was wrong. So the narrative framework of the book is interwoven with the poetic dialogues, and cannot easily be separated from them as an earlier folk tale. On the issue, see most recently Duck Woo Nam, *Talking about God: Job 42:7–9 and the Nature of God in the Book of Job* (Studies in Biblical Literature 49; New York: Peter Lang, 2003).

9 The friends, who have throughout the dialogues seen themselves as Job's moral superiors and theological instructors, have now to acknowledge themselves Job's inferiors, as sinners who need atonement for their wrong against God. They must take the place of clients of Job, depending on him for his prayer to avert the wrath of an angry God.

Job, for his part, having had a bad experience of the efficacy of sacrifice in respect of his children (1:5), will now experience God's blessing on his piety, as in the days when God watched over him and made his lamp shine over his head (29:2–3). This time, Job has only to offer his prayer and it will be accepted without further ado. It is unlikely that any contrast is intended between the inefficacy of his sacrifices and the efficacy of his prayer. It is not said that Yahweh accepted the friends' sacrifices, but we may assume that, supposing that they fall into the background as Job himself comes more sharply into focus.

10–17 This final segment of the narrative of the book contains three elements: (1) the restoration of Job's fortunes (vv 10–12), (2) the restored family of Job (vv 13–15), and (3) the later life of Job, and his death (vv 16–17). It depicts

Job's return to the idyllic existence he enjoyed before all his troubles came upon him. His lost possessions are restored to him twice over, he acquires a new family to replace his dead children, he is feted by his family and friends, and he dies at last in a ripe old age. But there are omissions from this perfect picture, which may or may not be significant: his restoration to health is not mentioned (though it is no doubt to be assumed). His wife is not referred to (though it must be she who is the mother of his new family of ten children), and there is not a word of any resumption of his role in civic affairs. The friends disappear from the scene without a farewell, and Job himself never utters another word, least of all on theological subjects. Perhaps all these omissions are to be set to the account of the falsely naïve style of the narrative framework of the book; or perhaps they are to be weighed and savored, as well.

10 The narrative of Job's restoration must wait upon the settlement of the friends' position. First their escape from the divine wrath must be arranged and executed (vv 7–9), and only then will we read of the reversal of Job's fortunes (vv 10–13). It is almost as if Job's restoration is dependent on his prayer on their behalf, as if his last trial of all will be to take his stand on the side of his "torturer-comforters." It is true that this prayer is the first selfless act that Job has performed since his misfortunes overtook him—not that we much begrudge him the self-centeredness that has dominated his speech throughout the book. Perhaps his renewed orientation to the needs of others is the first sign that he has abandoned his inward-looking mourning and is ready to accept consolation. In any case, in the very act of offering his prayer on the friends' behalf his own restoration is said to take effect: the Hebrew says, "Yahweh restored the fortunes of Job while he was praying for his friends" (not, as most versions, "when he had prayed for his friends"). Things that happen simultaneously, especially in the naïve world of this prose framework to the book, are likely to have an inner connection with one another.

On the other hand, Job's restoration does not come about overnight. Ten children have yet to be born to him over the course of a decade or more, and the vast herds of livestock will not miraculously appear on his grazing lands; they must accumulate according to the natural order of things, even though we may expect, remembering his footsteps bathed in curds and the rock flowing with streams of oil in his former existence (29:6), that Job's cattle will be exceptionally fecund. He still has 140 years in which to experience ever-increasing wealth. The clause "[Yahweh] gave him twice as much as he had had before" can only be a headline sentence, referring to the whole of his future life, his "later years" (v 12); it is not the narrative of an event that took place at a given moment, and especially not at the moment that Job prays for his friends—though that is no doubt how it is generally understood by readers. The language reaches forward into the distant future. Job cannot acquire his flocks and herds in the numbers of v 12 earlier than the end of his life, otherwise, given their natural increase over the years, Yahweh would, by the end of Job's life, have given him much more than twice as much as he had before.

At this moment, at any rate, Job does not know that Yahweh will restore his fortunes, and he does not know that he is destined to have back double what has been taken from him. He only knows, presumably, that his skin complaint is clearing up (though no mention is made of it), and that his approval by God has become public knowledge (we may suppose that the friends did not keep Yahweh's words to them in v 8 to themselves, though those words would not have been to their own credit).

11 Here there is depicted in narrative form the outcome of Job's announcement in v 6 that he will "accept consolation." He has publicly put an end to his period of mourning, so all his family and acquaintances know that it is the right time to visit him with tokens of his resumption of normal life. Sharing a meal is an obvious demonstration of Job's return to the ordinary daily round. To "eat bread, or, food, with someone" occurs also at Exod 18:12 (Aaron and the elders of Israel with Jethro).

The phrase "they showed grief (נוד) for him and consoled (נחם) him" is repeated from 2:11. It is not a little strange that they are showing grief (Gray renders נוד as "nod the head" or "rock to and fro") on the same occasion as they "console" (נחם) him. Newsom has stressed that the action of showing grief or sympathy is more suitable for the time immediately after the death or misfortune, while consolation, which consists rather of encouragement to resume a normal life, sometimes with quite severe reproaches to the sufferer, is a second phase in the duty of a comforter ("The Consolations of God"). That would make it seem that sympathy is out of place here, but so too—now that Job's fortunes have been restored (v 10)—would consolation be. So we must understand the narrative as a very general account of events, not as a step-by-step sequence. Whybray detects an ironic note, in that "the help that was not given to Job in his destitution is now pressed upon him when he no longer needs it."

The "coin" (קשיטה) is a piece of silver of guaranteed weight, not a coin as we envisage it. Although coinage was possibly in use by the time of the poet (it became usual in Palestine in the fifth century BCE), the story of Job is set in an ancient patriarchal age, when valuables were weighed rather than counted. A single "coin" is perhaps not a very precious gift (Jacob paid 100 "coins" for a piece of land [Gen 33:19; Josh 24:32]), and the gift is a token of Job's reintegration into the community rather than in itself a restoration of his former wealth, which consisted, then as now, in livestock (though Murphy thinks their gifts were part of his enrichment). As for gold rings, we know that they were worn by women in the nose (Gen 24:47 [half a shekel, i.e., 5.7 grams]; Isa 3:21; cf. Prov 11:22) and by men and women in the ears (Gen 35:4; Exod 32:2–3; Judg 8:24–26). A gold ring appears as a gift in Gen 24:22. Since Job is being presented with a ring by each of his family and friends, we may presume that he is not planning to wear all the jewelry, but that the rings are a substitute for money. On the other hand, since we know that Ishmaelite men were known for wearing gold earrings, an Uzite like Job may well have demonstrated his wealth by adorning himself with some at least of his jewelry.

The little phrase of the narrator's, "for all the misfortune that Yahweh had brought on him," lets slip the fact that neither Job nor his friends ever get to know anything of the events in heaven that precipitated his woes, or anything of the role played by the Satan. On the other hand, if they had known what readers know about the origins of Job's sufferings, they may still have been inclined to refer to them as "the misfortune that Yahweh had brought on him," since it was Yahweh who had no doubt been morally responsible for all that had transpired—despite the fact that the Satan was their immediate cause.

12 The numbers of Job's cattle after his restoration are exactly double what they were before (cf. 1:3). If Yahweh had given him the same numbers of cattle he would have been restoring to Job what he had lost; by giving him double he is paying compensation for the loss, according to the law of Exod 22:4; Andersen, for example, writes: "It is a wry touch that the Lord, like any thief who has been found out (Exod 22:4), repays Job double what he took from him." Even if there is not a reference to the Exodus passage, restoring to Job more than has been taken from him would seem to be an admission of a wrong done to him. Note too the apparent doubling of the years of Job's life in v 16.

If the significance of the doubling of Job's possessions is here rightly understood, it is far more than a "wry touch" (Andersen); it is critical for the narrative of the book. For it was Job's fundamental complaint—that he had been unjustly treated in being deprived of his possessions and his good name—that spurred the whole argument of the book. It has been an ethical problem for readers also, who, even if they have not been enmeshed in the doctrine of retribution as it was taught in Job's world, have not been able to accept the initial act of Yahweh's seizure of Job's possessions as justifiable (see also David J. A. Clines, "Job's Fifth Friend: An Ethical Critique of the Book of Job," *BibInt* 12 [2004] 233–50). Yahweh of course says nothing about the injustice of it, or that he is attempting to compensate for it, and the narrative gives no explicit hint of the huge significance of the doubling of Job's wealth. But it makes a difference to our reading of the book as a whole if we know that at the end of the day the wrong done to Job in chap. 1 is righted—even if it is not explicitly stated, even if there is no apology, even though Job's dead children cannot be replaced by his new family (and even though not a word is said about the replacement of his lost servants [1:3, 15–17]). Though the narrator has just now reminded us (v 11) that the harm Job suffered was indeed Yahweh's responsibility, Yahweh does not acknowledge in so many words that a wrong was done to Job. But his doubling of Job's possessions says it all.

How are we to imagine Job's restoration being effected? All his possessions were lost to him in a single day, but if they are restored to him in a single day we would be in the realm of the fairytale not the folktale. How long he must wait to see his flocks grow and his wealth accumulate we cannot know, but he will be a poor man for many years before the effects of his affliction will be undone. The narrative is less than candid on this topic, leaving us as it does with the impression that the wrong done to Job is simply and painlessly undone by divine fiat.

13 It is possible that the word for "seven" (שבעֻנה) is actually a dual form, thus "twice seven, fourteen" (see *Note* a). This would make the number of Job's sons fall under the rubric of "twice as much as before" (v 10), but that is perhaps not a very persuasive view when the number of Job's daughters did not double. Dhorme, however, remarked that "Daughters are not an index of wealth and status, hence their number is not doubled." There is, incidentally, one other biblical character, Heman, David's seer in 1 Chr 25:5, who had fourteen sons and three daughters, which was seen as a special gift from God, a "lifting up of his horn." On the significance of the numbers, see also *Comment* on 1:2.

14 Females are not usually named in the narratives of the Hebrew Bible unless they are going to be important for the plot, so this notation is out of the ordinary. It does not make the daughters prominent, however, but is another sign of the wealth and status of the patriarch Job. We may note that all three names are, like most female names in Hebrew society, what are known as "profane names," i.e., they are taken from objects in the everyday world rather than encapsulating a short prayer or theological statement as most male names do (e.g., Eliphaz, "my God is fine gold"); so Michael David Coogan, "Job's Children," in *Lingering over Words: Studies in Ancient Near Eastern Literature in Honor of William L. Moran* (ed. Tzvi Abusch, John Huehnergard, and Piotr Steinkeller; HSS 37; Atlanta: Scholars Press, 1990) 135–47.

The name Jemimah has been explained as the Arabic *yamāmat* "turtle-dove"; Dhorme remarked that Arabs "like to give their daughters the names of gracious beasts or birds." Keziah (קציעה) is cassia, a strongly aromatic spice made from the bark of the cassia tree (most commercial "cinnamon" is in fact cassia); in Ps 45:8 (9) cassia is one of the perfumes scenting the clothes of the queen. Keren-happuch means "horn of kohl, antimony," the black eye cosmetic. Presumably such a cosmetic was kept in a horn (as was anointing oil, 1 Sam 16:1, 13; 1 Kgs 1:39). The three names invoke three of the senses: Jemimah the hearing, Keziah the taste or the smell, and Karen-happuch the sight.

Job's wife is elided from the narrative. Not only unmentioned, she is not even said to name the daughters. In Hebrew society, it is always mothers who are said to name children (Gen 19:37, 38; 29:32; and six other examples in Genesis); this is the only place in the Hebrew Bible where a father names (men always name places, as in Gen 4:17; 32:2).

15 As in most cultures, females in Job's world are judged on their appearance rather than their qualities. Presumably the sons of Job were more or less as good-looking as their sisters, having the same father and mother. The daughters here have already been objectified to some extent by being given names of natural objects (v 14) rather than the inspirational or aspirational names we may suppose their brothers bore.

The two halves of the verse, about the daughters' beauty and about their inheritance, are connected by a simple "and" (ו), which leaves the relation of the two parts open to question. We saw in the prologue how the "and" suggests a causal connection: Job was blameless and upright "and" there were born to him seven sons and three daughters (1:1–2)—as if his piety were the reason for his perfect family. The same doubtless applies here: the daughters' beauty is the reason for their father's exceptional treatment of them.

The Israelite custom was that a daughter inherited from her father only if there was no son (Num 27:8). The fact that Job's daughters inherit along with his sons may simply indicate his extreme wealth, rather than reflecting any deliberate design to make female offspring the equivalent of males in matters of inheritance.

What is an "inheritance" (נחלה)? It is usually what is passed on to descendants after one's death. Milgrom has argued that sometimes it can be a gift made during the donor's lifetime, comparing Gen 25:6; 2 Chr 21:3; Ecclus 33:24; but Gen 25:6 refers to a "gift" (מתנה), 2 Chr 21:3 is not made while the donor is alive (and it is moreover a מתנה), and Ecclus 33:24 envisages making a נחלה when one is dying. So it is strange to have Job giving his daughters a נחלה and then going on to live another 140 years. The *Testament of Job* has him making the assignment of the inheritance three days before his death, omitting the note about Job's 140 years. Joseph Fleishman has suggested that the "inheritance" was more properly a dowry, and that the land given would not really have belonged to the daughters but only to their heirs ("'Their father gave them *nahala* "an estate" among their breth-ren'" (Job 42:15b): What Did Job Give His Daughters?," *ZAR* 13 (2007) 120–34). But why say that the inheritance was "among their brothers" if in the one impor-tant respect it was unlike their inheritances? In Job's world, all daughters might expect to be given dowries, so why should this gift be specially mentioned?

Some have thought that the inheritance of the daughters among the sons is an old epic motif (N. M. Sarna, "Epic Substratum in the Prose of Job," *JBL* 76 [1957] 13–25 [24]; Coogan, "Job's Children," 146–47). See further on inheri-tance by daughters Zafira Ben-Barak, "Inheritance by Daughters in the Ancient Near East," *JSS* 25 (1980) 22–33; Ze'ev Feliks, "ירושת הבת והאלמנה במקרא ובתלמוד," *Tarb* 23 (1951) 9–15; Pinhas Ne'eman, "ירושת הבת בתורה ובהלכה," *BMik* 47 (1971) 476–89; Jacob Milgrom, *Numbers* (The JPS Torah Commentary; Philadelphia: Jewish Publication Society, 1990) 230–33, 296–98, 482–84; Peter Machinist, "Job's Daughters and Their Inheritance in the Testament of Job and Its Biblical Congeners," in *The Echoes of Many Texts: Reflections on Jewish and Christian Traditions. Essays in Honor of Lou H. Silberman* (ed. William G. Dever and J. Edward Wright; Brown Judaic Studies 313; Atlanta: Scholars Press, 1997) 67–80.

Job's daughters are named (his sons are not) and are given an inheritance along with their brothers. These narrative traits have suggested to some readers that part of the rehabilitation of Job is a recovery from his former patriarchal mindset, with the consequent empowerment of the women in his family (cf. Joan Chittister, *Job's Daughters: Women and Power* [New York: Paulist Press, 1990]). But we should not forget that Job's wife, who will by now have endured twenty pregnancies, does not rate a mention in the narrative and that the daughters are not given an inheritance along with their brothers because of the obvious justice of such a settlement, but solely because of their beauty. William S. Morrow has pointed to the "thick ambivalence" here ("Toxic Religion and the Daughters of Job," *JR* 27 [1998] 263–76), one that reminds us yet again of the "false naivety" of the prologue to the book; cf. David J. A. Clines, "False Naivety in the Prologue to Job," *HAR* 9 (1985) 127–36 (= *Biblical and Other Studies in Memory of Shelmo Dov Goitein* [ed. Reuben Ahroni]); = *On the Way to the Postmodern: Old Testament Essays, 1967–1998* (JSOTSup 293; Sheffield: Sheffield Academic Press, 1998) 735–44. In the world of the text, Job's action arises from no proto-feminist impulse; it is no more than a signal of his delight in his restored family. It is an exceptional and unconventional act to make daughters inherit, but we have come to know Job as a man who does nothing by halves. Already in the prologue, his excessive scrupu-losity with sacrifices showed him to be something of an obsessive.

16 Job lives 140 years "after this," presumably after the events described in the book. This is the final doubling (cf. v 10) in Job's restored state, for 70 years is the normal life span (Ps 90:10). That Job lives for 140 years after his trials means that his life has been started again from scratch. The former life is effec-tively cancelled, and he is to live as if those days had not existed—which may not be exactly what we would expect a restoration to be. The LXX has 170 years, and adds "and all the years he lived were 248," implying that Job was already a senior citizen of some 78 years when his trials fell upon him (Gordis, however, argues that the Job of the dialogues is a man in his prime). Joseph is said to have lived 110 years, and to have seen his great-grandchildren (Gen 50:23). To see one's grandchildren is a blessing (Ps 128:6), and grandchildren are the "crown of the aged" (Prov 17:6).

If he lives to see his children and his grandchildren, how can that be "four generations"? Commentators usually think "grandchildren" must mean descendants in general, including great-grandchildren and later generations (thus, e.g., Gordis). Yet if he lives for 140 years, he might well expect to see five or six generations of his descendants even if their average age at marriage were only about 25. It may be that the "four generations" are to be counted as his own generation, the generation of his first family, who died, and two generations of his new family (Fohrer). We were not expecting to be reminded of the dead children of the first chapter at the very end of the book, when all seems to be going so well for Job. And in a way, we are not reminded, for the author says not a word about them. Yet, such is the way of this subtle writer, that if we linger a moment over the wording, the "four generations" may suggest that the dead children must not be forgotten, and even perhaps that nothing will compensate for their loss.

17 The expression "full of days" (שבע ימים lit. "satiated with days") is used elsewhere only of Isaac (Gen 35:29) and of David (1 Chr 29:28); Abraham died in a "good old age, an old man and satiated" (Gen 25:8); Jehoiada the priest "grew old and was satiated with days" (2 Chr 24:15).

Job's death, at such an age, is no calamity, but the natural and even desired end of a full and satisfied life. There will be ritual lamenting over him, of course, as on every occasion of death, but this last little sentence in the story of Job has its own profundity: death is the completion of Job, as it is of his story, and the end of his life is not a failing or a fading or a weakening but a filling up to the brim, a fullness, even a satiation (שבע), of days. It is also, *sotto voce,* something of a reassurance to the reader, who may have been wondering whether Job has been at any risk of another unexpected and undeserved calamity; if fire could fall from heaven on his flocks and herds one day, who is to know that it will never happen again in 140 years? It is a little naïve, is it not, to believe that lightning never falls in the same place twice.

The LXX adds a lengthy appendix to the book at this point: "And it is written that he will rise again with those whom the Lord raises up. This man [Job] is interpreted from the Syriac book as living in the land of Ausitis on the border of Idumea and Arabia, and previously his name was Jobab. He took an Arabian wife, and fathered a son, by name Ennon. He himself was the son of Zare, a descendant of Esau, and his mother was Bosorra; he was the fifth from Abraham. These are the kings who ruled in Edom, which country he himself also ruled: first Balak the son of Beor, and the name of his city was Dennaba; and after Balak Jobab, who is called Job, and after him Asom, who was a ruler from the country of Thaiman; and after him Adad the son of Barad, who cut down Madiam in the plain of Moab, and the name of his city was Geththaim. The friends who came to him were Eliphaz, of the sons of Esau, king of the Thaimanites, Baldad, the ruler of the Sauchites, and Sophar, the king of the Mineans." For explanation of the details of this supplement, see Annette Yoshiko Reed, "Job as Jobab: The Interpretation of Job in LXX Job 42:17b–e," *JBL* 120 (2001) 31–55.

Explanation

What, in the end, becomes of Job? After all he has endured, after all his vigor to clear his name, after the encounter with God that has proved so disappointing—and after his decision to "accept consolation" and resume his life

(42:6)—what becomes of him? He steps back into the world of the prologue to the book, the world of naïve folktale, and closes the door for ever on the world of intensity, intellectual struggle—and lucidity—that he has inhabited since the day of his curse on life (chap. 3).

Has that been a happy outcome for him? Well, he no longer is suffering from his irritating skin disease, we presume. He has heard, we suppose, at second hand, that Yahweh believes he has spoken what is right of him. Better still, he begins to become wealthy again, which is beneficial not only for its own sake but even more for the signal it sends to others that Job is not a sinner, as everyone had thought. Over the years, he acquires a new family of ten children, the daughters especially being a source of delight to him. Presumably he becomes again the "greatest of all the people of the East" as he was in 1:4 with only half the wealth.

Is that enough to constitute happiness? The patriarch Job—as we have learned from the dialogues—also has an interior life, one of feeling and intelligence, which is masked by the simple (or, falsely naïve) style of the opening and closing narratives. Is he engaged ever again in serious theological conversation, or is he from now on wholly occupied with domestic matters and animal husbandry? Above all, where in his life has the encounter with Yahweh gone? He never had satisfaction in his case against him, and the whole affair turned out quite dismally. He has 140 years to meditate on the significance of the divine speeches; can he be content through all those years with the disappointing conclusion to his grand arraignment of Yahweh? If the epilogue is all there is of Job after his restoration, it hardly seems to be a happy outcome.

And yet, in the world of the tale, in the land of Uz, what greater felicity is there than to live a full and prosperous life with one's family around one and the evident blessing of God upon one's house? We moderns can no doubt think of all kinds of deficiencies in such a life, but the character Job, according to the tale, lacks nothing, and when he dies, will be fully satisfied with life, replete with days (42:17).

The epilogue at least addresses two of the most momentous issues the book has raised. The first is Job's complaint that the world is not being governed in justice, in that neither the righteous nor the wicked receive their just deserts. On this subject, Yahweh now says that Job has spoken of him "what is right" (vv 7, 8). Now, in the divine speeches, Yahweh had castigated Job for obscuring the divine plan (38:2) in not recognizing that retribution is not built into the world order as designed by its creator. But now he allows that Job has been right in asserting that the principle of retribution does not operate. Job had thought it should, though it did not; Yahweh had intended that it should not, and of course it did not. So in one respect Yahweh and Job are at loggerheads, and in another they are in harmony. That is the simple resolution of the crucial issue that has so bedeviled the relations between Yahweh and Job. And it has crept up on the readers in the form of a subordinate clause in Yahweh's closing address to the friends ("as my servant Job has," vv 7, 8)! Whether Job is accepting that the principle of retribution is not fundamental to the structure of the world we cannot know; if he accepts it, his dispute with Yahweh is truly at an end; if he does not, it is cold comfort to know that he is "right" only because the worst he can say about God is in fact the truth.

The second major issue concerns not the governance of the world of humans in general, but Job's own unreasonable treatment by heaven. Job never gets to know what debate in the heavenly court lay behind Yahweh's affliction of him, but in the days and years after the lawsuit with Yahweh he does discover, at length, that his possessions are restored, to twice their original quantity (vv 10, 12). Whether he recognizes in this excess of wealth an implicit admission on Yahweh's part that he has wronged Job, and that what was taken from him was indeed a theft (a convicted thief is supposed to restore twice what he has stolen), is of course unknowable. But if readers recognize it, the initial ethical problem of the book that has never gone away is ameliorated. Even a doubling of Job's possessions, we might say, is no recompense for heaven's unprovoked attack on him; but at least it is a recognition of the injustice of it, such as had never been hinted at throughout the whole course of the book.

The epilogue to the book may then be seen as a tying up of two major loose ends in its narrative development. Those who are dissatisfied by the apparently simplistic happy ending have not usually seen its importance for the narrative and the philosophy of the book as a whole. And yet the epilogue perhaps has a significance of its own beyond its function in bringing closure to the narrative.

It is a final surprise of the epilogue that, in a very long life of 140 years, not another word of theology passes Job's lips, as far as the story goes. The epilogue manages very effectively to shift the focus from the grand designs of heaven to the petty domestic plane. The divine speeches have offered a heady vision of the universe and the principles that do or do not govern it. But then the final narrative narrows the focus astonishingly from the universal vision of chaps. 38–41 to a close-up of a doting father settling estates upon his daughters, of an amiable patriarch laying on banquets for those visits of his extended family and acquaintances, of a master of animal husbandry adding to his enormous flocks year by year and putting them no doubt to profitable use. With 22,000 animals and four generations of his own offspring to worry about, what time does he have left over for questions of cosmic theology? Has this great chatterbox Job (as Voltaire called him) now at last had a surfeit of theology, that he never speaks another theological word?

The focus for the author of the Book of Job seems to have modulated in this epilogue from such questions as "What is the meaning of the universe?" and "Is there justice?," to a new question, "What is important for an authentic human existence?" How to measure the relative value of a solution to the intellectual puzzle of the universe against the delight of dreaming up beautiful names for beautiful daughters? Where stands a claim for cosmic justice against the demands of sociability and familial harmony?

Even the fundamental questions about God and the universe, the author seems to be saying, however pressing, however distressing, have their own context, in a world where human life goes on regardless—eating, drinking, begetting, dying. There is more to life than justice—more perhaps even than theology in general—however insatiable the human spirit may be for answers, however oppressed it may be by injustice. Yet the big questions, that come of their own accord, will not go away. Can't live with them, can't live without them.

Chapter Bibliographies

Supplements to those in Volumes 1, 2, and 3

Chapters 1–2

Astell, Ann W. "Job's Wife, Walter's Wife, and the Wife of Bath." In *Old Testament Women in Western Literature.* Ed. Raymond-Jean Frontain and Jan Wojcik. Conway, AR: UCA Press, 1991. 92–107. **Barr, James, and Jeremy Hughes.** "Hebrew עַד, especially at Job 1:18 and Neh 7:3." *JSS* 27 (1982) 177–92. **Berges, Ulrich.** "Der Ijobrahmen (Ijob 1,1–2,10; 42,7–17): Theologische Versuche angesichts unschuldigen Leidens." *BZ* ns 39 (1995) 225–45. **Bollhagen, Lorenz David.** *Jobum liberos suos sanctificantem ... dissertatione theologica ... submittit Matthæus Wollitsch.* Greifswald, 1705. **Breitbart, Sidney.** "Implications of the Wager in the Book of Job." *JBQ* 28 (2000) 119–24. **Brenner, Athalya.** "Job the Pious? The Characterization of Job in the Narrative Framework of the Book." *JSOT* 43 (1989) 37–52. **Broc, Catherine.** "La femme de Job dans la prédication de Jean Chrysostome." In *Studia patristica.* Vol. XXXVII. *Papers Presented at the Thirteenth International Conference on Patristic Studies Held in Oxford 1999. Cappadocian Writers, Other Greek Writers.* Ed. M. F. Wiles and E. J. Yarnold. Louvain: Peeters, 2001. 396–403. **Coogan, Michael David.** "Job's Children." In *Lingering over Words: Studies in Ancient Near Eastern Literature in Honor of William L. Moran.* Ed. Tzvi Abusch, John Huehnergard, and Piotr Steinkeller. HSS 37. Atlanta: Scholars Press, 1990. 135–47. **Cooper, Alan.** "Reading and Misreading the Prologue to Job." *JSOT* 46 (1990) 67–79. **Cunchillos, J. L.** "Le dieu Mut, guerrier de El" [on the sons of God (Job 1–2; 38:7)]. *Syria* 62 (1985) 205–18. **Day, John.** "How Could Job Be an Edomite?" In *The Book of Job.* Ed. W. A. M. Beuken. BETL 114. Leuven: Leuven University Press, 1994. 392–99. **Day, Peggy Lynne.** *An Adversary in Heaven: Śaṭan in the Hebrew Bible.* HSM 43. Atlanta: Scholars Press, 1988. **Dimant, Devorah.** "Bible through a Prism: The Wife of Job and the Wife of Tobit." *Shnaton* 17 (2007) 201–11. **Dion, P.-E.** "Un nouvel éclairage [Fekherye] sur le contexte culturel des malheurs de Job." *VT* 34 (1984) 213–15. **Dochhorn, Jan.** "De iusto Job quando venerunt tres amici eius ut viderunt eum (Oxford, Bodleian Library, Holkham 24 [olim 90], 173v–175r)." *ZAC* 10,2 (2006) 187–94.

Ebach, Jürgen. "Ist es 'umsonst,' dass Hiob gottesfürchtig ist? Lexikographische und methodologische Marginalien zu *ḥinnām* in Hi 1,9." In *Die hebräische Bibel und ihre zweifache Nachgeschichte. Festschrift für Rolf Rendtorff zum 65. Geburtstag.* Ed. Erhard Blum. Neukirchen–Vluyn: Neukirchener Verlag, 1990. 319–35. **Elliger, Katharina.** "Ijob und seine Frau. Buch Ijob, Kapitel 1 und 2." In *Schön bist du und verlockend. Grosse Paare der Bibel.* Ed. Herbert Haag. Freiburg i.Br.: Herder, 2001. 162–66. **Fleming, David M.** *The Divine Council as Type Scene in the Hebrew Bible.* Diss. Southern Baptist Theological Seminary, 1989. **Fontaine, Carole R.** "Folktale Structure in the Book of Job: A Formalist Reading." In *Directions in Biblical Hebrew Poetry.* Ed. Elaine R. Follis. JSOTSup 40. Sheffield: JSOT Press, 1987. 205–32. **Fontinoy, Charles.** "Les noms du Diable et leur étymologie." In *Orientalia J. Duchesne-Guillemin emerito oblata. Acta iranica* 23 (1984) 164–66. **Forrest, Robert W. E.** "The Two Faces of Job: Imagery and Integrity in the Prologue." In *Ascribe to the Lord: Biblical and Other Studies in Memory of Peter C. Craigie.* Ed. Lyle M. Eslinger and Glen J. Taylor. JSOTSup 67. Sheffield: JSOT Press, 1988. 385–98. **Fournier, Christian.** "Augustin, Adnotationes in Job I, 29–31 (traduction d'après CSEL 28)." In *Le Livre de Job chez les Pères.* Ed. Centre d'Analyse et de Documentation Patristiques. Cahiers de Biblia patristica 5. Strasbourg: Centre d'Analyse et de Documentation Patristiques, 1996. 49–61. **Freund, Yosef.** "Were Job's Friends Gentiles?" *Dor* 18 (1989) 107–10. **Gillmayr-Bucher, Susanne.** "Rahmen und Bildträger. Der mehrschichtige Diskurs in den Prosatexten des Ijobbuchs." In *Das Buch Ijob: Gesamtdeutungen—Einzeltexte—zentrale Themen.* Ed. Theodor Seidl and Stephanie Ernst. Österreichische biblische Studien 31.

Frankfurt: Peter Lang, 2007. 139–64. **Gruber, Mayer I.** "The Rhetoric of Familiarity and Contempt in Job 2:9–10." *Scriptura* 97 (2004) 261–66. **Guillaume, Philippe.** "Caution: Rhetorical Questions!" *BN* 103 (2000) 11–16. **Hamilton, W. T.** "Difficult Texts from Job" [Job 1:12; 2:6]. In *Difficult Texts of the Old Testament Explained.* Ed. Wendell Winkler. Hurst, TX: Winkler Publications, 1982. 301–10. **Handy, Lowell K.** "The Authorization of Divine Power and the Guilt of God in the Book of Job: Useful Ugaritic Parallels." *JSOT* 60 (1993) 107–18. **Hicklin, Eddie, Jr.** "The Other Side of God" [Job 1:21]. *AME Zion Quarterly Review* 108/4 (1996) 110–15. **Hoffer, Victoria.** "Illusion, Allusion, and Literary Artifice in the Frame Narrative of Job." In *The Whirlwind: Essays on Job, Hermeneutics and Theology in Memory of Jane Morse.* Ed. Stephen L. Cook, Corrine L. Patton, and James W. Watts. Sheffield: Sheffield Academic Press, 2001. 84–99. **Hoop, Raymond de.** "The Frame Story of the Book of Job: Prose or Verse? Job 1:1–5 as a Test Case." In *Layout Markers in Biblical Manuscripts and Ugaritic Tablets.* Ed. Marjo C. A. Korpel and Josef M. Oesch. Pericope 5. Assen: Van Gorcum, 2005. 40–77.

Japhet, Sara. "The Trial of Abraham and the Test of Job: How Do They Differ?" *Henoch* 16 (1994) 153–72. **Jenks, Alan W.** "Theological Presuppositions of Israel's Wisdom Literature" [incl. Job 1–2]. *HBT* 7 (1985) 43–75. **Johnson, Timothy J.** "Critical Note on Job 2:8: Ash-Heap or Dung-Heap?" *Bulletin of the International Organization for Septuagint and Cognate Studies* 36 (2003) 87–92. **Kamp, Albert.** "Mit oder ohne Grund. Gottes- und Menschenbilder in Ijob 1–3." *Conc* 40 (2004) 375–83 [= "With or without a Cause: Images of God and Man in Job 1–3." *Conc* 40 (2004) 9–17; also in *Job's God.* Ed. Ellen van Wolde. London: SCM Press, 2004. 9–17]. **Kee, Min Suc.** "The Heavenly Council and Its Type-Scene." *JSOT* 31 (2007) 259–73. **Kermode, Frank.** "The Uses of Error" [Job 1–2]. *Theology* 89 (1986) 425–31 [= *The Uses of Error: Sermon before the University, King's College Chapel, 11 May 1986.* Cambridge: King's College Chapel, 1986. Included in his *The Uses of Error.* London: Collins; Cambridge, MA: Harvard University Press, 1991]. **Kinet, Dirk.** "The Ambiguity of the Concepts of God and Satan in the Book of Job." *Conc* 169 (1983) 30–35. **Klein, Lillian R.** "Job and the Womb: Text about Men, Subtext about Women." In *A Feminist Companion to Wisdom Literature.* Ed. Athalya Brenner. The Feminist Companion to the Bible 9. Sheffield: Sheffield Academic Press, 1995. 186–200 [= her *From Deborah to Esther: Sexual Politics in the Hebrew Bible.* Philadelphia: Fortress Press, 2003. 73–84]. **Knauf, Ernst Axel.** "Hiobs Heimat." *WO* 19 (1988) 65–83. ———. "Supplementa ismaelitica" [incl. on Job's homeland]. *BN* 22 (1983) 25–33. **Krieg, Matthias.** "Gegeben–genommen. Die Hiob-Novelle (Hiob 1–2 und 42)." In *Hiob. Ökumenischer Arbeitskreis für Bibelarbeit.* Ed. Regina Berger-Lutz. Bibelarbeit in der Gemeinde 7. Basel: F. Reinhardt, 1989. 97–127. **Kutsch, Ernst.** "Hiob und seine Freunde. Zu Problemen der Rahmenerzählung des Hiobbuches." In *Zur Aktualität des Alten Testaments: Festschrift für Georg Sauer zum 65. Geburtstag.* Ed. Siegfried Kreuzer and Kurt Lüthi. Frankfurt a.M.: Peter Lang, 1992. 73–83.

Langenhorst, Georg. "'Sieben Tage und sieben Nächte' (Hiob 2,13). Gelingender und scheiternder Trost im Buch Hiob." *LS* 57 (2006) 7–12. **Legaspi, Michael C.** "Job's Wives in the *Testament of Job*: A Note on the Synthesis of Two Traditions." *JBL* 127 (2008) 71–79. **Levin, S.** "Satan: Psychologist." *JBQ* 18 (1989–90) 157–64. **Lewis, Andrew Zack.** *The Second Adam: The Intertextual Relationship between the Prologue to Job and Genesis 1–3.* Diss. Regent College, 2005. **Linafelt, Tod.** "The Undecidability of BRK in the Prologue to Job and Beyond." *BibInt* 4 (1996) 154–72. **Lo, Alison.** "Device of Progression in the Prologue to Job." *BN* 130 (2006) 31–43. **Mack, Hananel.** "Were the Children of Job Sinners or Innocent Victims? The Issue of Their Death in Ancient Sources and in Medieval Jewish Exegesis." *Shnaton* 12 (2000) 221–39. **Magdalene, F. Rachel.** "Job's Wife as Hero: A Feminist-Forensic Reading of the Book of Job." *BibInt* 14 (2006) 209–58. **McGinnis, Claire Mathews.** "Playing the Devil's Advocate in Job: On Job's Wife." In *The Whirlwind: Essays on Job, Hermeneutics and Theology in Memory of Jane Morse.* Ed. Stephen L. Cook, Corrine L. Patton, and James W. Watts. Sheffield: Sheffield Academic

Press, 2001. 121–41. **Meade, Sonya R.** *Bless God and Die: An Examination of the Role of Job's Wife in the Masoretic Text of Job.* Diss. Memorial University of Newfoundland, 1997. **Meier, Sam.** "Job i–ii, a Reflection of Genesis i–iii." *VT* 39 (1989) 183–93. **Michel, Andreas.** "Ijob und Abraham. Zur Rezeption von Gen 22 in Ijob 1–2 und 42,7–17." In *Gott, Mensch, Sprache. Schülerfestschrift für Walter Gross zum 60. Geburtstag.* Ed. Andreas Michel and Hermann-Josef Stipp. ATSAT 58. St Ottilien: Eos Verlag, 2001. 73–98. **Moberly, R. W. L.** "Solomon and Job: Divine Wisdom in Human Life" [Job 1:1; 2:10]. In *Where Shall Wisdom Be Found? Wisdom in the Bible, the Church and the Contemporary World.* Ed. Stephen C. Barton. Edinburgh: T. & T. Clark, 1999. 3–17. **Moskala, Jiri.** "The God of Job and Our Adversary." *Journal of the Adventist Theological Society* 15 (2004) 107–17. **Nel, Philip J.** "The Conception of Evil and Satan in Jewish Traditions in the Pre-Christian Period." In *Like a Roaring Lion: Essays on the Bible, the Church and Demonic Powers.* Ed. Pieter G. R. De Villiers. Pretoria: University of South Africa, 1987. 1–21. **Newsom, Carol A.** "The 'Consolations of God': Assessing Job's Friends across a Cultural Abyss." In *Reading from Right to Left: Essays on the Hebrew Bible in Honour of David J. A. Clines.* JSOTSup 373. Ed. J. Cheryl Exum and H. G. M. Williamson. London: Sheffield Academic Press, 2003. 347–58. **Nielsen, Kirsten.** "Whatever Became of You, Satan? or, A Literary-Critical Analysis of the Role of Satan in the Book of Job." In *Goldene Äpfel in silbernen Schalen: Collected Communications to the XIIIth Congress of the International Organization for the Study of the Old Testament, Leuven 1989.* Ed. Klaus-Dietrich Schunck and Matthias Augustin. BEATAJ 20. Frankfurt a.M.: Peter Lang, 1992. 129–34. **Noort, E.** "JHWH und das Böse: Bemerkungen zu einer Verhältnisbestimmung [Gen 32:23ff; Ex 4:24ff; Deut 32; 2 Sam 24:1; 1 Chron 21:1; Job 2:3–7]." In *Prophets, Worship and Theodicy: Studies in Prophetism, Biblical Theology and Structural and Rhetorical Analysis and on the Place of Music in Worship: Papers Read at the Joint British–Dutch Old Testament Conference Held at Woudschoten, 1982.* OTS 23. Leiden: E. J. Brill, 1984. 120–36.

O'Connor, Daniel J. "The Keret Legend and the Prologue–Epilogue of Job." *ITQ* 55 (1989) 1–6. **O'Connor, Donal.** "'Bless God and die' (Job 2:9): Euphemism or Irony?" *PrIrBibAss* 19 (1996) 48–65. **Page, Sydney H. T.** "Satan: God's Servant." *JETS* 50 (2007) 449–65. **Pinker, Aron.** "The Core Story in the Prologue–Epilogue of the Book of Job." *Journal of Hebrew Scriptures* 6 (2006). **Pribnow, Hans.** "Der glaubende Mensch und die Welt" [Job 1]. In … *und fragten nach Jesus: Beiträge aus Theologie, Kirche und Geschichte: Festschrift für Ernst Barnikol zum 70. Geburtstag.* Ed. Udo Meckert, Günther Ott, and Bernt Satlow. Berlin: Evangelische Verlagsanstalt, 1964. **Rohan-Chabot, Claude de.** "Exégèse de Job 2:6 dans une homélie inédite de Basile de Séleucie." In *Studia patristica: Papers of the 1983 Oxford Patristics Conference.* Studia patristica 18/2. Ed. Elizabeth A. Livingstone. Kalamazoo: Cistercian Publications; Leuven: Peeters, 1989. 197–201. **Ruiten, Jacques van.** "Abraham, Job and the Book of Jubilees: The Intertextual Relationship of Genesis 22:1–19, Job 1:1–2:13 and Jubilees 17:15–18:19." In *The Sacrifice of Isaac: The Aqedah (Genesis 22) and Its Interpretations.* Ed. Edward Noort and Eibert Tigchelaar. Themes in Biblical Narrative. Jewish and Christian Traditions 4. Leiden: E. J. Brill, 2002. 58–85. **Runions, Erin.** "Ms Job and the Problem of God: A Feminist, Existentialist, Materialist Reading." In *From the Margins. I. Women of the Hebrew Bible and Their Afterlives.* Ed. Peter S. Hawkins and Lesleigh Cushing Stahlberg. Bible in the Modern World 18. Sheffield: Sheffield Phoenix Press, 2008. 159–74. **Sasson, Victor.** "The Literary and Theological Function of Job's Wife in the Book of Job." *Bib* 79 (1998) 86–90. **Schindler, Audrey.** "One Who Has Borne Most: The Cri de Coeur of Job's Wife." *AusBR* 54 (2006) 24–36. **Schmid, Konrad.** "Das Hiobproblem und der Hiobprolog." In *Hiobs Weg. Stationen von Menschen im Leid.* Ed. M. Oeming and K. Schmid. BThSt 45. Neukirchen–Vluyn: Neukirchener Verlag. 2001. 9–34. **Schreiner, Stefan.** "Der gottesfürchtige Rebell oder Wie die Rabbinen die Frömmigkeit Ijobs deuteten." *ZTK* 89 (1992) 159–71. **Schulze, Manfred.** "Der Hiob-Prediger: Johannes von Staupitz auf der Kanzel der Tübinger Augustinerkirche" [Job 1:1–2:10]. In *Augustine, the Harvest, and Theology: Essays Dedicated to Heiko Augustinus*

Oberman in Honor of His Sixtieth Birthday. Ed. Kenneth Hagen. Leiden: E. J. Brill, 1990. 60–88. **Schweitzer, Donald.** "'Curse God and die': Was Job's Wife Completely Wrong?" *Touchstone* 14/2 (1996) 32–38. **Schwienhorst-Schönberger, Ludger, and Georg Steins.** "Zur Entstehung, Gestalt und Bedeutung der Ijob-Erzählung (Ijob 1f; 42)." *BZ* ns 33 (1989) 1–24. **Seow, Choon-Leong.** "Job's Wife, with Due Respect …" In *Das Buch Hiob und seine Interpretationen: Beiträge zum Hiob-Symposium auf dem Monte Verità vom 14.–19. August 2005.* Ed. Thomas Krüger, Manfred Oeming, Konrad Schmid, and Christoph Uehlinger. ATANT 88. Zurich: Theologische Verlag Zürich, 2007. 351–73. **Shepherd, David.** "Rendering 'flesh and bones.' Pair Reversal and the Peshitta of Job 2.5." *Aramaic Studies* 3 (2005) 205–13. **Slotki, Judah J.** "Job i 6." *VT* 35 (1985) 229–30. **Strauss, Hans.** "Theologische, form- und traditionsgeschichtliche Bemerkungen zur Literargeschichte des (vorderen) Hiobrahmens (Hi 1–2)." *ZAW* 113 (2001) 553–65.

Tate, Marvin E. "Satan in the Old Testament." *RevExp* 89 (1992) 461–74. **Tidwell, N. L. A.** *"Wā'ōmar* (Zech 3:5) and the Genre of Zechariah's Fourth Vision" [1 Kgs 22; Isa 6, 40; Job 1, 2; Zech 1, 3, 6]. *JBL* 94 (1975) 343–55. **Vall, Gregory.** "The Enigma of Job 1,21a." *Bib* 76 (1995) 325–42. **Vogels, Walter.** "Job's Empty Pious Slogans (Job 1,20–22; 2,8–10)." In *The Book of Job.* Ed. W. A. M. Beuken. BETL 114. Leuven: Leuven University Press, 1994. 369–76. ———. "Job's Superficial Faith in His First Reactions to Suffering (Job 1:20–23; 2:8–10)." *EglTh* 25 (1994) 343–59. **Ward, Thomas R., Jr.** "Blessed be the name of the Lord" [Job 1:13–21]. *Sewanee Theological Review* 49 (2005) 9–10. **Watson, Wilfred G. E.** "Internal Parallelism in Classical Hebrew Verse." *Bib* 66 (1985) 365–84. **West, Gerald.** "Hearing Job's Wife: Towards a Feminist Reading of Job." *OTEss* 4 (1991) 107–31. **White, Marylyn Ellen.** *The Purpose and Portrayal of the śāṭān in the Old Testament.* Diss. Tyndale Seminary, Toronto, Ont., 2004. **White, Wade Albert.** "A Devil in the Making: Isomorphism and Exegesis in OG Job 1:8b." In *Septuagint Research: Issues and Challenges in the Study of the Greek Jewish Scriptures.* Ed. Wolfgang Kraus and R. Glenn Wooden. SBLSCS 53. Atlanta: Society of Biblical Literature, 2006. **Whybray, R. N.** "The Immorality of God: Reflections on Some Passages in Genesis, Job, Exodus and Numbers." *JSOT* 72 (1996) 89–120. **Wolde, Ellen van.** "A Text-Semantic Study of the Hebrew Bible, Illustrated with Noah and Job." *JBL* 113 (1994) 19–35. ———. *Meneer en mevrouw Job: Job in gesprek met zijn vrouw, zijn vrienden en God.* Baarn: Ten Have, 1991 [= *Mr and Mrs Job.* Trans. John Bowden. London: SCM Press, 1997]. ———. "The Development of Job: Mrs Job as Catalyst." In *A Feminist Companion to Wisdom Literature.* Ed. Athalya Brenner. The Feminist Companion to the Bible 9. Sheffield: Sheffield Academic Press, 1995. 201–21. **Wolpe, Gerald I.** "Health Care and Mrs Job: The Conflict of Personal Categories." In *Health Care: Right or Privilege? Moral and Religious Values in Health Care Reform* [= *Conservative Judaism* 51 (1999)] 31–39.

Chapter 3

Alter, Robert. "Structures of Intensification in Biblical Poetry." In *Judaic Perspectives on Ancient Israel.* Ed. Jacob Neusner, Baruch A. Levine, and Ernest S. Frerichs. Philadelphia: Fortress Press, 1985. 189–206 [= his *The Art of Biblical Poetry.* New York: Basic Books, 1981. 62–84]. **Althann, Robert.** "Job 3 after the Discussion between Mitchell Dahood and James Barr." In his *Studies in Northwest Semitic.* BibOr 45. Rome: Biblical Institute Press, 1997. 121–53. **Amu, Ifeoma C. M.** *Voice from Heaven and Earth: A Literary and Conceptual Exploration between Job 3 and 38:1–41:34.* Diss. Candler, Atlanta, 2000. **Aurivillius, Karl.** *Versus 3–10 cap. III libri Jobi explicati.* Uppsala: Edman, 1778. **Beuken, W. A. M.** "Job's Imprecation as the Cradle of a New Religious Discourse. The Perplexing Impact of the Semantic Correspondences between Job 3, Job 4–5 and Job 6–7." In *The Book of Job.* Ed. W. A. M. Beuken. BETL 114. Leuven: Leuven University Press, 1994. 4–78. **Bezuidenhout, Louis C.** "Semantiese ritme en beweging in Job 3. 'n ander benadering tot die waardering van die teks." *HervTS* 50 (1994) 236–45. **Blumenthal,**

Elke. "Hiob und die Harfnerlieder." *TLZ* 115 (1990) 721–30. **Boyse, Samuel.** "The III. Chapter of the Book of Job Translated" [in verse]. In his *Translations and Poems Written on Several Subjects.* Edinburgh: Thomas & Walter Ruddimans, 1731. **Bullock, C. Hassell.** "Abortion and Old Testament Prophetic and Poetic Literature" [Psalm 139; Job; Jeremiah]. In *Abortion: A Christian Understanding and Response.* Ed. James K. Hoffmeier. Grand Rapids: Baker Book House, 1987. 65–71. **Burns, John Barclay.** "Cursing the Day of Birth" [Iliad, Erra, Jeremiah, Job]. *PrGLM* 13 (1993) 11–22. **Chiolerio, M.** "Giobbe invoca la morte: paura o desiderio? (Gb 3,3–26)." *Ter* 43 (1992) 27–52. **Cho, Eun Suk.** "Creation in the Book of Job: An Exegetical Essay on Job 3 from a Korean Perspective." *AsiaJT* 17 (2003) 26–76. **Cooper, Alan.** "Narrative Theory and the Book of Job" [addendum on Job 3:3–10]. *SR* 11 (1982) 35–44. **Cox, Dermot.** "The Desire for Oblivion in Job 3." *SBFLA* 23 (1973) 37–49. **Duin, Kees van.** "Der Gegner Israels: Leviatan in Hiob 3:8." In *Give Ear to My Words: Psalms and Other Poetry in and around the Hebrew Bible. Essays in Honour of Professor N. A. van Uchelen.* Ed. Janet Dyk. Amsterdam: Societas hebraica amstelodamensis, 1996. 153–59. **Fokkelman, J. P.** *Major Poems of the Hebrew Bible: At the Interface of Hermeneutics and Structural Analysis. 1. Ex. 15, Deut. 32, and Job 3.* Studia semitica neerlandica 37. Assen: Van Gorcum, 1998.

Ha, Kyung-Taek. *Frage und Antwort: Studien zu Hiob 3 im Kontext des Hiob-Buches.* Herders biblische Studien 46. Freiburg i.Br.: Herder, 2005. **Jacobsen, Thorkild, and Kirsten Nielsen.** "'Cursing the Day'" [Mesopotamian and biblical examples]. *SJOT* 6 (1992) 187–204. **Japhet, Sara.** "Insights on Job 3, from a Medieval Commentary: Rabbi Samuel Ben Meir (Rashbam) on the Book of Job." In *Reading from Right to Left: Essays on the Hebrew Bible in Honour of David J. A. Clines.* JSOTSup 373. Ed. J. Cheryl Exum and H. G. M. Williamson. London: Sheffield Academic Press, 2003. 241–53. **Kamp, Albert.** "Mit oder ohne Grund. Gottes- und Menschenbilder in Ijob 1–3." *Conc* 40/4 (2004) 375–83 [= "With or without a Cause: Images of God and Man in Job 1–3." In *Job's God.* Ed. Ellen van Wolde. London: SCM Press, 2004. 9–17]. **Lugt, Pieter van der.** "Stanza-Structure and Word-Repetition in Job 3–14." *JSOT* 40 (1988) 3–38. **Luther, Johannes Andreas.** *Dissertatio philologica de* יום ארדי *sive maledictoribus diei a Iobo cap. III. com. 8 in subsidium evocatis.* Wittenberg: Formis Schroederianis, [1712]. **Michel, Walter L.** "Ṣlmwt, 'deep darkness' or 'shadow of death'?" [Job 3:5]. *BibRes* 29 (1984) 5–20. **Noegel, Scott B.** "Job iii 5 in the Light of Mesopotamian Demons of Time." *VT* 57 (2007) 556–62. **Parker, Simon B.** "The Birth Announcement." In *Ascribe to the Lord: Biblical and Other Studies in Memory of Peter C. Craigie.* Ed. Lyle M. Eslinger and Glen J. Taylor. JSOTSup 67. Sheffield: JSOT Press, 1988. 133–49. **Perdue, Leo G.** "Metaphorical Theology in the Book of Job: Theological Anthropology in the First Cycle of Job's Speeches (Job 3; 6–7; 9–10)." In *The Book of Job.* Ed. W. A. M. Beuken. BETL 114. Leuven: Leuven University Press, 1994. 129–56. **Pettys, Valerie Fortsman.** "Let There Be Darkness: Continuity and Discontinuity in the 'Curse' of Job 3." *JSOT* 98 (26/4) (2002) 89–104. **Schroer, Silvia.** "In die Enge getrieben—in die Weite geführt. Hiobs Klage und die erste Gottesrede (Hiob 3 und 38–39)." *Hiob. Ökumenischer Arbeitskreis für Bibelarbeit.* Ed. Regina Berger-Lutz. Bibelarbeit in der Gemeinde 7. Basel: F. Reinhardt, 1989. 128–60. **Tönsing, Detlev L.** "The Use of Creation Language in Job 3, 9 and 38 and the Meaning of Suffering." *Scriptura* 59 (1996) 435–49.

Chapters 4–5

Beuken, W. A. M. "Eliphaz: One among the Prophets or Ironist Spokesman? The Enigma of Being a Wise Man in One's Own Right (Job 4–5)." In *Das Buch Hiob und seine Interpretationen: Beiträge zum Hiob-Symposium auf dem Monte Verità vom 14.–19. August 2005.* Ed. Thomas Krüger, Manfred Oeming, Konrad Schmid, and Christoph Uehlinger. ATANT 88. Zurich: Theologische Verlag Zürich, 2007. 292–313. ———. "Job's Imprecation as the Cradle of a New Religious Discourse. The Perplexing Impact of the Semantic Correspondences between Job 3, Job 4–5 and Job 6–7." In *The Book of Job*. Ed. W. A. M. Beuken. BETL 114. Leuven: Leuven University Press, 1994. 41–78. **Brin, Gershon.** "Job v 3–Textual Test Case: The Translator's Limits of Consideration." *VT* 42 (1992) 391–93. **Burns, John Barclay.** "The Chastening of the Just in Job 5:17–23: Four Strikes of Erra." *PrGLM* 10 (1990) 18–30. ———. "The *šwṭ lšwn* in Job 5,21a as Metaphor and Irony." *BZ* 35 (1991) 93–96. **Chbeir, Tanios.** *Themata praecipua Job 4–5 in contextu prologi epilogi et theophaniae.* Diss. Gregorian, 1993. **Ciccarese, Maria Pia.** "Il formicaleone, il Fisiologo e l'esegesi allegorica di Gb 4,11." *Annali di storia dell'esegesi* 11 (1994) 545–69. **Cohen, Matty.** "Fauves et songe nocturne dans le premier discours d'Eliphaz." *Graphè* 6 (1997) 35–58. **Cooper, Marlene E.** "Meditation on Job 5:8–16." *Lutheran Theological Journal* 33 (1999) 69–71. **Cotter, David W.** *A Study of Job 4–5 in the Light of Contemporary Literary Theory.* SBLDS 124. Atlanta: Scholars Press, 1992 [= Diss. Gregorian, 1989]. **Fishbane, Michael.** "The Book of Job and Inner-Biblical Discourse." In *The Voice from the Whirlwind: Interpreting the Book of Job.* Ed. Leo G. Perdue and Clark Gilpin. Nashville: Abingdon Press, 1992. 86–98. **Fokkelman, J. P.** *Major Poems of the Hebrew Bible: At the Interface of Prosody and Structural Analysis.* II. *85 Psalms and Job 4–14.* Studia semitica neerlandica 41. Assen: Van Gorcum, 2000. 325–33. **Gammie, John G.** "The Angelology and Demonology in the Septuagint of the Book of Job." *HUCA* 56 (1985) 1–19. **Gibson, John C. L.** "Eliphaz the Temanite: Portrait of a Hebrew Philosopher." *SJT* 28 (1975) 259–72. **Gorringe, Timothy J.** "Job and the Pharisees." *Int* 40 (1986) 17–28. **Harding, James E.** "A Spirit of Deception in Job 4:15? Interpretive Indeterminacy and Eliphaz's Vision." *BibInt* 13 (2005) 137–66. **Hoffman, Y.** "The Use of Equivocal Words in the First Speech of Eliphaz (Job 4–5)." *VT* 30 (1980) 114–18. **Irwin, William H.** "Conflicting Parallelism in Job 5,13; Isa 30,28, Isa 32,7." *Bib* 76 (1995) 72–74. **Lugt, Pieter van der.** "Stanza-Structure and Word-Repetition in Job 3–14." *JSOT* 40 (1988) 3–38. **Lyserius (Lyser), Wilhelm.** *In Caput IV. Jobi. Quaestio I. Unde certo colligi posit, visionem aliquam vere divinam esse?* Wittenberg, 1631.

 Mastin, B. A. "A Re-Examination of an Alleged Orthographic Feature in 4Q Targum Job." *RevQ* 11 (1984) 583–84. **Miller, James E.** "The Vision of Eliphaz as Foreshadowing in the Book of Job." *PrGLM* 9 (1989) 98–112. **Orlinsky, H. M.** "Job 5,8, A Problem in Greek-Hebrew Mythology." *JQR* 25 (1935) 271–78. **Paul, Shalom M.** "Unrecognized Biblical Legal Idioms in the Light of Comparative Akkadian Expressions" [incl. Job 5:8]. *RB* 86 (1979) 231–39. **Pfister, Xaver.** "Zurechtgewiesen—nicht verstanden. Elifas und Hiob (Hiob 4–5 und 6–7)." In *Hiob. Ökumenischer Arbeitskreis für Bibelarbeit.* Ed. Regina Berger-Lutz. Bibelarbeit in der Gemeinde 7. Basel: F. Reinhardt, 1989. 161–80. **Pinker, Aron.** "Fear of Fear in Job 4:14." *BN* 130 (2006) 31–43. **Reifler, Erwin.** "Semantic Parallelisms in Job 5." *JBQ* 26 (1998) 143–48. **Robinson, Douglas Fred.** "A Strophic Analysis of Job 4–5." In *From Babel to Babylon: Essays on Biblical History and Literature in Honour of Brian Peckham.* Ed. Joyce Rilett Wood, John E. Harvey, and Mark Leuchter. LHB/OTS 455. New York; London: T. & T. Clark, 2006. 320–31. **Sasson, Victor.** "Two Unrecognized Terms in the Plaster Texts from Deir Alla" [tm; smr]. *PEQ* 117 (1985) 102–3. **Scherer, Andreas.** *Lästiger Trost. Ein Gang durch die Eliphas-Reden im Hiobbuch.* Biblisch-theologische Studien 98. Neukirchen–Vluyn: Neukirchener Verlag, 2008. **Smith, Gary V.** "Job iv 12–21: Is It Eliphaz's Vision?" *VT* 40 (1990) 453–63. **Snoek, J.** *Antwoorden op het lijden. Een bijdrage aan de discussie over contextueel bijbellezen: Job 4–5 in het licht van opvattingen van Nicaraguaanse pinkstergelovigen.* Gorinchem: Narratio, 2000. **Spicer, Tobias.** "Remarks on the Vision of Eliphaz" [Job 4:18; 15:15]. *Methodist Magazine* 7 (1824) 453–55. **Tsoi, Jonathan T. P.** "The Vision of Eliphaz (Job 4:12–21): An Irony of Human Life." *Theology and Life* 25 (2002) 155–82. **Waddle, Sharon Hels.** *Dubious Praise: The Form and Context of the Participial Hymns in Job 4–14* [5:9–16; 9:5–10; 12:13–25]. Diss. Vanderbilt, 1987. **Wolfers, David.** "A Note on Job v 3." *VT* 43 (1993) 274–76. ———. "Sparks Flying? Job 5:7." *JBQ* 23 (1995) 3–8.

Chapters 6–7

Altenbergerus, Christianus. *Commentarius rabbinicus in cap. VI et VII Hiobi* [translation of Gersonides' commentary]. Leipzig, 1705. **Beuken, W. A. M.** "Job's Imprecation as the Cradle of a New Religious Discourse. The Perplexing Impact of the Semantic Correspondences between Job 3, Job 4–5 and Job 6–7." In *The Book of Job*. Ed. W. A. M. Beuken. BETL 114. Leuven: Leuven University Press, 1994. 4–78. **Diewert, David A.** "Job 7:12: Yam, Tannin and the Surveillance of Job." *JBL* 106 (1987) 203–15. **Fishbane, Michael.** "The Book of Job and Inner-Biblical Discourse." In *The Voice from the Whirlwind: Interpreting the Book of Job*. Ed. Leo G. Perdue and Clark Gilpin. Nashville: Abingdon Press, 1992. 86–98. **Fokkelman, J. P.** *Major Poems of the Hebrew Bible: At the Interface of Prosody and Structural Analysis.* II. *85 Psalms and Job 4–14.* Studia semitica neerlandica 41. Assen: Van Gorcum, 2000. 333–42. **Girard, René.** "'The Ancient Trail Trodden by the Wicked.' Job as Scapegoat." *Semeia* 33 (1985) 13–41. **Gorea, M.** "Job 7,8: une contribution à la problématique des versets portant astérisque dans la Septante." In *The Book of Job*. Ed. W. A. M. Beuken. BETL 114. Leuven: Leuven University Press, 1994. 430–34. **Hagedorn, Ursula, and Dieter Hagedorn.** "Neue Fragmente des Hiobkommentars Didymos' des Blinden?" In *Miscellanea papyrologica in occasione del bicentenario dell'edizione della Charta Borgiana*. Ed. Mario Capasso, Gabriella Messeri Savorelli, and Rosario Pintaudi. Florence: Edizioni Gonnelli, 1990. 245–54. **Janzen, J. Gerald.** "Another Look at God's Watch over Job (7:12)." *JBL* 108 (1989) 109–14. **Klug, Eugene F.** "The Doctrine of Man: Christian Anthropology." *CTQ* 48 (1984) 141–52. **Lugt, Pieter van der.** "Stanza-Structure and Word-Repetition in Job 3–14." *JSOT* 40 (1988) 3–38. **Mettinger, Tryggve N. D.** "Intertextuality: Allusion and Vertical Context Systems in Some Job Passages" [Job 7; 16:7–17; 19:6–12]. In *Of Prophets' Visions and the Wisdom of Sages*. Ed. Heather A. McKay and David J. A. Clines. JSOTSup 162. Sheffield: JSOT Press, 1993. 257–80. **Perdue, Leo G.** "Job's Assault on Creation." *HAR* 10 (1987) 295–315. ———. "Metaphorical Theology in the Book of Job: Theological Anthropology in the First Cycle of Job's Speeches (Job 3; 6–7; 9–10)." In *The Book of Job*. Ed. W. A. M. Beuken. BETL 114. Leuven: Leuven University Press, 1994. 129–56. **Pfister, Xaver.** "Zurechtgewiesen—nicht verstanden. Elifas und Hiob (Hiob 4–5 und 6–7)." In *Hiob. Ökumenischer Arbeitskreis für Bibelarbeit*. Ed. Regina Berger-Lutz. Bibelarbeit in der Gemeinde 7. Basel: F. Reinhardt, 1989. 161–80. **Priest, John.** "Job and J.B.: The Goodness of God or the Godness of Good?" *Horizons* 12 (1985) 265–83. **Rozelaar, Marc.** "Het boek Job in nederlandse verzen" [Job 7]. *NedTTs* 39 (1985) 18–20. **Seidl, Theodor.** "Wunschsätze mit mi yittin im Biblischen Hebräisch." In *Sachverhalt und Zeitbezug. Semitistische und alttestamentliche Studien Adolf Denz zum 65. Geburtstag.* Ed. Rüdiger Bartelmus and Norbert Nebes. Jenaer Beiträge zum Vorderen Orient 4. Wiesbaden: Harrassowitz, 2001. 129–42. **Sutcliffe, E. F.** "Notes on Job, Textual and Exegetical. 6, 18; 11, 12; 31, 35; 34, 17. 20; 36, 27–33; 37, 1." *Bib* 30 (1949) 66–90. **Szpek, Heidi M.** "The Peshitta on Job 7:6: 'My Days Are Swifter (?) Than an אׇרִג'." *JBL* 113 (1994) 287–97. **Van Leeuwen, Raymond C.** "Psalm 8.5 and Job 7.17–18: A Mistaken Scholarly Commonplace?" In *The World of the Aramaeans*. I. *Biblical Studies in Honor of Paul-Eugène Dion*. Ed. P. M. Michèle Daviau, John W. Wevers, and Michael Weigl. JSOTSup 324. Sheffield: Sheffield Academic Press, 2001. 211–15. **Wedel, Theodore O.** "I hate myself" [Job 7:20]. *Int* 5 (1951) 427–31.

Chapter 8

Fokkelman, J. P. *Major Poems of the Hebrew Bible: At the Interface of Prosody and Structural Analysis.* II. *85 Psalms and Job 4–14.* Studia semitica neerlandica 41. Assen: Van Gorcum, 2000. 343–45. **Girard, René.** "'The Ancient Trail Trodden by the Wicked.' Job as Scapegoat." *Semeia* 33 (1985) 13–41. **Lugt, Pieter van der.** "Stanza-Structure and Word-Repetition in Job 3–14." *JSOT* 40 (1988) 3–38.

Chapters 9–10

Brown, William P. "Creatio corporis and the Rhetoric of Defense in Job 10 and Psalm 139." In *God Who Creates: Essays in Honor of W. Sibley Towner.* Ed. William P. Brown and S. Dean McBride. Grand Rapids: W. B. Eerdmans, 2000. 107–24. **Brueggemann, Walter.** "Theodicy in a Social Dimension" [Job]. *JSOT* 33 (1985) 3–25. **Carroll, Robert P.** "Theodicy and the Community: The Text and Subtext of Jeremiah 5:1–6" [incl. Job 9:22–24]. In *Prophets, Worship and Theodicy: Studies in Prophetism, Biblical Theology and Structural and Rhetorical Analysis and on the Place of Music in Worship.* OTS 23. Leiden: E. J. Brill, 1984. 19–38. **Chalmers, Aaron.** "'There is no deliverer (from my hand)': A Formula Analysis" [Job 10:5]. *VT* 55 (2005) 287–92. **Crenshaw, James L.** "The Influence of the Wise upon Amos: The Doxologies of Amos and Job 5:9–16, 9:5–10." *ZAW* 79 (1967) 42–52. **Egger-Wenzel, R.** *Von der Freiheit Gottes, anders zu sein. Die zentrale Rolle der Kapitel 9 und 10 für das Ijobbuch.* Forschung zur Bibel 83. Würzburg: Echter Verlag, 1998. **Fokkelman, J. P.** *Major Poems of the Hebrew Bible: At the Interface of Prosody and Structural Analysis.* II. *85 Psalms and Job 4–14.* Studia semitica neerlandica 41. Assen: Van Gorcum, 2000. 346–58. **Frevel, Christian.** "Die Entstehung des Menschen: Anmerkungen zum Vergleich der Menschwerdung mit der Kaseherstellung in Ijob 10,10." *BN* 130 (2006) 45–57. **Funke-Reuter, A.** *Septuaginta-exegetische Studien am Beispiel von Hiob 9 und 10.* Diss. Leipzig, 1992. **Jenks, Alan W.** "Theological Presuppositions of Israel's Wisdom Literature" [incl. Job 9:9–12]. *HBT* 7 (1985) 43–75. **Loader, James Alfred.** "Job 9:5–10 as a Quasi-Hymn." *OTEss* 14 (2001) 76–88. **Lugt, Pieter van der.** "Stanza-Structure and Word-Repetition in Job 3–14." *JSOT* 40 (1988) 3–38. **Michel, Walter L.** "Ṣlmwt, 'deep darkness' or 'shadow of death'?" [Job 10:21, 22]. *BibRes* 29 (1984) 5–20. **Perdue, Leo G.** "Metaphorical Theology in the Book of Job: Theological Anthropology in the First Cycle of Job's Speeches (Job 3; 6–7; 9–10)." In *The Book of Job.* Ed. W. A. M. Beuken. BETL 114. Leuven: Leuven University Press, 1994. 129–56. **Pope, Marvin H.** "The Word שחה in Job 9:31." *JBL* 83 (1964) 269–78. **Priest, John.** "Job and J.B.: The Goodness of God or the Godness of Good?" *Horizons* 12 (1985) 265–83. **Taguchi, Mayumi.** "A Middle English Penitential Treatise on Job 10:20–22, *Dimitte me, Domine ...*" *Mediaeval Studies* 67 (2005) 157–217. **Waddle, Sharon Hels.** *Dubious Praise: The Form and Context of the Participial Hymns in Job 4–14* [5:9–16; 9:5–10; 12:13–25]. Diss. Vanderbilt, 1987. **Wilson, Lindsay.** "Realistic Hope or Imaginative Exploration: The Identity of Job's Arbiter." *Pacifica* 9 (1996) 243–52.

Chapter 11

Fokkelman, J. P. *Major Poems of the Hebrew Bible: At the Interface of Prosody and Structural Analysis.* II. *85 Psalms and Job 4–14.* Studia semitica neerlandica 41. Assen: Van Gorcum, 2000. 359–61. **Lugt, Pieter van der.** "Stanza-Structure and Word-Repetition in Job 3–14." *JSOT* 40 (1988) 3–38. **Regt, L. J. de.** "Implications of Rhetorical Questions in Strophes in Job 11 and 15." In *The Book of Job.* Ed. W. A. M. Beuken. BETL 114. Leuven: Leuven University Press, 1994. 321–28. **Seidl, Theodor.** "Wunschsätze mit mi yittin im Biblischen Hebräisch ." In *Sachverhalt und Zeitbezug. Semitistische und alttestamentliche Studien Adolf Denz zum 65. Geburtstag.* Ed. Rüdiger Bartelmus and Norbert Nebes. Jenaer Beiträge zum Vorderen Orient 4. Wiesbaden: Harrassowitz, 2001. 129–42. **Sokolow, Moshe.** "*Ta'ufa kabboqer tihyeh:* The Vicissitudes of Rashi's Commentary to Job 11:17." *JANES* 18 (1986) 87–89. **Tur-Sinai, N. H. [Torczyner, H.].** "Hiob xi und die Sprache der Amarna-Briefe." *BO* 9 (1952) 162–63.

Chapters 12–14

Baillie, Joanna. "Job, XIII. 15." In *The Dramatic and Poetical Works of Joanna Baillie.* London: Longman, Brown, Green, & Longmans, 1851. **Brueggemann, Walter.**

"Theodicy in a Social Dimension" [Job]. *JSOT* 33 (1985) 3–25. **Chin, Catherine.** "Job and the Injustice of God: Implicit Arguments in Job 13:17–14:12." *JSOT* 64 (1994) 91–101. **Crenshaw, James L.** "Flirting with the Language of Prayer (Job 14.13–17)." In *Worship and the Hebrew Bible: Essays in Honour of John T. Willis.* Ed. M. Patrick Graham, Rick R. Marrs, and Steven L. McKenzie. JSOTSup 284. Sheffield: Sheffield Academic Press, 1999. 110–23 [= his *Prophets, Sages, and Poets.* St Louis, MO: Chalice Press, 2006. 6–13]. **Dahood, Mitchell J.** "Ugaritic *ušn,* Job 12,10 and 11QPs^aPlea 3–4." *Bib* 47 (1966) 107–8. **Dohm, Kurt.** "Ohne Gott leben? Text: Hiob 14,1–6." In *Gottesdienstpraxis.* Ed. Erhard Domay and Horst Nitschke. Gütersloh: Gütersloher Verlag, 2003. 105–10. **Fokkelman, J. P.** *Major Poems of the Hebrew Bible: At the Interface of Prosody and Structural Analysis.* II. *85 Psalms and Job 4–14.* Studia semitica neerlandica 41. Assen: Van Gorcum, 2000. 362–79. **Glazner, A.** "Job, ch. 12: A Bible Puzzle" [Heb.]. *BMik* 23 (1977–78) 483–95, 523. **Gollinger, Hildegard.** "'Wenn einer stirbt, lebt er dann wieder auf?' (Ijob 14,14): Zum alttestamentlich-jüdischen Hintergrund der Deutung der dem Kreuzestod nachfolgenden Erfahrung der Jünger mit dem Bekenntnis zur Auferweckung Jesu." In *Auferstehung Jesu–Auferstehung der Christen. Deutung des Osterglaubens.* Ed. Lorenz Oberlinner. Freiburg: Herder, 1986. **Griffiths, John G.** "The Idea of Posthumous Judgement in Israel and Egypt" [Job 14:7–10]. In *Fontes atque pontes. Eine Festgabe für H. Brunner.* Ed. M. Görg. Wiesbaden: Harrassowitz, 1983. 186–204. **Hamilton, W. T.** "Difficult Texts from Job" [Job 14:10–12]. In *Difficult Texts of the Old Testament Explained.* Ed. Wendell Winkler. Hurst, TX: Winkler Publications, 1982. 301–10. **Hecke, Pierre van.** "Job xii 18a: Text and Interpretation." *VT* 54 (2004) 269–73. **Heick, O. W.** "If a man die, shall he live again?" *LuthQ* 17 (1965) 99–110. **Jenks, Alan W.** "Theological Presuppositions of Israel's Wisdom Literature" [incl. Job 13:15]. *HBT* 7 (1985) 43–75.

Lang, Bernhard. "Afterlife: Ancient Israel's Changing Vision of the World Beyond." *BibRev* 4 (1988) 12–23. **Lugt, Pieter van der.** "Stanza-Structure and Word-Repetition in Job 3–14." *JSOT* 40 (1988) 3–38. **Michel, Walter L.** "Ṣlmwt, 'deep darkness' or 'shadow of death'?" [Job 12:22]. *BibRes* 29 (1984) 5–20. **Murphy, Roland E.** "Wisdom and Creation." *JBL* 104 (1985) 3–11. **Priest, John.** "Job and J.B.: The Goodness of God or the Godness of Good?" *Horizons* 12 (1985) 265–83. **Schmidt, Eva Renate.** "Hiob 14: Hiob-Träumer und Rebell." In *Feministisch gelesen.* 2. *Ausgewählte Bibeltexte für Gruppen und Gemeinden, Gebete für den Gottesdienst.* Ed. Eva Renate Schmidt, Mieke Korenhof, and Renate Jost. Stuttgart: Kreuz Verlag, 1989. 138–48. **Schnocks, Johannes.** "The Hope for Resurrection in the Book of Job." In *The Septuagint and Messianism.* Ed. Michael A. Knibb. BETL 195. Leuven: Leuven University Press, 2006. 291–99. **Seidl, Theodor.** "Wunschsätze mit mi yittin im Biblischen Hebräisch." In *Sachverhalt und Zeitbezug. Semitistische und alttestamentliche Studien Adolf Denz zum 65. Geburtstag.* Ed. Rüdiger Bartelmus and Norbert Nebes. Jenaer Beiträge zum Vorderen Orient 4. Wiesbaden: Harrassowitz, 2001. 129–42. **Stevenson, William B.** "Job 13:9–11: A New Interpretation." *ExpT* 62 (1950) 93. **Swanepoel, M. G.** "Job 12– An(other) Anticipation of the Voice from the Whirlwind?" *OTEss* ns 4 (1991) 192–205. **Waddle, Sharon Hels.** *Dubious Praise: The Form and Context of the Participial Hymns in Job 4–14* [5:9–16; 9:5–10; 12:13–25]. Diss. Vanderbilt, 1987. **Wolfers, David.** "'Greek' Logic in the Book of Job." *Dor* 15 (1986–87) 166–72. ———. "Reflections on Job xii." *VT* 44 (1994) 401–6. ———. "Science in the Book of Job" [incl. Job 14:18–19] *JBQ* 19 (1990–91) 18–21.

Chapter 15

Emerton, John A. "The Meaning of the Verb ḥāmas in Jeremiah 13,22" [Job 15:33]. In *Prophet und Prophetenbuch: Festschrift für Otto Kaiser zum 65. Geburtstag.* Ed. Volkmar Fritz. BZAW 185. Berlin: W. de Gruyter, 1989. 19–28. **Gammie, John G.** "The Angelology and Demonology in the Septuagint of the Book of Job." *HUCA* 56 (1985) 1–19. **Girard, René.** "'The Ancient Trail Trodden by the Wicked.' Job as Scapegoat." *Semeia* 33 (1985) 13–41. **Paul, Shalom M.** "A Double Entendre in Job 15:32 in the Light of Akkadian." In

Emanuel: Studies in Hebrew Bible, Septuagint, and Dead Sea Scrolls in Honor of Emanuel Tov. Ed. Shalom M. Paul, Robert A. Kraft, Lawrence H. Schiffman, and Weston W. Fields. Leiden: Brill, 2003. 755–57. **Regt, L. J. de.** "Implications of Rhetorical Questions in Strophes in Job 11 and 15." In *The Book of Job.* Ed. W. A. M. Beuken. BETL 114. Leuven: Leuven University Press, 1994. 321–28. **Scherer, Andreas.** *Lästiger Trost. Ein Gang durch die Eliphas-Reden im Hiobbuch.* Biblisch-theologische Studien 98. Neukirchen–Vluyn: Neukirchener Verlag, 2008. **Wolfers, David.** "Job 15,4–5: An Exploration." In *The Book of Job.* Ed. W. A. M. Beuken. BETL 114. Leuven: Leuven University Press, 1994. 382–86.

Chapters 16–17

Bastiaens, Jean Charles. "The Language of Suffering in Job 16–19 and in the Suffering Servant Passages in Deutero-Isaiah." In *Studies in the Book of Isaiah.* Ed. J. van Ruiten and M. Vervenne. BETL 132. Leuven: Leuven University Press, 1997. 421–32. **Blommerde, A. C. M.** "The Broken Construct Chain, Further Examples" [Job 17:11; 29:18; Isa 27:9]. *Bib* 55 (1974) 549–52. **Girard, René.** "'The Ancient Trail Trodden by the Wicked.' Job as Scapegoat." *Semeia* 33 (1985) 13–41. **Griffiths, John G.** "The Idea of Posthumous Judgement in Israel and Egypt" [Job 16:19–22]. In *Fontes atque pontes. Eine Festgabe für H. Brunner.* Ed. M. Görg. Wiesbaden: Harrassowitz, 1983. 186–204. **Gross, Carl D.** "Notes on the Meaning of Job 16:20." *BiTrans* 43 (1992) 236–41. **Kummerow, David.** "Job, Hopeful or Hopeless? The Significance of בֹּ in Job 16:19 and Job's Changing Conceptions of Death." *JHS* 5 (2004). **Mettinger, Tryggve N. D.** "Intertextuality: Allusion and Vertical Context Systems in Some Job Passages" [Job 7; 16:7–17; 19:6–12]. In *Of Prophets' Visions and the Wisdom of Sages.* Ed. Heather A. McKay and David J. A. Clines. JSOTSup 162. Sheffield: JSOT Press, 1993. 257–80. **Michel, Andreas.** "Herausstellungsstrukturen in den Streitreden des Ijob im Vergleich zu den Freunden (Ijob 3–25) im Ausgang von Ijob 16,7–14." In *Literatur- und sprachwissenschaftliche Beiträge zu alttestamentlichen Texten. Symposion in Hólar í Hjaltadal, 16.–19. Mai 2005. Wolfgang Richter zum 80. Geburtstag.* Ed. Sigurður Örn Steingrímsson and Kristinn Ólason. St Ottilien: Eos Verlag, 2007. 123–36. **Michel, Walter L.** "Ṣlmwt, 'deep darkness' or 'shadow of death'?" [Job 16:16]. *BibRes* 29 (1984) 5–20. **Priest, John.** "Job and J.B.: The Goodness of God or the Godness of Good?" *Horizons* 12 (1985) 265–83. **Wilson, Lindsay.** "Realistic Hope or Imaginative Exploration: The Identity of Job's Arbiter." *Pacifica* 9 (1996) 243–52.

Chapter 18

Bastiaens, Jean Charles. "The Language of Suffering in Job 16–19 and in the Suffering Servant Passages in Deutero-Isaiah." In *Studies in the Book of Isaiah.* Ed. J. van Ruiten and M. Vervenne. BETL 132. Leuven: Leuven University Press, 1997. 421–32. **Burns, J. Barclay.** "The Mythological Background to Job 18,5–61." *BeO* 33 (1991) 129–40. **Noegel, Scott B.** "Another Look at Job 18:2, 3." *JBQ* 23 (1995) 159–61. **Weymann, Volker.** "Verwehrte Klage-Wege ins Vertrauen. Bildad und Hiob (Hiob 18 und 19)." In *Hiob. Ökumenischer Arbeitskreis für Bibelarbeit.* Ed. Regina Berger-Lutz. Bibelarbeit in der Gemeinde 7. Basel: F. Reinhardt, 1989. 181–212. **Wolfers, David.** "Three Singular Plurals, Job 18:2, 3." *JBQ* 22 (1993–94) 21–25. **Wyatt, Nicolas.** "The Expression bĕkôr māwet in Job xviii 13 and Its Mythological Background." *VT* 40 (1990) 207–16. **Zuckerman, Bruce.** "For Your Sake: A Case Study in Aramaic Semantics" [11 QtgJob 1:7]. *JANES* 15 (1983) 119–29.

Chapter 19

Balentine, Samuel E. "Who Will Be Job's Redeemer?" *PerspRelSt* 26 (1999) 269–89. **Bastiaens, Jean Charles.** "The Language of Suffering in Job 16–19 and in the

Suffering Servant Passages in Deutero-Isaiah." In *Studies in the Book of Isaiah*. Ed. J. van Ruiten and M. Vervenne. BETL 132. Leuven: Leuven University Press, 1997. 421–32. **Ceballos Atienza, Antonio.** "La argumentación teológico-bíblica en la Biblia Parva de San Pedro Pascual." *EstBíb* ns 42 (1984) 89–136. **Chardonnens, Denis.** "L'espérance de la resurrection selon Thomas d'Aquin, commentateur du Livre de Job: 'Dans ma chair, je verrai Dieu' (Jb 19,26)." In *Ordo sapientiae et amoris: image et message de Saint Thomas d'Aquin à travers les récentes études historiques, herméneutiques et doctrinales. Hommage au professeur Jean Pierre Torrell, OP, à l'occasion de son 65e anniversaire*. Ed. Carlos J. Pinto de Oliveira. Freiburg, Switzerland: Universitätsverlag, 1993. 65–83. **Christo, Gordon E.** *The Eschatological Judgment in Job 19:21–29: An Exegetical Study*. Diss. Andrews, 1992 [abstract: *AUSS* 30 (1992) 157]. **Costard, George.** *Some Observations Tending to Illustrate the Book of Job; and in Particular the Words I Know That My Redeemer Liveth, &c. Job XIX. 25*. Oxford: Richard Clements, 1747. **Deuel, David C.** "Job 19:25 and Job 23:10 Revisited: An Exegetical Note." *MastSemJ* 5 (1994) 97–99. **Doukhan, Jacques.** "Radioscopy of a Resurrection. The Meaning of *niqqᵉpû zō't* in Job 19:26." *AUSS* 34 (1996) 187–93. **Ebach, Jürgen.** "Die 'Schrift' in Hiob 19,23." In *Prophetie und geschichtliche Wirklichkeit im alten Israel: Festschrift für Siegfried Herrmann zum 65. Geburtstag*. Ed. Rüdiger Liwak and Siegfried Wagner. Stuttgart: Kohlhammer, 1991. 99–121 [= his *Hiobs Post. Gesammelte Aufsätze zum Hiobbuch zu Themen biblischer Theologie und zur Methodik der Exegese*. Neukirchen–Vluyn: Neukirchener Verlag, 1995. 32–54]. **Gibson, J. C. L.** "I Know That My Redeemer Liveth." In *New Heaven and New Earth, Prophecy and the Millennium: Essays in Honour of Anthony Gelston*. Ed. P. J. Harland and C. T. R. Hayward. VTSup 77. Leiden: Brill, 1999. 53–60. **Gosling, Frank A.** "An Unsafe Investigation of Job 19:25." *JNSL* 24 (1998) 157–66. **Greenspoon, L. J.** "The Origins of the Idea of Resurrection." In *Traditions in Transformation: Turning Points in Biblical Faith* [Festschrift Frank Moore Cross]. Ed. Baruch Halpern and Jon D. Levenson. Winona Lake, IN: Eisenbrauns, 1981. 247–321. **Griffiths, John G.** "The Idea of Posthumous Judgement in Israel and Egypt" [Job 19:25–27]. In *Fontes atque pontes. Eine Festgabe für H. Brunner*. Ed. M. Görg. Wiesbaden: Harrassowitz, 1983. 186–204.

Hamilton, W. T. "Difficult Texts from Job" [Job 19:25]. In *Difficult Texts of the Old Testament Explained*. Ed. Wendell Winkler. Hurst, TX: Winkler Publications, 1982. 301–10. **Hermisson, Hans-Jürgen.** "'Ich weiss, dass mein Erlöser lebt' (Hiob 19,23–27)." In *Gott und Mensch im Dialog. Festschrift für Otto Kaiser zum 80. Geburtstag*. Ed. Markus Witte. BZAW 345/2. Berlin: de Gruyter, 2004. 2:667–88. **Holman, Jan.** "Does My Redeemer Live or Is My Redeemer the Living God? Some Reflections on the Translation of Job 19,25." In *The Book of Job*. Ed. W. A. M. Beuken. BETL 114. Leuven: Leuven University Press, 1994. 377–81. **Holmius, Jacobus.** *De B. Jobo satisfactionis a Christo in cruce præstandæ vateevangelico, Job. 19, v. 2*. 1763. **Hudal, A.** "Die Auslegung von Job 19,25–27 in der katholischen Exegese." *Katholik* 96 (1916) 331–45. **Jenks, Alan W.** "Theological Presuppositions of Israel's Wisdom Literature" [incl. Job 19:11]. *HBT* 7 (1985) 43–75. **Kessler, Rainer.** "'Ich weiss, dass mein Erlöser lebet': Sozialgeschichtlicher Hintergrund und theologische Bedeutung der Löser-Vorstellung in Hiob 19,25." *ZTK* 89 (1992) 139–58. **Kruger, Paul A.** "Job 18:11B: A Conceptualisation of the Emotion of Fear?" *JNSL* 28 (2002) 143–49. **Magdalene, F. Rachel.** "Who Is Job's Redeemer? Job 19:25 in Light of Neo-Babylonian Law." *ZAR* 10 (2004) 292–316. **Mende, Theresia.** "'Ich weiss, dass mein Erlöser lebt' (Ijob 19,25): Ijobs Hoffnung und Vertrauen in der Prüfung des Leidens." *TTZ* 99 (1990) 15–35. **Mettinger, Tryggve N. D.** "Intertextuality: Allusion and Vertical Context Systems in Some Job Passages" [Job 7; 16:7–17; 19:6–12]. In *Of Prophets' Visions and the Wisdom of Sages*. Ed. Heather A. McKay and David J. A. Clines. JSOTSup 162. Sheffield: JSOT Press, 1993. 257–80. **Michel, W. L.** "Confidence and Despair: Job 19,25–27 in the Light of Northwest Semitic Studies." In *The Book of Job*. Ed. W. A. M. Beuken. BETL 114. Leuven: Leuven University Press, 1994. 157–81. **Moore, Michael S.** "Job's Texts of Terror" [Job 19:29]. *CBQ* 55 (1993) 662–75. **Muñoz García de Iturrospe, M. Teresa.** "La Biblia y la epigrafía cristiana visigoda: Job 19,25–26." In *IV*

Simposio bíblico español (i Ibero-Americano). Biblia y culturas 1. Ed. J. R. Ayaso Martínez, V. Collado Bertomeu, L. Ferre Cano, et al. Valencia: Area de estudios hebreos, Universidad de Granada, 1993. 117–24.

Oblath, Michael D. "Job's Advocate: A Tempting Suggestion." *BulBibRes* 9 (1999) 189–201. **Ollenburger, Ben C.** "If Mortals Die, Will They Live Again? The Old Testament and Resurrection." In *Resurrection: Papers from the North Park Symposium on Theological Interpretation of Scripture, North Park Theological Seminary, Chicago, Illinois— October 8–10, 1993* [= *Ex auditu* 9 (1993)] 29–44. **Parry, R.** *A Defense of the Lord Bishop of London's Interpretation of the Famous Text in the Book of Job* [Job 19:25] … *against the Exceptions of the Bishop of Gloucester, and the "Examiner" of the Bishop of London's Principles*…. Northampton, 1760. **Pihringer, Christian.** *Das von Hiob in seinem Erlöser tröstlich ergriffene Erlösungs Recht: Einer Volck-reichen und ansehnlichen Trauer-Versamlung* [Job 19:25]. Altdorff: Schönnerstädts, 1685. **Ratner, Robert.** "The 'Feminine Takes Precedence' Syntagm and Job 19,15." *ZAW* 102 (1990) 238–51. **Rehefelden, Johann.** *Fester und unüberwindlicher Glaubens Schildt eines rechtschaffenen Christen auß den Worten Job., 19 v. 25, 26, 27 gefasset* … Erfurt, 1645. **Sato, Mariko.** *An Interpretation of Job 19:23–27.* Diss. Lancaster Bible College, 2003. **Schnocks, Johannes.** "The Hope for Resurrection in the Book of Job." In *The Septuagint and Messianism.* Ed. Michael A. Knibb. BETL 195. Leuven: Leuven University Press, 2006. 291–99. **Seidl, Theodor.** "Wunschsätze mit mi yittin im Biblischen Hebräisch." In *Sachverhalt und Zeitbezug. Semitistische und alttestamentliche Studien Adolf Denz zum 65. Geburtstag.* Ed. Rüdiger Bartelmus and Norbert Nebes. Jenaer Beiträge zum Vorderen Orient 4. Wiesbaden: Harrassowitz, 2001. 129–42. **Seow, Choon Leong.** "Job's *go'el*, Again." In *Gott und Mensch im Dialog: Festschrift für Otto Kaiser zum 80. Geburtstag.* Ed. Markus Witte. BZAW 345. Berlin: Walter de Gruyter, 2004. 2:689–709. **Tooley, Henry.** "Remarks on Job XIX." *MethRev* 10 (1827) 25–26. **Tremblay, Hervé.** *Job 19,25–27 dans la septante et chez les pères grecs. Unanimité d'une tradition.* Etudes bibliques ns 47. Paris: J. Gabalda, 2002. **Trudinger, Paul.** "The Misleading Consequences of Biblical Mistranslation: A Tale of Two Texts" [Job 19:25–27 and Isa 1:18 in KJV and RSV]. *Faith and Freedom* 52 (1999) 119–24. **Velthusen, Johann Kaspar.** *Exercitationes criticae in Jobi cap. XIX, 23–29. Accedit strictior expositio reliquarum ejusdem libri sententiarum quibus religionis antiquissimae vestigia produntur.* Lemgo: Meyer, 1772. **Weymann, Volker.** "Verwehrte Klage-Wege ins Vertrauen. Bildad und Hiob (Hiob 18 und 19)." In *Hiob. Ökumenischer Arbeitskreis für Bibelarbeit.* Ed. Regina Berger-Lutz. Bibelarbeit in der Gemeinde 7. Basel: F. Reinhardt, 1989. 181–212. **Wilson, Lindsay.** "Realistic Hope or Imaginative Exploration: The Identity of Job's Arbiter." *Pacifica* 9 (1996) 243–52. **Wolfers, David.** "Jot, Tittle and Waw (Job 19:25)." *Dor* 17 (1988–89) 230–36.

Chapter 20

Gammie, John G. "The Angelology and Demonology in the Septuagint of the Book of Job." *HUCA* 56 (1985) 1–19. **Pinker, Aron.** "On the Meaning of קשׁת נחושׁה" [Job 20:24]. *JHS* 5 (2004). **Priest, John.** "Job and J.B.: The Goodness of God or the Godness of Good?" *Horizons* 12 (1985) 265–83.

Chapter 21

Willi-Plein, Ina. "Hiobs immer aktuelle Frage." In *Der Herr ist einer, unser gemeinsames Erbe.* Ed. Karl-Johan Illman and Jukka Thurén. Åbo: Åbo Akademi, 1979. 122–36.

Chapter 22

Scherer, Andreas. *Lästiger Trost. Ein Gang durch die Eliphas-Reden im Hiobbuch.* Biblisch-theologische Studien 98. Neukirchen–Vluyn: Neukirchener Verlag, 2008.

Chapters 23–24

Egan, Claire Marie. *The Integrity of Job: A Contextual Study of Job Chapters 24–28.* Diss. Birmingham, 2002. **Grenzer, Matthias.** "Die Armenthematik in Ijob 24." In *Das Buch Ijob: Gesamtdeutungen—Einzeltexte—zentrale Themen.* Ed. Theodor Seidl and Stephanie Ernst. Österreichische biblische Studien 31. Frankfurt: Peter Lang, 2007. 229–78. **Jenks, Alan W.** "Theological Presuppositions of Israel's Wisdom Literature" [incl. Job 23:3–7, 12]. *HBT* 7 (1985) 43–75. **Seidl, Theodor.** "Wunschsätze mit mi yittin im Biblischen Hebräisch." In *Sachverhalt und Zeitbezug. Semitistische und alttestamentliche Studien Adolf Denz zum 65. Geburtstag.* Ed. Rüdiger Bartelmus and Norbert Nebes. Jenaer Beiträge zum Vorderen Orient 4. Wiesbaden: Harrassowitz, 2001. 129–42.

Chapters 25–26

Egan, Claire Marie. *The Integrity of Job: A Contextual Study of Job Chapters 24–28.* Diss. Birmingham, 2002. **Jenks, Alan W.** "Theological Presuppositions of Israel's Wisdom Literature" [incl. Job 26:14]. *HBT* 7 (1985) 43–75. **Slotki, Israel W.** "A Study of רעם" [Job 26:14; 37:4; 39:19]. *AJSL* 37 (1920–21) 149–55.

Chapter 27:1–6

Egan, Claire Marie. *The Integrity of Job: A Contextual Study of Job Chapters 24–28.* Diss. Birmingham, 2002. **Jenks, Alan W.** "Theological Presuppositions of Israel's Wisdom Literature" [incl. Job 27:2–6]. *HBT* 7 (1985) 43–75.

Chapter 27:7–23

Egan, Claire Marie. *The Integrity of Job: A Contextual Study of Job Chapters 24–28.* Diss. Birmingham, 2002. **Sasson, Victor.** "An Edomite Joban Text with a Biblical Joban Parallel" [Job 27:10–17]. *ZAW* 117 (2005) 601–15. **Smick, Elmer B.** "Architectonics, Structured Poems, and Rhetorical Devices in the Book of Job" [incl. 13:28–14:6; 27–31; 38–41]. In *A Tribute to Gleason Archer.* Ed. Walter C. Kaiser, Jr, and Ronald F. Youngblood. Chicago: Moody Press, 1986. 87–104.

Chapter 28

Bechmann, Ulrike, and Klaus Bieberstein. *Weisheit im Leiden: Ijobs Ringen und das Lied der Weisheit in Ijob 28.* Stuttgart: Katholisches Bibelwerk, 2007. **Egan, Claire Marie.** *The Integrity of Job: A Contextual Study of Job Chapters 24–28.* Diss. Birmingham, 2002. **Jenks, Alan W.** "Theological Presuppositions of Israel's Wisdom Literature" [incl. Job 28:12–13]. *HBT* 7 (1985) 43–75. **Lo, Alison.** *Job 28 as Rhetoric: An Analysis of Job 28 in the Context of Job 22–31.* VTSup 97. Leiden: Brill, 2003. **McKane, William.** "The Theology of the Book of Job and Chapter 28 in Particular." In *Gott und Mensch im Dialog: Festschrift für Otto Kaiser zum 80. Geburtstag.* Ed. Markus Witte. BZAW 345. Berlin: Walter de Gruyter, 2004. 2:711–22. **Müllner, Ilse.** "Der Ort des Verstehens. Ijob 28 als Teil der Erkenntnisdiskussion des Ijob-buchs." In *Das Buch Ijob: Gesamtdeutungen— Einzeltexte—zentrale Themen.* Ed. Theodor Seidl and Stephanie Ernst. Österreichischc biblische Studien 31. Frankfurt: Peter Lang, 2007. 57–83. **Pareau, Johann Hendrik.** *Commentatio de immortalitatis ac vitae futurae notitiis ab antiquissimo Jobi scriptore in suos usus adhibitis. Accedit sermo Jobi de sapientia mortuis magis cognita quam vivis, sive Jobeidis caput XXVIII, philologice et critice illustratum.* Deventer: L. A. Karsenbergh, 1807. **Viviers, Hendrik.** "Why Was Job 28 Included in the Book of Job? A Rhetorical-Critical

Investigation." *Ekklesiastikos pharos* 77 (1) (1995) 1–9. **Wendland, E. R.** "'Where in the world can *wisdom* be found?' (Job 28:12, 20). A Textual and Contextual Survey of Job 28 in Relation to Its Communicative Setting, Ancient (ANE) and Modern (Africa)." *JSem* 12 (2003) 1–33, 151–71. **Wolde, Ellen van.** "Ancient Wisdoms, Present Insights. A Study of Job 28 and Job 38." *SEÅ* 71 (2006) 55–74. ———. "Towards an 'Integrated Approach' in Biblical Studies, Illustrated with a Dialogue between Job 28 and Job 38." In *Congress Volume: Leiden, 2004*. VTSup 109. Ed. André Lemaire. Leiden: Brill, 2006. 355–80.

Chapters 29–31

Crenshaw, James L. "A Good Man's Code of Ethics (Job 31)." In his *Prophets, Sages, and Poets*. St Louis, MO: Chalice Press, 2006. 42–45. **Curtis, John Briggs.** "Reflections on Job 31:15." *PrGLM* 20 (2000) 73–79. **Janzen, J. Gerald.** "Job's Oath." *RevExp* 99 (2002) 597–605. **Neville, Richard W.** "A Reassessment of the Radical Nature of Job's Ethic in Job xxxi 13–15." *VT* 53 (2003) 181–200. **Rechenmacher, Hans.** "'taw' und 'sipr' in Ijob 31,35–37." In *Das Buch Ijob: Gesamtdeutungen—Einzeltexte—zentrale Themen*. Ed. Theodor Seidl and Stephanie Ernst. Österreichische biblische Studien 31. Frankfurt: Peter Lang, 2007. 165–80. **Seidl, Theodor.** "Wunschsätze mit mi yittin im Biblischen Hebräisch." In *Sachverhalt und Zeitbezug. Semitistische und alttestamentliche Studien Adolf Denz zum 65. Geburtstag*. Ed. Rüdiger Bartelmus and Norbert Nebes. Jenaer Beiträge zum Vorderen Orient 4. Wiesbaden: Harrassowitz, 2001. 129–42. **Smick, Elmer B.** "Architectonics, Structured Poems, and Rhetorical Devices in the Book of Job" [incl. 13:28–14:6; 27–31; 38–41]. In *A Tribute to Gleason Archer*. Ed. Walter C. Kaiser, Jr, and Ronald F. Youngblood. Chicago: Moody Press, 1986. 87–104.

Chapters 32–37

Carstensen, R. N. "The Persistence of the 'Elihu' Tradition in the Later Jewish Writings." *LTQ* 2 (1967) 37–46 [original, Diss. Vanderbilt, 1960]. **Clines, David J. A.** "Putting Elihu in His Place: A Proposal for the Relocation of Job 32–37." *JSOT* 29 (2005) 243–53. **Cox, Claude E.** "Origen's Use of Theodotion in the Elihu Speeches." *Second Century* 3 (1983) 89–98. **Lynch, Matthew J.** "Bursting at the Seams: Phonetic Rhetoric in the Speeches of Elihu." *JSOT* 30 (2006) 345–64. **McCant, Jerry W.** "Toward a Biblical Approach for Ministry to Older Adults" [Job 32:4–9]. *Christian Education Journal* 4/1 (1983) 26–37. **Müllner, Ilse.** "Literarische Diachronie in den Elihureden des Ijobbuchs (Ijob 32–37)." In *Das Manna fällt auch heute noch: Beiträge zur Geschichte und Theologie des Alten, Ersten Testaments. Festschrift für Erich Zenger*. Ed. Frank-Lothar Hossfeld and Ludger Schwienhorst-Schönberger. Herders biblische Studien 44. Freiburg i.Br.: Herder, 2004. 447–69. **Velthusen, Johann Caspar.** *Sermones Eliae Busitae, carminibus religiosis antiquissimis intertextorum ex Iobi capp. XXXII–XXXVII*. Rostock, c. 1770. **Vermeylen, Jacques.** "'Pour justifier mon créateur': les discours d'Elihou (Job 32–37) et leur histoire littéraire." In *Gott und Mensch im Dialog: Festschrift für Otto Kaiser zum 80. Geburtstag*. Ed. Markus Witte. BZAW 345. Berlin: Walter de Gruyter, 2004. 2:743–73. **Wolters, Al.** "Job 32–37: Elihu as the Mouthpiece of God." In *Reading and Hearing the Word from Text to Sermon: Essays in Honor of John H. Stek*. Ed. Arie C. Leder. Grand Rapids: Calvin Theological Seminary and CRC Publications, 1998. 107–23.

Chapter 34

Michel, Walter L. "Ṣlmwt, 'deep darkness' or 'shadow of death'?" [Job 34:22]. *BibRes* 29 (1984) 5–20.

Chapters 36–37

Flores, Randolf C. "Elihu's Critique of Power and Wealth. An Exegesis of Job 36:16–21." In *Scripture and the Quest for a New Society. Proceedings of the Sixth Annual Convention. Phinma Training Center, Tagaytay City, 22–24 July 2005.* Ed. Catholic Biblical Association of the Philippines. Manila, 2007. 91–111. **Gold, Sally L.** "Making Sense of Job 37.13: Translation Strategies in 11Q10, Peshitta and the Rabbinic Targum." In *Biblical Hebrews* [*sic*], *Biblical Texts: Essays in Memory of Michael P. Weitzman.* Ed. Ada Rapaport-Albert and Gillian Greenberg. JSOTSup 333. Sheffield: Sheffield Academic Press, 2001. 282–302. **Newsom, Carol A.** "Elihu's Sapiential Hymn (Job 36:24–37:13): Genre, Rhetoric and Moral Imagination." In *Relating to the Text: Interdisciplinary and Form-Critical Insights on the Bible.* Ed. Timothy J. Sandoval and Carleen Mandolfo. JSOTSup 384. London: T. & T. Clark International, 2003. **Slotki, Israel W.** "A Study of רעם" [Job 26:14; 37:4; 39:19]. *AJSL* 37 (1920–21) 149–55. **Wilk, Stephen R.** "The Meaning of the Thunderbolt" [lightning in physics and mythology]. *Parabola* 17 (1992) 72–79.

Chapter 42:7–17

Gillmayr-Bucher, Susanne. "Rahmen und Bildträger. Der mehrschichtige Diskurs in den Prosatexten des Ijobbuchs." In *Das Buch Ijob: Gesamtdeutungen—Einzeltexte—zentrale Themen.* Ed. Theodor Seidl and Stephanie Ernst. Österreichische biblische Studien 31. Frankfurt: Peter Lang, 2007. 139–64. **Langenhorst, Georg.** "'Die richtige Übersetzung …'? Georg Langenhorsts Replik auf 'Ihr habt nicht recht zu mir geredet'." *LS* 57 (2006) 15–16. **Michel, Andreas.** "Ijob und Abraham. Zur Rezeption von Gen 22 in Ijob 1–2 und 42,7–17." In *Gott, Mensch, Sprache. Schülerfestschrift für Walter Gross zum 60. Geburtstag.* Ed. Andreas Michel and Hermann-Josef Stipp. ATSAT 58. St Ottilien: Eos Verlag, 2001. 73–98.

General Bibliography

1. BIBLIOGRAPHIES OF WORKS ON JOB

This Section does not contain bibliographies on the influence of Job in later literature and culture; for such items, see Sections 8.a (Job and Its Influence), 8.f (Western Thinkers and Writers), 8.g (Literary Works Inspired by Job), 8.h (Job in Art), and 8.i (Job in Music).

Baker, J. A. "Commentaries on Job." *Theol* 66 (1963) 179–85. **Barr, J.** "The Book of Job and Its Modern Interpreters." *BJRL* 54 (1971–72) 28–46. **Bogaert, M.** "Report on the August 1993 Louvain Biblical Colloquium on the Book of Job." *RTL* 24 (1993) 529–30. **Borgonovo, Gianantonio.** *La notte e il suo sole. Luce e tenebre nel Libro di Giobbe: analisi simbolica.* AnBib 135. Rome: Pontifical Biblical Institute, 1995. 340–430. **Conte, Gino.** "Letture di Giobbe." *Protestantesimo* 39 (1984) 93–96. **Dailey, Thomas F.** *The Book of Job.* Bibliographies for Biblical Research. Old Testament series 13. Lewiston: Mellen Biblical Press, 1997. **Downing, Frederick L.** "Voices from the Whirlwind. Contemporary Criticism and the Biblical Book of Job." *PerspRelSt* 26 (1999) 389–404. **Fuchs, Gotthard.** "Hiob und seine Botschaften: Neue Literatur." *BLit* 71 (1998) 357–59. **Glatzer, Nahum H.** *The Dimensions of Job: A Study and Selected Readings.* New York: Schocken Books, 1969. **Hausen, Adelheid.** *Hiob in der französischen Literatur: Zur Rezeption eines alttestamentlichen Buches.* Europäische Hochschulschriften 13/17. Frankfurt: Peter Lang, 1972. 212–60. **Kaminka, A.** "Neueste Literatur zu den Hagiographen." *MGWJ* 71 (1927) 289–306. **Kegler, Jürgen.** "Hauptlinien der Hiobforschung seit 1956." In C. Westermann. *Der Aufbau des Buches Hiob.* 2nd ed. Stuttgart: Calwer, 1977. 9–25. **Kinet, Dirk.** "Der Vorwurf an Gott. Neuere Literatur zum Ijobbuch." *BK* 36 (1981) 255–59. **Kuhl, Curt.** "Neuere Literarkritik des Buches Hiob." *TRu* N.F. 21 (1953) 163–205, 257–317. ———. "Vom Hiobbuche und seinen Problemen." *TRu* N.F. 22 (1954) 261–316. **Lang, B.** "Neue Literatur zum Buch Ijob." *TTQ* 160 (1980) 40–42. **Lods, A.** "Recherches récentes sur le livre de Job." *RHPR* 14 (1934) 501–33. **Matthes, J. C.** *Het Boek Job, vertaald en verklaard, insonderheid naar aanleiding van de jongste buitenlandsche kommentaren.* Utrecht: Bosch, 1865. 205ff. **Mika'el, Moshe.** "ספר איוב באספקלריה של כתבי־עת משנת 1921 עד שנת 1950 [The Book of Job in Periodical Review 1921–1950]." *BMik* 76 (1978–79) 106–15; 77, 229–40; 78, 336–46. **Mills, Watson E.** *Ruth, Esther, Job.* Bibliographies for Biblical Research 7. Lewiston,

NY: Mellen Biblical Press, 2002. **Müller, Hans-Peter.** "Altes und Neues zum Buch Hiob." *EvTh* 37 (1977) 284–304. ———. *Das Hiobproblem: seine Stellung und Entstehung im alten Orient und im Alten Testament.* Erträge des Forschung 84. Darmstadt: Wissenschaftliche Buchgesellschaft, 1978; 3rd ed., 1995. **Newsom, Carol A.** "Re-considering Job." *CRBS* 5 (2007) 155–82. **Oorschot, Jürgen van.** "Tendenzen der Hiobforschung." *TRu* 60 (1995) 351–88. **Pakala, James C.** "A Librarian's Comments on Commentaries: 9 (Job and Ephesians)." *Presbyterion* 26 (2000) 26–31. **Radzinowicz, Mary Ann.** "How and Why the Literary Establishment Caught Up with the Bible: Instancing the Book of Job." *ChrLit* 39/1 (Autumn 1989) 77–89. **Robinson, T. R.** "The Ten Best Books on the Book of Job." *Exp* 9/4 (1925) 357–77. **Rodd, Cyril S.** "Which Is the Best Commentary? Part 4: Job." *ExpT* 97 (1986) 356–60. **Rogers, Robert William.** "Recent Commentaries on Job." *MethRev* 104 (1921) 966–71. **Sanders, Paul S. (ed.).** *Twentieth Century Interpretations of the Book of Job: A Collection of Critical Essays.* Englewood Cliffs, NJ: Prentice–Hall, 1968. **Schneider.** "Die neueste Studien über das Buch Hiob." *Deutsche Zeitschrift für christliche Wissenschaft* 27 (1859). **Tebbe, W.** "Predigthilfe aus Kommentaren. Neuere Literatur zum Buche Hiob." *MP* 43 (1954) 156–67. **Vold, K.** "Jobbokens problemer. Litteratur om Jobboken." *TTKi* 3 (1932) 41–56. **Waldow, H. E. von.** "Studien zum Buche Hiob." *VF* 20 (1960–62) 215–27. **Williams, Ronald J.** "Current Trends in the Study of the Book of Job." In *Studies in the Book of Job.* Ed. W. E. Aufrecht. SRSup 16. Waterloo, Ont.: Wilfrid Laurier University Press, 1985. 1–27.

2. COMMENTARIES AND TRANSLATIONS

This Section contains primarily commentaries (that is, works arranged to follow the sequence of Job) and translations of the book. In addition, there are some general works, and some special studies on commentaries, especially the ancient commentaries. General studies of the book are in Section 3 (The Book as a Whole).

a. Patristic

Baskin, Judith R. *Pharaoh's Counsellors: Job, Jethro and Balaam in Rabbinic and Patristic Tradition.* Brown Judaic Studies 47. Chico, CA: Scholars Press, 1983. **Bianco, Maria Grazia.** "Interpretazioni di Giobbe nella patristica delle origini." In *I volti di Giobbe: percorsi interdisciplinari.* Ed. Gilberto Marconi and Cristina Termini. Bologna: EDB, 2002. 101–25. **Centre d'Analyse et de Documentation Patristiques (ed.).** *Le livre de Job chez les Pères.* Cahiers de Biblia patristica 5. Strasbourg: Centre d'Analyse et de Documentation Patristiques, 1996. **Dhorme, E.** *A Commentary on the Book of Job.* Trans. H. Knight. London: Thomas Nelson, 1967. ccxxi–ccxxiv. **Guillaumin, Marie-Louise.** "Recherches sur l'exégèse patristique de Job." In *Studia Patristica* 12/1. Ed. Elizabeth A. Livingstone. Texte und Untersuchungen 115. Berlin: Akademie Verlag, 1975. 304–8. **Manley, Johanna (ed.).** *Wisdom, Let Us Attend: Job, the Fathers, and the Old Testament.* Menlo Park, CA: Monastery Books, 1997. **Simonetti, Manlio, and Marco Conti (eds.).** *Job.* Ancient Christian Commentary on Scripture 6. Downers Grove, IL: InterVarsity Press, 2006. **Vicchio, Stephen J.** "Job in Early Christianity: The First Four Centuries." In his *Job in the Ancient World.* Eugene, OR: Wipf & Stock, 2006. 139–57.

i. Greek

Anon. *To vivlio tou Iōv.* [Facsimile of Sinaitikos kōdikas 3 from St Catherine Monastery, Sinai.] 3 vols. Athens: Graphida, 2002. **Osieczkowska, C.** "Note sur un manuscrit grec du livre de Job, no 62 du Musée byzantin d'Athènes." *Byzantion* 6 (1931) 223–28.

Athanasius (c. 296–373). *Fragmenta in Job* [excerpts from the Greek catena]. *PG* 27:1343–48.

Basil of Seleucia (d. c. 458). *PG* 85:27–474. **Rohan-Chabot, Claude de.** "Exégèse de Job 2:6 dans une homélie inédite de Basile de Séleucie." *StPatr* 18,2 (1988–89) 197–201. **Chrysostom, John (c. 347–407).** Editions: *Fragmenta in beatum Job* [excerpts from the Greek catena]. *PG* 64:506–635. *In Job homilias IV*. *PG* 56:563–82. *Synopsis scripturae sacrae, Job*. *PG* 56:361–68. **Hagedorn, Ursula, and Dieter Hagedorn.** *J. Chrysostomos Kommentar zu Hiob*. PatrTStud 35. Berlin: de Gruyter, 1990. **Sorlin, Henri, and Louis Neyrand.** *Jean Chrysostom, Commentaire sur Job*. I (1–14), II (15–42). SC 346, 348. Paris: Cerf, 1988. *Homilia in poenitentiam Ninivitarum. Specimen expositionis in Jobum*. In Angelo Maria Bandini. *Graecae ecclesiae vetera monumenta*. II. Florence: Typis Caesaris, 1762–1764. See also **Aubineau, Michel Barhebraeus.** "Candélabre du sanctuaire 11, 5, 2: une citation identifiée de Jean Chrysostome." *JTS* ns 35 (1984) 480–82. **Broc, Catherine.** "La femme de Job dans la predication de Jean Chrysostome." In *Studia patristica*. XXXVII. *Papers Presented at the Thirteenth International Conference on Patristic Studies held in Oxford 1999. Cappadocian Writers, Other Greek Writers*. Ed. M. F. Wiles and E. J. Yarnold. Louvain: Peeters, 2001. 396–403. **Brottier, Laurence.** "L'actualisation de la figure de Job chez Jean Chrysostome." In *Le Livre de Job chez les Pères*. Ed. Centre d'Analyse et de Documentation Patristiques. Cahiers de Biblia patristica 5. Strasbourg: Centre d'Analyse et de Documentation Patristiques, 1996. 63–110. **Dieu, L.** "Le 'commentaire de S. Jean Chrysostome sur Job'." *RHE* 13 (1912) 640–58. **Hagedorn, Ursula, and Dieter Hagedorn.** "Chrysostomisches und Pseudo-chrysostomisches: Eine Analyse der Fragmente zu Hiob in PG 64,504–656." In *Philanthropia kai eusebeia: Festschrift für Albrecht Dihle zum 70. Geburtstag*. Ed. Glenn W. Most, Hubert Petersmann, and Adolf Martin Ritter. Göttingen: Vandenhoeck & Ruprecht, 1993. **Haidacher, S.** "Chrysostomus-Fragmente. A: Chrysostomus-fragmente zum Buche Hiob." In Χρυσοστομικα. *Studi e richerche intorno a S. Giovanni Crisostomo*. Rome: Pustet, 1908. 1:217–34. **Samir, K.** "Les sermons sur Job du Pseudo-Chrysostome (CPG 4564 = BHG 939d-g) retrouvés en arabe." *OLP* 8 (1977) 205–16. **Samir, K., and J. L. Scharpé.** "Les sermons sur Job du Pseudo-Chrysostome (CPG 4564 = BHG 939d-g) dans la version paléo-russe." *OLP* 9 (1978) 167–73.

Didymus the Blind (c. 313–398). Editions: *Fragmenta ex catenis in Job*. *PG* 39:1119–54. **Hagedorn, Dieter, Ursula Hagedorn, Albert Henrichs, and Ludwig Koenen.** *Kommentar zu Hiob (Tura-Papyrus). Didymus the Blind*. Mathaf al-Misri Papyrologische Texte und Abhandlungen 1–3, 33. Bonn: Habelt, 1968. **Hagedorn, Ursula, and Dieter Hagedorn.** "Neue Fragmente des Hiobkommentars Didymos' des Blinden?" In *Miscellanea papyrologica in occasione del bicentenario dell'edizione della Charta Borgiana*. Ed. Mario Capasso, Gabriella Messeri Savorelli, and Rosario Pintaudi. Florence: Gonnelli, 1990. 245–54. **Hagedorn, Ursula, Dieter Hagedorn, and Ludwig Koenen.** *Didymos der Blinde, Kommentar zu Hiob (Tura-Papyrus)*. Vols. 3, 4. Bonn: R. Habelt, 1985. **Henrichs, A.** *Didymos der Blinde. Kommentar zu Hiob (Tura-Papyrus)*. 2 vols. Papyrologische Texte und Abhandlungen 1, 2. Bonn: R. Habelt, 1968. See also **Hagedorn, Ursula, and Dieter Hagedorn.** "Zur Katenenüberlieferung des Hiobkommentars von Didymos dem Blinden." *Bulletin of the American Society of Papyrologists* 22 (1985) 55–58. **Marchal, Gerrit Wijnand.** *Didyme de blinde en zijn interpretatie van het boek Job*. Sneek: Doevendans, 1977. **Reventlow, Henning Graf.** "Hiob der Mann. Ein altkirchliches Ideal bei Didymus dem Blinden." In *Text and Theology. Studies in Honour of Prof. Dr Theol. Magne Sæbø*. Ed. Arvid Tangberg. Oslo: Verbum, 1994. 213–27.

Evagrius Ponticus (345–399). Casiday, A. M. "Notes on Job." In his *Evagrius Ponticus*. London: Routledge, 2006.

Greek Catena. Editions: **Comitolus, Paulus (Paolo Comitolo) (ed.).** *Catena in beatissimum Job absolutissima, e quatuor et viginti Graeciae doctorum explanationibus contexta, a Paulo Comitolo e graeco in latinum conversa*. Lyons: Antonius Tardif, 1586; Venice, 1587. **Hagedorn, Ursula, and Dieter Hagedorn.** *Die älteren griechischen Katenen zum Buch Hiob*. 4 vols. Patristische Texte und Studien 40, 48, 53, 59. Berlin: W. de Gruyter, 1994–2004.

Junius, P. [Young, Patrick] (ed.). *Catena graecorum patrum in beatum Job collectore Niceta Heracleae Metropolita ex duobus mss. Bibliothecae Bodleianae codicibus, graece, nunc primum in lucem edita et latine versa, opera et studio Patricii Junii Bibliothecarii Regii.* London, 1637 [= *PG* 64:505–635]. See also **Bertini, U.** "La catena greca in Giobbe." *Bib* 4 (1923) 129–42.

Greek Translators. Hagedorn, Ursula, and Dieter Hagedorn. "Nachlese zu den Fragmenten der jüngeren griechischen Übersetzer des Buches Hiob." In *Nachrichten von der Akademie der Wissenschaften in Göttingen.* Philologisch-Historische Klasse. Göttingen: Vandenhoeck & Ruprecht, 1991.

Hesychius of Jerusalem (fl. c. 300). Edition: **Renoux, Charles.** *Hesychius de Jérusalem, Homélies sur Job. Version arménienne.* PO 42/1–2. Turnhout: Brepols, 1983. **Tscherakian, C. (ed.).** *The Commentary on Job by Hesychius, presbyter of Jerusalem.* Venice, 1913. See also **Renoux, C.** "L'église de Sion dans les homélies sur Job d'Hésychius de Jérusalem." *REArmén* 18 (1984) 135–46.

Julian the Arian (4th cent.). Edition: **Hagedorn, Dieter.** *Der Hiobkommentar des Arianers Julian.* Patristische Texte und Studien 14. Berlin: de Gruyter, 1973. See also **Draguet, R.** "Un commentaire grec arien sur Job." *RHE* 24 (1924) 38–65. **Ferhat, P.** "Der Jobprolog des Julianos von Halicarnassus in einer armenischen Bearbeitung." *OrChr* 1 (1911) 26–31. **Vinel, Françoise.** "Job 38: le commentaire de Julien l'arien et les interprétations cappadociennes." In *Le Livre de Job chez les Pères.* Cahiers de Biblia patristica 5. Strasbourg: Centre d'Analyse et de Documentation Patristiques, 1996. 163–75.

Methodius (d. c. 311). *Commentary on Job* [not extant].

Olympiodorus of Alexandria (6th cent.). Editions: *Commentarium in beatum Job* [excerpts from the Greek catena]. *PG* 93:11–409. **Hagedorn, Ursula, and Dieter Hagedorn.** *Olympiodor, Diakon von Alexandria. Kommentar zu Hiob.* Patristische Texte und Studien 24. Berlin: de Gruyter, 1984.

Origen (c. 185–c. 254). Editions: *Ennarrationes in Job. PG* 17:57–106. *Ex Origene selecta in Job. PG* 12:1031–50. *Hexaplorum quae supersunt … Job. PG* 16/1:287–570. See also **Pazzini, D.** "Origene commenta Giobbe." *Parola, spirito e vita* 34 (1996) 289–98.

Porphyry (Neo-Platonist philosopher, c. 232–303). Hagedorn, Dieter, and Reinhold Merkelbach. "Ein neues Fragment aus Porphyrios Gegen die Christen." *VigChr* 20 (1966) 86–90.

Ps.-Julian of Halicarnassus (d. after 518). *Commentary on Job* [now ascribed to an unknown Arian author]. CPL 3:7125–27.

Ps.-Origen. Edition: *In Job commentarius. PG* 17:371–522 [known only in Latin]. *Origenis opera omnia quae graece vel latine tantum exstant et ejus nomine circumferuntur.* XVI. *Anonymi in Job commentarius adamantii de recta in Deum fide.* Ed. Carl Heinrich Eduard Lommatzsch. Berlin: Haude & Spener, 1844. **Dossey, Leslie.** "The Last Days of Vandal Africa: An Arian Commentary on Job and Its Historical Context" [Pseudo-Origen]." *JTS* 54 (2003) 60–138.

Theodore of Mopsuestia (c. 350–428). Edition: *In Jobum* [excerpts from the Greek catena]. *PG* 66:697–98.

Theodoret (c. 393–c. 458). Guinot, Jean-Noël. "Regard sur l'utilisation du Livre de Job dans l'oeuvre de Théodoret de Cyr." In *Le Livre de Job chez les Pères.* Ed. Centre d'Analyse et de Documentation Patristiques. Cahiers de Biblia patristica 5. Strasbourg: Centre d'Analyse et de Documentation Patristiques, 1996. 111–40.

Zeno (d. c. 375). Maraval, Pierre. "Job dans l'oeuvre de Zénon de Vérone." In *Le Livre de Job chez les Pères.* Ed. Centre d'Analyse et de Documentation Patristiques. Cahiers de Biblia patristica 5. Strasbourg: Centre d'Analyse et de Documentation Patristiques, 1996. 23–30.

ii. Latin

Ambrose (c. 339–397). Editions: *Liber de interpellatione Job et David. PL* 14:793–850. *De patriarchis. De fuga saeculi. De interpellatione Iob et David. = I patriarchi. La fuga dal mondo.*

La rimostranze di Giobbe e di Davide. Ed. Karl Schenkl. Introduzione, traduzione, note e indici di Gabriele Banterle. Tutte le opere di Sant'Ambrogio 4. Opera esegitiche. Milan: Biblioteca Ambrosiana; Rome: Città nuova, 1980. Translation: **McHugh, M. P.** *Seven Exegetical Works: Isaac, or the Soul, Death as Good, Jacob and the Happy Life, Joseph, The Patriarchs, Flight from the World, The Prayer of Job and David.* The Fathers of the Church 65. Washington, DC: Catholic University of America Press, 1972. See also **Baskin, Judith R.** "Job as Moral Exemplar in Ambrose." *VigChr* 35 (1981) 222–31. **Cazier, Pierre.** "Lectures du livre de Job chez Ambroise, Augustin et Grégoire le Grand." *Graphè* 6 (1997) 51–111. **Vicchio, Stephen J.** *Job in the Medieval World.* Eugene, OR: Wipf & Stock, 2006. 18–20.

    Anon. Edition: **Steinhauser, Kenneth B. (ed.).** *Anonymi in Iob commentarius.* CSEL 96. Vienna: Verlag der Österreichischen Akademie der Wissenschaften, 2006.

    Augustine (354–430). Editions: *Adnotationum in Job liber unus. PL* 34:825–86. *Sermo de eo quod scriptum est in Job, cap. 1,6. PL* 38:100–106. *Anotaciones al libro de Job; La concordancia de los evangelistas.* Obras completas 29. Madrid: BAC, 1992. *De patientia. PL* 40:615–16. *Opere esegetiche: testo latino dell'edizione maurina confrontato con il Corpus christianorum e con il Corpus scriptorum ecclesiasticorum latinorum. 3. Otto questioni dell'Antico Testamento; Annotazioni su Giobbe; Specchio di precetti morali dalla Sacra Scrittura. Introduzioni particolari di Luigi Carrozzi, Gaspare Mura, Czar Emmanuel Alvarez.* Nuova biblioteca agostiniana: Opere di Sant'Agostino 10,3. Rome: Città nuova, 1997. **Poujoulat, M., and M. l'Abbé Raulx (eds.).** *Oeuvres complètes de Saint Augustin. 4. Commentaires sur l'Ecriture: Doctrine chrétienne, Genèse, Heptateuque, Job.* Oeuvres complètes 4. Rodez: Librairie catholique et religieuse de B. Sasserre, 1886. **Zycha, Josephus (ed.).** *Sancti Aureli Augustini Quaestionum in Heptateuchum ad notationem libri VII. Adnotationum in Job liber unus.* CSEL 28/2. Vienna: F. Tempsky, 1895 [repr. New York: Johnson Reprint Corporation, 1970].

    See also **Cazier, Pierre.** "Lectures du livre de Job chez Ambroise, Augustin et Grégoire le Grand." *Graphè* 6 (1997) 51–111. **Dolbeau, François.** "Une citation non reconnue de Job 31, 11 (LXX), dans un sermon d'Augustin." *RevEtAug* 43 (1997) 309–11. **Folliet, G.** "Une citation scripturaire ambigüe dans les Confessions d'Augustin I,5,6: 'non iudicio contendo tecum,' allusion à Job 9,3 ou à Jérémie 2,29?" *Aug(L)* 53 (2003) 139–46. **Fournier, Christian.** "Augustin, Adnotationes in Job I, 29–31 (traduction d'après CSEL 28)." In *Le Livre de Job chez les Pères.* Ed. Centre d'Analyse et de Documentation Patristiques. Cahiers de Biblia patristica 5. Strasbourg: Centre d'Analyse et de Documentation Patristiques, 1996. 49–61. **Harrison, Carol.** "'Who is free from sin?' The Figure of Job in the Thought of Saint Augustine." In *Letture cristiane dei Libri Sapienziali: XX Incontro di studiosi della antichità cristiana, 9–11 maggio 1991.* Ed. Franco Bolgiani. Studia ephemeridis «Augustinianum» 37. Rome: Institutum Patristicum Augustinianum, 1992. 483–88. **Jackson, M. G. StA.** "Formica Dei: Augustine's Enarratio in Psalmum 66:3" [Job as "God's ant"]. *VigChr* 40 (1986) 153–68. **Steinhauser, Kenneth B.** "Job Exegesis: The Pelagian Controversy." In *Augustine: Biblical Exegete.* Ed. Frederick van Fleteren and Joseph C. Schnaubelt. New York: Peter Lang, 2001. 299–311. **Vincent, M.** "El libro de Job en la predicación de san Agustín." *Augustinus* 36 (1991) 355–60.

    Boethius (c. 480–c. 525). Astell, Ann W. *Job, Boethius, and Epic Truth.* Ithaca: Cornell University Press, 1994. **Relihan, Joel C.** *The Prisoner's Philosophy: Life and Death in Boethius's Consolation.* Notre Dame, IN: University of Notre Dame Press, 2006.

    Cassian, John (360–435). Sheridan, Mark. "Job and Paul. Philosophy and Exegesis in Cassian's Sixth Conference." *Studia monastica* 42 (2000) 271–94.

    Gregory the Great (c. 540–604). Editions: *Libri XXXV Moralium. PL* 75:515–1162; 76:9–782. *Excerpta ex commentario in Jobum* (attrib. Bede). *PL* 23:1470–80. **Adriaen, M. (ed.).** *S. Gregorii Magni Moralia in Iob.* 3 vols. CCSL 143, 143A, 143B. Turnhout: Brepols, 1979–85. **Adriaen, Marc, et al. (eds.).** *Grégoire le Grand: texte latin de Marc Adriaen; introduction par Carole Straw; traduction par les moniales de Wisques, notes par Adalbert de Vogüé* [*Moralia in Job,* French and Latin]. VI. Livres XXVIII–XXIX. SC 476. Paris: Editions du Cerf, 2003. **Bocognano, Aristide.** *Morales sur Job. Livres 11–14. Texte latin, introduction,* *traduction et notes.* SC 212. Paris: Cerf, 1974. ———. *Morales sur Job. Livres 15–16. Texte latin, introduction, traduction et notes.* SC 221. Paris: Cerf, 1975. **Gillet, R., A. de Gaudemaris, and A. Bocognano.** *Grégoire le Grand, Morales sur Job. Texte latin, introduction et notes.* 4 vols. SC 32, 32b, 212, 221. Paris: Cerf, 1950–75. Translations: **Bliss, James.** *Morals on the Book of Job, Translated with Notes and Indices.* 3 vols. in 4. Oxford: H. Parker, 1844–50. **O'Donnell, James J.** *Gregory the Great: Moralia in Iob. Books 1–5 in English.* [http://ccat. sas.upenn.edu/jod/gregory.html]. **Strata, Matteo Zanobio da.** *I Morali del pontefice S. Gregorio Magno sopra il libro di Giobbe volgarizzatida.* Rome: Corbeletti, 1714; Rome: Girolamo Mainardi, 1725; Naples: Giovanni di Simone, 1746.

See also **Astell, Ann W.** "Translating Job as Female" [Gregory's Moralia in Job and Chaucer's Patient Griselda]. In *Translation Theory and Practice in the Middle Ages.* Ed. Bernadette Beer. Kalamazoo, MI: Western Michigan University Press, 1997. 59–69. **Ayala, L. de.** *Las flores de los 'Morales de Job.' Introduzione, testo critico e note.* Florence: Le Monnier, 1963. **Baasten, Matthew.** *Pride according to Gregory the Great: A Study of the Moralia.* Studies in the Bible and Early Christianity 7. Lewiston: Edwin Mellen Press, 1986. **Braga, Gabriella.** "Le Sententiae morales super Job Ioannis abbatis: ricerche sulle epitomi altomedievali dei 'Moralia'." In *Studi sul medioevo cristiano offerti a Raffaello Morghen: per il 90. anniversario dell'Istituto storico italiano (1883–1973).* Rome: Istituto storico italiano per il medio evo, 1974. **Branciforti, Francesco.** *Las flores de los Morales de Job.* Biblioteca letteraria 7. Florence: Le Monnier, 1963. **Castaldelli, F.** "Il meccanismo psicologico del peccato nei 'Moralia in Job' di San Gregorio Magno." *Salesianum* 27 (1965) 563–605. **Cavallero, Pablo.** "La adaptación poética de los Moralia in Iob de San Gregorio en el Rimado de Palacio del canciller Ayala." *Hispania sacra* 38 (1986) 401–518. **Cazier, Pierre.** "Lectures du livre de Job chez Ambroise, Augustin et Grégoire le Grand." *Graphè* 6 (1997) 51–111. **Collon-Gevaert, Suzanne.** "Les moralia de saint Grégoire sur Job." In her *Etude sur les miniatures mosanes pré-gothiques: quatre manuscrits mosans de la Bibliothèque Nationale, Paris.* Bibliothèque nationale, Département des manuscrits, Académie royale de Belgique. Classe des beaux-arts. Brussels: Palais des Académies, 1948. **Foerster, Wendelin (ed.).** *Les dialogues du Pape Gregoire traduits en français du XIIe siècle accompagnés du texte latin suivis de Sermon sur la sapience et des fragments de Moralités sur Job, d'une étude sur la langue du texte, d'un commentaire et d'un glossaire.* Halle, Paris, 1876 [repr. Amsterdam: Rodopi, 1965]. **Greschat, Katharina.** *Die Moralia in Job Gregors des Grossen: ein christologisch-ekklesiologischer Kommentar.* Studien und Texte zu Antike und Christentum 31. Tübingen: Mohr Siebeck, 2005. **Hauber, Rose Marie.** *The Late Latin Vocabulary of the Moralia of Saint Gregory the Great: A Morphological and Semasiological Study.* Washington, DC: The Catholic University of America, 1938. **Hester, Kevin L.** *Eschatology and Pain in St Gregory the Great: The Christological Synthesis of Gregory's Morals on the Book of Job.* Milton Keynes: Paternoster, 2007. **Hidal, Sten.** "Hjältedikt eller själens resasynen pa Jobs bok i fornkyrkan." *SvTK* 62 (1986) 69–76. **Laporte, Jean B.** "Gregory the Great as a Theologian of Suffering." *Patristic and Byzantine Review* 1 (1982) 22–31. **López [Lope] de Ayala, Pedro [Pero] (1332–1407).** *Morales sobre el Libro de Job* [Spanish translation of Gregory the Great]. 1401 [see Giuseppina Grespi. *Traducciones castellanas de obras latinas e italianas contenidas en manuscritos del siglo XV en las bibliotecas de Madrid y El Escorial.* Madrid, 2004. 133]. **Meyvaert, Paul.** "Uncovering a Lost Work of Gregory the Great: Fragments of the Early Commentary on Job." *Traditio* 50 (1995) 55–74. **Morrison, Frederick Maclaurin.** *The Abbreviated Version of Ayala's Translation of the "Moralia" of St Gregory the Great: Edition and Study.* Diss. Michigan, 1984. **O'Hara, Mary L.** "Truth in Spirit and Letter: Gregory the Great, Thomas Aquinas, and Maimonides on the Book of Job." In *From Cloister to Classroom: Monastic and Scholastic Approaches to Truth.* Ed. E. Rozanne Elder. Kalamazoo, MI: Cistercian Publications, 1986. 47–79. **Romagnoli, A. B.** "Gregorio Magno davanti a Giobbe. Fondamenti di un'antropologia medioevale." In *I volti di Giobbe: percorsi interdisciplinari.* Ed. Gilberto Marconi and Cristina Termini. Bologna: EDB, 2002. 127–45. **Rudolph, Conrad.** *Violence and Daily Life: Reading, Art, and Polemics in the Cîteaux Moralia in Job.* Princeton: Princeton University Press, 1997.

Salmon, P. "Le texte de Job utilisé par S. Grégoire dans les 'Moralia'." In *Miscellanea biblica et orientalia R. P. Athanasio Miller O.S.B., secretario Pontificiae Commissionis Biblicae, completis LXX annis oblata*. Ed. Adalbert Metzinger. Studia anselmiana philosophica theologica 27–28. Rome: Orbis Catholicus, Herder, 1951. 187–94. **Schreiner, Susan E.** "The Role of Perception in Gregory's Moralia in Job." In *Papers Presented to the Eleventh International Conference on Patristic Studies Held in Oxford 1991*. Ed. Elizabeth A. Livingstone. Studia patristica 28. Louvain: Peeters, 1993. 87–95. **Siniscalco, Paolo (ed.).** *San Gregorio Magno: Commento morale a Giobbe*. Rome: Città Nuove, 1992–2001. **Smeets, Arnold.** "Une lettre comme don: une lecture sémiotique de la lettre de Gregoire dans les 'Moralia in Job'." In *Les lettres dans la Bible et dans la littérature: Actes du colloque de Lyon (3–5 juillet 1996)*. Ed. Louis Panier. Lectio divina 181. Paris: Cerf, 1999. 241–63. **Vicchio, Stephen J.** *Job in the Medieval World*. Eugene, OR: Wipf & Stock, 2006. 26–43. **Wasselynck, René.** "L'influence de l'exégèse de saint Grégoire le Grand sur les commentaires bibliques médiévaux." *RTAM* 32 (1965) 157–204. ———. "Le compilations des Moralia in Job du VIIe au XIIe siècle." *RTAM* 29 (1962) 5–33. ———. "Les Moralia in Job dans les ouvrages de morale du haut moyen âge latin." *RTAM* 31 (1964) 5–31. ———. *L'influence des Moralia in Job de S. Grégoire le Grand sur la théologie morale entre le VIIe et le XIIe siècle*. Diss. Lille, 1956. **Wiener, Claudia.** "Beobachtungen zur Überlieferung von Gregors "Moralia in Job" im späten achten Jahrhundert in Würzburg und Freising." *Würzburger Diözesangeschichtsblätter* 53 (1991) 5–14. **Wilken, Robert L.** "Interpreting Job Allegorically. The 'Moralia' of Gregory the Great." *Pro ecclesia* 10/2 (2001) 213–26.

Hilary (c. 315–67). Edition: *Tractatus in Job* [fragment]. *PL* 10:723–24. See also **Doignon, Jean.** "Versets de Job sur le péché de notre origine selon Hilaire de Poitiers." In *Le Livre de Job chez les Pères*. Ed. Centre d'Analyse et de Documentation Patristiques. Cahiers de Biblia patristica 5. Strasbourg: Centre d'Analyse et de Documentation Patristiques, 1996. 13–21. ———. "Corpora vitiorum materies. Une formule-clé du fragment sur Job d'Hilaire de Poitiers inspiré d'Origène et transmis par Augustin (Contra Iulianum 2,8,27)." *VigChr* 35 (1981) 209–21. ———. "'Rengaines' origéniennes dans les Homélies sur Job d'Hilaire de Poitiers." In *Le Livre de Job chez les Pères*. Ed. Centre d'Analyse et de Documentation Patristiques. Cahiers de Biblia patristica 5. Strasbourg: Centre d'Analyse et de Documentation Patristiques, 1996. 7–11.

Jerome (c. 342–420). Editions: *Commentarii in librum Job*. *PL* 26:619–802. *Liber Job* [a translation]. *PL* 28:1079–1122. *Liber Job. Altera versio*. *PL* 29:61–114. *Expositio interlinearis libri Job*. *PL* 23:1402–70 [attrib. to Jerome]. **Gasquet, Aidan.** *Hester et Iob: ex interpretatione Sancti Hieronymi; cum praefationibus et variis capitulorum seriebus*. Biblia sacra iuxta latinam vulgatam versionem ad codicum fidem 9. Rome: Typis Polyglottis Vaticanis, 1951. Translations: **Bareille, Jean-François (ed.).** *Oeuvres complètes de saint Jérôme, traduites en français par l'Abbé Bareille. 7. Commentaires sur Ezéchiel, livres vi–xiv. Commentaires sur Daniel, livres i–xiii. Commentaires sur Job, fragment. Homélies d'Origène, i–viii*. Paris: L. Vivès, 1879. ———. *Oeuvres complètes de saint Jérôme; traduites en français par l'Abbé Bareille. 11. Commentaire sur l'Epître à Tite. Commentaire sur l'Epître à Philémon. Appendice: Commentaire sur le livre de Job. Commentaire abrégé sur les Psaumes*. Paris: L. Vivès, 1884. ———. *Oeuvres complètes de saint Jérôme, traduites en français. 15. Libri Ruth, Samuelis, Malachim, Isaiae, Jeremiae, Ezechielis, Osée, Joel, Amos, Abdiae, Jonae, Michaeae, Nahum, Habacuc, Sophoniae, Aggaei, Zachariae, Malachiae, Job*. Paris: L. Vivès, 1884. ———. *Oeuvres complètes de saint Jérôme, traduites en français par l'Abbé Bareille. 16. Libri Psalmorum, Proverbium, Ecclesiastes, Danielis, Paralipomenon, Esdrae, Esther, Tobiae, Judith, Job, Psalmorum*. Paris: L. Vivès, 1884. See also **Lagarde, P. de.** "Des Hieronymus Übertragung der griechischen Übersetzung des Iob." In his *Mittheilungen*. Göttingen: Dieterich, 1887. 2:189–237. **Vicchio, Stephen J.** *Job in the Medieval World*. Eugene, OR: Wipf & Stock, 2006. 10–17.

Julian of Eclana (c. 386–454). Editions: **Amelli, A.** *PL Suppl.* 1:1573–1679. **Coninck, Lucas de, with Maria Josepha d'Hont.** *Iuliani Aeclanensis Expositio libri Iob; Tractatus prophetarum Osee, Iohel et Amos: accedunt operum deperditorum fragmenta post Albertum Bruckner denuo collecta aucta ordinata*. CCSL 88. Turnhout: Brepols, 1977. See also

Vaccari, Alberto. *Un commento a Giobbe di Giuliano di Eclana.* Rome: Pontifical Biblical Institute, 1915. **Weyman, Carl.** "Der Hiobkommentar des Julianus von Aeclanum." *TRev* (1916) 241–48.

Philip the Presbyter (d. 455/6). Edition: **Sichardus [Sickart], J. (ed.).** *Philippi Presbyteri viri longe eruditissimi in historiam Iob commentariorum libri tres.* Basel, 1527. See also **Ciccarese, Maria Pia.** "Sulle orme di Gerolamo: la 'Expositio in Iob' del presbitero Filippo." In *Motivi letterari ed esegetici in Gerolamo: atti del convegno tenuto a Trento il 5–7 dicembre 1995.* Ed. Claudio Moreschini and Giovanni Menestrina. Brescia: Morcelliana, 1997. 247–68. ———. "Una esegesi 'double face.' Introduzione all' 'Expositio in Iob' del presbitero Filippo." *Annali di storia dell'esegesi* 9 (1992) 483–92. **Fransen, Irénée.** *Le commentaire au Livre de Job du Prêtre Philippe: Etude sur le texte.* Lyon: Facultés catholiques, 1949. **Gorman, M.** "The Manuscript and Printed Editions of the Commentary on Job by Philippus." *RBen* 116,2 (2006) 193–232.

iii. Syriac

Bar Hebraeus (1226–1286). Editions: **Bernstein, G. H.** *Gregorius bar Hebraeus: Scholia in librum Iobi; ex codd. MSS. emendata, denuo edidit, difficiliorum locorum interpretatione illustravit, notis criticis instruxit.* Breslau: Typis Universitatis, 1858. *Scholia in Jobum.* In **Kirsch, G. G.** "Bar Hebraei scholia in Jobum ex ejus Horreo Mysteriorum, sec. cod. Bodl. A." In *Chrestomathie syriaque.* Leipzig: K. Knobloch, 1836. 186–210.

Ephrem (c. 306–373). Benedictus, P. *Scholies sur Job: Edition syriaque et traduction latine.* Opera syriaca. Rome, 1740. 2:1–20.

Ishodad of Merv (9th cent.). Schliebitz, J. *Išodadh's Kommentar zum Buche Hiob.* BZAW 11. Giessen, 1907. See also **Vosté, J. M.** "Mar Išo'dad de Merw sur Job." *Bib* 30 (1949) 305–13. **Van den Eynde, C.** *Commentaire d'Iso'dad de Merv sur l'Ancien Testament. 3: Livre des sessions.* CSCO 229–30. Scriptores syriaci 96–97. Louvain: Secrétariat du CSCO, 1962–63.

b. Jewish, before the 19th Century

i. General

Casper, Bernard M. *An Introduction to Jewish Bible Commentary.* New York: Thomas Yoseloff, 1960. **Delmaire, Jean-Marie.** "Les principaux courants de l'exégèse juive sur Job." *Graphè* 6 (1997) 59–79. **Eisen, Robert.** *The Book of Job in Medieval Jewish Philosophy.* New York: Oxford University Press, 2004. **Kalman, Jason.** "Repeating His Grandfather's Heresy: The Significance of the Charge That Job and Esau Denied the Resurrection of the Dead for Understanding Rabbinic Polemics." In *Midrash and Context: Proceedings of the 2004 and 2005 SBL Consultation on Midrash.* Ed. Lieve M. Teugels and Rivka Ulmer. Piscataway, NJ: Gorgias Press, 2007. 5–22. **Pfeffer, Jeremy I.** *Providence in the Book of Job: The Search for God's Mind.* Brighton: Sussex Academic Press, 2005. **Verdegaal, C. M. L.** *De Statenbijbel en de rabbijnen: Een onderzoek naar de betekenis van de rabbijnse traditie voor de vertaling van het boek Job.* Tilburg: Tilburg University Press, 1998. **Weinberg, Joanna.** "Job versus Abraham: The Quest for the Perfect God-Fearer in Rabbinic Tradition." In *The Book of Job.* Ed. W. A. M. Beuken. BETL 114. Leuven: Leuven University Press, 1994. 281–96. **Wiernikowski, Isaak.** *Das Buch Hiob nach der Auffassung der rabbinischen Litteratur in den ersten fünf nachchristlichen Jahrhunderten.* Breslau: H. Fleischmann, 1902.

ii. Authors

Abraham, Israel ben. ‏ספר איוב: עם העתקה אשכנזית ובאור‎. Prague, 1791.
Abraham, Zeeb Wolf ben. ‏זה ספר פשר דבר על מקרא איוב‎. Berlin, 1777.
Alshech (Alshich, Alshekh), Moses (d. c. 1601). ‏ספר איוב חלקת מחוקק: ביאור‎. *Portio legislatoris.* Venice, 1603 [= *The Book of Job: A Celestial Challenge.* Trans. Ravi Shahar. Jerusalem; Nanuet, NY: Feldheim Publishers, 1996].

Anon. *Bruchstücke eines rabbinischen Hiob-Commentars. Als Manuscript in einigen Exemplaren* (from 1295). Bonn: C. Georgi, 1874. ———. **[Ps.-Rashbam]. Rosen, M. S.** *An Anonymous Commentary on Job MS L778 Jewish Theological Seminary N.Y.: An Analysis of Its Authorship and an Assessment of Its Contents.* Diss. University College, London, 1995. ———.

Paper, Herbert H. "A Judeo-Persian Book of Job." In *Proceedings, The Israel Academy of Sciences and Humanities* 5/12. Jerusalem: Israel Academy of Sciences and Humanities, 1976.

Arama, Meir b. Isaac (1492–1556). ספר מאיר איוב. Thessalonica, 1516; Venice, 1567.

ben 'Ali, Yefet (10th cent.). Hussain, H. A. *Yefet ben 'Ali's Commentary on the Hebrew Text of the Book of Job i–x.* Diss. St Andrews, 1987.

ben Melech, Salomo. יפי מכלל. *Perfectio pulchritudinis, seu Commentarius in loca selecta vocesque et res difficiliores S. Scripturæ* [commentary on whole Bible]. Amsterdam, 1661.

Berechiah ben Natrona (Berechiah ben Natronai Naqdan). *A Commentary on the Book of Job, from a Hebrew Manuscript in the University Library, Cambridge.* Trans. S. A. Hirsch. Ed. William Aldis Wright. London: Williams & Norgate, 1905.

Cohen, Isaac (b. Shelomoh) [Isaac Ben Solomon ha-Kohen]. ספר איוב עם פרוש. *Commentarius in Iobum.* Constantinople, 1545.

Duran, Simon (1361–1444). ספר אהב משפט, with **Obadiah b. Jacob Sforno,** ספר משפט צדק. Venice: Z. Digarah, 1589 [the two commentaries in parallel columns].

Farissol (Perizol), Abraham ben Mardochai (c. 1470). *Commentary on Job.* In Venice Rabbinic Bibles (from 1517) and Buxtorf's Amsterdam editions (from 1724).

Gersonides [Ralbag] (1288–1344 [? 1370]). Editions: *Perush al Iyyov* [Commentary on Job] (Ferrara, 1477; Naples, 1487; Venice, 1524; Amsterdam, 1724–27; and in subsequent editions of the Miqra'ot Gedolot). *Commentarius R. Levi, f. Gersonis, in Libri* [sic] *Iobi.* Paris, 1623. In Venice and Amsterdam Rabbinic Bibles, from 1517 and 1724, respectively. *Commentaries on Proverbs, Job, Song of Songs, Ruth, Ecclesiastes, Esther and Daniel in Qehillot Mosheh* [Rabbinic Bible edited by Moses Frankfurter]. Amsterdam, 1724–27. **Altenbergerus, Christianus.** *Commentarius rabbinicus in cap. VI et VII Hiobi.* Leipzig, 1705. **Aquinas, Ludwig Heinrich.** *Commentarius R. Levi Filii Gersonis in Librum Iobi.* Paris, 1625. **Barfat, Zerah.** *Perush Iyyov be-Qizzur Muflag, beHalazah uve-Shir, Kefi Perusho shel ha-Ralbag (A Greatly Abbreviated Commentary on Job in Rhyme and Meter according to the Commentary of Gersonides).* Venice, 1543/4; Cracow, 1573/4. Translations: **Lassen, Abraham L.** *The Commentary of Levi ben Gersom (Gersonides) on the Book of Job.* Translated from the Hebrew with Introduction and Notes. New York: Bloch Publishing Co., 1946. **Stitskin, Leon.** "Ralbag's Introduction to the Book of Job." *Tradition* 6 (1963) 81–85 [= *A Treasury of Tradition.* Ed. Norman Lamm and Walter Wurzburger. New York: Hebrew Publishing Company, 1967. 370–74; *Studies in Honor of Dr Samuel Belkin.* Ed. L. Stitskin. New York: Ktav, 1974. 147–51]. See also **Burrell, David B.** "Maimonides, Aquinas and Gersonides on Providence and Evil." *RelStud* 20 (1984) 335–51. **Eisen, R.** "Gersonides' 'Commentary on the Book of Job'." *JJewThPhilos* 10 (2001) 239–88. **Kellner, Menachem M.** "Gersonides, Providence, and the Rabbinic Tradition." *JAAR* 42 (1974) 673–85. **Vicchio, Stephen J.** "Job in Maimonides and Gersonides." In his *Job in the Medieval World.* Eugene, OR: Wipf & Stock, 2006. 106–27.

ibn Bal'am, Judah ben Samuel (11th cent.). שער טעמי שלושה ספרים איוב משלי תהלים. *Abhandlung über die poetischen Accente der 3 Bücher Hiob, Sprüchen und Psalmen von R. Jehuda Ibn Balam: zum ersten male aus einer Hs. von Mercerus herausgegeven, Paris 1556.* Ed. G. I. Polak. Amsterdam: K. D. Props, 1858.

ibn Ezra (Abraham ben Meir) (c. 1089–1164). Editions: *Commentary on Job.* In Rabbinic Bibles, including Bomberg Rabbinic Bibles (Venice, 1525–1526) and Buxtorf's (Basel, 1618; Amsterdam, 1724). See also **Galliner, Julius.** *Abraham ibn Esra's Hiobkommentar auf seine Quellen untersucht.* Berlin: H. Itzkowski, 1901. **Gómez, Mariano.** "Aspectos científicos en el comentario de Abraham ibn Ezra al libro de Job." *Henoch* 23 (2001) 81–96.

Jabez, Isaac ben Shelomoh (16th cent.). יראת שדי [Fear of Shaddai]. *Commentary on Job.* In Amsterdam Rabbinic Bibles from 1724.

Jehuda, Abraham ben. חבורי לקט. *Chibbure Leket.* Lublin: Jafe, 1593, 1612.

Kimchi, David [Radak] (1160–1235). Edition: *Perush R. Mosheh Kimhi le-sefer Iyov* [commentary on Job]. Ed. Herbert W. Basser and Barry Walfish. South Florida Studies in the History of Judaism 64. Atlanta: Scholars Press, 1992. See also **Basser, Herbert W.** "A Conundrum in the Ms. Reading to Moses Kimhi's Job Commentary." In *Proceedings of the Tenth World Congress of Jewish Studies.* Div. A. Jerusalem: World Union of Jewish Studies, 1990. 183–90.

Maimonides, Moses (1135–1204). Burrell, David B. "Maimonides, Aquinas and Gersonides on Providence and Evil." *RelStud* 20 (1984) 335–51. **Carpentier, J.-M.** "L'interrogation de Job sur la toute-puissance de Dieu et la conversion de cette interrogation dans 'Le guide des égarés' de Maïmonide." *Mélanges de sciences religieuses* 53 (1996) 39–50. **Cohen, Mordechai Z.** "A Philosopher's Peshat Exegesis: Maimonides' Literary Approach to the Book of Job and Its Place in the History of Biblical Interpretation." *Shnaton* 15 (2005) 213–64. **Curley, Edwin.** "Maïmonide, Spinoza et le Livre de Job." In *Architectures de la raison. Mélanges offerts à Alexandre Matheron.* Ed. P.-F. Moreau. Fontenay-aux-Roses: ENS Editions, 1996. 103–35. **Dobbs-Weinstein, Idit.** "Medieval Biblical Commentary and Philosophical Inquiry as Exemplified in the Thought of Moses Maimonides and St Thomas Aquinas." In *Moses Maimonides and His Time.* Ed. Eric L. Ormsby. Studies in Philosophy and the History of Philosophy 19. Washington, DC: Catholic University of America Press, 1989. 101–20. **Herbst, Adrian.** "La filosofia juridica de Maimonides: un analisis del libro de Job." *CuadTe* 23 (2004) 289–304. **Kasher, Hannah.** "The Image and Views of Job in the *Guide of the Perplexed." Da'at* 15 (1985) 81–89. **Levinger, Jacob.** "Maimonides' Exegesis of the Book of Job." In *Creative Biblical Exegesis: Christian and Jewish Hermeneutics through the Centuries.* Ed. Benjamin Uffenheimer and Henning Graf Reventlow. Sheffield: JSOT Press, 1988. 81–88. **Nuriel, Avraham.** "Towards a Clarification of the Concept of Satan in the *Guide of the Perplexed"* [Heb.]. *Jerusalem Studies in Jewish Thought* 5 (1986) 83–91. **O'Hara, Mary L.** "Truth in Spirit and Letter: Gregory the Great, Thomas Aquinas, and Maimonides on the Book of Job." In *From Cloister to Classroom: Monastic and Scholastic Approaches to Truth.* Ed. E. Rozanne Elder. Kalamazoo, MI: Cistercian Publications, 1986. 47–79. **Vicchio, Stephen J.** "Job in Maimonides and Gersonides." In his *Job in the Medieval World.* Eugene, OR: Wipf & Stock, 2006. 106–27. **Yaffe, Martin D.** "Providence in Medieval Aristotelianism: Moses Maimonides and Thomas Aquinas on the Book of Job." In *The Voice from the Whirlwind: Interpreting the Book of Job.* Ed. Leo G. Perdue and Clark Gilpin. Nashville: Abingdon Press, 1992. 111–28.

Masnuth, Samuel b. Nissim (12th cent.). Edition: מעין גנים: פורש על ספר איוב. In Samuel Buber. *Commentar zu Job von Rabbi Samuel ben Nissim Masnuth.* Berlin, 1889.

Medieval Jewish Commentaries. *Tseror ḥibure ḳadmonim 'al sefer Iyov: Ma'ayan ganim … Midrash Iyov ha-ḳadum … Rabenu Bahīya 'al Iyov … Kur le-zahav …* Jerusalem: Mekhon Ketav, 2002.

Meir, Samuel ben (Rashbam) (c. 1085–c. 1158). Edition: **Japhet, Sara.** *Rashbam. Perush R. Shemu'el ben Me'ir (Rashbam) le-Sefer Iyov.* Jerusalem: Magnes Press, 2000. See also **Japhet, Sara.** "Insights on Job 3, from a Medieval Commentary: Rabbi Samuel Ben Meir (Rashbam) on the Book of Job." In *Reading from Right to Left: Essays on the Hebrew Bible in Honour of David J. A. Clines.* Ed. J. Cheryl Exum and H. G. M. Williamson. JSOTSup 373. London: Sheffield Academic Press, 2003. 241–53.

Meldola, J. H. ספר איוב [Hebrew text with Spanish version by Jacob Lombroso]. Livorno, 1778.

Menahem, Jacob U. S. F. בית יעקב אש: באיור נחמד ונעים על ספר איוב. Frankfurt an der Oder, 1765.

Midrash. Edition: מדרש איוב. Ed. S. A. Wertheimer. 2nd ed. Jerusalem, 1953.

Nachmanides, Moses (1194?–c. 1270). Editions: *Commentary on Job.* In Rabbinic Bibles, from Bomberg Venice edition of 1517 and Amsterdam edition from 1724.

Chavel, C. B. כתבי רבנו משה בן נחמן. Jerusalem, 1963. 1:19–28. See also **Silver, Daniel Jeremy.** "Nachmanides' Commentary on the Book of Job." *JQR* 60 (1969–70) 9–26.

Pikartei, Avroham ben Schemuel (fl. 1557). Edition: **Brünnel, Gabriele, Walter Röll, and Maria Fuchs (eds.).** *Die "Hiob"-Paraphrase des Avroham ben Schemuel Pikartei: In Handschriftenabdruck und Transkription.* Jidische schtudies 6. Hamburg: Buske, 1996. See also **Röll, Walter.** "Die Edition der ältesten erhaltenen Hiob-Übersetzung eines deutschen Juden." In *Editionsdesiderate zur Frühen Neuzeit: Beiträge zur Tagung der Kommission für die Edition von Texten der Frühen Neuzeit, [4.–7. Oktober 1994 in Wolfenbüttel].* Ed. Hans-Gert Roloff. Chloe 25. Amsterdam: Rodopi, 1997. 621–36.

Qara, Joseph (b. c. 1065). Edition: **Arend [Ahrend], Mosheh [Moshé Max].** *Pêrûs Rabbî Yôsef Qarâ le-séfer Iyyôv: al-pî kitvê-yad û-defûsîm, im mavô', sînnûyê nûsha'ôt, siyyûnê meqôrôt, hearôt û-vê'ûrîm we-nispahôt.* Jerusalem: Kook, 1988. ———. *Le commentaire sur Job de Rabbi Yoséph Qara'. Etude des méthodes philologiques et exégétiques.* Hildesheim: Gerstenberg, 1978. ———. "The Commentary of R. Joseph Kara on Job and Its Relationship to Rashi's Commentary." In *Studies in Bible and Exegesis: In memoriam Arie Toeg.* Ed. Ulrich E. Simon and Moshe H. Goshen-Gottstein. Ramat-Gan: Bar Ilan University Press, 1980. 183–207 [Heb]. **Japhet, Sara.** "The Nature and Distribution of Medieval Compilatory Commentaries in the Light of Rabbi Joseph Kara's Commentary on the Book of Job." In *The Midrashic Imagination: Jewish Exegesis, Thought, and History.* Ed. Michael Fishbane. Albany: State University of New York Press, 1993. 98–130.

Rashi (Yitzhaki, R. Shlomo) (1040–1105). Editions: In Rabbinic Bibles. **Breithaupt, Johann Friedrich.** *Commentarius hebraicus, latine versus, auctus et emendatus atque notis illustratus.* 3 vols. Gotha: Typis Reyherianis, 1713–14. **Shoshana, Abraham.** *Sefer Iyov mi-bet midrasho shel Rashi.* Jerusalem: Mekhon Ofek; Euclid, OH: Sifriyat Fridberg, 1999.

Saadia b. Joseph Gaon (882–942). Editions: **Goodman, L. E.** *The Book of Theodicy. Translation and Commentary on the Book of Job by Saadiah ben Joseph al-Fayyûmî, Translated from the Arabic with a Philosophic Commentary.* New Haven: Yale University Press, 1988. **Qapah, Yosef.** איוב: עם תרגום ופרוש רבנו סעדי הגאון [*Job, with the Translation and Commentary of Rabbi Sa'adia Gaon*]. Jerusalem, 1970. See also **Rosenthal, E. I. J.** "Saadya's Exegesis of the Book of Job." In his edited *Saadya Studies. In Commemoration of the One Thousandth Anniversary of the Death of R. Saadya Gaon.* Manchester: Manchester University Press, 1943. 177–205. **Stump, Eleonore.** "The God of Abraham, Saadia and Aquinas." In *Referring to God: Jewish and Christian Philosophical and Theological Perspectives.* Ed. Paul Helm. London: Curzon Press; New York: St Martin's Press, 2000. 95–119. ———. "Saadia Gaon on the Problem of Evil." *Faith and Philosophy* 14 (1997) 523–49. **Vajda, G.** "Quelques remarques en marge de la seconde rédaction du Commentaire de Saadia Gaon sur le livre de Job." *REJ* 135 (1976) 157–68. **Vicchio, Stephen J.** "Job in Saadiah Gaon and Early Medieval Judaism." In his *Job in the Medieval World.* Eugene, OR: Wipf & Stock, 2006. 87–105. **Weiss, R.** "Saadiah on Divine Grace and Human Suffering." *JJewThPhilos* 9 (2000) 155–71.

Sforno, Obadiah ben Jacob (1470–1550). משפט צדק. *Judicium justum* [commentary on Job]. Venice, 1590.

Tibbon, Samuel ibn (c. 1150–c. 1230). Commentary on Job in his *Ma'amar Yiqqavu Ha-Mayim.* Ed. M. L. Bisliches. Pressburg: A. fon Shmid, 1837. See **Eisen, Robert.** "Samuel Ibn Tibbon on the Book of Job." *AJS Review* 24 (1999) 263–300.

Yiddish Glosses. Röll, Walter. *Die jiddischen Glossen des 14.–16. Jahrhunderts zum Buch "Hiob" in Handschriftenabdruck und Transkription.* Texte und Textgeschichte 52. Tübingen: Niemeyer, 2005.

Zerahiah of Barcelona (13th cent.). Greenberg, Moshe. "Did Job Really Exist? An Issue of Medieval Exegesis." In *Shaarei Talmon: Studies in the Bible, Qumran, and the Ancient Near East Presented to Shemaryahu Talmon.* Ed. M. Fishbane, Emanuel Tov, and Weston W. Fields. Winona Lake, IN: Eisenbrauns, 1992, *3–*11.

Zohar (c. 13th cent.). Translation: *The Zohar.* Ed. Harry Sperling and Maurice Simon. 5 vols. London: Soncino Press, 1931–34. ———. *The Zohar: Translation and Commentary*

[Pritzker Edition]. Trans. Daniel C. Matt. 4 vols. to date. Stanford: Stanford University Press, 2004–2007. ———. *Zohar, the Book of Enlightenment.* Trans. Daniel Chanan Matt. New York: Paulist Press, 1983 [selections]. See also **Vicchio, Stephen J.** "Job in the Zohar." In his *Job in the Medieval World.* Eugene, OR: Wipf & Stock, 2006. 153–72.

c. Christian, Medieval and Pre-16th Century

i. General

Cornagliotti, Anna. "La situazione stemmatica vetero-testamentaria: i libri dell'Ecclesiastico e di Giobbe." In *La bibbia in italiano tra Medievo e Rinascimento.* Ed. Lino Leonardi. Florence: Galluzzo, 1998. 201–25. **Dochhorn, Jan.** "De iusto Job quando venerunt tres amici eius ut viderunt eum (Oxford, Bodleian Library, Holkham 24 [olim 90], 173v–175r)." *ZAC* 10,2 (2006) 187–94.

ii. Authors

Aelfric, abbot of Eynsham (c. 955–1022). Editions: **Grein, C. W. M.** *Älfrik, De vetere et novo Testamento, Pentateuch, Iosua, Buch der Richter und Hiob.* Bibliothek der angelsächsischen Prosa 1. Hamburg: H. Grand, and Kassel: Wigand, 1872; repr. 1921. **Clemoes, Peter, and Malcolm Godden.** *Ælfric's Catholic Homilies.* Early English Text Society 17–18. Oxford: Oxford University Press, 1979, 1997. Text: faculty.virginia.edu/ OldEnglish/ anthology/aelfric_job.html. See also **Brühl, Karl.** *Die Flexion des Verbums in Aelfrics Heptateuch und Buch Hiob.* Marburg: O. Ehrhardt, 1892. **Wilkes, J.** *Lautlehre zu Aelfrics Heptateuch und Buch Hiob.* Bonner Beiträge zur Anglistik 21. Bonn: Hanstein, 1905. **Wohlfahrt, Theodor.** *Die Syntax des Verbums in Aelfric's Uebersetzung des Heptateuch und des Buches Hiob: Ein Beitrag zur Grammatik des Angelsächsichen.* Munich: Theodor Reidel, 1886.

Albert the Great (c. 1200–1280). Edition: **Weiss, Melchior.** *Commentarii in Job: additamentum ad opera omnia B. Alberti, primum ex V. codicibus manuscriptis. Postillae super Job.* Freiburg i.Br.: Herder, 1904. See also **Coggi, R.** "Il significato del libro di Giobbe secondo S. Alberto Magno." *SacDoc* 26 (1981) 105–22. **Jutras, A.-M.** "Le Commentarius in Job d'Albert le Grand et la Disputatio." *Etudes et recherches* 9 (1955) 9–20. **Vicchio, Stephen J.** "Job in Albert the Great and Thomas Aquinas." In his *Job in the Medieval World.* Eugene, OR: Wipf & Stock, 2006. 128–52.

Anon. *Büchlein von dem heiligen Job.* Strassburg, 1498. ———. *Hijr begynt dat boeck Iob.* Augsburg, 1480. ———. *L'Hystore Job* (16th cent.). ———. *Mitteldeutsche Hiob-Paraphrase.* Teutonic Order, 1338. Edition: **Karsten, Torsten Evert (ed.).** *Die mitteldeutsche poetische Paraphrase des Buches Hiob; aus der Handschrift des Königlichen Staatsarchivs zu Königsberg herausgegeben.* Deutsche Texte des Mittelalters 21. Berlin: Weidmann, 1910.

Anon. *Mystère de la patience de Job* (15th cent.), in verse. Also known as *Mystère de Job* and *Pacience de Job.* Edition: **Meiller, Albert (ed.).** *La Pacience de Job, mystère anonyme du XVe siècle (ms. fr. 1774).* Bibliothèque française et romane. Série B, Editions critiques de textes 11. Paris: Klincksieck, 1971. Extracts and synopsis: **Parfaict, François, and Claude Parfaict.** *Histoire du théâtre françois depuis son origine jusqu'à present, avec la vie des plus célèbres poètes dramatiques, un catalogue exact de leurs pièces, et des notes historiques et critiques.* Paris, 1745–1749. 2:532–36.

Anon. *Paraphrase des Buches Hiob.* See **Müller, Walter.** *Über die mittelhochdeutsche Paraphrase des Buches Hiob. Ein Beitrag zur Geschichte der Sorache und Literatur des Deutschordenlandes.* Halle: Niemeyer, 1883.

Anon. *Pety Job.* 15th cent. [a version of the Job texts in the Office for the Dead, in verse]. See **Crawford, Karis Ann.** *The Middle English Pety Job: A Critical Edition with a Study of Its Place in Late Medieval Religious Literature.* Diss. Toronto, 1977. **Fein, Susanna Greer.** "Pety Job." In her *Moral Love Songs and Laments.* Kalamazoo, MI: Medieval Institute Publications, 1998. **Kail, J. (ed.).** *Twenty-Six Political and Other Poems (including 'Petty Job')* from the Oxford MSS. Digby 102 and Douce 322. Early English Text Society 124. London:

Kegan Paul, Trench, Trübner & Co., 1904. **Vicchio, Stephen J.** *Job in the Medieval World.* Eugene, OR: Wipf & Stock, 2006. 56–59.
   Aquinas, Thomas (c. 1225–1274). Editions: *Expositio in librum beati Job.* In *Sancti Thomae Aquinatis Doctoris angelici O.P. expositio in aliquot Veteris Testamenti libros et in Psalmos adjectis brevibus adnotationibus.* Parma: Fiaccadori, 1863. 1–145. *Expositio super Job ad litteram cura et studio Fratrum Praedicatorum.* Opera omnia 26. Rome: Ad Sanctae Sabinae, 1965. **Damico, Anthony, and Martin D. Yaffe.** *Thomas Aquinas, the Literal Exposition of Job: A Scriptural Commentary concerning Providence.* Trans. A. Damico, interpretative essay by M. Yaffe. Atlanta: Scholars Press, 1989. **Fretté, Stanislav Eduard (ed.).** *Doctoris angelici divi Thomae Aquinatis ... Expositiones in Job, in Psalmos Davidis, in canticum canticorum, in Isaiam prophetam.* Sancti Thomae de Aquino opera omnia 18. Paris: L. Vivès, 1876.
   See also **Burrell, David B.** "Maimonides, Aquinas and Gersonides on Providence and Evil." *RelStud* 20 (1984) 335–51. **Chardonnens, Denis.** "L'espérance de la résurrection selon Thomas d'Aquin, commentateur du Livre de Job: 'Dans ma chair, je verrai Dieu' (Jb 19,26)." In *Ordo sapientiae et amoris: image et message de Saint Thomas d'Aquin à travers les récentes études historiques, herméneutiques et doctrinales; hommage au professeur Jean-Pierre Torrell à l'occasion de son 65e anniversaire.* Ed. Carlos-Josaphat Pinto de Oliveira. Fribourg: Editions Université Fribourg, 1993. 65–83. ———. *L'homme sous le regard de la providence: providence de Dieu et condition humaine selon l'Exposition littérale sur le livre de Job de Thomas d'Aquin.* Bibliothèque thomiste 50. Paris: J. Vrin, 1997. **Coggi, R.** "L'insegnamento del libro di Giobbe. i. Sintesi dell'Expositio super Iob di S. Tommaso; ii. Validità perenne." *SacDoc* 27 (1982) 215–310. **Dahan, Gilbert.** "Les éditions des commentaires bibliques de saint Thomas d'Aquin: leur apport à la connaissance du texte de la Bible au XIIIe siècle." *RSPT* 89 (2005) 9–15. **Dobbs-Weinstein, Idit.** "Medieval Biblical Commentary and Philosophical Inquiry as Exemplified in the Thought of Moses Maimonides and St Thomas Aquinas." In *Moses Maimonides and His Time.* Ed. Eric L. Ormsby. Studies in Philosophy and the History of Philosophy 19. Washington, DC: Catholic University of America Press, 1989. 101–20. **Elders, L.** "El Commentario de Santo Tomás de Aquino sobre el Libro de Job." In *Miscellanea Brunero Gherardini.* Ed. Giacomo Campanile, Battista Mondin, and Leo J. Elders. Rome Vatican City: Libreria Editrice Vaticana, 1996. 39–64. **Gri i Casas, C. M.** "Man under the Eye of Providence. The Providence of God and the Human Condition according to the Literal Interpretation of the Book of Job by Thomas Aquinas." *StudMonast* 42 (2000). **Jackson, T. P.** "Must Job Live Forever? A Reply to Aquinas on Providence and Freedom, Evil and Immortality." In *Human and Divine Agency: Anglican, Catholic, and Lutheran Perspectives.* Ed. F. Michael McLain and W. Mark Richardson. Lanham, MD: University Press of America, 1999. 217–52 [= *Thomist* 62 (1998) 1–39]. **Kreit, J.** *Job, un homme pour notre temps, Saint Thomas d'Aquin, Exposition littérale sur le livre de Job.* Paris: Téqui, 1982. **Manzanedo, Marcos F.** "La antropología filosófica en el comentario tomaista al libro de Job." *Ang* 62 (1985) 419–71. ———. *La antropología filosófica en el comentario tomista al libro de Job.* Rome: Pontificia Università San Tommaso, 1987. **Michaud-Quantin, P.** "L'édition critique de l'Expositio super Job de S. Thomas d'Aquin." *RSPT* 50 (1966) 407–10. **O'Hara, Mary L.** "Truth in Spirit and Letter: Gregory the Great, Thomas Aquinas, and Maimonides on the Book of Job." In *From Cloister to Classroom: Monastic and Scholastic Approaches to Truth.* Ed. E. Rozanne Elder. Kalamazoo, MI: Cistercian Publications, 1986. 47–79. **Pandolfi, Carmelo.** "Il prologo al commento a Giobbe di San Tommaso d'Aquino." *Aquinas* 37 (1994) 597–622. ———. "Linee per una metafisica della sofferenza suggerite da Giobbe e dal Commento a Giobbe di San Tommaso." *Il cannocchiale* (May–August, 1998) 115–37. **Perotto, Lorenzo A.** "La mistica del dolore nel Commento di S. Tommaso al libro di Giobbe." In *S. Tommaso filosofo: ricerche in occasione di due centenari accademici.* Ed. Antonio Piolanti. Città del Vaticano: Libreria editrice vaticana, 1995. 191–203 [= *Divinitas* 46 (2003) 53–67]. **Pflibsen, T. P.** *Nicholas of Lyra's Use of St Thomas Aquinas' "Expositio super Iob ad litteram" in his Postillas on Job.* Diss. Marquette, 2006. **Saranyana,**

Jose I. "Sobre la tristeza. Santo Tomás comenta el libro de Job." *Scripta theologica* 6 (1974) 329–61. **Sommers, M. C.** "*Manifestatio:* The Historical Presencing of Being in Aquinas' *Expositio super Job.*" *Proceedings of the American Catholic Philosophical Association* 62 (1988) 147–56. **Stump, Eleonore.** "Aquinas on the Sufferings of Job." In *Reasoned Faith: Essays in Philosophical Theology in Honor of Norman Kretzmann.* Ed. Eleonore Stump. Ithaca: Cornell University Press, 1993. 328–57 [= *Human and Divine Agency: Anglican, Catholic, and Lutheran Perspectives.* Ed. F. Michael McLain and W. Mark Richardson. Lanham, MD: University Press of America, 1999. 191–215; *The Evidential Argument from Evil.* Ed. D. Howard Snyder. Bloomington: Indiana University Press, 1996. 49–68]. ———. "The God of Abraham, Saadia and Aquinas." In *Referring to God: Jewish and Christian Philosophical and Theological Perspectives.* Ed. Paul Helm. London: Curzon Press; New York: St Martin's Press, 2000. 95–119. **Vicchio, Stephen J.** "Job in Albert the Great and Thomas Aquinas." In his *Job in the Medieval World.* Eugene, OR: Wipf & Stock, 2006. 128–52. **Wright, J. H.** "Man under the Influence of Providence: Divine Providence and the Human Condition according to the 'Literal Exposition of the Book of Job' by Thomas Aquinas." *TS* 60 (1999) 548–49. **Yaffe, Martin D.** "Providence in Medieval Aristotelianism: Moses Maimonides and Thomas Aquinas on the Book of Job." In *The Voice from the Whirlwind: Interpreting the Book of Job.* Ed. Leo G. Perdue and Clark Gilpin. Nashville: Abingdon Press, 1992. 111–28. **Yocum, John P.** "Aquinas' Literal Exposition on Job." In *Aquinas on Scripture: An Introduction to His Biblical Commentaries.* Ed. Thomas G. Weinandy, Daniel A. Keating, and John P. Yocum. London: T. & T. Clark International, 2005. 21–42.

   Bede (673–735). See **Vaccari, A.** "Scripsitne Beda commentarium in Job?" *Bib* 5 (1924) 369–73.

   Bruno d'Asti (Bruno of Segni) (c. 1048–1123). Editions: **Bruno d'Asti.** *Expositio in Job. PL* 164:551–696. *Expositio in Jobum.* In *Opera ... aucta et adnotationibus illustrata ...* Rome: Joannes Zempel, 1789–91.

   Denis the Carthusian [Dionysius Cartusianus, Denys van Leeuwen, Denys Ryckel] (1402–71). Edition: *De causa diversitatis eventorum humanorum. Enarrationes in libros Job, Tobiae, Judith, Esther, Esdrae, Nehemiae, Machabaeorum.* Cologne, 1534. *Enarratio in librum Job.* In *Doctoris ecstatici D. Dionysii cartusiani opera omnia.* Monstrolii: de Pratis, 1897–98. 4:293–696.

   Dionysius Bar Salibi (d. 1171). Edition: **Jacobsen, Thorkild Peter Rudolph.** *The Commentary of Dionysius Bar Salibi on the Book of Job.* Diss. Chicago, 1929.

   Enikel, Jans der (13th cent.). "Job." In his *Weltchronik.* 13173–13456. In *History as Literature: German World Chronicles of the Thirteenth Century in Verse. Excerpts from: Rudolf von Ems, Weltchronik; The Christherre-Chronik; Jans Enikel, Weltchronik.* Ed. Graeme Dunphy. Medieval Texts in Bilingual Editions 3. Kalamazoo, MI: Western Michigan University Press, 2003.

   Francocordia, J. de. *Commentarius super librum Job.* 1441.

   Kulm, Tilo von (fl. 1331–1338). Editions: **Karsten, Torsten Evert.** *Die mitteldeutsche poetische Paraphrase des Buches Hiob; aus der Handschrift des Königlichen Staatsarchivs zu Königsberg herausgegeben.* Deutsche Texte des Mittelalters 21. Berlin: Weidmann, 1910. **Mueller, Walter.** *Ueber die mitteldeutsche poetische Paraphrase [by Tilo von Culm] des Buches Hiob: Ein Beitrag zur Geschichte der Sprache und Literatur des Deutschordenlandes.* Halle: E. Karras, 1882; Niemeyer, 1883.

   Lathcen [Laidcend, Laidgen] (d. 661). Edition: *Egloga quam scripsit Lathcen filius Baith de Moralibus Job quas Gregorius fecit.* Ed. M. Adriaen. CCSL 145. Turnhout: Brepols, 1969. See also **Wasselynck, R.** "Les Moralia in Job dans les ouvrages de morale du haut moyen âge latin." *RTAM* 31 (1964) 5–31.

   López de Ayala (1332–1407). Edition: **Pero Branciforti, Francesco.** *Pero López de Ayala, El libro de Job: Edizione critica con introduzione, note e glossario.* Università degli studi di Messina. Pubblicazioni della Facoltà di Magistere. Testi e documenti 1. Messina: G. D'Anna, 1962.

Macé de La Charité, curé de Cenquonis (13th cent.). *La Bible de Macé de La Charité.* IV. *Ruth, Judith, Tobie, Esther, Daniel, Job* [free translation of Petrus Riga's *Aurora*]. Ed. Hendrikus Cornelis Maria van der Krabben. Leidse romanistische reeks 10/4. Leiden: E. J. Brill, 1964. See also **Beichner, Paul E.** "The Old French Verse *Bible* of Macé de la Charité, a Translation of the *Aurora*." *Speculum* 22 (1947) 226–39. **Herzog, Eugen.** "Untersuchungen zu Macé de la Charité's altfranzösischer Übersetzung des Alten Testamentes." In *Sitzungsberichte der philosophisch-historische Classe der Kaiserlichen Akademie der Wissenschaften* 142. Vienna, 1900. **Paris, Gaston.** "Macé de la Charité, auteur d'une Bible en vers français." *Histoire littéraire de France* 28 (1881) 208–21.

Marquard von Lindau (14th cent.). Editions: **Greifenstein, Eckart.** *Der Hiob-Traktat des Marquard von Lindau. Überlieferung, Untersuchung und kritische Textausgabe.* Münchener Texte und Untersuchungen zur deutschen Literatur des Mittelalters 68. Munich: Artemis, 1979. **Palmer, Nigel F.** "Der Hiob-Traktat Marquards von Lindau in lateinischer Überlieferung." *Beiträge zur Geschichte der deutschen Sprache* 104 (1982) 48–83.

Matthew of Aquasparta (c. 1240–1302). *Postilla super librum Jobum* [unpublished].

Melitona, Wilhelm von (d. c. 1260). *Postilla super Iob.* Bordeaux, Bibliothèque Municipale, Ms 26–27 [unpublished].

Nicetas of Heraclea (11th cent.). Edition: **Junius, P. [Young, Patrick] (ed.).** *Catena Graecorum Patrum in beatum Job collectore Niceta Heracleae Metropolita ex duobus mss. Bibliothecae Bodleianae codicibus, graece, nunc primum in lucem edita et latine versa, opera et studio Patricii Junii Bibliothecarii Regii.* London, 1637 [= *PG* 64:505–635].

Nicholas of Lyra (c. 1270–1340). Edition: *Postillae perpetuae in Vetus et Novum Testamentum.* Cologne, 1478.

Odo [Odon] of Cluny (879–942). Editions: *Epitome moralium S. Gregorii in Job.* PL 133:105–512. **Marrier, Martin.** *Sancti Odonis ... Moralium in Job libri XXXV.* Paris: S. Cramoisy, 1617. See also **Wasselynck, R.** "Les Moralia in Job dans les ouvrages de morale du haut moyen âge latin." *RTAM* 31 (1964) 5–31.

Olivi, Petrus Ioannis (1248–1298). *Expositio in librum Iob.* Biblioteca Apostolica Vaticana, Vatican City. Ms Urb. lat. 480 [unpublished].

Peter of Blois (1135–1204). Editions: *Compendium in Job.* PL 207:795–826. *Insignia opera in unum volumen collecta et emendata ... Epistolae; Sermones; Tractatus in librum Job; Contra perfidiam Iudeorum; De confessione; De amicitia christiana ...* Paris: André Boucard, 1519. **Gildea, Joseph (ed.).** *L'Hystore Job: An Old French Verse Adaptation of Compendium in Job by Peter of Blois.* 2 vols. Liège: Vaillant-Carmanne; Villanova, PA: St Thomas Press, 1979. See also **Bates, R. C.** *L'hystore Job: adaptation en vers français du "Compend[i]um in Job" [of Peter of Blois].* Yale Romanic Studies. New Haven: Yale University Press, 1937.

Peter of Waltham, archdeacon of London (c. 1190–1196). Edition: **Gildea, Joseph (ed.).** *Remediarium conversorum. A Synthesis in Latin of Moralia in Job by Gregory the Great.* Villanova, PA: Villanova University Press, 1984. Translation: **Gildea, Joseph.** *Source Book of Self-Discipline: A Synthesis of Moralia in Job by Gregory the Great. A Translation of Peter of Waltham's Remediarium conversorum.* American University Studies. Series VII. Theology and Religion 117. New York: Peter Lang, 1991. See also **Wasselynck, R.** "Les Moralia in Job dans les ouvrages de morale du haut moyen âge latin." *RTAM* 31 (1964) 5–31.

Pico della Mirandola, Giovanni (Italian philosopher, 1463–1494). Wirszubski, Chaim. "Giovanni Pico's Book of Job" [using Gersonides on Job]. *Journal of the Warburg and Courtauld Institutes* 32 (1969) 171–99.

Riga, Peter of (c. 1140–1209). Edition: **Beichner, Paul E.** *Aurora: Petri Rigae Biblia versificata: A Verse Commentary on the Bible.* Publications in Mediaeval Studies, University of Notre Dame 19. Notre Dame: University of Notre Dame Press, 1965.

Roland of Cremona (13th cent.). *Commentarius in Iob.* Paris, Bibliothèque Nationale, Cod. lat. 405 [unpublished]. See also **Dondaine, A.** "Un commentaire scripturaire de Roland de Cremone: 'Le livre de Job'." *Archivum Fratrum Praedicatorum* 11 (1941) 109–37.

Rolle, Richard, of Hampole (1290–1329). Editions: *Explanationes in Job.* Oxford, 1483. **Moyes, Malcolm Robert.** *Richard Rolle's "Expositio super novem lectiones mortuorum"* [from Job]: *An Introduction and Contribution towards a Critical Edition.* 2 vols. Salzburg Studies in English Literature. Elizabethan and Renaissance Studies 92/2. Salzburg: Institut fur Anglistik und Amerikanistik, Universität Salzburg, 1988.

Rupert de Deutz (c. 1070–1129). Edition: *Super Job commentarius. PL* 168:963–1196.

Walafrid Strabo (c. 808–49) (attrib.). Edition: *Glossa ordinaria … In librum Job. PL* 113:747–840. See also **Datema, Cornelis.** "A Supposed Narratio on Job, BHG 939t." *AnBoll* 103 (1985) 303–4. **Stiglmayr, H.** "Der Jobkommentar von Monte Cassino." *ZTK* 43 (1919) 269–88.

Wycliffe [Wyclif], John (c. 1320–1384). Gruber, Annemarie. *Das Lehngut der WyclifBibel: Eine Untersuchung des Buches Hiob.* Diss. Zurich, 1998. **Meichtry, Annemarie.** *Die Sprache der Wyclif-Bibel: Die Verwendung von Lehnwörtern in den Büchern Baruch, Richter und Hiob.* Europäische Hochschulschriften 14/436. Berne: Peter Lang, 2007.

d. 16th to 18th Centuries

The items in this Section are arranged by decades of publication. At the end of the Section there is an index of the authors mentioned, with the dates of publication.

i. General

Beecher, Susan Godsil. *Sixteenth and Early Seventeenth-Century French and English Expositions of the Book of Job.* Diss. London, 1977. **Conques, Jeroni (Catalan author, 16th cent.).** *Llibre de Job: versió del segle XVI* [Catalan]. Ed. Jaume Riera i Sans. Biblioteca Nacional Biblioteca Torres Amat 3. Barcelona: Institut d'Estudio Catalans; Departament de Filologia, Universitat de Barcelona: Curial, 1976. **Cooper, Alan M.** "The Suffering Servant and Job: A View from the Sixteenth Century." In *"As those who are taught": The Interpretation of Isaiah from the LXX to the SBL.* Ed. Claire Mathews McGinnis and Patricia K. Tull. SBL Symposium Series 27. Atlanta: Society of Biblical Literature, 2006. 189–200. **John of the Cross (1542–1591).** See **Ruíz Pesce, Ramón Eduardo.** "Dios del pobre. Amor gratuito y sufrimiento del inocente. Leer el Libro de Job desde San Juan de la Cruz a Gustavo Gutiérrez." *Studium filosofía y teología* 5 (2002) 207–20. **Ludwig of Anhalt, Prince (1579–1650).** See **Trutta-Szabo, Diane.** *Prince Ludwig of Anhalt's Book of Job: An Example of Christian Hebraism during the Thirty Years' War (Germany).* Diss. Pittsburgh, 1998. **Staupitz, J. von (1460–1524).** See **Schulze, Manfred.** "Der Hiob-Prediger: Johannes von Staupitz auf der Kanzel der Tübinger Augustinerkirche" [Job 1:1–2:10]. In *Augustine, the Harvest, and Theology: Essays Dedicated to Heiko Augustinus Oberman in Honor of His Sixtieth Birthday.* Ed. Kenneth Hagen. Leiden: E. J. Brill, 1990. 60–88. **Ulrich, Jakob.** *Job, un drama engiadinais del 16. secul. nouvamaing publicho.* Societad Rhaetoromanscha. Annalas 12. Chur, 1886. **Zwingli, Ulrich (1484–1531).** See **Egli, Emil (ed.).** *Huldreich Zwinglis sämtliche Werke.* 13. *Exegetische Schriften.* 1. *Schriften zum Alten Testament, Erläuterungen zur Genesis, Erläuterungen zum Exodus, Hiob, die Psalmen.* Corpus reformatorum 100. Berlin: Schwetschke, 1963.

ii. Authors

1500s. Anon. *Liber beati Job. Si patientiam, si modestiam, si constantiam in tribulationibus, infirmitatibus et adversis, si denique celibem ac beatam vitam ducere cupis librum beati Job ydumie sive Arabiam legito* [the Latin text preceded by Jerome's prologue]. Paris, 1508.

1520s. Anon. *Contenta Libri Regum IIII libri Paralipoménon II libri Esdrae IIII liber Tobiae liber Judith liber Esther liber Job* [Vulgate]. Paris: Simon Colinaeus (de Colines), 1529. **Brentius [Brentz], Johann.** *Hiob cum piis et eruditis Iohannis Brentii commentariis ad hebrai-cam veritatem ita translatus, ut nulla porro obscuritas lectorem possit offendere.* Haguenau, 1527. **Bucer, M.** *Commentarii in librum Jobi.* Strasbourg, 1528. **Bugenhagen, J. [Iohannis**

Bugenhagius Pomeranus]. *Adnotationes in Jobum.* Strasbourg. 1526 [= Bibliotheca palatina Microfiche F1377. Munich: Saur, 1991]. **Dati, Juliano (Giuliano).** *Historia di Sancto Iob Propheta ... messa inversi vulgari.* 1520 (?). **Lausana, J. de.** *Moralitates in Iob.* Limoges, 1528. **Nebiensis, A. Justinianus.** *Liber beati Job: quem nuper hebraice veritati restituit* [Vulgate and the author's own translation]. Paris: Egidio de Gourmont, 1520.

   1530s. Brucioli, Antonio. *Il libro di Iob, tradotto dalla ebraica verita, in lingua italiana, & con nuovo commento dichiarato.* Venice, 1534. **Cajetan [Gaetanus], Tommaso de Vio.** *In librum Iob commentarii.* Rome: Antonio Blado, 1535. **Coverdale, Miles.** *Biblia: The Bible, That Is, the Holy Scripture of the Olde and New Testament, Faithfully and Truly Translated out of Douche and Latyn in to Englishe.* Cologne, 1535. **Oecolampadius, Johannes.** *In librum Iob exegemata. Opus admodum eruditum, ac omnibus divinae Scripturae studiosis utile.* Basel, 1532. **Pélerin, J. [Le Viateur].** *Texte de Hiob, translaté selon la verité hebraïque. Et bref commentaire du Viateur [Jean Pélerin] sur icelluy.* Paris, 1530.

   1540s. Anon. *Job* [fifth part of Hebrew Bible of 1539–44]. Paris: Robert Estienne, 1541. ———. *Proverbia Salomonis et Job.* Paris: Robert Estienne, 1545. **Linck, Wenzeslaus.** *Das ... theyl des Alten Testaments. 2. Annotation ... inn die Historische bücher der Bibel: Nämlich Josua, der Richter, Ruth, Samuelis, der Künig, Chronica, Essra, Nehemia, Esther, Hiob.* Strasbourg: Balthassar Beck, 1545 [= Bibliotheca palatina. Microfiche E1721–E1723. Munich: Saur, 1990]. **Lorichius, Johannes (d. 1569 [?]).** *Iobus: Patientiae spectaculum in comoedaiam et actum comicum nuper redactus* [also known as *Iobus comoedia*]. Marburg: Christian Egenolff, 1543. Ed. Edward Schröder. Marburg, 1897. **Narhamer, Johan.** *Historia Jobs.* Hof a.d. Saale, 1546. Ed. Barbara Könneker and Wolfgang F. Michael. Arbeiten zur mittleren deutschen Literatur 12. Berne: Lang, 1983. **Savonarola, Girolamo (Italian reformer, 1452–1498).** *Prediche sopra Giobbe* [1545]. In *Edizione nationale delle opere di G. Savonarola.* III/1–2. Ed. Roberto Ridolfi. Rome: A. Belardetti, 1957. **Stephanus, Robertus.** ספר איוב. *Job.* Paris, 1540. **Titelmans, Franciscus.** *Elucidatio paraphrastica in librum D. Iob.* Antwerp, Paris, 1547.

   1550s. Anon. *Bibliorum graecorum latinorumque pars secunda, continens Regum libros quatuor, & Paralipomenon duos, tum Esdram et Neemiam, Esther & Job, Davidis Psalterium, Solomonis Proverbia, Ecclesiasten & Canticum canticorum.* Basel: Nikolaus Brylinger, 1550. **Calvin, Jean.** *Sermons sur le livre de Job, recueillis fidèlement de sa bouche selon qu'il les preschoit.* 1554 [= *Johannis Calvini in librum Jobi conciones.* Geneva: Eustathius Vignon, 1593]. Editions: *Calvini opera.* Ed. G. Baum, E. Cunitz, and E. Reuss. Vols. 33–34. Braunschweig, 1887. See also **Schreiner, Susan E.** "Exegesis and Double Justice in Calvin's Sermons on Job." *Church History* 58 (1989) 322–38. ———. "Through a Mirror Darkly: Calvin's Sermons on Job." *CalvTJ* 21 (1986) 175–93. **Smid, T. D.** "Some Bibliographical Observations on Calvin's Sermons sur le livre de Job." *Free University Quarterly* (1960) 51–56. **Woudstra, Marten H.** "The Use of 'Example' in Calvin's Sermons on Job." In *Bezield verband: opstellen aangeboden aan prof. J. Kamphuis bij gelegenheid van zijn vijfentwintig-jarig ambtsjubileum als hoogleraar aan de Theologische Hogeschool van De Gereformeerde Kerken in Nederland te Kampen op 9 ap Bezield verband.* Ed. M. J. Arntzen, J. Boersema, and J. Bruggen. Kampen: Van den Berg, 1984. 344–51.| **d'Albiac, A. [A. du Plessis].** *Le livre de Iob: traduit en poésie françoise, selon la verité hébraïque.* Geneva, 1552. **Fer, J.** *Jobi historia docta et catholica explicatio in CXIIII conciones eleganter distributa.* Cologne, 1558. **Járava, Fernando de.** *Las liciones de Job en castellano.* Antwerp, 1550. **Lutz, Renhardus.** *Commentariorum, quibus beati viri Iob historia ... breviter explicatur, libri II.* Basel, 1559. **Wildt [Wild], Johann.** *Iobi historia Christlich vnd nützlich Predig weyss aussgelegt ... Durch Johan Wildt ... geprediget ... 1552.* Mainz, 1558.

   1560s. Anon. *Libri regum IIII. Paralipomenon, II. Esdrae, IIII. Tobiae, I. Judith, I. Esther, I. Job, I.* Antwerp: Christophe Plantin, 1563. **Borrhaus, Martin.** *Commentarius in Jobum et Ecclesiasten.* Basel, 1564. **Forerius, Franciscus.** *Commentarius in Job.* Antwerp, 1563. **Luther, M.** *Das Buch Hiob auffs new zugericht.* Erfurt, 1560 [repr. Bibliotheca palatina F1277. Munich, Saur, 1991]. See also **Vicchio, Stephen J.** *Job in the Medieval World.* Eugene, OR: Wipf & Stock, 2006. 173–83.| **Steuchus, Augustinus.** *Enarrationes in* *librum Jobi.* Venice, 1567; Paris, 1578. **Weller, Hieronymus.** *Das Buch Hiob ausgeleget.* [1.] *Die ersten XII. Capitel des Buchs Hiob. Allen betrubten hertzen zu dieser letzten Zeit tröstlich.* Nuremburg, 1563. II. *Der ander Theil des Buchs Hiob, darinnen begriffen ist die Auslegung vom dreyzehenden Capitel an bisz ins zwey vnnd zweintzigste.* Nuremburg, 1565 [repr. Bibliotheca palatina. Microfiche E 175–77, E637–38. Munich: Saur, 1990].

1570s. Belleau, R. *Traduction en vers du livre de Job.* 1576. **Beza, Théodore de.** *Ioannis Merceri regii quondam in academia parisiensi literarum hebraicarum professoris Commentarii in librum Iob. Aiecta est Theodori Bezae epistola, in qua de huius viri doctrina, & istorum Commentariorum utilitate disseritur.* Geneva: Eustathius Vignon, 1573. See also **Raitt, Jill.** "Beza, Guide for the Faithful Life (Lectures on Job, Sermons on Song of Songs, 1587)." *SJT* 39 (1986) 83–107.| **Calvin, John.** *Sermons upon the Booke of Job, translated out of French.* Trans. Arthur Golding. London, 1574 [= *Sermons on Job.* Edinburgh: Banner of Truth Trust, 1993; Carlisle, PA: Banner of Truth Trust, 1994]. See also **Vicchio, Stephen J.** *Job in the Medieval World.* Eugene, OR: Wipf & Stock, 2006. 183–93.| **León, Luis Ponce de.** *Exposición de Job* [1576]. Editions: **Alonso González, Alegría, and Jacobo Sanz Hermido (eds.).** *Obras propias y traducciones latinas, griegas, y italianas: con la paráfrasi de algunos psalmos, y capítulos de Job.* Madrid: Imprenta del Reino, 1631. **Anon (ed.).** *Exposición del libro de Job. Obra posthuma del Padre Fr. L. de Leon.* Madrid, 1779. **Merino, Antolín (ed.).** *Obras del P. Mtro Fr. Luis de León reconocidas y cotejadas con varios manuscritos auténticos por Merino.* I–II. Madrid: Compañia de Impresores y Libreros del Reino, 1885. **García, Félix (ed.).** *Obras completas castellanas de Fray Luis de León.* Biblioteca de autores cristianos 3. Madrid: BAC, 1951. 791–1287. **García Gual, Carlos (ed.).** *El Libro de Job / Fray Luis de León.* Madrid: Idea, 1987. **Lera, Javier San José (ed.).** *Exposición del libro de Job.* Textos recuperados 8. Salamanca: Universidad de Salamanca, 1992. See also **Arkin, Alexander Habib.** *La influencia de la exégesis hebrea en los comentarios bíblicos de Fray Luis de León.* Madrid: Consejo Superior de Investigaciones Científicas, Instituto Benito Arias Montano, 1966. 65–182. **Baruzi, J.** *Luis de León, interprète du livre de Job.* Cahiers de la RHPR. Paris: Presses Universitaires de France, 1966. **Urrutibe Heity, Amelia.** "Las referencias personales de Fray Luis de León en la 'Exposición del libro de Job'." In *Estudios de crítica literaria.* Serie Trabajos de alumnos 3. Buenos Aires: Universidad Nacional de La Plata, Facultad de Humanidades y Ciencias de la Educación, 1973. 25–37. **Valentí, José Ignacio.** *Apologia sobre la exposición que hizo el gran poeta lírico Fr. Luis de León acerca del Libro de Job.* Madrid: Imprenta de los Huérfanos, 1894.| **Mercerus [Mercier], J.** *Commentarii in librum Iob.* Geneva, 1573. **Oecolampadius, Johann.** *Commentarii omnes in libros prophetarum et Jobum.* Geneva, 1578. **Osorio, Hieronymus de.** *Paraphraseon in Job libri III.* Cologne, 1579. **Strigelius, Victorinus.** *Liber Iob, ad ebraicam veritatem recognitus et argumentis atque scholiis illustrata.* Leipzig, 1571.

1580s. Anon. *The Third Part of the Bible, (after Some Division) Conteining Five Excellent Bookes, Most Commodious for All Christians; Faithfully Translated out of the Ebrews, and Expounded with Most Profitable Annotation* [Job, Psalms, Proverbs, Ecclesiastes, and the Song of Solomon]. London: Christopher Barker, 1580. **Beza, Theodore de.** *Jobus commentario et paraphrasi illustratus.* Geneva, 1583. ———. *Iob Expounded by Theodore Beza, Partly in Manner of a Commentary, Partly in Manner of a Paraphrase. Faithfully Translated out of Latine into English.* Cambridge: John Legatt, 1589 (?) [= Early English books, 1475–1640, 275:16 = 179:3]. ———. *Jobus partim commentariis partim paraphrasi illustratus.* Geneva, 1589. **Huelga [Huerga], Cipriano de la.** *Commentaria in librum beati Job et in Cantica Canticorum Salomonis regis.* Alcalá: Complutum, 1582 [= *Obras completas.* III. *Comentarios al libro de Job.* Ed. Crescencio Miguélez Baños. Humanistas españoles 9. León: Secretariado de publicaciones de la Universidad, 1994]. **Lavater, Ludwig.** *Liber Iobi, homiliis CXLI ... germanica lingua explicatus ... ac recens ... latinitate donatus.* Zurich, 1585. **Morgan, William.** *Llyvyr Iob* [first Welsh translation]. London, 1588 [repr. Oxford: J. G. Evans, 1888]. **Zúñiga, D. de [Didacus a Stunica].** *In Iob commentaria, quibus triplex eius editio vulgata Latina, Hebraea, et Graeca septuaginta interpretum, necnon et Chaldaea explicantur et inter se cum diferre hae editiones videntur, conciliantur, et praecepta vitae cum virtute colendae literaliter* *deducuntur.* Toledo, 1584. See also **San José Lera, Javier.** "Fray Diego de Zúñiga, In Iob Commentaria, 1584." *La ciudad de Dios* 212 (1999) 149–82.

    1590s. Chassignet, J.-B. *Job ou de la fermeté* [verse paraphrase]. Bibliothèque Nationale, Ms. fr. 2381. 1592. See also **Müller, Armand.** *Un poète religieux du XVIe siècle: Jean-Baptiste Chassignet, 1578(?)–1635(?).* Paris: R. Foulon, 1951. **Whitten, Sara W.** *A Critical Edition of Jean-Baptiste Chassignet's Job ou de la fermeté.* Diss. Vanderbilt, 1968.| **Merlin, Pierre.** *Iiob Petri Merlini commentariis illustratus. Analytica methodo in gratiam studiosae iuventutis conscriptus.* Geneva: Eustathius Vignon, 1599 [= Bibliotheca palatina F4889/F4891. Munich: Saur, 1992]. **Roulliard, S.** *Job, ou Histoire de la patience de Job traduicte de la sacrée Bible en vers françois, divisée en quatre livres.* 2nd ed. Paris: Nicolas & Pierre Bonfons, 1599. **Thuanus [Thou], J. A. de.** *Metaphrasis poetica librorum aliquot sacrorum. Iobus, sive de constantia libri IIII poetica metaphrasi explicati.* Paris, 1588; Tours, 1592.

    1600s. Heneus, Andreas. *Jobus, carmine latino redditus.* Frankfurt, 1602. **Pineda, J. de.** *Commentariorum in Iob libri tredecim, adiuncta singulis capitibus sua paraphrasi, quae et longioris commentarii continet.* 2 vols. Madrid, 1600 [usually printed as the commentary on Job in editions of the biblical commentaries of Cornelius a Lapide]. See also **García Moreno, Antonio.** "Juan de Pineda y el libro de Job." *EstBíb* 35 (1976) 23–47, 165–85.
    ———. *El sentido del dolor en el libro de Job según Juan de Pineda.* Diss. Gregorian University, 1977 [= *Sentido del dolor en Job.* Toledo: Estudio Teológico de San Ildefonso, 1990].

    1610s. Bolducius [Bolduc], Jacobus. *Commentaria in librum Job.* 2 vols. Paris, 1619. **Jesús Maria, Juan de.** *Paraphrasis in Librum Job, cui subjicitur brevis expensio litteralis, vel tropologica, vel mixta.* Rome: Guglielmo Facciotti, 1611. **Mello de Sousa, Joâo de (Joannes Mellius de Sousa).** *In librum Job paraphrasis poetica.* Lyon: Horatius Cardon, 1615. **Piscator, Johannes.** *In librum Jobi commentarius. In quo, praeter novam versionem, versioni Tremellio-Junianae e regione adjectam, ordine & distincte proponuntur I. Analysis logica singulorum capitum; II. Scholia in singula capita; III. Observationes locorum doctrinae e singulis capitibus depromtae.* Herborn, 1612 [= Bibliotheca palatina; E1952/E1954. Munich: Saur, 1990]. **Rosapachius, Joannes Gulielmus.** *Jobus ligatus; h. e. Paraphrasis poetica historiae Divi Jobi, elegiaco carmine.* Hanover, 1613. **Scialach, Victorius.** *Libri justi Job ex Chaldaeo, sive Syro idiomate in Latinum nunc primum interpretatio in totius catholicae ecclesiae utilitatem edita.* Rome: Stefano Paolini, 1618. **Tuccius Lucensis [Stefano Tucci].** *Lectiones in Job.* Rome, 1617.

    1620s. Chasteignier de la Roche-Posai, Henri-Louis. *Exercitationes in librum Job.* Poitiers, 1628. **Estius, Gulielmus [Willem Hesselzoon Van Est].** *Annotationes in praecipua ac difficiliora Sacrae Scripturae loca. Annotationes in librum Job.* Douai, 1620. **Janssonius, Jacobus.** *In propheticum librum Job enarratio.* Louvain, 1623. **Sanctius [Sanchez], Gaspar.** *In librum Iob commentarii cum paraphrasi.* Leiden: Jacob Cardon and Pierre Cavellat, 1625.

    1630s. Anon. *Das Buch Hiob, nach der Hebreischen Grundsprache gottsfürchtiger und gelehrter Lehrer Auslegung: In zwölf vnd dreyzehen silbige deutsche Reime gesetzt, Sampt ... einer kurtzen erzehlung wer dieser heilige Mann gewesen und zu welcher Zeitt ere gelebet.* Wittenberg, 1638. **Aurelius, Abraham.** *Iobus, sive de patientia liber, poetica metaphrasi explicatus.* London, 1632. **Benserradde, I. de.** *Paraphrases sur les IX. leçons de Iob.* Paris, 1637. **Cermellus, Augustinus.** *Catena in Iob. Ex selectis antiquorum, et recentium Patrum sententijs, philosophorum testimonijs, Graecis, et Latinis Historijs ... concinnata. In qua vetus sapientum doctrina restauratur, nova illustratur, doctorum sensus expenduntur ...* Geneva: P. J. Calenzanus and J. M. Farronus, 1636. **Crommius, A.** *In Jobi historiam.* Louvain, 1632. **Drusius [van der Driesche], J.** *Nova versio et scholia in Iobum.* Amsterdam, 1636. **Duport, J. D.** ΘΡΗΝΟΘΡΙΑΜΒΟΣ. *Sive Liber Job graeco carmine redditus.* Cambridge, 1637. **Gordon, James.** *Biblia Sacra cum commentariis ad sensum literae et explicatione temporum, locorum, rerumque omnium quae in sacris codicibus habent obscuritatem.* Paris, 1632. 548–91. **Sandys, George.** *A Paraphrase upon the Divine Poems. A Paraphrase upon Job ...* London, 1638 [= *Selections from the Metrical Paraphrases on the Psalms, the Book of Job, and other portions of Holy Scripture, by George Sandys ... With a Memoir of His Life and Writings, by the Rev. Henry John Todd.* London: J. G. & F. Rivington, 1839]. **Senault, Jean-François.** *Paraphrase* *sur Job*. Paris, 1637. Rouen: Pierre de La Motte, 1667 [= *A Paraphrase upon Job, Written in French*. London: R. Bostock, 1648; *The Pattern of Patience in the Example of Holy Job: A Paraphrase upon the Whole Book*. London: Joseph Cranford, 1657]. **Sylvester, J.** *A Divine and True TragiComedy. Iob Triumphant in His Triall: or, The Historie of His Heroicall Patience, in a Measured Metaphrase*. In *The Second Session of the Parliament of Vertues Royall (Continued by Prorogation) for Better Propagation of All True Pietie and Utter Extirpation of Atheisme and Hypocrisie, Avarice and Crueltie, Pride and Luxurie*. In his *Du Bartas: His Diuine Weekes, and Workes*. London, 1633. 886–950. **Vavassor [Vavasseur], François [Franciscus].** *Jobus brevi commentario et metaphrasi poetica illustratus*. Paris. 1638 [? = *Francisci Vavasseur e societate Jesu Jobus: Carmen heroïcum*. Paris: Jean Camusat, 1638].

   1640s. Abbott, George. *The Whole Booke of Job Paraphrased, or, Made Easie for Any to Understand*. London: Edward Griffin for Henry Overton, 1640. **Cocceius (Coccejus, Coch), Johannes.** *Commentarius in librum Ijobi, synopticam rerum ac textus dispositionem, et expositionem verborum ac sententiarum ex Hebraismi proprietate ac emphasi usuque et analogia Scripturae continens atque ad linguae sanctae pleniorem intelligentiam, sensus perspicuitatem, lectionis facilitatem, meditationis ubertatem et certitudinem memoriaeque firmitatem adornatus*. Franeker, 1644. **Corderus [Corderius, Cordier], Balthasar.** *Iob elucidatus*. Antwerp, 1646 [= Cornelius a Lapide, *Commentaria in Scripturam Sacram*. III. *Balthasaris Corderi Commentaria in librum Job, quibus accedit nova totius libri ex hebraeo versio latina notis illustrata, auctore Augustino Crampon*. Paris: Vivès, 1861]. **Gallo, Joseph.** *Historia y diálogos de Job, con explicación literal y moral de todos sus capitulos, según las versiones de Vatablo, Pagnino, Parafraste y los setenta*. Burgos, 1644. **Garcia, J.** *Job evangélico*. Zaragoza, 1644. **Grotius [De Groot], H.** *Annotationes in Vetus Testamentum*. Paris, 1644. **Guillebert, Nicolas.** *Le Livre de Job paraphrasé*. Paris: P. Rocolet, 1641. **Hatcher, Robert.** "Jobi peroratio, pro triplici status sui colore, tribus capitulis distincta." In his *Funus corporis et animæ conjugium: sive Apomnemoneymata quorundam: fœlicis memoriæ, hominum qui per mortis dedecus in vitæ æternæ gloriam evaserunt*. London: T. R. & E. M., 1646. 89–112. **Quevedo [Quebedo] Villegas [y Villegas], Francisco [de] (Spanish Golden Age author, 1580–1645).** Editions: *La constancia y paciencia del Santo Job en sus peridas endermedades y persecucioues* (1641). First published 1713. Also in his *Obras completas*. Barcelona: Planeta, 1963. 1:1322–86. "Constance et patience du Saint Job: fragments." *Cahiers des saisons* 20 (1960) 548–52. See also Quevedo, 1700; and **Piero, R. A. del.** "Quevedo y Juan de Pineda." *Modern Philology* 56 (1958) 82–91. ———. "Two Notes en Quevedo's Job." *Romanic Review* 50 (1959) 9–24.

   1650s. Cappel[lus], Louis. *Critica sacra, sive de variis quae in sacris Veteris Testamenti libris occurrunt lectionibus libri sex*. Paris, 1650. **Caryl, Joseph.** *An Exposition with Practical Observations upon the Book of Job*. 12 vols. London, 1644–1666 [= *An Exposition with Practical Observations on the Book of Job*. 12 vols. Grand Rapids: Reformation Heritage Books, 2001]. **Codurcus, Philippus [Codurc, Philippe].** *Libri Job versio nova ex Hebraeo cum scholiis*. Paris: Savreux, 1652 [= *Annotationes in librum Job*. In *Critici sacri*. III. Ed. John Pearson. 1660]. **Drexel [Drexelius], Jeremias.** *Jobus divinae providentiae theatrum*. Munich: Wagner, 1653 [= *Operum Tomus ... huic novae editione accessere tractatus duo; Antigrapheus, sive conscientia; et Job*. Lyons: Huguetan, 1675; = *Operum Tomus*. Band 28. *Jobus divinae providentiae theatrum*. Cologne: Egmond, 1715]. **Jackson, Arthur.** *Annotations upon the Five Books Immediately Following the Historicall Part of the Old Testament (Commonly Called the Five Doctrinall or Poeticall Books): To Wit, the Book of Iob, the Psalms, the Proverbs, Ecclesiastes, and the Song of Solomon*. London: Roger Daniel, 1658. **Malvenda, Thomas de.** *Commentaria in S. Scripturam, una cum nova de verbo in verbum ex hebraeo translatione variisque lectionibus*. Lyons, 1650. **Manley, Thomas.** *The Affliction and Deliverance of the Saints: or, The Whole Booke of Iob, Composed into English Heroicall Verse, Metaphrastically*. London, 1652. **Mayer, John.** *A Commentary upon the Whole Old Testament, Added to That of the Same Author upon the Whole New Testament ...* London, 1653. **Mercerus, Johannes.** *Commentarii, in Jobum, et Salomonis Proverbia, Ecclesiasten, Canticum Canticorum. Opus ... nunc in unum corpus*

redactum, et à mendis Ebraicis ... purgatum. Amsterdam: L. Elsevier, 1651. **Reis, Gaspar dos.** *Lucerna concionatorum et sacræ scripturæ professorum. In tria volumina ... divisa ... II. Jobum, Sapientiales, ac Prophetales usque ad Machabæorum secundum.* Lisbon, 1658.
1660s. Anon. *Grabschrifft des gedultigen Jobs.* 1667 [= *Poetische Tafeln oder Gründliche Anweisung zur Teutschen Verskunst.* Ed. Joachim Dyck. Frankfurt: Athenäum, 1971. 155]. **Arias Montano, Benito.** *Liber Ijobi chaldaice et latine, cum notis. Item graece [sticheros], cum variantibus lectionibus.* Franeker: Johannes Wellens, 1663. **Brett, Arthur.** *Patientia victrix: or, The Book of Job, in Lyrick Verse.* London, 1661. **Broughton, Hugh.** *Iob. To the King. A Colon-Agrippina Studie of One Moneth, for the Metricall Translation: but of Many Yeres, for Ebrew Difficulties.* In his *The Works of the Great Albionean Divine, Renown'd in Many Nations for Rare Skill in Salems and Athens Tongues, and Familiar Acquaintance with All Rabbinical Learning.* London, 1662. 2:247–94. **Codurcus, Philippus [Codurc, Philippe].** *Annotationes in Jobum.* In *Critici sacri: sive clarissimorum virorum in sacro-sancta utriusque foederis Biblia doctissimae annotationes atque tractatus theologico-philologici.* Ed. John Pearson et al. London, 1660 [see also Codurcus, 1652]. **Hutcheson, George.** *An Exposition of the Book of Job. Being the Sum of cccxvi Lectures Preached in the City of Edenburgh.* London, 1669. **Jonghen, Hendrik de.** *Brevis elucidatio litteralis libri Jobi.* Antwerp, 1661. **Morillon, Gatien de.** *Paraphrase sur le livre de Iob, en vers françois.* Paris: Louis Billaine, 1668. **Olearius, Gottfried (1604– 1685).** *Das uhralte fürtreffliche Lehr- Trost- und Ermahnungsreiche Buch des heiligen Hiobs der christlichen Gemeinde zu in Sachsen in 55. Sermonen und kurtzen Predigten summarisch erkläret und fürgetragen.* Leipzig: Wittigau, 1663. **Olearius, Johannes (1611–1684).** *Beständiger Trost wider die schrecklichen Hiobs-Posten, und die männiglich, insonderheit aber gottselige Eltern den Todt der jenigen Kinder ... anzusehen, u. sich dabey ... gedultig zuerweisen haben.* Leipzig: Wittigau, 1668. **Terentius, Johannes, and Patrick Young.** *Liber Ijobi Chaldaice et Latine: cum notis. Item Graece sticheros, cum variantibus lectionibus.* Franeker: Johannes Wellens, 1663. **Trapp, John.** *Annotations upon the Old and New Testament. V. Ezra, Nehemiah, Esther, Job, and Psalms.* London, 1662.
1670s. Olearius, Johannes (1611–1684). *Darinnen nicht allein die übrigen Geschicht-Bücher Altes Testaments, Nehmlich Das 1. und 2. Buch Samuelis, Das 1. und 2. Buch der Könige, Das 1. und 2. Buch der Chronica, Das Buch Esdra, Das Buch Nehemia, Das Buch Esther, enthalten, Sondern auch das vortreffliche Haupt-Buch deß Heiligen Hiobs, ebenmässig Aus der Grundsprache deß Heiligen Geistes betrachtet, und mit nothwendiger Lehre ... vorgestellet wird.* Biblische Erklärung 2. Leipzig: Tarnoven, 1678. **Patrick, Symon.** *The Book of Job Paraphras'd.* London, 1679. **Pole, Matthew.** *Synopsis criticorum aliorumque scripturae interpretum.* London, 1671. 2:1–498. **Schmid [Schmidt], Sebastian.** *In librum Ijobi commentarius, in quo, cum optimis quibusque commentatoribus, tum Hebraeis tum Christianis, cohaerentia et vocabula diligenter expenduntur, et sensus studiose eruitur.* Strasbourg, 1670. **Spanheimius, Fridericus [Friedrich Spanheim].** *Historia Jobi, sive de obscuris historiae commentatio.* Leiden; Geneva: Peter Chouët, 1670.
1680s. Cappel[lus], Louis [Ludovicus]. *Commentarii et notae criticae in Vetus Testamentum.* Amsterdam: P. & J. Blaeu, 1689. **Hog [Hogaeus Scotus], William.** *Paraphrasis in Jobum poetica.* London, 1682. **Hottinger, Johann Heinrich.** *Liber Ijobh post textum hebraeum et versionem verbalem latinum, analysis simplex, sed accurata, omnium radicum.* Zurich, 1689. **Le Maistre de Sacy, Isaac Louis.** *Job traduit en françois: avec une explication tirée des Saints Pères et des auteurs ecclésiastiques.* Paris: Guillaume Desprez, 1688. **Pole [Poole], Matthew.** *Annotations upon the Holy Bible. Wherein the Sacred Text Is Inserted and Various Readings Annex'd, together with the Parallel Scriptures.* 2 vols. London, 1683–1685 [= *A Commentary on the Holy Bible.* 3 vols. London: Banner of Truth Trust, 1962].
1690s. Thwaites, Edward. *Heptateuchus, liber Job, et Evangelium Nicodemi: anglosaxonice. Historiae Judith fragmentum; dano-saxonice.* Oxford, 1698.
1700s. Baker, Daniel. *The History of Job: A Sacred Poem. In Five Books.* London: Robert Clavel, 1706. **Blackmore, R. A.** *Paraphrase on the Book of Job, as Likewise on the Songs of Moses, Deborah, David; on Four Select Psalms, Some Chapters of Isaiah, and the Third Chapter*

of Habakkuk [in verse]. London, 1700. **Henry, Matthew.** *An Exposition on the Old and New Testament: Wherein Each Chapter Is Summed up in Its Contents; the Sacred Text Inserted at Large in Distinct Paragraphs … Forming the Most Complete Family Bible Ever Published.* London, 1706 [many subsequent editions and abridgments; see also Henry, 1710, 1990; Eadie, 1859; Church, 1960; Peterman, 1992]. **Isham, Z.** *Divine Philosophy: Containing the Books of Job, Proverbs, and Wisdom, with Explanatory Notes.* London, 1706. **Kortum, Renato Andrea.** *Das Buch Hiob, aus dem hebräischen Grund-text auffs neue getreulich ins Teutsche übersetzt, nebst einer paraphrasi.* Leipzig, 1708. **Kromayer, Johann Abraham.** *Filia matri obstetricans, hoc est: De usu linguæ arabicæ in addiscenda ebræa, & explicanda Scriptura S. libelli duo: quorum prior usum illum, præceptis perspicuis & exemplis selectis, in genere tradit; posterior seorsim in libro Jobi … hæc ita applicat … ut supplementum omnium commentariorum im Jobum, hic libellus esse possit, & linguæ arabicæ ignaris quoque inserviat.* Frankfurt and Leipzig, 1707. **P., R., Minister of the Gospel.** *The Book of Job in Meeter, as to Several of Those Excellent Things Contain'd Therein, the Better to Familiarize Them, and to Bring Them the More into Use, for Peoples Benefit, to be Sung after the Ordinary, and Usual Tunes.* London, 1700. **Quevedo [Quebedo] Villegas [y Villegas], Francisco [de].** *La providencia de Dios, padecida de los que la niegan y gozada de los que la confiessan. Doctrina estudiada en los gusanos y persecuciones de Job.* Zaragoza, 1700. **Schultens, Albert.** *Animadversiones philologicae in Jobum, in quibus plurima … ope linguae Arabicae et affinium illustrantur.* Utrecht, 1708.

1710s. Egard [Egardus], Paul. *Erläuterung des Buches Hiob, Oder, Die Schule der leiblichen und geistlichen Anfechtungen, Welche Denen Gläubigen nach dem Willen Gottes in dem Lauf des Christenthums begegnen, im Bilde Hiobs gezeiget … Samt einer vorangesetzten Kurtzen Einleitung des Buchs Hiob von Io. Heinr. Michaelis …* Halle: Verlegung des Wäysenhauses, 1716. **Henry, Matthew.** *An Exposition of the Five Poetical Books of the Old Testament; viz. Job, Psalms, Proverbs, Ecclesiastes, and Solomon's Song.* London, 1710. **Laurens, Andreas.** *Libri Isaiae, Jeremiae, Job, psalmorum, prouerbiorum, sapientiae, ecclesiastes, cantici canticorum, ecclesiastici.* Lyons, 1716. **Guyon, Jeanne Marie Bouvières [Bouvier] de La Motte.** In **Le Maistre de Sacy, Isaac-Louis.** *La Sainte Bible, avec des explications et réflexions qui regardent la vie intérieure* [by Jeanne Marie Bouvières de la Motte-Guyon]. VII. *Le livre de Job.* Cologne: Jean de la Pierre, 1714 [= *Das Buch Hiobs erklärt von Madame Guion; in frantzösischer Sprach geschrieben und nun treulich ins Teutsche übersetzt.* Berlenburg: Regelein, 1743; repr. New Haven: Research Publications, 1973]. **Michaelis, Johann Heinrich.** *Kurtze Einleitung des Buchs Hiob. In Pauli Egardi … Erläuterung des Buches Hiob, oder, Die Schule der leiblichen und geistlichen Anfechtungen, Welche Denen Gläubigen nach dem Willen Gottes in dem Lauf des Christenthums begegnen, im Bilde Hiobs gezeiget … Samt einer vorangesetzten Kurtzen Einleitung des Buchs Hiob.* Halle: Verlegung des Wäysenhauses, 1716. **Patrick, Symon.** *The Books of Job, Psalms, Proverbs, Ecclesiastes, and the Song of Solomon, Paraphras'd: with Arguments to Each Chapter, and Annotations Thereupon.* London. 1710. **Presbyter of the Church of England, A.** *A Short Paraphrase on the Book of Job with Arguments to Each Chapter.* London, 1716. **Young, Edward.** *A Paraphrase on Part of the Book of Job.* London, 1719 [= *The Complaint; Or Night-Thoughts on Life, Death, and Immortality. To Which Are Added, Some Thoughts on the Late Rebellion, and a Paraphrase on Part of the Book of Job.* London, 1748].

1720s. Acher, Abraham. *Le livre de Job, traduit en francois sur l'original hebreu.* Rotterdam, 1729. **Calmet, Augustin.** *Commentaire litteral sur tous les livres de l'Ancien et du Nouveau Testament.* X. *Le livre de Job.* Paris: Emery, Saugrain & Martin, 1722 [= *Commentarius literalis in omnes libros Veteris et Novi Testamenti.* III. Lucca: Marescandoli, 1732. 537–714]. **Crinsoz [Crinsoz de Sottens], Theodore.** *Le Livre de Job, traduit en françois sur l'original hébreu avec des notes littérales pour éclaircir le texte.* Rotterdam: Abraham Acher, 1729. **Hardouin, J.** *Le livre de Job selon la Vulgate paraphrasé avec des remarques.* Paris, 1729. **Michaelis, Johann Heinrich.** *Notae in Jobum.* Halle, 1720. ———. *Uberiorum adnotationum philologico-exegeticarum in hagiographos Veteris Testamenti libros … 2. Adnotationes in Librum Jobi.* Halle: Sumptibus Orphanotrophei, 1720. **Quevedo [Quebedo] Villegas [y Villegas], Francisco [de].** "La constancia y paciencia del Santo Job." In *Obras posthumas*

y vida de Don Francisco de Quevedo y Villegas. Parte tercera. Madrid, 1729. **Thompson, William.** *A Poetical Paraphrase on Part of the Book of Job, in Imitation of the Style of Milton.* London: Thomas Worrall, 1726 [= microfilm ed., The Eighteenth Century, Reel 1345/43. Woodbridge, CT: Research Publications, Inc., 1985].
1730s. Boyse, Samuel. "The III. Chapter of the Book of Job Translated" [in verse]. In his *Translations and Poems Written on Several Subjects.* Edinburgh: Thomas & Walter Ruddimans, 1731. **Clericus [Le Clerc], Johannes [Jean].** *Vetus Testamentum. III. Veteris Testamenti libri hagiographi: Jobus, Davidis Psalmi, Salomonis Proverbia, Concionatrix & Canticum canticorum ex translatione Joannis Clerici; cum ejusdem commentario philologico in omnes memoratos libros, et paraphrasi in Jobum ac Psalmos.* Amsterdam: R. & J. Wetsten & W. Smith, 1731. **Duguet, J. J., and J. V. Bidel d'Asfeld.** *Explication du livre de Job où, selon la méthode des saints Pères, l'on s'attache à découvrir les mystères de Jésus-Christ et les règles des moeurs renfermées dans la lettre même de l'Ecriture.* Paris: F. Babuty, 1732. **Duguet, Jacques-Joseph.** *Préface sur le livre de Job.* Amsterdam: Michel-Charles Le Cène, 1734. **Fenton, Thomas.** *Annotations on the Book of Job, and the Psalms.* London: C. Rivington, 1732. **Hoffmann, J. A.** *Neue Erklärung des Buches Hiob, darin das Buch selbst aus der Grund-sprache mit den darin liegenden Nachdruck ins Teutsche übersetzt; hienächst aus denen Altherthümern und der morgenländischen Philosophie erläutert; überhaupt aber die darin verborgene tieffe Wiesheit geseiget wird. Jetzo nach des Verfassers seel. Abschiede mit Fliess ubersehen, und mit einer Paraphrasi, wie auch Vorbericht von Hiobs Person, Buche und dessen Auslegern vermehret.* Hamburg: T. C. Felginers Wittwe, 1734. **Johnston [Jonstonus], Arthur, John Ker [Kerrus], Patrick Adamson, and William Hog [Hogaeus].** *Poetarum scotorum musæ sacræ: sive, Quatuor Sacri Codicis scriptorum, Davidis & Solomonis, Jobi & Jeremiæ, poetici libri, per totidem Scotos, . . . latino carmine redditi* [incl. paraphrase of Job]. 2 vols. Edinburgh: T. & W. Ruddimans, 1739. **Koch, Jacob.** *Verschiedene vortrefliche bisher noch dunckel gewesene Schrift-Stellen vom Messia, vornemlich aus den Psalmen, Hiob und Mose.* Lemgo: Meyer, 1738. **Michaelis, Johann Heinrich.** *Kurtze Anleitung zum rechten Verstande des Predigers Salomonis und des Buchs Hiob.* Halle: Waisenhaus, 1737. **Schultens, Albert.** *Liber Iobi cum nova versione ad Hebraeum fontem et commentario perpetuo, in quo veterum et recensiorum interpretum cogitata praecipua expenduntur: genuinus sensus ad priscum linguae genium indagatur, atque ex filo, et nexu universo, argumenti nodus intricatissimus evolvitur.* Leiden: Joannes Luzac, 1737. **Wesley, Samuel.** *Dissertationes in librum Jobi.* London, 1736. **Will, Johannes Ludovicus.** *Dissertatio inauguralis exegetica qua sensus verborum Iobi cap. XVIIII a comm. XXV. usq. ad fin. eruitur.* Halle, [1735].
1740s. Bellamy, D. *A Paraphrase on the Sacred History, or Book of Job, with Observations from Various Authors.* London, 1748. **Garnett, John.** *A Dissertation on the Book of Job, Its Nature, Argument, Age and Author.* London, 1749. **Grey, Richard.** *Liber Jobi in versiculos metrice divisus, cum versione latina Alberti Schultens, notisque ex ejus commentario excerptis, quotquot ad divinum plane poema illustrandum (quoad vel argumenti materiam & filum, vel sensuum pathos & sublimitatem, vel styli copiam & elegantiam) necessariae videbantur.* London: W. Bowyer, 1742. **Guicciardi, Antonio Maria.** *Lezioni sacre e morali sopra i libri di Giobbe profeta santo, e pazientissimo, distribuite in tre parti, che contengono le azioni, e le virtu esercitate dal santo nel primo stato di felicita; nel secondo di estrema calamità; e nel terzo il suo risorgimento a vita piu fortunata, e gloriosa.* Venice: Giovani Battista Recurti, 1741. **Guyon, Jeanne Marie Bouvier de La Motte.** *Das Buch Hiobs erklärt; in frantzösischer Sprach geschrieben und nun treulich ins Teutsche übersetzt.* Berlenburg: Christoph Michael Regelein, 1743 [= German baroque literature, Harold Jantz collection no. 1257/247; *The Book of Job: With Explanations and Reflections Regarding the Interior Life.* Trans. Mrs M. W. Russell. Boston: B. B. Russell, 1887; Augusta, ME: Christian Books, 1985]. **Honert, Jan van den.** *Verklaring van de Geheele Heilige Schrift door eenigen van de voornaamste engelsche godgeleerden. 5. Uitbreiding en verklaring van het boek van Job: uit de Engelsche werken van de heeren Patrik, Polus, Wels . . .* Amsterdam: Tirion en Loveringh, 1743. **Parma, Orazio da.** *Esposizioni letterali, e morali sopra la Sacra Scrittura. 7. Tomo settimo, che comprende il libro di Giobbe, de' Salmi, e de' Proverbi.*

Venice: Francesco Pitteri, 1740. **Schultens, Henrik Albert.** *Le livre de Job traduit du Latin de Mr Schultens par E. de Joncourt, J. Sacrelaire, et J. Allamand.* Leiden: Jean Luzac, 1748. **Stemler, David.** *Jobum theologum tentationibus probatum.* Leipzig: Breitkopf, 1746. **1750s. Boullier, D. R.** *Observationes miscellaneae in librum Job.* Amsterdam, 1758. **Ceruti [Cerutti], Giacinto.** *Il libro di Giobbe recato dal testo ebreo in versi italiani.* Turin, 1759; Rome, 1773. **Chappelow, Leonard.** *A Commentary on the Book of Job, in Which Is Inserted the Hebrew Text and English Translation, with a Paraphrase from the Third Verse of the Third Chapter, Where It Is Supposed the Metre Begins, to the Seventh Verse of the Forty-Second Chapter, Where It Ends.* 2 vols. Cambridge: J. Bentham, 1752. **Durham, James.** *An Exposition of the Whole Book of Job, with Practical Observations.* Glasgow: J. Bryce and D. Paterson, 1759 [repr. *Lectures on Job.* Dallas: Naphtali Press, 1995]. **Erskine, Ralph.** *Job's Hymns; or, A Book of Songs upon the Book of Job.* Glasgow, 1753. **Heath, Thomas.** *An Essay towards a New English Version of the Book of Job, from the Original Hebrew, with a Commentary, and Some Account of His Life.* London: A. Miller and S. Baker, 1756. **Houbigant, Carolus Franciscus.** *Biblia Hebraica cum notis criticis et versione latina ad notas criticas facta* [unvocalized Heb. text, Latin translation, and notes]. 4 vols. Paris, 1753.

1760s. Bahrdt, Johann Friedrich. *Paraphrastische Erklärung des Buches Hiob.* 2 vols. Leipzig: Heinsius, 1764–1765. **Boysen, Friedrich Eberhard.** *Das Buch Hiob.* In his *Kritische Erleuterungen des Grundtextes der heiligen Schriften Altes Testaments.* Halle im Magdeburgischen: C. H. Hemmerde, 1762. **Bravi, Buonaventura Antonio.** *Parafrasi del sacro libro di Giobbe fatta in versi italiani.* Verona, 1763. **Cube, Johann David.** *Poetische und prosaische Übersetzung des Buches Hiob.* 3 vols. Berlin: Buchhandlung der Realschule, 1769–1771. **Grynaeus, Simon.** *Das Buch Hiob in einer poetischer Uebersetzung nach des Prof. Schultens Erklärung mit Anmerkungen von Simon Grynäus.* Basel, 1767. **Holden, Lawrence.** *A Paraphrase on the Books of Job, Psalms, Proverbs, and Ecclesiastes, with Notes Critical, Historical and Practical.* 4 vols. London, 1763. **Langhorne, William [John].** *Job. A Poem, in Three Books.* London, 1760. **León, Luis Ponce de.** *Obras proprias i traducciones de latin, griego, i toscano, con la parafrasi de algunos Salmos i capitulos de Job.* Valencia: J. T. Lucas, 1761. **Michaelis, Johann David.** "Das Buch Hiob." In his *Deutsche Übersetzung des Alten Testaments mit Anmerkungen für Ungelehrte.* Göttingen, 1765. See also **Anon.** *Schreiben an einen Freund die Uebersetzung des Buches Hiob, vom Herrn Hofrathe Michaelis betreffend.* Berlin, 1770. **Meintel, Johann Georg.** *Freund-schaftliche Antwort auf das in Berlin 1770 gedruckte Schreiben an einen Freund, die Übersetzung des Buches Hiob vom Herrn Hofrath Michaelis betreffend.* Frankfurt; Leipzig, 1771.| **Rezzano, Francesco.** *Il Libro di Giobbe, esposto in Italiana poesia, con annotazioni.* Rome: Giuseppe and Niccolo Grossi, 1760. **Schultens, Albert.** *Alberti Schultens Opera minora: animadversiones ejus in Jobum, et ad varia loca V.T. nec non varias dissertationes et orationes, complectentia.* Leiden, 1769. **Talleoni, Marcantonio.** *Volgarizzamento in terza rima del sacro libro di Giob.* Osimo, 1764; 2nd ed. Rome: Mordacchini, 1824. **Zampieri, Cammillo [Camillo].** *Giobbe esposto in ottava rima.* Piacenza: Niccolo Orcesi and Giuseppe Tedeschi, 1763.

1770s. Anon. *A Paraphrase of the 38th Chapter of Job.* Chesterfield: J. Bradley, 1778. ———. *A Commentary on the Holy Bible: Containing the Sacred Text of the Old and New Testaments, with Notes Explanatory, Historical, Critical, and Practical. Calculated to Assist the Christian Reader in Profitably Using the Most Valuable Book.* Bristol: William Pine, 1774. **Barbauld, Anna Laetitia.** *Devotional Pieces, Compiled from the Psalms and the Book of Job. To Which are Prefixed, Thoughts on the Devotional Taste, on Sects, and on Establishments.* London, 1775. **Devens, Richard.** *A Comment on Some Passages in the Book of Job.* 1773 [the first work on Job written and published in the USA]. **Döderlein, J. C.** *Scholia in libros Veteris Testamenti poeticos Jobum, Psalmos et tres Salomonis.* Halle: J. J. Curtius, 1779. **Eckermann, J. C. R.** *Versuch einer neuen poetischen Uebersetzung des Buches Hiob, nebst einigen Vorerinnerungen und einer nachstehenden Umschreibung.* Leipzig, 1778. **Fry, Francis.** *A Commentary on the Holy Bible: Containing the Whole Sacred Text of the Old and New Testaments: with Notes Explanatory,*

Historical Critical, and Practical: Calculated to Assist the Christian Reader in Profitably Using This Most Valuable Book. Bristol: William Pine, 1774. **Gill, John.** *An Exposition of the Whole Old Testament, Critical, Doctrinal and Practical.* 4 vols. London: George Keith, 1763–65. **Houbigant, Carolus Franciscus.** *Notae criticae in universos Veteris Testamenti libros cum hebraice, tum graecae scriptos cum integris ejusdem prolegomenis* [the notes only, an abbreviated form of those in his *Biblica Hebraica* of 1753]. 2 vols. Frankfurt: Varrentrapp Filius & Wenner, 1777. 2:155–218. **Le Maistre de Sacy, Isaac Louis.** *Sacra scrittura.* 16. *Giobbe giusta la vulgata in lingua latina e volgare colla spiegazione del senso litterale, e del senso spirituale tratta dai santi padri, e dagli autori ecclesiastici.* Venice: Lorenzo Baseggio, 1777. **Meintel, Johann Georg.** *Metaphrasis libri Jobi sive Jobus metricus.* Nuremberg, 1775. **Michaelis, Johann David.** "Anzeige der Varianten im Buch Hiob." In his *Orientalische und exegetische Bibliothek.* Frankfurt a.M.: J. G. Garbe, 7 (1774) 217–47; 8 (1775) 179–224. **Moldenhawer, Johann Heinrich Daniel.** *Uebersetzung und Erläuterung des Buchs Hiob.* Quedlinburg and Blankenburg: C. A. Reussner, 1778. **Reiske, Johann Jacob.** *Coniecturae in Jobum et Proverbia Salomonis, cum ejusdem oratione de studio arabicae linguae.* Leipzig, 1779. **Sanctis, Alessandro Fabiano de.** *L'interpretazione del libro di Giobbe.* Rome: Arcangelo Casaletti, 1774. **Schultens, Albert.** *Commentarius in librum Iobi. In compendium redegit et observationes criticas atque exegeticas adspersit G. I. L. Vogel.* Halle: J. J. Curt, 1773–1774. **Scott, Thomas.** *The Book of Job in English Verse, Translated from the Original Hebrew, with Remarks, Historical, Critical, and Explanatory.* London, 1771. **Società Clementina, Paris.** *Saggio sopra il Libro di Giobbe secondo la nuova versione fatta su l'ebreo da' PP. della Società Clementina di Parigi.* Milan, 1774.

1780s. Baur, Jacob Immanuel. *Animadversiones ad quaedam loca Iobi.* Diss. Tübingen, 1781. **Dathe, Johann August.** *Jobus, Proverbia Salomonis, Ecclesiastes, Canticum Canticorum ex recensione textus hebraei et versionum antiquarum latine versi notisque philologicis et criticis illustrati.* Halle: Sumtibus Orphanotrophei, 1789. 1–221. **Hufnagel, Wilhelm Friedrich.** *Hiob neu übersetzt mit Anmerkungen.* Erlangen, 1781. **Ilgen, Carolus David.** *Jobi antiquissimi carminis hebraici natura atque virtutes.* Leipzig, 1789. **Kessler [Keszler], Christian David.** *Hiob aus dem hebräischen Original neu übersetzt und mit erklärenden Anmerkungen versehen zum allgemeinen Gebrauche.* Tübingen, 1784. **Muntinghe, Herman.** *Het Boek Job, uit het Hebreeuwsch vertaald, met aanmerkingen, door H. A. Schultens ... uitgegeven en voltooid.* Amsterdam, 1794. **Sander, Heinrich.** *Das Buch Hiob zum allgemeinen Gebrauche.* Frankfurt, 1780.

1790s. Carpenter, William. *A Poetical Paraphrase on the Book of Job.* Rutland, VT, 1796. **Devens, Richard.** *A Paraphrase on Some Parts of the Book of Job* [in verse]. Boston, 1795. **Elliott, Ebenezer.** *A Paraphrase on the Book of Job, Agreeable to the Meaning of the Sacred Text.* Rotherham: John Crookes, 1792. **Fernandez de Palazuelos, A.** *La divina providencia o historia sacra poetica de Job. Versio de un filopatro expatriado, dedicada al principe de la paz.* Venice, 1795. **Garden, Charles.** *An Improved Version Attempted of the Book of Job: A Poem ... with a Preliminary Dissertation and Notes.* Oxford, 1796. **Greve, E. J.** *Ultima capita Libri Jobi: nempe cap. xxxviii, xxxix, xl, xli et capitis xlii pars ad Graecam versionem recensita, notisque instructa.* 2 vols. Steinfort, Luxembourg: J. H. Peck, 1791. **Pape, Samuel Christian.** *Hiob übersetzt: Ein Versuch. Begleitet mit einer Vorrede vom Herrn Hofrath Eichhorn.* Göttingen: Rosenbusch, 1797. **Priestley, T.** *The New Evangelical Family Bible; or, a Complete Paraphrase, Exposition, and Commentary on the Holy Scriptures.* London, 1793. **Schultens, Henrik Albert.** *Het Boek Job, uit het Hebreeuwsch vertaald, met aanmerkingen.* Amsterdam, 1794. **Schulz [Schulzius], Johann Christian Friedrich.** *Scholia in Vetus Testamentum.* VI. *Librum Iobi complectens.* Nuremburg: A. C. Grattenhauer, 1792. **Weidenbach, K. F.** *Das Buch Hiob aus dem hebräischen mit Anmerkungen von H. A. Schultens nach dessen Tode hrsg. und vollendet von H. Muntinghe. Aus dem holländischen mit Zusätzen und Anmerkungen des Herrn D. und Professor I. P. Berg.* Leipzig, 1797.

Index to Commentaries of 16th to 18th Centuries

Acher 1729
Anon. 1545, 1560, 1571, 1580,
　　1592, 1599, 1660, 1770, 1768
Arias Montano 1663
Aurelius 1632
Bahrdt 1764
Baker 1706
Barbauld 1775
Baur 1781
Bellamy 1748
Belleau 1576
Beza 1573, 1583, 1589
Blackmore 1700
Bolducius 1629
Boullier 1758
Boyse 1731
Boysen 1762
Bravi 1763
Brentius 1527
Brett 1661
Broughton 1662
Brucioli 1534
Bucer 1528
Bugenhagen 1526
Cajetan [Gaetanus] 1535
Calmet 1722
Calvin 1554, 1574
Cappellus 1650, 1689
Carpenter 1796
Caryl 1644
Cermellus 1636
Ceruti 1759
Chappelow 1752
Chasteignier de la
　　Roche-Posai 1628
Clericus 1731
Cocceius 1644
Codurcus 1652, 1695
Corderus 1646
Coverdale 1535
Crinsoz 1729
Crommius 1632
Cube 1769
d'Albiac 1552
Dathe 1789
Dati 1520
Devens 1795
Didacus a Stunica 1584
Döderlein 1779
Drexel 1653
Drusius 1636
Duguet 1732, 1734
Duport 1637
Durham 1759
Eckermann 1778
Egard 1716
Elliott 1792
Erskine 1753
Estius 1620
Fenton 1732
Fer 1558
Fernandez de Palazuelos 1795
Forerius 1563

Fry 1774
Gallo 1644
García 1644
Garden 1796
Garnett 1749
Gill 1778
Gordon 1632
Grey 1742
Grotius 1644
Grynaeus 1767
Guicciardi 1741
Guillebert 1641
Guyon 1743
Hardouin 1729
Hatcher 1646
Heath 1756
Heneus 1602
Henry 1706, 1710
Hoffmann 1734
Hog 1682
Holden 1763
Honert 1743
Hottinger 1689
Houbigant 1753, 1777
Huelga 1582
Hufnagel 1781
Hutcheson 1669
Ilgen 1789
Isham 1706
Jackson 1658
Janssonius 1623
Járava 1550
Jesús Maria 1611
Johannes a Jesu-Maria 1611
Johnston 1739
Jonghen 1661
Kessler 1784
Koch 1738
Kortum 1708
Kromayer 1707
Langhorne 1760
Laurens 1716
Lausana 1528
Lavater 1585
Le Maistre de Sacy 1688, 1714,
　　1777
Leon 1576, 1631, 1761
Lorichius 1543
Lowth 1753
Lutz 1559
Malvenda 1650
Manley 1652
Mayer 1653
Meintel 1771, 1775
Mello de Sousa 1615
Mercerus 1573
Merlin 1599
Michaelis, J. D. 1765, 1774
Michaelis, J. H. 1716, 1720, 1737
Moldenhawer 1778
Morgan 1588
Morillon 1668
Muntinghe 1784

Narhamer 1546
Nebiensis 1520
Oecolampadius 1532, 1578
Olearius, G. 1663
Olearius, J. 1678
Osorio 1579
P., R. 1700
Pape 1797
Parma 1740
Patrick 1679, 1710
Pélerin 1530
Peters 1751
Pineda 1600
Piscator 1612
Pole 1671, 1683
Presbyter 1716
Priestley 1793
Quevedo 1641, 1700
Reis 1658
Reiske 1779
Rezzano 1760
Rosapachius 1613
San José Lera 1584
Sanctis 1774
Sanctius 1625
Sander 1780
Sandys 1638
Savonarola 1545
Schmid 1670
Schultens, A. 1708, 1737, 1769,
　　1773
Schultens, H. A. 1748, 1794
Schulz 1792
Scialach 1618
Scott 1771
Senault 1637
Società Clementina 1774
Sotomayor 1610
Spanheimius 1670
Stemler 1746
Stephanus 1540
Steuchus 1567
Sylvester 1633
Talleoni 1764
Terentius 1663
Thompson 1726
Thou 1592
Thwaites 1698
Titelmans 1547
Trapp 1662
Tuccius Lucensis 1617
Vavassor 1638
Weidenbach 1797
Weller 1563
Wesley 1736
Wildt 1558
Will 1735
Worthington 1743
Wright 1792
Young 1719
Zampieri 1763
Zúñiga 1584

e. 19th to 21st Centuries

The items in this Section are arranged by decades of publication. At the end of the Section there is an index of the authors mentioned, with the dates of publication.

1800s. Abraham, Israel ben. ספר איוב עם באור ותרגום אשכנזי. Offenbach, 1807. **Anon.** *A Complete Family Bible: Comprising All the Sacred Text of the Old and New Testaments: with*

Valuable Notes and Annotations, the Whole Forming an Explanatory and Practical Commentary. New ed. Berwick: Lochhead, 1800. ———. *The Christian's New and Complete Family Bible: Being a New, Clear, Full, and Universal Exposition and Commentary … by Several Eminent Divines.* Halifax, 1800. **Bernard, V. L.** *A Sacred Poem in Four Books. Being a Paraphrase on the Book of Job.* Norwich: Stevenson & Matchett, 1800. **Burder, Samuel.** *The Scripture Expositor: A New Commentary, Critical and Practical, on the Holy Bible.* London: Albion Press, 1809. **Coke, Thomas.** *A Commentary on the Holy Bible.* London: A. Strahan and G. Whitfield, 1803. **Eichhorn, Johann Gottfried.** *Hiob.* Leipzig: Weidmann, 1800. **Gaab, J. F.** *Das Buch Hiob.* Tübingen: J. G. Cotta, 1809. **Hawker, Robert.** *The Poor Man's Commentary on the Bible.* London, 1805. **Kreyssig, Johann Gottlieb.** *Observationes criticae in Graecos Jobi interpretes.* Schneeberg: Typis Schillianis, 1808. **Lee, Chauncey.** *The Trial of Virtue: A Sacred Poem. Being a Paraphrase of the Whole Book of Job, and Designed as an Explanatory Comment upon the Divine Original, Interspersed with Critical Notes upon a Variety of its Passages. In Six Books, to Which Is Annexed, a Dissertation upon the Book of Job.* Hartford, CT: Lincoln & Gleason, 1806 [= Early American Imprints. Second series 10710. 1990]. **Ottensosser (Ottenzoser), D.** ספר איוב :כתובים. *Job: cum commentario Sal. Jarchi … et versione germanica* [Hebrew text, Yiddish translation, Hebrew commentary by Israel b. Abraham of Lissa]. Fürth: Zirendorf, 1805. **Polotak, P. ben Judah.** ספר איוב … גבעת פנחס. Vilna, 1808. **Rosenmüller, Ernst Friedrich Karl [E. F. C.].** *Scholia in Vetus Testamentum. V. Jobus latine vertit et annotatione perpetua illustravit.* Leipzig: J. A. Barth, 1806. **Stock, Joseph.** *The Book of Job, Metrically Arranged according to the Masora, and Newly Translated into English. With Notes Critical and Explanatory.* Bath: Richard Cruttwell, 1805. **Stuhlmann, Matthias Heinrich.** *Hiob, ein religiöses Gedicht. Aus dem Hebräischen neu übersetzt, geprüft und erläutert.* Hamburg: F. Perthes, 1804.

1810s. Bridel, J. Louis. *Le livre de Job, nouvellement traduit d'après le texte original non ponctué et les anciennes versions, notamment l'Arabe et la Syriaque; avec un commentaire imprimé à part.* Paris: Firmin Didot, 1818. **Brown, John.** *The Self-Interpreting Bible with an Evangelical Commentary.* London: Richard Evans, 1815. **Burder, Samuel.** *The Scripture Expositor: A New Commentary, Critical and Practical on the Holy Bible: in Which Difficult Passages Are Explained, Mistranslations Corrected, and Apparent Contradictions Reconciled … Incorporating an Historical Account of the Customs and Manners of the Nations of the East, in Which the Various Transactions Took Place Recorded in the Holy Scriptures.* London: Albion Press, 1811. **Campbell, George.** *The Holy Bible, with a Commentary and Evangelical Reflections Selected from the Writings of the Most Celebrated Commentators.* Newcastle upon Tyne: Mackenzie & Dent, 1813. **Clarke, Adam.** *The Holy Bible: Containing the Old and New Testaments, according to the Authorized Translation, with All the Parallel Texts and Marginal Readings: to Which Are Added, Notes and Practical Observations …* Liverpool: Nuttall, Fisher, & Dixon, 1813. **Good, John Mason.** *The Book of Job, Literally Translated from the Original Hebrew, and Restored to Its Natural Arrangement: with Notes Critical and Illustrative; and an Introductory Dissertation on Its Scene, Scope, Language, Author, and Object.* London: Black, Parry and Co., 1812. **Jones, Thomas.** *Sylwadau eglurhaol ac ymarferol; neu: Esponiad byr ar Lyfr Job, gydag Ysgrythyrau cyfeiriol aml ar ol yr adnodau: a fwriadwyd er mwyn y rhai nad oes ganddynt y fantais o ddarllen na deall esponiadau saesneg.* Caerfyrddin/Carmarthen: J. Evans, 1818. **Messchert van Vollenhoven, Jan.** *Het Boek Job, In Dichtmaat.* Amsterdam, 1812. **Rossi, G. Bernardo de.** *Il Libro di Giobbe tradotto dal testo originale.* Parma: Stamperia Imperiale, 1812. **Schärer [Scharer], Johann Rudolf.** *Das Buch Hiob, aus dem Grundtext metrisch übersetzt und erklärt.* Berne: L. R. Walthard, 1818. **Smith, Elizabeth.** *The Book of Job, Translated from the Hebrew … with a Preface and Annotations by the Rev. F. Randolph.* Bath: Richard Cruttwell, 1810 [repr. with an introduction by Maurice O'Sullivan. Delmar, NY: Scholars' Facsimiles & Reprints, 1996]. **Sutcliffe, Joseph.** *The Complete Family Bible: or, Christian's Divine Library: Containing the Sacred Text of the Old and New Testaments, Illustrated with Notes Theological, Historical, Critical, and Explanatory; Wherein the Mistranslations Are Corrected, the Seeming Contradictions Reconciled, the Difficult Passages Explained, and the Sacred Writings Displayed in*

Their Genuine Purity and Sacred Lustre, the Whole Forming a Copious Commentary ... Leeds: Davies & Co., 1813.

1820s. Anon. *Jesu Christi festum natalitium. Insunt observationes ad librum Jobi.* Tübingen, 1826. **Blumenfeld, B.** ובאור אשכנזי תרגום עם איוב ספר. Vienna: A. Strauss (Shtroys), 1826. **Böckel, Ernst Gottfried Adolf.** *Hiob für gebildete Leser bearbeitet.* Berlin: Rücker, 1821. **Carrières, [Louis] de.** *Sainte Bible en latin et en français, avec un commentaire littéral inséré dans la traduction française. IV. Les deux livres des Paralipomènes. Esdras. Néhémias. Tobie. Judith. Esther et Job.* Lyon: Ruisand, 1825. **Costa, Giuseppe.** *Il libro di Giobbe volgarizzato* [verse translation]. Rome: Tipografia della Società Editrice Romana, 1847. **Fry, John.** *A New Translation and Exposition of the Very Ancient Book of Job; with Notes, Explanatory and Philological.* London: James Duncan, 1827. **Hunt, George.** *The Book of Job. Translated from the Hebrew.* Bath: Wood & Cunningham, 1825. **Levavasseur, B. M. F.** *Le Livre de Job, traduit en vers français, avec le texte de la Vulgate en regard; suivi de notes explicatives, ainsi que des variantes tirées des plus célèbres interprètes de la Bible, et de quelques poésies françaises du traducteur.* Paris: P. Delaunay & G. Dentu, 1826. **Noyes, George R.** *An Amended Translation of the Book of Job, with an Introduction and Notes Chiefly Explanatory.* Cambridge, MA: Hilliard & Brown, 1827 [= *A New Translation of the Book of Job, with an Introduction and Notes Chiefly Explanatory.* 2nd ed. Boston: James Munroe & Co., 1838]. **Rowley, A.** *Ten Chapters of the Book of Job, Rendered from the Common Translation into Verse.* Boston: J. H. A. Frost, 1825. **Umbreit, Friedrich Wilhelm Carl.** *Das Buch Hiob: Übersetzung und Auslegung nebst Einleitung über Geist, Form und Verfasser des Buchs.* Heidelberg: J. C. B. Mohr, 1824; 2nd ed., 1832.

1830s. Arnheim, H. *Das Buch Hiob übersetzt und vollständig commentirt.* Glogau: H. Prausnitz, 1836. **Birch, Mrs Walter.** *Job; or, the Gospel Preached to the Patriarchs: Being a paraphrase of the Last Ten Chapters of the Book of Job. By the Widow of a Clergyman of the Church of England* [i.e., Mrs Walter Birch]. London: J. G. & F. Rivington, 1838. **Böckel, Ernst Gottfried Adolf.** *Das Buch Hiob, übersetzt und ... kurz erläutert ... mit einer Zugabe philologischer und exegetischer Anmerkungen.* 2nd ed. Hamburg, 1830. **Brentano, Dominik von, and Thaddäus Anton Dereser.** "Hiob." In their edited *Die Heilige Schrift des Alten Testaments.* II/3. Frankfurt a.M., 1833. **Cobbin, Ingram.** *The Condensed Commentary and Family Exposition of the Holy Bible: Containing the Most Valuable Criticisms of the Best Biblical Writers, with Practical Reflections; and Marginal References, Chronology, Indexes, etc.* London: Thomas Ward & Co., 1837. **Fischel, Simhah Aryeh ben Ephraim.** מחוקק חלקת זאת :מהכתובים איוב ספר. Lemberg: Matfusische Buchdruckerey, 1833. **Hirzel, Ludwig.** *Hiob erklärt.* KEH 2. Leipzig: Weidmann, 1839. **Holzhausen, Friedrich August.** *Uebersetzung des Buches Hiob.* Göttingen, 1839. **Köster, Friedrich Burchard.** *Das Buch Hiob und der Prediger Salomo's nach ihrer strophischen Anordnung übersetzt. Nebst Abhandlungen über den strophischen Character dieser Bücher. Zum Gebrauche bey akademischen Vorlesungen.* Schleswig: Königliches Taubstummen-Institut, 1831. **Laurens, Hippolyte.** *Job et les Psaumes. Traduction nouvelle d'après l'hébreu, les anciennes versions et les plus habiles interprètes, précédées de deux discours préliminaires et accompagnée d'arguments et de notes.* Paris: Gaume Frères, 1839. **Lee, Samuel.** *The Book of the Patriarch Job, Translated from the Original Hebrew as Nearly as Possible in the Terms and Style of the Authorised English Version; to Which Is Prefixed an Introduction on the History, Times, Country, Friends, and Book of the Patriarch; with Some Strictures on the Statements of Bishop Warburton, and of the Rationalists of Germany, on the Same Subjects; and to Which Is Appended a Commentary, Critical and Exegetical, Containing Elucidations of Many Other Passages of Holy Writ.* London: James Duncan, 1837. **Sarao, Antonio.** *Giobbe, poema eroico.* Messina: Pappalardo, 1831. **Umbreit, Friedrich Wilhelm Carl.** *A New Version of the Book of Job with Expository Notes, and an Introduction on the Spirit, Composition, and Author of the Book.* Trans. John Hamilton Gray. 2 vols. The Biblical Cabinet 16, 19. Edinburgh: Thomas Clark, 1836–37.

1840s. Anon. *The Illustrated Commentary on the Old and New Testaments: Chiefly Explanatory of the Manners and Customs Mentioned in the Sacred Scriptures; and Also of the History, Geography, Natural History, and Antiquities; Being a Republication of the Notes of The*

Pictorial Bible. III. London: C. Knight & Co., 1840. **Baour Lormian, L.-F.** *Le Livre de Job, traduit en vers français*. Paris: Lallemand–Lépine, 1847. **Barnes, Albert.** *Notes, Critical, Illustrative, and Practical, on the Book of Job*. Glasgow: Blackie & Son, 1847. **Boys, Thomas.** *Job: em nova ediçao: revista e reformada segundo o original hebraico*. London: Trinitarian Bible Society; London: A. Macintosh, 1845. **Brenner, [?].** *Noten zum hebräischen Texte des Alten Testaments, nebst einer Uebersetzung des Buches Hiob, und einem grammatischen Anhang*. Basel: J. G. Bahnmaier, 1841. **Cobbin, Ingram.** *The Portable Commentary: The Holy Bible Containing the Old and New Testaments: with the Most Approved Marginal References, and Explanatory Notes, Selected from the Most Distinguished Biblical Writers*. London: Partridge & Oakey, 1846. **Fockens, H. F. T.** *Pulchra Jobeïdis loca*. Amsterdam, 1844. ———. *Het Boek Job vertaald en opgehelderd ten dienste van beschaafde christenen*. Leeuwarden: Schierbeek, 1845. **Haupt, Leopold.** *Hiob. Ein Gespräch über die göttliche Vorsehung. Ins das Deutsche übertragen*. Leipzig, 1847. **Haweis, Thomas.** *The Evangelical Expositor: or, A Commentary on the Holy Bible Wherein the Text Is Inserted at Large, the Sense Explained, and the More Difficult Passages Elucidated, with Practical Observations, for the Use of Families and Private Christians of Every Denomination*. London: Edward and Charles Dilly, 1765–66 [later editions include the name of John Brown]. **Hawker, Robert.** *A Commentary on the Bible, with the Sacred Text at Large*. 3 vols. London: E. Spettigue, 1842–44. 51–104. **Heiligstedt, Augustus.** *Commentarius grammaticus historicus criticus im Jobum*. Leipzig: Renger, 1847. **Hosse, Friedrich.** *Hiob, ein erbauliches dramatisches Gedicht für unsere Zeit* [translated into iambic pentamenters]. Elberfeld: Hassel, 1849. **Hussey, T. J.** *The Holy Bible, Containing the Old and New Testaments, and the Apocrypha, Translated out of the Original Tongues … Accompanied throughout with a Brief Hermeneutic and Exegetical Commentary and Revised Version*. London: Henry Colburn, 1844. **Justi, Karl Wilhelm.** *Hiob, neu übersetzt und erläutert*. Kassel: J. J. Bohné (Bahne), 1840. **Lichtenstädter, Benjamin Wolf.** יחזקאל עד הנביאים איוב משלי תהלים התורה על … : בנימין אמתחת. Fürth, 1844. **Löwenthal, Moritz.** איוב. *Hiob: Praktische Philosophie oder klare Darstellung der im Buche Hiob obwaltenden Ideen, nebst wortgetreuer, rhythmisch gegliederter Übersetzung mit fortlaufendem Commentar*. Frankfurt a.M.: privately printed, 1846. **Margolfo, Pasquale.** *Lamentazioni di Giobbe e di Geremia, profeta*. Naples: Banzoli, 1840. **Peyromet, P.-D. de.** *Le livre de Job traduit en vars francais*. Paris, 1848. **Scott, Thomas.** *The Holy Bible, Containing the Old and New Testaments. With an Abridged Commentary*. London: Virtue, 1842. **Stickel, Johann Gustav.** *Das Buch Hiob rhythmisch gegliedert und übersetzt, mit exegetischen und kritischen Bemerkungen*. Leipzig: Weidmann, 1842. See also **Vaihinger, J. G.** "Zur Erklärung von Hiob 19, 23–29: mit Beziehung auf die Auslegung dieser Stelle in der Schrift des Herrn Prof. Stickel: Das Buch Hiob rhythmisch gegliedert und übersetzt u.s.w. Hamburg, 1843." *TSK* 16 (1843) 961–82.| **Vaihinger, Johann Georg.** *Das Buch Hiob, der Urschrift gemäss metrisch übersetzt und erläutert*. Stuttgart: Cotta, 1842. **Van Hagen, Mrs Henry.** *Evenings in the Land of Uz: A Comment on the Book of Job, Arranged for Family Reading*. London: W. W. Robinson, 1843 [– *Evenings in the Land of Uz. Short Expositions of the Book of Job, Arranged for Family Reading*. 1845]. **Welte, B.** *Das Buch Hiob, übersetzt und erklärt*. Freiburg i.Br.: Welter, 1849. **Wolfson, Jochanan.** איוב. *Das Buch Hiob. Mit Beziehung auf Psychologie und Philosophie der alten Hebräer neu übersetzt und kritisch erläutert*. Breslau: Joh. Urban Kern, 1843.

   1850s. Anon. *The Book of Job, Illustrated with Fifty Engravings from Drawings by John Gilbert, and with Explanatory Notes and Poetical Parallels*. London: J. Nisbet & Co., 1857. **Berkholz, C. A.** *Das Buch Hiob. Ein Versuch* [translation]. Riga: E. Götschel, 1859. **Cahen, Samuel.** *Bible: traduction nouvelle, avec l'hébreu en regard*. La Bible 15. Paris: privately printed, 1851. **Carey, Carteret Priaulx.** *The Book of Job Translated … on the Basis of the Authorized Version: Explained in a Large Body of Notes … and Illustrated by Extracts from Various Works … and a Map; with Six Preliminary Dissertations, an Analytical Paraphrase, and Meisner's and Doederlein's Selection of the Various Readings of the Hebrew Text*. London: Wertheim, Macintosh & Hunt, 1858. **Conant, Thomas Jefferson.** *The Book of Job. The Common English Version, the Hebrew Text, and the Revised Version of the American Bible Union, with Critical and Philological Notes*. New York: American Bible Union, 1856; London:

Trübner, 1856 [= *The Book of Job: A Translation from the Original Hebrew on the Basis of the Common and Earlier English Versions with an Introduction and Explanatory Notes for the English Reader*. New York: American Bible Union, 1856]. **Eadie, John.** *The Holy Bible, with the Commentaries of Scott and Henry*. Glasgow: McPhun, 1859. **Ebrard, [J. H.] August.** *Das Buch Hiob als poetische Kunstwerk übersetzt und erläutert für Gebildete*. Landau: Kaussler, 1858. **Ewald, Heinrich.** *Das Buch Ijob übersetzt und erklärt*. Die Dichter des Alten Testaments 3. Göttingen: Vandenhoeck & Ruprecht, 1854 [see also Ewald, 1882]. **Fischmann, N. I.** איוב עם פירוש הנקרא שפה לנאמנים. Lemberg, 1854. **Fox, S. H.** *A Metrical Version of the Book of Job*. Part 1 [chaps. 1–20]. London: C. Gilpin, 1852. **Gerlach, Otto von.** *Das Alte Testament nach Dr Martin Luthers Uebersetzung, mit Einleitungen und erklarenden Anmerkungen herausgegeben*. 4th ed. Berlin: Schlawitz, 1858. **Hahn, H. A.** *Commentar über das Buch Hiob*. Berlin: Wohlgemuth, 1850. **Hupfeld, Hermann.** *Quaestionum in Jobeidos locos vexatos specimen. Commentatio...* Halle: E. Anton, 1853. **Kemmler, G.** *Hiob oder die Weisheit der Urzeit* [verse translation with some notes]. Stuttgart–Bad Cannstatt: Bosheuye, 1856. **Kenrick, Francis Patrick.** *The Book of Job, and the Prophets: Translated from the Vulgate, and Diligently Compared with the Original Text, Being a Revised Edition of the Douay Version, with Notes, Critical and Explanatory*. Baltimore: Kelly, Hedian & Piet, 1859. **Landau, Moses Israel.** *Iyov: 'im perush Rashi ve-tirgum Ashkenazi [be-'otiyot 'Ivriyot] u-ve'ur meturgam u-mevo'ar*. Vilna, 1853. **Luzzatto, Samuel David.** *Il Libro di Giobbe volgarizzato ad uso degli Israeliti* [translation into Italian]. Trieste: F. Marenigh, 1853. **Merj, Serafino.** *Il libro di Giobbe: versione italiana col testo a fronte e con annotazioni*. Ascoli: Emidio Cesari, 1858. **Mosner, Heinrich.** *Hiob ins Deutsche übersetzt und mit hebräische Anmerkungen versehen* [Job 1:1–11:8]. Halle, 1858. **Olshausen, Justus.** *Hiob erklärt*. 2nd ed. KEH 2. Leipzig: S. Hirzel, 1852. **Ottoni, J. E.** *Job, traduzido em verso... Precedido primeiro, d'um discurso sobre a poesia em geral, e em particular no Brasil... Terceiro d'um prefacio extrahido de versão da Biblia por de Genoude*. Rio de Janeiro: F. M. Ferreira, 1852. **Porteous, M.** *Job Paraphrased: A Poem*. Maybole: The Author, 1854. **Schlottmann, Konstantin.** *Das Buch Hiob verdeutscht und erläutert*. Berlin: Wiegandt & Grieben, 1851. **Spiess, Moritz.** *Hiob metrisch übersetzt*. Buchholz: G. Adler, 1852. **Theile, C. G. G.** איוב. *Liber Jobi ex recensione C. G. G. Theile*. New York: American Bible Union, 1857.

    1860s. Adams, Henry W. *The Book of Job in Poetry; or, a Song in the Night*. New York: Robert Craighead, 1864. **Ahmad Khan, Sayidd.** *The Mohomedan Commentary on the Holy Bible*. Ghazeepore: The Author, 1865. **Bernard, Hermann Hedwig.** ספר איוב. *The Book of Job, as Expounded to His Cambridge Pupils by the Late Hermann Hedwig Bernard*. Ed. Frank Chance. London: Hamilton, Adams & Co., 1864. **Coleman, John Noble.** *The Book of Job, the Most Ancient Book in the Universe ... Translated from the Hebrew with Notes Explanatory, Illustrative, and Critical*. London: J. Nisbet & Co., 1869. **Crelier, H.-J.** *Le livre de Job vengé des interprétations fausses et impies de M. Ernest Renan*. Paris: Douniol, 1860 [see Renan, 1860]. **Davidson, A. B.** *A Commentary, Grammatical and Exegetical, on the Book of Job, with a Translation*. Vol. 1 [chaps. 1–14]. London: Williams & Norgate, 1862. **Delitzsch, Franz J.** *Das Buch Iob. Mit Beiträgen von Prof. Dr Fleischer und Consul Dr Wetzstein, nebst einer Karte und Inschrift*. Leipzig: Dörfling & Francke, 1864 [= *Biblical Commentary on the Book of Job*. Trans. F. Bolton. 2 vols. Edinburgh: T. & T. Clark, 1866]. **Dillmann, August.** *Hiob: für die dritte Auflage nach L. Hirzel und J. Olshausen neu bearbeitet*. 3rd ed. KEH 2. Leipzig: S. Hirzel, 1869. *Hiob*. 4th ed. Leipzig: S. Hirzel, 1891. **Eadie, John.** *The Practical and Devotional Family Bible ... with the Marginal Readings, and Original and Selected Parallel References ... and the Commentaries of Henry and Scott*. Glasgow: William Collins, 1868. **Greene, W. B.** *The Book of Job* [a translation]. Boston: G. C. Rand & Avery, 1866. **Hassoun, Rizq-Allah.** *The Poem of Poems: A Metrical Arabic Version of the Book of Job, &c.* London: Frederic Straker, 1869. **Heiligstedt, August.** *Praeparation zum Buche Hiob mit den nöthigen, die Uebersetzung und das Verstandniss des Textes erleichternden Anmerkungen*. Halle: Anton, 1869. **Jamieson, Robert, A. R. Fausset, and David Brown.** *A Commentary, Practical and Explanatory, on the Whole Bible*. Glasgow: William Collins, 1864–70. **Kamphausen, Adolf.** *Die Bibel, oder, die Schriften des Alten und Neuen Bundes nach den überlieferten Grundtexten übersetzt und für* *die Gemeinde erklärt.* III. *Die Schriften.* Ed. Christian Carl Josias Bunsen. Leipzig: F. A. Brockhaus, 1868. **Lees, Frederic Richard, and Dawson Burns.** *The Temperance Bible-Commentary: Giving at One View, Version, Criticism, and Exposition, in Regard to All Passages of Holy Writ Bearing on "Wine" and "Strong Drink," or Illustrating the Principles of the Temperance Reformation.* London: S. W. Partridge, 1868. 113–16. **Leroux, Pierre.** *Le véritable livre de Job, retrouvé par Pierre Leroux.* 2nd ed. Geneva: J. Leroux, 1867. ———. *Job, drame en cinq actes, avec prologue et épilogue, par le prophète Isaie, retrouvé, rétabli dans son integrité, et traduit littéralement sur le texte hébreu.* With Appendix, "Le Job des Eglises, et le Job de M. Renan" (pp. 201–389). Grasse, Paris: E. Dentu, 1866. See also Renan, 1860.| **Matthes, J. C.** *Het Boek Job, vertaald en verklaard, insonderheid naar aanleiding van de jongste buitenlandsche kommentaren.* Utrecht: Bosch, 1865. **Meikle, William.** *The Book of Job in Metre, according to the Most Approved Commentaries.* Falkirk: William Meikle, 1869. **Noyes, George R.** *A New Translation of Job, Ecclesiastes, and the Canticles.* 3rd ed. Boston: American Unitarian Association, 1867. **Odiosus (pseud.).** ‎ספר איוב‎. *Das Buch Ijob im engeren Anschluss an den masoretischen Urtext deutsch übersetzt und mit Erläuterungen versehen von Odiosus.* Lieferung 1 [chaps. 1–14]. Berlin: W. Adolf, 1863. **Renan, Ernest.** *Le livre de Job, traduit de l'hébreu.* [with] *Etude sur l'age et le caractère du poème.* Paris: Michel Lévy Frères, 1860 [repr. Paris: Arlea, 1991; in his *Oeuvres complètes.* VII. Paris: Calmann-Lévy, 1955; = *The Book of Job Translated from the Hebrew with a Study upon the Age and Character of the Poem.* Trans. A. F. G. [H. F. Gibbons] and W. M. T[homson]. London: W. M. Thomson, 1899; pp. xxxix–lvi reprinted as "The Cry of the Soul" in **Glatzer, Nahum H.** *The Dimensions of Job: A Study and Selected Readings.* New York: Schocken Books, 1969. 111–23]. See also Crelier, 1860; Leroux, 1866; Rosny, 1860.| **Rodwell, J. M.** ‎איוב‎. *The Book of Job, Translated from the Hebrew.* London: Williams & Norgate, 1864. **Rosny, Léon de.** *Le poëme de Job et le scepticisme sémi-tique* [review of E. Renan's *Le livre de Job traduit de l'hébreu*]. Paris: Challamel aîné, 1860. See also Renan, 1860.| **Saint-Maur, Hector de.** *Le livre de Job. Traduction en vers.* Paris: E. Dentu, 1861. **Schwarz, F. W. S.** *Das Buch Hiob. Ein Kreuz- und Trostbuch. Nach dem Holländischen des ten Kate unter Vergleichung des biblischen Textes deutsch bearbeitet.* Bremen: C. E. Müller, 1868. **Schwarz, Israel.** ‎תקוה אנוש: ספר איוב‎. Berlin, 1868 [repr. Jerusalem: Makor, 1969/1970; microfiche: Munich: K. G. Saur, 1990]. **Stather, W. C.** *The Book of Job in English Verse. Translated from the Original Hebrew, with Notes, Critical and Explanatory.* Bath: Binns & Godwin, 1860. **Trentepohl, Carl Friedrich Bernhard.** *Das Buch Hiob, übersetzt und metrisch bearbeitet.* Vechta: Fauvel, 1860. **Viani dalla Beata Chiara, Bonaventura.** *Il Libro di Giobbe, recato in versi italiani e corredato di note.* Rome: Osservatore Romano, 1865. **Winchilsea, Earl of [Finch Hatton, G. J.].** *The Poem of the Book of Job Done into English Verse.* London: Smith, Elder & Co., 1860. **Wolf, E. F. H.** *Het Boek Job, in dichtvorm gebracht en toegelicht voor het Nederlandsche volk.* Amsterdam, 1869. **Young, Robert.** *A Commentary on the Holy Bible, as Literally and Idiomatically Translated out of the Original Languages.* Edinburgh: A. Fullarton & Co.; New York: Fullarton, Macnab & Co., 1868. ———. *Concise Commentary on the Holy Bible, being a Companion to the New Translation of the Old and New Covenants: Specially Designed for Those Teaching the Word of God, whether Preachers, Catechists, Scripture Readers, District Visitors, Sabbath School Teachers, or Heads of Families.* Edinburgh: George Adam Young & Co., 1865.

1870s. Andreä, Hermann Victo. *Hiob. Classisches Gedicht der Hebräer. Aus dem Grundtexte neu übersetzt und mit Andeutungen zum tieferen Verständniss versehen.* Barmen: W. Laugewiesche, 1870. **Ashkenazi, Mosheh Yitshak.** *Ho'il Mosheh: be'ur hadash 'al sefer Iyov.* Padua: Francisco Sakito, 1876. **Barham, Francis.** *The Book of Job, Newly Translated from the Original. Printed both in Phonetic and in the Customary Spelling, as a Transition Book from Phonetic Reading to the Reading of Books as Now Commonly Printed.* London: Fred. Pitman and Bath: Isaac Pitman, 1871. **Consolo, Beniamino.** *Volgarizzamento del libro di Job, con spiegazione e commenti.* Florence: Cellini, 1874. **Cowles, H.** *The Book of Job, with Notes, Critical, Explanatory, and Practical ... With a New Translation Appended.* New York: D. Appleton & Co., 1877. **Elzas, A.** *The Book of Job, Translated from the Hebrew Text, with an Introduction and Notes, Critical and Explanatory.* London: Trübner & Co., 1872. **Fava,**

A. *Poesie bibliche voltate in versi italiani: Il libro di Giobbe; I Salmi; Cantici scritturali.* 2nd ed. Milan: V. Maisner, 1875. **Gray, James Comper.** *The Biblical Museum: A Collection of Notes Explanatory, Homiletic, and Illustrative, on the Holy Scriptures.* London: Elliott Stock, 1871–81. 5:145–384. **Halsted, O. S.** *The Book Called Job. From the Hebrew. With Footnotes.* Newark, NJ: The Author, 1875. **Hengstenberg, E. W.** *Das Buch Hiob erläutert.* Berlin: Schlawitz, 1870. Leipzig: J. C. Hinrichs, 1875. **Hitzig, Ferdinand.** *Das Buch Hiob übersetzt und ausgelegt.* Leipzig and Heidelberg: C. F. Winter, 1874. **Hutchinson, R. F.** *Thoughts on the Book of Job.* London: S. Bagster & Sons, 1875. **Kelly, William.** *Notes on the Book of Job, with a New Version.* London: G. Morrish, 1879. **Kemmler, G.** *Hiob; oder, Kampf und Sieg im Leiden. In dichterischen Form wiedergegeben.* Calw: Verlag der Vereinsbuchhandlung, 1877. **Le Hir, Arthur-Marie.** *Le livre de Job; Traduction sur l'hébreu et commentaire; précédé d'un Essai sur le rhythme chez les juifs; et suivi du Cantique de Debora et Psaume CX.* Paris: L. Hachette; Jouby & Roger, 1873. **Malbim [Meir Loeb ben Jehiel Michael].** "אִיּוֹב." In his נביאים וכתובים עם פירוש רש״י ופי׳ ... נקרא בשם מקרא קודש. Vol. 5. Warsaw: Y. Levenzohn, 1874. **Merx, Adalbert.** *Das Gedicht von Hiob: Hebräischer Text, kritisch bearbeitet und übersetzt, nebst sachlicher und kritischer Einleitung.* Jena: Mauke (Hermann Dufft), 1871. **Raymond, Rossiter W.** *The Book of Job: Essays, and a Metrical Paraphrase. With an Introductory Note by T. J. Conant, and the Text of the Revised Version Prepared by Dr Conant for the American Bible Union.* New York: D. Appleton & Co., 1878. **Reuss, Eduard.** *La Bible. 6. Ancien Testament. Philosophie religieuse et morale des Hébreux. Job, les Proverbes, l'Ecclésiaste, l'Ecclésiastique, la Sapience, Contes moraux, Baruch, Manassé. Traduction nouvelle avec introductions et commentaires.* Paris: Sandoz & Fischbacher, 1878. See also **Vincent, Jean Marcel.** "Edouard Reuss, traducteur et interprète du Livre de Job. À l'occasion du bicentenaire de la naissance de l'exégète strasbourgeois." *RHPR* 85 (2005) 337–64.| **Rosenfeld, Mordecai Jonah.** ספר איוב: עם פירוש חלק לשנים. Lemberg: J. Ehrenpreis, 1875. **Sternberg, S. Z.** ספר איוב: עם באור חקר שדי. 1872. **Stewart, Alexander.** *A Practical Bible Temperance Commentary.* Aberdeen: W. Lindsay, 1872. **Takamini, A. V.** *Il Libro di Giobbe. Versione poetica.* Venice, 1871. **Thomas, David.** *Problemata mundi. The Book of Job, Exegetically and Practically Considered. Critically Revised, with an Introduction, by Samuel Davidson.* London: Smith, Elder, & Co., 1878 [= *Book of Job: Expository and Homiletical Commentary.* Grand Rapids: Kregel, 1982]. **Wolff, J.** *Job, traduit et commenté.* Colmar: C. Decker, 1873. **Young, Robert Newton, and Adam Clarke.** *The Holy Bible, Authorized Translation, with a Commentary and Critical Notes: Condensed from the Original Work, with Occasional Notes Added.* 3 vols. London: W. Tegg, 1874. **Zöckler, Otto.** *Das Buch Job theologisch-homiletisch bearbeitet.* Theologisch-homiletisches Bibelwerk: Des Alten Testamentes 10. Bielefeld: Velhagen & Klasing, 1872 [= *The Book of Job.* Trans. L. J. Evans. Lange's Commentary on the Holy Scriptures. Edinburgh: T. & T. Clark, 1875]. **Zschokke, Hermann.** *Das Buch Job übersetzt und erklärt.* Vienna: Wilhelm Braumüller, 1875.

1880s. Barry, Alfred. "The Book of Job." In *The Old Testament according to the Authorised Version, with a Brief Commentary, by Various Authors.* II. *Poetical Books.* London: SPCK, 1886. 9–142. **Blunt, John Henry.** *The Annotated Bible, Being a Household Commentary upon the Holy Scriptures.* London: Rivingtons, 1882. **Böttcher, V.** *Das Buch Hiob nach Luther und der Probebibel aus dem Grundtext bearbeitet und mit Bemerkungen versehen.* Leipzig: J. Lehmann, 1885. **Bradley, George Granville.** *Lectures on the Book of Job Delivered in Westminster Abbey.* Oxford: Clarendon Press, 1887. **Clarke, H. J.** *The Book of Job. A Metrical Translation with Introduction and Notes.* London: Hodder & Stoughton, 1880. **Cook, F. C.** "Job: Commentary and Critical Notes." In *The Holy Bible ... with an Explanatory and Critical Commentary ... by Bishops and Other Clergy of the Anglican Church* [The Speaker's Bible]. Ed. F. C. Cook. London: John Murray, 1882. 4:1–145. ———. "Job: Commentary and Critical Notes." In *The Students' Commentary on the Holy Bible. Founded on the Speaker's Commentary.* London: John Murray, 1880. 3:1–92. **Cox, Samuel.** *A Commentary on the Book of Job, with a Translation.* London: Kegan, Paul & Co., 1880. **Curry, Daniel.** *The Book of Job (according to the Version of 1885), with an Expository and Practical Commentary.* New York: Phillips & Hunt, 1887. **Davidson, A. B.** *The Book of Job, with Notes, Introduction and Appendix.*

CamB. Cambridge: Cambridge University Press, 1884. ———. "Job." In *Encyclopaedia britannica*. 9th ed. Edinburgh: A. & C. Black, 1880. 697–703. **Ewald, Georg Heinrich August von [Heinrich Ewald].** *Commentary on the Book of Job, with Translation.* Trans. J. Frederick Smith. London: Williams & Norgate, 1882 [see also Ewald, 1854]. **Freund, Wilhelm, and Friedrich Marx.** *Präparation zum Buch Ruth und Buch Hiob.* Leipzig: Violet, 1886. **Gilbert, George H.** *The Book of Job as Poesy* [translation into English verse]. Rutland, VT: The Tuttle Co, 1886. ———. *The Poetry of Job.* Part I. *A Rhythmical Translation of Job.* Part II. *Interpretation of the Poem.* Chicago: A. C. McClurg, 1889. **Knabenbauer, Joseph.** *Commentarius in Librum Iob.* Cursus scripturae sacrae: Commentarii in Vetus Testamentum 2,1. Paris: P. Lethielleux, 1886. **Langer, J.** *Das Buch Job in neuer und treuer Uebersetzung nach der Vulgata, mit fortwährender Berücksichtigung des Urtextes.* Luxembourg: Brück, 1884. ———. *Das Buch Job und Das Hohelied.* Freiburg i.Br.: Herder, 1889. **Leathes, Stanley.** "The Book of Job." In *An Old Testament Commentary for English Readers.* Ed. Charles John Ellicott. 5 vols. London: Cassell & Co., 1882–84 [included in *The Complete Bible Commentary for English Readers.* 7 vols. London: Cassell, 1897]. 4:1–75. See also Bowdle, Donald N. (ed.). *Ellicott's Bible Commentary.*| **Lesêtre, H.** *Le livre de Job: introduction critique, traduction française et commentaires.* La sainte bible: texte de la vulgate 16. Paris: Lethielleux, 1886. **Malet, Arthur.** *The Book of Job in Blank Verse* [2146 lines]. Ashcott, Bridgwater, 1880. ———. *The Books of Job, Ecclesiastes, and Revelation Rendered into English Verse. Also, Solomon and His Bride: A Drama from the Song of Songs.* London: Nisbet & Co., 1883. **Millet, Adolphe.** *Le Livre de Job traduit en vers.* Lyons: Vitte & Perrussel, 1887. **Parker, Joseph.** *The Book of Job.* The People's Bible: Discourses upon Holy Scripture. London: Hazell, Watson & Viney, 1889. **Pierik, R. J.** *Het boek Job: naar 't Hebreeuwsch letterlijk vertaald ter vergelijking met de Vulgata.* Gulpen: Alberts, 1881. **Strashun, Abraham David Moses.** איוב ספר על באור :אדם תורת. Vilna: Rozenkrants & Shriftzettser, 1888. **Studer, Gottlieb Ludwig.** *Das Buch Hiob für geistliche und gebildete Laien übersetzt und kritisch erläutert.* Bremen: M. Heinsius, 1881. **Szold, Benjamin.** מחדש מבואר :איוב ספר. *Das Buch Hiob, nebst einem neuen Kommentar.* Baltimore: H. F. Siemers, 1886. **Ulrich, Jakob.** *Job, un drama engiadinais del 16. secul. nouvamaing publicho.* Societad Rhaetoromanscha. Annalas 12. Chur, 1886. **Vilmar, August Friedrich Christian.** *Collegium biblicum: Praktische Erklärung der heiligen Schrift Alten und Neuen Testaments. 3. Die Lehrbücher: Hiob bis Klagelieder Jeremiä.* Gütersloh: Bertelsmann, 1882. **Volck, W.** "Das Buch Hiob." In *Die poetischen Hagiographa (Buch Hiob, Prediger Salomo, Hohelied und Klagelied ausgelegt).* Ed. W. Volck and S. Oettli. KKAT. Nördlingen: C. H. Beck, 1889. 3–102. **White, G. Cecil.** *The Discipline of Suffering. Nine Short Readings on the History of Job* [incl. the text of Job in blank verse]. London: W. Skeffington & Son, 1880. **Wright, G. H. Bateson.** *The Book of Job. A New, Critically Revised Translation, with Essays on Scansion, Date, etc.* London: Williams & Norgate, 1883.

1890s. Baethgen, Friedrich. *Hiob deutsch, mit kurzen Anmerkungen für Ungelehrte.* Göttingen: Vandenhoeck & Ruprecht, 1898. **Barash, Abraham M. ha-Zayit.** *Perush 'al Iyov.* Berdichev: H. Y. Sheftil, 1895. **Barbaresi, Pasquale.** *Il Libro di Giobbe. Versione poetica.* Milan: A. Brocca, 1894. **Barelli, Vincenzo.** *Il libro di Giobbe, recato in versi italiani.* Como: F. Ostinelli, 1891. **Baxter, Elizabeth.** *Job.* London: Christian Herald, 1894. **Bickell, Gustav.** *Das Buch Job nach Anleitung der Strophik und der Septuaginta auf seine ursprüngliche Form zurückgeführt und in Versmasse des Urtextes übersetzt.* Vienna: Carl Gerold's Sohn, 1894. **Boileau, M.-J.** *Le livre inspiré de Job: discours de ce prince d'Idumée, des princes ses amis et de Dieu lui-même sur l'origine des souffrances et de la douleur ou du mal physique dans la vie terrestre. Paraphrase.* Paris: V. Retaux & Fils, 1893. **Budde, Karl.** *Das Buch Hiob übersetzt und erklärt.* GHAT 2/1. Göttingen: Vandenhoeck & Ruprecht, 1896; 2nd ed., 1913. **Cary, Otis.** *The Man Who Feared God for Nought, Being a Rhythmical Version of the Book of Job.* London: Elliot Stock, 1898. **Castelli, David.** *Il poema semitico del pessimismo. Il libro di Job. Tradotto e commentato.* Florence: Paggi, 1897. **Dillon, E. J.** *The Sceptics of the Old Testament. Job. Koheleth. Agur, with English Text Translated for the First Time from the Primitive Hebrew as Restored on the Basis of Recent Philological Discoveries.* London: Isbister

& Co., 1895 [repr. New York: Haskell House, 1973]. **Duhm, Bernhard.** *Das Buch Hiob erklärt.* KHC 16. Freiburg i.Br.: J. C. B. Mohr (Paul Siebeck), 1897. **Fenton, Ferrar.** *The Book of Job. Translated Direct from the Hebrew Text into English ... Rendered into the Same Metre as the Original Hebrew Word by Word and Line by Line.* London: Elliot Stock, 1898. **Ferguson, Dugald.** *Job and Other Sacred Poems.* Dunedin: J. Horsburgh, 1898. ———. *The Book of Job (with Reflections) in Rhyme.* Dunedin: J. Horsburgh, 1891. **Fielding, George Hanbury.** *The Book of Job: A Revised Text, with Introduction and Notes.* London: Elliot Stock, 1898. **Figueiredo, C. de.** *O Livro de Job em versos portuguezes.* Lisbon: Livraria Ferreira, 1894. **Genung, John F.** *The Epic of the Inner Life. Being the Book of Job, Translated Anew, and Accompanied with Notes and an Introductory Essay.* Boston: Houghton, Mifflin, 1891. **Gibson, E. C. S.** *The Book of Job, with Introduction and Notes.* WC. London: Methuen, 1899. **Granville Fell, Herbert, and Joseph Jacobs.** *The Book of Job.* London: J. M. Dent, 1896. **Hoffmann, Johann Georg Ernst [Georg].** *Hiob.* Kiel: C. F. Haeseler, 1891. **Hubbard, Elbert.** *The Book of Job as Translated from the Original by Rabbi Abraham Elzas; with Some Comments on the Poem by Elbert Hubbard.* East Aurora, NY: Roycroft, 1897. **Königsberger, Bernhard.** *Hiobstudien. Exegetische Untersuchungen zum Buche Hiob nebst einer Einleitung zum Buche.* Breslau: W. Koebner, 1896. **Le Blanc d'Ambonne, Prosper.** *Le Livre de Job allégoriquement expliqué: La grande tribulation de l'Eglise ...* [Vulgate and allegorical explanation in parallel columns]. Nantes: E. Grimaud, 1893. **Loisy, A.** *Le Livre de Job, traduit de l'hébreu avec une introduction.* Amiens: Rousseau-Leroy, 1892. **Maizel, Samuel.** ספר איוב: עם ספר דברי שבי"ם: הוא באור על ספר איוב. Warsaw: M. Y. Halter, 1899. **Montvaillant, A. de.** *Poètes bibliques. Le livre de Job mis en vers français.* Paris: Fischbacher, 1897. **Ratner, I.** ספר איוב עם פירוש... בשם דברי אמת. Warsaw, 1893. **Sadler, Ralph.** *The Book of Ayub: Known in the West as Job* [translation with notes]. London: Sheppard & St John, 1897. **Siegfried, C.** *The Book of Job. Critical Edition of the Hebrew Text.* SBOT. Baltimore: Johns Hopkins Press, 1893. **Solomon [Baba-Jan].** ספר איוב עם עתקה בלשון פרסי [the Book of Job with Persian translation]. Jerusalem: Zuckerman, 1895. **Strashun, A. D.** מישר נבוכים: והוא באור על ספר איוב עם מבוא. Vilna, 1897. **Sydenstricker, H. M.** *The Epic of the Orient: An Original Poetic Rendering of the Book of Job.* Hartford: Student Publishing Co., 1894. **Talmid.** *The Book of Job and the Song of Solomon. Translated into English Metre.* Edinburgh: James Thin, 1890. **Tattersall, John.** *The Poem of Job, Rendered in English Metre.* London: B. Quaritch, 1897. **Voigt, Clemens.** *Einige Stellen des Buches Hiob.* Leipzig: W. Drugulin. 1895. **Walls, A.** *The Oldest Drama in the World: The Book of Job, Arranged in Dramatic Form, with Elucidation.* New York: Hunt & Eaton, 1891. **Watson, Robert A.** *The Book of Job.* ExpB. London: Hodder & Stoughton, 1892. **Winterfeld, Ernst von.** *Commentar über das Buch Iob. Teil 1. Uebersetzung und sprachliche Analyse.* Anklam: Wolter, 1898. **Zuck, William Johnston.** *The Book of Job, with an Introduction and Notes.* Dayton, OH: United Brethren Publishing House, 1898.

1900s. Addis, W. E. *The Book of Job and the Book of Ruth.* The Temple Bible. London: J. M. Dent; Philadelphia: J. B. Lippincott, 1902. **Bullinger, E. W.** *The Book of Job. Part 1, The Oldest Lesson in the World. Part 2, A Rhythmical Translation* [in iambic pentameters], *with the Structure and Notes.* London: Eyre & Spottiswoode, 1903. **Davies, David.** *The Book of Job* [commentary]. 1. *Job I–XIV.* London: Simpkin, Marshall, Hamilton, Kent & Co., 1909. **Delitzsch, Friedrich.** *Das Buch Hiob, neu übersetzt und kurz erklärt. Ausgabe mit sprachlichem Kommentar.* Leipzig: J. C. Hinrichs, 1902. **Dillon, E. J.** *The Original Poem of Job Translated from the Restored Text.* London: T. Fisher Unwin, 1905. **Driver, S. R.** *The Book of Job in the Revised Version. Edited with Introductions and Brief Annotations.* Oxford: Clarendon Press, 1906. **Dummelow, John R. (ed.).** *A Commentary on the Holy Bible: Complete in One Volume, with General Articles.* London: Macmillan, 1908. 289–320. **Hauser, Otto.** *Das Buch Hiob. In der Übertragung von Otto Hauser.* Berlin: Julius Bard, 1909. **Herrmann, J.** *Das Buch Hiob. Aus dem Grundtext übersetzt und mit Erläuterungen versehen.* Leipzig: P. Reclam, 1900. **Hontheim, Joseph.** *Das Buch Hiob als strophisches Kunstwerk nachgewiesen, übersetzt und erklärt.* Biblische Studien 9/1–3. Freiburg i.Br.: Herder, 1904. **Lewis, Tayler.** *The Book of Job: A Rhythmical Version with Introduction and Annotations by Tayler Lewis; A Commentary by Otto Zöckler; Translated from the German, with Additions by L. J. Evans; together with a General*

Introduction to the Poetical Books by Philip Schaff. Commentary on the Holy Scriptures. Old Testament 8. Lange's Commentary 7. Edinburgh: T. & T. Clark, 1875; New York: Charles Scribner, 1902. **Ley, Julius.** *Das Buch Hiob nach seinem Inhalt, seiner Kunstgestaltung und religiösen Bedeutung. Für gebildete Leser dargestellt.* Halle: Waisenhaus, 1903. **Loch, Valentin, and Wilhelm Reischel.** *Die Heilige Schrift des Alten und Neuen Testaments.* II. Regensburg: Manz, 1905. **Maclaren, Alexander.** *The Books of Esther, Job, Proverbs, and Ecclesiastes.* New York: A. C. Armstrong & Son; London: Hodder & Stoughton, 1908. **Marshall, J. T.** *The Book of Job.* An American Commentary on the Old Testament. Philadelphia: American Baptist Publication Society, 1904. **Morgan, G. Campbell.** *The Analyzed Bible.* II. *Job–Malachi.* New York: Fleming H. Revell, 1908. **Moulton, Richard G.** *The Book of Job, Edited, with an Introduction and Notes.* The Modern Reader's Bible 7. New York: Macmillan, 1896. **Oettli, S.** *Das Buch Hiob erläutert für Bibelleser.* Stuttgart: Calwer, 1908. **Peake, Arthur S.** *Job: Introduction, Revised Version.* CB. London: T. C. &. E. C. Jack, 1904. **Pritchard, M.** *The Poem of Job, a Version … with Introduction and Notes.* London: Kegan Paul, Trench, Trübner & Co., 1903. **Vignolo, G. Maria.** *Il libro di Giobbe tradotto in versi sciolti.* Turin: P. Celanza, 1902. **Wilkinson, F. H.** *The Book of Job. Translated and Annotated.* London: Skeffington & Son, 1901.

1910s. Arnaudet, L. *Job, ou le drame de l'homme dans ses rapports avec Dieu et avec Satan. Tragédie en 4 actes, un prologue, un intermède et l'épilogue. Traduction française en vers rythmés à 12 et à 6 syllabes.* Paris, Bloud & Gay, 1914. **Barton, George A.** *Commentary on the Book of Job.* The Bible for Home and School. New York: Macmillan, 1911. **Beer, G.** "Iob." In *Biblica hebraica.* Ed. R. Kittel. 3rd ed. Stuttgart: Württembergische Bibelanstalt, 1913. 1105–54. **Castelli, D.** *Il libro di Job, tradotto dall'ebraico, con introduzione e note.* Cultura dell'anima 50. Lanciano: R. Crabba, 1916. **Dawidowicz, D.** קדם ... ספר איוב חידות מני קדם. *Hebräisches Kommentar zum Ijob-Buche. Mit einer deutschen Beilage: "Zur Auslegung des Ijob-Buches" von Prof. A. Berliner.* Berlin: L. Lamm, 1913. ———. ספר איוב. *Das Buch Hiob. Mit Uebersetzung und Erläuterung. Deutsche Bearbeitung des* חידות מני קדם *(Rätsel aus dem Morgenlande).* Berlin: A. Schwetschke & Sohn, 1919. **Delebecque, Edmée.** *Le Livre de Job. Traduit de l'hébreu.* Paris: E. Leroux, 1914. **Ehrlich, A. B.** *Randglossen zur hebräischen Bibel. VI. Psalmen, Sprüche, und Hiob.* Leipzig: J. C. Hinrichs, 1918 [repr. Hildesheim: Georg Olms, 1968]. 180–344. **Freegard, Edwin.** *The Book of Job: A Transcription.* St Louis: The Freegard Press, 1914. **Jennings, William.** *The Dramatic Poem of Job: A Close Metrical Translation, with Critical and Explanatory Notes.* London: Methuen, 1912. **King, Edward G.** *The Poem of Job, Translated in the Metre of the Original.* Cambridge: Cambridge University Press. 1914. **Lambert, Franz A.** *Das Buch Hiob übertragen und herausgegeben.* Berlin: Furche-Verlag, 1919. **Leimbach, Karl A.** *Das Buch Job übersetzt und kurz erklärt.* Biblische Volksbücher 8. Fulda: Fuldaer Actiendruckerei, 1911. **Luzzi, Giovanni.** *Giobbe, tradotto dall'ebraico e annotato.* Florence: Società "Fides et Amor," 1918. **McFadyen, John Edgar.** *The Wisdom Books (Job, Proverbs, Ecclesiastes); also Lamentations and the Song of Songs in Modern Speech and Rhythmical Form.* London: James Clarke, 1918. **Noyes, G. A.** *Job, a Translation in the Hebrew Rhythm.* London: Luzac, 1915. **Obronin, Avronin [Rabinowitz, A. Z.].** איוב. Jaffa, 1916. **Rabinowitz, A. Z.** See Obronin, Avronin. **Ridout, Samuel.** *The Book of Job: An Exposition.* New York: Loizeaux Brothers, 1918. **Runciman, Walter.** *The Book of Job* [verse translation, with additions]. East Sheen, London: Temple Sheen Press, 1918. **Schlögl, Nivard.** *Das Buch Hiob, aus dem kritisch hergestellten hebräisch Urtext ins Deutsche metrisch übersetzt und erläutert.* Vienna: Orionverlag, 1916. **Schmidt, Nathaniel.** *The Messages of the Poets: The Books of Job and Canticles and Some Minor Poems in the Old Testament, with Introductions, Metrical Translations, and Paraphrases.* New York: Scribners, 1911. **Sprague, Homer B.** *The Book of Job. The Poetic Portion Versified, with Due Regard to the Language of the Authorized Version, a Closer Adherence to the Sense of the Revised Versions, and a More Literal Translation of the Hebrew Original, with an Introductory Essay Advancing New Views and Explanatory Notes Quoting Many Eminent Authorities.* Boston: Sherman, French & Co., 1913. **Strahan, James.** *The Book of Job Interpreted.* Edinburgh: T. & T. Clark, 1913. **Teles [Telles], Bazilio.** *O livro de Job. Traducção em verso um estudo sobre o poema.* Porto: Livraria Chardron, 1912. **Volz,**

Paul. *Weisheit (Das Buch Hiob, Sprüche und Jesus Sirach, Prediger).* Göttingen: Vandenhoeck & Ruprecht, 1911. **Wilson, Peter.** *The Book of Job Translated into English Verse* [of various meters]. Edinburgh: James Thin, 1912.

1920s. Anon. *Das Buch Hiob. Mit 4 Urholzschnitten von F. R. Schwemmer.* Munich: Arche-Verlag, 1920. **Arndt, Augustin (ed.).** *Die Heilige Schrift des Alten und Neuen Testamentes aus der Vulgata mit Rücksichtnahme auf den Grundtext übersetzt und mit Anmerkungen erläutert.* Regensburg: Pustet, 1920. 1:1389–1586. **Ball, C. J.** *The Book of Job. A Revised Text and Version.* Oxford: Clarendon Press, 1922. **Bertie, Paul.** *Le poème de Job. Traduction nouvelle, introduction et notes.* Judaïsme 10. Paris: Rieder, 1929. **Bleeker, L. H. K.** *Job. Tekst en uitleg. Het Oude Testament.* Groningen: Wolters, 1926. **Buttenwieser, Moses.** *The Book of Job.* London: Hodder & Stoughton, 1922. **Caminero, Francisco Javier.** *El libro de Job. Versión directa del hebreo e introducción crítica.* Madrid: Voluntad, 1924. **Castera, Constantin (ed.).** *Scripta manent: Collection* [French translation]. Paris: Pot cassé, 1925. **Clow, W. McC., and W. G. Jordan.** *Job: A Little Library of Exposition, with New Studies.* London: Cassell & Co., 1928. **Davids, A. B.** *Het boek Job: met inleiding en aanteekeningen.* Amsterdam: Elsevier, 1923. **Davidson, A. B., and H. C. O. Lanchester.** *The Book of Job, with Notes, Introduction and Appendix. Adapted to the Text of the Revised Version with Some Supplementary Notes.* CamB. Cambridge: Cambridge University Press. 1926. **Dhorme, E.** *Le livre de Job.* Paris: Gabalda. 1926 [= *A Commentary on the Book of Job.* Trans. H. Knight. London: Thomas Nelson & Sons, 1967]. **Dimmler, E.** *Job übersetzt, eingeleitet und erklärt.* Mönchengladbach: Volksvereins-Verlag, 1922. **Driver, Samuel Rolles, and George Buchanan Gray.** *A Critical and Exegetical Commentary on the Book of Job, together with a New Translation.* ICC. Edinburgh: T. & T. Clark, 1921 [see also **Compston, H. F. B.** "Marginal Notes on Driver-Gray's 'Job'." *ExpT* 42 (1930–31) 92–93.]. **Franks, R. S.** "Job." In *A Commentary on the Bible.* Ed. Arthur S. Peake. London: T. C. & E. C. Jack, 1919. 346–65. **Fry, Carli.** *Il cudisch de Job, translataus per romontsch da Sur Carli Fry.* Sursum corda: lectura religiusa romontscha 1. Glion: M. Maggi, 1926. **Guillaume, Alfred.** "Job." In *A New Commentary on Holy Scripture, Including the Apocrypha.* Ed. Charles Gore, Henry Leighton Goudge, and Alfred Guillaume. London: SPCK, 1929. **Haghebaert, P.** *Het Boek Job, vertaald en uitgelegd.* New ed. Bruges: Bayaert, 1929. **Halley, Henry H.** *Pocket Bible Handbook: An Abbreviated Bible Commentary.* Chicago: Henry H. Halley, 1924; later editions entitled *Halley's Bible Handbook: An Abbreviated Bible Commentary.* Grand Rapids: Zondervan, 1962 [= *Il commentario biblico abbreviato.* Naples: Edizioni Centro biblico, 1964; *Biblejskij spravočnik.* St Petersburg: Genri Gellej, 1996; *Halley Manual Bíblico.* Grand Rapids: Vida, 2002]. **Irwin, Clarke Huston (ed.).** *The Universal Bible Commentary: With an Introduction to Each Book of the Bible.* London: The Religious Tract Society, 1928. **Jastrow, Morris.** *The Book of Job. Its Origin, Growth and Interpretation, together with a New Translation Based on a Revised Text.* Philadelphia: Lippincott, 1920. **Kahana, Abraham.** ספר איוב מפורש. Tel Aviv: Meqorot, 1928. **Kalt, Edmund.** *Das Buch Job übersetzt und erklärt.* Steyl: Missionsdrückerei, 1924. **König, Eduard.** *Das Buch Hiob eingeleitet, übersetzt und erklärt.* Gütersloh: C. Bertelsmann, 1929. **Lofthouse, W. F.** "The Book of Job." In *Abingdon Bible Commentary.* Ed. Frederick Carl Eiselen, Edwin Lewis, and David G. Downey. London: The Epworth Press; New York: Abingdon–Cokesbury, 1929. 483–508. **Montet, Edouard.** *Le livre de Job: traduction nouvelle.* Geneva: A. Kundig, 1926. **Mowinckel, Sigmund.** *Diktet om Ijob og hans tre venner.* Kristiania: Aschehoug, 1924. **Mumford, A. H.** *The Book of Job: A Metrical Version. With an Introductory Essay, "The Significance of the Book of Job," by A. S. Peake.* London: Hodder & Stoughton, 1923. **Obbink, H. T.** *De Bijbel (verkorte uitgave) opnieuw uit den grondtekst vert. door en onder leiding.* II. *Job tot Maleachi.* Amsterdam: Van Looy, 1924. **O'Neill, George.** *The World's Classic Job. Translation from Original Texts, with Introduction and Notes.* Milwaukee: Bruce Publishing, 1938. **Peters, Norbert.** *Das Buch Hiob übersetzt und erklärt.* EHAT. Münster: Aschendorff, 1928. **Rahlwes, Ferdinand.** *Die Bücher der Bibel. 7. Die Lehrdichtung: Die Sprüche, Hiob, der Prediger, Ruth, Jona, Esther, Daniel.* Monographien zur Wissenschaft des Judentums 1. Braunschweig: G. Westermann, 1923 [= Egelsbach: Hänsel–Hohenhausen, 1996]. **Ricciotti, Giuseppe.** *Il libro di Giobbe. Versione critica dal testo* *ebraico con introduzione e commento.* Turin: Marietti, 1924. **Riessler, Paul.** *Die Heilige Schrift des Alten Bundes nach dem Grundtext übersetzt.* II. *Weisheitsbücher, Psalmen, Propheten.* Mainz: Matthias-Grünewald-Verlag, 1928. 7–76. **Rocholl, Cornelie.** *Das Buch Hiob, neu gedichtet.* Stuttgart: Steinkopf, 1922. **Schmidt, Hans.** *Hiob. Das Buch vom Sinn des Leidens. Gekürzt und verdeutscht.* Tübingen: J. C. B. Mohr, 1927. **Schubert, L.** *Das Buch Hiob. Dichterische Übersetzung mit einer Erklärung.* Leipzig: Klein, 1927. **Simon, Matthias.** *Hiob übersetzt und herausgegeben.* Munich: Chr. Kaiser, 1925. **Steuernagel, Carl.** "Das Buch Hiob." In *Die Heilige Schrift des Alten Testaments.* Ed. E. Kautzsch and A. Bertholet. 4th ed. Tübingen: J. C. B. Mohr, 1923. 2:323–89. **Thilo, Martin.** *Das Buch Hiob neu übersetzt und aufgefasst.* Bonn: A. Marcus & E. Weber, 1925. **Torczyner, H. [Tur-Sinai, N. H.].** *Das Buch Hiob. Eine kritische Analyse des überlieferten Hiobtextes.* Vienna: R. Löwit, 1920. **Vaccari, Alberto.** *Il Libro di Giobbe e i Salmi, tradotti dai testi originali e annotati.* Rome: Pontifical Biblical Institute, 1925; 2nd ed., 1927. **Valente, Ferruccio.** *Giobbe: traduzione e note.* Turin: Società Editrice Internazionale, 1928. **Valera, Cipriano de.** *El Libro de Job.* Madrid: Deposito Central de la Sociedad Biblica, 1923. **Yellin, D.** חקרי־מקרא: באורים חדשים במקראות: איוב. Jerusalem: Tarpiz, 1927. **Yerushalmi, E.** ספר איוב: הקפה מדעת. Jerusalem: Eretz-Israel, 1927.

1930s. Anon. *Tobias, Judith, Ester, Job* [in Malayalam]. Alwaye: Jubilee Memorial Press, 1933. **Bückers, Hermann.** *Die Makkabäerbücher. Das Buch Job. Übersetzt und erklärt.* Die Heilige Schrift für das Leben erklärt 5. Freiburg i.Br.: Herder, 1939. **Busch, K. A.** *Hiob: Ein Lehrgedicht im Wechselgespräche aus dem Alten Testament in neuen deutschen Rhythmen.* Dresden: Sturm, 1935. **Buskes, J. J.** *Job.* Berne: Bosch & Kenning, 1935. **Crampon, A.** *La Sainte Bible, traduction d'après les textes originaux par le chanoine A. Crampon.* Paris: Desclée & Cie, 1939. **Dimnent, Edward Daniel.** *The Book of Job: The Poem, an Epic Version in English* [paraphrase]. New York: Fleming H. Revell, 1937. **Glotzbach, A.** *Het Boek Job. Het Hooglied.* Arnhem: Van Loghum Slaterus, 1938. **Gordon, S. L.** איוב תנך כתובים. Tel-Aviv: The Author, 1936. **Grün, Albert.** *Jób Könyvének egyik kommentár-töredéke.* Budapest: Gewürcz F., 1931. **Hamblen, Emily S.** *The Book of Job Interpreted, Illustrated with the Designs of William Blake* [commentary]. New York: Delphic Studios, 1933. **Hölscher, Gustav.** *Das Buch Hiob.* HAT 1/17. Tübingen: J. C. B. Mohr (Paul Siebeck), 1937; 2nd ed., 1952. **Kissane, Edward J.** *The Book of Job Translated from a Critically Revised Hebrew Text with Commentary.* Dublin: Browne & Nolan, 1939; New York: Sheed & Ward, 1946. **Kraeling, Emil G.** *The Book of the Ways of God* [commentary]. London: SPCK, 1938 [some pages reprinted as "A Theodicy—and More" in *The Dimensions of Job: A Study and Selected Readings.* Ed. Nahum H. Glatzer. New York: Schocken Books, 1969. 205–14]. **Martin, Hugh.** *The Teachers' Commentary [Teaching the Bible Stories to Children].* London: SCM Press, 1932 [later edition edited by Gwynne Henton Davies, Alan Richardson, and Charles L. Wallis, *The Twentieth Century Bible Commentary.* Rev. ed. New York: Harper, 1955]. **Montet, Edouard.** "Job." In *La Sainte Bible: traduction nouvelle d'après les meilleurs textes avec introductions et notes.* La Bible du Centenaire. Paris: Société biblique, 1947. 3:xi–xiii, 215–72. **Nairne, A.** *The Book of Job, Edited with an Introduction.* Cambridge: Cambridge University Press, 1935. **Nesfield, Vincent.** *Let Cockle Grow instead of Barley.* London: A. J. Davies, 1933. **Neumann, R.** *The Book of Job: A Metrical Translation, with a Critical Introduction.* Burlington, IA: The Lutheran Literary Board, 1934. **Richardson, Jacob W.** *Out of the Whirlwind. A Dramatized Version of the Book of Job. Based on Dr James Moffatt's Translation.* London: Epworth, 1936. **Szczygiel, Paul.** *Das Buch Job, übersetzt und erklärt.* HSAT 5/1. Bonn: Peter Hanstein, 1931. **Weiser, L.** *Das ungekürzte Buch Hiob. Deutsch von Lazarus Weiser. Jetzt ein Buch für jede Seele, die Kraft trinken kann vom alten starken Geiste Hiobs, früher bei dem gekürzten Urtext ein unverstandenes Buch.* Vienna: Ta'nach-Selbstverlag, 1931. **Wutz, Franz.** *Das Buch Job* [translation and commentary]. Eichstätter Studien 3. Stuttgart: Kohlhammer, 1939.

1940s. Chase, Mary Ellen. *The Book of Job, from the Translation Prepared at Cambridge in 1611 for King James I. With a Preface by Mary Ellen Chase and Illustrations by Arthur Szyk.* New York: The Limited Editions Club, 1946. **Fisher, Alfred Young.** *The Book of Job from the King James Bible, with Wood Engravings by Gustav Wolf and a Note by Alfred Young Fisher.*

[Cummington, MA:] The Cummington Press, 1944. **Fohrer, G.** *Das Buch Hiob übertragen und herausgegeben.* Krefeld: Scherpe-Verlag, 1948. **Hertzberg, Hans Wilhelm.** *Das Buch Hiob übersetzt und ausgelegt.* Bibelhilfe für die Gemeinde. Stuttgart: J. G. Oncken, 1949. **Hölscher, Gustav.** *Das Gedicht von Hiob und seinen drei Freunden übersetzt.* Wiesbaden: Insel-Verlag, 1948. **Hurwitz (Gurvits), Nathan.** *The Immortal Drama of Life (The Book of Job). The Mystery Book of More than 3000 Years, Translated from the Original.* Cape Town: Stewart Printing Co., 1944. **Kroeze, J. H.** *Paraphrase van het boek Job.* Franeker: Wever, 1946. **Kunstmann, Joseph.** *Job: Eine Auswahl aus dem biblischen Text. Eugen Nerdinger gestaltete… mit… zehn Langholzschnitten.* Augsburg: Dom-Verlag, 1945. **Lods, A., and L. Randon.** "Job." In *La Sainte Bible: traduction nouvelle d'après les meilleurs textes avec introductions et notes* (La Bible du Centenaire). III. Paris, 1947. **Minn, H. R.** *The Burden of This Unintelligible World: or, The Mystery of Suffering, Being a Rhythmical Version of the Book of Job, Annotated.* Auckland: Whitcombe & Tombs, 1942. **Pirot, Louis, and Albert Clamer.** *La Sainte Bible, texte latin et traduction française.* 4. *Paralipomènes; Esdras; Néhémie; Tobie; Judith; Esther; Job.* Paris: Letouzey & Ané, 1949. **Prosdij, A. C. G. van.** *Het Boek Job.* Amsterdam: S. J. B. Bakker, 1948. **Reichert, Victor E.** *Job with Hebrew Text and English Translation. Commentary.* Soncino Books of the Bible 11. Hindhead, Surrey: The Soncino Press, 1946; rev. ed., 1993. **Robin, E.** "Job traduit et commenté." In *La Sainte Bible.* Ed. L. Pirot and A. Clamer. Paris: Letouzey & Ané, 1949. 4:797–868. **Schröder, Rudolf Alexander.** *Das Buch Hiob mit Randbemerkungen.* Munich: R. Piper, 1948. **Snaith, Norman H.** *Notes on the Hebrew Text of Job 1–6.* London: Epworth Press, 1945. **Stevenson, William Barron.** *The Poem of Job: A Literary Study with a New Translation.* London: Oxford University Press, 1947. **Torczyner, H. [Tur-Sinai, N. H.].** ספר איוב מפורש. *The Book of Job Interpreted.* Jerusalem: Hebrew University Press, 1941. **Villa, Emilio.** *Antico teatro ebraico: Giobbe. Cantico dei cantici.* Milan: Poligono, 1947. **Warren, Charles B.** *A Paraphrase of Job's Dark Days* [poem]. New York: H. Harrison, 1941. **Weber, Jean-Julien.** *Le Livre de Job. L'Ecclésiaste. Texte et commentaire.* Paris: Desclée, 1947.

    1950s. Artom [Hartom], E. S. ספר איוב: מפרש. Tel Aviv: Yavneh, 1954; 2nd ed., 1967. **Augé, R.** *Job.* La Biblia. Versió… i Comentari 9. Montserrat: Monestir de Montserrat, 1959. **Bavinck, J. H., and A. H. Edelkoort (eds.).** *Bijbel met kanttekeningen. Het boek Job. Het boek der Psalmen. De Spreuken. Het boek Prediker. Het Hooglied.* Baarn: Bosch & Keuning, 1952. **Calvin, John.** *Sermons from Job.* Trans. Leroy Nixon. Grand Rapids: W. B. Eerdmans, 1952. **Clarke, W. K. Lowther.** "Job." In his *Concise Bible Commentary.* London: SPCK, 1952. 464–74. **Crampon, A.** *L'Ancien Testament, traduction du Chanoine Crampon. Revisée et annotée par J. Bonsirven.* In *La Sainte Bible du Chanoine Crampon. Traduction d'après les textes originaux.* Paris: Desclée & Cie, 1952. 593–627. **Davies, Gwynne Henton, Alan Richardson, and Charles L. Wallis (eds.).** *The Twentieth Century Bible Commentary.* Rev. ed. New York: Harper, 1955 [earlier edition edited by Hugh Martin, *The Teachers' Commentary [Teaching the Bible Stories to Children].* London: SCM Press, 1932]. **Dhorme, E.** "Job." In *La Bible de la Pléiade.* Paris: Gallimard, 1959. **Faraj, Murād.** *Ayyāb* [a prose version in rhymed Arabic]. Cairo: Al-'Alam al-'Arabi, 1950. **Freehof, S. B.** *The Book of Job: A Commentary.* New York: Union of American Hebrew Congregations, 1958. **Gans, A.** *Job vertaald en ingeleid.* Leiden: Sijthoff, 1952. **Gemser, B., et al. (eds.).** *Die Bybel met verklarende aantekeninge.* II. *Job tot Maleági.* Kaapstad: Verenigde Protestantse Uitgewers, 1958. **Hanson, A. T., and Miriam Hanson.** *The Book of Job. Introduction and Commentary.* Torch Bible Commentary. London: SCM Press, 1953. **Junker, Hubert.** *Das Buch Job.* EchB. Würzburg: Echter-Verlag, 1951. **Kaplan, J.** ספר איוב: מבוא ופירוש [*The Book of Job. Introduction and Commentary*]. Tel Aviv: Mahbarot Lisparot, 1951. **Lamparter, Helmut.** *Das Buch der Anfechtung, übersetzt und ausgelegt.* BotAT. Stuttgart: Calwer, 1951. **Larcher, C.** *Le Livre de Job, traduit.* BJ. La Sainte Bible. Paris: Cerf, 1950. **Liénart, Achille (ed.).** *La Sainte Bible, nouvelle édition publiée sous la direction de S. Em. le Cardinal Liénart par La Bible pour Tous.* Paris: Letouzey & Ané, 1956. 618–49. **Mowinckel, Sigmund.** "Diktet om Ijob." In *Det gamle Testament.* Trans. S. Michelet, Sigmund Mowinckel, and N. Messe. Oslo: H. Aschehoug & Co. (W. Nygaard), 1955. 4:293–384. **Murphy, Roland E.** "Job in the

New Confraternity Version." *AER* 133 (1955) 16–29. **Steinmann, Jean.** *Le Livre de Job.* Lectio Divina. Paris: Cerf, 1955. **Stier, Fridolin.** *Das Buch Ijjob hebräisch und deutsch. Übertragungen ausgelegt und mit Text- und Sacherläuterungen versehen.* Munich: Kösel, 1954. **Sutcliffe, E. F.** "Job." In *A Catholic Commentary on Holy Scripture.* Ed. Bernard Orchard, Edmund F. Sutcliffe, Reginald C. Fuller, and Ralph Russell. London: Thomas Nelson & Sons, 1953. 417–41. **Terrien, S. L., and P. Scherer.** "Job." *IB.* New York, Nashville: Abingdon Press, 1954. 3:877–1198. **Turoldo, David Maria.** *Da una casa di fango (Job).* Brescia: La Scuola, 1951 [commentary, with translation of A. Vaccari]. **Tur-Sinai, N. H. [Torczyner, H.].** חדש פירוש עם איוב ספר. Tel Aviv: Yavneh, 1954 [= *The Book of Job: A New Commentary.* Jerusalem: Kiryath-Sepher, 1957; 2nd ed., 1967]. See also **Gruber, Mayer I.** "Tur-Sinai's Job in the Jewish Liturgy." *Review of Rabbinic Judaism* 6 (2003) 87–100.| **Vischer, Wilhelm.** *Valeur de l'Ancien Testament. Commentaire des livres de Job, Esther, Ecclésiaste, le Second Isaïe.* Geneva: Labor & Fides, 1958. **Weiser, Artur.** *Das Buch Hiob übersetzt und erklärt.* ATD 13. Göttingen: Vandenhoeck & Ruprecht. 1951 [= *Giobbe: Traduzione e commento.* Brescia: Paideia, 1975]. **Weiser, Asher.** מפרש איוב ספר. Tel Aviv: Yehuda, 1950/51.

1960s. Blair, J. Allen. *Living Patiently: A Devotional Study of the Book of Job.* Neptune, NJ: Loizeaux Brothers, 1966. **Boer, P. A. H. de, et al.** *Zoals er gezegd is over Job.* Bijbelcommentaren voor de moderne mens 15. Hilversum: de Haan; Antwerp: Standaard, 1965. **Bourke, M. M.** *The Book of Job: Parts 1 & 2, with a Commentary.* New York Paulist Press, 1962–63. **Brates Cavero, J.** *Job. Traducción y comentario.* BAC 287. Madrid: Católica, 1969. 435–739. **Brown, Raymond E., Joseph A. Fitzmyer, and Roland E. Murphy (eds.).** *The Jerome Biblical Commentary.* London: Geoffrey Chapman, 1968. **Church, Leslie F. (ed.).** *Matthew Henry's Commentary on the Whole Bible in One Volume.* London: Marshall, Morgan & Scott, 1960. **Crawford, Harriet A.** *A Libretto for Job.* New York: Christopher Publishing House, 1963. **Donn, Thomas M.** *The Divine Challenge, Being a Metrical Paraphrase of the Book of Job in Four-Line Stanzas of Anapaestic Tetrameters in Rhyme.* Inverness: Robert Carruthers, 1963. **Drijvers, Pius, and Pé Hawinkels.** *Job. Prediker. Met commentaar en verklarende aantekeningen.* Baarn: Ambo, 1969. **Epping, W., and J. T. Nelis.** *Job.* BOT 7A. Roermond: J. J. Romen & Zonen, 1968. **Fohrer, Georg.** *Das Buch Hiob.* KAT 16. Gütersloh: Gütersloher Verlagshaus Gerd Mohn, 1963. **Fowler, David C.** "A Middle English Bible Commentary (Oxford Trinity College, MS 93)." *Manuscripta* 12/2 (1968) 67–78. **García Cordero, M.** "Libro de Job: introducción y comentario." In *Biblia comentada: texto de la Nácar-Colunga. 4. Libros sapienciales.* BAC 218. Madrid: BAC, 1962. 16–167. **Guillaume, Alfred.** *Studies in the Book of Job, with a New Translation.* ALUOS 2. Leiden: E. J. Brill, 1968. **Ḥakham, Amos.** מפורש איוב ספר. Jerusalem: Mosad ha-Rab Kook, 1969–70. **Harper, A. F. (ed.).** *Beacon Bible Commentary. III. Job, Psalms, Proverbs, Ecclesiastes, Song of Solomon.* Kansas City, MO: Beacon Hill Press, 1967. **Horst, Friedrich.** *Hiob.* I [chaps. 1–19]. BKAT 16/1. Neukirchen: Neukirchener Verlag, 1960–69. **Hulme, William E.** *Dialogue in Despair: Pastoral Commentary on the Book of Job.* Nashville: Abingdon Press, 1968. **Irwin, W. A.** "Job." In *Peake's Commentary on the Bible.* Ed. Matthew Black and H. H. Rowley. London: Thomas Nelson & Sons, 1962. 391–408. **Kelly, Balmer H.** *Ezra, Nehemiah, Esther, Job.* The Layman's Bible Commentaries 8. London: SCM Press, 1963 [= *The Book of Ezra; the Book of Nehemiah; the Book of Esther; the Book of Job.* The Layman's Bible Commentary 8. Richmond, VA: John Knox Press, 1962]. **Kline, Meredith G.** "Job." In *The Wycliffe Bible Commentary.* Ed. Charles F. Pfeiffer and Everett F. Harrison. Chicago, Moody Press, 1962; London: Oliphants, 1963. 459–90. **Kroeze, J. H.** *Het Boek Job, opnieuw uit de grondtekst vertaald en verklaard.* Korte verklaring der Heilige Schrift. Kampen: J. H. Kok, 1960. ———. *Het Boek Job.* Commentaar op het OT. Kampen: J. H. Kok, 1961. **Lamparter, Helmut.** *Das Buch Hiob. In der Übertragung von Helmut Lamparter. Mit 38 Weissschnitten von den Originalplatten von Kurt Passon. Einführung von Rainer Zimmermann.* Frankenau, Hessen: Siebenberg-Verlag, 1962. **Laurin, Robert B.** "Job." In *The Biblical Expositor: The Living Theme of the Great Book.* Ed. Carl F. H. Henry. Philadelphia: A. J. Holman; London: Pickering & Inglis, 1960. 13–33. **Lubsczyk, Hans.** *Das*

Buch Ijob erläutert. Geistliche Schriftlesung 1. Düsseldorf: Patmos Verlag, 1969 [= *Il libro di Giobbe.* Commenti spirituali dell'Antico Testamento 1. Rome: Città Nuovo, 1971]. **Luteijn, C. M.** *De boeken Ezra, Nehemia, Esther en Job.* Leeuwarden: A. Jongbloed, 1965. **MacBeath, Andrew.** *The Book of Job. A Study Manual.* Glasgow: Pickering & Inglis, 1967. **MacKenzie, R. A. F.** "Job." In *The Jerome Bible Commentary.* Ed. Raymond E. Brown, Joseph A. Fitzmyer, and Roland E. Murphy. Englewood Cliffs, NJ; London: Chapman, 1968. 511–33 [= "Giobbe." In *Grande commentario biblico.* Ed. A. Bonora. Brescia: Queriniana, 1973. 642–82]. **Meyer, F. B.** *Great Verses through the Bible: A Devotional Commentary on Key Verses.* London: Marshall, Morgan & Scott, 1974. **Minn, H. R.** *The Book of Job: A Translation with Introduction and Notes.* Auckland: University of Auckland, 1965. **Neil, William.** "Job." In his *One Volume Bible Commentary.* London: Hodder & Stoughton, 1962. 220–28. **Pascal, P.** *Le Livre de Job: épopée biblique en XLII chapitres paraphrasée en vers par P. Pascal, d'après les textes conjoints des LXX et de la Vulgate, embellié avec les XXI illustrations … que W. Blake consacra au plus sublime des livres poëtiques & sapientiaux … Le tout précédé de l'exégèse, écrite … par G. K. Chesterton, et puis d'une nouvelle paraphrase du psaume XXII.* Turin: Minerva medica, 1967. **Potter, R. D.** "Job." In *A New Catholic Commentary on Holy Scripture.* Ed. Reginald C. Fuller, Leonard Johnston, and Conleth Kearns. London: Nelson, 1969. 417–38. **Quevedo [Quebedo] Villegas [y Villegas], Francisco [de]** (Spanish Golden Age author, 1580–1645). "Constance et patience du Saint Job: fragments." *Cahiers des saisons* 20 (1960) 548–52. **Renassia, Daniel, and Joseph Ben Aaron.** *Le livre de Job orné de soixante-dix-huit gravures originales de Marc Dawtry* [original translation]. Nice: J. Pardo, 1961. **Schweitzer, René.** *Job.* La Bible et la vie 6. Paris: Ligel, 1966. **Steinmann, Jean.** *Job. Texte français, introduction et commentaires.* Connaître la Bible. Bruges, Paris: Desclée de Brouwer, 1961. ———. *Poésie biblique: Isaïe, Jérémie, Job, Cantique des cantiques: traduction et presentation de Jean Steinmann.* Paris: Colin, 1961. **Strange, Marcian.** *Job and Qoheleth: Introduction and Commentary.* Old Testament Reading Guide 27. Collegeville, MN: The Liturgical Press, 1968 [= *Job y Eclesiastés: introducción y comentario.* Bilbao: Mensajero, 1970]. **Terrien, Samuel.** *Job.* Commentaire de l'Ancien Testament 13. Neuchâtel: Delachaux & Niestlé, 1963; 2nd ed., Geneva: Labor & Fides, 2005. **Weitzner, Emil.** *The Book of Job: A Paraphrase.* New York, 1960.

1970s. Alonso Schökel, L., and J. L. Ojeda. *Job.* Los Libros Sagrados 16. Madrid: Ediciones Cristiandad, 1971 [Translation by Alonso Schökel and J. L. Ojeda, commentary by Alonso Schökel]. **Andersen, F. I.** *Job. An Introduction and Commentary.* TOTC. Leicester: Tyndale Press, 1976. **Anderson, Hugh.** "The Book of Job." In *The Interpreter's One-Volume Commentary on the Bible.* Ed. Charles M. Laymon. Nashville: Abingdon Press, 1972. 238–52. **Anon.** *Bible Today: The Jerusalem Version, with Commentary, Illustrations and Historical Notes.* London: Marshall Cavendish, 1970. ———. *En ce temps-là, la Bible.* III [Les Livres historiques. II. Esdras, Néhémie, Tobie, Judith, Esther, Les Maccabées. Les Livres poétiques et sapientiaux. I. Job, les Psaumes]. Brussels: «Femmes d'aujourd'hui»; Paris: Editions du Hennin, 1970. ———. *Le livre de Job: traduction oecuménique.* Paris: Les Bergers et les Mages: Editions du Cerf, 1971. **Blei, K.** *Job: Verklaring van een bijbelgedeelte.* Kampen: Kok, 1978. **Bonsels, Erich.** *Geläutert im Schmelztiegel Gottes: Betrachtungen über das Buch Hiob.* Hückeswagen: Christliche Schriftenverbreitung, 1979. **Bowdle, Donald N. (ed.).** *Ellicott's Bible Commentary in One Volume: A Verse-by-Verse Explanation.* Grand Rapids: Zondervan; London: Pickering & Inglis, 1971. 372–400 [see also Leathes, 1882–84]. **Bratcher, Robert G.** *Job for Modern Man: Today's English Version.* New York: American Bible Society, 1971. **Brière, Jean, Raymond Castanié, Vicent Chartier, and Michel Danchin.** *La Sagesse d'Israël.* [1]. *Le Livre des Proverbes, Job, l'Ecclésiaste* [extracts]. Ecouter la Bible 13. Paris: Desclée de Brouwer; Limoges: Droguet-Ardant, 1977. **Carlisle, T. J.** *Journey with Job* [versified commentary]. Grand Rapids: Eerdmans, 1976. **Ceronetti, Guido.** *Il libro di Giobbe.* Biblioteca Adelphi 41. Milan: Adelphi, 1972. **Chouraqui, A.** *Iyov.* La Bible traduite et présentée 15. Paris: Desclée de Brouwer, 1974. **Cook, Edward David.** *The Man Who Had Everything: Job* [Selections from Job in TEV]. Today's Good News. Illustrated by Annie Vallotton. [London]: Fount Paperbacks: Falcon Books, 1978.

Ellison, H. L. *From Tragedy to Triumph: The Message of the Book of Job.* London: Paternoster Press, 1958 [= *A Study of Job: From Tragedy to Triumph.* Grand Rapids: Zondervan, 1971]. **Fedrizzi, Pio.** *Giobbe: La Sacra Bibbia, traduta dai testi originali illustrata con note critiche e commentata.* Turin: Marietti, 1972. **García Cordero, M., and G. Pérez Rodríguez.** *Libro de Job. Introducción y comentario.* Madrid: BAC, 1972. **Garland, D. D.** *Job: A Study Guide.* Grand Rapids: Zondervan, 1971. **Gerleman, Gillis, and Johannes Fichtner.** *Iyov, Mishlei. Iob et Proverbia.* Biblia hebraica stuttgartensia 12. Stuttgart: Württembergische Bibelanstalt, 1974. **Gordis, Robert.** *The Book of Job: Commentary, New Translation, and Special Notes.* New York: Jewish Theological Seminary of America, 1978. **Gualandi, Dario.** *Giobbe: nuova versione critica.* Rome: Gregorian University, 1976. **Hakham, Amos.** ספר איוב מפורש [The Book of Job, A Commentary]. Jerusalem: Kook, 1970. **Habel, Norman C.** *The Book of Job. Commentary.* CamB. Cambridge: Cambridge University Press, 1975. **Heavenor, E. S. P.** "Job." In *The New Bible Commentary.* Ed. F. Davidson. London: Inter-Varsity Fellowship, 1953. 387–411 [= *New Bible Commentary Revised.* Ed. D. Guthrie et al. London: IVP, 1970. 421–45]. **Heinen, Karl.** *Der unverfügbare Gott. Das Buch Ijob.* Stuttgarter kleiner Kommentar: Altes Testament 18. Stuttgart: Katholisches Bibelwerk, 1979. **Hesse, Franz.** *Hiob.* Zürcher Bibelkommentar. Zurich: Theologischer Verlag, 1978. **Leahy, Desmond J.** *The Wisdom Literature* [Proverbs, Ecclesiastes, the Book of Wisdom, the Song of Songs, Job]. Mowbrays Mini-Commentaries 12. London: A. R. Mowbray, 1970. **McCarthy, Carmel, and Vitus Huonder.** *The Book of Job / Le livre de Job. Preliminary Report on the Hebrew Old Testament Project.* Vol. 3. Stuttgart: United Bible Societies, 1977. **Mitchell, Stephen.** *Into the Whirlwind: A Translation of the Book of Job.* Garden City, NY: Doubleday, 1979 [= *The Book of Job.* San Francisco: North Point Press, 1987; London: Kyle Cathie, revised ed., 1990]. **Moraldi, Luigi, Giovanni Boccali, and Florindo di Vincenzo.** *Giobbe, Ecclesiaste.* Milan: Garzanti, 1977. **Müller, Charlotte, and Gerhard Ising.** *Die niederdeutschen Bibelfrühdrucke: Kölner Bibeln (um 1478), Lübecker Bibel (1494), Halberstädter Bibel (1522).* IV. *Hiob–Jesaja.* Berlin: Akademie-Verlag, 1971. **Murphy, Roland Edmund.** *The Psalms, Job.* Proclamation Commentaries. Philadelphia: Fortress Press, 1977. **Neiman, David.** *The Book of Job: A Presentation of the Book with Selected Portions Translated from the Original Hebrew Text.* Jerusalem: Massada, 1972. **Osty, Emile, and Joseph Trinquet.** *Le Livre de Job—L'Ecclésiaste—Le Livre de la sagesse.* Lausanne, Paris: Rencontre, 1971. **Patrick, Dale.** *Arguing with God: The Angry Prayers of Job* [with translation]. St Louis: Bethany Press, 1977. **Pope, Marvin H.** *Job: Introduction, Translation and Notes.* AB 15. Garden City, NY: Doubleday, 1973; 2nd ed., 1965; 3rd ed., 1973 [an extract from the Introduction (p. lxxvii) is reprinted as "Viewed as a Whole" in *The Dimensions of Job: A Study and Selected Readings.* Ed. Nahum H. Glatzer. New York: Schocken Books, 1969. 276–77]. **Ravasi, Gianfranco.** *Giobbe. Traduzione e commento.* Commenti biblici. Rome: Borla, 1979; 2nd ed., 1984. **Rosenberg, David.** "Job." In his *A Poet's Bible: Rediscovering the Voices of the Original Text.* New York: Harper & Row, 1977. 81–168. ———. *Job Speaks: Interpreted from the Original Hebrew Book of Job.* New York: Harper & Row, 1977. **Rowley, H. H.** *Job.* NCB. London: Thomas Nelson & Sons, 1970. **Sekine, M.** *Yob-ki chu'mkai* [commentary on the Book of Job]. Tokyo: Kyombunkan, 1970 [Japanese]. **Speyr, Adrienne von.** *Job* [commentary]. Einsiedeln: Johannes-Verlag, 1972. **Watts, J. D. W., J. J. Owens, and M. E. Tate.** "Job." In *Broadman Bible Commentary.* Ed. Clifton J. Allen. Nashville: Broadman, 1971. 22–151. **Wilde, A. de.** *Het boek Job, ingeleid en vertaald.* Wageningen: Veenman, 1974. ———. *Het boek Job in westerse dichtvorm.* Lunteren: The Author, 1979. **Wright, J. Stafford.** "Ezra–Job." In *The Daily Commentary: Genesis–Job.* Ed. Arthur E. Cundall. London: Scripture Union, 1974. 412–45. **Zuck, Roy B.** *Job.* Everyman's Bible Commentary. Chicago: Moody Press, 1978.

1980s. Afanas'eva, Elena Vladimirovna. *K istorii teksta i jazyka drevnejsego slavjanskogo perevoda knigi Iova.* Diss. Leningrad, 1988. **Alonso Schökel, L., and J. L. Sicre Díaz.** *Job, comentario teológico y literario.* Nueva Biblia Española. Madrid: Ediciones Cristiandad, 1983; 2nd ed. 2002. **Anon.** *Sagesse du livre de Job* [extracts]. Méry-sur-Oise: Sator; Paris: Médiaspaul, 1988. ———. *The Book of Job: A New Translation according to the Traditional*

Hebrew Text. Philadelphia: Jewish Publication Society, 1980. **Bergant, Dianne.** *Job, Ecclesiastes.* Old Testament Message 18. Wilmington: Michael Glazier, 1982. **Bič, Miloš.** *Jób.* Komenského Bohosloveck 8. Prague: Kalich, 1981. **Bruges, W. E.** *The Book of Job* [translation in iambic pentameters]. Bognor Regis: New Horizon, 1983. **Cantalausa, J. de.** *Lo libre de Jòb (presentacion e causidas). Qohelèt: revirada integrala.* Illustrations by Martina Bedruna-Còsta [Occitan translation]. Toulouse: Centre Régional d'Etudes Occitanes, 1983. **Chouraqui, André.** *L'univers de la Bible.* V. *Douze inspirés (Petits prophètes); louanges (Psaumes); exemples (Proverbes); Iob (Job).* Paris: Lidis; Turnhout: Brepols, 1984. **Clines, David J. A.** "Job." In *A Bible Commentary for Today. Based on the Revised Standard Version.* Ed. G. C. D. Howley. London: Pickering & Inglis, 1979. 559–92 [= *The Pickering Bible Commentary for Today.* 1984; *Marshall Pickering Bible Commentary.* Basingstoke: Marshall, Morgan & Scott, 1986; *The New Layman's Bible Commentary.* Grand Rapids: Zondervan, 1979]. 2nd ed. based on the New International Version in *The International Bible Commentary.* Ed. F. F. Bruce. Basingstoke: Marshall Pickering; Grand Rapids: Zondervan, 1986. 520–51. ———. "Job." In *The Books of the Bible.* I. *The Old Testament/The Hebrew Bible.* Ed. Bernhard W. Anderson. New York: Charles Scribner's Sons, 1989. 181–201. ———. *Job 1–20.* WBC 17. Waco, TX: Word Books, 1989 [see also Clines, 2006]. **Davies, Glenn N.** *Job: A Mini-Commentary on the Book of Job.* Bible Probe. London: Scripture Union, 1989. **Edel, Reiner-Friedemann.** *Hebräisch-deutsche Präparation zum Buch Hiob.* Darmstadt: Lüdenscheid–Lobetal: Ökumenischer-Verlag, 1984. **Field, Filip.** *The Book of Job* = ‏ספר איוב‎. *A New Translation according to the Traditional Hebrew Text.* Philadelphia: Jewish Publication Society of America, 1980. **Gibson, J. C. L.** *Job.* Daily Study Bible. Edinburgh: St Andrews Press, 1985. **Good, Edwin M.** "Job." In *Harper's Bible Commentary.* Ed. James L. Mays. San Francisco: Harper & Row, 1988; 2nd ed., 1999. 407–32. **Greenberg, M., J. C. Greenfield, and N. M. Sarna.** *The Book of Job, a New Translation according to the Traditional Hebrew Text with Introductions.* Philadelphia: Jewish Publication Society of America, 1980. **Gringoire, Pedro.** *Archaeological Commentary on the Bible.* Garden City, NY: Doubleday, 1984. **Gross, Heinrich.** *Ijob.* Die neue Echter Bibel. Kommentar zum Alten Testament 13. Würzburg: Echter Verlag, 1986. **Guinan, Michael D.** *Job.* Collegeville Bible Commentary. Old Testament 19. Collegeville, MN: Liturgical Press, 1986. **Habel, Norman C.** *Job.* Knox Preaching Guides. Atlanta: John Knox, 1981. ———. *The Book of Job: A Commentary.* OTL. London: SCM Press; Philadelphia: Westminster Press, 1985 [see also **Cooper, Alan M.** "The Book of Job" [review article of Norman C. Habel, *The Book of Job*], *Theodolite. A Journal of Christian Thought and Practice* 7/7 (1986) 4–6]. **Hartley, John E.** *The Book of Job.* NICOT. Grand Rapids: Eerdmans, 1988. **Janzen, J. Gerald.** *Job.* Interpretation. Atlanta: John Knox, 1985. **Jérémie, Marc.** *Chaque jour les Ecritures.* 3ème année, *Job, Psaumes 1 à 41, Proverbes ch. 1 à 15, Esaïe, Matthieu, Jérémie, Lamentations.* Valence: Bibles et publications chrétiennes: La bonne semence, 1987. **Martínez Terrassa, José M.** *Job, la fe en conflicto: Comentario y reflexiones sobre el libro de Job.* Barcelona: Clie, 1982. **McKenna, David L.** *Job.* Communicator's Commentary 12. Waco, TX: Word Books, 1986. **Michel, Walter L.** *Job in the Light of Northwest Semitic.* 1. *Prologue and First Cycle of Speeches. Job 1:1–14:22.* BibOr 42/1. Rome: Biblical Institute Press, 1987. **Morgan, G. Campbell.** "Job." In his *An Exposition of the Whole Bible.* Westwood, NJ: Fleming H. Revell; London: Pickering & Inglis, 1959. 201–20. **Murphy, Roland E.** *Wisdom Literature: Job, Proverbs, Ruth, Canticles, Ecclesiastes, and Esther.* FOTL 11. Grand Rapids: Eerdmans, 1981. **Nicole, Jules-Marcel.** *Le livre de Job.* Commentaire évangelique de la Bible. Vaux-sur-Seine: Edifac, 1986–87. **Owens, Mary Frances.** *Ezra, Nehemiah, Esther, Job.* Layman's Bible Book Commentary 7. Nashville: Broadman Press, 1983. **Philip, George M.** *The Book of Job: A Detailed Exposition in the Form of Bible Reading Notes.* Aberdeen: Didasko Press, 1980. **Pixley, Jorge V.** *El libro de Job: comentario bíblico latino-americano.* San José, Costa Rica: Sebila, 1982. **Rosenberg, A. J.** *Job, A New English Translation of the Text and Rashi, with a Commentary Digest.* New York: Judaica Press, 1989. **Rozelaar, Marc.** *Mijn leven is een ademtocht. Het boek Job uit het Hebreeuws in Nederlandse verzen overgebracht en van een inleiding, toelichting en verantwoording.* Kampen: Kok, 1984. **Saithwell, Peter.** *Ezra–Job.*

London: Scripture Union, 1982. **Schroten, H.** *Het boek Job voor de gemeente verklaard.* The Hague: Boekencentrum, 1986. **Selms, Adrianus van.** *Job: een praktische bijbelverklaring. Tekst en toelichting.* Kampen: J. H. Kok, 1984 [= *Job, A Practical Commentary.* Trans. John Vriend. Grand Rapids: Eerdmans, 1985]. ———. *Job.* 2 vols. De Prediking van het Oude Testament. Nijkerk: Callenbach, 1982–83. **Simundson, Daniel J.** *The Message of Job: A Theological Commentary.* Minneapolis: Augsburg/Fortress Press, 1986. **Smick, Elmer B.** "Job." In *The Expositor's Bible Commentary, with the New International Version of the Holy Bible.* Ed. Frank E. Gaebelein. Grand Rapids: Regency Reference Library; London: Hodder & Stoughton, 1988. 4:843–1060. **Szirmai, Julia C.** *La Bible anonyme du Ms. Paris B.N., F. Fr. 763: édition critique.* Faux titre 22. Amsterdam: Rodopi, 1985. **Virgulin, Stefano.** *Giobbe: versione, introduzione, note.* Nuovissima Versione della Bibbia 17. Rome: Edizioni Paoline, 1980. **Vogels, Walter.** *Job. Belichting van het Bijbelboek.* Boxtel: Katholieke Bijbelstichting, 1989. **Wilde, A. de.** *Das Buch Hiob eingeleitet, übersetzt und erläutert.* OTS 22. Leiden: E. J. Brill, 1981. **Wood, Fred M.** *The Sunnier Side of Doubt: A Popular Commentary on the Book of Job.* Nashville: Broadman Press, 1984. **Zuck, Roy B.** "Job." In *The Bible Knowledge Commentary.* Ed. John B. Walvoord and Roy B. Zuck. Wheaton, IL: Victor Books, 1985. 715–77.

1990s. Alden, Robert L. *Job.* NAC 11. Nashville: Broadman & Holman, 1993. **Balentine, Samuel E.** "Job." In Watson E. Mills and Richard F. Wilson (eds.). *Mercer Commentary on the Bible.* Macon, GA: Mercer University Press, 1994. **Barker, Kenneth L., and John R. Kohlenberger.** *The NIV Bible Commentary.* I. *Old Testament.* London: Hodder & Stoughton, 1994. **Beall, Todd S., William A. Banks, and Colin Smith.** *Old Testament Parsing Guide. Job–Malachi.* Chicago: Broadman Press, 1991. **Bräumer, Hansjörg.** *Das Buch Hiob erklärt.* Wuppertaler Studienbibel: Altes Testament. Wuppertal: Brockhaus, 1992, 1994. **Brown, Raymond E., Joseph A. Fitzmyer, and Roland E. Murphy (eds.).** *The New Jerome Biblical Commentary.* London: Geoffrey Chapman. 1995. **Burton, James, and Thelma B. Coffman.** *Commentary on the Book of Job.* The James Burton Coffman Commentaries: The Wisdom Literature 1. Abilene, TX: ACU Press, Abilene Christian University, 1993. **Clines, David J. A.** "Job." In *New Bible Commentary Revised.* Ed. D. A. Carson, R. T. France, J. A. Motyer, and G. J. Wenham; Leicester: Inter-Varsity Press; Downers Grove, IL: InterVarsity Press, 21st Century Edition, 1994. 459–84. **Durand, Silas H.** *The Trial of Job.* Salisbury, MD: Welsh Tract Publications, 1997. **Eisenmann, Moshe.** *Iyov. Job. A New Translation with a Commentary Anthologized from Talmudic, Midrashic and Rabbinic Sources.* Brooklyn, NY: Mesorah Publications, 1994. **Farmer, William Reuben (ed.).** *The International Bible Commentary: A Catholic and Ecumenical Commentary for the Twenty-First Century.* Collegeville, MN: Liturgical Press, 1998. **Good, Edwin M.** *In Turns of Tempest: A Reading of Job, with a Translation.* Stanford: Stanford University Press, 1990. **Henry, Matthew.** "Job." In *The Definitive Bible Commentary.* Ed. Owen Collins. London: Marshall Pickering, 1998. 426–51 [see also Henry, 1706]. **Kumok, Iakov, and Ernst Neizvestnyi.** *Kniga Iova; Velichie iz prakha i pepla.* Moscow, 1999. **Lang, Walter.** *Job and Science: A Commentary on the Book of Job in the Bible.* Richfield, MN: Genesis Institute, 1991. **Lobato Fernández, Juan Bautista.** *El libro de Job: texto bíblico y comentario. El mensaje del Antiguo Testamento 18.* Salamanca: Sígueme, 1992. **Luzzatto, Amos.** *Il libro di Giobbe.* Milan: Feltrinelli, 1991. **Mende, Theresia.** *Das Buch Ijob erläutert.* 2 vols. Geistliche Schriftauslegung 14. Düsseldorf: Patmos, 1993–94. **Moore, Thomas.** *The Book of Job, with Commentary.* New York: Riverhead Books, 1998. **Murphy, Roland Edmund.** *The Book of Job: A Short Reading.* New York: Paulist Press, 1999. **Newsom, Carol A.** "Job." In *The Women's Bible Commentary.* Ed. Carol A. Newsom and Sharon H. Ringe. Louisville, KY: Westminster/John Knox Press, 1992. 130–36. **Peterman, Gerald W. (ed.).** "An Exposition, with Practical Observations, of the Book of Job." In *Matthew Henry's Commentary for the NIV: Genesis to Revelation. Based on the Broad Oak Edition Edited by Leslie F. Church.* Basingstoke: Marshall Pickering, 1992. 539–603 [see also Henry, 1706]. **Radermakers, Jean.** *Dieu, Job et la sagesse: lecture continue et texte. Avec 20 illustrations de Ghislaine Stas de Richelle.* Brussels: Lessius, 1998 [= *Il libro di Giobbe: Dio, l'uomo e* *la sapienza*. Bologna: EDB, 1999; *Deus, Job e a sabedoria*. Trans. Miriam Lopes. Lisbon: Instituto Piaget, 2004]. **Ravasi, Gianfranco.** *Il libro di Giobbe. Prefazione di Mario Luzi; traduzione e postfazione di Gianfranco Ravasi* [translation into Italian verse]. Collana "I classici" 4. Locarno: Dadò, 1996. **Reyburn, William D.** *A Handbook on the Book of Job*. New York: United Bible Societies, 1992. **Rizhskii, M. I.** *Kniga Iova: iz istorii bibleiskogo teksta* [Russian translation]. Akademiia nauk SSSR. Sibirskoe otdelenie. Institut istorii, filologii i filosofii. Novosibirsk: Nauka, 1991. **Rodd, Cyril S.** *The Book of Job*. Epworth Commentaries. London: Epworth Press, 1990. ———. *The Book of Job*. Narrative Commentaries. Philadelphia: Trinity Press International, 1990. **Sacks, Robert D.** "The Book of Job: Translation and Commentary." *IntJPolPhilos* 24 (1997) 135–69. ———. *The Book of Job with Commentary: A Translation for Our Time*. South Florida Studies in the History of Judaism 197. Atlanta: Scholars Press, 1999. **Sailhamer, John.** *NIV Compact Bible Commentary*. Grand Rapids: Zondervan; London: Hodder & Stoughton, 1994. 312–14. **San José Lera, Javier.** *Fray Luis de León. Exposición del Libro de Job. Estudio, edición y notas*. Textos recuperados 8. Salamanca: Universidad de Salamanca, 1991. **Scheindlin, Raymond P.** "Translation of Selected Chapters from the Book of Job" [3, 9, 10, 29, 30]. *Arion: A Journal of Humanities and the Classics* 4 (1997) 131–38. ———. *The Book of Job*. New York: W. W. Norton, 1998. **Schultz, Carl.** "Job." In *Evangelical Commentary on the Bible*. Ed. Walter A. Elwell. Grand Rapids: Baker Book House, 1989. 337–66 [= *The Marshall Pickering Commentary on the NIV*. London: Marshall Pickering, 1991]. **Strauss, Hans.** *Hiob*. 2. *19,1–42,17*. BKAT 16/2. Neukirchen–Vluyn: Neukirchener Verlag, 1995. **Taylor, David B.** *Job, a Rational Exposition*. Braunton, Devon: Merlin, 1990. **Tennant, Cyril.** *The Book of Job: "Hast thou considered my servant Job?"* Birmingham: The Christadelphian, 1991. **Thomas, Derek.** *The Storm Breaks: Job Simply Explained*. Welwyn Commentary Series. Durham: Evangelical Press, 1995. **Thomas, Mack.** *Gesprächsführer zur Bibel. Einstiegsfragen und Anregungen zu jedem Kapitel des Alten Testaments*. 1. *Mose–Hiob*. Dillenburg: Christliche Verlagsgesellschaft, 1998. **Vattioni, Francesco.** *Per il testo di Giobbe*. Istituto universitario orientale. Supplemento agli Annali, Istituto universitario orientale 89. Naples: Istituto universitario orientale, 1996. **Viviers, Hennie.** "Job." In *Die Bybellennium: Eenvolumekommentaar*. Ed. Wil Vosloo and Fika J. van Rensburg. Die Bybel uitgelê vir eietydse toepassing. Vereeniging: Christelike Uitgewersmaatskappy, 1999. 561–99. **Wharton, James A.** *Job*. Westminster Bible Companion. Louisville, KY: Westminster/John Knox Press, 1999. **Whybray, Norman.** *Job*. Readings. Sheffield: JSOT Press, 1998; 2nd ed. Sheffield: Sheffield Phoenix Press, 2008. **Wolfers, David.** *Deep Things out of Darkness. The Book of Job: Essays and a New English Translation*. Kampen: Kok Pharos; Grand Rapids: Eerdmans, 1995.

2000s. Alféri, Pierre, and Jean-Pierre Prévost. *Job: livre de Job. Traduction de Pierre Alféri et Jean-Pierre Prévost; introduction et notes par Jean-Pierre Prévost*. Collection Folio. Paris: Gallimard, 2004. **Balentine, Samuel E.** *Job*. Smyth & Helwys Bible Commentary. Macon, GA: Smyth & Helwys, 2006. **Bertram, Axel (ed.).** *Das Buch Hiob, nach der Übertragung von Martin Luther, mit den Marginalien von ihm selbst und vergleichenden Anmerkungen aus dem revidierten Text von 1964 … mit 68 Schabblättern versehen*. Leipzig: Faber & Faber, 2003. **Bräumer, Hansjörg.** *Die Bücher Esra und Nehemia, das Buch Esther, das Buch Hiob erklärt von Klaus vom Orde, Gerhard Maier and Hansjörg Bräumer*. Wuppertaler Studienbibel. Wuppertal: R. Brockhaus, 2005. **Clines, David J. A.** *Job 21–37*. WBC 18A. Dallas: Thomas Nelson, 2006 [see also Clines, 1989]. **Cotton, Bill.** *Will You Torment a Windblown Leaf? A Commentary on Job*. Fearn: Christian Focus, 2001. **Crenshaw, James L.** "Job." In *The Oxford Bible Commentary*. Ed. John Barton and John Muddiman. Oxford: Oxford University Press, 2001. 331–55. **Dell, Katharine J.** "Job." In *Eerdmans Commentary on the Bible*. Ed. J. D. G. Dunn and John W. Rogerson. Grand Rapids: W. B. Eerdmans, 2003. 337–63. **Fischl, Viktor (trans.).** "Kniha Job." In his *Poezie starého zákona*. Prague: Garamond, 2002. **Gradl, Felix.** *Das Buch Ijob*. Neuer Stuttgarter Kommentar: Altes Testament 12. Stuttgart: Verlag Katholische Bibelwerk, 2001. **Griffiths, Richard.** *The Bible in the Renaissance: Essays on Biblical Commentary and Translation in the Fifteenth and*

Sixteenth Centuries. Aldershot: Ashgate, 2001. **Gruber, Mayer.** "Job. Introduction and Annotations." In *The Jewish Study Bible.* Ed. Adele Berlin and Marc Zvi Brettler. Oxford: Oxford University Press, 2004. 1499–1562. **Gunnarssonar, Jóns.** "Jobs bók." In *Biblíurit.* 3. *Mósebók. Dómarabók. Jobsbók.* Reykjavík: Hid islenska Biblíufélag, 2001. **Jones, Hywel R.** *A Study Commentary on Job.* Darlington: Evangelical Press, 2007. **Kozyrev, F. N.** *Iskushenie i pobeda sviatogo Iova, poedinok Iakova.* Moscow: Dom nadezhdy, 2005. **Lawson, Steven J., and Kenneth O. Gange.** *Job.* Holman Old Testament Commentary. Nashville: Broadman & Holman, 2004. **Peters, Benedikt.** *Jób könyvének magyarázata: miért kell az igazaknak szenvedniük?* Budapest: Evangéliumi K., 2005. **Pfeffer, Jeremy I.** *The Book of Job Translated and Interpreted in the Light of the Commentary of Rabbi Meir Lebush Malbim.* Jersey City, NJ: Ktav Publishing House, 2003. **Piper, John.** *The Misery of Job and the Mercy of God* [poem]. Wheaton, IL: Good News Publishers, 2002. **Schwab, Shimon.** *Rav Schwab on Iyov: The Teachings of Rav Shimon Schwab on the Book of Job.* Brooklyn, NY: Mesorah Publications, 2005. **Wilson, Gerald H.** *Job.* New International Biblical Commentary 10. Peabody, MA: Hendrickson, 2007.

Index to Commentaries of 19th to 21st Centuries

Fischel 1833
Fischl 2002
Fischmann 1854
Fisher 1944
Fockens 1845
Fohrer 1948, 1963, 1968
Fox 1852
Franks 1920
Frazier 1999
Freegard 1914
Freehof 1958
Freund 1886
Fry, C. 1926
Fry, J. 1827
Gaab 1809
Gans 1952
Garcia Cordero 1962, 1972
Garland 1971
Gemser 1958
Genung 1891
Gerlach 1858
Gerleman 1974
Gibson, E. C. S. 1899
Gibson, J. C. L. 1985
Gilbert 1886, 1889
Glotzbach 1938
Good, E. M. 1988, 1990
Good, J. M. 1812
Gordis 1973
Gordon 1936
Gradl 2001
Graetz 1892
Grant 1963
Granville Fell 1896
Gray 1871
Greenberg 1980
Greene 1866
Griffiths 2001
Gringoire 1984
Gross 1986
Grube 2003, 2004
Grün 1931
Gualandi 1976
Guillaume 1928, 1968
Guinan 1986
Gunnarssonar 2001
Habel 1975, 1981, 1985
Haghebaert 1928
Hahn 1850
Ḥakham 1969, 1970
Halley 1924
Halsted 1875
Hamblen 1933
Hanson 1953
Harper 1967
Hartley 1988
Hartom 1954
Hassoun 1869
Haupt 1847
Hauser 1909
Haweis 1846
Hawkers 1805, 1842
Heavenor 1970
Heiligstedt 1847, 1869
Heinen 1979
Hengstenberg 1870
Henry 1833, 1860, 1877, 1998
Herrmann 1900
Hertzberg 1949
Hesse 1978
Hirzel 1839
Hitzig 1874
Hoffmann 1891
Hölscher 1937, 1948
Holzhausen 1839
Hontheim 1904
Horst 1960

Hosse 1849
Hubbard 1897
Hulme 1968
Hunt 1825
Hupfeld 1853
Hurwitz 1944
Hussey 1844
Hutchinson 1875
Irwin, C. H. 1928
Irwin, W. A. 1962
Jamieson 1864
Janzen 1985
Jastrow 1920
Jennings 1912
Jérémie 1987
Jones, H. R. 2007
Jones, T. 1818
Junker 1951
Justi 1840
Kahana 1928
Kalt 1924
Kamphausen 1868
Kaplan 1951
Karris 1989
Kelly, B. H. 1963
Kelly, W. 1879
Kemmler 1856, 1877
Kenrick 1859
King 1914
Kissane 1939
Kline 1962
Knabenbauer 1886
König 1928
Königsberger 1896
Köster 1831
Kozyrev 2005
Kraeling 1938
Kreyssig 1808
Kroeze 1946, 1960, 1962
Kumok 1999
Kunstmann 1945
Lambert 1919
Lamparter 1951, 1962
Landau 1853
Lang 1991
Langer 1884, 1889
Larcher 1950
Laurens 1839
Laurin 1960
Lawson 2007
Le Blanc d'Ambonne 1893
Le Hir 1873
Leahy 1970
Leathes 1882
Lee, C. 1806
Lee, S. 1837
Lees 1868
Leimbach 1919
Leroux 1866, 1867
Lesêtre 1886
Levavasseur 1826
Levi 1946
Lewis 1902
Ley 1903
Liénart 1956
Lobato Fernández 1992
Loch 1905
Lods 1947
Lofthouse 1928
Loisy 1892
Löwenthal 1846
Lubsczyk 1969
Luteijn 1965
Luyten 1986
Luzzatto, A. 1991
Luzzatto, S. 1853
Luzzi 1918

MacBeath 1967
MacKenzie 1968
Maclaren 1908
Maizel 1899
Malbim 1874
Malet 1880, 1883
Margolfo 1840
Marshall 1904
Martin 1932
Martínez Terrassa 1982
Matthes 1865
McCarthy 1977
McFadyen 1918
McGrath 1995
McKenna 1986
Meikle 1869
Mende 1993
Merj 1858
Merx 1871
Messchert van Vollenhoven 1812
Meyer 1966
Michel 1987
Millet 1887
Minn 1942, 1965
Mitchell 1979
Montet 1926, 1947
Montvaillant 1897
Moore 1886
Moraldi 1977
Morgan 1908, 1989
Mosner 1858
Moulton 1906
Mowinckel 1924, 1955
Mumford 1923
Murphy 1955, 1977, 1981, 1999
Nairne 1935
Neil 1962
Neiman 1972
Nesfield 1933
Neumann 1934
Newsom 1992
Nicole 1986
Noyes 1827, 1867, 1915
Obbink 1924
Obronin 1916
Odiosus 1863
Oettli 1908
Olshausen 1852
Osty 1971
Ottensosser 1805
Ottoni 1852
Owens 1983
Parker 1889
Pascal 1967
Patrick 1977
Patterson 1843
Peake 1904
Peterman 1992
Peters, B. 2005
Peters, N. 1928
Peyromet 1848
Philip 1980
Pierik 1881
Piper 2002
Pirot 1949
Pixley 1982
Polotak 1808
Pope 1973
Porteous 1854
Potter 1969
Pritchard 1903
Prosdij 1948
Rabinowitz 1916
Radermakers 1998
Rahlwes 1923
Ratner 1893
Ravasi 1979, 1996

Raymond 1878
Reichert 1946
Renan 1860
Renassia 1961
Reuss 1878
Reyburn 1992
Ricciotti 1924
Richardson 1936
Rizhskii 1991
Robin 1949
Roche 1964
Rocholl 1922
Rodd 1990
Rodwell 1864
Rosenberg 1977, 1989
Rosenfeld 1875
Rosenmüller 1806
Rosenthal 1960
Rosny 1860
Rossi 1812
Rowley, A. 1825
Rowley, H. H. 1970
Rozelaar 1984
Runciman 1918
Sacks 1997
Sadler 1897
Sailhamer 1994
Saint-Maur 1861
Saithwell 1982
San José Lera 1991
Sarao 1831
Schärer 1818
Scheindlin 1997, 1998
Schlögl 1916
Schlottmann 1851
Schmidt, H. 1927
Schmidt, N. 1911
Schröder 1948
Schroten 1986
Schubert 1927
Schultz 1991
Schwarz 1868
Schweitzer 1966
Scott 1842
Sekine 1970
Selms 1982, 1984
Siegfried 1893
Simon 1925
Simundson 1986
Smick 1988

Smith 1810
Snaith 1945
Solomon [Baba-Jan] 1895
Speyr 1972
Spiess 1852
Sprague 1913
Stather 1860
Steinmann 1955, 1961
Sternberg 1872
Steuernagel 1923
Stevenson 1947
Stewart 1872
Stickel 1842
Stier 1954
Stock 1805
Strahan 1913
Strange 1968
Strashun 1888, 1897
Strauss 1995
Studer 1881
Stuhlmann 1804
Sutcliffe, E. F. 1953
Sutcliffe, J. 1813
Sydenstricker 1894
Szczygiel 1931
Szirmai 1985
Szold 1886
Takamini 1871
Talmid 1890
Tattersall 1897
Taylor 1990
Teles 1912
Tennant 1991
Terrien 1954, 1963
Theile 1857
Thilo 1925
Thomas, David 1878
Thomas, Derek 1995
Thomas, M. 1998
Torczyner 1920, 1941
Trentepohl 1860
Tur-Sinai 1954, 1957
Turoldo 1951
Umbreit 1824, 1835
Vaccari 1927
Vaihinger 1842, 1843
Valente 1928
Valera 1923
Van Hagen 1845
Vattioni 1996

Viani dalla Beata Chiara 1865
Vignolo 1902
Villa 1947
Vilmar 1882
Vincent 2005
Virgulin 1980
Vischer 1958
Viviers 1999
Vogels 1989
Voigt 1895
Volck 1889
Volz 1911
Vuilleumier 1894
Walls 1891
Warren 1941
Watson 1892
Watts 1971
Weber 1947
Weiser, Artur 1951
Weiser, Asher 1950
Weiser, L. 1931
Weitzner 1960
Welte 1849
Wharton 1999
White 1880
Whybray 1998
Wilde 1974, 1979, 1981
Wilkinson 1901
Wilson, G. H. 2007
Wilson, P. 1912
Winchilsea 1860
Winterfeld 1898
Wolf 1869
Wolfers 1995
Wolff 1873
Wolfson 1843
Wood 1984
Wright, G. H. B. 1883
Wright, J. S. 1974
Wutz 1939
Yeger 1984
Yellin 1927
Yerushalmi 1927
Young, R. N. 1874
Young, Robert 1865, 1868
Zöckler 1872, 1875
Zschokke 1875
Zuck, R. B. 1978, 1985
Zuck, W. J. 1898

3. THE BOOK AS A WHOLE

The items in this Section are arranged by decades of publication. At the end of the Section there is an index of the authors mentioned, with the dates of publication.

In this Section are listed works which offer interpretations of the Book of Job as a whole but are not arranged according to the sequence of the book itself. Works that concern only a part of the Book of Job are listed in the bibliographies to the relevant chapters, and are not mentioned here.

1510s. Badis, Petrus de. "De sancto et patientissimo Job, edificatorius sermo." In *Sermones venerabilis ac devoti religiosi Magistri Johan[n]is Herolt.* Ed. Joannes Herolt. Haguenau, 1514. **Rolle, Richard.** *Explanationes notabiles devotissimi viri Richardi Hampole heremite super lectiones illas Beati Iob: que solent in exequijs defunctorum legi: qui non minus hystoriam quam tropologiam, et anagogiam ad studentium utilitatem exactissime annotavit.* Paris, 1510.

1560s. Borrhaus, Martin. *In sancti viri Iobi historiam salutari de mysterio crucis et de lege atque evangelio doctrina refertam.* Basel, 1564 [= Bibliotheca palatina C4081/C4084]. **Lutz, Renhardus.** *In historiam Jobi annotationes.* In his *Harmonia, seu historia de Christo Jesu juxta seriem atque concentum Evangelistarum.* Basel: Henricus Petrus, 1561.

1570s. Wild, Johann, and Tilmann Bredenbach. *Jobi historiae docta et catholica explicatio … non solum piam ac salutiferam christianae patientiae doctrinam, verumetiam orthodoxam Ecclesia de praecipuis religionis controversiis sententiam luculenta methodo complectens.* Cologne, 1574.

1580s. Bugati, Gaspare. *Libro et vita del beato Giobbe in pia comparatione della vita del Signor nostro per gli S. Euangeli.* Alessandria: Ercole Quintiano, 1586. **Zappi, Giovan Battista.** *Prato della filosofia spirituale doue si contiene la somma del viuer christiano. Con vn breue trattato dell'osseruanza delle feste, & d'alcuni sermoni, & espositioni sopra il Cantico di Zacharia profeta, della B. Vergine, di Simeone, & di Giobbe.* Venice: Franmcesco Senese, 1585.

1620s. Leon, Francisco de. *Privanca del hombre con Dios sobre el "parce mihi" Job, 7.* Pamplona, 1622.

1640s. Aguilar y Zúñiga, Esteban. *Combates de Job con el Demonio.* Madrid, 1642. **Marmet, Ezekiel.** *Dix-huict sermons sur Iob.* Geneva, 1641.

1650s. Leigh, Edward. *Annotations on Five Poetical Books of the Old Testament: (viz.) Job, Psalmes, Proverbs, Ecclesiastes, and Canticles.* London, 1657. **Oxinden, Henry.** *Iobus triumphans. Vincit qui patitur.* London, 1651.

1660s. Santeul, Pierre de. *Quaestio theologica: Quis solus est? Job.* Diss. Sorbonne, 1661. **Uythage, Cornelius.** *Solutiones, seu instantiae in Jobum prophetam. Contra Judaeorum objecta.* Leiden, 1664.

1680s. Clark, William. *The Grand Tryal, or, Poetical Exercitations upon the Book of Job: Wherein Suitable to Each Text of That Sacred Book, a Modest Explanation, and Continuation of the Several Discourses Contained in It, Is Attempted.* Edinburgh: Andrew Anderson, 1685 [= Early English Books, 1641–1700. 935/1].

1710s. Serpilius, Georg. *Lebensbeschreibungen der biblischen Scribenten, davon der VII. Theil praesentiret Personalia Jobi.* Regensburg, 1710.

1720s. Hardt, Hermann von der. *In Jobum, historiam populi Israelis in Assyriaco exilio, Samaria eversa, et regno extincto: tragoediam sacram admirandi decoris: partibus II. quibus sublimis et perelegans sermonum autoris Jobi indoles, pro gravi, nervoso et arguto priscorum autorum stilo, generatim declaratur: et illustrium poetarum Claudiani et Musaei …* Helmstadt: F. W. Meyer, 1728.

1730s. Petit de Montempuys, Jean-Gabriel. *Analyse sur le livre de Job.* Paris, 1734.

1740s. Eichler, Christian Gottlob. *Patientiam Jobi et finis Domini ad illustrandam et vindicandam historiam Jobaeam sistit Iac. 5,11.* Leipzig: Langenheim, 1744. **Grey, Richard.** *An Answer to Mr Warburton's Remarks on Several Occasional Reflections, so far as They Concern the Preface to a Late Edition of the Book of Job, in Which the Subject and Design of That Divine Poem Are Set in a … Clear Light.* London, 1744. **Joubert, F.** *Traité du caractère essentiel à tous les prophètes de ne rien dire que de vrai quand ils prophétisent, … avec un éclaircissement sur les discours de Job.* Paris, 1741. **Koch, Jacob.** *Kleine geographisch-historische Abhandlungen zur Erläuterung einiger Stellen Mosis und vornehmlich des ganzen Buchs Hiob.* Lemgo: Meyer, 1747. ———. *Rechtbeleuchtetes Buch Hiobs, mit vielen dabey gemachten neuen Entdeckungen, nöthigen Anmerkungen und erbaulichen Nutz-Anwendungen.* Lemgo: Meyer, 1743–47. **Worthington, William.** "A Dissertation on the Design and Argumentation of the Book of Job." In his *An Essay on the Scheme and Conduct, Procedure and Extent of Man's Redemption.* London, 1743. 463–527.

1750s. Hodges, Walter. *Elihu, or, An Enquiry into the Principal Scope and Design of the Book of Job.* London: J. Hodges. 1750. **Lowth, Robert.** "De poemati Jobi argumento et fine." Praelectio 37 in his *De sacra poesi hebraeorum. Praelectiones academicae.* Oxford: Clarendon Press, 1753 [= *Lectures on the Sacred Poetry of the Hebrews.* Trans. G. Gregory. London, 1789; Praelectio 33 is reprinted as "Of the Poem of Job" in *The Dimensions of Job: A Study and Selected Readings.* Ed. Nahum H. Glatzer. New York: Schocken Books, 1969. 132–40]. See also **Witte, Markus.** "Die literarische Gattung des Buches Hiob: Robert Lowth und seine Erben." In *Sacred Conjectures: The Context and Legacy of Robert Lowth and Jean Astruc.* New York: T. & T. Clark, 2007. 93–123.| **Peters, Charles.** *A Critical Dissertation on the Book of Job, Wherein the Account Given of That Book by the Author of The*

Divine Legation of Moses Demonstrated, &c. Is Particularly Considered; the Antiquity of the Book Vindicated; the Great Text (Chap. xix.25-) Explained; and a Future State Shewn to Have Been the Popular Belief of the Ancient Jews or Hebrews. London: E. Owen, 1751.

1760s. Poix, Louis de. *Essai sur le livre de Job.* Paris, 1768.

1790s. Granelli, Giovanni. *L'istoria santa dell'antico Testamento spiegata in lezioni morali, istoriche, critiche, e cronologiche, da Giovanni Granelli della Compagnia di Gesu con l'aggiunta delle lezioni sinora inedite sui libri di Giuditta, Ester, e Giobbe.* 11 vols. Venice: Antonio Zatta e figli, 1792.

1810s. Brink, Albertus. *Aanmerkingen voor ongeleerden over het boek Job.* Leeuwarden: J. W. Brouwe, 1815.

1820s. Autenrieth, Johannes Heinrich Ferdinand von. *Ueber das Buch Hiob.* Tübingen: Heinrich Laupp, 1823. **Blake, William.** *Illustrations of the Book of Job.* London: Published by William Blake, 1825.

1830s. Kaakebeen, D. M. *Leerredenen, over grootere en kleinere afdeelingen uit het Boek van Job.* Amsterdam: Willems, 1835. **Knobel, Augustus W.** *De carminis Jobi argumento, fine ac dispositione.* Bratislava: Richter, 1835. **Wemyss, Thomas.** *Job and His Times, or, A Picture of the Patriarchal Age: A New Version of That Most Ancient Poem, Accompanied with Notes and Dissertations.* London: Jackson & Walford, 1839.

1840s. Ewing, William. *Some Critical Observations on the Book of Job* [in reply to S. Lee's *Book of the Patriarch Job,* 1837]. London, 1844. **Gleiss, Wilhelm.** *Beiträge zur Kritik des Buches Hiob.* Horn bei Hamburg, 1845. **Le Roux de Lincy, [Antoine].** *Les Quatre Livres des Rois, traduits en français du XIIe siècle, suivis d'un fragment de Moralités sur Job, et d'un choix de sermons de Saint Bernard.* Collection de documents inédits sur l'histoire de France. 2e sér. Histoire des lettres et des sciences. Paris: Imprimerie royale, 1841. **Parisi, R.** *La divino libro di Giobbe esposto in lezioni teologico-critico-morali.* Palermo, 1843. **Pasquale Marinelli, Giuseppe.** *Job, Apocalypsis et Moysis cantica versibus expressa.* Ancona: Petrus Aurelius, 1846.

1850s. Darby, J. N. "Job." In *Synopsis of the Books of the Bible.* London: G. Morrish, 1857–67. 2:28–41. **Froude, J. A.** *The Book of Job.* London: J. Chapman, 1854 [= *The Westminster Review,* ns 8 (Oct. 1853); his *Essays in Literature and History.* Everyman's Library. London: J. M. Dent, 1906; **Hone, Ralph E.** *The Voice out of the Whirlwind: The Book of Job.* San Francisco: Chandler, 1960. 200–232]. See also **Vicchio, Stephen J.** *Job in the Modern World.* Eugene, OR: Wipf & Stock, 2006. 179–82.| **Hengstenberg, E. W.** *Ueber das Buch Hiob: Ein Vortrag gehalten im Auftrage der Evangelischen Vereins in Berlin.* Berlin: Schlawitz, 1856. **Hulbert, Charles Augustus.** *The Gospel Revealed to Job: or, Patriarchal Faith and Practice Illustrated, in Thirty Lectures on the Principal Passages of the Book of Job; with Explanatory, Illustrative, and Critical Notes.* London: Longman, Brown, Green, & Longmans, 1853.

1860s. Böttcher, Friedrich. *Neue exegetisch-kritische Aehrenlese zum Alten Testamente.* Leipzig: J. A. Barth, 1863 65. 3:39–76. **Hengstenberg, Ernst Wilhelm.** "The Book of Job." In his *Commentary on Ecclesiastes, with Other Treatises.* Clark's Foreign Theological Library 3/6. Edinburgh: T. & T. Clark, 1860. **Meunier-Palusson, J. B. C.** *Le livre de Job suivi du chant de Deborah et de l'âme exilée.* Paris: Didier, 1868. **Raebiger, Julius Ferdinand.** *De libri Iobi sententia primaria.* Bratislava; Hirtzig, 1860. **Reuss, Eduard.** *Das Buch Hiob: Vortrag gehalten in der Nicolaikirche, den 8. Februar 1869.* Strassburg: Treuttel & Würtz, 1869. **Rosseeuw Saint-Hilaire, Eugène François Achille.** "Le livre de Job." In his *Etudes religieuses et littéraires.* Paris: Dentu, 1863. **Seinecke, L. Chr. F. W.** *Der Grundgedanke des Buches Hiob.* Clausthal: Grosse, 1863. **Simson, August.** *Zur Kritik des Buches Hiob, eine alttestamentliche Studie.* Königsberg: Dalkowski, 1861.

1870s. Budde, Karl (Carl). *Beiträge zur Kritik des Buches Hiob. I. Die neuere Kritik und die Idee des Buches Hiob. II. Der sprachliche Charakter der Elihu-Reden.* Bonn: Adolph Marcus, 1876. **Cassel, David.** *Geschichte der jüdischen Literatur.* Berlin: L. Gerschel, 1872–73. **Demante, Henri.** *Conférences sur le livre de Job.* Paris: Sousens, 1879. **Godet, Frédéric.** "The Book of Job." In *Godet's Biblical Studies on the Old Testament.* Ed. W. H.

Lyttleton. Oxford: James Parker, 1875. 183–240. **Green, W. H.** *The Argument of the Book of Job Unfolded.* New York: Hurst & Co., 1873 [= *Conflict and Triumph: The Argument of the Book of Job Unfolded.* Edinburgh: Banner of Truth Trust, 1999]. **Kelly, William.** *Three Lectures on the Book of Job.* London: W. H. Broom, 1877 [= *Gods hand in het lijden: een over-denking over het bijbelboek Job.* The Hague: Voorhoeve, 1931]. **Layman of the Church, A.** *Truth Vindicated with Reference to the Book of Job.* Raleigh, NC: Biblical Recorder Publishing House, 1875. **Schmitz, Bernhard.** *Der Ideengang des Buches Hiob.* Greifswald: Kinike, 1870 [= *(Jahresbericht) des Städtisches Gymnasiums zu Greifswald.* 1869/70].

   1880s. Bickell, Gustav. *Job, Dialog über das Leiden des Gerechten.* In his *Dichtungen der Hebräer: Zum erstenmale nach dem Versmasse des Urtextes übersetzt.* II. Innsbruck: Wagner'sche Universitäts-Buchhandlung, 1882. **Böttcher, Viktor.** *Das Buch Hiob nach Luther und der Probebibel aus dem Grundtext bearbeitet und mit Bemerkungen versehen.* Leipzig: J. Lehmann, 1885. **Burr, J. K.** *Job, Proverbs, Ecclesiastes, and Solomon's Song.* New York: Hunt & Eaton; Cincinnati: Cranston & Stowe, 1881. **Cheyne, T. K.** *Job and Solomon, or, The Wisdom of the Old Testament.* London: Kegan Paul, Trench, 1887. **Latch, Edward B.** *Indications of the Book of Job.* Philadelphia: J. B. Lippincott, 1889. **Moore, T. W.** "The Book of Job—Revised Version Old Testament." *MethQR* 23 (1886) 261–71. **Preiss, Hermann.** *Zum Buche Hiob.* Theologische Studien und Skizzen aus Ostpreussen. Einzelausgabe 7. Königsberg: Hartung, 1889. **Rutherford, Mark [William Hale White; Reuben Shapcott]** (English author, 1831–1913). "Notes on the Book of Job." In his *The Autobiography of Mark Rutherford, Dissenting Minister. Edited by His Friend Reuben Shapcott.* London: Trübner, 1881 [repr. The World's Classics. Oxford: Oxford University Press, 1936]. **Wright, Charles H. H.** *Biblical Essays: or, Exegetical Studies on the Books of Job and Jonah, Ezekiel's Prophecy of Gog and Magog, St Peter's "Spirits in Prison," and the Key to the Apocalypse.* Edinburgh: T. & T. Clark, 1886.

   1890s. Anon. *Job's Conversion, or, God the Justifier.* London: G. Morrish, c. 1890. **Cheyne, T. K.** "Job." In *Encyclopaedia britannica.* 10th ed. **Conder, C. R.** "Illustrations of the Book of Job." *PEFQS* (1898) 254–61. **Cooke, J. Hunt.** *Job: An Appreciation.* London: S. H. Burrows & Co., 1899. **Davies, William Walter.** "The Integrity of the Book of Job." *MethRev* 72 (1890) 329–46. **Duhm, B.** "The Book of Job." *The New World* (1894) 328–44. **Horne, Charles Silvester.** *The Ordeal of Faith. Meditations on the Book of Job.* London: J. Clarke & Co., 1898. **Keener, John Christian.** "Job, a Prince of the East; and His Inspired Epic." *MethQR* 45 (1897) 321–41. **Ley, J.** "Das Problem im Buche Hiob und dessen Lösung." *Neue Jahrbuch für Philosophie und Pädagogie* (1896) 125ff. **Mandl, Armin.** *Die Peschittha zu Hiob: nebst einem Anhang über ihr Verhältniss zu LXX und Targum.* Budapest: L. Propper, 1892. **Meinhold, J.** "Das Problem des Buches Hiob." *NJDTh* 1 (1892) 63–109. **Vuilleumier, Henri.** *Le livre de Job* [conférence]. Lausanne, 1894. **Wilbur, Emma G.** "The Spiritual Teaching of the Book of Job." *MethQR* 38 (1894) 258–70. **Zahn, Johann Kleophas Adolph.** "Die Grundgedanken des Buches Hiob." In his *Ein Winter in Tübingen. Skizzen aus dem Leben einer deutschen Universitätsstadt, und Mitteilungen aus Vorlesungen über die Thora Moses im Lichte der heiligen Schrift.* Stuttgart: Greiner & Pfeiffer, 1896.

   1900s. Aitken, James. *The Book of Job.* Handbooks for Bible Classes. Edinburgh: T. & T. Clark, [1905]. **Bellett, J. G.** "The Book of Job." In *The Patriarchs: Being Meditations on Enoch, Noah, Abraham, Isaac, Jacob, Joseph, Job; The Canticles, Heaven and Earth.* London: G. Morrish, 1909. 204–42. **Brown, Charles Reynolds.** *The Strange Ways of God. A Study in the Book of Job.* Boston: The Pilgrim Press, 1908. **Chesterton, G. K.** *The Book of Job, with an Introduction by G. K. Chesterton and Illustrated in Colour by C. Mary Tongue.* London: S. Wellwood, 1907; London: Cecil Palmer & Hayward, 1916 [pp. ix–xxxvii (abridged) are reprinted as "Man Is Most Comforted by Paradoxes" in *The Dimensions of Job: A Study and Selected Readings.* Ed. Nahum H. Glatzer. New York: Schocken Books, 1969. 228–37]. **Cheyne, T. K.** "Job, Book of." In *EB* (1901) 2:2465–91. **Cornely, R.** *Historica et critica introductio in utriusque testamenti libros sacros.* II/2. Paris: Lethielleux, 1907. **Coutts, F. [B. T. M.] [Coutts-Nevill, F. B. T.].** *The Heresy of Job, with the Inventions of William Blake.* London: John Lane, 1907. **Davies, William Walter.** "Job of the Cuneiform Inscriptions."

MethRev 89 (1907) 307–10. **Foote, G. W.** "Poor Job." In *Bible Heroes*. London: Freethought Publishing Co., 1900. 37–44. **Gärtner, Hersch.** *Der dramatische Charakter des Buches Hiob und die Tendenz desselben.* Diss. Berne, 1900. Berlin: H. Itzkowski, 1909. **Harper, W. R.** *The Book of Job. A Study in the Problem of Suffering as Treated in the Old Testament.* Chicago: American Institute of Sacred Literature, 1908. **Hiller, Gustavus Emanuel.** "A Fresh Look at the Book of Job." *MethQR* 56 (1907) 663–71. **Klostermann, A.** "Hiob." *RE*. 3rd ed., 1900. 8:97–126. **Köberle, Justus.** *Das Rätsel des Leidens. Eine Einführung in das Buch Hiob.* Berlin–Lichterfelde: E. Runge, 1905. **Ley, J.** "Characteristik der drei Freunde Hiobs und der Wandlungen in Hiobs religiösen Anmerkungen." *TSK* (1900) 331–63. **Marshall, J. T.** *Job and His Comforters: Studies in the Theology of the Book of Job.* London: James Clarke & Co, 1905. **Müller, Eugen.** *Der echte Hiob.* Hanover: F. Rehtmeyer, 1902. **Nebel.** "Das Problem des Buches Hiob." *Zeitschrift für Philosophie und Pädagogik* 10 (1903) 214–26, 306–26. **Penn-Lewis, Jessie.** *The Story of Job: A Glimpse into the Mystery of Suffering.* London: Marshall Brothers, 1902 [repr. Fort Washington, PA: Christian Literature Crusade, 1996].

    1910s. Aked, Charles F. *The Divine Drama of Job.* Edinburgh: T. & T. Clark; New York: C. Scribner's Sons, 1913. **Anon.** *Das Buch Esther und das Buch Hiob. Urholzschnitte von Bruno Goldschmitt.* Die erzählenden Bücher des Alten Testaments 1. Munich: Knorr & Hirth, 1918. **Blake, Buchanan.** *The Book of Job and the Problem of Suffering.* London: Hodder & Stoughton, 1911 [= *The Problem of Human Suffering: A Study of the Book of Job.* New York: Hodder & Stoughton, 1911]. **Bode, William.** *The Book of Job and the Solution of the Problem of Suffering It Offers.* Grand Rapids: Eerdmans-Sevensma, 1914. **Cobern, Camden McCormack.** "A New Interpretation of the Book of Job." *MethRev* 95 (1913) 419–39. **Copeland, Theodore.** "Job—A Study." *MethQR* 66 (1917) 461–66. **Davidson, A. B., and C. H. Toy.** "Job." In *Encyclopædia britannica.* 11th ed. Cambridge: Cambridge University Press, 1910–11 [= **Hone, Ralph E.** *The Voice out of the Whirlwind: The Book of Job.* San Francisco: Chandler, 1960. 87–103]. **Hevesi, Simon.** *Der Grundgedanke des Buches Hiob. Vortrag, gehalten in Wien am 26. Februar 1914.* Budapest, 1914. **Hubbard, Elbert.** "The Book of Job." In his *The Liberators, Being Adventures in the City of Fine Minds.* East Aurora, NY: Roycroft, 1919. **Huffman, Jasper Abraham.** *Job, a World Example.* Introduction by Bud Robinson. New Carlisle, OH: Bethel, 1914. **Kelly, William.** *Eleven Lectures on the Book of Job.* London: F. E. Race, 1919. **Kent, Charles Foster.** "The Problem and Teachings of the Book of Job." In *The Makers and Teachers of Judaism, from the Fall of Jerusalem to the Death of Herod the Great.* New York: Charles Scribner's Sons, 1911. **Knott, John O.** "An Interpretation of the Book of Job." *MethQR* 59 (1910) 553–67. ———. "Job: The Soul's Pathfinder." In his *Seekers after Soul.* Boston: Sherman, French, 1911. **MacFadyen, John Edgar.** *The Problem of Pain: A Study in the Book of Job.* London: James Clarke & Co., 1917. **Martin, A. D.** "The Book of Job." *ExpT* 26 (1914) 75–81. **Pfeiffer, Robert Henry.** *Le problème du livre de Job.* Diss. Geneva, 1915. **Pladra, Oskar.** *Die dichterische und religiöse Bedeutung des Buches Hiob, ein Anregung zum Studium des Buches.* Langensalza: Beyer, 1914. **Portor, Laura Spencer.** "The Book of Job." In her *The Greatest Books in the World: Interpretive Studies. With Lists of Collateral Reading Helpful to the Study of Great Literature.* Boston and New York: Houghton Mifflin, 1913. **Robinson, H. Wheeler.** *The Cross of Job.* London: SCM Press, 1916 [reprinted in *The Cross in the Old Testament.* London: SCM Press, 1955]. **Royds, Thomas Fletcher.** *Job and the Problem of Suffering.* London: Wells Gardner & Co., 1911. **Sellin, Ernst.** *Das Problem des Hiobbuches. Vortrag gehalten auf dem theologischen Lehrkursus für Feldgeistliche in Riga am 13. März 1918.* Leipzig: A. Deichert, 1919. **Thrändorf, Ernst, and H. Meltzer.** *Der Religionsunterricht auf der Mittelstufe der Volksschule und in den Unterklassen höherer Schulen. 3. Der Prophetismus und das nachexilische Judentum (Hiob, Messianische Hoffnung, Jona, Makkabäerzeit, Psalmen): Präparationen.* Dresden-Blasewitz: Bleyl & Kaemmerer, 1911.

    1920s. Allen, Frank E. *Practical Lectures on the Book of Job.* New York: Revell, 1923. **Beet, W. E.** "The Message of the Book of Job." *ExpT* 48 (1922) 111–20. **Bigot, L.** "Job

(Livre de)." In *Dictionnaire de théologie catholique contenant l'exposé des doctrines de la théologie catholique, leurs preuves et leur histoire*. Ed. Jean-Michel-Alfred Vacant. Paris: Letouzey, 1925. 8:1458–86. **Blake, William.** *The Book of Job: The Eighteenth Book of the Old Testament.* London: E. Benn, 1927. **Bruston, E.** "La littérature sapientiale dans le livre de Job." *ETR* 3 (1928) 297–305. **Chambers, Oswald.** *Baffled to Fight Better: Talks on the Book of Job.* Oxford: Alden & Co, 3rd ed. 1923 [= *In finsteren Zeiten: Hiob und das Problem des Leidens.* Marburg an der Lahn: Francke, 1992]. **Dalzell, S. H.** *Lessons from the Book of Job.* London: Stockwell, 1922. **Devine, M.** *The Story of Job: A Sympathetic Study of the Book of Job in the Light of History and Literature.* London: Macmillan, 1921. **Dodd, Evelyn Baker.** "The Integrity of Job's Three Friends." *MethQR* 74 (1925) 127–30. **Farley, Fred Long.** "Two Old Men." *MethRev* 103 (1920) 699–711. **Jordan, W. G.** *The Book of Job: Its Substance and Spirit.* New York: Macmillan, 1929. **Knieschke, Wilhelm.** *Kultur- und Geisteswelt des Buches Hiob.* Zeit- und Streitfragen des Glaubens, der Weltanschauung und Bibelforschung 15/9–12. Berlin–Lichterfelde: E. Runge, 1925. **McKechnie, James.** *Job, Moral Hero, Religious Egoist, and Mystic.* Greenock: James McKelvie, 1925. **Quiller-Couch, Arthur.** "On Reading the Bible" [on Job]. In his *On the Art of Reading.* Cambridge: Cambridge University Press, 1920. **Ryckmans, G.** "De scopo auctoris sacri in libro Job." *ColctMech* 17 (1928) 674ff. **Smith, J. M. Powis.** "The Book of Job" [review of Buttenwieser, *The Book of Job,* and Ball, *The Book of Job. A Revised Text and Version*]." *JR* 3 (1923) 208–11. **Wray, N.** *The Book of Job, a Biblical Masterpiece Interpreted and Explained.* Boston: Hamilton Bors, 1929.

1930s. Baker, Albert E. *Prophets for an Age of Doubt* [Job, Socrates, Pascal, Newman]. London: The Centenary Press, 1934. **Baumgärtel, F.** *Der Hiobdialog. Aufriss und Deutung.* BZAW 4/9. Stuttgart: Kohlhammer, 1933. **Baumgartner, F.** "Das Buch Job im Religionsunterricht." *ChrPädBl* 54 (1931) 87–88. **Ben Meïr, Elieser.** *Menschenleid und Sünde? Das Buch Hiob im Lichte neuer Kommentare übersetzt und erklärt.* Frankfurt: Kauffmann, 1930. **Brunner, Robert.** *Der Gottesknecht: Eine Auslegung des Buches Hiob.* Basel: J. F. Reinhardt, 1938. **Calcar, J. D. van.** *Job: bijbels lekespel van strijd en bevrijding.* Assen: Van Gorcum, 1934. **Ceuppens, Franciscus.** *De libro Job quaestiones selectae.* Rome: Collegium Angelicum, 1932. **Compston, H. F. B.** "Marginal Notes on Driver–Gray's 'Job'." *ExpT* 42 (1930–31) 92–93. **Cruveilhier, P.** "Pour une connaissance plus parfaite du livre de Job." *RevApol* 53 (1931) 641–67; 54 (1932) 5–27. **Davis, H. G.** "The Message of the Book of Job for Today." *LCQ* 6 (1933) 131–46. **Drucker, A. P.** "The Book of Job." *The Open Court* 49 (1935) 65–78. **Duesberg, H.** *Les scribes inspirés: introduction aux livres sapientiaux de la Bible Proverbes, Job, Ecclésiaste, Sagesse, Ecclésiastique.* 2 vols. Paris: Desclée de Brouwer, 1938–39. **Eerdmans, B. D.** *Studies in Job.* Leiden: Burgersdijk & Niermans, 1939. **Feinberg, C. L.** "The Book of Job." *BSac* 91 (1934) 78–86. **Ferrin, Howard W.** *The Crucible: Brief Studies in the Book of Job.* Providence, RI: Providence Bible Institute, 1935. **Gelderen, C. van.** *De hoofdpunten des zielsgeschiedenis van Job.* Kampen: Kok, 1931. **Genung, John Franklin.** "Job," "Job, Book of." In *The International Bible Encyclopaedia.* Ed. James Orr. Grand Rapids: Eerdmans, 2nd ed. 1939. III. 1679–88 [revised by Melvin Grove Kyle]. **Hackmann, H.** "Das wahre Gesicht des Buches Hiob." *NedTTs* 19 (1930) 25–35. **Irwin, W. H.** "An Examination of the Progress of Thought in the Dialogue of Job." *JR* 13 (1933) 150–64. **Kellett, E. E.** "'Job': An Allegory?" *ExpT* 51 (1939–40) 250–51. **Krieger, Paul.** *Weltbild und Idee des Buches Hiob, verglichen mit dem altorientalischen Pessimismus.* Leipzig: Schwarzenberg & Schumann, 1930. **Levine, Israel.** "The Book of Job." In his *Faithful Rebels. A Study in Jewish Speculative Thought.* London: Soncino Press, 1936. **MacDonald, Duncan Black.** "The Book of Job as Lyric." In his *The Hebrew Philosophic Genius: An Interpretation. Being an Introduction to the Reading of the Old Testament.* Princeton: Princeton University Press, 1936. 2–32. **Mirandolle, Ludovicus.** *Het boek Job: tekst van een voordracht gehouden te Amsterdam en 's-Gravenhage.* Amsterdam, 1930. **Miskotte, Kornelis Heiko.** *Antwoord uit het onweer: Een verhandeling over het boek Job.* Amsterdam: Uitgevers-Maatschappij Holland, 1936. See also **Ridderbos, J.** "Dr Miskotte over het boek Job." *GerefTTs* 38 (1937) 57–72.| **Morgan, G. Campbell.** *The Answers of Jesus to Job.* London: Marshall, Morgan & Scott, 1934. **Obbink, H. T.** *Over het Boek Job.* Amsterdam: H. J.

Paris, 1935. **Phillips, T. W.** *Job, a New Interpretation*. London: Thomas Murby & Co., 1937. **Pollock, Seton.** *The Root of the Matter: Sketches on Job, with a New Dramatic Version*. London: Walters Bros., 1939. **Proskauer, Walter.** *Hiob—und wir: Schicksalsfragen und Gottesantwort. Gestern und heute 6*. Berlin: Brandus, 1937. **Rongy, H.** "Le dialogue poétique du livre de Job: le prologue du livre de Job." *RevEcclLiège* 25 (1933–34) 96–101, 168–71. **Seitz, Oskar.** *Hiob: Eine Betrachtung über das Leiden*. Berlin: Oskar Seitz, 1931. **Sellin, Ernst.** *Das Hiobproblem. Rede gehalten bei der Reichsgründungsfeier der Friedrich-Wilhelms-Universität Berlin am 18. Januar 1931*. Berlin: Preussische Druckerei, 1931. **Simon, M.** "Hiob." *Zeitwende* 7 (1931) 159–74. **Smith, J. M. Powis.** "A New Rendering of the Book of Job" [review of Bernie, *Le poème de Job. Traduction nouvelle, introduction et notes*]." *AJSL* 46 (1930) 213–14. **Steinberg, Milton.** "Job Answers God: Being the Religious Perplexities of an Obscure Pharisee." *JR* 12 (1932) 159–76. **White, E. W.** *Ancient Yet Modern: The Book of Job*. Toronto: United Church of Canada, 1939. **Wilson, George Louis Rosa.** *Job*. Balerno: Celandine Press, 1938. **Würtemberg, G.** "Das Hiobsproblem." *Philosophie und Schule* 2 (1930) 190–203. **Zorell, F.** "Ex disputatione Jobi cum amicis suis." *VD* 10 (1930) 265–68, 374–78; 11 (1931) 33–37.

1940s. Clarke, W. K. Lowther. *Job and His Friends: The Problem of Suffering*. London: SPCK, 1947. **Claudel, Paul.** *Le livre de Job* [essay]. Paris: Plon, 1946 [= *Das Buch Job*. Düsseldorf: Bastion-Verlag, 1948; "Un regard sur le livre de Job." In his *Le poète et la Bible*. Paris: Gallimard, 1998. 1:919–39]. **Cranfield, C. E. B.** "An Interpretation of the Book of Job." *ExpT* 54 (1943) 295–98. **Edelkoort, Albertus Hendrik.** *Het Boek Job en het probleem van het lijden*. Hague: J. V. Voorhoeve, 1946. **Flügel, Heinz.** *Mensch und Menschensohn: Vierzehn Essays*. Munich: Kösel, 1947. **Flügge, Theophil.** *Gott in der Hölle. Hiob's Klage, den Trotzigen und Verzweifelten zu Trost nacherzählt*. Berlin–Dahlem: Christlicher Zeitschriftenverlag, 1947. **Gordis, Robert.** "'All Men's Book.' A New Introduction to Job." *Menorah Journal* 37 (1949) 329–58 [= his *Poets, Prophets and Sages: Essays in Biblical Interpretation*. Bloomington, IN: Indiana University Press, 1971. 280–84]. **Hawthorne, R. R.** "Joban Theology." *BSac* 101 (1944) 64–75, 173–86, 290–303, 417–33; 102 (1945) 37–54. **Junker, Hermann.** *Jobs Leid, Streit und Sieg; oder Ein Mensch ringt mit dem Schicksal und mit Gott. Die biblische Schatzkammer*. Freiburg i.Br.: Herder, 1948. **Kaminka, A.** "Principles for Understanding the Speeches in the Book of Job" [Heb]. *Moznaim* 1 (1945). **Lande, Lawrence Montague.** *The Story of Stories: The Book of Job*. Montreal, 1946. **Lindblom, Johannes.** *Boken om Job och hans idande*. Lund: C. W. K. Gleerup, 1940. **Lippert, Peter.** *Et Job dit à Dieu. La vie intérieure*. Aubier: Editions Montaigne, 1945. **Paulsen, Anna.** *Hiob. Ein Buch der Bibel für unsere Zeit gedeutet*. Hamburg: Wittig, 1947. **Pollock, Seton.** *Stubborn Soil: A Study of the Hebrew Interpretation of Life, with Special Reference to, and New Versions of, the Books of Proverbs, Ecclesiastes and Job*. London: Sidgwick & Jackson, 1946 [pp. 104–8 are reprinted as "God and a Heretic" in *The Dimensions of Job: A Study and Selected Readings*. Ed. Nahum H. Glatzer. New York: Schocken Books, 1969. 268–72]. **Schrempf, Christoph.** *Menschenlos: Hiob, Ödipus, Jesus, homo sum … * Stuttgart: Frommann, 1948. **Schröder, Rudolf Alexander.** *Das Buch Hiob mit Randbemerkungen*. Munich: R. Piper, 1948. **Segal, M. H.** אױב ספר [The Book of Job]." *Tarb* 13 (1941–42) 73–91. **Slater, Robert Henry Lawson.** *God and Human Suffering, Considered with Special Reference to the Book of Job*. London: Epworth Press, 1941. **Spalding, P. A.** "The Poem of Job." *Congregational Quarterly* 18 (1940) 290–99. **Steele, Robert Benson.** "The Book of Job." *MethQR* 70 (1921) 523–34. **Steinmann, Jean.** *Job. Témoins de Dieu 8*. Paris: Cerf, 1946. **Stewart, Irma.** *Job: His Spiritual Value*. New York: North River Press, 2nd ed. 1943. **Straubinger, Johannes.** *Job, el libro del consuelo*. Buenos Aires: Guadalupe, 1945 [= *Job. Ein Trostbuch in schwerer Zeit. Betrachtungen über das Geheimnis des Übels und des Leidens*. Stuttgart: Katholisches Bibelwerk, 1949]. **Weill, R.** "Le livre du 'Désesperé.' Le sens, l'intention et la composition de l'ouvrage." *BIFAO* 45 (1947) 89–154.

1950s. Arienzo, Corrado da. "Il dolore di Giobbe." *PalCl* 37 (1958) 735–39. **Baab, O.** "The Book of Job." *Int* 5 (1951) 329–43. **Baumer, L.** "Das Buch Hiob, Versuch einer psychopathologischen Deutung." *Der Nervenarzt* 28 (1957) 546–50. **Blackwood, Andrew**

Watterson. *Devotional Introduction to Job.* Grand Rapids: Baker Book House, 1959.
Cocagnac, A. M. "Job sans beauté ni éclat." *VS* 422 (1956) 355–71. **Crook, Margaret
Brackenbury.** *The Cruel God: Job's Search for the Meaning of Suffering.* Boston: Beacon Press,
1959. **Daniélou, J.** "Les quatre visages de Job." *Etudes* (Sept. 1955) 145–56. ———. *Les
saints païens de l'Ancien Testament.* Paris: Le Seuil, 1956. 109–28 [= *Holy Pagans of the Old
Testament.* Trans. F. Faber. London: Longmans, Green & Co., 1957. 86–102; these pages
reprinted as "Job: The Mystery of Man and God" in *The Dimensions of Job: A Study and
Selected Readings.* Ed. Nahum H. Glatzer. New York: Schocken Books, 1969. 100–111].
Fichtner, Johannes. "Hiob in der Verkündigung unserer Zeit." *WuD* 29 (1950) 71–89
[= his *Gottes Weisheit. Gesammelte Studien zum Alten Testament.* Arbeiten zur Theologie
2/3. Stuttgart: Calwer, 1965. 52–66]. **Fohrer, Georg.** "'Nun aber hat mein Auge dich
geschaut.' Der innere Aufbau des Buches Hiob." *ThZ* 15 (1959) 1–21 [= "Der innere
Aufbau des Buches Hiob." In his *Studien zum Buche Hiob (1956–1979).* BZAW 159. Berlin:
de Gruyter, 1963. 2nd ed., 1983. 1–18]. **Gemüsch, Georg.** *Das Rätsel Hiob. Gemeinfassliche
Gedanken über das Buch Hiob.* Karlsruhe: C. F. Müller, 1958. **Ginsberg, H. L.** "עיונים בספר איוב.
Studies in the Book of Job." *Lesh* 21 (1956–57) 259–64. **Godet, Frédéric.** *Notes sur le livre
de Job et le Cantique des Cantiques.* Guebwiller: Ligue pour la lecture de la Bible, [?] 1950.
Gordis, Robert. "The Conflict of Tradition and Experience." In *Great Moral Dilemmas in
Literature, Past and Present.* Ed. R. M. McIver. New York: Institute for Religious and Social
Studies, 1956. 155–78. ———. "The Temptation of Job: Tradition versus Experience in
Religion." *Judaism* 4 (1955) 195–208 [= his *Poets, Prophets and Sages: Essays in Biblical Interpre-
tation.* Bloomington, IN: Indiana University Press, 1971. 305–24; a slightly abridged
version in *The Dimensions of Job: A Study and Selected Readings.* Ed. Nahum H. Glatzer.
New York: Schocken Books, 1969. 74–85]. **Humbert, Paul.** "A propos du livre de Job."
In his *Opuscules d'un hébraïsant.* Mémoires de l'Université de Neuchâtel 26. Neuchâtel:
Secrétariat de l'Université, 1958. 204–19. ———. "Le modernisme de Job." In *Wisdom in
Israel and in the Ancient Near East, Presented to Professor Harold Henry Rowley ... in Celebration
of His Sixty-Fifth Birthday.* Ed. M. Noth and D. Winton Thomas. VTSup 3. Leiden: E. J.
Brill, 1955. 150–61. **Jung, C. G.** *Antwort auf Hiob.* Zurich: Rascher, 1952 [= *Answer to Job:
Researches into the Relation between Psychology and Religion.* Trans. R. F. C. Hull. London:
Routledge & Kegan Paul, 1954]. **Knight, Harold.** "Job. Considered as a Contribution
to Hebrew Theology." *SJT* 9 (1956) 63–76. **Kuhl, Curt.** "Hiobbuch." *RGG.* 3rd ed. 1959.
3:355–61. **Kunz, Ulrich.** *Hiob.* Stuttgarter Bibelhefte. Stuttgart: Quell-Verlag, 1958.
Lande, Lawrence M. *Toward the Quiet Mind: A Guide to Self-Discovery through the Study of the
Book of Job.* Toronto: McClelland and Stewart, 1954. **Lovelock, Ralph Tweed.** *Job. A Study
of the Book and Its Message.* Birmingham: The Christadelphian, 1957. **Lusseau, H.** "Job."
In *Introduction à la Bible.* Ed. A. Robert and A. Feuillet. Freiburg: Herder, 1959. 1:642–
54. **Möller, Hans.** *Sinn und Aufbau des Buches Hiob.* Berlin: Evangelische Verlagsanstalt,
1955. **Müller, Heinrich.** *Durch Kreuz und Leid zur Herrlichkeit: Bibelstunden über das Buch
Hiob.* Lieme in Lippe: Evangelische landeskirchliche Volks- und Schriftenmission, 1959.
Popma, K. J. *De boodschap van het boek Job.* Goes: Oosterbaan & LeCointre, 1957. **Pury,
Roland de.** *Job, ou, l'homme révolté.* Les cahiers du renouveau 12. Geneva: Labor & Fides,
1955 [= *Hiob, der Mensch im Aufruhr.* Biblische Studien 15. Neukirchen Kreis Moers:
Buchhandlung der Erziehungsvereins, 1957; *Job: de mens in opstand.* Amsterdam: Ten
Have, 1957]. **Retief, Guillaume J.** *Hy het die geloof behou. Oordenkinge oor Job.* Kaapstad,
Pretoria, 1957. **Richter, H.** "Erwägungen zum Hiobproblem." *EvTh* 18 (1958) 202–24.
Richter, Heinz. *Studien zu Hiob. Der Aufbau des Hiobbuches, dargestellt an den Gattungen des
Rechtslebens.* Berlin: Evangelische Verlagsanstalt, 1959. **Robinson, Theodore H.** *Job and
His Friends.* London: SCM Press, 1954. **Roehrs, Walter R.** "The Theme of the Book of
Job." *CTM* 25 (1954) 298–302. **Samuel, J. B.** *The Prophetic Character of Job; or, the Solution
of a Great Problem.* Goodmayes, London: Hebrew Christian Testimony to Israel, 1954.
Schofield, John N. "Job in the Framework of His Time." *Modern Churchman* ns 1 (1958)
238–44. **Spadafora, F.** "Giobbe." *EC* 6 (1951) 407–13. **Stange, C.** "Das Problem Hiob's
und seine Lösung." *ZST* 24 (1955) 342–55. **Stewart, James.** *The Message of Job.* London:

Independent Press, 1959. **Studer, Gottfried.** *Gott redet in Wettersturm. Eine Auslegung des Buches Hiob.* Witten: Bundes-Verlag, 1954. **Sullivan, K.** "The Book of Job." *Worship* 29 (1954–55) 449–61. **Terrien, Samuel.** *Job: Poet of Existence.* Indianapolis: Bobbs Merrill Co., 1958. **Tournay, R.** "Le procès de Job ou l'innocent devant Dieu." *VS* 95 (1956) 339–54. **Treves, Marco.** "The Book of Job." *ZAW* 107 (1995) 261–72. **Ulanov, B.** "Job and His Comforters." *The Bridge* 3 (1958) 234–68. **Ward, William B.** *Out of the Whirlwind: Answers to the Problem of Suffering from the Book of Job.* Richmond: John Knox Press, 1958. **Welch, Charles H.** *Studies in the Book of Job.* London: Berean Publishing Trust, 1953 [= *The Book of Job.* London: Berean Publishing Trust, 1975]. **Wendt, A. Ernest.** *A New Look at Job.* Vol. 1. Boston: Christopher Publishing House, 1954; Vol. 2. New York: Greenwich Book Publishers, 1956. **Westermann, Claus.** *Der Aufbau des Buches Hiob.* Tübingen: J. C. B. Mohr (Paul Siebeck), 1956; 3rd ed., Stuttgart: Calwer Verlag, 1978 [= *The Structure of the Book of Job: A Form-Critical Analysis.* Trans. Charles A. Muenchow. Philadelphia: Fortress Press, 1981]. **Wielenga, J. L.** *Gevecht om God: korte overwegingen van enkele gedeelten uit het boek Job.* Kampen: Kok, 1959.

1960s. Anderson, H. "Another Perspective on the Book of Job." *TGUOS* 18 (1961) 43–46. **Augé, R.** "Job." *EncBib* 4 (1965) 569–78. **Baeyer, Walter von, and Helmut Kretz.** "Hiob heute." In *Wirklichkeit der Mitte: Beiträge zu einer Strukturanthropologie. Festgabe für August Vetter zum 80. Geburtstag.* Ed. Johannes Tenzler. Munich: Alber, 1968. 571–88. **Baker, Wesley C.** *More Than a Man Can Take: A Study of Job.* Philadelphia: Westminster Press, 1966. **Barth, Karl.** *Hiob. Herausgegeben und eingeleitet von Helmut Gollwitzer.* Biblische Studien 49. Neukirchen-Vluyn: Neukirchener Verlag, 1966 [= his *Kirchliche Dogmatik* 4/3,1]. **Barthélemy, D.** "Dieu méconnu par le vieil homme: Job." *VS* 105 (1961) 445–63. **Bloch, Ernst.** "Studien zum Buche Hiob." In *Für Margarete Susman: Auf gespaltenem Pfad.* Ed. Manfred Schlösser. Darmstadt: Erato, 1964. 85–102. **Bonnard, P. E.** "Job ou l'homme enfin exstasié." *LumVie* 13 (1964) 15–33. **Brandenburg, Hans.** *Das Buch Hiob: Der Mensch in der Anfechtung.* Das lebendige Wort 11. Giessen: Brunnen-Verlag, 1969. **Brandon, S. G. F.** "The Book of Job: Its Significance for the History of Religions." *History Today* 2 (1961) 547–54. **Breakstone, Raymond.** *Job: A Case Study.* New York: Bookman Associates, Inc., 1964. **Brook, Peggy M.** *Job: An Interpretation.* London: Foundational Book Co., 1967. **Carstensen, Roger N.** "The Scandal of Job and the Rabbinics." In *One Faith: Its Biblical, Historical, and Ecumenical Dimensions: A Series of Essays in Honor of Stephen J. England on the Occasion of His Seventieth Birthday.* Ed. Robert L. Simpson. Enid, OK: Phillips University Press, 1966. ———. *Job: Defense of Honor.* New York: Abingdon Pres, 1963. **Catmull, Joseph Fielding.** *An Interpretation of the Book of Job.* Diss. Utah, 1960. **Cook, Albert.** *The Root of the Thing: A Study of "Job" and "The Song of Songs."* Bloomington: Indiana University Press, 1968. **Crook, M. B., and S. A. Eliot.** "Tracing Job's Story." *HibJ* 60 (1962) 323–39. **Duesberg, Hilaire, and Irénée Fransen.** "Le plaid de Job contre la Tradition." In *Les scribes inspirés: introduction aux livres sapientiaux de la Bible. Proverbes, Job, Ecclésiaste, Sagesse, Ecclésiastique.* [Maredsous]: Editions de Maredsous, [1966]. 455–536. **Epp, Theodore H.** *Job, a Man Tried as Gold.* Lincoln, NE: Back to the Bible Publications, 1967. **Fohrer, Georg.** "Das Hiobproblem und seine Lösung." *WZ der Martin-Luther-Universität* 12 (1963) 249–58. ———. *Studien zum Buche Hiob.* BZAW 159. Gütersloh: Gerd Mohn, 1963 [2nd ed., *Studien zum Buche Hiob (1956–1979)*. Berlin: de Gruyter, 1983]. **Gibbs, P. T.** *Job and the Mysteries of Wisdom.* Nashville: Southern Publishing, 1967. **Glatzer, Nahum H.** "Knowest Thou? Notes on the Book of Job." *Studies in Rationalism, Judaism and Universalism in Memory of Leon Roth.* Ed. Raphael Loewe. London: Routledge & Kegan Paul, 1966. 73–86. **Goldsmith, Robert Hillis.** "Healing Scourge: A Study in Suffering and Meaning." *Int* 17 (1963) 271–79. **Goodheart, Eugene.** "Job and the Modern World." *Judaism* 10 (1961) 21–28 [= *Twentieth Century Interpretations of the Book of Job: A Collection of Critical Essays.* Ed. P. S. Sanders. Englewood Cliffs, NJ: Prentice–Hall, 1968. 98–106]. **Gordis, Robert.** *The Book of God and Man: A Study of Job.* Chicago: University of Chicago Press, 1965. ———. "The Lord out of the Whirlwind. The Climax and Meaning of 'Job'." *Judaism* 13 (1964) 48–63. **Gray, G. B.**

"The Purpose and Method of the Writer." In *Twentieth Century Interpretations of the Book of Job: A Collection of Critical Essays*. Ed. P. S. Sanders. Englewood Cliffs, NJ: Prentice–Hall, 1968. 36–45 [= Driver–Gray, xxv–l]. **Hempel, J.** "Das theologische Problem des Hiob." *ZST* 6 (1929) 621–89 [= his *Apoxysmata. Vorarbeitungen zu einer Religionsgeschichte und Theologie des Alten Testaments*. BZAW 81. Berlin: A. Töpelmann, 1961. 114–74]. **Hirsch, N. D.** "The Architecture of the Book of Job." *CCAR Journal* 16 (1969) 22–32. **Holmgren, Fredrick.** "Barking Dogs Never Bite, except Now and Then: Proverbs and Job." *ATR* 61 (1969) 341–53. **Hone, Ralph E.** *The Voice out of the Whirlwind: The Book of Job*. San Francisco: Chandler, 1960. **Irwin, W. H.** "Job." In *Dictionary of the Bible* [New Hastings]. 2nd ed. Edinburgh: T. & T. Clark, 1963. 501–5. **Jaspers, Karl.** "Hiob." In *Einsichten. Gerhard Krüger zum 60. Geburtstag*. Ed. Klaus Oehler and Richard Schaeffler. Frankfurt: Klostermann, 1962. 86–106. **Jepsen, Alfred.** *Das Buch Hiob und seine Deutung*. Aufsätze und Vorträge zur Theologie und Religionswissenschaft 28. Berlin: Evangelische Verlagsanstalt, 1963 [= *Arbeiten zur Theologie* 1,14. Ed. Alfred Jepsen, Otto Michel, and Theodor Schlatter. Stuttgart: Calwer Verlag, 1964]. **Johnstone, C. K.** "Poetic Statement in 'Job'." *RevUnivOtt* 32 (1962) 45–59. **Jones, Edgar.** *The Triumph of Job*. London: SCM Press, 1966. **Kent, H. Harold.** *Job Our Contemporary*. Grand Rapids: Eerdmans, 1968. **King, Horace Maybray.** *Songs in the Night. A Study of the Book of Job, with Illustrations by William Blake*. Gerrards Cross: Colin Smythe, 1968. **Kline, Meredith G.** "Job." In *The Zondervan Pictorial Bible Dictionary*. Ed. M. C. Tenney. Grand Rapids: Zondervan, 1963. 443–44. **Krinetski, L.** "Ich weiss, mein Anwalt lebt. Die Botschaft des Buches Job." *BK* 20 (1965) 8–12. **Kurzweil, Baruch.** *Ba-ma'avak 'al 'erkhey ha-Yahadut*. Tel 'Aviv, 1969. **Kusenberg, K.** "Das Buch Hiob. Stichworte bei meiner Lektüre." *Merkur* 23 (1969) 543–46. **Larcher, C.** "Job (Le Livre de)." *Catholicisme* 6,25 (1965) 899–907. **Lipiński, E.** "Le juste souffrant." *FoiTemps* 1 (1968) 329–42. **Luz Ojeda, José.** *El libro de Job*. Mexico City: Periodística, 1964.

Michel, Diethelm. "Hiob: Wegen Gott gegen Gott." In his *Israels Glaube im Wandel: Einführungen in die Forschung am Alten Testament*. Berlin: Verlag Die Spur, Dorbandt, 1968. 252–77. **Morgan, G. Campbell.** "Job, Proverbs, Ecclesiastes." In his *The Unfolding Message of the Bible: The Harmony and Unity of the Scriptures*. Westwood, NJ: Fleming H. Revell; London: Pickering & Inglis, 1961. 215–29. **Murphy, Joseph.** *Living without Strain. Inner Meaning of the Book of Job*. San Gabriel, CA: Willing, 1959 [= *Positiv leben ohne Stress: das Buch Hiob interpretiert für unsere Zeit*. Munich: Goldmann, 1990]. **Nelis, J.** "Job (Buch)." In *Bibel-Lexikon*. Ed. Herbert Haag. Zurich: Benzinger Verlag, 1968. 846–50. **Paterson, John.** *The Wisdom of Israel: Job and Proverbs*. Bible Guides 11. London: Lutterworth; Nashville: Abingdon Press, 1961. **Platt, Albert Thomas.** *The Argument of the Book of Job*. Diss. Dallas Theological Seminary, 1962. **Quintens, W.** "De boodschap van het boek Job." *ColBG* 15 (1969) 17–33. **Rexroth, Kenneth.** "The Book of Job." In *Twentieth Century Interpretations of the Book of Job. A Collection of Critical Essays*. Ed. P. S. Sanders. Englewood Cliffs, NJ: Prentice–Hall, 1968. 107–9 [= *Saturday Review* (April 23, 1966) 21]. **Rolla, Armondo.** "Il libro di Giobbe." In *Il messaggio della salvezza: Corso completo di studi biblici*. Ed. Giovanni Canfora. Turin–Leumann: Editrice Elle Di Ci, 1968. 3:535–57. **Rowley, H. H.** "The Book of Job and Its Meaning." *BJRL* 41 (1958–59) 167–207 [= his *From Moses to Qumran: Studies in the Old Testament*. London: Lutterworth, 1963. 139–83; pp. 175–83 reprinted as "The Intellectual versus the Spiritual Solution" in *The Dimensions of Job: A Study and Selected Readings*. Ed. Nahum H. Glatzer. New York: Schocken Books, 1969. 123–28]. **Rubenstein, Richard L.** "Job and Auschwitz." *USQR* 25 (1969–70) 421–37. **Schröder, Rudolf Alexander.** "Marginalien zum Buch Hiob." In his *Über die Liebe zum Menschen: Gedanken und Betrachtungen*. Munich: Siebenstern Taschenbuch Verlag, 1966. **Sewall, Richard B.** "The Book of Job." In *Twentieth Century Interpretations of the Book of Job. A Collection of Critical Essays*. Ed. P. S. Sanders. Englewood Cliffs, NJ: Prentice–Hall. 1968. 21–35 [= his *The Vision of Tragedy*. New Haven: Yale University Press, 1959. 9–24]. **Singer, Richard E.** *Job's Encounter*. New York: Bookman Associates, 1963. **Skehan, P. W.** "Job, Book of." *New Catholic Encyclopedia* 7 (1967) 999–1001 [= his *Studies in Israelite Poetry* *and Wisdom.* CBQMS 1. Washington, DC: Catholic Biblical Association, 1971. 78–82]. **Snaith, Norman H.** *The Book of Job: Its Origin and Purpose.* SBT 2/11. London: SCM Press; Naperville: Allenson, 1968. **Steinmann, Jean.** *Job, témoin de la souffrance humaine.* Foi vivante 120. Paris: Cerf, 1969. **Stockhammer, Morris.** *Das Buch Hiob. Versuch einer Theodizee.* Vienna: Europäischer Verlag, 1963. **Strolz, Walter.** *Hiobs Auflehnung gegen Gott.* Opuscula aus Glaube und Dichtung 30. Pfullingen: Neske, 1967. **Tsevat, Matitiahu.** "The Meaning of the Book of Job." *HUCA* 37 (1966) 73–106 [= his *The Meaning of the Book of Job and Other Biblical Studies: Essays on the Literature and Religion of the Hebrew Bible.* New York: Ktav, 1980. 1–37; *Studies in Ancient Israelite Wisdom: Selected with a Prolegomenon.* Ed. James L. Crenshaw. New York: Ktav, 1976. 341–74; *Sitting with Job: Selected Studies on the Book of Job.* Ed. Roy B. Zuck. Grand Rapids: Baker Book House, 1992. 189–218; also *The Fourth World Congress of Jewish Studies.* 1967. 1:177–80]. **Vischer, Wilhelm.** "God's Truth and Man's Lie. A Study of the Message of the Book of Job." *Int* 15 (1961) 131–46. **Wevers, John William.** *The Way of the Righteous: Psalms and the Books of Wisdom.* Philadelphia: Westminster Press, 1961. **Wood, James.** *Job and the Human Situation.* London: Geoffrey Bles, 1966. **Zika, C.** "Ijob." *Biblia Revuo* 4 (1968) 21–34.

1970s. Aalders, W. *Wet, tragedie, evangelie: een andere benadering van het boek Job.* The Hague: Voorhoeve, 1979. **Alonso Schökel, L.** "Toward a Dramatic Reading of the Book of Job." *Semeia* 7 (1977) 45–61. **Baker, J. A.** "The Book of Job: Unity and Meaning." In *Studia Biblica 1978: Sixth International Congress on Biblical Studies, Oxford 3–7 April 1978.* I. Ed. E. A. Livingstone. JSOTSup 11. Sheffield: JSOT Press, 1978. 17–26. **Barylko, J.** *Job.* Biblioteca popular judía. Colección Grandes figuras del judaísmo 58. Buenos Aires: Ejucativo Sudamericano del Congreso Judío Mondial, 1970. **Bennett, T. Miles.** "When a Righteous Man Suffers: A Teaching Outline of the Book of Job." *SWJT* 14 (1971) 57–64. ———. *When Human Wisdom Fails: An Exposition of the Book of Job.* Grand Rapids: Baker, 1971. **Bishop, Eric F. F.** *Job, the Patriarch of East Palestine: The Epic That Transjordan Gave to the Scriptures of the World.* Reigate, Surrey: George J. Hieatt & Son, 1973. **Bonnard, Pierre-Emile.** "Mes yeux t'ont vu [Job]." *Journal de la vie: Aujourd'hui la Bible* 139 (May 1973). **Bonora, Antonio.** *Il contestatore di Dio: Giobbe.* Turin: Marietti, 1978. **Callachor, P. J.** "A View of the Book of Job." *TBT* 68 (1973) 329–31. **Camhy, O.** *Une trilogie biblique sur le drame de la vie: un sujet, trois conceptions: Job, Qohéleth ou l'Ecclésiaste, Isaïe. Dessins de Maxa Nordau et Devi Tuszynski.* Paris: J. Grassin, 1973. **Carroll, Robert P.** "Postscript to Job." *Modern Churchman* 19 (1976) 161–66. **Cherchevsky, Jacques (Yaacov Sioni).** *Livre de Job.* Paris: J. Cherchevsky, 1970. **Cox, Dermot.** "Reason in Revolt: The Poetic Dialogues in the Book of Job." *SBFLA* 24 (1974) 317–28. ———. *The Triumph of Impotence: Job and the Tradition of the Absurd.* AnGreg 212. Rome: Università Gregoriana Editrice, 1978. **Dearlove, J. E.** "Job: The Artistry of Ambiguity." *ChrCent* 93 (1976) 484–87. **Dobson, John Hasleden.** *Out of the Storm: The Drama of Job in Poetry.* New York: Vantage Press, 1974. **Ehlinger, Charles (ed.).** *La Bible du peuple de Dieu. 2. Des hommes devant Dieu* [Chroniques, Esdras et Néhémie, Tobie, Judith, Esther, Maccabées, Job, Psaumes]. Paris: Le Cerf, 1971. **Ewing, Ward B.** *Job: A Vision of God.* New York: Seabury, 1976. **Francisco, C. T.** "A Teaching Outline of the Book of Job." *RevExp* 68 (1971) 511–20. **Frost, G. E.** *The Color of the Night: Reflections on the Book of Job.* Minneapolis: Augsburg, 1977. **Glazner, A.** "Introduction to the Book of Job" [Heb]. *BMik* 23 (1978) 189–202. **Good, E. M.** "Job and the Literary Task: A Response" [to David Robertson]. *Soundings* 56 (1973) 470–84. **Gordis, Robert.** "Observations on Problems and Methods in Biblical Research. Writing a Commentary on Job." *PrAmAcJewRes* 41–42 (1973–74) 105–35. **Gros Louis, Kenneth R.** "The Book of Job." In *Literary Interpretations of Biblical Narratives.* Ed. Kenneth R. R. Gros Louis. Nashville: Abingdon Press, 1974. 226–66. **Haag, Herbert.** *Ijobs Fragen an Gott.* Stuttgart: Katholisches Bibelwerk Verlag, 1972. **Hengstenberg, E. W.** "Interpreting the Book of Job." In *Classical Evangelical Essays in Old Testament Interpretation.* Ed. Walter C. Kaiser. Grand Rapids: Baker, 1973. 91–112. **Howard, David M.** *How Come, God? Reflections from Job about God and Puzzled Man.* Philadelphia: A. J. Holman, 1972 [= *Understanding God's Plan.* London: Scripture Union, 1973]. **Inch, Morris A.** *My Servant Job.* Grand Rapids: Baker,

1979. **Johnson, L. D.** *Out of the Whirlwind: The Major Message of Job.* Nashville: Broadman, 1971. **Kahn, Jack, with Hester Soloman.** *Job's Illness: Loss, Grief and Integration. A Psychological Interpretation.* Oxford: Pergamon, 1975. **Kapelrud, Arvid S.** *Job og hans problem, i fortid og i dag.* Oslo: Land og Kirche, 1976. **Karary, E.** "איוב ספר [The Book of Job]." *BMik* 51 (1972) 416–27, 530–31. **Kroeze, J. H.** *Geveg met God, die boek Job.* Pretoria: N. G. Kerkboekhandel, 1978. **Kuhn, Johannes.** *Warum bist du so, Gott? Hiob der Fragende.* Stuttgart: Quell, 1978. **Lacocque, André.** "Est-ce gratuitement que Job craint Dieu?" In *Mélanges A. Neher.* Ed. E. Amado Lévy-Valensi. Paris: Librairie d'Amérique et d'Orient, Adrien-Maisonneuve, 1975. 175–79. **Laurin, Robert.** "The Theological Structure of Job." *ZAW* 84 (1972) 86–89. **Levenson, Jon Douglas.** *The Book of Job in Its Time and in the Twentieth Century.* Cambridge, MA: Harvard University Press, 1972. **Lévêque, Jean.** *Job et son Dieu. Essai d'exégèse et de théologie biblique.* 2 vols. Paris: Gabalda, 1970. ———. "Job, ou l'espoir déraciné." *VS* 125 (1971) 287–304. **Lichtenstein, A.** "Toward a Literary Understanding of the Book of Job." *HS* 20–21 (1979–80) 34.

   MacKenzie, R. A. F. "The Transformation of Job." *BTB* 9 (1979) 51–57. **Maillot, Alphonse.** "Job, livre païen." *FoiVie* 69 (1970) 2–15. ———. "L'apologétique du livre de Job." *RHPR* 59 (1979) 567–76 [= *Prophètes, poètes et sages d'Israel: hommages à Edmond Jacob à l'occasion de son 70ème anniversaire par ses amis, ses collègues et ses élèves.* Paris: Presses Universitaires de France, 1979]. **Matheney, M. Pierce, Jr.** "Major Purposes of the Book of Job." *SWJT* 14 (1971) 17–42. **McKall, Duke K. (ed.).** "Book of Job." *RevExp* 68 (1971) 443–533. **McKeating, Henry.** "The Central Issue of the Book of Job." *ExpT* 82 (1971) 244–47. **Mendoza de la Mora, José, José María Valverde, José Luz Ojeda, and L. Alonso Schökel.** *Job.* Libros sagrados. Madrid: Ediciones Cristiandad, 1971. **Miles, John A., Jr.** "Gagging on Job, or The Comedy of Religious Exhaustion." *Semeia* 7 (1977) 71–126. See also **Polzin, R.** "John A. Miles on the Book of Job: A Response." *Semeia* 7 (1977) 127–33.| **Müller, Hans-Peter.** *Das Hiobproblem: seine Stellung und Entstehung im alten Orient und im Alten Testament.* Erträge des Forschung 84. Darmstadt: Wissenschaftliche Buchgesellschaft, 1978; 3rd ed., 1995. ———. *Hiob und seine Freunde: Traditionsgeschichtliches zum Verständnis des Hiobbuches.* Theologische Studien 103. Zurich: EVZ-Verlag, 1970. **Naylor, Robert E. (ed.).** "Studies in the Book of Job." *SWJT* 14 (1971) 5–78. **Nola, A. M. di.** "Giobbe, Libro de." *ERE* 3 (1971) 212–22. **Orelli, A. von.** "Hiob. Deutung eines biblischen Mythos." *Reform* 25 (1976) 74–82, 148–58. **Patrick, Dale.** "Job's Address of God." *ZAW* 91 (1979) 268–82. **Polzin, Robert, and David Robertson (eds.).** *Studies in the Book of Job.* Semeia 7. Missoula, MT: Scholars Press, 1977. **Reid, S. A.** "The Book of Job." *Psychoanalytic Review* 60 (1973) 373–91. **Richards, I. A.** *Beyond.* New York: Harcourt Brace Jovanovich, 1974. **Robertson, David.** "The Book of Job." In his *The Old Testament and the Literary Critic.* Guides to Biblical Scholarship. Philadelphia: Fortress Press, 1977. 33–54. ———. "The Book of Job: A Literary Study." *Soundings* 56 (1973) 446–69. **Rubinstein, R. L.** "Job and Auschwitz." *New Theology* 8 (1971) 107–14. **Ruckman, Peter S.** *The Book of Job.* Pensacola, FL: Pensacola Bible Institute, 1978. **Scafella, F.** "A Reading of Job." *JSOT* 14 (1979) 63–67. **Schaper, Robert N.** *Why Me, God? Wisdom from Job.* Glendale, CA: Regal Books, 1974. **Schapiro, D. S.** "A Study of the Book of Job." *Tradition* 13 (1972) 81–99. **Schreiber, Vernon R.** *My Servant Job: A Devotional Guide to the Book of Job, Including the Complete Text of Job for Modern Man, Today's English Version.* Minneapolis: Augsburg Publishing House, 1974. **Shapiro, David S.** "A Study of the Book of Job." *Tradition* 13 (1972) 81–99. **Slochower, Harry.** "The Hebrew Memory of a Chosen God: The Book of Job." In his *Mythopoesis: Mythic Patterns in the Literary Classics.* Detroit: Wayne State University Press, 1970. 47–66. **Smeets, J. R.** *La Bible de Jehan Malkaraume (Ms. Paris, B.N. Fr. 903)* [13th cent. French Bible]. 2 vols. Assen: Van Gorcum, 1978. **Smith, Ralph L.** "Introduction to the Book of Job." *SWJT* 14 (1971) 5–16. ———. *Job: A Study in Providence and Faith.* Nashville: Convention Press, 1971. **Sperka, Joshua S.** *The Book of Job. Mankind on Trial. A Modern Interpretation of the Most Perplexing Problem of All Ages.* New York: Bloch, 1979. **Still, W.** *God, Job and Satan.* [Aberdeen]: [The Author], [1978?]. **Stockhammer, Morris.** "Job's Problem." In *Faith and Reason: Essays* *in Judaism.* Ed. Robert Gordis and Ruth B. Waxman. New York: Ktav, 1973. 54–60. **Strauss, J. D.** *The Shattering of Silence: Job Our Contemporary.* Joplin, MO: College Press, 1976. **Usmiana, Renate.** "A New Look at the Drama of Job." *Modern Drama* 13 (1970) 191–200. **Weimer, James D.** *Job's Complaint: A Study of Its Limits and Form, Content and Significance.* Diss. Union Theological Seminary, New York, 1974. **Whedbee, J. William.** "The Comedy of Job." *Semeia* 7 (1977) 1–39 [= *On Humour and the Comic in the Hebrew Bible.* Ed. Yehuda T. Radday and Athalya Brenner. JSOTSup 92. Sheffield: JSOT Press, 1990. 217–49]. **Willi-Plein, Ina.** "Hiobs immer aktuelle Frage." In *Der Herr ist einer, unser gemeinsames Erbe.* Ed. Karl-Johan Illman and Jukka Thurén. Åbo: Åbo Akademi, 1979. 122–36. **Williams, J. G.** "'You have not spoken truth of me.' Mystery and Irony in Job." *ZAW* 83 (1971) 231–55. **Yates, K. M.** "Understanding the Book of Job." *RevExp* 68 (1971) 433–45. **Zenger, Erich, and Rupert Böswald.** *Durchkreuztes Leben: Besinnung auf Hiob.* Freiburg i.Br.: Herder, 1976. **Zimmermann, E. H.** "The Book of Job." *MethQR* 16 (1979) 703–16. **Zuckerman, B.** "Job, Book of." *IDBS* (1976) 479–81.

1980s. André, Gunnel. "Deuterojesaja och Jobsboken: En jämförande studie." *SEÅ* 54 (1989) 33–42. **Anon.** *Schweigt Gott? Sieben Texte aus dem Buch Ijob (Hiob, Job).* Ökumenische Arbeitshefte für die Bibelwoche 19. Stuttgart: Deutsche Bibelgesellschaft, 1983. **Archer, G. L.** *The Book of Job: God's Answer to the Problem of Undeserved Suffering.* Grand Rapids: Baker, 1982. **Aufrecht, W. E. (ed.).** *Studies in the Book of Job.* SRSup 16. Waterloo: Wilfrid Laurier University, 1985. **Ben-Chorin, Schalom.** "Hiob." In his *Schalom: Weil wir Brüder sind. Zum christlich-jüdischen Dialog heute.* Gerlingen: Bleicher Verlag, 1988. 59–64. **Bergant, Dianne.** "Things Too Wonderful for Me (Job 42:3): Facing the Incomprehensible." In *Scripture and Prayer: A Celebration for Carroll Stuhlmueller.* Ed. Carolyn Osiek and Donald Senior. Wilmington, DE: Glazier, 1988. ———. "Why Do I Suffer?" *TBT* 20 (1982) 341–46. **Berger-Lutz, Regina (ed.).** *Hiob. Ökumenischer Arbeitskreis für Bibelarbeit.* Bibelarbeit in der Gemeinde 7. Basel: F. Reinhardt, 1989. **Bezuidenhout, Louis Christiaan.** *Structure and Meaning of the Book of Job* [Afrikaans]. Diss. Pretoria, 1987. **Billheimer, Paul E.** *Adventure in Adversity.* Alresford, Hants.: Christian Literature Crusade and Kingsway, 1984. **Bizjak, Jurij.** *Job.* Ljubljana, 1989. **Bloem, Diane Brummel.** *Into the Midst of Suffering: A Woman's Workshop on Job. Leader's Manual.* Grand Rapids: Zondervan Publishing House, 1986. **Bloom, Harold (ed.).** *The Book of Job: Modern Critical Interpretations.* New York: Chelsea House Publishing, 1988. **Bos, Wijm.** *Mijn verdediger leeft: teksten uit het boek Job.* Boxtel: Stichting Vrienden van de Bijbel, 1988. **Brenner, Athalya.** "God's Answer to Job." *VT* 31 (1981) 129–37. **Brodsky, Beverly.** *The Story of Job Retold and Illustrated* [for children]. New York: G. Braziller, 1986. **Buckey, Donald R.** "Three Ways in Text Interpretation" [of Job] [reply to M. Fox, D. Pellauer, and A. Lacocque]. *Semeia* 19 (1981) 91–97. **Casalis, Georges, and Laurent Gagnebin.** "La révolte: lecture apologétique et herméneutique" [on R. de Pury's *Job ou L'homme révolté,* 1955]. *ETR* 57 (1982) 165–84. **Clines, David J. A.** "The Arguments of Job's Three Friends." In *Art and Meaning: Rhetoric in Biblical Literature.* Ed. David J. A. Clines, David M. Gunn, and Alan J. Hauser. JSOTSup 19. Sheffield: JSOT Press, 1982. 199–214 [= his *On the Way to the Postmodern: Old Testament Essays, 1967–1998.* JSOTSup 293. Sheffield: Sheffield Academic Press, 1998. 2:719–34]. ———. "The Wisdom Books." In *Creating the Old Testament: The Emergence of the Hebrew Bible.* Ed. Stephen Bigger. Oxford: Basil Blackwell, 1989. 269–91. **Cooper, Alan M.** "The Book of Job" [review article of Norman C. Habel, *The Book of Job*], *Theodolite. A Journal of Christian Thought and Practice* 7/7 (1986) 4–6. **Cooper, Burton Z.** "Why, God? A Tale of Two Sufferers" [Russell Baker, Job]. *TTod* 42 (1986) 423–24. **Cox, Dermot.** "A Rational Inquiry into God: Chapters 4–27 of the Book of Job." *Greg* 67 (1986) 621–58. **Craigie, P. C.** "Biblical Wisdom in the Modern World. III. Job." *Crux* 16 (1980) 7–10. **Crenshaw, James L.** "God's Answer to Job." *Conc* 169 (1983) 45–51. ———. "The Twofold Search: A Response to Luis Alonso Schökel." *Conc* 169 (1983) 63–69. **Croatto, S.** "El libro de Job como clave hermenéutica de la teología." *RBibArg* 43 (1981) 33–45. **Dell, Katharine J.** *The Book of Job as Sceptical Literature.* Diss. Oxford, 1988. **Deselaers, Paul, et al.** *Sehnsucht nach dem lebendigen*

Gott: Das Buch Ijob. Bibelauslegung für die Praxis 8. Stuttgart: Verlag Katholisches Bibelwerk, 1983. **Eaton, J. H.** *Job*. Old Testament Guides 5. Sheffield: JSOT Press, 1985. **Ebach, Jürgen.** "Hiob/Hiobbuch." *TRE* 15 (1986) 360–80. **Eisenberg, Josy, and Elie Wiesel.** *Job, ou Dieu dans la tempête*. Paris: Fayard, 1986 [= *Giobbe, o Dio nella tempesta*. Turin: Società editrice internazionale, 1989; *Job of God in storm en wind*. Hilversum: Gooi & Sticht, 1989]. **Festorazzi, Franco (ed.).** *Gli "scritti" dell'Antico Testamento*. Il messaggio della salvezza 5. Turin–Leumann: Editrice Elle Di Ci, 1985. 14–28, 52–182. **Feuer, Lewis S.** "The Book of Job: The Wisdom of Hebrew Stoicism." In *Biblical v. Secular Ethics*. Ed. R. Joseph Hoffmann and Gerald A. Larue. Buffalo, NY: Prometheus Books, 1988. 79–97. **Fiedler, Leslie.** "Job." In *Congregation: Contemporary Writers Read the Jewish Bible*. Ed. David Rosenberg. San Diego: Harcourt Brace Jovanovich, 1987. 331–45. **Fisch, Harold.** "Job: Tragedy Is Not Enough." In his *Poetry with a Purpose: Biblical Poetics and Interpretation*. Bloomington: Indiana University Press, 1988. 26–42. **Flender, Helmut.** *Ein Mensch ringt mit Gott: Sieben Abschnitte aus dem Buch Hiob*. Zur 46. Bibelwoche 1983/84. Arbeitsheft zur Bibelwoche. Gladbeck, Westfalen: Schriftmissions-Verlag, 1983. **Ford, L. S.** "The Whirlwind Addresses Job." *StLuke* 24 (1980–81) 217–21. **Freedman, David Noel.** "Is It Possible to Understand the Book of Job?" *BibRev* 4 (Apr. 1988) 26–33, 44. **Gaulmyn, M. de.** "Dialogue avec Job." *SémBib* 52 (1988) 1–14. **Genuyt, François.** "Job et la condition humaine." *SémBib* 56 (1989) 37–41. **Gerber, Israel J.** *Job on Trial: A Book for Our Times*. Gastonia, NC: E. P. Press, 1982. **Girard, René.** *La route antique des hommes pervers*. Paris: Bernard Grasser & Fasquelle, 1985 [= *De aloude weg der boosdoeners*. Kampen: Kok Agora, 1987; *Job, the Victim of His People*. London: Athlone, 1988; *Hiob–ein Weg aus der Gewalt*. Zurich: Benziger, 1990; *L'antica via degli empi*. Trans. C. Giardino. Saggi NS 14. Milan: Adelphi, 1994]. **Gmehling, Otto.** *Mein Bruder Hiob*. Hamburg: Saatkorn-Verlag, 1984. **Goguel, Anne-Marie.** "Livre de Job: une nouvelle lecture." *Réforme* (15 June 1985). **Goldingay, John.** *Understanding Poetry and Wisdom Today: Eight Bible Studies for Students and Young Adults Groups on Job, Psalms, Proverbs, Ecclesiastes, Song of Songs and Daniel*. Understanding the Bible Today. Swindon: Bible Society, 1987. **Gual, Carlos.** *Fray Luís de Leon: El libro de Job*. Madrid: Ediciones de La Idea, 1987. **Gutiérrez, Gustavo.** "But Why, Lord: On Job and the Suffering of the Innocent." *Other Side* 23 (1987) 18–23. ———. *Hablar de Dios desde el sufrimiento del inocente*. Lima: Centro de Estudios y Publicaciones, 1986 [= *On Job. God-Talk and the Suffering of the Innocent*. Trans. M. J. O'Connell. Maryknoll, NY: Orbis. 1987; *Von Gott sprechen in Unrecht und Leid*. Munich: Kaiser, 1988]. **Hermisson, Hans-Jürgen.** "Notizen zu Hiob." *ZTK* 86 (1989) 125–39 [= his *Studien zu Prophetie und Weisheit: Gesammelte Aufsätze*. FAT 23. Tübingen: J. C. B. Mohr, 1998. 286–99]. **Höffken, P.** "Hiob in exegetischer Sicht." *EvErz* 36 (1984) 509–26. **Hoffman, Yair.** "The Mutual Relation between the Prologue and the Dialogues in the Book of Job" [Heb.]. In *Proceedings of the Seventh World Congress of Jewish Studies*. Jerusalem: World Union of Jewish Studies, 1981. 53–61. ———. "The Relation between the Prologue and the Speech Cycles in Job: A Reconsideration." *VT* 31 (1981) 160–70. **Hunter, A. G.** "Could Not the Universe Have Come into Existence 200 Yards to the Left? A Thematic Study of Job." In *Text as Pretext: Essays in Honour of Robert Davidson*. Ed. Robert P. Carroll. JSOTSup 138. Sheffield: JSOT Press, 1982. 140–59. **Jaffin, David.** "Hiob, der Gottesknecht." In his *Warum brauchen wir das Alte Testament?* Bad Liebenzell: Verlag der Liebenzeller Mission, 1986. 42–61. **Job, John.** *Where Is My Father? Studies in the Book of Job*. London: Epworth, 1977 [= *Job Speaks to Us Today*. Atlanta: John Knox, 1980]. **Kidner, Derek.** *Wisdom to Live By: An Introduction to the Old Testament's Wisdom Books of Proverbs, Job and Ecclesiastes, with Some Notes on the Teachings of Israel's Neighbours and of the Old Testament Apocrypha*. Leicester: Inter-Varsity Press, 1985. **Klever, Peter.** *Es soll nicht dunkel bleiben: Gedanken im Leid–Hiob*. Lahr: Kaufmann, 1985. **Kreeft, Peter.** *Three Philosophies of Life: Ecclesiastes—Life as Vanity, Job—Life as Suffering, Song of Songs—Life as Love*. San Francisco: Ignatius Press, 1989. **Kutsch, Ernst.** "Hiob und seine Freunde. Zu Problemen der Rahmenerzählung des Hiobbuches." In *Zur Aktualität des Alten Testaments: Festschrift für Georg Sauer zum 65. Geburtstag*. Ed. Siegfried Kreuzer and

Kurt Lüthi. Frankfurt a.M.: Peter Lang, 1992. 73–83. **Lacocque, André.** "Job or the Impotence of Religion and Philosophy." *Semeia* 19 (1981) 33–52. **Lande, Lawrence M.** *A Man Called Job. Illustrated by Brad Jernigan.* Montreal: Jewish Educational Council of Greater Montreal, 1984. **Lévêque, Jean.** *Job, le livre et le message.* Cahiers Evangile 53. Paris: Cerf, 1985. **Loader, James A.** "Job—Answer or Enigma?" *OTEss* 2 (1984) 1–38. ———. "Job—antwoord of enigma." *Theologia evangelica* 16/2 (1983) 15–31. **Lockyer, Herbert.** *God's Book of Faith: Meditations from Job.* Nashville: Thomas Nelson, 1984. **Long, T. G.** "Job: Second Thoughts in the Land of Uz." *TTod* 45 (1988) 5–20 [= "Ijob: Quere Gedanken im Lande Uz." *TGegw* 32 (1989) 11–23]. **Luther, Martin.** "Vorrede zum Buch Hiob." In *Luthers Vorreden zur Bibel.* Ed. Heinrich Bornkamm. Frankfurt: Insel, 1983. 59–61. **Luyten, Jos.** "A New Commentary on the Book of Job." *Louvain Studies* 11 (1986) 60–69. **Maag, Victor.** *Hiob. Wandlung und Verarbeitung des Problems in Novelle, Dialogdichtung und Spätfassungen.* FRLANT 128. Göttingen: Vandenhoeck & Ruprecht, 1982. **Mack, Ulrich.** *O Herr! Psalmen und Weisheitsschriften.* Stuttgarter Bibelkurs. Stuttgart: Deutsche Bibelgesellschaft, 1988. **MacKenzie, R. A. F.** "The Cultural and Religious Background of the Book of Job." *Conc* 169 (1983) 3–7. **MacKenzie, Roderick, et al.** *Job en het zwijgen van God: een controversieel boek in de bijbel dat vragen oproept die in de theologie en de verkondiging amper aan bod komen.* Hilversum: Gooi en Sticht, 1983. **Marböck, J.** *Das Buch Hiob. Illustrationen von Hans Fronius. Einleitung von J. Marböck.* Klosterneuburg: Österreichisches Katholisches Bibelwerk, 1980 [12 charcoal sketches]. **Melamed, Ezra Zion.** *Hikre Mikra. Kitve David Yelin.* Kerekh 6. Jerusalem: R. Mas, 1983. **Michaud, Robert.** *La littérature de sagesse: histoire et théologie. 1. Proverbes et Job.* Paris: Cerf, 1984. **Miller, Ward S.** "The Structure and Meaning of Job." *ConcJ* 15 (1989) 103–20. **Mitchell, Christopher.** "Job and the Theology of the Cross." *ConcJ* 15 (1989) 156–80. **Mitchell, Stephen.** *The Book of Job* [spiritual formation theme]. *Tikkun* 1/1 (1986) 56–64. **Müller, Hans-Peter.** "Neue Aspekte der Anfragen Hiobs." In *Schöpfung und Befreiung: für Claus Westermann zum 80. Geburtstag.* Ed. Rainer Albertz, Friedemann W. Golka, and Jürgen Kegler. Stuttgart: Calwer Verlag, 1989. 178–88. **Müller, Petra Ritter.** "Gott antwortet Ijob: Eine Auslegung." *Entschluss* 53 (1988) 12–13. **Nash, Jesse.** "Images of Job." *RRel* 42 (1983) 28–33. **Nützel, Johannes M.** *Menschen vor Gott: Elija, Jeremia, Ijob.* Schriftenreihe zur Meditation 48. Munich: Kaffke, 1982. **O'Connor, Daniel J.** "The Hybris of Job." *ITQ* 55 (1989) 1–6, 125–41, 240–42.

Parsons, Gregory W. "The Structure and Purpose of the Book of Job." *BSac* 138 (1981) 139–57 [= *Sitting with Job: Selected Studies on the Book of Job.* Ed. Roy B. Zuck. Grand Rapids: Baker Book House, 1992. 17–34]. **Philip, George M.** *Lord from the Depths I Cry: A Study in the Book of Job.* Didasko series. Glasgow: Gray, 1986. **Plank, Karl A.** "Raging Wisdom: A Banner of Defiance Unfurled." *Judaism* 36 (1987) 323–30. **Poirot-Delpech, Bertrand.** "Job ou le grand remède de la haine unanime." *Le Monde* (29 March 1985) 18. **Radzinowicz, Mary Ann.** "How and Why the Literary Establishment Caught Up with the Bible: Instancing the Book of Job." *ChrLit* 39/1 (Autumn 1989) 77–89. **Rathert, Donna R., and Dennis Jones.** *The Book of Job for Children.* Arch Books. Concordia, 1988. **Renouvin, Bertrand, Philippe Cailleux, Julien Betbèze, Alain Flamand, and Patrice Le Roué.** "Les malheurs de Job: Un mythe biblique enfin rendu clair." *Royaliste* 426 (1–14 May 1985) 426–27. **Riebl, Maria.** *In Krise und Hoffnung: Eines Arbeitsheft zum Buch Ijob.* Gespräche zur Bibel 12. Klosterneuburg: Österreichisches Katholisches Bibelwerk, 1981. **Riley, William.** "The Book of Job and the Terrible Truth about God." *Scripture in Church* 18 (Dublin 1988) 322–26. **Rutler, George W.** *The Impatience of Job.* La Salle, IL: Sugden, 1982. **Šalabi, Maḥmūd.** *Hayāt Aiyūb.* Beirut: Dar al-Gil, 1980. **Seitz, Christopher R.** "Job: Full-Structure, Movement and Interpretation." *Int* 43 (1989) 5–17. **Sicre, J. L.** "El libro de Job (entrevista con su autor)." *RazF* 211 (1985) 621–29. **Silberman, Lou H.** "The Question of Job's Generation: She'elat doro shel "Iyob": Buber's Job." In *Judaic Perspectives on Ancient Israel.* Ed. Jacob Neusner, Baruch A. Levine, and Ernest S. Frerichs. Philadelphia: Fortress Press, 1987. 261–69. **Silbermann, Alphons.** "Soziologische Anmerkungen zum Buch Hiob." *ZRGG* 41 (1989) 1–11. **Smick,**

Elmer B. "Semeiological Interpretation of the Book of Job." *WTJ* 48 (1986) 135–49. **Smith, J. Alfred.** *Making Sense of Suffering: A Message to Job's Children. A Guide to Teaching and Preaching the Book of Job.* George Washington Williams Collection of Afro-American Studies. Elgin, IL: Progressive National Baptist Convention, Board of Education, 1988. **Smits, C.** *De wortel der zaak: 11 bijbellezingen over het boek Job.* Zwijndrecht: Van den Berg, 1981. **Snell, P.** "A Journey of Faith." *TBT* 20 (1982) 334–37. **Stadelmann, L.** "O livro de Jó; a propósito de um 'comentário bíblico latino-americano'." *PerspT* 15 (1983) 407–12. **Stedman, Ray C.** *Expository Studies in Job: Behind Suffering.* Waco: Word, 1981. **Thiele, Edwin, and Margaret Thiele.** *Job and the Devil.* Boise, ID: Pacific, 1988. **Unen, Chaim van.** *Job: dwarsligger of verbondgenoot? Een nieuwe kijk op een oud boek.* Kampen: Kok, 1987 [= *Op ooghoogte: Job en het establishment.* Delft: Eburon, 2003]. **Urbrock, William J.** "Job as Drama: Tragedy or Comedy?" *CurTM* 8 (1981) 35–40. **Vawter, Bruce.** *Job and Jonah: Questioning the Hidden God.* New York: Paulist Press, 1985. **Vermeylen, J.** *Job, ses amis et son Dieu. La légende de Job et ses relectures postexiliques.* Studia biblica 2. Leiden: E. J. Brill, 1981. **Vogels, Walter.** "Job a parlé correctement. Une approche structurale du livre de Job." *NRT* 102 (1980) 835–52. ———. *Reading and Preaching the Bible: A New Semiotic Approach.* Background Books 4. Wilmington, DE: Michael Glazier, 1986. 80–106. **Voser, Marty.** "Vom Umgang mit Hiob-Texten in der Gruppenarbeit." In *Hiob. Ökumenischer Arbeitskreis für Bibelarbeit.* Ed. Regina Berger-Lutz. Bibelarbeit in der Gemeinde 7. Basel: F. Reinhardt, 1989. 244–60. **Vries, S. de.** *Wegwijs in Job: voor bijbelstudie.* Hattem: Filippus, 1979. **Warner, Martin.** *Philosophical Finesse: Studies in the Art of Rational Persuasion.* Oxford: Clarendon Press, 1989. **Westermann, Claus.** "The Two Faces of Job." *Conc* 169 (1983) 15–22 [= *Job and the Silence of God.* Ed. Christian Duquoc and Casiano Floristán. Edinburgh: T. & T. Clark, 1983]. **Weyer, Christian.** *Hiobs-Botschaft.* Stuttgart: Radius-Verlag, 1983. **Wharton, James A.** "The Unanswerable Answer: An Interpretation of Job." In *Texts and Testaments: Critical Essays on the Bible and Early Church Fathers … in Honor of Stuart Dickson Currie.* Ed. W. Eugene March. San Antonio: Trinity University Press, 1980. 37–69. **Whedbee, J. William.** *The Bible and the Comic Vision.* Cambridge: Cambridge University Press, 1988. 242–45. **Whybray, R. N.** *Two Jewish Theologies: Job and Ecclesiastes.* Hull: University of Hull, 1980. **Williams, J. Tudno.** *Problem dioddefaint a Llyfr Job.* Caernarfon: Gwasg Pantycelyn, 1980. **Williams, James G.** "Job's Vision: The Dialectic of Person and Presence." *HAR* 8 (1984) 259–72 [= *Biblical and Other Essays in Honor of Sheldon H. Blank.* Ed. Reuben Ahroni]. **Williams, Ronald J.** "Current Trends in the Study of the Book of Job." In *Studies in the Book of Job.* Ed. Walter E. Aufrecht. SRSup 16. Waterloo, Ont.: Wilfrid Laurier University Press, 1985. 1–27. **Zenger, Erich.** "Ijob—ein Lebensbuch für Leidende und Mitleidende." *Lebendige Katachese* 5 (1983) 106–10.

1990s. Alexander, Jon. "Job Considered as a Conversion Account." *Spirituality Today* 42 (1990) 126–39. **Andersen, Francis I., and A. Dean Forbes.** *A Key-Word-in-Context Concordance to Psalms, Job, and Proverbs.* The Computer Bible 34. Wooster, OH: Biblical Research Associates, 1991. **André, G.** *Job.* Pour les jeunes croyants: Personnages bibliques. Valence: Bibles et publications chrétiennes, 1991. **Anon.** *Le livre de Job.* Graphè 6. Villeneuve-d'Ascq: Graphè, Centre de recherches Lectures de l'Ecriture, 1997. **ApRoberts, Ruth.** *The Biblical Web.* Ann Arbor: University of Michigan Press, 1994. **Astell, Ann W.** *Job, Boethius, and Epic Truth.* Ithaca: Cornell University Press, 1994. **Asurmendi, Jésus María.** *Job.* La Bible tout simplement. Paris: Atelier, 1999 [= **Asurmendi Ruiz, Jesús M.** *Job: experiencia del mal, experiencia de Dios.* Trans. José Pérez Escobar. Estella, Navarra: Verbo Divino, 2001]. **Atkinson, David.** *The Message of Job: Suffering and Grace.* The Bible Speaks Today. Leicester: Inter-Varsity Press, 1991. **Backhouse, Robert.** *C. H. Spurgeon's Commentary on the Bible.* London: Hodder & Stoughton, 1997. **Bakon, Shimon.** "God and Man on Trial." *JBQ* 21 (1993) 226–35. **Balchin, Jack.** *Sitting with Job: Reflections on the Man and the Book.* Oswestry, Salop.: Rhoswiel Books, 1998. **Balentine, Samuel E.** "'What are human beings, that you make so much of them?' Divine Disclosure from the Whirlwind: 'Look at Behemoth'." In *God in the Fray: A Tribute to Walter Brueggemann.* Ed. Tod Linafelt and Timothy K. Beal. Minneapolis: Fortress Press, 1998. 259–78. **Basser,**

Herbert W., and Barry Walfish. *Peyrush R. Mosheh Qimhi le-sefer 'Iyov.* South Florida Studies in the History of Judaism 64. Atlanta: Scholars Press, 1992. **Bechtel, Lyn M.** "A Feminist Approach to the Book of Job." In *A Feminist Companion to Wisdom Literature.* Ed. Athalya Brenner. The Feminist Companion to the Bible 9. Sheffield: Sheffield Academic Press, 1995. 222–51. **Becker, Hansjakob (ed.).** *Warum? Hiob interdisziplinär diskutiert.* Mainzer Universitätsgespräche Wintersemester 1997/98. Vorträge von Hansjakob Becker, Jürgen Ebach, Herbert Jochum, Georg Langenhorst, Józef Niewiadomski, Willi Oelmüller, and Wilhelm Pesch. Mainz: Studium Generale der Universität Mainz, 1998. **Beek, A. van de.** *Rechtvaardiger dan God: gedachten bij het boek Job.* Nijkerk: Callenbach, 1992. **Ben-Chorin, Schalom, and Michael Langer.** *Die Tränen des Hiob.* Bilder von Hans-Günther Kaufmann. Innsbruck: Tyrolia-Verlag, 1994. **Benfold, Gary.** *Why Lord? The Book of Job for Today.* Epsom: Day One, 1998. **Bernières, Louis de.** "The Impatience of Job." In *The Book of Job: Authorised King James Version.* Edinburgh: Canongate, 1998. **Beuken, Willem A. (ed.).** *The Book of Job.* BETL 114. Leuven: Leuven University Press, 1994. **Beuken, W. A. M.** "The Book of Job" [Colloquium biblicum lovaniense XLII (1993)]. *ETL* 69 (1993) 509–11. **Bezuidenhout, L. C.** "A Context to Frame the Book of Job." *OTEss* 9 (1996) 9–19. **Bjerkem-Hirtz, Emmanuelle.** *Ijob und Sprichwörter.* Stuttgart: Katholisches Bibelwerk, 1999. **Blumenthal, Fred.** "The Book of Job: A Prelude to Prophecy." *JBQ* 27 (1999) 222–30. **Boadt, Lawrence (ed.).** *The Book of Job: Why Do the Innocent Suffer?* Foreword by Alice Thomas Ellis. The Classic Bible Series. New York: St Martin's Press, 1997. **Bochinger, Erich.** *Wie kann Gott das zulassen? Geschichten von Hiob, Erfahrungen von heute. Mit Zeichnungen und Holzschnitte von Gerhard Grimm.* Reutlingen: Diakonie-Verlag, 1995 **Borchert, R.** "Ijobs Auseinandersetzung mit Gott." *Reformierte Kirchenzeitung* 138 (1997) 465–68. **Bovon, Francois.** *Les trois récits sur Job.* Geneva: Labor & Fides, 1996. **Brändle, Werner.** "Hiob—ein tragischer Held? Überlegungen zur Theodizeethematik der Hiobdichtung." *KuD* 39 (1993) 282–92. **Brenner, Athalya.** *A Feminist Companion to Wisdom Literature.* Feminist Companion to the Bible 9. Sheffield: Sheffield Academic Press, 1995. **Brown, William P.** "Introducing Job: A Journey of Transformation." *Int* 53 (1999) 228–38. ———. *Character in Crisis: A Fresh Approach to the Wisdom Literature of the Old Testament.* Grand Rapids: Wm. B. Eerdmans, 1996. 50–119. **Bühler, Christian.** "Hiob. Ein Zugang für die Sekundarstufe II." *EvErz* 48 (1996) 162–78. ———. *Die Bibel macht Schule: Biblische Texte im Unterricht mit Jugendlichen und Erwachsenen.* Wittingen: Erev-Rav, 2nd ed., 1998. **Caesar, Lael O.** "Job: Another New Thesis." *VT* 49 (1999) 435–47. **Cazier, Pierre.** *Le cri de Job. Approche biblique, mythologique et littéraire du problème de la souffrance du juste.* Collection «Etudes littéraires et linguistiques». Arras: Artois Presses Université, 1996. **Champy, Harry Doyle III.** *The Meaning of the Book of Job: A Literary Approach.* Diss. New Orleans Baptist Theological Seminary, 1995. **Chapalain, Claude.** "Cheminer avec le libre de Job." *SémBib* 89 (1998) 51–56. **Chauvin, Jacques.** *Job l'insoumis: Dieu n'est jamais celui qu'on croit.* Aubonne: Editions du Moulin, 1994. **Cheney, Michael.** *Dust, Wind and Agony. Character, Speech and Genre in Job.* Coniectanea biblica. Old Testament Series 36. Stockholm: Almqvist & Wik-sell, 1994. **Chieregatti, Arrigo.** *Giobbe: lettura spirituale.* Conversazioni bibliche. Bologna: Dehoniane, 1995. **Ciholas, Paul.** *Consider My Servant Job: Meditations on Life's Struggles and God's Faithfulness.* Peabody, MA: Hendrickson, 1998. **Ciobanu, Mircea.** *La capatul puterilor: însemnari pe Cartea lui Iov.* Bucharest: Vitruviu, 1997. **Clines, David J. A.** "Deconstructing the Book of Job." In *The Bible as Rhetoric: Studies in Biblical Persuasion and Credibility.* Ed. Martin Warner. Warwick Studies in Philosophy and Literature. London: Routledge, 1990. 65–80 [= his *What Does Eve Do to Help? and Other Readerly Questions to the Old Testament.* JSOTSup 94. Sheffield: JSOT Press, 1990. 106–23; *BibRev* 11/2 (April, 1995) 30–35, 43–44 (abbreviated)]. ———. "Job." In *The Oxford Companion to the Bible.* Ed. Bruce M. Metzger and Michael D. Coogan. New York: Oxford University Press, 1993. 368–70. ———. "Why Is There a Book of Job, and What Does It Do to You if You Read It?" In *The Book of Job.* Ed. W. A. M. Beuken. BETL 114. Leuven: Leuven University Press, 1994. 1–20 [= his *Interested Parties: The Ideology of Writers and Readers of the Hebrew Bible.* JSOTSup 205. Sheffield: JSOT

Press, 1995. 122–44]. **Clines, David J. A.** (ed.). *The Poetical Books.* Biblical Seminar 41. Sheffield: Sheffield Academic Press, 1997. **Cooper, Alan.** "The Sense of the Book of Job." *Prooftexts* 17 (1997) 227–44. **Cox, Dermot.** *Man's Anger and God's Silence: The Book of Job.* Slough: St Paul Publications, 1990. **Crenshaw, James L.** "Job," "Job as Drama," "Job the Silent or Job the Affirmer?" In his *Urgent Advice and Probing Questions: Collected Writings on Old Testament Wisdom.* Macon, GA: Mercer University Press, 1995. 426–48, 477–80, 449–54. ———. "The Search for Divine Presence: Job." In his *Old Testament Wisdom: An Introduction.* Louisville: Westminster John Knox Press, 1998. 89–115. **Croft, Joy Granite.** *Twentieth Century Perspective on the Book of Job.* Diss. Glasgow, 1992. **Dailey, Thomas F.** "Job as an Icon for Theology." *PerspRelSt* 23 (1996) 247–54. ———. "Seeing He Repents: Contemplative Consciousness and the Wisdom of Job." *AmBenRev* 46 (1995) 87–101. ———. "The Book of Job as Optimistic Wisdom." *Journal of Theta Alpha Kappa* 18/1 (1994) 3–16. ———. *The Repentant Job: A Ricoeurian Icon for Biblical Theology.* Lanham, MD: University Press of America, 1994. **Dailey, Thomas F., and Janet Yeager.** "Job's World: A Chaotic Conundrum." *Encounter* 56 (1995) 175–89. **Davidson, Robert.** *Sounding the Silence: Ideological Tensions within the Wisdom Literature of the Hebrew Bible.* The Hastie Lectures, 1997. Glasgow: Trinity St Mungo Press, 1999. **Dell, Katharine J.** *Shaking a Fist at God: Understanding Suffering through the Book of Job.* London: Fount, 1995. ———. *The Book of Job as Sceptical Literature.* BZAW 197. Berlin: de Gruyter, 1991. **Dennis, Trevor.** *Face to Face with God: Moses, Eluma and Job.* London: SPCK, 1999. **Dietrich, Luis José.** *O grito de Jó.* São Paulo: Pia Sociedade Filhas de São Paulo, 1996 [= *El grito de Job.* Trans. Teodoro Nieto. Mexico City: Ediciones Dabar, 2003]. **Duarte Castillo, Raúl.** "¿Qué pretendía el autor del libro de Job? Nuevo intento de respuesta." In *IV Simposio bíblico español (i Ibero-Americano).* Biblia y culturas 1. Ed. J. R. Ayaso Martínez, V. Collado Bertomeu, L. Ferre Cano, et al. Granada: Area de estudios hebreos, Universidad de Granada, 1993. 101–12. **Ebach, Jürgen.** "Hiob. Der 'Fall Hiob' und das 'Hiob-Problem' in der Bibel." *Musik und Kirche* 67 (1997) 276–80 [= "Der 'Fall Hiob' und das 'Hiobproblem'." In *Warum? Hiob interdisziplinär diskutiert.* Mainzer Universitätsgespräche Wintersemester 1997/98. Vorträge von Hansjakob Becker, Jürgen Ebach, Herbert Jochum, Georg Langenhorst, Józef Niewiadomski, Willi Oelmüller, and Wilhelm Pesch. Mainz: Studium Generale der Universität Mainz, 1998. 7–34]. ———. *Hiobs Post. Gesammelte Aufsätze zum Hiobbuch zu Themen biblischer Theologie und zur Methodik der Exegese.* Neukirchen–Vluyn: Neukirchener Verlag, 1995. ———. *Streiten mit Gott: Hiob.* 2 vols. Kleine biblische Bibliothek. Neukirchen–Vluyn: Neukirchener Verlag, 1995–96. **Edwards, Cliff.** "Trespassing a Monument: A Lacanian Visit to Uz" [Job and Oedipus]. *Religious Education* 85 (1990) 279–94. **Encarnación Varela, María.** "Ultimas preguntas sobre Job." In *IV Simposio bíblico español (i Ibero-Americano).* Biblia y Culturas 1. Ed. J. R. Ayaso Martínez. Granada: Area de estudios hebreos, Universidad de Granada, 1993. 189–94. **Farmer, Kathleen A.** "The Wisdom Books: Job, Proverbs, Ecclesiastes." In *The Hebrew Bible Today: An Introduction to Critical Issues.* Ed. Steven L. McKenzie and M. Patrick Graham. Louisville, KY: Westminster John Knox Press, 1998. 129–51. **Fleming, Daniel E.** "Job: The Tale of Patient Faith and the Book of God's Dilemma." *VT* 44 (1994) 468–82. **Fox-Düvell, Gisela, and Adelheid Bienmüller.** *Und Dunkelheit wird wie der Morgen sein: Bilder und Texte zu Ijob.* Munich: Don-Bosco-Verlag, 1994. **Freedman, David Noel.** "The Book of Job." In *The Hebrew Bible and Its Interpreters.* Ed. William Henry Propp, Baruch Halpern, and David Noel Freedman. Winona Lake, IN: Eisenbrauns, 1990. 26–33. **Fyall, Robert S.** *How God Treats His Friends* [cover title: *How Does God Treat His Friends?*]. Fearn: Christian Focus, 1995. **Garbini, Giovanni.** "Le ricchezze di Giobbe." In *Meilenstein: Festgabe für Herbert Donner zum 16. Februar 1995.* Ed. Manfred Weippert und Stefan Timm. Wiesbaden: Harrassowitz, 1995. 27–32. **Gariepy, Henry.** *Portraits of Perseverance: 100 Meditations from the Book of Job.* Wheaton, IL: Victor Books, 1991. **Gerlach, Heinz.** *Hiob lebt noch—Fragen suchen Antwort: Ein Gemeinde-Seminar.* Arolsen: Gerlach, 1993. **Gladson, Jerry A.** "Job." In *A Complete Literary Guide to the Bible.* Ed. Leland Ryken and Tremper Longman III. Grand Rapids: Zondervan, 1993. 230–43. **Goldstein, Clifford.** *Warum schweigst du,*

Gott? Hamburg: Saatkorn-Verlag, 1993. **Gowan, Donald E.** "Reading Job as a 'Wisdom Script'." *JSOT* 55 (1992) 85–96. **Greenberg, Moshe.** "Job." In his *Studies in the Bible and Jewish Thought.* Philadelphia: Jewish Publication Society, 1995. 335–57. ———. "Job." In *The Literary Guide to the Bible.* Ed. Robert Alter and Frank Kermode. Cambridge, MA: The Belknap Press of Harvard University Press, 1994. 283–304. **Greenstein, Edward L.** "In Job's Face/Facing Job." In *The Labour of Reading: Desire, Alienation, and Biblical Interpretation.* Ed. Fiona C. Black, Roland T. Boer, and Erin Runions. Semeia Studies. Atlanta: Society of Biblical Literature, 1999. 301–17. **Grill, Ingrid.** *Aber meine Augen werden ihn schauen … : Hiob.* 1. *Ein Versuch zum Themenbereich "Die Bibel als Grundlage des Glaubens" für die 11. Jahrgangsstufe.* 2. *Ein Lesebuch zur Wirkungsgeschichte der Hiobgestalt in Philosophie, Theologie und Kunst.* Arbeitshilfe für den evangelischen Religionsunterricht an Gymnasien: Themenfolge 97. Erlangen: Gymnasialpädagogische Materialstelle der Evangelisch-Lutherischen Kirche in Bayern, 1994. **Haar, Murray J.** "Job after Auschwitz." *Int* 53 (1999) 265–75. **Häussler, Manfred (ed.).** *Materialien Hiob—der Mensch im Leid: Sekundarstufe.* I. Stuttgart: Klett-Verlag für Wissen und Bildung, 1995. **Hartley, John E.** "From Lament to Oath: A Study of Progression in the Speeches of Job." In *The Book of Job.* Ed. W. A. M. Beuken. BETL 114. Leuven: Leuven University Press, 1994. 79–100. **Hoffman, Yair.** *A Blemished Perfection: The Book of Job in Context.* JSOTSup 213. Sheffield: Sheffield Academic Press, 1996 [= ספר איוב ורקעו: שלמות פגומה. Jerusalem: Bialik, 1995]. **Holbert, John C.** *Preaching Job.* St Louis: Chalice Press, 1999. **Holm-Nielsen, Svend.** "Is Job a Scapegoat?" In *In the Last Days: On Jewish and Christian Apocalyptic and Its Period.* Ed. Knud Jeppesen. Aarhus: Aarhus University Press, 1994. 128–35. **Honsey, Rudolph E.** *Job.* People's Bible. St Louis: Concordia Publishing House, 1992. **Hubble, Rosemary A.** *Conversation on the Dung Heap: Reflections on Job.* Collegeville, MN: Liturgical Press, 1998. **Illman, Karl-Johan.** "Job's Radicalism and God's Replies." In *Approaches to Ancient Judaism.* Vol. 9 ns. South Florida Studies in the History of Judaism 136. Atlanta: Scholars Press, 1996. 43–60. **Jagersma, H. (ed.).** *Job. Studies over en rondom een bijbelboek.* Kampen: Kok, 1990. **Jiménez Hernández, Emiliano.** *Job, crisol de la fe.* Biblioteca Mercaba: Colección Trípode. Baracaldo: Grafite, 1999. **Jobsen, Aarnoud.** "Job op het leesrooster." *Interpretatie* 6/1 (1998) 4–6. **Jochum, Herbert.** "Hiob und die Shoah." In *Warum? Hiob interdisziplinär diskutiert.* Mainzer Universitätsgespräche Wintersemester 1997/98. Vorträge von Hansjakob Becker, Jürgen Ebach, Herbert Jochum, Georg Langenhorst, Józef Niewiadomski, Willi Oelmüller, and Wilhelm Pesch. Mainz: Studium Generale der Universität Mainz, 1998. 101–20. **Kis, Antonija Zaradija.** *Knjiga o Jobu u hrvatskoglagoljskoj knjizevnosti.* Hrvatsko Filolosko Drustvo: Znanstvena biblioteka Hrvatskog Filoloskog Drustva 28. Zagreb: HFD, 1997. **Köhlmoos, Melanie.** *Das Auge Gottes: Textstrategie im Hiobbuch.* Forschungen zum Alten Testament 25. Tübingen: Mohr Siebeck, 1999. **Künzli, Arnold.** *Gotteskrise: Fragen zu Hiob: Lob der Agnostizismus.* Rowohlts Enzyklopädie 55596. Reinbek bei Hamburg: Rowohlt, 1998. **Lacocque, André.** "Job and Religion at its Best." *BibInt* 4 (1996) 131–53. **Lamb, Jonathan.** *The Rhetoric of Suffering: Reading the Book of Job in the Eighteenth Century.* Oxford: Clarendon Press, 1995. **Lawrie, Douglas G.** "The Dialectical Grammar of Job and Qohelcth: A Burkean Analysis." *Scriptura* 66 (1998) 217–34. **Leiter, Karin.** "Hiobsbotschaft oder Botschaft des Hiob." *TPQ* 143 (1995) 41–44. **Lévêque, J.** "L'enseignement des Sages (Job, Les Proverbes)." In *Les Psaumes et les autres écrits.* Ed. Joseph Auneau. Petite bibliothèque des sciences bibliques: Ancien Testament 5. Paris: Desclée, 1990. 89–143. ———. "Le thème du juste souffrant en Mésopotamie et la problématique du livre de Job." *Graphè* 6 (1997) 11–33. **Lévêque, Jean, et al.** *Le livre de Job* [extract from *Graphé, lectures de l'écriture* 6 (1997)]. Lille: Centre de recherches de l'Université Charles-de-Gaulle-Lille, 1997. **Louwerse, Bert.** *Mijn naam is Job: teksten naar aanleiding van het boek Job.* Velp: Bond van Vrije Evangelische Gemeenten in Nederland, 1998. **Luebering, Carol.** *A Retreat with Job and Julian of Norwich: Trusting That All Will Be Well.* Cincinnati: St Anthony Messenger Press, 1995. **Madanu, Francis.** *Why the Innocent Suffer: Job and Harischandra: Biblical and Puranic Expression.* Ramanthpur, Hyderabad: St John's

Regional Seminary, 1998. **Maier, Christl, and Silvia Schroer.** "Das Buch Ijob. Anfragen an das Buch vom leidenden Gerechten." In *Kompendium. Feministische Bibelauslegung.* Ed. Luise Schottroff and Marie-Theres Wacker. Gütersloh: Kaiser, 1998. 192–207 [= "What about Job? Questioning the Book of 'the Righteous Sufferer'." In *Wisdom and Psalms.* Ed. Athalya Brenner and Carole R. Fontaine. The Feminist Companion to the Bible. Second Series 2. Sheffield: Sheffield Academic Press, 1988. 175–204]. **Malter, Rudolf.** "Schöpfergott und Theodizee: Eine philosophische Meditation über den 73. Psalm und das Buch Hiob." In *Gott—das bleibende Geheimnis.* Ed. Peter Reifenberg. Würzburg: Echter Verlag, 1996. 68–88. **Marnewick, J. C., and A. P. B. Breytenbach.** "Die boek Job gelees vanuit 'n Ou-Testamentiese verbondsperspektief." *HervTS* 50 (1994) 923–35. **Martini, Carlo Maria.** *Avete perseverato con me nelle mie prove.* Milan: Centro Ambrosiano, Casale Monferrato, 1990 [= *Perseverance in Trials: Reflections on Job.* Trans. Matthew J. O'Connell. Collegeville, MN: Liturgical Press, 1992; *Wer in der Prüfung bei mir bleibt: Von Ijob zu Jesus.* Freiburg i.Br.: Herder, 1991; *Epreuve et persévérance: méditations sur le livre de Job.* Paris: Editions du Cerf, 1993]. **Mason, Mike.** *The Gospel according to Job.* Wheaton, IL: Crossway Books, 1994. **McCann, J. Clinton.** "Wisdom's Dilemma: The Book of Job, the Final Form of the Book of Psalms, and the Entire Bible." In *Wisdom, You Are My Sister. Studies in Honor of Roland E. Murphy, O. Carm., on the Occasion of His Eightieth Birthday.* Ed. Michael L. Barré. CBQMS 29. Washington, DC: Catholic Biblical Association of America, 1997. 18–30. **McKibben, Bill.** *The Comforting Whirlwind: God, Job, and the Scale of Creation.* Grand Rapids: W. B. Eerdmans, 1994. **Meier, Samuel A.** "Job and the Unanswered Question." *Prooftexts* 19 (1999) 265–76. **Mettinger, Tryggve N. D.** "The Enigma of Job: The Deconstruction of God in Intertextual Perspective." *JNSL* 23 (1997) 1–19. **Mies, Françoise.** "Est-il sage d'espérer en Dieu? L'énigme de Job." In *Toute la sagesse du monde: hommage à Maurice Gilbert, S.J., pour le 65e anniversaire de l'exégète et du recteur.* Ed. Françoise Mies. Le livre et le rouleau 7. Brussels: Lessius, 1999. 385–41. ———. "Le livre de Job: de l'excès du mal à l'altérité du mal?" *NRT* 121 (1999) 177–96. **Millard, M.** "Das Hiobbuch. Skizzen zur Interpretation eines Buches der Schriften." *WuD* 22 (1993) 27–37. **Myerson, George.** "The Book of Job." In his *The Argumentative Imagination: Wordsworth, Dryden, Religious Dialogues.* Manchester: Manchester University Press, 1992. **Neizvestny, Ernst.** *Kniga Iova.* Moscow: Izdatelstvo Kogelet, 1999. **Nemo, Philippe.** *Job et l'excès du mal.* Paris: B. Grasset, 1978 [= *Job and the Excess of Evil.* Trans. Michael Kigel. Pittsburgh: Duquesne University Press, 1998]. **Newsom, Carol A.** "Considering Job." *CRBS* 1 (1993) 87–118. ———. "Job and Ecclesiastes." In *Old Testament Interpretation, Past, Present and Future. Essays in Honour of Gene M. Tucker.* Ed. James Luther Mays, David L. Petersen, and Kent Harold Richards. Nashville: Abingdon Press, 1995. 177–94. ———. "Job and His Friends: A Conflict of Moral Imaginations." *Int* 53 (1999) 239–53. ———. "The Book of Job. Introduction, Commentary, and Reflections." In *The New Interpreter's Bible.* Ed. Leander Earl Keck. Nashville: Abingdon Press, 1996. 4:317–637. **Niccacci, A.** "The Meaning of the Book of Job." *Studium Biblicum Franciscanum Essays* 1 (1998) 1–6. **O'Connor, Donal J.** *Job, His Wife, His Friends and His God.* Maynooth Bicentenary Series. Blackrock, Co. Dublin: Columba Press, 1995. **Odell, Margaret S.** "History or Metaphor: Contributions to the Old Testament Theology in the Works of Leo G. Perdue." *RelSRev* 24 (1998) 241–45. **Oesch, Josef-M.** "Ijob—Ein Buch der Reichen." *ZTK* 121 (1999) 281–90. **Oorschot, Jürgen van.** "Gott in der Dunkelheit: Hiobgestalten und ihr Beitrag zu einer Grundfrage." *Zeitwende* 68 (1998) 6–42. **Oosthuizen, M. J.** "Divine Insecurity and Joban Heroism: A Reading of the Narrative Framework of Job." *OTEss* 4 (1991) 295–315. **Parsons, Greg W.** "Guidelines for Understanding and Proclaiming the Book of Job." *BSac* 151 (1994) 393–413. **Patterson, Ben.** *Waiting: Finding Hope When God Seems Silent.* Downers Grove, IL: InterVarsity Press, 1990. **Penchansky, David.** *The Betrayal of God: Ideological Conflict in Job.* Literary Currents in Biblical Interpretation 1. Louisville: Westminster/John Knox Press, 1990. **Perdue, Leo G.** *Wisdom in Revolt: Metaphorical Theology in the Book of Job.* JSOTSup 112. Bible and Literature Series 20. Sheffield: Almond Press, JSOT Press, 1991. **Perdue, Leo G., and Clark Gilpin (eds.).**

The Voice from the Whirlwind: Interpreting the Book of Job. Nashville: Abingdon Press, 1992. **Pesch, Wilhelm.** "Hiob: Trostbuch in der Begleitung Schwerkranker." In *Warum? Hiob interdisziplinär diskutiert. Mainzer Universitätsgespräche Wintersemester 1997/98.* Vorträge von Hansjakob Becker, Jürgen Ebach, Herbert Jochum, Georg Langenhorst, Józef Niewiadomski, Willi Oelmüller, and Wilhelm Pesch. Mainz: Studium Generale der Universität Mainz, 1998. 147–65. **Peterson, Eugene H.** *The Message: Job: Led by Suffering to the Heart of God.* Colorado Springs, CO: NavPress, 1996. **Pifano, P.** *La luce di Giobbe: tra teologia e dramma.* Treviso: Santi Quaranta, 1994. **Poma, Andrea.** *Avranno fine le parole vane? Una lettura del libro di Giobbe.* Dimensioni dello spirito 35. Cinisello Balsamo, Milan: San Paolo, 1998. **Potter, Harry.** "Rebel against the Light: Job or God?" *ExpT* 103 (1992) 198–201. **Quillo, Ronald.** "Naked Am I: Psychological Perspectives on the Unity of the Book of Job." *PerspRelSt* 18 (1991) 213–22.

 Rader, Dick, and Sue Rader. *A Road beyond Suffering: An Experimental Journey through the Book of Job.* Franklin, TN: Providence House, 1997. **Ralph, Margaret Nutting.** *Discovering Prophecy and Wisdom: The Books of Isaiah, Job, Proverbs, Psalms.* Discovering the Living Word 4. New York: Paulist Press, 1993. **Rhoades, R. E.** *Job: A Comparative Study of Job and Paul.* Gainesville, FL: Maranatha Publications, 1996. **Robertson, David.** "Job and Ecclesiastes." *Soundings* 73 (1990) 257–72. **Römer, Thomas.** *La sagesse dans l'Ancien Testament: Proverbes, Job, Qohéleth.* Cahiers bibliques 3. Aubonne: Editions du Moulin, 1991 [= *Les chemins de la sagesse: Proverbes, Job, Qoheleth.* Poliez-le-Grand: Moulin, 1999]. **Rouillard-Bonraisin, Hedwige.** "Le livre de Job et ses vrais-faux dialogues." In *La controverse religieuse et ses formes.* Ed. Alain Le Boulluec. Patrimoines: Religions du Livre. Paris: Editions du Cerf, 1995. **Rozik, E.** "'The Book of Job': A Dialogue between Cultures." In *Hellenic and Jewish Arts: Interaction, Tradition and Renewal.* Ed. Asher Ovadiah. Howard Gilman International Conferences 1. Tel Aviv: Ramot/Tel Aviv University, 1998. 369–84. **Ruiz, Jean-Pierre.** "Contexts in Conversation: First World and Third World Readings of Job." *JHisp/LatTh* 2 (1995) 5–29. **Safire, William.** *The First Dissident: The Book of Job in Today's Politics.* New York: Random House, 1992. **Schreiner, Susan Elizabeth.** *Where Shall Wisdom Be Found? Calvin's Exegesis of Job from Medieval and Modern Perspectives.* Chicago: University of Chicago Press, 1994. **Seng, Gunther.** *Das Buch Hiob, eine Einführung in die Heilsgeschichte.* Fellbach: AT-Verlag, 1994. **Shelton, Pauline.** "Making a Drama out of a Crisis? A Consideration of the Book of Job as a Drama." *JSOT* 83 (1999) 69–82. **Sigmund, Helga.** *Biblische Bildergeschichten* [illustrated by Gerhard Hauck]. Frankfurt a.M.: Bischoff, 1995. **Simian-Yofre, Horacio.** "Giobbe (libro di)." In *Dizionario di omiletica.* Ed. Manlio Sodi and Achille M. Triacca. Turin–Leumann: Edizioni Di Ci, 1998. 628–31. **Simundson, Daniel J.** "Job and His Ministers." *Word and World Suppl.* 1 (1992) [= *All Things New: Essays in Honor of Roy A. Harrisville.* Ed. Arland J. Hultgren, Donald H. Juel, and Jack Dean Kingsbury] 33–41. **Smith, Gary V.** "Is There a Place for Job's Wisdom in Old Testament Theology?" *TrinJ* 13 (1992) 3–20. **Smoke, Andrew B.** "A Survey of Wisdom Literature: Job, Ecclesiastes, Proverbs, Psalms." *AME Zion Quarterly Review* 108/4 (1996) 43–58. **Souzenelle, Annick de.** *Job sur le chemin de la lumière.* Spiritualités vivantes 168. Paris: Albin Michel, 1999. **Spek-Begeman, G. A. V. D.** *Job, het troostboek voor Israël. Een bijbelstudie.* The Hague: Boekencentrum, 1991. **Steinmann, Andrew E.** "The Structure and Message of the Book of Job." *VT* 46 (1996) 85–100. **Stek, John H.** "Job: An Introduction." *CalvTJ* 32 (1997) 443–58. **Strauss, Hans.** "Die 'Freunde' Hiobs—ein Kreis frommer Weiser im Hintergrund des Hiobbuches." *BN* 95 (1998) 71–78. **Susaimanickam, Jebamalai.** *Commitment to the Oppressed: A Dalit Reading of the Book of Job.* Diss. Gregorian, 1996. **Swados, Elizabeth.** "Job: He's a Clown." In *Out of the Garden: Women Writers on the Bible.* Ed. Christina Büchmann and Celina Spiegel. New York: Fawcett Columbine, 1994; London: Pandora, 1995. 204–20. **Tafferner, Andrea.** "Das Buch Ijob lesen." *Entschluss* 53 (1998) 8–9. **Tamez, Elsa.** "Ijob: 'Schrei' ich: Gewalt!, wird mir keine Antwort'." *Conc* 33 (1997) 632–39. **Theobald, Gerd.** *Hiobs Botschaft: Die Ablösung der metaphysischen durch die poetische Theodizee.* Gütersloh: Kaiser, 1993 [= *Hiobs Prozess und Gottes Gericht: Die poetische Theodizee des Welttheaters.* Diss. Heidelberg, 1991].

Tompkins, Iverna, and Judson Cornwall. *On the Ash Heap with No Answers.* Lake Mary, FL: Creation House, 1992 [= *Out of the Whirlwind.* Eastbourne: Kingsway, 1993]. **Tomson, Charles.** *Job the Bold.* Worthing: Churchman Publishing, 1990. **Trevi, Mario, and Amos Luzzatto.** *Il libro di Giobbe.* Milan: Feltrinelli, 1991. **Turoldo, David Maria.** *La parabola di Giobbe. L'inevitabile mia storia* ... Quaderni di ricerca 41. Cernusco sul Naviglio: CENS, 1992. **Varenne, Susan B., and John F. Thornton (eds.).** *The Book of Job, with a Preface by Cynthia Ozick.* New York: Vintage Books, 1998. **Vauthier, Geneviève (ed.).** *Une sagesse pour les nations: Proverbes, Qohélet, Cantique, Job, Jonas, Tobit, Daniel, Esther, Siracide.* Première lecture de l'Ancien Testament 4. Paris: OEIL, 1991. **Vogels, Walter.** *Job, l'homme qui a bien parlé de Dieu.* Lire la Bible 104. Paris: Editions du Cerf, 1995 [= *Giobbe: uomo che ha parlato bene di Dio.* Cinisello Balsamo: San Paolo, 2001]. **Wasserzug-Traeder, Gertrud.** *Bewährt durch Leiden: Ein Wort zu dem Buche Hiob.* Bad Teinach–Zavelstein: Schriftenmission Bibel- und Erholungsheim Haus Felsengrund, 1998. **West, Gerald.** "Hearing Job's Wife: Towards a Feminist Reading of Job." *OTEss* 4 (1991) 107–31. **Wiesel, Elie.** "Job." In *Peace, in Deed: Essays in Honor of Harry James Cargas.* Ed. Zev Gerber and Richard Libowitz. South Florida Studies in the History of Judaism 162. Atlanta: Scholars Press, 1998. 119–34. **Wilcox, John T.** *The Bitterness of Job: A Philosophical Reading.* Ann Arbor: University of Michigan Press, 1994. **Williams, James G.** "Job and the God of Victims." In *The Voice from the Whirlwind: Interpreting the Book of Job.* Ed. Leo G. Perdue and Clark Gilpin. Nashville: Abingdon Press, 1992. 208–31. ———. "On Job and Writing: Derrida, Girard, and the Remedy–Poison." *SJOT* 7 (1993) 32–50. **Wittenberg, G. H.** "Job the Farmer: The Judean *am-haretz* and the Wisdom Movement." *OTEss* 4 (1991) 151–70. **Wolde, Ellen van.** "A Text-Semantic Study of the Hebrew Bible, Illustrated with Noah and Job." *JBL* 113 (1994) 19–35. ———. *Meneer en mevrouw Job: Job in gesprek met zijn vrouw, zijn vrienden en God.* Baarn: Ten Have, 1991 [= *Mr and Mrs Job.* Trans. John Bowden. London: SCM Press, 1997]. **Wolfers, David.** "Job: A Universal Drama." *JBQ* 21 (1992–93) 13–23, 80–89. ———. "The Book of Job: Its True Significance." *JBQ* 24 (1996) 3–8. **Zuck, Roy B. (ed.).** *Sitting with Job: Selected Studies on the Book of Job.* Grand Rapids: Baker Book House, 1992. **Zuckerman, Bruce.** *Job the Silent: A Study in Historical Counterpoint.* New York: Oxford University Press, 1991.

2000s. Ahrens, Theodor. "Ijob und seine Berater. Zu den Bildern dieses Heftes." *RHS* 50 (2007) 300–305. **Allerton, John.** "The Koan of Job." *Faith and Freedom* 54 (2001) 46–57. **Anon.** *Das Weisheit des Alten Testaments mit Andachten von Frauen für Frauen: Das Buch Hiob, die Psalmen, die Sammlung der Sprüche, der Prediger Salomo, das Lied von der Liebe.* Asslar: Lydia-Verlag, 2001. **Ash, Christopher.** *Out of the Storm: Grappling with God in the Book of Job.* Leicester: Inter-Varsity Press, 2004. **Asurmendi Ruiz, Jesús M.** *Job: experiencia del mal, experiencia de Dios.* Trans. José Pérez Escobar. Estella, Navarra: Verbo Divino, 2001 [see Asurmendi, 1999]. **Auel, Hans-Helma.** "Hiob." *PastBl* 144 (2004) 823–27. **Balentine, Samuel E.** "Have You Considered My Servant Job?" *RevExp* 99 (2002) 495–501. **Basset, Lytta.** *Holy Anger: Jacob, Job, Jesus.* Grand Rapids: Eerdmans, 2007. **Bätz, Kurt, and Heinrich Schmidt.** *Von Gottes Hand gepackt: Der Prophet Jeremia, das Buch Hiob.* Biblisches Arbeitsbuch 8. Lahr: Kaufmann, 2007. **Beauchamp, Paul.** *Biblische Lebensbilder.* Stuttgart: Verlag Katholisches Bibelwerk, 2002. **Beck, Eleonore, and Fridolin Stier.** *Das Buch Ijob.* Katholisches Bibelwerk, 2004. **Bernières, Louis de.** "Book of Job." In *Revelations: Personal Responses to the Books of the Bible.* Introduction by Richard Holloway. Edinburgh: Canongate, 2005. **Berrigan, Daniel.** *Job: And Death No Dominion.* With art by Robert McGovern. Franklin, WI: Sheed & Ward, 2000. **Black, Hugh B., with Alison H. Black.** *Till I See You Clearly.* Greenock: New Dawn, 2002. **Branch, R. G.** "Space for Joy: Another Look at the Book of Job and Job Himself in the Light of Some Principles of Wisdom Literature." *JSem* 14 (2005) 384–412. **Brettler, Marc Zvi.** "Being but Dust and Ashes: Reading Job." In his *How to Read the Bible.* Philadelphia: Jewish Publication Society, 2005. **Buhre, Traugott.** *Traugott Buhre liest Das Buch Hiob.* Berlin: Argon-Verlag, 2007. **Campbell, Antony F.** "The Book of Job: Two Questions, One Answer." *AusBR* 51 (2003) 15–25. **Canepa-Anson, Robert Nicholas.**

The Book of Job, Narration and Knowledge: A Post "Wisdom Thesis" Reading. Diss. Birmingham, 2000. **Carreira das Neves, Joaquim.** "A actualidade da pergunta de Job." *Itin* 51,181/183 (2005) 363–70. **Chilongani, D. D.** *Reading the Book of Job with an African Eye: A Reinterpretation of the Book of Job from an African Traditional Religious Perspective, with Special Reference to the Wagogo of Central Tanzania.* Diss. Bristol, 2004. **Chirpaz, François.** *Job: la force d'espérance.* Paris: Editions du Cerf, 2001. **Cixous, Hélène.** "Stigmata, or Job the Dog." In her *Stigmata: Escaping Texts.* London: Routledge, 2005. **Claassens, Juliana M.** "A Dialogue of Voices: Job, Socrates and the Quest for Understanding." *OTEss* 19 (2006) 1106–23. **Cook, Stephen L., Corrine L. Patton, and James W. Watts (eds.).** *The Whirlwind: Essays on Job, Hermeneutics and Theology in Memory of Jane Morse.* JSOTSup 336. London: Sheffield Academic Press, 2001. **Cooper, Alan M.** "The Suffering Servant and Job: A View from the Sixteenth Century." In *"As those who are taught": The Interpretation of Isaiah from the LXX to the SBL.* Ed. Claire Mathews McGinnis and Patricia K. Tull. SBL Symposium Series 27. Atlanta: Society of Biblical Literature, 2006. 189–200. **Crenshaw, James L.** "Some Reflections on the Book of Job." *RevExp* 99 (2002) 589–95. **David, Pascal.** *Job ou l'authentique théodicée.* Paris: Bayard, 2004. **Dell, Katharine.** "Job: Sceptics, Philosophers and Tragedians." In *Das Buch Hiob und seine Interpretationen: Beiträge zum Hiob-Symposium auf dem Monte Verità vom 14.–19. August 2005.* Ed. Thomas Krüger, Manfred Oeming, Konrad Schmid, and Christoph Uehlinger. ATANT 88. Zurich: Theologische Verlag Zürich, 2007. 1–19. **Desnitskogo, A. S.** "Kniga Iova." In *Pritchi.* Moscow: Izdatelstvo Rossiskogo, 2000. **Dumbrell, William J.** "The Purpose of the Book of Job." In *The Way of Wisdom: Essays in Honor of Bruce K. Waltke.* Ed. J. I. Packer and Sven Soderlund. Grand Rapids: Zondervan, 2000. 91–105. **Edwards, Cliff.** "Greatest of All the People in the East. Venturing East of Uz." *RevExp* 99 (2002) 529–40. **Eskenazi, Tamara Cohn.** "Song of Songs as an 'Answer' to Clines's Book of Job." In *Reading from Right to Left: Essays on the Hebrew Bible in Honour of David J. A. Clines.* Ed. J. Cheryl Exum and H. G. M. Williamson. JSOTSup 373. London: Sheffield Academic Press, 2003. 128–40. **Estes, Daniel J.** *Handbook on the Wisdom Books and Psalms: Job, Psalms, Proverbs, Ecclesiastes, Song of Songs.* Grand Rapids: Baker Academic, 2005. **Forster, Roger.** *Suffering and the Love of God: The Book of Job.* London: Push Publishing, 2006. **Fox, Michael V.** "Job the Pious." *ZAW* 117 (2005) 351–66. **Geeraerts, Dirk.** "Caught in a Web of Irony: Job and His Embarrassed God." In *Job 28: Cognition in Context.* Ed. Ellen van Wolde. Biblical Interpretation Series 64. Leiden: Brill, 2003. 37–55. **Gilbert, Maurice.** *Les cinq livres des sages: Proverbes, Job, Qohélet, Ben Sira, Sagesse.* Lire la Bible 129. Paris: Cerf, 2003. **Godwin, Gail.** "Turning to Job." *RevExp* 99 (2002) 505–27. **Green, Douglas J.** "The Good, the Bad and the Better: Psalm 23 and Job." In *The Whirlwind: Essays on Job, Hermeneutics and Theology in Memory of Jane Morse.* Ed. Stephen L. Cook, Corrine L. Patton, and James W. Watts. JSOTSup 336. Sheffield: Sheffield Academic Press, 2001. 69–83. **Grimm, Markus.** "'Dein Auftritt, Ijob!' oder: wie Ijob aus seinem Buch spaziert und sich auf die Bühne stellt." In *Vom Ausdruck zum Inhalt, vom Inhalt zum Ausdruck. Beiträge zur Exegese und Wirkungsgeschichte alttestamentlicher Texte. Festschrift der Schülerinnen und Schüler für Theodor Seidl zum 60. Geburtstag.* Ed. Maria Häusl and David Volgger. ATSAT 75. St Ottilien: Eos Verlag, 2005. 211–23. **Grzesikowski, Stefan, and Stefanie Müller.** *Das Buch Hiob in der hebräischen Bibel und der Umgang mit Hiob und dem Hiobproblem in den drei grossen Offenbarungsreligionen Judentum, Christentum und Islam.* Munich: Grin Verlag, 2008. **Haas, Siegfried, and Julia Dieter.** *Warum gerade ich? Die Hiob-Geschichte: Arbeitsmaterialien für die Sekundarstufen.* Mülheim an der Ruhr: Verlag an der Ruhr, 2004. **Hecke, Pierre van.** "From Conversation about God to Conversation with God: The Case of Job." In *Theology and Conversation: Towards a Relational Theology.* Ed. J. Haers and P. De Mey. BETL 172. Leuven: Leuven University Press; Uitgeverij Peeters, 2003. 115–24. **Heckner, William J., and Willie Young.** "Extending the Circle of Study: Job and Scriptural Reasoning in the Undergraduate Setting." *Journal of Scriptural Reasoning* 4/1 (2004). **Heuser, August.** "Hiob—eine Auseinandersetzung im Bild." In *Wohin du auch gehst. Festschrift für Franz Josef Stendebach OMI.* Ed. Thomas Klosterkamp and Norbert Lohfink. Stuttgart: Verlag

Katholisches Bibelwerk, 2005. 43–47. **Hohensee, Wolfgang.** *Zum Beispiel: Hiob: mit Menschen der Bibel Lebenskrisen überwinden.* Gütersloh: Quell, 2002. **Hostetter, Edwin C.** "The Antitheodicy of a Man in the Land of Uz." *ExpT* 116 (2005) 336–37. **Janatuinen, Mailis.** *Der Herr hat's genommen. Das Buch Hiob verstehen. Ein Buch für Sie, wenn Sie genau das verloren haben, was Ihr Leben ausgemacht hat.* Trans. Anne-Kathrin Braun. Holzgerlingen: Hänssler, 2007. **Janzen, J. Gerald.** "Job and the Lord of the East Wind." *HBT* 26,2 (2004) 2–47. **Kaiser, Gerhard.** "Wo ist der Vater? Hiob sucht den Vatergott." *GeistL* 80 (2007) 412–22. **Kaiser, Gerhard, and Hans-Peter Mathys.** *Das Buch Hiob. Dichtung als Theologie.* Biblisch-theologische Studien 81. Neukirchen–Vluyn: Neukirchener Verlag, 2006. **Kalas, J. Ellsworth.** *When Suffering Comes: A Study of Job.* Nashville: Abingdon, 2001. **Keller, Catherine.** "'Recesses of the deep': Job's Comi-Cosmic Epiphany." In her *Face of the Deep: A Theology of Becoming.* London: Routledge, 2003. 124–40. **Kepnes, Steven.** "Job and Post-Holocaust Theodicy." In *Strange Fire: Reading the Bible after the Holocaust.* Ed. Tod Linafelt. The Biblical Seminar 71. Sheffield: Sheffield Academic Press, 2000. 252–66. ———. "Rereading Job as Textual Theodicy." In *Suffering Religion.* Ed. Robert Gibbs and Elliot R. Wolfson. London: Routledge, 2002. 36–55. **Kermani, Navid.** *Der Schrecken Gottes: Attar, Hiob und die metaphysische Revolte; mit sechs Kalligraphien von Karl Schlamminger.* Munich: Beck, 2005. **Klinger, Bernhard.** *Im und durch das Leiden lernen. Das Buch Ijob als Drama.* BBB 155. Hamburg: Philo, 2007. **Knauf, Ernst Axel, and Philippe Guillaume.** "Job." In *Introduction à l'Ancien Testament.* Ed. Thomas Römer and Jean-Daniel Macchi. Le Monde de la Bible 49. Geneva: Labor & Fides, 2004. 500–10. **Koch, Hermann.** *Aus der Tiefe rufe ich: Hiob, der Mann, der an Gott festhielt.* Leinfelden–Echterdingen: Verlag Junge Gemeinde, 2003. **Krabill, Merrill, and Eric Massanari.** "Answer Me: Reflections on the Book of Job." *Mennonite Life* 55 (2000). **Krüger, Thomas, Manfred Oeming, Konrad Schmid, and Christoph Uehlinger (eds.).** *Das Buch Hiob und seine Interpretationen: Beiträge zum Hiob-Symposium auf dem Monte Verità vom 14.–19. August 2005.* ATANT 88. Zurich: Theologische Verlag Zürich, 2007. **Kühlwein, Klaus.** *Schöpfung ohne Sinn? Gott und das Leid.* Düsseldorf: Patmos, 2003. **Leicht, Robert.** "Hiob–oder: Das Hohelied der absurden Treue (Hiob 1ff)." In *Huren, Helden, Heilige: Biblische Porträts aus prominenter Feder.* Ed. Stephan Dorgerloh, Jörg Göpfert, and Wolfgang Thierse. Gütersloh: Gütersloher Verlagshaus. 2004. 94–97. **Lienhard, Simon.** *Gott im Leid: das Buch Hiob und seine Impuls für die heutige Seelsorge.* Diss. Freiburg im Breisgau Universität, 2004. **Limbeck, Meinrad.** *Alles Leid ist gottlos: Ijobs Hoffnung contra Jesu Todesschrei.* Stuttgart: Verlag Katholisches Bibelwerk, 2005. **Linden, Nico ter.** *Es wird erzählt. 5. Die Psalmen, Hiob, das Hohelied und andere Schriften.* Gütersloh: Gütersloher Verlagshaus, 2004. **Lipe, David. L. (ed.).** *When We Hurt: Tragedy and Triumph in Job.* Henderson, TN: Freed–Hardeman University, 2003. **Lohse, Timm H.** *Hiob: die glaubwürdige Geschichte eines aufrichtigen Menschen, nach der biblischen Erzählung getextet.* Neukirchen–Vluyn: Neukirchener Verlag, 2005. **Maceina, Antanas.** *Drama Iova perevod s litovskogo T. F. Korneevoi-Matseinene.* Issledovaniia po istorii russkoi mysli. St Petersburg: Izdvo Aleteiia, 2000. **Madsen, Peter.** *Historien om Job tegnet og fortalt.* Copenhagen: Danske Bibelselskab, 2000. **Magdalene, F. Rachel.** "Job's Wife as Hero: A Feminist-Forensic Reading of the Book of Job." *BibInt* 14 (2006) 209–58. **Marconi, Gilberto, and Cristina Termini (eds.).** *I volti di Giobbe: percorsi interdisciplinari.* Bologna: EDB, 2002. **Margalioth, Rachel.** איוב־כמו שהוא. *The Original Job: Discussion and Proofs of Its Antiquity and Singular Authorship.* Jerusalem: Mass, 2007. **Martens, Elmer A.** "The Purpose of the Book of Job." In *The Way of Wisdom: Essays in Honor of Bruce K. Waltke.* Ed. J. I. Packer and Sven Soderlund. Grand Rapids: Zondervan, 2000. **Mayer, Yvette.** *Ein kostbarer Fund: Begegnungen mit Hiob* [photographs by Jürgen Richter]. Leipzig: Thomas-Verlag, 2001. **McKane, William.** "The Theology of the Book of Job and Chapter 28 in Particular." In *Gott und Mensch im Dialog: Festschrift für Otto Kaiser zum 80. Geburtstag.* Ed. Markus Witte. BZAW 345. Berlin: Walter de Gruyter, 2004. 2:711–22. **Meyer, Ockert.** *God se antwoord is 'n vraag: oor God, lyding en die lewe in die lig van die boek Job.* Wellington, South Africa: Lux Verbi, 2005. **Mink, Paul-Gerhard.** *Hiob—ein Mann im*

Schmelztiegel Gottes. Hirzenhain: Maranatha-Mission, 2003. **Mukenge, André Kabasele.** "Une lecture populaire de la figure de Job au Congo." *Bulletin for Old Testament Studies in Africa* 16 (2004) 2–6. **Newsom, Carol A.** "The Book of Job as Polyphonic Text." *JSOT* 97 (2002) 87–108. ———. *The Book of Job: A Contest of Moral Imaginations.* Oxford: Oxford University Press, 2003. **Nicole, Emile.** "La théologie des amis de Job." *Théologie évangélique* 4,1 (2005) 3–17. **Oeming, Manfred.** "Leidige Tröster seid ihr alle (Hiob 16, 2). Das Hiobbuch als provokativer poimenischer Traktat." In *Auf dem Weg zu einer seelsorglichen Kirche. Theologische Bausteine Christian Möller zum 60. Geburtstag.* Ed. Manfred Josuttis, Heinz Schmidt, and Stefan Scholpp. Göttingen: Vandenhoeck & Ruprecht, 2000. 211–22. **O'Sullivan, Maurice J.** *The Books of Job.* Newcastle: Cambridge Scholars Publishing, 2007. **Pereira, Américo.** "O crisol da bondade. Do ser, para aquém do bem e do mal (breve comentário ao "Livro de Job")." *Itin* 49,177 (2003) 499–536. **Perrin, Louis.** "Une lecture du livre de Job." *SémBib* 114 (2004) 3–19; 115 (2004) 29–40. **Philip, George M.** *Faith in the Dark: Daily Bible Readings from Job.* Edinburgh: Rutherford House, 2001. **Rammler, Stephan.** "'Hiob von heute.' Genese und Gestaltung von Mobilität: sozialwissenschaftliche Überlegungen zu Theorie und Praxis des modernen Verkehr." In *Verkehrsgenese: Entstehung von Verkehr sowie Potenziale und Grenzen der Gestaltung einer nachhaltigen Mobilität.* Studien zur Mobilitäts- und Verkehrsforschung 5. Mannheim: MetaGIS Infosysteme, 2004. 71–90. **Ravasi, Gianfranco.** *Hiob: der Mensch im Leid.* Munich: Verlag Neue Stadt, 2005. **Reiss, Moshe.** "The Fall and Rise of Job the Dissenter." *JBQ* 33 (2005) 257–66. **Rödszus-Hecker, Marita.** "Hiob in Karlsruhe." In *Kleine Transzendenzen: Festschrift für Hermann Timm zum 65. Geburtstag.* Ed. Klaas Huizing. Münster: Lit, 2003. 229–45. **Rohr, Richard.** *Job and the Mystery of Suffering: Spiritual Reflections.* Leominster: Gracewing, 1996 [= *Hiobs Botschaft: Vom Geheimnis des Leidens.* Munich: Claudius, 2000]. **Samuel, James R.** "Job: A Perfect Man in an Imperfect World." *AME Zion Quarterly Review* 116 (2004) 11–16. **Sasson, Victor.** "In Defence of Job." *UF* 32 (2000) 465–74. **Schmid, Konrad.** "Das Hiobproblem und der Hiobprolog." In *Hiobs Weg. Stationen von Menschen im Leid.* Ed. Manfred Oeming and Konrad Schmid. BThSt 45. Neukirchen-Vluyn: Neukirchener Verlag. 2001. 9–34. **Schreiner, Stefan.** "Das Leid des Gerechten: das Buch Hiob in jüdischer Auslegung." In *Hiob: mit Beiträgen aus Judentum, Christentum, Islam, Literatur, Kunst.* Ed. Klara Butting and Gerard Minnaard. Wittingen: Erev-Rav, 2003. 84–89. **Schroer, Silvia.** "A Feminist Reading of the Book of Job." *TDig* 53 (2006) 239–42 [= "Das Buch Hiob feministisch lesen?" *BK* 50 (2004) 73–77]. **Schultheiss, Andreas.** "Wenn Hiob berührt worden ware ..." In *Zeichen und Gesten: Heilpädagogik als Kulturthema.* Ed. Heinrich Greving. Giessen: Psychosozial-Verlag, 2004. 165–281. **Schwienhorst-Schönberger, Ludger.** "Die Bücher der Weisheit. Das Buch Ijob." In *Einleitung in das Alte Testament.* Ed. Erich Zenger. 5th ed. Stuttgart: Kohlhammer, 2004. 335–47. ———. "Ijob: Vier Modelle der Interpretation." In *Das Buch Ijob: Gesamtdeutungen—Einzeltexte—zentrale Themen.* Ed. Theodor Seidl and Stephanie Ernst. Österreichische biblische Studien 31. Frankfurt: Peter Lang, 2007. 21–37. ———. *Ein Weg durch das Leid: Das Buch Ijob.* Freiburg: Herder, 2007. **Seidl, Theodor.** "'Gedicht von Anfang bis zu Ende' (Herder). Zur Einführung." In *Das Buch Ijob: Gesamtdeutungen—Einzeltexte—zentrale Themen.* Ed. Theodor Seidl and Stephanie Ernst. Österreichische biblische Studien 31. Frankfurt: Peter Lang, 2007. 9–18. **Seidl, Theodor, and Stephanie Ernst (eds.).** *Das Buch Ijob: Gesamtdeutungen— Einzeltexte—zentrale Themen.* Österreichische biblische Studien 31. Frankfurt: Peter Lang, 2007. **Shchedrovitski, D.** *Besedy o Knige Iova.* Moscow: Oklik, 2005. **Sitaramayya, K. B.** *The Marvel and the Mystery of Pain: A New Interpretation of the Book of Job.* Bangalore: M. C. C. Publications, 2001. **Smith, Percy Rawle.** *The Dragon Which Gave Power unto the Beast, with an Analysis of the Book of Job.* Winnipeg: Distant Speck, 2004. **Snoek, J.** *Antwoorden op het lijden. Een bijdrage aan de discussie over contextueel bijbellezen: Job 4–5 in het licht van opvattingen van Nicaraguaanse pinkstergelovigen.* Gorinchem: Narratio, 2000. **Sorge, Bob.** *Pain, Perplexity and Promotion.* Greenwood: Oasis House, 2001 [= *Du bist der Herr, der mein Haupt erhebt: eine prophetische Auslegung des Buches Hiob.* Solingen: Bernard, 2002; *Van beproeving tot heerlijkheid: een* *profetische uitleg van het boek Job.* [Ommen]: Kingdom Ministries Publishing, 2005]. **Stedman, Ray C.** *Let God Be God: Life-changing Truths from the Book of Job.* Ed. James D. Denney. Grand Rapids: Discovery House, 2007. **Susaimanickam, J.** "An Indian Problem of Evil: The Caste System. A Dalit Reading of the Book of Job." In *Indian Interpretation of the Bible: Festschrift in Honour of Prof. Dr Joseph Pathrapankal.* Ed. Augustine Thottakara. Bangalore: Dharmaram Publications, 2000. 181–200. **Syring, Wolf-Dieter.** *Hiob und sein Anwalt: Die Prosatexte des Hiobbuches und ihre Rolle in seiner Redaktions- und Rezeptionsgeschichte.* BZAW 336. Berlin: de Gruyter, 2004. **Tausky, Robert.** *Hiob: ein Mann im Lande Utz und seine Wege durch die Welt.* Würzburg: Königshausen & Neumann, 2004. **Ticciati, Susannah.** "Does Job Fear God for Naught?" *ModTh* 21 (2005) 353–66. **Tshikendwa Matadi, Ghislain.** *Suffering, Belief, Hope: The Wisdom of Job for an AIDS-stricken Africa.* Trans. Joseph P. Newman with Robert E. Czerny. Nairobi: Paulines Publications Africa, 2007. ———. "De l'epreuve à la sagesse. Une lecture du livre de Job dans le contexte afric-ain." *Telema* 123,4 (2005) 7–24. **Veijola, Timo.** "Abraham und Hiob. Das literarische und theologische Verhältnis von Gen 22 und der Hiob-Novelle." In his *Offenbarung und Anfechtung. Hermeneutisch-theologische Studien zum Alten Testament.* Ed. Walter Dietrich and Marko Marttila. Biblisch-theologische Studien 89. Neukirchen–Vluyn: Neukirchener Verlag, 2007. 134–57. **Vincent, Jean Marcel.** "Edouard Reuss, traducteur et interprète du Livre de Job. À l'occasion du bicentenaire de la naissance de l'exégète strasbour-geois." *RHPR* 85 (2005) 337–64. **Volgger, David.** "Das Buch Ijob als skeptische oder seelsorgliche Literatur? Oder: Das Buch Ijob und die wahre Gottesfurcht." In *Das Buch Ijob: Gesamtdeutungen—Einzeltexte—zentrale Themen.* Ed. Theodor Seidl and Stephanie Ernst. Österreichische biblische Studien 31. Frankfurt: Peter Lang, 2007. 39–55. **Watts, James W.** "The Unreliable Narrator of Job." In *The Whirlwind: Essays on Job, Hermeneutics and Theology in Memory of Jane Morse.* Ed. Stephen L. Cook, Corrine L. Patton, and James W. Watts. JSOT Supplement 336. Sheffield: Sheffield Academic Press, 2001. 168–80. **Weil, Gabriele.** *Der Fall Hiob im Zeitalter des Wassermanns.* Frankfurt a.M.: Cornelia-Goethe-Literaturverlag, 2003. **Weinreb, Friedrich.** *Die Freunden Hiobs. Eine Deutung des Buches Hiob nach jüdischer Überlieferung.* Zurich: Verlag der Friedrich-Weinreb-Stiftung, 2006. **Wierenga, Lambert.** *"Job": het leed, het vuil en de laster: de prozasecties van "Job" gelezen als routeplanner voor het boek "Job."* Kampen: Kok, 2004. **Williams, Peter.** *From Despair to Hope: Insights into the Book of Job.* Epsom: Day One, 2002. **Williamson, Robert, Jr.** "Reading Job from the Margins: Dialogical Exegesis and Theological Education." *SBL Forum* [cited June 2008, http://sbl-site.org/Article.aspx?ArticleID=777]. **Wilson, Leslie S.** *The Book of Job: Judaism in the 2nd Century BCE. An Intertextual Reading.* Lanham, MD: University Press of America, 2006. **Wolde, Ellen van.** "Questions about a World without Justice." *Conc* 40/4 (2004) 7–8. **Zeller, Dankwart Paul.** *Abschied von Hiob. Ein ausgefallenes Wiedersehen in der Galerie Kneipe.* Berlin: Teetz, 2006. **Zhang, Ying.** *Divine Justice and Divine Providence in Tension: A Dual Rhetoric in the Book of Job.* Diss. Chinese University of Hong Kong, 2007.

Index to Works on the Book as a Whole

Baumgärtel 1933
Baumgartner 1931
Beauchamp 2002
Bechtel 1995
Beck 2004
Becker 1998
Beek 1992
Beet 1922
Bellett 1909
Ben Meïr 1930
Ben-Chorin 1988, 1994
Benfold 1998
Bennett 1971
Bergant 1982, 1988
Berger-Lutz 1989
Bernières 1998, 2005
Berrigan 2000
Beuken 1993, 1994
Bezuidenhout 1987, 1996
Bickell 1882
Bigot 1925
Billheimer 1984
Bishop 1973
Bizjak 1989
Bjerkem-Hirtz 1999
Black 2002
Blackwood 1959
Blake, B. 1911
Blake, W. 1825, 1927
Bloch 1964
Bloem 1986
Bloom 1988
Blumenthal 1999
Boadt 1997
Bochinger 1995
Bode 1914
Bonnard 1964, 1973
Bonora 1978
Borchert 1997
Borrhaus 1564
Bos 1988
Böttcher 1863
Bovon 1996
Branch 2005
Brandenburg 1969
Brändle 1993
Brandon 1961
Breakstone 1964
Brenner 1981, 1995
Brettler 2005
Brink 1815
Brodsky 1986
Brook 1967
Brown, C. R. 1908
Brown, W. P. 1996, 1999
Brunner 1938
Bruston 1928
Buckey 1981
Budde 1876
Bugati 1586
Bühler 1996, 1998
Buhre 2007
Burr 1881
Caesar 1999
Calcar 1934
Callachor 1973
Camhy 1973
Campbell 2003
Canepa-Anson 2000
Carreira das Neves 2003
Carroll 1976
Carstensen 1963, 1966
Casalis 1982
Catmull 1960
Cazier 1996
Ceuppens 1932

Chambers 1923
Champy 1995
Chapalain 1998
Chauvin 1994
Cheney 1994
Cherchevsky 1970
Chesterton 1907
Cheyne 1887, 1901
Chieregatti 1995
Chilongani 2004
Chirpaz 2001
Ciholas 1998
Ciobanu 1997
Cixous 2005
Claassens 2006
Clark 1685
Clarke 1947
Claudel 1946
Clines 1982, 1989, 1990, 1993,
    1994, 1997
Cobern 1913
Cocagnac 1956
Conder 1898
Cook, A. 1968
Cook, S. L. 2001
Cooke 1899
Cooper, A. M. 1986, 1997, 2006
Cooper, B. Z. 1986
Copeland 1917
Cornely 1907
Coutts 1907
Cox 1978, 1974, 1986, 1990
Craigie 1980
Cranfield 1943
Croatto 1981
Croft 1992
Crook 1962
Cruveilhier 1931
Dailey 1994, 1995, 1996
Dalzell 1922
Daniélou 1955, 1957
Darby 1857
David 2004
Davidson, A. B. 1910
Davidson, R. 1999
Davies 1890, 1907
Davis 1933
Dearlove 1976
Dell 1988, 1991, 1995, 2007
Demante 1879
Dennis 1999
Deselaers 1983
Desnitskogo 2000
Devine 1921
Dietrich 1996
Dobson 1974
Dodd 1925
Drucker 1935
Duarte Castillo 1993
Duesberg 1938, 1966
Duhm 1894
Dumbrell 2000
Eaton 1985
Ebach 1986, 1995, 1998
Edelkoort 1946
Edwards 1990, 2002
Eerdmans 1939
Ehlinger 1971
Eichler 1744
Eisenberg 1986
Encarnación Varela 1993
Epp 1967
Eskenazi 2003
Estes 2005
Ewing, W. 1844
Ewing, W. B. 1976

Farley 1920
Farmer 1998
Feinberg 1934
Ferrin 1935
Festorazzi 1985
Feuer 1988
Fichtner 1950
Fiedler 1987
Fisch 1988
Fleming 1994
Flender 1983
Flügel 1947
Flügge 1947
Fohrer 1959, 1963
Foote 1900
Ford 1980
Forster 2006
Fox 2005
Fox-Düvell 1994
Francisco 1971
Freedman 1988, 1990
Frost 1977
Froude 1853
Fyall 1995
Garbini 1995
Gariepy 1991
Gärtner 1909
Gaulmyn 1988
Geeraerts 2003
Gelderen 1931
Gemüsch 1958
Genung 1939
Genuyt 1989
Gerber 1982
Gerlach 1993
Gibbs 1967
Gilbert 2003
Ginsberg 1956
Girard 1988
Gladson 1993
Glatzer 1966
Glazner 1978
Gleiss 1845
Gmehling 1984
Godet 1875, 1950
Godwin 2002
Goguel 1985
Goldingay 1987
Goldsmith 1963
Goldstein 1993
Good 1973
Goodheart 1961
Gordis 1949, 1955, 1956, 1964,
    1965
Gowan 1992
Granelli 1792
Gray 1968
Green, D. J. 2001
Green, W. H. 1873
Greenberg 1994, 1995
Greenstein 1999
Grey 1744
Grill 1994
Grimm 2005
Gros Louis 1974
Grzesikowski 2008
Gutiérrez 1986, 1987
Haag 1972
Haar 1999
Haas 2004
Hackmann 1930
Hardt 1728
Harper 1908
Hartley 1994
Häussler 1995
Hawthorne 1944

Hecke 2003
Heckner 2004
Hempel 1961
Hengstenberg 1856, 1869, 1973
Hermisson 1989
Heuser 2005
Hevesi 1914
Hiller 1907
Hirsch 1969
Hodges 1750
Höffken 1984
Hoffman 1981, 1996
Hohensee 2002
Holbert 1999
Holm-Nielsen 1994
Holmgren 1969
Hone 1960
Honsey 1992
Horne 1898
Hostetter 2005
Howard 1972
Hubbard 1919
Hubble 1998
Huffman 1914
Hulbert 1853
Humbert 1955. 1958
Hunter 1982
Illman 1996
Inch 1979
Irwin 1933, 1963
Jaffin 1986
Jagersma 1990
Janatuinen 2007
Janzen 2004
Jaspers 1962
Jepsen 1963
Jiménez Hernández 1999
Job 1980
Jobsen 1998
Jochum 1998
Johnson 1971
Johnstone 1962
Jones 1966
Jordan 1928
Joubert 1741
Jung 1954
Junker 1948
Kaakebeen 1835
Kahn 1975
Kaiser 2007
Kalas 2001
Kaminka 1945
Kapelrud 1976
Karary 1972
Keener 1897
Keller 2003
Kellett 1939
Kelly 1877, 1919
Kent, C. F. 1911
Kent, H. H. 1968
Kepnes 2000, 2002
Kermani 2005
Kidner 1985
King. 1968
Kis 1997
Klever 1985
Kline 1963
Klinger 2007
Klostermann 1900
Knauf 2004
Knieschke 1925
Knight 1956
Knobel 1835
Knott 1910, 1911
Köberle 1905

Koch, H. 2003
Koch, J. 1743, 1747
Köhlmoos 1999
Krabill 2000
Kreeft 1989
Krieger 1930
Krinetski 1965
Kroeze 1978
Krüger 2007
Kuhl 1959
Kühlwein 2003
Kuhn 1978
Kunz 1958
Künzli 1998
Kurzweil 1969
Kusenberg 1969
Kutsch 1986
Lacocque 1975, 1981, 1996
Lamb 1995
Lande 1946, 1954, 1984
Larcher 1965
Latch 1889
Laurin 1972
Lawrie 1998
Layman of the Church 1875
Le Roux de Lincy 1841
Leicht 2004
Leigh 1657
Leiter 19959
Leon 1622
Levenson 1972
Lévêque 1970, 1971, 1985, 1990,
    1997
Levine 1936
Ley 1896, 1900
Lichtenstein 1978
Lienhard 2004
Limbeck 2005
Lincy 1841
Lindblom 1940
Linden 2004
Lipe 2003
Lipiński 1968
Lippert 1945
Loader 1983, 1984
Lockyer 1984
Lohse 2005
Long 1988
Louwerse 1998
Lovelock 1957
Luebering 1995
Lusseau 1959
Luther 1983
Lutz 1561
Luz Ojeda 1964
Maag 1982
MacDonald 1936
Maceina 2000
MacFadyen 1917
Mack 1988
MacKenzie 1979, 1983
Madanu 1998
Madsen 2000
Magdalene 2006
Maier 1998
Maillot 1970, 1979
Malter 1996
Mandl 1892
Marböck 1980
Marconi 2002
Margalioth 2007
Marmet 1641
Marnewick 1994
Marshall 1905
Martens 2000

Martin 1914
Martini 1990
Mason 1994
Matadi 2005
Matheney 1971
Mayer 2001
McCann 1997
McKall 1971
McKane 2004
McKeating 1971
McKechnie 1925
McKibben 1994
Meier 1999
Meinhold 1892
Melamed 1983
Mendoza de la Mora 1971
Mettinger 1997
Meunier-Palusson 1868
Meyer 2005
Michaud 1984
Michel 1968
Mies 1999
Miles 1977
Millard 1993
Miller 1989
Mink 2003
Mirandolle 1930
Miskotte 1936
Mitchell, C. 1989
Mitchell, S. 1986
Möller 1955
Morgan 1934, 1961
Mukenge 2004
Müller, H. 1959
Müller, H.-P. 1970, 1978, 1989
Müller, P. R. 1988
Murphy 1961
Myerson 1992
Nash 1983
Naylor 1971
Nebel 1903
Neizvestny 1999
Nelis 1968
Nemo 1998
Newsom 1993, 1995, 1996, 1999,
    2002, 2003
Niccacci 1998
Nicole 2005
Nola 1971
Nützel 1982
Obbink 1935
O'Connor, Daniel J. 1989
O'Connor, Donal J. 1995
Odell 1998
Oeming 2000
Oesch 1999
Oorschot 1987, 1998
Oosthuizen 1991
Orelli 1976
O'Sullivan 2007
Oxinden 1651
Parisi 1843
Parsons 1981, 1994
Pasquale Marinelli 1846
Paterson 1961
Patrick 1979
Patterson 1990
Paulsen 1947
Penchansky 1990
Penn-Lewis 1902
Perdue 1991, 1992
Pereira 2003
Perrin 2004
Pesch 1998
Peterson 1996

Petit de Montempuys 1734
Pfeiffer 1915
Philip, G. M. 1986, 2001
Philips, T. W. 1937
Pifano 1994
Pladra 1914
Plank 1987
Platt 1962
Poirot-Delpech 1985
Poix 1768
Polzin 1977
Poma 1998
Pope 1973
Popma 1957
Portor 1913
Potter 1992
Preiss 1889
Proskauer 1937
Pury 1955
Quiller-Couch 1920
Quillo 1991
Quintens 1969
Rader 1997
Radzinowicz 1989
Raebiger 1860
Ralph 1993
Rammler 2004
Rathert 1988
Ravasi 2005
Reid 1973
Reiss 2008
Renouvin 1985
Retief 1957
Reuss 1869, 1878
Rexroth 1966
Rhoades 1996
Richards 1974
Richter 1958, 1959
Ridderbos 1937
Riebl 1981
Riley 1988
Robertson 1973, 1977, 1990
Robinson, H. W. 1916
Robinson, T. H. 1954
Rödszus-Hecker 2003
Roehrs 1954
Rohr 2000
Rolla 1968
Rolle 1510
Römer 1991
Rongy 1933
Rosseeuw Saint-Hilaire 1863
Rouillard-Bonraisin 1995
Rowley 1963
Royds 1911
Rozik 1998
Rubenstein 1969, 1971
Ruckman 1978
Ruiz 1995
Rutherford 1881
Rutler 1982
Ryckmans 1928
Safire 1992
Šalabi 1980
Samuel, J. B. 1954
Samuel, J. R. 2004
Santeul 1661
Sasson 2000
Scafella 1979
Schaper 1993
Schapiro 1972
Schmid 2001
Schmitz 1870
Schofield 1958
Schreiber 1974

Schreiner, S. 2003
Schreiner, S. E. 1994
Schrempf 1948
Schröder 1948, 1966
Schultheiss 2004
Schwienhorst-Schönberger 2004, 2007
Segal 1941
Seidl 2007
Seinecke 1863
Seitz, C. R. 1989
Seitz, O. 1931
Sellin 1991, 1931
Seng 1994
Serpilius 1710
Sewell 1968
Shapiro 1972
Shchedrovitski 2005
Shelton 1999
Sicre 1985
Sigmund 1995
Silberman 1987
Silbermann 1989
Simian-Yofre 1998
Simon 1931
Simson 1861
Simundson 1992
Singer 1963
Sitaramayya 2001
Skehan 1967
Slater 1941
Smeets 1978
Smick 1986
Smith, G. V. 1992
Smith, J. A. 1988
Smith, J. M. P. 1923, 1930
Smith, P. R. 2004
Smith, R. L. 1971
Smits 1981
Smoke 1996
Snaith 1968
Snell 1982
Snoek 2000
Sorge 2001
Souzenelle 1999
Spadafora 1951
Spalding 1940
Spek-Begeman 1991
Sperka 1979
Stadelmann 1983
Stange 1955
Stedman 1981, 2007
Steele 1944
Steinberg 1932
Steinmann, A. E. 1996
Steinmann, J. 1946, 1969
Stek 1997
Stewart, I. 1943
Stewart, J. 1959
Still 1978
Stockhammer 1963, 1973
Strata 1714
Straubinger 1945
Strauss, H. 1998
Strauss, J. D. 1976
Strolz 1967
Studer 1954
Sullivan 1954
Susaimanickam 1996, 2000
Swados 1995
Syring 2004
Tafferner 1998
Tamez 1997
Tausky 2004
Terrien 1958

Theobald 1993
Thiele 1988
Thrändorf 1911
Ticciati 2005
Tompkins 1992
Tomson 1990
Torczyner 1920
Tournay 1956
Treves 1955
Trevi 1991
Tsevat 1966
Tshikendwa Matadi 2007
Tur-Sinai 1941, 1957
Turoldo 1992
Ulanov 1958
Unen 1987
Urbrock 1981
Usmiana 1970
Uythage 1664
Varenne 1998
Vauthier 1991
Vawter 1985
Veijola 2007
Vermeylen 1986
Vischer 1961
Vogels 1980, 1986, 1995
Volgger 2007
Voser 1989
Vries 1980
Ward 1958
Warner 1989
Wasserzug-Traeder 1998
Watts 2001
Weil 2003
Weill 1947
Weimer 1974
Weinreb 2006
Welch 1953
Wemyss 1839
Wendt 1954
West 1991
Westermann 1956, 1983
Wevers 1961
Weyer 1983
Wharton 1980
Whedbee 1977, 1988
White 1939
Whybray 1980
Wielenga 1959
Wierenga 2004
Wiesel 1998
Wilbur 1894
Wilcox 1994
Wild 1574
Willi-Plein 1979
Williams, J. G. 1971, 1984, 1992, 1993
Williams, P. 2002
Williams, R. J. 1985
Williamson 2008
Wilson, L. S. 2006
Wilson, G. L. R. 1938
Wittenberg 1991
Wolde 1991, 1994, 2004
Wolfers 1993, 1996
Wood 1966
Wright 1886
Würtemberg 1930
Yates 1971
Zhang 2007
Zimmermann 1979
Zorell 1930
Zuck 1992
Zuckerman 1976, 1991

4. PHILOLOGY, TEXT CRITICISM

Adini, U. "A Biblical Hapax Legomenon in Modern Hebrew." *HS* 20–21 (1979–80) 12–16. **Althann, Robert.** "Reflections on the Text of the Book of Job." In *Sôfer mahîr: Essays in Honour of Adrian Schenker.* Ed. Yohanan A. P. Goldman, Arie van der Kooij, and Richard D. Weis. VTSup 110. Leiden: Brill, 2006. 7–14. ———. *Studies in Northwest Semitic.* BibOr 45. Rome: Editrice Pontificio Istituto Biblico, 1997. **Anon.** *Jobus hebraice, ad optimas editiones accuratissime exscriptus.* Berlin: G. Eichler, 1864. **Aufrecht, W. E.** "Aramaic Studies and the Book of Job." In *Studies in the Book of Job.* Ed. W. E. Aufrecht. SRSup 16. Waterloo: Wilfrid Laurier University Press, 1985. 54–66. **Baer, S.** ‏ספר איוב‎. *Liber Iobi. Textum masoreticum collatis praestantibus codicibus instauravit atque ex fontibus masorae illustravit.* Leipzig: Tauchnitz, 1875. **Banks, William A.** *Old Testament Parsing Guide: Job–Malachi.* Chicago: Moody Press, 1990. **Barr, J.** "Hebrew Orthography and the Book of Job." *JSS* 30 (1985) 1–33. ———. "Philology and Exegesis. Some General Remarks, with Illustrations from Job." In *Questions disputées d'Ancien Testament. Méthode et théologie.* Ed. C. Brekelmans. BETL 33. Leuven: Leuven University Press, 1989. 39–61. ———. "Hebrew Orthography and the Book of Job" [reply to D. N. Freedman, *EI* 9 (1969) 35–44]. *JSS* 30 (1985) 1–33. **Barton, George A.** "Some Text-Critical Notes on Job." *JBL* 42 (1923) 29–32. **Beer, Georg.** *Der Text des Buches Hiob.* 2 vols. Marburg: N. G. Elwert, 1895–97. ———. "Textkritische Studien zum Buche Hiob." *ZAW* 16 (1886) 297–314; 17 (1897) 97–122; 18 (1898) 257–86. **Bertrand, Daniel A.** "Le bestiaire de Job. Notes sur les versions grecques et latines." In *Le Livre de Job chez les Pères.* Cahiers de Biblia patristica 5. Strasbourg: Centre d'Analyse et de Documentation Patristiques, 1996. 215–58. **Bickell, Gustavus.** *Carmina Veteris Testamenti metrice. Notas criticas et dissertationem de re metrica Hebraeorum adjecit* [Job, Psalms, Proverbs, Song of Solomon, Lamentations, with poems contained in other books]. Innsbruck: Libraria Academica Wagneriana, 1882. 151–87. ———. "Kritische Bearbeitung des Jobdialogs." *WZKM* 6 (1892) 136–47, 241–57, 327–34; 7 (1893) 1–20, 153–68; 8 (1894) 121. **Blommerde, Anton C. M.** *Northwest Semitic Grammar and Job.* Rome: Pontifical Biblical Institute, 1969. **Boadt, L.** "A Re-Examination of the Third-Yodh Suffix in Job." *UF* 7 (1975) 59–72. **Bobzin, Hartmut.** *Die "Tempora" im Hiobdialog.* Diss. Marburg, 1974. **Brockington, L. H.** *The Hebrew Text of the Old Testament: The Readings Adopted by the Translators of the New English Bible.* London: Oxford University Press, 1973. **Brongers, H. A.** "Miscellanea exegetica" [incl. notes on Job]. In *Übersetzung und Deutung: Studien zum Alten Testament und seiner Umwelt Alexander Reinard Hulst gewidmet von Freunden und Kollegen.* Nijkerk: F. Callenbach, 1977. 30–47 (42–46). **Buber, Martin.** "Zur Verdeutschung des Buches Ijob (Hiob)." In his *Werke.* II. *Schriften zur Bibel.* Munich: Kösel, 1964. 2:1170–74. **Byington, S. T.** "Hebrew Marginalia." *JBL* 60 (1941) 279–88. ———. "Hebrew Marginalia II: Job 28." *JBL* 61 (1942) 205–7. ———. "Hebrew Marginalia III." *JBL* 64 (1945) 339–55. ———. "Some Bits of Hebrew. IV. Texts in Job." *ExpT* 57 (1945–46) 110–11. **Clarke, E. C.** "Marginal Notes on Driver–Gray's Job (I.C.C.)." *ExpT* 42 (1930–31) 92–93. ———. "Reflections on Some Obscure Hebrew Words in the Biblical Job in the Light of XI Q Tg Job." In *Studies in Philology in Honour of Ronald James Williams: A Festschrift.* Ed. Gerald E. Kadish and Geoffrey E. Freeman. SSEA 3. Toronto: Benben Publications, 1982. 17–30. **Clodius, Johann Christian.** *Theoria et praxis linguae arabicae, i.e. grammatica arabica.* II. *Du usu linguae arabicae in libri Jobi seorsim.* Leipzig: Gross, 1729. 68–230. **Compston, H. F. B.** "The Accentuation of *wayyomar* in Job." *JTS* 13 (1912) 426–27. **Craigie, Peter C.** "Job and Ugaritic Studies." In *Studies in the Book of Job.* Ed. W. E. Aufrecht. SRSup 16. Waterloo, Ont.: Wilfrid Laurier University Press, 1985. 28–35.

Dahan, Gilbert. "Les éditions des commentaires bibliques de saint Thomas d'Aquin: leur apport à la connaissance du texte de la Bible au XIIIe siècle." *RSPT* 89 (2005) 9–15. **Dahood, M.** "Chiasmus in Job: A Text-Critical and Philological Criterion." In *A Light unto My Path: Old Testament Studies in Honor of Jacob M. Myers.* Ed. H. N. Bream et al. Philadelphia: Temple University Press, 1974. 119–30. ———. "Northwest Semitic Philology and Job." In

The Bible in Current Catholic Thought. Gruenthaner Memorial Volume. Ed. J. L. McKenzie. St Mary's Theological Studies 1. New York: Herder & Herder, 1962. 55–74. ———. "Some Northwest-Semitic Words in Job." *Bib* 38 (1957) 306–20. ———. "Some Rare Parallel Word Pairs in Job and Ugaritic." In *The Word in the World: Essays in Honor of Frederick L. Moriarty.* Ed. Richard J. Clifford and George W. MacRae. Cambridge, MA: Weston College Press, 1973. 19–34. **DeCaen, Vincent.** "Moveable Nun and Intrusive Nun. The Nature and Distribution of Verbal Nunation in Joel and Job." *JNWSL* 29 (2003) 121–32. **Díez Macho, Alejandro.** "Un manuscrito protobabilónico de los libros poéticos de la Biblia." *EstBib* 18 (1959) 323–56. ———. "Un manuscrito hebreo protomasoretico y nueva teoria acerca de los llamados Mss. Ben Naftali." *EstBib* 15 (1956) 187–222. **Díez Macho, Alejandro, and Angeles Navarro Peiró (eds.).** *Biblia babilónica: fragmentos de Salmos, Job y Proverbios (ms. 508 A del Seminario Teológico Judío de Nueva York).* Consejo Superior de Investigaciones Científicas Textos y Estudios "Cardenal Cisneros" 42. Madrid: Consejo Superior de Investigaciones Científicas, Instituto de Filología, Departamento de Filología Biblica y de Oriente Antiguo, 1987. **Driver, G. R.** "Problems in Job." *AJSL* 52 (1935–36) 160–70. ———. "Problems in Job and Psalms Reconsidered." *JTS* 40 (1939) 391–94. ———. "Problems in the Hebrew Text of Job." In *Wisdom in Israel and in the Ancient Near East, Presented to Professor Harold Henry Rowley.* Ed. M. Noth and D. Winton Thomas. VTSup 3. Leiden: E. J. Brill, 1955. 72–93. ———. "Studies in the Vocabulary of the Old Testament. VIII." *JTS* 36 (1935) 293–301. **Ehrlich, A. B.** *Randglossen zur hebräischen Bibel. VI. Psalmen, Sprüche, und Hiob.* Leipzig: J. C. Hinrichs, 1918 [repr. Hildesheim: Georg Olms, 1968]. 180–344. **Eitan, I.** "Biblical Studies. 4. Notes on Job." *HUCA* 14 (1939) 9–13. **Foster, F. H.** "Is the Book of Job a Translation from an Arabic Original?" *AJSL* 49 (1932–33) 21–45. **Freedman, D. N.** "Orthographical Peculiarities in the Book of Job." *EI* 9 [= W. F. Albright Volume] (1969) 35–44.

Gold, Sally L. "Targum or Translation. New Light on the Character of Qumran Job (11Q10) from a Synoptic Approach." *Journal for the Aramaic Bible* 3 (2001) 101–20. **Gosling, F. A.** *The Syntax of Hebrew Poetry: An Examination of the Use of Tense in Poetry with Particular Reference to the Book of Job 3:1–42:6.* Diss. Saint Andrews, 1992. **Grabbe, Lester L.** *Comparative Philology and the Text of Job: A Study in Methodology.* SBLDS 34. Chico, CA: Scholars Press, 1977. **Graetz, H.** "Lehrinhalt der 'Weisheit' in den biblischen Büchern." *MGWJ* 35 (1886) 289–99, 402–10, 544–49 (pp. 402–10, 544–49 often cited as "Register der corrumpierten Stellen in Hiob und Vorschläge zur Verbesserung"). **Gray, G. B.** "Critical Notes on the Text of Job." *AJSL* 35 (1919–20) 95–102. **Greef, J.** "'n Beoordeling van pogings vanuit Ugaries, Aramees en Arabies om sekere cruces interpretum in die boek Job op te los." *NedGTT* 23 (1982) 6–17. **Greenstein, Edward L.** "Features of Language in the Poetry of Job." In *Das Buch Hiob und seine Interpretationen: Beiträge zum Hiob-Symposium auf dem Monte Verità vom 14.–19. August 2005.* Ed. Thomas Krüger, Manfred Oeming, Konrad Schmid, and Christoph Uehlinger. ATANT 88. Zurich: Theologische Verlag Zürich, 2007. 81–96. **Grimme, H.** "Metrisch-kritische Emendationen zum Buche Hiob." *TQ* 80 (1898) 295–304, 421–32; 81 (1899) 112–18, 259–77. **Guillaume, A.** *Hebrew and Arabic Lexicography: A Comparative Study.* Leiden: E. J. Brill, 1965. ———. *Studies in the Book of Job, with a New Translation.* ALUOSSup 2. Leiden: E. J. Brill, 1968. ———. "The Arabic Background of the Book of Job." In *Promise and Fulfilment: Essays Presented to Professor S. H. Hooke.* Ed. F. F. Bruce. Edinburgh: T. & T. Clark, 1963. 106–27. ———. "The First Book to Come out of Arabia." *Islamic Studies* 3 (1964) 152–66. **Herz, N.** "Some Difficult Passages in Job." *ZAW* 20 (1900) 160–63. **Hoffmann, Georg.** "Ergänzungen und Berichtigungen zu Hiob." *ZAW* 49 (1931) 141–45, 270–73. **Houtsma, M. T.** *Textkritische Studien zum Alten Testament. I. Das Buch Hiob.* Leiden: Brill, 1925. **Jeffrey, J.** "The Massoretic Text and the Septuagint Compared, with Special Reference to the Book of Job." *ExpT* 36 (1924–25) 70–73. **Jongeling, Bastiaan.** "L'expression *my ytn* dans l'Ancien Testament." *VT* 24 (1974) 32–40. **Joüon, P.** "Notes de lexicographie hébraïque." *Bib* 18 (1937) 205–6. ———. "Notes philologiques sur le texte hébreu de Job." *Bib* 11 (1930) 322–24. **Kaltner, John.** *The Use of Arabic in Biblical Hebrew Lexicography: The Book of Job in Context.* Washington, DC:

Catholic Biblical Association of America, 1996. **Kassan, Shalom.** *Hapax Legomena in the Book of Job.* Diss. Chicago, 1931. **Kennicott, Benjamin.** *Remarks on Select Passages in the Old Testament.* Oxford: Prince & Cooke, 1787. 151–72. **King, Edward G.** "Some Notes on the Text of Job." *JTS* 15 (1914) 74–81. **Kis, A. Zaradija.** "Particularités des traductions de l'Ancien Testament dans le glagolisme croate (Job 38–39)." In *The Interpretation of the Bible: The International Symposium in Slovenia.* Ed. Jože Krašovec. JSOTSup 289. Sheffield: Sheffield Academic Press, 1998. 1015–29. **Kromayer, Johann Abraham.** *Filia matri obstetricans, hoc est: De usu linguæ arabicæ in addiscenda ebræa, & explicanda Scriptura S. libelli duo: quorum prior usum illum, præceptis perspicuis & exemplis selectis, in genere tradit; posterior seorsim in libro Jobi … hæc ita applicat … ut supplementum omnium commentariorum im Jobum, hic libellus esse possit, & linguæ arabicæ ignaris quoque inserviat.* Frankfurt and Leipzig, 1707. **Kutsch, Ernst.** "Die Textgliederung im hebräischen Ijobbuch sowie in 4QTgJob und in 11QTgJob." *BZ* 27 (1983) 221–28. **Lipiński, E.** "Notes lexicographiques et stylistiques sur le livre de Job." *FolOr* 21 [= *Studia biblica Alexius Klawek oblata*] (1980) 65–82. **Michaelis, Johann David.** "Anzeige der Varianten im Buche Hiob." In his *Orientalische und exegetische Bibliothek.* Theil 7. Frankfurt a.M.: Johann Gottlieb Garbe, 1774. 217–47. Theil 8. Frankfurt a.M.: Johann Gottlieb Garbe, 1775. 175–224. **Michel, Walter L.** *Job in the Light of Northwest Semitic.* 1. *Prologue and First Cycle of Speeches. Job 1:1–14:22.* BibOr 42/1. Rome: Biblical Institute Press, 1987. ———. *The Ugaritic Texts and the Mythological Expressions in the Book of Job, Including a New Translation and Philological Notes on the Book.* Diss. Wisconsin–Madison, 1970. **Muhsin, S. R.** *A Comparative Study of the Hebrew Text and Arabic Versions of the Book of Job.* Diss. Manchester, 1986. ———. *The Language of the Book of Job in the Light of Pre-Islamic North Arabic.* Diss. Manchester, 1982.

Oort, H. *Textus hebraici emendationes quibus in Vetere Testamento neerlandice vertendo usi sunt A. Kuenen, I. Hooykaas, W. H. Kosters, H. Oort.* Leiden: Brill, 1900. **Oudenrijn, M. A. van den.** "Scholia in locos quosdam libri Job." *Ang* 13 (1936) 228–40. **Palache, J. L.** "Drie plaatsen uit het boek Job" *TTijd* (1916) 348–56. **Parchon, ibn [Solomon ben Abraham].** *Lexicon hebraicum.* Ed. S. G. Stern. Pressburg, 1844. **Perani, M.** "Rilievi sulla terminologia temporale nel libro di Giobbe." *Hen* 5 (1983) 1–28. **Pérez Castro, F.** "Corrigedo y correcto. El MS B 19a (Leningrado) frente al MS Or 4445 (Londres) y al Códice de los Profetas de El Cairo." *Sef* 14 (1955) 3–20. **Perles, Felix.** *Analekten des Alten Testaments.* Munich: Ackermann, 1895. ———. *Analekten zur Textkritik des Alten Testaments. Neue Folge.* Leipzig: Engel, 1922. ———. "Neue Analekten zur Textkritik des Alten Testaments." In *Orientalische Studien: Fritz Hommel zum sechzigsten Geburtstag am 31. Juli 1914 gewidmet von Freunden, Kollegen und Schülern.* MVAG 21–22. Leipzig: Hinrichs, 1917. 125–35. **Peters, N.** "Textkritisches zu Hiob." *TQ* 83 (1901) 208–18, 389–96. ———. "Vertikale Doppelschreibung als Fehlerquelle im Buche Job." *TGl* 14 (1922) 106–10. **Prijs, J.** "Über Ben Naftali-Bibelhandschriften und ihre paläographischen Besonderheiten. Unter Berücksichtigung eines Ben Naftali Fragments der Universitätsbibliothek Basel." *ZAW* 69 (1957) 171–84. **Qafiḥ, J.** "The Accents of Job, Proverbs, and Psalms in Yemenite Tradition" [Heb]. *Tarb* 31 (1961–62) 371–76. **Reider, Joseph.** "Contributions to the Scriptural Text" [incl. Job]. *HUCA* 24 (1952–53) 85–106. **Richter, Georg.** *Erläuterungen zu dunkeln Stellen im Buche Hiob.* BZAW 11. Leipzig: Hinrichs, 1912. ———. *Textstudien zum Buche Hiob.* BWANT 3/7. Stuttgart: W. Kohlhammer, 1927. **Richter, Wolfgang.** *Biblia Hebraica transcripta: BHt; das ist das ganze Alte Testament transkribiert, mit Satzeinteilungen versehen und durch die Version tiberisch-masoretischer Autoritäten bereichert, auf der sie gründet.* 12. *Ijob. Sprüche.* Arbeiten zu Text und Sprache im Alten Testament 33,12. St Ottilien: EOS-Verlag, 1993. **Rignell, L. G.** "Comments on Some *cruces interpretum* in the Book of Job." *ASTI* 11 (1978) 111–18.

Sarna, Nahum M. "Notes on the Use of the Definite Article in the Poetry of Job." In *Texts, Temples, and Traditions: A Tribute to Menahem Haran.* Ed. Michael V. Fox, Victor Avigdor Hurowitz, and Avi Hurvitz. Winona Lake, IN: Eisenbrauns, 1996. 279–84. ———. "Some Instances of the Enclitic *-m* in Job." *JJS* 6 (1955) 108–10. ———. *Studies in the Language of Job.* Diss. Dropsie College, 1955. **Schwally, F.** "Einige Bemerkungen zum

Buche Hiob." *ZAW* 20 (1900) 44–48. **Segert, Stanislav.** "Vorarbeiten zur hebräischen Metrik." *ArOr* 21 (1953) 481–542. **Snaith, Norman H.** "The Introductions to the Speeches in the Book of Job, Are They in Prose or in Verse?" *Textus* 8 (1973) 133–37. ———. *Notes on the Hebrew Text of Job 1–6.* London: Epworth Press, 1945. **Steurer, Rita Maria.** *Das Alte Testament: Interlinearübersetzung hebräisch-deutsch und Transkription des hebräischen Grundtextes nach der Biblia Hebraica stuttgartensia 1986.* 4. *Die 12 kleinen Propheten—Hiob—Psalmen.* Neuhausen–Stuttgart: Hänssler, 1999. **Stevenson, William Barron.** *Critical Notes on the Hebrew Text of the Poem of Job.* Aberdeen: Aberdeen University Press, 1951. **Sutcliffe, E. F.** "Further Notes on Job, Textual and Exegetical." *Bib* 31 (1950) 365–78. ———. "Notes on Job, Textual and Exegetical. 6, 18; 11, 12; 31, 35; 34, 17. 20; 36, 27–33; 37, 1." *Bib* 30 (1949) 66–90. **Ulrich, Eugene, and Sarianna Metso.** "A Preliminary Edition of 4QJob[a]." In *Antikes Judentum und frühes Christentum. Festschrift für Hartmut Stegemann zum 65. Geburtstag.* BZNW 97. Berlin: Walter de Gruyter, 1999. 29–38. **Vetter, Paul.** *Die Metrik des Buches Hiob.* Biblische Studien 2. Freiburg i.Br., 1897. **Voigt, Clemens.** *Einige Stellen des Buches Hiob.* Leipzig: W. Drugulin, 1895. **Webber, H. J.** "Material for the Construction of a Grammar of the Book of Job." *AJSL* 15 (1898–99) 1–32. **Weber, Henry Jacob.** *Linguistic Peculiarity of the Book of Job.* Diss. Pennsylvania, 1895. **Weitzman, Michael.** "Hebrew and Syriac Texts of the Book of Job." In *Congress Volume: Cambridge 1995.* Ed. J. A. Emerton. VTSup 66. Leiden: Brill, 1997. 381–99. **Whitley, C. F.** "Has the Particle םא an Asseverative Force?" *Bib* 55 (1974) 394–96. **Wickes, William.** *A Treatise on the Accentuation of the Three So-Called Poetical Books of the Old Testament, Psalms, Proverbs, and Job. With an Appendix Containing the Treatise, Assigned to R. Jehuda Ben-Bil'am, on the Same Subject, in the Original Arabic.* Oxford: Clarendon Press, 1881. **Zijl, J. B. van.** "Structural Linguistics and Textual Criticism." In *Text and Context: Old Testament and Semitic Studies for F. C. Fensham.* Ed. W. Claassen. JSOTSup 48. Sheffield: JSOT Press, 1988. 209–16.

5. THE ANCIENT VERSIONS

a. Septuagint and Other Greek Versions

Bertrand, Daniel A. "Le bestiaire de Job. Notes sur les versions grecques et latines." In *Le Livre de Job chez les Pères.* Cahiers de Biblia patristica 5. Strasbourg: Centre d'Analyse et de Documentation Patristiques, 1996. 215–58. **Bickell, Gustav.** *Das Buch Job nach Anleitung der Strophik und der Septuaginta auf seine ursprüngliche Form zurückgeführt und in Versmasse des Urtextes übersetzt.* Vienna: Carl Gerold's Sohn, 1894. ———. *De indole ac ratione versionis alexandrinae in interpretando libro Jobi.* Marburg: G. Elwert, 1862. ———. "Der ursprüngliche Septuagintatext des Buches Hiob." *ZTK* 10 (1886) 557–64. **Cimosa, Mario.** "La preghiera d'intercessione nel testo greco di Giobbe." In his *La preghiera nella Bibbia greca: studi sul vocabolario dei LXX.* Collana biblica. Rome: Edizioni Dehoniane, 1992. **Cook, Johann.** "Aspects of the Relationship between the Septuagint Versions of Proverbs and Job." In *IX Congress of the International Organization for Septuagint and Cognate Studies, Cambridge, 1995.* Ed. Bernard A. Taylor. Septuagint and Cognate Studies 45. Atlanta: Scholars Press, 1997. 309–28. **Cooper, Alan M.** "The Suffering Servant and Job: A View from the Sixteenth Century." In *"As those who are taught": The Interpretation of Isaiah from the LXX to the SBL.* Ed. Claire Mathews McGinnis and Patricia K. Tull. SBL Symposium Series 27. Atlanta: Society of Biblical Literature, 2006. 189–200. **Cox, Claude E.** "Job's Concluding Soliloquy: chh. 29–31." In *VII Congress of the International Organization for Septuagint and Cognate Studies.* SBLSCS 31. Ed. Claude E. Cox. Atlanta: Scholars Press, 1987. 325–39. ———. "Methodological Issues in the Exegesis of LXX Job." In *VI Congress of the International Organization for Septuagint and Cognate Studies. Jerusalem, 1986.* SBLSCS 23. Atlanta: Scholars Press, 1987. 79–89. ———. "Origen's Use of Theodotion in the Elihu Speeches." *Second Century* 3 (1983) 89–98. ———. "Tying It All Together: The Use of Particles in Old Greek Job." *BIOSCS* 38 (2005) 41–54. ———.

"Vocabulary for Wrongdoing and Forgiveness in the Greek Translation of Job." *Textus* 15 (1990) 119–30. **Dafni, Evangelia G.** "BROTOS. A Favourite Word of Homer in the Septuagint Version of Job." *Verbum et ecclesia* 28 (2007) 35–65. **De Lange, N. R. M.** "Some New Fragments of Aquila on Malachi and Job." *VT* 30 (1980) 291–94. **Dieu, Léon.** "Le texte de Job du Codex Alexandrinus et ses principaux témoins." *Le Muséon* ns 13 (1912) 223–74. **Dolbeau, François.** "Une citation non reconnue de Job 31, 11 (LXX), dans un sermon d'Augustin." *RevEtAug* 43 (1997) 309–11. **Fernandez-Marcos, Natalio.** "The Septuagint Reading of the Book of Job." In *The Book of Job.* Ed. W. A. M. Beuken. BETL 114. Leuven: Leuven University Press, 1994. 251–66. **Field, Frederick.** *Origenis Hexapla quae supersunt; sive veterum interpretum Graecorum in totum VT fragmenta.* Oxford: Clarendon Press, 1871–75. 2:4–82. **Frankl, P. F.** "Die Zusätze in der LXX zu Hiob." *MGWJ* 21 (1872) 306–15. **Funke-Reuter, A.** *Septuaginta-exegetische Studien am Beispiel von Hiob 9 und 10.* Diss. Leipzig, 1992. **Gailey, James Herbert.** *Jerome's Latin Version of Job from the Greek, Chapters 1–26. Its Texts, Character and Provenance.* Diss. Princeton, 1945. **Gammie, John G.** "The Angelology and Demonology in the Septuagint of the Book of Job." *HUCA* 56 (1985) 1–19. ———. "The Septuagint of Job: Its Poetic Style and Relationship to the Septuagint of Proverbs." *CBQ* 49 (1987) 14–31. **Gard, Donald H.** "The Concept of Job's Character according to the Greek Translator of the Hebrew Text." *JBL* 72 (1953) 182–86. ———. "The Concept of the Future Life according to the Greek Translator of the Book of Job." *JBL* 73 (1954) 137–43. ———. *The Exegetical Method of the Greek Translator of the Book of Job.* SBLMS 8. Philadelphia: Society of Biblical Literature, 1952. **Gehman, H. S.** "The Theological Approach of the Greek Translator of Job 1–15." *JBL* 68 (1949) 231–40. **Gentry, Peter J.** "The Asterisked Materials in the Greek Job and the καιγε Recension." *Textus* 19 (1998) 141–56. ———. "The Place of Theodotion-Job in the Textual History of the Septuagint." In *Origen's Hexapla and Fragments. Papers Presented at the Rich Seminar on the Hexapla, Oxford Centre for Hebrew and Jewish Studies, 25th–3rd August* [sic] *1994.* Ed. Alison Salvesen. Texte und Studien zum antiken Judentum 58. Tübingen: J. C. B. Mohr Siebeck, 1998. 199–230. ———. *The Asterisked Materials in the Greek Job.* SBLSCS. 38. Atlanta: Scholars Press, 1995. **Gerleman, Gillis.** *Studies in the Septuagint.* I. *The Book of Job.* LUÅ 1/43.2. Lund: C. W. K. Gleerup, 1946. **Gorea, M.** "Job 7,8: une contribution à la problématique des versets portant astérisque dans la Septante." In *The Book of Job.* Ed. W. A. M. Beuken. BETL 114. Leuven: Leuven University Press, 1994. 430–34. **Graetz, H. H.** "Das Zeitalter der griechischen Übersetzung des Buches Hiob." *MGWJ* 26 (1877) 83–91. **Gray, G. B.** "The Additions in the Ancient Greek Version of Job." *Exp* 46 (1920) 422–38. **Gray, J.** "The Massoretic Text of the Book of Job, the Targum and the Septuagint Version in the Light of the Qumran Targum (11Qtarg Job)." *ZAW* 86 (1974) 331–50. **Guey, J.** "Une glose pseudonumismatique incluse dans Job xliii. 11 (LXX)." *BullSocFranNumis* 19 (1964) 320–31.

Heater, Homer, Jr. *A Septuagint Translation Technique in the Book of Job.* CBQMS 11. Washington, DC: Catholic Biblical Association, 1982. **Janowski, Bernd.** "Sündenvergebung »um Hiobs willen«: Fürbitte und Vergebung in 11QtgJob 38:2f und Hi 42:9f LXX." *ZNW* 73 (1982) 251–80. **Jeffrey, J.** "The Massoretic Text and the Septuagint Compared, with Special Reference to the Book of Job." *ExpT* 36 (1924–25) 70–73. **Jenkins, R. G.** "Hexaplaric Marginalia and the Hexapla-Tetrapla Question." In *Origen's Hexapla and Fragments. Papers Presented at the Rich Seminar on the Hexapla, Oxford Centre for Hebrew and Jewish Studies, 25th–3rd August* [sic] *1994.* Ed. Alison Salvesen. Texte und Studien zum antiken Judentum 58. Tübingen: J. C. B. Mohr Siebeck, 1998. 73–87. **Kalman, Jason.** "Job Denied the Resurrection of Jesus? A Rabbinic Critique of the Church Fathers' Use of Exegetical Traditions Found in the Septuagint and the Testament of Job." In *The Changing Face of Judaism, Christianity and Other Greco-Roman Religions in Antiquity: Presented to James H. Charlesworth on the Occasion of His 65th Brithday.* Ed. Ian H. Henderson and Gerbern S. Oegema. Studien zu den jüdischen Schriften aus hellenistisch-römischer Zeit 2. Gütersloh: Gütersloher Verlagshaus, 2006. 371–97. **Katz, P.** "Notes on the LXX: IV, ἔα δέ 'let alone' in Job." *JTS* 47 (1946) 168–69.

————. Notes on the LXX: V, Job xv:2; VI, Some Further Passages in Job." *JTS* 48 (1947) 194–96. **Klostermann, Erich.** *Analecta zur Septuaginta, Hexapla und Patristik.* Leipzig: Deichert, 1895. **Köhler, L.** "Die LXX-Vorlage von Hi. xv: 28." *ZAW* 31 (1911) 155–56. **Kreyssig, Joannes Gottlieb.** *Observationes criticae in graecos Jobi interpretes.* Schneeberg: Schillian, 1808. **Küchler, Max.** "Gott und seine Weisheit in der Septuaginta (Ijob 28; Spr 8)." In *Monotheismus und Christologie: Zur Gottesfrage im hellenistischen Judentum und im Urchristentum.* Ed. Hans-Josef Klauck. Quaestiones disputatae 138. Freiburg i.Br.: Herder, 1992. 118–43. **Kutz, Karl V.** "Characterization in the Old Greek of Job." In *Seeking out the Wisdom of the Ancients: Essays Offered to Honor Michael V. Fox on the Occasion of His Sixty-Fifth Birthday.* Ed. Ronald L. Troxel, Kelvin G. Friebel, and Dennis R. Magary. Winona Lake, IN: Eisenbrauns, 2005. 345–55. ————. "The Old Greek of Job: A Study in Early Biblical Exegesis." *BIOSCS* 30 (1997) 24–25. ————. *The Old Greek of Job: A Study in Early Biblical Exegesis.* Diss. Wisconsin–Madison, 1997.

Lagarde, P. de. "Des Hieronymus Übertragung der griechischen Übersetzung des Iob." In his *Mittheilungen.* Göttingen: Dieterich, 1887. 2:189–237. **Lange, N. R. M. de.** "Some New Fragments of Aquila on Malachi and Job?" *VT* 30 (1980) 291–94. **Liebreich, Leon J.** "Notes on the Greek Version of Symmachus." *JBL* 63 (1944) 397–403. **Mandl, Armin.** *Die Peschittha zu Hiob: nebst einem Anhang über ihr Verhältniss zu LXX und Targum.* Budapest: L. Propper, 1892. **Nuland, J. van.** *Semantiek en Bijbel: Studie van het vocabularium van het lijden in de Septuaginta van het Boek Job.* 1969. **Origen.** *Hexaplorum quae supersunt … Job.* PG 16/1:287–570. **Orlinsky, Harry M.** *An Analysis of the Relationship between the Septuagint and Masoretic Text of the Book of Job.* Diss. Dropsie, 1935. ————. "ἀποβαίνω and ἐπιβαίνω in the Septuagint of Job." *JBL* 56 (1937) 361–67. ————. "Some Corruptions in the Greek Text of Job." *JQR* 26 (1935–36) 133–45. ————. "Studies in the Septuagint of the Book of Job." *HUCA* 28 (1957) 53–74; 29 (1958) 229–71; 30 (1959) 153–57; 32 (1961) 239–68; 33 (1962) 119–51; 35 (1964) 57–78; 36 (1965) 37–47. ————. "The Hebrew and Greek Texts of Job 14:12." *JQR* ns 28 (1937–38) 57–68. **Philonenko, Marc.** "Romains 7,23, une glose qoumrânisante sur Job 40,32 (Septante) [Engl. 41:8] et trois textes qoumrâniens." *RHPR* 87 (2007) 257–65. **Prijs, Leo.** *Jüdische Tradition in der Septuaginta: Die grammatische Terminologie des Abraham Ibn Esra.* Leiden: E. J. Brill, 1948 [repr. Hildesheim: Georg Olms, 1987]. **Rahlfs, Alfred.** "Iob-Fragmente." *Mitteilungen der Septuaginta-Unternehmens* 1 (1915) 398–404. ————. *Septuaginta. II. Libri poetici et prophetici.* Stuttgart: Privilegierte Württembergische Bibelanstalt, 5th ed. 1952. 271–345. **Reed, Annette Yoshiko.** "Job as Jobab: The Interpretation of Job in LXX Job 42:17b–e." *JBL* 120 (2001) 31–55.

Schaller, B. "Das Testament Hiobs und die Septuaginta-Übersetzung des Buches Hiob." *Bib* 61 (1980) 377–406. **Schnocks, Johannes.** "The Hope for Resurrection in the Book of Job." In *The Septuagint and Messianism.* Ed. Michael A. Knibb. BETL 195. Leuven: Leuven University Press, 2006. 291–99. **Stegmüller, Otto.** *Berliner Septuagintafragmente.* Berlin: Weidmann, 1939. **Szpek, Heidi M.** "On the Influence of the Septuagint on the Peshitta." *CBQ* 60 (1998) 251–66. **Thompson, J. David.** *A Critical Concordance to the Septuagint: Job.* 2 vols. The Computer Bible 69. Wooster, OH: Biblical Research Associates, 1999. **Tisserant, E.** "Note additionelle sur le manuscrit palimpsestes de Job." *RB* ns 16 (1919) 500–505. ————. "Nouvelles notes sur le manuscrit palimpseste de Job." *RB* ns 16 (1919) 89–105. ————. "Un manuscrit palimpseste de Job." *RB* ns 9 (1912) 481–503. **Wahrendorff, David Otto.** *De resurrectione speciatim Jobi cum sotere facta ad finem libri Jobi secundum Septuaginta meditationes.* Göttingen: Vandenhoeck, 1738. **Wevers, J. W.** "Septuagintaforschungen." *TRu* 22 (1954) 85–138, 171–90. **White, Wade Albert.** "A Devil in the Making: Isomorphism and Exegesis in OG Job 1:8b." In *Septuagint Research. Issues and Challenges in the Study of the Greek Jewish Scriptures.* Ed. Wolfgang Kraus and R. Glenn Wooden. SBLSCS 53. Atlanta: Society of Biblical Literature, 2006. **Witte, Markus.** "The Greek Book of Job." In *Das Buch Hiob und seine Interpretationen: Beiträge zum Hiob-Symposium auf dem Monte Verità vom 14.–19. August 2005.* Ed. Thomas Krüger, Manfred Oeming, Konrad Schmid, and Christoph Uehlinger. ATANT 88. Zurich:

Theologische Verlag Zürich, 2007. 33–54. **Wolters, Al.** "Text and Script of the LXX Vorlage of Job 40:17b." *Textus* 17 (1994) 101–15. **Wutz, Franz.** *Systematische Wege von der LXX zum hebräischen Text.* Stuttgart: W. Kohlhammer, 1937. **Ziegler, J.** "Der textkritische Wert der Septuaginta des Buches Hiob." In *Miscellanea Biblica B. Ubach.* Ed. Romualdo M. Díaz. Montserrat, 1953. 2:277–96 [= his *Sylloge: Gesammelte Aufsätze zur Septuaginta.* Göttingen: Vandenhoeck & Ruprecht, 1971. 9–28]. ———. *Beiträge zum griechischen Job.* MittSeptU 18. Göttingen: Vandenhoeck & Ruprecht, 1985. ———. *Iob.* Septuaginta gottingensis 11,4. Göttingen: Vandenhoeck & Ruprecht, 1982. **Zimmermann, L.** "The Septuagint Appendix to Job." *The Scotist* (1960) 48–59.

b. Targums

Andersen, F. I. "The Qumran Targum of Job." *BurHist* 10/3 (1974) 77–84. **Arias Montano, Benito.** *Liber Ijobi chaldaice et latine, cum notis. Item graece [sticheros], cum variantibus lectionibus.* Franeker: Johannes Wellens, 1663. **Aufrecht, W. E.** "Aramaic Studies and the Book of Job." In *Studies in the Book of Job.* Ed. W. E. Aufrecht. SRSup 16. Waterloo, Ont.: Wilfrid Laurier University Press, 1985. 54–66. **Bacher, W.** "Das Targum zu Hiob." *MGWJ* 20 (1871) 208–23, 283–84. **Boyarin, D.** "Aramaic Notes I: Column 36 of 11QTg Job." *JANES* 6 (1974) 29–33. **Brownlee, W. H.** "The Cosmic Role of Angels in the 11Q Targum of Job." *JSJ* 8 (1977) 83–84. **Caquot, A.** "Un écrit sectaire de Qoumrân: Le 'Targoum de Job'." *RHR* 185 (1974) 9–27. **Clarke, E. C.** "Reflections on Some Obscure Hebrew Words in the Biblical Job in the Light of XI Q Tg Job." In *Studies in Philology in Honour of Ronald James Williams: A Festschrift.* Ed. Gerald E. Kadish and Geoffrey E. Freeman. SSEA 3. Toronto: Benben Publications, 1982. 17–30. **Delcor, M.** "Le Targum de Job et l'araméen du temps de Jésus." In *Exégèse biblique et judaïsme* [= *RSR* 47 (1973)]. Ed. J.-E. Ménard. Leiden: E. J. Brill, 1973. 78–107. **Díez Macho, Alejandro.** "Le Targum de Job dans la tradition sefardie." In *De la Tôrah au Messie. Etudes d'exégèse et d'herméneutique bibliques offerts à Henri Cazelles.* Ed. M. Carrez, Joseph Dore, and Pierre Grelot. Paris: Desclée, 1981. 545–56. **Díez-Merino, Luis.** "Manuscritos del Targum de Job." *Hen* 4 (1982) 41–64. ———. *Targum de Job. Edición principe del Ms. Villa-Amil n. 5 de Alfonso Zamora.* Bibliotheca hispana bíblica 8. Biblia poliglota complutense, tradición sefardí de la Biblia Aramea IV, 2. Madrid: Consejo Superior de Investigaciones Científicas, Instituto "Francisco Suárez," 1984. **Dupont-Sommer, A.** "Sur 11QtgJob, col. XXXIII." *Sem* 15 (1965) 70–74. **Epstein, Elias L.** *A Critical Analysis of Chapters 1–26 of the Targum to the Book of Job.* Diss. Chicago, 1941. **Fernández Vallina, Francisco J.** *El Targum de Job.* Diss. Madrid, 1982. **Fernández Vallina, Javier.** "Targum y exégesis contemporánea: algunos problemas metodológicos" [on the Targum to Job]. In *Simposio Bíblico Español (Salamanca, 1982).* Ed. N. Fernandez Marcos, J. Trebolle Barrera, and J. Fernández Vallina. Madrid: Editorial de la Universidad Complutense, 1984. 513–21. **Fitzmyer, J. A.** "Some Observations on the Targum of Job from Qumran Cave 11." *CBQ* 36 (1974) 503–24 [= "The First-Century Targum of Job from Qumran Cave XI." In his *A Wandering Aramean: Collected Aramaic Essays.* SBLMS 25. Missoula, MT: Scholars Press, 1979. 161–82]. **Fohrer, G.** "4QOrNab, 11QTgJob und die Hioblegende." *ZAW* 34 (1963) 93–97.

García Martínez, F. "Nuevas lecturas de 11QtgJob." *Sef* 36 (1976) 241–49. **Gray, J.** "The Massoretic Text of the Book of Job, the Targum and the Septuagint Version in the Light of the Qumran Targum (11Qtarg Job)." *ZAW* 86 (1974) 331–50. **Greenfield, J. C., and Shaul Shaked.** "Three Iranian Words in the Targum of Job from Qumran." *ZDMG* 122 (1972) 37–45. **Janowski, Bernd.** "Sündenvergebung »um Hiobs willen«: Fürbitte und Vergebung in 11QtgJob 38:2f und Hi 42:9f LXX." *ZNW* 73 (1982) 251–80. **Jongeling, B.** "Contributions of the Qumran Job Targum to the Aramaic Vocabulary." *JSS* 17 (1972) 191–97. ———. "Détermination et indétermination dans 11QTgJob." In *Qumran. Sa piété, sa théologie et son milieu.* Ed. M. Delcor. BETL 46. Gembloux: Duculot,

1978. 131–36. ———. *Een aramees Boek Job (11QtgJob) uit de bibliotheek van Qumrân.* Exegetica N.R. 3. Amsterdam: Bolland, 1974. ———. "La colonne XVI de 11QtgJob." *RevQ* 8 (1974) 415–16. ———. "The Job Targum from Qumran Cave 11 (11QtgJob)." *FolOr* 15 (1974) 181–86. **Jongeling, B., C. J. Labuschagne, and A. S. van der Woude.** "The Job Targum from Cave II." In *Aramaic Texts from Qumran, with Translation and Annotations.* Semitic Study Series ns 4. Leiden: E. J. Brill, 1976. **Kaufman, S. A.** "The Job Targum from Qumran." *JAOS* 93 (1973) 317–27. **Kutsch, Ernst.** "Die Textgliederung im hebräischen Ijobbuch sowie in 4QTgJob und in 11QTgJob." *BZ* 27 (1983) 221–28. **Lewin, Moritz.** *Targum und Midrasch zum Buche Hiob in ihrem gegenseitigen Verhältnis.* Berne: J. Wirth, 1895. **Lübbe, John C.** "Describing the Translation Process of 11QtgJob: A Question of Method." *RevQ* 13 (1988) 583–93. ———. *Toward an Evaluation of the Translation Process in 11Qtg Job: A Study in Methodology.* Diss. UNISA, 1987. **Mangan, Céline.** "Blessing and Cursing in the Prologue of Targum Job." In *Targum and Scripture. Studies in Aramaic Translations and Interpretation in Memory of Ernest G. Clarke.* Ed. Paul V. M. Flesher. Leiden: Brill, 2002. 225–29. ———. "Some Observations on the Dating of Targum Job." In *Back to the Sources: Biblical and Near Eastern Studies in Honour of Dermot Ryan.* Ed. Kevin J. Cathcart and John F. Healey. Dublin: Glendale, 1989. 67–78. ———. "Some Similarities between Targum Job and Targum Qohelet." In *The Aramaic Bible: Targums in Their Historical Context.* Ed. D. R. G. Beattie and M. J. McNamara. JSOTSup 166. Sheffield: JSOT Press, 1994. 349–53. ———. "The Attitude to Women in the Prologue of Targum Job." In *Targumic and Cognate Studies: Essays in Honour of Martin McNamara.* Ed. Kevin J. Cathcart and Michael Maher. JSOTSup 230. Sheffield: Sheffield Academic Press, 1996. 100–10. ———. "The Interpretation of Job in the Targums." In *The Book of Job.* Ed. W. A. M. Beuken. BETL 114. Leuven: Leuven University Press, 1994. 267–80. **Mangan, Céline, John F. Healey, and Peter S. Knobel.** *The Targum of Job. The Targum of Proverbs. The Targum of Qohelet.* The Aramaic Bible 15. Wilmington, DE: Glazier; Edinburgh: T. & T. Clark, 1991. **Margain, Jean.** "11QtgJob et la langue targumique: A propos de la particule BDYL." *RevQ* 13 (1988) 525–28. **Mastin, B. A.** "A Re-Examination of an Alleged Orthographic Feature in 4Q Targum Job." *RevQ* 11 (1984) 583–84. **Milik, J. T.** "Targum de Job." In *Discoveries in the Judean Desert.* IV. *Qumrân Grotte 4.* Oxford: Clarendon Press, 1977. 90. **Moravkeh, T.** "On the Language of the Job Targum from Qumran." In *Proceedings of the 6th World Congress of Jewish Studies.* Jerusalem: World Union of Jewish Studies, 1977–1980. 159–65. **Morrow, Francis J.** "11 Q Targum Job and the Massoretic Text." *RevQ* 8 (1972–75) 253–56. **Muraoka, T.** "Notes on the Old Targum of Job from Qumran Cave XI." *RevQ* 9 (1977) 117–25. ———. "On the Aramaic of the Targum of Job from Qumran." In *Proceedings of the Sixth World Congress of Jewish Studies.* I/A. Ed. Avigdor Shinan. Jerusalem: World Union of Jewish Studies, 1977. 159*–65*. **Ploeg, J. P. M. van der.** *Le Targum de Job de la Grotte 11 de Qumran (11QtgJob). Première communication.* Akademie van Wetenschappen, Amsterdam. Mededelingen. Afd. Letterkunde. N.R. 25/9. Amsterdam: Noord-Hollandsche Uitgevers Maatschappij, 1962. **Ploeg, J. P. M. van der, and A. S. van der Woude.** *Le targum de Job de la grotte XI de Qumran.* Leiden: Brill, 1971. **Ribera-Florit, Josep.** "Los targumes de Job: algunos aspectos textuales y literarios." *EstBíb* 62 (2004) 77–86. **Ringgren, Helmer.** "Some Observations on the Qumran Targum of Job." *ASTI* 11 (1978) 119–26. **Shepherd, David.** *11QAramaic Job: The Qumran Targum as an Ancient Aramaic Version of Job.* Diss. Edinburgh, 2000. ———. "Before Bomberg: The Case of the Targum of Job in the Rabbinic Bible and the Solger Codex (MS Nürnberg)." *Bib* 79 (1998) 360–80. ———. "MN QDM: Deferential Treatment in Biblical Aramaic and the Qumran Targum of Job." *VT* 50 (2000) 401–404. ———. "Will the Real Targum Please Stand Up? Translation and Coordination in the Ancient Aramaic Versions of Job." *JJS* 51 (2000) 88–116. **Sokoloff, Michael.** *The Targum to Job from Qumran Cave XI.* Bar Ilan Studies in Near Eastern Languages and Cultures. Ramat-Gan, Jerusalem: Bar-Ilan University, 1974. **Stec, David M.** *The Text of the Targum of Job. An*

Introduction and Critical Edition. Arbeiten zur Geschichte des antiken Judentums und des Urchristentums 20. Leiden: E. J. Brill, 1994. ———. "The Recent English Translation of the Targumim to Job, Proverbs and Qohelet: A Review." *JSS* 39 (1994) 161–81.

Tuinstra, Evert Willem. *Hermeneutische aspecten van de targum van Job uit grot XI van Qumrân.* Diss. Groningen, 1970. **Vasholz, Robert I.** "4Q Targum Job versus 11Q Targum Job." *RevQ* 11 (1982) 109. ———. "A Further Note on the Problem of Nasalisation in Biblical Aramaic, 11QtgJob, and 1QApGn." *RevQ* 10 (1979) 95–96. ———. "An Additional Note on the 4QEnoch Fragments and 11QtgJob." *Maarav* 3 (1982) 115–18. ———. "Two Notes on 11QtgJob and Biblical Aramaic." *RevQ* 10 (1979) 93–94. **Vicchio, Stephen J.** "Job in the Dead Sea Scrolls." In his *Job in the Ancient World.* Eugene, OR: Wipf & Stock, 2006. 177–96. **Vivian, Angelo.** "Il targum di Giobbe: analisi concettuale contrastiva di TgGb 1–4." *Henoch* 10 (1988) 293–334. **Weiss, A.** *De libri Job paraphrasi chaldaica.* Breslau, 1873. **Weiss, R.** איוב לספר הארמי התרגום. *The Aramaic Targum of Job.* Diss. Hebrew University, Jerusalem, 1974 [= *The Aramaic Targum of Job.* Tel-Aviv: Tel-Aviv University, 1979]. ———. "Divergences from the MT Reflected in the Qumran Targum of Job" [Heb]. In *Studies in the Text and Language of the Bible.* Jerusalem: Magnes Press, 1981. 240–44. ———. "Further Notes on the Qumran Targum of Job." *JSS* 19 (1974) 13–18. ———. "Recensional Variations between the Aramaic Translation of Job from Qumran Cave 11 and the Masoretic Text." *Shnaton* 1 (1975) 123–27. ———. "The Aramaic Targum of Job from Qumran Cave 11." In *Proceedings of the Sixth World Congress of Jewish Studies.* Volume 1. Division A. Ed. Avigdor Shinan. Jerusalem: World Union of Jewish Studies, 1977. 101*–10*. **Wilson, E. Jan.** "11QtgJob and the Peshitta Job." In *The Dead Sea Scrolls, Fifty Years after Their Discovery: Proceedings of the Jerusalem Congress, July 20–25, 1997.* Ed. Lawrence H. Schiffman, Emanuel Tov, and James C. VanderKam. Jerusalem: Israel Exploration Society, 2000. 411–17. **Woude, A. S. van der.** "Das Hiobtargum aus Qumran Höhle XI." In *Congress Volume, Bonn 1962.* VTSup 9. Leiden: E. J. Brill, 1962. 322–31. **York, Anthony D.** "11QTgJob XXI 4–5 (Job 32:13)." *RevQ* 9 (1977) 127–29. ———. "רומאה זרע as an Indication of the Date of 11QTg Job?" *JBL* 93 (1974) 445–46. **Zuckerman, Bruce E.** *The Process of Translation in 11QtgJob, a Preliminary Study.* Diss. Yale, 1980. ———. "The Date of 11Q Targum Job: A Paleographic Consideration of Its Vorlage." *JSP* 1 (1987) 57–78. ———. "Two Examples of Editorial Modification in 11QtgJob" [Job 36,14; 34,31; 13,15]. In *Biblical and Near Eastern Studies: Essays in Honor of William Sanford LaSor.* Ed. Gary A. Tuttle. Grand Rapids: Eerdmans, 1978. 269–75.

c. Vulgate and Other Latin Versions

Anon. *Biblia Sacra juxta latinam Vulgatam versionem. IX. Libri Hester et Job.* Rome: Typis Polyglottis Vaticanis, 1951. ———. *Wenzelsbibel. 9. Die nichtilluminierten Bücher* [Jesaias, Jeremias, Judith, Esther und Hiob; Codex Vindobonensis 2762, Fol. 1–211]. Facsimile. Codices selecti 70. Graz: Akademisches Druck- und Verlagsanstalt, 1991. **Barret, L.** *Job selon la Vulgate.* Toulon: J. d'Arc, 1925. **Caspari, Carl Paul.** *Das Buch Hiob (1,1–38,16) in Hieronymus's Übersetzung aus der alexandrinischen Version nach einer St Gallener Handschrift, saec. VIII.* Christiania Videnskabs-selskabs forhandlinger 1893, 4. Christiania: J. Dybwad, 1893. **Erbes, P. J.** *Die Job-Übersetzung des hl. Hieronymus.* Diss. Freiburg im Breisgau, 1951. **Gailey, J. H.** *Jerome's Latin Version of Job from the Greek, Chapters 1–26: Its Text, Character and Provenience.* Diss. Princeton, 1945. **Hewitt, Arthur Wentworth.** "Job and Psalms in the Vulgate." *RL* 18 (1948–49) 66–78. **Sabatier, Pierre.** *Bibliorum sacrorum latinæ versiones antiquæ: seu vetus italica, et cæteræ quæcunque in codicibus mss. et antiquorum libris reperiri potuerunt: quæ cum vulgata latina, & cum textu græco comparantur.* 3 vols. Paris: Franciscus Didot, 1751; Reims: Reginald Florentin, 1753 [= Microfiche. Leiden: IDC, 2001]. 1:826–910. **Salmon, P.** "De quelques leçons du texte du Job dans la nouvelle édition de la Vulgate." In *Miscellanea biblica B. Ubach.* Ed. Romualdo M. Diaz. Montserrat: Casa Provincial de Caridad, 1953. 177–84. ———. "Le texte de Job utilisé par S. Grégoire dans les 'Moralia'." In *Miscellanea biblica et orientalia R. P. Athanasio Miller O.S.B., secretario Pontificiae Commissionis Biblicae, completis LXX annis oblata.* Ed. Adalbert Metzinger. Studia anselmiana philosophica theologica 27–28. Rome: Orbis Catholicus, Herder, 1951. 187–94. **Verdejo Sánchez, M. Dolores.** "Los adverbios en las notas marginales del libro de Job de la Vetus Latina." *Helmantica: Revista de filología clásica y hebrea Universidad Pontificia de Salamanca* 40 (1987–89) 463–73. **Wahl, Otto.** "Der Codex Rupefucaldinus—ein bedeutsamer Textzeuge des Ijobs-textes der Sacra Parallela." In *Theologie und Leben. Festgabe für George Söll zum 70. Geburtstag.* Ed. Anton Bodem and Alois M. Kothgasser. Biblioteca di scienze religiose 58. Rome: Libreria Ateneo salesiano, 1983. 25–30. **Ziegler, J.** "Randnoten aus der Vetus Latina des Buches Job in spanischen Vulgatabibeln." In *Sitzungberichte der Bayerische Akademie der Wissenschaften.* Phil.-hist. Kl. 1980. Heft 2. Munich: Bayerische Akademie der Wissenschaften, 1980.

d. Peshitta and Other Syriac Versions

Baumann, E. "Die Verwendbarkeit der *Pešita* zum Buche Hiob für die Textkritik." *ZAW* 18 (1898) 305–38; 19 (1899) 15–95, 288–309; 20 (1900) 177–201, 264–307. **Ceriani, Antonio Maria (ed.).** *Codex Syro-Hexaplaris Ambrosianus.* Monumenta sacra et profana 7. Mediolani: Impensis Bibliothecae Ambrosianae, 1874. ———. *Translatio Syra Pescitto Veteris Testamenti ex codice Ambrosiano sec. fere VI, photolithographice edita.* Milan: Angelus della Croce & J. B. Poglianus; London: Williams & Norgate, 1876. **Goréa-Autexier, Maria.** "La bible des syriens à la lumière des citations de Job." *RB* 106 (1999) 481–510. ———. "The 'Peshitta'—A Syriac Translation in Light of Biblical Text References in the 'Book of Job': An Examination of Cultural Bilingualism between the 4th and 9th Centuries BCE." *RB* 106 (1999) 481–510. **Gosling, F. A.** *The Peshitta of Job: An Examination of the Translator's Technique with Particular Reference to the Book of Job 3:1–10:22.* Diss. St Andrews, 1994. **Lee, S.** *Vetus Testamentum syriace recognovit et ad fidem codicum MSS. emendavit.* London: BFBS, 1823.

Mandl, Armin. *Die Peschittha zu Hiob: nebst einem Anhang über ihr Verhältniss zu LXX und Targum.* Budapest: L. Propper, 1892. **Middeldorpf, Henricus.** *Codex syriaco-hexaplaris. IV. Regum, Jesaias, Duodecim Prophetae Minores, Proverbia, Jobus, Canticum, Threni, Ecclesiastes.* Berlin: Enslin, 1835. ———. *Curae hexaplares in Jobum: e codice syriaco-hexaplari ambrosiano-mediolanensi.* Bratislava: A. W. Holaeufer, 1817. **Rignell, Gösta, and Karl-Erik Rignell.** *The Peshitta to the Book of Job, Critically Investigated with Introduction, Translation, Commentary and Summary.* Kristianstad: Monitor Forlaget, 1994. **Rignell, L. G.** *Job.* The Old Testament in Syriac according to the Peshiṭta Version 2/1a. Leiden: Brill, 1982. ———. "Notes on the Peshitta of the Book of Job." *ASTI* 9 (1973) 98–106. **Shepherd, David.** "Rendering 'flesh and bones.' Pair Reversal and the Peshitta of Job 2.5." *Aramaic Studies* 3 (2005) 205–13. **Smith Lewis, Agnes.** *A Palestinian Syriac Lectionary Containing Lessons from the Pentateuch, Job, Proverbs, Prophets, Acts and Epistles.* Studia sinaitica 6. London: C. J. Clay & Sons, 1897. **Stenij, Edvard.** *De syriaca libri Jobi interpretatione quae Peschîta vocatur.* Helsingfors: Frenckell, 1887. **Szpek, Heidi M.** "An Observation on the Peshiṭta's Translation of *šdy* in Job." *VT* 47 (1997) 550–53. ———. "On the Influence of the Septuagint on the Peshitta." *CBQ* 60 (1998) 251–66. ———. "The Peshitta on Job 7:6: 'My days are swifter (?) than an אֶרֶג'." *JBL* 113 (1994) 287–97. ———. *Translation Technique in the Peshitta to Job: A Model for Evaluating a Text with Documentation from the Peshitta to Job.* SBLDS 137. Atlanta: Scholars Press, 1992. **Vicchio, Stephen J.** "Job in the Peshitta." In his *Job in the Ancient World.* Eugene, OR: Wipf & Stock, 2006. 197–216. **Vosté, J.-M.** "Les deux versions syriaques de la Bible d'après Mar Išōdad de Merw (c. 850)." *Bib* 33 (1952) 235–36. **Wilson, E. Jan.** "11QtgJob and the Peshitta Job." In *The Dead Sea Scrolls, Fifty Years after Their Discovery: Proceedings of the Jerusalem Congress, July 20–25, 1997.* Ed. Lawrence H. Schiffman, Emanuel Tov, and James C. VanderKam. Jerusalem: Israel Exploration

Society, 2000. 411–17. **Zimmermann, Frank.** *A Syriac–Hebrew and Hebrew–Syriac Index to the Book of Job.* Diss. Dropsie, 1935.

e. Arabic

Bacher, Wilhelm. *Moses b. Samuel Hakohez ibn Chiquitilla: Arabische Übersetzung zum Buche Hiob nebst arabischem Kommentar.* Budapest, 1909. ———. *Version arabe du livre de Job de R. Saadia ben Iosef al-Fayyoūmî, publiée avec des notes hébraïques par W. Bacher. Accompagnée d'une traduction française d'après l'arabe par J. Derenbourg et H. Derenbourg.* Paris: Leroux, 1899 [= *Œuvres complètes: publiées sous la direction de J. Derenbourg.* V. Hildesheim: Georg Olms Verlag, 1979]. **Baudissin, W. W. von.** *Translationis antiquae arabicae libri Jobi quae supersunt ex apographo codicis Musei Britannici.* Leipzig: Dörffling & Franks, 1870. **Blackburn, Steven P.** *The Early Arabic Versions of Job (First Millennium C.E.).* Diss. St Andrews, 1998. **Cohn, John.** אלמלקב בכתאב אלתעדיל: כתאב איוב. *Das Buch Hiob, übersetzt und erklärt von Gaon Saadia. Nach Handschriften der Bodlejana und der Königlichen Bibliothek in Berlin, herausgegeben und mit Anmerkungen versehen.* Altona: Gebrüder Bonn, 1889. ———. *Kitāb Ajjūb al-mulaqqab bi-Kitāb at-ta'dīl: Das Buch Hiob* [translation of and commentary on chaps. 1–5 of Saadia's translation]. Altona: Gebrüder Bonn, 1882. **Ecker, Roman.** *Die arabische Job-Übersetzung des Gaon Sa'adja ben Josef al-Fajjumi nach ihrer Eigenart untersucht: Ein Beitrag zur Geschichte der Übersetzung des Alten Testaments.* SANT 4. Munich: Kösel Verlag, 1962. **Ewald, Heinrich, and Leopold Dukes.** *Beiträge zur Geschichte der ältesten Auslegung und Spracherklärung des Alten Testamentes.* 3 vols. Stuttgart: A. Krabbe, 1844. 1:75–115 [Saadia's Job]. **Lagarde, P. de.** *Psalterium, Job, Proverbia arabice.* Göttingen: W. F. Kaestner, 1876. **Ulback, E.** "An Arabic Version of the Book of Job." *The Open Court* 46 (1932) 782–86.

f. Ethiopic

Pereira, Francesco Maria Esteves. *Le livre de Job. Version éthiopienne publiée et traduite.* PO 2. Paris: Firmin-Didot, 1907. 561–688.

g. Coptic

Ciasca, Augustinus. *Sacrorum Bibliorum fragmenta copto-sahidica musei borgiana issue et sumptibus S. Congregationis de propaganda fide studio P. Augustini Ciasca ordinis eremitarum S. Augustini.* II. Rome: S. Congregatio de propaganda fide, 1889. **Dieu, L.** "Nouveaux fragments préhexaplaires du livre de Job en copte sahidique." *Le Muséon* (1912) 147–85. **Porcher, E.** *Le livre de Job. Version copte bohairique.* PO 87. Paris: Firmin-Didot, 1924. Repr. Turnhout: Brepols, 1974. **Schleifer, J.** *Sahidische Bibel-Fragmente aus dem British Museum zu London.* 3 vols. Sitzungsberichte der Kaiserlichen Akademie der Wissenschaften in Wien. Philosophisch-historische Klasse 162/6, 164/6, 173/5. Vienna: A. Hölder, 1909–14. **Tattam, H.** *The Ancient Coptic Version of the Book of Job the Just. Translated into English and Edited.* London: W. Straker, 1846.

h. Armenian

Cox, Claude E. "Text Forms and Stemmatics in the Armenian Text of Job." In *Armenian Texts, Tasks, and Tools.* Ed. Henning J. Lehmann and J. J. S. Weitenberg. Aarhus: Aarhus University Press, 1993. 38–43. ———. *Armenian Job: Reconstructed Greek Text, Critical Edition of the Armenian with English Translation.* Hebrew University Armenian Studies 8. Leuven: Peeters, 2006.

6. LITERARY ASPECTS

Ahroni, R. "An Examination of the Literary Genre of the Book of Job" [Heb.]. *Tarb* 49 (1979–80) 1–13. **Alter, Robert.** *The Art of Biblical Poetry.* New York: Basic Books, 1985. 95–110. **Antolín, T.** "El género literario del libro de Job." *EstBíb* 6 (1947) 449–50. **Bezuidenhout, Louis C.** "Semantiese ritme en beweging in Job 3. 'n ander benadering tot die waardering van die teks." *HervTS* 50 (1994) 236–45. **Borgonovo, Gianantonio.** "Per 'tradire' (o tradurre) senza inganno: annnotazioni ad una traduzione di Giobbe." In L. Alonso Schökel and J. L. Sicre Díaz, *Giobbe: Commento teologico e letterario.* Trans. and ed. G. Borgonovo. Commenti biblici. Rome: Borla, 1985. 682–741. **Bowes, Paula J.** "The Structure of Job." *TBT* 20 (1982) 329–33. **Brenner, Athalya.** "Job the Pious? The Characterization of Job in the Narrative Framework of the Book." *JSOT* 43 (1989) 37–52. **Bruno, Arvid.** *Das Hohe Lied. Das Buch Hiob. Eine rhythmische und textkritische Untersuchung nebst einer Einführung in das Hohe Lied.* Stockholm: Almqvist & Wiksell, 1956. **Burden, J. J.** "Decision by Debate: Examples of Popular Proverb Performance in the Book of Job." *OTEss* 4 (1991) 37–65. **Ceresko, A. R.** "The A:B::B:A Word Pattern in Hebrew and Northwest Semitic with Special Reference to the Book of Job." *UF* 7 (1976) 73–88. **Clines, David J. A.** "On the Poetic Achievement of the Book of Job." In *Palabra, prodigio, poesía: in memoriam P. Luis Alonso Schökel, S.J.* Ed. Vicente Collado Bertomeu. AnBib 151. Rome: Editrice Pontificio Istituto Biblico; Jávea, Alicante: Huerto de Enseñanzas (ALAS), 2003. 243–53. **Cooper, Alan.** "Narrative Theory and the Book of Job." *SR* 11 (1982) 35–44. **Cotter, David W.** *A Study of Job 4–5 in the Light of Contemporary Literary Theory.* SBLDS 124. Atlanta: Scholars Press, 1992 [= Diss. Gregorian, 1989]. **Course, John E.** *Speech and Response: A Rhetorical Analysis of the Introductions to the Speeches of the Book of Job (chapters 4–24).* CBQMS 25. Washington, DC: Catholic Biblical Association of America, 1994 [= Diss. University of St Michael's College, Toronto, 1990]. **Cox, Dermot.** "The Book of Job as 'Bi-Polar Mašal': Structure and Interpretation." *Ant* 62 (1987) 12–25. **Crenshaw, James L.** "Impossible Questions, Sayings and Tasks." In *Gnomic Wisdom.* Ed. John Dominic Crossan. Semeia 17. Atlanta: Scholars Press, 1980. 19–34 [= "Questions, dictons et épreuves impossibles." In *La sagesse de l'Ancien Testament.* Ed. M. Gilbert et al. BETL 51. Gembloux: Duculot; Leuven: Leuven University Press, 1979. 96–111].

Dahood, M. "Chiasmus in Job: A Text-Critical and Philological Criterion." In *A Light unto My Path: Old Testament Studies in Honor of Jacob M. Myers.* Ed. H. N. Bream et al. Philadelphia: Temple University Press, 1974. 119–30. **Dion, P.-E.** "Formulaic Language in the Book of Job: International Background and Ironical Distortions." *SR* 16 (1987) 187–93. **Dobson, J. H.** "Translating Job—Prose or Poetry?" *BiTrans* 23 (1972) 243–44. **Driver, G. R.** "Hebrew Poetic Diction." In *Congress Volume, Copenhagen 1953.* VTSup 1. Leiden: E. J. Brill, 1953. 26–39. **Engljähringer, Klaudia.** *Theologie im Streitgespräch: Studien zur Dynamik der Dialoge des Buches Ijob.* Stuttgarter Bibelstudien 198. Stuttgart: Verlag Katholisches Bibelwerk, 2003. **Feinberg, C. L.** "The Poetic Structure of the Book of Job and the Ugaritic Literature." *BSac* 103 (1946) 283–92. **Fohrer, Georg.** "Dialog und Kommunikation im Buche Hiob." In *La sagesse de l'Ancien Testament.* Ed. M. Gilbert et al. BETL 51. Leuven: Leuven University Press, 1979. 219–30 [= his *Studien zum Buch Hiob (1956–1979).* BZAW 159. Berlin: de Gruyter, 1963, 2nd ed. 1983. 135–46]. ———. "Form und Funktion in der Hiobdichtung." *ZDMG* 109 (1959) 31–49 [= his *Studien zum Buche Hiob (1956–1979).* BZAW 159. Berlin: de Gruyter, 1963; 2nd ed. 1983. 60–77]. **Fontaine, Carole R.** "Folktale Structure in the Book of Job: A Formalist Reading." In *Directions in Biblical Hebrew Poetry.* Ed. Elaine R. Follis. JSOTSup 40. Sheffield: JSOT Press, 1987. 205–32. ———. "Wounded Hero on a Shaman's Quest: Job in the Context of Folk Literature." In *The Voice from the Whirlwind: Interpreting the Book of Job.* Ed. Leo G. Perdue and Clark Gilpin. Nashville: Abingdon Press, 1992. 70–85. **Frye, J. B.** "The Use of *mašal* in the Book of Job." *Semitics* 5 (1977) 59–66. **Gitay, Yehoshua.** "The Failure of Argumentation in the Book of Job: Humanistic Language versus Religious Language."

JNWSL 25 (1999) 239–50. ———. "Theories of Literature and the Question of (Hebrew) Biblical Theology: A Prolegomenon." *SJOT* 10 (1996) 61–68. **Goodchild, Philip.** "Job as Apologetic: The Role of the Audience." *Religion* 30 (April 2000) 149–67. **Gordis, Robert.** "Quotations as a Literary Usage in Biblical, Oriental and Rabbinic Literature." *HUCA* 22 (1949) 157–219. ———. "Virtual Quotations in Job, Sumer and Qumran." *VT* 31 (1981) 410–27. **Greenstein, Edward L.** "The Language of Job and Its Poetic Function." *JBL* 122 (2003) 651–66. **Grimm, Markus.** *"Dies Leben ist der Tod": Vergänglichkeit in den Reden Ijobs. Entwurf einer Textsemantik.* Arbeiten zu Text und Sprache im Alten Testament 62. St Ottilien: EOS-Verlag, 1998.

Habel, Norman C. "Appeal to Ancient Tradition as a Literary Form" [example of Job]. In *Society of Biblical Literature Seminar Papers*. I. Ed. G. MacRae. Cambridge, MA: Society of Biblical Literature, 1973. 34–54 [= *ZAW* 88 (1976) 253–72]. ———. "The Narrative Art of Job. Applying the Principles of Robert Alter." *JSOT* 27 (1983) 101–11. **Hertzberg, H. W.** "Der Aufbau des Buches Hiob." In *Festschrift Alfred Bertholet zum 80. Geburtstag gewidmet von Kollegen und Freunden.* Ed. Walter Baumgartner, Otto Eissfeldt, Kurt Elliger, and Leonhard Rost. Tübingen: J. C. B. Mohr (Paul Siebeck), 1950. 233–58. **Herz, J.** "Formgeschichtliche Untersuchungen zum Problem des Hiobbuches." In *Festschrift: Albrecht Alt zum 70. Geburtstag gewidmet.* Ed. Georg Mayer. Leipzig: Karl-Marx-Universität, 1954. 107–12 [= WZ der Karl-Marx-Universität, Leipzig. Gesellschafts- und Sprachwissenschaftliche Reihe 3 (1953–54) 157–62]. **Hirsch, N. D.** "The Architecture of the Book of Job." *CCAR Journal* 16 (1969) 22–32. **Hoffer, Victoria.** "Illusion, Allusion, and Literary Artifice in the Frame Narrative of Job." In *The Whirlwind: Essays on Job, Hermeneutics and Theology in Memory of Jane Morse.* Ed. Stephen L. Cook, Corrine L. Patton, and James W. Watts. JSOTSup 336. Sheffield: Sheffield Academic Press, 2001. 84–99. **Hoffman, Yair.** "Ancient Near Eastern Literary Conventions and the Restoration of the Book of Job." *ZAW* 103 (1991) 399–411. ———. "Irony in the Book of Job." *Immanuel* 17 (1983–84) 7–21 [= "Irony in the Book of Job" (Heb.). In *Bible Studies: Y. M. Grintz in Memoriam.* Ed. B. Uffenheimer. Te'uda 2. Tel Aviv: Hakibbutz Hameuchad, 1982. 157–94, 393]. **Holbert, John C.** *The Function and Significance of the "Klage" in the Book of Job with Special Reference to the Incidence of Formal and Verbal Irony.* Diss. Southern Methodist University, 1975. **Holland, J. A.** "On the Form of the Book of Job." *AJBA* 1 (1972) 160–77. **Hontheim, Joseph.** *Das Buch Hiob als strophisches Kunstwerk nachgewiesen, übersetzt und erklärt.* Biblische Studien 9/1–3. Freiburg i.Br.: Herder, 1904. **Hoop, Raymond de.** "The Frame Story of the Book of Job: Prose or Verse? Job 1:1–5 as a Test Case." In *Layout Markers in Biblical Manuscripts and Ugaritic Tablets.* Ed. Marjo C. A. Korpel and Josef M. Oesch. Pericope 5. Assen: Van Gorcum, 2005. 40–77. **Irwin, W. A.** "Poetic Structure in the Dialogue of Job." *JNES* 5 (1946) 26–39. **Johnstone, C. K.** "Poetic Statement in 'Job'." *RevUnivOtt* 32 (1962) 45–59. **Joosten, Jan.** "La macrostructure du livre de Job et quelques parallèles (Jérémie 45; 1 Rois 19)." In *The Book of Job.* Ed. W. A. M. Beuken. BETL 114. Leuven: Leuven University Press, 1994. 400–404. **Kissane, Edward J.** "The Metrical Structure of Job." In *Twentieth Century Interpretations of the Book of Job: A Collection of Critical Essays.* Ed. Paul S. Sanders. Englewood Cliffs, NJ: Prentice-Hall. 1968. 78–85 [= his *The Book of Job Translated from a Critically Revised Hebrew Text with Commentary.* Dublin: Browne & Nolan, 1939; New York: Sheed & Ward, 1946. l–lx]. **Koops, Robert.** "Rhetorical Questions and Implied Meaning in the Book of Job." *BiTrans* 39 (1988) 415–23.

Lawrie, Douglas G. "The Dialectical Grammar of Job and Qoheleth: A Burkean Analysis." *Scriptura* 66 (1998) 217–34. **Ley, J.** "Die metrische Beschaffenheit des Buches Hiob." *TSK* (1895) 635–92; (1897) 7–42. **Lichtenstein, A.** "Irony in the Book of Job." *Dor* 13 (1984–85) 41–42. **Lo, Alison.** "Device of Progression in the Prologue to Job." *BN* 130 (2006) 31–43. **Loader, James Alfred.** "Job and Cognition in Context—Impressions and Prospects from the Perspective of Exegesis." In *Job 28: Cognition in Context.* Biblical Interpretation Series 64. Leiden: Brill, 2003. 321–29. **Löhr, M.** "Beobachtungen zur Strophik im Buche Hiob." In *Abhandlungen zur semitischen Religionskunde und*

Sprachwissenschaft Wolf Wilhelm Grafen von Baudissin zum 26 Sept. 1917 überreicht von Freunden und Schülern. Ed. W. Frankenberg and F. Küchler. BZAW 33. Giessen: A. Töpelmann, 1918. 303–21. **Loyd, Douglas Emory.** *Patterns of Interrogative Rhetoric in the Speeches of the Book of Job.* Diss. Iowa, 1986. **Lugt, Pieter van der.** *Rhetorical Criticism and the Poetry of the Book of Job.* OTS 32. Leiden: E. J. Brill, 1995. "Speech-Cycles in the Book of Job: A Response to James E. Patrick." *VT* 56 (2006) 554–57. ———. "Stanza-Structure and Word-Repetition in Job 3–14." *JSOT* 40 (1988) 3–38. ———. "Strophes and Stanzas in the Book of Job: A Historical Survey." In *The Structural Analysis of Biblical and Canaanite Poetry.* Ed. Willem van der Meer and J. C. de Moor. JSOTSup 74. Sheffield: JSOT Press, 1988. 235–64. **Magary, Dennis R.** "Answering Questions, Questioning Answers: The Rhetoric of Interrogatives in the Speeches of Job and His Friends." In *Seeking out the Wisdom of the Ancients: Essays Offered to Honor Michael V. Fox on the Occasion of His Sixty-Fifth Birthday.* Ed. Ronald L. Troxel, Kelvin G. Friebel, and Dennis R. Magary. Winona Lake, IN: Eisenbrauns, 2005. 283-98. **Masini, F.** "Observaciones al rededor de la poesía del Viejo Testamento y del libro de Job en particular." *Davar* 69 (1957) 46–53. **Mettinger, Tryggve N. D.** "Intertextuality: Allusion and Vertical Context Systems in Some Job Passages" [Job 7; 16:7–17; 19:6–12]. In *Of Prophets' Visions and the Wisdom of Sages: Essays in Honour of R. Norman Whybray on His Seventieth Birthday.* Ed. Heather A. McKay and David J. A. Clines. JSOTSup 162. Sheffield: JSOT Press, 1993. 257–80. ———. "The Enigma of Job: The Deconstruction of God in Intertextual Perspective." *JNWSL* 23 (1997) 1–19. **Michel, Andreas.** "Herausstellungsstrukturen in den Streitreden des Ijob im Vergleich zu den Freunden (Ijob 3–25) im Ausgang von Ijob 16,7–14." In *Literatur- und sprachwissenschaftliche Beiträge zu alttestamentlichen Texten. Symposion in Hólar í Hjaltadal, 16.–19. Mai 2005. Wolfgang Richter zum 80. Geburtstag.* Ed. Sigurður Örn Steingrímsson and Kristinn Ólason. St Ottilien: Eos Verlag, 2007. 123–36. **Mies, Françoise.** "Le genre littéraire du livre de Job." *RB* 110 (2003) 336–69. **Nel, P. J., and N. F. Schmidt.** "The Rhetoric of the Theophany of Job." *OTEss* 16 (2003) 79–95. **Newsom, Carol A.** "Dramaturgy and the Book of Job." In *Das Buch Hiob und seine Interpretationen: Beiträge zum Hiob-Symposium auf dem Monte Verità vom 14.–19. August 2005.* Ed. Thomas Krüger, Manfred Oeming, Konrad Schmid, and Christoph Uehlinger. ATANT 88. Zurich: Theologische Verlag Zürich, 2007. 375–93. **Nicholls, P. H.** *The Structure and Purpose of the Book of Job.* Diss. Hebrew University, Jerusalem, 1982. **Noegel, Scott B.** "Janus Parallelism in Job and Its Literary Significance." *JBL* 115 (1996) 313–20. ———. *Janus Parallelism in the Book of Job.* JSOTSup 223. Sheffield: Sheffield Academic Press, 1996.

    O'Connor, Michael Patrick. "The Pseudo-Sorites in Hebrew Verse." In *Perspectives on Language and Text: Essays and Poems in Honor of Francis I. Andersen's Sixtieth Birthday, July 28, 1985.* Ed. Edgar W. Conrad and Edward G. Newing. Winona Lake, IN: Eisenbrauns, 1987. 239–53. **Painter, Rick.** "Cycle Theory and the Dialogue Cycle of Job." *PrGLM* 25 (2005) 59–68. **Palmer, Earle Fenton.** *An Inductive Study of the Metaphorical Language in the Book of Job.* Diss. New York, 1906. **Parsons, Gregory W.** "Literary Features of the Book of Job." *BSac* 138 (1981) 213–29. **Patrick, James E.** "The Fourfold Structure of Job. Variations on a Theme." *VT* 55 (2005) 185–206. **Peake, A. S.** "The Art of the Book." In *Twentieth Century Interpretations of the Book of Job. A Collection of Critical Essays.* Ed. P. S. Sanders. Englewood Cliffs, NJ: Prentice–Hall, 1968. 109–13 [= Peake, *Job.* 41–45]. **Polak, Frank H.** "On Prose and Poetry in the Book of Job." *JANES* 24 (1996) 61–97. **Polzin, Robert.** *Biblical Structuralism. Method and Subjectivity in the Study of Ancient Texts.* Semeia Supplements. Philadelphia: Fortress Press, 1977. 57–125. ———. "The Framework of the Book of Job." *Int* 28 (1974) 182–200. **Power, William Joseph Ambrose.** *A Study of Irony in the Book of Job.* Diss. Toronto, 1962. **Pyeon, Yohan.** *You have not spoken what is right about me: Intertextuality and the Book of Job.* Studies in Biblical Literature 45. New York: Peter Lang, 2003. **Rau [Ravius], Sebald Fulco Johannes.** *De l'excellence et de la perfection du talent poétique, considérées dans les trois poètes du premier ordre: l'auteur du livre de Job, Homère et Ossian.* n.d. ———. *Orationes duae. Altera de poeseos Hebraicae prae Arabum poesi praestantia ... altera de poeticae facultatis excellentia ... spectata in tribus poetarum principibus, scriptore Jobi,*

Homero et Ossiano. Leiden: Luchtmans, 1800. **Rechenmacher, Hans.** "Artikelsetzung in Poesie. Beobachtungen zu den Büchern Ijob und Psalmen." In *Literatur- und sprachwissenschaftliche Beiträge zu alttestamentlichen Texten. Symposion in Hólar í Hjaltadal, 16.–19. Mai 2005. Wolfgang Richter zum 80. Geburtstag.* Ed. Sigurður Örn Steingrímsson and Kristinn Ólason. St Ottilien: Eos Verlag, 2007. 199–218. ———. "Repetition und Variation von Präpositionen im Parallelismus membrorum, untersucht am Beispiel der Ijob-Poesie." In *"Erforsche mich, Gott, und erkenne mein Herz!" Beiträge zur Syntax, Sprechaktanalyse und Metaphorik im Alten Testament. Schülerfestschrift für Hubert Irsigler zum 60. Geburtstag.* Ed. Carmen Diller, Martin Mulzer, and Kristinn Olason. ATSAT 76. St Ottilien: Eos Verlag, 2005. 1–14. **Reed, W. L.** "Dimensions of Dialog in the Book of Job, a Topology according to Bakhtin." *Texas Studies in Literature and Language* 34 (1992) 177–96. **Regt, Lénart J. de.** "Discourse Implications of Rhetorical Questions in Job, Deuteronomy and the Minor Prophets." In *Literary Structure and Rhetorical Strategies in the Hebrew Bible.* Ed. Lénart J. de Regt, J. de Waard, and J. P. Fokkelman. Assen: Van Gorcum, 1996. 51–78. ———. "Functions and Implications of Rhetorical Questions in the Book of Job." In *Biblical Hebrew and Discourse Linguistics.* Ed. Robert D. Bergen. Summer Institute of Linguistics. Winona Lake, IN: Eisenbrauns, 1994. 361–73. **Rensburg, J. F. J. van.** "Wise Men Saying Things by Asking Questions: The Function of the Interrogative in Job 3 to 14." *OTEss* ns 4 (1991) 227–47. **Reynolds, Roberta M.** *Piety and Paradox. A Rhetorical Analysis of the King James Version of the Book of Job.* Diss. Oregon, 1984. **Richter, Heinz.** *Studien zu Hiob. Der Aufbau des Hiobbuches, dargestellt an den Gattungen des Rechtslebens.* Berlin: Evangelische Verlagsanstalt, 1959. **Robertson, David.** "The Book of Job." In his *The Old Testament and the Literary Critic.* Guides to Biblical Scholarship. Philadelphia: Fortress Press, 1977. 33–54. ———. "The Book of Job: A Literary Study." *Soundings* 56 (1973) 446–69.

Sarna, Nahum M. "Epic Substratum in the Prose of Job." *JBL* 76 (1957) 13–15. **Sawyer, J. F. A.** "The Authorship and Structure of the Book of Job." In *Studia Biblica 1978.* I. *Papers on Old Testament and Related Themes.* Ed. E. A. Livingstone. JSOTSup 11. Sheffield: JSOT Press, 1979. 253–57. **Schlobin, Roger C.** "Prototypic Horror: The Genre of the Book of Job." *Semeia* 60 (1992) 23–38. **Schorlemmer, Helmut.** *Hiob auf der Bühne: Die dramatischen und theatralen Elemente des alttestamentarischen Buches Hiob.* Diss. Munich, 1983. **Seitz, Christopher R.** "Job: Full-Structure, Movement and Interpretation." *Int* 43 (1989) 5–17. **Selms, Adrianus van.** "A Composition Device in the Book of Job." *Semitics* 10 (1989) 1–9. ———. "Motivated Interrogative Sentences in the Book of Job." *Semitics* 6 (1978) 28–35. **Seybold, Klaus.** "Psalmen im Buch Hiob. Eine Skizze." In his *Studien zur Psalmenauslegung.* Stuttgart: Kohlhammer, 1998. 270–87. **Sievers, Eduard.** *Metrische Studien.* I. *Studien zur hebräischen Metrik* [Job 3–7]. Abhandlungen der Sächsischen Gesellschaft der Wissenschaften, philologisch-historischen Klasse 21. Leipzig: S. Hirzel, 1901. **Skehan, P. W.** "Strophic Patterns in the Book of Job." *CBQ* 23 (1961) 125–42 [= his *Studies in Israelite Poetry and Wisdom.* CBQMS 1. Washington, DC: Catholic Biblical Association, 1971. 96–113]. **Smick, Elmer B.** "Architectonics, Structured Poems, and Rhetorical Devices in the Book of Job" [incl. 13:28–14:6; 27–31; 38–41]. In *A Tribute to Gleason Archer.* Ed. Walter C. Kaiser, Jr, and Ronald F. Youngblood. Chicago: Moody Press, 1986. 87–104. ———. "Semeiological Interpretation of the Book of Job." *WTJ* 48 (1986) 135–49. **Smyser, William Emory.** "A Literary Study of the Book of Job." *MethRev* 82 (1900) 849–68. **Snaith, Norman H.** "The Introductions to the Speeches in the Book of Job, Are They in Prose or in Verse?" *Textus* 8 (1973) 133–37. **Steinmann, Andrew E.** "The Graded Numerical Saying in Job." In *Fortunate the Eyes That See: Essays in Honor of David Noel Freedman in Celebration of His Seventieth Birthday.* Ed. Astrid B. Beck, Andrew H. Bartelt, Paul R. Raabe, and Chris A. Franke. Grand Rapids: Eerdmans, 1995. 288–97. ———. "The Structure and Message of the Book of Job." *VT* 46 (1996) 85–100. **Stordalen, Terje.** "Dialogue and Dialogism in the Book of Job." *SJOT* 20 (2006) 18–37. **Strauss, Hans.** "Motiv und Strukturen von Umkehrungssprüchen in Ägypten und im Alten Testament (Buch Hiob)." *ZAW* 115 (2003) 25–37. **Toorn, Karel van der.** "The Ancient Near Eastern

Literary Dialogue as a Vehicle of Critical Reflection." In *Dispute Poems and Dialogues in the Ancient and Mediaeval Near East: Forms and Types of Literary Debates in Semitic and Related Literatures*. Ed. G. L. Reinink and H. L. J. Vanstiphout. OLA 42. Leuven: Departement oriëntalistiek, 1991. 59–75. **Trebolle Barrera, Julio.** "Paralelismo de género en la poesía hebrea bíblica. La mujer del 'Cantar de los Cantares' y el hombre del libro de 'Job'." *'Ilu* 10 (2005) 225–47. **Tur-Sinai, N. H. [Torczyner, H.].** שירת איוב כיצרה כפרותית" [The Poem of Job as a Literary Creation]." *Hen* 25 (1954) 300–305. **Urbrock, William J.** "Oral Antecedents to Job: A Survey of Formulas and Formulaic Systems." *Semeia* 5 (1976) 111–37. ———. "Formula and Theme in the Song-Cycle of Job." *Society of Biblical Literature, 1972 Proceedings*. Ed. Lane C. McGaughy. Missoula, MT: Society of Biblical Literature, 1972. 2:459–87. ———. "Job as Drama: Tragedy or Comedy?" *CurTM* 8 (1981) 35–40.

Vetter, P. *Die Metrik des Buches Hiob*. Biblische Studien 2. Freiburg i.Br., 1897. **Vogels, Walter.** "Job a parlé correctement. Une approche structurale du livre de Job." *NRT* 102 (1980) 835–52. **Warner, Martin.** *Philosophical Finesse: Studies in the Art of Rational Persuasion*. Oxford: Clarendon Press, 1989. **Watters, William R.** *Formula Criticism and the Poetry of the Old Testament*. BZAW 138. Berlin: Walter de Gruyter, 1976. **Watts, James W.** "The Unreliable Narrator of Job." In *The Whirlwind: Essays on Job, Hermeneutics and Theology in Memory of Jane Morse*. Ed. Stephen L. Cook, Corrine L. Patton, and James W. Watts. JSOTSup 336. Sheffield: Sheffield Academic Press, 2001. 168–80. **Webster, Edwin C.** "Strophic Patterns in Job 3–28." *JSOT* 26 (1983) 33–60. ———. "Strophic Patterns in Job 29–42." *JSOT* 30 (1984) 95–109. **Westermann, Claus.** *Der Aufbau des Buches Hiob*. Tübingen: J. C. B. Mohr (Paul Siebeck), 1956; 3rd ed. Stuttgart: Calwer Verlag, 1978 [= *The Structure of the Book of Job: A Form-Critical Analysis*. Trans. Charles A. Muenchow. Philadelphia: Fortress Press, 1981]. **Whedbee, J. William.** *The Bible and the Comic Vision*. Cambridge: Cambridge University Press, 1988. 242–45. ———. "The Comedy of Job." *Semeia* 7 (1977) 1–39 [= *On Humour and the Comic in the Hebrew Bible*. Ed. Yehuda T. Radday and Athalya Brenner. JSOTSup 92. Sheffield: JSOT Press, 1990. 217–49]. **Williams, James G.** "Comedy, Irony, Intercession: A Few Notes in Response." *Semeia* 7 (1977) 135–45. ———. "On Job and Writing: Derrida, Girard, and the Remedy-Poison." *SJOT* 7 (1993) 32–50. ———. "'You have not spoken truth of me.' Mystery and Irony in Job." *ZAW* 83 (1971) 231–55. **Wilson, Gerald H.** "Preknowledge, Anticipation, and the Poetics of Job." *JSOT* 30 (2005) 243–56. **Witte, Markus.** "Die literarische Gattung des Buches Hiob: Robert Lowth und seine Erben." In *Sacred Conjectures: The Context and Legacy of Robert Lowth and Jean Astruc*. New York: T. & T. Clark, 2007. 93–123. **Wolde, Ellen van.** "A Text-Semantic Study of the Hebrew Bible, Illustrated with Noah and Job." *JBL* 113 (1994) 19–35.

7. Topics

This is not a complete index to the literature on the topics mentioned below; the chapter *Bibliographies* where the subject is discussed should also be consulted.

abortion. Bullock, C. Hassell. "Abortion and Old Testament Prophetic and Poetic Literature" [Psalm 139; Job; Jeremiah]. In *Abortion: A Christian Understanding and Response*. Ed. James K. Hoffmeier. Grand Rapids: Baker Book House, 1987. 65–71.

absurd. Russotto, Mario. "Il non senso della vita: l'esperienza di Giobbe." *Presenza pastorale* 67 (1997) 593–607. **Taradach, Madeleine.** "De la 'modernité' de l'absurde chez Job à la lumière de l'absurde chez Camus." *EstFranc* 81 (1980) 155–68.

afterlife. See **resurrection**.

alienation. Thompson, K. T. "Out of the Whirlwind. The Sense of Alienation in the Book of Job." *Int* 14 (1960) 51–63.

animals. Riede, Peter. "'Ein Spinnenhaus ist sein Vertrauen' (Hi 8,14). Tiere in der Bildsprache der Hiobdialoge. Teil II: Der Frevler und sein Geschick." "'Ich bin ein Bruder der Schakale' (Hi 30,29). Tiere als Exponenten der gegenmenschlichen Welt in der Bildsprache der Hiobdialoge." In his *Im Spiegel der Tiere. Studien zum Verhältnis von Mensch und Tier im alten Israel.* OBO 187. Freiburg, Switzerland: Universitätsverlag; Göttingen: Vandenhoeck & Ruprecht, 2002. 133–52, 120–32.

anthropocentrism. Sponheim, Paul R. "Against Anthropocentrism: A Jobian Appeal to Science on Theology's Behalf." *Dialog* 46 (2007) 255–62.

argumentation. Adams, Nicholas. "The Goodness of Job's Bad Arguments." *Journal of Scriptural Reasoning* 4/1 (2004) [http://etext.lib.virginia.edu/journals/ssr/issues/volume4/number1/ssr04-01-e03.html].

astronomy. Ammon, Franz. *Über die Bedeutung der im Buche Hiob vorkommenden Sternnamen: Ein Beitrag zur Astrognosie.* Passau, 1838. **Halpern, Baruch.** "Assyrian and Pre-Socratic Astronomies and the Location of the Book of Job." In *Kein Land für sich allein: Studien zum Kulturkontakt in Kanaan, Israel/Palästina und Ebirnari für Manfred Weippert zum 65. Geburtstag.* Ed. Ulrich Hübner and Ernst Axel Knauf. OBO 186. Freiburg, Switzerland: Universitätsverlag; Göttingen: Vandenhoeck & Ruprecht, 2002. 255–64.

belief. Bloch, Ernst. "Grenze der Geduld, Hiob oder Exodus nicht in, sondern aus der Jahwevorstellung selber, Schärfe des Messianismus." In *Atheismus im Christentum: zur Religion des Exodus und des Reichs.* Frankfurt a.M.: Suhrkamp, 1968. 148–66 [= *Atheism in Christianity: The Religion of the Exodus and the Kingdom.* New York: Herder & Herder, 1972].

betrayal. Lévêque, J. "Tradition and Betrayal in the Speeches of the Friends." *Conc* 169 (1983) 39–44.

blood. Vattioni, Francesco. "La sangue nella fonte di Giobbe." In his edited *Sangue e antropologia nella teologia: atti della 6. Settimana, Roma, 23–28 novembre 1987.* Rome: Pia Unione Preziosissimo Sangue, 1989. 691–708, 871–87.

body. Viviers, H. "Body and Nature in Job." *OTEss* 14 (2001) 510–24.

chaos. Cepeda Calzada, P. "El Leviatán, símbolo bíblico. El Caos frente a la idea de ley en Job." *Crisis* 21 (1974) 49–68.

children. Coogan, Michael David. "Job's Children." In *Lingering over Words: Studies in Ancient Near Eastern Literature in Honor of William L. Moran.* Ed. Tzvi Abusch, John Huehnergard, and Piotr Steinkeller. HSS 37. Atlanta: Scholars Press, 1990. 135–47.

Christology. Haught, J. F. "The Significance of Job for Christology." *AER* 166 (1972) 579–86.

comedy. Urbrock, William J. "Job as Drama: Tragedy or Comedy?" *CurTM* 8 (1981) 35–40. **Whedbee, J. William.** *The Bible and the Comic Vision.* Cambridge: Cambridge University Press, 1988. 242–45. ———. "The Comedy of Job." *Semeia* 7 (1977) 1–39 [= *On Humour and the Comic in the Hebrew Bible.* Ed. Yehuda T. Radday and Athalya Brenner. JSOTSup 92. Sheffield: JSOT Press, 1990. 217–49]. **Williams, J. G.** "Comedy, Irony, Intercession: A Few Notes in Response." *Semeia* 7 (1977) 135–45.

comfort. Langenhorst, Georg. "'Sieben Tage und sieben Nächte' (Hiob 2,13). Gelingender und scheiternder Trost im Buch Hiob." *LS* 57 (2006) 7–12. **O'Connor, Daniel.** "The Comforting of Job." *ITQ* 53 (1987) 245–57.

contemplation. Dailey, Thomas F. "Seeing He Repents: Contemplative Consciousness and the Wisdom of Job." *AmBenRev* 46 (1995) 87–101.

contextual interpretation. Berges, Ulrich. "Hiob in Lateinamerika. Der leidende Mensch und der aussätzige Gott." In *The Book of Job.* Ed. W. A. M. Beuken. BETL 114. Leuven: Leuven University Press, 1994. 297–317. **Chilongani, D. D.** *Reading the Book of Job with an African Eye: A Reinterpretation of the Book of Job from an African Traditional Religious Perspective, with Special Reference to the Wagogo of Central Tanzania.* Diss. Bristol, 2004. **Matadi, Ghislain Tshikendwa.** "De l'epreuve à la sagesse. Une lecture du livre de Job dans le contexte africain." *Telema* 123,4 (2005) 7–24. **Mukenge, André Kabasele.** "Une lecture populaire de la figure de Job au Congo." *Bulletin for Old Testament Studies in Africa* 16 (2004) 2–6. **Snoek, J.** *Antwoorden op het lijden. Een bijdrage aan de discussie over contextueel bijbellezen: Job 4–5 in het licht van opvattingen van Nicaraguaanse pinkstergelovigen.*

Gorinchem: Narratio, 2000. **Susaimanickam, Jebamalai.** *Commitment to the Oppressed: A Dalit Reading of the Book of Job.* Diss. Gregorian, 1996. ———. "An Indian Problem of Evil: The Caste System. A Dalit Reading of the Book of Job." In *Indian Interpretation of the Bible: Festschrift in Honour of Prof. Dr Joseph Pathrapankal.* Ed. Augustine Thottakara. Bangalore, Dharmaram Publications, 2000. 181–200. **Tshikendwa Matadi, Ghislain.** *Suffering, Belief, Hope: The Wisdom of Job for an AIDS-stricken Africa.* Trans. Joseph P. Newman with Robert E. Czerny. Nairobi: Paulines Publications Africa, 2007. **Weber, Burkhard.** *Ijob in Lateinamerika. Bedeutung und Bewältigung von Leid in der Theologie der Befreiung.* Mainz: Grünewald, 1999.

convergence. Ticciati, Susannah. "Convergence and Divergence: Differing Jobs." *Journal of Scriptural Reasoning* 4/1 (2004) [http://etext.lib.virginia.edu/journals/ssr/issues/ volume4/number1/ssr04-01-f01.html].

cosmology. Habel, Norman C. "The Inverse Cosmology of Job: An Option to Celebrate?" In *The Bright Side of Life.* Ed. Ellen van Wolde. Concilium 2000/4. London: SCM Press, 2000 [= "Ijobs Umkehr der Kosmologie—eine feiernswerte Option?" *Conc* 36 (2000) 394–402]. **Perdue, Leo G.** "Cosmology and Social Order in the Wisdom Tradition." In *The Sage in Israel and the Ancient Near East.* Ed. John G. Gammie and Leo G. Perdue. Winona Lake, IN: Eisenbrauns, 1990. 457–78.

counseling. Becker, D. "Der Grundgedanke des Buches Job. Biblische Lehr- und Trostgedanken zur praktischen Seelsorge." *TPM* 29 (1918–19) 109–17. **Mickel, Tobias.** *Seelsorgerliche Aspekte im Hiobbuch: Ein Beitrag zur biblischen Dimension der Poimenik.* Berlin: Evangelische Verlagsanstalt, 1990.

creation. Albertz, R. *Weltschöpfung und Menschenschöpfung, untersucht bei Deuterojesaja, Hiob und im den Psalmen.* Calwer Theologische Monographien A3. Stuttgart: Calwer, 1974. **Cho, Eun Suk.** "Creation in the Book of Job: An Exegetical Essay on Job 3 from a Korean Perspective." *AsiaJT* 17 (2003) 26–76. **Clifford, Richard J.** "Creation in the Hebrew Bible." In *Physics, Philosophy, and Theology.* Ed. Robert J. Russell, William R. Stoeger, and George V. Coyne. Vatican City: Vatican Observatory, 1988. 151–70. **Eberhardt, Rodney.** "Preaching on Job: Creation and Cross." *Lutheran Forum* 36 (2002) 28–31. **Forrest, Robert William Edward.** *The Creation Motif in the Book of Job.* Diss. McMaster University, 1975. **Fyall, Robert S.** *Now My Eyes Have Seen You: Images of Creation and Evil in the Book of Job.* Leicester: Apollos, 2002. **Janzen, J. Gerald.** "Creation and the Human Predicament in Job." *Ex auditu* 3 (1987) 45–53. **Lévêque, Jean.** "L'argument de la création dans le livre de Job." In *La création dans l'orient ancien. Congrès de l'Association Catholique Française pour l'Etude de la Bible.* Ed. Louis Derousseaux and Fabien Blanquart. Lectio divina 127. Paris: Les Editions du Cerf, 1987. 261–99.

Mahlmann, Theodor. "Das eschatologische Faktum der Schöpfung." In *Ernst Blochs Vermittlungen zur Theologie.* Ed. Hermann Deuser and Peter Steinacker. Munich: Kaiser, 1983. 144–85. **Malter, Rudolf.** "Schöpfergott und Theodizee: Eine philosophische Meditation über den 73. Psalm und das Buch Hiob." In *Gott—das bleibende Geheimnis.* Ed. Peter Reifenberg. Würzburg: Echter Verlag, 1996. 68–88. **Martin-Achard, Robert.** *Et Dieu crée le ciel et la terre: Trois études: Esaïe 40—Job 38–42—Genèse I.* Essais bibliques 2. Geneva: Editions Labor et Fides, 1979. **McKibben, Bill.** "Climate Change and the Unraveling of Creation." *ChrCent* 116 (1999) 1196–99. **O'Connor, Kathleen M.** "Job Uncreates the World." *BiTod* 34 (1996) 4–8. ———. "Wild, Raging Creativity: Job in the Whirlwind." In *Earth, Wind, and Fire: Biblical and Theological Perspectives on Creation.* Ed. Barbara E. Bowe, Carol J. Dempsey, and Mary Margaret Pazdan. Collegeville, MN: Liturgical Press, 2004. 171–79. **Perdue, Leo G.** "Creation in the Dialogues between Job and His Opponents." In *Das Buch Hiob und seine Interpretationen: Beiträge zum Hiob Symposium auf dem Monte Verità vom 14.–19. August 2005.* Ed. Thomas Krüger, Manfred Oeming, Konrad Schmid, and Christoph Uehlinger. ATANT 88. Zurich: Theologische Verlag Zürich, 2007. 197–216. ———. "Job's Assault on Creation." *HAR* 10 (1987) 295–315. **Prado, Juan.** "La creación, conservación y gobierno del universo en el libro de Job." *Sef* 11 (1951) 259–88. **Reimer, Haroldo.** "Gerechtigkeit und Schöpfung: ein Beitrag zum Verständnis des

Hiobbuches." In *Freiheit und Recht: Festschrift für Frank Crüsemann zum 65. Geburtstag*. Ed. Christof Hardmeier, Rainer Kessler, and Andreas Ruwe. Gütersloh: Kaiser, 2003. 414–28. **Rowold, Henry Lawrence.** *The Theology of Creation in the Yahweh Speeches of the Book of Job as a Solution to the Problem Posed by the Book of Job*. Diss. Concordia Seminary in Exile (Seminex), 1977. **Schifferdecker, Kathryn.** *Out of the Whirlwind: Creation Theology in the Book of Job*. Harvard Theological Studies 58. Cambridge, MA: Harvard University Press, 2007 [= Diss. Harvard, 2005; see *HTR* 98 (2005) 489–506]. **Schmidt, P.** "Sinnfrage und Glaubenskrise. Ansätze zu einer kritischen Theologie der Schöpfung im Buche Hiob." *GeistL* 45 (1972) 348–63. **Sekine, Masao.** "Schöpfung und Erlösung im Buche Hiob." In *Von Ugarit nach Qumran: Beiträge zur alttestamentlichen und altorientalischen Forschung. Otto Eissfeldt zum 1. September 1957 dargebracht von Freunden und Schülern*. BZAW 77. Berlin: A. Töpelmann, 1958. 213–23. **Strolz, Walter.** "Schöpfungsweisheit im Buch Ijob." *Diakonia* 21 (1990) 314–22. **Tönsing, Detlev L.** "The Use of Creation Language in Job 3, 9 and 38 and the Meaning of Suffering." *Scriptura* 59 (1996) 435–49. **Wagner, S.** "'Schöpfung' im Buche Hiob." *ZZ* 34 (1980) 93–96. **Yeager, Janet, and Thomas F. Dailey.** "Job's World: A Chaotic Conundrum!" *Enc* 56 (1995) 175–87. **Zakovitch, Yair.** "מדרש בריאה: בראשית תהלים איוב תהלים." In *Creation and Re-Creation in Jewish Thought: Festschrift in Honor of Joseph Dan on the Occasion of His Seventieth Birthday*. Ed. Rachel Elior and Peter Schäfer. Tübingen: Mohr Siebeck, 2005. *7–*14.

   crisis. Löhr, Max. *Seelenkämpfe und Glaubensnöte vor 2000 Jahren*. Religionsgeschichtliche Volksbücher. 2. Reihe, Die Religion des Alten Testaments 1. Halle a. Saale: Gebauer-Schwetschke, 1904.

   cultural politics. Newsom, Carol A. "Cultural Politics and the Reading of Job." *BibInt* 1 (1993) 119–38.

   curse. Young, D. M. *Fencing with the Promises. Report of a Project on Proper and Faithful Cursing: A Study of the Book of Job with Senior High Youth*. Diss. Boston University, 1981.

   darkness. Galbiati, E. R. "The Night and Its Sun. Light and Darkness in the Book of Job. Symbolic Analyses." *Aevum* 73 (1999) 199–202.

   death. Bobrinskoy, B. "La vieillesse et la mort, drame ou benediction: pointe de vue de la tradition orthodoxe." In *In necessariis unitas: mélanges offerts à Jean-Louis Leuba*. Ed. Richard Stauffer. Paris: Editions du Cerf, 1984. 25–33. **Christ, Marie-Paul du.** "Job et le mystère de la mort." *VS* 422 (1956) 392–406. **Crouch, Walter B.** *Death and Closure in Biblical Narrative*. Frankfurt a.M.: Peter Lang, 2000. **Crumbach, K. H.** "Splitter zum Problem des Todes." *GeistL* 43 (1970) 325–38. **Kummerow, David.** "Job, Hopeful or Hopeless? The Significance of מוֹ in Job 16:19 and Job's Changing Conceptions of Death." *JHS* 5 (2004). **Mathewson, Dan.** *Death and Survival in the Book of Job: Desymbolization and Traumatic Experience*. LHB/OTS 450. New York: T. & T. Clark, 2006. **Michel, W. L.** "Death in Job." *Dialog* 11 (1972) 183–89. **Muntingh, L. M.** "Life, Death and Resurrection in the Book of Job." *OTWSA* 17–18 (*Old Testament Essays: Studies in the Pentateuch*. Ed. W. C. van Wyk) (1974–75) 32–44. **Perani, M.** "Giobbe di fronte alla morte." In *Gesù e la sua morte: Atti della XXVII Set-timana dell'Associazione Biblica Italiana, Roma 13–17 settembre 1982*. Ed. G. Boggio, A. Bonora, S. Cipriani, et al. Brescia: Paideia, 1984. 267–91. **Sauer, Georg.** "Der Mensch vor der Aporie des Todes: Gilgamesch–Hiob." In *Gott und Mensch im Dialog: Festschrift für Otto Kaiser zum 80. Geburtstag*. Ed. Markus Witte. BZAW 345/2. Berlin: de Gruyter, 2004. 2:655–65. **Smith, David L.** "The Concept of Death in Job and Ecclesiastes." *Didaskalia* 4/1 (1992) 2–14. **Strauss, Hans.** "Tod (Todeswunsch; 'Jenseits'?) im Buch Hiob." In *Gottes Recht als Lebensraum: Festschrift für Hans Jochen Boecker*. Ed. Peter Mommer, Werner H. Schmidt, and Hans Strauss. Neukirchen–Vluyn: Neukirchener Verlag, 1993. 239–49. **Tromp, Nicholas J.** *Primitive Conceptions of Death and the Nether World in the Old Testament*. BibOr 21. Rome: Pontifical Biblical Institute, 1969.

   demons. Chastain, K. "The Dying Art of Demon-Recognition: Victims, Systems, and the Book of Job." In *Power, Powerlessness, and the Divine: New Inquiries in Bible and Theology*. Ed. Cynthia L. Rigby. Atlanta: Scholars Press, 1997. 161–78 [reply by F. Keshgegian, pp.

199–205]. **Duquoc, C.** "Demonism and the Unexpectedness of God." In C. Duquoc and C. Floristán. *Job and the Silence of God.* Concilium 169. Edinburgh: T. & T. Clark, 1983. 81–87.

dialogue. Fischer, Georg. "Heilendes Gespräch—Beobachtungen zur Kommunikation im Ijobbuch." In *Das Buch Ijob: Gesamtdeutungen—Einzeltexte—zentrale Themen.* Ed. Theodor Seidl and Stephanie Ernst. Österreichische biblische Studien 31. Frankfurt: Peter Lang, 2007. 183–200. **Fohrer, G.** "Dialog und Kommunication im Buche Hiob." In *La sagesse de l'Ancien Testament.* Ed. M. Gilbert et al. BETL 51. Leuven: Leuven University Press, 1979. 219–30 [= his *Studien zum Buch Hiob (1956–1979).* BZAW 159. Berlin: de Gruyter, 1963, 2nd ed., 1983. 135–46]. **Gruber, Mayer I.** "Three Failed Dialogues from the Biblical World" [incl. Job 3–37]. *JPsychJud* 22 (1998) 51–64. **Hecke, Pierre van.** "From Conversation about God to Conversation with God: The Case of Job." In *Theology and Conversation: Towards a Relational Theology.* Ed. J. Haers and P. De Mey. BETL 172. Leuven: Leuven University Press; Uitgeverij Peeters, 2003. 115–24. **Müllner, Ilse.** "Erkenntnis im Gespräch. Zur Bedeutung der (verbalen) Begegnung im Ijobbuch." In *Auf den Spuren der schriftgelehrten Weisen. Festschrift für Johannes Marböck anlässlich seiner Emeritierung.* Ed. Irmtraud Fischer, Ursula Rapp, and Johannes Schiller. BZAW 331. Berlin: Walter de Gruyter, 2003. 167–80. **Ticciati, Susannah.** "Job, Debate, and the Shaping of Lives." *Journal of Scriptural Reasoning* 4/1 (2004). **Würthwein, E.** "Gott und Mensch in Dialog und Gottesreden des Buches Hiob." In his *Wort und Existenz: Studien zum Alten Testament.* Göttingen: Vandenhoeck & Ruprecht, 1970. 217–95. ———. *Gott und Mensch in Dialog und Gottesreden des Buches Hiob.* Habilitationsschrift, Tübingen, 1938.

disability. Raphael, Rebecca. "Things Too Wonderful. A Disabled Reading of Job." *PerspRS* 31 (2004) 399–424.

doubt. Dietzel, Gabriele. "Hiob—Trauer und Verzweiflung." *DPB* 100/3 (2000) 118–19. **Israel, Martin.** *Doubt: The Way of Growth.* London: Mowbray, 1997. **Schimmel, Solomon.** "Job and the Psychology of Suffering and Doubt." *JPsychJud* 11 (1987) 239–49.

drama. Kennedy, Andrew. "Myth and the Drama of the Soul." In *Theatre and Holy Script.* Ed. Shimon Levy. Brighton: Sussex Academic Press, 1999. 238–46. **Usmiana, Renate.** "A New Look at the Drama of Job." *Modern Drama* 13 (1970) 191–200.

dream. Erny, P. "La rêve dans le livre de Job." *Présence orthodoxe* 74 (1987) 30–39.

dust. Conerly, Rodrick Evan. *An Examination of the Hebrew Term* עפר *in the Book of Job: A Rhetorical and Anthropological Analysis.* Diss. New Orleans Baptist Theological Seminary, 2000.

ecology. Gordis, Robert. "Job and Ecology (and the Significance of Job 40:15)." *HAR* 9 (1985) 189–202 [= *Biblical and Other Studies in Memory of Shelmo Dov Goitein.* Ed. Reuben Ahroni. Columbus, OH]. **Habel, Norman C.** "Earth First: Inverse Cosmology in Job." In *The Earth Story in Wisdom Traditions.* Ed. Norman C. Habel and Shirley Wurst. The Earth Bible 3. Sheffield: Sheffield Academic Press, 2001. 65–77. **Hart, John.** "Job, Injustice, and Dynamic Nature." In his *Sacramental Commons: Christian Ecological Ethics.* Lanham, MD: Rowman & Littlefield, 2006. 159–77. **Maarschalk, R.** "Die Godsredes in die boek Job: ideologie en eko-teologie." *VerbEccl* 23 (2002) 125–40.

education. Langer, Michael. "Alte Weisheiten für junge Menschen: Gedanken zum Buch Hiob im Religionsunterricht der gymnasialen Oberstufe." In *Steht nicht geschrieben? Studien zur Bibel und ihrer Wirkungsgeschichte. Festschrift für Georg Schmuttermayr.* Ed. Johannes Frühwald-König, Ferdinand R. Prostmeier, and Reinhold Zwick. Regensburg: Pustet, 2001. 457–80. **Melchert, Charles F.** "The Book of Job: Education through and by Diversity." *Religious Education* 92 (1997) 9–23.

eschatology. Royer, Jakob. *Die Eschatologie des Buches Job.* Regensburg: G. J. Manz, 1892 [= *Die Eschatologie des Buches Job unter Berücksichtigung der vorexilischen Prophetie.* Biblische Studien 6/5. Freiburg i.Br.: Herder, 1901].

ethics. Clines, David J. A. "Job's Fifth Friend: An Ethical Critique of the Book of Job." *BibInt* 12 (2004) 233–50. **Ehrlich, Bernard.** "The Book of Job as a Book of Morality."

JBQ 34 (2006) 30–38. **Eising, H.** "Alttestamentliche Sittenlehre im Buche Hiob." *Kirche in der Welt* (Munich) (1952) 255–58. **Faur, J.** "Reflections on Job and Situation-Morality." *Judaism* 19 (1970) 219–25. **Hamilton, W. T.** "Difficult Texts from Job." In *Difficult Texts of the Old Testament Explained.* Ed. Wendell Winkler. Hurst, TX: Winkler Publications, 1982. 301–10. **Maston, T. B.** "Ethical Content in Job." *SWJT* 14 (1971) 43–56. **Newsom, Carol A.** "The Moral Sense of Nature: Ethics in the Light of God's Speech to Job." *PrSemBull* 15 (1994) 9–27. **Oeming, Manfred.** "Ethik in der Spätzeit des Alten Testaments am Beispiel von Hiob 31 und Tobit 4." In *Altes Testament: Forschung und Wirkung: Festschrift für Henning Graf Reventlow.* Ed. Peter Mommer and Winfried Thiel. Frankfurt a.M.: Peter Lang, 1994. 159–73. **Raurell, Frederic.** "Ètica de Job i llibertat de déu." *RCatalT* 4 (1979) 5–24; *Butlletí de l'Associació Bíblica de Catalunya* 10 (1979) 12–19 [= "Job's Ethic and God's Freedom." *TDig* 29 (1981) 133–37]. **Stockhammer, Morris.** "Theorie der Moralprobe." *ZRGG* 22 (1970) 164–67. **Strauss, Hans.** "Juridisches im Buch Hiob." In *Recht und Ethos im Alten Testament—Gestalt und Wirkung: Festschrift für Horst Seebass zum 65. Geburtstag.* Ed. Stefan Beyerle, Günter Mayer, and Hans Strauss. Neukirchen–Vluyn: Neukirchener Verlag, 1999. 83–90.

    evil. Böhles, M. "Von der Macht und Ohnmacht des Bösen." *OrdKor* 18 (1977) 129–46. **Burrell, David B.** "Maimonides, Aquinas and Gersonides on Providence and Evil." *RelStud* 20 (1984) 335–51. **Cameron, Brian K.** "A Critique of Marilyn McCord Adams' 'Christian Solution' to the Existential Problem of Evil." *AmCathPhilQ* 73 (1999) 419–34. **Carson, D. A.** "Job: Mystery and Faith." In his *How Long, O Lord? Reflections on Suffering and Evil.* Grand Rapids: Baker Academic, 2006. **Clifford, Paul Rowntree.** "Omnipotence and the Problem of Evil." *JR* 41(1961) 118–28. **Corey, Michael Anthony.** *Job, Jonah, and the Unconscious: A Psychological Interpretation of Evil and Spiritual Growth in the Old Testament.* Lanham, MD: University Press of America, 1995. **Dewey, Rosemary.** "Qoheleth and Job: Diverse Responses to the Enigma of Evil." *Spirituality Today* 37 (1985) 314–25. **Elkins, William Wesley.** "'Suffering Job': Scriptural Reasoning and the Problem of Evil." *Journal of Scriptural Reasoning* 4/1 (2004). **Foucher, Daniel.** *Job et le mystère du mal.* Réponses aux questions 2. La Chapelle Montligeon: Editions de Montligeon, 1997. **Friedman, R. Z.** "Evil and Moral Agency." *International Journal for Philosophy of Religion* 24 (1988) 3–20. **Fyall, Robert S.** *Now My Eyes Have Seen You: Images of Creation and Evil in the Book of Job.* Leicester: Apollos, 2002. **Gibson, John C. L.** "On Evil in the Book of Job" [as represented by Leviathan and Behemoth]. In *Ascribe to the Lord: Biblical and Other Studies in Memory of Peter C. Craigie.* Ed. Lyle M. Eslinger and Glen J. Taylor. JSOTSup 67. Sheffield: JSOT Press, 1988. 399–419. **Good, Edwin M.** "The Problem of Evil in the Book of Job." In *The Voice from the Whirlwind: Interpreting the Book of Job.* Ed. Leo G. Perdue and Clark Gilpin. Nashville: Abingdon Press, 1992. 50–69. **Guillaume Taubmann, Florence.** *Job: le mal et la lettre.* Diss. Montpellier, 1992. **Kelly, Joseph F.** *The Problem of Evil in the Western Tradition: From the Book of Job to Modern Genetics.* Collegeville, MN: Liturgical Press, 2002. **King, Albion Roy.** *The Problem of Evil: Christian Concepts and the Book of Job.* New York: Ronald Press, 1952. **Lacocque, A.** "Job and the Symbolism of Evil." *BibRes* 24–25 (1979–80) 7–19. **Lafont, G.** "L'excès du malheur et la reconnaissance de Dieu." *NRT* 101 (1979) 724–39. **Leaman, Oliver.** *Evil and Suffering in Jewish Philosophy.* Cambridge Studies in Religious Traditions 6. Cambridge: Cambridge University Press, 1995. **Leduc-Fayette, Denise.** *Pascal et le mystère du mal: la clef de Job.* Cogitatio fidei 198. Paris: Editions du Cerf, 1996. **Lévêque, J.** "Le mal de Job." In *Le mystère du mal, péché, souffrance et rédemption.* Ed. M.-B. Borde. Toulouse: Carmel, 2001. 27–48.

    Mattioli, A. "Le ultime ragioni dell'esistenza del male e della sofferenza in Giobbe." *La sapienza della croce oggi* 3 (1976) 157–87. **Mies, Françoise.** "Job et l'altérité du mal." In *Imaginaires du mal.* Ed. Myriam Watthee-Delmotte and Paul-Augustin Deproost. Paris, Cerf, 2000 141–50. **Nash, R. T.** *Job's Misconception: A Critical Analysis of the Problem of Evil in the Philosophical Theology of Charles Hartshorne.* Diss. Leuven, 1991. **Nel, Philip J.** "The Conception of Evil and Satan in Jewish Traditions in the Pre-Christian Period." In *Like a Roaring Lion: Essays on the Bible, the Church and Demonic Powers.* Ed. by Pieter G. R. De

Villiers. Pretoria: University of South Africa, 1987. 1–21. **Nemo, Philippe.** *Job et l'excès du mal.* Paris: B. Grasset, 1978 [= *Job and the Excess of Evil.* Trans. Michael Kigel. Pittsburgh: Duquesne University Press, 1998]. ———. "Job et l'excès du mal." In *La confession de la foi chrétienne.* Ed. Claude Bruaire. Paris: Fayard, 1977. **Ravasi, Gianfranco.** "Giobbe: male fisico e male morale." *ParSpV* 19 (1989) 83–94. **Rella, Franco.** "Auschwitz, Libro di Giobbe, Satana." In his *Figure del male.* Milan: Feltrinelli, 2002. **Seeskin, Kenneth R.** "Job and the Problem of Evil." *Philosophy and Literature* 11 (1987) 226–41. **Shapiro, D. S.** "The Problem of Evil and the Book of Job." *Judaism* 5 (1956) 46–52. **Siegwalt, Gerard.** "Le mal et Dieu: contribution à la question de la trinité ou quaternité de Dieu." *RSR* 80 (2006) 481–97. **Slater, Peter.** "Evil and Ultimacy." *SR* 4 (1974–75) 137–46. **Susaimanickam, J.** "An Indian Problem of Evil: The Caste System. A Dalit Reading of the Book of Job." In *Indian Interpretation of the Bible: Festschrift in Honour of Prof. Dr Joseph Pathrapankal.* Ed. Augustine Thottakara. Bangalore: Dharmaram Publications, 2000. 181–200. **Vicchio, Stephen J.** *The Voice from the Whirlwind: The Problem of Evil and the Modern World.* Westminster, MD: Christian Classics, 1989. **Weiss, Paul.** "God, Job, and Evil: The Eternal Tension between Man and God." *Commentary* 6 (1948) [reprinted in *The Dimensions of Job: A Study and Selected Readings.* Ed. Nahum H. Glatzer. New York: Schocken Books, 1969. 181–93]. **Wright, John H.** "Problem of Evil, Mystery of Sin and Suffering." *CommSpok* 6 (1979) 140–56.

exile. Kammerer, Gabriele. "'Aus dem beschädigten Leben': Das Exil als Erfahrungshintergrund von Margarete Susmans Hiobdeutung—entdeckt mit Theodor W. Adornos Hilfe." In *Knospen und Früchtchen: Ein studentischer Geburtstagstrauss für Friedrich-Wilhelm Marquardt.* Ed. Thorsten Becker. Berlin: Wissenschaftlicherverlag, 1998. 37–49.

existentialism. Canfield, Craig. "Response to Fred Johnson's 'A Phonological, Existential Analysis of the Book of Job'." *JRelHealth* 45 (2006) 619–27. **Di Lella, A.** "An Existential Interpretation of Job." *BTB* 15 (1985) 49–55. **Ehrenberg, Hans.** *Hiob der Existentialist: Fünf Dialoge in zwei Teilen.* Heidelberg: Lambert Schneider, 1952 [pp. 45–52 reprinted as "Elihu the Theologian" in *The Dimensions of Job: A Study and Selected Readings.* Ed. Nahum H. Glatzer. New York: Schocken Books, 1969. 93–100]. **Johnson, Fred R.** "A Phonological Existential Analysis to the Book of Job." *JRelHealth* 44 (2005) 391–401. **Kardong, T.** "The True Image of Job—An Existentialist Who Searches Deeper Conversion." *ColcTFu* 59 (1984) 1–14.

faith. Brandt, Hans-Martin. *Der Hiob in uns: Vertrauen im Zweifeln.* Göttingen: Vanden-hoeck & Ruprecht, 1986. **Carney, Glandion, and William Long.** *Trusting God Again: Regaining Hope after Disappointment or Loss.* Illustrations by Julie Bosacker. Downers Grove, IL: InterVarsity Press, 1995. **Carson, Donald A.** "Job: Mystery and Faith." *Southern Baptist Convention* 4/2 (2000) 38–55. **Egger-Wenzel, Renate.** "'Faith in God' rather than 'Fear of God' in Ben Sira and Job: A Necessary Adjustment in Terminology and Understanding." In *Intertextual Studies in Ben Sira and Tobit: Essays in Honor of Alexander A. Di Lella, O.F.M.* Ed. Jeremy Corley and Vincent Skemp. Washington, DC: Catholic Biblical Association of America, 2005. 211–26. **Jong, Aad T. H. M. de.** *Weerklank van Job; over geloofstaal in bijbellessen.* Diss. Nijmegen, 1990. **Scammon, John F.** *If I Could Find God: Anguish and Faith in the Book of Job.* Valley Forge, PA: Judson Press, 1974.

fear of God. Ararat, N. "Concerning Job's 'Fear of God'" [Heb]. *BMik* 29 (1983–84) 263–78. **Wilson, Lindsay.** "The Book of Job and the Fear of God." *TynB* 46 (1995) 59–79.

friends. Bauks, Michaela. *Die Feinde des Psalmisten und die Freunde Ijobs: Untersuchungen zur Freund-Klage im Alten Testament am Beispiel von Ps 22.* Stuttgarter Bibelstudien 203. Stuttgart: Verlag Katholisches Bibelwerk, 2004. **Freund, Yosef.** "Were Job's Friends Gentiles? *Dor* 18 (1989) 107–10. **Habel, Norman.** "'Only the jackal is my friend': On Friends and Redeemers in Job." *Int* 31 (1977) 227–36. **Knellwolf, Ulrich.** "Hiobs Nächster: Frage und Antwort, Klage und Trost." *NZSysTh* 45 (2003) 263–75. **Siebald, Manfred.** "Job's Comforters." In *A Dictionary of Biblical Tradition in English Literature.* Ed. David Lyle Jeffrey. Grand Rapids: Eerdmans, 1992. 404–5. **Waldner, E.** "Das todeswürdige Verbrechen der Freunde Jobs." *Seelsorger* 7 (1930–31) 181–84.

gift. Ki, Wing-Chi. "Gift Theory and the Book of Job." *TS* 67 (2006) 723–49.
God. Balentine, Samuel E. "Job's 'Struggle for the Last Truth about God'." *RevExp* 99 (2002) 579–80. **Barthélemy, D.** "Dieu méconnu par le vieil homme: Job." *VS* 105 (1961) 445–63. **Barucq, André.** "Dieu chez les sages d'Israël." In *La notion biblique de Dieu: le Dieu de la Bible et le Dieu des philosophes.* Ed. J. Coppens, J. Villot, and B. A. Alfrink. Gembloux: J. Duculot, 1976. 169–89. **Bemporad, Jack.** "Man, God, and History." In his edited *A Rational Faith: Essays in Honor of Levi A. Olan.* New York: Ktav, 1977. **Berg, W.** "Gott und der Gerechte in der Rahmenerzählung des Buches Ijob." *MTZ* 32 (1981) 206–21. **Berges, Ulrich.** "Hiob in Lateinamerika. Der leidende Mensch und der aussätzige Gott." In *The Book of Job.* Ed. W. A. M. Beuken. BETL 114. Leuven: Leuven University Press, 1994. 297–317. **Beuken, W. A. M.** "Job's Imprecation as the Cradle of a New Religious Discourse. The Perplexing Impact of the Semantic Correspondences between Job 3, Job 4–5 and Job 6–7." In *The Book of Job.* Ed. W. A. M. Beuken. BETL 114. Leuven: Leuven University Press, 1994. 4–78. **Bovey, W.** "The Unjust God: God's Problem and Ours." *HibJ* 36 (1937–38) 353–64. **Clines, David J. A.** "Job's God." *Conc* 40 (2004) 39–51 [= "Ijobs Gott" *Conc* 40 (2004) 403–15; "Jobs God." In *De Gott van Job.* Ed. Ellen van Wolde. Zoetermeer: Uitgeverij Meinema, 2005. 74–92]. **Cranford, William Jefferson.** *The Doctrine of God in the Book of Job and the Systematic Theology of Paul Tillich.* Diss. Baylor, 1981. **Crenshaw, James L.** "The Concept of God in Old Testament Wisdom." In *In Search of Wisdom: Essays in Memory of John G. Gammie.* Ed. Leo G. Perdue, Bernard Brandon Scott, and William Johnston Wiseman. Louisville: Westminster/John Knox Press, 1993. 1–18. **Cross, R. N.** "Shall We Reason with God?" *HibJ* 46 (1948) 125–28. **Dunbar, Scott.** "On God and Virtue." *RelStud* 18 (1982) 489–502. **Duquoc, C., and C. Floristán.** *Job and the Silence of God.* Concilium 169. Edinburgh: T. & T. Clark, 1983. **Eerdmans, B. D.** *Studies in Job.* Leiden: Burgersdijk & Niermans, 1939. **Fretheim, Terence E.** "God in the Book of Job." *CTM* 26 (1999) 85–93.

Gibert, Pierre. "Dieu sage." In *Dieu, vingt-six portraits bibliques.* Ed. Pierre Gibert and Daniel Marguerat. Paris: Bayard, 2002. 16–72. **Gomez-Géraud, Marie-Christine.** "Dieu qui voit tout." In *Dieu, vingt-six portraits bibliques.* Ed. Pierre Gibert and Daniel Marguerat. Paris: Bayard, 2002. 204–12. **Habel, Norman C.** "He Who Stretches out the Heavens." *CBQ* 34 (1972) 417–30. ———. "In Defense of God the Sage." In *The Voice from the Whirlwind: Interpreting the Book of Job.* Ed. Leo G. Perdue and Clark Gilpin. Nashville: Abingdon Press, 1992. 21–38. ———. "The Verdict on/of God at the End of Job." *Conc* 40/4 (2004) 27–38 [= "Das Urteil Gottes. Über Gott am Schluss des Buches Ijob." *Conc* 40/4 (2004) 391–402]. **Harris, R. L.** "The Book of Job and Its Doctrine of God." *GJ* 13 (1972) 3–33 [= *Presbyterion* 7 (1981) 5–33]. **Hecke, Pierre van.** "'Ich aber will zum Allmächtigen reden' (Ijob 13,3). Die Aussagen Ijobs und seiner Freunde über Gott." *Conc* 40/4 (2004) 383–91 [= "'But I, I would converse with the Almighty' (Job 13.3): Job and His Friends on God." *Conc* 40/4 (2004) 18–26; also in *Job's God.* Ed. Ellen van Wolde. London: SCM Press, 2004. 18–26]. **Hyman, Frieda Clark.** "Job, or The Suffering of God." *Judaism* 42 (1993) 218–28. **Janssens, Mark.** *Onbegrijpelijk! God in het boek Job.* Zoetermeer: Boekencentrum, 1998. **Kellenberger, James.** "God's Goodness and God's Evil." *RelStud* 41 (2005) 23–37. **Kinet, Dirk.** "The Ambiguity of the Concepts of God and Satan in the Book of Job." *Conc* 169 (1983) 30–35. **Klehr, Franz Josef.** "Ijob und der Gott seiner Verfolger: Bericht über eine Tagung der Diözesanakademie am 2./3. März 1991 in Weingarten." *BK* 46 (1991) 186–88. **Klein, Joseph P.** "How Job Fulfills God's Word to Cain." *BibRev* 9/3 (1993) 40–43. **Köppel, M.** "Jahwes Allmacht und Gerechtigkeit in den Reden Hiobs." *ZAW* 29 (1909) 204–14. **Langenhorst, Georg (ed.).** *Hiobs Schrei in die Gegenwart. Ein literarisches Lesebuch zur Frage nach Gott im Leid.* Religion und Ästhetik. Mainz: Matthias-Grünewald-Verlag, 1995. **Marcus, Ralph.** "Job and God." *RR* 14 (1949–50) 5–29. **Mettinger, Tryggve N. D.** "The God of Job: Avenger, Tyrant, or Victor?" In *The Voice from the Whirlwind: Interpreting the Book of Job.* Ed. Leo G. Perdue and Clark Gilpin. Nashville: Abingdon Press, 1992. 39–49. **Michel, Diethelm.** "Hiob—oder: der inhumane Gott." In *Humanität heute.* Ed. Heinrich Foerster. Berlin: Lutherisches

Verlagshaus, 1970. 37–50. **Möller, M.** "Die Gerechtigkeit Gottes des Schöpfers in der Erfahrung seines Knechtes Hiob." *TVers* 6 (1975) 25–36. **Moskala, Jiri.** "The God of Job and Our Adversary." *Journal of the Adventist Theological Society* 15 (2004) 107–17. **Murphy, Roland E.** "The Last Truth about God." *RevExp* 99 (2002) 581–87. **O'Malley, W. J.** "The Untamable God of Job." *America* 176/18 (1997) 18–24.

Stockhammer, Morris. "Job's Problem" [and the infinity of God]. *Judaism* 2 (1953) 247–53. **Strauss, Hans.** "Bemerkungen zu Gebrauch und Bedeutung von אל in der Hiobdichtung und -gesamtkomposition." In *Altes Testament: Forschung und Wirkung: Festschrift für Henning Graf Reventlow.* Ed. Peter Mommer and Winfried Thiel. Frankfurt a.M.: Peter Lang, 1994. 95–101. **Tilley, Terrence W.** "God and the Silencing of Job." *Modern Theology* 5 (1989) 257–70. **Viganò, Lorenzo.** *Nomi e titoli di YHWH alla luce del semitico del Nordouest.* BibOr 31. Rome: Biblical Institute Press, 1976. **Watté, P.** "La logique de Dieu [apropos R. Girard]." *RevNouv* 83 (1986) 177–80. **Wendel, Saskia.** "'We cannot fathom the Almighty.' The Relationship between Transcendence and Immanence in the Light of 'Job's God'." *Conc* 40/4 (2004) 52–66 [= "'Den Allmächtigen ergründen wir nicht ...' Zur Verhältnisbestimmung von Transzendenz und Immanenz angesichts von 'Ijobs Gott'." *Conc* 40/4 (2004) 416–28]. **Whybray, R. N.** "The Immorality of God: Reflections on Some Passages in Genesis, Job, Exodus and Numbers." *JSOT* 72 (1996) 89–120. ———. "Wisdom, Suffering and the Freedom of God in the Book of Job." In *In Search of True Wisdom: Essays in Old Testament Interpretation in Honour of Ronald E. Clements.* Ed. Edward Ball. JSOTSup 300. Sheffield: Sheffield Academic Press, 1999. 231–45. **Wolde, Ellen van.** "Different Perspectives on Faith and Justice: The God of Jacob and the God of Job." In *The Many Voices of the Bible.* Ed. Seán Freyne and Ellen van Wolde. London: SCM Press, 2002. 17–23 [= *Conc* 38/1 (2002); "Der Gott Jakobs und der Gott Ijobs: Unterschiedliche Perspektiven zu Glaube und Gerechtigkeit." *Conc* 38/1 (2002) 10–17].

grief. Funke, Johannes G. "Hiobs Klage im Zeichen des Jona: Eine psychospirituelle Betrachtung von Trauer und was sie trösten kann." *DPB* 104 (2004) 305–6, 311–12. **Lyon, D. S.** "Before Kubler-Ross: Lessons about Grief from the Book of Job." *Obstetrics and Gynecology* 96 (2000) 151–52.

happiness. Denker, Rolf, and Uwe Bernhardt (eds.). *Hiob—oder die Schwere des Glücks: ein philosophisches Lesebuch über Leben und Lebenlassen.* Philosophie: Forschung und Wissenschaft 8. Münster: Lit Verlag, 2003. **Marcuse, Ludwig.** "Hiobs Recht auf Glück." In *Die Philosophie des Glücks: Von Hiob bis Freud.* Meisenheim am Glan: Hain, 1949 [= *Die Philosophie des Glücks: Zwischen Hiob und Freud.* Munich: List, 1962; *Die Philosophie des Glücks: Von Hiob bis Freud.* Zurich: Diogenes-Verlag, 1972. 24–41].

health care. Wolpe, Gerald I. "Health Care and Mrs Job: The Conflict of Personal Categories." In *Health Care: Right or Privilege? Moral and Religious Values in Health Care Reform* [= *Conservative Judaism* 51 (1999)] 31–39.

hero. Davidson, Jo Ann. "'Even if Noah, Daniel, and Job' (Ezekiel 14:14, 20)—Why These Three?" *Journal of the Adventist Theological Society* 12 (2001) 132–44.

HIV/AIDS. Dyk, Peet van. "The Tale of Two Tragedies: The Book of Job and HIV/AIDS in Africa." *Bulletin for Old Testament Studies in Africa* 16 (2004) 7–13. **Masenya, Madipoane J.** "Between Unjust Suffering and the 'Silent' God: Job and HIV/AIDS Sufferers in South Africa." *Missionalia* 29 (2001) 186–99. **Nadar, Sarojini.** "Re-reading Job in the Midst of Suffering in the HIV/AIDS Era: How Not to Talk of God." *OTEss* 16 (2003) 343–57. **Tshikendwa Matadi, Ghislain.** *Suffering, Belief, Hope: The Wisdom of Job for an AIDS-stricken Africa.* Trans. Joseph P. Newman with Robert E. Czerny. Nairobi: Paulines Publications Africa, 2007. **West, Gerald, and Bongi Zengele.** "Reading Job 'Positively' in the Context of HIV/AIDS in South Africa." *Conc* 40/4 (2004) 112–24 [= "Eine 'positive' Auslegung Ijobs im Kontext von HIV/AIDS in Südafrika." *Conc* 40/4 (2004) 471–83]. **Wittenberg, Gunther.** "Counselling AIDS Patients: Job as a Paradigm." *JThSAfr* 88 (1994) 61–68.

holocaust. See Section 8.c (Contemporary Jewish).

hope. Boorer, Suzanne. "Job's Hope. A Reading of the Book of Job from the Perspective of Hope." *Colloquium* 30 (1998) 101–22. **Brates, L.** "La esperanza en el libro de Job." In *XXX Semana Bíblica Española.* Madrid, 1972. 21–34. **Hervella Vázquez, José.** "'Post tenebras spero lucem' (Job 17,12). La esperanza y el mito de Pandora en la catedral de Orense." In *La Biblia en el arte y en la literatura. V Simposio Bíblico Español. 2. Arte.* Ed. Javier Azanza. Valencia: Universidad de Navarra, 1999. 443–54.

humanity. Barron, Mary Catherine. "Sitting It out with Job: The Human Condition." *RRel* 38 (1979) 489–96. **Bergant, Dianne.** *An Historico-Critical Study of the Anthropological Traditions and Motifs in Job.* Diss. St Louis University, 1975. **Eising, Hermann.** "Das Menschenleben im Buche Ijob." In *Memoria Jerusalem: Freundesgabe Franz Sauer zum 70. Geburtstag.* Ed. Johannes B. Bauer and Johannes Marböck. Graz: Akademische Druck- und Verlagsanstalt, 1977. 43–57. **Habel, Norman C.** "'Naked I Came …': Humanness in the Book of Job." In *Die Botschaft und die Boten. Festschrift für Hans Walter Wolff zum 70. Geburtstag.* Ed. J. Jeremias and L. Perlitt. Neukirchen–Vluyn: Neukirchener Verlag, 1981. 373–92. **Krüger, Thomas.** "'Wie der Wind verfliegt meine Würde …' (Hiob 30,15): Elend und Würde des Menschen in alttestamentlicher Sicht." In *Menschenbild und Menschenwürde.* Ed. Ellert Herms. Gütersloh: Chr. Kaiser, 2001. 271–87. **Oorschot, Jürgen van.** "Menschenbild, Gottesbild und Menschenwürde: ein Beitrag des Hiobbuches." In *Menschenbild und Menschenwürde.* Ed. Eilert Herms. Gütersloh: Kaiser, 2001. 320–43. **Remus, Martin.** *Menschenbildvorstellungen im Ijob-Buch: Ein Beitrag zur alttestamentlichen Anthropologie.* BEATAJ 21. Frankfurt a.M.: Peter Lang, 1993. **Thelen, Mary Frances.** "J. B., Job, and the Biblical Doctrine of Man." *JBR* 27 (1959) 201–5.

identity. Seybold, Klaus. "Das Hiobproblem als Ausdruck einer Identitätskrise." In *Ein Inuk sein. Interdisziplinäre Vorlesungen zum Problem der Identität.* Ed. Gaetano Benedetti and Louis Wiesemann. Göttingen: Vandenhoeck & Ruprecht, 1986. 125–37. **Ticciati, Susannah.** *Job and the Disruption of Identity: Reading beyond Barth.* London: T. & T. Clark, 2005.

illness. Bühlmann, Walter. "Der von Krankheit geschlagene Mensch—Ijob heute." *BK* 59 (2004) 95–98. **González, Á.** "Giobbe, il malato." *Conc* 12 (1976) 1475–82. **Fohrer, Georg.** "Man and Disease according to the Book of Job." In *Koroth. Proceedings of the Second International Symposium on Medicine in Bible and Talmud, Jerusalem, December 18–20, 1984.* Ed. Samuel S. Kottek. Jerusalem: The Israel Institute of the History of Medicine, 1985. 43–48 [= his *Studien zum Alten Testament (1966–1988).* BZAW 196. Berlin: de Gruyter, 1991. 80–84]. **Lindskoog, Kathryn.** "What Do You Say to Job?" [chronic disease]. *Leadership* 6/2 (1985) 90–95. **Magdalene, F. Rachel.** "The ANE Legal Origins of Impairment as Theological Disability and the Book of Job." *PerspRelSt* 34 (2007) 23–60. **Renié, J.** "La maladie de Job." *RevApol* 60 (1935) 365–67. See also HIV/AIDS.

imagery. Vall, Gregory Robert. *From Womb to Tomb: Poetic Imagery and the Book of Job.* Diss. Catholic University of America, 1993.

innocence. Kutsch, Ernst. "Unschuldsbekenntnis und Gottesbegegnung. Der Zusammenhang zwischen Hiob 31 und 38ff." In his *Kleine Schriften zum Alten Testament.* Ed. Ludwig Schmidt and Karl Eberlein. BZAW 168. Berlin: Walter de Gruyter, 1986. 308–35.

inspiration. Payne, John Barton. "Inspiration in the Words of Job." In *The Law and the Prophets. Old Testament Studies Prepared in Honor of Oswald Thompson Allis.* Ed. J. H. Skilton. Nutley, NJ: Presbyterian & Reformed Publishing Company, 1974. 319–36.

integrity. Davis, Ellen F. "Job and Jacob: The Integrity of Faith." In *Reading between Texts: Intertextuality and the Hebrew Bible.* Ed. Danna Nolan Fewell. Louisville: Westminster/John Knox Press, 1992. 203–24. ———. "Job and Jacob: The Integrity of Faith." In *The Whirlwind: Essays on Job, Hermeneutics and Theology in Memory of Jane Morse.* Ed. Stephen L. Cook, Corrine L. Patton, and James W. Watts. JSOTSup 336. Sheffield: Sheffield Academic Press, 2001. 100–120.

intercession. Ivanski, Dariusz. *The Dynamics of Job's Intercession.* AnBib 161. Rome: Pontifical Biblical Institute, 2006.

irony. Pixley, Jorge V. "La ironía, antesala de la teología de la liberación: el libro de Job." *CuadTe* 3 (1973) 57–80. **Williams, J. G.** "Comedy, Irony, Intercession: A Few Notes in Response." *Semeia* 7 (1977) 135–45. ———. "'You have not spoken truth of me.' Mystery and Irony in Job." *ZAW* 83 (1971) 231–55.

Israel. Feinberg, C. L. "Job and the Nation Israel." *BSac* 96 (1935) 405–11; 97 (1940) 27–33, 211–16. **Ouweneel, Willem J.** *Het Jobslijden van Israel—Israels lijden oplichtend uit het boek Job.* Vaassen: Uitgeverij Medema, 2000.

Israelite. Kleinert, P. "Das spezifisch Hebräische im Buche Job." *TSK* 59 (1886) 267–300.

Israelite religion. Janzen, J. Gerald. "The Place of the Book of Job in the History of Israel's Religion." In *Ancient Israelite Religion: Essays in Honor of Frank Moore Cross.* Ed. Patrick D. Miller, Paul D. Hanson, and S. Dean McBride. Philadelphia: Fortress Press, 1987. 523–37.

Jewish interpretation. See Section 8.c (Contemporary Jewish).

Job. Alonso Díaz, J. "La experiencia de Job en la órbita del amor de Dios." *BibFe* 1 (1975) 66–81. **Begg, Christopher T.** "Comparing Characters: The Book of Job and the Testament of Job." In *The Book of Job.* Ed. W. A. M. Beuken. BETL 114. Leuven: Leuven University Press, 1994. 435–45. **Bloch, E.** "L'uomo Giobbe." *De homine* 24–25 (1967–68) 3–18. **Bogert, Elizabeth A.** "Desolation and Solitude of Job." *Muslim World* 52 (1962) 322–30. **Brenner, Athalya.** "Job the Pious? The Characterization of Job in the Narrative Framework of the Book." *JSOT* 43 (1989) 37–52. **Brinkman, Martien E.** "Als ik Job niet had." *GerefTTs* 98 (1998) 20–25. **Caquot, André.** "Traits royaux dans le personnage de Job." In *maqqél shâqédh, La branche d'amandier. Hommage à Wilhelm Vischer.* Montpellier: Causse, Graille, Castelnau, 1960. 32–45. **Chow, See-Wing.** "Job, a Believer Searching for Deeper Conversion." *ColcTFu* 85 (1990) 349–56. **Christensen, D. L.** "Job and the Age of the Patriarchs in Old Testament Narrative." *PerspRelSt* 13 (1986) 225–28. **Cocagnac, A. M.** "Job sans beauté ni éclat." *VS* 422 (1956) 355–71. **Cocorda, Dante.** *Le problème du livre de Job et la personnalité de l'auteur: étude de psychologie religieuse.* Geneva: Société Générale d'Imprimerie, 1908. **Engelmann, F.** *Gerecht durch Gott. Hiobs Leidenweg durch Drangsal zur Freude.* Licht des Neuen Testaments im Alten. Wittenberg: Bundes-Verlag, 1933. **Jackson, T. P.** "Must Job Live for Ever? A Reply to Aquinas on Providence." *The Thomist* 62 (1998) 1–39. **Keulen, E. J.** "Van acceptatie tot rebellie. Job als paradigmatisch gelovige." *Schrift* 218 (2005) 55–59. **Kieffer, René.** "Frimodiga och uthålliga människor i bibeln." *SEÅ* 70 (2005) 133–44.

Macaluso, G. *Profeti e màrtiri. 1. Giobbe come uomo e come Cristo. 2. Il messaggio del Mahatma Gandhi.* Rome: Edizione "Pensiero & Azione," 1970. **MacKenzie, R. A. F.** "The Transformation of Job." *BTB* 9 (1979) 51–57. **Moore, R. D.** "The Integrity of Job." *CBQ* 45 (1983) 17–31. **Neher, André.** "Job: The Biblical Man." *Judaism* 13 (1964) 37–47 [= "L'homme biblique: Job." In his *L'existence juive: solitude et affrontements.* Paris: Editions du Seuil, 1962. 60–72]. **Newell, B. Lynne.** "Job: Repentant or Rebellious?" *WTJ* 46 (1984) 298–316 [= *Sitting with Job: Selected Studies on the Book of Job.* Ed. Roy B. Zuck. Grand Rapids: Baker Book House, 1992. 441–56]. **Nigg, Walter.** *Drei grosse Zeichen: Elias, Hiob, Sophia.* Olten: Walter-Verlag, 1972. **Rood, Lydia.** *Het boek Job: portret van een man met autisme.* Amsterdam: Singel Pockets, 2007. **Rouillard, P.** "The Figure of Job in the Liturgy: Indignation, Resolution or Silence?" *Conc* 169 (1983) 8–12. **Ruegg, Ulrich.** "Job réhabilité. Témoignage—méditation." *RevEthThéolMor* 209 (1999) 102–16. **Schramm, Jonas Conrad.** *Dissertatio præliminaris qua Jobum Talmudicum e Bava Batra cap. i examinat veriorique addita Jobi descriptione.* Helmstadt, 1716. **Southwick, Jay S.** "Job, an Exemplar for Every Age." *Enc* 45 (1984) 373–91. **Urbano Delgado, María C.** "El itinerario de Job y el creyente de hoy." *VyV* 58/229 (2000) 541–54. **Walker, C. C.** *Job: 'Hast thou considered my servant Job?' (Job 1:8; 2:3). An Attempted 'Consideration' in the Light of the Later Work of God* *in Christ.* Birmingham: Christadelphian, 1955. **Westermann, Claus.** "The Two Faces of Job." *Conc* 169 (1983) 15–22 [= *Job and the Silence of God.* Ed. Christian Duquoc and Casiano Floristán. Edinburgh: T. & T. Clark, 1983]. **Wittenberg, G. H.** "Job the Farmer: The Judean *am-haretz* and the Wisdom Movement." *OTEss* 4 (1991) 151–70. **Wolde, Ellen van.** "The Development of Job: Mrs Job as Catalyst." In *A Feminist Companion to Wisdom Literature.* Ed. Athalya Brenner. The Feminist Companion to the Bible 9. Sheffield: Sheffield Academic Press, 1995. 201–21. **Wolfers, David.** "Is Job after All Jewish?" *Dor* 14 (1985–86) 39–44.

Job and Jesus. Fischer, W. "Hiob, ein Zeuge Jesu Christ." *ZZ* 12 (1932–33) 386–414. **Gilbert, Maurice.** "Job et Jésus dans la tradition chrétienne." In his *Il a parlé par les prophètes: thèmes et figures bibliques.* Le livre et le rouleau 2. Brussels: Lessius, 1998. 233–48. **Harrison, William Pope.** "Christ in the Book of Job." *MethQR* 27 (1888) 390–400. **Morris, James C.** "The Book of Job and the Revelation of the Messiah." *MethQR* 52 (1903) 498–506. **Vischer, Wilhelm.** *Hiob. Ein Zeuge Jesu Christi.* Bekennende Kirche 8. Munich: Kaiser, 1934. **Wyckoff, Rufus J.** "Job and the Man of the Sermon on the Mount." *MethRev* 93 (1911) 257–63.

Judaism. Green, William Scott. "Stretching the Covenant. Job and Judaism." *RevExp* 99 (2002) 569–77.

justice. Brawley, Robert L. "Paul, Job, and the New Quest for Justice." In *Character Ethics and the New Testament: Moral Dimensions of Scripture.* Ed. Robert L. Brawley. Louisville: Westminster/John Knox Press, 2007. **Cepeda Calzada, P.** "El problema de la justicia en Job. Personalidad, ley y justicia en el libro de Job." *Crisis* 20 (1973) 243–90. ———. *El problema de la justicia en Job.* Madrid: Prensa Española, 1975. **Crenshaw, James L.** "Popular Questioning of the Justice of God in Ancient Israel." *ZAW* 82 (1970) 380–93. **Gitay, Yehoshua.** *The Human Search for Justice: The Case of Hebrew Literature.* Cape Town: University of Cape Town, 1994. **Hart, John.** "Job, Injustice, and Dynamic Nature." In his *Sacramental Commons: Christian Ecological Ethics.* Lanham, MD: Rowman & Littlefield, 2006. 159–77. **Hoare, Henry William.** *The Book of Job and Plato's Dialogue on Justice* [an article extracted from the *Fortnightly Review,* 1875]. **Lasine, Stuart.** "Bird's-Eye and Worm's-Eye Views of Justice in the Book of Job." *JSOT* 42 (1988) 29–53. **Lichtenstein, M. H.** "The Poetry of Poetic Justice: A Comparative Study in Biblical Imagery." *JANES* 5 (1974) 255–65. **Passaro, A.** "Domande e risposte sulla giustizia in Giobbe." *Ricerche storico bibliche* 14 (2002) 19–136 [= *La giustizia in conflitto. 36. Settimana biblica nazionale (Roma, 11–15 settembre 2000).* Ed. Rinaldo Fabri. Bologna: EDB, 2002]. **Scholnick, Sylvia Huberman.** "The Meaning of *mišpaṭ* in the Book of Job." *JBL* 101 (1982) 521–29 [= Roy B. Zuck (ed.). *Sitting with Job: Selected Studies on the Book of Job.* Grand Rapids: Baker Book House, 1992. 349–58]. **Schultz, Carl.** "The Cohesive Issue of *mišpaṭ* in Job." In *"Go to the land I will show you": Studies in Honor of Dwight W. Young.* Ed. Joseph E. Coleson and Victor H. Matthews. Altertumskunde des Vorderen Orients 4. Winona Lake, IN: Eisenbrauns, 1996. 159–75. **Zhang, Ying.** *Divine Justice and Divine Providence in Tension: A Dual Rhetoric in the Book of Job.* Diss. Chinese University of Hong Kong, 2007.

knowledge. Shackelford, Robert Donald. *The Concept of Knowledge in the Book of Job.* Diss. New Orleans Baptist Theological Seminary, 1977.

lament. Berges, Ulrich. "Ijob: Klage und Anklage als Weg der Befreiung?" *BLit* 71 (1998) 321–26. **Fuchs, G.** "»Du bist mir zum Trugbach geworden.« Verwandte Motive in den Konfessionen Jeremias und den Klagen Hiobs." *BZ* 41 (1997) 212–28; 42 (1998) 19–38. ———. "Die Klage des Propheten. Beobachtungen zu den Konfessionen Jeremias im Vergleich mit den Klagen Hiobs (Erster Teil)." *BZ* NF 41 (1997) 212–28. **Fuchs, Gotthard (ed.).** *Angesichts des Leids an Gott glauben? Zur Theologie der Klage.* Frankfurt a.M.: Knecht, 1996. **Holbert, John C.** *The Function and Significance of the "Klage" in the Book of Job with Special Reference to the Incidence of Formal and Verbal Irony.* Diss. Southern Methodist University, 1975. **Margolfo, Pasquale.** *Lamentazioni di Giobbe e di Geremia, profeta.* Naples: Banzoli, 1840. **Rusche, Helga.** "Warum starb ich nicht vom Mutterschoss weg? Mit Ijob klagen lernen." *Entschluss* 40 (1985) 32, 34–35. **Tamez, Elsa.** "Job: 'Even when I cry out "violence!" I am not answered'." In *The Return of the Plague*. Ed. José-Oscar Beozzo and Virgil Elizondo. London: SCM Press; Maryknoll, NY: Orbis Books, 1997. 55–62.

law. Zenger, Erich. "Die späte Weisheit und das Gesetz." In *Literatur und Religion des Frühjudentums: Eine Einführung*. Ed. Johann Maier and Josef Schreiner. Würzburg: Echter Verlag, 1973. 43–56.

lawsuit. Erikson, Gösta, and Kristina Jonasson. "Jobsbokens juridiska grundmönster." *SvTK* 65 (1989) 64–69. **Frye, J. B.** *The Legal Language of the Book of Job.* Diss. King's College, London, 1973. **Harrison, G.** "Legal Terms in Job." *The Biblical Illustrator* 13 (1987) 13–15. **Hoffman, Yair.** "The Book of Job as a Trial: A Perspective from a Comparison to Some Relevant Ancient Near Eastern Texts." In *Das Buch Hiob und seine Interpretationen: Beiträge zum Hiob-Symposium auf dem Monte Verità vom 14.–19. August 2005.* Ed. Thomas Krüger, Manfred Oeming, Konrad Schmid, and Christoph Uehlinger. ATANT 88. Zurich: Theologische Verlag Zürich, 2007. 21–31. **Jacobson, Richard.** "Satanic Semiotics, Jobian Jurisprudence." *Semeia* 19 (1981) 63–71. **Kiss, K.** "Ein Dokument der altisraelitischen Rechtsprechung: Das Buch Hiob." *ThSz* 23 (1980) 73–79. **Many, Gaspard.** *Der Rechtsstreit mit Gott (rîb) im Hiobbuch.* Diss. Munich, 1970. **Roberts, J. J. M.** "Job's Summons to Yahweh: The Exploitation of a Legal Metaphor." *RestQ* 16 (1973) 159–65. **Scholnick, Sylvia Huberman.** *Lawsuit Drama in the Book of Job.* Diss. Brandeis, 1975.

Leviathan. Eerdmans, B. D. *Studies in Job.* Leiden: Burgersdijk & Niermans, 1939. **Gordon, C. H.** "Leviathan: Symbol of Evil." In *Biblical Motifs: Origins and Transformations.* Ed. A. Altmann. Philip W. Lown Institute of Advanced Judaic Studies. Studies and Texts 3. Cambridge, MA: Harvard University Press, 1966. 1–10.

liberation. Gutiérrez, Gustavo. "Song and Deliverance" [Book of Job and Latin American liberation theology]. In *Voices from the Margin: Interpreting the Bible in the Third World.* Ed. R. S. Sugirtharajah. Maryknoll, NY: Orbis Books, 1995. 129–46 [previously published in author's *On Job: God-Talk and the Suffering of the Innocent.* Maryknoll, NY: Orbis Books, 1987].

liberation theology. Cox, Harvey G. "Complaining to God: Theodicy and the Critique of Modernity in the Resurgence of Traditional Religion—Latin American Liberation Theology." *Archivio di filosofia* 56 (1988) 311–25. **Weber, Burkhard.** *Ijob in Lateinamerika. Bedeutung und Bewältigung von Leid in der Theologie der Befreiung.* Mainz: Grünewald, 1999.

life. Augustin, Matthias. "Sinn des Lebens—Sinn des Leidens. Betrachtungen zur marxistischen Hiob-Interpretation von Milan Machovec als Beitrag zum alttestamentlich-philosophischen Dialog." In *Schöpfung und Befreiung. Festschrift für Claus Westermann zum 80. Geburtstag.* Ed. Rainer Albertz, Friedemann W. Golka, and Jürgen Kegler. Stuttgart: Calwer Verlag, 1989. 166–77. **Boorer, Suzanne.** "A Matter of Life and Death: A Comparison of Proverbs 1–9 and Job." In *Prophets and Paradigms: Essays in Honor of Gene M. Tucker.* Ed. Stephen Breck Reid. JSOTSup 229. Sheffield: Sheffield Academic Press, 1996. 187–204. **Cosser, W.** "The Meaning of 'Life' (*hayyîm*) in Proverbs, Job, Qoheleth." *TGUOS* 15 (1955) 48–53. **D'Alario, Vittoria.** "La réflexion sur le sens de la vie en Sg 1–6: une réponse aux questions de Job et de Qohélet." In *Treasures of Wisdom: Studies in Ben Sira and the Book of Wisdom. Festschrift M. Gilbert.* Ed. Nuria Calduch-Benages and Jacques Vermeylen. BETL 143. Leuven: Leuven University Press; Louvain: Peeters, 1999. 313–29. **Deselaers, Paul.** "Lebensbuch Ijob." *Entschluss* 53 (1988) 5–6. **Dussaud, R.** "La néphesh et la rouah dans le 'Livre de Job'." *RHR* 129 (1945) 17–30. **Gese, H.** "Die Frage nach dem Lebenssinn: Hiob und die Folgen." *ZTK* 79 (1982) 161–79. **Janzen, J. Gerald.** "Lust for Life and the Bitterness of Job." *TTod* 55 (1998) 152–62. **Schmitt, Ernst.** *Leben in den Weisheitsbüchern, Job, Sprüche und Jesus Sirach.* Freiburger theologische Studien 66. Freiburg i.Br.: Herder, 1954. **Wood, J.** "The Idea of Life in the Book of Job." *TGUOS* 18 (1959–60) 29–37.

light. Blumenberg, H. "Licht als Metapher der Wahrheit: Im Vorfeld der philosophischen Befgriffsbildung." *StGen* 10 (1957) 432–47. **Borgonovo, Gianantonio.** *La notte e il suo sole. Luce e tenebre nel Libro di Giobbe: analisi simbolica.* AnBib 135. Rome: Pontifical Biblical Institute, 1995. **Galbiati, E. R.** "The Night and Its Sun. Light and Darkness in the Book of Job. Symbolic Analyses." *Aevum* 73 (1999) 199–202.

maturity. Beck, Harrell F. "Maturity, Spirituality, and the Bible: Job's Search for Integrity." In *Maturity and the Quest for Spiritual Meaning.* Ed. C. Kao. Lanham, MD: University Press of America, 1988. 53–63. **Herbst, Adrian.** "El libro de Job y la madurez religiosa." *CuadTe* 19 (2000) 49–57.

medicine. Jacob, Wolfgang. "Die Hiob-Frage in der Medizin." In *Die Grenze der machbaren Welt: Festschrift der Klopstock-Stiftung anlässlich ihres 20-jährigen Bestehens.* Ed. E. Benz. Leiden: E. J. Brill, 1975. 46–66.

meteorology. Garbini, Giovanni. "La meteorologia di Giobbe." In *In onore di Mons. Enrico Galbiati nel suo 80o compleanno.* Ed. G. Ghiberti. *RivBib* 43 (1995) 85–91.

misfortune. Baird, Robert M. "On Bad Luck: Job and Jesus." *JRelHealth* 33 (1994) 305–12.

missiology. Allen, Wayne W. "The Missionary Message of Job: God's Universal Concern for Healing." *Caribbean Journal of Evangelical Theology* 6 (2002) 18–31. **Zyl, Danie C. van.** "Missiological Dimensions in the Book of Job." *International Review of Mission* 91/360 (2002) 24–30.

monotheism. Koch, Klaus. "Saddaj: zum Verhältnis zwischen israelitischer Monolatrie und nordwest-semitischem Polytheismus." *VT* 26 (1976) 299–332.

monsters. Beal, Timothy K., and Tod Linafelt. "Beowulf's Bible." In *Relating to the Text: Interdisciplinary and Form-Critical Insights into the Bible.* Ed. Timothy Sandoval and Carleen Mandolfo. JSOTSup 384. London and New York: T. & T. Clark, 2003. 275–89. **Beal, Timothy K.** *Religion and Its Monsters.* New York: Routledge, 2002.

mortality. Dafni, Evangelia G. "BROTOS. A Favourite Word of Homer in the Septuagint Version of Job." *VerbEccl* 28 (2007) 35–65.

music. Heymel, Michael. "Hiob und die Musik. Zur Bedeutung der Hiobgestalt für eine musikalische Seelsorge." In *Das Alte Testament und die Kunst. Beiträge des Symposiums "Das Alte Testament und die Kultur der Moderne" anlässlich des 100. Geburtstags Gerhard von Rads (1901–1971), Heidelberg, 18.–21. Oktober 2001.* Ed. John Barton, J. Cheryl Exum, and Manfred Oeming. Altes Testament und Moderne 15. Münster: Lit Verlag, 2005.

mystery. Robinson, H. Wheeler. *The Religious Ideas of the Old Testament.* London: Duckworth, 1913 [pp. 174–76 are reprinted as "Life: A Mystery" in *The Dimensions of Job: A Study and Selected Readings.* Ed. Nahum H. Glatzer. New York: Schocken Books, 1969. 245–46]. **Williams, J. G.** "'You have not spoken truth of me.' Mystery and Irony in Job." *ZAW* 83 (1971) 231–55.

mythology. Smick, Elmer B. "Mythology and the Book of Job." *JETS* 13 (1970) 101–8.

nationalism. Gonzalo Maeso, D. "Sentido nacional en el libro de Job." *EstBib* 9 (1950) 67–81.

nature. Asano, Junichi. "Nature in the Book of Job" [Japanese, with English summary]. In *Studies in Saint Paul for T. Matsumoto.* Ed. K. Ishiwara et al. 1961. **Deloche, René.** *Les sciences physiques et naturelles dans le livre de Job.* Nîmes: A. Chastanier, 1909. **Fischer, Georg.** "Spuren des Schöpfers. Zur Rolle der Natur im Ijobbuch." In *Auf den Spuren der schriftgelehrten Weisen: Festschrift für Johannes Marböck anlässlich seiner Emeritierung.* Ed. Irmtraud Fischer, Ursula Rapp, and Johannes Schiller. BZAW 331. Berlin: Walter de Gruyter, 2003. 157–66. **Kessler, Rainer.** "Die Welt aus den Fugen: Natur und Gesellschaft im Hiobbuch." In *Gott und Mensch im Dialog: Festschrift für Otto Kaiser zum 80. Geburtstag.* Ed. Markus Witte. BZAW 345. Berlin: Walter de Gruyter, 2004. 2:639–54. **Loader, J. A.** "Seeing God with Natural Eyes: On Job and Nature." *OTEss* 5 (1992) 346–60. **Malchow, B.** "Nature from God's Perspective, Job 38–39." *Dialog* 21 (1982) 130–33. **Palm, J. H. van der.** *Verhandeling over eenige dichterlijke Natuurbeschrijvingen uit het boek Job.* In *Werken der Bataafsche maatschappij van taalen dichtkunde.* II. Amsterdam,

1807. 1–34. **Richter, Heinz.** "Die Naturweisheit des Alten Testaments in Buche Hiob" *ZAW* 70 (1958) 1–20. **Schwarz, W.** "Naturschau im Buch Hiob." *Frankfurter israelitische Gemeindeblätter* 9 (1930–31) 337–40. **Viviers, H.** "Body and Nature in Job." *OTEss* 14 (2001) 510–24.

night. Bleeker, C. J. "La signification religieuse de la nuit." In his *The Sacred Bridge: Researches into the Nature and Structure of Religion.* Numen Supplements 7. Leiden: E. J. Brill, 1963. 72–82.

opposites. Urbrock, William J. "Reconciliation of Opposites in the Dramatic Ordeal of Job." *Semeia* 5 (1976) 111–37.

order. May, Nicholas. "Job and Jeremiah. Understanding the Divine Moral Order through Lament and Response." *JBibSt* 3 (2003) 22–26. **Weiser, A.** "Das Problem der sittlichen Weltordnung im Buche Hiob. Unter Berücksichtigung seiner Entwicklung bei den Griechen und in der israelitischen Religion." *ThBl* 2 (1923) 157–64 [= his *Glaube und Geschichte im Alten Testament und andere ausgewählte Schriften.* Göttingen: Vandenhoeck & Ruprecht, 1961. 9–19].

orthodoxy. Sutherland, Martin. "'Bringing their gods in their hands.' Job and Absolute Orthodoxy." *Pacifica* 14 (2001) 144–58.

paradox. Lévêque, Jean. "Sagesse et paradoxe dans le livre de Job." In *La sagesse biblique de l'ancien au Nouveau Testament.* Ed. Jacques Trublet. Lectio divina 160. Paris: Cerf, 1995. 99–128. **Reynolds, Roberta M.** *Piety and Paradox. A Rhetorical Analysis of the King James Version of the Book of Job.* Diss. Oregon, 1984.

past. Grimm, Markus. *"Dies Leben ist der Tod": Vergänglichkeit in den Reden Ijobs. Entwurf einer Textsemantik.* Arbeiten zu Text und Sprache im Alten Testament 62. St Ottilien: EOS-Verlag, 1998.

pastoral theology. Gibson, J. C. L. "The Book of Job and the Cure of Souls." *SJT* 42 (1989) 303–17. **Louw, Daniel Johannes.** "'Hóóp-volle perspektiewe vir die pastoraat aan die lydende vanuit die boek Job." In *Die Ou Testament vandag.* Ed. D. H. Odendaal, B. A. Müller and H. J. B. Combrink. Kaapstad: NG Kerkuitgewers, 1979. **Mickel, Tobias.** *Seelsorgerliche Aspekte im Hiobbuch: Ein Beitrag zur biblischen Dimension der Poimenik.* Theologische Arbeiten 48. Berlin: Evangelische Verlagsanstalt, 1990. **Möller, Christian (ed.).** *Geschichte der Seelsorge in Einzelporträts.* 1. *Von Hiob bis Thomas von Kempen.* Göttingen: Vandenhoeck & Ruprecht, 1994. **Schäfer, Dierk.** "Nachtcafé: Hiob und seine Freunde. Notfallseelsorge-Tagung, November 1999." *DPB* 100/3 (2000) 115–17. **Thijs, L.** "Het verhaal van Job in het pastoraat." *PrakT* 17 (1990) 251–71. **Williams, Michael S.** "The Book of Job as a Reflection on the Practice of Ministry." *JRelThought* 54–55 (1998) 53–59.

patience. Fine, H. A. "The Tradition of a Patient Job." *JBL* 74 (1955) 28–32. **Garrett, Susan R.** "The Patience of Job and the Patience of Jesus." *Int* 53 (1999) 254–64. **Ghidelli, Carlo.** *La pazienza di Giobbe.* Per capire la Bibbia. Rome: AVE, 1994. **Ginsberg, H. L.** "Job the Patient and Job the Impatient." In *Congress Volume: Rome, 1968.* VTSup 17. Leiden: E. J. Brill, 1968. 88–111 [= *ConsJud* 21 (1966) 12–28]. **Hancock, E. L.** "The Impatience of Job." In *Spinning a Sacred Yarn: Women Speak from the Pulpit.* New York: Pilgrim Press, 1982. 98–106. **Marconi, Gilberto.** "La nascita della pazienza di Giobbe, I." In *I volti di Giobbe: percorsi interdisciplinari.* Ed. i Gilberto Marconi and Cristina Termini. Bologna: EDB, 2002. 69–80. **Scarpa, A. M.** "La nascita della pazienza di Giobbe, II." In *I volti di Giobbe: percorsi interdisciplinari.* Ed. Gilberto Marconi and Cristina Termini. Bologna: EDB, 2002. 81–99. **Schwienhorst-Schönberger, Ludger.** "Zwischen Demut und Rebellion: Der Ijob der Bibel." *RHS* 50 (2007) 270–75. **Seitz, Christopher R.** "The Patience of Job in the Epistle of James." In *Konsequente Traditionsgeschichte. Festschrift für Klaus Baltzer zum 65. Geburtstag.* Ed. Rüdiger Bartelmus, Thomas Krüger, and Helmut Utzschneider. OBO 126. Freiburg, Switzerland: Universitätsverlag, 1993. 373–82. **Young, W. W., III.** "The Patience of Job: Between Providence and Disaster." *HeythJ* 48 (2007) 593–613. **Zens, Jon.** "You Have Heard of Job's Perseverance: Perspectives for the Heart in Times of Affliction." *Searching Together* 14/3 (1985) 12–15.

Pentateuchal traditions. Frye, J. B. "The Use of Pentateuchal Traditions in the Book of Job." *OTWSA* 17–18 (1977) 13–20.

perfection. Egger-Wenzel, Renate. "Der Gebrauch von TMM bei Ijob und Ben Sira: ein Vergleich zweier Weisheitsbücher." In *Freundschaft bei Ben Sira: Beiträge des Symposions zu Ben Sira, Salzburg, 1995.* Ed. Friedrich V. Reiterer. BZAW 244. Berlin: Walter de Gruyter, 1996. 203–38.

pessimism. Krieger, Paul. *Weltbild und Idee des Buches Hiob, verglichen mit dem altorientalischen Pessimismus.* Leipzig: Schwarzenberg & Schumann, 1930.

piety. Humfrey, Richard. *Iob's Pietie, or, The Patterne of a Perfect Man: Containing an Absolute Historie of All the Excellencies Which Ought to Be in a Perfect Man: and Being Drawne from Diuine Writ, May Serue as a Patterne for Euery Reasonable Bodie, Whether Reall or Representatiue, Being Eyther Mightie or Meane, Rich or Poore. A Worke Worthie the Consideration of All Men; euen from the Kings Pallace, to the Poore Mans Cottage; from the High House of Parliament, to the Lowest Seat of the Meanest Magistrate; and from the Greatest Generall, to the Humblest Launce-pessado That Euer Commanded in Armies.* London, 1624.

poor. Ceresko, Anthony R. "The Option for the Poor." *IndTSt* 26 (1989) 105–21. ———. *Introduction to Old Testament Wisdom: A Spirituality for Liberation.* Maryknoll, NY: Orbis Books, 1999. **Grenzer, Matthias.** "Die Armenthematik in Ijob 24." In *Das Buch Ijob: Gesamtdeutungen—Einzeltexte—zentrale Themen.* Ed. Theodor Seidl and Stephanie Ernst. Österreichische biblische Studien 31. Frankfurt: Peter Lang, 2007. 229–78. **Madanu, Francis.** *Understanding of the Poor in Job in the Context of Biblical Wisdom Literature.* Ramanthpur, Hyderabad, India: St John's Regional Seminary, 1997. **Ruíz Pesce, Ramón Eduardo.** "Dios del pobre. Amor gratuito y sufrimiento del inocente. Leer el Libro de Job desde San Juan de la Cruz a Gustavo Gutiérrez." *Studium filosofía y teología* 5 (2002) 207–20. **Said, D. H.** *Longing for Justice: A Study on the Cry and Hope of the Poor in the Old Testament* [incl. Job 24:1–12]. Diss. Edinburgh, 1988.

post-mortem judgment. Griffiths, John G. "The Idea of Posthumous Judgement in Israel and Egypt." In *Fontes atque pontes. Eine Festgabe für H. Brunner.* Ed. M. Görg. Wiesbaden: Harrassowitz, 1983. 186–204.

power. Glasberg, R. "Power in Western Civilization: The Book of Job and Primo Levi's 'Survival in Auschwitz'." *CanRevCompLit* 19 (1992) 597–614.

prayer. Bergant, Dianne. "Things Too Wonderful for Me (Job 42:3): Facing the Incomprehensible." In *Scripture and Prayer: A Celebration for Carroll Stuhlmueller.* Ed. Carolyn Osiek and Donald Senior. Wilmington, DE: M. Glazier, 1988. 62–75. **Dohmen, Christoph.** "Gott seis geklagt ... Vom Verlust einer biblischen Gebetsform." *Renovatio* 61/1 (2005) 53–63. **Gilbert, Maurice.** "La prière des sages d'Israel." In *L'expérience de la prière dans les grandes religions: actes du colloque de Louvain-la-Neuve et Liège, 22–23 novembre 1978.* Ed Henri Limet and Julien Ries. Homo religiosus 5. Louvain-la-Neuve: Centre d'histoire des religions, 1980. 227–43. **Guiler, Myron.** "Prayers of Job." In *Biblical Prayers: Messages on Prayer.* Ed. A. Hickok et al. Greenville, SC: Bob Jones University, 1976. **Levoratti, Armando J.** "Las preguntas de Job." *RBibArg* 55 (1993) 1–53. **McDonagh, Kathleen.** "Job and Jeremiah: Their Approach to God." *TBT* 18 (1980) 331–35. **Moore, Rickie.** "Raw Prayer and Refined Theology: 'You have not spoken straight to me, as my servant Job has.'" In *The Spirit and the Mind: Essays in Informed Pentecostalism.* Ed. Terry L. Cross and Emerson B. Powery. Lanham, MD: University Press of America, 2000. 35–48.

preaching. Fichtner, Johannes. "Hiob in der Verkündigung unserer Zeit." *WuD* 29 (1950) 71–89 [= his *Gottes Weisheit. Gesammelte Studien zum Alten Testament.* Arbeiten zur Theologie 2/3. Stuttgart: Calwer, 1965. 52–66]. **Holbert, John C.** "The Book of Job and the Task of Preaching." *Journal for Preachers* 13 (1990) 13–22. ———. *Preaching Job.* St Louis: Chalice Press, 1999. **Nusstein, Bernhard.** *"Ist nicht Kriegsdienst des Menschen Leben auf der Erde?" (Ijob 7,1): Der Beitrag von Predigtkritik und Predigtanalyse zu einem verantwortlicheren homiletischen Umgang mit der Leidfrage.* Würzburg: Echter, 2001. **Schlafer, David J.** "Exempla XIV: The Book of Job and the Tao te ching as Antidotes to 'Preachy' Preaching." *ATR* 74 (1992) 370–75. **Schlegel, Beth A.** "Preaching on Job:

A Type of Christ and the Church." *Lutheran Forum* 36 (2002) 31–34. **Steiger, Lothar.** "Die Wirklichkeit Gottes in unserer Verkündigung." In *Auf dem Wege zu schriftgemässer Verkündigung: Hermann Diem zum 65. Geburtstag am 2. Februar 1965.* Ed. Martin Honecker and Lothar Steiger. BEvTh 39. Munich: Kaiser, 1965. 143–77.

primal man. Callender, Dexter Eugene, Jr. *The Significance and Use of Primal Man Traditions in Ancient Israel.* Diss. Harvard, 1995.

prophetic elements. Bardtke, H. "Prophetische Züge im Buche Hiob." In *Das ferne und nahe Wort. Festschrift für Leonard Rost.* BZAW 105. Ed. F. Maass. Berlin: Töpelmann, 1967. 1–10.

providence. Burrell, David B. "Maimonides, Aquinas and Gersonides on Providence and Evil." *RelStud* 20 (1984) 335–51. **Charles, M.** "The Book of Job and God's Hand in All Things." In *Women and Christ: Living the Abundant Life: Talks Selected from the 1992 Women's Conference Sponsored by Brigham Young University and the Relief Society.* Ed. Dawn Hall Anderson, Susette Fletcher Green, and Marie Cornwall. Salt Lake City: Deseret Book Co., 1993. **Cruveilhier, P.** "La conduite de la Providence selon l'auteur du livre de Job." *RevApol* 52 (1931) 150–68. **Zhang, Ying.** *Divine Justice and Divine Providence in Tension: A Dual Rhetoric in the Book of Job.* Diss. Chinese University of Hong Kong, 2007.

psychology. See Section 8.n (Job in Psychology).

questions. Crenshaw, James L. "Impossible Questions, Sayings and Tasks." In *Gnomic Wisdom.* Semeia 17. Atlanta: Scholars Press, 1980. 19–34.

rationality. Giannotto, C. (ed.). *La domanda di Giobbe e la razionalità sconfitta.* Trento: Università degli Studi di Trento, 1995.

reader. Pyper, Hugh S. "The Reader in Pain: Job as Text and Pretext" [reader's suffering in Muriel Sparks's *The Only Problem*]. In *Text as Pretext: Essays in Honour of Robert Davidson.* Ed. Robert P. Carroll. JSOTSup 138. Sheffield: JSOT Press, 1982. 234–55 [= *LitTheol* 7 (1993) 111–29].

rebel. Parmentier, Martien. "Job the Rebel: From the Rabbis to the Church Fathers." In *Saints and Role Models in Judaism and Christianity.* Ed. Marcel Poorthuis and Joshua Schwartz. Jewish and Christian Perspectives 7. Leiden: Brill, 2004. 227–42.

rebellion. Hamilton, Mark W. "Critiquing the Sovereign. Perspectives from Deuteronomy and Job." *RestQ* 47 (2005) 237–49. **Morrow, William S.** *Protest against God: The Eclipse of a Biblical Tradition.* Hebrew Bible Monographs 4. Sheffield: Sheffield Phoenix Press, 2006. **Schreiner, Stefan.** "Der gottesfürchtige Rebell oder wie die Rabbinen die Frömmigkeit Ijobs deuteten." *ZTK* 89 (1992) 159–71. **Susaimanickam, Jebamalai.** "Protest: The Language of Prophecy." *Journal of Dharma* 26 (2001) 311–35.

redemption. Sekine, Masao. "Schöpfung und Erlösung im Buche Hiob." In *Von Ugarit nach Qumran: Beiträge zur alttestamentlichen und altorientalischen Forschung. Otto Eissfeldt zum 1. September 1957 dargebracht von Freunden und Schülern.* BZAW 77. Berlin: A. Töpelmann, 1958. 213–23.

religion. Dunkmann, Karl. *Das Buch Hiob in religiösen Betrachtungen: für das moderne Bedürfnis.* Gütersloh: Bertelsmann, 1913. **Lacocque, André.** "Job and Religion at Its Best." *BibInt* 4 (1996) 131–53. ———. "Job or the Impotence of Religion and Philosophy." *Semeia* 19 (1981) 33–52. **Loader, J. A.** "Job's Sister: Undermining an Unnatural Religiosity." *OTEss* 6 (1993) 312–29. **Morrow, William S.** "Toxic Religion and the Daughters of Job." *SR* 27 (1998) 263–76. **Schraub, J. Jonathan.** "For the Sin We Have Committed by Theological Rationalizations: Rescuing Job from Normative Religion." *Soundings* 86 (2003) 431–62.

responsibility. Häring, Hermann. "Who Is Responsible?" *Conc* 40/4 (2004) 67–82 [= "Wer trägt die Verantwortung?" *Conc* 40/4 (2004) 429–43].

resurrection. Althann, Robert. "Job and the Idea of the Beatific Afterlife." *OTEss* 4 (1991) 316–26. **Ancessi, Victor.** *Job et l'Egypte: le rédempteur et la vie future dans les civilisations primitives.* Paris: Ernest Leroux, 1877. **Benamozegh, E.** "L'immortalità dell'anima in Giobbe e nei Proverbi." *AnStEbr* 8 (1975–76) 145–72. **García Cordero, M.** "Corporal Resurrection in Job." *TDig* 2 (1954) 90–94. ———. "La esperanza de la resurrección corporal en Job." *CiTom* 80 (1953) 1–23. ———. "La tesis de la sanción moral y la espe-ranza de la resurrección en el libro de Job." In *XII Semana bíblica española: la encíclica Humani generis (24–26 Sept. 1951).* Madrid [Burgos: Aldecoa], 1952. 571–94. **Greenspoon, L. J.** "The Origins of the Idea of Resurrection." In *Traditions in Transformation: Turning Points in Biblical Faith* [Festschrift Frank Moore Cross]. Ed. Baruch Halpern and Jon D. Levenson. Winona Lake, IN: Eisenbrauns, 1981. 247–321. **Lang, Bernhard.** "Afterlife: Ancient Israel's Changing Vision of the World Beyond." *BibRev* 4 (1988) 12–23. **Lavater, Ludwig.** *Beati Iobi fides et confessio de resurrectione mortuorum, novissime iudicio, et vita aeterna, homilia L. Lauerteri ... illustrata; nunc primum ex Germanico ... conversa.* Zurich, 1587. **Levenson, Jon D.** "Are Abraham, Moses, and Job in Sheol?" In his *Resurrection and the Restoration of Israel: The Ultimate Victory of the God of Life.* New Haven: Yale University Press, 2006. **Long, T. J.** "Life after Death, the Biblical View." *BiTod* 20 (1982) 347–53. **Muntingh, L. M.** "Life, Death and Resurrection in the Book of Job." *OTWSA* 17–18 (*Old Testament Essays: Studies in the Pentateuch.* Ed. W. C. van Wyk) (1974–75) 32–44. **Pareau, Johann Hendrik.** *Commentatio de immortalitatis ac vitae futurae notitiis ab antiquissimo Jobi scriptore in suos usus adhibitis. Accedit sermo Jobi de sapientia mortuis magis cognita quam vivis, sive Jobeidis caput XXVIII, philologice et critice illustratum.* Deventer: L. A. Karsenbergh, 1807. **Plantz, Samuel.** "Doctrine of the Future Life in the Book of Job." *MethRev* 78 (1896) 45–59. **Rongy, H.** "La résurrection est-elle enseignée dans Job?" *RevEcclLiège* 25 (1983–84) 25–30. **Schnocks, Johannes.** "The Hope for Resurrection in the Book of Job." In *The Septuagint and Messianism.* Ed. Michael A. Knibb. BETL 195. Leuven: Leuven University Press, 2006. 291–99. **Vawter, B.** "Intimations of Immortality in the Old Testament." *JBL* 91 (1972) 158–71. **Vidal, J. M.** "L'idée de résurrection dans Job." *Revue du clergé français* 57 (1909) 295ff., 672ff. **Wahrendorff, David Otto.** *De resurrectione speciatim Jobi cum sotere facta ad finem libri Jobi secundum Septuaginta meditationes.* Göttingen: Vandenhoeck, 1738.

retribution. **Charue, A.** "Job et le problème des rétributions dans l'Ancien Testament." *Collationes namurcenses* 33 (1939) 251–71. **Fischer, S.** "How God Pays Back: Retributive Concepts in the Book of Job." *AcTheol* 20 (2000) 26–41. **Koch, K.** "Gibt es ein Vergeltungsdogma im Alten Testament?" *ZTK* 52 (1955) 1–42. ———. *Um das Prinzip der Vergeltung in Religion und Recht des Alten Testaments.* Wege der Forschung 125. Darmstadt: Wissenschaftliche Buchgesellschaft, 1972. **Krašovec, Jože.** "God's Requital in General and in Job" [Slovenian]. *Bogoslovni Vestnik* 45 (1985) 3–22. **Lindblom, C. J.** "Die Vergeltung Gottes im Buche Hiob. Eine ideenkritische Skizze." In *In piam memoriam Alexander von Bulmerincq Gedenkschrift zum 5. Juni 1938, dem 70. Geburtstage des am 29. März 1938 Entschlafenen.* Ed. Rudolf Abramowski. Abhandlungen der Herder-Gesellschaft und der Herder-Instituts zu Riga 6/3. 1938. 80–97. **Loader, J. A.** "Different Reactions of Job and Qoheleth to the Doctrine of Retribution." *OTWSA* 15 (= *Studies in Wisdom Literature.* Ed. W. C. van Wyk) (1972) 43–48. **Niekerk, M. J. H. van.** "Response to J. A. Loader's 'Different Reactions of Job and Qoheleth to the Doctrine of Retribution'." *OTEss* 4 (1991) 97–105.

reverence. **O'Connor, D. J.** "Reverence and Irreverence in Job." *ITQ* 51 (1985) 85–104.

righteousness. **Baltzer, Klaus, and Thomas Krüger.** "Die Erfahrung Hiobs. 'Konnektive' und 'distributive' Gerechtigkeit nach dem Hiob-Buch." In *Problems in Biblical Theology: Essays in Honor of Rolf Knierim.* Ed. Henry T. C. Sun and Keith L. Eades. Grand Rapids: William B. Eerdmans, 1997. 27–37. **Berg, W.** "Gott und der Gerechte in der Rahmenerzählung des Buches Ijob." *MTZ* 32 (1981) 206–21. **Bič, M.** "Le juste et l'impie dans le livre de Job." In *Volume du congrès: Genève 1965.* VTSup 15. Leiden: E. J. Brill, 1966. 33–43. **Cox, Dermot.** "*Ṣedāqâ* and *mišpāṭ*: The Concept of Righteousness in Later Wisdom [Job, Proverbs, Qoheleth]." *SBFLA* 27 (1977) 33–50. **Holm-Nielsen, Svend.** "Die Verteidigung für die Gerechtigkeit Gottes." *SJOT* 2 (1987) 69–89. **Klassen, Randy.** "Job's Thirst for Righteousness: A Parable of Post Modernism." *Direction* 25 (1996) 44–53. **Oorschot, Jürgen van.** "Gottes Gerechtigkeit und Hiobs Leid." *ThBeitr*

30 (1999) 202–13. **Reimer, Haroldo.** "Gerechtigkeit und Schöpfung: ein Beitrag zum Verständnis des Hiobbuches." In *Freiheit und Recht: Festschrift für Frank Crüsemann zum 65. Geburtstag.* Ed. Christof Hardmeier, Rainer Kessler, and Andreas Ruwe. Gütersloh: Kaiser, 2003. 414–28. **Ruppert, Lothar.** *Jesus als der leidende Gerechte? Der Weg Jesu im Lichte eines alt- und zwischentestamentlichen Motivs.* Stuttgarter Bibelstudien 59. Stuttgart: Verlag Katholisches Bibelwerk, 1972. **Ruprecht, Eberhard.** "Leiden und Gerechtigkeit bei Hiob." *ZTK* 73 (1976) 424–45. **Scherer, Andreas.** "Relative Gerechtigkeit und absolute Vollkommenheit bei Hiob: Überlegungen zu Spannungsmomenten im Hiobbuch." *BN* 101 (2000) 81–99. **Stamm, Johann Jakob.** "Gottes Gerechtigkeit, das Zeugnis des Hiobbuches." *Der Grundriss. Schweizerische Reformierte Monatsschrift* 5 (1943) 1–13. **Stockhammer, Morris.** "The Righteousness of Job." *Judaism* 7 (1958) 64–71. **Thieberger, F.** "Jona, Hiob, und das Problem der Gerechtigkeit." *Der Morgen* 2 (1926) 128–40.

sacrifice. Bakan, D. "Das Opfer im Buche Hiob." In *Psychoanalytische Interpretationen biblischer Texte.* Ed. Yorick Spiegel. Munich: Kaiser, 1972. 152–66. ———. "Sacrifice and the Book of Job." In his *Disease, Pain and Sacrifice: Toward a Psychology of Suffering.* Chicago: University of Chicago Press, 1968. 95–128. **Heim, S. Mark.** "The Voice of Job: Sacrifice Revealed and Contested." In his *Saved from Sacrifice: A Theology of the Cross.* Grand Rapids: William B. Eerdmans, 2006. 64–104. **Lux, Rüdiger.** "Der leidende Gerechte als Opfer und Opferherr in der Hiobnovelle." *Leqach* 5 (2004) 41–57.

salvation. Rohr Sauer, A. von. "Salvation by Grace: The Heart of Job's Theology." *CTM* 37 (1966) 259–70.

Satan. Brockway, R. W., and P. J. Hordern. "The Devil and Job." *Faith and Freedom* 36/1 (1982) 41–44. **Kinet, Dirk.** "The Ambiguity of the Concepts of God and Satan in the Book of Job." *Conc* 169 (1983) 30–35. **Laudon, Barbara Elaine.** *Light and Darkness Imagery and the Demonic Element in Mixail Bulgakov's "The Master and Margarit"* [Satan in Job]. Diss. Wisconsin–Madison, 1983. **Levin, S.** "Satan: Psychologist." *JBQ* 18 (1989–90) 157–64. **Maldaner, Plínio R.** "Deus e o diabo na roça: explicação popular do mal e seu embate teológico no meio: confronto com o livro de Jó." *EstBíb* 74 (2002) 65–69. **Moskala, Jiri.** "The God of Job and Our Adversary." *Journal of the Adventist Theological Society* 15 (2004) 107–17. **Nielsen, Kirsten.** "Whatever Became of You, Satan? or, A Literary-Critical Analysis of the Role of Satan in the Book of Job." In *Goldene Äpfel in silbernen Schalen: Collected Communications to the XIIIth Congress of the International Organization for the Study of the Old Testament, Leuven 1989.* Ed. Klaus-Dietrich Schunck and Matthias Augustin. BEATAJ 20. Frankfurt a.M.: Peter Lang, 1992. 129–34. **Schärf, Rivka R.** "Die Gestalt des Satans im Alten Testament." In C. G. Jung, *Symbolik des Geistes.* Zurich: Rascher Verlag, 1948 [= Rivka R. Scharf Kluger. *Satan in the Old Testament.* Trans. H. Nagel. Evanston: Northwestern University Press, 1967]. **Schramm, Brooks.** "God and Satan in Job." *Lutheran Theological Seminary Bulletin* 78 (1998) 35–48. **Toynbee, A. J.** "Challenge and Response: The Mythological Clue." In *Twentieth Century Interpretations of the Book of Job. A Collection of Critical Essays.* Ed. P. S. Sanders. Englewood Cliffs, NJ: Prentice–Hall. 1968. 86–97 [= his *A Study of History* (abridged ed.). New York: Oxford University Press, 1947. 60–67; *A Study of History* (original ed.). New York: Oxford University Press, 1934. 1:293–98]. **White, Marylyn Ellen.** *The Purpose and Portrayal of the sāṭān in the Old Testament.* Diss. Tyndale Seminary, 2004.

scapegoat. Girard, René. "Job as Failed Scapegoat." In *The Voice from the Whirlwind: Interpreting the Book of Job.* Ed. Leo G. Perdue and Clark Gilpin. Nashville: Abingdon Press, 1992. 185–207. ———. "'The ancient trail trodden by the wicked.' Job as Scapegoat." *Semeia* 33 (1985) 13–41. ———. "Job et le bouc émissaire." *BCPE* 35 (1983) 3–33. **Holm-Nielsen, Svend.** "Is Job a Scapegoat?" In *In the Last Days: On Jewish and Christian Apocalyptic and Its Period.* Ed. Knud Jeppesen. Aarhus: Aarhus University Press, 1994. 128–35.

science. Lang, Walter. *Job and Science: A Commentary on the Book of Job in the Bible.* Richfield, MN: Genesis Institute, 1991. **Morris, Henry M.** *The Remarkable Record of Job: The Ancient Wisdom, Scientific Accuracy, and Life-Changing Message of an Amazing Book.*

Grand Rapids: Baker, 1988 [= *Der estaunliche Bericht des Hiob: Alttestamentliche Weisheit, moderne Naturwissenschaft und lebendige Botschaft.* Dillenburg: Christliche Verlagsgesellschaft, 1995]. **Wolfers, David.** "Science in the Book of Job." *JBQ* 19 (1990–91) 18–21.

sea. Janzen, J. Gerald. "On the Moral Nature of God's Power: Yahweh and the Sea in Job and Deutero-Isaiah." *CBQ* 56 (1994) 458–78.

sex. Brown, William P. "On Matters of Sex, What Kind of 'Textual Orientation' Does the Wisdom Literature Provide?" [http://www.covenantnetwork.org/FAQ-pdfs/brown.pdf].

Shaddai. Nielsen, Eduard. "Shadday in the Book of Job." In *Living Waters: Scandinavian Orientalistic Studies Presented to Frede Løkkegaard on His Seventy-Fifth Birthday, January 27th 1990.* Ed. Egon Keck, Svend Søndergaard, and Ellen Wulff. Copenhagen: Museum Tusculanum Press, 1990. 249–58.

silence. Dunn, R. P. "Speech and Silence in Job." *Semeia* 19 (1981) 99–103. **Gutridge, Coralie A.** "The Sacrifice of Fools and the Wisdom of Silence: Qoheleth, Job and the Presence of God." In *Biblical Hebrew, Biblical Texts. Essays in Memory of Michael P. Weitzman.* Ed. Ada Rapoport-Albert and Gillian Greenberg. JSOTSup 333. Sheffield: Sheffield Academic Press, 2001. 83–99. **Olson, Alan M.** "The Silence of Job as the Key to the Text." *Semeia* 19 (1981) 113–19. **Patriquin, Allan.** "Deconstruction, Plurivocity, and Silence" [reply to R. Jacobson, "Satanic Semiotics, Jobian Jurisprudence"]. *Semeia* 19 (1981) 121–23. **Pleins, J. David.** "'Why Do You Hide Your Face?' Divine Silence and Speech in the Book of Job." *Int* 48 (1994) 229–38. **Steins, Georg (ed.).** *Schweigen wäre gotteslästerlich: Die heilende Kraft der Klage.* Würzburg: Echter, 2000. **Wiesel, Elie.** "Job ou le silence révolutionnaire." In *Célébration biblique: portraits et légendes.* Paris: Editions du Seuil, 1975. 179–99 [= *Messengers of God: Biblical Portraits and Legends.* New York: Summit Books, 1976; "Der das revolutionäre Schweigen." In *Adam oder das Geheimnis des Anfangs: Brüderliche Urgestalten.* Freiburg i.Br.: Herder, 1980. 207–32]. **Woodin, Ataloa-Snell.** "Speak, O Lord: The Silence of God in Human Suffering." *Direction* 25 (Spr 1996) 29–54.

sin. Brown, Walter E. *The Nature of Sin in the Book of Job.* Diss. New Orleans Baptist Theological Seminary, 1983. **Goldin, Paul-Rakita.** "Job's Transgressions: Luis Alonso Schökel and Jose Luz Ojeda." *ZAW* 108 (1996) 378–90. **Milgrom, Jacob.** "The Cultic שגגה and Its Influence in Psalms and Job." *JQR* 58 (1967) 115–25. **Nimmo, Peter W.** "Sin, Evil and Job: Monotheism as a Psychological and Pastoral Problem." *Pastoral Psychology* 42 (1994) 427–39.

skepticism. Anderson, William H. U. "What Is Scepticism and Can It Be Found in the Hebrew Bible?" *SJOT* 13 (1999) 225–57. **Crenshaw, James L.** "The Birth of Skepticism in Ancient Israel." In his *The Divine Helmsman: Studies on God's Control of Human Events, Presented to Lou H. Silberman.* Ed. James L. Crenshaw and Samuel Sandmel. New York: Ktav, 1980. 1–19.

social theology. Anderson, D. G. L. *The Book of Job and the Construction of a Critical Theory of Soteriological Social Theology: A Habermasian Reading.* Diss. Sheffield, 1998.

society. Aimers, Geoffrey J. "The Rhetoric of Social Conscience in the Book of Job." *JSOT* 91 (2000) 99–107. **Berg, Werner.** "Arbeit und Soziales im Buch Ijob." In *Glaube in Politik und Zeitgeschichte.* Paderborn: Ferdinand Schoningh, 1995. 151–68. **Nyström, Samuel.** "Übriges nachexilisches Schrifttum und das Wüstenleben mit besonderer Rücksicht auf das Buch Hiob." In his *Beduinentum und Jahwismus: Eine soziologisch-religionsgeschichtliche Untersuchung zum Alten Testament.* Lund: C. W. K. Gleerup, 1946. 201–17. **Silbermann, Alphons.** "Soziologische Anmerkungen zum Buch Hiob." *ZRGG* 41 (1989) 1–11. **Stordalen, Terje.** "Tsunami and Theology: The Social Tsunami in Scandinavia and the Book of Job." *ST* 60 (2006) 3–20. **Whybray, R. N.** "The Social World of the Wisdom Writers." In *The World of Ancient Israel: Sociological, Anthropological, and Political Perspectives.* Ed. R. E. Clements. Cambridge: Cambridge University Press, 1989. 227–50.

solitude. Vinton, Patricia. "Radical Aloneness: Job and Jeremiah." *TBT* 99 (1978) 143–49.

spirituality. Dailey, Thomas F. "The Wisdom of Irreverence: Job as an Icon for Postmodern Spirituality." *Int* 53 (1999) 276–89. **Ochs, Carol.** *Song of the Self: Biblical Spirituality and Human Holiness.* Valley Forge, PA: Trinity Press International, 1994.

stress. Murphy, Joseph. *Living without Strain. Inner Meaning of the Book of Job.* San Gabriel, CA: Willing, 1959 [= *Positiv leben ohne Stress: das Buch Hiob interpretiert für unsere Zeit.* Munich: Goldmann, 1990].

sublime. Linafelt, Tod. "The Wizard of Uz: Job, Dorothy, and the Limits of the Sublime." *BibInt* 14 (2006) 94–109.

suffering. Archer, G. L. *The Book of Job: God's Answer to the Problem of Undeserved Suffering.* Grand Rapids: Baker, 1982. **Balentine, Samuel E.** "'Let love clasp grief lest both be drowned'." *PerspRelSt* 30 (2003) 381–97. **Balla, E.** "Das Problem des Leides in der Geschichte der israelitisch-jüdischen Religion." In ΕΥΧΑΡΙΣΤΗΡΙΟΝ: *Studien zur Religion und Literatur des Alten und Neuen Testaments Hermann Gunkel zum 60. Geburtstage ... dargebracht.* Ed. Hans Schmidt. FRLANT 19. Göttingen: Vandenhoeck & Ruprecht, 1923. 1:214–60. **Barry, Wendy Elizabeth.** *A Cipher to Lend Significance: Pain, Suffering and Narrative in the Book of Job, Clarissa, and David Copperfield.* Diss. Vanderbilt, 1999. **Bastiaens, Jean Charles.** "The Language of Suffering in Job 16–19 and in the Suffering Servant Passages in Deutero-Isaiah." *In Studies in the Book of Isaiah.* Ed. J. van Ruiten and M. Vervenne. BETL 132. Leuven: Leuven University Press, 1997. 421–32. **Batley, J. Y.** *The Problem of Suffering in the Old Testament.* Cambridge: Deighton, Bell & Co., 1916. **Beel, A.** "De causis tribulationum juxta librum Job. De historica existentia personae Job. Interpretatio Job 7,11–21." *ColBG* 38 (1933) 321–26, 349–53; 34 (1934) 89–94. **Berges, Ulrich.** "Hiob in Lateinamerika. Der leidende Mensch und der aussätzige Gott." In *The Book of Job.* Ed. W. A. M. Beuken. BETL 114. Leuven: Leuven University Press, 1994. 297–317. **Blake, Buchanan.** *The Book of Job and the Problem of Suffering.* London: Hodder & Stoughton, 1911 [= *The Problem of Human Suffering: A Study of the Book of Job.* New York: Hodder & Stoughton, 1911]. **Boadt, Lawrence (ed.).** *The Book of Job: Why Do the Innocent Suffer?* Foreword by Alice Thomas Ellis. The Classic Bible Series. New York: St Martin's Press, 1997. **Bode, William.** *The Book of Job and the Solution of the Problem of Suffering.* Diss. Temple, 1913. **Böning, Adalbert.** *Das Buch Ijob oder Gott und das Leid: Kommentar zu Texten aus dem Buch Ijob, der jüdischen Tradition und zum Problem der Theodizee, für den Hebräischunterricht.* Munich: Literaturhandlung, 1997. **Bonora, Antonio.** *Giobbe: il tormento di credere. Il problema e lo scandalo del dolore.* Fratelli nostri 5. Padua: Gregoriana, 1990. **Booker, David James.** *A Sovereign God and a Suffering World: A Study in the Book of Job.* Diss. Biola, 1993. **Bormuth, Lotte.** *Meine Trauer muss der Freude weichen: Gedanken zum Buch Hiob.* Marburg: Francke, 1995. **Brown, David.** "Job and Innocent Suffering." In his *Discipleship and Imagination: Christian Tradition and Truth.* Oxford: Oxford University Press, 2004. **Cabodevilla, J. M.** *La impaciencia de Job: estudio sobre el sufrimiento humano.* Madrid: B.A.C., 1967. **Carson, D. A.** "Job: Mystery and Faith." In his *How Long, O Lord? Reflections on Suffering and Evil.* Grand Rapids: Baker Academic, 2006. **Caspar, J.** "Job, ein Held in Leid." *BLit* 10 (1935–36) 497–98. **Cazier, Pierre.** *Le cri de Job: approche biblique, mythologique et littéraire du problème de la souffrance du juste.* Arras: Artois Presses Université, 1996. **Clarke, W. K. Lowther.** *Job and His Friends: The Problem of Suffering.* London: SPCK, 1947. **Clines, David J. A.** "Does the Book of Job Suggest That Suffering Is Not a Problem?" In *Weisheit in Israel: Beiträge des Symposiums "Das Alte Testament und die Kultur der Moderne" anlässlich des 100. Geburtstags Gerhard von Rads (1901–1971), Heidelberg, 18.–21. Oktober 2001.* Ed. David J. A. Clines, Hermann Lichtenberger, and Hans-Peter Müller. Altes Testament und Moderne 12. Münster: Lit Verlag, 2003. 93–110. **Croatto, J. S.** "El problema del dolor." *RivB* 24 (1962) 129–35. **Crook, Margaret Brackenbury.** *The Cruel God: Job's Search for the Meaning of Suffering.* Boston: Beacon Press, 1959. **Crossan, John Dominic.** "Pattern and Particularity in Suffering and Story." *Journal of Supervision and Training in Ministry* 9 (1987) 211–16.

Dell, Katharine J. *Shaking a Fist at God: Understanding Suffering through the Book of Job.* London: Fount, 1995. **Dijk, K.** *Lijden en loven: het boek Job in schriftoverdenkingen.* Kampen: Kok, 1924. **Dumoulin, Pierre.** *Job: une souffrance féconde.* Petits traités spirituels. Série VIII, Ecriture sainte. Nouan-le-Fuzelier: Pneumathèque, 1998. **Dussel, E.** "The People of El Salvador: The Communal Sufferings of Job." *Conc* 169 (1983) 61–68. **Elman, Yaakov.** "The Suffering of the Righteous in Palestinian and Babylonian Sources." *JQR* 80 (1989–90) 315–39. **Fabry, Heinz-Josef.** "Das Buch Ijob und die Fragen nach dem Leid des Menschen." In *Leiden: 27. Internationaler Fachkongress für Moraltheologie und Sozialethik (September 1995–Köln/Bonn).* Ed. Gerhard Höver. Münster: Lit, 1997. 13–32. **Fleischer, Theodore E.** "Suffering Reclaimed: Medicine according to Job." *Perspectives in Biology and Medicine* 42 (1999) 475–88. **Fuente Adánez, Alfonso de la.** "Job y el siervo de Yahvé: Dos interpretaciones del sufrimiento." *RevEspTeol* 51 (1991) 237–51. **Garofalo, S.** "Il peso di Dio e l'angoscia dell'uomo Giobbe." *EuntDoc* 2 (1949) 3–30. **Gruber, Mayer I.** "The Book of Job as Anthropodicy." *BN* 136 (2007) 59–71. **Gutiérrez, G.** "But Why, Lord: On Job and the Suffering of the Innocent." *Other Side* 23 (1987) 18–23. **Hammer, R.** "Two Approaches to the Problem of Suffering" [Job, Ruth]. *Judaism* 35 (1986) 300–305. **Häring, Hermann.** "Ijob in unserer Zeit: Zum Problem des Leidens in der Welt." In *Vorsehung und Handeln Gottes.* Ed. Theodor Schneider and Lothar Ullrich. Freiburg: Herder, 1988. 168–91. **Häussler, Manfred.** *Stundenblätter Hiob–der Mensch im Leid: Sekundarstufe.* I. Stuttgart: Klett-Verlag für Wissen und Bildung, 1994. **Harrison, Roland K.** "The Problem of Suffering and the Book of Job." *EvQ* 25 (1953) 18–27. **Haubold, Peter.** *Die Botschaften des Hiob: Ratlos im Leid* [TV program video]. Glut unter der Asche 3. Munich: BMG-Video, 2000. **Hoang-van-Doan, F.** *Le sens de la souffrance dans le livre de Job.* Diss. Paris, 1944. Paris: Letouzey et Ané, [1946]. **Homann, Ursula.** "Hiobs Frage und die Unbegreiflichkeit des Leids." *ZeichZt* 3/3 (2000) 15–18. **Hora, R., and D. M. Robinson.** "Does the Book of Job Offer an Adequate Pastoral Response to Suffering?" In *Church Divinity 1981.* Ed. John H. Morgan. Notre Dame, IN: J. H. Morgan, 1981. 67–73. **Humbert, Paul.** *L'Ancien Testament et le problème de la souffrance.* Lausanne: La Concorde, 1918. **Hung, Emmanuel.** "God, Job and Friends: The Ethics of Suffering." *Hill Road* 9 (2006) 69–83. **Kaiser, Otto.** "Leid und Gott: Ein Beitrag zur Theologie des Buches Hiob." In *Sichtbare Kirche: für Heinrich Laag zu seinem 80. Geburtstag.* Ed. Ulrich Fabricius und Rainer Volp. Gütersloh: Mohn, 1973. 13–21 [= his *Der Mensch unter dem Schicksal: Studien zur Geschichte, Theologie und Gegenwartsbedeutung der Weisheit.* BZAW 161. Berlin: W. de Gruyter, 1985. 54–62]. **Kausemann, Josef.** *Hiob: Geheimnis des Leidens.* Dillenburg: Christliche Verlagsgesellschaft, 1990. **Kimball, Charles.** "Why Christians Suffer: Job's Story." *Preaching* 14 (May–June 1999) 38–41. **Kock, Manfred.** "Warum ein Leben voller Bitterkeit und Mühe? Die dunklen und die hellen Seiten Gottes im Buch Hiob." In *Glauben nach Ground Zero.* Ed. Margot Kässmann. Stuttgart: Kreuz Verlag, 2003. 15–23. **König, Eduard.** "The Problem of Suffering in the Light of the Book of Job." *ExpT* 32 (1920–21) 361–63. ———. "The Problem of Suffering and the Book of Job." *MethRev* 110 (1927) 582–86. **Koepp, W.** "Vom Hiobthema und der Zeit als Leiden." *TLZ* 74 (1949) 389–96. **Krieger, Hermann.** *Das Leiden des Gerechten im Buche Hiob und im Lichte des Neuen Testamentes.* Beilage zum Jahresbericht des Königlichen Gymnasiums zu Wehlau. Wehlau, 1902. **Krüger, Thomas.** "Gott und das Leid: Hiobs Botschaft." In his *Kritische Weisheit: Studien zur weisheitlichen Traditionskritik im Alten Testament.* Zurich: Pano, 1997. 215–25. **Kubina, Veronica.** "Ja-Sagen zur Wirklichkeit: Leiden und Leidbewältigung im Buche Ijob." *KatBl* 107 (1982) 743–53. **Küng, Hans.** *Gott und das Leid.* Theologische Meditationen 18. Einsiedeln: Benziger, 1968. **Kushner, Harold S.** "Why Bad Things Happen: Lessons from the Book of Job." *Areopagus* 7/1 (1994) 10–12 [repr. from his *When Bad Things Happen to Good People,* 1981]. **Kutsch, Ernst.** "Hiob: leidender Gerechter–leidender Mensch." *KuD* 19 (1973) 197–214 [= his *Kleine Schriften zum Alten Testament.* Ed. Ludwig Schmidt and Karl Eberlein. BZAW 168. Berlin: Walter de Gruyter, 1986. 290–307]. ———. "Von Grund und Sinn des Leidens nach dem Alten

Testament." In his *Kleine Schriften zum Alten Testament*. Ed. Ludwig Schmidt and Karl Eberlein. BZAW 168. Berlin: Walter de Gruyter, 1986. 336–47. **Lamb, Jonathan**. *The Rhetoric of Suffering: Reading the Book of Job in the Eighteenth Century*. Oxford: Clarendon Press, 1995. **Lang, Bernhard**. "Ein Kranker sieht seinen Gott. Leidenswelt und Leidenswende im Buch Ijob [38–41]." In *Der Mensch unter dem Kreuz: Wegweisung, Erfahrungen, Hilfen*. Ed. Reinhold Bärenz. Regensburg: Pustet, 1980. 35–48 [= "Ein Kranker sieht scinen Gott." In Bernhard Lang. *Wie wird man Prophet in Israel? Aufsätze zum Alten Testament*. Düsseldorf: Patmos Verlag, 1980. 137–48]. **Lange, Albert de, and Onno Zijlstra**. *Als ik Job niet had: tien denkers over God en het lijden*. Zoetermeer: Meinema, 1997. **Langenhorst, Georg (ed.)**. *Hiobs Schrei in die Gegenwart. Ein literarisches Lesebuch zur Frage nach Gott im Leid*. Religion und Ästhetik. Mainz: Matthias-Grünewald-Verlag, 1995. ———. "Lehrmeister Hiob. Hiobsweisheiten im Umgang mit Leiden." *RPäB* 41 (1999) 129–42. **Leaman, Oliver**. *Evil and Suffering in Jewish Philosophy*. Cambridge Studies in Religious Traditions 6. Cambridge: Cambridge University Press, 1995. **Lévêque, J.** "Le sens de la souffrance d'après le livre de Job." *RTL* 6 (1975) 438–59. ———. "Sofferenza e metamorfosi. Una lettura del libro di Giobbe." *Communio* 33 (1977) 4–16. **Lumire, J. P.** "Tout au long de mon été" [reflections on suffering]. *Flambeau* 59 (1980) 393–96. **Lytle-Vieira, Jane E.** "Job and the Mystery of Suffering." *Spiritual Life* (Washington, DC) 44 (1968) 76–86. **Macleod, William B.** *The Afflictions of the Righteous as Discussed in the Book of Job and the New Light of the Gospel*. London: Hodder & Stoughton, 1911. **Madanu, Francis.** "Hope in Suffering: Job as a Model (A Study on an Innocent Sufferer)." *BibBash* 24 (1998) 253–71. ———. *Why the Innocent Suffer: Job and Harischandra: Biblical and Puranic Expression*. Ramanthpur, Hyderabad, India: St John's Regional Seminary, 1998. **Magonet, J.** "The Problem of Suffering in the Bible." *Month* 244 (1982) 311–16. **Masenya, Madipoane J.** "Between Unjust Suffering and the 'Silent' God: Job and HIV/AIDS Sufferers in South Africa." *Missionalia* 29 (2001) 186–99. **Meves, Christa.** "Vom Sinn des Leidens—Lebenshilfe durch Hiob." *Theologisches* 26 (1996) 172–78. **Moriconi, Bruno.** *Giobbe: il peso della sofferenza, la forza della fede*. Turin: Edizioni camilliane, 2001. **Mura, Gaspare.** *Angoscia ed esistenza, da Kierkegaard a Moltmann; Giobbe e la 'sofferenza di Dio'*. Rome: Città nuova, 1982. **Nowell-Rostron, Sydney.** *The Challenge of Calamity: A Study of the Book of Job*. London: RTS–Lutterworth, 1939. **Nuland, J. van.** *Semantiek en Bijbel: Studie van het Vocabularium van het Lijden in de Septuaginta van het Boek Job*. 1969. **O'Brien, George Dennis.** "Prolegomena to a Dissolution to the Problem of Suffering." *HTR* 57 (1964) 301–23. **Oelmüller, Willi.** "Philosophische Fragen und Antworten zu Leiden und Katastrophen." In *Warum? Hiob interdisziplinär diskutiert*. Mainzer Universitätsgespräche Wintersemester 1997/98. Vorträge von Hansjakob Becker, Jürgen Ebach, Herbert Jochum, Georg Langenhorst, Józef Niewiadomski, Willi Oelmüller, and Wilhelm Pesch. Mainz: Studium Generale der Universität Mainz, 1998. 73–100. **Oeming, Manfred, and Konrad Schmid.** *Hiobs Weg: Stationen von Menschen im Leid*. Biblisch-theologische Studien 45. Neukirchen–Vluyn: Neukirchener Verlag, 2001. **Oorschot, Jürgen van.** "Gottes Gerechtigkeit und Hiobs Leid." *ThBeitr* 30 (1999) 202–13. **Pandolfi, Carmelo.** "Linee per una metafisica della sofferenza suggerite da Giobbe e dal Commento a Giobbe di San Tommaso." *Il cannocchiale* (May–August, 1998) 115–37. **Parente, Pascal P.** "The Book of Job. Reflexions on the Mystic Value of Human Suffering." *CBQ* 8 (1946) 213–19. **Parkoff, Eliezer.** *Fine Lines of Faith: A Study of the Torah's Outlook on Human Suffering, Based on Malbim's Commentary to Iyov*. Spring Valley, NY: Feldheim, 1994. **Paulus, J.** "Le thème du juste souffrant dans la pensée grecque et hébraïque." *RHR* 121 (1940) 18–66. **Peake, Arthur S.** *The Problem of Suffering in the Old Testament*. London: Robert Bryant, 1904; repr. London: Epworth Press, 1947 [pp. 89–102 reprinted as "Job's Victory" in *The Dimensions of Job: A Study and Selected Readings*. Ed. Nahum H. Glatzer. New York: Schocken Books, 1969. 197–205]. **Peters, Benedikt.** *Das Buch Hiob: warum müssen die Gerechten leiden?* Dillenburg: Christliche Verlagsgesellschaft, 2002. **Peters, Norbert.** *Die Leidensfrage im Alten Testament*. Biblische Zeitfragen

11/3–5. Münster: Aschendorff, 1923. **Pipes, Buddy Rogers.** *Christian Response to Human Suffering: A Lay Theological Response to the Book of Job.* Diss. Drew, 1981. **Poinsett, Brenda.** *When Saints Sing the Blues: Understanding Depression through the Lives of Job, Naomi, Paul, and Others.* Grand Rapids: Baker Books, 2006. **Pollard, Edward John.** *The Problem of Suffering as Dealt with in the Book of Job.* Diss. Claremont, 1960. **Ponthot, J.** "Le scandale de la souffrance du juste selon le livre de Job." *Revue diocésaine de Tournai* 13 (1958) 271–75. **Pröpper, T.** "Warum gerade ich? Zur Frage nach dem Sinn vom Leiden." *KatBl* 108 (1983) 253–74.

Raabe, Paul R. "Human Suffering in Biblical Context." *ConcJ* 15 (1989) 139–55. **Ravasi, Gianfranco.** "'Le lacrime da nessuno consolate.' Il giusto sofferente in Giobbe e Qohelet." *ParSpV* 34 (1996) 85–95. **Ravi-Booth, Vincent.** *Why Do the Good Suffer? A Meditation Suggested by the Book of Job.* Boston: Gorham Press, 1920. **Robinson, H. Wheeler.** *The Cross of Job.* London: SCM Press, 1916 [reprinted in his *The Cross in the Old Testament.* London: SCM Press, 1955]. ———. *Suffering Human and Divine.* London: SCM Press, 1940. **Royds, Thomas Fletcher.** *Job and the Problem of Suffering.* London: Wells Gardner & Co., 1911. **Rubenstein, Richard L.** "Job and Auschwitz." In *Strange Fire: Reading the Bible after the Holocaust.* Ed. Tod Linafelt. The Biblical Seminar 71. Sheffield: Sheffield Academic Press, 2000. 233–51. **Ruprecht, Eberhard.** "Leiden und Gerechtigkeit bei Hiob." *ZTK* 73 (1976) 424–45. **Salguero, J.** "El dolor constituye una prueba saludable para el hombre." *CuBíb* 20 (1963) 280–99. **Sanders, James Alvin.** *Suffering as Divine Discipline in the Old Testament and Post-Biblical Judaism.* Rochester Divinity School Bulletin 28 (1955). **Schimmel, Solomon.** "Job and the Psychology of Suffering and Doubt." *JPsychJud* 11 (1987) 239–49. **Schwarzwäller, Klaus.** "'Nun hat mein Auge dich gesehen': Leiden als Grundproblem der Theologie." In *Einfach von Gott reden: ein theologischer Diskurs. Festschrift für Friedrich Mildenberger zum 65. Geburtstag.* Ed. Jürgen Roloff and Hans G. Ulrich. Stuttgart: Kohlhammer, 1994. 190–225. **Schwienhorst-Schönberger, Ludger.** "Das Buch Ijob: Ein Weg durch das Leid." In *Wo war Gott, als er nicht da war?* Ed. Hans Mendl, Ludger Schwienhorst-Schönberger, and Hermann Stinglhammer. Glauben und Leben 33. Münster: Lit Verlag, 2006. 5–28. **Seitz, Oskar.** *Hiob: Eine Betrachtung über das Leiden.* Berlin: Oskar Seitz, 1931. **Sheldon, Mark.** "Job, Human Suffering and Knowledge: Some Contemporary Jewish Perspectives." *Enc* 41 (1980) 229–35. **Slater, Robert Henry Lawson.** *God and Human Suffering, Considered with Special Reference to the Book of Job.* London: Epworth Press, 1941. **Sockman, Ralph W.** *The Meaning of Suffering.* Nashville: Abingdon Press, 1961. **Splett, Jörg.** "Ist Gott gut, wenn wir leiden müssen? Das Denken vor der Ijobs-Frage." *Katholische Bildung* 100 (1999) 440–47. **Stadler, Alisa M.** *Hiob: Der Mensch in seinem Leid.* Innsbruck: Tyrolia-Verlag, 1992. **Stefani, Piero.** "Metto la mano sulla bocca (Gb 40,4): Quando il dolore diventa innocente?" In *Il Crocifisso e le religioni: compassione di Dio e sofferenze dell'uomo nelle religioni monoteiste.* Ed. Piero Coda and Mariano Crociata. Rome: Città nuova, 2002. 113–23. **Sutcliffe, Edmund F.** *Providence and Suffering in the Old and New Testaments.* London: Thomas Nelson, 1955 [= *Der Glaube und das Leiden nach den Zeugnissen des Alten und Neuen Testamentes.* Freiburg: Herder, 1958]. **Swain, L.** "Suffering in Job." *CleR* 51 (1966) 624–31. **Tai, Nicholas H. F., and Peter K. H. Lee.** "A Dialogue: Job, Paul and the Chinese Sages on Suffering." *Theology and Life* 17–19 (1996) 179–95. **Tengbom, Mildred.** *Sometimes I Hurt: Reflections and Insights from the Book of Job.* Nashville: Nelson, 1980. **Thomason, Bill.** *God on Trial: The Book of Job and Human Suffering.* Collegeville, MN: Liturgical Press, 1997. **Villiers, H. Montagu.** *Perfect through Suffering: Being Thoughts on the Book of Job Taken from Addresses Given at S. Paul's, Knightsbridge.* London: Longmans, Green & Co., 1909. **Vugdelija, Marijan.** "Job i problemi patnje." *Bogoslovska smotra* 64 (1994) 219–48. **Wagner, S.** "Leiderfahrung und Leidbewältigung im biblischen Ijobbuch." In *Gottes Ehre erzählen: Festschrift für Hans Seidel zum 65. Geburtstag.* Ed. Matthias Albani and Timotheus Arndt. Leipzig: Thomas-Verlag, 1994. 185–210. **Waters, Larry J.** "Reflections on Suffering from the Book of Job." *BSac* 154 (1997) 436–51. **Webster, Douglas D.** "Reflections on Suffering." *Crux* 20/2 (1984) 2–8. **West, Marjory S.** "The Book of Job and the Problem of Suffering." *ExpT* 40

(1928–29) 358–64. **White, G. Cecil.** *The Discipline of Suffering. Nine Short Readings on the History of Job* [incl. the text of Job in blank verse]. London: W. Skeffington & Son, 1880. **Whybray, R. Norman.** "Wisdom, Suffering and the Freedom of God in the Book of Job." In *In Search of True Wisdom: Essays in Old Testament Interpretation in Honour of Ronald E. Clements.* Ed. Edward Ball. JSOTSup 300. Sheffield: Sheffield Academic Press, 1999. 231–45. **Wiesel, Elie.** "The Eternal Question of Suffering." In *Proceedings of the Center for Jewish-Christian Learning.* Jay Phillips Center for Jewish-Christian Learning, St Paul, MN. Vol. 3 (1987). **Williams, James G.** "Job and the God of Victims." In *The Voice from the Whirlwind: Interpreting the Book of Job.* Ed. Leo G. Perdue and Clark Gilpin. Nashville: Abingdon Press, 1992. 208–31. **Witte, Markus.** "Betrachtungen zum Verhältnis von Zeit und Leid im Buch Ijob." In *Beiträge zum Verständnis der Bibel und ihrer Botschaft: Festschrift für Rudolf Mosis zum 70. Geburtstag.* Ed. Franz Sedlmeier. Würzburg: Echter, 2003. 399–414. **Yancey, Philip.** "Riddles of Pain: Clues from the Book of Job." *ChrTod* 29/18 (1985) 80. **Zahrnt, Heinz.** *Wie kann Gott das zulassen? Hiob, der Mensch im Leid.* Munich: Piper, 1985; Leipzig: Evangelische Verlagsanstalt, 2000. **Zobel, Hans Jürgen.** "Schuld und Leiden in der Auseinandersetzung mit Gott nach der Hiob Dichtung." *TVers* 18 (1993) 13–26. **Zurhellen-Pfleiderer, E.** "Das Hiobproblem. Vom Sinn des Leidens." *Christentum und Wirklichkeit* 10 (1932) 111–18, 131–38, 154–61.

suffering servant. **Kuenen, A.** "Job en de lijdende knecht van Jahveh." *TTijd* 7 (1873) 540–41.

teaching. **Penzenstadler, Joan.** "Teaching the Book of Job with a View to Human Wholeness." *Religious Education* 89 (1994) 223–31.

technology. **Strong, David.** "The Promise of Technology versus God's Promise in Job." *TTod* 48 (1991) 170–81.

theodicy. **Brändle, Werner.** "Hiob—ein tragischer Held? Überlegungen zur Theodizeethematik der Hiobdichtung." *KuD* 39 (1993) 282–92. **Bravo, Galo Severo Sánchez.** *Sofrer sem motivo: teodicéia da moldura narrativa do livro de Jó.* Diss. Pontificia Universidade Católica do Rio de Janeiro, 1999. **Brueggemann, Walter.** "Theodicy in a Social Dimension" [Job]. *JSOT* 33 (1985) 3–25. **Burrell, David B., with A. H. Johns.** *Deconstructing Theodicy: Why Job Has Nothing to Say to the Puzzled Suffering.* Grand Rapids: Brazos Press, 2008. **Cox, Harvey G.** "Complaining to God: Theodicy and the Critique of Modernity in the Resurgence of Traditional Religion—Latin American Liberation Theology." *Archivio di filosofia* 56 (1988) 311–25. **Greenstein, Edward L.** "Truth or Theodicy? Speaking Truth to Power in the Book of Job." *PrincSemBull* 27 (2006) 238–58. **Häring, Hermann.** "Ijob und die Theodizee. Systematisch-theologische Perspektiven." *RHS* 50 (2007) 283–90. **Hastoupis, A. P.** "The Problem of Theodicy in the Book of Job" [Greek]. *Theologia* (1951) 657–68. **Horne, Milton P.** *Theodicy and the Problem of Human Surrender in Job.* Diss. Oxford, 1989. **Illman, Karl-Johan.** "Theodicy in Job." In *Theodicy in the World of the Bible.* Ed. Antti Laato and Johannes C. de Moor. Leiden: Brill, 2003. 304–33. **Jans, Jan.** "'Neither Punishment nor Reward': Divine Gratuitousness and Moral Order." *Conc* 40 (2004) 83–92. **Keulen, Emke Jelmer.** *God-Talk in the Book of Job. A Biblical, Theological and Systematic Theological Study into the Book of Job and Its Relevance for the Issue of Theodicy.* Diss. Groningen, 2007. **Kraeling, Emil G.** "A Theodicy—and More." In *The Dimensions of Job: A Study and Selected Readings.* Ed. Nahum H. Glatzer. New York: Schocken Books, 1969. 205–14 [reprinted from his *The Book of the Ways of God.* London: SPCK, 1938. 241–55 (abridged)]. **Langenhorst, Georg.** "Von der Theodizee zum Trost: Ijob im Unterricht." *RHS* 50 (2007) 306–13. **Link, Christian.** "Die Überwindung eines Problems: Bemerkungen zur Frage der Theodizee." In *Wenn nicht jetzt, wann dann? Aufsätze für Hans-Joachim Kraus zum 65. Geburtstag.* Ed. Hans-Georg Geyer. Neukirchen-Vluyn: Neukirchener Verlag, 1983. 339–51.

Malter, Rudolf. "Schöpfergott und Theodizee: Eine philosophische Meditation über den 73. Psalm und das Buch Hiob." In *Gott—das bleibende Geheimnis.* Ed. Peter Reifenberg. Würzburg: Echter Verlag, 1996. 68–88. **Moretto, Giovanni.** "Teodicea, storia e Jobismo." *Archivio di filosofia* 56 (1988) 245–71. **Müller, Hans-Peter.** "Die Theodizee und das Buch

Hiob." *NZSysTh* 2 (1997) 140–56. ———. Theodizee? Anschlusserörterungen zum Buch Hiob." *ZTK* 89 (1992) 249–79. ———. "Tun-Ergehens-Zusammenhang, Klageerhörung und Theodizee im biblischen Hiobbuch und in seinen babylonischen Parallelen." In *The Wisdom Texts from Qumran and the Development of Sapiential Thought*. Ed. Charlotte Hempel, Hermann Lichtenberger, and Armin Lange. Leuven: Leuven University Press, 2002. 153–71. **Müller, K.** "Die Auslegung der Theodizeeproblems im Buche Hiob." *ThBl* 1 (1922) 73–79. ———. "Theodizee nach Ijob: Eine systematisch-geistliche Betrachtung." *Theologie der Gegenwart* 38 (1995) 211–22. **Nicholson, E. W.** "The Limits of Theodicy as a Theme of the Book of Job." In *Wisdom in Ancient Israel: Essays in Honour of J. A. Emerton*. Ed. John Day, Robert P. Gordon, and H. G. M. Williamson. Cambridge: Cambridge University Press, 1995. 71–82. **Procksch, O.** "Die Theodizee im Buche Hiob." *Allgemeine evangelisch-lutherische Kirchenzeitung* 58 (1925) 722–24, 739–42, 763–65. **Schweitzer, Don.** "The Dialectic of Understanding and Explanation in Answers to Questions of Theodicy." *SR* 34 (2005) 251–68. **Sparn, W.** "Mit dem Bösen leben: Zur Aktualität des Theodizeeproblems." *NZSysTh* 32 (1990) 207–25. **Stockhammer, Morris.** *Das Buch Hiob. Versuch einer Theodizee*. Vienna: Europäischer Verlag, 1963. **Terrien, S. L.** "The Babylonian Dialogue on Theodicy and the Book of Job." *JBL* 63 (1944) vi. **Theobald, Gerd.** *Hiobs Prozess und Gottes Gericht. Die poetische Theodizee des Welttheaters*. Diss. Heidelberg, 1991. **Yancey, Philip.** "When the Facts Don't Add Up: A Just, Loving, and Powerful God Should Follow Certain Rules, Shouldn't He?" [Job]. *ChrTod* 30/9 (1986) 19–22.

theological geography. **Görg, Manfred.** "Ijob aus dem Lande Us: ein Beitrag zur 'theologischen Geographie'." *BN* 12 (1980) 7–12.

theology. **Adams, Marilyn McCord.** "Posing the Problems: Beginning with Job." In her *Christ and Horrors: The Coherence of Christology*. Cambridge: Cambridge University Press, 2006. **Alonso Díaz, José.** "La muerte de Josías en la redacción deuterocanónica del Libro de los Reyes como anticipo de la teología del Libro de Job." In *Homenaje a Juan Prado: miscelánea de estudios bíblicos y hebráicos*. Ed. L. Alvarez Verdes and E. J. Alonso Hernández. Madrid: Consejo Superior de Investigaciones Científicas, Instituto Benito Arias Montano de Estudios Hebráicos, Sefardies y Oriente Próximo, 1975. **Bennett, W. H.** *Modern Problems in the Book of Job*. The Deansgate Lecture. Manchester: Thos. Griffiths & Co., n.d. **Dailey, Thomas F.** "Job as an Icon for Theology." *PerspRelSt* 23 (1996) 247–54. **Gilkey, Langdon.** "Power, Order, Justice, and Redemption: Theological Comments on Job." In *The Voice from the Whirlwind: Interpreting the Book of Job*. Ed. Leo G. Perdue and Clark Gilpin. Nashville: Abingdon Press, 1992. 159–71. **Greenberg, Moshe.** "Reflections on Job's Theology." In his *Studies in the Bible and Jewish Thought*. Philadelphia: Jewish Publication Society, 1995. 327–33. **Hawthorne, R. R.** "Joban Theology." *BSac* 101 (1944) 64–75, 173–86, 290–303, 417–33; 102 (1945) 37–54. **Hempel, J.** "Was nicht im Buche Ijob steht." In *Festschrift für Emanuel Hirsch zu seinem 75. Geburtstag*. Ed. Hayo Gerdes. Itzehoe: Verlag "Die Spur," 1963. 134–36. ———. "Das theologische Problem des Hiob." *ZST* 6 (1929) 621–89 [= his *Apoxysmata. Vorarbeitungen zu einer Religionsgeschichte und Theologie des Alten Testaments*. BZAW 81. Berlin: A. Töpelmann, 1961. 114–74]. **Jenks, Alan W.** "Theological Presuppositions of Israel's Wisdom Literature." *HBT* 7 (1985) 43–75. **Larue, Gerald A.** "The Book of Job on the Futility of Theological Discussion." *The Personalist* 45 (1964) 72–79. **Laurin, Robert.** "The Theological Structure of Job." *ZAW* 84 (1972) 86–89. **Linder, Karl.** "Zur Theologie des Buches Hiob." In *Aus Schrift und Geschichte: Theologische Abhandlungen und Skizzen Herrn Prof. D. Conrad von Orelli zur Feier seiner 25-jährigen Lehrthätigkeit in Basel von Freunden und Schülern gewidmet*. Basel: R. Reich, 1898. **Noort, Edward.** *Een duister duel: over de theologie van het boek Job*. Kampen: Kok, 1986. **Perdue, Leo G.** "Metaphorical Theology in the Book of Job: Theological Anthropology in the First Cycle of Job's Speeches (Job 3; 6–7; 9–10)." In *The Book of Job*. Ed. W. A. M. Beuken. BETL 114. Leuven: Leuven University Press, 1994. 129–56. **Pixley, Jorge V.** "Jó, ou o diálogo sobre a razão teológica." *PerspT* 15 (1983) 407–12; 16 (1984) 333–43. **Simundson, Daniel J.** "The Case of Job: An Experiential Critique of

Traditional Theology." *Word and World Supplement* [= *God, Evil, and Suffering: Essays in Honor of Paul R. Sponheim.* Ed. Terence E. Fretheim and Curtis L. Thompson] 4 (2000) 75–84. **Theobald, Gerd.** "Von der Biblischen Theologie zur Buch-Theologie: Das Hiobbuch als Vorspiel zu einer christlichen Hermeneutik." *NZSysTh* 35 (1993) 276–302.

    theophany. Forrest, Robert W. E. "Theophany in Job and the Bhagavad-Gita." *Journal of Studies in the Bhagavadgita* 2 (1982) 25–43. **Lillie, William.** "The Religious Significance of the Theophany in the Book of Job." *ExpT* 68 (1956–57) 355–58.

    time. Rodríguez Ochoa, J. M. "Estudio de la dimensión temporal en Proverbios, Job y Qohélet. El eterno volvar a comenzar en Qohelet." *EstBíb* 22 (1963) 33–67. **Witte, Markus.** "Betrachtungen zum Verhältnis von Zeit und Leid im Buch Ijob." In *Beiträge zum Verständnis der Bibel und ihrer Botschaft: Festschrift für Rudolf Mosis zum 70. Geburtstag.* Ed. Franz Sedlmeier. Würzburg: Echter, 2003. 399–414.

    tolerance. Herrmann, S. "Grenzen der Toleranz im Alten Testament: Die Bücher Deuteronomium, Jeremia und Hiob." In *Glaube und Toleranz, das theologische Erbe der Aufklärung.* Ed. Trutz Rendtorff. Gütersloh: Mohn, 1982. 180–90.

    tradition. Waldman, Nahum M. "Tradition and Experience in the Book of Job." In *Studies in Jewish Education and Judaica in Honor of Louis Newman.* Ed. Alexander M. Shapiro and Burton I. Cohen. New York: Ktav, 1984. 157–68.

    tragedy. Fisch, Harold. "Job: Tragedy Is Not Enough." In his *Poetry with a Purpose: Biblical Poetics and Interpretation.* Bloomington: Indiana University Press, 1988. 26–42. **Kurzweil, Baruch.** "Job and the Possibility of Biblical Tragedy." In *Arguments and Doctrines: A Reader of Jewish Thinking in the Aftermath of the Holocaust.* Ed. Arthur A. Cohen. New York: Harper & Row, 1970. 323–44. **Poltkin, Frederick.** "Judaism and Tragic Theology." *Judaism* 18 (1969) 492–97. **Raphael, D. D.** "Tragedy and Religion." In *Twentieth Century Interpretations of the Book of Job. A Collection of Critical Essays.* Ed. P. S. Sanders. Englewood Cliffs, NJ: Prentice–Hall. 1968. 46–55 [= his *The Paradox of Tragedy.* Bloomington: Indiana University Press, 1960. 37–61]. **Sewall, Richard B.** *The Vision of Tragedy: Tragic Themes in Literature from the Book of Job to O'Neill and Miller.* New York: Paragon House, 1990. **Urbrock, William J.** "Job as Drama: Tragedy or Comedy?" *CurTM* 8 (1981) 35–40.

    trial. Kline, M. G. "Trial by Ordeal." In *Through Christ's Word. A Festschrift for Dr Philip E. Hughes.* Phillipsburg, NJ: Presbyterian & Reformed Publishing Co., 1985. 81–93.

    vain, in. Klopfenstein, Martin. "*ḥinnam* im Hiobbuch." In *"Lasset uns Brücken bauen ..." Collected Communications to the XVth Congress of the International Organization for the Study of the Old Testament, Cambridge, 1995.* Ed. Klaus-Dietrich Schunck and Matthias Augustin. BEATAJ 42. Frankfurt a.M.: Peter Lang, 1998. 287–90.

    victim. Hamerton-Kelly, Robert. "The Mob and the Victim in the Psalms and Job." *Contagion* 8 (2001) 151–60.

    violence. Kessler, Edward. "Reasoning with Violent Scripture: With a Little Help from Job." *Journal of Scriptural Reasoning* 4/1 (2004). **Michel, Andreas.** "Das Gewalthandeln Gottes nach den Ijobreden." In *Das Buch Ijob: Gesamtdeutungen—Einzeltexte—zentrale Themen.* Ed. Theodor Seidl and Stephanie Ernst. Österreichische biblische Studien 31. Frankfurt: Peter Lang, 2007. 201–27. **Rowlett, Lori.** "My Papa Was Called Bubba, but His Real Name Was Leroy: Violence, Social Location and Job." In *Autobiographical Biblical Criticism: Between Text and Self.* Ed. Ingrid Rosa Kitzberger. Leiden: Deo, 2002.

    wealth. Ortiz de Urtaran, F. "Un rico amigo de Dios." *Lumen* 34 (1985) 289–313.

    wicked. García de la Fuente, O. "La prosperidad del malvado en el libro de Job y en los poemas babilónicas del 'Justo Paciente'." *EstEcl* 34 (1960) 603–16. **Schreiner, Susan E.** "Why Do the Wicked Live? Job and David in Calvin's Sermons on Job." In *The Voice from the Whirlwind: Interpreting the Book of Job.* Ed. Leo G. Perdue and Clark Gilpin. Nashville: Abingdon Press, 1992. 129–43. **Vermeylen, Jacques.** "Le méchant dans les discours des amis de Job." In *The Book of Job.* Ed. W. A. M. Beuken. BETL 114. Leuven: Leuven University Press, 1994. 101–27.

wisdom. Aiura, T. "Wisdom Motifs in the Joban Poem." *Kwansei Gakuin University Annual Studies* 15 (1966) 1–20. **Albertz, Rainer.** "The Sage and Pious Wisdom in the Book of Job: The Friends' Perspective." In *The Sage in Israel and the Ancient Near East.* Ed. John G. Gammie and Leo G. Perdue. Winona Lake, IN: Eisenbrauns, 1990. 243–61. **Asurmendi, Jesus.** "La sabiduria, entre experiencia y doctrina." *EstBíb* 57 (1999) 83–95. **Bridieu-Linières, Roger-Antoine de.** *Quis posuit in visceribus hominis sapientiam? Job.* Diss. Sorbonne, 1655. **Crenshaw, James L.** "In Search of Divine Presence: Some Remarks Preliminary to a Theology of Wisdom." *RevExp* 74 (1977) 353–69. ———. "Wisdom and Authority: Sapiential Rhetoric and Its Warrants." In *Congress Volume: Vienna, 1980.* Ed. John A. Emerton. VTSup 32. Leiden: E. J. Brill, 1981. 10–29. **Dailey, Thomas F.** "The Book of Job as Optimistic Wisdom." *Journal of Theta Alpha Kappa* 18/1 (1994) 3–16. ———. "Seeing He Repents: Contemplative Consciousness and the Wisdom of Job." *AmBenRev* 46 (1995) 87–101. ———. "The Wisdom of Job: Moral Maturity or Religious Reckoning." *USQR* 51 (1997) 45–55. **Gruber, Mayer I.** "Human and Divine Wisdom in the Book of Job." In *Boundaries of the Ancient Near Eastern World: A Tribute to Cyrus H. Gordon.* Ed. Meir Lubetski, Claire Gottlieb, and Sharon Keller. JSOTSup 273. Sheffield: Sheffield Academic Press, 1998. 88–102. **Guillaume, Philippe.** "Job le nudiste ou la genèse de la sagesse." *BN* 88 (1997) 19–26. ———. "The Demise of Lady Wisdom and of 'homo sapiens'." An Unwise Reading of Genesis 2 and 3 in Light of Job and Proverbs." *ThRev* 25,2 (2004) 20–38. **Habel, Norman C.** "Of Things beyond Me: Wisdom in the Book of Job." *CurTM* 10 (1983) 142–54. **Hill, Robert C.** "Job in Search of Wisdom." *ScrB* 23 (1993) 34–38. **Lévêque, Jean.** "Sagesse et paradoxe dans le livre de Job." In *La sagesse biblique de l'ancien au Nouveau Testament.* Ed. Jacques Trublet. Lectio divina 160. Paris: Cerf, 1995. 99–128.

Moberly, R. W. L. "Solomon and Job: Divine Wisdom in Human Life." In *Where Shall Wisdom Be Found? Wisdom in the Bible, the Church and the Contemporary World.* Ed. Stephen C. Barton. Edinburgh: T. & T. Clark, 1999. 3–17. **Perani, M.** "Crisi della Sapienza e ricerca di Dio nel libro di Giobbe." *RivB* 28 (1980) 157–84. **Perdue, Leo G.** "Wisdom in the Book of Job." In *In Search of Wisdom: Essays in Memory of John G. Gammie.* Ed. Leo G. Perdue, Bernard Brandon Scott, and William Johnston Wiseman. Louisville: Westminster/John Knox Press, 1993. 73–98. **Sanders, Jack T.** "Wisdom, Theodicy, Death, and the Evolution of Intellectual Traditions." *JSJ* 36 (2005) 263–77. **Smith, Gary V.** "Is There a Place for Job's Wisdom in Old Testament Theology?" *TrinJ* 13 (1992) 3–20. **Terrien, Samuel.** "Job as a Sage." In *The Sage in Israel and the Ancient Near East.* Ed. John G. Gammie and Leo G. Perdue. Winona Lake, IN: Eisenbrauns, 1990. 231–42. **Thomas, D.** "Types of Wisdom in the Book of Job." *IndJT* 20 (1971) 157–65. **Whybray, R. Norman.** "Wisdom, Suffering and the Freedom of God in the Book of Job." In *In Search of True Wisdom: Essays in Old Testament Interpretation in Honour of Ronald E. Clements.* Ed. Edward Ball. JSOTSup 300. Sheffield: Sheffield Academic Press, 1999. 231–45. **Zerafa, Peter Paul.** *The Wisdom of God in the Book of Job.* Rome: Herder, 1978. **Ziener, G.** "Die altorientalische Weisheit als Lebenskunde: Israels neues Verständnis und Kritik der Weisheit." In *Wort und Botschaft: Eine theologische und kritische Einführung in die Probleme des Alten Testaments.* Ed. J. Schreiner. Würzburg: Echter Verlag, 1967. 258–71.

witness. Mies, Françoise. "L'herméneutique du témoignage en philosophie: littérature, mythe et Bible." *RSPT* 81 (1997) 3–20. **Vischer, Wilhelm.** "Hiob, ein Zeuge Jesu Christi." *ZZ* 11 (1963) 386–414.

women. Chittister, Joan. *Job's Daughters: Women and Power.* New York: Paulist Press, 1990. **Klein, Lillian R.** "Job and the Womb: Text about Men, Subtext about Women." In *A Feminist Companion to Wisdom Literature.* Ed. Athalya Brenner. The Feminist Companion to the Bible 9. Sheffield: Sheffield Academic Press, 1995. 186–200 [= her *From Deborah to Esther: Sexual Politics in the Hebrew Bible.* Philadelphia: Fortress Press, 2003].

work. Berg, Werner. "Arbeit und Soziales im Buch Ijob." In *Glaube in Politik und Zeitgeschichte.* Paderborn: Ferdinand Schoningh, 1995. 151–68. **David, M.** "Travaux et service dans l'Epopée de Gilgamesh et le livre de Job." *RevPhil* 147 (1957) 341–49. **Negri, Antonio.** *Il lavoro di Giobbe: il famoso testo biblico come parabola del lavoro umano.* Milan: Sugarco, 1990. **world. Bauer, J. B.** *Das Weltbild im Buche Job.* Diss. Vienna, 1951. **Getcha, Job.** "La transfiguration du monde." *Irénikon* 80/1 (2007) 23–35. **writing. Williams, James G.** "On Job and Writing: Derrida, Girard, and the Remedy–Poison." *SJOT* 7 (1993) 32–50. **Williamson, A.** *Physiques of Inscription* [Job as context for writing as a trace of the body]. Diss. Sussex, 1997.

8. JOB AND ITS INFLUENCE

a. General

Allen, Margaret J. *The Book of Job in Middle English Literature (1100–1500).* Diss. King's College, London, 1970. **Alonso de las Heras, César.** *El libro de Job: el hombre frente a Dios.* Biblioteca de estudios paraguayos 57. Asunción, Paraguay: Universidad Católica Nuestra Señora de la Asunción, 1998. **ApRoberts, Ruth.** *The Biblical Web.* Ann Arbor: University of Michigan Press, 1994.

Barine, Arvède. "Le nouveau Job." *La revue politique et littéraire* 8/42 (April 19, 1879) 996–98. **Bauschinger, Sigrid.** "Hiob und Jeremias: Biblische Themen in der deutschen Literatur des 20. Jahrhunderts." In *Akten des VI. Internationalen Germanisten-Kongresses, Basel, 1980.* Ed. Heinz Rupp and Hans-Gert Roloff. Berne: P. Lang, 1980–81. 3:466–72. **Beheim-Schwarzbach, Martin.** "Hiob." In his *Die Geschichten der Bibel.* Hamburg: Claassen, 1952. 18–22. **Berger, Alan L.** *Children of Job: American Second-Generation Witnesses to the Holocaust.* Albany: SUNY Press, 1997. **Berry, D. L.** "Scripture and Imaginative Literature Focus on Job." *Journal of General Education* 19 (1967) 49–79. **Besserman, Lawrence L.** "Job." In *A Dictionary of Biblical Tradition in English Literature.* Ed. David Lyle Jeffrey. Grand Rapids: Eerdmans, 1992. 403–4. ———. *The Legend of Job in the Middle Ages.* Cambridge, MA: Harvard University Press, 1979. **Bochet, Marc.** *Job après Job: destinée littéraire d'une figure biblique.* Le livre et le rouleau 9. Brussels: Lessius, 2000. ———. "Job, figure inspiratrice du théâtre du absurde." *Graphè* 17 (1998) 165–71. ———. "Job in Literature." In *Job and the Silence of God.* Ed. Christian Duquoc and Casiano Floristán. Edinburgh: T. & T. Clark, 1983 [= *Conc* 169 (1983)] 73–77 [= "Jó na literatura." *Conc* 189 (1983) 96–102]. ———. *Présence de Job dans le théâtre d'après-guerre II en France.* Berne: Peter Lang, 1988. **Bocian, Martin.** *Lexikon der biblischen Personen, mit ihrem Fortleben in Judentum, Christentum, Islam, Dichtung, Musik und Kunst.* Stuttgart: A. Kröner, 1989. 159–69. **Böswald, Rupert.** "Hiob in moderner Dichtung." In *Durchkreuztes Leben: Besinnung auf Hiob.* Ed. Erich Zenger and Rupert Böswald. Freiburg: Herder, 1976. 89–129. **Boitani, Piero.** *The Bible and Its Rewritings.* Trans. Anita Weston. Oxford: Oxford University Press, 1999. **Butting, Klara (ed.).** *Hiob, mit Beiträgen aus Judentum, Christentum, Islam, Literatur, Kunst.* Wittingen: Erev-Rav, 2003.

Campbell, Karen Mills. *Poetry as Epitaph: A Study of Representation and Poetic Language* [Job, Herbert, Wordsworth, Dickinson]. Diss. State University of New York at Buffalo, 1982. ———. "Poetry as Epitaph." *Journal of Popular Culture* 14 (1981) 657–68. **Castagna, Edoardo.** *L'uomo di Uz: Giobbe e la letteratura del Novecento.* Milan: Medusa, 2007.

Daemmrich, Horst S., and Ingrid Daemmrich. "Hiob." In *Themen und Motive in der Literatur: Ein Handbuch.* Munich: Francke, 1987. 175. **Daiches, David.** "The Book of Job: God under Attack." In his *God and the Poets.* Oxford: Clarendon Press, 1984. 1–25. **Dov Lerner, Berel.** "Faith, Fiction and the Jewish Scriptures." *Judaism* 39 (1990) 215–20.

Eltz-Hoffmann, Liselotte von. "Hiob in der Dichtung." *Wege zum Menschen: Monatsschrift für Seelsorge, Psychotherapie und Erziehung* 19 (1967) 184–94.

Fava Guzzetta, Lia. "La figura di Giobbe in alcune pagine di letteratura moderna." In *I volti di Giobbe. Percorsi interdisciplinari.* Ed. Gilberto Marconi and Cristina

Termini. Bologna: EDB, 2002. 229–38. **Fisch, Harold.** "Job as Modern Archetype." *Hebrew University Studies in Literature and the Arts* 11/1 (1983) 102–14. **Flügel, Heinz.** "Hiob in der Gegenwartsliteratur." In *"Sie werden lachen, die Bibel": Erfahrungen mit dem Buch der Bücher.* Ed. Hans Jürgen Schultz. Munich: Deutscher Taschenbuch-Verlag, 1985. 204–17. **Francisco, Nancy A.** "Job in World Literature." *RevExp* 68 (1971) 521–33. **Frenzel, Elisabeth.** "Hiob." In *Stoffe der Weltliteratur: Ein Lexikon dichtungsgeschichtlicher Längsschnitte.* Stuttgart: Alfred Kröner, 1962. 276–79 [6th ed. 1983. 323–26]. **Friedman, Maurice S.** *Problematic Rebel: An Image of Modern Man.* New York: Random House, 1963; rev. ed. *Problematic Rebel: Melville, Dostoievsky, Kafka, Camus.* Chicago: University of Chicago Press, 1970.

Geyer, C.-F. "Das Hiobbuch im christlichen und nachchristlichen Kontext. Anmerkungen zur Rezeptionsgeschichte." *Kairos* 28 (1986) 174–95. **Glatzer, Nahum H.** *The Dimensions of Job: A Study and Selected Readings.* New York: Schocken Books, 1969. **Glutsch, Karl Heinz.** *Die Gestalt Hiobs in der deutschen Literatur des Mittelalters.* Diss. Karlsruhe, 1972. **Goldschmidt, Hermann Levin.** "Hiob einst und immer." In *Israel hat dennoch Gott zum Trost: Festschrift für Schalom Ben-Chorin.* Ed. Gotthold Müller. Trier: Paulinus-Verlag, 1978. 20–30. **Goodheart, Eugene.** "Job and Romanticism." *Reconstructionist* 24 (1958) 7–12. ———. "Job and the Modern World." *Judaism* 10 (1961) 21–28 [= *Twentieth Century Interpretations of the Book of Job: A Collection of Critical Essays.* Ed. P. S. Sanders. Englewood Cliffs, NJ: Prentice–Hall, 1968. 98–106]. **Grimm, Gunter E., and Hans-Peter Bayerdörfer (eds.).** *Im Zeichen Hiobs: Jüdische Schriftsteller und deutsche Literatur im 20. Jahrhundert.* Königstein: Athenäum, 1985. **Günther, Johann Christian.** *Sämtliche Werke in sechs Bänden.* Darmstadt: Wissenschaftliche Buchgesellschaft, 1964.

Hartman, Michelle. *Jesus, Joseph and Job. Reading Rescriptings of Religious Figures in Lebanese Women's Fiction.* Wiesbaden: Reichert Verlag, 2002. **Hausen, Adelheid.** *Hiob in der französischen Literatur: Zur Rezeption eines alttestamentlichen Buches.* Europäische Hochschulschriften 13/17. Frankfurt: Peter Lang, 1972. **Hügelsberger, Josef.** *Der Dulder Hiob in der deutschen Literatur: Ein Beitrag zur Geschichte der biblischen Stoffe in Deutschland.* Diss. Graz, 1930.

Knobelsdorff, Kristina. *Re-readings of the Book of Job in American Life and Letters: Debate and Dissent within Bounds (Gatta, Higonnet, Tilton).* Diss. University of Connecticut, 2005. **Krieg, Matthias.** "Das wandernde Hiobmotiv: Ein Kapitel Literaturgeschichte." In *Hiob. Ökumenischer Arbeitskreis für Bibelarbeit.* Ed. Regina Berger-Lutz. Bibelarbeit in der Gemeinde 7. Basel: F. Reinhardt, 1989. 63–86.

Labin, Linda L. *The Whale and the Ash-Heap: Transfigurations of Jonah and Job in Modern American Fiction—Frost, MacLeish, and Vonnegut.* Diss. Kent State University, 1980. **Langenhorst, Georg.** *Hiob unser Zeitgenosse: Die literarische Hiob-Rezeption im 20. Jahrhundert als theologische Herausforderung.* Theologie und Literatur 1. Mainz: Matthias–Grünewald–Verlag, 1994; 2nd ed. 1995. ———. "Ijob—Vorbild in Demut und Rebellion." In *Die Bibel in der deutschsprachigen Literatur des 20. Jahrhunderts.* II. *Personen und Figuren.* Ed. Heinrich Schmidinger. Mainz: Matthias-Grünewald-Verlag, 1999. 259–80. ———. "'Sein haderndes Wort' (Paul Celan)—Hiob in der Dichtung unserer Zeit." In *Das Buch Ijob: Gesamtdeutungen—Einzeltexte—zentrale Themen.* Ed. Theodor Seidl and Stephanie Ernst. Österreichische biblische Studien 31. Frankfurt: Peter Lang, 2007. 279–306. ———. "Zuviel 'Warum?' gefragt? Hiob in der Literatur des 20. Jahrhunderts." In *Warum? Hiob interdisziplinär diskutiert.* Mainzer Universitätsgespräche Wintersemester 1997/98. Vorträge von Hansjakob Becker, Jürgen Ebach, Herbert Jochum, Georg Langenhorst, Józef Niewiadomski, Willi Oelmüller, and Wilhelm Pesch. Mainz: Studium Generale der Universität Mainz, 1998. 121–45. **Lemann, Nicholas.** "Political Applications of the Book of Job." *New York Times* 142 (November 5, 1992) 10. **Levenson, Jon D.** *The Book of Job in Its Time and in the Twentieth Century.* Cambridge, MA: Harvard University Press, 1972. **Link, Franz.** "The Bible in Twentieth-Century Jewish Literature (German, English, and French)." *Literatur in Wissenschaft und Unterricht* 24 (1991) 321–38. **Lüth, E.** "Das

Buch Hiob und die Deutschen." In *Auf gespaltenem Pfad. Festschrift Margarete Susman.* Ed. M. Schlössner. Darmstadt: Erato-Presse, 1964. 63–67. **MacLean, Hector.** "The Job Drama in Modern Germany." *Journal of the Australasian Universities Modern Language Association* 2 (1954) 13–20. **Mastag, Horst Dieter.** *The Transformations of Job in Modern German Literature.* Diss. University of British Columbia, 1990. **Matthews, Marjorie Swank.** *Issues and Answers in the Book of Job and Joban Issues and Answers in Three Twentieth Century Writers: Carl Jung, Robert Frost, and Archibald MacLeish.* Diss. Florida State University, 1976. **May, J. E.** "Early Eighteenth-Century Paraphrases of the Book of Job." In *Man, God, and Nature in the Enlightenment.* Ed. Donald C. Mell, Jr, Theodore E. D. Braun, and Lucia M. Palmer. East Lansing, MI: Colleagues Press; Woodbridge: Boydell & Brewer, 1988. 151–61. **Mazor, Lea (ed.).** ‫איוב במקרא, בהגות, באמונות‬. *Job in the Bible, Philosophy, and Art.* Jerusalem: Magnes Press, 1995. **Mura, G.** "Giobbe e il pensiero contemporaneo; l'esilio della parola." *Nuova umanità* 1,6 (1979) 23–44; 2,7 (1980) 36–61; 2,10–11 (1980) 29–62.

Neher, André. "Hiob als Thema der modernen jüdischen und der Welt-Literatur." *Ariel: A Quarterly Review of the Arts and Sciences in Israel* 42 (1976) 65–77. **Nicole, Emile.** "Trois lecteurs de Job contemporains." *Théologie évangélique* 1,1 (2002) 3–14.

Oberhänsli-Widmer, Gabrielle. *Hiob in jüdischer Antike und Moderne: Die Wirkungs-geschichte Hiobs in der jüdischen Literatur.* Neukirchen–Vluyn: Neukirchener Verlag, 2003. **Owen, John.** *The Five Great Skeptical Dramas of History* [Aeschylus, *Prometheus vinctus,* Job, *Faust, Hamlet,* Calderón, *El magico prodigioso*]. London: S. Sonnenschein, 1896.

Painter, Mark Andrew. *The Word and Tragedy: The Revelation of Divine Mystery in the Portrayal of Man as Language* [Genesis, Job, Oedipus, Lear]. Diss. North Texas, 1988. **Pifano, P.** "Nel grido di Giobbe il grido dell'uomo contemporaneo." *Asprenas* 31 (1984) 497–524. **Pinell, J.** "El Canto de los 'Threni' en las Misas cuaresmales de la antigua liturgia hispanica." In *Eulogia miscellanea liturgica in onore di P. Burkhard Neunheuser O.S.B.* Ed. M. Arranz. Studia anselmiana 68; Analecta liturgica 1. Rome: Editrice ansel-miana, 1979. 317–66.

Rabory, Joseph. *Le livre de la souffrance. Le livre de Job, dans l'histoire, la théolo-gie, la liturgie.* Paris: Téqui, 1917. **Ravasi, Gianfranco.** "Giobbe, nostro contempo-raneo." In his *Giobbe, traduzione e commento.* Rome: Borla, 1984. 185–255. **Roth, J.** ‫היחס אל ספר איוב בתחום התרבות היהודית והנוצרית‬ [Attitudes towards the Book of Job as Reflected by Jewish and Christian Thinkers. A Survey]." *BMik* 50 (1972) 306–9, 381–82.

Sanders, Paul S. (ed.). *Twentieth Century Interpretations of the Book of Job: A Collection of Critical Essays.* Englewood Cliffs, NJ: Prentice–Hall, 1968. **Savory, Jerold.** *Caged Light* [Job in literature]. Valley Forge, PA: Judson Press, 1973. **Schrader, Ulrike.** *Die Gestalt Hiobs in der deutschen Literatur seit der frühen Aufklärung.* Europäische Hochschulschriften: Reihe 1, Deutsche Sprache und Literatur 1294. Frankfurt a.M.: Peter Lang, 1992. **Schrempf, Christoph.** *Menschenlos: Hiob, Ödipus, Jesus, homo sum …* Stuttgart: Frommann, 1948. **Schubert, Beatrix.** "Vom Umgang mit dem menschlichen Leiden: Ein Versuch über Ijob in der modernen Literatur." *ErbAuf* 60 (1984) 356–75. **Sewall, Richard B.** *The Vision of Tragedy: Tragic Themes in Literature from the Book of Job to O'Neill and Miller.* New York: Paragon House, 1990. **Siger, Leonard.** *The Image of Job in the Renaissance.* Diss. John Hopkins University, 1960. **Spitzer, Gary Michael.** *The Book of Job in Contemporary Literature.* Diss. Syracuse, 1970. **Steinwendtner, Brita.** *Hiobs Klage heute: Die biblische Gestalt in der Literatur des 20. Jahrhunderts.* Innsbruck: Tyrolia-Verlag, 1990. 37–62. **Stern, Guy.** "Job as Alter Ego: The Bible, Ancient Jewish Discourse, and Exile Literature." *The German Quarterly* 63 (1990) 199–210. **Stock, E.** "'Masque of Reason' and 'J. B.': Two Treatments of the Book of Job." *Modern Drama* 3 (1961) 378–86. **Stora-Sandor, Judith.** *L'humour juif dans la littérature: de Job à Woody Allen.* Paris: Presses Universitaires de France, 1984. **Strolz, Walter.** "Die Hiob-Interpretation bei Kant, Kierkegaard und Bloch." *Kairos* 23 (1981) 75–87.

Theobald, Gerd. *Hiobs Prozess und Gottes Gericht. Die poetische Theodizee des Welttheaters.* Diss. Heidelberg, 1991. **Treichel, Dietmar M.** *In extremis: Modelle der Todeserfahrung im englischen Roman des 19. Jahrhunderts (Scott, Emily Bronte, Dickens) unter Berücksichtigung des Buches Hiob.* Diss. Heidelberg, 1987.

Uellenberg, Gisela. "Hiob-Buch." In *Kindlers Literatur-Lexikon.* Ed. Wolfgang von Einsiedel. Munich: Kindler, 1974. 11:4453–55. **Usmiana, Renate.** "A New Look at the Drama of Job." *Modern Drama* 13 (1970) 191–200.

Wielandt, Ulf. *Hiob in der alt- und mittelhochdeutschen Literatur.* Diss. Freiburg i.Br. Bamberg: R. Rodensbusch, 1970.

b. Early Jewish

i. General

Baring-Gould, Sabine. *Legends of Old Testament: Characters from the Talmud and Other Sources.* London: Macmillan, 1871. 52–59. **Baskin, Judith R.** *Pharaoh's Counsellors: Job, Jethro and Balaam in Rabbinic and Patristic Tradition.* Brown Judaic Studies 47. Chico, CA: Scholars Press, 1983. ———. "Rabbinic Interpretations of Job." In *The Voice from the Whirlwind: Interpreting the Book of Job.* Ed. Leo G. Perdue and Clark Gilpin. Nashville: Abingdon Press, 1992. 101–10. **Caquot, André.** "Léviathan et Béhémoth dans la troisième «Parabole» d'*Hénoch.*" *Sem* 25 (1975) 111–22. **Carnevale, Laura.** "Note per la ricostruzione di tradizioni giobbiche tra Oriente e Occidente." *VetChr* 44 (2007) 225–38. **Carstensen, R. N.** "The Persistence of the 'Elihu' Tradition in the Later Jewish Writings." *LTQ* 2 (1967) 37–46. **Chesnutt, Randall D.** "Revelatory Experiences Attributed to Biblical Women in Early Jewish Literature." In *Women like This: New Perspectives on Jewish Women in the Greco-Roman World.* Ed. Amy-Jill Levine. Atlanta: Scholars Press, 1991. 107–25. **D'Alario, Vittoria.** "La réflexion sur le sens de la vie en Sg 1–6: une réponse aux questions de Job et de Qohélet." In *Treasures of Wisdom: Studies in Ben Sira and the Book of Wisdom. Festschrift M. Gilbert.* Ed. Nuria Calduch-Benages and Jacques Vermeylen. BETL 143. Leuven: Leuven University Press; Louvain: Peeters, 1999. 313–29. **Dimant, Devorah.** "Bible through a Prism: The Wife of Job and the Wife of Tobit." *Shnaton* 17 (2007) 201–11. **Ehrlich, Ernst Ludwig.** "Hiob in der jüdischen Tradition." In *Und dennoch ist von Gott zu reden: Festschrift für Herbert Vorgrimler.* Ed. Matthias Lutz-Bachmann. Freiburg i.Br.: Herder, 1994. 38–55. **Fine, H. A.** "The Tradition of a Patient Job." *JBL* 74 (1955) 28–32. **Glatzer, Nahum H.** "The Book of Job and Its Interpreters" [mainly medieval Jewish]. In *Biblical Motifs. Origins and Transformations.* Ed. A. Altmann. Philip W. Lown Institute of Advanced Judaic Studies. Studies and Texts 3. Cambridge, MA: Harvard University Press, 1966. 197–220. ———. "Jüdische Ijob-Deutungen in den ersten christlichen Jahrhunderten." *FreibRu* 26 (1974) 31–34. **Gorringe, Timothy J.** "Job and the Pharisees." *Int* 40 (1986) 17–28. **Hanson, A. T.** "Job in Early Christianity and Rabbinic Judaism." *CQ* 2 (1969) 147–51. **Jacobs, Irving.** *The Book of Job in Rabbinic Thought.* Diss. University College, London, 1971.

Kalman, Jason. "Job Denied the Resurrection of Jesus? A Rabbinic Critique of the Church Fathers' Use of Exegetical Traditions Found in the Septuagint and the Testament of Job." In *The Changing Face of Judaism, Christianity and Other Greco-Roman Religions in Antiquity. Presented to James H. Charlesworth on the Occasion of His 65th Birthday.* Ed. Ian H. Henderson and Gerbern S. Oegema. Studien zu den jüdischen Schriften aus hellenistisch-römischer Zeit 2. Gütersloh: Gütersloher Verlagshaus, 2006. 371–97. **Kraus Reggiani, Clara.** "La figura di Giobbe in tre documenti del giudaismo ellenistico." *VetChr* 36 (2000) 165–92. **Leibowitz, Joseph H.** *The Image of Job as Reflected in Rabbinic Writings.* Diss. Berkeley, 1987. **Lewin, Moritz.** *Targum und Midrasch zum Buche Hiob in ihrem gegenseitigen Verhältnis.* Berne: J. Wirth, 1895. **Mack, Hananel.** אלא משל היה: איוב בספרות הבית השני ובעיני חז״ל. *Job and the Book of Job in Rabbinic Literature.* Ramat-Gan: Bar-Ilan University Press, 2004. **Ravenna, A.** "Il caso Giobbe e la tradizione talmudica." *RivB* (1959) 61–63. **Schramm, Jonas Conrad.** *Dissertatio præ-liminaris qua Jobum Talmudicum e Bava Batra cap. i examinat veriorique addita Jobi descriptione.* Helmstadt, 1716. **Schreiner, Stefan.** "Der gottesfürchtige Rebell oder Wie die Rabbinen die Frömmigkeit Ijobs deuteten." *ZTK* 89 (1992) 159–71. **Sel, M.** "Job, in Rabbinical Literature." *JewEnc* 7:195. **Szpek, Heidi M.** "On the Influence of Job on Jewish Hellenistic Literature." In *Seeking out the Wisdom of the Ancients: Essays Offered to Honor Michael V. Fox on the Occasion of His Sixty-Fifth Birthday.* Ed. Ronald L. Troxel, Kelvin G. Friebel, and Dennis R. Magary. Winona Lake, IN: Eisenbrauns, 2005. 357–70. **VanderKam, James C.** "Intertestamental Pronouncement Stories." *Semeia* 20 (1981) 65–72. **Vicchio, Stephen J.** "Job in the Talmud and Midrash." In his *Job in the Ancient World.* Eugene, OR: Wipf & Stock, 2006. 158–76. **Whitney, Kenneth William, Jr.** *Two Strange Beasts: A Study of Traditions concerning Leviathan and Behemoth in Second Temple and Early Rabbinic Judaism.* Diss. Harvard, 1992. Cf. *HTR* 85 (1992) 503–4. **Wiernikowski, Isaac.** *Das Buch Hiob nach der Auffassung der rabbinischen Literatur in den ersten fünf nachchristlichen Jahrhunderten.* Breslau: H. Fleishmann, 1902. ———. *Das Buch Hiob nach der rabbinischen Agada.* Frankfurt, 1893.

ii. Texts

Aristeas the Exegete. Life of Job (a lost work, attested by Eusebius in his *Praeparatio evangelica* 9.25). See **Doran, R.** "Aristeas the Exegete." In *The Old Testament Pseudepigrapha.* Ed. James H. Charlesworth. London: Darton, Longman & Todd, 1985. 2:855–59.

Enoch. Caquot, André. "Leviathan et Béhémoth dans la troisième «Parabole» d'*Hénoch*." *Sem* 25 (1975) 111–22.

Haggadah. Kaufmann, Hermann Ezechiel. *Die Anwendung des Buches Hiob in der rabbinischen Agadah.* Frankfurt a.M.: Slobotzky, 1893. **Wiernikowski, Isaac.** *Das Buch Hiob nach der rabbinischen Agada.* Frankfurt, 1893.

Testament of Abraham. See **Allison, Dale C., Jr.** "Job in the Testament of Abraham." *JSP* 12 (2001) 131–47.

Testament of Job. See **Begg, Christopher T.** "Comparing Characters: The Book of Job and the Testament of Job." In *The Book of Job.* Ed. W. A. M. Beuken. BETL 114. Leuven: Leuven University Press, 1994. 435–45. **Brock, S. P., and J.-C. Picard.** *Testamentum Iobi. Apocalypsis Baruchi graece.* Pseudepigrapha Veteris Testamenti Graece 2. Leiden: E. J. Brill, 1967. **Carnevale, Laura.** "Il caso di Giobbe tra persistenze bibliche e trasformazioni. Il ruolo del 'Testamentum Iobi'." *ASEs* 23,1 (2006) 225–56. **Carstensen, R. N.** "The Persistence of the 'Elihu' Tradition in the Later Jewish Writings." *LTQ* 2 (1967) 37–46 [original, Diss. Vanderbilt, 1960]. **Collins, John J.** "Structure and Meaning in the Testament of Job." In *Society of Biblical Literature: 1974 Seminar Papers.* Ed. G. MacRae. Cambridge, MA: Society of Biblical Literature, 1974. 1:35–52. ———. "Testaments" [incl. *Testament of Job*]. In *Jewish Writings of the Second Temple Period: Apocrypha, Pseudepigrapha, Qumran Sectarian Writings, Philo, Josephus.* Ed. Michael E. Stone. Assen: Van Gorcum, 1984. 325–55. **Delcor, M.** "Le Testament de Job, la prière de Nabonide et les traditions targoumiques." In *Bibel und Qumran. Beiträge zur Erforschung der Beziehungen zwischen Bibel und Qumranwissenschaft, Hans Bardtke zum 22.9.1966.* Ed. S. Wagner. Berlin: Evangelische Haupt-Bibelgesellschaft, 1968. 57–74. **Garrett, Susan R.** "The 'Weaker Sex' in the Testament of Job." *JBL* 112 (1993) 55–70. **Gray, Patrick.** "Points and Lines: Thematic Parallelism in the Letter of James and the Testament of Job." *NTS* 50 (2004) 406–24. **Haas, Cees.** "Job's Perseverance in the Testament of Job." In *Studies on the Testament of Job.* Ed. Michael A. Knibb and Pieter W. van der Horst. SNTSMS 66. Cambridge: Cambridge University Press, 1989. 117–54. **Horst, Pieter W. van der.** "Images of Women in the Testament of Job." In *Studies on the Testament of Job.* Ed. Michael A. Knibb and Pieter W. van der Horst. SNTSMS 66. Cambridge: Cambridge University Press, 1989. 101–14. ———. "The Role of Women in the Testament of Job." *NedTTs* 40 (1986) 273–89. **Jacobs, I.** "Literary Motifs in the Testament of Job." *JJS* 21 (1970) 1–10. **James, Montague Rhodes.**

Apocrypha anecdota. Second Series. Cambridge: Cambridge University Press, 1897. 104–37. **Kee, H. C.** "Satan, Magic, and Salvation in the Testament of Job." In *Society of Biblical Literature: 1974 Seminar Papers.* Ed. G. MacRae. Cambridge, MA: Society of Biblical Literature, 1974. 1:53–76. **Kirkegaard, Bradford A.** "Satan in the Testament of Job: A Literary Analysis." In *Of Scribes and Sages: Early Jewish Interpretation and Transmission of Scripture.* Ed. Craig A. Evans. London: T. & T. Clark International, 2004. 4–19. **Knibb, Michael A., and Pieter W. van der Horst (eds.).** *Studies on the Testament of Job.* SNTSMS 66. Cambridge: Cambridge University Press, 1989. **Kohler, K.** "The Testament of Job: An Essene Midrash on the Book of Job." In *Semitic Studies in Memory of Rev. Dr Alexander Kohut.* Ed. George Alexander Kohut. Berlin: S. Calvary, 1897. 264–338. **Kraft, Robert A., with Harold Attridge, Russell Spittler, and Janet Timbie.** *The Testament of Job according to the SV Text* [Greek text and English translation]. Texts and Translations 5. Pseudepigrapha Series. Missoula, MT: Scholars Press, 1974. **Kugler, Robert A., and Richard L. Rohrbaugh.** "On Women and Honor in the Testament of Job." *JSP* 14 (2004) 43–62. **Machinist, Peter.** "Job's Daughters and Their Inheritance in the Testament of Job and Its Biblical Congeners." In *The Echoes of Many Texts: Reflections on Jewish and Christian Traditions. Essays in Honor of Lou H. Silberman.* Ed. William G. Dever and J. Edward Wright. Brown Judaic Studies 313. Atlanta: Scholars Press, 1997. 67–80. **Mai, Angelo.** "Iobi testamentum, scriptum apocryphum, sed valde antiquum." In his *Scriptorum veterum nova collectio e vaticanis codicibus.* Rome, 1826–38. **Nicholls, P. H.** *The Structure and Purpose of the Testament of Job.* Diss. Hebrew University, 1982. **Philonenko, Marc.** "Le Testament de Job et les Thérapeutes." *Sem* 8 (1958) 51–53. ———. *Le Testament de Job: Introduction, traduction et notes.* Semitica 18. Paris: Librairie d'Amérique et d'Orient Adrien-Maisonneuve, 1968. **Schaller, Berndt.** *Das Testament Hiobs.* JüdSHRZ 3/3. Gütersloh: Gütersloher Verlagshaus Gerd Mohn, 1979. 305–87. ———. "Das Testament Hiobs und die Septuaginta-Übersetzung des Buches Hiob." *Bib* 61 (1980) 377–406. ———. "Zur Komposition und Konzeption des Testaments Hiobs." In *Studies on the Testament of Job.* Ed. Michael A. Knibb and Pieter W. van der Horst. SNTSMS 66. Cambridge: Cambridge University Press, 1989. 46–92. **Schenderling, J. G.** *Het Testament van Job: Een document van joodse vroomheid uit het begin van onze jaartelling.* Kampen: J. H. Kok, 1990. **Spitta, Friedrich.** *Die Versuchung Jesu: Lücken im Markusevangelium; Das Testament Hiobs und das Neue Testament.* Göttingen: Vandenhoeck & Ruprecht, 1907. **Spittler, Russell P.** "Testament of Job." In *The Old Testament Pseudepigrapha.* Ed. James H. Charlesworth. London: Darton, Longman & Todd, 1983. 1:829–68. ———. *The Testament of Job.* Diss. Harvard, 1971. **Sutter Rehmann, Luzia.** "Das Testament des Hiob." *BK* 59 (2004) 78–82. **Thornhill, R.** "The Testament of Job." In *The Apocryphal Old Testament.* Oxford: Clarendon Press, 1984. **Wills, Lawrence M. (ed. and trans.).** "Testament of Job." In his *Ancient Jewish Novels: An Anthology.* Oxford: Oxford University Press, 2002.

Tobit. Dimant, Devorah. "Bible through a Prism: The Wife of Job and the Wife of Tobit." *Shnaton* 17 (2007) 201–11. **Portier-Young, Anathea.** "'Eyes to the Blind': A Dialogue between Tobit and Job." In *Intertextual Studies in Ben Sira and Tobit: Essays in Honor of Alexander A. Di Lella, O.F.M.* Ed. Jeremy Corley and Vincent Skemp. CBQMS 38. Washington, DC: Catholic Biblical Association of America, 2004. 14–27.

Wisdom. D'Alario, Vittoria. "La réflexion sur le sens de la vie en Sg 1–6: une réponse aux questions de Job et de Qohélet." In *Treasures of Wisdom: Studies in Ben Sira and the Book of Wisdom. Festschrift M. Gilbert.* Ed. Nuria Calduch-Benages and Jacques Vermeylen. BETL 143. Leuven: Leuven University Press; Louvain: Peeters, 1999. 313–29.

c. Contemporary Jewish

Bonola, Gianfranco. "Giobbe ad Auschwitz: la Sho'ah e la teodicea ebraica." In *La Sho'ah. Tra interpretazione e memoria.* Ed. Paolo Amodio. Naples: Vivarium, 1999. 551–86. **Dedmon, R.** "Job as Holocaust Survivor." *StLuke* 26 (1982–83) 165–85. **Goldschmidt,**

Hermann Levin. "Hiob in neuzeitlichen Judentum." In *Weltliche Vergegenwärtigungen Gottes: Zum Problem der Entmythologisierung.* Ed. Karl Kerényi et al. Weltgespräch 2. Freiburg: Herder, 1967. 41–55. **Haar, Murray J.** "Job after Auschwitz." *Int* 53 (1999) 265–75. **Jochum, Herbert.** "Hiob und die Shoah." In *Warum? Hiob interdisziplinär diskutiert.* Mainzer Universitätsgespräche Wintersemester 1997/98. Vorträge von Hansjakob Becker, Jürgen Ebach, Herbert Jochum, Georg Langenhorst, Józef Niewiadomski, Willi Oelmüller, and Wilhelm Pesch. Mainz: Studium Generale der Universität Mainz, 1998. 101–20. **Kepnes, Steven.** "Job and Post-Holocaust Theodicy." In *Strange Fire: Reading the Bible after the Holocaust.* Ed. Tod Linafelt. The Biblical Seminar 71. Sheffield: Sheffield Academic Press, 2000. 252–66. **Neher, André.** "Job: The Biblical Man." *Judaism* 13 (1964) 37–47 [= "L'homme biblique: Job." In his *L'existence juive: solitude et affrontements.* Paris: Editions du Seuil, 1962. 60–72]. **Oberhänsli-Widmer, Gabrielle.** "Ijob: Streiflichter einer jüdischen Lektüre." *RHS* 50 (2007) 291–99. **Sheldon, Mark.** "Job, Human Suffering and Knowledge: Some Contemporary Jewish Perspectives." *Enc* 41 (1980) 229–35. **Susman, Margarete.** *Das Buch Hiob und das Schicksal des jüdischen Volkes.* Zurich: Steinberg Verlag, 1946. 2nd ed. Basel: Herder, 1968. **Trutwin, Werner.** "Eine neuzeitliche Ijobsgeschichte: Gott, die Shoa und das Judentum." *Religionsunterricht an höheren Schulen* 38 (1995) 236–47. **Watté, P.** "Job à Auschwitz: Deux constats de la pensée juive." *RTL* 4 (1973) 173–90. **Zafrani, H.** "Une histoire de Job en judéo-arabe du Maroc." *RevEtIsl* 36 (1968) 279–315.

d. Islam and Other Religions

i. Islam

Apt, Naftali. *Die Hiobserzählung in der arabischen Literatur.* 1. Teil. *Zwei arabische Hiobhandschriften der Kgl. Bibliothek zu Berlin.* Kirchhain N.-L.: Schmersow, 1913. **Arnold, Thomas W.** *The Old and New Testaments in Muslim Religious Art.* London: Oxford University Press, 1932. **Busse, Heribert.** "Die bedeutenden biblischen Gestalten im Koran. Welches Profil erhalten sie im Islam?" *Welt und Umwelt der Bibel* 15 (2000) 51–59. **Castillo Castillo, C.** "Job en la leyenda musulmana." *CiuD* 195 (1982) 115–30. **Declais, Jean-Louis.** *Les premiers musulmans face à la tradition biblique: trois récits sur Job.* Paris: Harmattan, 1996. **Grünbaum, M.** *Neue Beiträge zur semitischen Sagenkunde.* Leiden: E. J. Brill, 1893. 264–71 [a summary of the Moroccan story of Job]. **Guillen Robles, F.** "La estoria y recontiamento de Ayub, de sus pruebas y de su paciencia." In *Leyendas moriscas, sacadas de varios manuscritos existentes en las bibliotecas Nacional, Real y de D. P. de Gayangos.* Colección de escritores castellanos novelistas 25. Madrid: M. Tello, 1885–86. 1:225–63 [a Moroccan Spanish story of Job from an Arabic original]. **Jeffery, A.** "Ayyub." In *Encyclopédie de l'Islam.* Ed. H. A. R. Gibb et al. Leiden: Brill, 1965. 13:318. **Johns, Anthony H.** "Aspects of the Prophet Job (salla Allahu 'alayhi wa-sallam) in the Qur'an: A Rendering of Tabari's Exegesis of Surah al-Anbiya (XXI:83–84)." *Hamdard islamicus* 28 (2005) 7–51. **Kohlbrugge, Hanna.** *De tijding van Job in de Bijbel en in de Koran.* The Hague: J. N. Voorhoeve, 1981. ———. *Hiob in der Bibel und Koran.* Wiesbaden: Orientdienst, 1976. **MacDonald, D. B.** "Some External Evidence on the Original Form of the Legend of Job." *AJSL* 14 (1897–88) 137–63. **Tayara, Kamal.** "Job dans le Coran." *Graphè* 6 (1997) 113–34. **Vicchio, Stephen J.** "Job in the Qur'an and Later Islam." In his *Job in the Medieval World.* Eugene, OR: Wipf & Stock, 2006. 67–86. **Wheeler, Brannon M.** "Job." In his *Prophets in the Quran: An Introduction to the Quran and Muslim Exegesis.* London: Continuum, 2002. **Yazicioglu, Isra Umeyye.** "Affliction, Patience and Prayer: Reading Job (P) in the Qur'an." *JScrReas* 4/1 (2004).

ii. Other Religions

Clines, David J. A. "In Search of the Indian Job." *VT* 33 (1983) 398–418 [= his *On the Way to the Postmodern: Old Testament Essays, 1967–1998.* JSOTSup 293. Sheffield: Sheffield

Academic Press, 1998. 2:770–91]. **Fortes, Meyer.** *Oedipus and Job in West African Religion.* Cambridge: Cambridge University Press, 1959 [= *Oedipe et Job dans les religions ouest-africaines.* Bibliothèque repères. Sciences humaines-idéologies 15. Tours: Mame, 1974]. **Rao, S., and M. Reddy.** "Job and His Satan–Parallels in Indian Scripture." *ZAW* 91 (1979) 416–22. **Scaltriti, G.** "Giobbe tra Cristo e Zaratustra." *PalCl* 34 (1955) 673–82, 721–28.

e. Early Christian

Brawley, Robert L. "Paul, Job, and the New Quest for Justice." In *Character Ethics and the New Testament: Moral Dimensions of Scripture.* Ed. Robert L. Brawley. Louisville, KY: Westminster John Knox Press, 2007. **Burchard, Christoph.** "Hiob unter den Propheten. Ein biblisches Exempel im Jakobusbrief (5,11)." *DBAT* 30 (1999) 13–18. **Dassmann, Ernst.** "Akzente frühchristlicher Hiobdeutung." *JAC* 31 (1988) 40–56. **Geerlings, W.** "Hiob und Paulus: Theodizee und Paulinismus in der lateinischen Theologie am Ausgang des vierten Jahrhunderts." *JAC* 24 (1981) 56–66. **Gilbert, Maurice.** "Job et Jésus dans la tradition chrétienne." In his *Il a parlé par les prophètes: thèmes et figures bibliques.* Le livre et le rouleau 2. Brussels: Lessius, 1998. 233–48. **Hainthaler, Theresia.** *Von der Ausdauer Ijobs habt ihr gehört" (Jak 5,11): Zur Bedeutung des Buches Ijob im Neuen Testament.* Europäische Hochschulschriften. Reihe 23: Theologie 337. Frankfurt a.M.: Peter Lang, 1988. **Hanson, A. T.** "Job in Early Christianity and Rabbinic Judaism." *CQ* 2 (1969) 147–51. **Hanson, R. P. C.** "St Paul's Quotations from the Book of Job." *Theol* 54 (1950) 250–53. **Hay, David M.** "Job and the Problem of Doubt in Paul." In *Faith and History: Essays in Honor of Paul W. Meyer.* Ed. John T. Carroll, Charles H. Cosgrove, and E. Elizabeth Johnson. Homage series. Atlanta: Scholars Press, 1990. 208–22. **Michael, J. H.** "Paul and Job. A Neglected Analogy." *ExpT* 36 (1924–25) 67–70. **Perraymond, Myla.** *La figura di Giobbe nella cultura paleocristiana tra esegesi patristica e manifestazioni iconografiche.* Città del Vaticano: Pontificio istituto di archeologia cristiana, 2002. **Philonenko, Marc.** "Romains 7,23, une glose qoumrânisante sur Job 40,32 (Septante) [Engl. 41:8] et trois textes qoumrâniens." *RHPR* 87 (2007) 257–65. **Richardson, Kurt Anders.** "Job as Exemplar in the Epistle of James." In *Hearing the Old Testament in the New Testament.* Ed. Stanley E. Porter. Grand Rapids: William B. Eerdmans, 2006. 213–29. **Schaller, B.** "Zum Textcharakter der Hiobzitate im paulinischen Schrifttum." *ZNW* 71 (1980) 21–26 [= his *Fundamenta judaica: Studien zum antiken Judentum und zum Neuen Testament.* Ed. Lutz Doering and Annette Steudel. SUNT 25. Göttingen: Vandenhoeck & Ruprecht, 2001]. **Seitz, Christopher R.** "The Patience of Job in the Epistle of James." In *Konsequente Traditionsgeschichte. Festschrift für Klaus Baltzer zum 65. Geburtstag.* Ed. Rüdiger Bartelmus, Thomas Krüger, and Helmut Utzschneider. OBO 126. Freiburg, Switzerland: Universitätsverlag, 1993. 373–82.

f. Western Thinkers and Writers

i. General

Bizzotto, Mario. *Il grido di Giobbe: l'uomo, la malattia, il dolore nella cultura contemporanea.* Cinisello Balsamo, Milan: San Paolo, 1995. **Gaiffi, Francesco.** "Giobbe nella teologia contemporanea." In *I volti di Giobbe. Percorsi interdisciplinari.* Ed. Gilberto Marconi and Cristina Termini. Bologna: EDB, 2002. 287–69. **Ghini, Giuseppe, Gian Michele Tortolone, Aldo Bodrato, and Piero Stefani.** *Le provocazioni di Giobbe: una figura biblica nell'orizzonte letterario. Convegno [organizzato dalla] Fondazione Collegio San Carlo.* 1989 [cassettes]. **Grill, Ingrid.** *Aber meine Augen werden ihn schauen ...: Hiob. 1. Ein Versuch zum Themenbereich "Die Bibel als Grundlage des Glaubens" für die 11. Jahrgangsstufe. 2. Ein Lesebuch zur Wirkungsgeschichte der Hiobgestalt in Philosophie, Theologie und Kunst.* Arbeitshilfe für den evangelischen Religionsunterricht an Gymnasien: Themenfolge 97. Erlangen: Gymnasialpädagogische Materialstelle der Evangelisch-Lutherischen Kirche in Bayern, 1994. **Jauss, Hans Robert.** "Job's Questions and Their Distant Reply: Goethe, Nietzsche, Heidegger." *Comparative Literature* 34 (1982) 193–207. **Lamb, Jonathan.** *The Rhetoric of Suffering: Reading the Book of Job in the Eighteenth Century.* Oxford: Clarendon Press, 1995. **Lemann, Nicholas.** "Political Applications of the Book of Job." *New York Times* 142 (November 5, 1992) 10. **Mertin, Jörg.** *Hiob—religionsphilosophisch gelesen: Rezeptionsgeschichtliche Untersuchungen zur Hioblektüre Herders, Kants, Hegels, Kierkegaards und zu ihrer Bedeutung für die Hiobexegese des 18. und 19. Jahrhunderts.* Diss. Paderborn, 1991. **Moretto, Giovanni.** *Giustificazione e interrogazione: Giobbe nella filosofia.* Filosofia e sapere storico. Napoli: Guida, 1991. **Salvati, Giuseppe Marco.** "Giobbe e il parlare di Dio." In *I volti di Giobbe. Percorsi interdisciplinari.* Ed. Gilberto Marconi and Cristina Termini. Bologna: EDB, 2002. 311–18. **Steinmann, Jean.** *Le Livre de Job.* Lectio Divina. Paris: Cerf, 1955. 323–79. **Vicchio, Stephen J.** *Job in the Ancient World.* Eugene, OR: Wipf & Stock, 2006. ———. *Job in the Medieval World.* Eugene, OR: Wipf & Stock, 2006. ———. *Job in the Modern World.* Eugene, OR: Wipf & Stock, 2006. **Vogler, Thomas.** "Eighteenth-Century Logology and the Book of Job." *RelLit* 20 (1988) 25–47. **Zenger, Erich.** "Ein Beispiel. Die Rezeption des Buches Ijob/Hiob." In his edited *Lebendige Welt der Bibel. Entdeckungsreise in das Alte Testament.* Freiburg i.Br.: Herder, 1997. 59–65.

ii. Authors

Baczko, Bronislav [Bronislaw] (Polish philosopher and author, b. 1924). *Job, mon ami: promesses du bonheur et fatalité du mal.* NRF essais. Paris: Gallimard, 1997 [= Hiob, mój przyjaciel: bietnice szczęścia i nieuchronności zła. Warszaw: Wydawn. Naukowe PWN, 2001].

Baeck, Leo (German-Polish Jewish scholar, 1873–1956). *Dieses Volk: jüdische Existenz.* Frankfurt a.M.: Europäische Verlagsanstalt, 1955 [= *This People Israel: The Meaning of Jewish Existence.* Trans. Albert H. Friedlander. London: W. H. Allen, 1965; pp. 95–100 reprinted as "Job and Kohelet: Books of Wisdom" in *The Dimensions of Job: A Study and Selected Readings.* Ed. Nahum H. Glatzer. New York: Schocken Books, 1969. 51–56].

Barrett, William (US philosopher, 1913–1922). "Hebraism and Hellenism." In his *Irrational Man: A Study in Existential Philosophy.* New York: Doubleday, 1958 [pp. 64–68 are reprinted as "The Hebraic Man of Faith" in *The Dimensions of Job: A Study and Selected Readings.* Ed. Nahum H. Glatzer. New York: Schocken Books, 1969. 272–76].

Barth, Karl (Swiss theologian, 1886–1968). See **Migliore, Daniel L.** "Barth and Bloch on Job: A Conflict of Interpretations." In *Understanding the Word: Essays in Honor of Bernhard W. Anderson.* JSOTSup 37. Ed. James T. Butler, Edgar W. Conrad, and Ben C. Ollenburger. Sheffield: JSOT Press, 1985. 265–79. **Schulweis, Harold M.** "Karl Barth's Job: Morality and Theodicy." *JQR* 65 (1975) 156–67. **Sherman, Robert J.** "Reclaiming a Theological Reading of the Bible: Barth's Interpretation of Job as a Case Study." *IntJSysTheol* 2 (2000) 175–88. **Ticciati, Susannah.** *Job and the Disruption of Identity: Reading beyond Barth.* London: T. & T. Clark, 2005.

Bloch, Ernst (German Marxist philosopher, 1885–1977). See **Bondolfi, Alberto.** "Giobbe o Prometeo: la concezione blochiana del fatto morale a confronto con le concezioni teologiche." In *La fondazione della norma morale nella riflessione teologica e marxista contemporanea. VII Congresso nazionale dei teologi moralisti.* Collana Studi e ricerche 29. Bologna: EDB, 1979. **Chirpaz, François.** "Ernst Bloch and Job's Rebellion." *Conc* 169 (1983) 23–29 [= "Ernst Bloch und die Rebellion Ijobs." *Conc* 19 (1983) 686–92]. **Gerbracht, D.** "Aufbruch zu sittlichem Atheismus. Die Hiob-Deutung Ernst Blochs." *EvTh* 35 (1975) 223–37. **Mottu, H.** "Job dans l'oeuvre de Bloch." In *Utopie, marxisme selon Ernst Bloch: un système de l'inconstructible. Hommages à Ernst Bloch pour son 90ème anniversaire.* Ed. Gérard Raulet. Paris: Payot, 1976. 233–38. ———. "La figure de Job chez Bloch." *RTP* 27 (1977) 307–20. **Neher, André.** "Job dans l'oeuvre d'Ernst Bloch." In

Utopie, marxisme selon Ernst Bloch: un système de l'inconstructible. Hommages à Ernst Bloch pour son 90ème anniversaire. Ed. Gérard Raulet. Paris: Payot, 1976. 233–38. **Neumann, Peter H. A.** *Theodizee zwischen Hiob und Ernst Bloch—oder vom Verhalten im Leid.* Religion-Studienstufe 11. Stuttgart: Calwer, 1974. **Raurell, Frederic.** "Job llegit per E. Bloch." *EstFranc* 81 (1980) 403–27 [= *Butlletí de l'Associació Bíblica de Catalunya* 15 (1980) 27–43]. **Strolz, Walter.** "Die Hiob-Interpretation bei Kant, Kierkegaard und Bloch." *Kairos* 23 (1981) 75–87. **Zecchi, Stefano.** "Hiob und Müntzer. Die Utopie als Spur ethischer Bedeutung." In *Ernst Bloch.* Ed. Heinz Ludwig Arnold. Munich: Edition Text + Kritik, 1985.

Brod, Max (Jewish Czech author, 1884–1968). See **Flügel, Heinz.** "Hiobs Prozess mit Gott." In *Max Brod 1884–1968. Ein Gedenkbuch.* Ed. Hugo Gold. Tel Aviv: Olamenu, 1969. 47–59.

Brown, Thomas (English satirist, 1663–1704). "An Epigram upon Job." In *The Works of Mr Thomas Brown, Serious, Moral, Comical and Satyrical.* London: Samuel Briscoe, 1715–20. 4:85. ———. "As Moody Job, in Shirtless Case." In *The Works of Mr Thomas Brown, Serious, Moral, Comical and Satyrical.* London: Samuel Briscoe, 1715–20.

Buber, Martin (Austrian Jewish scholar, 1878–1965). תורת הנביאים. Tel-Aviv: Mosad Bialik, 1950 [= *The Prophetic Faith.* Trans. Carlyle Witton-Davies. New York: Macmillan, 1949; pp. 188–97 reprinted as "A God Who Hides His Face" in *The Dimensions of Job: A Study and Selected Readings.* Ed. Nahum H. Glatzer. New York: Schocken Books, 1969. 56–65]. See also **Silberman, Lou H.** "The Question of Job's Generation: She'elat doro shel 'Iyob': Buber's Job." In *Judaic Perspectives on Ancient Israel.* Ed. Jacob Neusner, Baruch A. Levine, and Ernest S. Frerichs. Philadelphia: Fortress Press, 1987. 261–69.

Bultmann, Rudolf (German theologian, 1884–1976). See **Schmidt, Ernst-Walter.** "Hiob, Jung und Bultmann." *Neue deutsche Hefte* 9 (1954) 699–705.

Calvin, John (French Protestant theologian, 1509–1564). See **Clines, David J. A.** "Job and the Spirituality of the Reformation" [on Luther and Calvin]. In *The Bible, the Reformation and the Church: Essays in Honour of James Atkinson.* Ed. W. P. Stephens. JSNTSup 105. Sheffield: Sheffield Academic Press, 1995. 49–72 [= his *Interested Parties: The Ideology of Writers and Readers of the Hebrew Bible.* JSOTSup 205. Gender, Culture, Theory 1. Sheffield: Sheffield Academic Press, 1995. 145–71]. **Halter, Didier.** "Job et Calvin: Réflexions sur le livre de Job au travers des prédications de Calvin." *FoiVie* 97 (1998) 25–37. **Jeschke, Dieter Walter.** *Die Weltaktualität Gottes: Providenz und Theodizee nach Calvins Predigten über das Buch Hiob.* Diss. Wuppertal, 1999 [= Microfiche ed.: Rosbach vor der Höhe: Ulshöfer, 1999]. **Miln, P.** *Hommes d'une bonne cause: Calvin's Sermons on the Book of Job.* Diss. Nottingham, 1989. **Potgieter, Pieter C.** "Perspectives on the Doctrine of Providence in Some of Calvin's Sermons on Job." In *Proceedings of the Fifth South African Congress on Calvin Research, 1995.* Ed. Andries G. Van Aarde. *HervTS* 54 (1998) 36–49. **Schreiner, Susan E.** "Calvin as an Interpreter of Job." In *Calvin and the Bible.* Ed. Donald K. McKim. Cambridge: Cambridge University Press, 2006. 53–84. ———. "Exegesis and Double Justice in Calvin's Sermons on Job." *Church History* 58 (1989) 322–38. ———. *Where Shall Wisdom Be Found? Calvin's Exegesis of Job from Medieval and Modern Perspectives.* Chicago: University of Chicago Press, 1994. ———. "Why Do the Wicked Live? Job and David in Calvin's Sermons on Job." In *The Voice from the Whirlwind: Interpreting the Book of Job.* Ed. Leo G. Perdue and Clark Gilpin. Nashville: Abingdon Press, 1992. 129–43. **Thomas, D. W. H.** *Incomprehensibilitas Dei: Calvin's Pastoral Theology in the Sermons on Job.* Diss. Lampeter, 1999.

Chesterton, G. K. (English Catholic author, 1874–1936). *The Book of Job, with an Introduction by G. K. Chesterton and Illustrated in Colour by C. Mary Tongue.* London: S. Wellwood, 1907; London: Cecil Palmer & Hayward, 1916.

Cioran, Emile Michel (Romanian philosopher, 1911–1995). See **Poupin, Roland.** *Cioran, entre Job et catharisme: les pouvoirs dépositaires de l'universel et la prière non-conçue.* Diss. Montpellier, 1994.

Cixous, Hélène (French writer and philosopher, b. 1937). See **Pyper, Hugh S.** "'Job the Dog': Hélène Cixous on Wounds, Scars and the Biblical Text." *BibInt* 11 (2003) 438–48.

Conant, James B. (US scientist, 1893–1978). "Science and Spiritual Values." In his *Modern Science and Modern Man.* New York: Columbia University Press, 1952 [pp. 88–92 are reprinted as "Job: The Twofold Answer" in *The Dimensions of Job: A Study and Selected Readings.* Ed. Nahum H. Glatzer. New York: Schocken Books, 1969. 247–50].

Cramer, Friedrich (German biologist, b. 1923). *Wie Hiob leben: Erinnerungen.* Stuttgart: Deutsche Verlags-Anstalt, 1999.

Ehrenberg, Hans (Jewish-Christian theologian, 1883–1958). *Hiob der Existentialist: Fünf Dialoge in zwei Teilen.* Heidelberg: Lambert Schneider, 1952 [pp. 45–52 reprinted as "Elihu the Theologian" in *The Dimensions of Job: A Study and Selected Readings.* Ed. Nahum H. Glatzer. New York: Schocken Books, 1969. 93–100].

Frye, Northrop (Canadian literary critic, 1912–1991). See **Dolzani, M.** "The Ashes of the Stars: Northrop Frye and the Trickster-God." *Semeia* 89 (2002) 59–73.

Girard, René (French philosopher and literary critic, b. 1923). "The Ancient Trail Trodden by the Wicked: Job as Scapegoat" [excerpt from his *La route antique des hommes pervers*]. *Semeia* 33 (1985) 13–41. See also **Atlan, Henri.** "Founding Violence and Divine Referent." In *Violence and Truth: On the Work of René Girard.* Ed. Paul Dumouchel. London: Athlone Press, 1988. 192–208 [= "Violence fondatrice et référent divin." In *Violence et vérité: Autour de René Girard.* Ed. Paul Dumouchel. Colloque de Cerisy. Paris: Grasset, 1985. 434–49]. **Arenilla, Louis.** "Le destin de Job." *La quinzaine littéraire* 441 (June 1985) 22–23. **Bonora, Antonio.** "Giobbe, capro espiatorio secondo R. Girard." *Teologia* 2 (1989) 138–42. **Jaccard, Roland.** "Job, victime et antihéros." *24 heures* (May 28, 1985) 51. **Levine, Baruch.** "René Girard on Job: The Question of the Scapegoat." *Semeia* 33 (1985) 125–33. **McKenna, Andrew J. (ed.).** *René Girard and Biblical Studies.* Decatur, GA: Scholars Press [= *Semeia* 33 (1985)]. **Niewiadomski, Józef.** "Das 'Hiobproblem' in den Religionen: Ein Versuch im Kontext der Perspektive von René Girard." In *Warum? Hiob interdisziplinär diskutiert.* Mainzer Universitätsgespräche Wintersemester 1997/98. Vorträge von Hansjakob Becker, Jürgen Ebach, Herbert Jochum, Georg Langenhorst, Józef Niewiadomski, Willi Oelmüller, and Wilhelm Pesch. Mainz: Studium Generale der Universität Mainz, 1998. 53–72. **Palaver, Wolfgang.** "Rezension zu 'Hiob—ein Weg aus der Gewalt,' von René Girard." *Die Zeit im Buch* 44 (1990) 178–79. **Poirot-Delpech, Bertrand.** "Job ou le grand remède de la haine unanime." *Le Monde* (29 March 1985) 18. **Renouvin, Bertrand, Philippe Cailleux, Julien Betbèze, Alain Flamand, and Patrice Le Roué.** "Les malheurs de Job: Un mythe biblique enfin rendu clair." *Royaliste* 426 (May 1–14, 1985) 426–27.

Goritschewa, Tatjana (Goritcheva, Tatiana) (Russian feminist philosopher, b. 1947). *Hiobs Töchter.* Freiburg i.Br.: Herder, 1988 [= *Filles de Job.* Paris: Nouvelle cité, 1989].

Gramsci, Antonio (Italian political philosopher, 1891–1937). See **Medici, Rita.** *Giobbe e Prometeo: filosofia e politica nel pensiero di Gramsci.* Studi e ricerche, Alinea 2. Florence: Alinea, 2000.

Greenberg, Hayim (Russian-born US Zionist thinker, 1889–1953). *The Inner Eye: Selected Essays.* New York: Jewish Frontier Association, 1953 [pages on Job reprinted as "In Dust and Ashes" in *The Dimensions of Job: A Study and Selected Readings.* Ed. Nahum H. Glatzer. New York: Schocken Books, 1969. 217–24].

Gutiérrez, Gustavo (Peruvian theologian, b. 1928). *Hablar de Dios desde el sufrimiento del inocente.* Lima: Centro de Estudios y Publicaciones, 1986 [= *On Job. God-Talk and the Suffering of the Innocent.* Trans. M. J. O'Connell. Maryknoll, NY: Orbis. 1987; *Von Gott sprechen in Unrecht und Leid.* Munich: Kaiser, 1988]. See also **Cooper, L. L.** *The Book of Job: A Foundation for Testimony in the Writings of Gustavo Gutiérrez, Elie Wiesel, Archibald MacLeish, and Carl Gustav Jung.* Diss. Oxford, 1994. **Feliciano, Juan G.** "Gustavo Gutiérrez'

Liberation Theology: Toward a Hispanic Epistemology and Theology of the Suffering of the Poor." *Apuntes* 13 (1993) 151–61. **Habel, Norman C.** "Gutiérrez on Job: A Review Essay" [*On God: God-Talk and the Suffering of the Innocent*. 1987]. *Lutheran Theological Journal* 22 (1988) 37–40. **Rayan, Samuel.** "Wrestling in the Night" [Gutiérrez's *On Job*, the Bhagavadgita and the Poems of Gitanjali]. In *The Future of Liberation Theology: Essays in Honor of Gustavo Gutiérrez*. Ed. Marc H. Ellis and Otto Maduro. Maryknoll, NY: Orbis Books, 1989. 450–69. **Ruíz Pesce, Ramón Eduardo.** "Dios del pobre. Amor gratuito y sufrimiento del inocente. Leer el Libro de Job desde San Juan de la Cruz a Gustavo Gutiérrez." *Studium filosofía y teología* 5 (2002) 207–20.

Halley, Edmond (English astronomer, 1656–1742). See **Dietrich, Johann David.** *Jobum non esse scepticum adversus Observatorem Halensem*. Wittenberg: Litteris Viduae Gerdesiae, 1726 [?].

Hamann, Johann Georg (German philosopher, 1730–1768). "Hiob einst und immer." In his *Sämtliche Werke*. I. *Tagebuch eines Christen*. Ed. F. Blanke and K. Gründer. Vienna: Herder, 1949. 141–49.

Hartshorne, Charles (US philosopher, 1897–2000). See **Nash, R. T.** *Job's Misconception: A Critical Analysis of the Problem of Evil in the Philosophical Theology of Charles Hartshorne*. Diss. Leuven, 1991.

Hegel, Georg Wilhelm Friedrich (German philosopher, 1770–1831). *Vorlesungen über die Philosophie der Religion*. Berlin, 1832 [= *Lectures on the Philosophy of Religion*. Ed. Peter C. Hodgson. Oxford: Clarendon Press, 2007; II:193–94 are reprinted as "Confidence" in *The Dimensions of Job: A Study and Selected Readings*. Ed. Nahum H. Glatzer. New York: Schocken Books, 1969. 251–52]. See also **Mertin, Jörg.** *Hiob—religionsphilosophisch gelesen: Rezeptionsgeschichtliche Untersuchungen zur Hioblektüre Herders, Kants, Hegels, Kierkegaards und zu ihrer Bedeutung für die Hiobexegese des 18. und 19. Jahrhunderts*. Diss. Paderborn, 1991. **Sichirollo, Livio.** "Fede e sapere. Giobbe e gli amici. Riflessioni in tema di filosofia, religione e filosofia della religione in Kant e in Hegel." In *Filosofia, storia, istituzioni. Saggi e conferenze*. Milan: Guerini e Associati, 1990. 183–226. **Vicchio, Stephen J.** *Job in the Modern World*. Eugene, OR: Wipf & Stock, 2006. 116–22.

Hobbes, Thomas (English philosopher, 1588–1629). *Leviathan, or The Matter, Forme and Power of a Common-Wealth Ecclesiasticall and Civil*. London, 1651. See also **Braun, Dietrich.** *Der sterbliche Gott, oder Leviathan gegen Behemoth*. I. *Erwägungen zu Ort, Bedeutung und Funktion der Lehre von der Königsherrschaft Christi in Thomas Hobbes' "Leviathan."* Diss. Basel, 1960. Basler Studien zur historischen und systematischen Theologie 2. Zurich: EVZ-Verlag, 1963. **Cooke, Paul D.** *Hobbes and Christianity: Reassessing the Bible in Leviathan*. Lanham, MD: London: Rowman & Littlefield, 1996. **Laserson, Max M.** "Power and Justice: Hobbes versus Job." *Judaism* 2 (1953) 52–60. **Palaver, Wolfgang.** "Thomas Hobbes' Umgang mit der Bibel: Eine Interpretation aus der Sicht der Theorie von René Girard." *ZKT* 114 (1992) 257–73. **Schmitt, Carl.** *Der Leviathan in der Staatslehre des Thomas Hobbes. Sinn und Fehlschlag eines politischen Symbols*. Cologne: Hohenheim Verlag, 1938. **Taubes, Jacob.** "Statt einer Einleitung: Leviathan als sterblicher Gott. Zur Aktualität von Thomas Hobbes." In *Religionstheorie und politische Theologie*. Ed. Jacob Taubes. Paderborn: Schöningh, 1983. 1:9–15. **Vicchio, Stephen J.** *Job in the Modern World*. Eugene, OR: Wipf & Stock, 2006. 30–34.

Jaspers, Karl (German philosopher, 1883–1969). "Die persönliche Gott unter Anklage." In *Der philosophische Glaube angesichts der Offenbarung*. Munich: R. Piper, 1962. 331–51. ———. "Hiob." in *Einsichten. Gerhard Krüger zum 60. Geburtstag*. Ed. Klaus Oehler and Richard Schaeffler. Frankfurt: Klostermann, 1962. 86–106.

John of the Cross, St (Spanish mystic, 1542–1591). See **Anon.** "Job et S. Jean de la Croix, choix de textes." *VS* 422 (1956) 372–91.

Jonas, Hans (German philosopher, 1903–1993). See **Manganaro, P.** "Dio: la coscienza occidentale contemporanea di fronte al divino ovvero il grido di Giobbe nella riflessione di Hans Jonas." *Aquinas* 41 (1998) 647–54.

Juhan, Deane (Esalen Institute masseur). *Job's Body: A Handbook for Bodywork.* New York: Station Hill Press, 1987.
Jung, Carl G. (Swiss psychiatrist and philosopher, 1875–1961). *Antwort auf Hiob.* Zurich: Rascher, 1952 [= *Answer to Job: Researches into the Relation between Psychology and Religion.* Trans. R. F. C. Hull. London: Routledge & Kegan Paul, 1954]. See also **Amado Lévy-Valensi, Eliane.** *Job, réponse à Jung.* Parole présente. Paris: Editions du Cerf, 1991. **Bishop, Paul.** *Jung's Answer to Job: A Commentary.* Hove, East Sussex: Brunner–Routledge, 2002. **Boorer, Suzanne.** "The Dark Side of God? A Dialogue with Jung's Interpretation of the Book of Job." *Pacifica* 10 (1997) 277–97. **Broadribb, D.** "Carl Jung kaj la Biblio." *Biblia revuo* 1 (1964) 13–45. **Collins, Brendan.** "Wisdom in Jung's Answer to Job." *BTB* 21 (1991) 97–101. **Cooper, L. L.** *The Book of Job: A Foundation for Testimony in the Writings of Gustavo Gutiérrez, Elie Wiesel, Archibald MacLeish, and Carl Gustav Jung.* Diss. Oxford, 1994. **Cummins, Jaqueline Mary.** *Inner Conflict: The Problem of Evil in C. G. Jung's Answer to Job.* Diss. Goldsmiths College, London, 1994. **Desplanque-Vez, Agnès.** *C. G. Jung et la théodicée: présentation critique de "réponse à Job."* Montpellier: Institut protestant de théologie, 1986. **Devescovi, Pier Claudio.** "La centralità della coscienza. Riflessioni su 'Riposta a Giobbe' di C. G. Jung." In *Jung e l'ebraismo.* Ed. Patrizia Puccioni. Florence: Giuntina, 2001. 29–39. **Edinger, Edward F., and Lawrence W. Jaffe (eds.).** *Transformation of the God-Image: An Elucidation of Jung's Answer to Job.* Studies in Jungian Psychology by Jungian Analysts 54. Toronto: Inner City Books, 1992. **Griffin, R.** "Jung's Science in 'Answer to Job' and the Hindu Matrix of Form." *Tem* 23 (1987) 35–44. **Hedinger, Ulrich.** "Reflexionen zu C. G. Jungs Hiobinterpretation." *TZ* 23 (1967) 340–52. **Marco, N. di.** "Dio come Padre nella 'Riposta a Giobbe' di C. G. Jung." *Aquinas* 27 (1984) 33–74. **Matthews, Marjorie Swank.** *Issues and Answers in the Book of Job and Joban Issues and Answers in Three Twentieth Century Writers: Carl Jung, Robert Frost, and Archibald MacLeish.* Diss. Florida State University, 1976. **Michaëlis, Edgar.** "Le livre de Job interpreté par C. G. Jung." *RTP* 3 (1953) 182–95. ———. "Ist Satan die vierte Person der Gottheit?" *Zeitwende* 25 (1954) 368–77. **Pascal, E.** "Risposta a Jung (A proposito di C. G. Jung, Risposta a Giobbe)." *Prot* 21 (1966) 215–22. **Philp, Howard L.** *Jung and the Problem of Evil.* London: Rockliffs, 1958; New York: R. M. McBride. 133–71. **Ryan, Penelope J.** *An Interpretive and Critical Analysis of Carl Jung's "Answer to Job" as It Reflects His Psychological Theory, His Religious Understanding and Statements in Light of Christian Tradition.* Diss. Fordham, New York, 1983. **Ryce-Menuhin, Joel.** *A New Look at Jung's "Answer to Job."* Guild of Pastoral Psychology Guild Lecture 237. London: Guild of Pastoral Psychology, 1991. ———. "Jung's Answer to Job in the Light of the Monotheisms." In his edited *Jung and the Monotheisms: Judaism, Christianity and Islam.* London: Routledge, 1994. 111–24. **Sanford, John A.** *C. G. Jung and the Problem of Evil: The Strange Trial of Mr Hyde.* Boston: Sigo, 1993. **Scheffler, E. H.** "Jung's Answer to Job: A Reappraisal." *OTEss* ns 4 (1991) 327–41. **Schmidt, Ernst-Walter.** "Hiob, Jung und Bultmann." *Neue deutsche Hefte* 9 (1954) 699–705. **Schwartz-Salant, Nathan.** "Patriarchy in Transformation: Judaic, Christian, and Clinical Perspectives." In *Jung's Challenge to Contemporary Religion.* Ed. Murray Stein and Robert L. Moore. Wilmette, IL: Chiron Publications, 1987. 41–71. **Vaydat, P.** "Kant et Carl Gustave Jung lecteurs du Livre de Job." *Graphè* 6 (1997) 157–73. **Welland, Malcolm.** "Active Imagination in Jung's Answer to Job." *SR* 26 (1997) 297–308. **White, Victor.** "Jung et son livre sur Job." *VS Suppl* 37 (1956) 199–209. **Wildberger, H.** "Das Hiobproblem und seine neueste Deutung." *Reformatio* 3 (1954) 355–63, 439–48 [= *Jahwe und sein Volk: Gesammelte Aufsätze zum Alten Testament zu seinem 70. Geburtstag am 2. Januar 1980.* Ed. Hans Heinrich Schmid and Odil Hannes Steck. Munich: Chr. Kaiser, 1979. 9–27].

Kant, Immanuel (German philosopher, 1724–1804). "Über das Misslingen aller philosophischem Versuche in der Theodizee" (1791). In his *Werke.* Ed. Ernst Cassirer. Berlin: B. Cassirer, 1914. 6:119–38. See also **Loades, Ann L.** "Job's Comforters." In *New Studies in Theology, 1.* Ed. Stephen Sykes and Derek Holmes. London: Duckworth, 1980.

119–38. ———. *Kant and Job's Comforters.* Newcastle upon Tyne: Avero, 1985. **Mertin, Jörg.** *Hiob—religionsphilosophisch gelesen: Rezeptionsgeschichtliche Untersuchungen zur Hioblektüre Herders, Kants, Hegels, Kierkegaards und zu ihrer Bedeutung für die Hiobexegese des 18. und 19. Jahrhunderts.* Diss. Paderborn, 1991. **Sichirollo, Livio.** "Fede e sapere. Giobbe e gli amici. Riflessioni in tema di filosofia, religione e filosofia della religione in Kant e in Hegel." In *Filosofia, storia, istituzioni. Saggi e conferenze.* Milan: Guerini e Associati, 1990. 183–226. **Strolz, Walter.** "Die Hiob-Interpretation bei Kant, Kierkegaard und Bloch." *Kairos* 23 (1981) 75–87. **Tomasoni, Francesco.** "Giobbe modello di fede razionale in Kant." *Humanitas* 45 (1991) 267–69. **Vaydat, P.** "Kant et Carl Gustave Jung lecteurs du Livre de Job." *Graphè* 6 (1997) 157–73. **Venturelli, Domenico.** "Forme del male e interrogazione jobica nella filosofia di Kant." In *La domanda di Giobbe e la razionalità sconfitta.* Ed. C. Giannotto. Trento: Università degli Studi di Trento, 1995. 117–47.

Kaufman, Yehezkel (Israeli biblical scholar, 1889–1963). תולדות האמונה הישראלית. Tel Aviv: Mosad Byalik, 1937–1956. Abridged as *The Religion of Israel: From Its Beginnings to the Babylonian Exile.* Trans. Moshe Greenberg. London: Allen & Unwin, 1961 [pp. 334–38 reprinted as "Job the Righteous Man and Job the Sage" in *The Dimensions of Job: A Study and Selected Readings.* Ed. Nahum H. Glatzer. New York: Schocken Books, 1969. 65–70].

Kaufmann, Walter (German-born US philosopher and poet, 1921–1980). *The Faith of a Heretic.* New York: Doubleday, 1959 [pp. 162–68, 180–81 are reprinted as "An Uncanny World" in *The Dimensions of Job: A Study and Selected Readings.* Ed. Nahum H. Glatzer. New York: Schocken Books, 1969. 237–46].

Kierkegaard, Søren (Danish philosopher and theologian, 1813–1855). "'The Lord gave, and the Lord hath taken away'." In *Opbyggelige taler i forskjellig aand [Edifying Discourses in Diverse Spirits].* Copenhagen, 1847 [= *Four Edifying Discourses.* 1843. In *Edifying Discourses.* Trans. David F. and Lillian M. Swenson. Minneapolis: Augsburg, 1942; some pages on Job are reprinted as "The Lord Gave, and the Lord Hath Taken Away" in *The Dimensions of Job: A Study and Selected Readings.* Ed. Nahum H. Glatzer. New York: Schocken Books, 1969. 253–68]. ———. **[Constantinus, Constantin, pseud.].** *Gjentagelsen, et forsøg i den experimenterende psychologi.* Copenhagen, 1843 [= *Repetition. An Essay in Experimental Psychology.* 1843. In *Fear and Trembling.* Ed. Howard V. and Edna H. Hong. Princeton: Princeton University Press. 1983. 125–231. ———. *Christelige Taler.* Copenhagen, 1848 [= *Christian Discourses, and The Lilies of the Field and the Birds of the Air, and Three Discourses at the Communion on Fridays.* Trans. Walter Lowrie. London: Oxford University Press, 1939; *Christian Discourses: The Crisis and a Crisis in the Life of an Actress.* Trans. Howard V. Hong and Edna H. Hong. Princeton, NJ: Princeton University Press, 1997]. See also **Hayashi, Tadayoshi.** "Kierkegaard über Hiob." *Kwansei Gakuin University Humanities Review* 1 (1996) 72–81. **Mertin, Jörg.** *Hiob—religionsphilosophisch gelesen: Rezeptionsgeschichtliche Untersuchungen zur Hioblektüre Herders, Kants, Hegels, Kierkegaards und zu ihrer Bedeutung für die Hiobexegese des 18. und 19. Jahrhunderts.* Diss. Paderborn, 1991. **Mooney, Edward F.** "Kierkegaard's Job Discourse: Getting Back the World." *International Journal for Philosophy of Religion* 34 (1993) 151–69. **Müller, Hans-Peter.** "Welt als 'Wiederholung': Sören Kierkegaards Novelle als Beitrag zur Hiob-Interpretation." In *Werden und Wirken des Alten Testaments: Festschrift C. Westermann.* Ed. Rainer Albertz. Göttingen: Vandenhoeck & Ruprecht, 1980. 335–72. **Müller, Paul.** "Sören Kierkegaards forståelse af teodicéproblemet, belyst ud fra hans skildring af Job-skikkelsen." *DTT* 32 (1969) 199–217. **Mura, Gaspare.** *Angoscia ed esistenza, da Kierkegaard a Moltmann; Giobbe e la "sofferenza di Dio."* Rome: Città nuova, 1982. **Strolz, Walter.** "Die Hiob-Interpretation bei Kant, Kierkegaard und Bloch." *Kairos* 23 (1981) 75–87. **Taylor, Mark Lloyd.** "Ordeal and Repetition in Kierkegaard's Treatment of Abraham and Job." In *Foundations of Kierkegaard's Vision of Community: Religion, Ethics, and Politics in Kierkegaard.* Ed. George Connell and C. Stephen Evans. Atlantic Highlands, NJ: Humanities Press, 1992. 33–53. **Wahl, Jean.** "Sören Kierkegaard et le livre de Job." In

L'homme. 2. Metaphysique et conscience de soi. Ed. Emile Bréhier, Pierre Thévenaz, et al. Etre et penser 27. Neuchâtel: La Baconnière, 1948. 147–66.

Korczak, Janusz [Henryk Goldszmit, pseud.] (Jewish Polish author, 1877–1942). See **Koch, Ursula.** *Hiob, mein Bruder: Begegnungen mit Tilman Riemenschneider, Janusz Korczak, Katharina von Henot u.a.* Giessen: Brunnen-Verlag, 1990.

Leibowitz, Isaïe (Yeshayahou) (Jewish philosopher, 1903–1994). *Israël et judaïsme: ma part de vérité. Suivi de Job et Antigone: entretiens avec Michaël Shashar.* Paris: Desclée de Brouwer, 2nd ed. 1996.

Leopardi, Giacomo (Italian poet and philosopher, 1798–1837). See **Marcon, Loretta.** *La notte oscura dell'anima: Giobbe e Leopardi.* Strumenti e ricerche 32. Napoli: Guida, 2005.

Lessing, Gotthold Ephraim (German writer and philosopher, 1729–1781). See **Fetscher, Justus.** "Hiob in Gath: deutsch-jüdische Lektüren von Lessings "Nathan der Weise." *ZRGG* 57 (2005) 209–31. **Strohschneider-Kohrs, Ingrid.** "Lessings Hiob-Deutungen im Kontext des 18. Jahrhunderts." *Edith-Stein-Jahrbuch* 8 (2002) 255–68.

Levi, Primo (Italian writer, 1919–1987). See **Luca, Vania de.** *Tra Giobbe e i buchi neri: le radici ebraiche dell'opera di Primo Levi.* Studium lucis 1. Naples: Istituto grafico editoriale italiano, 1991.

Luther, Martin (German theologian and reformer, 1483–1546). *Das Buch Hiob auffs new zugericht.* Erfurt, 1560 [repr. Bibliotheca palatina F1277. Munich, Saur, 1991]. ———. "Vorrede zum Buch Hiob." In *Luthers Vorreden zur Bibel.* Ed. Heinrich Bornkamm. Frankfurt: Insel, 1983. 59–61. See also **Böttcher, V.** *Das Buch Hiob nach Luther und der Probebibel aus dem Grundtext bearbeitet und mit Bemerkungen versehen.* Leipzig: J. Lehmann, 1885. **Clines, David J. A.** "Job and the Spirituality of the Reformation" [on Luther and Calvin]. In *The Bible, the Reformation and the Church: Essays in Honour of James Atkinson.* Ed. W. P. Stephens. JSNTSup 105. Sheffield: Sheffield Academic Press, 1995. 49–72. **Sutter, Franz.** *Die Geschichte von Hiob, dem rechtschaffenen Mann, seinen Prüfungen und seinem Streit mit Gott, in der Übertragung von Martin Luther.* Zurich: Diogenes 1985.

Machovec, Milan (Czech philosopher, 1925–2003). See **Augustin, Matthias.** "Sinn des Lebens—Sinn des Leidens. Betrachtungen zur marxistischen Hiob-Interpretation von Milan Machovec als Beitrag zum alttestamentlich-philosophischen Dialog." In *Schöpfung und Befreiung. Festschrift für Claus Westermann zum 80. Geburtstag.* Ed. Rainer Albertz, Friedemann W. Golka, and Jürgen Kegler. Stuttgart: Calwer Verlag, 1989. 166–77.

Maimonides, Moses (Jewish philosopher and writer, 1135–1204). See **Kravitz, L. S.** "Maimonides and Job: An Enquiry as to the Method of the Moreh." *HUCA* 38 (1967) 149–58. **Laks, H. Joel.** "The Enigma of Job. Maimonides and the Moderns." *JBL* 83 (1964) 345–64. **Oberhänsli-Widmer, Gabrielle.** "Ist auch Hiob unter den Philosophen? Maimonides' Interpretation des Hiob." *Kirche und Israel* 17 (2002) 62–75. **Pfaff, Konrad.** *Salomon Maimon: Hiob der Aufklärung. Mosaiksteine zu seinem Bildnis.* Philosophische Texte und Studien 41. Hildesheim: Olms, 1995.

Moltmann, Jürgen (German theologian, b. 1926). See **Mura, Gaspare.** *Angoscia ed esistenza, da Kierkegaard a Moltmann; Giobbe e la "sofferenza di Dio."* Rome: Città nuova, 1982.

Murray, Gilbert (Australian-born British classical scholar, 1866–1957). *Aeschylus: The Creator of Tragedy.* Oxford: Clarendon Press, 1940 [pp. 91–95 reprinted as "Beyond Good and Evil" in *The Dimensions of Job: A Study and Selected Readings.* Ed. Nahum H. Glatzer. New York: Schocken Books, 1969. 194–97].

Nietzsche, Friedrich Wilhelm (German philosopher, 1844–1900). See **Jauss, Hans Robert.** "Job's Questions and Their Distant Reply: Goethe, Nietzsche, Heidegger." *Comparative Literature* 34 (1982) 193–207.

Orthodox writers. Reardon, Patrick Henry. *The Trial of Job: Orthodox Christian Reflections on the Book of Job.* Ben Lomond, CA: Conciliar Press, 2005.

Otto, Rudolf (German theologian and philosopher of religion, 1869–1937). "The Numinous of the Old Testament." Chapter 8 in his *Das Heilige: über das Irrationale in der Idee des Göttlichen und sein Verhältnis zum Rationalen.* Breslau: Trewendt & Granier, 1917 [= *The Idea of the Holy: An Inquiry into the Non-Rational Factor in the Idea of the Divine and Its Relation to the Rational.* Trans. John W. Harvey. London: Oxford University Press, 1923; pp. 93–96 reprinted as "The Elements of the Mysterious" in *The Dimensions of Job: A Study and Selected Readings.* Ed. Nahum H. Glatzer. New York: Schocken Books, 1969. 225–28].

Pascal, Blaise (French philosopher and writer, 1623–1662). *Pensées ... sur la religion et sur quelques autres sujets.* Paris, 1670. See **Leducfayette, D.** "Proposing a Key to the Book of Job: Blaise Pascal on Freedom." *RevPhil* 119 (1994) 181–94. **Stern, Esther Hannah.** *Pascal and the Jews* [influence of prophets, Job]. Diss. City University of New York, 1981. **Vicchio, Stephen J.** *Job in the Modern World.* Eugene, OR: Wipf & Stock, 2006. 36–38.

Popular European Tradition. Kretzenbacher, Leopold. *Hiobs-Erinnerungen zwischen Donau und Adria: Kulträume, Patronate, Sondermotive der Volksüberlieferungen um Job und sein biblisches und apokryphes Schicksal in den Südost-Alpenländern.* Bayerische Akademie der Wissenschaften, philosophisch-historische Klasse: Sitzungsberichte 1987, 1. Munich: Verlag der Bayerischen Akademie der Wissenschaften, 1987.

Ragaz, Leonhard (Swiss theologian, 1868–1945). *Die Bibel. Eine Deutung.* 7 vols. Zurich: Diana Verlag, 1947–1950 [4:255–59 reprinted as "God Himself Is the Answer" in *The Dimensions of Job: A Study and Selected Readings.* Ed. Nahum H. Glatzer. New York: Schocken Books, 1969. 128–31].

Ricoeur, Paul (French philosopher, 1913–2005). See **Bolton, Frederick J.** "The Sense of the Text and a New Vision" [reply to D. Pellauer, "Reading Ricoeur Reading Job"]. *Semeia* 19 (1981) 87–90. **Crossan, J. D. (ed.).** *The Book of Job and Ricoeur's Hermeneutics.* Semeia 19. Chico, CA: Scholars Press. 1981. **Dailey, Thomas F.** *The Repentant Job: A Ricoeurian Icon for Biblical Theology.* Lanham, MD: University Press of America, 1994. **Dornisch, Loretta.** "The Book of Job and Ricoeur's Hermeneutics." *Semeia* 19 (1981) 3–21. **Lowe, Walter J.** "Cosmos and Covenant" [Ricoeur and Job]. *Semeia* 19 (1981) 107–12. **Pellauer, David.** "Reading Ricoeur Reading Job." *Semeia* 19 (1981) 73–83.

Roth, Leon (Israeli philosopher, 1896–1963). *Judaism: A Portrait.* London: Faber & Faber, 1960 [pp. 227–30 reprinted in *The Dimensions of Job: A Study and Selected Readings.* Ed. Nahum H. Glatzer. New York: Schocken Books, 1969. 71–74].

Royce, Josiah (US philosopher, 1855–1916). *Studies of Good and Evil: A Series of Essays upon Problems of Philosophy and of Life.* New York: D. Appleton & Co., 1898 [pages on Job are reprinted in **Hone, Ralph E.** *The Voice out of the Whirlwind: The Book of Job.* San Francisco: Chandler, 1960. 233–53. Pp. 1–28 are reprinted as "The Oneness of God with the Sufferer" in *The Dimensions of Job: A Study and Selected Readings.* Ed. Nahum H. Glatzer. New York: Schocken Books, 1969. 156–74]. See also **Vicchio, Stephen J.** *Job in the Modern World.* Eugene, OR: Wipf & Stock, 2006. 182–85.

Savater, Fernando (Spanish philosopher, b. 1947). *Diario de Job.* Alfaguara bolsillo 80. Madrid: Alfaguara, 1997.

Schopenhauer, Arthur (German philosopher, 1788–1860). "Parerga und Paralipo mena." In his *Sämtliche Werke.* V. Ed. Wolfgang Freiherr von Löhneysen. Leipzig: Brockhaus, 1874.

Shestov [Chestov], Lev (Ukrainian Jewish existentialist philosopher, 1866–1938). *In Job's Balances: On the Sources of the Eternal Truths.* Trans. Camilla Coventry and C. A. Macartney. London: Dent, 1932 [repr. Athens, OH: Ohio University Press, 1975] [= *Sur la balance de Job, pérégrinations à travers les âmes.* In his *Œuvres.* IV. Paris: Flammarion, 1971].

Spinoza, Baruch [Benedict] (Jewish Dutch philosopher, 1632–1677). *Tractatus theologico-politicus.* Amsterdam, 1670. See also **Curley, Edwin.** "Maïmonide, Spinoza et le Livre de Job." In *Architectures de la raison. Mélanges offerts à Alexandre Matheron.* Ed. P.-F. Moreau. Fontenay-aux-Roses: ENS Editions, 1996. 103–35. **Vicchio, Stephen J.** *Job in the Modern World.* Eugene, OR: Wipf & Stock, 2006. 34–36.

Susman, Margarete (German philosopher and poet, 1872–1966). *Das Buch Hiob und das Schicksal des jüdischen Volkes.* Zurich: Steinberg Verlag, 1946. 2nd ed. Basel: Herder, 1968. ———. "Früheste Dichtung Frank Kafkas." In her *Gestalten und Kreise.* Zurich: Diana Verlag, 1954. 348–66 [= "Franz Kafka." *The Jewish Frontier* (Sept. 1956); reprinted in part as "God the Creator" in *The Dimensions of Job: A Study and Selected Readings.* Ed. Nahum H. Glatzer. New York: Schocken Books, 1969. 86–92]. See also Susman, Margarete, in Section g.i (Poetry), below; and **Kammerer, Gabriele.** "'Aus dem beschädigten Leben': Das Exil als Erfahrungshintergrund von Margarete Susmans Hiobdeutung—entdeckt mit Theodor W. Adornos Hilfe." In *Knospen und Früchten: Ein studentischer Geburtstagsstrauss für Friedrich-Wilhelm Marquardt.* Ed. Thorsten Becker. Berlin: Wissenschaftlicherverlag, 1998. 37–49. **Rammstedt, Angela.** "'... die Sonne Homers' und 'Hiobs ew'ge leidgequälte Frage ...' Zeichen der Nähe und Distanz bei Gertrud Kantorowicz und Margarete Susman." In *Der abgerissene Dialog. Die intellektuelle Beziehung Gertrud Kantorowicz–Margarete Susman oder die Schweizer Grenze bei Hohenems als Endpunkt eines Fluchtversuchs.* Ed. Petra Zudrell. Innsbruck: StudienVerlag, 1999. 81–100.

Teilhard de Chardin, Pierre (French philosopher and priest, 1881–1955). See **Franco, R.** "Job y Teilhard de Chardin sobre el problema del mal." *Proyección* 32 (1985) 27–41.

Tillich, Paul (German and US theologian, 1886–1965). See **Cranford, William Jefferson.** *The Doctrine of God in the Book of Job and the Systematic Theology of Paul Tillich.* Diss. Baylor, 1981.

Voltaire [François Marie Arouet] (French philosopher, 1694–1778). "Job." In his *Dictionnaire philosophique.* 1767–1769. In *Oeuvres complètes de Voltaire.* Paris: Garnier, 1879. 19:504–7. ———. "Histoire des voyages de Scarmentado." In his *Romans, et contes philosophiques.* London, 1776. In *Oeuvres complètes de Voltaire.* XLIII. Paris: P. Dupont, 1824 [= *The History of the Voyages of Scarmentado. A Satire.* London: Paul Vaillant, 1757]. ———. *Poemes sur la loi naturelle ... et sur le désastre de Lisbonne.* Geneva, 1756. See also Voltaire, in Section g.iii (Fiction), below; and **Foulet, Alfred.** "Zadig and Job." *Modern Language Notes* 75 (1960) 421–23. **Senior, Nancy.** "Voltaire and the Book of Job." *French Review* 47 (1973) 340–47. **Vicchio, Stephen J.** *Job in the Modern World.* Eugene, OR: Wipf & Stock, 2006. 66–71. **Weinrich, Harald.** "Voltaire, Hiob und das Erdbeben von Lissabon." In *Aufsätze zur portugiesischen Kulturgeschichte.* Münster: Aschendorff, 1966. 4:96–104.

Weil, Simone (French philosopher and Christian mystic, 1909–1943). *Attente de Dieu. Lettres et réflexions.* Paris: La Colombe, 1950 [= *Waiting for God.* Trans. Emma Crawford. New York: Putnam, 1951]. ———. *La pesanteur et la grâce.* Paris: Plon, 1947 [= *Gravity and Grace.* Trans. Emma Craufurd. London: Routledge & Kegan Paul, 1952. Trans. Arthur Wills. Lincoln, NE: University of Nebraska Press, 1997]. See **Fuchs, Gotthard.** "Unglück und Schönheit: Die Gestalt Hiobs bei Simone Weil." *BK* 59 (2004) 83–88.

Weiss, Paul (US philosopher, 1901–2002). "God, Job, and Evil: The Eternal Tension between Man and God." *Commentary* 6 (1948) [reprinted as "God, Job, and Evil" in *The Dimensions of Job: A Study and Selected Readings.* Ed. Nahum H. Glatzer. New York: Schocken Books, 1969. 181–93].

Wesley, John (founder of Methodism, 1703–1791) and **Charles Wesley (early Methodist and hymn writer, 1707–1788).** See **Maser, Frederick E.** "The Wesleys and Job." *Methodist History* 37 (1999) 266–70.

Wiesel, Elie (Hungarian and US Jewish writer, b. 1928). See **Cooper, L. L.** *The Book of Job: A Foundation for Testimony in the Writings of Gustavo Gutiérrez, Elie Wiesel, Archibald MacLeish, and Carl Gustav Jung.* Diss. Oxford, 1994. **Mies, Françoise.** "Job dans la tourmente: de l'intrigue biblique à Elie Wiesel." In *Bible et littérature: l'homme et Dieu mis en intrigue.* Brussels: Lessius; Namur: Presses Universitaires de Namur, 1999. 75–121.

Zapffe, Peter Wessel (Norwegian author and philosopher, 1899–1990). *Om det tragiske.* Oslo: Gyldendal, 1941.

g. Literary Works Inspired by Job

i. Poetry

Abati, Antonio (Italian poet, c. 1600–1667). "Il Giobbe: Oratorio per musica." "Giobbe che si lamenta." In his *Poesie postume.* Bologna: Giovanni Recaldini, 1671; Venice: F. Busetto, 1676.

Adler, Hermann (Jewish poet, Poland and Switzerland, 1911–1951). *Balladen der Gekreuzigten, der Auferstandenen, Verachteten.* Zurich: Verlag Oprecht, 1946.

Allman, John (US poet, b. 1935). "On Hugh Mesibov's Job." In his *Scenarios for a Mixed Landscape.* New York: New Directions Publishing, 1986.

Anon. *A Godly Ballad of the Just Man Job.* 1654–55. In *The Pepys Ballads.* Ed. W. G. Day. Cambridge: Brewer, 1987.

Anon. *Hiobs männlicher Muth in einem weiblichen Leibe.* In *Benjamins Neukirchs Anthologie: Herrn von Hoffmannswaldau und anderer Deutschen bissher noch nie zusammengedruckter Gedichte.* V. Glückstadt, 1705 [= Ed. Erika Metzger and Anita Holz. Neuwied; Berlin: M. Niemeyer, 1962. 5:261].

Anon. *L'hystore Job.* **Bates, Robert Champan.** *L'hystore Job: adaptation en vers français du "Compend[i]um in Job" [of Peter of Blois].* Yale Romanic Studies. New Haven: Yale University Press, 1937.

Anon. *Mystère de la patience de Job* (15th cent.), in verse. Also known as *Mystère de Job, Pacience de Job.* Extracts and synopsis: **Parfaict, François, and Claude Parfaict.** *Histoire du théâtre françois depuis son origine jusqu'à present, avec la vie des plus célébres poëtes dramatiques, un catalogue exact de leurs piéces, et des notes historiques et critiques.* Paris, 1745–49. 2:532–36.

Anon. *Paraphrase of the Book of Job* (14th cent.). Edition: **Karsten, Torsten Evert (ed.).** *Die mitteldeutsche poetische Paraphrase des Buches Hiob; aus der Handschrift des Königlichen Staats-archivs zu Königsberg herausgegeben.* Deutsche Texte des Mittelalters 21. Berlin: Weidmann, 1910. See also **Dunphy, Graeme.** "Rabengefieder—Elefantengezisch: Naturdeutung in der mitteldeutschen Hiob-Paraphrase." In *Natur und Kultur in der deutschen Literatur des Mittelalters.* Proceedings of the 1997 Exeter Colloquium. Ed. Alan Robertshaw and Gerhard Wolf. Tübingen: Niemeyer, 1999. 91–102.

Anon. *Phoenix, The* [Old English poem, 9th cent., a translation of *De ave phoenice,* attributed to Lactantius; refers to Job 29:18].

Anon. "Utendi wa Ayubu (Job)." In *Tendi: Six Examples of a Swahili Classical Verse Form with Translations and Notes.* Ed. J. W. T. Allen. Nairobi and London: Heinemann, 1971.

Aue, Hartmann von (c. 1170–c. 1210). *Der arme Heinrich.* Editions: **E. Martin.** *Lieder und Büchlein und des Armen Heinrich.* Leipzig: S. Hirzel, 1881; Kurt Gärtner. *Der arme Heinrich.* Tübingen: M. Niemeyer, 16th ed. 2001. See also **Datz, Günther.** *Die Gestalt Hiobs in der kirchlichen Exegese und der "Arme Heinrich" Hartmanns von Aue.* Göppinger Arbeiten zur Germanistik. Göppingen: A. Kümmerle, 1973. **Hauptmann, Gerhart.** *Der arme Heinrich. Eine deutsche Sage.* Berlin: Fischer, 1902. **Hunter, J. A.** "'Sam Joben den Richen': Hartmann's 'Der arme Heinrich' and the Book of Job." *The Modern Language Review* 68 (1973) 358–66.

Baillie, Joanna (Scottish poet and dramatist, 1762–1851). "Job, XIII. 15." In *The Dramatic and Poetical Works of Joanna Baillie.* London: Longman, Brown, Green, & Longmans, 1851.

Balossardi, Marco (pseudonym of Olindo Guerrini, Italian poet, 1845–1916). *Giobbe* [poem]. Milan: Treves, 1882. See also *Giobbe: serena concezione di Marco Balossardi.* Memoria bibliografica 21. Manziana, Rome: Vecchiarelli, 1994.

Barton, Bernard (English poet, 1784–1849). "To Job's Three Friends" [sonnet]. In his *Household Verses.* London: George Virtue, 1845.

Bauer, Walter (German and Canadian poet and novelist, 1904–1976). *Stimme aus dem Leunawerk: Verse und Prosa.* Berlin: Malik-Verlag, 1930.

Becher, Johannes Robert (German poet and essayist, 1891–1958). "Hiob." In *Gesammelte Werke*. Vol. 6, *Gedichte, 1949–1958*. Berlin: Aufbau, 1973.

Belleau, Rémi [Remy] (French poet, 1528–1577). *Les Cantiques du Sieur de Valagre et les cantiques du sieur de Maizonfleur… avec quelques autres cantiques [prières et sainctes doléances de Job par R. Belleau, cantiques de Phil. Desportes T. de Sautemont, J. du Bellay, Ronsard, de l'inconstance et vanité du monde par A.Z.; Les quatrains du Seigneur de Pybrac… avec les plaisirs de la vie rustique extraits d'un sien… poème]*. Paris, 1587.

Benserade, Isaac de (French poet, 1613–1691). *Sur Job. Sonnet*. In *Poésies de Benserade*. Ed. Octave Uzanne. Paris: Librairie des bibliophiles, 1875. 107.

Bethge, Eberhard Gilbert (German poet, 1876–1946). *Hiob Christ: Dichtung in drei Teilen*. Frankfurt a.M.: Haag & Herchen, 1992.

Blackmore, Roger A. *Paraphrase on the Book of Job, as Likewise on the Songs of Moses, Deborah, David; on Four Select Psalms, Some Chapters of Isaiah, and the Third Chapter of Habakkuk* [in verse]. London, 1700. See also Thomas Brown, below.

Blank, Renold J. (Swiss theologian and writer, b. 1941). "Hiob, und keine Frage mehr." In *Heller kann kein Himmel sein: Ausgewählte Gedichte aus dem Wettbewerb für christliche Literatur*. Graz: Styria, 1984. 19.

Borchardt, Rudolf (German poet and author, 1877–1945). *Geschichte des Heimkehrenden: Das Buch Joram* [prose poem]. Basel: Schweizerischen Verlags Druckerei, 1905 [= *Das Buch Joram*. Leipzig: Insel-Verlag, 1907].

Bosschère, Jean de (French illustrator and poet, 1878–1953). *Job le pauvre, avec un portrait par Wyndham Lewis, traduction des poèmes en anglais, et quatorze gravures noires*. Collection d'Art "La Cible." Paris: Jacques Povolozky; London: John Lane, Bodley Head, 1922.

Boye, Karin Maria (Swedish poet and novelist, 1900–1941). *De sju dødssynderna: och andra efterlæmnade dikter* [The Seven Deadly Sins]. Stockholm: Bonnier, 1941 [in her *Complete Poems*. Trans. David McDuff. Newcastle-upon-Tyne: Bloodaxe, 1994].

Boyse, Samuel (Irish and Scottish writer, 1708–1749). "The III. Chapter of the Book of Job Translated" [in verse]. In his *Translations and Poems Written on Several Subjects*. Edinburgh: Thomas & Walter Ruddimans, 1731.

Brewster, Elizabeth W. "Footnotes to the Book of Job" [poem]. *Fiddlehead* 178 (1994) 23–32.

Broome, William (English poet, 1689–1745). "Part of the 38th and 39th Chapters of Job: A Paraphrase." In his *Poems on Several Occasions*. London: Henry Lintot, 2nd ed. 1739.

Brown, Thomas (English satirist, 1663–1704). "An Epigram, Occasion'd by the News that Sir R—— Bl——re's [Roger Blackmore's] Paraphrase upon Job Was in the Press." In *The Works of Mr Thomas Brown, Serious, Moral, Comical and Satyrical*. London: Samuel Briscoe, 1715–20. ———. "On Job Newly Travestied by Sir R—— B——re." In *The Works of Mr Thomas Brown, Serious, Moral, Comical and Satyrical*. London: Samuel Briscoe, 1715–20. 1:138–39.

Bruin, Hein de (Friesland poet and writer, pseudonymously H. van Drielst, 1899–1947). *Job: Herdichting naar het Bijbelboek* [epic poem]. Baarn: Bosch & Keuning, 1943 [clandestinely published].

Brunner, Sebastian. *Der deutsche Hiob*. Regensburg: G. J. Manz, 1846.

Byron, George Gordon (Lord Byron, English Romantic poet, 1788–1824). "From Job: A Spirit Passed before Me." In his *Hebrew Melodies*. London: John Murray, 1815. See **Ashton, Thomas L.** *Byron's Hebrew Melodies*. London: Routledge & Kegan Paul, 1972. 145. **Clines, David J. A.** "Job 4,13: A Byronic Suggestion." *ZAW* 92 (1980) 289–91. **Vicchio, Stephen J.** *Job in the Modern World*. Eugene, OR: Wipf & Stock, 2006. 92–95.

Cathlin, Léon (French poet, 1882–1963). *Les treize paroles du pauvre Job. Le paludéen de Salonique. La terre sonne et autres proses de ténèbres et de guerre*. Paris: Perrin, 1920.

Centeno Güell, Fernando (Costa Rican poet, 1907–1993). *Las danzas de Job: Poema coreográfico, en un prólogo, tres movimientos y un epílogo*. San José: Editorial Costa Rica, 1977.

Chaucer, Geoffrey (English author, c. 1343–1400). *The Canterbury Tales.* 4.932–34. *The Wife of Bath's Tale.* 3.433–36. See also **Astell, Ann W.** "Job's Wife, Walter's Wife, and the Wife of Bath." In *Old Testament Women in Western Literature.* Ed. Raymond-Jean Frontain and Jan Wojcik. Conway, AR: UCA Press, 1991. 92–107. ———. "Translating Job as Female" [Gregory's Moralia in Job and Chaucer's Patient Griselda]. In *Translation Theory and Practice in the Middle Ages.* Ed. Jeanette Beer. Kalamazoo, MI: Western Michigan University Press, 1997. 59–69. **Shaw, Harry B.** *Similarities between The Clerk's Tale and The Book of Job.* Diss. Illinois State University at Normal, 1965.

Claudel, Paul (French poet and dramatist, 1868–1955). "Réponse à Job." In his *Oeuvres complètes.* Paris: Gallimard, 1952. 2:373–74. See also **Espiau de la Maestre, André.** "Hiob und die Claudelsche Anthropodizee." In his *Das göttliche Abenteuer. Paul Claudel und sein Werk.* Salzburg: O. Müller, 1968. 258–75. ———. "Job et le problème du mal dans l'oeuvre de Claudel." In *Entretiens sur Paul Claudel.* Ed. Georges Cattaui and Jacques Madaule. Paris: Mouton, 1969. 301–27. **Steinwendtner, Brita.** *Hiobs Klage heute: Die biblische Gestalt in der Literatur des 20. Jahrhunderts.* Innsbruck: Tyrolia-Verlag, 1990. 63–96. **Van den Heede, Philippe.** "La présence de Job et Qohélet dans 'Tête d'Or' de Paul Claudel." *RTL* 31 (2000) 362–93.

Cremer, Drutmar (German writer and theologian, b. 1930). "Tränen aus Herzmitte." In *Dein Atemzug holt Zeiten heim: Gedichte zu Bildern der Bibel von Marc Chagall, mit biblischen Texten und Hinweisen.* Limburg: Lahn-Verlag, 1984. 69–72.

Cruchaga Santa María, Angel (Chilean poet, 1893–1964). *Job: poema.* 1922. Santiago de Chile: Editorial Luz, 1933.

Curzon, David (Australian Jewish poet). "Job: A Summary." In his *Dovchik.* In *The Wild Life.* By David Curzon, Philip Hammial, Coral Hull, and Stephen Oliver. Ringwood, Victoria: Penguin Books, 1996. 102–3.

Cynewulf (c. 9th cent.). *The Ascension (Christ II).* Exeter Book, fol. 14a–20b. See **S. A. J. Bradley (ed. and trans.).** *Anglo-Saxon Poetry: An Anthology of Old English Poems in Prose Translation with Introduction and Headnotes.* London: Dent, 1982.

Dante Alighieri (Florentine poet, 1265–1321). See **Baur, Gustav Adolf Ludwig.** *Das Buch Hiob und Dantes Göttliche Komödie. Eine Parallele.* Giessen, 1850 [= *TSK* 29 (1856) 583–652].

David, Jakob Julius (Austrian Jewish poet, 1859–1906). "Hiob." In *Gesammelte Werke.* Ed. Ernst Heilborn and Erich Schmidt. Munich, Leipzig: Piper, 1908. 1:68–71 [= *Die Bibel im deutschen Gedicht des 20. Jahrhunderts. Unvergängliches Gedankengut der Bibel in der Sprache zeitgenössischer deutscher Dichter.* Ed. Hermann Hakel. Basel: B. Schwabe, 1958. 50–52].

Delogu, I. (Italian poet). "Racconto di Giobbe e della maga" [poem]. *La grotta della vipera: Rivista trimestrale di cultura* 75 (Summer 1996).

Desportes, Philippe (French poet, 1546–1606). *Poesies chrestiennes.* Paris. 1598 [including 'Plainte de l'Autheur durant une sienne longue maladie']. See also **Pensec, H.** "Philippe Desportes' Poésies chrestiennes and the Book of Job." *Res publica litterarum* 6 (1983) 265–73.

Diamond, Leon. "Job, Man of Uz" [poem]. *Judaism* 29 (1980) 432–39.

Dickinson, Emily (US poet, 1830–1886). See **Herndon, Jerry A.** "A Note on Emily Dickinson and Job." *ChrLit* 30 (1981) 45–52.

Domin, Hilde (pseudonym of Hilde Palm, German lyric poet, 1909–2002). "Lieder zur Ermutigung III." In her *Gesammelte Gedichte.* Frankfurt a.M.: S. Fischer, 1987. 223.

Donne, John (English metaphysical poet, 1572–1631). See **Duclow, Donald F.** "Into the Whirlwind of Suffering: Resistance and Transformation" [on Job, A. Camus, *The Plague,* J. Donne, *Devotion*]. *Second Opinion* 9 (1998) 11–27. **Vicchio, Stephen J.** *Job in the Medieval World.* Eugene, OR: Wipf & Stock, 2006. 202–8.

Eliot, Thomas Stearns (US and British poet and author, 1888–1965). See **Moyle, Joanna.** *Towards a Common Style:* Four Quartets *and Biblical Wisdom Poetry.* Diss. Oxford, 2004.

Enriquez Basurto, Diego (Spanish playwright and poet, 17th cent.). See **Rauchwarger, Judith.** "Seventeenth-Century Epic, Diego Enriquez Basurto's El triumpho de la virtud y paciencia de Job." *Sef* 40 (1980) 99–119.

Enriquez Gómez, Antonio (Spanish dramatist and poet of Portuguese-Jewish origin, c. 1601–c. 1661). See **Rauchwarger, Judith.** "Antonio Enriquez Gómez: Epistolas tres de Job. A Matter of Racial Atavism?" *REJ* 138 (1979) 69–87.

Erskine, Ralph (Scottish minister and poet, 1685–1752). *Job's Hymns; or, A Book of Songs upon the Book of Job.* Glasgow, 1753.

Eschenbach, Wolfram von (German epic poet, 1170–1220). See **Gietmann, G.** *Parzival, Faust, Job und einige verwandte Dichtungen.* Klassische Dichter und Dichtungen 1. Freiburg i.Br.: Herder, 1887.

Espriu i Castelló, Salvador (Catalan poet, 1913–1985). See **Cornadó i Teixidó, Maria-Pau.** *The Influence of the Bible in the Work of Salvador Espriu* [Job, Qoheleth]. Diss. Universitat Autonoma de Barcelona, 1990. **Kulin, Katalin.** "The Myth of Job in the Works of Juan Carlos Onetti and Salvadore Espriu." In *Evolution of the Novel. Proceedings of the IXth Congress of the International Comparative Literature Association, Innsbruck, 1979.* Ed. Zoran Konstantinovic, Eva Kushner, and Béla Köpeczi. Innsbruck: Institut für Sprachwissenschaft der Universität Innsbruck, 1981. 397–402.

Fasel, Ida. "Hard Times for Job" [poem]. *Christianity and Literature* 48 (1998) 44.

Fritz, Walter Helmut (German poet, b. 1929). "Sie alle lesen." In *Mit einer Feder aus den Flügeln des Ikarus: Ausgewählte Gedichte und Prosagedichte.* Frankfurt a.M.: Fischer, 1989.

Frost, Robert (US poet, 1874–1963). *A Masque of Reason.* New York: Henry Holt, 1945. ———. *A Sequel to Job.* In *Complete Poems of Robert Frost.* New York: Holt, Rinehart & Winston, 1964. 600. See also **Labin, Linda L.** *The Whale and the Ash-Heap: Transfigurations of Jonah and Job in Modern American Fiction—Frost, MacLeish, and Vonnegut.* Diss. Kent State University, 1980. **Levenson, Jon Douglas.** *The Book of Job in Its Time and in the Twentieth Century.* Cambridge, MA: Harvard University Press, 1972. 55–70. **Matthews, Marjorie Swank.** *Issues and Answers in the Book of Job and Joban Issues and Answers in Three Twentieth Century Writers: Carl Jung, Robert Frost, and Archibald MacLeish.* Diss. Florida State University, 1976. **Stock, E.** "'Masque of Reason' and 'J. B.': Two Treatments of the Book of Job." *Modern Drama* 3 (1961) 378–86.

Gex, Amélie (Savoyard, French poet and writer, 1835–1883). *Feuilles mortes: Job, Pages vécues, Poèmes satiriques, Ibo!* Chambéry: Ménard, 1894.

Glawischnig, Gerhard (Austrian poet, b. 1906). *Und morgen wird Hiob anders heissen: Gedichte.* Vienna: Bergland Verlag, 1963.

Goethe, Johann Wolfgang von (German writer and poet, 1749–1832). *Faust: der Tragödie erster Teil.* 1808. Rev. 1828–1829. *Faust: der Tragödie zweiter Teil.* 1832. See also **Adler, Lazar.** "Das Buch Hiob und Göthes Faust oder Über Optimismus und Pessimismus." In his *Zwei Vorträge zur Förderung der Humanität.* Kassel: Klaunig, 1876. **Alt, Carl.** "Der Gedanke der Theodicee in Goethes Faust." *Preussische Jahrbücher* 108 (1902) 112–24. **Biese, Alfred.** "Prometheus, Hiob und Faust." *Allgemeine Zeitung* 8.11.1883. **Carrière, Ludwig.** "Satan, Mephisto und die 'Wetten' bei Hiob und 'Faust'." *Goethe: Neue Folge des Jahrbuchs der Goethe-Gesellschaft* 20 (1958) 285–87. **Durrani, Osman.** *Faust and the Bible: A Study of Goethe's Use of Scriptural Allusions and Christian Religious Motifs in Faust I and II.* Europäische Hochschulschriften. Reihe I, Deutsche Literatur und Germanistik 208. Frankfurt a.M.: Peter Lang, 1977. **Gensichen, Martin.** "Hiob und Faust. Eine Parallele, Vortrag." *Evangelische Kirchenzeitung* 1 (1889) 15–17; 3 (1889) 45–50; 5 (1889) 91–96; 6 (1889) 11–114. **Gietmann, G.** *Parzival, Faust, Job und einige verwandte Dichtungen.* Freiburg i.Br.: Herder, 1887. **Hebensperger, Johann Nepomuk.** "Faust's Mephistopheles und der Satan Jobs." *Neues Abendland* (Augsburg) 2/4 (1947) 103–7. **Jauss, Hans Robert.** "Job's Questions and Their Distant Reply: Goethe, Nietzsche, Heidegger." *Comparative Literature* 34 (1982) 193–207 [= "Hiobs Fragen und ihre ferne Antwort: Goethe, Nietzsche, Heidegger." *Poetica* 13 (1981) 1–15]. **Landsberger, Julius.** *Das Buch Hiob und Goethes Faust.* Darmstadt: G. Jonghaus, 1882. **Levi, Raphael.** "Faust und Hiob." *Nord und Süd* 37 (1913) 82–96. **Matenko, Percy, and Samuel Sloan.** *Two Studies in Yiddish Culture.* I. *The Aqedath Jishaq: A Sixteenth Century Yiddish Epic.* II. *Job and Faust: A Study and Translation of Ch. Zhitlowsky's Essay by Percy Matenko.* Leiden: E. J. Brill, 1968. 75–162. **Melzer, Friso.** "Faust und Hiob." *Neubau* (Munich) 1 (1946) 194–96. **Meynert, Hermann.** "Faust und Hiob." *Die Dioskuren* 24 (1894) 35–44. **Muenzer, Clark S.** "Das Buch 'Hiob' und Goethes Naturbegriff." In *Goethe und die Bibel.* Arbeiten zur Geschichte und Wirkung der Bibel 6. Ed. Johannes Anderegg and Edith Anna Kunz. Stuttgart: Deutsche Bibelgesellschaft, 2005. 161–71. **Oettingen, Herbert von.** *Gott in der Faust? Ein Versuch, der bibellesenden Gemeinde das Buch Hiob verständlich und lebendig zu machen.* Neukirchen Kreis Moers: Buchhandlung des Erziehungsvereins, c. 1935. **Petsch, Robert.** "Faust und Hiob." *Chronik der Wiener Goethe-Vereins* 20/3 (1906) 13–16. **Rhoades, Winfred Chesney.** "Job and Faust." *MethRev* 85 (1903) 373–87. **Schlossmacher, Joseph.** "Goethes Faust und das Buch Hiob." *Deutsches Heim* (Berlin) 8 (1884) 252–53. **Schrader, Hans-Jürgen.** "'Hiob' in deutscher Dichtung ('Faust'–Joseph Roth–Lyrik nach der Schoah) Muster des Menschen–des jüdischen Leids–der Frage nach Theodizee." In *Religio in litteris: Vier Interpretationen deutscher Dichtung zwischen Aufklärung und Moderne in ihrer Beziehung zum Religiösen.* Vorträge anlässlich des 70. Geburtstags von Dr. Rudolf Mohr im Rahmen der Jahrestagung 2003 des Vereins für Rheinische Kirchengeschichte. Bonn: R. Habelt, [2004]. 1–32. ———. "Modell des Menschen: Hiob im Goetheschen 'Faust'." *Colloquium helveticum* 34 (2003) 159–91. **Schütze, Alfred.** "Ein Vorläufer der Faustgestalt." *Die Kommenden* (Freiburg i.Br.) 1/19 (1947) 3–4. **Van der Laan, James M.** "Job Retold." In his *Seeking Meaning in Goethe's Faust.* London: Continuum, 2007. **Zhitlowsky, C. [Zitlobsqi, Hajjim].** *Job and Faust. Translated with Introduction and Notes by P. Matenko.* Leiden: Brill, 1966 [= "Job and Faust." *Die Zukunft* (1919)].

Goll, Yvan (German poet and writer, 1891–1950). "Hiob, erste Fassung. Hiobs Revolte"; "Hiob" [zweite Fassung]. In his *Dichtungen: Lyrik, Prosa, Drama.* Darmstadt: H. Luchterhand, 1960. 372–39, 588. See also **Berg, Phyllis.** *Jüdische Themen und das Hiob-Schicksal im Werke Yvan Golls.* Diss. Cincinnati, 1976. **Schwandt, Erhard.** "Mythische Selbstdarstellung in der Lyrik Yvan Golls. Der neue Orpheus, Jean sans Terre, Hiob." *Colloquia germanica* 4 (1970) 232–47.

Graves, Michael P. "Job the Rhetor" [poem]. *ChrCent* 109 (1992) 455.

Gryphius, Christian (German poet, 1649–1706). *Aus den Worten Hiobs XXV.4.* In his *Poetische Wälder.* Frankfurt, 1698. 56–57.

Günther, Johann Christian (German poet, 1695–1723). See **Stenzel, Jürgen.** "Ein anderer Hiob. Johann Christian Günthers Klagegedicht 'Als er durch innerlichen Trost bey der Ungedult gestarket wurde'." In *Gedichte und Interpretationen.* Ed. Volker Meid. Stuttgart: Reclam, 1982. 1:405–14.

Gütersloh, Albert Paris (Austrian poet, 1887–1973). "Spruch des Hiobs"; "Des neuen Hiob Klage." In *Musik zu einem Lebenslauf: Gedichte.* Vienna: Bergland Verlag, 1957. 68.

Gutl, Martin (Austrian poet, 1940–1994). *Der tanzende Hiob.* Graz: Styria, 1981.

Habchi, Sobhi (Lebanese poet and critic, living in France, b. 1948). *Au nom de Job.* Poètes des cinq continents 229. Paris: l'Harmattan, 1999.

Hajnal, Gábor (Hungarian poet, 1912–1987). "Job bin nich." In *Gedichte und Nachdichtungen.* Ed. Franz Fühmann. Rostock: Hinstorff Verlag, 1978. 261.

Heine, Heinrich (German poet, 1797–1856). "Hebräische Melodien." Book 3 of *Romanzero.* In his *Sämtliche Werke.* Ed. H. Kaufmann. Munich: Kindler, 1964. 3:117–64. See also **Ellermeier, Friedrich.** "Randbemerkung zur Kunst des Zitierens: welches Buch der Bibel nannte Heinrich Heine das Hohelied der Skepsis?" *ZAW* 77 (1965)

93–94. Eörsi, István. *Hiob und Heine: Passagiere im Niemandsland.* Trans. Gregor Mayer. Klagenfurt: Wieser, 1999 [= *Utasok a senkiföldjén: Jóbok könyve.* Budapest: Palatinus, 1998]. **Kraft, Werner.** "Heine und die Hiobsfrage." In his *Augenblicke der Dichtung.* Munich: Kösel, 1964. 41–45. **Neuss, Christina.** "Heines Verhältnis zum Tod als Schlüssel zur Interpretation der 'Lazarus'—Gedichte—sein Weg von Lazarus zu Hiob." *Berliner theologische Zeitschrift* 13 (1996) 111–32.

Henisch, Peter (Austrian writer, b. 1943). *Hamlet, Hiob, Heine: Gedichte.* Salzburg: Residenz-Verlag, 1989. 66–94. ———. *Mir selbst auf der Spur/Hiob. Gedichte.* Baden, Vienna: Grasl, 1977. 143–65. See also **Steinwendtner, Brita.** *Hiobs Klage heute: Die biblische Gestalt in der Literatur des 20. Jahrhunderts.* Innsbruck: Tyrolia-Verlag, 1990. 63–96.

Herder, Johann Gottfried von (German philosopher and poet, 1744–1803). *Vom Geist der Ebräischen Poesie. Eine Anleitung für die Liebhaber derselben, und der ältesten Geschichte des menschlichen Geistes.* Dessau, 1782–83 [= *The Spirit of Hebrew Poetry.* Trans. James Marsh. Burlington, VT: Edward Smith, 1833; Dialogue IV, pp. 80–98, is reprinted as "God and Nature in the Book of Job" in *The Dimensions of Job: A Study and Selected Readings.* Ed. Nahum H. Glatzer. New York: Schocken Books, 1969. 141–56]. See also **Mertin, Jörg.** *Hiob—religionsphilosophisch gelesen: Rezeptionsgeschichtliche Untersuchungen zur Hioblektüre Herders, Kants, Hegels, Kierkegaards und zu ihrer Bedeutung für die Hiobexegese des 18. und 19. Jahrhunderts.* Diss. Paderborn, 1991. **Vicchio, Stephen J.** *Job in the Modern World.* Eugene, OR: Wipf & Stock, 2006. 82–86.

Holz, Joseph Michael. *'Iyov be-derek shir* [Yiddish]. Zloczów [Zolochiv], Ukraine: Hamhaber, 1904.

Jerome, Judson (US writer and poet, 1927–1991). *Jonah and Job: Two Poems and an Afterword.* Santa Barbara, CA: J. Daniel, 1991.

Kaléko, Miguel. "Enkel Hiobs." *Aufbau* 6 (1940/1) 1.

Kate, Jan Jacob Lodewijk ten (Dutch theologian and poet, 1819–1889). *De jobeïde: het boek Job in nederduitschen dichtform overgebracht en toegelicht.* 2nd ed. Leiden: Sijthoff, 1869 [= *Das Buch Hiob: ein Kreuz- und Trostbuch.* Trans. F. W. S. Schwarz. Bremen: Müller, 1868].

Klabund (Alfred Henschke, German poet, 1891–1928). *Gesammelte Gedichte: Lyrik, Balladen, Chansons.* Vienna: Phaidon, 1930.

Klopstock, Friedrich Gottlieb (German poet, 1724–1803). *Der Messias.* Vienna, 1751–56 [= *The Messiah. Attempted from the German.* Trans. Joseph Collyer. London, 1763]. See also **Vicchio, Stephen J.** *Job in the Ancient World.* Eugene, OR: Wipf & Stock, 2006. 244–45.

Koch, W. "Dein Zeitbruder Hiob." In *3 Stasi-Haftpoeme.* Hamburg: Europrint, 1992.

Köster [Koester], Hans. *Hiob. Episches Gedicht in zwölf Gesängen. Die Bergpredigt. Biblische Idyll in fünf Gesängen.* Bielefeld: Velhagen & Klasing, 1885. 360

Kunert, Günter (German writer, b. 1929). *Unterwegs nach Utopia: Gedichte.* Munich: Hanser, 1977.

Lamartine, Alphonse de (French poet and politician, 1790–1869). "Job lu dans le désert." In his *Philosophie et littérature.* Paris: A. Lemerre, 1894. ———. *Cours familier de littérature.* Paris, 1856–69. 2:441. See also **Vicchio, Stephen J.** *Job in the Modern World.* Eugene, OR: Wipf & Stock, 2006. 89–90.

Lauwaert, Guido. *Job en Jaweh: een poëtische monoloog naar het Boek Job uit de Bijbel.* Antwerp: Soethoudt, 1977.

Le Cordier, Hélie (Normandy poet, 17th cent.). *L'illustre souffrant ou Job: poëme.* Paris: Jean Cochart, 1667.

Leivick, Halper (Yiddish writer, 1886–1962). *In di leg fun Job. Dramatishe Poeme.* New York: Grenich Printing Corporation, 1953.

Leonhard, Rudolf (German poet and writer, 1889–1953). "Furunkulose." In his *Ausgewählte Werke in Einzelausgaben.* Berlin: Verlag der Nation, 1961. 1:191.

Leopardi, Giacomo (Italian poet, 1798–1837). See **Marcon, Loretta.** *La notte oscura dell'anima: Giobbe e Leopardi.* Naples: Guida, 2005. **Niccoli, Elena, and Brunetto**

Salvarani. *In difesa di "Giobbe e Salomon": Leopardi e la Bibbia.* Il castello di Atlante 14. Reggio Emilia: Diabasis, 1988.

Lienhard, Hermann (Austrian poet, b. 1922). "Hiob." In his *Die Verwandlung: Gedichte.* Klagenfurt: Kleinmayr, 1948.

Lomonosov, Mikhail Vasilevich (Russian writer and educationist, 1711–1765). "Ode from the Book of Job." Trans. Dean Furbish. *Metamorphoses: A Journal of Literary Translation* 6 (April, 1998) 2, 96.

Lydgate, John (monk and poet, Bury St Edmunds, c. 1370–c. 1451). *Story of Holy Job, The.* Also *The Life of Holy Job.* See Henry N. McCracken. "Lydgatiana, the Life of Holy Job." *Archiv für das Studium der neuern Sprachen* ns 26, 65 (1911) 365.

Marti, Kurt (Swiss poet and pastor, b. 1921). "ich habe die guten tage genossen." In *Leichenreden.* Darmstadt: Luchterhand, 1969. 36–37.

Merezhkovsky, Dmitry Sergeyevich (Russian symbolist poet, 1865–1941). *Sobranie stikhov, 1883–1910: Selected Poems.* Letchworth: Bradda Books, 1969 [orig. St Petersburg, 1910].

Milton, John (English poet, 1608–1674). See **Budick, Sanford.** "Milton's Joban Phoenix in *Samson Agonistes.*" *Early Modern Literary Studies* 11/2 (2005) 5.1–15. **Fisch, Harold.** "Creation in Reverse: The Book of Job and Paradise Lost." In *Milton and Scriptural Tradition: The Bible into Poetry.* Ed. James H. Sims and Leland Ryken. Columbia: University of Missouri Press, 1984. 104–16. **Fulton, Pauline Robinson.** *Milton's Use of the Book of Job in "Paradise Regained" and "Samson Agonistes."* Diss. University of North Carolina, 1984. **Lewalski, Barbara Kiefer.** *Milton's Brief Epic: The Genre, Meaning, and Art of 'Paradise Regained.'* Providence, RI: Brown University Press, 1966. **Steadman, John M.** "Eyelids of the Morn: A Biblical Convention" [use in Milton]. *HTR* 56 (1963) 159–67. **Teunissen, John James.** *Of Patience and Heroic Martyrdom. The Book of Job and Milton's Conception of Patient Suffering in "Paradise Regained" and "Samson Agonistes."* Diss. Rochester, 1967. **Vicchio, Stephen J.** *Job in the Modern World.* Eugene, OR: Wipf & Stock, 2006. 42–59.

Modlmayr, Jörg (Austrian poet). *Hiob immer: Gedichte 1941–1946.* Hopfen am See: Ed. Margaretha Modlmayr, 1978.

Mok, Maurits (Dutch poet, 1907–1989). *Job: een tragedie.* Amsterdam: Athenaeum-Polak en Van Gennep, 1969. ———. "Met Job geleefd." 1972. In his *Gedichten van zestig tot zeventig.* Amsterdam: De Bezige Bij, 1977.

Monaco, Giuseppe (Italian poet, 17th cent.). *L' Eustachio ouero Il secondo Giobbe. Poema sagro.* Naples: Carlo Porsile, 1692.

Montale, Eugenio (Italian poet, 1896–1981). "Per un nuovo Giobbe." *La Stampa,* December 31, 1988.

Morse, Kenneth I. "Whisper and Word" [poem]. *Brethren Life and Thought* 5 (1960) 2.

Müller, Johann Wilhelm. *Hiob. Dramatisches Gedicht.* Braunschweig: Westermann; New Orleans: L. Schwarz, 1850.

Nesson, Pierre de (French poet, 1383–1473). "Paraphrase des IX leçons de Job." In *Pierre de Nesson et ses oeuvres. Documents artistiques du XVe siècle.* Ed. A. Piaget and E. Droz. Paris: G. Jeanbin, 1925 [= Geneva: Slatkine, 1977]. 20–25. ———. *Les vigiles des morts (XVe s.).* Ed. Alain Collet. Paris: Champion, 2002. See also **Collet, Alain.** "La cause de l'homme: le recours au Livre de Job dans les Vigiles des morts de Pierre de Nesson." In *Le recours à l'Ecriture: polémique et conciliation du XVe siècle au XVIIe siècle.* Ed. M.-J. Louison-Lassablière. Saint-Etienne: Publications de l'Université de Saint-Etienne, 2000. 139–49.

Ohse, Traugott. *Hiob: Ein Gedichtzyklus. Mit Holzschnitte von Peter Opitz.* Berlin: Evangelische Verlag-Anstalt, 1959.

Pagis, Dan (Israeli poet, 1930–1986). *Erdichter Mensch. Gedichte hebräisch/deutsch. Aus dem Hebräischen übertragen und mit einem Nachwort versehen von Tuvia Rübner.* Frankfurt a.M.: Jüdischer Verlag, 1993. 84–85. ———. *An beiden Ufern der Zeit. Ausgewählte Gedichte und Prosa hebräisch-deutsch. Aus dem Hebräischen übertragen von Anne Birkenhauer.* Straelen: Straelener Manuskript Verlag, 2003.

Prudentius, Aurelius (Roman Christian poet, 348–c. 413). *Psychomachia.* PL 60:11–90.

Pushkin, Alexander Sergeyevich (Russian poet, 1799–1837). See Yureva, I. Y. "The Book of Job in Pushkin Writings." *Russkaia literatura* 1 (1995) 184–88 [Russian].

Quarles, Francis (English poet, 1592–1644). *Iob Militant: With Meditations Diuine and Morall.* London, 1624 [= "Job Militant." In his *Divine Poems: Containing the History of Ionah, Ester, Iob, Sampson: Sions Sonets, Elegies.* London, 1642].

Rapisardi, Mario (Sicilian poet and author, 1844–1912). "Il Giobbe" [poem]. In *Opere.* IV. Catania: N. Giannotta, 1896.

Rennert, Jürgen (German poet, b. 1943). "Hiobs Botschaft." In *Dialog mit der Bibel: Malerei und Grafik aus der DDR zu biblischen Themen.* Stuttgart: Kreuz, 1986 [= *Verlorene Züge.* Norderstedt: Books on Demand, 2001].

Riedel, Franz Xaver (Austrian poet, 1738–1773). *Das Buch Hiob in zwölf Gesängen.* Pressburg, 1779.

Rietmann, J. J. *Hiob oder Das alte Leid im neuen Liede.* St Gallen: Huber, 1843.

Rosenthal, Fritz [Schalom Ben-Chorin] (German Jewish philosopher and writer, 1913–1999). *Das Mal der Sendung: der Lieder des ewigen Brunnens neue Folge.* Munich: Heller, 1935. 10.

Rothenfelder, Franz. *Der Mann den Gott schlug: Verse zum Buche Hiob.* Berlin [privately printed], 1928.

Sachs, Nelly (German Jewish poet and playwright, living in Sweden, 1891–1970). "O die Schornsteine," "Hiob," "Landschaft aus Schreien." In *Fahrt ins Staublose: Die Gedichte der Nelly Sachs.* Frankfurt a.M.: Suhrkamp, 1961. ———. "Job" [poem]. In *Eclipse of the Stars.* Trans. Michael Hamburger et al. In Abba Kovner and Nelly Sachs, *Selected Poems.* Harmondsworth: Penguin, 1971. 91. See also **Kuschel, Karl-Josef.** "Hiob und Jesus. Die Gedichte der Nelly Sachs als theologische Herausforderung." *Stimmen der Zeit* 211 (1993) 804–18. **Lenzen, Verena.** "Hiob–'O Du Windrose der Qualen' (Nelly Sachs): Literarische Lesung." In *Leiden. 27. Internationaler Fachkongress für Moraltheologie und Sozialethik (September 1995, Köln/Bonn).* Ed. Gerhard Höver. Münster: Lit, 1997. 33–41. **Lermen, Birgit Johanna.** "Die Hiob-Gestalt in der Lyrik von Nelly Sachs." *TGegw* 32,1 (1989) 3–10. **Steinwendtner, Brita.** *Hiobs Klage heute: Die biblische Gestalt in der Literatur des 20. Jahrhunderts.* Innsbruck: Tyrolia-Verlag, 1990. 63–96.

Schacht, Ulrich (German writer, b. 1951). *Scherbenspur: Gedichte.* Zurich: Ammann, 1983.

Singu, Yesudasan. *Yobu caritramu: harikatha rupamu* [a Telugu harikatha in mixed verse and prose, on the biblical story of Job]. Candragiri, 1926.

Stanwood, Eunice H. (US poet). *The Story of Job, Showing the True Perfection Which God Requires Attainable on Earth.* Boston: McDonald, Gill & Co., 1885.

Susman, Margarete (Swiss Jewish philosopher and writer, 1872–1966). *Aus sich wandelnder Zeit: Gedichte.* Zurich: Diana Verlag, 1953. See also Susman, Margarete, in Section f.ii (Authors) above.

Telschow, Wilhelm (Polish poet, 1809–1872). "Hiob's Todesschauer." Set to music by Johann Karl Gottfried Loewe (1796–1869). "Hiob's Todessang," 1848.

Torga, Miguel [Adolfo Correia da Rocha] (Portuguese writer and poet, 1907–1995). *O outro livro de Job.* Coimbra: Coimbra Editora, 1936.

Trebosch, Tilo. "Fragen an Hiob." In his *Fragen an Hiob: Das Gottesbild in uns.* Munich: Schobert, 1986.

Turoldo, David Maria (Italian priest and poet, 1916–1992). *Gli occhi miei lo vedranno (Job., XIX, 27): Poesie.* Milan: A. Mondadori, 1955.

Untermeyer, Jean Starr (US poet, 1886–1970). *Job's Daughter.* New York: W. W. Norton, 1967.

Villon, François (French poet, 1431–1463). See **Sargent-Baur, Barbara Nelson.** *Brothers of Dragons: Job Dolens and François Villon.* Garland Monographs in Medieval Literature 3. New York: Garland Publishing, 1990.

Werfel, Franz (Austrian Jewish writer, 1890–1945). "Verwundeter Storch." In *Das lyrische Werk*. Frankfurt a.M.: Fischer, 1967. 234.

Wolfskehl, Karl (German Jewish poet and writer, emigré to New Zealand, 1869–1948). *Hiob, oder Die vier Spiegel. Gedichte*. Hamburg: Claassen-Verlag, 1950 [= *Gesammelte Werke. Dichtungen, Dramatische Dichtungen*. Ed. Margot Ruben and Klaus Victor Bock. Hamburg: Claassen-Verlag, 1960. 1:203–15]. See also **Berg, Phyllis.** *Das Hiobthema im Werke Karl Wolfkehls*. Diss. Cincinnati, 1970. **Grimm, Gunter.** *Karl Wolfskehl: Die Hiob-Dichtung*. Abhandlungen zur Kunst-, Musik- und Literaturwissenschaft 116. Bonn: Bouvier, 1972. **Jasper, Willi.** "Hiob und Ahasver: Karl Wolfskehl und Robert Neumann." In *Deutsch-jüdischer Parnass: Literaturgeschichte eines Mythos*. Ed. Willi Jasper. Berlin: Propyläen, 2004. 419–24. **Steinwendtner, Brita.** *Hiobs Klage heute: Die biblische Gestalt in der Literatur des 20. Jahrhunderts*. Innsbruck: Tyrolia-Verlag, 1990. 63–96.

Young, A. J. (Scottish poet and clergyman, 1885–1971). *The Adversary* [poem]. London: John G. Wilson, 1923.

Zeller, Eva (German poet and novelist, b. 1923). "Hiob." In *Sage und schreibe: Gedichte*. Stuttgart: Deutsche Verlagsanstalt, 1971.

ii. Drama

Adler, Leopold (b. 1850). *Das Buch Hiob. Schauspiel in einem Aufzug*. Leipzig: Reclam, 1891 [adapted from the play by Hermann Holtz; see also Willy Schäffer, *Das Buch Hiob*, in Section 8.i (Music)].

Andreyev, Leonid (Russian playwright, 1871–1919). *Anathema: A Tragedy in Seven Scenes*. Trans. Herman Bernstein. New York: Macmillan, 1910 [original, 1909].

Angioletti, Giovanni Battista (Italian writer, 1896–1961). *Giobbe, uomo solo* [drama]. Milan: Bompiani, 1955.

Anon. *Job. Ün drama engiadinais del XVI. secul. Nouvamaing publicho da Dr J. Ulrich* [drama in Romansch]. Chur: Societad Rhaetoromanscha. Annalas. 11 (1886).

Artoud, Antonin (French playwright, 1895–1948). See **Bochet, Marc.** *Présence de Job dans le théâtre d'après-guerre II en France*. Berne: Peter Lang, 1988. 52–56.

Aspenström, Werner (Swedish writer and dramatist, 1918–1997). *Stackars Job: en andlig revy*. Stockholm: Proprius, 1971 [= *Pauvre Job: théâtre*. Théâtre hors la France. Paris: P. J. Oswald, 1974].

Bailey, Loretto Carroll (US playwright, 20th cent.). *Job's Kinfolks, a Play of the Mill People in Three Acts*. Boston: Walter H. Baker, 1930.

Beckett, Samuel (Irish playwright and author, 1906–1989). *En attendant Godot*. Paris: Editions de Minuit, 1952 [=*Waiting for Godot: A Tragicomedy in Two Acts*. New York: Grove Press, 1954]. See also **Beckmann, Heinz.** *Godot oder Hiob: Glaubensfragen in der modernen Literatur*. Hamburg: Furche-Verlag, 1965. **Bochet, Marc.** "Beckett: La prostration de Belacqua." In his *Présence de Job dans le théâtre d'après-guerre II en France*. Berne: Peter Lang, 1988. 71–77. **Castagna, Edoardo.** *L'uomo di Uz: Giobbe e la letteratura del Novecento*. Milan: Medusa, 2007. 27–34. **Magny, Olivier de.** "Samuel Beckett ou Job abandonné." *Monde nouveau-paru* 97 (Feb. 1956) 91–99.

Bertaut (Bertault), François (French playwright, 17th cent.). *Le jugement de Job et d'Uranie* [comedy]. 1653. In *Petites comédies rares et curieuses du XVIIe siècle*. I. Ed. Victor Fournel. Paris: A. Quantin, 1884.

Bertesius, Johann (German dramatist, 1598–1606). *Hiob: Tragicomoedia. Ein schön newes geistliches spiel, darinnen der Gedult ein sondermercklich Exempel wird fürgestellet*. Erfurt, 1603.

Biale, Noam, Daveed Diggs, and Ben Watson-Lamprey. *The Book of Job, by God!* 2002. Production Workshop, Brown University.

Billetdoux, François (French playwright and novelist, 1927–1991). *Comment va le monde, môssieu? Il tourne, môssieu! etc.: Comédie en quatre actes*. Paris, 1964 [= *Comment va le monde, môssieu? Il tourne, môssieu: Comédie*. Paris: Actes Sud-Papiers, 1990]. See also

Bochet, Marc. "Billetdoux: Le monde comme il va." *Présence de Job dans le théâtre d'après-guerre II en France.* Berne: Peter Lang, 1988. 95–99.

Borchert, Wolfgang (German author and playwright, 1921–1947). *Draussen vor der Tür: Ein Stück, das kein Theater spielen und kein Publikum sehen will* [radio and stage play, first performed 1947]. Hamburg: Rowohlt, 1948 [chamber opera by Xaver Paul Thoma, 1994].

Calderón de la Barca y Henao, Pedro (Spanish Golden Age dramatist, 1600–1681). "El príncipe constante." 1629. In *Autos sacramentales completos de Calderón: edición crítica.* Ed. Ignacio Arellano and Ángel L. Cilveti. Pamplona: Universidad de Navarra, 1992.

Chanceral, Léon. "Job 1941." In *Répertoire des Comédiens routiers.* 2nd ed. Paris: La Hutte, 1941. See also **Dorcy, Jean.** *A la rencontre de la mime et des mimes Decroux, Barrault, Marceau. Suivi de textes inédits.* Neuilly-sur-Seine: Cahiers de danse et culture, 1958.

Gignoux, Hubert. *Histoire d'une famille théatrale: Jacques Copeau–Léon Chancerel: les comédiens-routiers, la décentralisation dramatique.* Lausanne: Editions de l'Aire, 1984.

Chartreux, Bernard (French dramatist, b. 1942). *Un homme pressé: d'après le livre de Job. Théâtrales.* Paris: Edilig, 1987.

Clements, Colin C. (US playwright). *Job: A Play in One Act.* New York: Samuel French, 1923.

Corey, Orlin. *The Book of Job Arranged for Stage.* Anchorage, KY: Children's Theatre Press, [1960].

Création Avignon. *Le Livre de Job* [drama]. Avignon, 1997.

Debluë, Henri (Swiss dramatist, 1924–1988). *La passion de Job: drame.* Vevey: Editions B. Galland, 1981.

Dunning, Alfred. *Job: A Dramatic Version.* London, 1928.

Eggers, Kurt (National Socialist author, 1905–1943). *Das Spiel von Job dem Deutschen: Ein Mysterium.* Berlin-Südende: Volkschaft-Verlag für Buch, Bühne und Film, 1933.

Eörsi, István (Hungarian poet and author, 1931–2005). *Hiob proben* [drama]. Trans. Hans Skirecki. Frankfurt a. M.: Verlag der Autoren, 1999.

Faure, Alexander. *Hiob: Ein biblisches Spiel.* Münchener Laienspiele 23. Munich: Kaiser, 1926. 2nd ed. 1936.

Ferguson, John. *Job* [a play, in verse]. Proscenium Plays. London: Epworth, 1961.

Fontana, Oskar Maurus (Austrian playwright and author, 1889–1969). *Hiob der Verschwender: Komödie.* Leipzig: Schauspiel-Verlag, 1925.

Forsyth, James. See **Dunkel, Wilbur D.** "Theology in the Theater" [recent Broadway plays by A. MacLeish, J. Forsyth, G. Greene, E. O'Neill, and others]. *TTod* 16 (1959) 65–73.

Geiger, Hannsludwig. *Ein Mensch wie Hiob.* Spiele der Zeit 141. Munich: Kaiser, 1960.

Gelber, S. Michael. *Job Stands Up: The Biblical Text of the Book of Job Arranged for the Theater.* New York: Union of American Hebrew Congregations, 1975.

Ghéon, Henri. "Job: Tragédie biblique en trois actes." *La vie intellectuelle* 5/19 (1933) 38–67, 318–37.

Godínez, Felipe (Spanish dramatist, 1588–1637). *La gran comedia de los trabajos de Job.* Barcelona: Jayme Romeu, 1638. Edition: *Felipe Godínez: Aún de noche alumbra el sol. Los trabajos de Job.* Ed. Piedad Bolaños Donoso and Pedro M. Piñero Ramírez. Teatro del siglo de oro. Ediciones críticas 27. Kassel: Reichenberger, 1991.

Goetz [Götz], Kurt (Swiss-German writer, actor and director, 1888–1960). *Dr. med. Hiob Prätorius, Facharzt für Chirurgie und Frauenleiden: eine Geschichte ohne Politik, nach alten, aber guten Motiven neuerzählt.* Rostock: Carl Hinstorff, 1951. See also in Section k.ii (Film), Curt Goetz, Carl Hoffmann, and Joseph L. Mankiewicz.

Grüb, Willy (German playwright, 1912–1998). *"Ich heisse Hiob": Eine Komödie in 3 Akten.* Donaueschingen: Rohrbacher, 1949.

Grumberg, Jean-Claude (French playwright, b. 1939). *Sortie de théâtre, suivi de Une vie de "On," Un nouveau Job, Bon saint Etienne priez pour nous, Mystère de Noël et du Jour de l'an.* Arles: Actes Sud, 2000.

Haecker, Hans-Joachim (German writer, 1910–1994). *Hiob: Ein Spiel von Adams und Evas Schuld, von Hiobs Heimsuchung und der Auferstehung des Herrn.* Berlin: Furche-Verlag, 1937.

Haerten, Theodor (National Socialist dramatist and writer, 1898–1968). *Die Hochzeit von Dobesti: Ein Drama.* Berlin: Bondi, 1937] [= Bücherei der dramatischen Dichtung 6. Berlin: Langen & Müller, 1939].

Haranburu Altuna, Luis (Basque dramatist, b. 1947). *Job.* Donostia: Kriselu, 1975.

Henneman, Annet (director). *La pazienza di Giobbe.* Secondo spettacolo del progetto Teatro Reportage sul popolo Kurdo. Teatro Nazionale d'Arte della Toscana, 2000.

Henz, Rudolf (Austrian poet and playwright, 1897–1987). "Herr Job." In his *Tollhaus Welt: Fünf neue Dramen.* Vienna: Österreichische Verlagsanstalt, 1970.

Hilbert, Jaroslav (Czech dramatist and writer, 1871–1936). *Job: Hra o trech dejstvích.* Prague: ĝeskomoravské podniky tisk. a vydav., 1928.

Hochhuth, Rolf (German playwright, b. 1931). See **Freiman-Morris, Sarah.** "Faust and Job in Rolf Hochhuth's *The Deputy.*" *LitTheol* 21,2 (2007) 214–26.

Horne, R. H. *Bible Tragedies* [in prose and verse]. *John the Baptist; or, the Valour of the Soul* [in two acts]. *Rahman. The Apocryphal Book of Job's Wife. Judas Iscariot, a Mystery* [in two acts]. London: Newman & Co., 1881.

Icard, Renaud (French playwright, 1886–1971). *Théâtre inédit: Job.* Marseille: Les Cahiers du Sud, 1941.

Ionesco, Eugène (Romanian and French playwright and dramatist, 1909–1994). See **Bochet, Marc.** "Ionesco: L'enlisement dans la vase et les débris du souvenir." In his *Présence de Job dans le théâtre d'après-guerre II en France.* Berne: Peter Lang, 1988. 65–70.

Kafka, Franz (Czech writer, 1883–1924). See **Bochet, Marc.** *Présence de Job dans le théâtre d'après-guerre II en France.* Berne: Peter Lang, 1988. 43–52. **Friedman, Maurice S.** *Problematic Rebel: An Image of Modern Man.* New York: Random House, 1963; revised ed. *Problematic Rebel: Melville, Dostoievsky, Kafka, Camus.* Chicago: University of Chicago Press, 1970.

Kokoschka, Oskar (Austrian artist and writer, 1886–1980). *Sphinx und Strohmann.* 1907. Reissued as *Hiob.* 1917 [= "Job, a Drama." In *An Anthology of German Expressionist Drama.* Ed. W. H. Sokel. New York: Anchor, 1963. 159–71]. ———. *Vier Dramen: Orpheus und Eurydike; Der brennende Dornbusch; Mörder, Hoffnung der Frauen; Hiob.* Berlin: P. Cassirer, 1919 [= *Schrei und Bekenntnis. Expressionistisches Theater.* Ed. Karl Otten. Darmstadt: Hermann Luchterhand, 1959. 466–83]. See also **Denkler, Horst.** "Textvarianten zwischen der Erstausgabe und der Ausgabe letzter Hand des Dramas 'Hiob' von Oskar Kokoschka—Ein Nachtrag." *Deutsche Vierteljahrsschrift für Literaturwissenschaft und Geistesgeschichte* 42 (1968) 303–5. **Kerr, Alfred.** "Oskar Kokoschka: 'Der brennende Dornbusch'—'Hiob'." In *Mit Schleuder und Harfe: Theaterkritiken aus drei Jahrzehnten.* Berlin: Henschelverlag, 1981. 154–59. **Schvey, Henry I.** *Oskar Kokoschka: The Painter as Playwright.* Detroit: Wayne State University Press, 1982. 67–88, 145–50. **Steinwendtner, Brita.** *Hiobs Klage heute: Die biblische Gestalt in der Literatur des 20. Jahrhunderts.* Innsbruck: Tyrolia-Verlag, 1990. 7–36.

Lanner, Alois. *Job: Ein biblisches Drama in 5 Akten.* Breslau: Aderholz, 1913. ———. *Job, ein biblisches Drama.* Innsbruck: Vereinsbuchhandlung und Buchdruckerei, 1925.

Lauckner, Rolf (German playwright and poet, 1887–1954). "Hiob." In his *Gesammelte Werke.* Darmstadt: Stichnote, 1952. 303–62.

Laya, Leon (French playwright, 1811–1872). *Le duc Job: comédie en quatre actes et en prose.* Paris: Lévy, 1860.

Leroux, Pierre (French philosopher, 1797–1871). *Job, drame en cinq actes, avec prologue et épilogue, par le prophète Isaie, retrouvé, rétabli dans son integrité, et traduit littéralement* *sur le texte hébreu.* With Appendix, "Le Job des Eglises, et le Job de M. Renan" (pp. 201–389). Grasse, Paris: E. Dentu, 1866.

Levin, Hanoch (Israeli dramatist, 1943–1999). "The Sorrows of Job." In *Modern Israeli Drama in Translation.* Ed. Michael Taub. Portsmouth, NH: Heinemann, 1993 [= *The Sorrows of Job.* Tel-Aviv: Hebrew Book Club, c. 1980]. See also **Caspi, Zahava.** "Sources of Pleasure in the Theatre of Hanoch Levin." *Theatre Research International* 32 (2007) 263–77.

MacLeish, Archibald (US playwright, 1892–1982). *J.B. A Play in Verse.* London: Samuel French, 1956 [= *Spiel um Job.* Trans. Eva Hesse. Frankfurt a.M.: Suhrkamp, 1958]. See also **Bieman, E.** "Faithful to the Bible in Its Fashion: MacLeish's J.B." *CSRBull* 3/5 (1972) 26. **Cooper, L. L.** *The Book of Job: A Foundation for Testimony in the Writings of Gustavo Gutiérrez, Elie Wiesel, Archibald MacLeish, and Carl Gustav Jung.* Diss. Oxford, 1994. **Dunkel, Wilbur D.** "Theology in the Theater" [recent Broadway plays by A. MacLeish, J. Forsyth, G. Greene, E. O'Neill, and others]. *TTod* 16 (1959) 65–73. **Fuzzard, Carol Jane.** *Job in the 20th Century. Beyond the Whirlwind: Piety in the Book of Job and A. MacLeish's J.B.* Diss. Candler, Atlanta, 1995. **Labin, Linda L.** *The Whale and the Ash-Heap: Transfigurations of Jonah and Job in Modern American Fiction—Frost, MacLeish, and Vonnegut.* Diss. Kent State University, 1980. **Levenson, Jon Douglas.** *The Book of Job in Its Time and in the Twentieth Century.* Cambridge, MA: Harvard University Press, 1972. 40–54. **Matthews, Marjorie Swank.** *Issues and Answers in the Book of Job and Joban Issues and Answers in Three Twentieth Century Writers: Carl Jung, Robert Frost, and Archibald MacLeish.* Diss. Florida State University, 1976. **Priest, John.** "Job and J.B.: The Goodness of God or the Godness of Good?" *Horizons* 12 (1985) 265–83. **Siebald, Manfred.** "Archibald MacLeishs J. B. und das Buch Hiob." In *Paradeigmata: Literarische Typologie des Alten Testaments.* Ed. Franz H. Link. Berlin: Duncker & Humblot, 1989. 759–74. **Steinwendtner, Brita.** *Hiobs Klage heute: Die biblische Gestalt in der Literatur des 20. Jahrhunderts.* Innsbruck: Tyrolia-Verlag, 1990. 63–96. **Stock, E.** "'Masque of Reason' and 'J. B.': Two Treatments of the Book of Job." *Modern Drama* 3 (1961) 378–86. **Terrien, Samuel.** "J.B. and Job." *ChrCent* (January 7, 1959) 9–11. **Thelen, Mary Frances.** "J. B., Job, and the Biblical Doctrine of Man." *JAAR* 27 (1959) 201–5.

Meigs, Charles Hardy (US dramatist). *The Man of Uz: A Drama in Three Acts.* New York, London: G. P. Putnam's Sons, 1933.

Mönnich, Horst. *Hiob im Moor* [play for radio, 1953]. Hamburg: Baken-Verlag, 1966.

Morax, René (Swiss playwright, 1873–1963). *Job le vigneron, mystère en trois actes.* Sierre: Editions des treize étoiles, 1953.

Narhamer, Johan (16th cent.). *Historia Jobs* [drama]. Hof a.d. Saale, 1546. Ed. Barbara Könneker and Wolfgang F. Michael. Arbeiten zur mittleren deutschen Literatur 12. Berne: Lang, 1983. 366

Nobili, Francesco (Francesco de' Nobili, Italian dramatist, 17th cent.). *Il Giobbe: nell'inuitta patienza di Santa Rosa di Santa Maria Limana dell'ordine de Predicatori. Opera sacroscenica del sig. marchese Francesco de' Nobili.* Bologna: Giacomo Monti, 1678.

Nortel, Jean-Pierre (French dramatist and impresario). *Le manteau de Job.* Paris: Les éditions ouvrières, 1986.

Obaldia, René de (French playwright and poet, b. 1918). *Et à la fin était le bang. Comédie héroïque* [a play]. In his *Théâtre.* Paris: Grasset, 1975. 6:1–194. See also **Bochet, Marc.** "Obaldia: Les larmes des témoins." In his *Présence de Job dans le théâtre d'après-guerre II en France.* Berne: Peter Lang, 1988. 108–13.

O'Neill, Eugene (US playwright, 1868–1953). *Lazarus Laughed: A Play for an Imaginative Theatre* (1925). New York: Boni & Liveright, 1927.

Petermann, Margit (German writer, 1906–1956). "Job: Ein Opfer." In *Zwei Spiele.* Freiburg i.Br: Caritasverlag, 1936.

Ponholzer, Bartholomäus. *Job, der fromme Dulder: Religiöses Schauspiel in 5 Akten mit Prolog und lebenden Bildern* [drama, 1862]. Bonn: A. Heidelmann, 1927.

Racine, Jean (French dramatist, 1639–1699). "Annotations du livre de Job." In his *Oeuvres complètes.* Ed. Raymond Picard. Paris: Gallimard, 1960. 2:699–705.

Radcliffe, Ralph [Robert]. *Job's Afflictions* [drama]. c. 1550.

Richards, I. A. (English literary critic and poet, 1893–1979). "Job's Comforting." In his *Internal Colloquies: Poems and Plays.* New York: Harcourt Brace Jovanovich, [1971].

Riebold, Fritz. *Hiob: Ein biblisches Verkündigungsspiel.* Stuttgart: Oncken, 1947.

Roblot, René (pseudonym of Jacques Dubout, French priest and playwright, 1872–1939). *Job, maître d'école libre; comédie dramatique en 3 actes.* Paris, G. Enault, 1932.

Rössler, Max. *Job: Ein Spiel von der geprüften Liebe* [childrens' drama]. Würzburg: Echter-Verlag, 1946.

Rouville, Odile de. "Job dépose son bilan: lecture biblique marginale" [dramatic dialogue]. *FoiVie* 84/6 (1985) 57–66.

Ruf, Jakob (Swiss surgeon and dramatist, 1500–1558). *Hiob* [drama]. Zurich, c. 1535.

Sachs, Hans (the Meistersinger, German poet and playwright, 1494–1576). *Ein comedi, mit neuzehen personen, der Hiob* [drama]. Nuremberg, 1547 [= his *Werke*. Ed. Adelbert von Keller. Stuttgart: Litterarischer Verein, 1872. 6:29–55].

Sackler, Howard O. (US screenwriter and playwright, 1929–1982). *The Book of Job* [sound recording]. Caedmon TC 1076. 1957.

Schimmel, Hendrik Jan (Dutch poet and novelist, 1823–1906). "Het boek Job." In his *Dramatische werken.* II. Schiedam: Roelants, 1897.

Seidel, Jürgen. *Zum Teufel mit Hiob: Kriminalhörspiel* [radio play]. Westdeutscher Rundfunk, 1987.

Shakespeare, William (English dramatist, 1564–1616). See **Eaton, Thomas Ray.** *Shakespeare and the Bible: Showing How Much the Great Dramatist Was Indebted to Holy Writ for His Profound Knowledge of Human Nature.* London: James Blackwood, 1860. **Ellis, Charles.** *Shakespeare and the Bible: Shakespeare, A Reading from the Merchant of Venice; Shakespeariana; Sonnets, with Their Scriptural Harmonies.* London: Houlston & Sons, 1897. **Marx, Steven.** "'Within a Foot of the Extreme Verge': The Book of Job and *King Lear*." In his *Shakespeare and the Bible.* Oxford: Oxford University Press, 2000. 59–78. **Thomas, Frank Morehead.** "Hamlet and Job." *MethQR* 68 1 (1919) 3–16. **Truesdale, Barbara L.** *The Problem of Suffering: The Questions of Job in "King Lear," "Moby-Dick," and "The Sound and the Fury."* Diss. Ohio State University, 1991.

Simon, Neil. *God's Favorite: A New Comedy.* New York: Random House, 1975.

Sorge, Reinhard Johannes (German playwright, 1892–1916). "Hiob" [dramatic poem]. In his *Werke, eingeleitet und herausgegeben von Hans Gerd Rötzer.* Nuremburg: Glock & Lutz, 1962–67. 3:178–82.

Stalberg, Ruth Roberta. *Hiob: Ein Spiel.* Munich: Höfling, 1950.

Steinhoff, Peter A. *Der arme Hiob: Drama in 5 Akten.* Berlin-Grunewald: Herbig, [1948].

Stevens, James S. *A Dramatization of the Book of Job: The Problem of Human Suffering.* Boston: Stratford, 1917.

Stoltz, Kevin. *From out of the Whirlwind: A One-Act Play on the Book of Job.* Kansas City, MO: Lillenas Publishing Co., 1994.

Strindberg, August (Swedish playwright, 1849–1912). See **Paul, Fritz.** "Ismael, Hiob, Jakob: alttestamentarische Typologie bei August Strindberg." In *Paradeigmata: literarische Typologie des Alten Testaments.* Ed. Franz Link. Berlin: Duncker & Humblot, 1989. 1:465–86

Tabori, Georg (Hungarian and German author and playwright, 1914–2007). See **Würmser, Rudolf.** "Fragen zu Hiob. Aspekte der Theaterarbeit George Taboris." In *Religion–Literatur–Künste II. Ein Dialog.* Ed. Peter Tschuggnall. Anif, Salzburg: Müller-Speiser, 2002. 81–90.

Wahltuch, Marco. *Giobbe, tragedia in cinque atti …, con figure simboliche de caratteri* *principali, tracciate secondo il nuovo sistema di filosofia intitolato Psicografia* [five-act tragedy]. Milan: Guglielmini, 1872.

Weege, Fritz (1880–1945). *Das Spiel Hiob* [play]. Die Schatzgräberbühne 37. Berlin: Bühnenvolksbundverlag, 1926; Munich: G. D. W. Callwey, 1927.

Weinrich, Franz Johannes (German playwright, 1897–1978). *Das Gastmahl des Job.* 1948.

Welti, Albert Jakob (Swiss dramatist, 1894–1965). *Hiob der Sieger: Vier Akte.* Zurich, Munich: Dreiflammen Verlag, 1954.

Wiechert, Ernst (German writer, 1887–1950). *Das Spiel vom deutschen Bettelmann* [originally a radio play]. Munich: A. Langen, G. Müller, 1933.

Wilder, Thornton (US playwright and novelist, 1897–1975). "Hast Thou Considered My Servant Job?" In *The Angel That Troubled the Waters and Other Plays.* New York: Coward McCann; London: Longmans, 1928. 129–33. ———. "Leviathan." In *The Angel That Troubled the Waters and Other Plays.* New York: Coward McCann; London: Longmans, 1928.

Winawer, Bruno (Polish playwright and author, 1883–1944). *The Book of Job, A Satirical Comedy.* Trans. Joseph Conrad. London: J. M. Dent, 1931 [orig. *Ksiega Hjoba*].

Wojtyla, K. (Pope John Paul II, 1920–2005). "Job." In *The Collected Plays and Writings on Theater. Karol Wojtyla. Translated with Introductions by Boleslaw Taborski.* Berkeley: University of California Press, 1987. See also **Fantuzzi, V.** "Il 'Giobbe' di Karol Wojtyla a San Miniato." *CivCat* 136 (1985) 500–504. **Gatta, E.** "Il Giobbe di Papa Wojtyla." *CiVit* 40 (1985) 403–48.

Wulf, Berthold (German priest and writer, b. 1926). *Hiob, der Wanderer: Drama in fünf Akten.* St Michael: J. G. Bläschke, 1983. ———. *Hiob: Szenische Dichtung in 7 Bildern.* Zurich: Christengemeinschaft, 1971.

Zapf, Adolf Philipp (1825–1872). *Hiob. Ein dramatisch-didactisches Bild aus dem Morgenlande. Mit einem Anhang von Sonetten* [drama in two acts, with poems]. Brooklyn, NY; Münchberg, Bavaria, 1866.

Zawieyski, Jerzy (Polish writer, 1902–1969). *Maz doskolany* [The Perfect Husband]. In his *Dramaty.* Warsaw: Pax, 1985 [orig. 1945].

Zech, Paul (German poet and author, 1881–1946). *Zuletzt bleibt Hiob. Ein alltägliches Spiel in fünf Akten.* Berlin: Oesterheld, 1928.

iii. Fiction

Aguado, Emiliano (Spanish writer, b. 1907). *Job estaba solo.* Colección Ensayo 4. Madrid: Editora Nacional, 1963.

Altendorf, Wolfgang (German writer, 1921–2007). *Hiob im Weinberg: Erzählung.* Freudenstadt–Wittlensweiler: The Author, 1962.

Arthur, Randall. *Jordan's Crossing.* Portland, OR: Multnomah Press, 1993 [= *Die Erbin des Hiob: Roman.* Asslar: GerthMedien, 2006]. ———. *Wisdom Hunter.* Portland, OR: Multnomah Press, 1993 [= *Die Enkelin des Hiob. Roman.* Wiesbaden: Projektion-J-Buch- und Musikverlag, 1995; Asslar: GerthMedien, 2006].

Baum, L. Frank (US author, 1856–1919). *The Wonderful Wizard of Oz.* Chicago: George M. Hill, 1900. See also **Linafelt, Tod.** "The Wizard of Uz: Job, Dorothy, and the Limits of the Sublime." *BibInt* 14 (2006) 94–109.

Baumann, Emile (French Catholic novelist, 1868–1942). *Job le prédestiné, roman.* Paris: B. Grasset, 1922.

Bayer-Fichter, Gussla. *Die Flöte Hiobs: Roman.* Stuttgart: Cotta, 1963.

Beaulieu, Victor-Lévy (French Canadian writer, b. 1945). *Sagamo Job J: cantique.* Montréal: VLB, 1977.

Brecht, Bertolt. "Der blinde." In *Gesammelte Werke.* Prosa, Vol. 1. Ed. Herta Ramthun and Klaus Völker. Frankfurt a.M.: Suhrkamp, 1967.

Brenner, Y. H. (Ukrainian-born Israeli novelist, 1881–1921). See **Brinker, M.** "On the Ironic Use of the Myth of Job in Y. H. Brenner's *Breakdown and Bereavement.*" In *Biblical Patterns in Modern Literature.* Ed. D. Hirsch and N. Aschkenasy. Brown Judaic Studies 77. Chico, CA: Scholars Press, 1984. 115–26.

Britting, Georg (German poet and writer, 1891–1964). *Der verlachte Hiob* [short story]. Traisa-Darmstadt: Arkadenverlag, 1921 [= *Sämtliche Werke. I. Frühe Werke: Prosa, Dramen, Gedichte, 1920 bis 1930.* Ed. Walter Schmitz. Munich: Süddeutscher Verlag, 1987, 117–19]. See also **Steinwendtner, Brita.** *Hiobs Klage heute: Die biblische Gestalt in der Literatur des 20. Jahrhunderts.* Innsbruck: Tyrolia-Verlag, 1990. 7–36.

Bulgakov, Mikhail (Russian novelist and playwright, 1891–1940). *The Master and Margarita.* Trans. Michael Glenny. London: Collins, 1967 [original, 1966]. See **Laudon, Barbara Elaine.** *Light and Darkness Imagery and the Demonic Element in Mixail Bulgakov's "The Master and Margarita"* [Satan in Job]. Diss. Wisconsin–Madison, 1983.

Campfranc, M. Du (pseudonym of Marie-Simone Coutance). *Pauvre Job* [novel]. Paris: H. Gautier, 1905.

Camus, Albert (Algerian-born French novelist and philosopher, 1913–1960). *La peste.* Paris: Gallimard, 1947 [= *The Plague.* Trans. Stuart Gilbert. London: Hamish Hamilton, 1948]. See also **Castagna, Edoardo.** *L'uomo di Uz: Giobbe e la letteratura del Novecento.* Milan: Medusa, 2007. 15–26. **Duclow, Donald F.** "Into the Whirlwind of Suffering: Resistance and Transformation" [on Job, A. Camus, *The Plague,* J. Donne, *Devotion*]. *Second Opinion* 9 (1998) 11–27. **Friedman, Maurice S.** *Problematic Rebel: An Image of Modern Man.* New York: Random House, 1963; revised ed. *Problematic Rebel: Melville, Dostoievsky, Kafka, Camus.* Chicago: University of Chicago Press, 1970. 413–36. **Taradach, Madeleine.** "De la 'modernité' de l'absurde chez Job à la lumière de l'absurde chez Camus." *EstFranc* 81 (1980) 155–68.

Cardoso Pires, José (Portuguese writer, 1925–1998). *O hóspede de Job: Romance* [The Guest of Job]. Lisbon: Arcádia, 1963] [= *L'ospite di Giobbe.* Milan: Lerici Editori, 1963; *El huésped de Job.* Barcelona: Seix Barral, 1972; *L'invité de Job.* Paris: Editions Autrement, 2000].

Chedid, Andrée (Lebanese poet and novelist, living in France, b. 1920). *La femme de Job. Récit.* Paris: M. Sell, Calmann-Lévy, 1993 [= *Die Frau des Ijob. Erzählung.* Limburg: Lahn-Verlag, 1995].

Demélier, Jean (French writer and painter, b. 1940). *Le rêve de Job* [novel]. *Le Chemin.* Paris: Gallimard, 1971.

Dickens, Charles (English novelist, 1812–1970). See **Barry, Wendy Elizabeth.** *A Cipher to Lend Significance: Pain, Suffering and Narrative in the Book of Job,* Clarissa, and David Copperfield. Diss. Vanderbilt, 1999.

Döblin, Alfred (German expressionist novelist, 1878–1957). *Berlin Alexanderplatz: Die Geschichte vom Franz Biberkopf* [novel] Berlin: S. Fischer, 1929 [= *Alexanderplatz Berlin: The Story of Franz Biberkopf.* Trans. Eugene Jolas. London: Martin Secker, 1931]. See also **Fromm, Georg.** "Hiobs Wachhund. Die erste Hiob-Paraphrase in Alfred Döblins *Berlin Alexanderplatz.*" In *Internationales Alfred Döblin-Kolloquium, Paris 1993.* Ed. Michel Grunewald. Berne: Peter Lang, 1995, 213–26. **Steinwendtner, Brita.** *Hiobs Klage heute: Die biblische Gestalt in der Literatur des 20. Jahrhunderts.* Innsbruck: Tyrolia-Verlag, 1990. 63–96.

Dostoevsky, Fyodor Mikhailovich (Russian novelist, 1821–1881). *Crime and Punishment* [original, 1866]. *The Brothers Karamosov* [original, 1880]. See also **Castagna, Edoardo.** *L'uomo di Uz: Giobbe e la letteratura del Novecento.* Milan: Medusa, 2007. 53–58. **Friedman, Maurice S.** "The Modern Job: On Melville, Dostoievsky and Kafka." *Judaism* 12 (1963) 436–55. ———. *Problematic Rebel: An Image of Modern Man.* New York: Random House, 1963; revised ed. *Problematic Rebel: Melville, Dostoievsky, Kafka, Camus.* Chicago: University of Chicago Press, 1970. 151–284. **Kirk, Irina.** "The Myth of the Devil in Dostoevksy's *Crime and Punishment.*" In *Evolution of the Novel. Proceedings of*

the IXth Congress of the International Comparative Literature Association, Innsbruck, 1979.
Ed. Zoran Konstantinovic, Eva Kushner, and Béla Köpeczi. Innsbruck: Institut für
Sprachwissenschaft der Universität Innsbruck. 403–8. **Vicchio, Stephen J.** *Job in the
Modern World.* Eugene, OR: Wipf & Stock, 2006. 142–51.

   Doyon, Jacques-René (b. 1938). *Yob ou la mort de Yob.* Paris: Mercure de France, 1970
[= *Hiob oder der Tod Hiobs.* Berlin: Verlag Volk und Welt, 1973].

   Eeden, Frederik van (Dutch writer and psychiatrist, 1860–1932). *Van de koele
meren des doods* [novel]. Amsterdam: W. Versluys, 1900 [= *The Deeps of Deliverance.* Trans.
Margaret Robinson. London: T. Fisher Unwin, 1902].

   Eliot, George (pseudonym of Mary Ann Evans, English novelist, 1819–1880). See
Murayama, H. *George Eliot and the Bible.* Diss. Newcastle upon Tyne, 2003.

   Farrère, Claude (French novelist, 1876–1957). *Job, siècle XX: Roman.* Paris:
Flammarion, 1949.

   Faulkner, William (US novelist, 1897–1962). See **Truesdale, Barbara L.** *The Problem of Suffering: The Questions of Job in "King Lear," "Moby-Dick," and "The Sound and the Fury."*
Diss. Ohio State University, 1991.

   Fehrbrügge, Michael. "Die Geige des Hiobs. Ein Märchen." *Das Goldene Tor:
Monatsschrift für Literatur und Kunst* 5 (1950) 53–62.

   Féval, Paul (French novelist, 1817–1887). "Job misère" [short story]. In his *Contes
de Bretagne.* Paris: Waille, 1844 [= "Job le rôdeur." In his *Job le Rôdeur.* Paris: G. Roux &
Cassanet, 1857].

   Franco Ruiz, Mario (Colombian writer). *Los hijos de Job.* Bogotá: Editorial Cosmos,
1960.

   Franke, Herbert W. (German science-fiction author, b. 1927). *Hiobs Stern: Science-
Fiction-Roman.* Frankfurt a.M.: Suhrkamp, 1988.

   Franzos, Karl Emil (Jewish writer, 1848–1904). *Der Hiob von Unterach und andere
Geschichten* [short story]. Stuttgart, Berlin: Cotta, 1913. 7–26.

   Gernhardt, Robert (German writer and painter, 1937–2006). "Das Buch Ewald."
In *Kippfigur: Erzählungen.* Zurich: Haffmans Verlag, 1986. 9–27 [= *Der Rabe* 3 (1962)
116–30].

   Gide, André (French novelist, 1869–1951). *L'immoraliste.* 1902. See **Oliver, Andrew.**
Intertextualité de la lecture dans "L'immoraliste" de Gide: Michel, Job, Pierre, Paul. Archives des
lettres modernes. Archives André Gide 4. Paris Lettres modernes, 1979.

   Goldsmith, Oliver (Irish novelist, 1730–1774). *The Vicar of Wakefield.* London, 1766.
See also **Lehmann, James H.** "The Vicar of Wakefield: Goldsmith's Sublime, Oriental
Job." *ELH* 46/1 (1979) 97–121.

   Green, Julien (French-born US author, 1900–1998). *Léviathan. Roman.* Paris:
Plon, 1929 [= *The Dark Journey.* Trans. Vyvyan Holland. London: W. Heinemann,
1929; *Leviathan. Ein Roman.* Trans. Gina Hermann Kesten. Berlin: Kiepenheuer &
Witsch, 1930; *Leviathan, novela.* Barcelona: La Pléyade, 1943; *Leviatan: romanzo.* Milan:
Mondadori, 1946]. See also **Doering, Bernard.** "Jacques Maritain, George Bernanos
and Julien Green on the Mystery of Suffering." *RelLit* 17 (1985) 317–55.

   Gregor-Dellin, Martin (German writer, 1926–1989). *Möglichkeiten einer Fahrt:
Erzählungen.* Munich: Carl Hanser, 1964.

   Guzmán, Jorge (Chilean author, b. 1930). *Job-Boj: Novela.* Barcelona: Seix Barral,
1968.

   Hansen, Joseph (US mystery writer, 1923–2004). *Job's Year* [novel]. New York: Holt,
Reinhart & Winston, 1983.

   Hauptmann, Gerhart (German dramatist, 1862–1946). *Buch der Leidenschaft:
Roman einer Ehe.* 2 vols. Berlin: S. Fischer, 1930 [= *Das erzählerische Werke.* Frankfurt:
Ullstein, 1982. 8:7–335].

   Heinlein, Robert A. (US science-fiction author, 1907–1988). *Job, a Comedy of Justice.*
New York: Ballantine Books, 1984.

Heissenbüttel, Helmut (German avant-garde novelist and poet, 1921–1996). "Hiobsbotschaft." 1964. In his *Das Textbuch*. Neuwied: Luchterhand, 1970. 143–45.

Hertz, Henri (French poet and writer). "Ceux de Job" [short story]. In his *Tragédies des temps volages: contes et poèmes 1906–1954*. Paris: Pierre Seghers, 1955.

Herzberg, Abel J. (Dutch Jewish writer and poet, 1893–1989). *Drie rode rozen: een novelle*. Amsterdam: Querido, 1975.

Hill, Grace Livingston (US Christian romantic novelist, 1865–1947). *Job's Niece*. Philadelphia, London: J. B. Lippincott Company, [1927].

Humphrey, William (US novelist, 1924–1997). "A Job of the Plains." In his *A Time and a Place: Stories of the Red River Country*. New York: Knopf, 1968 [= "Hiob in Oklahoma." In his *Zur Zeit von Bonnie und Clyde. Geschichten aus Texas*. Frankfurt: G. B. Fischer, 1970. 61–88].

Kafka, Franz (Czech writer, 1883–1924). *Der Prozess. Roman*. Berlin: Die Schmiede 1925 [= *The Trial*. Trans. Willa and Edwin Muir. London: V. Gollancz, 1937]. See also **Bochet, Marc.** *Présence de Job dans le théâtre d'après-guerre II en France*. Berne: Peter Lang, 1988. 43–52. **Brod, Max.** "Franz Kafka und Hiob." *Jüdische Revue* 2 (1937) 622–26. **Castagna, Edoardo.** *L'uomo di Uz: Giobbe e la letteratura del Novecento*. Milan: Medusa, 2007. 59–76. **Friedman, Maurice S.** *Problematic Rebel: An Image of Modern Man*. New York: Random House, 1963; revised ed. *Problematic Rebel: Melville, Dostoievsky, Kafka, Camus*. Chicago: University of Chicago Press, 1970. ———. "The Modern Job: On Melville, Dostoievsky and Kafka." *Judaism* 12 (1963) 436–55. **Kartiganer, Donald M.** "Job and Joseph K. Myth in Kafka's 'The Trial'." *Modern Fiction Studies* 8 (1962) 31–43. **Lasine, Stuart.** "The Trials of Job and Kafka's Josef K." *German Quarterly* 63 (1990) 187–98. ———. "Job and His Friends in the Modern World: Kafka's *The Trial*." In *The Voice from the Whirlwind: Interpreting the Book of Job*. Ed. Leo G. Perdue and Clark Gilpin. Nashville: Abingdon Press, 1992. 144–55. **Léger, François.** "De Job à Kafka." *Cahiers du sud* 32 (1945) 161–65. **Ries, Wiebrecht.** "Kafka und Hiob. Zur Hiob-Situation des religiösen Denkens." In his *Transzendenz als Terror. Eine religionsphilosophische Studie über Franz Kafka*. Heidelberg: Schneider, 1977. 123–46. **Steinwendtner, Brita.** *Hiobs Klage heute: Die biblische Gestalt in der Literatur des 20. Jahrhunderts*. Innsbruck: Tyrolia-Verlag, 1990. 7–36. **Susman, Margarete.** "Der Hiobproblem bei Franz Kafka." *Der Morgen* 5 (1929) 31–49. **Suter, Rudolf.** *Kafkas "Prozess" im Lichte des "Buches Hiob."* Europäische Hochschulschriften 1/169. Frankfurt: P. Lang, 1976.

Kalechofsky, Roberta (US feminist and animal rights activist and writer, b. 1931). "Job Enters a Pain Clinic" [short story]. 2002. www.samizdat.com/micah/job.html.

Koch, N. K. *Baumann—Hiob's kleiner Bruder* [novel]. Zurich: Editions à la Carte, 2004.

Kołakowski, Leszek (Polish philosopher, b. 1927). "Job, or The Contradictions of Virtue." In his *The Key to Heaven: Edifying Tales from Holy Scripture to Serve as Teaching and Warning: Conversations with the Devil*. New York: Grove Press, 1972 [= *Tales from the Kingdom of Lailonia, and, The Key to Heaven*. Trans. Salvator Attansio and Agnieszka Kolakowska. Chicago: Chicago University Press, 1989; "Hiob—oder die Widersprüche der Tugend." In *Der Himmelsschlüssel: Erbauliche Geschichten*. Frankfurt a.M.: Suhrkamp, 1969; original, *Klucz niebieski albo opowieści budujące z historii świętej zaczerpnięte ku pouczeniu i przestrodze*. Warsaw: Panstwowy Instytut Wydawniczy, 1964].

Kolitz, Zwi. "Jossel Rackower rechnet mit Gott." *Stimmen der Zeit* 159 (1956–57) 161–68.

Kroneberg, Eckart (German novelist, b. 1930). *Keine Scherbe für Hiob: Roman*. Munich: R. Piper, 1964.

Kunert, Günter (German writer, b. 1929). "Hiob gut bürgerlich." *Akzente. Zeitschrift für Literatur* 18 (1971) 69–70.

Kyser, Hans (German writer and filmmaker, 1882–1940). *Der Blumenhiob: Roman*. Berlin: S. Fischer, 1909.

La Touche-Espé, Albert (pseudonym of Albert Caro). *Job, roman*. Gisors: Imprimerie régionale, 1938 [= *Mercure universel, revue mensuelle* (March–April, 1938)].

Laederach, Jürg (Swiss writer, b. 1945). *Passion: Ein Geständnis. Roman.* Frankfurt a.M.: Suhrkamp, 1993.

Landgrebe, Erich (Austrian poet and writer, 1908–1979). *Narr des Glücks: Roman.* Hamburg: Wegner, 1962.

Levi, Primo (Italian Jewish writer, 1919–1987). *Se questo è un uomo.* Turin: F. de Silva, 1947 [memoirs] [= *If This Is a Man.* Trans. Stuart Woolf. London: Orion Press, 1959; (in USA) *Survival in Auschwitz: The Nazi Assault on Humanity.* New York: Macmillan, 1958]. See also **Glasberg, R.** "Power in Western Civilization: The Book of Job and Primo Levi's 'Survival in Auschwitz'." *CanRevCompLit* 19 (1992) 597–614.

Limentani, Giacoma (Italian Jewish author, b. 1927). *Le grande seduto.* Milan: Adelphi, 1979.

Linscheid, John. "Jobia versus God: The Book of Job revisited" [short story]. *Other Side* 23 (1987) 24–27.

Mack, Lorenz. *Hiob und die Ratten: Roman.* Zurich, Stuttgart: Artemis Verlag, 1961 [= *Jób és a patkányok: Regény.* Budapest: Európa Könyvkiadó, 1972; *Job in podgane: Roman.* Maribor: Zalozba Obzorja, 1971; *Jov i pluchovete: Roman.* Sofia: Narodna Kultura, 1967].

Malamud, Bernard (US Jewish author, 1914–1986). *God's Grace.* London: Chatto & Windus, 1982. See also **Brown, Peter Craig.** *The Promise of Malamud's Fiction* [Job and Malamud's *God's Grace*]. Diss. Emory, 1993.

Mann, Thomas (German novelist, 1875–1955). *Doktor Faustus. Das Leben des deutschen Tonsetzers Adrian Leverkühn, erzählt von einem Freunde.* Stockholm: Bermann-Fischer, 1947 [= *Doctor Faustus: The Life of the German Composer, Adrian Leverkühn, as Told by a Friend.* Trans. H. T. Lowe-Porter. New York: A. A. Knopf, 1948; London: Minerva, 1949]. See also **Busch, Stefan.** "Nachleben im Zitat: Joseph Roths 'Hiob' und Thomas Manns 'Doktor Faustus'." In *Verlorenes Lachen: blasphemisches Gelächter in der deutschen Literatur von der Aufklärung bis zur Gegenwart.* Ed. Stefan Busch. Tübingen: Niemeyer, 2004. 168–78. **Stockhammer, Morris.** "Thomas Mann's Job–Jacob." *Judaism* 8 (1959) 242–46.

Melville, Herman (US novelist and writer, 1819–1891). *Moby Dick, or, The Whale.* New York: Harper & Brothers, 1851. ———. *The Confidence Man: His Masquerade.* New York: Dix, Edwards, 1857. See also **Baumann, Uwe.** "Herman Melvilles 'Moby-Dick' und das Alte Testament." In *Paradeigmata. Literarische Typologie des Alten Testaments.* Ed. Franz Link. Berlin: Duncker & Humblot, 1989. 1:411–29. **Behnken, Eloise M.** "Joban Theme in Moby Dick." *Iliff Review* 33 (1976) 37–48. **Friedman, Maurice S.** *Problematic Rebel: An Image of Modern Man.* New York: Random House, 1963; revised ed. *Problematic Rebel: Melville, Dostoievsky, Kafka, Camus.* Chicago: University of Chicago Press, 1970. 51–150. ———. "The Modern Job: On Melville, Dostoievsky and Kafka." *Judaism* 12 (1963) 436–55. **Holman, C. Hugh.** "The Reconciliation of Ishmael, Moby Dick and the Book of Job." *South Atlantic Quarterly* 57 (1958) 477–90. **Holstein, Jay A.** "Melville's Inversion of Job in Moby Dick." *Iliff Review* 37 (Winter 1980) 13–19. **Stout, Janis P.** "Melville's Use of the Book of Job." *Nineteenth-Century Fiction* 25 (1970) 69–83. **Truesdale, Barbara L.** *The Problem of Suffering: The Questions of Job in "King Lear," "Moby-Dick," and "The Sound and the Fury."* Diss. Ohio State University, 1991. **Vicchio, Stephen J.** *Job in the Modern World.* Eugene, OR: Wipf & Stock, 2006. 133–41. **Wright, Nathalia.** "Moby Dick: Jonah's or Job's Whale?" *American Literature* 37 (1965) 190–95. **Young, W. A.** "Leviathan in the Book of Job and Moby-Dick." *Soundings* 65 (1983) 388–401.

Mombert, Alfred (Jewish German poet, 1872–1942). *Sfaira der Alte: Mythos.* 2 vols. Berlin, Winterthur: Schocken Verlag, 1936–42.

Montmajour, Pierre. *Un homme appelé Job.* Pont-Anthou: Daumas, 1943.

Mynona (pseudonym of Salomo Friedlaender, German Dadaist writer, 1871–1946). "Der lachende Hiob." In *Der lachende Hiob und andere Grotesken.* Paris: Editions du Phénix, 1935. 51–64.

Ned, Edouard (Luxembourgian poet and novelist, 1873–1949). *Job le glorieux, roman.* Brussels: Durendal; Courtrai: Jos. Vermaut; Paris, P. Lethielleux, 1933.

Nowlin, Stephen Dudley. *Petroburg* [novel]. Diss. Stephen F. Austin State University, 1992.

Onetti, Juan Carlos (Uruguayan novelist, 1909–1984). See **Kulin, Katalin.** "El libro de Job y la obra de J. C. Onetti." *Annales sectio philologica moderna* 11 (1980) 109–17. ———. "The Myth of Job in the Works of Juan Carlos Onetti and Salvadore Espriu." In *Evolution of the Novel. Proceedings of the IXth Congress of the International Comparative Literature Association, Innsbruck, 1979.* Ed. Zoran Konstantinovoc, Eva Kushner, and Béla Köpeczi. Innsbruck: Institut für Sprachwissenschaft der Universität Innsbruck, 1981–82. 397–402.

Osorio Lizarazo, José Antonio (Colombian novelist, 1900–1964). "Job." In *Tres cuentistas jóvenes: Manuel García Herreros, J. A. Osorio Lizarazo, E. Arias Suárez.* Biblioteca aldeana de Colombia 17. Bogotá: Minerva, 1936.

Polgar, Alfred (German writer, 1873–1955). *Hiob:* In his *Hiob. Ein Novellenband.* Munich: Langen, 1912. 7–21.

Posch, Günter. *Hiobs chaotisches Lesebuch.* Constance: Posch, 1989.

Rast, Severin, and Oliver Hoffmann. *Hiobs Botschaft, Jubiläumsausgabe* [science fiction]. Mannheim: Feder & Schwert, 2004.

Reinke, Siegfried. *Hiob. Roman.* Munich: Albert Langen, 1922.

Reiser, Werner. *Hiob: Ein Rebell bekommt recht.* Stuttgart: Quell-Verlag, 1991.

Risse, Heinz (German writer, 1898–1989). "Dein Bruder Hiob." In *Die Grille: Erzählungen.* Bremen: Schünemann, 1953.

Roth, Joseph (Austrian novelist, 1894–1939). "Der Leviathan." In his *Der Leviathan. Erzählungen.* Amsterdam: Querido, 1940. 168–96. ———. *Hiob: Roman eines einfachen Mannes.* Berlin: G. Kiepenheuer, 1930 [= *Job: The Story of a Simple Man.* Trans. Dorothy Thompson. London: William Heinemann, 1932; *Job: roman d'un simple juif.* Paris: Valois, 1931; *Giobbe: Romanzo di un uomo semplice.* Milan: Treves, Treccani, Tumminelli, 1932]. See also **Blanke, Hans-Jürgen.** *Joseph Roth, Hiob: Interpretation.* Oldenbourg-Interpretationen 58. Munich: Oldenbourg, 1993. **Bohn, Ursula.** "'Beinahe ein Heiliger'. Joseph Roth, sein Hiob-Roman und das Ostjudentum." *Veröffentlichungen aus dem Institut Kirche und Judentum* 13 (1981) 68–83. **Busch, Stefan.** "Nachleben im Zitat: Joseph Roths 'Hiob' und Thomas Manns 'Doktor Faustus'." In *Verlorenes Lachen: blasphemisches Gelächter in der deutschen Literatur von der Aufklärung bis zur Gegenwart.* Ed. Stefan Busch. Tübingen: Niemeyer, 2004. 168–78. **Butler, G. P.** "It's the Bitterness That Counts. Joseph Roth's 'Most Jewish' Novel [*Hiob*] Reconsidered." *German Life and Letters* 41,3 (1988) 227–34. **Castagna, Edoardo.** *L'uomo di Uz: Giobbe e la letteratura del Novecento.* Milan: Medusa, 2007. 35–52. **Eckhoff, Astrid.** *Joseph Roth, Hiob: Eine Interpretation.* Schriften des Germanistischen Instituts der Universität Bergen 9. Bergen: Germanistisches Institut, 1987. **Fisch, Harold.** "Being Possessed by Job" [Job as literary archetype in Joseph Roth and others]. *LitTheol* 8 (1994) 280–95. **Fricke-Roth, Almut.** *Eine textsemantische Untersuchung des Buches Hiob von Joseph Roth unter dem Aspekt des soziokulturellen Hintergrundwissens.* Frankfurt a.M.: Peter Lang, 2005. **Göggel, Emil.** *Lektürehilfen Joseph Roth, "Hiob."* Klett-Lektürehilfen. Stuttgart: Klett-Verlag für Wissen und Bildung, 1997. **Heide-Koch, Marlies.** *Hiob oder Die Auflehnung des Einzelnen gegen das Schicksal: Joseph Roth: "Die Rebellion" und "Hiob."* Diss. Salzburg, 1991. **Hofe, Gerhard vom.** "'Reigen aus Mühsal' und 'Schwere des Glücks.' Joseph Roths Hiob-Deutung." In *"Die Schwere des Glücks und die Grösse der Wunder": Joseph Roth und seine Welt.* Ed. Michael Nüchtern. Karlsruhe: Verlag Evangelischer Presseverband für Baden, 1994. 66–91. **Horch, Hans Otto.** "Zeitroman, Legende, Palimpsest. Zu Joseph Roths 'Hiob'-Roman im Kontext deutsch-jüdischer Literaturgeschichte." *Germanisch-romanische Monatsschrift* 39,2 (1989) 210–26. **Klaghofer-Treitler, Wolfgang.** *Zwischen Hiob und Jeremia: Stefan Zweig und Joseph Roth am Ende der Welt.* Frankfurt a.M.: Lang, 2007. **Kleinschmidt, Erich.** "Poetik der Auflösung: Zur Funktion der Hiob-Mythe in Texten Oskar Kokoschkas, Joseph Roths und Karl Wolfskehls." In *Paradeigmata: Literarische Typologie des Alten*

Testaments. Vol. 2. Ed. Franz Link. Berlin: Duncker & Humblot, 1989. 511–26. **Lowsky, Martin.** *Erläuterungen zu Joseph Roth, Hiob: Roman eines einfachen Mannes.* Hollfeld: Bange, 2005. **Mazellier-Grunbeck, Catherine.** "Le poids de la grace de Joseph Roth: reduction parodique et condensation mythique." In *Le héros et l'héroïne bibliques dans la culture.* Montpellier: Université Paul-Valéry de Montpellier, 1997. 171–82. **Robertson, Ritchie.** "Roth's 'Hiob' and the Traditions of Ghetto Fiction." In *Co-Existent Contradictions: Joseph Roth in Retrospect. Papers of the 1989 Joseph Roth Symposium at Leeds University to Commemorate the 50th Anniversary of His Death.* Ed. Helen Chambers. Riverside, CA: Ariadne Press, 1991. 185–200. **Rosenfeld, Sidney.** "Joseph Roth's 'Hiob': Glaube und Heimat im Bild des Raumes." *Journal of English and Germanic Philology* 66 (1967) 489–500. **Schmidjell, Christine.** *Joseph Roth, Hiob.* Stuttgart: Reclam, 2004. **Schrader, Hans-Jürgen.** "'Hiob' in deutscher Dichtung ('Faust'–Joseph Roth–Lyrik nach der Schoah) Muster des Menschen–des jüdischen Leids–der Frage nach Theodizee." In *Religio in litteris: Vier Interpretationen deutscher Dichtung zwischen Aufklärung und Moderne in ihrer Beziehung zum Religiösen.* Vorträge anlässlich des 70. Geburtstags von Dr. Rudolf Mohr im Rahmen der Jahrestagung 2003 des Vereins für Rheinische Kirchengeschichte. Bonn: R. Habelt, [2004]. 1–32. **Shaked, Gershon.** "Wie jüdisch ist ein jüdisch-deutscher Roman? Über Joseph Roths 'Hiob. Roman eines einfachen Mannes'." In *Juden in der deutschen Literatur. Ein deutsch-israelisches Symposium.* Ed. Stéphane Moses and Albrecht Schöne. Frankfurt: Suhrkamp, 1986, 281–92. **Steinwendtner, Brita.** *Hiobs Klage heute: Die biblische Gestalt in der Literatur des 20. Jahrhunderts.* Innsbruck: Tyrolia-Verlag, 1990. 37–62. **Verrienti, Virginia.** "Joseph Roth: il Giobbe di Zuchnow." In *I volti di Giobbe. Percorsi interdisciplinari.* Ed. Gilberto Marconi and Cristina Termini. Bologna: EDB, 2002. 253–69. **Voges, Michael.** "Literatur und Film. Michael Kehlmanns Verfilmung von Joseph Roths Roman 'Hiob'." In *Joseph Roth. Interpretation, Kritik, Rezeption.* Ed. Michael Kessler and Fritz Hackert. Tübingen: Stauffenburg Verlag, 1990. 385–94. **Voss, Oda.** "'Hiob-Roman eines einfachen Mannes.' Joseph Roth und das Ostjudentum." *Exil* 9,2 (1989) 19–41. **Zimmer, Michael.** *Joseph Roth, Hiob: Interpretationen und Materialen.* Analysen und Reflexionen 83. Hollfeld: Beyer, 1998.

Roy, Gabrielle (French Canadian novelist, 1909–1983). *Alexandre Chenevert: caissier.* Paris: Flammarion, 1954. [= *The Cashier.* Trans. Harry Binsse. Toronto: McClelland and Stewart, 1955]. See also **Drummond, Dennis.** "Alexandre Chenevert and the Book of Job." *Essays in French Literature* 27 (1990) 46–63.

Sacher-Masoch, Leopold von (Austrian novelist, 1836–1895). *Der neue Hiob: Roman.* Stuttgart: Cotta, 1872 [= *Le nouveau Job: Le laid.* Paris: Librairie Hachette, 1879; *The New Job.* Trans. H. L. Cohen. New York: Cassell Publishing Co., 1891].

Schaper, Edzard (German writer, 1908–1984). *Die Söhne Hiobs.* Cologne, Olten: Hegner, 1962.

Schmidt, Alfred Paul (Austrian writer, b. 1941). *Hiob zweiter Klasse: Roman. Was hatte ich an mir, dass man auf mich so einschlagen musste?* Vienna: Aarachne Verlag, 1995.

Schmidt, Arno (German dystopian author, 1914–1979). "Leviathan oder Die Beste der Welten" (1949). In his *Leviathan und Schwarze Spiegel.* Frankfurt: Fischer, 1987. 7–39. See also **Thomé, Hort.** "Wissenschaft und Spekulation in Arno Schmidts 'Leviathan'." In *Gebirgslandschaft mit Arno Schmidt. Grazer Symposion 1980.* Ed. Jörg Drews. Munich: Text und Kritik, 1982. 9–29.

Schneider, Rolf (German novelist, b. 1932). *Das Glück.* Darmstadt: Luchterhand, 1976.

Schnell, Robert Wolfgang (German painter, dramatist and writer, 1916–1986). *Das verwandelte Testamente: Hiob bekommt Bohnen; Drei Männer im Feuer; Der gute Kain; David spielt vor Saul; Susanna und Daniel.* Wuppertal: Hammer, 1973. 7–33.

Shaw, George Bernard (Irish dramatist and writer, 1856–1950). *The Adventures of the Black Girl in Her Search for God. Designed and Engraved by John Farleigh.* London: Constable & Co., 1932.

Shaw, Jean. *Job's Wife: A Novel.* Brentwood, TN: Wolgemuth & Hyatt, 1990.

Singer, Isaac Bashevis (Polish-born US Jewish author, 1902–1991). See **Reyer, William Robert.** *Biblical Figures in Selected Short Fiction of Isaac Bashevis Singer* [Abraham and Sarah, Job, Hosea]. Diss. Bowling Green State University, 1988.

Spark, Muriel (Scottish novelist, 1918–2006). *The Only Problem.* London: The Bodley Head, 1984 [= *Das einzige Problem: Roman.* Zurich: Diogenes, 1985]. See also **Pyper, Hugh S.** "The Reader in Pain: Job as Text and Pretext" [reader's suffering in Muriel Sparks's *The Only Problem*]. In *Text as Pretext: Essays in Honour of Robert Davidson.* Ed. Robert P. Carroll. JSOTSup 138. Sheffield: JSOT Press, 1982. 234–55 [= *LitTheol* 7 (1993) 111–29].

Sterne, Laurence (Irish-born English novelist, 1713–1768). *The Life and Opinions of Tristram Shandy, Gentleman.* London, 1759–62. See also **Lamb, Jonathan.** "The Job Controversy, Sterne, and the Question of Allegory." *Eighteenth-Century Studies* 24 (1990) 1–19.

Stoner, George Raymond (US writer, 1884–1958). *A Throne of Ashes: A Narrative Interpretation of the Life of Job.* Orange, CA: The Author, 1951.

Tan, Amy (Chinese US novelist, b. 1952). See **Kuan, Jeffrey K.** "Reading Amy Tan Reading Job." In *Relating to the Text: Interdisciplinary and Form-Critical Insights on the Bible.* Ed. Timothy J. Sandoval and Carleen Mandolfo. JSOTSup 384. London: T. & T. Clark International, 2003. 263–74.

Ulsen, Henk van (Dutch actor, b. 1927). *Job op Schokland.* Kampen: Kok, 1992.

Vargas Vila, José María (Colombian author, 1860–1933). *La demencia de Job: Novela.* Madrid: A. Rubinos, 1916 [= *Obras completas.* I. *Aura.* Buenos Aires: Biblioteca Nueva, 1946?].

Vialar, Paul (French novelist, 1898–1996). *Job: Roman.* Paris: Denoël, 1946.

Voltaire (pseudonym of François-Marie Arouet, French author and philosopher, 1694–1778). *Candide, ou l'optimisme.* London, 1759 [= *Candid: or, All for the Best.* London, 1759]. See also Voltaire, in Section f.ii (Authors) above.

Vonnegut, Kurt (US novelist, 1922–2007). *Breakfast of Champions, or, Goodbye Blue Monday.* New York: Delacorte Press, 1973 [= *Frühstück für starke Männer.* Reinbek, Hamburg: Rowohlt, 1987]. See also **Labin, Linda L.** *The Whale and the Ash-Heap: Transfigurations of Jonah and Job in Modern American Fiction—Frost, MacLeish, and Vonnegut.* Diss. Kent State University, 1980.

Walsh, William Thomas (US historical novelist, 1891–1949). *Out of the Whirlwind.* New York: R. M. McBride, 1935.

Wassmo, Herbjorg (Norwegian novelist, b. 1942). See **Paulson, Sarah Jeanette Root.** *Reflections in a Shattered Mirror: The Voices of Herbjorg Wassmo and Dina.* Diss. Wisconsin–Madison, 1993.

Wells, H. G. (English novelist, 1866–1946). *Mr Britling Sees It Through.* London: Cassell, 1916 [= *The Works of H. G. Wells.* Vol. 22. Atlantic Edition. London: T. Fisher Unwin, 1925.]. ———. *The Undying Fire: A Contemporary Novel.* London: Cassell & Co., 1919 [= *The Works of H. G. Wells.* Atlantic Edition. London: T. Fisher Unwin, 1925. 11:1–172; *Undying Fire: A Novel Based on the Book of Job.* Chicago: Summit Publishing, 1997; *Unsterbliches Feuer.* Frankfurt: Ullstein, 1985]. ———. *God the Invisible King.* London: Cassell, 1917. See also **Levenson, Jon Douglas.** *The Book of Job in Its Time and in the Twentieth Century.* Cambridge, MA: Harvard University Press, 1972. 30–39.

Werfel, Franz (Austrian Jewish writer, 1890–1945). "Die arge Legende von gerissenen Galgenstrick." In *Erzählungen aus zwei Welten.* Frankfurt a.M.: S. Fischer, 1954. 3:7–27 [orig. 1938].

Wiechert, Ernst (German Catholic novelist, 1887–1950). See **Steinwendtner, Brita.** *Hiobs Klage heute: Die biblische Gestalt in der Literatur des 20. Jahrhunderts.* Innsbruck: Tyrolia-Verlag, 1990. 63–96.

Williams, Walter Jon (US science-fiction writer, b. 1953). *Voice of the Whirlwind* [novel]. London: Futura, 1989.

Wolfe, Thomas (US novelist, 1900–1938). "God's Lonely Man." In *The Hills Beyond.* New York, London: Harper & Brothers, 1941 [= "Der Einsame Gottes." In his *Hinten jenen Bergen. Erzählungen.* Hamburg: Rowohlt, 1956. 135–43].

Zweig, Stefan (Austrian novelist, 1881–1942). See **Klaghofer-Treitler, Wolfgang.** *Zwischen Hiob und Jeremia: Stefan Zweig und Joseph Roth am Ende der Welt.* Frankfurt a.M.: Lang, 2007.

iv. Other literature

Allen, Woody (US filmmaker, b. 1935). See **Speidell, Todd H.** "God, Woody Allen, and Job." *ChrSchRev* 29 (2000) 551–61. **Stora-Sandor, Judith.** *L'humour juif dans la littérature: de Job à Woody Allen.* Paris: Presses Universitaires de France, 1984.

Borges, Jorge Luis (Argentinian writer, 1899–1986). "El libro de Job." *Conferencias.* Buenos Aires: Istituto de Intercambio Cultural Argentino Israeli [= "The Book of Job." In *Borges and His Successors: The Borgesian Impact on Literature and the Arts.* Ed. Edna Aizenberg. Columbia: University of Missouri Press, 1989. 267–75].

Buisset, Ariane (French yoga professor). "Le chien de Job." In *Le dernier tableau de Wang Wei: contes de l'éveils.* Paris: A. Michel, 1988.

Burton, Robert (English writer, 1577–1640). *The Anatomy of Melancholy: What It Is.* Oxford, 1621–51. See also **Vicchio, Stephen J.** *Job in the Modern World.* Eugene, OR: Wipf & Stock, 2006. 26–28.

Chanteur, Janine (French philosopher). *Les petits-enfants de Job: chronique d'une enfance meurtrie.* Paris: Editions du Seuil, 1990 [= *Chronique d'une enfance meurtrie: Les petits-enfants de Job.* Paris: France loisirs, 1991; *Los hijos de Job: crónica de una infancia dolorida.* Estella: Verbo Divino, 1993; *Giobbe, perche? Dialogo di una madre.* Assisi: Cittadella, 1992].

Colombo, Felipe (Peruvian priest and writer, 1623–1684). *El Job de la ley de gracia, retratado en la admirable vida del siervo de Dios venerable padre fray Pedro Urraca, del real, y militar orden de Nuestra Señora de la Merced, redencion de cqutivos, nacido al mundo en la villa de Xadraque, a la religion en el convento de la ciudad de Quito, al cielo en el de la ciudad de Lima en el Peru.* Madrid: Pedro Marin, 1790.

DeMatteis, Marc, Paul Jenkins, and John Kuramoto. *The Book of Job.* Part 1: *The End of All Things!* Part 2: *Termineus/Terminus* [graphic novel]. Strange Tales 4/2. New York: Marvel Comics, 1998.

Dysart, Joshua D. *Violent Messiahs: Volume One: The Book of Job* [graphic novel]. Orange, CA: Image Comics. 2002.

Freeman, Joseph. *Job: The Story of a Holocaust Survivor* [biography]. Westport, CT: Praeger, 1996.

Gardner, John C. (American author, 1933–1982). See **Ventura, Sally.** "John Gardner's Dialogue with the Book of Job." *Midwest Quarterly* 37 (1995) 80–91.

Kägi, Ulrich. *Am Ende—am Anfang: Gespräche mit Hiob. Erfahrungen nach einem Hirnschlag.* Stäfa: Rothenhäusler-Verlag, 1992.

Kaniuk, Yoram. *Hiob, Pebble und der Elefant.* Frankfurt a.M.: Alibaba-Verlag, 1993 [retelling for children; trans. from Hebrew].

Lange, Günther. *Grenzgänger wie Hiob: Unwirkliche Tatsachenberichte.* Stuttgart: Urachhaus, 1982.

Lazare, Bernard. *Le fumier de Job.* Paris: Rieder, 1928 [repr. Saulzures: Circé, 1996] [= *Job's Dungheap: Essays on Jewish Nationalism and Social Revolution.* Trans. Harry Lorin Binsse. New York: Schocken Books, 1948; *El muladar de Job.* Buenos Aires: M. Gleize, 1945; *Il letame di Giobbe.* Milan: Medusa, 2004].

Lhuillier, Claude. *Sur les pas de Job: carnets d'un prisonnier de guerre.* L'Evangile au vingtième siècle. Paris: Editions du Cerf, 1980.

Maeterlinck, Maurice (Belgian playwright and essayist, 1862–1949). "Job" [essay]. In his *L'ombre des ailes.* Paris: Fasquelle, 1936.

McLelland, Joseph C. *The Clown and the Crocodile.* Richmond: John Knox Press, 1970.

Meidinger-Geise, Inge (ed.) (German writer, b. 1923). *Hiob kommt nach Himmerod: Ein Lesebuch.* Himmerod: Himmerod-Drucke, 1974.

Mitchell, Stephen A. *Job in Female Garb: Studies on the Autobiography of Agneta Horn* [Swedish noblewoman, 1629–1672]. Gothenburg: Litteraturvetenskapliga institutionen vid Göteborgs universitet, 1985.

Molzahn, Ilse. "Hiobs Versuchung." *Goldene Tor: Monatsschrift für Literatur und Kunst* 4 (1949) 194–201.

Schröder, Rudolf Alexander (German writer and poet, 1878–1962). "Marginalien zum Buch Hiob." In his *Gesammelte Werke.* Vol. 3. Frankfurt a.M.: Suhrkamp, 1952. 439–78.

Tamez, Elsa. "A Letter to Job." In *New Eyes for Reading: Biblical and Theological Reflections by Women from the Third World.* Ed. J. Pobee and B. Wartenberg-Potter. Quezon City, Philippines: Claretian, 1987. 50–52 –––. "Dear Brother Job–A Letter from the Dump." *Sojourners* 12 (1983) 23.

Tepl, Johann von (Bohemian author, 1350–1414). *Der Ackermann aus Böhmen* [first popular printed German book, 1461; = **Knieschek, J. (ed.).** *Der Ackermann aus Boehmen.* Bibliothek der mittelhochdeutschen Literatur in Boehmen 2. Prague: Brockhaus, 1877; *Death and the Ploughman: An Argument and a Consolation from the Year 1400.* Trans. K. W. Maurer. London: Langley, 1947]. See **Winston, Carol Anne.** *The "Ackermann aus Böhmen" and the Book of Job.* Diss. Kansas, 1979.

Wells, Leon Weliczker (Holocaust survivor, b. 1925). *The Janowska Road.* New York: Macmillan, 1963 [= *The Death Brigade: The Janowska Road.* New York: Holocaust Library, 1978; *Ein Sohn Hiobs.* Munich: Hanser, 1963; *Pour que la terre se souvienne.* Paris: A. Michel, 1962].

Wiesel, Elie. "Job ou le silence révolutionnaire." In *Célébration biblique: portraits et légendes.* Paris: Editions du Seuil, 1975. 179–99 [= *Messengers of God: Biblical Portraits and Legends.* New York: Summit Books, 1976; "Hiob oder das revolutionäre Schweigen." In *Adam oder das Geheimnis des Anfangs: Brüderliche Urgestalten.* Freiburg i.Br.: Herder, 1980. 207–32].

Wolff, Karin (ed.). *Hiob 1943: Ein Requiem für das Warschauer Getto.* Neukirchen–Vluyn: Neukirchener Verlag, 1983.

Zorn, Fritz (pseudonym of Fritz Angst, 1944–1976). *Mars.* Munich: Kindler, 1977 [= *Mars.* London: Picador, 1982].

h. Job in Art

In the lists of themes and of artists, cross-references are given where possible to certain standard works. Balentine = **Balentine, Samuel E.** *Job.* Smyth & Helwys Bible Commentary. Macon, GA: Smyth & Helwys, 2006. Besserman = **Besserman, Lawrence L.** *The Legend of Job in the Middle Ages.* Cambridge, MA: Harvard University Press, 1979. Denis = **Denis, V.** "Saint Job, patron des musiciens." *Revue belge d'archéologie et d'histoire d'art* 21 (1952) 253–98. Hulst = **Hulst, Roger-Adolf d'.** *Rubens: The Old Testament.* London: Harvey Miller, 1969. Karcher = **Karcher, Eva.** *Otto Dix, 1891–1969: Leben und Werk.* Cologne: Benedikt Taschen Verlag, 1988. Meyer = **Meyer, Kathi.** "St Job as a Patron of Music." *Art Bulletin* (New York) 36 (1954) 21–31. Pigler = **Pigler, Andor.** *Barockthemen. Eine Auswahl von Verzeichnissen des 17. und 18. Jahrhunderts.* 3 vols. Budapest: Akadémiai Kiadó, 1974. Terrien = **Terrien, Samuel L.** *The Iconography of Job through the Centuries: Artists as Biblical Interpreters.* University Park, PA: Pennsylvania State University

Press, 1996. Vicchio = **Vicchio, Stephen, and Lucinda Dukes Edinberg.** *The Sweet Uses of Adversity: Images of the Biblical Job.* Baltimore, MD: IPP Press, 2002.

i. General

Baumstark, A. "Die byzantische Job-Illustration und ihre Grundlagen." *OrChr* 31 (1964) 261–67. **Bochet, Marc.** "L'expressionisme et le cri de Job." *Etudes* 388/1 (1998) 89–97. **Budde, Rainer.** "Job." In *Lexikon der christlichen Ikonographie.* Ed. Engelbert Kirschbaum. Rome: Herder, 1970. 2:407–14. **Carles, Chaffrey.** "Job dans les arts." *Gazette des beaux-arts* no. 880 (Sept.–Oct. 1936). **Coolen, Chanoine.** "La confrérie de Monsieur Saint Job." *Bulletin de la société des antiquaires de la Morinie* 16 (1942) 208 [Job as patron saint of syphilitics]. **Deremble, Jean-Paul.** "Jalons iconographiques du thème de Job: du premier siècle au début de la Renaissance." *Graphè* 6 (1997) 135–55. **Durand, Jannic.** "Note sur une iconographie méconnue: le 'saint roi Job'." *CahArch* 32 (1984) 113–35. ———. *Recherches sur l'iconographie de Job des origines de l'art chrétien jusqu'au XIIIe siècle.* Diss. L'Ecole des Chartes, Paris, 1981. **Gaillard, G.** "Le chapiteau de Job aux musées de Toulouse et de Pampelune." *Revue des arts* 10 (1960) 146–56. **Gallo, Marco.** "Giobbe 'rursus resurrecturus cum quibus dominus resurgit.' Note sull'iconografia della Discesa di Cristo agl'inferi e sulla figura di Giobbe in area veneta tra la fine del XV e l'inizio del XVI secolo." In *I volti di Giobbe. Percorsi interdisciplinari.* Ed. Gilberto Marconi and Cristina Termini. Bologna: EDB, 2002. 183–216. **Gallottini, Angela.** "Ma Giobbe era solo paziente? L'iconografia paleocristiana di Giobbe." In *I volti di Giobbe. Percorsi interdisciplinari.* Ed. Gilberto Marconi and Cristina Termini. Bologna: EDB, 2002. 171–82. **Gitay, Zefira.** "The Portrayal of Job's Wife and Her Representation in the Visual Arts." In *Fortunate the Eyes That See: Essays in Honor of David Noel Freedman in Celebration of His Seventieth Birthday.* Ed. Astrid B. Beck, Andrew H. Bartelt, Paul R. Raabe, and Chris A. Franke. Grand Rapids: Ecrdmans, 1995. 516–26. **Grill, Ingrid.** *Aber meine Augen werden ihn schauen … : Hiob. 1. Ein Versuch zum Themenbereich "Die Bibel als Grundlage des Glaubens" für die 11. Jahrgangsstufe. 2. Ein Lesebuch zur Wirkungsgeschichte der Hiobgestalt in Philosophie, Theologie und Kunst.* Arbeitshilfe für den evangelischen Religionsunterricht an Gymnasien: Themenfolge 97. Erlangen: Gymnasialpädagogische Materialstelle der Evangelisch-Lutherischen Kirche in Bayern, 1994. **Huber, Paul.** *Hiob. Dulder oder Rebell? Byzantinische Miniaturen zum Buche Hiob in Patmos, Rom, Venedig, Sinai, Jerusalem und Athos.* Düsseldorf: Patmos, 1986. **Kritter, Ulrich von, and Karl Arndt (eds.).** *Das Buch Hiob in der Kunst des 20. Jahrhunderts.* Göttingen: Goltze, 1987. **Lannois, Maurice, and J. Lacassagne.** "Quelques représentations sculpturales du Saint Job." *Æsculape* 28 (1938) 32–46. **Le Blant, E.** "D'une représentation inédite de Job sur un sarcophage d'Arles." *RevArch* (1860-B) 36–44. **Leclerq, H.** "Job." *DAC* 7:2554–70. **Osten, Gert von der.** "Job and Christ: The Development of a Devotional Image." *Journal of the Warburg and Courtauld Institutes* 16 (1953) 153–58. **Papadaki-Okland, Styliani.** *The Illustration of the Byzantine Job-Manuscript: A Preliminary Study on Its Origin and Development.* Diss. Heidelberg, 1980. **Perraymond, Myla.** "Giobbe: annotazioni icongrafiche e tradizione esegetica." *SMSR* 67 (2001) 229–52. ———. *La figura di Giobbe nella cultura paleocristiana tra esegesi patristica e manifestazioni iconografiche.* Città del Vaticano: Pontificio istituto di archeologia cristiana, 2002. **Pigler, Andor.** *Barockthemen. Eine Auswahl von Verzeichnissen des 17. und 18. Jahrhunderts.* 3 vols. Budapest: Akadémiai Kiadó, 1974. 1:204–6. **Poesch, Jessie.** "The Beasts from Job in the Liber Floridus Manuscripts." *Journal of the Warburg and Courtauld Institutes* 33 (1970) 41–51. **Ravasi, Gianfranco.** *Giobbe. Traduzione e commento.* Commenti biblici. Rome: Borla, 1979; 2nd ed. 1984. 258–74. **Réau, Louis.** *Iconographie de l'art chrétien.* II. *Iconographie de la Bible.* I. *Ancien Testament.* Paris: Presses Universitaires de France, 1956. 310–18. **Sindermann-Lange, Anke.** *Die Hiob-Ikonographie des 15.–17. Jahrhunderts im deutsch-niederländischen Kulturraum.* Diss. Karlsruhe, 1999. **Sparrow, Walter Shaw (ed.).** *Joshua to Job, Being a Continuation of "The Old Testament in Art" and a Companion Volume to "The Gospels in Art" and "The Apostles in Art."* London: Hodder &

Stoughton, 1906. **Terrien, Samuel L.** *The Iconography of Job through the Centuries: Artists as Biblical Interpreters.* University Park, PA: Pennsylvania State University Press, 1996. **Vásquez de Parga, Luis.** "La historia de Job en un capitel románico de la catedral de Pamplona." *Archivo español de arte* 14 (1941) 410–11. **Vicchio, Stephen, and Lucinda Dukes Edinberg.** *The Sweet Uses of Adversity: Images of the Biblical Job.* Baltimore, MD: IPP Press, 2002. **Walbrodt, Friedemann.** *Buch-Malerei zum Buche Hiob.* Berlin–Dahlem: F. Walbrodt, 2007. **Weisbach, Werner.** "L'histoire de Job dans les arts: A propos du tableau de Georges de La Tour au musée d'Epinal." *Gazette des beaux-arts* 78/2 (1936) 102–12. **Westerhoff-Sebald, Ingrid.** *Zur Ikonographie des Hiob in der französischen Kathedralskulptur.* Diss. Frankfurt am Main, 1987.

ii. Topics

Behemoth and Leviathan. Drewer, Lois. "Leviathan, Behemoth and Ziz: A Christian Adaptation." *Journal of the Warburg and Courtauld Institutes* 44 (1981) 148–56. **Gutmann, Joseph.** "Leviathan, Behemoth and Ziz: Jewish Messianic Symbols in Art." *HUCA* 39 (1968) 219–30.

Job as the Patron Saint of Musicians. Balentine, Samuel E. "The Church of Saint Job." *RevExp* 96 (1999) 501–18. **Cuttler, Charles D.** "Job–Music–Christ: An Aspect of the Iconography of Job." *Institut royal du patrimoine artistique* (Brussels), *Bulletin* 15 (1975) 87–96. **Declerq, P.** "Verering van Sint Job te Nieuwpoort." *Biekorf* 56 (1956) 360–62. **Denis, V.** "Saint Job, patron des musiciens." *Revue belge d'archéologie et d'histoire d'art* 21 (1952) 253–98. **Erens, A.** "De Eeredienst van Sint Job te Wezemaal." In *Eigen Schoon en De Brabander* (1939) 1–12. **Hoq, Marcel.** "Médailles de S. Job vénéré à Wesemael." *Revue belge de numismatique et de la sigilographie* 89 (1942) 19–42. **Lannois, Maurice.** "Job, sa femme et les musiciens." *Æsculape* 29 (1939) 194–207. **Meyer, Kathi.** "St Job as a Patron of Music." *Art Bulletin* (New York) 36 (1954) 21–31. **Nicholson, J. W.** "Job." In *The New Grove Dictionary of Music and Musicians.* Ed. Stanley Sadie. London: Macmillan, 1980. 9:655–56. **Vötterle, Karl.** "Hiob als Schutzpatron der Musiker." *Musik und Kirche* 23 (1953) 225–32.

Job Relieved of His Pain by Water and Music. Brown, Marguerite L. "The Subject Matter of Duerer's Jabach Altar." *Marsyas* 1 (1941) 55–68. **Kaufmann, Hans.** "Albrecht Dürer's Dreikönigs-Altar." *Westdeutsches Jahrbuch für Kunstgeschichte, Wallraf-Richartz Jahrbuch* 10 (1938) 166–78. **Weiszäcker, Heinrich.** "Der sogennante Jabachsche Altar und die Dichtung des Buches Hiob." In *Kunstwissenschaftliche Beiträge: August Schmarshow gewidmet zum fünfzigsten Semester seiner akademischen Lehrtätigkeit.* Leipzig: K. W. Hiersmann, 1907. 153–62.

iii. By Theme and Period

Adam, the Gardener, Buries Job. *20th cent.* **Kokoshka, Oskar.** Drawing. 1917 [Terrien 240].

Anima and the Dying Job. *20th cent.* **Kokoshka, Oskar.** Drawing. 1917 [Terrien 241].

Banquet of King Job and His Queen. *14th cent.* **Fredi, Bartolo di.** c. 1367. Fresco. Basilica Collegiata di S. Maria Assunta, San Gimignano [Terrien 98].

Behemoth. *13th cent.* **Anon.** Miniature. From Northern France. British Museum, London. Ms. add. 11639, fear of the Lord. 519r.

Behemoth and Leviathan. *8th/9th cent.* **Anon.** Miniature. Codex Patmos, 171. St John's Monastery, Patmos. *19th cent.* **Blake, William.** In *Illustrations of the Book of Job.* 1823–1825, 17 [Terrien 215; Balentine 682].

Behemoth Ridden by the Devil. *12th cent.* **Anon.** Illumination. *Liber Floridus.* Centraale Bibliotheek van der Rijksuniversiteit, Ghent [Terrien 46; Balentine 683].

Death of Job's Children. *12th cent.* **Anon.** Romanesque capital. Cathedral of Pamplona [Terrien 66]. **Anon.** Romanesque capital. La Daurade Priory. Musée des Augustins, Toulouse [Terrien 69]. *14th cent.* **Fredi, Bartolo di.** *A Hurricane Kills Job's*

Children. c. 1367. Fresco. Basilica Collegiata di S. Maria Assunta, San Gimignano [Terrien 99]. **Gaddi, Taddeo.** Fresco. c. 1350. Camposanto, Pisa [LCI 411]. *16th cent.* **Orley, Bernart van.** Altarpiece, central panel. Oil on canvas. 1521–1525. Musées Royaux de Beaux-Arts, Brussels [Terrien 161]. *19th cent.* **Blake, William.** *Death of Job's Children.* Also known as *Job's Sons and Daughters Overwhelmed by Satan.* In *Illustrations of the Book of Job.* 1823–1825. 3 [Terrien 198].

Demons Attack Job with Leprosy. *12th cent.* **Anon.** Miniature. Winchester School. Bodleian Library, Oxford. Ms. Auct.E.infra I, fol. 304.

Elihu. *19th cent.* **Blake, William.** *Elihu Points to the Stars.* Also known as *The Wrath of Elihu.* In *Illustrations of the Book of Job.* 1823–1825. 12 [Terrien 210].

Eliphaz, Vision of. *19th cent.* **Blake, William.** In *Illustrations of the Book of Job.* 1823–1825. 9 [Terrien 207].

Fountain of Job, The. *19th cent.* **Haghe, Louis.** *The Fountain of Job–The Holy Land.* Lithograph with hand coloring. Fine Arts Museums of San Francisco.

God and Satan. *12th cent.* **Anon.** Miniature. Gumpert Bible. Universitätsbibliothek, Erlangen. Codex 121, fol. 247v. *14th cent.* **Gaddi, Taddeo.** 1366. Fresco. Camposanto, Pisa [Terrien 93; Balentine 711].

Job. *11th cent.* **Anon.** Miniature. In Gregory, *Moralia.* Staatsbibliothek, Vienna. Cod. 673. *12th cent.* **Anon.** Fresco. Before 1149. Benedictine Abbey, Brauweiler. **Anon.** Title page to John's Gospel in the Floresse Bible. c. 1125. British Museum, London. Add. ms. 17738, fol. 3v.

14th cent. **Anon.** Illustration. In Hebrew Hymnal. c. 1300. Library, Jewish Theological Seminary, Cincinnati. Ms 0017. **Bonaiuto, Andrea di.** Fresco. Spanish chapel in Santa Maria Novella, Florence. c. 1365. **Martini, Simone.** Papal Palace, Avignon [Meyer 25]. **Nardo di Ciotte, after.** 1365. Triptychon, Santa Croce, Florence.

15th cent. **Anon.** Window. Sainte Chapelle, Paris. See **Hinkle, William M.** *The Portal of the Saints of Reims Cathedral: A Study in Mediaeval Iconography.* New York: College Art Association of America, 1965. Fig. 88. ———. Window. St Patrice, Rouen [Meyer 28]. **Bartolommeo, Fra.** *Study for "Job."* Pen and ink on paper. Courtauld Institute of Art Gallery, London. **Bellini, Filippo.** Painting. Oratorio della Carità Fabriano [Pigler 204]. **Bellini, Giovanni.** *Madonna and Child, Three Musical Angels, and SS. Francis, John the Baptist, Job, Dominic, Sebastian, and Louis of Toulouse,* known as the *St Job Altarpiece (Pala di San Giobbe).* c. 1487. Tempera on panel. Galleria dell'Accademia, Venice [Terrien 133]. **Carpaccio, Vittorio.** *Meditation on the Passion.* Tempera on wood. c. 1495. Metropolitan Museum of Art, New York [Terrien 136].

16th cent. **al-Nishapur, Ibrahim.** Illumination in Persian manuscript of *Qisas al Anbiya* (*Legends of the Prophets*). 1580. Spencer Collection, New York Public Library. Persian MS 46, fol. 109 [Vicchio 56]. **Anon.** Predella. Stadtkirche, Bitterfeld. c. 1520. **Bartolommeo, Fra.** Engraving by Gerard René Le Vilain (1740–1836), Baltimore Museum of Art: Garrett Collection, BMA 1946.112.3155 [Vicchio 62]. **Bellini, Giovanni.** Sacra allegoria. Oil on canvas. c. 1504–1505. Uffizi, Florence [Terrien 129]. **Carpaccio, Vittore.** *Job and the Dead Christ.* Tempera on wood. c. 1505–1510. Staatliche Museen zu Berlin, Preussischer Kulturbesitz Gemäldegalerie [Terrien 138]. **Cranach, Lucas.** Sketch. c. 1510. Marienkirche, Frankfurt [Meyer 29]. **Meldolla, Andrea (Schiavone).** Drawing. Musée du Louvre, Paris [Pigler 204]. **Pencz, Georg.** Engraving [Pigler 204].

17th cent. **Anon.** *Saint Job.* Wood sculpture. 17th or 18th cent. New Mexico Santo. Taylor Museum of Southwestern Studies of the Colorado Springs Fine Arts Center [Terrien 157]. **Anon.** *St Job with Sunburst Halo.* Wood sculpture. Old Bolderbergkerk, Limburg [Terrien 156]. **Borzone, Luciano.** *Job (?).* Painting. Private Collection, Genoa [Pigler 204]. **Brentana, Simone.** Painting. S. Niccolò, Verona [Pigler 205]. **Callot, Jacques.** *St Job, Prophet, May 10.* In *Les Images de tous les saincts et saintes de l'année, suiuant le martyrologe romains . . . Mises en lumiere par Israel Henriet.* Paris, 1636. ———. *St Job, Prophet.* Etching. National Gallery of Art, Washington, DC. **Franck, Franz Friedrich.** Painting. Evangelisches Waisenhaus, Augsburg [Pigler 206]. **Heuvel, Antoon van den.** Painting.

Church of Puivelde near Beisele, Belgium [Pigler 206]. **Holzmair, Johann Wilhelm.** Painting. Church, Bergkirchen, Upper Bavaria [Pigler 206]. **Langetti, Giovanni Battista.** Oval Painting. Galerie Schönborn, Pommersfelden, Bamberg [Pigler 205]. **Loth, Johann Carl (Carlotto).** Painting. Baron von Obermayr Collection, Munich. ———. Painting. Palazzo Morosini, Venice. **Preti, Mattia.** Painting. Palazzo Dragonetti Cappelli, Aquila, Italy [Pigler 205]. **Ribera, Jusepe de.** *Job [Job in Prayer]*. 1640. Galleria nazionale, Parma [Terrien 184; Balentine 4]. **Ricci, Sebastiano.** Painting. Formerly Collection Sipriot, Marseilles. ———. Drawing. Windsor Castle, England [Pigler 205]. **Sacchi, Andrea.** Painting. Wilton House, Salisbury, England [Pigler 204]. **Velázquez, Diego (?).** *Seated Job in Profile.* c. 1618–1630. Oil on canvas. The Art Institute of Chicago [Terrien 180].

18th cent. **Appiani, Giuseppe.** Painting and oil sketch. Germanisches National- museum, Nuremburg [Pigler 205]. **Deshayes, Jean-Baptiste-Henri.** Painting. 1751 [Pigler 206]. **Guglielmi, Gregorio.** Oval painting. Cappella Colleoni, Bergamo [Pigler 205]. **Polazzo, Francesco.** Painting. 1743. S. Alessandro della Croce, Bergamo [Pigler 205].

19th cent. **Blake, William.** *Job* (separate plate). 1st state c. 1793. Keynes Collection, Fitzwilliam Museum, Cambridge. 2nd state c. 1820–1826. The British Museum, London. **Gilbert, John.** *The Patriarch. Illustration to the Book of Job.* Wood engraving. Museum of Fine Arts, Boston. **Legros, Alphonse.** *Job.* Drypoint and etching. National Gallery of Art, Washington, DC [Vicchio 72]. **Stölzel, Christian Ernst.** Etching and engraving, after Gustav Marie Jäger (1808–1871). Philadelphia Museum of Art. 1985-052-15920 [Vicchio 70]. **Strang, William.** *Job.* Print. 1882. P.8861-R. Fitzwilliam Museum, Cambridge.

20th cent. **Baskin, Leonard.** *Job.* Etching. c. 1970. Museum of Fine Arts, Boston. **Ben-Zion.** Etching. In his portfolio, *The Book of Ruth—Job—Song of Songs.* 1954. The Jewish Museum, New York [Vicchio 87]. **Ben-Shmuel, Ahron.** Bronze sculpture. 1942. Philadelphia Museum of Art [Vicchio 81]. **Braque, George.** *Job.* Drypoint and etch- ing. 1911. Fine Arts Museums of San Francisco. ———. *Job.* Etching on Arches paper. 1911. National Gallery of Art, Washington, DC. **Chagall, Marc.** *Job with Background of Geometricized Christ à la Cimabuë.* 1975. Oil on canvas. Private collection, St Paul de Vence [Terrien color plate 4]. **Dix, Otto.** Tempera on plywood. 1946. Otto-Dix-Stiftung, Vaduz [Karcher 224]. **Fuchs, Ernst.** *Hiob.* Etching and aquatint. 1963. Fine Arts Museums of San Francisco. **Gruber, Francis.** Oil on canvas. 1944. Tate Gallery, London [Terrien 250; Balentine 361]. **Kohn, Misch.** Woodcut. Library of Congress, Washington, DC [Vicchio 90]. **Kulhanek, Oldrich.** *Job.* 2002. Galerie Art Chrudim, Czech Republic. **Levin, Julo.** Painting. Oil on linen. 1933/34. Stadtmuseum, Düsseldorf [Kempel 297]. **Rattner, Abraham.** *Job #9.* Oil on canvas. 1959. Kennedy Galleries, New York [Terrien color plate 3]. **Spruance, Benton Murdoch.** *The Word and Job.* Woodcut. 1951. Philadelphia Museum of Art [Vicchio 83]. **Wachter, Emil.** In *Biblische Portraits. Lithographien mit Texten von Friedrich Weinreb.* Munich, 1982. 107. **Whelan, Michael.** *Job, a Comedy of Justice* [cover illustration for the novel by Robert A. Heinlein]. Acrylic. 1984. The Kelly Collection of American Illustration [Vicchio 95].

Job Afflicted by Satan. *11th cent.* **Anon.** Miniature. Ms Vat. lat. 5729, fol. 162. *16th cent.* **Beham, Hans Sebald.** Woodcut, in his *Biblisch Historien, figürlich fürgebildet.* Frankfurt a.M., 1533 [Vicchio 52].

Job and a Prancing Demon. *20th cent.* **Chagall, Marc.** Tinted drawing. 1960 [Terrien 258].

Job and Elihu. *8th/9th cent.* **Anon.** Illumination. St John Monastery, Patmos [Terrien 36; Balentine 525].

Job and His Daughters. *19th cent.* **Blake, William.** *Job and His Daughters.* 1799/1800. National Gallery of Art. Washington, DC. ———. *Job and His Daughters.* Pencil sketch. c. 1821. Rosenwald Collection, National Gallery of Art, Washington, DC. ———. *Job and His Daughters.* Tempera painting. c. 1799–1800. National Gallery of Art, Washington, DC. ———. *Job and His Daughters.* Watercolor. c. 1821–1827. Private collection, USA.

———. *Job and His Daughters.* Copper engraving, 1823–1826. Tate Britain, London. ———. *The Beauty of Job's Daughters.* Also known as *Job and His Daughters.* In *Illustrations of the Book of Job.* 1823–1825, 20 [Terrien 223; Balentine 716].

Job and His Family. *19th cent.* **Blake, William.** In *Illustrations of the Book of Job.* 1823–1825. 1 [Terrien 196; Balentine 50]. **Jaeckel, Willy.** *Das Buch Hiob.* Lithograph. 1917. The Jewish Museum, New York [Vicchio 80]. **Tissot, James Jacques Joseph.** c. 1896–1902. Gouache on paper. The Jewish Museum, New York [Vicchio 73].

Job and His Friend. *20th cent.* **Michelson, Leo.** *Job and His Friend* [cf. Terrien 246].

Job and His Friends (see also Job's Friends). *8th/9th cent.* **Anon.** Miniature. Codex Patmos, 171. St John's Monastery, Patmos. *12th cent.* **Anon.** *Job and His Three Friends.* Bas relief on capital of twin columns. c. 1165–1175. Musée des Augustins, Daurade Monastery (Benedictine priory of Notre-Dame de la Daurade), Toulouse [Terrien 70].

13th cent. **Anon.** Bas-relief in West Doorway representing the Last Judgment. Notre Dame, Paris.

14th cent. **Anon.** Monastic Psalter, 1300. Walters Art Museum, Baltimore [Vicchio 47]. **Anon.** Bible, historiated initial V. c. 1300. Walters Art Museum, Baltimore. W151, fol. 239 [Vicchio 48]. **Fredi, Bartolo di.** Fresco. c. 1367. Basilica Collegiata di S. Maria Assunta, San Gimignano [Terrien 100]. **Gaddi, Taddeo.** c. 1355. Fresco. Camposanto, Pisa [Terrien 96].

15th cent. **Anon.** French Book of Hours. 1400. Library of Congress, Washington, DC [Vicchio 49]. **Anon.** Misericord in church of Champeaux, Seine-et-Marne. **Fouquet, Jean.** *Job and His False Comforters.* c. 1452–1460. Miniature from the Book of Hours of Etienne Chevalier. Musée Condé, Chantilly [Terrien 103; Balentine 484].

16th cent. **Beham, Barthel.** *Job Conversing with His Friends.* Engraving. Fine Arts Museums of San Francisco. **Beham, Hans Sebald.** Engraving. 1547. Philadelphia Museum of Art [Vicchio 54]. **Bosch, Hieronymus.** Douai Museum. **Bourdichon, School of.** Illumination, *Book of Hours of Henri IV.* Ms lat. 1171, fol. 58v. Bibliothèque Nationale, Paris [Terrien 116]. **Dietenberger, Johann.** *Biblia, beider Allt vnnd [unnd] Newen Testamenten, fleissig, treülich vn[d] Christlich, nach alter, inn Christlicher kirchen gehabter Translation, mit ausslegunng etlicher dunckeler ort, vnnd besserung viler verrückter wort und Sprüch.* Cologne: Quentel; Mainz: Jordan, 1534. **Falaise, Robert.** *Job's Friends in Dunce Cap.* Wood sculpture, stalls of the Collegium of Champeaux [Terrien 125; Balentine 202].

17th cent. **Bramer, Leonaert.** Drawing. National Museum, Warsaw [Pigler 206]. **Giordano, Luca.** *Job and His Comforters.* Oil on canvas. c. 1680. Sacristia del Monasterio de San Lorenzo, L'Escorial, Madrid [Terrien 186]. **Il Calabrese.** *Job, His Wife, His Friends, the Devil, and an Angel.* Oil on canvas. 1690. Musée Royal des Beaux-Arts, Brussels [Terrien 185]. **Loth, Johann Carl (Carlotto).** Painting. Galerie Schönborn, Pommersfelden. ———. Painting. Gemäldegalerie Alte Meister, Dresden. Kat. 1905, Nr 2005. **Preti, Mattia.** Painting. Suermondt Museum, Aachen [Pigler 205]. **Rosa, Salvator.** *Giobbe [Job, His Friends, and an Armored Warrior].* Oil on canvas. c. 1665. Vasari Corridor, Uffizi, Florence [Terrien 170].

18th cent. **Barry, James.** *Job Reproved by His Friends.* Etching, line-engraving and aquatint on paper. 1777. Tate Gallery, London. **Lama, Giulia.** Painting. Location unknown [Pigler 205].

19th cent. **Blake, William.** *Job and His Friends.* Pencil sketch in Blake's Notebook, c. 1790–1792. British Library, London. **Bourne, Herbert.** Engraving, after Paul Falconer Poole (1807–1879). Jewish Theological Seminary of America, New York. Special Collections F74.2.2 [Vicchio 71]. **Goldschmitt, Bruno.** *Hiob.* Wood engraving. In *Portfolio Die Bibel (The Bible).* Plate 17. Fine Arts Museums of San Francisco. **Grassi, Nicola.** Painting. Formerly Sammlung Haberstock, Berlin [Pigler 205]. **Repin, Ilya.** Oil on canvas. 1869. The Russian Museum, St Petersburg. **Rogers, John.** Engraving after Denis Auguste Marie Raffet. Jewish Theological Seminary of America, New York [Vicchio 78]. **Strang, William.** *Job and His Comforters.* 1884. P.8895-R. Fitzwilliam

Museum, Cambridge. **Tissot, James Jacques Joseph.** Gouache on paper. The Jewish Museum, New York [Vicchio 76]. **Wächter, Eberhard Georg Friedrich.** Painting. Staatsgalerie, Stuttgart [Pigler 207].

    20th cent. **Ben-Zion.** Etching. In his portfolio, *The Book of Ruth—Job—Song of Songs.* 1954. The Jewish Museum, New York [Vicchio 85]. **Eichenberg, Fritz** (German and US engraver, 1901–1990). *The Book of Job.* Wood engraving. 1955. National Gallery of Art, Washington, DC [Vicchio 88]. **Karsch, Joachim.** Gypsum sculpture. 1919. Lost (?) [Barron, Pl. 25]. **Ratner, Philip.** *Job.* 1998. Israel Bible Museum. **Zadkine, Ossip.** Wood sculpture. 1914. Koninklik Museum voor Schone Kunsten, Antwerp [Barron, Pl. 24].

    Job and His Neighbors. *19th cent.* **Blake, William.** *Every Man Also Gave Him a Piece of Money* (Alternative Composition). Watercolor. c. 1821–1823. Tate Britain, London.

    Job and His Wife. *3rd cent.* **Anon.** Fresco. Catacombs of the Via Dino Compagni, Rome. **Anon.** Fresco. Catacombs of Santi Marcellino e Pietro, Rome. *4th cent.* **Anon.** Fresco. New Catacomb. Via Latina, Rome [Terrien 20]. **Anon.** Sarcophagus of Junius Bassus. Museum of the Treasury, St Peter's Basilica, Rome [Terrien 25; Balentine 292]. See also **Malbon, Elizabeth Struthers.** *The Iconography of the Sarcophagus of Junius Bassus.* Princeton, NJ: Princeton University Press, 1990. *8th cent.* **Anon.** Bas relief, sarcophagus. Arles [Terrien 28]. *13th cent.* **Anon.** Franco-Flemish (probably Lille). **Anon.** Illustration. Bible. c. 1238. Hessische Landes- und Hochschulbibliothek, Darmstadt. Ms 825, fol. 166r [Besserman 116]. *15th cent.* **Anon.** German Bible, hand-colored illustrations. Nuremberg, 1483. Printed by Anton Koberger (1445–1513). Library of Congress, Washington, DC [Vicchio 50]. *16th cent.* **Anon.** Stalls of the Cathedral, Amiens. **Anon.** Windows of St Patrice and of St Romain. Rouen. **Dürer, Albrecht.** *Jabach Altarpiece.* Also known as *Job's Wife Pours Water on His Neck.* c. 1504. Städelschen Kunstinstitut, Frankfurt [Terrien 140–41]. **Huys, Peter.** Douai Museum. *17th cent.* **La Tour, Georges de.** *Job and His Wife.* Also known as *Job Mocked by His Wife.* c. 1650. Oil on canvas. Musée départemental des Vosges, Epinal, France. Cat. 1929, no. 152 [Terrien 167; Balentine 65]. **Loth, Johann Carl (Carlotto).** Painting. Galleria dell'Accademia, Venice. Inv. 437. ———. Painting. Palazzo Casilini Rovigo. ———. Painting. Vienna. Kat. Nr. 157. **Meyer, Rudolf.** Drawing. Albertina, Vienna [Pigler 206]. **Murillo, Bartolomé Esteban.** Parma Pinocoteca. *19th cent.* **Anon.** *Job in Deep Distress.* Engraving. Jewish Theological Seminary of America, New York [Vicchio 79]. *20th cent.* **Kokoshka, Oskar.** *Job's Wife Pours Water on His Neck.* Drawing. 1917 [Terrien 238]. **Wachter, Emil.** In *Biblische Portraits. Lithographien mit Texten von Friedrich Weinreb.* Munich, 1982. 109.

    Job and Musicians. *14th cent.* **Anon.** Illumination. Catena on Job [21:12]. Ms Gr. 1231, fol. 285. Bibliothèque Nationale, Paris [Terrien 113].

    15th cent. **Anon.** *Frightened Job and Maleficent Musicians.* Illumination. Ms lat. 1381, fol. 62. Bibliothèque Nationale, Paris [Terrien 113]. **Anon.** *Job and Musicians.* Ivory reliquary. Musée de Cluny, Paris [Terrien 120]. **Anon.** *Job and Musicians.* Painting. Dutch. c. 1495–1500. Church in Hattern [Denis 296]. **Anon.** *Job and Three Musicians.* Miniature. In Pierre de Nesson, *Paraphrase dea IX. Leçons de Job ou les Vigiles des morts.* Bibliothèque Nationale, Paris. Fonds français 1226, fol. 40. **Anon.** *Job Offers a Gold Piece to Three Musicians.* Illumination. Ms fr. 1226, fol. 40. Bibliothèque Nationale, Paris [Terrien 115]. **Bosch, Hieronymus.** Groeninge Museum, Bruges. **Mandyn, Jan.** *Job, His Wife, and Musicians.* Oil on canvas. c. 1470–1500. Musée de la Chartreuse, Douai [Terrien 121]. **Friesach, Konrad von.** *Christ as Job Tortured by the Devil and Musicians.* Painting on cloth. Lenten curtain. Gurk Cathedral, Carinthia [Terrien 114]. **Master of the Saint Barbara Legend.** Painting. c. 1470–1500. Wallraf-Richartz Museum, Cologne [Terrien 118–19].

    16th cent. **Anon.** *Job and Two Musicians.* Flemish. Wallfahrtsmünze, Wezemaal [Denis, Pl. VII]. **Anon.** *Job and Two Musicians.* French engraving. Title page, *Patience de Job.* Paris (Simon Calvarin). c. 1570 [Denis, fig. 19]. **Anon.** *Job and Two Musicians.* French engraving. In *Textus Bibliae.* Lyons, 1527 [Denis, fig. VIII]. **Anon.** *Job, Two Musicians and a Putto.* In *La Saincte Bible translatée de Latin.* Louvain, 1550 [Denis, fig. XVII]. **Anon.**

Netherlands, first quarter, 16th century. Poznan NM (ex Breslau, Children's Hospital). **Bosch, Hieronymus (after).** *Job and Three Musicians.* Painting. Ashmolean Museum, Oxford [Denis, Pl. XII]. **Dürer, Albrecht.** *Two Musicians Comfort Job.* Detail of *Jabach Altarpiece.* 1504–1510. Wallraf-Richartz Museum, Cologne. **Falaise, Robert.** *Misericord.* Wood sculpture. 1522. Collegium of Champeaux [Terrien 122]. **Leyden, Lucas van.** *Job and Three Musicians.* Also known as *Job and His Comforters.* Painting. Oil on panel. c. 1510. Collection of Viscount Lee of Fareham. Courtauld Institute of Art Gallery, London [Denis, Pl. XIII]. **Leyden, Lucas van, School of.** *Job and Three Musicians.* Painting. Private collection, Portugal [Denis, Pl. XIV].

17th cent. **Oost, Jacob van.** *Job and Musicians Comforting Him.* Painting. Archbishop's Palace, Olomouc, Czech Republic [Pigler 206].

Job and Patience. *9th cent.* **Anon.** Illustration. Prudentius, *Psychomachia.* Bürgerbibliothek Bern (MS 264, pp. 80, 81).

Job and Satan. *14th cent.* **Gaddi, Taddeo.** Fresco. c. 1355. Camposanto, Pisa [Terrien 93]. *17th cent.* **Herrera, Francisco de.** Painting. Musée Rouen [Pigler 295].

Job and the Angel of Death. *20th cent.* **Chagall, Marc.** Tinted drawing. 1960 [Terrien 259].

Job and the Messengers. *12th cent.* **Anon.** *The Three Messengers of Misfortune.* Chapter House of Pamplona Cathedral. *13th cent.* **Anon.** Tympanon of the Calixtus Portal, Reims Cathedral. See **Hinkle, William M.** *The Portal of the Saints of Reims Cathedral: A Study in Mediaeval Iconography.* New York: College Art Association of America, 1965. Figs. 79, 86, 87, 90. *14th cent.* **Anon.** *Job's Messengers.* Fresco. St Stephen's Chapel, Westminster Abbey. c. 1350/60. Now in British Museum, London. *16th cent.* **Anon.** *The Three Messengers of Misfortune.* Fresco. Camposanto, Pisa. **Hirschvogel, Augustin.** *Job Learns of His Misfortunes.* Etching. 1549. National Gallery of Art, Washington, DC [Vicchio 55]. *19th cent.* **Blake, William.** *The Messengers of Woe.* In *Illustrations of the Book of Job.* 1823–1825. 4 [Terrien 200]. **Tissot, James Jacques Joseph.** *Job Hears Bad Tidings.* c. 1896–1902. Gouache on paper. The Jewish Museum, New York [Vicchio 74].

Job and the Rubber Man. *20th cent.* **Kokoshka, Oskar.** Lithograph in black on laid paper. 1916/17. National Gallery of Art, Washington, DC.

Job and the Sabeans. *14th cent.* **Gaddi, Taddeo.** Fresco. c. 1355. Camposanto, Pisa [Terrien 95].

Job and the Savior. *12th cent.* **Anon.** Miniature. In *Bible moralisée.* Bodleian, Oxford. Ms 270b, fol. 218r.

Job as a Gypsy. *20th cent.* **Yoors, Jan.** Gouache. 1962. Private collection [Terrien 255].

Job as a Live Byzantine Mosaic. *20th cent.* **Corey, Orlin.** Mask, New York World's Fair, 1964 [Terrien 254].

Job as King. *12th cent.* **Anon.** Illumination. *Tuscan Bible.* Plut. 125.13, c. 285. Bibliotheca Medicea-Laurenziana, Florence [Terrien 53]. *13th cent.* **Anon.** Illumination. *Fécamp Bible.* MS A4, fol. 199v. Bibliothèque Municipale, Rouen [Terrien 49]. **Anon.** Illumination. *Bible de la Sauve Majeure.* Ms lat. 1. Fol. 250v. Bibliothèque de Bordeaux, Bordeaux [Terrien 52]. *14th cent.* **Anon.** Narthex of Chora Church, Constantinople.

Job as King, with His Daughters. *7th cent.* **Anon.** Illustration. Coptic biblical fragment. Biblioteca Nazionale Neapolitana, mss I.B.18, fol. 4v.

Job as King, with His Sons and His Daughters. *11th cent.* **Anon.** Illumination. *Bible of Stavelot.* Ms Add. 28107. II, fol. 4v. British Library, London [Terrien 51].

Job as Lazarus. *16th cent.* **Orley, Bernat van.** Altarpiece (closed), left panel. Oil on canvas. 1521–1525. Musées Royaux de Beaux-Arts, Brussels [Terrien 163].

Job as Patriarch. *15th cent.* **Anon.** Hebrew manuscript from North Italy. 1470. In Rothschild Miscellany. Israel Museum, Jerusalem. Ms 180/51, fol. 55 [*EncJud* 114].

Job as Priest. *16th cent.* **Anon.** Wood sculpture. Church of St Martin, Wezemaal, Belgium [Terrien 150]. **Anon.** Wood sculpture. Mayer van der Bergh Museum, Antwerp [Terrien 151].

Job as Prophet. *17th cent.* **Anon.** Wood sculpture. Chapel of All Saints, Diest, Brabant [Terrien 152].

Job as Prophet of the Resurrection. *18th cent.* **Anon.** Icon. Monastery of St John, Patmos [Huber 55, Pl. 18].

Job as Prototype of Patience. *19th cent.* **Anon.** Miniature. *Bamberg Apocalypse.* 983–1002. Staatsbibliothek Bamberg. Cod. lat. 140, fol. 60.

Job as Sage. *17th cent.* **Anon.** Wood sculpture. Vrouw Kerk, Veerle, Belgium [Terrien 154].

Job as Warrior (leading army against Satan). *10th cent.* **Anon.** Vatican Library.

Job Assailed by Evil Spirits. *17th cent.* **Saftleven, Cornelis.** Painting. Kunsthalle, Karlsruhe [Schulz 514].

Job at Prayer. *20th cent.* **Chagall, Marc.** Tinted drawing. 1960 [Terrien 260].

Job at the Capture of Leviathan. *12th cent.* **Anon.** Window representing the Crucifixion, Cathedral of Chalons-sur-Marne.

Job Comforted by an Angel. *12th cent.* **Anon.** Romanesque capital. La Daurade Priory, Toulouse. Musée des Augustins, Toulouse [Terrien 70].

Job Confessing His Presumption to God Who Answers from the Whirlwind. *19th cent.* **Blake, William.** Pen, ink, and watercolor over pencil on paper. 1803–1805. National Gallery of Scotland, Edinburgh.

Job Curses the Day of His Birth. *19th cent.* **Blake, William.** Also known as *Job's Despair.* In *Illustrations of the Book of Job.* 1823–1825. 8 [Terrien 205; Balentine 85].

Job Cycle. *8th/9th cent.* **Anon.** Forty-three miniatures. Codex Patmos, 171. Pp. 448–511. St John's Monastery, Patmos. See also **Jacopi, Giulio.** "Le miniature dei Codici di Patmo: Elenco delle illustrazione del libro di Giobbe." *Clara Rhodos* 9–7/3 (1932–33) 584–87. *9th cent.* **Anon.** Miniatures. Codex Vaticanus graecus 749. Rome. **Anon.** Miniatures. John of Damascus. *Sacra parallela.* Codex Parisinus graecus 923, fol. 256v, 257r. *10th cent.* **Anon.** Ms Marcianus graecus 538. 904/905. Bibliotheca Marciana, Venice.

11th cent. **Anon.** Miniatures. Codex Sinaiticus graecus 3. St Catherine's Monastery. *12th cent.* **Anon.** Miniatures. In Olympiodorus, *Commentary on Job.* Codex Vatopedion 590. Vatopedi, Mount Athos.

13th cent. **Anon.** One hundred seventeen miniatures. Codex Panhagion Taphon 5. Codex Sancti Sepulchri Job hierosolymitanus graecus [Huber 200–241]. **Anon.** One hundred forty-five miniatures. Bibliotheca vaticana, Rome. Codex vaticanus graecus 1231 [Huber 200–241]. **Anon.** Grosse Lavra B/100. Mount Athos [Huber 250]. **Anon.** Miniatures. In *Job Catena.* Bodleian Library, Oxford. Ms Barocci 201. **Anon.** Miniatures. In Olympiodorus, *Commentary on Job.* Ms par. gr. 134. Bibliothèque Nationale, Paris [Huber 251]. **Anon.** Tympanon of the Sixtus Door, Reims Cathedral [Lannois/Lacassagne, figs. 11, 12].

14th cent. **Anon.** Miniatures. 1362. Ms par. gr. 135. Bibliothèque Nationale, Paris [Huber 251]. *15th cent.* **Anon.** Flemish. *Scenes from the Life of Job.* c. 1480–90. Altarpiece, oak panel. Wallraf-Richartz Museum, Cologne.

16th cent. **Anon.** *Story of Job.* Dutch. Sketch. c. 1510. Museo Civico, Cremona [Denis, Pl. XV]. **Heemskerck, Maerten van.** Album of Job prints, including *Job Receiving Gifts* (1563), *Job Receiving the Ill-News of His Misfortunes* (1563), *Job Sacrificing for the Sins of His Children* (1563), *Job Sitting on the Dunghill* (1563), *Satan Challenging the Lord to Remove His Protection from Job* (1563), *Satan Smiting Job with Boils* (1563), *The Sons of God, Satan amongst Them, Present Themselves before the Lord* (1563), *The Lord Answering Job* (1563), *The Triumph of Job* (1559). Philip Galle, printmaker. Fitzwilliam Museum, Cambridge. **Orley, Bernard van.** *The Story of Job.* 1521. Altarpiece, central panel (Triptych of Virtue of Patience, Job, and Lazarus). Oil on canvas. 1521–1525. Musées Royaux de Beaux-Arts, Brussels [Terrien 161]. **Scarsella, Ippolito (Lo Scarsellino, 1551–1620).** Eight paintings. c. 1600. Landesmuseum Hanover. Kat. 1954, Nr. 348–55 [Novell, Pls. 38–41]. **Sichem, Christopher van.** *Two Biblical Scenes from the Book of Job: Wherefore hidest thou thy face, and holdest me for thine enemy? Job 13. Before I go whence I shall not return. Job 10.* Woodcuts in

Dutch Bible. Fine Arts Museums of San Francisco. **Stimmer, Tobias.** *Das Buch Job.* In *Neue künstliche Figuren biblischer Historien.* Basel, 1576.
18th cent. **Sigrist, Franz.** Germanisches Nationalmuseum, Nuremburg. Inv. 11312 [Pigler 206].
20th cent. **Bosschère, Jean de.** *Job le pauvre, avec un portrait par Wyndham Lewis, traduction des poèmes en anglais, et quatorze gravures noires.* Paris: Jacques Povolozky, Collection d'Art "La Cible," 1922; London: John Lane, Bodley Head, 1922. **Fox-Düvell, Gisela, and Adelheid Bienmüller.** *Und Dunkelheit wird wie der Morgen sein: Bilder und Texte zu Ijob.* Munich: Don-Bosco-Verlag, 1994. **Heidenheim, Hanns H.** (b. 1922). *Holzschnitte zur Bibel.* I. *Ijob.* Düsseldorf: Ursus Press, 1965. **Henriques, Anna Ruth.** *The Book of Mechtilde* [forty-page illuminated manuscript]. Ink, gouache and paint on paper. 1992. The Jewish Museum, New York [Vicchio 96–99]. **Rattner, Abraham.** *Job in Agony* [cf. Terrien 246]. **Uecker, Günther.** *Das Buch Hiob.* Forty-seven prints in silkscreen and Terragraph. Jaffa: Har-El, 2007.
Job Dejected. *19th cent.* **Vermeylen, François.** Plaster statue. c. 1880. Museum voor Religieuze Kunst en Cultuur, Leuven [Terrien 232].
Job Distributes Alms to the Poor. *13th cent.* **Anon.** Miniature. In Gregory the Great, *Moralia in Job.* c. 1260. Chorherrenstift Herzogenburg, Austria. Cod. 54, fol. 173v [LCI 408]. *19th cent.* **Marshall, William Calder.** *"Unto me men gave ear and waited, and kept silence at my counsel" (Job 29).* 1863. South nave aisle, St Paul's Cathedral, London.
Job Haunted by Nightmares. *19th cent.* **Blake, William.** *Job Is Haunted by Nightmares.* In *Illustrations of the Book of Job.* 1823–1825 [Terrien 209; Balentine 135].
Job Hunting. Anon. *3rd cent.* Fresco. Dura-Europos synagogue [Terrien 5].
Job in Dereliction. *16th cent.* **Anon.** Lantern of the Dead. 1508–1510. Waging, Bavaria [Terrien 85].
Job in Despair. *20th cent.* **Ben-Zion.** Etching. In his portfolio, *The Book of Ruth—Job—Song of Songs.* 1954. The Jewish Museum, New York [Vicchio 86].
Job in the History of Salvation. *13th cent.* **Pisano, Niccolo.** 1260. Pillar, Baptistery, Pisa.
Job Intercedes for His Friends. *14th cent.* **Gaddi, Taddeo.** 1366. Fresco. Camposanto, Pisa [Terrien 93; Balentine 711]. *19th cent.* **Blake, William.** Also known as *Job's Sacrifice.* In *Illustrations of the Book of Job.* 1823–1825. 18 [Terrien 221].
Job Interrupts God. *12th cent.* **Anon.** Illumination. Greek codex of Job, Gr. 1231, fol. 19v. Rome, Vatican Museum [Terrien 267; Balentine 699].
Job Is Haunted by Nightmares. *19th cent.* **Blake, William.** Also known as *Job's Evil Dreams.* In *Illustrations of the Book of Job.* 1823–1825. 11 [Terrien 209; Balentine 135].
Job Mocked. *13th cent.* **Anon.** Flemish. c. 1270. Getty Museum, Los Angeles. **Anon.** Miniature. In Gregory the Great, *Moralia in Job.* c. 1260. Chorherrenstift Herzogenburg, Austria. Cod. 54, fol. 42 [LCI 411]. *16th cent.* **Anon.** *Spinola Hours.* Flemish Book of Hours. c. 1510–1520. Getty Museum, Los Angeles. Ms Ludwig IX 18, fol. 18. **Bosch, Hieronymus.** Painting. c. 1514. Musée Communal, Douai [Denis, Pl. XXI]. *19th cent.* **Blake, William.** *Job Laughed to Scorn.* Also known as *Job Rebuked by His Friends.* In *Illustrations of the Book of Job.* 1823–1825. 10 [Terrien 208; Balentine 231].
Job Mocked by His Wife. *13th cent.* **Anon.** *Job Derided by His Wife.* Franco-Flemish. Historiated initial V as first letter of the Book of Job. Tempera and gold leaf on parchment. Marquette Bible. c. 1270. Getty Museum, Los Angeles. *17th cent.* **La Tour, Georges de.** *Job and His Wife.* Also known as *Job Mocked by His Wife.* c. 1650. Oil on canvas. Musée départemental des Vosges, Epinal, France. Cat. 1929, no. 152 [Terrien 167; Balentine 65]. **Ricci, Sebastiano.** Painting. Musei Belluno. *18th cent.* **Mariotti, Giambattista.** Painting. SS. Simone e Taddeo, Verona [Pigler 205].
Job Mocked by His Wife and Tormented by Demons. *14th cent.* **Anon.** *Job Assailed by Satan and Railed at by His Wife.* Illumination. *Mirror of Human Salvation.* Ms 139/1363, fol. 22r. Musée Condé, Chantilly [Besserman 128]. *16th cent.* **Anon.** Miniature. Prayerbook. Cardinal Albrecht von Brandenburg, fol. 154. c. 1530. Private collection [Winckler,

fig. 256]. **Heemskerck, Maerten van.** *Job Tormented by a Demon, and Job and His Wife.* Drawing. Albertina, Vienna [Pigler 204]. *17th cent.* **Anon.** Engraving (after Rubens, St Nicolaas triptych, left panel). Rubenianum, Antwerp [Hulst, Pl. 130]. ———. Painting (after Rubens, St Nicolaas triptych, left panel). Alte Pinakothek, Munich. Cat. 1908, no. 805 [Hulst 381]. ———. Painting (after Rubens, St Nicolaas triptych, left panel). Musée du Louvre. Cat. 1979, No. M.I. 968) [Hulst 381]. ———. Painting (after Rubens, St Nicolaas triptych, left panel). Musée Municipal, Louvain [Hulst, Pl. 133]. ———. Painting (after Rubens, St Nicolaas triptych, left panel). R. Werner Collection, Berchem-Antwerp. [Hulst 381]. **Dyck, Anthony van.** Drawing (after Rubens, St Nicolaas triptych, left panel). Cabinet des dessins, Musée du Louvre, Paris [Hulst, Pl. 128]. *17th cent.* **Barburen, Dirk van.** Painting. National Museum, Warsaw [Pigler 206]. **Vorsterman, Lucas Emil** (after Peter Paul Rubens). Oil on canvas. 1620. Musées Royaux des Beaux-Arts, Brussels [Terrien 188]. ———. Engraving. c. 1620. Philadelphia Museum of Art [Vicchio 59]. ———. *Job Tormented by Demons and Abused by His Wife.* Engraving. National Gallery of Art, Washington, DC. *18th cent.* **Delacroix, Eugène.** Painting. Musée Bonnat, Bayonne. Cat. 1908, no. 70 [Hulst 381].

Job Mourning. *4th cent.* Fresco. Catacombs of Santi Marcellino e Pietro, Rome. Rome.

Job on the Ashheap [in Christian art, a prefiguration of Christ awaiting crucifixion]. *3rd cent.* **Anon.** Frescoes in Catacombs of Santi Marcellino e Pietro, Rome. **Anon.** Frescoes of Synagogue, Dura-Europos. *4th cent.* **Anon.** Sarcophagus of Junius Bassus. Museum of the Treasury, St Peter's Basilica, Rome [Balentine 292]. *12th cent.* **Anon.** *Job Scraping Himself with Potsherds.* Miniature. In Gregory, *Moralia.* Bibliothèque Nationale, Paris. Ms lat. 15675, fol. 4-712. *13th cent.* **Anon.** North Door of Chartres Cathedral. **Anon.** Door depicting the Last Judgment, Notre Dame, Paris. *15th cent.* **Anon.** Woodcut. *Strassburg Bibel* (Grueninger). 1485 [Meyer, fig. 6]. **Anon.** *Job on the Ashheap, with Three Musicians.* Woodcut. In *Heures à l'usage de Rouen* (Pigouchet). c. 1496. Bibliothèque Nationale, Paris. Ms lat. 13181, fol. 62 [Lannois 197]. **Bourdichon, Jean.** *Job on the Dung Heap.* c. 1480–1485. Getty Museum, Los Angeles. **Fouquet, Jean.** Heures d'Etienne Chevalier, Musée Condy, Chantilly.

16th cent. **Dohany Master.** *Job on the Dung-Heap, with Friends.* Illumination. Book of Hours. 1520–1530. Ms 134, p. 174. Fitzwilliam Museum, Cambridge. **Heemskerck, Maerten van.** *Job Sitting on the Dunghill.* Album of Job prints. 1563. Fitzwilliam Museum, Cambridge. **Lindtmayer, Daniel.** *Job on the Dung Heap.* 1581. Pen and black ink with gray wash. Getty Museum, Los Angeles.

17th cent. **Anon.** *Job on the Ashheap, with His Friends and His Wife.* Engraving, after Peter Paul Rubens. Philadelphia Museum of Art [Vicchio 61]. **Anon.** Wood sculpture. Collection Jean Lacassagne [Lannois/Lacassagne, Pl. 6]. **Assereto, Giovacchino.** *Job in Distress.* Szepmiuveszeti Museum, Budapest. **Goltzius, Hendrick.** *Job in Distress.* 1616. Oil on panel. Private collection, New York. **Loth, Johann Carl (Carlotto).** Painting. Freiherr Joseph Leopold von Castell Collection, Mannheim. **Ribera, Jusepe de (Lo Spagnoletto).** *Job on the Ash Heap.* Oil on canvas. c. 1630. **Rubens, Peter Paul.** *Job on the Dunghill* (1612), presented to the musicians' guild of Antwerp. **Seghers, Gerard.** *The Patient Job.* c. 1625. Oil on canvas. National Gallery, Prague. *18th cent.* **Krafft, Jan Lauwrijn.** Engraving [Hulst, Pl. 121]. **Querena, Lactanzio.** S. Giobbe, Venice. *19th cent.* **Bonnat, Léon.** *Job.* 1880. Oil on canvas. Musée Bonnat, Bayonne [Balentine 548]. ———. Musée du Luxembourg, Paris. **Brown, Ford Madox.** *Job on the Ash-heap.* 1837. **Tissot, James Jacques Joseph.** *Job Lying on the Heap of Refuse.* c. 1896–1902. Gouache on paper. The Jewish Museum, New York [Vicchio 74].

Job on the Tortoise. *16th cent.* **Heemskerck, Maerten van.** *Job op de mestvaalt/Job on the Tortoise* [symbol of patience], also known as *The Triumph of Job.* 1548. Pen and brown ink with traces of chalk on laid paper. National Gallery of Art, Washington, DC [Vicchio 57].

Job Overcome by Guilt. *20th cent.* **Bishop, Raymond.** Drawing. c. 1928 [Terrien 245].

Job Praying. *15th cent.* **Egerton Master (French illustrator, fl. 1405–1420), follower of.** *Job in Prayer.* French. 1410. Getty Museum, Los Angeles.

Job Praying for His Friends. *14th cent.* **Gaddi, Taddeo.** c. 1355. Camposanto, Pisa.

Job Prepares to Fight with God. *8th/9th cent.* **Anon.** Miniature. Greek codex of Job, Patmos 171. St John Monastery, Patmos [Terrien 38; Balentine 644].

Job Ready to March On. *15th cent.* **Syrlin, Jörg.** Wood carving, choir stall. 1469–1474. Ulm Münster.

Job Receiving Gifts. *16th cent.* **Heemskerck, Maerten van.** Album of Job prints. 1563. Fitzwilliam Museum, Cambridge.

Job Receiving the Ill-News of His Misfortunes. *16th cent.* **Heemskerck, Maerten van.** Album of Job prints. 1563. Fitzwilliam Museum, Cambridge.

Job Restored. *12th cent.* **Anon.** Romanesque capital. La Daurade Priory. Musée des Augustins, Toulouse [Terrien 71]. *14th cent.* **Gaddi, Taddeo.** Fresco. c. 1350. Camposanto, Pisa. *16th cent.* **Anon.** *Die gantze Bibel: das ist alle Bücher vnnd neüws Testaments den vrsprünglichen spraachen nach auffs aller treüwlichest verteütschet.* Zurich: Christoff. Froschouer, 1534. **Heemskerck, Maarten van.** *The Triumph of Job.* 1559. *17th cent.* **La Hyre, Laurent de.** *Job Restored to Prosperity.* Chrysler Museum of Art, Norfolk, VA. *19th cent.* **Blake, William.** *God Blesses Job and His Wife.* Also known as *The Vision of Christ.* In *Illustrations of the Book of Job.* 1823–1825. 17 [Terrien 219]. ———. *Job's Latter End.* Also known as *Job and His Family Restored to Prosperity.* In *Illustrations of the Book of Job.* 1823–1825. 21 [Terrien 225]. ———. *Job and His Family Restored to Prosperity.* Also known as *Job's Latter End.* Pen and ink with watercolor over graphite. 1821. Rosenwald Collection. National Gallery of Art, Washington, DC. **Tissot, James Jacques Joseph.** *Job Joins His Family in Happiness.* c. 1896–1902. Gouache on paper. The Jewish Museum, New York [Vicchio 77]. *20th cent.* **Ben-Zion.** *Job Reconciled.* Oil. 1957. Ben-Zion Collection, New York [Vicchio 89]. **Spruance, Benton Murdoch.** *After Blake's Job.* Lithograph in black and gray. 1966. National Gallery of Art, Washington, DC [Vicchio 94].

Job Sacrificing. *16th cent.* **Heemskerck, Maerten van.** *Job Sacrificing for the Sins of His Children.* Album of Job prints. 1563. Fitzwilliam Museum, Cambridge. *19th cent.* **Blake, William.** *Job's Sacrifice.* Watercolor, c. 1821. City Art Gallery, Leeds. **Linnell, John.** *Job Offering a Sacrifice on His Return to Prosperity.* Painting. Oil on panel. 1845. Fitzwilliam Museum, Cambridge.

Job Seated. *3rd cent.* **Anon.** Fresco. Cemetery of Domitilla, Rome [Terrien 19]. *4th cent.* **Anon.** Fresco. Cemetery of Apronianus, Rome [Terrien, color plate 2].

Job Standing Erect. *20th cent.* **Harootian, Koren der.** Stone sculpture. c. 1950 [Terrien 251].

Job with Cloak. *3rd cent.* **Anon.** Fresco. Catacombs of St Calixtus, Rome.

Job Wooing Anima, with Satan's Blessing. *20th cent.* **Kokoschka, Oskar.** Drawing. 1917 [Terrien 236].

Job Wrestling. *20th cent.* **Somervile, Beatrice.** *Wrestling Job.* Needlepoint. 1982 [Terrien 263].

Job's Friends. *16th cent.* **Falaise, Robert.** *Job's Friends in Dunce Cap.* Wood engraving, stalls of the Collegium of Champeaux [Terrien 124, Balentine 202].

Job's Prosperity. *15th cent.* **Anon.** Miniature (full page). In Rothschild Miscellany 24. Israel Museum, Jerusalem. Ms 180/51, fol. 65 [*EncJud* 108].

Job's Servants Assailed by Satan. *12th cent.* **Master of the Harding Bible.** *Moralia in Job.* 1111. Bibliothèque publique, Dijon. Ms 173, fol. 47v.

Job's Trials. *11th cent.* **Anon.** Illumination. Plut. 7 dex. 11, c. 8v. Bibliotheca Medicea-Laurenziana, Florence [Terrien 60]. *13th cent.* **Anon.** *Job, His Wife, His Friends, and the Devil.* c. 1220. North Transept, West Portal, Chartres Cathedral [Terrien 74–81; Balentine 244]. **Anon.** *The Devil Laying His Hand on Job.* North Transept, Calixtus portal,

c. 1225–1230. Reims Cathedral. *14th cent.* Breviary of Martin of Aragon, Bibliothèque Nationale de France. Frescoes from St Stephen's Chapel, Westminster, now in British Museum. *15th cent.* **Master of the Legend of St Barbara.** *The Story of Job.* 1480–1483. Cologne, Wallraf-Richartz Museum. **Sorg, Anton.** *Hie vahet an das Register uber die bibeln des alten testaments.* Pitts Theology Library, Emory University, Atlanta. *16th cent.* **Anon.** *Die gantze Bibel: das ist alle Bücher allts vnnd neüws Testaments den vrsprünglichen spraachen nach auffs aller treüwlichest verteütschet.* Zurich: Christoff. Froschouer, 1536. **Anon.** Window of Troyes Cathedral. **Bosch, Hieronymus, follower of.** *Trials of Job.* Painting. 1514. Heirs of Max de Coninck, Diegem, Belgium [Denis, Pl. XXII]. See also **Hellerstedt, Kahren Jones.** "The Blind Man and His Guide in Netherlandish Painting." *Simiolus* 13 (1983) 163–81.| **Hugo, Peter** (or Jan Mandyn). *Les épreuves de Job.* Douai Museum. **Rubens, Peter Paul.** Altarpiece. 1612–1613. Church of St Nicholas, Brussels (destroyed in 1695). See copies by Anthony van Dyck, Gaspar de Crayer, Abraham van Diepenbeek, Nicolaas van der Horst, Cornelis Saftleven, and Lucas Emil Vorsterman. *17th cent.* **Anon.** Dutch. Engraving. *Patientiam Hiob audiuistis (The Affliction of Job).* From a group of biblical illustrations printed by C. J. or Nicolaes Visscher, Engraving. Fine Arts Museums of San Francisco. **Bramer, Leonaert.** *Afflictions of Job.* Pen and ink on paper. Courtauld Institute of Art Gallery, London. **Goltzius, Hendrick.** *Job in Distress.* 1616. Oil on panel. Private collection, New York. **Lievens, Jan.** *Job in His Misery/Job sur son fumier.* 1631. Ottawa, National Gallery of Canada. **Merian, Matthaeus the Elder.** *The Misfortunes of Job.* 1625–1630. Engraving in Melchior Küsel, *Icones biblicae.* Vienna, 1679. *19th cent.* **Blake, William.** *Satan Smiting Job with Boils.* 1826. Watercolor. Tate Gallery, London. *20th cent.* **Mesibov, Hugh.** *Job in the Wilderness.* Charcoal. 1972. ———. *Job's Agony.* Acrylic collage. 1969. ———. *Job in the Wilderness.* Charcoal. 1972. ———. *Book of Job Mural.* Temple Beth El, Spring Valley, NY. Canvas, acrylic and charcoal. 1971.

Job, Anima, Eros, and the Dogs. *20th cent.* **Kokoshka, Oskar.** Drawing. 1917 [Terrien 238].

Job, God, and Dancing Devil. *16th cent.* **Anon.** Wood sculpture, Dean's throne. c. 1508. Amiens Cathedral [Terrien 86–87].

Job, His Family, God, and Satan. *12th cent.* **Anon.** Romanesque capital. Cathedral of Pamplona [Terrien 64].

Job, His Wife, and Cappadocian Fathers. *9th cent.* **Anon.** Illumination. Ms Gr. 510, fol. 285. Bibliothèque Nationale, Paris [Terrien 54].

Job, His Wife, and Christ in Blessing. **Anon.** *11th cent.* Miniature. In *Theodore Psalter.* Before 1066. British Museum, London. Ms add. 19.352, fol. 154r.

Job, His Wife, and Demons. *15th cent.* **Anon.** *Job, His Wife, a Demon, a Musician, and Two Plague Sufferers.* Colored woodcut. 1490–1500. Kupferstichkabinett, Berlin [Lannois 196]. *17th cent.* **Flemish School.** Oil on canvas. c. 1620. Chapel of the Beguines, Louvain [Terrien 189]. **Vanni, Raffaello.** *Job, His Wife, and a Demon.* Painting. S. Rocca, Siena [Pigler 204]. *18th cent.* **Anon.** Flemish engraving. *Job, His Wife, a Demon, and Musical Instruments.* 1720. Jahresgabe der Hiobs-Bruderschaft von Antwerpen an ihre Mitglider [Denis, Pl. XX]. **Schoonjans, Anthoni.** Painting. 1710 [Pigler 204].

Job, His Wife, and His Friends. *3rd cent.* **Anon.** Fresco. Catacombs, Viale Manzoni, Rome. **Anon.** *Job, His Wife, and Three Youths.* Fresco. Hypogeum of the Viale Marconi, Rome [Terrien, color plate 1].

7th cent. **Anon.** Miniature. *Syriac Bible.* Bibliothèque Nationale, Paris, ms syr. 341, fol. 46r [Terrien 56]. *9th cent.* **Anon.** Miniature. In Gregory Nazianzus. *Homilies.* (Ms Par. gr. 510, fol. 71v). Paris. *10th cent.* **Anon.** Miniature. Bible of Patrikios Leon. c. 900. Vat. regin. gr. 1, fol. 17v. *11th cent.* **Anon.** Miniature. c. 1000. Par. lat. 6, fol. 63.

12th cent. **Anon.** Illumination. *Admont Bible,* Cod. ser nov. 2701, fol. 252v. Bild-Archiv der Östereichischen Nationalbibliothek, Vienna [Terrien 58].

13th cent. **Anon.** Illustration. *Job, His Wife, and Four Friends.* Bible. c. 1240. Staatsbibliothek Preussischer Kulturbesitz, Berlin. Ms. Theol. lat. 379, fol. 221r [Besserman 117].

14th cent. **Anon.** *Job, His Wife, and Two Friends.* Illumination, letter Q. In *German Paraphrase of Job.* Staatliche Archivlager Preussischen Kulturbesitz, Göttingen. Ms 1, fol. 421 [Besserman 118].

16th cent. **Anon.** French. *Book of Hours.* 1524. Library of Congress, Washington [Vicchio 51]. **Beham, Hans Sebald.** Woodcut. In his *Biblisch Historien, figürlich fürgebildet.* Frankfurt a.M., 1533 [Pigler 204]. **Cardi, Ludovici (Il Cigoli).** Painting. Formerly Galleria Feroni, Florence [Pigler 204]. **Holbein, Hans, the Younger.** In his *Icones historiarum Veteris Testamenti.* 1547. Wood engraving by Hans Lützelburger (1495?–1526). Basel. c. 1542 [Vicchio 53].

17th cent. **Anon.** Painting. Notre Dame de Saint Omer [Hulst 381]. **Crayer, Gaspar de.** Painting (after Rubens, St Nicolaas triptych). Musée de Beaux-Arts, Toulouse. Cat. 438 [Hulst, Pl. 126]. **Diepenbeek, Abraham van** (after Rubens, St Nicolaas triptych). Drawing, for title page of Balthasar Corderius, *Jobus elucidatus.* Antwerp, 1646. Hermitage, St Petersburg. Inv. 25322. **Horst, Nicolaas van der** (after Rubens, St Nicolaas triptych). Drawing. N. de Boer Foundation, Amsterdam [Hulst, Pl. 124]. **Loth, Johann Carl (Carlotto).** *Job, His Wife, His Friends, and a Child.* Painting. Gemäldegalerie Alte Meister, Dresden. Kat. 1905, Nr 2006. **Rijn, Rembrandt van.** *Job, His Wife, and Two Friends.* Drawing. Dr Tobias Christ Collection, Basel [Pigler 206]. **Rubens, Peter Paul (after).** Painting. Oil on canvas. c. 1635. Institut royal du patrimoine artistique, Brussels [Terrien 190]. **Saftleven, Cornelis** (after Rubens, St Nicolaas triptych). Painting. Museum Mayer van der Bergh, Antwerp. Inv. 479 [Schulz 1187]. **Veen, Otto van.** *Job, His Friends, His Wife, and Her Attendants.* Altarpiece, panels closed. c. 1620. St Jacobskerk, Antwerp [Terrien 191].

18th cent. **Bergl, Johann.** Painting. 1752. Germanisches Nationalmuseum, Nuremburg. Inv. 1312 [Pigler 206].

19th cent. **Blake, William.** *Job, His Wife, and Friends.* Also known as *Job's Comforters.* In *Illustrations of the Book of Job.* 1823–1825, 7 [Terrien 204; Balentine 69]. ———. *Job, His Wife and His Friends: The Complaint of Job* (recto); *Job's Wife and Other Sketches* (verso). Pen and ink and wash on paper, pencil on paper. c. 1785. Tate Gallery, London. ———. *The Complaint of Job.* Gray wash on thin wove paper. c. 1786. Fine Arts Museums of San Francisco. **Decamps, Alexandre-Gabriel.** Oil on canvas. c. 1855. Minneapolis Institute of Arts.

Job, His Wife, and Musicians. *15th cent.* **Anon.** *Job's Wife Brings Three Musicians to Job.* Miniature. *Book of Hours,* Henry IV. c. 1450. Bibliothèque Nationale, Paris. Ms lat. 1171, fol. 58v [Lannois 206–7]. *16th cent.* **Anon.** *Job, His Wife, and Two Musicians.* German. Panel of the Riestadt Altar. c. 1510. Landessmuseum, Hanover. Kat. 1954, Nr. 247 [Denis, Pl. III]. **Anon.** *Job, His Wife, and a Musician.* Carpet design. 1550. Collection F. S. Powell, London [Denis, Pl. VII]. **Bourdichon, School of.** Illumination. Ms lat. 1171, fol. 58v. Bibliothèque Nationale, Paris [Terrien 117]. **Glockenton, Albrecht.** *Job, His Wife, and Two Musicians.* In Prayerbook of Prince Wilhelm IV of Bavaria. 1535. Nationalbibliothek, Vienna. Ms 1880, fol. 83v [Denis, fig. VI].

Job, His Wife, and Neighbors. *19th cent.* **Blake, William.** Also known as *Every Man Also Gave Him a Piece of Money.* In *Illustrations of the Book of Job.* 1823–1825. 19 [Terrien 222].

Job, His Wife, and Satan. *10th cent.* **Anon.** Miniature. In Bible of Isidore. 960. Kollegiatstift Léon. Fol. 182r. *12th cent.* **Anon.** Capital. Notre Dame des Doms. Musée Calvet, Avignon. **Anon.** *Job, His Wife, Satan, and a Beggar.* Romanesque capital. Eglise Saint-André-le-Bas, Vienne. Musée de Vienne (Isère) [Terrien 72–73]. *14th cent.* **Anon.** Altarpiece. 1360–66. Doberan Abbey, Mecklenburg, Germany [Terrien 82].

Job, His Wife, and Servants. *12th cent.* **Anon.** Illustration. In Bible. St Edmunds Abbey, Bury St Edmunds. 1121–1141. Corpus Christi College, Cambridge. Ms 2, fol. 344v.

Job, Old Man Sitting with Raised Arm. *20th cent.* **Barlach, Ernst.** 1909. Drawing. Pl. 40 in his *Zwischen Erde und Himmel: 45 Handzeichnungen.* Munich: Piper, 1964.

Job, Scraping His Boils. *12th cent.* **Anon.** Marble capital. Andreas Kirche (Romanian Orthodox), Vienna.

Job, the Young Women, and Death. *20th cent.* **Kokoschka, Oskar.** Drawing. 1917 [Terrien 237].

John the Baptist as Job. *14th cent.* **Anon.** Mosaic. 1350, Baptistery. San Marco, Venice [Terrien 91].

Leviathan. *12th cent.* **Anon.** *Leviathan Ridden by the Devil.* Ms laud. gr. 86. 407. Bodleian Library, Oxford. **Anon.** *Leviathan with Antichrist Seated.* Illumination. **Anon.** (?). MS 93, fol. 62v. Bibliotheek van der Rijksuniversiteit, Ghent. *13th cent.* **Anon.** Miniature. From Northern France. British Library, London. Ms. add. 11639, fol. 518v [Gutmann]. *14th cent.* **Anon.** *Leviathan.* Spanish. In *Golden Haggadah.* c. 1320. Ms. Add. 27210. *20th cent.* **Spruance, Benton Murdoch.** *Book of Job: The Leviathan, or The Blue Whale.* Lithograph. 1966. Philadelphia Museum of Art [Vicchio 93].

Pleiades, Sweet Influences of the. *19th cent.* **Blake, William.** Also known as *When the Morning Stars Sang Together.* In *Illustrations of the Book of Job.* 1823–1825. 14 [Terrien 213].

Raid on Job's Herds and Flocks. *12th cent.* **Anon.** Romanesque capital. Cathedral of Pamplona [Terrien 65]. *16th cent.* **Orley, Bernat van.** *The Raid on Job's Flocks and Herds.* Altarpiece (closed), right panel. Oil on canvas. 1521–1525. Musées Royaux de Beaux-Arts, Brussels [Terrien 163].

Satan. *16th cent.* **Heemskerck, Maerten van.** *Satan Smiting Job with Boils.* Album of Job prints. 1563. Fitzwilliam Museum, Cambridge. *19th cent.* **Blake, William.** *Satan Falls from Heaven.* Also known as *The Fall of Satan.* In *Illustrations of the Book of Job.* 1823–1825. 16 [Terrien 218]. ———. *Satan Smites Job.* Also known as *Satan Smites Job with Boils.* In *Illustrations of the Book of Job.* 1823–1825. 6 [Terrien 202]. ———. *Satan Smiting Job with Sore Boils.* c. 1826. Pen and ink and tempera on mahogany support. Tate Gallery, London. *20th cent.* **Kokoshka, Oskar.** *Satan Throws Anima on Job.* Drawing. 1917 [Terrien 239].

Satan and Yahweh. *16th cent.* **Heemskerck, Maerten van.** *Satan Challenging the Lord to Remove His Protection from Job.* Album of Job prints. 1563. Fitzwilliam Museum, Cambridge. ———. *The Sons of God, Satan amongst Them, Present Themselves before the Lord.* Album of Job prints. 1563. Fitzwilliam Museum, Cambridge. *19th cent.* **Blake, William.** *Satan before God's Throne.* In *Illustrations of the Book of Job.* 1823–1825. 2 [Terrien 197]. ———. *Satan Going Forth from the Presence of the Lord and Job's Charity.* Also known as *Satan's Wager with God.* In *Illustrations of the Book of Job.* 1823–1825. 5. ———. *Satan's Wager with God.* In *Illustrations of the Book of Job.* 1823–1825 [Terrien 201]. *20th cent.* **Spruance, Benton Murdoch.** *Book of Job, or, Jehovah and Satan.* Color woodcut. 1951. Philadelphia Museum of Art [Vicchio 84].

Triumph of Job. *16th cent.* **Coornhert, Dirck Volckertz.** Engraving, after Maerten van Heemskerck's *Job op de mestvaalt/Job on the Tortoise* [symbol of patience]. National Gallery of Art, Washington, DC [Vicchio 58]. **Heemskerck, Maerten van.** *The Triumph of Job.* Album of Job prints. 1559. Fitzwilliam Museum, Cambridge. *17th cent.* **Reni, Guido.** Etching by Giuseppe Maria Mitelli. 1679. Philadelphia Museum of Art [Vicchio 60].

Virgin and Child with Sts John the Baptist and Job. *16th cent.* **Franciabigio, Marcantonio.** 1516. Museo di S. Salvi, Florence.

Woman and Man. *20th cent.* **Kokoschka, Oskar.** Poster used for *Job: A Drama.* 1909. [Terrien 234].

Yahweh's Answer to Job. *16th cent.* **Collaert, Adriaen.** *The Lord's First Answer to Job.* Print in album. c. 1689. P.4290-R-166. Fitzwilliam Museum, Cambridge. **Heemskerck, Maerten van.** *The Lord Answering Job.* Album of Job prints. 1563. Fitzwilliam Museum, Cambridge. *19th cent.* **Blake, William.** *Out of the Whirlwind.* Also known as *The Lord*

Answering Job out of the Whirlwind. In *Illustrations of the Book of Job.* 1823–1825. 13 [Terrien 212].

iv. By Artist

al-Nishapur, Ibrahim. Job. Illumination in Persian manuscript of *Qisas al Anbiya* (*Legends of the Prophets*). 1580. Spencer Collection, New York Public Library. Persian MS 46, fol. 109 [Vicchio 56].

Angelo, Valenti. *The Book of Job, according to the Authorized Version of MDCXI, Following the Arrangement of the Temple Bible* [illustrated by Valenti Angelo]. San Francisco: Edwin and Robert Grabhorn, 1926.

Appiani, Giuseppe (Italian painter, 1701–1786). *Job.* Painting and oil sketch. Germanisches Nationalmuseum, Nuremburg [Pigler 205].

Assereto [Axareto], Giovacchino [Gioacchino] (Italian painter, 1600–1649). *Job in Distress.* Szepmiuveszeti Museum, Budapest.

Barburen, Dirk van (Dutch painter, 1595–1624). *Job Mocked by His Wife.* Painting. National Museum, Warsaw [Pigler 206].

Barlach, Ernst (German expressionist sculptor, printmaker, and writer, 1870–1938). *Job, Old Man Sitting with Raised Arm.* 1909. Pl. 40 in his *Zwischen Erde und Himmel: 45 Handzeichnungen.* Munich: Piper, 1964.

Barry, James (Irish painter, 1741–1806). *Job Reproved by His Friends.* Etching, line-engraving, and aquatint on paper. 1777. Tate Gallery, London.

Bartolommeo, Fra (Italian painter, 1472–1517). *Job.* Engraving by Gerard René Le Vilain (1740–1836), Baltimore Museum of Art: Garrett Collection, BMA 1946.112.3155 [Vicchio 62]. ———. *Study for "Job."* Pen and ink on paper. Courtauld Institute of Art Gallery, London.

Baskin, Leonard (US artist, 1922–2000). *Job.* Etching. c. 1970. Museum of Fine Arts, Boston.

Bedruna-Còsta, Martina. *Lo libre de Jòb (presentacion e causidas).* Qohelèt: revirada integrala. Illustrations by Martina Bedruna-Còsta [Occitan translation]. Toulouse: Centre Régional d'Etudes Occitanes, 1983.

Beham, Barthel (German engraver, miniaturist, and painter, 1502–1540). Engraving. *Job Conversing with His Friends.* Fine Arts Museums of San Francisco.

Beham, Hans Sebald (1500–1550). *Job Afflicted by Satan.* Woodcut, in his *Biblisch Historien, figürlich fürgebildet.* Frankfurt a.M., 1533 [Vicchio 52]. ———. *Job and His Friends.* Engraving. 1547. Philadelphia Museum of Art [Vicchio 54]. ———. *Job Conversing with His Friends.* Engraving. 1547. National Gallery of Art, Washington, DC. ———. *Job, His Wife, and Three Friends.* Woodcut, in his *Biblisch Historien, figürlich fürgebildet.* Frankfurt a.M., 1533 [Pigler 204].

Bellini, Filippo (Italian painter, 1550/55–1603). *Job.* Painting. Oratorio della Carità Fabriano [Pigler 204].

Bellini, Giovanni (Italian painter, 1430–1516). *Madonna and Child, Three Musical Angels, and SS. Francis, John the Baptist, Job, Dominic, Sebastian, and Louis of Toulouse,* known as the *St Job Altarpiece* (*Pala di San Giobbe*). c. 1487. Tempera on panel. Galleria dell'Accademia, Venice [Terrien 133]. ———. *Sacra allegoria.* Oil on canvas. c. 1504–1505. Uffizi, Florence [Terrien 129]. See also **Hornik, Heidi J.** "The Venetian Images by Bellini and Carpaccio. Job as Intercessor or Prophet?" *RevExp* 99 (2002) 541–68. **Hubala, Erich.** *Giovanni Bellini: Madonna mit Kind, die Pala di San Giobbe.* Werkmonographien zur bildenden Kunst 133. Reclams Universal-bibliothek B9133. Stuttgart: Reclam, 1969.

Bening, Simon (Flemish illustrator, 1483–1561). *Job Mocked by His Wife and Tormented by Two Devils.* 1525–1530. Tempera colors, gold paint, gold leaf, and ink on parchment. The Getty Center, Los Angeles.

Ben-Shmuel, Ahron (US sculptor, 1903–1984). *Job.* Bronze sculpture. 1942. Philadelphia Museum of Art [Vicchio 81].

Ben-Zion (Ukrainian and US artist, 1897–1987). *Job*. Etching. In his portfolio, *The Book of Ruth—Job—Song of Songs*. 1954. The Jewish Museum, New York [Vicchio 87]. ———. *Job and His Friends*. Etching. In his portfolio, *The Book of Ruth—Job—Song of Songs*. 1954. The Jewish Museum, New York [Vicchio 85]. ———. *Job in Despair*. Etching. In his portfolio, *The Book of Ruth—Job—Song of Songs*. 1954. The Jewish Museum, New York [Vicchio 86]. ———. *Job Reconciled*. Oil. 1957. Ben-Zion Collection, New York [Vicchio 89].

Bergl, Johann (Czech painter, 1718–1789). *Job, His Wife, and Three Friends*. Painting. 1752. Germanisches Nationalmuseum, Nuremburg. Inv. 1312 [Pigler 206].

Bertram, Axel (German artist, b. 1936). In *Das Buch Hiob, nach der Übertragung von Martin Luther, mit den Marginalien von ihm selbst und vergleichenden Anmerkungen aus dem revidierten Text von 1964 … mit 68 Schabblättern vers. von Axel Bertram*. Leipzig: Faber & Faber, 2003.

Binyon, Laurence (English poet and art scholar, 1869–1943). In *Illustrations of the Book of Job, with a General Introduction*. London: Methuen & Co., 1906.

Bishop, Raymond. *Job Overcome by Guilt*. Drawing. c. 1928 [Terrien 245].

Blake, William (English artist, 1757–1827). *Illustrations of the Book of Job, in Twenty-one Plates, Invented and Engraved by W. B.* Twenty-one engraved prints. London, 1826. Based on a set of watercolors on the same themes. 1805–1810. A second series, 1821. ———. *Illustrations of the Book of Job: Six Proof Engravings with Marginal Drawings*. Plates in series with pencil sketches. c. 1823–1826. Rosenwald Collection, National Gallery of Art, Washington, D.C. ———. *Sketchbook Containing Twenty-Seven Drawings for the Engraved Illustrations to The Book of Job together with Other Drawings*. Pencil, a few touched with watercolor. 1823. Fitzwilliam Museum, Cambridge. ———. *Twenty-One Illustrations to the Book of Job*. The Butts Set. Watercolors. c. 1805–1806 and c. 1821–1827. Morgan Library and Museum, New York. ———. *Twenty-One Illustrations to the Book of Job*. The Linnell Set. Watercolors. 1821. Designs 1, 4–20: Fogg Art Museum, Harvard University, Cambridge, MA. Design 2: American private collection, Paris. Design 21: National Gallery of Art, Washington, DC. ———. *The Book of Job: The Eighteenth Book of the Old Testament, with the Twenty-Two Engravings of William Blake*. New York: Henry Holt, 1927. ———. *Illustrations of the Book of Job: Reproduced in Facsimile from the Original "New Zealand" Set Made about 1823–4, in the Possession of Philip Hofer*. London: J. M. Dent & Sons, 1937.

———. *Beauty of Job's Daughters, The*. Also known as *Job and His Daughters*. In *Illustrations*. 20 [Terrien 223; Balentine 716]. ———. *Behemoth and Leviathan*. In *Illustrations*. 17 [Terrien 215; Balentine 682]. ———. *The Complaint of Job* (recto); *Standing Figure* (verso). Monochrome wash drawing (recto); pencil (verso), c. 1785. Private collection, San Francisco. ———. *Death of Job's Children*. Also known as *Job's Sons and Daughters Overwhelmed by Satan*. In *Illustrations*. 3 [Terrien 198]. ———. *Elihu Points to the Stars*. Also known as *The Wrath of Elihu*. In *Illustrations*. 12 [Terrien 210]. ———. *Every Man Also Gave Him a Piece of Money* (Alternative Composition). Watercolor. c. 1821–1823. Tate Britain, London. ———. *Sketch for Alternative Composition*. Monochrome wash drawing, c. 1821–1823. British Museum, London. ———. *God Blesses Job and His Wife*. Also known as *The Vision of Christ*. In *Illustrations*. 17 [Terrien 219]. ———. *Job* (separate plate). 1st state c. 1793. Keynes Collection, Fitzwilliam Museum, Cambridge. 2nd state c. 1820–1826. The British Museum, London. ———. *Job and His Daughters*. 1799/1800. National Gallery of Art. Washington, DC. ———. *Job and His Daughters*. Pencil sketch. c. 1821. Rosenwald Collection, National Gallery of Art, Washington, DC. ———. *Job and His Daughters*. Tempera painting. c. 1799–1800. National Gallery of Art, Washington, DC. ———. *Job and His Daughters*. Watercolor. c. 1821–1827. Private collection, USA. ———. *Job and His Daughters*. Copper engraving, 1823–1826. Tate Britain, London. ———. *Job and His Family*. In *Illustrations*. 1 [Terrien 196; Balentine 50]. ———. *Job and His Family Restored to Prosperity*. Also known as *Job's Latter End*. Pen and ink with watercolor over graphite. 1821. Rosenwald Collection. National Gallery of Art, Washington, DC. ———. *Job and His Friends*. Pencil sketch in Blake's Notebook, c. 1790–1792. British Library, London. ———. *Job Confessing His Presumption to God Who Answers from the Whirlwind*. Pen, ink, and watercolor over pencil on paper. 1803–1805. National Gallery of Scotland, Edinburgh. ———. *Job Curses the Day of His Birth*. Also known as *Job's Despair*. In *Illustrations*. 8 [Terrien 205; Balentine 85]. ———. *Job Intercedes for His Friends*. Also known as *Job's Sacrifice*. In *Illustrations*. 18 [Terrien 221]. ———. *Job Is Haunted by Nightmares*. Also known as *Job's Evil Dreams*. In *Illustrations*. 11 [Terrien 209; Balentine 135]. ———. *Job Laughed to Scorn*. Also known as *Job Rebuked by His Friends*. In *Illustrations*. 10 [Terrien 208; Balentine 231]. ———. *Job, His Wife, and His Friends: The Complaint of Job* (recto); *Job's Wife and Other Sketches* (verso). Pen and ink and wash on paper, pencil on paper. c. 1785. Tate Gallery, London. ———. *Job, His Wife, and Friends*. Also known as *Job's Comforters*. In *Illustrations*. 7 [Terrien 204; Balentine 69]. ———. *Job, His Wife, and Neighbours*. Also known as *Every Man Also Gave Him a Piece of Money*. In *Illustrations*. 19 [Terrien 222]. ———. *Job's Latter End*. Also known as *Job and His Family Restored to Prosperity*. In *Illustrations*. 21 [Terrien 225]. ———. *Job's Sacrifice*. Watercolor, c. 1821. City Art Gallery, Leeds. ———. *Job's Sons and Daughters Overwhelmed by Satan*. Also known as *Death of Job's Children*. ———. *Messengers of Woe, The*. In *Illustrations*. 4 [Terrien 200]. ———. *Out of the Whirlwind*. Also known as *The Lord Answering Job out of the Whirlwind*. In *Illustrations*. 13 [Terrien 212]. ———. *Satan before God's Throne*. In *Illustrations*. 2 [Terrien 197]. ———. *Satan Falls from Heaven*. Also known as *The Fall of Satan*. In *Illustrations*. 16 [Terrien 218]. ———. *Satan Going Forth from the Presence of the Lord and Job's Charity*. Also known as *Satan's Wager with God*. In *Illustrations*. 5 [Terrien 201]. ———. *Satan Smites Job with Boils*. In *Illustrations*. 6 [Terrien 202]. ———. *Satan Smiting Job with Sore Boils*. c. 1826. Pen and ink and tempera on mahogany support. Tate Gallery, London. ———. *Sweet Influences of the Pleiades*. Also known as *When the Morning Stars Sang Together*. In *Illustrations*. 14 [Terrien 213]. ———. *Vision of Eliphaz, The*. In *Illustrations*. 9 [Terrien 207].

See also **Bindman, David.** *Blake as an Artist*. Oxford: Phaidon, 1977. ———. *Colour Versions of William Blake's Book of Job Designs from the Circle of John Linnell*. London: The William Blake Trust, 1987. ———. *William Blake's Illustrations of the Book of Job. The Engravings and Related Material*. London: William Blake Trust, 1987. **Bryant, Shelle Wilson.** *A Synthesis of the Interpretation of William Blake's Illustrations of the Book of Job*. Diss. Candler, 1993. **Burwick, F.** "Blake's Laocoön and Job: or, On the Boundaries of Painting and Poetry." In *The Romantic Imagination: Literature and Art in England and Germany*. Ed. Frederick Burwick and Jürgen Klein. Amsterdam: Rodopi, 1997. 125–55. **Cormack, Malcolm.** *William Blake: Illustrations of the Book of Job*. Richmond, VA: Virginia Museum of Fine Arts, 1998. **Damon, S. Foster.** *Blake's Job: William Blake's Illustrations of the Book of Job*. Providence: Brown University Press, 1966. ———. *William Blake: His Philosophy and Symbols*. London: Constable; Boston: Houghton, Mifflin, 1924. **Davis, Patricia Elizabeth.** "Revelation in Blake's Job." *Philological Quarterly* 65 (1986) 447–77. **Edinger, Edward F.** *Encounter with the Self: A Jungian Commentary on William Blake's Illustrations of the Book of Job*. Toronto: Inner City Books, 1986. **Emslie, John Adam.** *The Imagination of William Blake: A Study of the Illustrations of the Book of Job*. Diss. Regis College, 2000. **Essick, Robert N.** "Blake's Job: Some Unrecorded Proofs and Their Inscriptions." *Blake: An Illustrated Quarterly* 19 (1985–86) 96–102. **Frye, Northrop.** "Blake's Reading of the Book of Job." In *William Blake: Essays for S. Foster Damon*. Ed. Alvin H. Rosenfeld. Providence, RI: Brown University Press, 1969. 221–34 [= *Collected Works of Northrop Frye*. Ed. Alvin A. Lee. Toronto: University of Toronto Press, 1996. 366–77]. **Gillespie, Diane Filby.** "A Key to Blake's Job: Design XX." *Colby Library Quarterly* 19 (1983) 59–68. **Hamblen, Emily S.** *The Book of Job Interpreted, Illustrated with the Designs of William Blake* [commentary]. New York: Delphic Studios, 1933. **Hiles, David.** "Jung, William Blake, and Our Answer to Job." Paper presented to the Collegium Jungianum Brunense, April 25, 2001, Brno, Czech Republic [MM14]. **Keynes, Geoffrey.** *Blake Studies: Essays on His Life and Work*. Oxford: Clarendon Press, 1971. **Lindberg, Bo.** *William Blake's Illustrations to the Book of Job*. Acta academiae aboensis, Series A: Humaniora 46. Åbo: Åbo akademi, 1973. **Marqusee, Michael.** *The Book of Job Illustrated by William Blake, with a New Introduction by Michael Marqusee*. New York: Paddington, 1976. **Minney, Penelope.** *Job's Gethsemane:*

Tradition and Imagination in William Blake's Illustrations for the Book of Job. Diss. Durham, 1997. **Moskal, Jeanne.** "Friendship and Forgiveness in Blake's Illustrations of Job." *South Atlantic Review* 55/2 (1990) 15–31. **Nuckels, Rosa Turner.** *Visions of Light in the Poetry of William Blake and Emily Dickinson* [typological interpretation of Job]. Diss. North Texas, 1996. **Paley, Morton D.** "The World without Imagination: Blake's Visions of Leviathan and Behemoth." In his *Energy and the Imagination: A Study of the Development of Blake's Thought.* Oxford: Clarendon Press, 1970. 171–99. ———. *The Traveller in the Evening: The Last Works of William Blake.* Oxford: Oxford University Press, 2007. **Patchen, Kenneth** (introductory note). *Job, Invented and Engraved.* New York: United Book Guild, 1947. **Perry-Lehmann, Meira (Peri-Lehman, Me'irah).** *Ish hayah be-erets 'Uts: iyure Vilyam Blaik le-sefer Iyov. There Was a Man in the Land of Uz: William Blake's Illustrations to the Book of Job.* Jerusalem: Israel Museum, 1992. **Raine, Kathleen.** *The Human Face of God. William Blake and the Book of Job.* London: Thames & Hudson, 1982. **Shabetai, Karen.** *Blake's Perception of Evil.* Diss. University of California, San Diego, 1984. **Simmons, Robert E.** "A Way of Teaching Job" [Blake's illustrations]. In *Approaches to Teaching the Hebrew Bible as Literature in Translation.* Ed. Barry N. Olshen and Yael S. Feldman. New York: Modern Language Association of America, 1989. 124–26. **Solomon, Andrew.** *Blake's Job: A Message for Our Time.* London: Palamabron Press, 1993. **Sung, M.-Y.** *Technical and Material Studies of William Blake's Engraved Illustrations of The Book of Job (1826).* Diss. Nottingham Trent, 2005. **Van Pelt, William Vern.** *"The Gates of Paradise": A Study of Images of Desire in the Poetry and Illustrations of William Blake.* Diss. University of California, Santa Cruz, 1983. **Vicchio, Stephen J.** "Job in William Blake." In his *Job in the Modern World.* Eugene, OR: Wipf & Stock, 2006. 100–115. **Wicksteed, Joseph H.** *Blake's Vision of the Book of Job, with Reproductions of the Illustrations: A Study.* London: J. M. Dent & Sons, 1910. **Wright, Andrew.** *Blake's "Job": A Commentary.* Oxford: Clarendon Press, 1972.

Bonaiuto, Andrea di (Florentine painter, 14th cent.). *Job.* Fresco. Spanish chapel in Santa Maria Novella, Florence. c. 1365.

Bonnat, Léon (French painter, 1833–1922). *Job.* 1880. Oil on canvas. Musée Bonnat. Bayonne [Balentine 548].

Borzone, Luciano (Italian Baroque painter, 1590–1643). *Job* (?). Painting. Private Collection, Genoa [Pigler 204].

Bosch, Hieronymus (Netherlandish painter, c. 1450–1516). *Job and Musicians.* Musée Communal (Groeninge Museum), Bruges [Denis, Pl. XXIII]. ———. *Job Reviled.* Painting. 1514. Sammlung Max de Coninck, Diegem [Denis, Pl. XXII]. ———. *Job Reviled.* Painting. c. 1514. Musée Communal, Douai [Denis, Pl. XXI].

Bosch, Hieronymus, follower of (16th cent.). *Job and Three Musicians.* Painting. Ashmolean Museum, Oxford [Denis, Pl. XII]. ———. *Trials of Job.* Painting. 1514. Heirs of Max de Coninck, Diegem, Belgium [Denis, Pl. XXII]. See also **Hellerstedt, Kahren Jones.** "The Blind Man and His Guide in Netherlandish Painting." *Simiolus* 13 (1983) 163–81.

Bosschère, Jean de (French illustrator and poet, 1878–1953). *Job le pauvre, with English translation, avec un portrait par Wyndham Lewis, traduction des poèmes en anglais, et quatorze gravures noires.* Paris: Jacques Povolozky, Collection d'Art "La Cible," 1922. London: John Lane, Bodley Head, 1922.

Bourdichon, Jean (French illuminator, 1457–1521). *Job on the Dung Heap.* c. 1480–1485. Getty Museum, Los Angeles.

Bourdichon, School of. *Job and His Friends.* Illumination, *Book of Hours of Henri IV.* Ms lat. 1171, fol. 58v. Bibliothèque Nationale, Paris [Terrien 116]. ———. *Job's Wife and Musicians.* Illumination. Ms lat. 1171, fol. 58v. Bibliothèque Nationale, Paris [Terrien 117].

Bourne, Herbert (1820–1885). *Job and His Friends.* Engraving, after Paul Falconer Poole (English painter, 1807–1879). Jewish Theological Seminary of America, New York. Special Collections F74.2.2 [Vicchio 71].

Bramer, Leonaert (Dutch painter, 1596–1674). *Job and His Three Friends.* Drawing. National Museum, Warsaw [Pigler 206]. ———. *Afflictions of Job.* Pen and ink on paper. Courtauld Institute of Art Gallery, London.

Brangwyn, Sir Frank (Welsh artist, 1867–1956). *The Book of Job, with 33 Original Signed Etchings.* Leigh-on-Sea: F. Lewis, 1948.

Braque, George (French artist, 1882–1962). *Job.* Drypoint and etching. 1911. Fine Arts Museums of San Francisco. ———. *Job.* Etching on Arches paper. 1911. National Gallery of Art, Washington, DC.

Brentana, Simone (Italian painter, 1637–1706). *Job.* Painting. S. Niccolò, Verona [Pigler 205].

Brown, Ford Madox (English painter, 1821–1893). *Job on the Ash-heap.* 1837.

Brussel-Smith, Bernard (US wood engraver, 1914–1989). *The Book of Job.*

Callot, Jacques (French engraver, 1592–1635). *St Job, Prophet, May 10.* In *Les Images de tous les saincts et saintes de l'année, suiuant le martyrologe romain . . . Mises en lumiere par Israel Henriet.* Paris, 1636. ———. *St Job, Prophet.* Etching. National Gallery of Art, Washington, DC.

Cardi, Ludovici (Il Cigoli, Italian painter, 1559–1613). *Job, His Wife, and His Friends.* Painting. Formerly Galleria Feroni, Florence [Pigler 204].

Carpaccio, Vittore (Italian painter, c. 1460–1525/1526). *Job and the Dead Christ.* Tempera on wood. c. 1505–1510. Staatliche Museen zu Berlin, Preussischer Kulturbesitz Gemäldegalerie [Terrien 138]. ———. *Meditation on the Passion.* Tempera on wood. c. 1495. Metropolitan Museum of Art, New York [Terrien 136]. See also **Hartt, Frederick.** "Carpaccio's Meditation on the Passion." *Art Bulletin* 22 (1940) 25–35. **Hornik, Heidi J.** "The Venetian Images by Bellini and Carpaccio. Job as Intercessor or Prophet?" *RevExp* 99 (2002) 541–68.

Celesti, Andrea (Italian Baroque painter, 1637–1706). *Job and His Wife.* Painting. Formerly Barbisoni Collection, Brescia [Pigler 205].

Chagall, Marc (Russian-Belarusian-French painter, 1887–1985). *Job.* 1975. Private collection [Balentine 365]. ———. *Job and a Prancing Demon.* Tinted drawing. 1960 [Terrien 258]. ———. *Job and the Angel of Death.* Tinted drawing. 1960 [Terrien 259]. ———. *Job at Prayer.* Tinted drawing. 1960 [Terrien 260]. ———. *Job with Background of Geometricized Christ à la Cimabuë.* 1975. Oil on canvas. Private collection, St Paul de Vence [Terrien color plate 4].

Ciotte, Nardo di (active 1343–1366), follower of. *Job.* 1365. Triptychon, Santa Croce, Florence.

Collaert, Adriaen (Flemish printmaker, c. 1560–1618). *The Lord's First Answer to Job.* Print in album. c. 1689. P.4290-R-166. Fitzwilliam Museum, Cambridge.

Coornhert, Dirck Volckertz (Dutch engraver, 1522–1590). *The Triumph of Job.* Engraving, after Maerten van Heemskerck's *Job op de mestvaalt/Job on the Tortoise* [symbol of patience]. National Gallery of Art, Washington, DC [Vicchio 58].

Corey, Irene (costume designer). See **Hill, Carale Manning.** *"Light in Her Hands": A Biography of Irene Corey.* Diss. Texas Tech, 1995.

Corey, Orlin. *Job as a Live Byzantine Mosaic.* Mask, New York World's Fair, 1964 [Terrien 254].

Cranach, Lucas (German painter and printmaker, 1472–1553). *Job.* Sketch. c. 1510. Marienkirche, Frankfurt [Meyer 29].

Crayer, Gaspar de (Flemish painter, 1582–1669). *Job, His Wife, and His Friends* (after Rubens, St Nicolaas triptych). Painting. Musée de Beaux-Arts, Toulouse. Cat. 438 [Hulst, Pl. 126].

Dawtry, Marc, Daniel Renassia, and Joseph Ben Aaron. *Le livre de Job orné de soixante-dix-huit gravures originales de Marc Dawtry* [original translation]. Nice: J. Pardo, 1961.

Decamps, Alexandre-Gabriel (French painter, 1803–1860). *Job, His Wife and His Friends.* Oil on canvas. c. 1855. Minneapolis Institute of Arts [Terrien 230].

Delacroix, Eugène (French painter, 1798–1863). *Job Mocked by His Wife and Tormented by Demons.* Painting. Musée Bonnat, Bayonne. Cat. 1908, no. 70 [Hulst 381].

Delcloche, Paul-Joseph (Flemish painter, 1716–1755). *Job, His Wife and Hostile Friends.* Charcoal drawing. c. 1758. Musée de Beaux-Arts, Liège [Terrien 192].

Deshayes, Jean-Baptiste-Henri (1729–1765). *Job.* Painting. 1751 [Pigler 206].

Diepenbeek, Abraham van (Flemish painter, 1596–1675). *Job, His Wife, and His Friends* (after Rubens, St Nicolaas triptych). Drawing, for title page of Balthasar Corderus, *Jobus elucidatus.* Antwerp, 1646, Hermitage, St Petersburg. Inv. 25322.

Dix, Otto (German painter and printmaker, 1891–1969). *Job.* Tempera on plywood. 1946, Otto-Dix-Stiftung, Vaduz [Karcher 224].

Doberan Abbey (Cistercian monastery in Mecklenburg, Germany). See **Jensen, Jens Christian.** "Der Lettneraltar der Zisterzienserabtei Doberan." *Niederdeutsche Beiträge zur Kunstgeschichte* 3 (1964) 229–74.

Dohany Master (French illuminator, 15th cent.). *Job on the Dung-Heap, with Friends.* Illumination. Book of Hours. 1520–1530. Ms 134, p. 174. Fitzwilliam Museum, Cambridge.

Dürer, Albrecht (German painter and printmaker, 1471–1528). Engravings in *Die Psalmen Davids. Das Buch Hiob. Die Sprüche Salomos. Der Prediger Salomo. Das Hohelied Salomos.* Die Dürer-Bibel 2. Munich: Einhorn-Verlag, [1910]. ———. *Jabach Altarpiece.* c. 1504. Städelschen Kunstinstitut, Frankfurt and Cologne Museum [Terrien 140–41]. ———. *Job and His Wife.* c. 1504. Oil on panel. Städelsches Kunstinstitut, Frankfurt. See also **Weizsäcker, Heinrich.** "Der sogenannte Jabachsche Altar und die Dichtung des Buches Hiob. Ein Beitrag zur Geschichte von Albrecht Dürers Kunst." In *Kunstwissenschaftliche Beiträge August Schmarsow gewidmet.* Leipzig: Hiersemann, 1907. 153–62.

Dyck, Anthony van (Flemish Baroque painter living in England, 1599–1641). *Job Mocked by His Wife and Tortured by Demons.* Drawing (after Rubens, St Nicolaas triptych, left panel). Cabinet des dessins, Musée du Louvre, Paris [Hulst, Pl. 128].

Eichenberg, Fritz (German and US engraver, 1901–1990). *The Book of Job.* Wood engraving. 1955. National Gallery of Art, Washington, DC [Vicchio 88].

Falaise, Robert (French sculptor, 16th cent.). *Job and Musicians.* 1522. Misericord, wood sculpture. Collegium of Champeaux [Terrien 122]. ———. *Job's Friends in Dunce Cap.* Wood sculpture, stalls of the Collegium of Champeaux {Terrien 125; Balentine 202].

Flemish School (Netherlandish). *Job, His Wife, and Demons.* Oil on canvas. c. 1620. Chapel of the Beguines, Louvain [Terrien 189]. See **Ceuleneer, Adolf de.** "Les épreuves de Job: Triptyche d'un peintre flamand de la fin du 15e ou du commencement du 16e siècle, conservé à Turin dans la famille Prensa." *Bulletin de l'Académie Royale de Belgique* 5 (1922) 20–25. **Herck, Jozef van.** "Het retabel van Sint-Job te Schoonbroek." *Noordgouw: Cultureel tijdschrift van de Province Antwerpen* 5 (1965) 89–108. **Fouquet, Jean (French miniaturist, c. 1420–c. 1480).** *Job and His False Comforters.* c. 1452–1460. Miniature from the Book of Hours of Etienne Chevalier. Musée Condé, Chantilly [Balentine 484].

Fox-Düvell, Gisela, and Adelheid Bienmüller. *Und Dunkelheit wird wie der Morgen sein: Bilder und Texte zu Ijob.* Munich: Don-Bosco-Verlag, 1994.

Franciabigio, Marcantonio (Italian painter, 1482–1525). *Virgin and Child with Sts John the Baptist and Job.* 1516. Museo di S. Salvi, Florence.

Franck, Franz Friedrich (German painter, 1627–1687). *Job.* Painting. Evangelisches Waisenhaus, Augsburg [Pigler 206].

Fredi, Bartolo di (Italian painter, c. 1330–1410). *A Hurricane Kills Job's Children.* Fresco. c. 1367. Basilica Collegiata di S. Maria Assunta, San Gimignano [Terrien 99]. ———. *Banquet of King Job and His Queen.* Fresco. c. 1367. Basilica Collegiata di S. Maria Assunta, San Gimignano [Terrien 98]. ———. *Job and His Friends.* Fresco. c. 1367. Basilica Collegiata di S. Maria Assunta, San Gimignano [Terrien 100].

Friesach, Konrad von (German painter, fl. 1440–1460). *Christ as Job Tortured by the Devil and Musicians.* Painting on cloth. Lenten curtain. Gurk Cathedral, Carinthia [Terrien 114].

Fronius, Hans (Austrian painter and illustrator, 1903–1988). Twelve charcoal sketches. In **Marböck, J.** *Das Buch Hiob. Illustrationen von Hans Fronius. Einleitung von J. Marböck.* Klosterneuberg: Österreichisches Katholisches Bibelwerk, 1980.

Fuchs, Ernst (Austrian artist, b. 1930). *Hiob.* Etching and aquatint. 1963. Fine Arts Museums of San Francisco.

Gaddi, Taddeo (Italian painter, c. 1300–1366). *Job and His Friends.* c. 1355. Fresco. Camposanto, Pisa [Terrien 96]. ——. *Job and Satan.* Fresco. c. 1355. Camposanto, Pisa [Terrien 93]. ——. *Job and the Sabeans.* c. 1355. Fresco. Camposanto, Pisa [Terrien 95]. ——. *Job Distributes Alms to the Poor.* c. 1355. Fresco. Camposanto, Pisa. ——. *Job Restored.* Fresco. c. 1350. Camposanto, Pisa. ——. *Job Intercedes for His Friends.* c. 1355. Fresco. Camposanto, Pisa [Terrien 97; Balentine 711].

Gilbert, John (English painter, 1817–1897). *The Patriarch. Illustration to the Book of Job.* Wood engraving. Museum of Fine Arts, Boston.

Giordano, Luca (Italian Baroque painter and printmaker, 1634–1705). *Job and His Comforters.* Oil on canvas. c. 1680. Sacristia del Monasterio de San Lorenzo, L'Escorial, Madrid [Terrien 186].

Glockenton, Albrecht (German painter, fl. 1479–1491). *Job, His Wife, and Two Musicians.* In Prayerbook of Prince Wilhelm IV of Bavaria. 1535. Nationalbibliothek, Vienna. Ms 1880, fol. 83v [Denis, fig. VI].

Goldschmitt, Bruno (German artist, 1881–1964). *Hiob.* Wood engraving. In *Portfolio Die Bibel (The Bible).* Plate 17. Fine Arts Museums of San Francisco. ——. In *Das Buch Esther und das Buch Hiob. Urholzschnitte von Bruno Goldschmitt.* Die erzählenden Bücher des Alten Testaments 1. Munich: Hans von Weber, 1918. ——. *Die Bibel: Eine Folge von 30 Original-Holzschnitten von Bruno Goldschmitt.* Munich: F. Bruckmann, c. 1925.

Goltzius, Hendrick (Dutch painter, 1558–1617). *Job in Distress.* 1616. Oil on panel. Private collection, New York. See also **Nichols, Lawrence W.** "'Job in Distress,' a Newly-Discovered Painting by Hendrick Goltzius." *Simiolus: Netherlands Quarterly for the History of Art* 13, 3/4 (1983) 182–88.

Gothein, Werner (German artist, 1890–1968). *Hiob.* Woodcut. Schwenningen, Neckar: Ziegler, 1953.

Granville Fell, Herbert (English art nouveau artist, 1872–1951). In **Granville Fell, Herbert, and Joseph Jacobs.** *The Book of Job.* London: J. M. Dent, 1896.

Grassi, Nicola (Italian painter, 1682–1748). *Job and His Three Friends.* Painting. Formerly Sammlung Haberstock, Berlin [Pigler 205].

Grimm, Gerhard (German artist, b. 1927). In **Bochinger, Erich.** *Wie kann Gott das zulassen? Geschichten von Hiob, Erfahrungen von heute. Mit Zeichnungen und Holzschnitte von Gerhard Grimm.* Reutlingen: Diakonie-Verlag, 1995.

Gruber, Francis (French painter, 1912–1948). *Job.* Oil on canvas. 1944. Tate Britain, London [Terrien 250; Balentine 361].

Guglielmi, Gregorio (Italian painter, 1714–1773). *Job.* Oval painting. Cappella Colleoni, Bergamo [Pigler 205].

Haghe, Louis (English artist, 1806–1885). *The Fountain of Job—The Holy Land.* Lithograph with hand coloring. Fine Arts Museum of San Francisco.

Harootian, Koren der (Armenian-born artist, living in Jamaica and US, 1909–1991). *Job Standing Erect.* Stone sculpture. c. 1950 [Terrien 251].

Heemskerck, Maerten van (Marten, or Maarten, Jacobszoon Heemskerk van Veen; Dutch draftsman and painter, 1498–1574). *Job Tormented by a Demon, and Job and His Wife.* Drawing. Albertina, Vienna [Pigler 204]. ——. *Job op de mestvaalt/Job on the Tortoise* [symbol of patience]. 1559. Pen and brown ink with traces of chalk on laid paper. National Gallery of Art, Washington, DC [Vicchio 57]. ——. Album of Job prints, including *Job Receiving Gifts* (1563), *Job Receiving the Ill-News of His Misfortunes* (1563),

Job Sacrificing for the Sins of His Children (1563), *Job Sitting on the Dunghill* (1563), *Satan Challenging the Lord to Remove His Protection from Job* (1563), *Satan Smiting Job with Boils* (1563), *The Sons of God, Satan amongst Them, Present Themselves before the Lord* (1563), *The Lord Answering Job* (1563), *The Triumph of Job* (1559). Philip Galle, printmaker. Fitzwilliam Museum, Cambridge.

Heidenheim, Hanns H. (b. 1922). *Holzschnitte zur Bibel.* I. *Ijob.* Düsseldorf: Ursus Press, 1965. ———. "Ijob" [design]. *Zeichen der Hoffnung* 9/10 (Patmos Verlag, 2002) 93.

Henriques, Anna Ruth (Jamaican artist and writer, b. 1967). *The Book of Mechtilde* [forty-page illuminated manuscript]. Ink, gouache, and paint on paper. 1992. The Jewish Museum, New York [Vicchio 96–99].

Heuvel, Antoon van den (c. 1600–1677). *Job.* Painting. Church of Puivelde near Beisele, Belgium [Pigler 206].

Hirschvogel, Augustin (1503–1533). *Job Learns of His Misfortunes.* Etching. 1549. National Gallery of Art, Washington, DC [Vicchio 55].

Holbein, Hans, the Younger (c. 1497–1543). *Job, His Wife, and His Friends.* In his *Icones historiarum Veteris Testamenti.* 1547. Wood engraving by Hans Lützelburger (1495?–1526). Basel. c. 1542 [Vicchio 53].

Holzmair, Johann Wilhelm (fl. 1620–1660). *Job.* Painting. Church, Bergkirchen, Upper Bavaria [Pigler 206].

Horst, Nicolaas van der (1598–1646). *Job on the Ashheap, His Wife, and His Friends* (after Rubens, St Nicolaas triptych). Drawing. N. de Boer Foundation, Amsterdam [Hulst, Pl. 124].

Huys, Peter (Flemish painter, c. 1519–c. 1581). *The Trials of Job.*

Il Calabrese (Italian painter, 1615–1675). *Job, His Wife, His Friends, the Devil, and an Angel.* Oil on canvas. 1690. Musée Royal des Beaux-Arts, Brussels [Terrien 185].

Jaeckel, Willi (German Expressionist painter and printmaker, 1888–1944). *Das Buch Hiob.* Lithograph. 1917. The Jewish Museum, New York [Vicchio 80].

Jernigan, Brad. In **Lande, Lawrence M.** *A Man Called Job. Illustrated by Brad Jernigan.* Montreal: Jewish Educational Council of Greater Montreal, 1984.

Karsch, Joachim. *Job and His Friends.* Gypsum sculpture. 1919. Lost (?) [Barron, Pl. 25].

Kaufmann, Hans-Günther. In **Ben-Chorin, Schalom, and Michael Langer.** *Die Tränen des Hiob. Bilder von Hans-Günther Kaufmann.* Innsbruck: Tyrolia-Verlag, 1994.

Kohn, Misch (US artist, 1916–2003). *Job.* Woodcut. Library of Congress, Washington, DC [Vicchio 90].

Kokoschka, Oskar (Austrian artist, 1886–1980). *Adam, the Gardener, Buries Job.* Drawing. 1917 [Terrien 240]. ———. *Anima and the Dying Job.* Drawing. 1917 [Terrien 241]. ———. *Job and the Rubber Man.* Lithograph in black on laid paper. 1916/17. National Gallery of Art, Washington, DC. ———. *Job Wooing Anima, with Satan's Blessing.* Drawing, 1917 [Terrien 236]. ———. *Job, Anima, Eros, and the Dogs.* Drawing. 1917 [Terrien 238]. ———. *Job, the Young Women, and Death.* Drawing. 1917 [Terrien 237]. ———. *Job's Wife Pours Water on His Neck.* Drawing. 1917 [Terrien 238]. ———. *Satan Throws Anima on Job.* Drawing. 1917 [Terrien 239]. ———. *Woman and Man* (poster used for *Job: A Drama*, 1909) [Terrien 234]. See also **Kleinschmidt, Erich.** "Poetik der Auflösung: Zur Funktion der Hiob-Mythe in Texten Oskar Kokoschkas, Joseph Roths und Karl Wolfskehls." In *Paradeigmata: Literarische Typologie des Alten Testaments.* Ed. Franz Link. Berlin: Duncker & Humblot, 1989. 2:511–26.

Krafft, Jan Lauwrijn (b. 1694). *Job on the Ash Heap.* Engraving [Hulst, Pl. 121].

Kulhanek, Oldrich (Czech artist, b. 1940). *Job.* 2002. Galerie Art Chrudim, Czech Republic.

La Hyre [Hire], Laurent de (French Baroque painter, 1606–1656). *Job Restored to Prosperity.* Chrysler Museum of Art, Norfolk, VA.

La Tour, Georges de (French painter, 1593–1652). *Job and His Wife.* Also known as *Job Mocked by His Wife.* c. 1650. Oil on canvas. Musée départemental des Vosges, Epinal,

France. Cat. 1929, no. 152 [Terrien 167; Balentine 65]. See also **Weisbach, Werner.** "L'histoire de Job dans les arts: A propos du tableau de Georges de La Tour au musée d'Epinal." *Gazette des beaux-arts* 78/2 (1936) 102–12.

Lama, Giulia (Italian painter, 18th cent.). *Job and His Three Friends.* Painting. Location unknown [Pigler 205].

Langetti, Giovanni Battista (Italian painter, 1635–1676). *Job.* Oval painting. Galerie Schönborn, Pommersfelden [Pigler 205].

Legros, Alphonse (French painter, 1830–1911). *Job.* Drypoint and etching. National Gallery of Art, Washington, DC [Vicchio 72].

Lehnerer, Thomas (German artist, 1955–1995). *Hiob* [installation]. Essen: Kunstverein Ruhr, 1992.

Levin, Julo (German artist, 1901–1943). *Job.* Oil on linen. 1933/34. Stadtmuseum, Düsseldorf [Kempel 297].

Leyden, Lucas van (Dutch engraver and painter, 1494–1533). *Job and Three Musicians.* Also known as *Job and His Comforters.* Painting. Oil on panel. c. 1510. Collection of Viscount Lee of Fareham. Courtauld Institute of Art Gallery, London [Denis, Pl. XIII].

Leyden, Lucas van, School of (16th cent.). *Job and Three Musicians.* Painting. Private collection, Portugal [Denis, Pl. XIV].

Lievens, Jan (Dutch painter, 1607–1674). *Job in His Misery/Job sur son fumier.* 1631. National Gallery of Canada, Ottawa.

Lindtmayer, Daniel (Swiss artist, 1552–1602). *Job on the Dung Heap.* 1581. Pen and black ink with gray wash. Getty Museum, Los Angeles.

Linnell, John (British artist, 1792–1882]. *Job Offering a Sacrifice on His Return to Prosperity.* Painting. Oil on panel. 1845. Fitzwilliam Museum, Cambridge.

Loth, Johann Carl (Carlotto; German painter, 1632–1698). *Job.* Painting. Baron von Obermayr Collection, Munich. ———. *Job.* Painting. Palazzo Morosini, Venice. ———. *Job and His Friends.* Painting. Galerie Schönborn, Pommersfelden. ———. *Job and His Friends.* Painting. Gemäldegalerie Alte Meister, Dresden. Kat. 1905, Nr 2005. ———. *Job and His Wife.* Painting. Galleria dell'Accademia, Venice. Inv. 437. ———. *Job and His Wife.* Painting. Palazzo Casilini Rovigo. ———. *Job and His Wife.* Painting. Vienna. Kat. Nr. 157. ———. *Job on the Ash Heap.* Painting. Freiherr Joseph Leopold von Castell Collection, Mannheim.

Mandyn, Jan (Dutch painter, 1500–1560). *Job, His Wife, and Musicians.* Oil on canvas. c. 1470–1500. Musée de la Chartreuse, Douai [Terrien 121].

Máranová, Jarmila (Czech artist). *Das Buch Hiob* [illustrations]. Stuttgart: Müller & Schindler, 1971.

Mariotti, Giambattista (Italian artist, c. 1685–1765). *Job Mocked by His Wife.* Painting. SS. Simone e Taddeo, Verona [Pigler 205].

Marshall, William Calder (Scottish sculptor, 1813–1894). *"Unto me men gave ear and waited, and kept silence at my counsel" (Job 29).* 1863. South nave aisle, St Paul's Cathedral, London.

Martini, Simone (Italian painter, 1284–1344). *Job.* Papal Palace, Avignon [Meyer 25].

Master of the Saint Barbara Legend (Netherlandish painter, 15th cent.). *Job and Musicians.* Painting. c. 1470–1500. Wallraf-Richartz Museum, Cologne [Terrien 118–19].

McGovern, Robert (US artist). In **Berrigan, Daniel.** *Job: And Death No Dominion. With Art by Robert McGovern.* Franklin, WI: Sheed & Ward, 2000.

Meldolla, Andrea (Schiavone; Dalmatian artist living in Venice, c. 1510–1563). *Job.* Drawing. Musée du Louvre, Paris [Pigler 204].

Merian, Matthaeus the Elder (Swiss engraver, 1593–1650). *The Misfortunes of Job.* 1625–1630. Engraving in Melchior Küsel, *Icones biblicae.* Vienna, 1679 [repr. Hildesheim: Georg Olms, 1968].

Mesibov, Hugh (US artist, b. 1933). *Book of Job Mural.* Temple Beth El, Spring Valley,

NY. Canvas, acrylic and charcoal. 1971. ———. *Job in the Wilderness*. Charcoal. 1972. ———. *Job's Agony*. Acrylic collage. 1969.

Mestrovic, Ivan (Croatian sculptor, 1883–1962). *Job*. 1945. Bronze maquette. Syracuse University Art Collection [Vicchio 82].

Meyer, Rudolf (Swiss artist, 1605–1638). *Job and His Wife*. Drawing. Albertina, Vienna [Pigler 206].

Michelson, Leo (Latvian-born US artist, 1887–1978). *Job and His Friend* [cf. Terrien 246].

Murillo, Bartolomé Esteban (Spanish painter, 1617–1682). *Job and His Wife*. Parma Pinocoteca.

Nerdinger, Eugen (German artist, 1910–1991). In **Kunstmann, Joseph.** *Job: Eine Auswahl aus dem biblischen Text. Eugen Nerdinger gestaltete ... mit ... zehn Langholzschnitten.* Augsburg: Dom-Verlag, 1945.

Nordau, Maxa (French illustrator, 1897–1991). In **Camhy, O.** *Une trilogie biblique sur le drame de la vie: un sujet, trois conceptions: Job, Qohéleth ou l'Ecclésiaste, Isaïe. Dessins de Maxa Nordau et Devi Tuszynski.* Paris: J. Grassin, 1973.

Oost, Jacob van (Flemish painter, 1601–1671). *Job and Musicians Comforting Him*. Painting. Archbishop's Palace, Olomouc, Czech Republic [Pigler 206].

Orley, Bernart van (Flemish painter, c. 1487–1541). *Death of Job's Children*. Altarpiece, central panel (Triptych of Virtue of Patience, Job and Lazarus). Oil on canvas. 1521–1525. Musées Royaux de Beaux-Arts, Brussels [Terrien 161]. ———. *Job as Lazarus*. Altarpiece (closed), left panel (Triptych of Virtue of Patience, Job and Lazarus). Oil on canvas. 1521–1525. Musées Royaux de Beaux-Arts, Brussels [Terrien 163]. ———. *The Raid on Job's Flocks and Herds*. Altarpiece (closed), right panel (Triptych of Virtue of Patience, Job and Lazarus). Oil on canvas. 1521–1525. Musées Royaux de Beaux-Arts, Brussels [Terrien 163].

Pagani, Paolo (Italian artist, 1661–1716). *Job*. Drawing. Accademia Carrara, Bergamo [Pigler 205].

Passon, Kurt (Polish-born artist, b. 1929). In **Lamparter, Helmut.** *Das Buch Hiob. In der Übertragung von Helmut Lamparter. Mit 38 Weissschnitten von den Originalplatten von Kurt Passon. Einführung von Rainer Zimmermann.* Frankenau, Hessen: Siebenberg-Verlag, 1962.

Pencz, Georg (German engraver and painter, c. 1500–1550). *Job*. Engraving [Pigler 204].

Pisano, Niccolo (Italian sculptor, 1225–1287). *Job in the History of Salvation*. c. 1260. Pillar, Baptistery, Pisa.

Polazzo, Francesco (Italian painter, 1683–1753). *Job*. Painting. 1743. S. Alessandro della Croce, Bergamo [Pigler 205].

Preti, Mattia (Italian artist, 1613–1699). *Job*. Painting. Museum, Brussels. ———. *Job*. Painting. Palazzo Dragonetti Cappelli, Aquila [Pigler 205]. ———. *Job and His Three Friends*. Painting. Suermondt Museum, Aachen [Pigler 205].

Ratner, Philip (Jewish US artist). *Job*. 1998. Israel Bible Museum.

Rattner, Abraham (US painter, 1893–1978). *Job in Agony* [cf. Terrien 246]. ———. *Job #9*. Oil on canvas. 1959. Kennedy Galleries, New York [Terrien color plate 3].

Reni, Guido (Italian painter, 1575–1642). *Triumph of Job*. Etching by Giuseppe Maria Mitelli. 1679. Philadelphia Museum of Art [Vicchio 60].

Repin, Ilya (Russian painter, 1844–1930). *Job and His Friends*. 1869. Oil on canvas. The Russian Museum, St Petersburg.

Ribera, Jusepe de (Lo Spagnoletto; Spanish painter, 1591–1652). *Job in Prayer*. 1640. Galleria nazionale, Parma [Terrien 184; Balentine 4]. ———. *Job on the Ash Heap*. Oil on canvas. c. 1630.

Ricci, Sebastiano (Italian painter, 1659–1734). *Job*. Painting. Formerly Collection Sipriot, Marseilles. ———. *Job*. Drawing. Windsor Castle, England [Pigler 205]. ———. *Job Mocked by His Wife*. Painting. Musei Belluno.

Richter, Jürgen (photographer). In **Mayer, Yvette.** *Ein kostbarer Fund: Begegnungen mit Hiob* [photographs by Jürgen Richter]. Leipzig: Thomas-Verlag, 2001.

Riemenschneider, Tilman (German sculptor and woodcarver, 1455–1531). See **Koch, Ursula.** *Hiob, mein Bruder: Begegnungen mit Tilman Riemenschneider, Janusz Korczak, Katharina von Henot u.a.* Giessen: Brunnen-Verlag, 3rd ed., 1999.

Rijn, Rembrandt van (Dutch painter and etcher, 1606–1669). *Job, His Wife, and Two Friends.* Drawing. Dr Tobias Christ Collection, Basel [Pigler 206].

Rodlein, Hans (German sculptor, 17th cent.). See **Borchers, Jörg-Michael.** "Hiob im Elend: Zwei Reliefdarstellungen Hans Rodleins und ihre Vorlagen." *Wertheimer Jahrbuch* 1991/92 (1992) 59–80.

Rogers, John (English engraver, 1808–1888?). *Job and His Friends.* After Denis Auguste Marie Raffet (French painter, 1804–1860). Engraving. Jewish Theological Seminary of America, New York [Vicchio 78].

Rosa, Salvator (Italian painter, 1615–1673). *Giobbe.* Also known as *Job, His Friends, and an Armored Warrior.* Oil on canvas. c. 1665. Vasari Corridor, Uffizi, Florence [Terrien 170, 172].

Rose, Robert T. (illustrator). *The Book of Job.* London: George Bell & Sons; Edinburgh: The Abbey Press, 1902.

Rubens, Peter Paul (Flemish painter, 1577–1640). *Job's Trials.* Altarpiece (St Nicolaas triptych). 1612–1613. Church of St Nicholas, Brussels (destroyed in 1695). See copies by Anthony van Dyck, Gaspar de Crayer, Abraham van Diepenbeek, Nicolaas van der Horst, Cornelis Saftleven, and Lucas Emil Vorsterman. See also **Hulst, Roger Adolf d', and M. Vandenven.** *Rubens: The Old Testament.* London: Harvey Miller, 1968.

Rubens, Peter Paul, follower of. *Job, His Wife (?), and Comforters.* Oil on canvas. c. 1635. Institut royal du patrimoine artistique, Brussels [Terrien 190].

Sacchi, Andrea (Italian painter, 1590–1661). *Job.* Painting. Wilton House, Salisbury [Pigler 204].

Saftleven, Cornelis (Dutch painter, 1607–1681). *Job Assailed by Evil Spirits.* Painting. Kunsthalle, Karlsruhe [Schulz 514]. ———. *Job, His Wife, and His Friends* (after Rubens, St Nicolaas triptych). Painting. Museum Mayer van der Bergh, Antwerp. Inv. 479 [Schulz 1187].

Scarsella, Ippolito (Lo Scarsellino, Italian painter, 1551–1620). Eight paintings. c. 1600. Landesmuseum Hanover. Kat. 1954, Nr. 348–55 [Novell, Pls. 38–41].

Schoonjans, Anthoni (Belgian painter, 1655–1726). *Job, His Wife, and Demons.* Painting. 1710 [Pigler 206].

Schwemmer, Friedrich Rudolf (German artist). In *Das Buch Hiob. Mit 4 Urholzschnitten von F. R. Schwemmer.* Munich: Arche-Verlag, 1920.

Seghers, Gerard (Flemish painter, 1591–1651). *The Patient Job.* c. 1625. Oil on canvas. National Gallery, Prague.

Sichem, Christopher van (Dutch artist, b. 1550). *Two Biblical Scenes from the Book of Job: Wherefore hidest thou thy face, and holdest me for thine enemy? Job 13. Before I go whence I shall not return. Job 10.* Woodcuts in Dutch Bible. Fine Arts Museums of San Francisco.

Somervile, Beatrice. *Wrestling Job.* Needlepoint. 1982 [Terrien 263].

Spruance, Benton Murdoch (US artist, 1904–1967). *After Blake's Job.* Lithograph in black and gray. 1966. National Gallery of Art, Washington, DC [Vicchio 94]. ———. *Book of Job, or, Jehovah and Satan.* Color woodcut. 1951. Philadelphia Museum of Art [Vicchio 84]. ———. *Book of Job: The Leviathan, or The Blue Whale.* Lithograph. 1966. Philadelphia Museum of Art [Vicchio 93]. ———. *The Word and Job.* Woodcut. 1951. Philadelphia Museum of Art [Vicchio 83].

Stas de Richelle, Ghislaine (Belgian illustrator). In **Radermakers, Jean.** *Dieu, Job et la sagesse: lecture continue et texte. Avec 20 illustrations de Ghislaine Stas de Richelle.* Brussels: Lessius, 1998 [= *Il libro di Giobbe: Dio, l'uomo e la sapienza.* Bologna: EDB, 1999; *Deus, Job e a sabedoria.* Trans. Miriam Lopes. Lisbon: Instituto Piaget, 2004].

Steengracht, Dominica (Dutch illustrator). *Job, geschilderd door Dominica Steengracht.* London: Red Lion House, 1999.

Stimmer, Tobias (Swiss painter and illustrator, 1539–1584). *Das Buch Job.* Woodcuts. In *Neue künstliche Figuren biblischer Historien.* Basel, 1576.

Stölzel, Christian Ernst (1792–1837). *Job.* Etching and engraving, after Gustav Marie Jäger (1808–1871). Philadelphia Museum of Art. 1985-052-15920 [Vicchio 70].

Strang, William (British artist, 1859–1921). *Job.* Print. 1882. P.8861-R. Fitzwilliam Museum, Cambridge. ———. *Job and His Comforters.* 1884. P.8895-R. Fitzwilliam Museum, Cambridge.

Syrlin, Jörg (the Elder, German woodcarver, 1425–1491). *Job Ready to March On.* Wood carving, choir stall. 1469–1474. Ulm Münster. See also **Gropp, David.** *Das Ulmer Chorgestühl und Jörg Syrlin der Ältere.* Berlin: Deutscher Verlag für Kunstwissenschaft, 1999.

Szyk, Arthur (political cartoonist and illustrator, 1894–1951). In **Chase, Mary Ellen.** *The Book of Job, from the Translation Prepared at Cambridge in 1611 for King James I. With a Preface by Mary Ellen Chase and Illustrations by Arthur Szyk.* New York: The Limited Editions Club, 1946.

Tissot, James Jacques Joseph (French painter, 1836–1902). *Job and His Family.* c. 1896–1902. Gouache on paper. The Jewish Museum, New York [Vicchio 73]. ———. *Job and His Three Friends.* c. 1896–1902. Gouache on paper. The Jewish Museum, New York [Vicchio 76]. ———. *Job Hears Bad Tidings.* c. 1896–1902. Gouache on paper. The Jewish Museum, New York [Vicchio 74]. ———. *Job Joins His Family in Happiness.* c. 1896–1902. Gouache on paper. The Jewish Museum, New York [Vicchio 77]. ———. *Job Lying on the Heap of Refuse.* c. 1896–1902. Gouache on paper. The Jewish Museum, New York [Vicchio 74].

Tongue, C. Mary (British illustrator). In **Chesterton, G. K.** *The Book of Job, with an Introduction by G. K. Chesterton and Illustrated in Colour by C. Mary Tongue.* London: S. Wellwood, 1907; London: Cecil Palmer & Hayward, 1916.

Tuszynski, Devi (Jewish Polish miniaturist). In **Camhy, O.** *Une trilogie biblique sur le drame de la vie: un sujet, trois conceptions: Job, Qohéleth ou l'Ecclésiaste, Isaïe. Dessins de Maxa Nordau et Devi Tuszynski.* Paris: J. Grassin, 1973.

Uecker, Günther (German sculptor, op artist and installation artist, b. 1930). *Das Buch Hiob.* Forty-seven prints in silkscreen and Terragraph. Jaffa: Har-El, 2007.

Uhrig, Helmuth (German painter, 1906–1997). *Hiob. Eine Bildexegese in 15 Federzeichnungen.* Kassel: J. Stauda, 1954.

Vallotton, Annie (Swiss artist). In **Cook, Edward David.** *The Man Who Had Everything: Job* [Selections from Job in GNB]. *Today's Good News. Illustrated by Annie Vallotton.* [London]: Fount Paperbacks: Falcon Books, 1978.

Vanni, Raffaello (Italian painter, 1587–1673). *Job, His Wife, and a Demon.* Painting. S. Rocca, Siena [Pigler 204].

Veen, Otto van (Dutch painter, 1556–1629). *Job, His Friends, His Wife, and Her Attendants.* Altarpiece, panels closed. c. 1620. St Jacobskerk, Antwerp [Terrien 191].

Velázquez, Diego (Spanish painter, 1599–1660). *Seated Job in Profile.* c. 1618–1630. Oil on canvas. The Art Institute of Chicago [Terrien 180].

Vermeylen, François (Belgian sculptor, 1824–1888). *Job Dejected.* Plaster statue. c. 1880. Museum voor Religieuze Kunst en Cultuur, Leuven [Terrien 232].

Vorsterman, Lucas (Belgian engraver, 1595–1675). *Job Mocked by His Wife and Tortured by Demons* (after Peter Paul Rubens). Oil on canvas. 1620. Musées Royaux des Beaux-Arts, Brussels [Terrien 188]. Engraving. c. 1620. Philadelphia Museum of Art [Vicchio 59]. ———. *Job Tormented by Demons and Abused by His Wife.* Engraving. National Gallery of Art, Washington, DC.

Wächter, Eberhard Georg Friedrich (German artist, 1762–1852). *Job and His Friends.* Painting. Staatsgalerie, Stuttgart [Pigler 207].

Wachter, Emil (German artist, b. 1921). *Job. Job's Wife.* In *Biblische Portraits. Lithographien mit Texten von Friedrich Weinreb.* Munich, 1982. 107, 109.

Wagner, Roger Curtis (British illustrator, b. 1943). *Out of the Whirlwind: Illustrations to the Book of Job.* Carlisle: Solway, 1997.

Whelan, Michael (US illustrator, b. 1950). In **Heinlein, Robert A.** *Job, a Comedy of Justice.* Cover illustration. Acrylic. 1984. The Kelly Collection of American Illustration [Vicchio 95].

Wolf, Gustav (illustrator, 1887–1947). In **Fisher, Alfred Young.** *The Book of Job from the King James Bible, with Wood Engravings by Gustav Wolf and a Note by Alfred Young Fisher.* Cummington, MA: The Cummington Press, 1944.

Yoors, Jan (Flemish and US artist, 1922–1977). *Job as a Gypsy.* Gouache. 1962. Private collection [Terrien 255].

Zadkine, Ossip (Belarusian artist and sculptor, 1890–1967). *Job and His Friends.* Wood sculpture. 1914. Koninklik Museum voor Schone Kunsten, Antwerp [Barron, Pl. 24].

i. Job in Music

i. General

Brennecke, Wilfried. "Hiob als Musikheiliger." *Musik und Kirche* 24 (1954) 257–61. **Cebulj, Christian.** "Warum? Ijob zwischen Händel und Brahms." *KatBl* 130 (2005) 427–35. **Hammerstein, R.** "Hiob." In *Musik in Geschichte und Gegenwart.* Sachteil 4. Kassel: Bärenreiter, 1996. 297–301. **Heymel, Michael.** "Hiob als Schutzpatron der Musik. Die seelsorgerliche Bedeutung der Musik." *Pastoraltheologie* 89 (2000) 206–18. ———. "Hiob und die Musik." *BK* 59 (2004) 89–94. ———. "Hiob und die Musik. Zur Bedeutung der Hiobgestalt für eine musikalische Seelsorge." In *Das Alte Testament und die Kunst. Beiträge des Symposiums "Das Alte Testament und die Kultur der Moderne" anlässlich des 100. Geburtstags Gerhard von Rads (1901–1971), Heidelberg, 18.–21. Oktober 2001.* Ed. John Barton, J. Cheryl Exum, and Manfred Oeming. Altes Testament und Moderne 15. Münster: Lit Verlag, 2005. ———. *Trost für Hiob: Musikalische Seelsorge.* Munich: Strube, 1999. **Loader, James Alfred.** "Noomi und Hiob, Schubert und Mahler. Überlegungen zu einem alttestament-lichen Beitrag in Wien." In *Vielseitigkeit des Alten Testaments. Festschrift für Georg Sauer zum 70. Geburtstag.* Ed. James Alfred Loader and Hans Volker Kieweler. Frankfurt a.M.: Peter Lang, 1999. 149–63. **Seidel, Hans.** "Hiob, der Patron der Musiker." In *Alttestamentlicher Glaube und biblische Theologie Festschrift für Horst Dietrich Preuss zum 65. Geburtstag.* Ed. Jutta Hausmann and Hans-Jürgen Zobel. Stuttgart: Kohlhammer, 1992. 225–32.

ii. Composers

Adler, Hugo Chaim (Belgian-born and US cantor and composer, 1894–1955). *Hiob.* Oratorio. 1933.

Adorno, Theodor W. (German philosopher and composer, 1903–1969). *Lied der Kammerjungfer (zu Hiob von Oskar Kokoschka).* In *Sechs Bagatellen für Singstimme und Klavier, Op. 6.* In his *Kompositionen.* Ed. Heinz Klaus Metzger and Rainer Riehm. Munich, 1980. 1:71–72.

Albergati Capacelli, Pirro (Italian nobleman and composer, 1663–1735). *Giobbe: Oratorio.* Libretto by Giovanni Battista Neri. Bologna: Giacomo Monti, 1688.

Andriessen, Louis (Dutch composer, b. 1939). *Canzone 3. Utinam.* For soprano and piano. 1972.

Anon. *A Godly Ballad of the Just Man Job.* 1654–1655. In *The Pepys Ballads.* Ed. W. G. Day. Cambridge: Brewer, 1987.

Anon. *Il Giobbe: Oratorio per musica.* Text by Antonio Abati, in his *Poesie postume.* Bologna: Giovanni Recaldini, 1671.

Anon. *Vom dem gedultigen Job und seinem bösen Weib. Volkslied einer Augsburger Lieder-sammlung.* In Ernst Otto Lindner. *Geschichte des deutschen Liedes im 18. Jahrhundert.* Ed. Ludwig Erk. Beilage 2:33. Leipzig, 1871.

Bach, Johann Christian (German composer, youngest son of J. S. Bach, 1735–1782). *Lectio del officio per gli morti I–III.* Funeral music for two or three solo voices, chorus, and orchestra. E7–9.

Bach, Johann Christoph (German composer, cousin once removed of J. S. Bach, 1642–1703). *Der Mensch, vom Weibe geboren . . .* [Job 14:1–2]. Motet for five voices.

Bach, Johann Michael (German composer, father-in-law of J. S. Bach, 1648–1694). *Ich weiss, dass mein Erlöser lebt . . .* [Job 19:25–27]. Motet.

Bach, Johann Sebastian (German composer, 1685–1750). *Cantata 160. Ich weiss, dass mein Erlöser lebt* [now attrib. to Georg Philipp Telemann]. 1725 (?). ———. *Unser Leben ist ein Schatten . . .* [Job 8:9]. Motet.

Barahona, Juan Esquivel de (Spanish composer, c. 1560–c. 1615). *Responde mihi* [Job 33:5]. In his *Officium defunctorum.* 1613.

Barry, Ivo (French musician, 16th cent.). *Parce mihi Domine* [Job 7:16–21]. Motet. 1541.

Bartulis, Vidmantas (Lithuanian composer, b. 1954). *"Nelaimelis Jobas" ["Ill-fated Job"].* Oratorio for Soloists, Choir, and Orchestra. 2003.

Bergis, Cornelius Rigo de (composer, 16th cent.). *Cum audisset Job nuntiorum verba* [Job 1:20]. Antiphon. Florence, Biblioteca del Conservatorio di Musica Luigi Cherubini, MS Basevi 2439.

Berlinski, Herman (Polish-born US composer, 1910–2001). *Hiob: dramatisches Oratorium nach Texten der Bibel, des Buches Hiob und Gedichten von Nelly Sachs.* 1998. Leipzig: MDR, 1998 [cassette].

Bitgood, Roberta (US composer, 1908–2007). *Job: Cantata for Mixed Voices with Soprano, Tenor and Bass Solos.* New York: H. W. Gray Co., 1948.

Bittlinger, Clemens (German pastor and songwriter, b. 1959). "Hiob." In *Finger-spitzengefühle: Bearbeitung für Chor und Gitarre.* Gross-Bieberau, Rodau: Sanna Sound, 2004 [music score].

Blair, Hugh (English composer and organist, 1864–1932). *The Order for the Burial of the Dead, for Treble Voices* [Job 1:21; 14:1–2; 19:25–27].

Blume, Jürgen (German composer and musicologist, b. 1946). *Hiob: Vom Leiden guter Menschen. Oratorium in drei Akten für Soli, gemischten Chor, Streichorchester und Schlagzeug.* Munich: Strube, 2000.

Bornefeld, Helmut (German organist and composer, 1906–1990). *Motette nach Worten des Buches Hiob: für fünfstimmigen Chor [SSATB] a cappella.* In his *Studien zu seinem "Choralwerk," mit einem Verzeichnis seiner Werke.* Ed. Joachim Sarwas. Frankfurt a.M.: Peter Lang, 1991. 377–88.

Boyce, William (English composer, 1711–1779). *Burial Service in E Minor* [Job 14:1–2]. ———. *O where shall wisdom be found?* [Job 28:12]. Anthem.

Brahms, Johannes (German composer, 1833–1897). *Warum ist das Licht gegeben dem Mühseligen . . .* [Job 3:20–23]. Motet for unaccompanied five-part choir. Op. 74, No. 1. 1877. See also **Beller-McKenna, Daniel.** *Brahms, the Bible, and Post-Romanticism: Cultural Issues in Johannes Brahms's Later Setting of Biblical Texts, 1877–1896.* Diss. Harvard, 1994. ———. "The Great 'Warum?' Job, Christ, and Bach in a Brahms Motet" [*Warum ist das Licht gegeben?* Op. 74, No. 1, and Bach cantata BWV 106]. *Nineteenth-Century Music* 19 (1995–96) 234–36.

Brito, Estevão de (Portuguese composer, 1570–1641). *Homo natus de muliere* [Job 14:1–6]. ———. *Parce mihi Domine* [Job 7:16–21]. ———. *Responde mihi* [Job 33:5]. ———. *Spiritus meus attenuabitur* [Job 17: 1–3, 11–15]. In his *Officium defunctorum.* 1600.

Britten, Benjamin (English composer, 1913–1976). *Job's Curse* [Job 3]. Realization of Henry Purcell, *Job's Curse.*

Brossard, Sebastien (French composer, 1655–1730). *Manus tuae, Domine, fecerunt me* [Job 10:8–12]. ———. *Parce mihi Domine* [Job 7:16–21]. ———. *Taedet animam meam* [Job 10:1–7]. ———. *Responde mihi* [Job 33:5]. In his *Quatre leçons des morts.* Motets for two voices and three instruments. 1696/97.

Brun, Fritz (Swiss composer, 1878–1959). *Aus dem Buch Hiob.* Tone poem. 1906.

Büsser, Henri (French composer, 1872–1973). *Miseremini mei.* For Violin, Cello, Double Bass, Harp [Job 19:21].

Bungert, August (German composer, 1845–1915). *Warum? Woher? Wohin? Mysterium in drei Teilen nach Worten der Bibel, insbesondere des Buches Hiob. Für Soli, Chor und Orchester. Op. 60.* Leipzig: Bungert, 1908.

Burck, Joachim à (German composer, 1546–1610). "Ich weiss dass mein Erlöser lebt ob ich schon hie auff Erden" [Job 19:25–27]. In his *Deutsche Leidlein.* 1575.

Byrd, William (English composer, c. 1534–1623). *Cunctis diebus* [Job 14:14]. Motet for six voices. In his *Cantiones Sacrae.* In *The Byrd Edition.* Ed. P. Brett. III: *Cantiones sacrae (1591).* Ed. A. Brown. London: Stainer & Bell, 1981. 232–44.

Carissimi, Giacomo (Italian composer, 1605–1674). *Historia di Job* [oratorio]. c. 1650. Istituto italiano per la storia della musica. Monumenti III/1. Rome: Istituto italiano per la storia della musica, 1951.

Cazzati, Maurizio (Italian composer, 1616–1677). *Manus tuae, Domine, fecerunt me* [Job 10:8–12]. ———. *Parce mihi Domine* [Job 7:16–21]. ———. *Taedet animam meam* [Job 10:1–7]. In his *Messa concerta a 5.* 1663.

Charpentier, Marc-Antoine (French composer, 1643–1704). *Miseremini mei* [Job 19:21]. Motet.

Chiaromonte, Francesco (Italian composer, 1809–1886). *Job.* Drame biblique en trois actes. Poëme de J. Guilliaume. Leipzig: Breitkopf & Härtel, 1881.

Chipp, Edmund Thomas (English composer, 1823–1866). *Job: An Oratorio. The Words Selected from the Old Testament.* London, 1875.

Clemens non Papa, Jacobus (Flemish composer, c. 1510–c. 1555). *Job tonso capite* [Job 1:20]. Motet. ———. *Ne abscondas me* [Job 13:20–22]. Motet for four voices. ———. *Si bona suscepimus* [Job 2:10]. Responsorium. Motet for four voices.

Colombani, Ernesto (Italian composer, 1854–1921). *1. Notturno nell'ufficio dei morti: 1. 2. 3. lezione di Giobbe per baritono e coro con accompagnamento di grande orchestra: Op. 30.* Bologna: C. Venturi, n.d.

Complies Cisterciennes (Gregorian choir of the Abbaye de Fontfroide, south-western France). *Livre de Job.* 2007 [CD].

Converse, Frederick Shepherd (US composer, 1871–1940). *Job: Dramatic Poem for Solo Voices, Chorus and Orchestra. Op. 24.* London: Novello; New York: H. W. Gray, 1907 [English translation from the Vulgate by J. A. Macy].

Crecquillon, Thomas (Franco-Flemish composer, c. 1505–1557). *Job tonso capite* [Job 1:20]. In *Opera omnia.* XI. *Motetta quattuor vocum Thomasii Crequillonis.* Ed. Barton Hudson and Mary Tiffany Ferer. American Institute of Musicology. Neuhausen-Stuttgart: Hänssler-Verlag, 1997.

Croft, William (English composer, 1678–1727). *The Burial Service* [Job 14:1–2]. 1724 [used at state funerals in the UK].

Dallapiccola, Luigi (Italian composer, 1904–1975). *Giobbe: una sacra rappresentazione* [oratorio, also for stage performance; libretto based on William Blake's *Illustrations from the Book of Job*]. Milan: Suvini Zerboni, 1950. First performance: Rome, 1950. See also **Schomerus, Ute.** *Ecce homo: Die* Sacra Rappresentazione *Job von Luigi Dallapiccola.* Zwischen/Töne 13. Hamburg: von Bockel, 1998.

Davies, Peter Maxwell (British composer, b. 1934). *Job* [oratorio]. Vancouver, B.C.: The Turtle Press, 1997 [text from Stephen Mitchell. *The Book of Job*].

Distler, Hugo (German composer, 1908–1942). *Der Mensch, vom Weib geboren...* [Job 14:1–2]. Motet for soprano and two altos.

Dittersdorf, Karl Ditters von (Austrian composer, 1739–1799). *Giob.* Oratorio. 1786.

Eben, Petr (Czech composer, 1929–2007). *Job.* Suite for organ. Wiesbaden: Cappella Musikproduktion, 1994 [first performed at Ripon Cathedral, 1987]. See also **Bretschneider, Wolfgang.** "'Hinter die Grenzen des Lebens schauen': Petr Eben, Hiob. Eine Einführung in den Orgelzyklus." *Religionsunterricht an höheren Schulen* 47 (2004) 3–9.

Engel, Lehman (US composer, 1910–1982). *Four Excerpts from "Job"* [for voices and chamber orchestra]. Op. 3. In *Etude in Mixed Accents*. Ed. Ruth Crawford (Seeger). New Music 6/1. San Francisco: New Music Society of California, 1932.

Evans, Winsome (Australian composer, b. 1941). *Job's Jig.* In her *Testament: Archangels' Banquet/Shepherds' Delight*. CD Celestial Harmonies 14179.

Feroci, Francesco (Italian composer, 1673–1750). *Credo quod Redemptor meus* [Job 19:25–27]. In his *Officium defunctorum*.

Fietz, Siegfried (German songwriter, b. 1945). *Fragen nach dem Leben.* Greifenstein: Abakus-Musik, 2005 [songs and music].

Franck, Melchior (German composer, c. 1580–1639). *Ich weiss, dass mein Erlöser lebt* [Job 19:25–27]. Motet.

Franco, Fernando (Hernando) (Mexican composer, 1532–1585). *Parce mihi, Domine* [Job 7:16–21]. Motet. Ed. H. Ross. New York: Peer International, 1953.

Frederichs, Henning (German composer, 1936–2003). *Drei Oratorien: Textbücher und Erläuterungen zu: Petrus, Passionserzählung der Maria Magdalena, Hiob.* Gelnhausen: TRIGA-Verlag, 1996. ———. *Khinah, ein Klagegesang. Trio für Gitarre, Oboe und Violoncello.* 1990. Evangelische Statdtkirche, Remscheid. ———. *Ostinato* [for solo organ, from the oratorio *Hiob*]. Cologne-Rheinkassel: Musikverlag Dohr, 1996.

Gallus [Handl], Jacobus (Slovenian composer, 1550–1591). *Missa pro defunctis* [incl. motet].

Garro, Francisco de (Spanish composer, c. 1556–1623). *Parce mihi, Domine* [Job 7:16–21].

Gesius, Bartholomäus (German composer and hymn-writer, 1555–1631 or 1621). *Habn wir das Gut empfangen . . .* [Job 1:21; 2:10]. Motet. SATB.

Gherardeschi, Filippo Maria (Italian composer, 1738–1808). *Credo quod Redemptor meus* [Job 19:25–27]. Responsorium in his *Requiem e responsori per la morte di Ludovico I di Borbone*. 1803.

Gohl, Ulrich (German composer, b. 1930). *Hiob: Gottes armer Mensch: für Kinder- oder Jugendchor, Einzelstimmen, Sprecher und Tasteninstrument, ad libitum mit Melodie- und Rhythmusinstrumenten (auch Orff-Instrumentarium)* [choral score]. Stuttgart: Carus-Verlag, 2003.

Gombert, Nicolas (Flemish composer, c. 1495–c. 1557). *Si bona suscepimus* [Job 2:10]. Motet for six voices. c. 1521.

Goss, John (English composer, 1800–1860). *Burial Service in E Minor* [Job 1:21; 14:1–2; 19:25–27].

Granato, Dante (French organist and composer, 1910–2007). *Ex libro Job.* Motet. 1984.

Greene, Maurice (English composer and organist, 1696–1755). *Acquaint Thyself with God. Job 22, a Free Paraphrase of vv. 21–30. Anthem for Alto (or Tenor) Solo, Chorus, and Organ.* Novello Early Church Music 23. Borough Green, London: Novello & Co., 1971.

Guerrini, Guido (Italian composer, 1890–1965). *Il lamento di Job, per voce de basso, archi, pianoforte e tam-tam. Riduzione dall'autore per canto e pianoforte.* 1938. Milan: G. Ricordi, 1939.

Händel [Handel], Georg Frideric (German-born composer, living in England, 1685–1759). "I Know That My Redeemer Liveth." Aria in *Messiah* (1742).

Hatzis, Christos (Canadian Greek composer, b. 1953). *From the Book of Job.* For soprano and large orchestra. 2001. ———. *Tetragrammaton.* For soprano and tape. 1995.

Hennig, Walter (German composer, 1903–1967). *Ich weiss, dass mein Erlöser lebet...* [Job 19:25–27]. Motet.

Hensel-Mendelssohn, Fanny (German composer, 1805–1847). *Hiob: Kantate für Soli, Chor und Orchester.* 1831. Kassel: Furore-Editionen, 1992.

Herder, Ronald (US composer and arranger, b. 1930). *The Job Elegies* [choral].

Herrera, Juan de (Colombian composer, c. 1665–1738). *Parce mihi Domine* [Job 7:16–21]. Motet for seven voices.

Hiller, H. C. *Job's Wedding Day. Song, Words and Music.* London: D. Davidson, 1882.

Hoddinott, Alun (Welsh composer, 1929–2008). *Job.* Oratorio, with the libretto in Welsh, for bass, SATB chorus, and orchestra. 1963.

Huber, Klaus (Swiss composer, b. 1924). *Hiob 19. Für Chorstimmen und neun Instrumentalisten.* 1971. Mainz: Ars Viva Verlag, 1974.

Jacobi, Frederick (US Jewish composer, 1891–1952). *Hagiographa* [musical portraits of Job, Ruth, and Joshua]. 1938.

Jenkins, David (Welsh composer, 1848–1915). *Job: An Oratorio for Soli, Chorus, Organ and Orchestra.* Aberystwyth: [D. Jenkins], 1903.

Josquin [Josquin des Prez, Josquin Desprez, Josquinus Pratensis] (Franco-Flemish composer, 1450/55–1521). *Absolon, fili mi* [motet, includes Job 7:16; also ascribed to Pierre de la Rue]. ———. *Cutis mea aruit* [Job 7:5]. ———. *Miseremini mei* [Job 19:21]. ———. *Posuisti in nervo pedem meum* [Job 13:27]. ———. *Responde mihi* [Job 33:5]. ———. *Si dormiero.* [Job 7:4]. In *The Collected Works of Josquin des Prez.* 14. *Motets on Texts from the Old Testament ... Samuel, Job, The Song of Songs, Ecclesiasticus.* Ed. Richard Sherr. Utrecht: Vereniging voor Nederlandse Muziekgeschiedenis, 2002.

Kapp, Artur (Estonian composer, 1878–1952). *Hiob/Job.* 1929 [= *Hiob: Oratorium in zwei Teilen für Solisten, gemischten Chor, Männerchor, Frauen- oder Kinderchor Orgel und Orchester.* Lilienthal–Bremen: Eres Edition, 1997].

Kósa, György (Hungarian composer, 1897–1984). *Hiob.* Cantata. 1933.

Kosse, Lothar (German songwriter, guitarist and singer, b. 1959). *Ich weiss dass mein Erlöser lebt* [Job 19:25–27]. 2004.

Kühnl, Claus (German composer, b. 1957). *Die Klage des Hiob: Fünf dramatische Szenen für grosse Orgel, Klavier und Sprecher ad libitum.* Kammermusik-Bibliothek 2186. Wiesbaden: Breitkopf & Härtel, 1983.

La Rue, Pierre de (Franco-Flemish composer, 1452–1518). *Missa de Sancto Job.* In *Missa de Sancta Cruce; Missa de Sancto Antonio; Missa de Sancto Job; Missa de septem doloribus; Missa de virginibus.* Ed. Nigel St John Davison, J. Evan Kreider, and T. Herman Keahey. Corpus mensurabilis musicae 97. American Institute of Musicology; Neuhausen–Stuttgart: Hänssler-Verlag, 1992.

Lassus [Lasso], Orlando di (Franco-Flemish composer, 1532–1594). *Sacrae lectiones ex Propheta Iob* (c. 1560); *Lectiones sacrae novem, ex libris Hiob excerptae* [also known as *Lamentationes de Job*] (c. 1582). In *Two Motet Cycles for Matins for the Dead.* Ed. Peter Bergquist. Recent Researches in the Music of the Renaissance 55. Madison, WI: A-R Editions, 1983. ———. *Si bona suscepimus* [Job 2:10]. Motet for five voices. 1571. ———. *Taedet animam meam* [Job 10:1–7]. Motet for five voices. 1562.

Lechner, Leonhard (German composer, 1553–1606). *Nackend bin ich...* [Job 1:21]. Motet for soprano, mezzo-soprano, alto, tenor, bass. ———. *Si bona suscepimus* [Job 2:10]. Motet for five voices. 1581.

Leeuw, Ton [Antonius Wilhemus Adrianus] de (Dutch composer, 1926–1996). *Job.* Oratorio. 1956.

Lindberg, Oskar Fredrik (Swedish composer, 1887–1955). *Music for the Book of Job.* 1928.

Lobo, Alonso (Spanish composer, c. 1555–1617). *Credo quod Redemptor meus* [Job 19:25–27]. Motet for four voices in his *Officium defunctorum,* c. 1602. ———. *Versa est in luctum* [Job 30:31]. Motet for six voices in his *Officium defunctorum,* c. 1602.

Loewe, Carl (German composer, 1796–1869). *Hiob: Oratorium in drei Teilen für Soli, Chor und Orchester; erste Aufführung der Rekonstruktion nach den Original-Stimmen von 1848/49.* Bad Dürkheim: Soft Sound Music, 2005.

Loewe, Johann Karl Gottfried (German composer, 1796–1869). *Hiob's Todessang* [text by Wilhelm Telschow]. 1848.

Maconchy, Elizabeth (Anglo-Irish composer, 1907–1994). *Variations on a Theme from Vaughan Williams' "Job" for Unaccompanied Violoncello.* London: Alfred Lengnick & Co., 1960.

Mándoki, Leslie [László] (Hungarian musician and producer, b. 1953). *Hiob.* Music for readings from the Book of Job by Jan Josef Liefers. In *MusikBibel. IV. Die Propheten; Hiob.* Gütersloh: Gütersloher Verlag-Haus, 2007.

Manneke, Daan (Dutch composer and organist, b. 1939). *Job.* Cantata for men's choir and instrumentalists. 1976.

Maxwell Davies, Peter (English composer, b. 1934). *Job, for Soprano, Alto, Tenor and Bass Soli, Chorus and Orchestra.* Oratorio. 1997. London: Chester Music, 1999.

Metzger, Hans-Arnold (German composer, 1913–1977). *Gott tut grosse Dinge…* [Job 9:10]. Motet. SATB.

Micheelsen, Hans Friedrich (German organist and composer, 1902–1973). *Ich weiss, dass mein Erlöser lebt…* [Job 19:25–26]. Solo cantata for mezzo-soprano and organ.

Milhaud, Darius (French composer, 1892–1974). *Cantate de Job.* Cantata from Job: for baritone solo, mixed chorus and organ. Bryn Mawr: Presser, 1967.

Mitchell, Joni (Canadian musician and songwriter, b. 1953). "The Sire of Sorrow (Job's Sad Song)." In her CD *Turbulent Indigo.* 1994.

Monte, Philippe de (Flemish composer, 1521–1603). *Taedet animam meam* [Job 7:16–21]. Motet. 1564.

Morales, Christobal [Cristóbal] de (Spanish composer, 1500–1553). *Parce mihi Domine* [Job 7:16–21]. ———. *Taedet animam meam* [Job 10:1–7]. In his *Officium defunctorum.* For four voices. ———. *Parce mihi Domine* [Job 7:16–21}. Motet in his *Missa da Requiem.* c. 1553. ———. *Si bona suscepimus* [Job 2:10]. 1544.

Morley, Thomas (English composer, 1557–1602). *Burial Sentences* [Job 1:21; 14:1–2; 19:25–27]. 1559.

Nabokov, Nicolas (Russian and US composer, 1903–1978). *Job.* Oratorio. 1932. Text by Jacques Maritain.

Nivers, Guillaume Gabriel (French composer, 1632–1714). *Credo quod Redemptor meus* [Job 19:25–27]. Motet. In his *Officium defunctorum.* 1685.

Ochando, Tomás (Mexican composer, 18th cent.). *Parce mihi Domine* [Job 7:16–21].

Parry, C. Hubert H. (English composer, 1848–1918). *Job: An Oratorio for Treble, Tenor, Baritone and Bass Soli, Chorus and Orchestra.* 1892. London: Novello, 1892.

Pérez de la Parra, Ginés (Spanish composer, c. 1548–1600). *Parce mihi, Domine* [Job 7:16-21]. In his *Officium defunctorum.* 1590.

Petker, Allan Robert (US composer of church music). *I Will Follow Your Call* [SATB]. San Pedro, CA: Pavane Publishing, 2003.

Phinney, Kurt Werner (US composer). *Job.* Oratorio for soprano, contralto, tenor, baritone, and bass soloists, mixed chorus, and orchestra. Diss. Columbia, 1992.

Porpora, Nicola Antonio (Italian composer, 1686–1768). *Notturni per i defunti.* Includes Lessons from Job.

Purcell, Henry (English composer, 1659–1695). *Ah! Few and full of sorrow* [Job 14:1]. Text by George Sandys. Z130. c. 1680. ———. *Let the Night Perish (Job's Curse)* [Job 3:3]. Hymn. Verse paraphrase by Jeremy Taylor. Z191. 1688. ———. *Man that is born of a woman* [Job 14:1–2]. Anthem. Z027. c. 1680–1682. In his *Funeral Music for Queen Mary.* 1695. ———. *O, I'm sick of life* [Job 7:15–16]. Hymn. Text by George Sandys. Z140. c. 1680.

Rabaud, Henri (French composer, 1873–1949). *Deuxième poème lyrique sur le livre de Job pour baryton solo et orchestre (op. 11). Paroles tirées du texte l'Ancien Testament (d'après la* *traduction d'Ernest Renan).* Paris: Choudens, 1905. ———. *Job. Oratorio. Poème de Charles Raffali et Henri de Gorsse.* Paris, 1900.

Reger, Max (German composer, 1873–1916). *Haben wir Gutes empfangen* [Job 1:21; 2:10]. Motet. ———. *Ich weiss, dass mein Erlöser lebet* [Job 19:25–27]. Motet.

Reimann, Aribert (German composer, b. 1936). *Requiem.* Includes Lessons from Job. 1982.

Richafort, Jean (Franco-Flemish composer, c. 1480–c. 1547). *Miseremini mei* [Job 19:21].

Rogier, Philippe (Flemish composer, 1561–1596). *Taedet animam meam* [Job 10:1–7]. Motet for six voices. c. 1595.

Rore, Cipriano (Franco-Flemish composer, 1515/16–1565). *Parce mihi Domine* [Job 7:16–21]. Motet. In his *Sacrae cantiones.* Venice, 1595.

Russell, William (English organist and composer, 1777–1813). *Job, a Sacred Oratorio, in Three Parts.* London: T. Davison, 1814.

Rutini, Giovanni Marco (Italian composer, 1723–1797). *Il Giobbe: oratorio sacro per musica.* Florence: Francesco e Pietro Allegrini, 1780.

Sallinen, Aulis (Finnish composer, b. 1935). *Barabbas Dialogues.* Op. 84. 2002.

Samuel, Rhian (Welsh composer, b. 1944). *Fel Blodeuyn. Like a Flower. For Organ* [Job 14:2]. London: Stainer & Bell, 1997.

Schaffer, Willy. *Das Buch Hiob.* Opera in two acts, text by Leopold Adler, adapting a play by Hermann Holtz. 1912.

Schneider, Enjott (German composer, b. 1950). *Hiob.* Organ concerto. 2007.

Schütz, Heinrich (German composer, 1585–1672). *Ich weiss, dass mein Erlöser lebt* [Job 19:25–27]. Cantata in his *Geistliche Chor-Musik.* 1648. SWV 437.

Schumann, Georg (German composer, 1866–1952). *Gesängen Hiobs.* Three motets for mixed choir and organ, Op. 60. 1914.

Senfl [Sennfl, Sennfli, Senfelius, Senphlius], Ludwig (Swiss composer, c. 1486–c. 1542). *Cum aegrotasset Job.* Antiphon.

Sermisy, Claudin de (French composer, c. 1490–1562). Settings of the nine Lessons from Job in his *Liber II: Missa IX lectionum.* 1532.

Sheriff, Noam (Israeli conductor and composer, b. 1935). *The Sorrows of Job.* Opera. 1988. Libretto by Hanoch Levin. Frankfurt a.M.: Peters, 1990.

Tavares, Manuel de (Portuguese composer, 1585–1638). *Parce mihi Domine* [Job 7:16–21].

Telemann, Georg Philipp (German composer, 1681–1767). *Ich weiss, dass mein Erlöser lebt* [Job 19:25–27]. Cantata; formerly attrib. J. S. Bach as Cantata 160. 1725.

Thoma, Xaver Paul (German composer, b. 1953). *Draussen vor der Tür.* Chamber opera, based on Wolfgang Borchert's *Draussen vor der Tür: Ein Stück, das kein Theater spielen und kein Publikum sehen will.* Radio and stage play, first performed 1947. Bühl, Baden: Antes Edition, 1995.

Thompson, Randall (American composer, 1899–1984). *The Morning Stars* [Job 38:1–2, 4, 6–7]. SATB and piano. 1983 [revised from 1978 version with orchestral accompaniment].

Tomkins, Thomas (Welsh composer, 1572–1656). *Burial Sentences.*

Tomorsky, Dennis Fabyan (b. 1953). *The Book of Job.*

Turchant, Hermanus de (composer, fl. c. 1500). *Parce mihi Domine* [Job 7:16–21]. Motet. 1545.

Utendal, Alexander (Franco-Flemish composer, c. 1540–1581). *Scio, quod Redemptor meus vivit* [Job 19:25–27]. Motet for six voices. c. 1573.

Vásquez, Juan (Spanish composer, c. 1500–c. 1560). *Credo quod Redemptor meus* [Job 19:25–27]. ———. *Homo natus de muliere* [Job 14:1–6]. ———. *Manus tuae, Domine, fecerunt me* [Job 10:8–12]. ———. *Parce mihi Domine* [Job 7:16–21]. ———. *Pelli meae, consumptis carnibus, adhaesit os meum* [Job 19:20–27]. ———. *Quare de vulva eduxisti me?* [Job 20:18–22].

———. *Quis mihi hoc tribuat* [Job 14:13–16]. ———. *Responde mihi* [Job 33:5]. ———. *Taedet animam meam* [Job 10:1–7]. ———. *Spiritus meus attenuabitur* [Job 17:1–3, 11–15]. Motets. In his *Agenda defunctorum, Ad Matutinum.* 1556.

Vaughan Williams, Ralph (English composer, 1872–1958). *Job. A Masque for Dancing: Founded on Blake's Illustrations to the Book of Job, by Geoffrey Keynes and Gwendolen Raverat; Music by R. Vaughan Williams.* London: Oxford University Press, 1931. ———. *The Voice out of the Whirlwind: Motet for Chorus (S.A.T.B.) and Organ.* London: Oxford University Press, 1947. See also **Maconchy, Elizabeth (1907–1994).** *Variations on a Theme from Vaughan Williams' "Job" for Unaccompanied Violoncello.* London: Alfred Lengnick & Co., 1960. **Wiles, Patricia Joyce Wade.** *A Study of "Job, A Masque for Dancing" by Ralph Vaughan Williams.* Diss. Texas Tech, 1988.

Verdelot, Philippe (French composer, c. 1480–c. 1530). *Si bona suscepimus* [Job 2:10].

Victoria, Tomás Luis de (Spanish composer, 1548–1611). *Taedet animam meam* [Job 10:1–7]. ———. *Versa est in luctum* [Job 30:31]. Motets. In his *Requiem,* or *Officium defunctorum: in obitu et obsequiis sacrae imperatricis.* 1605.

Vincentino, Nicola (Italian composer, 1511–c. 1576). *Parce mihi Domine* [Job 7:16–21]. Motet. c. 1571.

Werner, Gregor Joseph (Austrian composer, 1693–1766). *Parce mihi Domine* [Job 7:16–21]. In his *Requiem in G Minor.* 1745.

Willaert, Adrian (Belgian composer, c. 1488–1562). *Spiritus meus attenuabitur* [Job 17: 1–3, 11–15]. Motet for four voices. 1539.

Zarlino, Gioseffo (Italian composer, 1517–1590). *Parce mihi Domine* [Job 7:16–21]. Motet. 1563.

Zeisl, Eric (Austrian composer, 1905–1959). *Job.* Opera, libretto by Hans Kafka after novel by Joseph Roth. ———. *Menuhim's Song.* Violin solo with piano accompaniment, from the opera *Job.* New York: Mills Music, 1949. ———. *Organ Prelude, Orchestral Suite,* and *To the Promised Land* [orchestral suite], from the opera *Job.* See also **Cole, Malcolm S.** "Eric Zeisl's 'Hiob': The Story of an Unsung Opera." *Opera Quarterly* 9 (1992) 52.

Zelenka, Jan [Johann] Dismas (Czech composer, 1679–1745). *Lectiones* from the *Officium defunctorum* for Elector Friedrich August I. Lectiones I–III for STB and orchestra. Z47.

Zillinger, Erwin (German composer, 1893–1974). *Hiob (Mensch und Schicksal).* Oratorium für 7 Soli, Chor, grosses Orchester und Orgel. Lübeck: Bibliothek der Hansestadt Lübeck, 2004.

j. Job in Dance

Beaumont, C. W. *Complete Book of Ballet: A Guide to the Principal Ballets of the Nineteenth and Twentieth Centuries.* London: Putnam, repr. 1951. 931–35. **Dorfman, David.** *Job.* Dance in performance at the American Dance Festival July 8 and 9, 1997 [videorecording]. Duke Library, Durham, NC, 1997. **Valois, Ninette de.** *Job (Being Blake's Vision of the Book of Job). A Masque for Dancing in Eight Scenes* [Book: Geoffrey Keynes and Gwendolen Raverat. Music: Ralph Vaughan Williams]. London, 1931. See also **Lawson, Joan et al.** *Job and The Rake's Progress.* Sadler's Wells Ballet Books 2. London: Bodley Head, 1949.

k. Job in Film

i. General

Reinhartz, Adele. "Cape Fear and the Devil as Savior (Job)." In her *Scripture on the Silver Screen.* Louisville, KY: Westminster John Knox Press, 2003. 67–80. **Rosenberg,**

Joel. "What the Bible and Old Movies Have in Common." *BibInt* 6 (1998) 266–91.
Vicchio, Stephen J. "The Biblical Book of Job in Film." In his *Job in the Modern World.* Eugene, OR: Wipf & Stock, 2006. 234–47.

ii. Directors

Allen, Woody. *Annie Hall.* 1977. *Manhattan.* 1979. *Star Dust and Memory.* 1980. *Broadway Danny Rose.* 1984. *Interiors.* 1978. *Crimes and Misdemeanors.* 1989. *Match Point.* 2005.
Bergman, Ingmar. *Through a Glass Darkly.* 1961. *The Communicants.* 1962. *The Silence.* 1963. *Fanny and Alexander.* 1982. *Cries and Whispers.* 1972. See also **Collet, Jan.** "From Job to Bergman: Anguish and Challenge." *Conc* 169 (1983) 69–72.
Brower, Otto. *Sins of Man.* 1936. A loose adaptation of Joseph Roth's novel, *Hiob: Roman eines einfachen Mannes.* 1930.
Capra, Frank. *It's a Wonderful Life.* 1946. With James Stewart.
Cosmatos, George Pan. *Leviathan* [science fiction]. 1989.
Fassbinder, Rainer W. *Berlin Alexanderplatz* (TV series). 1980. Remake of Piel Jutzi's film.
Frankenheimer, John. *The Fixer.* 1968. With Alan Bates, Dirk Bogarde. German version: *Ein Mann wie Hiob.*
Goetz, Curt. *Dr Med. Hiob Praetorius.* 1949. Film adaptation of Goetz's play of the same name. See also Carl Hoffman. See also Curt Goetz in Section g.ii (Drama) above.
Gorlitz, Christian. *Hiob* [thriller]. 2002.
Hoffmann, Carl. *Dr Med. Hiob Praetorius.* 1965. Remake of Curt Goetz's film of 1949.
Jones, David. *The Trial.* 1993. Based on Harold Pinter's screenplay adaptation of Franz Kafka's novel *The Trial.* See also Orson Welles.
Jutzi, Piel. *Berlin Alexanderplatz.* 1931. Adapted from Alfred Döblin's novel *Berlin Alexanderplatz: Die Geschichte vom Franz Biberkopf.* 1929. See also Rainer W. Fassbinder.
Kabay, Barna. *Job lazadasa* (*The Revolt of Job*). Writers: Imre Gyöngyössy, Katalin Gyöngyössy. 1983.
Kehlmann, Michael (Austrian filmmaker, 1927–2005). *Hiob, von Joseph Roth.* Vienna, 1978. TV series.
Mankiewicz, Joseph L. *People Will Talk.* Producer: Darryl F. Zanuck. 1951. With Cary Grant. Adapted from the play of Curt Goetz, *Dr Med. Hiob Praetorius.*
Morris, Errol. *The Thin Blue Line.* 1988.
Scorsese, Martin. *Cape Fear.* 1991. Remake of J. Lee Thompson's 1962 film. With Nick Nolte, Jessica Lange, Robert De Niro.
Thompson, J. Lee. *Cape Fear.* 1962. Screenplay: James R. Webb. With Gregory Peck, Robert Mitchum. Based on the novel *Cape Fear* by John D. MacDonald. Greenwich, CT: Fawcett, 1958. Originally published under the title *The Executioners.* New York: Simon & Schuster, 1958. See also Martin Scorsese.
Vettermann, Willy. *Hiob. Filmdichtung.* 1928. Chemnitz: M. Müller, 1928.
Welles, Orson. *The Trial.* 1962. With Anthony Perkins. Adaptation of Franz Kafka's novel *The Trial.* See also David Jones.

l. Job in Bibliodrama

Calcar, J. D. van. *Job: bijbels lekespel van strijd en bevrijding.* Assen: Van Gorcum, 1935. **Cartwright, Jeffrey Neal.** *Religious Drama within the Local Church* [Job and suffering]. Diss. Wesley Theological Seminary, 1992. **Eaton, J. H., and Frances M. Young.** *My Servant Job: The Book of Job Translated, Abridged and Adapted as a Drama with Music and Participating Audience.* Old Testament Texts as Drama 2. Birmingham: Department of Theology, University of Birmingham, 1986. **Gerritsen, Arthur.** "Bibliodrama about Job: Some Preliminary Notes." In *Current Issues in the Psychology of Religion: Third Symposium on the Psychology of Religion in Europe.* Ed. J. A. van Belzen and J. M. van der

Lans. Amsterdam: Rodopi, 1986. 112–23. **Klinger, Bernhard.** *Im und durch das Leiden lernen. Das Buch Ijob als Drama.* BBB 155. Hamburg: Philo, 2007. **Sauer, Charlotte.** *Hiob.* Verkündigungsspiele der Gemeinde. Berlin: Evangelische Verlagsanstalt, 1953.

m. Job in Liturgy

Several texts from Job have formed a traditional part of Christian liturgy. In the Roman Catholic rite, the official set of daily prayers is termed the Liturgy of the Hours (also called Divine Office, *Liturgia horarum*). The Night Office within that liturgy consists of three Nocturns, in which nine Lessons (readings) from Job are incorporated: In the First Nocturn: Lesson 1: Job 7:16–21 (*Parce mihi Domine,* Spare me, O Lord). Lesson 2: 10:1–7 (*Taedet animam meam,* My soul is weary). Lesson 3: 10:8–12 (*Manus tuae, Domine, fecerunt me,* Thy hands, O Lord, have made me). In the Second Nocturn: Lesson 4: Job 13:22–28 (*Responde mihi,* Answer thou me). Lesson 5: Job 14:1–6 (*Homo natus de muliere,* Man born of woman). Lesson 6: Job 14:13–16 (*Quis mihi hoc tribuat,* Who will grant me this). In the Third Nocturn: Lesson 7: Job 17:1–3, 11–15 (*Spiritus meus attenuabitur,* My spirit shall be weakened). Lesson 8: Job 19:20–27 (*Pelli meae, consumptis carnibus, adhaesit os meum,* The flesh being consumed, my bone hath cleaved to my skin). Lesson 9: Job 20:18–22 (*Quare de vulva eduxisti me?* Wherefore then hast thou brought me forth out of the womb?).

These medieval Lessons also formed part of services for the dead, the Office for the Dead (*Officium pro defunctis,* or, *Officium defunctorum*), and were often set to music, usually as motets (unaccompanied singing by a choir of several voices), by composers such as Lassus, Morales, and Victoria (see Section 8.i [Job in Music] above). However, settings of the whole Office for the Dead (Requiems) do not usually contain the Lessons. The Lessons from Job were omitted from the Office for the Dead after the Second Vatican Council (1962–1965).

The Joban Lessons, as part of the Office for the Dead, were usually included in Books of Hours, illuminated manuscripts used especially by individuals, and many illustrations of the story of Job can be found in them. See Section 8.h (Job in Art) above.

In the Church of England, the Joban Lessons were replaced by Cranmer's Burial Sentences, some of which may be sung. Settings were composed by Boyce, Croft, Morley, and Tomkins (see Section 8.i [Job in Music] above). The Sentences from Job are: I know that my Redeemer Liveth (Job 19:25–27), The Lord gave, and the Lord hath taken away (Job 1:21), Man that is born of a woman (Job 14:1–2).

Becker, Hansjakob (ed.). "Hiobsbotschaften—Hiobs Botschaften: Ein Beitrag zum Verhältnis von Bibel, Liturgie und Pastoral." In *Warum? Hiob interdisziplinär diskutiert.* Mainzer Universitätsgespräche Wintersemester 1997/98. Vorträge von Hansjakob Becker, Jürgen Ebach, Herbert Jochum, Georg Langenhorst, Józef Niewiadomski, Willi Oelmüller, und Wilhelm Pesch. Mainz: Studium Generale der Universität Mainz, 1998. 22–25. **Dassmann, Ernst.** "Hiob." In *RAC* 15 (1991) 366–442. **Gruber, Mayer I.** "Tur-Sinai's Job in the Jewish Liturgy." *Review of Rabbinic Judaism* 6 (2003) 87–100. **Kniaseff, A.** "The Theodicy of Job in the Byzantine Offices of Holy Week" [Greek]. *Theologia* (1955) 107–23. **Rouillard, P.** "The Figure of Job in the Liturgy: Indignation, Resolution or Silence?" *Conc* 169 (1983) 8–12. **Vicchio, Stephen J.** *Job in the Medieval World.* Eugene, OR: Wipf & Stock, 2006. 44–56.

n. Job in Sermons

i. The Book as a Whole

Barsotti, Divo. *Meditazione sul libro di Giobbe.* Bibbia e liturgia 40. Brescia: Queriniana, 2001. **Chappell, Clovis Gillham.** *Sermons from Job.* Nashville: Abingdon

Press, 1957. **Dijkstra, R.** *De aangevochtene en wat hij niet verstond: zestien preeken over het boek Job.* Wageningen: Veenman, 1930. **Ferris, Theodore Parker.** *Four Sermons on Job.* Boston: Trinity Church, 1959. **Goetz, Ronald.** "Job: Man of Sorrows" [Lenten meditation]. *ChrCent* 105 (1988) 204–6. **Hofman, A.** *De verdraagzaamheid van Job en het einde des Heeren: 7 preken uit het boek Job.* Goes: Hoekman, 1975. **Jetter, Werner.** *Warum verbirgst Du Dein Anlitz? Sechs Predigten über das Zeugnis des Buches Hiob.* Stuttgart: Quell Verlag, 1955. **Jörns, Klaus-Peter (ed.).** *Predigtmeditationen zu Continuatexten: Markuspassion— Hiob—Jona.* Göttinger Predigtmeditationen: Beiheft [N.F.] 1. Göttingen: Vandenhoeck & Ruprecht, 1985. **Knippenberg, M. van.** "Preken over Job; pastoraaltheologische reflekties." *PrakT* 17 (1990) 251–71, 272–83.

Maillot, Alphonse. *Job: pour rien. Prédications sur le livre de Job.* Pibrac: Editions Oméga International, 1994. **MacLeish, Archibald.** "God Has Need of Man." Sermon, 1945. In *The Dimensions of Job: A Study and Selected Readings.* Ed. Nahum H. Glatzer. New York: Schocken Books, 1969. 278–86. **Mason, Mike.** "The Wizard of Uz: Meditations on Job." *Crux* 27 (1991) 35–43. **Nelson, Christine.** "Job: The Confessions of a Suffering Person." In *Spinning a Sacred Yarn: Women Speak from the Pulpit.* New York: Pilgrim Press, 1982. 144–48. **Plumptre, James.** *A Popular Commentary on the Bible in a Series of Sermons: Following, in the Old Testament, the Course of the First Lessons at Morning and Evening Service on Sundays: Designed for Parish Churches, or for Reading in Private Families.* London: C. & J. Rivington, 1827. **Proosdij, Cornelis van.** *"Mijn knecht Job": een twaalftal predikatiën.* Leiden: Donner, 1904. **Reith, Wigbert.** *Job.* Alttestamentliche Predigten 1, 8, 17. Paderborn: Schöningh, 1917. **Sachse, Rudolf.** *Iobs und aller frommen Wohlthäter zu Zeitz und in der gantzen Christenheit, d. i. Christliche Auslegung und Erklerung von Iob 10 und 12 in einer Danksagungspredigt.* Leipzig, 1638. **Sietsma, Kornelis.** *De zelfrechtvaardiging Gods: zeven preeken uit het boek Job.* Amsterdam: Bakker, 1939 [= *The Self-Justification of God in the Life of Job.* Neerlandia, Alberta; Pella, IA: Inheritance Publications, 2001]. **Snoep, H.** *Job, aanklager en gedaagde.* The Hague: Boekencentrum, 1980.

Támez, Elsa. "Vom Vater der Waisen zum Bruder der Schakale und Gefährten der Strausse. Meditation über Ijob." *Conc* 40/4 (2004) 463–70 [= "From Father to the Needy Brother of Jackals and Companion of Ostriches: A Meditation on Job." *Conc* 40/4 (2004) 103–11; also in *Job's God.* Ed. Ellen van Wolde. London: SCM Press, 2004. 103–11]. **Thomas, Derek.** *Mining for Wisdom: A Twenty-Eight-Day Devotional Based on the Book of Job.* Darlington: Evangelical Press, 2002. **Torrance, James B.** "Why Does God Let Men Suffer? A Sermon on Job." *Int* 15 (1961) 157–63. **Verhoeks, Willem.** *Mijn verlosser leeft: negen preken over het boek Job.* Rumpt: De Schatkame, 2004. **Villiers, H. Montagu.** *Perfect through Suffering: Being Thoughts on the Book of Job Taken from Addresses Given at S. Paul's, Knightsbridge.* London: Longmans, Green & Co., 1909. **Wiersbe, Warren W.** *Be Patient, Job: Waiting on God in Difficult Times.* Wheaton, IL: Victor Books, 1991 [= *Sei geduldig. In schwierigen Zeiten auf Gottes Handeln warten (Hiob und Klagelieder).* Dillenburg: Christliche Verlagsgesellschaft, 2008].

ii. By Chapters

1. Eddy, G. Thackray. "No Carrion Comfort" [sermon on Job 1:1; 2:1–10]. *ExpT* 108 (1997) 369–70. **Edwards, Jonathan.** "The Nakedness of Job" [Job 1:21]. In *The Works of Jonathan Edwards.* Ed. Perry Miller and John E. Smith. New Haven, CT: Yale University Press, 1957–1998. 10:403–12. **Hastings, James.** "The Unselfishness of True Religion" [Job 1:9]. In his edited *The Great Texts of the Bible.* Edinburgh: T. & T. Clark, 1913. 3:1–17. **Hoare, Robert.** *A Funeral Sermon [on Job i. 21] ... on the ... death of Misses C. and L. Evans.* New York: Protestant Episcopal Press, 1833. **Holland, Henry.** *The Christian Exercise of Fasting, Priuate and Publike ... Hereunto Also are Added Some Meditations on the 1. and 2. Chapters of Iob, to Comfort and Instruct All Such as Be Afflicted with Any Crosse, either Inwardly in Minde, or Outwardly in Bodie.* London, 1596. **McCracken, Robert J.** "The Use and Abuse of Religion" [Job 1:9]. *USQR* 12 (1957) 3–8. **Palmer, Benjamin Morgan.** "Submission" [Job 1:21]. In his *Sermons.* New Orleans: First Presbyterian Church, 1875–76. 1:621–30 [=

Harrisonburg, VA: Sprinkle Publications]. **Spurgeon, C. H.** "Job i." In *The Metropolitan Tabernacle Pulpit.* LVII. London: Passmore & Alabaster, 1912 [repr. Pasadena, TX: Pilgrim Publications, 1979]. 34–36. ———. "A Merry Christmas [Job 1:4–5]." In *The New Park Street and Metropolitan Tabernacle Pulpit.* VII. London: Alabaster, Passmore & Sons, 1862 [repr. Pasadena, TX: Pilgrim Publications, 1969]. 33–40. ———. "Fifteen Years After! [Job 1:21]." In *The Metropolitan Tabernacle Pulpit.* LIII. London: Passmore & Alabaster, 1908 [repr. Pasadena, TX: Pilgrim Publications, 1978]. 61–72. ———. "Job i.6–22." In *The Metropolitan Tabernacle Pulpit.* XLII. London: Passmore & Alabaster, 1897 [repr. Pasadena, TX: Pilgrim Publications, 1976]. 142–44. ———. "Job's Resignation [Job 1:20–22]." In *The Metropolitan Tabernacle Pulpit.* XLII. London: Passmore & Alabaster, 1897 [repr. Pasadena, TX: Pilgrim Publications, 1976]. 133–42. ———. "Patient Job, and the Baffled Enemy [Job 1:22]." In *The Metropolitan Tabernacle Pulpit.* XXXVI. London: Passmore & Alabaster, 1891 [repr. London: Banner of Truth Trust, 1970]. 603–12. ———. "Satan Considering the Saints [Job 1:8]." In *The Metropolitan Tabernacle Pulpit.* London: Alabaster, Passmore & Sons, 1866 [repr. Pasadena, TX: Pilgrim Publications, 1970]. 11:193–204.

2. **Coleman, Thomas.** *Hopes Deferred and Dashed: Observed in a Sermon to the Honourable House of Commons ... July 30, 1645* [Job 2:20]. London: Christopher Meredith, 1645 [= Early English Books, 1641–1700, 1185/12]. **Holland, Henry.** *The Christian Exercise of Fasting, Priuate and Publike ... Hereunto Also Are Added Some Meditations on the 1. and 2. Chapters of Iob, to Comfort and Instruct All Such as Be Afflicted with Any Crosse, either Inwardly in Minde, or Outwardly in Bodie.* London, 1596. **Hooke, William.** *New Englands Teares, for Old Englands Feares: Preached in a Sermon on July 23, 1640: Being a Day of Publike Humiliation, Appointed by the Churches in Behalfe of Our Native Countrey in Time of Feared Dangers* [Job 2:13]. London: John Rothwell and Henry Overton, 1641 [= Early English Books, 1641–1700, 261 E.208/5]. **Jay, William, and John Kemp.** *The Value of Life: A Sermon Delivered May 8th, 1803, before the Correspondent Board in London of the Society in Scotland (incorporated by Royal Charter) for the Propagation of Christian Knowledge in the Highlands and Islands* [Job 2:4]. Society in Scotland for Propagating Christian Knowledge. Bath: S. Hazard, 1803. **McCormick, S.** "Someone HAD to Speak! A Sermon on Job 2:13." *Int* 20 (1966) 211–17. **Rodd, Cyril S.** "Those Who Are Not Healed" [Job 2:1–10; Acts 3:1–10; Lk 5:12–26]. *ExpT* 106 (1995) 116–17. **Spinner, Lukas.** "Hiobs Frau: Hiob 2,9." In his *"Bist du Elia, so bin ich Isebel!" Was Frauen sagten. 50 Predigten.* Zurich: TVZ, 2005. 142–47.

3. **MacKenzie, John.** "The Peace of the Grave" [Job 3:17–19]. *The Scotch Preacher* 3 (1775). **Reymond, Philippe.** "Notes bibliques de prédication pour les temps du Carême, de la Passion et de Pâques" [Job 3; 7; 9; 12:1–9]. *Verbum caro* 15 (1961) 99–104. **Roberts, J. J. M.** "A Future with Hope" [Job 3:20–26; Jer 31:15–17; Isa 56:3–7]." *PrSemBull* ns 14 (1993) 162–64. **Spurgeon, C. H.** "The Sorrowful Man's Question [Job 3:23]." In *The Metropolitan Tabernacle Pulpit.* XLVI. London: Passmore & Alabaster, 1901 [repr. Pasadena, TX: Pilgrim Publications, 1977]. 121–32. **Wesley, John.** "The Trouble and Rest of Good Men" [Job 3:17]. Sermon 127.

4. **Melvill, Henry.** "The Spectre's Sermon a Truism" [Job 4:15–17]. In his *Sermons on Some of the Less Prominent Facts and References in Sacred Story.* London: Rivingtons, 1872. 2:60–85. **Warham, Francis.** *The Crosse Lined That It Gall Not, or, A Sermon Preached Octob. 14, 1657 in Aldermanbury Church, London* [Job 4:5]. London: Thomas Ratcliffe, 1658 [Early English Books, 1641–1700, 1319/16].

5. **Ashe, Nicholas.** *A Funeral Sermon, Preached in the Parish Church of Maynooth, the 28th October, 1804* [on the occasion of the death of William Robert, Duke of Leinster] [Job 5:6]. Dublin: J. & J. Carrick, 1804. **Ball, Nathaniel.** *The Devices of the Crafty, Disappointed: or, A Discourse upon Job, Vth Chapter, Verse 12th, Preached at St James's Church in Westminster, the 5th of Nov. 1763.* London, 1763. **Broadfoot, William.** *The Christian Ripe for Eternity: A Sermon, Preached in Wells Street Chapel, Oxford Street, London, on Sabbath, December 23, 1827, Occasioned by the Death of the Rev. Alexander Waugh, D.D. ...* [Job 5:26]. London: Hamilton, Adams, & Co., 1828. **Dawes, William.** *A Sermon Preach'd before the King at Whitehall, Novemb.*

5, 1696 [Job 5:12]. London: Thomas Speed, 1696 [= Early English Books, 1641–1700, 1401/12]. **Lambe, John.** *A Sermon Preach'd before the King at Kensington, January 13, 1694/5* [Job 5:2]. London: Walter Kettilby, 1695 [= Early English Books, 1641–1700, 792/25]. **Shower, John.** *Of Long Life and Old Age: A Funeral Sermon, Occasion'd by the Death of the Much Honour'd Mrs Jane Papillon, Who Departed This Life, July 12th, 1698. AEtat. 72* [Job 5:26]. London: J. Fawkner, 1698 [= Early English Books, 1641–1700, 1049/12]. **Smith, George.** *The Christian Matured for Heaven: A Sermon, Occasioned by the Death of George Green, Esquire, Preached in Trinity Chapel, Poplar, on Sunday, March 4, 1849* [Job 5:26]. London: John Snow, 1849. **Spurgeon, C. H.** "'So It Is' [Job 5:27]." In *The Metropolitan Tabernacle Pulpit.* XXXVI. London: Passmore & Alabaster, 1891 [repr. London: Banner of Truth Trust, 1970]. 637–48.

6. Spurgeon, C. H. "A Cure for Unsavoury Meats; or, Salt for the White of an Egg [Job 6:6]." In *The Metropolitan Tabernacle Pulpit.* XXIX. London: Passmore & Alabaster, 1884 [repr. London: Banner of Truth Trust, 1971]. 385–96. ———. "Concealing the Words of God [Job 6:10]." In *The Metropolitan Tabernacle Pulpit.* London: Passmore & Alabaster, 1880 [repr. Pasadena, TX: Pilgrim Publications, 1980]. 25:241–52.

7. Duke, Paul D. "First Prayer from the Ashes. A Sermon on Job 7:7–21." *RevExp* 99 (2002) 615–19. **Jüngel, Eberhard.** "Hiob 7,11–21." In his *Weil es ein gesprochen Wort war…* Stuttgart: Radius-Verlag, 2003. 17–26. ———. "Hiob 7,17–21." In his *Zum Staunen geboren.* Stuttgart: Radius-Verlag, 2004. 31–38. **Reymond, Philippe.** "Notes bibliques de prédication pour les temps du Carême, de la Passion et de Pâques" [Job 3; 7; 9; 12:1–9]. *Verbum caro* 15 (1961) 99–104. **Spurgeon, C. H.** "'Am I a Sea, or a Whale?' [Job 7:12]." In *The Metropolitan Tabernacle Pulpit.* XXXVII. London: Passmore & Alabaster, 1892 [repr. London: Banner of Truth Trust, 1970]. 289–300. ———. "Job vii." In *The Metropolitan Tabernacle Pulpit.* XLVI. London: Passmore & Alabaster, 1901 [repr. Pasadena, TX: Pilgrim Publications, 1977]. 597–99. ———. "The Hand of God in the History of a Man" [Job 7:1]. In *The Metropolitan Tabernacle Pulpit.* London: Passmore & Alabaster, 1876 [repr. Pasadena, TX: Pilgrim Publications, 1971]. 21:565–76. ———. "Why Some Sinners are Not Pardoned [Job 7:21]." In *The Metropolitan Tabernacle Pulpit.* XLVI. London: Passmore & Alabaster, 1901 [repr. Pasadena, TX: Pilgrim Publications, 1977]. 589–97. **Watson, Richard.** "Man Magnified by the Divine Regard: A Sermon" [Job 7:17]. *Methodist Magazine* 7 (1824) 3–13.

8. Spurgeon, C. H. "A Sermon from a Rush [Job 8:11–13]." In *The Metropolitan Tabernacle Pulpit.* XI. London: Alabaster, Passmore & Sons, 1866 [repr. Pasadena, TX: Pilgrim Publications, 1970]. 529–40. ———. "The Beginning, Increase, and End of the Divine Life [Job 8:7]." In *The New Park Street Pulpit.* VI. London: Alabaster, Passmore & Sons, 1861 [repr. London: Banner of Truth Trust, 1964]. 197–204.

9. Chalmers, Thomas. "An Estimate of the Morality That Is without Godliness" [Job 9:30–33]. In his *Sermons and Discourses.* New York: Robert Carter & Bros., 1873. 2:32–37 [= *Sermons Preached in the Tron Church, Glasgow.* 1819. 100–121]. ———. "The Necessity of a Mediator between God and Man" [Job 9:33]. In his *Sermons and Discourses.* New York: Robert Carter & Bros., 1873. 2:44–48 [= *Sermons Preached in the Tron Church, Glasgow.* 1819. 151–66]. **Ferguson, John.** *A Sermon … Occasioned by the Death of Mr E. Daggett* [Job 9:12]. Dedham, MA, 1832. **Maguire, Robert.** *Sermons prêchés à Exeter Hall, 1858* [Job 9.33]. Toulouse, 1861. **Reymond, Philippe.** "Notes bibliques de prédication pour les temps du Carême, de la Passion et de Pâques" [Job 3; 7; 9; 12:1–9]. *Verbum caro* 15 (1961) 99–104. **Spurgeon, C. H.** "A Blow at Self-Righteousness [Job 9:20]." In *The New Park Street and Metropolitan Tabernacle Pulpit.* VII. London: Alabaster, Passmore & Sons, 1862 [repr. Pasadena, TX: Pilgrim Publications, 1969]. 17–24. ———. "False Justification and True [Job 9:20]." In *The Metropolitan Tabernacle Pulpit.* LI. London: Passmore & Alabaster, 1906 [repr. Pasadena, TX: Pilgrim Publications, 1978]. 193–202. ———. "The Great Arbitration Case [Job 9:33]." In *The Metropolitan Tabernacle Pulpit.* XI. London: Alabaster, Passmore & Sons, 1866 [repr. Pasadena, TX: Pilgrim Publications, 1970]. 649–60. ———. "Washed to Greater Foulness [Job 9:30–31]." In *The Metropolitan Tabernacle Pulpit.* XXXII. London: Passmore & Alabaster, 1887 [repr. London: Banner of Truth Trust, 1969]. 361–72. ———. "Washed to Greater Foulness [Job 9:30–31]." In *The Metropolitan Tabernacle Pulpit*. XXXV. London: Passmore & Alabaster, 1890 [repr. London: Banner of Truth Trust, 1970]. 433–44.

10. Bowerman, Scott. "Honest To God" [Job 10:1–4, 8–9, 15–22; Mk 15:25–34]. *Preaching* 13 (1998) 43–45. **Dominican Friar, A.** *A Sermon Preached on the Occasion of a Funeral at Gabuly in Ireland by a Dominican Fryer* [Job 10:10]. London, 1689 [= Early English Books, 1641–1700, 1069/14]. **Heywood, Oliver.** *Job's Appeal. Being a Funeral Discourse Delivered at Northonnam in Yorkshire, upon Occasion of the Death of Mr Jonathan Denton, Wherein a Christian's State Is Stated before God, and His Sufferings from the Hand of God Cleared. Grounded upon Job X.7.* London: B. Aylmer, 1695. **Spurgeon, C. H.** "A Song and a Solace [Job 10:12–13]." In *The Metropolitan Tabernacle Pulpit*. XLVI. London: Passmore & Alabaster, 1901 [repr. Pasadena, TX: Pilgrim Publications, 1977]. 313–24. ———. "The Sweet Uses of Adversity [Job 10:2]." In *The New Park Street Pulpit*. V. London: Alabaster, Passmore & Sons, 1860 [repr. London: Banner of Truth Trust, 1964]. 465–72. ———. "Three Blessings of the Heavenly Charter [Job 10:12]." In *The Metropolitan Tabernacle Pulpit*. XXXIX. London: Passmore & Alabaster, 1894 [repr. Pasadena, TX: Pilgrim Publications, 1975]. 301–12.

11. Byfield, Adoniram. *A Brief View of Mr Coleman His New-Modell of Church Government: Delivered by Him in a Late Sermon, upon Job 11.20.* London, 1645. **Friederich, Anselm.** "Osterpredigt: Hiob 11,12–18." *Zeitschrift für Gottesdienst und Predigt* 21 (2003) 32–33. **Gillespie, George.** *A Sermon Preached before the Right Honourable the House of Lords in the Abbey Church at Westminster, upon the 27th of August, 1645: Being the Day Appointed for Solemne and Publique Humiliation; Whereunto Is Added a Brotherly Examination of Some Passages of Mr Colemans Late Printed Sermon upon Job 11.20, in Which He Hath Endeavoured to Strike at the Root of All Church-Government.* London: Robert Bostock, 1645 [= English revolution series 1/18. repr. London: Cornmarket Press, 1971]. **Hastings, James.** "The Deeps of God" [Job 11:7]. In his edited *The Great Texts of the Bible*. Edinburgh: T. & T. Clark, 1913. 3:19–34. **Spurgeon, C. H.** "Comfort from the Future [Job 11:16]." In *The Metropolitan Tabernacle Pulpit*. XLVI. London: Passmore & Alabaster, 1901 [repr. Pasadena, TX: Pilgrim Publications, 1977]. 241–50. ———. "Job xi." In *The Metropolitan Tabernacle Pulpit*. XLVI. London: Passmore & Alabaster, 1901 [repr. Pasadena, TX: Pilgrim Publications, 1977]. 250–52.

12. Reymond, Philippe. "Notes bibliques de prédication pour les temps du Carême, de la Passion et de Pâques" [Job 3; 7; 9; 12:1–9]. *Verbum caro* 15 (1961) 99–104. **Spurgeon, C. H.** "Everywhere and Yet Forgotten [Job 12:9–10]." In *The New Park Street Pulpit*. VI. London: Alabaster, Passmore & Sons, 1861 [repr. London: Banner of Truth Trust, 1964]. 317–24.

13. Hastings, James. "Trust Inextinguishable" [Job 13:15]. In his edited *The Great Texts of the Bible*. Edinburgh: T. & T. Clark, 1913. 3:35–53. **Newman, John Henry.** "Peace and Joy amid Chastisement" [Job 13:15]. Sermon 8 in *Parochial and Plain Sermons*. London: Rivingtons, 1868. 117–32 [= **Hone, Ralph E.** *The Voice out of the Whirlwind: The Book of Job*. San Francisco: Chandler, 1960. 152–62]. **Spurgeon, C. H.** "A Frail Leaf [Job 13:25]." In *The Metropolitan Tabernacle Pulpit*. LVII. London: Passmore & Alabaster, 1912 [repr. Pasadena, TX: Pilgrim Publications, 1979]. 457–65. ———. "Faith Tried and Triumphing [Job 13:15]." In *The Metropolitan Tabernacle Pulpit*. LVII. London: Passmore & Alabaster, 1912 [repr. Pasadena, TX: Pilgrim Publications, 1979]. 409–18. ———. "Faith's Ultimatum [Job 13:15]." In *The Metropolitan Tabernacle Pulpit*. XXI. London: Passmore & Alabaster, 1876 [repr. Pasadena, TX: Pilgrim Publications, 1971]. 397–408. ———. "How to Converse with God [Job 13:22]." In *The Metropolitan Tabernacle Pulpit*. XXI. London: Passmore & Alabaster, 1876 [repr. Pasadena, TX: Pilgrim Publications, 1971]. 529–40. ———. "Struggles of Conscience [Job 13:23]." In *The New Park Street Pulpit*. VI. London: Alabaster, Passmore & Sons, 1861 [repr. London: Banner of Truth Trust, 1964]. 397–406.

14. G., R. *A Sermon of Mortalitie: Preached at the Funerals of Mr Thomas Man at Kingston in Surrey Feb. XXI, 1649* [Job 14:14]. London: Richard Constable, 1650 [= Early English Books, 1641–1700, 1688/1]. **Hastings, James.** "Life beyond Death" [Job 14:14]. In his edited *The Great Texts of the Bible.* Edinburgh: T. & T. Clark, 1913. 3:55–69. **Hoffmann, Willi.** "Predigt am 6. November 1994: Drittletzter Sonntag im Kirchenjahr; Hiob 14,1–6." *PastBl* 134 (1994) 617–22. **Horst, Reinhard.** "Hiob 14,1–3/19,25–26." In his *Nimm und lies: gepredigter Glaube im Kirchenjahr.* Göttingen: Cuvillier, 2003. 197–200. **M'Cheyne, Robert Murray.** "Death's Lessons" [Job 14:1–2]. In *Additional Remains of … Robert Murray M'Cheyne, Sermons and Lectures.* Edinburgh: John Johnstone, 1847. 353–57. **Prattant, Robert.** *A Sermon Preached at Rolesbye in Norfolk, on Wednesday the 12th of January 1680/81, at the Funeral of Madam Anna Gleane, the Late Wife of Thomas Gleane, Esq., the Only Son of Sir Peter Gleane of Hardwick in Norfolk, Baronet* [Job 14:14]. London: Joanna Brome, 1682 [= Early English Books, 1641–1700, 847/39]. **Spurgeon, C. H.** "A Voice from the Hartley Colliery [Job 14:14]." In *The Metropolitan Tabernacle Pulpit.* VIII. London: Alabaster, Passmore & Sons, 1863 [repr. Pasadena, TX: Pilgrim Publications, 1969]. 61–72. ———. "Our Life, Our Work, Our Change [Job 14:14]." In *The Metropolitan Tabernacle Pulpit.* XIII. London: Alabaster, Passmore & Sons, 1868 [repr. Pasadena, TX: Pilgrim Publications, 1970]. 433–44. **Toy, John.** *A Sermon Preached in the Cathedrall Church of Worcester the Second of Febr. Last Being Candlemas Day, at the Funerall of Mtis Alice Tomkins Wife unto Mr Thomas Tomkins One of the Gentlemen of His Majesties Chappell Royall* [Job 14:14]. London, 1642 [Early English Books, 1641–1700, 252: E.154/47]. **Waker, Nathaniel.** *A Sermon Preached at the Funerall of Mr Lucas Lucie, Merchant, October 23, 1663* [Job 14:1]. London: R. Royston, 1664 [Early English Books, 1641–1700, 402/24]. **Watson, Thomas.** "An Alarm to Sinners, or, The Last and Great Change" [Job 14:14]. In his *The Mischief of Sin, It Brings a Person Low.* London, 1671. 80–90. **Wilson, Harry Bristow.** *Two Sermons on the Death of Children* [Job 14:2; Ps 103:15–18]. London, 1810.

15. Spurgeon, C. H. "Restraining Prayer [Job 15:4]." In *The Metropolitan Tabernacle Pulpit.* LI. London: Passmore & Alabaster, 1906 [repr. Pasadena, TX: Pilgrim Publications, 1978]. 325–35. ———. "Concerning the Consolations of God [Job 15:11]." In *The Metropolitan Tabernacle Pulpit.* XXXIV. London: Passmore & Alabaster, 1889 [repr. London: Banner of Truth Trust, 1970]. 97–108.

16. Boston, Thomas. "The Shortness of Human Life" [Job 16:22]. In *The Complete Works of the Late Rev. Thomas Boston, Ettrick.* Wheaton, IL: Richard Owen Roberts, 1980. 4:67–71. **Lyon, Geri.** "God's Love Endures Forever [Job 16–18, Lk 10:25–37]." *Christian Ministry* 30 (1999) 26–28. **Spurgeon, C. H.** "Man's Scorn and God's Succour [Job 16:20]." In *The Metropolitan Tabernacle Pulpit.* LIX. London: Passmore & Alabaster, 1914 [repr. Pasadena, TX: Pilgrim Publications, 1979]. 457–66. ———. "Our Last Journey [Job 16:22]." In *The Metropolitan Tabernacle Pulpit.* XXIII. London: Passmore & Alabaster, 1878 [repr. Pasadena, TX: Pilgrim Publications, 1979]. 505–16.

17. Lyon, Geri. "God's Love Endures Forever [Job 16–18, Lk 10:25–37]." *Christian Ministry* 30 (1999) 26–28. **Spurgeon, C. H.** "The Final Perseverance of the Saints [Job 17:9]." In *The Metropolitan Tabernacle Pulpit.* XXIII. London: Passmore & Alabaster, 1878 [repr. Pasadena, TX: Pilgrim Publications, 1979]. 361–72. ———. "The Righteous Holding on His Way [Job 17:9]." In *The Metropolitan Tabernacle Pulpit.* XIII. London: Alabaster, Passmore & Sons, 1868 [repr. Pasadena, TX: Pilgrim Publications, 1970]. 253–64.

18. Lyon, Geri. "God's Love Endures Forever [Job 16–18, Lk 10:25–37]." *Christian Ministry* 30 (1999) 26–28. **Spurgeon, C. H.** "The Hunger-Bite [Job 18:12]." In *The Metropolitan Tabernacle Pulpit.* XXIV. London: Passmore & Alabaster, 1880 [repr. Pasadena, TX: Pilgrim Publications, 1980]. 702–8.

19. Brown, Richard. *Job's Expectations of a Resurrection Considered: Three Sermons Preached before the University at Oxford, at St Mary's, on Sunday October 19. Oct. 26. 1746 and Febr. 22. 1747.* Oxford: Richard Clements, 1747. **Crane, Thomas.** *Job's Assurance* *of the Resurrection: A Sermon at Winwick in the County Palatine of Lancaster, June 25, 1689 at the Funeral of the Reverend Richard Sherlock D.D.* London: Philip Burton, 1690. **Gill, John.** *Job's Creed or, Confession of Faith: A Sermon Occasioned by the Death of the Reverend Mr. Edward Wallin ... June 12, 1733 ... Preached June 18* [Job 19:25–27]. London: Aaron Ward and H. Whitridge, 1733. **Hastings, James.** "I Know That My Redeemer Liveth" [Job 19:25–27]. In his edited *The Great Texts of the Bible.* Edinburgh: T. & T. Clark, 1913. 3:71–96. **Hoffmann, Johann Georg.** *Ma'yānôt Oculissima Durchlauchtigster Augentrost: Bey Verblichener Augen-Lust ... Am Sontage Oculi, M DC LXXXVI. den VII. Martii In das Erb-Begräbnis Solte gebracht werden in einer Vorbereitungs-Predigt Und der Schloß-Kirche, aus Hiob. XIX. 25.26.27.* Weissenfels, 1686. **Horst, Reinhard.** "Hiob 14,1–3/19,25–26." In his *Nimm und lies: gepredigter Glaube im Kirchenjahr.* Göttingen: Cuvillier, 2003. 197–200. **Newton, John.** "Job's Faith and Expectation" [Job 19:25–26]. In *The Works of the Rev. John Newton.* London: J. Johnson & J. Smith, 1808–9. 4:435–47 (Sermon 39 in his series on the texts of Handel's *Messiah*). **Pawson, John.** *The Substance of a Sermon, Occasioned by the Death of Mr Alexander Mather, Minister of the Gospel: Preached in the Methodist Chapel, in York, August 26, 1800* [Job 19:23–27]. Leeds: Edward Baines, 1800. **Rodd, Cyril S.** "Bleak Confidence" [Job 19:23–27a; Lk 20:27–38]. *ExpT* 110 (1998) 16–17. **Spurgeon, C. H.** "Cleansing—Wrong or Right? [Job 19:30–31]." In *The Metropolitan Tabernacle Pulpit.* LIII. London: Passmore & Alabaster, 1908 [repr. Pasadena, TX: Pilgrim Publications, 1978]. 589–600. ———. "I Know That My Redeemer Liveth [Job 19:25–27]." In *The Metropolitan Tabernacle Pulpit.* IX. London: Alabaster, Passmore & Sons, 1864 [repr. Pasadena, TX: Pilgrim Publications, 1975]. 205–16. ———. "The Root of the Matter [Job 19:28]." In *The Metropolitan Tabernacle Pulpit.* IX. London: Alabaster, Passmore & Sons, 1864 [repr. Pasadena, TX: Pilgrim Publications, 1975]. 217–28. ———. "The Substance of True Religion [Job 19:28]." In *The Metropolitan Tabernacle Pulpit.* XXVII. London: Passmore & Alabaster, 1882 [repr. London: Banner of Truth Trust, 1971]. 269–80.

21. Mitchell, William. "Why the Wicked Are Suffered to Live: Sermon LXXXVIII" [Job 21:7]. *The National Preacher* 5/4 (Sept. 1830). **Spurgeon, C. H.** "Not Now, but Hereafter [Job 21:29–31]." In *The New Park Street and Metropolitan Tabernacle Pulpit.* VII. London: Alabaster, Passmore & Sons, 1862 [repr. Pasadena, Text: Pilgrim Publications, 1969]. 497–504.

22. Hastings, James. "Acquaintance with God" [Job 22:21]. In his edited *The Great Texts of the Bible.* Edinburgh: T. & T. Clark, 1913. 3:97–110. **Spurgeon, C. H.** "A Message to the Glad and the Sad [Job 22:29]." In *The Metropolitan Tabernacle Pulpit.* XLIII. London: Passmore & Alabaster, 1898 [repr. Pasadena, TX: Pilgrim Publications, 1976]. 577–86. ———. "A Word in Season [Job 22:29]." In *The Metropolitan Tabernacle Pulpit.* XIII. London: Alabaster, Passmore & Sons, 1868 [repr. Pasadena, TX: Pilgrim Publications, 1970]. 39–48. ———. "Delight in the Almighty [Job 22:26]." In *The Metropolitan Tabernacle Pulpit.* XXXI. London: Passmore & Alabaster, 1886 [repr. London: Banner of Truth Trust, 1971]. 253–64. ———. "The Old Way of the Wicked [Job 22:15–17]." In *The Metropolitan Tabernacle Pulpit.* XV. London: Passmore & Alabaster, 1870 [repr. Pasadena, TX: Pilgrim Publications, 1970]. 133–44.

23. Bain, J. *Faith's Reply to a Most Important Question: A Sermon, Preached at Holloway Chapel, on the 10th March, 1805, from Job XXIII v. 6 "Will he plead against me with his great power? No." By J. Bain, Minister of Potter Street Baptist Church, Harlow.* Transcribed by Stephen Hulcoop. Harlow: S.H. Publishing, 2001. **Cole Turner, Ronald.** "QuickVerse" [Job 23:1–9]. *MemphThSemJ* 33 (1995) 36–40. **Craner, Thomas.** *The Righteous Man Exemplified in the Character of Job: The Substance of Two Sermons on Job XXIII. 7. Preached on the Lord's Day, January 31, 1768.* London, 1768. **Knight, William.** *Seeking after God: A Sermon: Preached in Portland Street Church, London, May 26, 1872* [Job 23:3]. Glasgow: James Maclehose, 1872. **Spurgeon, C. H.** "Job xxiii.6–33." In *The Metropolitan Tabernacle Pulpit.* XLII. London: Passmore & Alabaster, 1897 [repr. Pasadena, TX: Pilgrim Publications, 1976]. 95–96. ———. "Job xxiii." In *The Metropolitan Tabernacle Pulpit.* XLIII. London: Passmore & Alabaster, 1898 [repr. Pasadena, TX: Pilgrim Publications,

1976]. 586–88. ———. "Longing to Find God [Job 23:3]." In *The Metropolitan Tabernacle Pulpit*. XXXVIII. London: Passmore & Alabaster, 1893 [repr. Pasadena, TX: Pilgrim Publications, 1970]. 421–29. ———. "Order and Argument in Prayer [Job 23:3–4]." In *The Metropolitan Tabernacle Pulpit*. XII. London: Alabaster, Passmore & Sons, 1867 [repr. Pasadena, TX: Pilgrim Publications, 1970]. 385–96. ———. "The Anxious Enquirer [Job 23:3]." In *The Metropolitan Tabernacle Pulpit*. XLV. London: Passmore & Alabaster, 1900 [repr. Pasadena, TX: Pilgrim Publications, 1977]. 97–108. ———. "The Fair Portrait of a Saint [Job 23:11–12]." In *The Metropolitan Tabernacle Pulpit*. XXVI. London: Passmore & Alabaster, 1881 [repr. London: Banner of Truth Trust, 1971]. 145–56. ———. "The Infallibility of God's Purpose [Job 23:13]." In *The New Park Street and Metropolitan Tabernacle Pulpit*. VII. London: Alabaster, Passmore & Sons, 1862 [repr. Pasadena, Text: Pilgrim Publications, 1969]. 465–72. ———. "The Question of Fear and the Answer of Faith [Job 23:6]." In *The New Park Street Pulpit*. III. London: Alabaster, Passmore & Sons, 1858 [repr. London: Banner of Truth Trust, 1964]. 9–16. ———. "Whither Goest Thou? [Job 23:10]." In *The Metropolitan Tabernacle Pulpit*. XXXV. London: Passmore & Alabaster, 1890 [repr. London: Banner of Truth Trust, 1970]. 421–32. **Stillingfleet, Edward.** *A Sermon Preached before the King, February 15, 1683/4* [Job 23:15]. London: Henry Mortlock, 1684 [Early English Books, 1641–1700, 515/32; 802/19]. **Whyte, Alexander.** "Job, Groping" [Job 23:3]. In his *Lord, Teach Us to Pray; Sermons on Prayer*. London: Hodder & Stoughton, 1937. 78–89.

24. Alley, Jerome. *A Sermon Preached at the Parish Church of Saint Mary, Islington, in the County of Middlesex, on Sunday Morning, November 16, 1817: Occasioned by the Death of Her Royal Highness the Princess Charlotte of Wales and Saxe Cobourg, &c.* [Job 34:18–20]. London: F. C. & J. Rivington, 1817.

26. Williams, Michael E. "Preaching as Storytelling" [sample, Job 26:7–14]. In *Journeys toward Narrative Preaching*. Ed. Wayne Bradley Robinson. New York: Pilgrim Press, 1990. 114–15.

27. Edwards, Jonathan. "Hypocrites Deficient in the Duty of Prayer" [Job 27:10]. In *The Works of Jonathan Edwards*. Ed. Perry Miller and John E. Smith. New Haven, CT: Yale University Press, 1957–. 2:71–77. **Spurgeon, C. H.** "A Vexed Soul Comforted [Job 27:2]." In *The Metropolitan Tabernacle Pulpit*. XLIV. London: Passmore & Alabaster, 1899 [repr. Pasadena, TX: Pilgrim Publications, 1976]. 85–93. ———. "Job xxvii." In *The Metropolitan Tabernacle Pulpit*. XLIV. London: Passmore & Alabaster, 1899 [repr. Pasadena, TX: Pilgrim Publications, 1976]. 93–96. ———. "The Touchstone of Godly Sincerity [Job 27:10]." In *The Metropolitan Tabernacle Pulpit*. XVII. London: Passmore & Alabaster, 1872 [repr. Pasadena, TX: Pilgrim Publications, 1971]. 205–16.

28. Liddon, H. P. "The Moral Groundwork of Clerical Training" [Job 28:12]. In *Clerical Life and Work: A Collection of Sermons with an Essay*. London: Longmans, Green & Co., 1894. 73–92. **Scattergood, Samuel.** *A Sermon Preached before the King at New-Market, April 2, 1676* [Job 28:28]. Cambridge: John Hayes, 1676 [Early English Books, 1641–1700, 333/3]. **Tillotson, John.** *The Wisdom of Being Religious: A Sermon Preached at St Pauls* [Job 28:28]. London: S. Gellibrand, 1664 [Early English Books, 1641–1700, 518/4]. **Young, Edward.** *A Sermon concerning the Wisdom of Fearing God: Preach'd at Salisbury, on Sunday, July XXX, 1693, Being the Time of the Assizes* [Job 28:28]. London: Walter Kettilby, 1693 [Early English Books, 1641–1700, 589/10].

29. Bradley, Thomas. *A Sermon Preached at the Minster in Yorke: at the Assizes There Holden, the Thirtieth Day of March, 1663* [Job 29:14–17]. York: Alice Broade, 1663 [= Early English Books, 1641–1700; 1565:3]. **Hunt, George.** *A Sermon Preached before the Grateful Society … on … the Anniversary of the Nativity of … E. Colston* [Job 29:16]. Bristol: J. Lansdown, 1809. **Spurgeon, C. H.** "Comfort for the Desponding [Job 29:2]." In *The New Park Street Pulpit*. I. London: Passmore & Alabaster, 1856 [repr. London: Banner of Truth Trust, 1963]. 387–94. ———. "Freshness [Job 29:20]." In *The Metropolitan Tabernacle Pulpit*. XXVIII. London: Passmore & Alabaster, 1883 [repr. London: Banner of Truth Trust, 1971]. 145–56. ———. "Job's Regret and Our Own [Job 29:2–4]." In *The Metropolitan Tabernacle*

Pulpit. XVII. London: Passmore & Alabaster, 1872 [repr. Pasadena, TX: Pilgrim Publications, 1971]. 517–28. **Stokes, David.** *A Sermon upon Job 29, 15: Preached before the Judges at a General Assise in Hertford when That Good and Charitable Person Rowland Hales, Esquire, Was High-Sheriff of That Shire.* Oxford: Richard Davis, 1667 [Early English Books, 1641–1700, 1213/27]. **Wilson, James.** *The Importance of Charity: A Sermon Preached in the Church of Falkirk … for the Benefit of the Public Kitchen in That Town* [Job 29:11,12]. Falkirk, 1800.

30. Boston, Thomas. "Death" [Job 30:23]. In his *Man's Fourfold State,* in *The Complete Works of the Late Rev. Thomas Boston, Ettrick.* Wheaton, IL: Richard Owen Roberts, 1980. 8:232–45. **Graham, John.** *A Sermon* [Job 30:23]. Dumfries: R. Jackson. 1821. **Riveley, Benedict.** *A Sermon Preach'd at the Cathedral of Norwich upon the Annual Solemnity of the Mayors Admission to His Office, Being June 17, 1679* [Job 30:23]. London: Samuel Lownds, 1679 [Early English Books, 1641–1700, 367/13]. ———. *A Sermon Prech'd in the Cathedral Church of Norwich, at the Funeral of the Right Reverend Father in God, Edward, Lord Bishop of Norwich, Who Departed This Life, July 28, 1676* [Job 30:23]. London: Samuel Lowndes & William Oliver, 1677 [Early English Books, 1641–1700, 546/13]. **Schnelle, Udo.** "Predigt am Sonntag, den 26. Oktober 2003, 'Ich schreie, aber du antwortest mir nicht!': Predigttext: Hiob 30, 20–27." *Hallesche Universitätspredigten* 7 (2004) 85–91. **Spurgeon, C. H.** "Christian Sympathy—A Sermon for the Lancashire Distress [Job 30:25]." In *The Metropolitan Tabernacle Pulpit.* V.III. London: Alabaster, Passmore & Sons, 1863 [repr. Pasadena, TX: Pilgrim Publications, 1969]. 625–36. ———. "Concerning Death [Job 30:23]." In *The Metropolitan Tabernacle Pulpit.* XXXII. London: Passmore & Alabaster, 1887 [repr. London: Banner of Truth Trust, 1969]. 529–40.

31. Chalmers, Thomas. "On the Love of Money" [Job 31:24–28]. In his *Sermons and Discourses.* New York: Robert Carter & Bros., 1873. 2:169–75. **Hartcliffe, John.** *A Sermon Preached before the Right Honourable the Lord Mayor and Court of Alderman, at St Bride's Church, on Wednesday in Easter-Week, April 11th, 1694* [Job 31:19]. London: Charles Harper, 1694 [= Early English Books, 1641–1700, 534/7]. **Rogers, Samuel.** *The Poore's Pension, a Sermon Preached in Gregories Church in Sudbury in the County of Suffolke, May 12, 1643: upon Occasion of the Charitable Reliefe That Yearly Then and There Is Given towards the Covering or Clothing of a Hundred Poore People, according to the Will of the Donour M Martine Cole, Late of the Towne Aforesaid Deceased* [Job 31:19]. London: Edward Brewster, 1644 [= Early English Books, 1641–1700, 229:E.10/2].

32. Anon. *The Doom of Britain* [Job 32:10]. Montrose: Alexander Rodgers, 1855. **Spurgeon, C. H.** "The Voices of Our Days [Job 32:7]." In *The Metropolitan Tabernacle Pulpit.* LVIII. London: Passmore & Alabaster, 1913 [repr. Pasadena, TX: Pilgrim Publications, 1979]. 1–9.

33. Mead, Matthew. *A Funeral Sermon Preached upon the Sad Occasion of the Death of That Eminent and Faithful Servant of Christ, Mr Thomas Rosewell, Who Departed This Life February the 4th …* [Job 33:23–24]. London: John Lawrence, 1692 [= Early English Books, 1641–1700, 541/2]. **Poole, Matthew.** "How Ministers or Christian Friends May and Ought to Apply Themselves to Sick Persons, for Their Good, and the Discharge of Their Own Conscience" [Job 33:23–24]. In *The Morning Exercises at Cripplegate.* Ed. S. Annesley. London, 1677. 1:111–21. **Resbury, Nathanael.** *A Sermon Preached before the Queen at White-Hall, August 21, 1692* [Job 33:22–24]. London: Thomas Bennet, 1692 [= Early English Books, 1641–1700, 1192/19]. **Spurgeon, C. H.** "An Old-Fashioned Conversion [Job 33:29, 30]." In *The Metropolitan Tabernacle Pulpit.* XIX. London: Passmore & Alabaster, 1874 [repr. Pasadena, TX: Pilgrim Publications, 1971]. 145–56. ———. "Footsteps of Mercy [Job 33:23–24]." In *The Metropolitan Tabernacle Pulpit.* XV. London: Passmore & Alabaster, 1870 [repr. Pasadena, TX: Pilgrim Publications, 1970]. 685–96. ———. "A Hard Case [Job 33:14–18]." In *The Metropolitan Tabernacle Pulpit.* XLII. London: Passmore & Alabaster, 1897 [repr. Pasadena, TX: Pilgrim Publications, 1976]. 85–95. ———. "Deliverance from the Pit [Job 33:24]." In *The Metropolitan Tabernacle Pulpit.* XLIII. London: Passmore & Alabaster, 1898 [repr. Pasadena, TX: Pilgrim Publications,

1976]. 85–94. ———. "Job xxxiii." In *The Metropolitan Tabernacle Pulpit*. XLIII. London: Passmore & Alabaster, 1898 [repr. Pasadena, TX: Pilgrim Publications, 1976]. 94–96.
   34. Curtois, John. *A Sermon Preach'd in the Cathedral of Lincoln, July XXIX, 1683* [Job 34:29]. London: Joseph Lawson, 1684 [= Early English Books, 1641–1700, 1613/19]. **M'Cheyne, Robert Murray.** "The Improvement of Affliction" [Job 34:31–32]. In his *A Basket of Fragments, Being the Substance of Sermons.* Aberdeen: King, 1854. 37–39. **Spurgeon, C. H.** "Job xxxiv." In *The Metropolitan Tabernacle Pulpit*. XLVI. London: Passmore & Alabaster, 1901 [repr. Pasadena, TX: Pilgrim Publications, 1977]. 177–80. ———. "For the Sick and Afflicted [Job 34:31–32]." In *The Metropolitan Tabernacle Pulpit*. XXII. London: Passmore & Alabaster, 1877 [repr. Pasadena, TX: Pilgrim Publications, 1981]. 37–48. ———. "God-All in All [Job 34:29]." In *The Metropolitan Tabernacle Pulpit*. XIII. London: Alabaster, Passmore & Sons, 1868 [repr. Pasadena, TX: Pilgrim Publications, 1970]. 109–20. ———. "Pride Catechized [Job 34:33]." In *The Metropolitan Tabernacle Pulpit*. XLVI. London: Passmore & Alabaster, 1901 [repr. Pasadena, TX: Pilgrim Publications, 1977]. 169–77. **Warner, James.** דרך שלום לשלום בצוק העתים. *Or, The Surest Way to the Safest Peace, in Troublous Times: Delivered in a Sermon Preached before the Right Honourable Sr John Eyles, Kt, then Lord Mayor of the City of London, on September 30, 1688* [Job 34:29]. London: Thomas Parkhurst, 1688 [Early English Books, 1641–1700, 480/15].
   35. Echternacht, Helmut Friedbert Richard Siegfried. "Predigt über Hiob 35, 9–11." *Homiletische Monatshefte*. 1974. **Hastings, James.** "Songs in the Night [Job 35:10]." In his edited *The Great Texts of the Bible*. Edinburgh: T. & T. Clark, 1913. 3:111–27. **Spurgeon, C. H.** "Questions Which Ought to be Asked [Job 35:10–11]." In *The Metropolitan Tabernacle Pulpit*. XXVI. [London: Passmore & Alabaster, 1881 [repr. London: Banner of Truth Trust, 1971]. 1–4. ———. "Songs in the Night [Job 35:10]." In *The Metropolitan Tabernacle Pulpit*. XLIV. London: Passmore & Alabaster, 1899 [repr. Pasadena, TX: Pilgrim Publica-tions, 1976]. 97–108.
   36. Gould, William. *The Primitive Christian Justified and Jack Presbyter Reproved, or, A Scrip-ture Demonstration, That to Be Innocent and Persecuted Is More Eligible Than to Be Prosperously Wicked: Delivered in a Sermon in the Abby-Church of Bath* [Job 36:21]. London: R. Royston, 1682 [= Early English Books, 1641–1700, 939/15]. **Hog, James.** *An Abstract of Sundry Discourses on Job XXXVI. 8, 9, 10*. Edinburgh, 1714. **Melvill, Henry, and Henry Thomas.** *The Dissolution of All Things, and God Instructing by His Providence. Two Sermons Preached on Sun-day, Nov. 7, 1841, in the Royal Chapel of St Peter ad Vincula on the Occasion of the Late Calami-tous Fire in the Tower of London* [1 Pet 3:11; Job 36:22]. London: J. G. F. & J. Rivington, 1841. **Palmer, Benjamin Morgan.** "The Law, the Rule of Christ's Kingdom" [Job 36:17]. In his *Sermons*. New Orleans: First Presbyterian Church, 1875–76. 1:3–12 [= Harrisonburg, VA: Sprinkle Publications]. **Resbury, Nathanael.** *A Sermon Preached before the Queen, at White-Hall, on Sunday, Aug. 16, 1691* [Job 36:8]. London: Thomas Bennet, 1691 [= Early English Books, 1641–1700, 749/24]. **Spurgeon, C. H.** "God's Advocates Breaking Silence [Job 36:2]." In *The Metropolitan Tabernacle Pulpit*. XXIV. London: Passmore & Alabaster, 1879 [repr. Pasadena, TX: Pilgrim Publications, 1972]. 145–56. ———. "Speaking on God's Behalf [Job 36:2]." In *The Metropolitan Tabernacle Pulpit*. LXII. London: Passmore & Alabaster, 1917 [repr. Pasadena, TX: Pilgrim Publications, 1980]. 601–12.
   38. Callahan, Jim. "Weatherproof" [Job 38:1–11]. *ChrCent* 117 (2000) 643. **Dewe, Samuel.** *The Sudden Change: A Sermon Preached in the Parish Church of Aspeden, Herts, on the Day of the Late Public Fast, March 10, 1813* [Job 38:23]. London: Black, Parry, & Co, 1813. **Falwell, Jerry.** "Your Day of Trouble" [Job 38:23] *FundJ* 1/2 (1982) 40–41. **Gannett, Ezra S.** *The Atlantic Telegraph: A Discourse delivered in the First Church, August 8, 1858* [Job 38:35]. Boston: Crosby, Nichols, 1858. **Hess, Margaret B.** "The Labyrinth of Life" [Job 38:1–11]. *ChrCent* 114 (1997) 557. **Leininger, David.** "Remembering Charlie" [Job 38:1–18; 40:1–4]. *Christian Ministry* 23 (Jan.–Feb. 1992) 24–25. **Rodd, Cyril S.** "From an Alien World" [Job 38:1–18; Acts 14:8–17]. *ExpT* 105 (1994) 376–77. **Roscher, Helmut.**

"Flutgottesdienst des Alten Landes am 16.2.2002: Hiob 38,4–11." *Homiletische Monatshefte* 78 (2003) 165–68. **Sölle, Dorothee, and Fulbert Steffensky.** "Wider den Geist der Kaufmannschaft: Hiob 38 + 40. Predigt am 6. April 2003 im Berliner Dom." In Sölle's *Löse die Fesseln der Ungerechtigkeit. Predigten.* Stuttgart: Kreuz, 2004. 155–64. **Spurgeon, C. H.** "Rain and Grace—A Parallel [Job 38:25–27]." In *The Metropolitan Tabernacle Pulpit.* XLIV. London: Passmore & Alabaster, 1899 [repr. Pasadena, TX: Pilgrim Publications, 1976]. 385–96. ———. "The Doors of the Shadow of Death [Job 38:17]." In *The Metropolitan Tabernacle Pulpit.* LI. London: Passmore & Alabaster, 1906 [repr. Pasadena, TX: Pilgrim Publications, 1978]. 13–21. ———. "The Pleiades and Orion [Job 38:31]." In *The Metropolitan Taberna-cle Pulpit.* XIV. London: Passmore & Alabaster, 1869 [repr. Pasadena, TX: Pilgrim Publica-tions, 1970]. 361–72. **Taylor, Barbara Brown.** "On Not Being God." *RevExp* 99 (2002) 609–13.

40. DeWitt, Calvin B. "The Beauty of the Beast: Behemoths and Batrachians in the Eye of God: A Meditation on Job 40:15–24." *Green Cross* 4 (1998) 8–9. **Leininger, David.** "Remembering Charlie" [Job 38:1–18; 40:1–4] [sermon]. *Christian Ministry* 23 (Jan.–Feb. 1992) 24–25. **Sölle, Dorothee, and Fulbert Steffensky.** "Wider den Geist der Kauf-mannschaft: Hiob 38 + 40. Predigt am 6. April 2003 im Berliner Dom." In Sölle's *Löse die Fesseln der Ungerechtigkeit. Predigten.* Stuttgart: Kreuz, 2004. 155–64. **Spranger, R. J.** *Behe-moth: or, The Children of Wrath.* Confirmation Lectures 6. 1860. **Spurgeon, C. H.** "Indwelling Sin [Job 40:3–4]." In *The New Park Street Pulpit.* II. London: Passmore & Alabaster, 1857 [repr. London: Banner of Truth Trust, 1963]. 233–40.

42. Anon. *A Sermon Preached in the Parish Church of Stockton-on-Tees, On Tuesday, Sept. 11th, 1839, Being a Day Set Apart for the Purpose of Divine Worship, on Account of the Destructive Pestilence Which Had Recently Prevailed in That Town* [Job 42:5–6]. Stockton-upon-Tees, 1832. **Hastings, James.** "Hearsay and Experience" [Job 42:5–6]. In his edited *The Great Texts of the Bible.* Edinburgh: T. & T. Clark, 1913. 3:145–64. **King, Edward.** *"What Is Comfort?" A Sermon Preached to Men at S.S. Philip & James' Church, during Lent, 1876* [Job 42:5–6]. Oxford: H. C. Spackman, 1876. **Logan, James C.** "Homiletical Resources: Exegesis of Four Propers Following Pentecost" [Job 42:1–6; Gen 2:18–24; 3:18–19; Isa 53:7–12]." *Quarterly Review* 5 (Fall 1985) 71–94. **Pippin, Tina.** "Between Text and Sermon: Job 42:1–6, 10–17." *Int* 53 (1999) 299–303. **Scott, Hew.** *Reflections on the Death of Job: A Sermon, Preached at Crail, on the 11th February, 1827, Being the First Sunday after the Interment of Mrs Elizabeth Inglis.* Edinburgh: Oliver & Boyd, 1827. **Spurgeon, C. H.** "Intercessory Prayer [Job 42:10]." In *The New Park Street and Metropolitan Tabernacle Pulpit.* VII. London: Alabaster, Passmore & Sons, 1862 [repr. Pasadena, TX: Pilgrim Publications, 1969]. 449–56. ———. "The Turning of Job's Captivity [Job 42:10]." In *The Metropolitan Tabernacle Pulpit.* XXI. London: Passmore & Alabaster, 1876 [repr. Pasadena, TX: Pilgrim Publications, 1971]. 613–24. **Witherspoon, John.** "A View of the Glory of God Humbling to the Soul" [Job 42:5–6]. In *The Works of J. W. … with His Lectures … Speeches in the American Congress, etc.* Edinburgh: Ogle, 1804–1805. 3:119–38.

o. Job and Psychology

Andresen, Jeffry J. "Biblical Job: Changing the Helper's Mind." *Contemporary Psychoanalysis* 27 (1991) 454–81. **Bakan, D.** "Das Opfer im Buche Hiob." In *Psychoanalytische Interpretationen biblischer Texte.* Ed. Yorick Spiegel. Munich: Kaiser, 1972. 152–66. ———. "Sacrifice and the Book of Job." In his *Disease, Pain and Sacrifice: Toward a Psychology of Suffering.* Chicago: University of Chicago Press, 1968. 95–128. **Baumer, L.** "Das Buch Hiob, Versuch einer psychopathologischen Deutung." *Der Nervenarzt* 28 (1957) 546–50. **Breakstone, Raymond (ed.).** *Job: A Case Study.* New York: Bookman Associates, 1964. **Byrne, Patricia Huff.** "Give Sorrow Words: Lament—Contemporary Need for Job's Old Time Religion." *Journal of Pastoral Care and Counseling* 56 (2002) 255–64. **Carlin, Nathan.** "The Book of Job and Male Melancholia: A Bizarre Story about

Hating Mother God and the Maternal Jesus, Featuring Mel Gibson." *PastPsych* 56 (2007) 121–41. **Drodge, Edward N.** "A Cognitive-Embodiment Approach to Emotioning and Rationality, Illustrated in the Story of Job." *IntJPsychRel* 10 (2000) 187–99. **Gerber, Israel J.** *A Psychological Approach to the Book of Job.* Diss. Boston University School of Theology, 1950. ———. *The Psychology of the Suffering Mind.* New York: Jonathan David, 1951. **Goitein, Lionel.** "The Importance of the Book of Job for Analytic Thought." *American Imago* 11 (1954) 407–15.

Hamman, Jacobus Johannes. *The Restoration of Job: A Study Based on D. W. Winnicott's Theory of Object Usage and Its Significance for Pastoral Theology.* Diss. Princeton Theological Seminary, 2000. **Hulme, William E.** *Christian Caregiving: Insights from the Book of Job.* St Louis: Concordia Publishing House, 1992. ———. "Pastoral Counseling in the Book of Job." *ConcJ* 15 (1989) 121–38. **Kahn, Jack, with Hester Soloman.** *Job's Illness: Loss, Grief and Integration. A Psychological Interpretation.* Oxford: Pergamon, 1975. **Kapusta, M. A., et al.** "The Book of Job and the Modern View of Depression." *AnnInternMed* 86 (1977) 667–72. **Keady, Richard E.** "Depression, Psychophysiology and Concepts of God." *Encounter* 41 (1980) 263–77. **Kutz, Ilan.** "Job and His 'Doctors': Bedside Wisdom in the Book of Job." *British Medical Journal* 321: 7276 (2000) 1613–15. **Maas, Jeannette P.** "A Psychological Assessment of Job." *PacJT* ns 2 (1989) 55–68. **Ney, P.** "A Psychiatrist's Discussion of Job." *Crux* 17 (1981) 2–3. **Nimmo, Peter W.** "Sin, Evil and Job: Monotheism as a Psychological and Pastoral Problem." *Pastoral Psychology* 42 (1994) 427–39. **Or-Bach, Israel.** "Job—A Biblical Message about Suicide." *Journal of Psychology and Judaism* 18 (1994) 241–47. **Osband, Beverly Ann.** *Fate, Suffering, and Transformation.* Diss. Pacifica Graduate Institute, Carpinteria, CA, 2000. **Quillo, Ronald.** "Naked Am I: Psychological Perspectives on the Unity of the Book of Job." *PerspRelSt* 18 (1991) 213–22. **Raguse, Hartmut.** "Psychoanalytische Erwägungen zum Hiob-Buch." *Wege zum Menschen* 53 (2001) 19–35. **Reid, S. A.** "The Book of Job." *Psychoanalytic Review* 60 (1973) 373–91. **Renik, O.** "The Biblical Book of Job: Advice to Clinicians." *Psychoanalytic Quarterly* 60 (1991) 596–606. **Reynierse, James H.** "A Behavioristic Analysis of the Book of Job." *JPsychTheol* 3 (1975) 75–81. ———. "Behavior Therapy and Job's Recovery." *Journal of Psychology and Theology* 3 (1975) 187–94. **Roy, Arlin.** "The Book of Job: A Grief and Human Development Interpretation." *JRelHealth* 30 (1991) 149–59.

Schimmel, Solomon. "Job and the Psychology of Suffering and Doubt." *JPsychJud* 11 (1987) 239–49. **Schultz, Karl A.** *The Art and Vocation of Caring for People in Pain.* New York: Paulist Press, 1993. **Schwab, George M., Sr.** "The Book of Job and Counsel in the Whirlwind." *Journal of Biblical Counseling* 17 (1998) 31–43. **Schwartz-Salant, Nathan.** "Patriarchy in Transformation: Judaic, Christian, and Clinical Perspectives." In *Jung's Challenge to Contemporary Religion.* Ed. Murray Stein and Robert L. Moore. Wilmette, IL: Chiron Publications, 1987. 41–71. **Taylor, W. S.** "Theology and Therapy in Job." *TTod* 12 (1955–56) 451–63. **Tsai, Allan.** "When Bad Things Happen to Good People (and Other Lessons from the Book of Job)" [Jungian reflections on suffering]. *Sojourners* 28 (1999) 32–36. **Van Praag, Herman M.** "Job's Agony: A Biblical Evocation of Bereavement and Grief." *Judaism* 37 (1988) 173–87. **Viljoen, Jaco.** "'n psigologiese verstaan van die boek Job. 'n beskouing van W. Brueggemann se bydrae tot 'n psigologiese verstaan van die boek Job, in die gesprek rondom psigologiese skriftverstaan." *OTEss* 11 (1998) 115–27. **Villiers, Francois T. de.** "Symptoms of Depression in Job. A Note on Psychological Exegesis." *OTEss* 17 (2004) 9–14. **Vogels, Walter.** "The Inner Development of Job: One More Look at Psychology and the Book of Job." *ScEs* 35 (1983) 227–30. ———. "The Spiritual Growth of Job: A Psychological Approach to the Book of Job." *BTB* 11 (1981) 77–80. **Volgger, David.** "Das Buch Ijob als skeptische oder seelsorgliche Literatur? Oder: Das Buch Ijob und die wahre Gottesfurcht." In *Das Buch Ijob: Gesamtdeutungen—Einzeltexte—zentrale Themen.* Ed. Theodor Seidl and Stephanie Ernst. Österreichische biblische Studien 31. Frankfurt: Peter Lang, 2007. 39–55. **Wohlgelernter, Devora K.** "Death Wish in the Bible." *Tradition* 19 (181) 131–40. ———. "Goal Directedness:

Understanding the Development of the Book of Job." *Individual Psychology: Journal of Adlerian Theory, Research and Practice* 44 (1988) 296–306.

p. Job in Botany

Job's Tears (*Coix lacryma-jobi*). Arber, Agnes. *The Gramineae: A Study of Cereal, Bamboo, and Grass.* New York: Wheldon & Wesley, 1965. **Armstrong, W. P.** "Job's Tears." *Ornament* 18/1 (1994) 104–5. ———. "Botanical Jewelry." *Herbalgram* 29 (1993) 26–33. **Arora, R. K.** "Job's Tears (*Coix lacryma-jobi*): A Minor Food and Fodder Crop of Northeastern India." *Economic Botany* 31 (1977) 358–66. **Francis, Peter, Jr.** "Plants as Human Adornment in India." *Economic Botany* 38/2 (1984) 194–209. **Venkateswarlu, J., and Raju S. K. Chaganti.** "Job's-tears (*Coix lacryma-jobi* L.)." *I.C.A.R. Technical Bulletin (Agric.)* 44. New Delhi: Indian Council of Agricultural Research, 1973.

9. Sources and Composition

Albertz, R. "Der sozialgeschichtliche Hintergrund des Hiobbuches und der 'Babylonischen Theodizee' [*Ludlul bēl nēmeqi*]." In *Die Botschaft und die Boten. Festschrift für Hans Walter Wolff.* Ed. J. Jeremias and L. Perlitt. Neukirchen–Vluyn: Neukirchener Verlag, 1981. 349–72. **Alt, A.** "Zur Vorgeschichte des Buches Hiob." *ZAW* 55 (1937) 265–68. **Brandwein, C.** "אגדת איוב לשלביה השונים [The Legend of Job according to Its Various Stages]." *Tarb* 35 (1965–66) 1–17, i–ii. **Buhl, F.** "Zur Vorgeschichte des Buches Hiob." In *Vom Alten Testament. Karl Marti zum siebzigsten Geburtstage gewidmet von Freunden, Fachgenossen und Schülern.* Ed. Karl Budde. BZAW 41. Giessen: Töpelmann, 1925. 52–61. **Curtis, John B.** "Elihu and Deutero-Isaiah: A Study in Literary Dependence." *PrGLM* 10 (1990). Ed. Terrance Callan. 31–38. **Fohrer, G.** "Überlieferung und Wandlung der Hioblegende." In *Friedrich Baumgärtel zum 70. Geburtstag 14. Januar 1958 gewidmet von den Mitarbeitern am Kommentar zum Alten Testament.* Ed. Johannes Herrmann. Erlangen: Universitätsbund Erlangen, 1959. 41–62 [= his *Studien zum Buche Hiob (1956–1979).* BZAW 159. Berlin: de Gruyter, 1963; 2nd ed. 1983. 37–59]. ———. "Vorgeschichte und Komposition des Buches Hiob." *TLZ* 81 (1956) 333–36. ———. "Zur Vorgeschichte und Komposition des Buches Hiob." *VT* 6 (1956) 249–67 [= his *Studien zum Buche Hiob (1956– 1979).* BZAW 159. Berlin: de Gruyter, 1963; 2nd ed. 1983. 19–36]. **Foster, F. H.** "Is the Book of Job a Translation from an Arabic Original?" *AJSL* 49 (1932–33) 21–45. **Fullerton, Kember.** "The Original Conclusion to the Book of Job." *ZAW* 42 (1924) 116–35. **Grill, W.** *Zur Kritik der Komposition des Buches Hiob.* Tübingen: Fues'sche Buchdruckerei, 1890. **Guillaume, A.** "The Unity of the Book of Job." *ALUOS* 4 (1962) 26–46.

Halpern, Baruch. "Assyrian and Pre-Socratic Astronomies and the Location of the Book of Job." In *Kein Land für sich allein: Studien zum Kulturkontakt in Kanaan, Israel/Palästina und Ebirnâri für Manfred Weippert zum 65. Geburtstag.* Ed. Ulrich Hübner and Ernst Axel Knauf. OBO 186. Freiburg, Switzerland: Universitätsverlag; Göttingen: Vandenhoeck & Ruprecht, 2002. 255–64. **Hoffman, Yair.** "Ancient Near Eastern Literary Conventions and the Restoration of the Book of Job." *ZAW* 103 (1991) 399–411. ———. "The Relation between the Prologue and the Speech Cycles in Job: A Reconsideration." *VT* 31 (1981) 160–70. **Hoffmann, R. E.** "Eine Parallele zur Rahmenerzählung des Buches Hiob in 1 Chr 7,20–29?" *ZAW* 92 (1980) 120–32. **Hoonacker, A. van.** "Une question touchant la composition du livre de Job." *RB* 12 (1903) 161–89. **Kautzsch, Karl.** *Das sogenannte Volksbuch von Hiob und der Ursprung von Hiob cap. I. II. XLII, 7–17: Ein Beitrag zur Frage nach der Integrität des Buches Hiob.* Tübingen: J. C. B. Mohr, 1900. **Kutsch, Ernst.** "Hiob und seine Freunde. Zu Problemen der Rahmenerzählung des Hiobbuches." In *Zur Aktualität des Alten Testaments: Festschrift für Georg Sauer zum 65. Geburtstag.* Ed. Siegfried Kreuzer and Kurt Lüthi. Frankfurt a.M.: Peter Lang, 1992. 73–83. **Landersdorfer, Simon.** *Eine babylonische Quelle für das Buch Job? Eine literar-geschichtliche Studie.* Biblische Studien

16,2. Freiburg i.Br.: Herder, 1911. **Laue, Ludwig.** *Die Composition des Buches Hiob: Ein litterar-kritischer Versuch.* Halle: J. Krause, 1896. **Lawrie, Douglas.** "How Critical Is It to Be Historically Critical? The Case of the Composition of the Book of Job." *JNSL* 27 (2001) 121–46. **Lindblom, Johannes.** "Joblegenden traditionshistoriskt undersökt." *SEÅ* 5 (1940) 29–42. ———. *La composition du livre de Job.* Lund: C. W. K. Gleerup, 1945. **Maag, Victor.** *Hiob. Wandlung und Verarbeitung des Problems in Novelle, Dialogdichtung und Spätfassungen.* FRLANT 128. Göttingen: Vandenhoeck & Ruprecht, 1982. **MacDonald, Duncan Black.** "Some External Evidence on the Original Form of the Legend of Job." *AJSL* 14 (1897–98) 137–63. ———. "The Original Form of the Legend of Job." *JBL* 14 (1895) 63–71. **Müller, Hans-Peter.** *Das Hiobproblem: seine Stellung und Entstehung im alten Orient und im Alten Testament.* Erträge des Forschung 84. Darmstadt: Wissenschaftliche Buchgesellschaft, 1978; 3rd ed. 1995. ———. *Hiob und seine Freunde: Traditionsgeschichtliches zum Verständnis des Hiobbuches.* Theologische Studien 103. Zurich: EVZ-Verlag, 1970. **Oesterley, W. O. E., and T. H. Robinson.** "The Three Stages of the Book." In *The Dimensions of Job: A Study and Selected Readings.* Ed. Nahum H. Glatzer. New York: Schocken Books, 1969. 214–17 [pp. 175–78 reprinted from their *An Introduction to the Books of the Old Testament.* London: SPCK, 1934]. **Pfeiffer, R. H.** "Edomitic Wisdom." *ZAW* 3 (1926) 13–24. **Reddy, M. P.** "The Book of Job—A Reconstruction." *ZAW* 90 (1978) 59–94. **Reventlow, Henning Graf.** "Skepsis und Klage. Zur Komposition des Hiobbuches." In *Verbindungslinien: Festschrift für Werner H. Schmidt zum 65. Geburtstag.* Ed. Axel Graupner, Holger Delkurt, and Alexander B. Ernst. Neukirchen–Vluyn: Neukirchener Verlag, 2000. 281–94. **Roper, L. A.** "The Social Context of the Book of Job." *VerbEccl* 26 (2005) 756–72. **Sarna, Nahum M.** "Epic Substratum in the Prose of Job." *JBL* 76 (1957) 13–15. **Schwienhorst-Schönberger, Ludger, and Georg Steins.** "Zur Entstehung, Gestalt und Bedeutung der Ijob-Erzählung (Ijob 1f; 42)." *BZ* ns 33 (1989) 1–24. **Stockton, E.** "Literary Development of the Book of Job." *AusCathRec* 49 (1972) 137–43. **Studer, G. L.** "Über die Integrität des Buches Hiob." *JPTh* 1 (1875) 688–723. **Terrien, S. L.** "Le poème de Job: drame para-rituel du nouvel-an?" In *Congress Volume. Rome 1968.* VTSup 17. Leiden: E. J. Brill, 1969. 220–35. **Thils, G.** "De genere litterario et fontibus libri Job." *ColctMech* 31 (1946) 37–40. **Torczyner, H. [Tur-Sinai, N. H.].** "Hiobdichtung und Hiobsage." *MGWJ* 69 (1925) 234–48, 717–33. **Vermeylen, J.** *Job, ses amis et son Dieu. La légende de Job et ses relectures postexiliques.* Studia biblica 2. Leiden: E. J. Brill, 1981. **Voorst, Dirk Cornelis van.** *De oudheid van het boek Job verdedigd, tegen Hufnagel en Doederlein.* Amsterdam, 1798. **Wahl, Harald Martin.** "Noah, Daniel und Hiob in Ezechiel xiv 12–20 (21–23): Anmerkungen zum traditionsgeschichtlichen Hintergrund." *VT* 42 (1992) 542–53. **Weimar, Peter.** "Literarkritisches zur Ijobnovelle." *BN* 12 (1980) 62–80. **Whybray, R. N.** "The Social World of the Wisdom Writers." In *The World of Ancient Israel: Sociological, Anthropological, and Political Perspectives.* Ed. R. E. Clements. Cambridge: Cambridge University Press, 1989. 227–50. **Wolfers, David.** "The Speech-Cycles in the Book of Job" [critique of conjectured third cycle]. *VT* 43 (1993) 385–402.

10. DATE AND AUTHORSHIP

Anon. "Job a-t-il existé? Son livre n'est-il qu'un conte pieux pour montrer un beau modèle de patience?" *AmiCl* 53 (1936) 131–33. **Bachar, Shlomo.** "על מועד כתיבת ספר איוב [When Was the Book of Job Written?]." *BMik* 76 (1978–79) 75–76, 122. **Barth, Jakob.** *Die Entstehungszeit des Buches Hiob.* Jahres-Bericht des Rabbiner-Seminars zu Berlin. Berlin: Rabbiner-Seminar, 1876 [= *Die Entstehungszeit des Buches Hiob: Beiträge zur Erklärung des Buches Job.* Leipzig, 1876]. **Beel, A.** "Auctor et tempus conscriptionis libri Job. Analysis libri Job. De indole libri Job." *ColBG* 33 (1922) 189–93, 241–47, 268–70. **Berger, Haim.** "האם היתה חורן מולדתו של איוב [Was Hauran the Birthplace of Job?]." *BMik* 53 (1973) 228–29, 274. **Beveridge, H.** "The Date of the Book of Job." *JRAS* (1919) 234. **Brenner, Athalya.** "The Language of the Book of Job as an Index to the Time of Its Composition" [Heb.].

BMik 24 (1978) 396–405. **Dhorme, E.** "Le pays de Job." *RB* 20 (1911) 102–7. **Endemann, K.** "Über den Verfasser des Buches Hiob." *Nach den Gesetz und Zeugnis* 26 (1926) 127–36. **Hurvitz, Avi.** "לשׁוּוּ שֶׁל סִיפּוּר־הַמִסגָרת בספר איוב במקומה בתולדות העברית המוראית." *RethM* 20 (1974–75) 457–72 [= "The Date of the Prose-Tale of Job Linguistically Re-considered." *HTR* 67 (1974) 17–34]. **Isaacson, Israel.** *Job. Is the Book Canonical?* London, c. 1905. **Knight, George Alexander Francis.** "The Egyptian Origin of the Book of Job." In his *Nile and Jordan: Being the Archaeological and Historical Inter-Relations between Egypt and Canaan from the Earliest Times to the Fall of Jerusalem in A.D. 70.* London: J. Clarke, 1921. 379–405. **Lévêque, Jean.** "La datation du livre de Job." In *Congress Volume: Vienna 1980.* VTSup 32. Ed. J. A. Emerton. Leiden: Brill, 1981. 206–19. **Ley, J.** "Die Abfassungszeit des Buches Hiob. Eine Abhandlung." *TSK* 71 (1898) 34–70. **Maisler, B.** *The Genealogy of the Sons of Nahor and the Historical Background of the Book of Job.* Jerusalem: Zion, 1946. **Naish, J. P.** "The Book of Job and the Early Persian Period." *ExpT* 9 (1925) 34–39, 94–104. **Pfeiffer, R. H.** "The Priority of Job over Is. 40–55." *JBL* 46 (1927) 202–6. **Richter, Carl Friedrich.** *De aetate libri Iobi definienda.* Leipzig, 1799. **Schmitt, G.** "Die Heimat Hiobs." *ZDPV* 101 (1985) 56–63. **Seyring, Friedrich.** *Die Abhängigkeit der Sprüche Salomos Kap. i–ix von Hiob auf Grund des Sprachlichen und Realen.* Halle a.S.: C. A. Kaemmerer, 1889. **Slotki, Judah J.** "The Origin of the Book of Job." *ExpT* 39 (1927–28) 131–34. **Strack, Hermann.** "Die Priorität des Buches Hiob gegenüber den Einleitungsreden zu den Sprüchen Salomons." In *Studien und Kritiken.* Berlin, 1896. **Vargon, Shmuel.** "The Date of Composition of the Book of Job in the Context of S. D. Luzzatto's Attitude to Biblical Criticism." *JQR* 91 (2001) 377–94. **Weinberg, J.** "Was Elihu, the Son of Berachel, the Author of the Book of Job? A Hypothesis." *Transeuphratène* 16 (1998) 149–66. **Williams, Walter George.** "Relative Dating of Additions to Job." *Iliff Review* 17 (1960) 11–14.

11. THE ANCIENT LITERARY CONTEXT

a. The Hebrew Bible

Altheim, Franz, and Ruth Stiehl. "Hiob und die prophetische Überlieferung." In their *Geschichte Mittelasiens im Altertum.* Berlin: de Gruyter, 1970. 131–42. **André, Gunnel.** "Deuterojesaja och Jobsboken: En jämförande studie." *SEÅ* 54 (1989) 33–42. **Bachar, S.** "The Significance of the Reflections of Proverbs in Job." *BMik* 25 (1980) 349–55. **Bastiaens, Jean Charles.** "The Language of Suffering in Job 16–19 and in the Suffering Servant Passages in Deutero-Isaiah." *In Studies in the Book of Isaiah.* Ed. J. van Ruiten and M. Vervenne. BETL 132. Leuven: Leuven University Press, 1997. 421–32. **Beerta, J.** *Ecclesiastes of de Prediker: benevens eenige natuur- en dichtkundige spreuken uit het Boek Job, verkort in dichtmaat gebragt.* Groningen: Wouters, 1814. **Bjerkem-Hirtz, Emmanuelle.** *Ijob und Sprichwörter.* Stuttgart: Katholisches Bibelwerk, 1999. **Boorer, Suzanne.** "A Matter of Life and Death: A Comparison of Proverbs 1–9 and Job." In *Prophets and Paradigms: Essays in Honor of Gene M. Tucker.* Ed. Stephen Breck Reid. JSOTSup 229. Sheffield: Sheffield Academic Press, 1996. 187–204. **Branch, R. G.** "Space for Joy: Another Look at the Book of Job and Job Himself in the Light of Some Principles of Wisdom Literature." *JSem* 14 (2005) 384–412. **Bruston, E.** "La littérature sapientiale dans le livre de Job." *ETR* 3 (1928) 297–305. **Caquot, André.** "Traits royaux dans le personnage de Job." In *maqqél shâqédh, La branche d'amandier. Hommage à Wilhelm Vischer.* Montpellier: Causse, Graille, Castelnau, 1960. 32–45. **Cheyne, T. K.** *Job and Solomon, or, The Wisdom of the Old Testament.* London: Kegan Paul, Trench, 1887. **Cooper, Alan M.** "The Suffering Servant and Job: A View from the Sixteenth Century." In *"As those who are taught": The Interpretation of Isaiah from the LXX to the SBL.* Ed. Claire Mathews McGinnis and Patricia K. Tull. SBL Symposium Series 27. Atlanta: Society of Biblical Literature, 2006. 189–200. **Corey, Michael Anthony.** *Job, Jonah, and the Unconscious: A Psychological Interpretation of Evil and Spiritual Growth in the Old Testament.* Lanham, MD:

University Press of America, 1995. **Crenshaw, James L.** "The Wisdom Literature." In *The Hebrew Bible and Its Modern Interpreters.* Ed. Douglas A. Knight and Gene M. Tucker. Philadelphia: Fortress Press, 1985. 369–407. **Crüsemann, F.** "Hiob und Kohelet: Ein Beitrag zum Verständnis des Hiobbuches." In *Werden und Wirken des Alten Testaments. Festschrift C. Westermann.* Ed. R. Albertz. Göttingen: Vandenhoeck & Ruprecht, 1980. 373–93. **Curtis, John B.** "Elihu and Deutero-Isaiah: A Study in Literary Dependence." *PrGLM* 10 (1990). Ed. Terrance Callan. 31–38.

Davidson, Jo Ann. "Even If Noah, Daniel, and Job" (Ezekiel 14:14, 20)–Why These Three?" *Journal of the Adventist Theological Society* 12 (2001) 132–44. **Delcor, M.** "Les sources du Deutéro-Zacharie et ses procédés d'emprunt." *RB* 59 (1952) 385–411 (390–92). **Dewey, Rosemary.** "Qoheleth and Job: Diverse Responses to the Enigma of Evil." *Spirituality Today* 37 (1985) 314–25. **Dhorme, E.** "Ecclésiaste ou Job?" *RB* 32 (1922) 5–27. **Egger-Wenzel, Renate.** "Der Gebrauch von TMM bei Ijob und Ben Sira: ein Vergleich zweier Weisheitsbucher." In *Freundschaft bei Ben Sira: Beiträge des Symposions zu Ben Sira, Salzburg, 1995.* Ed. Friedrich V. Reiterer. BZAW 244. Berlin: Walter de Gruyter, 1996. 203–38. ———. "'Faith in God' rather than 'Fear of God' in Ben Sira and Job: A Necessary Adjustment in Terminology and Understanding." In *Intertextual Studies in Ben Sira and Tobit: Essays in Honor of Alexander A. Di Lella, O.F.M.* Ed. Jeremy Corley and Vincent Skemp. Washington, DC: Catholic Biblical Association of America, 2005. 211–26. **Eskenazi, Tamara Cohn.** "Song of Songs as an 'Answer' to Clines's Book of Job." In *Reading from Right to Left: Essays on the Hebrew Bible in Honour of David J. A. Clines.* Ed. J. Cheryl Exum and H. G. M. Williamson. JSOTSup 373. London: Sheffield Academic Press, 2003. 128–40. **Festorazzi, F.** "Giobbe e Qohelet: crisi della sapienza." In *Problemi e prospettive di scienze bibliche.* Ed. Rinaldo Fabris. Brescia: Queriniana, 1981. 233–58. **Fishbane, Michael.** "The Book of Job and Inner-Biblical Discourse." In *The Voice from the Whirlwind: Interpreting the Book of Job.* Ed. Leo G. Perdue and Clark Gilpin. Nashville: Abingdon Press, 1992. 86–98. **Frye, J. B.** "The Use of Pentateuchal Traditions in the Book of Job." *OTWSA* 17–18 (1977) 13–20. **Fuchs, G.** "»Du bist mir zum Trugbach geworden.« Verwandte Motive in den Konfessionen Jeremias und den Klagen Hiobs." *BZ* 41 (1997) 212–28; 42 (1998) 19–38. ———. "Die Klage des Propheten. Beobachtungen zu den Konfessionen Jeremias im Vergleich mit den Klagen Hiobs (Erster Teil)." *BZ* NF 41 (1997) 212–28. **Fuente Adanez, Alfonso de la.** "Job y el siervo de Yahvé: Dos interpretaciones del sufrimiento." *RevEspTeol* 51 (1991) 237–51.

Gese, Hartmut. *Lehre und Wirklichkeit in der alten Weisheit. Studien zu den Sprüchen Salomos und zu dem Buche Hiob.* Tübingen: Mohr, 1958. ———. "Wisdom Literature in the Persian Period." In *The Cambridge History of Judaism.* Ed. W. D. Davies and Louis Finkelstein. Cambridge: Cambridge University Press, 1984. 189–218. **Gordis, Robert.** "Wisdom and Job." In *Old Testament Issues.* Ed. S. Sandmel. London: SCM Press, 1969. 213–41 [= his *The Book of God and Man: A Study of Job.* Chicago: University of Chicago Press, 1965. 31–52]. **Goshen-Gottstein, M. H.** "Ezekiel und Ijob. Zur Problemgeschichte von Bundestheologie und Gott–Mensch-Verhältnis." In *Wort, Lied und Gottesspruch. Festschrift für Joseph Ziegler.* Ed. Josef Schreiner. Würzburg: Echter Verlag, 1972. 2:155–70. **Green, Douglas J.** "The Good, the Bad and the Better: Psalm 23 and Job." In *The Whirlwind: Essays on Job, Hermeneutics and Theology in Memory of Jane Morse.* Ed. Stephen L. Cook, Corrine L. Patton, and James W. Watts. JSOTSup 336. Sheffield: Sheffield Academic Press, 2001. 69–83. **Greenstein, Edward L.** "Jeremiah as an Inspiration to the Poet of Job." In *Inspired Speech: Prophecy in the Ancient Near East. Essays in Honor of Herbert B. Huffmon.* Ed. J. Kaltner and Louis Stulman. London: T. & T. Clark, 2004. 98–110. **Hamilton, Mark W.** "Critiquing the Sovereign. Perspectives from Deuteronomy and Job." *RestQ* 47 (2005) 237–49. **Holmgren, F.** "Barking Dogs Never Bite, except Now and Then: Proverbs and Job." *ATR* 61 (1969) 341–53. **Japhet, Sara.** "The Trial of Abraham and the Test of Job: How Do They Differ?" *Henoch* 16 (1994) 153–72. **Johnson, L. D.** *Israel's Wisdom: Learn and Live.* Nashville: Broadman Press, 1975. **Kidner, Derek.** *Wisdom* *to Live By: An Introduction to the Old Testament's Wisdom Books of Proverbs, Job and Ecclesiastes, with Some Notes on the Teachings of Israel's Neighbours and of the Old Testament Apocrypha.* Leicester: Inter-Varsity Press, 1985. **Köster, Friedrich Burchard.** *Das Buch Hiob und der Prediger Salomo's nach ihrer strophischen Anordnung übersetzt. Nebst Abhandlungen über den strophischen Character dieser Bücher. Zum Gebrauche bey akademischen Vorlesungen.* Schleswig: Königliches Taubstummen-Institut, 1831. **Kreeft, Peter.** *Three Philosophies of Life: Ecclesiastes—Life as Vanity, Job—Life as Suffering, Song of Songs—Life as Love.* San Francisco: Ignatius Press, 1989. **Kuenen, A.** "Job en de lijdende knecht van Jahveh." *TTijd* 7 (1873) 540–41. **Lewis, Andrew Zack.** *The Second Adam: The Intertextual Relationship between the Prologue to Job and Genesis 1–3.* Diss. Regent College, 2005.

Mack, Ulrich. *O Herr! Psalmen und Weisheitsschriften.* Stuttgarter Bibelkurs. Stuttgart: Deutsche Bibelgesellschaft, 1988. **MacKenzie, R. A. F.** "The Cultural and Religious Background of the Book of Job." *Conc* 169 (1983) 3–7. **Maggioni, Bruno.** *Giobbe e Qohelet, la contestazione sapienziale nella Bibbia.* Assisi: Cittadella, 1979 [= *Job y Cohélet: la contestación sapiencial en la Biblia.* Bilbao: Desclée de Brouwer, 1993]. **Mandolfo, Carleen.** "A Generic Renegade: A Dialogic Reading of Job and Lament Psalms." In *Diachronic and Synchronic: Reading the Psalms in Real Time. Proceedings of the Baylor Symposium on the Book of Psalms.* Ed. Joel S. Burnett, W. H. Bellinger, Jr, and W. Dennis Tucker, Jr. LHB/OTS 488. London: T. & T. Clark International, 2008. 45–66. **McDonagh, Kathleen.** "Job and Jeremiah: Their Approach to God." *TBT* 18 (1980) 331–35. **Michel, Andreas.** "Ijob und Abraham. Zur Rezeption von Gen 22 in Ijob 1–2 und 42,7–17." In *Gott, Mensch, Sprache. Schülerfestschrift für Walter Gross zum 60. Geburtstag.* Ed. Andreas Michel and Hermann-Josef Stipp. ATSAT 58. St Ottilien: EOS Verlag, 2001. 73–98. **Neher, André.** "Au-delà de l'épreuve: Job et Abraham: des épreuves identiques." In המקרא והתולדות ישראל. *Studies in Bible and Jewish History Dedicated to the Memory of Jacob Liver.* Ed. B. Uffenheimer. Tel Aviv: University of Tel Aviv, 1971/72. 124–28, xvi. **Nestle, E.** "David in the Book of Job." *ExpT* 22 (1910) 90. **Newsom, Carol A.** "Job and Ecclesiastes." In *Old Testament Interpretation, Past, Present and Future. Essays in Honour of Gene M. Tucker.* Ed. James Luther Mays, David L. Petersen, and Kent Harold Richards. Nashville: Abingdon Press, 1995. 177–94. **Noth, M.** "Noah, Daniel und Hiob in Ezekiel xiv." *VT* 1 (1950) 251–60. **Oberforcher, Robert.** "Abraham, Jeremia, Ijob. Typen des von Gott beanspruchtens Menschen." *BLit* 52 (1979) 183–91. **Perdue, Leo G.** "Cosmology and Social Order in the Wisdom Tradition." In *The Sage in Israel and the Ancient Near East.* Ed. John G. Gammie and Leo G. Perdue. Winona Lake, IN: Eisenbrauns, 1990. 457–78. **Pfeiffer, R. H.** "The Dual Origin of Hebrew Monotheism" [Job and Deutero-Isaiah]. *JBL* 46 (1927) 202–6.

Ravasi, Gianfranco. "'Le lacrime da nessuno consolate.' Il giusto sofferente in Giobbe e Qohelet." *ParSpV* 34 (1996) 85–95. **Reiterer, Friedrich V.** "Das Verhältnis Ijobs und Ben Siras." In *The Book of Job.* Ed. W. A. M. Beuken. BETL 114. Leuven: Leuven University Press, 1994. 405–29. **Roberts, J. J. M.** "Job and the Israelite Religious Tradition." *ZAW* 89 (1977) 107–14. **Robertson, David.** "Job and Ecclesiastes." *Soundings* 73 (1990) 257–72. **Rodríguez Ochoa, J. M.** "Estudio de la dimensión temporal en Proverbios, Job y Qohélet. El eterno volvar a comenzar en Qohélet." *EstBíb* 22 (1963) 33–67. **Ruiten, Jacques van.** "Abraham, Job and the Book of Jubilees: The Intertextual Relationship of Genesis 22:1–19, Job 1:1–2:13 and Jubilees 17:15–18:19." In *The Sacrifice of Isaac: The Aqedah (Genesis 22) and Its Interpretations.* Ed. Edward Noort and Eibert Tigchelaar. Themes in Biblical Narrative. Jewish and Christian Traditions 4. Leiden: E. J. Brill, 2002. 58–85. **Sanders, James A.** "Comparative Wisdom: l'oeuvre [Samuel] Terrien." In *Israelite Wisdom: Theological and Literary Essays in Honor of Samuel Terrien.* Ed. John G. Gammie. Missoula, MT: Scholars Press, 1978. 3–14. **Segal, M. Z.** המקבילות ספר איוב [Parallels to the Book of Job]." *Tarb* 20 (1949) 35–48. **Seyring, Friedrich.** *Die Abhängigkeit der Sprüche Salomos Kap. i–ix von Hiob auf Grund des Sprachlichen und Realen.* Halle a.S.: C. A. Kaemmerer, 1889. **Shapiro, D. S.** "The Book of Job and the Trial of Abraham." *Tradition* 4 (1962) 210–20. **Skorka, Abraham.** "Job y el Eclesiastes." *CuadTe* 23 (2004) 23–30. **Smith, David L.** "The Concept of Death in Job and Ecclesiastes." *Didaskalia*

4/1 (1992) 2–14. **Smith, Gary V.** "Is There a Place for Job's Wisdom in Old Testament Theology?" *TrinJ* 13 (1992) 3–20. **Spiegel, Shalom.** "Noah, Daniel and Job: Touching on Canaanite Relics in the Legends of the Jews." In *Louis Ginzberg Jubilee Volume. On the Occasion of His Seventieth Birthday.* New York: American Academy for Jewish Research, 1945. 1:305–35.
Terrien, S. "Quelques remarques sur les affinités de Job avec le Deutéro-Esaïe." In *Vol·ume du Congrès: Genève 1965.* VTSup 15. Leiden: E. J. Brill, 1965. 295–310. **Thieberger, F.** "Jona, Hiob, und das Problem der Gerechtigkeit." *Der Morgen* 2 (1926) 128–40. **Vawter, Bruce.** *Job and Jonah: Questioning the Hidden God.* New York: Paulist Press, 1985. **Veijola, Timo.** "Abraham und Hiob. Das literarische und theologische Verhältnis von Gen 22 und der Hiob-Novelle." In his *Offenbarung und Anfechtung. Hermeneutisch-theologische Studien zum Alten Testament.* Ed. Walter Dietrich and Marko Marttila. Biblisch-theologische Studien 89. Neukirchen–Vluyn: Neukirchener Verlag, 2007. 134–57. **Vinton, Patricia.** "Radical Aloneness: Job and Jeremiah." *TBT* 99 (1978) 143–49. **Whybray, R. N.** *Two Jewish Theologies: Job and Ecclesiastes.* Hull: University of Hull, 1980. **Wittenberg, G. H.** "Job the Farmer: The Judean *am-haretz* and the Wisdom Movement." *OTEss* 4 (1991) 151–70. **Zenger, Erich.** "Die späte Weisheit und das Gesetz." In *Literatur und Religion des Frühjudentums: Eine Einführung.* Ed. Johann Maier and Josef Schreiner. Würzburg: Echter Verlag, 1973. 43–56. **Ziener, G.** "Die altorientalische Weisheit als Lebenskunde: Israels neues Verständnis und Kritik der Weisheit." In *Wort und Botschaft: Eine theologische und kritische Einführung in die Probleme des Alten Testaments.* Ed. J. Schreiner. Würzburg: Echter Verlag, 1967. 258–71. **Zoller, J.** "Giobbe e il servo di Dio." *RicR* 8 (1932) 223–33.

b. The Ancient Near East

Albertson, R. G. "Job and Ancient Near Eastern Wisdom Literature." In *Scripture in Context.* II. Ed. W. W. Hallo, J. Moyer, and L. Perdue. Winona Lake, IN: Eisenbrauns, 1983. 213–30. **Albertz, R.** "Der sozialgeschichtliche Hintergrund des Hiobbuches und der 'Babylonischen Theodizee' [*Ludlul bēl nēmeqi*]." In *Die Botschaft und die Boten. Festschrift für Hans Walter Wolff.* Ed. J. Jeremias and L. Perlitt. Neukirchen–Vluyn: Neukirchener Verlag, 1981. 349–72. **Assmann, Jan.** "Der 'leidende Gerechte' im alten Ägypten: zum Konflikt-potential der ägyptischen Religion." In *Loyalitätskonflikte in der Religionsgeschichte: Festschrift für Carsten Colpe.* Ed. Christoph Elsas and Hans G. Kippenberg. Würzburg: Königshausen & Neumann, 1990. 203–24. **Ayuso Marazuela, T.** "Los elementos extrabíblicos de Job y del Salterio." *EstBib* 5 (1946) 429–58. **Baldacci, Massimo.** "Studi ugaritici e poesia biblica." *BeO* 32 (1990) 95–101. **Blumenthal, Elke.** "Hiob und die Harfnerlieder." *TLZ* 115 (1990) 721–30. **Craigie, Peter C.** "Job and Ugaritic Studies." In *Studies in the Book of Job.* Ed. W. E. Aufrecht. SRSup 16. Waterloo, Ont.: Wilfrid Laurier University Press, 1985. 28–35. **David, M.** "Travaux et service dans l'Epopée de Gilgamesh et le livre de Job." *RevPhil* 147 (1957) 341–49. **Davies, William Walter.** "Job of the Cuneiform Inscriptions." *MethRev* 89 (1907) 307–10. **Dick, Michael B.** "The Neo-Assyrian Royal Lion Hunt and Yahweh's Answer to Job." *JBL* 125 (2006) 243–70. **Dion, P.-E.** "Un nouvel éclairage [Fekherye] sur le contexte culturel des malheurs de Job." *VT* 34 (1984) 213–15. **Feinberg, C. L.** "The Poetic Structure of the Book of Job and the Ugaritic Literature." *BSac* 103 (1946) 283–92. **Ferguson, Paul.** "Nebuchadnezzar, Gilgamesh, and the 'Babylonian Job'." *JETS* 37 (1994) 321–32. **Finkelstein, C.** "ספר איוב וחכמה המזרח הקדמון [The Book of Job and the Wisdom of the Ancient Near East]." *BMik* 51 (1972) 428–38, 532. **Fohrer, G.** "4QOrNab, 11QTgJob und die Hioblegende." *ZAW* 34 (1963) 93–97. **Fuchs, Gisela.** *Mythos und Hiobdichtung: Aufnahme und Umdeutung altorientalischer Vorstellungen.* Stuttgart: W. Kohlhammer, 1993.
García de la Fuente, O. "La prosperidad del malvado en el libro de Job y en los poemas babilónicas del 'Justo Paciente'." *EstEcl* 34 (1960) 603–16. **Gray, J.** "The Book

of Job in the Context of Near Eastern Literature." *ZAW* 82 (1970) 251–69. **Griffiths, John G.** "The Idea of Posthumous Judgement in Israel and Egypt." In *Fontes atque pontes. Eine Festgabe für H. Brunner.* Ed. M. Görg. Wiesbaden: Harrassowitz, 1983. 186–204. **Handy, Lowell K.** "The Authorization of Divine Power and the Guilt of God in the Book of Job: Useful Ugaritic Parallels." *JSOT* 60 (1993) 107–18. **Hoffman, Yair.** "Ancient Near Eastern Literary Conventions and the Restoration of the Book of Job." *ZAW* 103 (1991) 399–411. ———. "The Book of Job as a Trial: A Perspective from a Comparison to Some Relevant Ancient Near Eastern Texts." In *Das Buch Hiob und seine Interpretationen: Beiträge zum Hiob-Symposium auf dem Monte Verità vom 14.–19. August 2005.* Ed. Thomas Krüger, Manfred Oeming, Konrad Schmid, and Christoph Uehlinger. ATANT 88. Zurich: Theologische Verlag Zürich, 2007. 21–31. **Hoop, Raymond de.** "The Frame Story of the Book of Job: Prose or Verse? Job 1:1–5 as a Test Case." In *Layout Markers in Biblical Manuscripts and Ugaritic Tablets.* Ed. Marjo C. A. Korpel and Josef M. Oesch. Pericope 5. Assen: Van Gorcum, 2005. 40–77. **Horne, Charles F.** *The Ancient Babylonian Story of Job.* Whitefish, MT: Kessinger Publishing [= *Sacred Books and Early Literature of the East.* 1. *Babylonia and Assyria.* New York: Parke, Austin, & Lipscomb, 1917]. **Hoyos, H.** "Un texto original de los Sumerios con entonaciones del libro de Job." *RBibIt* 1 (1956) 36–37. **Humbert, Paul.** *Recherches sur les sources égyptiennes de la littérature sapientiale d'Israël.* Mémoires de l'Université de Neuchâtel 7. Neuchâtel: Secrétariat de l'Université, 1929. **Israel, Saul.** "Hiob: Prometheus in Judäa." *Antaios* 9 (1967) 369–84 [= "Giobbe, Prometeo in Giudea." In *Miscellanea di studi in memoria di D. Disegni.* Ed. M. E. Artom. Turin: Istituto di Studi Ebraici, 1969]. **Jastrow, Morris.** "A Babylonian Parallel to the Story of Job." *JBL* 25 (1906) 135–91. **Keller, Sharon R.** "Written Communications between the Human and Divine Spheres in Mesopotamia and Israel." In *The Biblical Canon in Comparative Perspective.* Ed. K. Lawson Younger, Jr, William W. Hallo, and Bernard F. Batto. Scripture in Context 4. Lewiston, NY: E. Mellen Press, 1983. 299–313. **Knieschke, Wilhelm.** *Kultur- und Geisteswelt des Buches Hiob.* Zeit- und Streitfragen des Glaubens, der Weltanschauung und Bibelforschung 15/9–12. Berlin–Lichterfelde: E. Runge, 1925. **Kramer, Samuel Noah.** "Man and His God: A Sumerian Variation on the 'Job' Motif." In *Wisdom in Israel and in the Ancient Near East, Presented to Professor Harold Henry Rowley.* VTSup 3. Ed. M. Noth and D. Winton Thomas. Leiden: E. J. Brill, 1955. 170–82. **Krieger, Paul.** *Weltbild und Idee des Buches Hiob, verglichen mit dem altorientalischen Pessimismus.* Leipzig: Schwarzenberg & Schumann, 1930.

Landersdorfer, Simon. *Eine babylonische Quelle für das Buch Job? Eine literar-geschichtliche Studie.* Biblische Studien 16,2. Freiburg i.Br.: Herder, 1911. **Lévêque, Jean.** "Le thême du juste souffrant en Mésopotamie et la problématique du livre de Job." *Graphè* 6 (1997) 11–33. **Limet, H.** "La pensée religieuse des sumériens et le Livre de Job." *Transeuphratène* 22 (2001) 115–27. **Loffreda, S.** "Raffronto fra un testo ugaritico (*2 Aqhat VI, 42–25*) e Giobbe 40, 9–12." *BibOr* 8 (1966) 103–16. **Mack-Fisher, Loren R.** "The Scribe (and Sage) in the Royal Court at Ugarit." In *The Sage in Israel and the Ancient Near East.* Ed. John G. Gammie and Leo G. Perdue. Winona Lake, IN: Eisenbrauns, 1990. 109–15. **Magdalene, F. Rachel.** "The ANE Legal Origins of Impairment as Theological Disability and the Book of Job." *PerspRelSt* 34 (2007) 23–60. ———. "Who Is Job's Redeemer? Job 19:25 in Light of Neo-Babylonian Law." *ZAR* 10 (2004) 292–316. ———. *On the Scales of Righteousness: Neo-Babylonian Trial Law and the Book of Job.* Brown Judaic Studies 348. Providence, RI: Brown Judaic Studies, 2007. **Matthews, Victor H., and Don C. Benjamin.** "Job, Ecclesiastes; Declarations of Innocence." In *Old Testament Parallels: Laws and Stories from the Ancient Near East.* New York: Paulist Press, 2006. **Mattingly, Gerald L.** "The Pious Sufferer: Mesopotamia's Traditional Theodicy and Job's Counselors." In *The Bible in Light of Cuneiform Literature.* Ed. William W. Hallo. Scripture in Context 3. Lewiston, NY: Mellen, 1990. 305–48. **Moor, Johannes C. de.** "Ugarit and the Origin of Job." In *Ugarit and the Bible: Proceedings of the International Symposium on Ugarit and the Bible, Manchester, September 1992.* Ed. George Brooke, Adrian H. W. Curtis, and John F. Healey. Ugaritisch-biblische Literatur 11. Münster: Ugarit-Verlag, 1994. 225–57. **Moran, W. L.** "Rib-Hadda: Job at Byblos?" In *Biblical and Related Studies Presented to Samuel Iwry*. Ed. Ann Kort and Scott Morschauer. Winona Lake, IN: Eisenbrauns, 1985. 173–81. **Müller, Hans-Peter.** *Das Hiobproblem: seine Stellung und Entstehung im alten Orient und im Alten Testament.* Erträge des Forschung 84. Darmstadt: Wissenschaftliche Buchgesellschaft, 1978; 3rd ed. 1995. ———. "Die Hiobrahmenerzählung und ihre altorientalischen Parallelen als Paradigmen einer weisheitlichen Wirklichkeitswahrnahme." In *The Book of Job*. Ed. W. A. M. Beuken. BETL 114. Leuven: Leuven University Press, 1994. 21–39. ———. "Keilschriftliche Parallelen zum biblische Hiobbuche. Möglichkeit und Grenze das Vergleichs." *Or* ns 47 (1978) 360–75 [= his *Mythos—Kerygma—Wahrheit: Gesammelte Aufsätze zum Alten Testament in seiner Umwelt und zur biblischen Theologie.* BZAW 200. Berlin: W. de Gruyter, 1991. 136–51; *Babylonien und Israel: Historische, religiöse und sprachliche Beziehungen.* Ed. Hans-Peter Müller. Wege der Forschung 633. Darmstadt: Wissenschaftliche Buchgesellschaft, 1991. 400–419]. **Murberg, Johan.** *Jobus ad res ægyptias alludens.* Uppsala, 1763. **Murtagh, J.** "The Book of Job and the Book of the Dead." *ITQ* 35 (1968) 166–73.

Negoiţă, A. "Un Iov babilonean? Ceva din teodicea akkadiana." *StTh* 29 (1977) 436–49. **Nougayrol, J.** "(Juste) souffrant (R.S. 25.460)." *Ugaritica* 5 (1968) 265–83. ———. "Une version ancienne du 'juste souffrant'." *RB* 59 (1952) 237–50. **O'Connor, Daniel J.** "The Keret Legend and the Prologue–Epilogue of Job." *ITQ* 55 (1989) 1–6. **Preuss, Horst Dietrich.** "Jahwes Antwort an Hiob und die sogenannte Hiobliteratur des alten Vorderen Orients." In *Beiträge zum alttestamentlichen Theologie: Festschrift für W. Zimmerli zum 70. Geburtstag.* Ed. Herbert Donner, Robert Hanhart, and Rudolf Smend. Göttingen: Vandenhoeck & Ruprecht, 1977. 323–43. **Schmökel, H.** "Hiob in Sumer." *FF* 30 (1956) 74–76. **Schneider, Thomas.** "Hiob 38 und die demotische Weisheit (Papyrus Insinger 24)." *TZ* 47 (1991) 108–24. **Sedlmeier, Franz.** "Ijob und die Auseinandersetzungsliteratur im alten Mesopotamien." In *Das Buch Ijob: Gesamtdeutungen—Einzeltexte—zentrale Themen.* Ed. Theodor Seidl and Stephanie Ernst. Österreichische biblische Studien 31. Frankfurt: Peter Lang, 2007. 85–136. **Speiser, E. A.** "The Case of the Obliging Servant." *JCS* 8 (1954) 98–105. **Terrien, S. L.** "The Babylonian Dialogue on Theodicy and the Book of Job." *JBL* 63 (1944) vi. **Toorn, Karel van der.** "The Ancient Near Eastern Literary Dialogue as a Vehicle of Critical Reflection." In *Dispute Poems and Dialogues in the Ancient and Mediaeval Near East: Forms and Types of Literary Debates in Semitic and Related Literatures.* Ed. G. L. Reinink and H. L. J. Vanstiphout. OLA 42. Leuven: Departement oriëntalistiek, 1991. 59–75. **Weinfeld, Moshe.** "Job and Its Mesopotamian Parallels—A Typological Analysis." In *Text and Context: Old Testament and Semitic Studies for F. C. Fensham.* Ed. W. Claassen. JSOTSup 48. Sheffield: JSOT Press, 1988. 217–25. **Williams, R. J.** "Theodicy in the Ancient Near East." *CJT* 2 (1956) 14–26. **Wiseman, D. J.** "A New Text of the Babylonian Poem of the Righteous Sufferer." *AnatSt* 30 (1980) 101–7.

c. Greek Literature

Alvárez de Miranda, A. "Job y Prometeo, o religión y irreligión." *Anthologia annua* 2 (1954) 207–37. **Biese, Alfred.** "Prometheus, Hiob und Faust." *Allgemeine Zeitung*, November 8, 1883. **Bussler, E.** *Hiob und Prometheus, zwei Vorkämpfer der göttlicher Gerechtigkeit.* Hamburg: J. F. Richter, 1897. **Claassens, Juliana M.** "A Dialogue of Voices: Job, Socrates and the Quest for Understanding." *OTEss* 19 (2006) 106–23. **Edwards, Cliff.** "Trespassing a Monument: A Lacanian Visit to Uz" [Job and Oedipus]. *Religious Education* 85 (1990) 279–94. **Friedländer, Moritz.** *Griechische Philosophie im Alten Testament. Eine Einleitung in die Psalmen- und Weisheitsliteratur: Psalmen, Proverbien, Hiob, Koheleth, Sirach, Pseudo-Salomo, und Anhang der Bücher Jona und Ruth; mit kritischen Anmerkungen, Nachweisen und Zitaten.* Berlin: G. Reimer, [= 1904 [repr. Amsterdam: Philo Press, c. 1974]. **Fries, Karl.** *Das philosophische Gespräch von Hiob bis Plato.* Tübingen: J.

C. B. Mohr, 1904. **Hidal, Sten.** "Israel och hellas: två världar eller en enda verklighet?" *STK* 61 (1985) 49–58. **Hoare, Henry William.** "The Book of Job and Plato's Dialogue on Justice." *Fortnightly Review* (1875). **Irwin, W. A.** "Prometheus and Job." *JR* 30 (1950) 90–108. **Kallen, Horace M.** *The Book of Job as a Greek Tragedy Restored.* New York: Moffat, Yard & Co., 1918 [= *Job: een tragedie*. Trans. Maurits Mok. Amsterdam: Athenaeum–Polak en Van Gennep, 1969; pp. 68–78 are reprinted as "Job the Humanist" in *The Dimensions of Job: A Study and Selected Readings.* Ed. Nahum H. Glatzer. New York: Schocken Books, 1969. 175–81]. **Kaufmann, U. Milo.** "Expostulation with the Divine: A Note on Contrasting Attitudes in Greek and Hebrew Piety." In *Twentieth Century Interpretations of the Book of Job. A Collection of Critical Essays.* Ed. P. S. Sanders. Englewood Cliffs, NJ: Prentice–Hall, 1968. 66–77.

   Laeuchli, Samuel, and Arvind Sharma. "The Problem of Job: An Eastern Response" [Buddhist and Hindu]. *ARC* 22 (1994) 83–90. **Lindblom, J.** "Job and Prometheus. A Comparative Study." In *Dragma. Martino P. Nilsson A.D. IV Id. Iul. anno MCMXXXIX dedicatum.* Acta Instituti Romani Regni Sueciae 2/1. Lund: H. Ohlssons, 1939. 280–87. **Lichtenstein, Anton August Heinrich.** *Disquisitio num liber Jobi cum Odyssea Homeri comparari possit?* Helmstadt, 1773. **May, Herbert Gordon.** "Prometheus and Job. The Problem of the God of Power and the Man of Wrath." *ATR* 34 (1952) 240–46. **Montefiore, C. G.** "The Book of Job as a Greek Tragedy Restored." *HTR* 12 (1919) 219–24. **Murray, Gilbert.** "Prometheus and Job." In *Twentieth Century Interpretations of the Book of Job. A Collection of Critical Essays.* Ed. P. S. Sanders. Englewood Cliffs, NJ: Prentice–Hall. 1968. 56–65 [= his *Aeschylus: The Creator of Tragedy.* Oxford: Clarendon Press, 1940. 87–110]. **Neyrand, J.** "Le livre de Job et les poèmes d'Homère." *Etudes* 59 (1922) 129–51. **Paulus, J.** "Le thème du juste souffrant dans la pensée grecque et hébraïque." *RHR* 121 (1940) 18–66. **Ronen, Miriam.** *The Hebrew "Apologia": Job in the Light of Socrates.* Diss. New York University, 1991. **Simon, Ulrich.** "Job and Sophocles." In *Images of Belief in Literature.* Ed. David Jasper. London: Macmillan, 1984. 42–51. **Vogel, A.** *Quod de fato senserint Judaei et Graeci, "Jobo" et Sophocli "Philoctete" probatur.* Diss. Rostock, 1869. **Weiser, A.** "Das Problem der sittlichen Weltordnung im Buche Hiob. Unter Berücksichtigung seiner Entwicklung bei den Griechen und in der israelitischen Religion." *ThBl* 2 (1923) 157–64 [= his *Glaube und Geschichte im Alten Testament und andere ausgewählte Schriften.* Göttingen: Vandenhoeck & Ruprecht, 1961. 9–19]. **Wolfson, E. R.** "The Dialectic of Faith and Doubt in the Philosophy of Socrates and Piety of Job." *Dor* 8 (1979–80) 197–200.

d. Other World Literature

   Forrest, Robert W. E. "Theophany in Job and the Bhagavad-Gita." *Journal of Studies in the Bhagavadgita* 2 (1982) 25–43. **Göring.** "Karmagedanken im Hiob." *Sphinx* 21 (1895) 232–33. **Smet, R. V. de.** "Job's 'Insufferable Comforters' and the Law of Karma." *Vidyajyoti* 58 (1994) 308–18. **Tai, Nicholas H. F., and Peter K. H. Lee.** "A Dialogue: Job, Paul and the Chinese Sages on Suffering." *Theology and Life* 17–19 (1996) 179–95.

Corrigenda to Volumes 1 and 2

Volume 1

Throughout the volume, *read* Sicre Díaz *for* Sicre Diaz.

p. 71, line 2: after rousers of *insert* (from עוּר)

p. 117, note 15.a, line 2: *read* sword from their mouth *for* sword of their mouth

p. 117, note 15.a, line 7: *read* mouth *for* tongue

p. 154, 2nd new paragraph, line 2: *read* encouragement

p. 158, note 3.b, line 1: *read* לעֵץ *for* לוֹעֵ

p. 163, note 4.d, line 4: *read* that מִדַּד־עֶרֶב is to be understood as meaning "from the breast of evening"

p. 220, note 31.a, line 1: *read* שַׁחַת *for* שַׁחַה

p. 232, line 6 from end: *read* Neukir-chen

p. 281, note 10b, line 1: *read* secret *for* sever

p. 283, note 6.a: *delete* for this context ... proper place).

p. 320, line 3: *read* אִיּוֹב

p. 336, line 9: *delete* be

p. 375, note 15.a, line 7: *delete* hence NEB *and insert* The NEB translation "piety" is apparently dependent on the view of G. R. Driver, "Notes on Joshua," in *The Seventy-Fifth Anniversary Volume of the JQR*, ed. A. A. Neuman and S. Zeitlin (Philadelphia: Jewish Quarterly Review, 1967) 149–65 (153 n. 14).

p. 406, note 12.c, line 2: *for* 1953 *read* 1954

p. 431, note 20.b (iii), line 2: *read* ǵauru(n) *for* ǵaru(n)

p. 473, note 3.b, line 6: *read* Ravasi *for* Ravisi

p. 475, note 18.d: *read* III *for* II.

p. 479, note 28.a, line 4: *read* יָבָל *for* יְבָל

Volume 2

p. 505, note 2.b, line 3: *read* חֵם II *for* חמה

p. 508, note 12.b, line 3: *read* כָּתִיף *for* כְּתִיף

p. 517, note 34.a, line 2: *read* חֵם II *for* חמה

p. 540, note 7.a, line 1: *delete* comma *after* water

p. 586, note 12.e: *insert before the end of the sentence*; so too M. Dahood (*Psalms II*, 194).

p. 620, *Translation*, v 13b: *read* fleeing *for* twisting

p. 694, note 14.b, line 3: *delete* similarly and *insert at the end of the sentence* following G. R. Driver in taking it from שׂרר IV "affirm" ("Difficult Words in the Hebrew Prophets," in *Studies in Old Testament Prophecy Presented to Professor Theodore H. Robinson*, ed. H. H. Rowley [Edinburgh: T. & T. Clark, 1950] 52–72 [68]).

p. 703, note 27.a, 3rd paragraph, line 10: *read* 123–61 (132) *for* 25–61 (32)

p. 752, note 20.f, line 9: *delete* Tur-Sinai reads עֲרִי, "he drives out."

p. 817, note 16.b, line 4: *insert space after* Perhaps

p. 823, note 21.b, 3rd paragraph, line 5: *read* עֶלְוָה *for* עַלְוָה

p. 828, note 31.c, 3rd paragraph, line 2: *read* זוֹן *for* זוֹן

p. 840, note 9.d, line 3: *read* Mezarim *for* Mazzarim

p. 840, note 9.d, line 10: *read* Schiaparelli *for* Schiaperelli

p. 878, line 4: *read* Mezarim *for* Mazzarim

p. 903, note 18.d, line 14: *read* Torczyner *for* Torzcyner

p. 953, note 17.e, line 9: *read* עֲרָק *for* עֲרָק

p. 969, note 11.d, 2nd paragraph, line 8: *read* פְּלִילִי *for* פליל

p. 998, 2nd new paragraph, line 4: *insert period after* accustomed to

Index of Emendations, Re-arrangements of Verses, and Adoptions of "New Words"

"New Words," marked with *, are words not mentioned in Brown–Driver–Briggs. All "new words" mentioned appear in the *Dictionary of Classical Hebrew* and the *Concise Dictionary of Classical Hebrew*. *Adoptions of Qere as against Kethiv and vice versa are not included.*

1

1:18   For MT עַד "until," read עוֹד or עֹד "while."

3

3:6   For MT יִחַדְּ "Let it [not] rejoice," read יֵחַד "let it [not] be joined."

4

4:6   For MT תִּקְוָתְךָ וְתֹם דְּרָכֶיךָ "your hope and the perfection of your ways," read וְתִקְוָתְךָ תֹם דְּרָכֶיךָ "and [is not] your hope the perfection of your ways."

4:16   Take דְּמָמָה not as דְּמָמָה I "silence" (from דמם I "be silent") but as *דְּמָמָה II "roaring" (from *רמם II "roar").

5

5:5   For MT וְאֶל־מִצִּנִּים יִקָּחֵהוּ "and unto from sheaves he takes it [?]," read וַאֲלֻמִּים צְנֻמִים יִקַּח הוּא "and their withered sheaves he takes away."

5:5   For MT צַמִּים "snares," read צְמֵאִים "the thirsty."

5:7   For MT יוּלָּד "is born," read יוֹלִיד "begets."

5:15   For MT מֵחֶרֶב מִפִּיהֶם "from the sword from their mouth," read מֵחֶרֶב פִּיהֶם "from the sword of their mouth."

5:21   For MT בְּשׁוֹט "in the scourging," read מִשּׁוֹט "from the scourging."

6

6:2   For MT הַיָּתִי "my life [?]," read Qr הַוָּתִי "my calamity."

6:10   Take וַאֲסַלְּדָה not from סלד I "spring up," but from *סלד IV "recoil."

6:14   For MT לַמָּס מֵרֵעֵהוּ חָסֶד "to the despairing kindness [should be shown] by his friend," read לֹא מָאַס מֵרֵעַ חָסֶד "a friend does not refuse his loyalty."

6:16   For MT יִתְעַלֶּם "is hidden," read יִתְעָרֵם "is swollen."

6:21   For MT כִּי "for" and לֹא "not," read כֵּן "thus" and לִי "to me."

7

7:20   For MT עָלַי "to myself," read עָלֶיךָ "to you."

8

8:17   For MT יֶחֱזֶה "sees," read יֹחַז (= יֹאחַז) "grasps," from אחז.

8:19   For MT מְשׂוֹשׂ דַּרְכּוֹ "the joy of his way," read מְסוֹס דַּרְכּוֹ "the dissolution of his way."

8:21   For MT עַד "unto," read עֹד "again."

9

9:8   Take בָּמֳתֵי יָם not as "the heights of the sea" (בָּמָה I "high place") but as "the back of Sea" (*בָּמָה II "back").

9:17   For MT בִּשְׂעָרָה "with a tempest," read בְּשַׂעֲרָה "for a hair, a trifle."

9:19   For MT יוֹעִידֵנִי "shall arraign me," read יוֹעִידֶנּוּ "shall arraign him."

9:24   For MT אִם־לֹא אֵפוֹא מִי־הוּא "if not, then who?," read אִם־לֹא הוּא אֵפוֹא מִי or אִם־לֹא הוּא אֵפוֹא מִי־הוּא "if not he, then who?"

9:27   For MT אִם־אָמְרִי "if my saying [?]," read אִם־אָמַרְתִּי "if I say."

9:30   For MT Qr בְמֵי־שֶׁלֶג "with snow water," read, in accord with MT Kt, בְמוֹ־שָׁלֶג "in snow."

9:33   For MT לֹא יֵשׁ "there is not," read לָא יֵשׁ or לוּ יֵשׁ "would that there were."

10

10:5 For MT כִּימֵי "days of," read שְׁנוֹת "years of."

10:8 For MT יַחַד סָבִיב "together round about," read אַחַר תָּסֹב "then you turned."

10:15 Take וּרְאֵה not from ראה I "see," but from *ראה II "be satiated" (= רוה).

10:16 For MT וְיִגְאֶה "and it is proud, lifts itself up," read וְאֶגְאֶה "and I am proud, lift myself up."

10:17 For MT עֵדֶיךָ "your witnesses," read עֶדְיְךָ "your hostility" (from *עדה II "attack").

10:20 For MT Kt יחדל "let it cease, it will cease," read MT Qr וַחֲדָל "and cease!"
        For MT Kt ישית "it will put [?]," read MT Qr וְשִׁית "and put."

11

11:6 For MT כִפְלַיִם "double," read פְּלָאִים "wonders."

11:8 For MT גָּבְהֵי שָׁמַיִם "heights of heaven," read גְּבֹהָה מִשָּׁמַיִם "higher than heaven."

11:18 For MT וְחָפַרְתָּ "and you shall search" (from חפר I "search"), read וְחֻפַּרְתָּ "and you shall be protected" (from *חפר III "protect").

13

13:11 For MT שְׂאֵתוֹ "his majesty," read שַׁאֵתוֹ "his fear."

13:12 Take גַּב in לְגַבֵּי־חֹמֶר גַּבֵּיכֶם not as גַּב I "back, defense," but as *גַּב II "answer," i.e., "your answers [would become] answers of clay."

13:14 Delete עַל־מָה "wherefore" as a dittograph of עָלַי מָה at the end of the previous verse.

13:15 Read MT Kt לֹא (= לֹא "not"), not Qr לוֹ "to him."

14

14:5 Read Kt חֻקוֹ (= חֻקּוֹ "his limit"), not Qr חֻקָּיו "his limits."

14:6 For MT וְיֶחְדָּל "that he may desist [?]," read חֲדַל "desist!"

14:19 For MT סְפִיחֶיהָ "its aftergrowths," read סְחִיפָה "rainstorm."

15

15:12 Take יִרְזְמוּן not from רזם I "wink, flash," but from *רזם II "fail."

15:18 For MT כִּחֲדוּ מֵאֲבוֹתָם "they have hidden from their fathers," read כִּחֲדוּם אֲבוֹתָם "their fathers have hidden" (with enclitic *mem* at the end of the verb).

15:23 For MT נֹדֵד הוּא לַלֶּחֶם אַיֵּה "he wanders for bread; where is it?," read נֻדַּד הוּא לְלֶחֶם אַיָּה "he is cast out (as) food for the vultures."
        For MT בְּיָדוֹ "in his hand," read פִּידוֹ "his ruin."
        Transfer יוֹם־חֹשֶׁךְ "the day of darkness" to the beginning of v 24.

15:24 For MT יְבַעֲתֻהוּ "they terrify him," read יְבַעֲתֵהוּ "it terrifies him."

15:27 Take וַיַּעַשׂ not from עשה I "do," but from *עשה II "cover."

15:29 For MT מִנְלָם "their gain [?]," read מְנֻלָם "their possession" or מְנֻלִים "[their] possessions," from מְנֻלֹה "possession."

15:30 For MT וְיָסוּר "and he shall turn away," read וְיֻסַּר "and he will be driven away."
        For MT פִּיו "his mouth," read פִּרְחוֹ "his blossom."

15:31 For MT תְּמוּרָתוֹ "his recompense," read זְמֹרָתוֹ "his branch."

15:32 For MT תִּמָּלֵא "will be paid in full," read תִּמַּל "it will wither."

16

16:4 Take אַחְבִּירָה not from חבר I "join," but from *חבר II "mutter, harangue."

16:11 For MT עֲוִיל "boy," read עַוָּל "evildoer."

16:20 For MT מְלִיצַי "my spokesmen," read מְלִיצִי "my spokesman."
        Take דָּלְפָה not from דלף II "leak," but from *דלף I "be sleepless."

17

17:2 For MT תָּלַן עֵינִי "my eye dwells," read תִּלְאֶן עֵינַי (= תִּלְאֶינָה) "my eyes are tired."

17:3 For MT עָרְבֵנִי "be surety for me," read עֲרֻבְנִי "my pledge."

17:6 For MT לִמְשֹׁל "to be a byword," read לְמֹשֵׁל "for a byword of."

17:7 For MT כֻּלָּם "all of them," read כָּלִים "are wasting" (from כלה).

17:11 Take מוֹרָשֵׁי not from מוֹרָשׁ I "possession," but from *מוֹרָשׁ II "desire."

17:15 For MT וְתִקְוָתִי "and my hope," read וְטוֹבָתִי "and my happiness."

17:16 For MT בַּדֵּי שְׁאֹל "the poles of Sheol [?]," read הַעִמָּדִי שְׁאֹל "[will they descend] with me to Sheol?"

For MT נָחַת "rest," read נֵחַת "we shall descend."

18

18:2   Take קִנְצֵי not from קֵץ I "trap," but from *קָנֵץ II "end."

18:3   For MT בְּעֵינֵיכֶם "in your (pl) eyes," read בְּעֵינֶיךָ "in your (sg) eyes."

18:13   For MT בַּדֵּי "parts of," read בְּדָוֵי "by disease."

          For MT יֹאכַל "devours," read יֵאָכֵל "is devoured."

18:14   For MT וְתַצְעִדֵהוּ "and she marches him [?]," read וְתִצְעָדֵהוּ "and they march him."

18:15   For MT מִבְּלִי־לוֹ "what is not his," read *מַבֵּל "fire."

19

19:3   Take תַּהְכְּרוּ not from הכר I "make to wonder," but from *הכר II "attack."

19:6   For MT וּמְצוּדוֹ "and his net," read וּמְצוּרוֹ "and his siegeworks."

19:11   For MT כְּצָרָיו "like his enemies," read כְּצָרוֹ "like his enemy."

19:14   Transfer גָּרֵי בֵיתִי "those who dwell in my house" from the beginning of v 15 to the end of v 14 as the subject of שְׁכֵחוּנִי "they have forgotten me."

19:18   Take וַיְדַבְּרוּ not from דבר I "speak," but from *דבר II "turn the back."

19:29   For MT שַׁדּוּן (Qr) "[?]," read שֶׁדִּין "that [there is] a judgment."

20

20:17   For MT פַּלְגוֹת נַהֲרֵי "streams of rivers of," read פַּלְגוֹת יִצְהָר "streams of oil."

20:23   For MT בִּלְחוּמוֹ "against his flesh," read בְּלַחְמוֹ "as his food."

20:25   For MT מִגֵּוָה "from the back," read מִגֵּוֹה "from his back."

20:26   For MT תְּאָכְלֵהוּ "consumes him," read תֹּאכְלֵהוּ "consumes him."

20:28   For MT יִגֶל "may it go into exile" (from גלה), read יִגֹּל "will roll away" (from גלל).

          For MT יְבוּל "produce," read יָבֵל "stream, flood."

          Take נִגָּרוֹת not as "things poured away [?]," but as "torrents" (from *נִגְרַת).

21

21:3   For MT תַּלְעִיג "mock on (sg)!," read תַּלְעִיגוּ "mock on (pl)!"

21:8   Delete עִמָּם "with them."

21:12   Take יִשְׂאוּ not from נשא I "lift up," but from *שאה I "rejoice."

21:13   For MT Kt יבלו "they consume," read MT Qr יְכַלּוּ "they complete."

          Take וּבְרֶגַע not from רֶגַע I "moment," but from *רֶגַע II "tranquillity."

          For MT יֵחָתּוּ "they are frightened" (from חתת), read יֵחָתוּ "they go down" (from נחת).

22

22:17   For MT לָמוֹ "to them," read לָנוּ "to us."

22:20   For MT קִימָנוּ "our hostility [?]," read יְקָמָם "their possessions."

22:21   For MT תְּבוֹאַתְךָ "will come [?]," read תְּבוֹאֲךָ "will come."

22:24   For MT וְשִׁית "and set!," read וְתָשִׁית "and you will set."

22:29   For MT הִשְׁפִּילוּ וַתֹּאמֶר גֵּוָה "when they are low, you will say, 'Pride' [?]," read הִשְׁפִּיל מִתְאַמֵּר גֵּוָה "he humbles the one who boasts in pride."

22:30   For MT אִי־נָקִי "not innocent," read אִישׁ נָקִי "an innocent man."

          For MT וְנִמְלַט "and he is delivered," read וְנִמְלַטְתָּ "and you will be delivered."

23

23:7   For MT וַאֲפַלְּטָה "and I should deliver," read וְאֶפָּלְטָה "and I should escape."

          For MT מִשֹּׁפְטִי "from my judge," read מִמְּשַׂפְטִי "from my adversary."

23:9   For MT בַּעֲשׂוֹתוֹ " in his working," read בְּקַשְׁתִי "I seek him."

          For MT יַעְטֹף "he turns," read אֶעֱטֹף "I turn."

23:12   For MT מֵחֻקִּי "from my statute [?]," read בְּחֵקִי "in my heart."

23:13   For MT וְהוּא בְאֶחָד "and he is in one [?]," read וְהוּא בָחָר "and he has decided."

23:17   Delete לֹא "not" before נִצְמָתִּי "I am annihilated."

          For MT וּמִפָּנַי "and from my face," read וּפָנַי "[and thick darkness covers] my face."

24

24:2   Insert רְשָׁעִים "the wicked" at the beginning of the line.

24:6   For MT בְּלִילוֹ "his fodder," read בְּלִי־לוֹ "what is not his."

Take יִלְקָשׁוּ, apparently "they despoil," from *לקשׁ "glean."

24:9   For MT וְעַל־עָנִי "and upon the poor," read וְעֻל־עָנִי "and the child of the poor."

24:12   For MT מְתִים "men," read מֵתִים "the dying."

24:14   For MT יְהִי "let him be," read יְהַלֵּךְ "goes about," and move וּבַלַּיְלָה יְהַלֵּךְ כַּגַּנָּב "and in the night he goes about as a thief" to the beginning of v 16.

24:18–24   Move to follow 27:17, as part of Zophar's third speech.

24:20   Take מְתָקוֹ, apparently "is sweet to him," from *מתק II "suck."

24:21   For MT רֹעֶה "he grazes on," read הֵרַע "he wrongs" (from רעע "do wrong").

24:24   For MT כַּכֹּל "like the totality [?]," read כַּמַּלּוּחַ "like the mallow."

26

26:1–4   Move to follow 25:1, and delete וַיַּעַן אִיּוֹב וַיֹּאמַר "and Job answered and said."

26:9   Take מְאַחֵז, apparently "he seizes," from *אחז II "cover."

26:10   For MT חֹק־חָג "he has drawn a boundary," read חָג חֻק "he has drawn a circle."

26:13   For MT בְּרוּחוֹ שָׁמַיִם שִׁפְרָה "by his wind the heavens were clearness," read בְּרוּחוֹ שָׁמַיִם שָׁפְרוּ "by his wind the heavens became clear."

26:14   For Kt דָּרְכוֹ "his way," read Qr דְּרָכָיו "his ways."

27

27:7–10   Move to follow 27:12 as the beginning of a third speech of Zophar.

27:7   Insert at the beginning of the verse וַיַּעַן צוֹפַר הַנַּעֲמָתִי וַיֹּאמַר "and Zophar the Naamathite answered and said."

27:8   For MT יִבְצַע "cuts off," read יִבָּצַע "is cut off."

        For MT יֵשֶׁל "extracts," read יִשְׁאַל "requires."

27:11–12   Move to follow 27:6, as the end of Job's ninth speech.

27:18–23   Move to follow 27:7–10, 13–17; 24:18–24, as the end of Zophar's third speech.

27:18   Take עָשׁ, apparently "moth," as *עָשׁ II "bird's nest."

27:19   For MT יֵאָסֵף "he is gathered," read יֹסִף "he adds."

27:22   For MT וְיַשְׁלֵךְ "and let him cast," read וְיַשְׁלִךְ "and he casts."

28

28:4   For MT נַחַל מֵעִם־גָּר "a shaft from with one who sojourns [?]," read חֲלָמִים עַם גָּר "a foreign people [has pierced] shafts."

        Take דַּלּוּ from *דלל II "hang down, dangle."

28:11   For MT חִבֵּשׁ "he bound up," read חִבֵּשׁ "he sought," taking it from *חבשׁ piel "seek."

        For MT מִבְּכִי "from weeping," read מִבְּכֵי "the sources of," taking it from *מַבָּךְ "source of waters, fountain."

        For MT תַּעֲלֻמָהּ "its secret," read תַּעֲלֻמָה "the secret."

28:12   For MT מֵאַיִן "whence," read אַיִן "where."

28:13   For MT עֶרְכָּהּ "its order, value," read דַּרְכָּהּ "its way."

28:15   For MT סְגוֹר "gold [?]," read *סָגוּר "gold."

28:18   Take מֶשֶׁךְ from *מֶשֶׁךְ II "pouch."

29

29:4   For MT בְּסוֹד "in the council of," read בְּסֹךְ or בְּשׂוֹךְ "when he covered, protected."

29:6   Delete עִמָּדִי "with me," and for יָצוּק "poured out," read יָצֹק "pours out."

29:7   For MT שַׁעַר עֲלֵי־קָרֶת "the gate upon the town," read עֲלֵי־שַׁעַר קֶרֶת "to the gate of the town."

29:18   For MT כַחוֹל "like the sand," read כְּחוּל "like the phoenix."

29:25   Delete כַּאֲשֶׁר אֲבֵלִים יְנַחֵם "like one who comforts mourners."

30

30:5   Take גֵּו from *גֵּו II "community, society."

30:6   Take עֲרוּץ from *עֲרוּץ II "gully."

30:13   Take נְתִיבָתִי from נְתִיבָה III "defense."

30:18   For MT יִתְחַפֵּשׂ "it is disguised [?]," read יִתְפֹּשׂ "he seizes."

30:24   For MT לֹא־בְעִי יִשְׁלַח־יָד אִם־בְּפִידוֹ לָהֶן שׁוּעַ "one does not stretch out a hand to a ruin, or in his calamity a cry for help to these things [?]," read לֹא־בְעֶנִי אֶשְׁלַח־יָד אִם־בְּפִידוֹ לִי יֶשַׁע "I did not stretch out [my] hand against any needy person, if they cried out to me in their calamity."

30:28   For MT בְּלֹא חַמָּה "without the sun," read בְּלֹא נֶחָמָה "without comfort."

31

31:15   For MT וַיְכֻנֶנּוּ "and prepared him," read וַיְכוֹנְנֵנוּ "and made us."

31:18   For MT גְדֵלַנִי "he grew up to me [?]," read אֲגַדְּלֶנּוּ "I brought him up."

31:21   Take הֲנִיפוֹתִי from *נוף V "raise."

31:38–40b   Move to precede 31:35.

31:39   For MT בְּעָלֶיהָ "its lords," read בֹּעֲלָיו "its workers," from *בעל II "do."

32

32:1–37:24   Move to precede 28:1, making 28:1–28 the conclusion of Elihu's fourth speech.

32:9   For MT רַבִּים "many," read שָׂבִים "the gray-haired."

33

33:13   For MT דְּבָרָיו "his words," read דְּבָרַי "my words."

33:16   For MT יַחְתֹּם "he seals," read יְחִתָּם "he dismays them."

     For MT וּמֹסָרָם "and their discipline," read וּבְמֹרָאִים "and by apparitions."

33:17   For MT מַעֲשֶׂה "deed," read מִמַּעֲשֵׂהוּ "from his deed."

     For MT יְכַסֶּה "he hides," read יְכַסֵּחַ "he cuts away."

33:24   For MT פְּדָעֵהוּ "[?]," read פְּדָהוּ "redeem him."

33:27   For MT יָשֹׁר "he looks" (from שׁור), read יָשִׁר "he sings" (from שׁיר).

34

34:20   For MT עָם "people," read שׁוֹעַ "nobles."

34:23   For MT עוֹד "yet," read מוֹעֵד "time."

34:26   For MT רְשָׁעִים "wicked ones," read רִשְׁעָם "their wickedness."

34:31   For MT הֶאָמַר "has he said?," read אָמֹר "say!"

     For MT נָשָׂאתִי "I have lifted up," read נִשֵּׁאתִי "I have been led astray" (from נשׁא II).

34:37   Take יִסְפּוֹק from *ספק II "doubt."

35

35:15   For MT אַיִן פָּקַד אַפּוֹ "because he has not visited [in] his anger [?]," read אֵין אַפּוֹ פֹּקֵד "his anger does not punish."

     For MT פַּשׁ "folly [?]," read פֶּשַׁע "transgression."

36

36:5   For MT אֶל כַּבִּיר וְלֹא יִמְאָס כַּבִּיר כֹּחַ לֵב "God is mighty and he does not reject, mighty of strength of heart," read אֵל כַּבִּיר כֹּחַ וְלֹא יִמְאָס בְּבַר לֵב "God is mighty in strength, and he will not reject the pure of heart."

36:12   For MT כִּבְלִי "as without [?]," read בִּבְלִי "without."

36:14   For MT קְדֵשִׁים "prostitutes [?]," read קְדֹשִׁים "Holy Ones."

36:16   For MT וְנַחַת שֻׁלְחָנְךָ מָלֵא דָשֶׁן "and the calm of your table was full of fat [?]," read וְנַחַת שֻׁלְחָנְךָ מָלֵא דָשֶׁן "and an abundance of fat weighed down your table."

36:18   For MT חֵמָה "fury," read חֲמֵה "see, beware!"

36:19   For MT שׁוּעֲךָ "your cry," read שׁוֹעֲךָ, from *שׁוע III "wealth."

36:21   For MT בָּחַרְתָּ "you have chosen," read בְּחַרְתָּ "you have been tested," from *בחר III "test."

36:25   Take רָב not as רב I "great," but as *רב V "showers."

36:27   For MT יָזֹקּוּ "they refine," read יָזֹק "he refines."

     For MT לְאֵדוֹ "to his mist," read מֵאֵד "from the mist."

36:30   Take MT כִּסָּה "he covers" as a privative piel, "he exposes."

36:31   Move v 31 to follow v 28.

     For MT יָדִין "he judges," read יָזוּן "he nourishes."

36:32   For MT מַפְגִּיעַ "assailant [?]," read מִפְגָּע "target."

36:33   For MT רֵעוֹ "his shout [?]," read רַעְמוֹ "his thunder."

     For MT עָלָיו "concerning him," read וְעֶמוֹ "his wrath."

     For MT מִקְנֶה "cattle," read מִקְנָה "passion of," from *מִקְנָה II "wrath."

     For MT עוֹלֶה "one coming up [?]," read עַוְלָה "iniquity."

37

37:3   Take יְשָׁרֵהוּ from *שׁרה II "flash."

37:4   Move v 4c to follow v 6.

37:5   Bracket v 5a as not original.

37:6   For MT וְגֶשֶׁם מָטָר וְגֶשֶׁם מִטְרוֹת עֻזּוֹ "and rain of shower and rain of showers, his strength," read וּלְגֶשֶׁם מִטְרוֹת עֹז "and to the rain of showers, Be strong!"

37:7   For MT בְּיַד "in the hand of," read בַּעַד "upon."
        For MT אֲנָשֵׁי "men of," read אֱנוֹשׁ "human."

37:11   For MT אוֹרוֹ "his light," read אֵד "torrent(s)."

37:13   For MT יַמְצִאֵהוּ "he makes them overtake [?]," read יוֹצִיאֵם "he sends them out."

37:15   For MT אֱלוֹהַּ עֲלֵיהֶם "God upon them," read אֵל פְּעָלָיו "God [ordained] his works."

37:20   Take יְבֻלָּע from *בלע III "communicate."

37:22   Bracket v 22b as a marginal comment.

37:23   For MT שַׂגִּיא־כֹחַ וּרֹב־צְדָקָה לֹא יְעַנֶּה "great in power and justice and multitude of righteousness, he does not afflict," read שַׂגִּיא־כֹחַ וְרֹב־צְדָקָה וּמִשְׁפָּט לֹא יְעַוֵּת "great in power and mighty in righteousness, and he does not pervert justice"

37:24   For MT יְרֵאוּהוּ "they feared him," read יִרָאֻהוּ "they fear him."
        For MT לֹא־יִרְאֶה "he does not see," read יִרְאֻ "they fear him," and take לֹא as *לֹא II "indeed."

38

38:8   For MT וַיָּסֶךְ "and [who] shut in?" (from סכך), read מִי סָךְ "who shut up?" (from סוך).

38:10   Take וָאֶשְׁבֹּר, apparently "and I broke," from *שׁבר II "measure."

38:11   For MT יָשִׁית "will set [?]," read יִשְׁבֹּת "must cease."
        For MT בִּגְאוֹן "in the pride of," read גְּאוֹן "the pride of [your waves]."

38:13   Take רְשָׁעִים, apparently "the wicked," as רְשָׁעִים "Dog-stars."

38:14   For MT וְיִתְיַצְּבוּ, apparently "and they stand," read וְתִצְטַבַּע hithp or וְתִצָּבַע niph "and it [the earth] is dyed" (from *צבע).

38:17b For MT שַׁעֲרֵי "gates of," read שֹׁעֲרֵי "gatekeepers of."

38:18   Take כֻּלָּהּ, apparently "all of it," from *כלל III "measure, extent," hence "its extent."

38:19   Take הַדֶּרֶךְ, apparently "the way," from *דֶּרֶךְ II "realm."

38:20   For MT תָּבִין "you discern" revocalize to תְּבִיֵן (defective spelling of תְּבִיאֵנּוּ) "you should bring it."

38:21   For MT אָז "then," read מֵאָז "from of old."

38:24   Take דֶּרֶךְ, apparently "way," from *דֶּרֶךְ II "realm."

38:24   Take יֵחָלֶק, apparently "is divided" (from חלק I "divide"), from *חלק VI "create."

38:24   For MT אוֹר "light," revocalize to *אוּר II "heat."

38:27   For MT מֹצָא "source," read מִצָּמֵא "from the thirsty (land)."

38:31   For MT מַעֲדַנּוֹת (i.e. מֵעֲדַן II "bond, chain"), read מַעֲרָכֹת "company, group."

38:34   For MT תְּכַסֶּךָ "shall cover you," read תַּעֲנֶךָ "shall answer you."

38:36   Take טֻחוֹת, apparently "inward parts," from *טֻחוֹת III "ibis."
        Take שֶׂכְוִי, apparently "celestial appearance, phenomenon [?]," from *שֶׂכְוִי I "cock."

38:37   Take יְסַפֵּר, apparently "can number," from a *סַפֵּר II "disperse."

38:41   For MT יִתְעוּ "wander" (from תעה), read יָתְעוּ "twitter, croak" (from תעע II).

39

39:1   Delete עֵת and read הֲיָדַעְתָּ לֶדֶת יַעֲלֵי־סָלַע "do you know the birthing of the mountain goats?"

39:7   Read שְׁאוֹן, as in *BHK. BHS* שֹׁאֵן "one drawing near" is a mistake.

39:8   For MT יְתוּר "range [of the mountains] [?]," read יָתוּר "it ranges."

39:13   For MT אֶבְרָה "pinion," read אֵבְרַת "pinion of."
        For MT נֹצָה "plumage," read נֵצָה "falcon" (fem of נֵץ).

39:18   Take תַּמְרִיא, apparently "beats [the air with her wings]," from *מרא V "wing up," thus "spreads [her plumes] aloft."

39:19   Take רַעְמָה "vibration [?]," from *רַעְמָה I "mane."

39:20   Take וַחֲרוֹ from *חרה "neigh."

39:25   For MT בְּדֵי "whenever [?]," read בְּדוּי "at the sound of," from *דְּוִי "echo, sound."

40

40:2   For MT רֹב "will he contend [?]," read רָב "one contending."

40:5   For MT אֶעֱנֶה "I will answer," read אָשֻׁנֶה "I will speak again."

40:20   For MT הָרִים "mountains," read נְהָרִים "rivers."

40:23   Take יַעְשֹׁק, apparently "oppresses," from *עשׁק II "gush."

40:24   For MT בְּעֵינָיו "by its eyes," read בְּשִׁנַּים "by a meat fork."

                  For MT בְּמוֹקְשִׁים "with snares," read בְּקַמּוֹשִׁים "with hooks."

40:25 (41:1)   Take תַּקְשִׁיעַ, apparently "will you press down?," from *שׁקע II "bind."

41

41:1 (9)   For MT הֲגַם "is it also?," read גַּם "even."

41:3 (11)   For MT הִקְדִּימַנִי "has confronted me," read הִקְדִּימוֹ "has confronted it."

                  For MT וַאֲשַׁלֵּם "that I should repay," read וַיִּשְׁלָם "and remained safe."

                  For MT לִי־הוּא "it is mine," read לֹא אֶחָד "not one."

41:4 (12)   For MT וּדְבַר־גְּבוּרוֹת "and the word of might," read וַאֲדַבֵּר גְּבוּרָתוֹ "and I will tell of its might."

                  For MT וְחִין עֶרְכּוֹ "the grace of its frame [?]," read אֵין עֵרֶךְ "without compare."

41:5 (13)   For MT רִסְנוֹ "its jaw, or, bridle," read סִרְיֹנוֹ "its coat of mail."

41:7 (15)   For MT גַּאֲוָה "pride," read גֵּוֹה "its back."

41:12 (20)   For MT וְאַגְמֹן "and rushes," read וְאָגֵם "and seething."

41:18 (26)   For MT מַשִּׂיגֵהוּ "one reaching it," read תַּשִּׂיגֵהוּ "reaches it."

41:26 (34)   For MT אֵת־כָּל־גָּבֹהַּ יִרְאֶה "it sees all that is proud," read אֹתוֹ כָּל־גָּבֹהַּ יִירָא "all that are lofty fear it."

42

42:8   For MT אִם "if," read אֶת־ (sign of the direct object).

Classified Index of the Book of Job

A. The Supernatural World

God

Almighty (Shaddai) 5:17; 6:4, 14; 8:5; 15:25; 21:15, 20; 22:3, 17, 23, 25, 26; 23:16; 24:1; 27:2, 10, 11, 13; 29:5; 31:2, 35; 32:8; 33:4; 34:10, 12, 17; 35:13; 37:23; 40:2 — Destroyer 15:21 — Eloah 19:21, 26 — God 1:1, 5, 6, 8, 16, 22; 2:1, 3, 9, 10; 3:4, 23; 4:9, 17, 18; 5:8, 17; 6:4, 8, 9; 8:3, 13, 20; 9:2, 13, 24, 34; 10:2; 11:4, 5, 6, 7; 12:4, 6; 13:3, 7, 8, 20; 15:4, 8, 11, 13, 15, 25; 16:11, 20, 21; 17:3; 18:21; 19:6, 22; 20:15, 23, 28, 29; 21:9, 14, 19, 22; 22:2, 12, 13, 26, 29; 23:16; 24:12, 22; 25:4; 27:2, 3, 8, 9, 10, 11, 13; 28:23; 29:2, 4; 30:11; 31:2, 6, 14, 23, 28; 32:2, 13; 33:4, 6, 12, 14, 26, 29; 34:5, 9, 10, 12, 31, 37; 35:2, 10, 13; 36:2, 5, 22, 26; 37:5, 10, 14, 15, 22; 38:7, 41; 39:17; 40:2, 9, 19 — Holy One 5:1 — King 18:14 — Lord (Yahweh) 28:28 — Maker 4:17; 9:9; 32:22; 35:10; 36:3; 40:19 — Man-Watcher 7:20 — Righteous One 34:17 — Shaddai 11:7 — teacher 36:22 — Watcher 7:20 — Yahweh 1:6, 7, 8, 9, 12, 19; 2:1, 2, 3, 4, 6, 7; 12:9; 38:1; 40:1, 6; 42:1, 7, 9, 9, 10, 11, 12

actions abandon 8:4; 16:11 — accept 42:8, 9 — acquit 10:14 — affright 7:14 — allot fate 20:29 — allow to rest 24:23 — answer 23:5; 30:20; 31:35; 33:13; 35:12; 38:1; 40:1, 6 — appall 16:17 — appraise 28:27 — approach 40:19 — arrange 37:15 — ask 42:3 — assault 16:8 — assay 23:10 — assign place 38:12 — assign weight 28:25 — banish 14:20 — bar way 19:8 — batter down 16:14 — be at work 37:7 — be exalted 36:22 — be great 36:26 — be informed 37:20 — be marveled at 10:16 — be minded 34:14 — be quiet 34:19 — begin proceedings 13:10 — behold 28:24 — bid 36:32 — bind 38:31 — bind rope 12:18 — bind up 5:18 — bless 1:10; 42:12 — blindfold 9:24 — breath 4:9; 27:3; 32:8; 33:4; 34:14; 37:10 — bring back 33:30 — bring clouds 37:13 — bring into dispute 14:3 — bring out 10:18; 38:32 — bring to light 12:22 — bring to ruin 12:19 — bring upon 34:11; 38:26; 42:11 — call 14:15 — call to account 11:10 — call up 38:12 — care little 35:15 — carry out plan 23:14 — charge 4:18; 24:12 — clasp tight 30:18 — clothe 10:11; 39:19 — command 9:7; 36:10 — conceal 14:13 — conduct 36:23 — contend 23:6 — council 15:8 — count 39:2 — count as enemy 13:24; 19:11 — count steps 14:16 — cover 14:17; 26:9 — crush 6:9; 9:17; 26:12 — curdle 10:10 — cut 38:25 — cut away 33:17 — cut off 6:9 — dash to pieces 16:12 — decide 6:9; 23:13 — declare 36:9. 33 — deliver 22:29; 36:15 — deny justice 27:2 — deprive 12:20, 24 — desire 23:13 — destroy 10:8; 12:14, 23; 14:19 — determine 28:25; 38:33 — disfigure 14:20 — dismay 23:16; 33:16 — disperse 12:23; 38:37 — dissolve 30:22 — distill 36:27 — do 9:12; 12:9; 23:13; 33:29; 37:5; 42:2 — do wickedness 34:10 — do wrong 34:10, 12 — drag away 24:22 — draw circle 26:10 — draw up drops 36:27 — drive 12:17 — endow 38:36 — ensnare 5:13 — enquire 31:14 — enter into judgment 22:4 — establish 28:27; 38:33 — examine 13:9 — expose roots of sea 36:30 — fashion 10:8; 31:15 — fathom 28:27 — favor 10:12; 33:26; 34:19 — fill 8:21; 20:23; 22:18 — fill hands 36:32 — find occasion 33:10 — fix dimensions 38:5 — fix eyes 14:3 — flash lightning 37:3 — fury 4:9; 40:11 — gain 22:3 — gaze 7:19 — give 1:21; 36:31; 38:36; 39:6, 19; 42:10 — give justice 36:6 — give life 33:4 — give share 39:17 — give songs 35:10 — gnash teeth 16:9 — go his way 22:14 — govern 22:13 — grant 6:8; 13:20 — grip garment 30:18 — guide 38:32 — hammer out sky 37:18 — hand over 30:23 — hatred 16:9 — heal 5:18 — hear 22:27; 27:9; 34:28 — hedge 3:23 — hide 13:24; 14:13; 34:29 — hold back 12:15 — hold innocent 9:28 — humble 22:29 — humiliate 30:11 — hunt 10:16; 38:39 — impose peace 25:2 — imprison 12:14 — increase wrath 10:17 — inspect 7:18 — keep back 33:18 — keep days 24:1 — keep pledge 17:3 — keep silence 40:12 — keep under guard 7:12 — keep watch 13:27; 24:23 — kindle anger 19:11 — knit together 10:11 — know 10:7; 22:13; 23:10; 28:23; 31:6; 34:25; 39:1, 2 — lay foundation 38:4 — lead 12:23 — lead away 12:17, 19 — leave alone 10:20 — leave to stagger 12:25 — leave to wander 12:24 — let be 7:19; 14:6 — let go free 39:5 — let live 36:6 — let loose 6:9; 12:15 — lift 5:11 — lift voice 38:34 — listen 9:16; 23:6; 35:13; 42:4 — live 27:2 — load with moisture 37:11 — look 28:24 — look away 14:6 — look down 22:12 — loose bonds 39:5 — loosen belt 12:18; 38:31 — loosen cord 30:11 — make 10:8 — make, create 31:15; 33:4; 40:15 — make a target 16:12 — make answer 38:34 — make decree 28:26 — make drink 9:18 — make flash 37:15 — make forget 39:17 — make garment 38:9 — make great 12:23 — make inherit 13:26 — make lamp shine 29:3 — make much of 7:17 — make overflow 37:11 — make path 28:26 — make quiver 39:20 — make ride 30:22 — make to disgorge 20:15 — make weak 23:16 — make wise 35:11 — mark 11:11 — mistrust 4:18 — mold 10:9 — mouth 22:22; 23:12; 37:2 — move 9:5, 11 — nourish 36:31 — number steps 31:4 — open ear

B. THE NATURAL WORLD

offspring 39:3; young 39:3, 4 — jackal 30:29 — kid 39:1 — lamb 21:11; 31:20 — Leviathan 3:8; 41:1–34; its back 41:15; breath 41:21; chest 41:24; corselet 41:13; eye 41:18; face 41:14; head 41:7; hide 41:7; jaw 41:2; limb 41:12; might 41:12; mouth 41:19, 21; neck 41:22; nose 41:2; nostril 41:20 ; outer garment 41:13 – row of teeth 41:14; sneeze 41:18; splash 41:25; tongue 41:1; tooth 41:14; underbelly 41:23; word 41:3 — lion 4:10, 11; 10:16; 28:8; 38:39–40; its cub 38:39; den 38:40; growl 4:10; mane 4:10; roar 4:10; thicket 38:40; whelp 4:11; young 4:10 — locust 39:20 — maggot 25:6 — moth 4:19; 13:28 — onager 24:5; 39:5; its (non-existent) bonds 39:5; dwelling 39:6 — ox 1:3, 14; 6:5; 40:15 — oxen, yoke of 42:12 — ram 42:8 — serpent 26:13 — she-ass 42:12 — sheep 1:3; 42:12 — snake 20:16 — spider 8:14 — wild animal 39:15; 40:20 — wild ass 6:5; 11:12; 39:5–8 — wild beast 5:22, 23; 39:9 — wild ox 39:9–12; its strength 39:11 — worm 17:14; 21:26; 24:20; 25:6

Birds

bird 12:7; 27:18; 28:7, 21; 35:11; 41:5; its egg 39:14; eye 39:29; nest 27:18; prey 9:26; 39:29; wing 20:8; 39:13, 26; young 39:30 — bird of prey 28:7 — cock 38:36 — eagle 9:26; 39:27; its eyes 39:29; eyrie 39:28; nest 39:27; young 39:30 — falcon 28:7; 39:13 — hawk 39:26; its wing 39:26 — ibis 38:36 — nestling 29:18 — ostrich 30:29; 39:13–18; its chicks 39:16; eggs 39:14; labor 39:16; plumes 39:18; wings 39:13 — phoenix 29:18 — raven 38:41; its young 38:41 — stork 39:13 — vulture 15:23 — fly 5:7 — pinion 39:13 — plume 39:18

Earth

broad place 36:16 — circle 26:10 — cliff 14:18; 39:28 — clod 21:33; 38:38 — corner of earth 37:3 — crag 39:28 — desert 6:18; 12:24; 24:5; 38:26 — dimensions 38:5 — dirt 30:19 — dust 2:12; 4:19; 7:22; 14:8; 16:15; 17:16; 20:11; 21:26; 22:24; 27:16; 30:19; 39:14; 40:13; 42:6 — earth 1:7; 2:2, :3; 5:10, 25; 7:1; 8:9; 9:6; 11:9; 12:8, 15; 16:18; 18:4; 19:25; 20:4, 27; 26:7; 28:5, 24; 30:6; 34:13; 35:11; 37:3, 6, 12, 17; 38:4, 13, 18, 24, 33; 38:38; 41:33 — earthquake 9:6 — end of the earth 28:24 — extent 38:18 — fleck 24:18; 28:6 — flood of waters 20:28; 22:11, 16; 27:20; 38:34 — garden 8:16 — gully 30:6 — height 5:11 — hill 15:7; 39:8 — lake 14:11 — land 1:10; 9:24; 14:19; 15:19, 29; 22:8; 24:4, 18, 19; 28:13; 30:8; 31:38; 37:13; 38:26, 27; 42:15 — marsh 8:11 — mass 38:38 — measure 28:25 — mire 10:9; 30:19 — mountain 9:5; 14:18; 24:8; 28:9 — mud 34:15 — mound 22:25 — order 10:22; 40:8 — pasture 39:8 — pile 27:16 — plain 39:10, 21 — pillar of earth 9:6 — pillar of heaven 26:11 — river 28:11; 33:18; 40:20, 22, 23 — rock 8:17; 18:4; 19:24; 24:8; 28:2, 5, 9, 10; 29:6; 30:6; 41:24 — saltings 39:6 — sand 6:3 — soil 5:6; 14:19; 28:2; 38:38 — source of river 28:11 — stream 14:11; 20:17; 29:6 — steppe 39:6 — stone 5:23; 6:12; 8:17; 14:19; 22:24; 38:30 — swamp 40:21 — thicket 38:40 — thorn 31:40 — torrent 14:19; 20:17, 28; 37:11; 38:25; 40:23 — valley 21:33 — wadi 6:15; 22:24; 30:6 — wilderness 1:19; 24:5 — world 15:7; 18:18; 34:13

Heavenly Bodies

Aldebaran 38:32 — Bear 9:9 — cluster 38:31 — Dog-stars 38:13, 15 — eclipse 3:5; 9:7 — Mazzaroth 38:32 — moon 25:5; 31:26 — Navigator's Line 38:15 — Orion 9:9; 38:31 — Pleiades 9:9; 38:31 — southern stars 9:9 — sun 8:16; 9:7; 31:26 — vault of heaven 22:14

Materials

ash 2:8; 13:12; 42:6 — brimstone 18:15 — bronze 6:12; 20:24; 40:18; 41:27 — clay 4:19; 10:9; 13:12; 27:16; 33:6; 38:14 — coals 41:21 — copper 28:2 — fire 18:5, 15; 20:26; 22:20; 28:5; 31:12; 41:19; its sparks 41:19 — fire-fuel 20:7 — flame 15:30; 18:5; 41:21 — flint 28:9 — iron 19:24; 20:24; 28:2; 40:18; 41:27 — lead (n.) 19:24 — lye 9:30 — metal 37:18 — ore 28:3 — silver 3:15; 22:25; 27:16, 17; 28:1, 15 — steam 41:20 — water 3:24; 5:10; 6:19; 8:11; 12:15; 14:9, 11, 19; 15:16; 22:7, 11; 24:18, 19; 26:5, 8, 10; 28:25; 29:19; 34:7; 36:27; 37:10; 38:30, 34; 41:31; its scent 14:9 — wood 41:27

Numbers

first 42:14 — five hundred 1:3 — four 1:19 — fourteen thousand 42:12 — fourth 42:16 — hundred and forty 42:16 — number 5:9; 21:21; 25:3; 31:4; 36:26; 38:21 — once 9:3; 14:20; 23:7; 40:5 — one 2:10; 4:2; 9:22; 21:23; 33:14, 23; 37:21 — second 42:14 — seven 1:2; 2:13; 42:8, 13 — seventh 5:19 — seven thousand 1:3 — six 5:19 — six thousand 42:12 — third 42:14 — thousand 9:3; 42:12 — three 1:2, 4, 17; 2:11; 32:1, 3, 5; 33:29; 42:13 — three thousand 1:3 — twice 33:29; 40:5 — two 13:20; 42:7

Plants and Trees

blossom 15:30, 33 – branch 15:31, 32; 18:16; 29:19 – broom 30:4 – bush 30:4, 7 – cedar 40:17 – flower 8:12; 14:2 – fruit 20:18 – leaf 13:25 – lotus 40:21, 22 – nettles 30:7 – olive rows 24:11 – olive tree 15:33 – papyrus 8:11 – plant 8:12, 16; 14:9; 40:20 – poplar 40:22 – reed 8:11; 9:26; 40:21; 41:2 – root 8:17; 14:8; 18:16; 19:10, 28; 28:9; 29:19; 30:4; 31:12; 36:30 – sheaf 5:5, 26; 24:10 – shoots 8:16; 14:7, 9; 15:30 – sprout 5:6 – stinkweed 31:40 – straw 13:25; 21:18; 41:27, 29 – stump 14:8 – tree 14:7; 24:20 – vine 15:33

Poisons

poison 6:4; 9:18; 20:16 – gall 16:13 – venom 20:14

Precious Stones

coral 28:18 – cornelian 28:16 – gold 3:15; 22:24, 25; 23:10; 28:1; 6, 15, 16, 17, 19; 31:24; 42:11 – jewel 28:17 – lapis 28:6, 16 – olivine 28:19 – rock crystal 28:18 – rubies 28:18

Roads

path 3:23; 13:27; 18:10; 19:8; 22:15, 28; 23:11; 24:13; 28:7, 26; 30:13; 33:11; 38:20, 25 – road 16:22; 21:29; 24:4 – way 17:9; 19:8; 22:14; 23:10,11; 24:13, 23; 28:13, 23; 29:25; 31:4, 7; 34:21

Sea

depth of abyss 20:26; 38:16 – deep 38:30; 41:31, 32 – ocean deep 28:14 – sea 6:3; 11:9; 12:8; 26:12; 28:14; 36:30; 38:8, 16 – wake in sea 41:32 – wave 30:14; 38:11 – wave, pride 38:11

Sky

chaos 26:7 – darkness 3:4; 5:14; 10:22; 11:17; 12:25; 15:22, 24, 30; 16:16; 17:12, 13; 18:18; 19:8; 20:26; 22:11; 23:17; 24:16, 17; 26:10; 28:3; 29:3; 33:20; 37:19; 38:9, 17, 19 – darkness, deep 3:6; 20:26; 30:26; 34:22 – daylight 5:14 – expanse 38:18 – fire of God 1:16 – gloom 28:3; 34:22 – glow 37:22 – heaven 1:16; 9:8; 11:8; 14:12; 15:15; 20:6, 27; 22:12, 14; 25:2; 26:11, 13; 28:24; 35:5, 11; 37:3; 38:37; 41:11 – height of heaven 22:12; 25:2 – laws of heaven 38:33 – light 3:4, 9, 16, 20, 23; 10:22; 11:17; 12:25; 17:12; 18:6, 18; 22:28; 24:13, 16; 25:3; 26:10; 28:11; 29:3; 30:26; 33:28, 30; 36:30; 38:15, 19; 41:18 – nothing 26:7 – shade 40:22 – shadow 7:2; 8:9; 14:2; 17:7; 24:17 – sky 12:7; 28:21; 37:18 – star 3:9; 9:7; 22:12; 25:5; 38:7

Time

ancient times 20:4; 38:21 – dawn 3:9; 4:20; 7:4; 38:12; 41:18 – day 1:6, 13; 2:1, 13; 3:1, 3, 4, 6, 8; 7:1, 6, 16; 8:9; 9:25; 10:5, 20; 12:12; 14:5, 6; 15:20; 17:1, 11, 12; 20:28; 21:13; 24:1, 16; 27:6; 29:2, 4, 18; 30:16, 27; 32:7; 33:25; 36:11; 38:12, 21, 23; 42:17 – daybreak 24:14 – dusk 4:20 – evening 7:2 – eyelids of morning 3:9 – future 8:7 – middle of night 34:20 – moment 20:5; 24:24; 27:10; 34:20; 37:21 – month 3:6; 7:3; 14:5; 21:21; 29:2; 39:2 – morning 1:5; 3:9; 7:18; 11:17; 24:17; 38:12 – night 2:13; 3:3, 6, 7; 4:13; 5:14; 7:3, 4; 17:12; 20:8; 24:7, 14; 27:20; 30:17; 33:15; 34:20, 25; 35:10; 36:20; 39:9, 28 – noonday 5:14; 11:17 – perpetuity 19:24 – prime of life 29:4 – season 5:26; 38:32 – time 14:13; 15:32; 22:16; 27:19; 34:23; 38:23; 39:2 – twilight 24:15 – year 3:6; 15:20; 16:22; 32:6, 7; 36:11, 26; 42:12, 16 – yesterday 8:9 – youth 31:18; 33:25; 36:13

Weather

air 2:12 – breath of air 41:16 – chamber of tempest 37:9 – channel for rain 38:25 – cloud 3:5; 7:8; 20:6; 22:13, 14; 26:8, 9; 30:15; 35:5; 36:28, 29; 37:11, 13, 15, 16, 21; 38:9, 34, 37 – cold (n.) 24:7; 37:9 – dew 29:19 – dewdrop 38:28 – downpour 30:22; 37:6 – drop 36:27 – drought 12:15; 24:19 – force of wind 27:22 – hail 38:22 – heat 6:17; 24:19; 30:30; 38:24 – hoar-frost 38:29 – ice 6:16; 37:10 – lightning 36:32; 37:3, 15 – lightning bolt 38:35 – mist 36:27 – moisture 37:11 – rain 5:10; 24:8; 28:26; 29:23; 36:27; 37:6; 38:25, 28 – rain, late 29:23 – rime 38:29 – shower 36:28 – sirocco 38:24 – snow 6:16; 24:19; 37:6; 38:22 – south wind 37:17 – spreading of clouds 36:29; 37:16 – storm 21:18 – sunlight 37:21 – tempest 27:20; 37:9; 38:1; 40:6 – thunder 26:14; 36:33; 40:9 – thunderbolt 28:26; 38:25 – whirlwind 4:15 – wind 1:19; 4:9, 15; 8:2; 13:25; 15:30; 21:18; 26:13; 28:25; 30:15, 22; 37:9, 21 – wind, east 15:2; 27:21 – wind, hand of 27:23

C. THE HUMAN WORLD

Body

arm 15:25; 25:2; 31:22; 40:9 – back 9:34; 19:17; 20:25 – being, inmost 19:27; 33:28 – belly 15:2; 20:15, 20, 23; 32:19 – blood 16:18; 39:30 – blubber 15:27 – body 4:15; 30:27 – bone 2:5; 4:14; 10:11; 19:20; 20:11; 21:24; 30:17, 30; 33:21 – breast 3:12; 24:9 – breath 7:7, 16; 9:18; 32:18 – cheeks 16:10 – crown (head) 2:7 – ear 4:12; 12:11; 15:21; 29:11; 33:1, 16; 34:2; 34:3; 36:10, 15; 42:5 – eye 2:12; 3:10; 4:16; 7:7, 8; 10:4; 11:20; 15:12; 16:9; 17:2, 7; 19:27; 20:9; 21:8; 20; 24:15; 27:19; 28:7, 10, 21; 29:11, 15; 31:1, 7, 16; 32:1; 42:5 – eyelid 16:16; 41:18 – face 4:15; 6:28; 11:15; 15:27; 16:16; 21:31; 23:17; 24:15, 18; 26:10; 37:12, 30 – flesh 2:5; 6:12; 7:5; 10:11; 13:14; 19:20, 26; 21:6; 33:21, 25 – foot 2:7; 12:17; 13:27; 23:11; 29:15; 31:5; 33:11; 39:15 – footprints 13:27 – footstep 29:6 – hand 1:10; 2:5; 4:3; 5:12, 15; 9:30, 33; 10:3, 7, 8; 11:13, 14; 13:14; 17:9; 20:10; 22:30; 23:2; 28:9; 29:9, 20; 30:2, 21, 24; 31:7, 21, 25, 27; 35:7; 40:4; 41:8 – hand, right 30:12; 40:14 – head 1:20; 2:7, 12; 16:4; 19:9; 20:6; 22:26; 29:2; 31:36 – heart 1:5; 17:11; 22:22; 23:12; 27:6; 29:13; 30:25; 31:7, 1,9, 27, 33; 33:3; 36:5; 37:1, 24 – heel 18:11 – height 15:31; 20:6 – jawbone 29:17 – kidneys 16:13 – knee 3:12; 4:4, 20 – limbs 17:7; 18:13 – lip 2:10; 8:21; 15:6; 16:5; 27:4; 32:20; 33:3 – liver 20:25 – loins 12:18; 15:27; 31:20; 38:3; 40:7 – neck 16:12; 39:19 – nostril 27:3 – palate 6:30; 12:11; 20:13; 29:10; 34:3 – palms 16:17 – presence 30:11; 34:37 – pus 7:5 – scab 7:5 – shoulder 31:22, 36 – shoulder-blade 31:22 – shoulder-socket 31:22 – sight 26:9; 30:10; 41:9 – sinews 10:11 – skin 2:4; 7:5; 10:11; 16:15; 19:20, 26; 30:30 – sole 2:7 – sore (noun) 5:18 – soul 7:11; 10:1; 21:25; 24:12 – spirit 3:20; 6:4; 7:11; 17:1; 21:4; 29:10; 33:2; 39:15 – spittle 7:19 – stomach 20:14 – stride 18:7 – teeth 13:14; 19:20; 29:17 – tongue 5:21; 6:30; 20:12; 20:16; 27:4; 29:10; 33:2 – vision 4:13; 7:14; 20:8; 33:15 – voice 2:12; 4:16; 29:10; 30:31; 38:34; 37:2 – womb 1:21; 3:10, 11; 10:18, 19; 15:35; 31:15, 18; 38:8, 29

Clothing

belt 12:18, 21; 38:31 – clothes 9:31; 37:17 – clothing 22:6; 24:7; 27:16; 31:19 – corselet 41:13 – covering 24:7; 31:19 – garment 13:28; 30:18; 38:9, 14; 41:13 – mantle 1:20 – neck of tunic 30:18 – robe 2:12; 29:14 – sackcloth 16:15 – swaddling band 38:9 – tunic 30:18 – turban 29:14; 31:36

Commerce

account 40:4 – asset 22:3 – balance 31:6 – barter 6:27 – bribe 6:22 – bribery 15:34 – caravan 6:18, 19 – coin 42:11 – commerce 20:18 – gain 4:21; 20:18; 21:15 – gift 6:22 – guild 41:6 – lots 6:27 – merchant 41:6 – payment 31:39 – pledge 17:3; 22:6; 24:3, 9 – portion 24:18, 19; 27:13; 31:2 – possessions 5:5; 15:29; 22:20 – price 28:15 – profit 33:27; 34:9; 35:3 – ransom money 36:18 – ransom 33:24 – redeem 33:28 – repay 34:11 – riches 15:29 – scales 6:2 – seal 38:14; 41:15 – seal on stars 9:7 – signature 31:35 – substance 1:10 – surety 17:3 – wages 7:2 – wealth 6:22; 15:29; 20:15; 22:20; 27:19; 31:25; 36:19

Dwellings

abode 8:6 – corner 1:19 – door 3:10; 31:9, 2; 31:34; 37:7; 38:10; 41:14 – dwell 4:19; 11:14; 15:28; 21:28; 30:6 – dwelling 5:24; 18:15 , 21; 20:9; 38:19; 39:6 – home 2:11; 5:3; 7:10; 17:13; 38:20; 39:6 – house 1:4, 10, 13, 18, 19; 3:15; 4:19; 8:14, 15; 15:28; 20:19, 28; 21:9, 28; 22:18; 24:16; 27:18; 42:11 – meetinghouse 30:23 – pavilion 36:29 – shelter 18:14; 24:8; 37:8 – square 29:7; 31:32 – tent 8:22; 11:14; 12:6; 15:34; 18:6, 14, 15; 19:12; 20:26; 21:28; 22:23; 31:31

Emotions

anger 5:2; 15:13; 19:29 – angry 32:2, 3, 5 – anguish 6:2; 7:11; 15:24 – appetite 33:20; 38:39 – arrogance 36:9 – assurance 24:22 – cheerfulness 9:27 – confidence 4:6; 6:20; 8:14; 31:24 – contentment 20:20; 36:11 – delight 3:22; 22:26; 23:10; 31:26 – desire 17:11; 19:26; 20:20; 23:13; 31:16; 33:32 – despair 6:26; 11:20 – disappointment 6:20; 41:1 – dread 3:25; 9:35; 7:14; 13:11, 25; 23:15; 25:2 – encouragement 15:11; 16:5 – fear 3:25; 5:21, ; 9:35; 11:15; 13:21; 21:9; 31:23, 34; 33:7; 39:16, 22 – fear of God 1:1, 8; 2:3; 6:14; 9:34, 35; 15:11 – feeling 14:22; 20:2 – fright 3:5; 6:21; 7:14; 18:11; 22:10 – frustration 6:20 – fury 40:11 – grief 14:22; 17:7; 30:25; 42:11 – happiness 17:15; 21:25 – happy 5:17   hate 31:29; 34:17 – haughty 40.11, 12 – hope 4:7; 5:16; 6:8, 19; 11:18; 17:15; 19:10; 27:8; 41:9 – horror 18:20 – joy 3:7; 8:21; 9:25; 14:6; 20:17; 29:13; 33:26; 38:7 – laugh 16:10; 22:19; 39:18, 22; 41:29 – laughter 8:21 – longing 7:2; 19:27; 36:20 – pleasure 10:3; 20:18; 21:6; 34:9 – pride 33:17; 35:12; 38:11 – quivering 4:15; 21:6 – rage 3:17; 18:4; 37:2 – rejoicing 3:22; 20:5; 31:25, 29; 38:7 – relief 14:14; 32:20 – resentment 5:2 – restlessness 7:4 – sadness 9:27 – shame 10:15; 11:3; 18:3 – sympathy 2:11 – terror 4:14; 6:4; 7:14; 13:11; 15:24; 18:11; 20:25; 22:10; 23:15; 24:17; 26:5;

30:15; 31:23, 34; 33:7; 41:22, 25 — torment 15:20; 19:2 — trembling 4:14; 19:29; 37:1 — trust 4:18; 8:14; 15:31; 31:24

Ethical Qualities

conduct 21:31; 22:3; 34:11 — deceit 15:35; 27:4; 31:5 — deceptive 36:4 — err 6:24 — evil (n.) 28:28; 30:26; 31:29 — evil 1:1, 9; 2:3; 20:12 — evil-doer 8:20; 18:21; 22:15; 34:8; 34:22 — evil men 16:11 — falsehood 6:30; 31:5 — fault 19:4 — folly 4:18 — fool 5:2; 5:3; 30:8 — foolish 2:10 — godless 8:13; 15:34; 20:5; 27:8; 34:30; 36:13 — good 2:10; 34:4; 30:26 — guilt 8:4; 10:14; 20:27; 31:33; power of guilt 8:4 — guilty 9:29; 10:2, 7 — iniquity 4:8; 6:29; 10:6; 11:14; 22:5; 31:3; 36:10, 21, 33 — integrity 2:3, 9; 6:29; 27:6; 31:6 — irreverence 1:22 — lie 6:28; 34:6 — loyalty 6:14; 10:12; 37:13 — mercy 20:10; 27:22; 41:3 — offense 31:11 — partiality 32:21 — perfidy 21:34 — right 8:3; 32:2; 33:23, 27; 34:4; 40:8; 42:7, 8 — righteous 4:17; 17:9; 22:19; 27:17; 32:1; 35:2, 7; 36:7 — righteousness 29:14; 33:26; 35:8; 37:23 — sin 1:5, 22; 2:10; 7:20, 21; 8:4; 10:6, 14; 14:16; 15:5; 31:30, 33; 33:27; 34:37; 35:6 — stain 31:7 — ungodly 17:8 — unrighteous 29:17; 31:3 — upright 4:7; 17:8; 23:7 — uprightness 33:3 — wicked 3:17; 8:22; 9:22, 24; 10:3; 11:20; 15:20; 16:11; 18:5; 20:5, 23, 29; 21:7, 16, 17, 28, 30; 22:18; 24:2, 6, 9, 11; 27:13; 34:8, 18, 36; 36:5, 17; 40:12 — wickedness 22:5, 23; 24:20; 34:10, 26; 35:8, 12, 15 — wrong 24:12; 27:4; 32:3; 33:9; 34:10, 12, 32; 36:23; 40:8 — wrongdoer 27:7 — wrongdoing 15:16

Events and Experiences

affliction 5:6; 30:27; 36:8, 15, 21 — birthday 1:4 — blessing 1:10, 21; 29:11, 13; 31:20; 42:12 — calamity 5:19; 6:21; 9:23; 21:17, 30; 30:24; 31:3; 38:23 — confusion 8:22 — constraint 36:16 — contempt 31:34 — death 3:5, 21; 4:20; 5:20; 7:15; 9:23; 16:16; 24:17, 17; 29:13; 30:23; 33:18, 22; 36:12; 38:17 — defend 36:19 — desolation 30:3 — destruction 5:21; 30:3 — die 1:19; 2:9; 3:11; 4:21; 10:18; 12:2; 14:8, 10, 14; 21:23, 25; 24:12; 26:5; 29:18; 34:20; 36:12; 42:17 — disaster 15:35; 31:3 — dismay 4:5 — dissolution 8:19 — distress 15:24; 20:22; 36:15, 16, 19 — dream 7:14; 20:8; 33:15 — dying, the 24:12 — escape 1:15, 16, 7, 19; 5:24 — exertion 36:19 — existence 36:14 — expectation 8:13 — exterminate 4:20 — fate 8:13; 18:20; 20:29 — fortune 42:10 — funeral procession 21:33 — good fortune 7:7 — grave 5:26; 10:19; 21:32; 27:15 — graveyard 17:1 — groaning 3:24; 23:2; 24:12 — harm 2:10; 5:19 — health 21:23 — help 5:4; 19:7; 24:12; 25:2, 4; 30:15, 28; 31:21; 35:9 — hiding 24:4 — life 2:4, 6; 3:20; 4:7; 6:11; 7:7, 16; 8:19; 9:21; 10:1, 12; 11:17; 19:17; 24:22; 27:2, 3; 27:8; 30:16; 31:30; 33:4, 18, 20, 22, 28, 30; 36:13; 41:4; 42:12 — living, the 28:13; 30:23 — marvel 37:16 — memory 18:17 — mischief 4:8; 15:35 — misery 7:3; 30:16 — misfortune 2:11; 6:2; 20:22; 42:11 — mockery 16:10; 17:2; 36:18 — mocking song 30:9 — mourning 30:31 — mystery 11:6, 7 — occasion 33:10 — oppression 10:3; 35:9 — pain 6:10; 14:22; 16:5, 6; 33:19 — pity 33:24 — plague 9:23; 27:15 — pressure 33:7 — prosperity 20:21; 21:13, 16; 22:18, 21; 24:22; 36:11 — protection 29:4 — repose 3:26 — restraint 30:11 — rest 3:12, 17, 26; 30:17 — retribution 21:30 — safety 5:11 — salvation 40:14 — scourge 21:9 — security 24:23 — silence 31:34; 41:12 — sleep 3:12 — sleep, deep 4:13; 33:15 — step 14:16; 31:4, 7, 37; 34:21 — strangling 7:15 — success 5:12 — suffering 2:13; 5:6, 7; 21:17 — tranquillity 3:13 — treachery 6:15 — trouble 3:10; 19:28; 27:9 — turmoil 3:26 — vigor 4:3; 20:11; 30:2; 33:25 — work 1:10; 10:3; 24:5; 34:19; 39:11

Family

acquaintance 16:7; 19:13; 42:11 — boy 3:3 — brother 1:13, 18; 6:15; 19:17; 30:29; 42:11, 15 — child 1:5; 3:16; 5:4; 17:5; 19:17; 20:10; 21:8, 11, 19; 24:5; 24:9; 27:14; 30:8; 42:16 — clansman 19:14 — daughter 1:2, 13, 18; 42:13, 15 — descendant 5:25 — family 21:21 — father 8:8; 15:10, 18; 17:14; 29:16; 30:1; 31:18; 38:28; 42:15 — fatherless 24:3, 9; 29:12; 31:21 — fellow 35:8 — firstborn 18:13 — friend 2:11; 6:14, 27; 16:21; 17:5; 19:21; 24:17; 32:3; 35:4; 42:7, 10 — generation 8:8; 42:16 — girl 41:5 — grandchild 42:16 — heritage 27:13 — infant 3:16 — inheritance 20:29; 31:2; 42:15 — intimates 19:14, 19 — kin 31:34 — kinsfolk 18:19; 19:13; 22:6 — lad 29:5 — man 1:1, 9; 4:13, 17; 5:7, 17; 10:4, 5; 14:10, 12, 14; 20:4; 38:3; 40:7 — mother 1:21; 3:12; 17:14; 31:18; 38:29 — offspring 5:25; 21:8; 27:14 — orphan 6:27; 22:9; 31:17 — posterity 18:19 — progeny 18:19 — retainers 19:14 — sister 1:4; 17:14; 42:11 — son 1:2, 13, 18; 5:7; 8:4; 14:21; 42:13 — widow 22:9; 24:3, 21; 27:15; 29:13; 31:16 — wife 2:9; 31:10; 39:4 — woman 2:10; 14:1; 15:14; 25:4; 31:9; 42:15 — woman, young 31:1 — young 1:19; 21:11; 29:8; 30:1; 32:6

Farming

booth 27:18 — burden 7:20 — chaff 21:18; 41:28 — famine 5:20 — farmlands 18:17 — fat 15:27 — field 5:10, 23; 24:6 — fleece 31:20 — fodder 6:5 — furrow 31:38; 39:10 — grass 5:25; 6:5; 40:15; 3:22 — graze 1:14 — grazing lands 18:17 — ground 1:20; 2:13; 5:6; 8:19; 14:8; 16:13; 30:3; 38:27; 39:14, 24 — harrow 39:10 — harvest 4:8; 31:12 — heads of grain 24:24 — hedge 1:10 — labor 39:16 — plow 1:14

— sowing 4:8; 5:5 — spear, fishing 41:7 — stall 39:9 — storehouse 38:22 — threshing floor 5:26; 39:12 — threshing sledge 41:30 — vineyard 24:6, 18, 19 — yield 31:39

Food and Drink

barley 31:40 — bread 3:24; 22:7 — cheese 10:10 — cream 20:17; 29:6 — crops 31:8 — drink 1:4, 13, 18 — eat 1:4, 13, 18; 5:5; 6:6; 20:21; 27:14; 31:8, 17, 39 — fatness 36:16 — feast 1:4, 5; 17:5 — food 6:6, 7; 20:23; 24:5; 28:5; 31:17; 33:20; 34:3; 36:31; 38:41 — grain 24:24; 39:12 — grape 15:33 — honey 20:17 — hunger 30:3 — hungry 5:5; 22:7 — mallow 6:6; 24:24; 30:4 — marrow 21:24 — meal 42:11 — meat 31:31 — milk 10:10; 21:24 — nourishment 38:41 — oil 20:17; 24:11; 29:6 — prey of unrighteous 29:17 — produce 40:20 — provisions 24:5 — salt 6:6 — want (n.) 30:3 — wheat 31:40 — wine 1:13, 18; 32:19

Law

assize 24:1 — case 13:18; 23:3; 35:14 — cause 29:16; 31:13; 30:6 — champion 16:14; 19:25 — claim 31:13 — court 9:32 — crime 31:11, 28 — declaration 19:23 — decree 28:26 — defend 9:15; 13:15 — deposition 42:3 — disputant 40:2 — evidence 19:5 — indictment 31:35 — injunction 31:1 — injustice 5:16 — innocence 27:5 — innocent 4:7; 9:20, 23, 28; 10:15; 12:4; 15:14; 17:8; 22:19, 30; 25:4; 27:17; 33:9; 34:5, 6 — judge 9:24; 12:17; 23:7 — judgment 19:29; 22:4; 24:1; 34:6, 23; 36:17 — justice 8:3; 19:7; 27:2; 29:14; 32:9; 34:12, 17; 35:2; 36:3, 5; 36:17; 37:23 — justify 9:2 — ordinance 6:10 — pact 41:4 — proceedings 13:10 — protest 7:11 — protestation 7:13 — punishment 21:19 — rights 34:5 — testimony 21:29 — transgression 14:17; 33:9; 34:37; 36:9 — witness 16:8, 19

Manufactures

assay 23:10 — band 1:17; 15:34 — bar 38:10; 40:18 — base 38:6 — bed 7:13; 27:19; 33:15, 19 — bond 36:8; 39:5 — bound 38:10 — boundary 26:10 — boundary-stone 24:2 — cauldron 41:31 — capstone 38:6 — channel in rocks 28:10 — chisel 19:24 — cord 30:11 — cord, measuring 38:5 — couch 7:13; 17:13 — crown 19:9 — fetter 36:8 — fishhook 41:1 — fork 40:24 — foundation 4:19; 22:16; 38:4 — fragment 4:12 — glass 28:17 — hook 40:24; 41:2 — lamp 18:5, 6; 21:17; 29:2 — leash 41:5 — millstone 41:24 — mine 28:1 — mirror 37:18 — monument 19:23 — mould 10:9 — ointment pot 41:31 — pail 21:24 — pot 41:20 — potsherd 2:8; 41:30 — pouch 14:17; 28:18 — prison 11:10; 12:14 — rope 39:10 — rubble 15:28 — ruin 5:13, 22; 21:20; 31:29 — shaft 28:4 — shuttle 7:6 — skiff 9:26 — stocks 13:27; 33:11 — table 36:16 — tent-cord 4:21 — thread 7:6 — tomb 21:32 — torch 41:19 — treasure 3:21; 20:26 — tube 40:18 — vent 32:19 — wall 30:14 — water jar 38:37 — weight 26:8; 28:25 — wine press 24:11 — wineskin 13:28; 32:19

Musical Instruments

flute 21:12; 30:31 — harp 21:12; 30:31 — timbrel 21:12 — trumpet 39:24, 25

Occupations

adulterer 24:15 — adversary 10:2 — advocate 16:19 — assailant 27:7 — brigand 6:23; 12:6 — chief 29:25 — counselor 12:17 — courier 9:25 — critic 40:2 — curser 3:8 — defender 5:4 — donkey-driver 39:7 — door-keeper 38:17 — drunkard 12:25 — fisher 41:6 — hero 15:25; 41:25 — hired laborer 7:1; 14:6 — liar 6:30 — messenger 1:14, 16, 17, 18 — mourner 29:25 — murderer 24:14 — opponent 31:35 — oppressor 27:13 — physician 13:4 — rebel 24:13 — rider 39:18 — sage 15:18; 22:2 — scoundrel 34:18 — servant 1:3, 8, 15, 16, 17, 2.3, 4.18; 7:2; 19:15; 31:13; 42:7, 8 — sinner 24:19 — slave 3:19; 7:2; 41:4 — slavedriver 3:18 — spokesman 16:20 — stranger 15:19; 19:16, 27; 29:16 — thief 24:14; 30:5 — traveler 6:19; 28:4; 31:32 — watchman 27:18 — weaver 7:6 — worker 31:39

Persons

Adam 31:33 — Barachel 32:2, 6 — Bildad 2:11; 8:1; 18:1; 25:1; 42:9 — Buzite 32:2; 32:6 — Chaldeans 1:17 — Cush 28:19 — Elihu 32:5; 32:6; 35:1; 36:1; 32:2; 32:4; 34:1 — Eliphaz 2:11; 4:1; 15:1; 22:1; 42:7, 9 — Jemimah 42:14 — Job 1:1, 5, 8, 9, 13, 14, 20, 22; 2:3, 7, 8, 10, 11; 3:1, 2; 6:1; 9:1; 12:1; 16:1; 19:1; 21:1; 23:1; 26:1; 27:1; 29:1; 31:40; 32:1, 2, 3, 4, 12; 33:1, 31; 34:5, 7, 35, 36; 35:16; 37:14; 38:1; 40:1, 3, 6; 42:1, 7, 8, 9, 10, 12, 15, 16, 17 — Karen-happuch 42:14 — Keziah 42:14 — Ram 32:2 — Sabeans 1:15 — Zophar 2:11; 11:1; 20:1; 27:7; 42:9

Places

city 3:14; 39:7 — country 12:24 — direction 37:12 — distance 2:12 — domain 38:20 — gate 5:4; 29:7; 31:21; 38:17 — place 7:10; 8:18; 18:21; 27:21, 23; 28:1, 12, 20, 23; 34:24; 37:1; 38:12, 19 — realm 38:24 — seat 29:7 — town 15:28; 24:12; 29:7 — Naamah 2:11 — Naamathite 11:1; 20:1; 27:7; 42:9

– Ophir 22:24; 28:16 – Sheba 6:19 – Shuah 2:11 – Shuhite 18:1; 42:9 – Tema 6:19 – Teman 2:11 – Temanite 4:1; 15:1; 22:1; 42:7, 9 – Uz 1:1 – east 1:3; 18:20; 23:8 – west 18:20; 23:8 – north 23:9; 26:7; 37:22 – south 23:9; 39:26

Qualities and States

abundance 20:22; 25:3; 36:31; 37:23 – accursed 5:3; 24:18 – afflicted 34:28; 36:15 – afraid 9:28 – aged 12:12; 32:6, 9 – alien 19:15; 31:32 – awesome 37:22 – barren 24:21 – beautiful 42:15 – bereaved 5:11 – bitter 3:20 – bitterness 7:11; 10:1; 21:25 – black 30:28, 30 – blameless 8:20; 9:22; 15:14 – blessed 1:21 – blight 5:22 – blind 29:15 – boastful 22:29 – cleanness 22:30 – command 23:12; 37:12; 39:27 – craftiness 5:13 – crafty 5:12; 15:5 – cruel 30:21 – crushed 5:16 – cunning (adj.) 5:13 – dignity 40:10 – dreadful 25:22 – ease 3:18 – effort 34:20 – false 31:28 – favor 8:5; 29:24 – fearful 9:35 – fierce 41:10 – firm 41:24 – force 19:12; 20:19 – free 3:19 – frozen 37:10 – full 42:17 – futility 7:3 – glory 29:20; 40:10 – golden 37:22 – great 3:19; 36:26; 37:5; 38:21 – green 39:8 – greenness 38:27 – grievous 2:7 – hard 37:10, 16, 18; 38:30; 41:23 – honor 17:4; 19:9; 30:15 – humble 36:5 – lame 29:15 – lofty 41:34 – lowly 5:11; 22:29 – majesty 37:22; 39:20; 40:10 – mighty 5:15; 12:21; 24:22; 34:20, 24; 35:9 – naked 1:21; 24:10 – nakedness 24:7 – needy 24:4, 14; 30:24 – old 29:2, 8; 32:4, 9; 42:17 – old age 5:26 –perfect 37:16 – poor 5:15; 20:10, 19; 24:4, 9, 10, 14; 29:12, 16; 30:25; 31:16, 19; 34:19, 28 – power 3:17; 6:13; 9:24; 14:10; 21:16; 26:2; 35:9; 37:23 – powerful 22:8 – powerless 25:2 – precious 28:10, 16 – privileged 22:8 – proud 41:34 – pure 4:17; 33:9; 36:5 – quiet 3:26 – rich 3:15; 27:19 – rooted 5:3 – ruthless 15:20 – secret 4:12; 13:10; 31:27 – secure 5:24 – skilled 3:8 – slain 39:30 – small 3:19 – splendor 31:26; 40:10 – stillborn 3:16 – strength 6:11, 12; 20:10, 22; 21:7; 22:9; 30:2; 36:5; 39:11, 21; 40:16; 41:22 – stupid 5:2 – supreme 37:23 – terrible 39:20; 41:14 – thirst 24:11 – thirsty 5:5 – troubled 3:20 – true 5:27 – weary 22:7 – wily 5:13 – wise 15:2; 17:10; 32:9; 34:2, 34; 35:11; 37:24 – wonder 5:9 – wonderful 37:5; 37:14; 42:3 – wounded 24:12

Religion

bless 1:10, 21; 29:11, 13; 31:20; 42:12 – curse 1:5, 11; 2:5, 9; 3:1, 8; 5:3; 24:18; 31:30 – fear of God 1:1, 8; 2:3; 6:14; 9:34, 35; 15:11 – hallow 1:5 – kiss hand 31:27 – obeisance 1:20 – offering, burnt 42:8 – piety 4:6; 22:4 – prayer 5:8; 8:5; 16:17; 21:15; 22:27; 42:8, 10 – priest 12:19 – reverence 1:22; 15:4 – sacrifice 1:5 – spell 3:8 – vow 22:27

Social World

assembly 30:28 – companion 30:29 – company 16:7; 34:8 – covenant 5:23 – elders 12:20 – foreign 28:4 – high-ranking 34:19 – human 5:9; 7:17; 15:7; 21:4; 22:2; 25:4; 28:4, 13, 21; 32:8, 13; 33:12, 17, 19, 23; 34:11; 35:8; 36:25, 28 – humanity 15:16; 34:15 – humankind 15:14; 28:28 – individual 34:29 – king 3:14; 12:18; 15:24; 29:25; 34:18; 36:7; 41:34 – master 3:19 – mediator 9:33; 33:23 – minister of state 3:14 – mob 30:12 – mortal 10:5; 16:21; 25:6; 33:14, 15, 16, 29; 34:21; 36:24 – multitude 31:34; 32:7 – name 1:21; 18:17; 32:21; 42:14, 14, 14 – nameless 30:8 – nations 12:23; 34:29; 36:20 – neighbor 31:9 – noble 12:21; 29:10; 34:18, 20 – people 17:6; 34:30; 36:31 – prince 3:15; 21:28; 29:9; 31:37; 34:19 – rule (n.) 38:33 – society 30:5 – throne 26:9; 36:7 – throng 21:33 – title 32:22 – train 38:32

Speech and Mental Activity

address 5:8 – answer 5:1; 20:2; 32:3, 5, 6; 40:2 – argument 23:4; 24:25 – attention 32:12; 35:13 – blessing 29:13 – byword 17:6; 30:9 – calumny 19:22 – comfort 2:11; 21:2, 34 – complaint 10:1; 23:2 – consolation 6:10; 42:6, 11 – correction 37:13 – counsel 5:13; 18:7; 29:21 – cry 27:9; 34:28 – derision 27:23 – discipline 5:17 – discover 5:27 – discovery 8:8 – enquiry 34:24 – entice 31:27 – hearing 33:8 – hearsay 28:22 – hiss 27:23 – idea 36:4 – impulse 20:3 – insight 25:3; 34:35; 38:4 – inspiration 25:4 – instruct 4:3 – instruction 20:3; 22:22; 36:10 – intelligence 38:36 – know 5:25; 5:27 – knowledge 21:22; 34:35; 35:16; 36:3, 12; 37:16; 38:2; 42:3 – language 15:5 – lash (tongue) 5:21 – learning 34:2 – mind 11:13; 17:4 – moaning 9:27 – mock 5:22 – neighing 39:20 – opinion 32:10, 17 – order of words 33:5 – plan 10:3; 17:11; 21:16; 22:18; 23:14; 38:2 – plea 35:13 – plot 5:12 – purpose 42:2 – reckoning 5:9 – recognize 2:12 – reply 20:3; 21:34; 34:36 – reproof 6:25 – response 32:11 – schemes 21:27 – scoffing 34:7 – scorn 22:19 – shout 3:18; 8:21; 39:7; 39:25 – sigh 3:24 – song 35:10; 36:24 – sound 33:8; 37:4 – speech 5:8; 15:2, 11; 32:14; 33:1 – splash 41:25 – talk (n.) 11:1; 15:3; 18:2; 27:12; 35:16 – thought 15:12; 20:2; 21:27; 23:15; 37:19 – thunder (humans) 39:25 – thundering 36:29 – triumph cry 20:5 – tumult 39:7 – understanding 8:10; 15:9; 20:3; 28:12, 20, 28; 32:8; 34:10, 16, 34; 39:17, 26; 42:3 – utterance 7:11 – warning 33:16 – whisper 26:14

— wisdom 4:3, 21; 11:6; 15:8; 25:3; 28:12, 18, 20, 28; 32:7, 13; 33:33; 38:36; 39:17; its secrets 11:6
— wise saying 32:11 — word 2:13; 4:2, 4, 12; 6:3, 25, 26; 15:5, 13; 16:3; 19:2; 20:3; 21:2; 23:12; 25:4; 29:22; 31:40; 32:11, 12, 14, 15, 18; 33:1, 3, 5, 8, 13; 34:2, 3, 16, 35, 37; 35:16; 38:2

Traps
gin 18:10 — lattice 18:8 — net 18:8 — noose 18:10; 41:1 — pit 9:31 — snare 18:9; 22:10 — trap 18:9

Warfare
arsenal 38:22 — battle 5:20; 38:23; 39:21; 39:25 — bowman 16:13 — breach 30:14 — captain 39:25
— captive 3:18 — enemy 6:23; 8:22; 13:24; 16:9; 19:11; 27:7; 33:10 — hard service 7:1; 14:14 — mark
36:32; 41:30 — peace 5:23; 15:21; 21:13; 22:21; 25:2 — raid 1:17 — rampart 19:12 — refuge 24:8
— siege 19:12 — siege-ramp 30:12 — siegeworks 19:6 — strife 33:19 — stroke 5:20 — struggle 41:8 —
survivor 18:19; 20:26; 27:15 — target 7:20; 16:12 — troops 19:12; 25:3; 29:25 — violence 19:7

Weapons
arrow 6:4; 20:24; 34:6; 39:23; 41:28; rattle of 39:23 — arrowhead 20:25 — javelin 39:23; 41:26, 29 —
club 41:29 — dart 41:7; 41:26 — bow 29:20 — quiver 4:15; 39:23 — shield 15:26; 41:15 — sling-stone
41:28 — spear 39:23; 41:26 — sword 1:15, 17; 5:15, 20; 15:22; 19:29; 27:14; 39:22; 40:19; 41:26 —
weapon 20:24

Index of Hebrew Words

This index of 1445 words contains references to (1) words whose meaning receives a substantial discussion in the commentary, (2) words used in Job in a special or unusual sense, (3) the 852 new words (not mentioned in BDB but registered in *DCH*) referred to in the commentary.

Hebrew		Meaning	Page
עֵשׁ IV *		night watchman	659
עֹשֶׂה *		evil deed	696
עָשָׁן I		vapor	1166
עשק II *		gush, pour	1155
עשק III *		come and go	1155
עֶשְׁתְּרוֹת *		lust, sexual desire	1069
עֶשְׁתָּרֹת		off-spring	1069
עתק II *		thrive	506
עתר I		make supplication	738
פ *		and	217, 218, 371, 701, 949
פגע		ptcp assailant, one aiming	833
פוץ III *		crush	405
פַּח I		trap	415
פַּחַד I		terror	357
פַּחַד III *		flock	1076
פַּחַד V *		testicle	1150, 1151
פחה *		quench	479
פִּטְדָה		peridot, olivine	903, 919
פִּיךְ *		jar	691
פִּין *		urinate	405
פלא		be wonderful	250
פלא		niph ptcp difficult	1206
פלא		niph ptcp wonder	144
פֶּלֶג I		stream	984
פלח II *		open	1070
פלט II *		bring forth	577
פְּלִילִי II *		assessable	963
פלל II *		expect	943
פלל V *		cut off	963
פלש II *		piercing	845
פלש III *		strew, sprinkle	845, 1210
פלש V *		pierce	845
פֶּלֶשׁ *		spreading out	845
פֶּן II *		not	686
פִּנָּה		capstone	1053
פְּנִינִים		corals, rubies	903
פקד I		inspect	192
פֶּרֶא I		zebra	158, 1071
פֶּרַח		offspring, brood, chick	949, 1076
פרץ IV *		cut, incise	896
פרץ IX *		cut, slit	897
פֶּרֶץ I		excavation	897
פֶּרֶץ I		torrent	951
פרר III *		hiph banish	342
פרר IV *		shake	371
פֶּשׁ II *		arrogance	792
פֶּשׁ III *		abundance	792
פתה I		piel (attempt to) deceive	962
פתח I		strip off	949
פֶּתִי I		inexperienced	138
פֶּתֶן		venomous serpent	490
פתק *		form, shape	656
צֶאֱלִים III *		mud	1155
צֹאן		flocks	14
צֶאֱצָא I		produce, crops	962
צָבָא I		hard service	183
צבע		dye	1057
צהר II *		spend the noon	585
צַוָּאר II *		hauberk	343
צוֹפַר		Zophar	59
צוּר I		olive press	984
צוּר I		rock	606
צוּר IX *		back, top	1165
צוּר VIII *		pebble, flint	545
צלם II *		be dark	69
צַלְמָוֶת		darkness of death	69, 223, 1058
צלע II *		stray	406
צלע III *		emerge	833
צְלָצַל II		fish-hook	1160
צְלָצַל III *		boat, ship	1160
צַמִּים I		snare	415
צַמִּים		robbers	116
צמת II *		be silent	580
צמת III *		dry up	580
צמת IV *		hem in	580
צמת V *		dismay	581
צמת VI *		flee	581
צמת VII *		complete	581
צמת VIII *		cut off	581
צָפוֹן I		north	636, 885
צָפוֹן III *		hiding	849
צֹר VII *		blade	370
צָרַעַת		skin disease	48
צרר I		wrap up	636
קבב I		curse	86
קבב I		despise, show contempt	115, 140
קבב II *		protrude	1158
קבב III *		dry up	115
קבל		accept	54
קָדוֹשׁ		prostitute	861
קדם I		piel ptcp herald	834
קָדְשִׁים *		adolescence	815
קהל III *		indict	255
קֹהֶל II *		voice	959
קוב *		be uprooted	115
קוה V *		cry out	958
קוט I		loathe	244
קֹלֵל		thunder	836
קֹל *		sound	1081
קוּם		begin to	937
קרץ II *		cut off	284
קטט II *		cut	199
קטט III *		be short	199
קים III *		possession	543
קַל II *		light	670
קלל I		be light	1139
קלל I		curse	79

Index of Authors